VOID IF DETACHED FROM BOOK OR ALTERED

AMERICAN HISTORIC I N N S
INCORPORATED

Certificate

redeemable for

One Free Night at a Bed & Breakfast or Country Inn

Compliments of
American Historic Inns, Inc. and
participating Bed & Breakfasts
and Country Inns.

This certificate entitles the bearer
to one free night at any one of the more
than 1,500 Bed & Breakfasts and Country Inns
included in this book when the bearer buys the first
night at the regular rate.
See back for requirements.

VOID IF DETACHED FROM BOOK OR ALTERED

AMERICAN HISTORIC INNS
I N C O R P O R A T E D

This section should be completed by the innkeeper when the certificate is redeemed.
MAIL COMPLETED CERTIFICATE TO:
AMERICAN HISTORIC INNS, INC.
PO BOX 669, DANA POINT, CA 92629-0669

_____
Name of Guest

_____
Guest Home Address

_____
Guest City/State/Zip

_____
Guest Home Phone

_____
Name of Bed & Breakfast/Inn

_____
Signature of Innkeeper

Certificate is good for one (1) free consecutive night when you purchase the first night at the regular rate. Offer not valid at all times. Contact inn in advance for availability, rates, reservations, meal plans, cancellation policies and other requirements. Offer valid only at participating inns featured in this Bed & Breakfast Guide. Not valid during holidays. Minimum 2-night stay. Certificate is for no more than two people and no more than one room. Other restrictions may apply. Bed tax, sales tax and gratuities not included. American Historic Inns, Inc. is not responsible for any changes in individual inn operation or policy. By use of this certificate, consumer agrees to release American Historic Inns, Inc. from any liability in connection with their travel to and stay at any participating Inn. This certificate may not be reproduced and cannot be used in conjunction with any other promotional offers. Certificate must be redeemed at participating inn by December 31, 2001. Void where prohibited.

Certificate Expires December 31, 2001

Media Comments

"…lighthouses, schoolhouses, stage coach stops, llama ranches … There's lots to choose from and it should keep B&B fans happy for years." – Cathy Stapells, Toronto Sun.

"Pay for one night at a nearby country inn and get the second night free…Among them is the very fine L'Auberge Provencale…The goal of the program, sponsored by the Association of American Historic Inns, is to introduce first-timers to inn stays but frequent inn guests also are eligible for the bargain."
– James Yenckel, Washington Post.

"Anytime you can get superb accommodations AND a free night, well that's got to be great, and it is … I've used this book before, and I must tell you, it's super … The news, information and facts in this book are all fascinating." – On the Road With John Clayton, KKGO, Los Angeles radio.

"…helps you find the very best hideaways (many of the book's listings appear in the National Register of Historic Places.)" – Country Living.

"I love your book!" – Lydia Moss, Travel Editor, McCall's.

"Delightful, succinct, detailed and well-organized. Easy to follow style…"
– Don Wudke, Los Angeles Times.

"Deborah Sakach's Bed & Breakfasts and Country Inns continues to be the premier Bed & Breakfast guide for travelers and tourists throughout the United States." – Midwest Book Review.

"One of the better promotions we've seen." – Baton Rouge Advocate.

"…thoughtfully organized and look-ups are hassle-free…well-researched and accurate…put together by people who know the field. There is no other publication available that covers this particular segment of the bed & breakfast industry – a segment that has been gaining popularity among travelers by leaps and bounds. The information included is valuable and well thought out." – Morgan Directory Reviews.

"Readers will find this book easy to use and handy to have. An excellent, well-organized and comprehensive reference for inngoers and innkeepers alike."
– Inn Review, Kankakee, Illinois.

"This guide has become the favorite choice of travelers and specializes only in professionally operated inns and B&Bs rather than homestays (lodging in spare bedrooms)." – Laguna Magazine.

"This is the best bed and breakfast book out. It outshines them all!"
– Maggie Balitas, Rodale Book Clubs.

"Most of us military families have lived all over the world, so it takes an unusual book, service or trip to excite us! As I began to look through the book, my heart beat faster as I envisioned what a good time our readers could have visiting some of these very special historic bed and breakfast properties." – Ann Crawford, Military Living.

"Absolutely beautiful!" – KQIL talk show radio.

"This is a great book. It makes you want to card everything." – KBRT Los Angeles radio talk show.

"All our lines were tied up! We received calls from every one of our 40 stations (while discussing your book.)" – Business Radio Network.

"For a delightful change of scenery, visit one of these historical inns. (Excerpts from Bed & Breakfasts and Country Inns follow.) A certificate for one free consecutive night (minimum two nights stay) can be found in the book" – Shirley Howard, Good Housekeeping.

Comments From Innkeepers

"The guests we receive from the Buy-One-Night-Get-One-Night-Free program are some of the most wonderful people. Most are first time inngoers and after their first taste of the inn experience they vow that this is the only way to travel." – Innkeeper, Mass.

"Guests that were staying here last night swear by your guide. They use it all the time. Please send us information about being in your guide." – Innkeeper, Port Angeles, Wash.

"The people are so nice! Please keep up the great program!"
– K. C, Avon Manor Inn, Avon-By-the-Sea, N.J.

"We would like to express our appreciation for the Free Night programs. We had an excellent response to the certificates. It has helped us fill our vacancies during the weekdays and in the slower time of the season. Keep up the good work!" – Hacienda Vargas, Sante Fe, N.M.

"Your book is so widely distributed that we booked up a room all the way from Japan!"
– Rose Inn, Ithaca, N.Y.

"We've just received the new edition. Congratulations on this magnificent book. You've done it again!" – Gilbert House, Charleston, W. V.

"We want to tell you how much we love your book. We have it out for guests to use. They love it! Each featured inn stands out so well. Thank you for the privilege of being in your book."
– Fairhaven Inn, Bath, Me.

"American Historic Inns is wonderful! We are proud and delighted to be included. Thank you for creating such a special guidebook." – The Heirloom, Ione, Calif.

"Your new edition has maintained the fine quality of previous editions and we are very pleased to be included." – The Victoriana 1898, Traverse City, Mich.

"We tell all our guests about the Free Night promotion and how to participate. However, we also remind them to visit with us again. Almost 100% said they will–and do so! We must be doing something right. Thanks again for this unique opportunity." – Alynn's Butterfly Inn B&B, Warrensburg, N.Y.

"We've had guests return two or three times after discovering us through your book. They have turned into wonderful guests and friends." – Port Townsend, Wash.

"The response to your book has been terrific and the guests equally terrific! Many are already returning. Thanks for all your hard work." – Rockport, Mass.

"We love your book and we also use it. Just went to New Orleans and had a great trip."
– Gettysburg, Pa.

"This has been one of the best B&B programs we have done and the guests have been delightful. Thanks!" – Eastern Shore, Md.

"We have been thrilled with our relationship with American Historic Inns for many years. Many of the travelers you've led to us had never visited our area before. Many of them, likewise, have returned."
– J.O., Thorpe House, Metamora, Ind.

"We are grateful that so many of our old friends and new guests have found us through your book. We always recommend your publications to guests who wish to explore other fine country inns of New England."
– Georgette & Albert Levis, Vermont innkeepers.

Comments About
Bed & Breakfasts and Country Inns

"Our office went crazy over this book. The quality of the inns and the quality of the book is phenomenal! Send us 52 books." – M.B., Westport, Conn.

"Outstanding! We were offering a variety of inn guide books, but yours was the only one guests bought." – J.A., White Oak Inn, Ohio

"My husband and I have really enjoyed our Bed & Breakfast free night for the past two summers. Such a good offer. Thanks!" – B.C., Houston, Texas

"The 300 women who attended my 'Better Cents' seminar went wild for the free-night book. I brought my copy and showed them the value of the free-night program. They all wanted to get involved. Thank you so much for offering such a great value." – R.R., Making Cents Seminars, Texas.

"Thank you for offering this special! It allowed us to get away even on a tight budget." – D.L., Pittsburgh, Pa.

"I'm ordering three new books. We've never stayed in one we didn't like that was in your book!" – M.R., Canton, Ohio

"My husband and I enjoyed the ambiance and delicious breakfasts! This is a lovely inn and a great offer. Thanks for making it possible for us to enjoy." – J.D., Woodbury, N.J.

"This made our vacation a lot more reasonable. We got the best room in a beautiful top-drawer inn for half the price." – L.A., Irvine, Calif.

"I used your book and free night offer and took my 17-year-old daughter. It was our first B&B visit ever and we loved it. (We acted like friends instead of parent vs. teenager for the first time in a long time.) It was wonderful!" – B.F., Clinton, N.J.

"Thanks! Do we love your B&B offer! You betcha! The luxury of getting a two-day vacation for the cost of one is Christmas in July for sure. Keep up the good work." – R.R., Grapevine, Texas.

"What a great idea for gifts. I'm ordering five to use as birthday, housewarming and thank-you gifts." – J.R., Laguna Niguel, Calif.

"The best thing since ice cream – and I love ice cream!" – M.C., Cape May, N.J.

"The 50% savings on a memorable three-day getaway makes this deal one we cannot pass up!" – P.T., Lafayette, Calif.

"After 44 years, it's hard to come up with something new … In the middle of hustle and bustle, we found a peaceful time to enjoy (and keep the memory always)." – B.K. Palm Harbor, Fla.

"Out of 25 products we presented to our fund raising committee your book was No. 1 and it generated the most excitement." – H.U., Detroit, Mich.

To Carson

American Historic Inns™

Bed & Breakfasts
and
Country Inns

by Deborah Edwards Sakach

Published by

AMERICAN
HISTORIC
INNS
INCORPORATED

PO Box 669
Dana Point
California
92629-0669
www.bnbinns.com

Bed & Breakfasts and Country Inns

FRONT COVER:
The White Inn, Fredonia, N.Y.
Photo by George W. Gardner

BACK COVER:
The author visits a bed & breakfast in Maine
Photo by American Historic Inns

Grand Victorian B&B Inn, Bellaire, Mich.
Photo by Don Rutt

Victoria-On-Main B&B, Whitewater, Wis.
Photo by Peter Hlavacek

Castle Inn Riverside, Wichita, Kansas

L'Auberge Provencale, White Post, Va.
Photo by Esther and Frank Schmidt

COVER DESIGN:
David Sakach

PRODUCTION MANAGER:
Joshua Prizer

ASSISTANT EDITORS:
Pamela Barrus, Tiffany Crosswy, Erika Jester, Jan Lynn,
Lucy Poshek, Patricia Purvis, Stephen Sakach

OPERATIONS MANAGER:
Sandy Imre

DATABASE ASSISTANT:
Molly Thomson

PROGRAMMING AND CARTOGRAPHY:
Tim Sakach

SCANNING:
Brionne Longfellow, Marissa Nunez, Suzanne Sakach

PROOFREADING:
Jordan Mullikin, Nathan Prenovost, Chaya Prizer

Publisher's Cataloging in Publication Data
Sakach, Deborah Edwards
American Historic Inns, Inc.
Bed & Breakfasts and Country Inns

1. Bed & Breakfast Accommodations - United States, Directories, Guide Books.
2. Travel - Bed & Breakfast Inns, Directories, Guide Books.
3. Bed & Breakfast Accommodations - Historic Inns, Directories, Guide Books.
4. Hotel Accommodations - Bed & Breakfast Inns, Directories, Guide Books.
5. Hotel Accommodations - United States, Directories, Guide Books.
I. Title. II. Author. III Bed & Breakfast, Bed & Breakfasts and Country Inns.

American Historic Inns is a trademark of American Historic Inns, Inc.

ISBN: 1-888050-12-8
Softcover
Printed in the United States of America.
10 9 8 7 6 5 4 3 2 1

Table Of Contents

How To Make A Reservation

1. **You must make ADVANCE reservations.**
    The FREE night offer is only valid by making
    reservations in advance directly with the par-
    ticipating lodging establishment AND when
    you identify yourself as having a Certificate
    from this guide.

2. **You must identify yourself FIRST as hold-
    ing a Certificate from this guide, or the
    innkeeper is not obligated to honor the
    Certificate.**

3. All FREE nights are <u>subject to availability.</u>
    This may mean that the lodging establish-
    ment has rooms but is projecting that those
    rooms will be filled with full-fare customers.
    Most hotels consider they are at full occupan-
    cy when they are about 80% filled and then
    cut off all reduced-fare programs at that time.
    Smaller properties such as bed & breakfast
    homes and inns may use different formulas.
    Some set aside a specific number of rooms or
    suites for Certificate holders and then will
    not accept any more reservations for the pro-
    motion after those rooms are filled. Others
    will accept Certificate holders at the last
    minute when they project that they will have
    rooms available.

4. Try to obtain a confirmation number, confir-
    mation letter or the name of the person taking
    your reservation.

5. If you have children or pets coming with you,
    or if you smoke, be sure to tell the innkeeper
    in advance. Most bed & breakfasts and coun-
    try inns are non-smoking. Accommodations
    for children or pets may be limited or non-
    existent.

6. Understand the cancellation policy. A number
    of bed & breakfasts and country inns require
    a two-week or more notice of cancellation in
    order to refund your deposit. You should find
    out what the policy is at the same time you
    make your reservations.

7. **All holidays are excluded.** There may be
    other periods of time that are excluded as
    well.

8. This is a two-night minimum program and
    the two nights MUST BE CONSECUTIVE,
    i.e. "Monday and Tuesday," or "Sunday and
    Monday." You can stay longer, of course.
    Please read each inn's specific restrictions.

9. Always find out what meals, if any, are includ-
    ed in the rates and whether you will have to
    pay for meals. Not every establishment partic-
    ipating in this program provides a free break-
    fast.

10. Some locales require that bed tax be collect-
    ed, even on FREE nights. If you have a ques-
    tion, check with the innkeeper, chamber of
    commerce or city hall serving the area in
    which you wish to stay.

11. For more information, request a brochure from
    participating inns before you make your reser-
    vations or look up the inn on **bnbinns.com**.

12. Don't forget to take this book with the
    Certificate along with you.

    The FREE night is given to you as a gift directly
from the innkeeper in the hope that you and your
friends will return and share your discovery with
others. **The inns are not reimbursed by
American Historic Inns, Inc.**

How To Use This Book

You hold in your hands a delightful selection of America's best bed & breakfasts and country inns. The innkeeper of each property has generously agreed to participate in our FREE night program. **They are not reimbursed for the second night, but make it available to you in the hope that you will return to their inn or tell others about your stay.**

Most knowledgeable innkeepers enjoy sharing regional attractions, local folklore, history, and pointing out favorite restaurants and other special features of their areas. They have invested much of themselves in creating an experience for you to long remember. Many have personally renovated historic buildings, saving them from deterioration and often, the bulldozer. Others have infused their inns with a unique style and personality to enliven your experience with a warm and elegant environment. Your innkeepers are a tremendous resource. Treat them kindly and you will be well rewarded.

Accommodations

You'll find bed & breakfasts and country inns in converted schoolhouses, stone castles, lighthouses, 18th-century farmhouses, Queen Anne Victorians, adobe lodges and more.

Many are listed in the National Register of Historic Places and have preserved the stories and memorabilia from their participation in historical events such as the Revolutionary or Civil wars.

The majority of inns included in this book were built in the 17th, 18th and 19th centuries. We have stated the date each building was constructed at the beginning of each description.

No inn paid to be featured in this guidebook. All costs for the production of the book have been absorbed by American Historic Inns. The selection of inns for this guidebook was made as carefully as possible from among the many that wanted to be included. American Historic Inns, as publishers, produced and financed the project. Inns did not pay advertising fees to be in the book.

They did, however, agree to honor the certificate for the free night when the first night is purchased. We hope you enjoy the choices we made, and we encourage you to suggest new inns that you discover.

A Variety of Inns

A **Country Inn** generally serves both breakfast and dinner and may have a restaurant associated with it. Many have been in operation for years; some, since the 18th century as you will note in our "Inns of Interest" section. Although primarily found on the East Coast, a few country inns are in other regions of the nation. Always check as to what meals are provided.

A **Bed & Breakfast** facility's primary focus is lodging. It can have from three to 20 rooms or more. The innkeepers usually live on the premises. Breakfast is the only meal served and can be a full-course, gourmet breakfast or a simple buffet. Many B&B owners pride themselves on their culinary skills.

As with country inns, many B&Bs specialize in providing historic, romantic or gracious atmospheres with amenities such as canopied beds, fireplaces, spa tubs, afternoon tea in the library and scenic views.

Some give great attention to recapturing a specific historic period, such as the Victorian or Colonial eras. Many display antiques and other furnishings from family collections.

A **Homestay** is a room available in a private home. It may be an elegant stone mansion in the best part of town or a charming country farm. Homestays have one to three guest rooms. Because homestays are often operated as a hobby-type business and open and close frequently, only a very few unique properties are included in this publication.

Area Codes

Although we have made every effort to update area codes throughout the book, new ones pop up from time to time. The phone companies provide recordings for several months after a change, but beyond that point, it can be difficult to reach an inn or B&B.

Although they are listed by state or province, the new codes were added only in certain sections of the state or province. For example, the new 845 area code in New York applies only to certain areas in the Hudson Valley and Catskill Region.

The following list includes the most recent area code changes that were available at press time.

State/Province	Old Code	New Code	Effective Date of Change
California	760	442	10/21/00
California	707	369	12/2/00
California	707	627	10/13/01
California	818	747	TBD
California	909	951	TBD
California	619	935	TBD
Georgia	912	478	8/1/00
Georgia	912	229	8/1/00
Iowa	515	641	7/9/00
Kentucky	606	859	4/1/00
Minnesota	612	763	2/27/00
Minnesota	612	952	2/27/00
Michigan	517	989	TBD
New York	914	845	6/5/00
Tennessee	423	865	TBD
Texas	409	936	2/19/00
Texas	409	979	2/19/00
Utah	801	385	12/31/00
Wisconsin	414	262	TBD
California	760	442	10/21/00

Baths

Not all bed & breakfasts and country inns provide a private bath for each guest room. We have included the number of rooms and the number of private baths in each facility. If you must have a private bath, make sure the room reserved for you provides this.

Beds

K, **Q**, **D**, **T**, indicates King, Queen, Double or Twin beds available at the inn.

Credit cards/Payments

MC	MasterCard	**VISA**	Visa
DC	Diner's Club	**CB**	Carte Blanche
AX	American Express	**DS**	Discover
TC	Traveler's checks	**PC**	Personal checks

Meals

Continental breakfast: Coffee, juice, toast or pastry.

Continental-plus breakfast: A continental breakfast plus a variety of breads, cheeses and fruit.

Full breakfast: Coffee, juice, breads, fruit and an entree.

Full gourmet breakfast: May be an elegant four-course candlelight offering or especially creative cuisine.

Teas: Usually served in the late afternoon with cookies, crackers or other in-between-meal offerings.

Meal Plans

AP: American Plan. All three meals may be included in the price of the room. Check to see if the rate quoted is for two people or per person.

MAP: Modified American Plan. Breakfast and dinner may be included in the price of the room.

EP: European Plan. No meals are included. We have listed only a few historic hotels that operate on an EP plan.

Always find out what meals, if any, are included in the rates. Not every establishment participating in this program provides breakfast, although most do. Inns offering the second night free may or may not include a complimentary lunch or dinner with the second night. Occasionally an innkeeper has indicated MAP and AP when she or he actually means that both programs are available and you must specify which program you are interested in.

Please do not assume meals are included in the rates featured in the book.

Rates

Rates are usually listed in ranges, i.e., $65-175. The LOWEST rate is almost always available during off-peak periods and may apply only to the least expensive room. Rates always are subject to change and are not guaranteed. You always should confirm the rates when making the reservations. Rates for Canadian listings usually are listed in Canadian dollars. Rates are quoted for double occupancy for two people.

Breakfast and other meals MAY or MAY NOT be included in the rates and may not be included in the discount.

Smoking

The majority of country inns and B&Bs in historic buildings prohibit smoking; therefore, if you are a smoker we advise you to call and specifically check with each inn to see if and how they accommodate smokers.

Rooms

Under some listings, you will note that suites are available. We typically assume that suites include a private bath.

Additionally, under some listings, you will note a reference to cottages. A cottage may be a rustic cabin tucked in the woods, a seaside cottage or a private apartment-style accommodation.

Fireplaces

When fireplaces are mentioned in the listing they may be in guest rooms or in common areas. A few have fireplaces that are non-working because of city lodging requirements. Please verify this if you are looking forward to an intimate, fireside chat in your room.

State maps

The state maps have been designed to help travelers

find an inn's location quickly and easily. Each city shown on the maps contains one or more inns.

As you browse through the guide, you will notice coordinates next to each city name, i.e. C3. The coordinates designate the location of inns on the state map.

Media coverage

Some inns have provided us with copies of magazine or newspaper articles written by travel writers about their establishments, and we have indicated that in the listing. Articles written about the inns may be available either from the source as a reprint, through libraries or from the inn itself.

Comments from guests

Over the years, we have collected reams of guest comments about thousands of inns. Our files are filled with these documented comments. At the end of some descriptions, we have included a guest comment received about that inn.

Inspections

Each year we travel across the country visiting hundreds of inns. Since 1981, we have had a happy, informal team of Inn travelers and prospective innkeepers who report to us about new Bed & Breakfast discoveries and repeat visits to favorite inns.

Although our staff usually sees hundreds of inns each year, inspecting inns is not the major focus of our travels. We visit as many as possible, photograph them and meet the innkeepers. Some inns are grand mansions filled with classic, museum-quality antiques. Others are rustic, such as reassembled log cabins or renovated barns or stables. We have enjoyed them all and cherish our memories of each establishment, pristine or rustic.

Only rarely have we come across a truly disappointing inn poorly kept or poorly managed. This type of business usually does not survive because an inn's success depends upon repeat guests and enthusiastic word-of-mouth referrals from satisfied guests. We do not promote these types of establishments.

Traveler or tourist

Travel is an adventure into the unknown, full of surprises and rewards. A seasoned "traveler" learns that even after elaborate preparations and careful planning, travel provides the new and unexpected. The traveler learns to live with uncertainty and considers it part of the adventure.

To the "tourist," whether "accidental" or otherwise, new experiences are disconcerting. Tourists want no sur-

prises. They expect things to be exactly as they had envisioned them. To tourists we recommend staying in a hotel or motel chain where the same formula is followed from one locale to another.

We have found that inngoers are travelers at heart. They relish the differences found at these unique bed & breakfasts and country inns. This is the magic that makes traveling from inn to inn the delightful experience it is.

Minimum stays

Many inns require a two-night minimum stay on weekends. A three-night stay often is required during holiday periods.

Cancellations

Cancellation policies are individual for each bed & breakfast. It is not unusual to see 7- to 14-day cancellation periods or more. Please verify the inn's policy when making your reservation.

What if the inn is full?

Ask the innkeeper for recommendations. They may know of an inn that has opened recently or one nearby but off the beaten path. Call the local Chamber of Commerce in the town you hope to visit. They also may know of inns that have opened recently. Please let us know of any new discoveries you make.

We want to hear from you!

We've always enjoyed hearing from our readers and have carefully cataloged all letters and recommendations. If you wish to participate in evaluating your inn experiences, use the **Inn Evaluation Form** in the back of this book. You might want to make copies of this form prior to departing on your journey.

We hope you will enjoy this book so much that you will want to keep an extra copy or two on hand to offer to friends. Many readers have called to purchase our Free Night Certificate book for hostess gifts, birthday presents, or for seasonal celebrations. It's a great way to introduce your friends to America's enchanting country inns and bed & breakfasts.

Visit us online at bnbinns.com!

Would you like more information about the inns listed in this book? For color photos, links to the inns' web sites and more, search our web site at **bnbinns.com**. You'll find thousands of inns from the United States and Canada. We think you'll agree it's "the only online bed & breakfast guide you will ever need.™"

How to Read an Inn Listing

Anytown ❶ *G6*

An American Historic Inn

❷ 123 S Main St
Anytown, VT 12345-6789
(123)555-1212 (800)555-1212 Fax:(123)555-1234

❸ **Circa 1897.** Every inch of this breathtaking inn offers something special. The interior is decorated to the hilt with lovely furnishings, plants, beautiful rugs and warm, inviting tones. Rooms include four-poster and canopy beds combined with the modern amenities such as fireplaces, wet bars and stocked ❹ refrigerators. Enjoy a complimentary full breakfast at the inn's gourmet restaurant. The chef offers everything from a light breakfast of fresh fruit, cereal and a bagel to heartier treats such as pecan peach pancakes and Belgium waffles served with fresh fruit and crisp bacon.

❺ Innkeeper(s): Blayne & Brianna Marks. $125-195. MC, VISA, AX, DS, PC, TC.
❽ 13 rooms with PB, 4 with FP, 1 suite and 1 conference room. Breakfast and afternoon tea included in rates. ❾Types of meals: full breakfast, gourmet breakfast and early coffee/tea. Dinner, picnic lunch, gourmet lunch, banquet service, catering service and room service available. Restaurant on premises.
❿ Beds: KQTC. ⓫Phone, air conditioning, turndown service, ceiling fan, TV and VCR in room. Fax, copier and bicycles on premises. Handicap access. Antiques, fishing, parks, shopping, theater and watersports nearby.
⓬ Location: One-half mile from Route 1A.
⓭ Publicity: *Beaufort, Southern Living, Country Inns, Carolina Style, US Air, Town & Country.*

⓮ *"A dream come true!"*

⓯ **Certificate may be used:** December, January and February, Sunday through Wednesday night only. Good only for four rooms which have a rate of $175.

① Map coordinates
Easily locate an inn on the state map using these coordinates.

② Inn address
Mailing or street address and all phone numbers for the inn.

③ Description of inn
Descriptions of inns are written by experienced travel writers based on visits to inns, interviews and information collected from inns.

④ Drawing of inn
Many listings include artistic renderings.

⑤ Innkeepers
The name of the innkeeper(s).

⑥ Rates
Rates are quoted for double occupancy. The rate range includes off-season rates and is subject to change.

⑦ Payment types accepted
MC-MasterCard, VISA, DS-Discover, AX-American Express, DC-Diner's Club, CB-Carte Blanche, TC-Traveler's Check, PC-Personal Check.

⑧ Rooms
Number and types of rooms available. PB=Private Bath

⑨ Types of meals
This section lists the types of meals that the inn offers. These meals may or may not be included in the rates.

⑩ Beds
King, Queen, Double, Full, Twin, Rollaway, Crib

⑪ Amenities and activities
Information included here describes the meals that might be included in the rates and other amenities or services available at the inn. Nearby activities also are included.

⑫ Location
Type of area where inn is located

⑬ Publicity
Newspapers, magazines and other publications which have featured articles about the inn.

⑭ Guest comments
Comments about the inn from guests.

⑮ Certificate dates
Indicates when inn has agreed to honor the Buy-One-Night-Get-One-Night-Free Certificate™. Always verify availability of discount with innkeeper.

Alabama

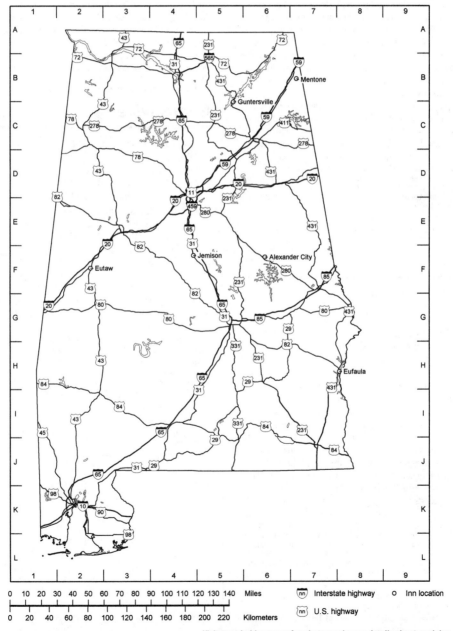

0 10 20 30 40 50 60 70 80 90 100 110 120 130 140 Miles

0   20   40   60   80   100 120 140 160 180 200 220 Kilometers

(nn) Interstate highway   o Inn location

(nn) U.S. highway

Visit www.bnbinns.com for photos and more details about each inn.   1

Alexander City   F6

Mistletoe Bough

497 Hillabee St
Alexander City, AL 35010
(256)329-3717 (877)330-3707
Internet: www.bbonline.com/al/mistletoe

Circa 1890. When Jean and Carlice Payne purchased this three-story Queen Anne Victorian, it had been in the Reuben Herzfeld family for 103 years. Surrounded by two acres of lawns, tall oak and pecan trees as well as a tulip tree, Victorian Pearl bushes, camellias and brilliant azaleas, the home has a three-story turret and cupola, balconies, stained-glass windows and a wraparound porch. The porch ceiling is painted sky blue. A gracious foyer features tung-and-groove wainscoting and opens to a ladies' parlor on one side and a gentlemen's parlor on the other. Fresh flowers, antiques and lace curtains are mixed with traditional and antique Victorian and European furnishings. Upon arrival, guests are pampered with refreshments and homemade cookies (frequently with ingredients from Mistletoe's fruit trees and Carlice's herb garden). Other goodies are always on hand. A four-course breakfast is served in the formal dining room with fine china, crystal and silver. The home is in the National Register.

Innkeeper(s): Jean & Carlice Payne. $85-120. PC, TC. 5 rooms with PB. Breakfast and snacks/refreshments included in rates. Type of meal: Full bkfst. Beds: KQD. Cable TV, phone, turndown service and ceiling fan in room. Air conditioning. Badminton and croquet on premises. Antiquing, golf, shopping and water sports nearby.

Location: City.

Certificate may be used: Jan. 10 through Dec. 10, Sunday through Thursday. Based on availability. Void during holidays and special events.

Eufaula   H8

Kendall Manor Inn

534 W Broad St
Eufaula, AL 36027-1910
(334)687-8847 Fax:(334)616-0678
Internet: www.bbonline.com/al/kendallmanor
E-mail: kmanorinn@mindspring.com

Circa 1872. At night, the lights through the Italianate mansion's floor-to-ceiling windows promise a warm welcome. In the National Register, the home's elaborate facade includes columns around the veranda and etched ruby glass. Sixteen-foot ceilings, French gold-leaf cornices, gleaming wood floors, wallpapers, Oriental carpets and appropriate antiques create a comfortable yet elegant decor. Breakfast in the formal dining room may include poached pears in raspberry sauce, pumpkin apple bread, Sunrise Eggs and cranberry coffee cake. Candlelight dinners are available by advance reservation. You may wish to add your name along with those of guests as far back as 1894 onto the walls of the belvedere after enjoying a tour of the home by the gracious hosts.

Innkeeper(s): Barbara & Tim Lubsen. $99-149. MC, VISA, AX, DS, PC, TC. 6 rooms with PB, 6 with FP. Breakfast included in rates. Types of meals: Full gourmet bkfst, cont plus and early coffee/tea. Beds: KQD. Cable TV, phone, turndown service and ceiling fan in room. Air conditioning. Fax, copier, bicycles and library on premises. Antiquing, fishing, golf, bird watching, parks, shopping, tennis and water sports nearby.

Location: Small town.

Publicity: *Named one of the top Country Inns by Travel Holiday, Country Inns, Travel & Leisure and Southern Living.*

Certificate may be used: Jan. 30-Nov. 30, Sunday-Thursday.

Eutaw   F2

Kirkwood Plantation

111 Kirkwood Dr
Eutaw, AL 35462-1101
(205)372-9009

Located on more than eight acres of green lawns, pecan trees and azaleas, this is a stately antebellum Greek Revival plantation house. There are eight Ionic columns on the front and side of the house and inside, Italian Carrara marble mantels adorn the fireplaces. Massive mirrors and a Waterford crystal chandelier add to the elegance of the inn's furnishings, most of which are original to the house. The innkeeper gives tours of the plantation along with a mini history lesson on the Civil War and its influence on Kirkwood Plantation.

Innkeeper(s): Sherry Vallides. $99. 6 rooms with PB. Breakfast included in rates. Type of meal: Full bkfst. Air conditioning.

Certificate may be used: Based upon availability.

Guntersville   C5

Lake Guntersville B&B

2204 Scott St
Guntersville, AL 35976-1120
(256)505-0133 Fax:(256)505-0133
Internet: www.bbonline.com/al/lakegunthersville/

Circa 1910. It's just a short walk from this bed & breakfast to Alabama's largest lake where guests can enjoy fishing, boating and more than 900 miles of shoreline. The early turn-of-the-century home is decorated with a variety of antiques. There are lake views from several rooms, and if weather permits, breakfast is served on the veranda  where guests can enjoy the scenery. The veranda also offers wicker chairs and a hammock for those who wish to relax.

Innkeeper(s): Carol Dravis. $55-125. MC, VISA, AX, DS, PC, TC. 8 rooms. Breakfast included in rates. Types of meals: Full gourmet bkfst and early coffee/tea. Beds: KQDT. Cable TV, phone and ceiling fan in room. Air conditioning. Fax and conference areas on premises. Handicap access. Antiquing, fishing, golf, walking trails, live theater, parks, shopping, sporting events, tennis and water sports nearby.

Location: Peninsula.

Publicity: *Huntsville Times, Sun Herald, Mobile Press, Advertiser Gleam and Birmingham News.*

Certificate may be used: Sunday-Thursday, year-round, excluding holidays.

Jemison   *F4*

The Jemison Inn Bed & Breakfast and Gardens

212 Hwy 191
Jemison, AL 35085
(205)688-2055
Internet: www.bbonline.com/al/jemison
E-mail: theinn@scott.net

Circa 1920. Shaded by tall oak trees, this gabled brick home offers flowers and fountains in the inn's gardens, created by the innkeeper, a certified Master Gardener. The arched, wraparound porch is furnished with white antique wicker and plants. Inside, heirloom quality, turn-of-the-century Victorian furnishings fill the rooms. There are marble top tables and collections of vintage musical instruments, Roseville and Waterford crystal. Whirlpool tubs are available, and an inviting swimming pool is open to guests in summer.

Innkeeper(s): Nancy Ruzicka. $75-135. MC, VISA, AX, DC, CB, DS, PC, TC. 3 rooms with PB. Breakfast included in rates. Type of meal: Full bkfst. Beds: KQT. Cable TV, VCR and one whirlpool tub in room. Swimming on premises.

Publicity: *Southern Living, Birmingham News, Prime Time and Birmingham Post-Herald.*

"I've never had a better breakfast anywhere."

Certificate may be used: Jan. 1-Dec. 31, Sunday-Thursday.

Mentone   *B7*

Mentone Inn

Hwy 117, PO Box 290
Mentone, AL 35984
(205)634-4836 (800)455-7470

Circa 1927. Mentone is a refreshing stop for those in search of the cool breezes and natural air conditioning of the mountains. Here antique treasures mingle with modern-day conveniences. Sequoyah Caverns, Little River Canyon and DeSoto Falls are moments away.

Innkeeper(s): Frances & Karl Waller. $70-125. MC, VISA, AX, DS, TC. 12 rooms with PB. Breakfast and afternoon tea included in rates. Types of meals: Full bkfst and early coffee/tea. Beds: QT. TV and ceiling fan in room. Air conditioning. VCR on premises. Antiquing, parks, downhill skiing and water sports nearby.

Location: Mountains.

Publicity: *Birmingham News, Gadsden Times, Daily Sentinel; Jackson County, Weekend Getaways Magazine and Montgomery Advertiser.*

Certificate may be used: Year round, subject to availability.

Alaska

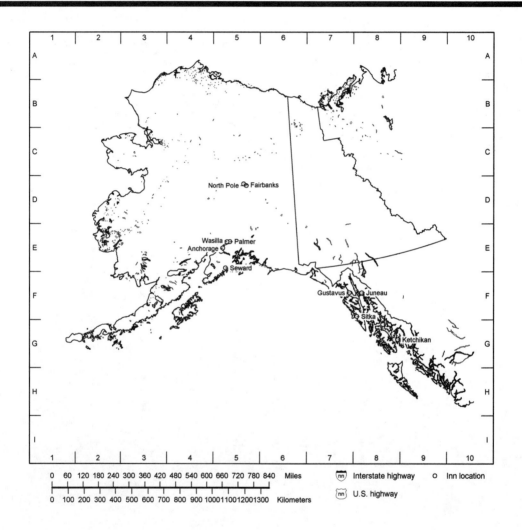

1	2	3	4	5	6	7	8	9	10

North Pole ⊙⊙ Fairbanks

Wasilla ⊙⊙ Palmer
Anchorage ⊙
⊙ Seward

Gustavus ⊙ ⊙⊙ Juneau
⊙ Sitka
⊙ Ketchikan

| Miles | 0 | 60 | 120 | 180 | 240 | 300 | 360 | 420 | 480 | 540 | 600 | 660 | 720 | 780 | 840 |
| Kilometers | 0 | 100 | 200 | 300 | 400 | 500 | 600 | 700 | 800 | 900 | 1000 | 1100 | 1200 | 1300 |

(nn) Interstate highway   ○ Inn location

(nn) U.S. highway

Anchorage   E5

Elderberry B&B

8340 Elderberry St
Anchorage, AK 99502-4245
(907)243-6968 Fax:(907)243-6968

Circa 1974. This homestay bed & breakfast is located in a quiet Anchorage residential neighborhood and offers three homey rooms with comfortable furnishings. It's not unusual to see moose walking around the neighborhood. The home is close to the airport, as well as shops and restaurants.

Innkeeper(s): Norm & Linda Seitz. $60-90. MC, VISA, PC, TC. 3 rooms with PB. Breakfast included in rates. Types of meals: Full bkfst, cont plus, cont and early coffee/tea. Beds: QDT. Phone and VCR in room. Fax, copier and 45" surround sound TV system on premises. Fishing, live theater, parks, shopping, downhill skiing, cross-country skiing and water sports nearby.

Location: City.

"A friendly face, a lovely breakfast, and a good bed made our stay in your wonderful state more enjoyable."

Certificate may be used: Sept. 15-May 15, Sunday-Thursday.

Glacier Bear B&B

4814 Malibu Rd
Anchorage, AK 99517-3274
(907)243-8818 Fax:(907)248-4532
Internet: www.touristguide.com/b&b/alaska/glacierbear
E-mail: gbear@alaska.net

Circa 1986. This cedar-sided contemporary home is located just three blocks from the world's largest float plane lake. The B&B is decorated with a mix of Oriental and Victorian pieces. One bedroom includes a pencil canopy bed, while another offers an antique king bed and a fireplace. The landscaped grounds include an eight-person spa surrounded by ferns, trees and wild berry bushes. The innkeepers offer both a hearty full breakfast or continental fare. Freshly ground coffee, tea, soft drinks and freshly baked cookies are available throughout the day. The innkeepers provide a courtesy van to and from the airport.

Innkeeper(s): Marge Brown & Georgia Taton. $59-100. MC, VISA, AX, DS, PC, TC. 5 rooms, 3 with PB, 1 with FP. Breakfast included in rates. Types of meals: Full gourmet bkfst and early coffee/tea. Beds: KQT. Phone in room. VCR, fax, spa, bicycles and library on premises. Antiquing, fishing, float plane lake, biking, nature walks, parks, shopping, downhill skiing, cross-country skiing, sporting events and water sports nearby.

Location: City.

Certificate may be used: Oct. 1-April 1.

North Country Castle B&B

PO Box 111876, 14600 Joanne Cir
Anchorage, AK 99511
(907)345-7296 Fax:(907)345-7296

Circa 1986. While this modern, Victorian cottage-style home is not actually a castle, guests are treated like royalty. The innkeepers offer two rooms with mountain views, and the Turnagain View Suite, which features a fireplace, double Jacuzzi and private deck. The home, which is surrounded by woods, rests in the foothills of the Chugach Mountains. The innkeepers serve a hearty, traditional breakfast with Alaskan blueberry pancakes or baked French toast, or specialty egg dishes and fresh fruit, juice and reindeer sausage.

Innkeeper(s): Cindy & Wray Kinard. $79-179. MC, VISA, AX, DS, PC, TC. 3 rooms, 1 with FP and 1 suite. Breakfast included in rates. Types of meals: Full gourmet bkfst, cont plus and cont. Beds: QT. Turndown service in room. Fax, copier and library on premises. Fishing, bird sanctuary, wilderness mountain trails, live theater, parks, shopping, downhill skiing, cross-country skiing and sporting events nearby.

Location: Foothills.

Publicity: *Country.*

Certificate may be used: Sept. 15-Oct. 14, April 15-May 15.

The Oscar Gill House

1344 W 10th Ave
Anchorage, AK 99501-3245
(907)258-1717 Fax:(907)258-6613

Circa 1913. This clapboard, Craftsman-style home was built in Knik, Alaska, but later disassembled and moved to Anchorage in 1916. The home is the city's oldest, and the innkeepers have kept the decor simple and comfortable, with antiques here and there, as well as vintage furnishings from the '30s and '40s. Down comforters and bathrooms stocked with toiletries are a few of the special touches guests will find. Breakfasts are served up in the cheery dining room, which features panoramic photos of Anchorage and the home in its original location. Innkeeper Susan Lutz prepares a variety of entrees for the morning meal, including items such as sourdough French toast or Mexican egg casseroles accompanied by freshly ground coffee, a selection of teas and homemade hot chocolate.

Innkeeper(s): Mark & Susan Lutz. $75-95. MC, VISA, AX, PC. 3 rooms, 1 with PB. Breakfast included in rates. Type of meal: Full bkfst. Beds: QDT. Phone, robes and body shop products in room. Fax, bicycles, child care and skis on premises. Fishing, courthouse, tennis, hockey, live theater, parks, downhill skiing, cross-country skiing and sporting events nearby.

Location: Downtown park-Rose Garden.

Certificate may be used: Jan. 2-April 1, Oct. 1 through Nov. 22, Nov. 28 through Dec. 22.

Swan House

6840 Crooked Tree Dr
Anchorage, AK 99516-6805
(907)346-3033 (800)921-1900 Fax:(907)346-3535
Internet: www.alaska.net/~swan1
E-mail: swan1@alaska.net

Circa 1985. If you can plan early, reward yourself by booking the Swan House, a uniquely designed Northwest home offering sweeping views of the city and Mt. McKinley. There's golden oak woodwork, a sunken living room and a dining room filled with Irish country antiques. Moose sometimes wander onto the yard. The innkeepers also offer a waterfront home in Seldovia where you can watch sea otters and bald eagles and fish for salmon.

Innkeeper(s): Judy & Jerry Swanson. $129-179. MC, VISA, AX, DS, PC, TC. 2 rooms with PB. Breakfast included in rates. Types of meals: Full gourmet bkfst and early coffee/tea. Beds: KQT. Cable TV and phone in room. VCR, fax and copier on premises. Golf and parks nearby.

Location: Mountains.

Certificate may be used: Nov. 15-March 15, Sunday-Thursday.

Fairbanks D5

7 Gables Inn

4312 Birch Ln
Fairbanks, AK 99709
(907)479-0751 Fax:(907)479-2229
Internet: www.7gablesinn.com
E-mail: gables7@alaska.net

Circa 1982. Located within walking distance to the University of Alaska and the Chena River, this modern Tudor-style inn, on an acre and a half, has 14 gables. A seven-foot waterfall inside the foyer is the first hint of a memorable stay. There's a two-story, flower-filled solarium and a meeting room. In season, enjoy the spectacular aurora borealis or a white fantasy of snow flakes and dog mushing, then come home to a steaming Jacuzzi tub in your room. If visiting in summer, canoe the river under the midnight sun. The innkeepers received the city's Golden Heart Award for exceptional hospitality.

Innkeeper(s): Paul & Leicha Welton. $50-150. MC, VISA, AX, DC, CB, DS, PC, TC. 15 rooms, 9 with PB, 4 suites, 2 cottages, 2 cabins and 1 conference room. Breakfast and snacks/refreshments included in rates. Type of meal: Full gourmet bkfst. Beds: KQT. Cable TV, phone, VCR and fireplaces in room. Fax, bicycles and library on premises. Antiquing, bicycling, fishing, golf, hiking, museums, parks, shopping, downhill skiing and cross-country skiing nearby.

Location: City.

Certificate may be used: Oct. 1-April 30.

Chena River B&B

1001 Dolly Varden Dr
Fairbanks, AK 99709-3229
(907)479-2532

Located on 10 acres along the Chena River, this inn offers spectacular views of the Northern Lights. Two of the rooms feature views of the river, woodlands and flower garden. (In the winter, moose are frequent visitors to the garden where they nibble its remnants.) The inn features hardwood floors, Oriental rugs and an enormous collection of books, many about Alaska. The innkeeper is a native Alaskan and has extensive knowledge about his home state. Breakfast features sourdough pancakes, bacon, sausage, eggs and fresh fruit salad. Guests are welcome to use the kitchen for snacks. Fairbanks is four miles. University museum, Riverboat Discovery and historic Chena Pump House are close-by.

Innkeeper(s): Steve Mease. $40-100. 5 rooms, 1 with PB. Breakfast included in rates. Type of meal: Full bkfst. Beds: QDT. TV in room.

Publicity: *Washington Post and Northwest Living.*

"Felt just like home, but the food was better."

Certificate may be used: September through May.

Frog Pond B&B

131 Frog Pond Cir
Fairbanks, AK 99712
(907)457-4006 (888)457-4006 Fax:(907)457-4020
Internet: frogpondbb.com
E-mail: frogpondbb@usa.net

Circa 1983. Shaded by birch trees, this split-level, ranch-style home offers two rooms and one bath and is sometimes available as an apartment. The owners offer a country breakfast, but there is a full kitchen and laundry in the apartment. This homestay accommodation is convenient for families with chil-

dren, located in the country a few minutes from Fairbanks.

Innkeeper(s): Dave & Kerinda Johnson. $70-185. MC, VISA, TC. 4 rooms and 1 suite. Breakfast included in rates. Type of meal: Full bkfst. Beds: QT. VCR, fax and copier on premises. Shopping, downhill skiing and sporting events nearby.

Location: City.

Certificate may be used: Oct. 1-April 30, all.

Gustavus F7

Glacier Bay's Bear Track Inn

PO Box 255
Gustavus, AK 99826
(907)697-3017 (888)697-2284 Fax:(907)697-2284
Internet: www.beartrackinn.com
E-mail: beartrac@aol.com

Circa 1997. This handsomely designed log inn offers a huge lobby with inspiring views of the water, mountains, forests and meadows. There are suede couches, a walk-around fireplace and moose antler chandeliers. Attractively furnished guest rooms are in keeping with the log decor and offer views and great comfort. Among the inn's specialities are Dungeness Crab, Alaskan spotted prawns, salmon and halibut. Favorite activities include a wide variety of chartered fishing excursions, whale watching, hiking, glacier tours, kayaking, "flight-seeing," golf and mountain biking. In addition, helicopter tours, mini-cruise ship excursions and bear viewing can be arranged by the innkeepers. The inn is family owned and operated.

Innkeeper(s): Mike Olney & Alice Park. $293. MC, VISA, AX, DS, PC, TC. 14 rooms with PB and 1 conference room. Breakfast, afternoon tea, dinner, snacks/refreshments and picnic lunch included in rates. Types of meals: Full bkfst and early coffee/tea. Beds: Q. Turndown service and hair dryer in room. VCR, fax, copier, library, child care, croquet, horse shoes, volleyball and badminton on premises. Handicap access. Fishing, golf, Glacier Bay National Park, parks, shopping and water sports nearby.

Pets allowed: Notify in advance, $100 deposit.

Location: Country.

Certificate may be used: May 13 to July 1, Sunday-Saturday.

Juneau F8

Alaska Wolf House

1900 Wickersham Ave, PO Box 21321
Juneau, AK 99802
(907)586-2422 (888)586-9053 Fax:(907)586-9053
Internet: www.alaskawolfhouse.com
E-mail: akwlfhs@ptialaska.neb

Circa 1972. With cedar log construction, this home offers a quiet location one mile from the downtown area. Antiques, art and a fireplace are features. Guest rooms offer sea and mountain views. Alaskan omelets and other Northwest cuisine are served in the Glassroom and Greatroom. The innkeepers provide day tours on their wooden yacht, the M/V Peregrine, by advance arrangement.

Innkeeper(s): Philip & Clovis Dennis. $65-145. MC, VISA, PC, TC. 6 rooms, 1 with PB, 1 with FP and 3 suites. Breakfast, afternoon tea and snacks/refreshments included in rates. Type of meal: Full gourmet bkfst. Beds: QT. Cable TV, ceiling fan and VCR in room. Fax, copier, spa, bicycles and library on premises. Handicap access. Antiquing, fishing, golf, museums, live theater, parks, shopping, downhill skiing, cross-country skiing, tennis and water sports nearby.

Location: Mountains.

Certificate may be used: October-March, Sunday-Friday.

Pearson's Pond Luxury Inn & Garden Spa

4541 Sawa Cir
Juneau, AK 99801-8723
(907)789-3772 (888)658-6358 Fax:(907)789-6722
Internet: www.juneau.com/pearsons.pond
E-mail: pearsons.pond@juneau.com

Circa 1985. From this award-winning B&B resort, guests can view glaciers, visit museums and chance their luck at gold-panning streams, or simply soak in a hot tub surrounded by a lush forest and nestled next to a picturesque duck pond. Blueberries hang over the private decks of the guest rooms. A full, self-serve breakfast is provided each morning in the kitchenettes. Nearby trails offer excellent hiking, and the Mendenhall Glacier is within walking distance. The sports-minded will enjoy river rafting or angling for world-class halibut and salmon.

Innkeeper(s): Steve & Diane Pearson. $89-249. MC, VISA, AX, DC, CB, DS, PC, TC. 3 rooms with PB, 3 with FP and 2 suites. Breakfast, afternoon tea and snacks/refreshments included in rates. Types of meals: Cont plus and early coffee/tea. Beds: Q. Cable TV, phone and VCR in room. Fax, copier, spa, bicycles, library and boats on premises. Antiquing, fishing, live theater, parks, shopping, downhill skiing, cross-country skiing and water sports nearby.

Location: Glacier/lake.

Publicity: *Good Housekeeping, Cross Country Skier, Alaska Journal of Commerce, Senior Voice, Sunset, Atlantic Monthly, Pacific Northwest, Style and Cooking Light.*

"A definite 10!"

Certificate may be used: October through April, Monday through Thursday.

Silverbow Inn & Restaurant

120 2nd St
Juneau, AK 99801-1215
(907)586-4146 (800)586-4146 Fax:(907)586-4242
Internet: www.silverbowinn.com
E-mail: silverbo@alaska.net

Circa 1914. For more than 100 years, Alaska's oldest operating bakery has been located here. The innkeepers, an architect and urban planner, have brought the building to life with a luxurious lobby and romantic restaurant. The inn offers B&B and European-style pension rooms. Freshly made bagels, breads and pastries are served at breakfast. Within two blocks are the state capitol, convention center, waterfront and shopping district.

Innkeeper(s): Jill Ramiel/Ken Alper. $78-135. MC, VISA, AX. 6 rooms with PB and 2 conference rooms. Breakfast, afternoon tea and snacks/refreshments included in rates. Types of meals: Cont and early coffee/tea. Beds: QT. Cable TV, phone and VCR in room. Fax, copier, library, social hour with wine and cheese and bakery on premises. Antiquing, fishing, live theater, parks, shopping, downhill skiing and cross-country skiing nearby.

Location: Urban, historic district.

Publicity: *Travel & Leisure, Destinos and Frommers Choice 2000.*

Certificate may be used: Oct. 1-April 1.

Ketchikan   G8

D & W's "Almost Home" B&B

412 D-1 Loop Rd N
Ketchikan, AK 99901-9202
(907)225-3273 (800)987-5337 Fax:(907)247-5337
Internet: www.ktn.net/krs/
E-mail: krs@ktn.net

Circa 1981. These rural B&B accommodations, located a few minutes' drive north of Ketchikan, provide guests with a completely outfitted apartment. Guests can choose from two- or

three-bedroom units. Each offers linens, phone, cable TV, washer and dryer and a gas barbecue grill. A special welcome is extended to fishing parties. Ketchikan is known for its excellent salmon and halibut fishing and offers several fishing derbies each summer.

Innkeeper(s): Darrell & Wanda Vandergriff. $75. MC, VISA, AX, DS, PC, TC. 4 cottages. Breakfast included in rates. Type of meal: Cont plus. Beds: KDT. Cable TV, phone, gas BBQ-Full outfitted kitchen and laundry facility in room. Fishing, totem poles and native culture, live theater, parks, shopping and water sports nearby.

Location: Wooded secluded lot.

Certificate may be used: Oct. 1-March 31.

North Pole   D5

Birch Tree B&B

3104 Dyke Rd
North Pole, AK 99705-6801
(907)488-4667 Fax:(907)488-4667

Few people can boast that they've weathered the rugged North Pole country. At this modern-style B&B, however, visitors can enjoy the wilderness of Alaska in pleasant, inviting surroundings. The innkeepers offer four individually decorated rooms, one includes a hide-a-bed and separate dressing area. The den offers plenty of amenities, including a fireplace, books about Alaska and a pool table. Guests are invited to use the inn's barbecue grill and picnic table. The stunning Northern Lights often are visible from the home, and it's not unusual to see a moose or two roaming the grounds.

Innkeeper(s): Pat Albrecht. $50-75. MC, VISA. 4 rooms. Breakfast included in rates. Type of meal: Full bkfst.

Certificate may be used: October-April (anytime).

Palmer   E5

Colony Inn

325 E Elmwood
Palmer, AK 99645-6622
(907)745-3330 Fax:(907)746-3330

Circa 1935. Historic buildings are few and far between in Alaska, and this inn is one of them. The structure was built to house teachers and nurses in the days when President Roosevelt

 was sending settlers to Alaska to establish farms. When innkeeper Janet Kincaid purchased it, the inn had been empty for some

time. She restored the place, including the wood walls, which now create a cozy ambiance in the common areas. The 12 guest rooms are nicely appointed, and 10 include a whirlpool tub. Meals are not included, but the inn's restaurant offers breakfast and lunch. The inn is listed in the National Register.

Innkeeper(s): Janet Kincaid. $80. MC, VISA, AX, DS, PC, TC. 12 rooms with PB. Type of meal: Full bkfst. Beds: QDT. Cable TV and phone in room. Handicap access. Antiquing, fishing, golf, parks, shopping, downhill skiing, cross-country skiing and tennis nearby.

Location: City.

"Love the antiques and history."

Certificate may be used: Oct. 1-May 1.

Seward
E5

The Farm B&B Inn

PO Box 305
Seward, AK 99664-0305
(907)224-5691 Fax:(907)224-5698
Internet: www.alaskan.com/thefarm/
E-mail: thefarm@ptialaska.net

Circa 1906. The main house of this bed & breakfast is located on 20 acres of farm-like setting with plenty of fields to enjoy. Rooms are spacious and comfortable, one includes a king-size, canopied bed. The innkeepers also offer sleeping cottages. A three-room, economy bungalow and kitchenette suites are available, as well. Guests may use the laundry facilities. The home is three miles outside of Seward.

$65-105. MC, VISA, DS. 15 rooms, 11 with PB and 2 suites. Breakfast included in rates. Type of meal: Cont plus. Beds: KQT. Cable TV and phone in room. VCR and fax on premises. Handicap access. Fishing, parks, shopping, cross-country skiing and water sports nearby.

Pets Allowed.

Certificate may be used: September-May.

Sitka
F8

Alaska Ocean View B&B

1101 Edgecumbe Dr
Sitka, AK 99835-7122
(907)747-8310 Fax:(907)747-3440
Internet: www.sitka-alaska-lodging.com
E-mail: alaskaoceanview@gci.net

Circa 1986. This Alaska-style all-cedar home is located in a quiet neighborhood just one block from the seashore and the Tongass National Forest. Witness the spectacular Alaska sunsets over Sitka Sound and surrounding islands. On clear days, view Mt. Edgecumbe, which is an extinct volcano located on Kruzoff Island and resembles Mt. Fuji. Binoculars are kept handy for guests who take a special treat in viewing whales and eagles.

Innkeeper(s): Carole & Bill Denkinger. $99-159. MC, VISA, AZ, PC, TC. 3 rooms with PB, 2 suites and 1 conference room. Breakfast, afternoon tea and snacks/refreshments included in rates. Types of meals: Continental-plus breakfast, full breakfast, full gourmet breakfast and early coffee/tea. Beds: King, Queen, double and twin. Cable TV, phone, turndown service, ceiling fan, VCR and microwave in room. Fax, copier, spa and library on premises. Antiquing, fishing, hiking, whale watching, historical attractions, wild life viewing, live theater, parks, shopping and water sports nearby.

Pets allowed: Kept outdoors in kennel only.

Location: Mountains.

Certificate may be used: October through March, except sell out convention dates if any, and Dec. 24 through Jan. 1 not valid.

Wasilla
E5

Wasilla Lake B&B

961 N Shore Dr
Wasilla, AK 99654-6546
(907)376-5985 Fax:(907)376-5985
E-mail: ginc@ttialaska.net

Circa 1974. This bed and breakfast offers mountain views, an award-winning garden and a location on the north shore of Wasilla Lake. Overlooking the lake is a two-story cottage with a circular stairway, or you can choose from three guest rooms in the main house or a private apartment with fireplace and living room. Art and antiques enhance the decor and views. The inn has a dock, and guests can arrange for a pontoon boat tour or salmon fishing. Anchorage is 45 miles away.

Innkeeper(s): Laverne & Arlene Gronewald. $65-130. MC, VISA. 7 rooms, 3 with PB, 1 with FP, 1 suite and 1 cottage. Breakfast included in rates. Types of meals: Full gourmet bkfst, cont and early coffee/tea. Beds: KQDT. Cable TV, phone and VCR in room. Fax, copier, swimming and bicycles on premises. Antiquing, fishing, golf, national and State parks, live theater, parks, shopping, downhill skiing, cross-country skiing and water sports nearby.

Location: Mountains.

Certificate may be used: January to January.

Arizona

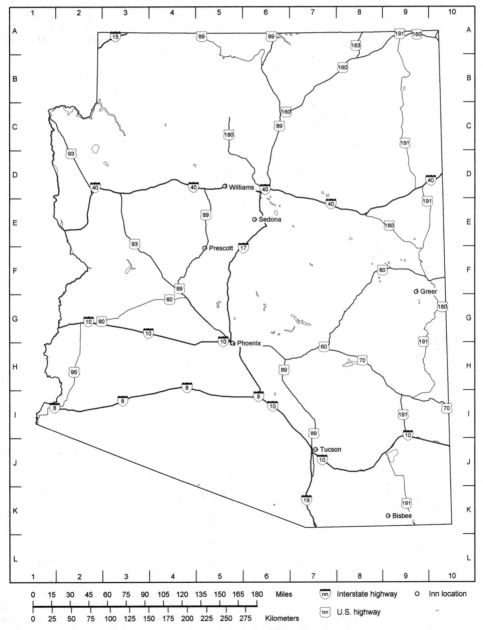

0 15 30 45 60 75 90 105 120 135 150 165 180 Miles

0 25 50 75 100 125 150 175 200 225 250 275 Kilometers

nn Interstate highway   o Inn location

nn U.S. highway

Bisbee   K9

Bisbee Grand Hotel, A B&B Inn

61 Main Street, Box 825
Bisbee, AZ 85603
(520)432-5900 (800)421-1909
Internet: www.bisbeegrand.com

Circa 1906. This National Register treasure is a stunning example of an elegant turn-of-the-century hotel. The hotel originally served as a stop for mining executives, and it was restored back to its Old West Glory in the 1980s. Each of the rooms is decorated with Victorian furnishings and wallcoverings. The suites offer special items such as clawfoot tubs, an antique Chinese wedding bed, a fountain or four-poster bed. The Grand Western Salon boasts the back bar fixture from the Pony Saloon in Tombstone. After a full breakfast, enjoy a day touring the Bisbee area, which includes mine tours, museums, shops, antiquing and a host of outdoor activities.

Innkeeper(s): Bill Thomas. $55-175. MC, VISA, AX, DS. 9 rooms and 5 suites. Breakfast included in rates. Type of meal: Full bkfst.
Certificate may be used: Excluding Jan. 15-May 15, excluding weekends and holidays. Offer does not apply to suites.

Greer   F9

White Mountain Lodge

PO Box 143
Greer, AZ 85927-0143
(520)735-7568 (888)493-7568 Fax:(520)735-7498

Circa 1892. This 19th-century lodge affords views of Greer meadow and the Little Colorado River. The guest rooms are individually decorated in a Southwestern or country style. The common rooms are decorated with period antiques,

Southwestern art and Mission-style furnishings. The Lodge's living room is an ideal place to relax with its stone fireplace. While dining on the hearty breakfasts, guests not only are treated to entrees that range from traditional country fare to the more gourmet, they also enjoy a view from the picture window. The cookie jar is always filled with homemade goodies and hot drinks are available throughout the day. Small pets are allowed, although certain restrictions apply. The inn is near excellent hiking trails.

Innkeeper(s): Charles & Mary Bast. $85-145. MC, VISA, AX, DC, DS, PC, TC. 7 rooms with PB, 1 with FP, 6 cabins and 1 conference room. Breakfast and snacks/refreshments included in rates. Types of meals: Full gourmet bkfst, country bkfst, veg bkfst and early coffee/tea. Beds: KQD. TV, ceiling fan, VCR and jetted tubs in room. Fax, copier and spa on premises. Antiquing, art galleries, fishing, golf, hiking, museums, shopping, downhill skiing and cross-country skiing nearby.
Pets allowed: One small pet per unit. Must not be left unattended in room.
Location: Mountains.
Publicity: Independent & Arizona Republic, Arizona Foothills. and Channel 3.
Certificate may be used: Sunday-Thursday (no holidays).

Phoenix   H5

The Harmony House B&B Inn

7202 N 7th Ave
Phoenix, AZ 85021
(602)331-9554 (877)331-9554 Fax:(602)395-0528
Internet: www.bbonline.com/az/harmony
E-mail: harmonybb2@aol.com

Circa 1934. In a Tudor style set back on a shaded green lawn, this bed and breakfast was built as a doctor's home, once surrounded by 60 acres of citrus trees. Most rooms are decorated in antiques. Ask for the Rose Room for a rose-carved, king-size bed, crystal chandelier and Victorian decor. French toast and homemade banana bread are frequently served for breakfast, presented in the dining room.

Innkeeper(s): Don & Fito. $65-115. MC, VISA. 5 rooms with PB and 1 suite. Breakfast and snacks/refreshments included in rates. Type of meal: Full bkfst. Beds: KQD. Cable TV in room. Air conditioning. VCR, fax and copier on premises. Handicap access. Amusement parks, golf, live theater, parks, shopping, sporting events and water sports nearby.
Location: City.

"The house has great character. I wish we had more time to spend here. Will definitely recommend Harmony House to friends."
Certificate may be used: April 15 to Dec. 30, Sunday to Thursday.

Maricopa Manor

15 W Pasadena Ave
Phoenix, AZ 85013
(602)274-6302 (800)292-6403 Fax:(602)266-3904
Internet: www.maricopamanor.com
E-mail: mmanor@getnet.com

Circa 1928. The secluded Maricopa Manor stands amid palm trees on an acre of land. The Spanish-style house features four graceful columns in the entry hall, an elegant living room with a marble mantel and a music room. The spacious suites are decorated with satins, lace, antiques and leather-bound books. Guests may relax on the deck, on the patio, by the pool or in the gazebo spa.

Innkeeper(s): Mary Ellen & Paul Kelley. $89-229. MC, VISA, AX, DS, PC, TC. 6 suites, 3 with FP. Breakfast included in rates. Type of meal: Cont plus. Beds: KQ. Cable TV, phone, ceiling fan and VCR in room. Air conditioning. Fax, copier, spa, swimming and library on premises. Handicap access. Amusement parks, antiquing, golf, live theater, parks, shopping, sporting events, tennis and water sports nearby.
Location: City.
Publicity: Arizona Business Journal, Country Inns, AAA Westways, San Francisco Chronicle, Focus and Sombrero.

"I've stayed 200+ nights at B&Bs around the world, yet have never before experienced the warmth and sincere friendliness of Maricopa Manor."
Certificate may be used: June 1-Aug. 31.

Prescott   F5

Dolls & Roses B&B

109 N Pleasant St
Prescott, AZ 86301
(520)776-9291 (800)924-0883 Fax:(520)778-2642
Internet: www.fourcorners.com/az/inns/dollsroses

Circa 1883. Each of the guest rooms at this historic Victorian is decorated with a rose theme. The English Rose is a spacious room with a sitting area decorated with a love seat and antique rocker. The Rose Garden has an antique clawfoot tub. In addition to the four rooms in the main house, guests can stay in the guest house. The historic home is decorated in Victorian style with antiques and a collection of porcelain dolls. A full breakfast is served each morning featuring specialty egg dishes, freshly baked pastries, homemade muffins and fresh fruit.

Innkeeper(s): Daryl & Pam O'Neil. $89-109. MC, VISA, PC, TC. 5 rooms with PB, 1 cottage and 1 conference room. Breakfast included in rates. Types of meals: Full bkfst and cont. Beds: KQ. Ceiling fan in room. Air conditioning. VCR on premises. Antiquing, art galleries, bicycling, fishing, golf, hiking, horseback riding, live theater, museums, parks, shopping, tennis and water sports nearby.

Location: Mountains.

Certificate may be used: Monday-Thursday, excluding holidays and special events.

Juniper Well Ranch

PO Box 11083
Prescott, AZ 86304-1083
(520)442-3415

Circa 1991. A working horse ranch sits on the front 15 acres of this 50-acre, wooded property, which is surrounded by the Prescott National Forest. Guests are welcome to feed the horses, and children have been known to take a ride on a tractor with innkeeper David Bonham. Two log cabins and the ranch house sit farther back on the land where families can enjoy nature, "unlimited" hiking and seclusion. A summer house is available for ranch guests. It has no walls, a sloping roof with skylights and a fire pit. Guest pets, including horses, are welcome on an individual basis.

Innkeeper(s): David Bonham & Gail Ball. $100. MC, VISA, AX, DC, DS, PC, TC. 3 cabins with PB, 3 with FP. Type of meal: Full bkfst. Beds: QDT. Ceiling fan and full kitchen in room. Stables, library, pet boarding, child care, working horse ranch, unlimited hiking, horse feeding and summer house on premises. Handicap access. Antiquing, fishing, golf, live theater, parks, shopping and cross-country skiing nearby.

Pets allowed: Well mannered guest pets, including horses, welcome on an individual basis.

Location: Ranch.

Certificate may be used: Sunday through Thursday, all year. Holidays excluded.

Mount Vernon Inn

204 N Mount Vernon Ave
Prescott, AZ 86301-3108
(520)778-0886 Fax:(520)778-7305
Internet: prescottlink.com/mtvrnon/index.htm
E-mail: mtvrnon@primenet.com

Circa 1900. This turn-of-the-century inn, listed in the National Register, is known as one of Prescott's "Victorian Treasures." There are four spacious guest rooms in the main house. There are three country cottages, as well. The inn is just a few blocks from the town square.

Innkeeper(s): Michele & Jerry Neumann. $95-125. MC, VISA, DS, TC. 4 rooms with PB and 3 cottages. Beds: QDT. Phone and cottages with kitchens and cable TV in room. Collection of movies on premises. Handicap access. Antiquing, restaurants, live theater, parks and shopping nearby.

Location: Small town USA.

Certificate may be used: Nov. 1-March 31. Sunday through Thursday only. Exclude holidays.

Pleasant Street Inn

142 S Pleasant St
Prescott, AZ 86303-3811
(520)445-4774 (877)226-7128

Pleasant Street Inn was moved to its present site, in the heart of historic Prescott, in an effort to save the home from demolition. Rooms at this quaint, Victorian inn are decorated with a touch of whimsy with floral prints and chintz fabrics. The PineView Suite boasts a sitting room and fireplace. Another suite includes a sitting room and private, covered deck. Prescott, which served twice as the state capital, offers a variety of museums and art galleries to explore, as well as the historic Court House Square. Nearby Prescott National Forest is a perfect place to enjoy hiking, climbing and other outdoor activities.

Innkeeper(s): Donna & Bruce Chadderdon. $89-135. MC, VISA, AX, DS, TC. 4 rooms with PB. Breakfast included in rates. Type of meal: Full bkfst. Beds: KQT.

Certificate may be used: Nov. 1-March 31, Sunday through Thursday, excluding holidays and special events.

Prescott Pines Inn

901 White Spar Rd
Prescott, AZ 86303-7231
(520)445-7270 (800)541-5374 Fax:(520)778-3665
Internet: www.prescottpinesinn.com
E-mail: info@prescottpinesinn.com

Circa 1934. A white picket fence beckons guests to the veranda of this comfortably elegant country Victorian inn, originally the Haymore Dairy. There are masses of fragrant pink roses, lavenders and delphiniums, and stately ponderosa pines that tower above the inn's three renovated guesthouses, which were once shelter for farm hands. A three-bedroom, two-bath on-site chalet that sleeps up to eight guests is perfect for a family or group. Eight of the eleven rooms are equipped with kitchenettes and three have fireplaces. The acre of grounds includes a garden fountain and romantic tree swing. A full breakfast is offered at an additional charge.

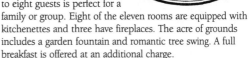

Innkeeper(s): Jean Wu & Michael Acton. $65-249. MC, VISA. 11 rooms with PB, 3 with FP and 1 guest house. Types of meals: Full bkfst and early coffee/tea. Beds: KQ. Cable TV, phone and ceiling fan in room. Air conditioning. Fax and copier on premises. Antiquing, hiking, hiking, live theater, parks and shopping nearby.

Location: Mountains.

Publicity: Sunset, Arizona Republic News and Arizona Highways.

"The ONLY place to stay in Prescott! Tremendous attention to detail."

Certificate may be used: Sept. 15 to June 15; Sunday to Thursday (exclude holidays and Ponderosa Guesthouse rooms). Subject to availability other time periods.

Sedona E6

A Touch of Sedona

595 Jordan Rd
Sedona, AZ 86336-4143
(520)282-6462 (800)600-6462 Fax:(520)282-1534
Internet: www.touchsedona.com
E-mail: touch@sedona.net

Circa 1989. This California ranch-style inn offers red rock views from its great room or deck. The innkeepers serve full breakfasts of eggs Florentine, Belgian waffles or Sedona Toast.

After trying one of the area attractions such as a swoosh down Slide Rock, a visit to the ancient cliff dwellings, hiking or biking, come home to a room such as the Roadrunner. It features a king-size lodge-pole four-poster bed, kitch-enette, fireplace and views of Wilson Mountain. The B&B is within walking distance to galleries, restaurants, shops, museums and trails.

Innkeeper(s): Sharon & Bill Larsen. $129-159. MC, VISA, AX, DS, PC, TC. 5 rooms, 1 with FP. Breakfast included in rates. Types of meals: Full gourmet bkfst and early coffee/tea. Beds: KQ. Cable TV and ceiling fan in room. Air conditioning. Fax and library on premises. Antiquing, fishing, golf, hiking, biking, live theater, parks, shopping and tennis nearby.

Location: Mountains.

Certificate may be used: All year, Sunday through Thursday only, excluding holiday periods.

The Graham B&B Inn/Adobe Village

150 Canyon Circle Dr
Sedona, AZ 86351-8676
(520)284-1425 (800)228-1425 Fax:(520)284-0767
Internet: www.sedonasfinest.com
E-mail: graham@sedona.net

Circa 1985. If the stunning Sedona scenery isn't enough to draw you to this popular Arizona getaway spot, this four-star, four-diamond bed & breakfast is sure to entice you. Theme rooms, suites and casitas are decorated in a variety of styles from Southwest to Victorian.

Amenities include Jacuzzis, bath fireplaces, waterfall showers, private balconies or decks, bread makers and CD players. Bathrooms are stocked with bubble bath and lotions, and there are irons, hair dryers, curling irons and robes. The innkeepers get the day off to a perfect start with a bountiful breakfast. The creative breakfast menus include items such as fanned pears with almond sauce, breakfast wraps, pecan waffles with praline sauce, bread pudding muffins and freshly ground and brewed coffee. Afternoon refreshments are served and in the evening a cookie jar is filled.

Innkeeper(s): Roger & Carol Redenbaugh. $169-369. MC, VISA, AX, DS, PC, TC. 10 rooms with PB, 10 with FP, 1 suite, 4 cottages and 1 conference room. Breakfast, afternoon tea and snacks/refreshments included in rates.

Types of meals: Full bkfst and early coffee/tea. Beds: KQT. Cable TV, phone, turndown service, ceiling fan, VCR, robes, ironing board, iron and dryer in room. Air conditioning. Fax, copier, spa, swimming, bicycles and library on premises. Antiquing, fishing, golf, sedona views, jeep tours, Indian ruins, live theater and shopping nearby.

Location: Sedona Red Rock Country.

Publicity: *Bon Appetit, Honeymoon Magazine, National Geographic Traveler, Country Inns and Travel & Leisure.*

Certificate may be used: Jan. 2-Feb. 1; July 5-Aug. 30; Dec. 1-20, Sunday through Thursday.

Territorial House, An Old West B&B

65 Piki Dr
Sedona, AZ 86336-4345
(520)204-2737 (800)801-2737 Fax:(520)204-2230
Internet: www.oldwestbb.sedona.net
E-mail: oldwest@sedona.net

Circa 1970. This red rock and cedar two-story ranch home, nestled in the serene setting of Juniper and Cottonwood, is a nature lover's delight. Guests can see families of quail march through the landscape of cacti, plants and red rock or at night hear the call of coyotes. More than 40 western movies were filmed in Sedona.

Innkeeper(s): John & Linda Steele. $115-165. MC, VISA, AX. 4 rooms with PB, 1 with FP and 1 suite. Breakfast and snacks/refreshments included in rates. Type of meal: Full bkfst. Beds: KQ. Cable TV, phone and VCR in room. Air conditioning. Spa and bicycles on premises. Antiquing, fishing, live theater, parks, shopping, downhill skiing and water sports nearby.

Certificate may be used: July-August, December-January. Sunday-Thursday. No holidays. $160 for best room available.

Tucson J7

Agave Grove B&B Inn

800 West Panorama Rd
Tucson, AZ 85704-3912
(520)797-3400 (888)822-4283 Fax:(520)797-0980
Internet: www.bbchannel.com/bbc/p602873.esp
E-mail: agavebb@azstarnet.com

Circa 1976. This private home is built in a hacienda style with courtyard, waterfall-fed swimming pool in view of the mountains, putting green and gazebo-like ramada on its two acres. There is a flagstone fireplace in the family room and guests enjoy playing billiards and board games. One of the guest rooms offers a Jacuzzi. Breakfast specialties may include caramelized French toast, fruit and sausage. Drive to the University of Arizona's observatory and museums as well as many other area attractions.

Innkeeper(s): John & Denise Kiber. $60-165. MC, VISA, AX, DS, PC, TC. 5 rooms, 1 with PB and 3 suites. Breakfast and snacks/refreshments included in rates. Types of meals: Full gourmet bkfst and early coffee/tea. Beds: KQ. Cable TV, phone, ceiling fan and microwaves in suites in room. Air conditioning. VCR, fax, copier, spa, swimming, library, child care and billiard table on premises. Handicap access. Amusement parks, antiquing, golf, botanical gardens, day trips, live theater, parks, shopping, downhill skiing, sporting events and tennis nearby.

Location: Suburban desert estate.

Publicity: *Arizona Daily Star.*

Certificate may be used: May 1-Oct. 31.

Jeremiah Inn B&B

10921 E Snyder Rd
Tucson, AZ 85749-9066
(520)749-3072 (888)750-3072
Internet: www.bbonline.com/az/jeremiah

Circa 1995. The Catalina Mountains serve as a backdrop for this modern Santa Fe-style home. There are five guest rooms, four offer a sitting area, and all are decorated in Southwestern style. Guest rooms have a private entrance, and there is a refrigerator for guest use. Breakfast at the inn is an event. The menu might include a lavish selection of fresh fruit, a Southwestern-style potato saute and homemade cinnamon toast. Guests enjoy use of a pool and a spa. Guests can spend the day hiking, golfing, shopping or exploring the scenic area on horseback.

Innkeeper(s): Bob & Beth Miner. $90-120. MC, VISA, AX, PC, TC. 5 rooms with PB. Breakfast included in rates. Type of meal: Early coffee/tea. Beds: Q. TV, phone, ceiling fan, table and chairs and VCR available in room. Air conditioning. VCR, spa, swimming and private outside entry to guest wing on premises. Antiquing, golf, live theater, parks and tennis nearby.

Location: Suburban ranch.

"We felt like honored guests at your inn-truly an oasis in the desert."
Certificate may be used: May 1 to Jan. 1, holidays excluded.

The Suncatcher

105 N Avenida Javalina
Tucson, AZ 85748-8928
(520)885-0883 (877)775-8355 Fax:(520)885-0883

Circa 1991. From the picture window in your opulent guest room, you'll enjoy views of mountains and desert scenery. The bedchambers include beautiful furnishings, such as a bed draped in a luxurious canopy. A fireplace or double Jacuzzi tub are options. Guests enjoy the use of a heated pool and hot tub in the backyard patio, as well as use of four acres. All of Tucson's sites and shops are nearby.

Innkeeper(s): JC & Carleen Carlson. $80-145. MC, VISA, AX, PC. 4 rooms with PB, 1 with FP. Breakfast included in rates. Type of meal: Full bkfst. Beds: Q. Cable TV, phone, turndown service and VCR in room. Air conditioning. Fax, copier, spa, swimming and bar on premises. Handicap access. Golf, hiking, birding, parks and shopping nearby.

Location: Mountains.

Certificate may be used: July 1-Sept. 1.

Williams   D5

The Sheridan House Inn

460 E Sheridan Ave
Williams, AZ 86046
(520)635-9441 (888)635-9345 Fax:(520)635-1005
Internet: www.thegrandcanyon.com/sheridan/
E-mail: egardner@primenet.com

Circa 1988. This two-story house offers porches and decks from which to enjoy its two acres of ponderosa forest. For a queen-size bed and views of pine trees ask for the Willow Room or for sunset views the Cedar Room is the best choice. It also features a bay widow. CD stereo systems and cable TV are in all the rooms. Full breakfasts are served, often on the upstairs deck. A fitness room and den with pool table and piano are open to guests, and there is a seasonally available hot tub, as well. The Grand Canyon is 45 minutes away and the Grand Canyon Railroad is within a half mile.

Innkeeper(s): Steve & Evelyn Gardner. $95-225. MC, VISA, AX, DS, PC, TC. 11 rooms, 8 with PB, 2 suites and 1 conference room. Breakfast and snacks/refreshments included in rates. Beds: KQDT. Cable TV, phone, ceiling fan and VCR in room. Fax, copier, spa, library and hiking trail on premises. Antiquing, fishing, golf, horseback riding, Grand Canyon Railroad, parks, shopping, downhill skiing, cross-country skiing and tennis nearby.

Pets allowed: Must not be left alone.

Location: Mountains.

Publicity: *Williams Grand Canyon News and KPAZ Flagstaff.*

Certificate may be used: Feb. 15 to April 30, any day in that period of time.

Arkansas

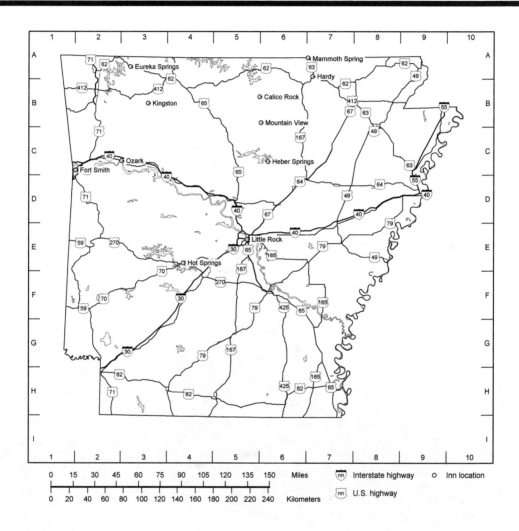

0 15 30 45 60 75 90 105 120 135 150 Miles

0 20 40 60 80 100 120 140 160 180 200 220 240 Kilometers

Interstate highway   O   Inn location

U.S. highway

Calico Rock   B5

Happy Lonesome Log Cabins

HC 61, Box 72
Calico Rock, AR 72519-9102
(870)297-8764
Internet: www.bbonline.com/ar/hlcabins
E-mail: hlcabins@centuryinter.net

Circa 1988. The two rustic log cabins are located on a wooded, 194-acre property on the bluff above White River. The interiors are simple and comfortable and include a sleeping loft, small kitchen and wood stove. Continental fare is placed in the kitchenette so guests may enjoy a light breakfast at their leisure. The favorite activity is relaxing on the porch and enjoying the views of river and woodland. Calico Rock is an interesting historic town nearby, and there are plenty of old buildings and shops to browse. Explore the Ozark National Forest, Blanchard Springs Caverns, or try one of the area's popular river activities, such as float trips, canoeing or fishing.

Innkeeper(s): Carolyn & Christian J. Eck. $65-95. MC, VISA, AX, DS, PC, TC. 4 rooms, 2 with PB. Breakfast included in rates. Type of meal: Cont plus. Beds: QD. Ceiling fan and kitchenette in room. Air conditioning. Amusement parks, antiquing, fishing, golf, live theater, parks, shopping, tennis and water sports nearby.

Location: Forest.

Certificate may be used: Sunday through Thursday.

Eureka Springs   A3

1884 Bridgeford House B&B

263 Spring St
Eureka Springs, AR 72632-3154
(501)253-7853 (888)567-2422 Fax:(501)253-5497
Internet: www.bridgefordhouse.com
E-mail: bridgefordbb@earthlink.net

Circa 1884. Victorian charm abounds at this Queen Anne-Eastlake-style home, located in the heart of the historic district. The Southern hospitality begins upon arrival as guests are treat-

ed to homemade pecan pralines. Fresh flowers add extra romance to rooms that include a variety of amenities. Several rooms include double jacuzzis, a fireplace and decks. Gourmet breakfasts are served on antique china and silver. The bed & breakfast is just a few blocks from gift bou-

tiques, antique shops, spas, restaurants and much more. The innkeepers offer discounted rates for those who wish to enjoy a spa treatment.

Innkeeper(s): Henry & Linda Thornton. $85-200. MC, VISA, AX, DS. 5 rooms with PB and 2 suites. Breakfast included in rates. Types of meals: Full bkfst and early coffee/tea. Beds: KQ. Cable TV and fans in room. Air conditioning. VCR on premises. Antiquing, fishing, golf, live theater, shopping and water sports nearby.

Location: Less than one hour from Branson, MO.

Publicity: *Times Echo Flashlight, Arkansas National Tour Guide and Country Almanac.*

"You have created an enchanting respite for weary people."

Certificate may be used: Jan. 1-Oct. 1; Nov. 1-Dec. 31, Sunday-Thursday.

A Cliff Cottage & The Place Next Door, A Bed & Breakfast Inn

42 Armstrong St
Eureka Springs, AR 72632-3608
(501)253-7409 (800)799-7409
Internet: www.cliffcottage.com
E-mail: cliffctg@aol.net

Circa 1892. In the heart of Historic Downtown, this Painted Lady Eastlake Victorian is listed in the National Register of Historic Places. A favorite among honeymooners, accommodations also are available in a Victorian replica named The Place Next Door. Guest rooms include a double Jacuzzi, mini-refrigerator stocked with complimentary champagne and beverages, and all rooms have private decks. The inn offers gourmet candlelight dinners, Victorian picnic lunches and sunset dinner cruises served aboard a 24-foot pontoon boat, which explores the area's romantic coves. Guests enjoy golf and tennis privileges at Holiday Island, which is located five miles away. The inn recently received the "Garden of the Season" award.

Innkeeper(s): Sandra Smith. $120-195. MC, VISA, PC. 5 rooms with PB, 1 with FP, 3 suites and 1 cottage. Breakfast included in rates. Types of meals: Full gourmet bkfst and early coffee/tea. Beds: KQ. Cable TV, ceiling fan and VCR in room. Air conditioning. Library on premises. Amusement parks, antiquing, fishing, golf, live theater, parks, shopping, tennis and water sports nearby.

Pets allowed: small dogs only, $20 charge.

Location: Mountains.

Publicity: *Arkansas Democrat Gazette, Country Inns, Modern Bride and Southern Living.*

Certificate may be used: Jan. 2 to Feb. 28, Monday to Thursday; Nov. 1 to Dec. 15, Monday to Thursday.

Arsenic & Old Lace B&B Inn

60 Hillside Ave
Eureka Springs, AR 72632-3133
(501)253-5454 (800)243-5223 Fax:(501)253-2246
Internet: www.eureka-usa.com/arsenic
E-mail: arseniclace@prodigy.net

Circa 1992. This bed & breakfast is a meticulous reproduction of Queen Anne Victorian style, and it offers five guest rooms decorated with antique Victorian furnishings. Popular with honeymooners, the guest rooms offer whirlpool tubs, balconies and fireplaces. The inn's gardens complement its attractive exterior, which includes a wraparound veranda and stone wall. Its location in the historic district makes it an excellent starting point for a sightseeing stroll or shopping.

Innkeeper(s): Gary & Phyllis Jones. $140-185. MC, VISA, AX, DS, PC, TC. 5 rooms with PB, 5 with FP and 2 suites. Breakfast and snacks/refreshments included in rates. Type of meal: Full gourmet bkfst. Beds: KQT. Cable TV, ceiling fan, VCR, private patios, robes and five with Jacuzzi in room. Air conditioning. Fax, copier and library on premises. Handicap access. Antiquing, fishing, golf, music festivals, car festivals, Passion Play, live theater, parks, shopping, tennis and water sports nearby.

Location: City.

Publicity: *Gail Greco's Romance of Country Inns, Houston Chronicle, Kiplinger's Personal Finance Magazine, Oklahoma Living. and KLSM-TV.*

"It was well worth the 1,000 miles we traveled to share your home for a short while...thanks for a four-star vacation."

Certificate may be used: Jan. 20-Sept. 30, Sunday through Thursday only. November-December, Sunday through Thursday only.

Candlestick Cottage

6 Douglas St
Eureka Springs, AR 72632-3416
(501)253-6813 (800)835-5184
Internet: www.candlestickcottageinn.com
E-mail: candleci@ipa.net

Circa 1888. Woods and foliage surround this scenic country home, nestled just a few blocks from Eureka Springs historic district. Guests are sure to discover a variety of wildlife strolling by the home, including an occasional deer. Breakfasts are served on the tree-top porch, which overlooks a waterfall and fish pond. The morning meal begins with freshly baked muffins and fresh fruit, followed by an entree. Innkeepers Bill and Patsy Brooks will prepare a basket of sparkling grape juice and wine glasses for those celebrating a special occasion. Guest rooms are decorated in Victorian style, and some include two-person Jacuzzis.

Innkeeper(s): Bill & Patsy Brooks. $65-109. MC, VISA, AX, DS, TC. 6 rooms with PB. Breakfast included in rates. Type of meal: Full bkfst. Beds: Q. Cable TV and Jacuzzi in room. Air conditioning. Antiquing, fishing, parks and shopping nearby.

Location: City.

Certificate may be used: Jan. 1-March 31, Sunday-Thursday.

Heart of The Hills Inn

5 Summit St
Eureka Springs, AR 72632
(501)253-7468 (800)253-7468

Circa 1883. Two suites and a Victorian cottage comprise this antique-furnished homestead located just four blocks from downtown. Suites have been restored and decorating in an 1880s style. The cottage is located beside the inn and is decorated in Victorian-country style. The cottage also offers a private deck that overlooks the garden. The village trolley stops at the inn, but the inn is within walking distance of town.

Innkeeper(s): James & Kathy Vanzandt. $80-119. MC, VISA, AX, PC, TC. 3 rooms with PB, 2 suites and 1 cottage. Breakfast and snacks/refreshments included in rates. Types of meals: Full gourmet bkfst, cont and early coffee/tea. Beds: KD. Cable TV in room. Air conditioning. Spa, library, private decks, double Jacuzzi and quiet garden area on premises. Handicap access. Antiquing, art galleries, fishing, golf, live theater, shopping and water sports nearby.

Location: Historic Loop.

Publicity: *Carroll County Tribune's Peddler and KHOG (ABC) Fayetteville/Fort Smith.*

"The decor and atmosphere of your inn was breathtaking; we were able to relax and not want for a thing."

Certificate may be used: November through September, Sunday through Thursday (may call at last minute).

The Heartstone Inn & Cottages

35 King's Hwy
Eureka Springs, AR 72632-3534
(501)253-8916 (800)494-4921 Fax:(501)253-5361
Internet: www.heartstoneinn.com
E-mail: heartinn@ipa.net

Circa 1903. A white picket fence leads to this spacious Victorian inn and its pink and cobalt blue wraparound porch filled with potted geraniums and Boston ferns. Located on the Eureka Springs historic loop the inn offers English country antiques, private entrances and pretty linens. Private Jacuzzis, refrigerators and VCRs are available. Pamper your self in the inn's massage therapy studio. Walk to shops, restaurants and

galleries or hop on the trolley to enjoy all the pleasures of the town. Golf privileges at a private club are extended to guests. The New York Times praised the inn's cuisine as the "Best Breakfast in the Ozarks."

Innkeeper(s): Rick & Cheri Rojek. $75-129. MC, VISA, AX, DS, PC, TC. 12 rooms with PB, 1 with FP, 3 suites and 2 cottages. Breakfast included in rates. Type of meal: Full gourmet bkfst. Beds: KQ. Cable TV and ceiling fan in room. Air conditioning. Fax, spa, massage therapy and gift shop on premises. Amusement parks, antiquing, fishing, golf, restaurants, live theater, parks, shopping and water sports nearby.

Location: Historic town.

Publicity: *Innsider, Arkansas Times, New York Times, Arkansas Gazette, Southern Living, Country Home, Country Inns and USA Today.*

"Extraordinary! Best breakfasts anywhere!"

Certificate may be used: Sunday through Wednesday arrivals during November through April. Other times, last minute only.

Pond Mountain Lodge & Resort

1218 Hwy 23 South
Eureka Springs, AR 72632-9709
(501)253-5877 (800)583-8043 Fax:(501)253-9087
Internet: www.eureka-usa.com/pondmtn/

Circa 1954. There's no shortage of activities for guests to enjoy at this lodge, built as a family summer retreat for the inventor of the Toni Home Permanent. Try fishing at one of the two ponds, enjoy horseback riding, use the swimming pool, shoot pool in the game room or hike along trails within the 150 acres. There are five suites, each individually decorated with contemporary, comfortable furnishings. Four suites include a fireplace, and all have a Jacuzzi tub. There also is a two-bedroom cabin with a Jacuzzi and a fireplace.

Innkeeper(s): Judy Jones. $100-140. MC, VISA, DS, PC, TC. 5 suites, 4 with FP and 2 cabins. Types of meals: Full gourmet bkfst, country bkfst and early coffee/tea. Beds: KQ. TV, ceiling fan, VCR, jacuzzis, microwaves and original arts in room. Air conditioning. Swimming, stables, library, video library and kitchens on premises. Handicap access. Antiquing, fishing, golf, passion play, national forests, rivers, live theater, shopping, sporting events and water sports nearby.

Location: Mountains.

Publicity: *Eureka Springs Times-Echo.*

Certificate may be used: Monday, Tuesday, Wednesday, Nov. 10 through Feb. 28, (excepting Dec. 23-Jan. 2).

Taylor-Page Inn

33 Benton St
Eureka Springs, AR 72632-3501
(501)253-7315

Within easy walking distance of downtown restaurants, shopping and trolley, this turn-of-the-century Square salt-box inn features Victorian and country decor in its three suites and rooms. Guests often enjoy relaxing in the inn's two sitting rooms. The suites offer ceiling fans, full kitchens and sun decks. The inn offers convenient access to antiquing, fishing, museums and parks.

Innkeeper(s): Jeanne Taylor. $85-100. MC, VISA. 3 suites. Breakfast included in rates. Type of meal: Cont. Cable TV, phone and ceiling fan in room. Air conditioning. Antiquing and shopping nearby.

Location: City.

Certificate may be used: January-March, anytime. April through December, Sunday through Thursday. Children welcome.

Fort Smith
C2

Thomas Quinn Apartment Suites

815 N B St
Fort Smith, AR 72901-2129
(501)782-0499

Circa 1863. Nine suites with kitchenettes are available at this inn, which in 1916 added a second story and stately columns to its original structure. Located on the perimeter of Fort Smith's historic district, it is close to the art center, historic sites, museums and restaurants. Several state parks are within easy driving distance. Early morning coffee and tea are served.

Innkeeper(s): Melody Conley. $65-100. MC, VISA, AX, DC, CB, DS, TC. 9 suites. Type of meal: Early coffee/tea. Cable TV, phone and VCR in room. Air conditioning. Hot tub on premises. Amusement parks, antiquing, fishing, parks, shopping and water sports nearby.

Pets allowed: Inquire first.

Certificate may be used: All year.

Hardy
A7

Hideaway Inn B&B

84 W Firetower Rd
Hardy, AR 72542-9598
(870)966-4770 (888)966-4770
Internet: www.bbonline.com/ar/hideaway/

Circa 1980. For those seeking solitude, this contemporary home is an ideal place to hide away, surrounded by more than 370 acres of Ozark wilderness. There are walking trails, a private fishing pond, swimming pool and playground area on the premises for guests to enjoy. There are three guest rooms in the house, and for those needing even more privacy, the innkeeper offers a private log cabin with two bedrooms, two bathrooms and a room that serves as a living, dining and kitchen area. The gourmet breakfasts include such items as homemade granola, freshly baked breads and peach upside-down French toast. For those celebrating a special occasion, the innkeeper can create unique packages.

Innkeeper(s): Julia Baldridge. $55-125. MC, VISA, AX, DS, PC, TC. 5 rooms, 3 with PB and 1 cabin. Breakfast and snacks/refreshments included in rates. Types of meals: Full bkfst, cont and early coffee/tea. Beds: Q. Ceiling fan in room. VCR, swimming and fishing pond on premises. Antiquing, fishing, live theater, parks, shopping and water sports nearby.

Location: Rural Area.

Publicity: *Southern Living.*

"This is a great place to look at the stars without the interference of the city lights."

Certificate may be used: Jan. 1-Dec. 31, Sunday-Thursday.

The Olde Stonehouse B&B Inn

511 Main St
Hardy, AR 72542-9034
(870)856-2983 (800)514-2983 Fax:(870)856-4036
Internet: www.bbonline.com/ar/stonehouse/
E-mail: oldestonehouse@centurytel.net

Circa 1928. The stone fireplace gracing the comfortable living room of this former banker's home is set with fossils and unusual stones, including an Arkansas diamond. Lace tablecloths, china and silver make breakfast a special occasion. Each room is decorated to keep the authentic feel of the Roaring

'20s. The bedrooms have antiques and ceiling fans. Aunt Jenny's room boasts a clawfoot tub and a white iron bed, while Aunt Bette's room is filled with Victorian-era furniture. Spring River is only one block away and offers canoeing, boating and fishing. Old Hardy Town caters to antique and craft lovers. The innkeepers offer "Secret Suites," located in a nearby historic home. These romantic suites offer plenty of amenities, including a Jacuzzi for two. Breakfasts in a basket are delivered to the door each morning. The home is listed in the National Register. Murder-mystery weekends, romance packages, golf, canoeing and fly-fishing are available.

Innkeeper(s): Peggy Volland. $69-125. MC, VISA, AX, DS, PC, TC. 6 rooms with PB and 2 suites. Breakfast and snacks/refreshments included in rates. Types of meals: Full bkfst and early coffee/tea. Beds: QDT. Ceiling fan in room. Air conditioning. VCR, fax, copier, spa, bicycles, library, guest refrigerator, coffee service and phones on premises. Antiquing, fishing, museums, fly fishing school and guide available, murder mystery weekends, live theater, parks, shopping and water sports nearby.

Location: Small town.

Publicity: *Memphis Commercial Appeal, Jonesboro Sun and Vacations.*

"For many years we had heard about 'Southern Hospitality' but never thought it could be this good. It was the best!"

Certificate may be used: November-April, anytime except special events. May-October, Sunday-Thursday.

Heber Springs
C6

Anderson House Inn

201 E Main ST
Heber Springs, AR 72543-3116
(501)362-5266 (800)264-5279 Fax:(501)362-2326
Internet: www.bbonline.com/Ar/Anderson
E-mail: innkeeper@cswnet.com

Circa 1880. The original section of this welcoming two-story inn was built by one of Heber Springs' founding citizens. The main structure of the inn was built to house a theater, and the home also has enjoyed use as a schoolhouse, doctor's clinic and, when the second story was added, a hotel. Rooms are decorated in a cozy, country motif with bright colors and handmade prints. Historic Spring Park is just across the street offering pleasant scenery for the inn's guests as well as a variety of activities.

Innkeeper(s): Terry Bryant. $75-120. MC, VISA, AX, DS, PC, TC. 16 rooms with PB, 1 with FP and 2 conference rooms. Breakfast included in rates. Types of meals: Full bkfst and early coffee/tea. Beds: QDT. Ceiling fan in room. Air conditioning. VCR, fax and library on premises. Antiquing, fishing, parks, shopping and water sports nearby.

Location: Ozark Foothills, River & Lake.

Publicity: *Arkansas Democrat, Arkansas Times, Sun-Times, ESPN (The Fishing Hole) and KAIT 8.*

Certificate may be used: Year-round, excluding holidays.

Hot Springs E4

Stitt House B&B Inn

824 Park Ave
Hot Springs, AR 71901
(501)623-2704 Fax:(501)623-2704
Internet: www.bbonline.com/ar/stitthouse/
E-mail: stittbb@hsnp.com

Circa 1875. Two acres of gardens and greenery surround this 6,000-square-foot Victorian, the oldest home in Hot Springs. Fine antiques decorate the library, parlor and other public areas of the house. Guest room offerings include a king-size canopy bed and Jacuzzi tub. Breakfast is served in your room or on the veranda or dining room. There is a heated swimming pool.

Innkeeper(s): Linda & Horst Fischer. $95-110. MC, VISA, AX, DS. 4 rooms, 3 with PB and 1 suite. Breakfast included in rates. Types of meals: Full gourmet bkfst and early coffee/tea. Beds: K. Cable TV, turndown service, ceiling fan, robes and ironing board in room. Air conditioning. VCR, fax, copier, swimming and library on premises. Antiquing, fishing, golf, art galleries, live theater, parks, shopping, tennis and water sports nearby.

Location: Mountains.

Publicity: *Southern Living and Dallas Morning News.*

"The atmosphere was charming and we were spoiled with the breakfast in bed."

Certificate may be used: Sunday-Wednesday.

Kingston B3

Fool's Cove Ranch B&B

HCR 30 Box 198
Kingston, AR 72742-9608
(501)665-2986 Fax:(501)665-2372
E-mail: klobster@aol.com

Circa 1979. Situated in the Ozarks' Boston Mountain range, this 6,000-square-foot farmhouse, part of a family farm, offers 160 acres of field, meadow and forest. Guests who have had their horses test negative on a Coggins test may bring them along and utilize the farm's corrals. Guests may angle for bass or catfish in the pond. Favorite gathering spots are the roomy parlor and the outdoor hot tub. Guests can check out the stars at the ranch's observatory. Area attractions include the Buffalo National River, and several fine fishing spots.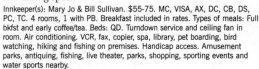

Innkeeper(s): Mary Jo & Bill Sullivan. $55-75. MC, VISA, AX, DC, CB, DS, PC, TC. 4 rooms, 1 with PB. Breakfast included in rates. Types of meals: Full bkfst and early coffee/tea. Beds: QD. Turndown service and ceiling fan in room. Air conditioning. VCR, fax, copier, spa, library, pet boarding, bird watching, hiking and fishing on premises. Handicap access. Amusement parks, antiquing, fishing, live theater, parks, shopping, sporting events and water sports nearby.

Pets allowed: Must make prior arrangements.

Location: Country.

Certificate may be used: May 1 to Dec. 15.

Little Rock E5

The Empress of Little Rock

2120 Louisiana St
Little Rock, AR 72206-1522
(501)374-7966 (877)374-7966 Fax:(501)375-4537
Internet: www.theEmpress.com
E-mail: hostess@theEmpress.com

Circa 1888. Day lilies, peonies and iris accent the old-fashioned garden of this elaborate, three-story Queen Anne Victorian. A grand center hall opens to a double staircase, lit by a stained-glass skylight. The 7,500 square feet includes a secret card room at the top of the tower. The original owner kept a private poker game going here and he paid local boys to keep an eye out for the authorities, who might close down his gambling  activities. The Hornibrook Room features a magnificent Renaissance Revival bedroom set with a high canopy. The Tower room mini-suite has an Austrian king-size bed. The two-course gourmet breakfasts are served in the dining room. Enjoy a relaxing and romantic soak in the gazebo hot tub in Eve's Garden.

Innkeeper(s): Sharon Welch-Blair & Robert Blair. $115-175. MC, VISA, AX, PC. 5 rooms, 2 with PB, 1 with FP, 3 suites and 1 conference room. Breakfast and snacks/refreshments included in rates. Types of meals: Full gourmet bkfst, cont, veg bkfst and early coffee/tea. Beds: KQDT. Cable TV, phone, turndown service, ceiling fan, luxury robes, complimentary liquors and antique stove w/gas logs in room. Central air. VCR, fax, copier, library, feather beds and complimentary liquor on premises. Antiquing, art galleries, bicycling, fishing, golf, hiking, horseback riding, live theater, museums, parks, shopping, sporting events, tennis and water sports nearby.

Location: Historic district.

Publicity: *National Geographic Traveler, Nation's Business, Victorian Home, Victorian Decorator & Life Styles, Southern Living and Home and Garden Television.*

"Staying at the Empress of Little Rock was a 'dream come true!' We've read about and admired it for years. It was definitely a trip to a more gracious time—one that we should all try to implement more in our daily lives."

Certificate may be used: Jan. 4-March 31 and June 15-Aug. 15, selected rooms only, any night, no holidays.

Hotze House

1619 Louisiana St
Little Rock, AR 72206-1429
(501)376-6563

Circa 1900. Upon its completion, this grand neoclassic mansion was noted as one of the state's finest homes. Opulent restored woodwork, a fireplace and a staircase carved from a South American mahogany tree grace the impressive front entrance. The home is filled with elegant, period pieces and traditional furnishings. Four of the guest rooms include fireplaces, and despite the turn-of-the-century authenticity, modern amenities of television, telephone and climate control are in each room. The innkeepers strive to make their National Register inn a place for both business travelers and those in search of romance or relaxation. Delectables such as frittatas, poached pears and Belgian waffles are served each morning either in the dining room or conservatory. The innkeepers keep a snack area stocked with hot water, soft drinks, herbal tea, hot chocolate, cheese, fruit and the like.

Innkeeper(s): Suzanne & Steve Gates. $95. MC, VISA, AX, DC, DS, PC, TC. 5 rooms with PB, 4 with FP and 2 conference rooms. Breakfast included in rates. Types of meals: Full bkfst and early coffee/tea. Beds: KQ. Cable TV, phone, turndown service, ceiling fan and computer hookups in room. Air conditioning. VCR, fax, copier and library on premises. Amusement parks, antiquing, live theater, parks, shopping and sporting events nearby.

Certificate may be used: Anytime, based on availability.

Mammoth Spring   A7

Roseland Inn B&B

570 Bethel, PO Box 4
Mammoth Spring, AR 72554-0004
(870)625-3378

Tucked away in a picturesque country town, this Colonial Revival home is just a stone's throw from one of the world's largest natural springs. Innkeeper Jean Pace, a former Mammoth Spring mayor, has decorated her National Register inn with antiques, collectibles and bright flower arrangements. With its reception hall, large front porch and gazebo, the home has served as a site for parties and weddings. Spring River and Mammoth Spring State Park are nearby, and Jean will refrigerate your daily catch.

Innkeeper(s): Jean Pace. $40-45. 4 rooms. Breakfast included in rates. Type of meal: Full bkfst.

Certificate may be used: Monday through Thursday, year round.

Mountain View   B6

Ozark Country Inn

PO Box 1201
Mountain View, AR 72560-1201
(870)269-8699 (800)379-8699

Circa 1906. This historic two-story Federal-style inn is located within a block of Courthouse Square and downtown eateries and shops. A full breakfast is served at 8 a.m. before guests

head out to explore the many attractions offered in the surrounding area, including Blanchard Springs Caverns and the Ozark Folk Center.

Innkeeper(s): Sissie & Don Jones. $55-65. MC, VISA. 6 rooms with PB. Breakfast included in rates. Type of meal: Full bkfst. Beds: QDT. Cable TV and tV in common room in room. Air conditioning. VCR on premises. Antiquing, fishing, ozark Folk Center and Blanchard Springs Caverns, shopping and water sports nearby.

Certificate may be used: March 1-Dec. 1, Sunday through Thursday.

Ozark   C3

1887 Inn B&B

100 E Commercial St
Ozark, AR 72949-3210
(501)667-1121

Circa 1885. At the foot of the Ozarks, this Queen Anne Victorian inn has been lovingly restored to its natural beauty. The inn's accommodations feature names such as the Anniversary Suite, the Rose Room, the Magnolia Room and the Country Room. Each room includes a queen-size bed, with the exception of the Magnolia Room. This bedchamber includes two double beds. The decor features antique Victorian and country furnishings. Receptions, special events and weddings are popular here. With advance reservations, a special candlelight dinner can be arranged. Less than two blocks away is the Arkansas River.

Innkeeper(s): Kay & Dewayne Jones. $60-75. MC, VISA. 4 rooms. Breakfast included in rates. Types of meals: Full bkfst and early coffee/tea. Beds: QD. Antiquing and shopping nearby.

Location: Mountains.

Certificate may be used: Anytime based on availability.

California

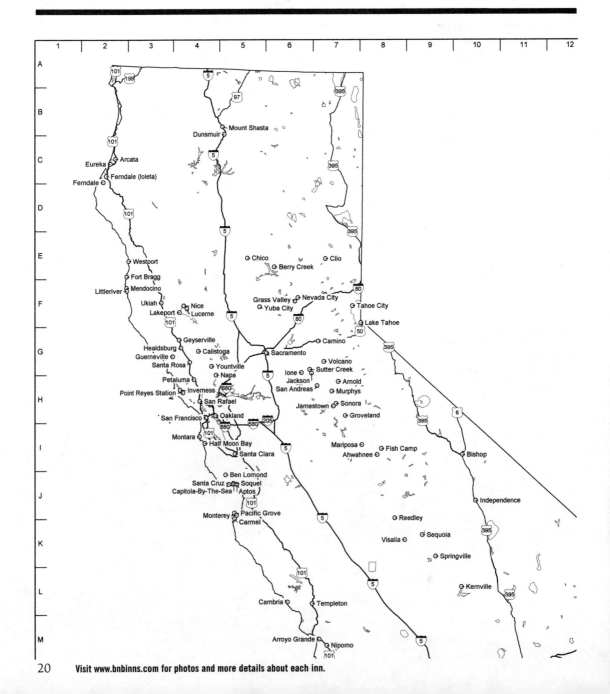

Visit www.bnbinns.com for photos and more details about each inn.

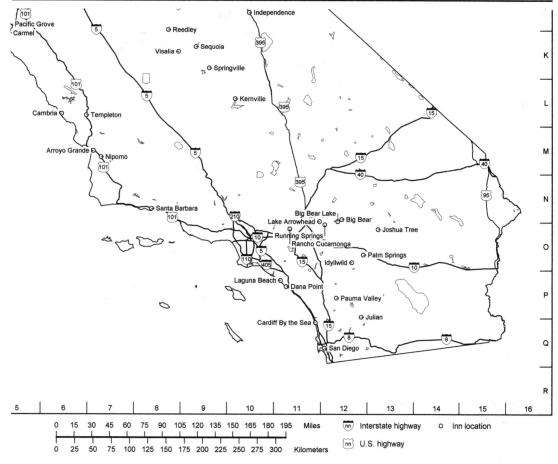

Pacific Grove
Carmel
Independence
Reedley
Sequoia
Visalia
Springville
Kernville
Cambria Templeton
Arroyo Grande Nipomo
Santa Barbara
Big Bear Lake
Lake Arrowhead Big Bear
Running Springs Joshua Tree
Rancho Cucamonga
Palm Springs
Idyllwild
Laguna Beach
Dana Point
Pauma Valley
Julian
Cardiff By the Sea
San Diego

| 5 | 6 | 7 | 8 | 9 | 10 | 11 | 12 | 13 | 14 | 15 | 16 |

| 0 | 15 | 30 | 45 | 60 | 75 | 90 | 105 | 120 | 135 | 150 | 165 | 180 | 195 | Miles |
| 0 | 25 | 50 | 75 | 100 | 125 | 150 | 175 | 200 | 225 | 250 | 275 | 300 | | Kilometers |

nn Interstate highway   o Inn location
nn U.S. highway

Ahwahnee   I8

Apple Blossom Inn B&B

44606 Silver Spur Tr
Ahwahnee, CA 93601
(559)642-2001 (888)687-4281
Internet: www.sierranet.net/web/apple/
E-mail: lhays@sierranet.net.

Circa 1991. A bountiful organic apple orchard surrounds this inn, an attractive country cottage a short distance from Yosemite National Park. Visitors choose either the Red Delicious Room, with its queen and day beds and private entrance, or the Granny Smith Room, with queen bed and private balcony. Both rooms feature ceiling fans, private bath and sitting areas. Guests enjoy the inn's wood-burning stove and the spa overlooking the woods.

Innkeeper(s): Lance, Lynn & Kody Hays. $96-165. MC, VISA, DS, TC. 3 rooms, 2 with PB. Breakfast, afternoon tea and snacks/refreshments included in rates. Types of meals: Full bkfst and early coffee/tea. Beds: QD. TV, turndown service, ceiling fan and VCR in room. Air conditioning. Spa on premises. Antiquing, fishing, live theater, parks, shopping, downhill skiing, cross-country skiing and water sports nearby.

Location: Mountains.

Certificate may be used: Nov. 1-March 30, Sunday-Thursday. Holidays excluded.

Aptos   J5

Bayview Hotel

8041 Soquel Dr
Aptos, CA 95003-3928
(831)688-8654 (800)422-9843 Fax:(831)688-5128
Internet: www.bayviewhotel.com
E-mail: lodging@bayviewhotel.com

Circa 1878. This Victorian hotel is the oldest operating inn on the Monterey Coast. Each of the rooms is decorated with local art, antiques, sitting areas, and some have fireplaces. The inn is just half a mile from beautiful beaches, and a redwood forest is nearby. This inn is an ideal spot for those seeking relaxation or those on a coastal trip. Monterey and San Jose are less than an hour from the hotel, and San Francisco is 90 miles north. Breakfast is served in the inn's dining room, and there is also has an on-site restaurant where weddings, small meetings, family reunions and seminars can be hosted. The hotel is close to an abundance of outdoor activities, as well as Nisene Marks State Park.

Innkeeper(s): Gwen Burkhard. $90-160. MC, VISA, AX, TC. 11 rooms with PB, 2 with FP and 1 suite. Breakfast included in rates. Types of meals: Cont plus and early coffee/tea. Beds: KQD. Cable TV, phone, turndown service and VCR in room. Fax on premises. Amusement parks, antiquing, parks, shopping and water sports nearby.

Publicity: *Mid-County Post and Santa Cruz Sentinel.*

"Thank you so much for all of your tender loving care and great hospitality."

Certificate may be used: Sunday-Thursday nights, all year, excludes holidays and special events.

Mangels House

570 Aptos Creek Rd
Aptos, CA 95003
(831)688-7982
Internet: www.innaccess.com/mangels
E-mail: mangels@cruzio.com

Circa 1886. Claus Mangels made his fortune in sugar beets and built this house in the style of a Southern mansion. The inn, with its encircling veranda, stands on four acres of lawns and orchards. It is bounded by the Forest of Nisene Marks, 10,000 acres of redwood trees, creeks and trails. Monterey Bay is three-quarters of a mile away.

Innkeeper(s): Jacqueline Fisher. $125-165. MC, VISA. 6 rooms with PB, 1 with FP and 1 conference room. Breakfast included in rates. Types of meals: Full bkfst and early coffee/tea. Beds: KQT. Refrigerator and phone available on premises. Antiquing, golf, whale watching, elephant seals, live theater, water sports and wineries nearby.

Location: Mountains.

Publicity: *Inn Serv and Innviews.*

"Compliments on the lovely atmosphere. We look forward to sharing our discovery with friends and returning with them."

Certificate may be used: All year, Sunday-Thursday, (holidays, Christmas etc, excepted) whenever we have other guests staying.

Arcata   C2

Hotel Arcata

.708 9th St
Arcata, CA 95521-6206
(707)826-0217 (800)344-1221 Fax:(707)826-1737
Internet: www.hotelarcata.com

Circa 1915. This historic landmark hotel is a fine example of Beaux Arts-style architecture. Several rooms overlook Arcata's downtown plaza, which is just outside the front door. A variety of rooms are available, each decorated in turn-of-the-century style. All rooms include pedestal sinks and clawfoot tubs. The hotel offers a full-service, renown Japanese restaurant, offering  excellent cuisine, and there are many other fine restaurants within walking distance. Guests also enjoy free use of a nearby full-scale health club. The starting point of Arcata's architectural homes tour is within walking distance of the hotel.

Innkeeper(s): Virgil Moorehead. $90-180. MC, VISA, AX, DC, CB, DS, TC. 31 rooms with PB, 7 suites and 1 conference room. Breakfast included in rates. Type of meal: Cont. Beds: KQT. Cable TV and phone in room. Fax, copier and free health club privileges on premises. Handicap access. State parks, beaches, redwoods, rivers, theater nearby, parks and shopping nearby.

Location: City.

Certificate may be used: Subject to availability.

Arnold   H7

Lodge at Manuel Mill B&B

PO Box 998
Arnold, CA 95223-0998
(209)795-2622

Circa 1950. Overlooking a three-acre lake that comes right up to the wraparound deck, this log lodge was once the site of a 19th-century lumber mill. Some structures on the property are a century old. The 43 acres of woods include sugar cone pines with 18-inch cones, dogwood and wild blackberries, and traces of the mill's narrow gauge rail system. Sounds of the 24-foot waterfall that cascades over rocks may be heard from the rooms that open to the deck. The Lottie Crabtree Room, named for a spirited performer in the Gold Rush days, is a peaceful, cozy retreat. The Mr. Manuel Room basks in 19th-century ambiance with an oak canopy bed and Victorian decor. The innkeepers prepare a hearty breakfast and present guests with a bottle of wine upon arrival. Martha Stewart-type weddings are popular here. Calaveras Big Trees State Park, known for its giant sequoias, is nearby.

Innkeeper(s): Linda Johnson. $100-140. MC, VISA. 5 rooms with PB and 1 suite. Breakfast included in rates. Type of meal: Full bkfst. Beds: KQD. Swimming on premises. Fishing, downhill skiing, cross-country skiing and water sports nearby.

Certificate may be used: Sunday-Thursday, November-April, excludes holidays.

Arroyo Grande   M7

Arroyo Village Inn

407 El Camino Real
Arroyo Grande, CA 93420
(805)489-5926 (800)563-7762
Internet: www.virtualcities.com\ons\ca\c\cac2701.htm

Circa 1984. The travel section of the Los Angeles Times has featured many rave reviews of this award-winning inn, a replica of an English farmhouse, located 15 minutes away from San Luis Obispo. The decor, highlighted by Laura Ashley prints and antiques, is welcoming and nostalgic. In-room spas, fireplaces and VCRs are available in some rooms. Skylights, window seats and balconies combine with country wreaths, baskets and candles to create a romantic ambiance. Rooms are decorated in garden themes, with names such as Forget-Me-Not, Callalily and Spring Bouquet. The gourmet breakfasts feature such items as frittatas, Mexican quiche, Dutch apple pancakes and blackberry cream cheese coffee cake. Complimentary homemade birthday cakes are given to guests who are celebrating, and there's always champagne for anniversaries. Among the many nearby attractions are Hearst Castle, wineries, beautiful beaches and horseback riding.

Innkeeper(s): John & Adriana. $139-375. MC, VISA, AX, DS. 7 suites. Breakfast and snacks/refreshments included in rates. Types of meals: Full gourmet bkfst and early coffee/tea. Beds: KQ. Cable TV, turndown service, robes, hair dryers, ironing boards and some with spas and fireplaces in room. Air conditioning. Hearst Castle, quaint historic villages, 2 miles to the beach, 15 minutes to San Luis Obispo and wineries nearby.

Publicity: *Los Angeles Times, Strictly Business and Telegram Tribune.*

Certificate may be used: Sunday through Thursday, excluding holidays, $198+ suites only.

Ben Lomond J5

Chateau Des Fleurs

7995 Highway 9
Ben Lomond, CA 95005-9715
(408)336-8943 (800)291-9966
Internet: www.chateaudesfleurs.com
E-mail: laura@chateaudesfleurs.com

Circa 1879. Once the home of the Bartlett pear family, this house offers gables, porches and gardens. The Rose Room has an antique clawfoot tub. A private deck is part of the Orchid Room, which features wicker furnishings and orchid watercolors. Breakfast is in the formal dining room and includes entrees such as cheese blintzes and egg dishes. In the early evening wine and hors d'oeuvres are served in the Gallery.

Innkeeper(s): Lee & Laura Jonas. $110-145. MC, VISA, DS, PC, TC. 3 rooms with PB, 2 with FP and 1 suite. Breakfast included in rates. Types of meals: Full bkfst and early coffee/tea. Beds: KQ. Ceiling fan in room. Air conditioning. VCR, fax and copier on premises. Handicap access. Amusement parks, antiquing, fishing, golf, live theater, parks, shopping, sporting events, tennis and water sports nearby.

Location: Mountains.

Certificate may be used: Nov. 1 to May 1, Sunday through Thursday.

Fairview Manor

245 Fairview Ave
Ben Lomond, CA 95005-9347
(831)336-3355 (800)553-8840

Circa 1924. The Santa Cruz Mountains serve as a backdrop at Fairview Manor, set on more than two acres of woods and lush grounds. The tranquil, parklike setting includes little paths that wind through the grounds and you'll find lily ponds and the San Lorenzo River. The home rests on the former site of the Ben Lomond Hotel, which was destroyed by fire in 1906. A prominent San Francisco attorney chose this spot to build his summer home, and the manor stayed in the family until the 1980s when the current innkeepers purchased it. The cozy guest rooms are decorated with antiques. The innkeepers serve a full, country breakfast in a dining room that overlooks the river. Restaurants and the beach are just minutes away.

Innkeeper(s): Nancy Glasson. $119-129. MC, VISA. 5 rooms with PB and 1 conference room. Breakfast and snacks/refreshments included in rates. Type of meal: Full bkfst. Beds: KQ. Sitting area in room. Refrigerator-complimentary drinks on premises. Handicap access. Antiquing, fishing, parks, shopping and water sports nearby.

Location: Mountains.

Certificate may be used: Sunday through Thursday.

Berry Creek E6

Lake Oroville Bed and Breakfast

240 Sunday Dr
Berry Creek, CA 95916-9640
(916)589-0700 (800)455-5253 Fax:(916)589-5313
Internet: lakeoroville.com/lakeoroville
E-mail: lakeinn@cncnet.com

Circa 1970. Situated in the quiet foothills above Lake Oroville, this country inn features panoramic views from the private porches that extend from each guest room. Two favorite rooms are the Rose Petal Room and the Victorian Room, both with lake views and whirlpool tubs. The inn's 40 acres are studded

with oak and pine trees. Deer and songbirds abound.

Innkeeper(s): Cheryl & Ron Damberger. $75-145. MC, VISA, AX, DS, PC, TC. 6 rooms with PB and 1 conference room. Breakfast included in rates. Types of meals: Full bkfst and early coffee/tea. Beds: KQ. Cable TV, phone, turndown service, ceiling fan, VCR, whirlpool tubs and tape player in room. Air conditioning. Fax, copier, spa, library, pet boarding and child care on premises. Handicap access. Antiquing, fishing, golf, live theater, parks, shopping, tennis and water sports nearby.

Pets allowed: On approval.

Location: Lake and valley views.

Publicity: *Oroville Mercury-Register, Chronicle, San Joe Mercury and Most Romantic Weekends.*

Certificate may be used: Sunday-Thursday (except holidays). All year.

Big Bear N12

Gold Mountain Manor Historic B&B

1117 Anita, PO Box 2027
Big Bear, CA 92314
(909)585-6997 (800)509-2604 Fax:(909)585-0327
Internet: www.goldmountainmanor.com
E-mail: info@goldmountainmanor.com

Circa 1928. This spectacular log mansion was once a hideaway for the rich and famous. Eight fireplaces provide a roaring fire in each room in fall and winter. The Lucky Baldwin Room offers a hearth made from stones gathered in the famous Lucky Baldwin mine nearby. In the Clark Gable room is the fireplace Gable and Carole Lombard enjoyed on their honeymoon. Gourmet country breakfasts and afternoon hors d'oeuvres are served. In addition to the guest rooms, there are home rentals.

Innkeeper(s): Trish & Jim Gordon. $125-200. MC, VISA, DS. 6 rooms with PB, 6 with FP, 2 suites and 1 conference room. Afternoon tea and snacks/refreshments included in rates. Types of meals: Full gourmet bkfst and early coffee/tea. Beds: Q. Ceiling fan and jacuzzi in suites in room. VCR, fax, spa, bicycles, library and pool table on premises. Fishing, hiking/forest, parks, downhill skiing, cross-country skiing, sporting events and water sports nearby.

Location: Forest at end of street.

Publicity: *Best Places to Kiss, Fifty Most Romantic Places and Kenny G holiday album cover.*

"A majestic experience! In this magnificent house, history comes alive."

Certificate may be used: January-Dec. 20, non-holiday, Sunday-Thursday.

Big Bear Lake N12

Eagle's Nest B&B

41675 Big Bear Blvd, Box 1003
Big Bear Lake, CA 92315
(909)866-6465 Fax:(909)866-6025
Internet: www.bigbear.com/enbb/
E-mail: enbb@bigbear.com

Circa 1983. Named for the more than 50 American bald eagles that nest in and around Big Bear, this lodgepole pine inn features a river rock fireplace in the parlor. Antiques, bronzed eagles and baskets of flowers provide a warm mountain setting. Surrounded by tall pine trees, the property also includes several cottage suites.

Innkeeper(s): Mark & Vicki Tebo. $75-170. MC, VISA, AX, PC. 10 rooms, 5 with PB, 5 suites and 5 cottages. Breakfast, afternoon tea and snacks/refreshments included in rates. Types of meals: Full bkfst and early coffee/tea. Beds: Q. Cable TV, phone, ceiling fan, microwave and coffee maker in room. VCR and fax on premises. Antiquing, fishing, golf, live theater, parks, shopping, downhill skiing, cross-country skiing and water sports nearby.
Pets allowed: One cottage allows pets.
Location: Mountains.
Publicity: *Los Angeles Times, Sun Living and AM Los Angeles.*
"Each breakfast was delicious and beautiful. A lot of thought and care is obvious in everything you do."
Certificate may be used: Anytime except holidays, subject to availability.

Knickerbocker Mansion Country Inn

869 Knickerbocker Rd
Big Bear Lake, CA 92315
(909)878-9190 (877)423-1180 Fax:(909)878-4248
Internet: www.knickerbockermansion.com
E-mail: knickmail@aol.com

Circa 1920. The inn is one of the few vertically designed log structures in the United States. The inn was built of local lumber by Bill Knickerbocker, the first dam keeper of Big Bear. The inn includes two historic buildings set on two-and-a-half wooded acres, backing to a national forest. Although, the inn offers a secluded setting, the village of Big Bear Lake is within walking distance. The village offers shopping, restaurants, fishing, hiking, mountain biking and excellent downhill skiing.
Innkeeper(s): Stanley Miller & Thomas Bicanic. $110-280. MC, VISA, AX, DS. 9 rooms with PB, 2 suites and 1 conference room. Types of meals: Full bkfst and early coffee/tea. Beds: KQ. TV, phone and VCR in room. Antiquing, bicycling, fishing, hiking, live theater, shopping, downhill skiing and cross-country skiing nearby.
Location: Mountains.
Publicity: *Los Angeles Magazine and Yellow Brick Road.*

"Best breakfast I ever had in a setting of rustic elegance, a quiet atmosphere and personal attention from the innkeepers. The moment you arrive you will realize the Knickerbocker is a very special place."
Certificate may be used: Jan. 30-Nov. 10, Sunday-Thursday.

Truffles, A Special Place

43591 Bow Canyon Rd
Big Bear Lake, CA 92135
(909)585-2772

Romance abounds at this mountain inn, which is decorated in a whimsical, English-country style. Rooms include four-poster or antique beds topped with luxurious feather mattresses. The Queen's Legacy room includes a soaking tub, while the Lady Rose offers a cozy alcove sitting area. Other rooms include special features such as a Palladian window or iron bed decorated with cherubs. Ever true to the inn's name, a truffle is placed on each pillow during the nightly turndown service. Those celebrating special occasions might find flowers or champagne in their rooms. The innkeepers deliver morning coffee or tea to their guests, and serve a lavish breakfast, afternoon tea and desserts in the evenings.
Innkeeper(s): Marilyn Kane. $115-150. MC, VISA. 5 rooms. Breakfast included in rates. Type of meal: Full bkfst.
Certificate may be used: March 1-June 30, Sunday-Thursday, holidays excepted.

Bishop   I10

The Matlick House

1313 Rowan Ln
Bishop, CA 93514-1937
(760)873-3133 (800)898-3133

Circa 1906. This gray and pink home with a double veranda was built by Alan Matlick, one of the area's pioneers. The spacious parlor features a clawfoot settee with massive curved arms, antique recliner, European burled-wood armoire and original cherry-wood fireplace. Rooms boast special pieces such as the white iron bed, Eastlake chair and quilted settee in the Lenna room. Guests will enjoy the home's views of both the Sierra Nevadas and the White Mountains. A hearty American breakfast with eggs, bacon and homemade biscuits is served in the dining room. The Eastern Sierras provide a wealth of activities, year-round catch-and-release fly fishing is within 20 minutes from the home.
Innkeeper(s): Ray & Barbara Showalter. $75-85. MC, VISA, AX, DS, TC. 5 rooms with PB. Breakfast and snacks/refreshments included in rates. Types of meals: Full bkfst, cont plus and early coffee/tea. Beds: QT. Phone and ceiling fan in room. Air conditioning. VCR and fax on premises. Antiquing, fishing, parks, shopping, downhill skiing and cross-country skiing nearby.
Location: Rural.
Publicity: *Inyo Register and Sunset.*

"Like sleeping on a nice pink cloud after our Rock Creek Horse drive."
Certificate may be used: Anytime except last two weeks of May (Mule Days).

Calistoga   G4

Foothill House

3037 Foothill Blvd
Calistoga, CA 94515-1225
(707)942-6933 (800)942-6933 Fax:(707)942-5692
Internet: www.foothillhouse.com
E-mail: gusgus@aol.com

Circa 1892. This country farmhouse overlooks the western foothills of Mount St. Helena. Graceful old California oaks and pockets of flowers greet guests. Each room features country  antiques, a four-poster bed, a fireplace and a small refrigerator. Breakfast is served in the sun room or is delivered personally to your room in a basket. Three rooms offer private Jacuzzi tubs.
Innkeeper(s): Doris & Gus Beckert. $165-300. MC, VISA, AX, DS, PC, TC. 4 suites, 4 with FP. Breakfast and snacks/refreshments included in rates. Types of meals: Full gourmet bkfst and early coffee/tea. Beds: KQT. Cable TV, phone, turndown service, ceiling fan, VCR, robes, bottled water, coffee and tea in room. Air conditioning. Fax, copier and library on premises. Amusement parks, antiquing, fishing, wineries, balloon rides, glider port, health spas, parks, shopping and water sports nearby.
Location: Country, Napa wine region.
Publicity: *Sunset Magazine, San Francisco Examiner, Herald Examiner and Baltimore Sun.*

"Gourmet treats served in front of an open fire. Hospitality never for a moment flagged."
Certificate may be used: December-January, Sunday through Thursday, holidays excluded.

Cambria   L6

The Squibb House

4063 Burton Dr
Cambria, CA 93428-3001
(805)927-9600 Fax:(805)927-9606

Circa 1877. A picket fence and large garden surround this
Victorian inn with its Italianate and Gothic Revival architecture.
Guests may relax in the main parlor, stroll the gardens or sit
and rock on the porch. The home was built by a Civil War veteran and young school teacher. The downstairs once was used
as a classroom while an addition was being made in the town's
school. Each guest room has a fire stove.

Innkeeper(s): Martha. $95-155. MC, VISA, PC, TC. 5 rooms with PB, 5 with
FP. Breakfast included in rates. Types of meals: Cont plus and cont. Beds: Q.
Retail shop in historic 1885 carpentry shop on premises. Antiquing, fishing,
golf, Hearst Castle, wine tasting, galleries, parks and shopping nearby.

Location: Pine covered hills.

Publicity: *Cambrian.*

Certificate may be used: Sunday-Thursday only, November-March, not valid
during holiday weeks.

Camino   G7

The Camino Hotel-Seven Mile House

4103 Carson Rd, PO Box 1197
Camino, CA 95709-1197
(530)644-7740 (800)200-7740 Fax:(530)647-1416

Circa 1888. Once a barracks for the area's loggers, this inn now
caters to visitors in the state's famed gold country. Just east of
Placerville, historic Camino is on the Old Carson Wagon Trail in
Apple Hill. Nine guest rooms are available, including the E.J.
Barrett Room, a
favorite with honey-
mooners. Other
rooms feature names
such as Pony Express,
Stage Stop and Wagon
Train. The family-ori-
ented inn welcomes children, and a local park offers a handy

site for their recreational needs. Popular area activities include
apple picking, antiquing, hot air ballooning, white-water rafting,
llama trekking and wine tasting. The inn also offers a Romance
Package, on-site wine tasting and an in-house masseuse.

Innkeeper(s): Paula Nobert. $65-95. MC, VISA, AX, DS, PC, TC. 9 rooms, 3
with PB and 1 conference room. Breakfast and snacks/refreshments included
in rates. Types of meals: Full bkfst and early coffee/tea. Beds: QDT. Turndown
service and coolers in all rooms in room. Antiquing, fishing, wine tasting,
white-water rafting, hot air ballooning, live theater, parks, shopping, downhill
skiing, cross-country skiing and water sports nearby.

Location: Small agricultural town.

Publicity: *Better Homes & Gardens.*

Certificate may be used: Year-round except Saturday in September, October,
November and December.

Capitola-by-the-Sea   J5

Inn at Depot Hill

250 Monterey Ave
Capitola-by-the-Sea, CA 95010-3358
(831)462-3376 (800)572-2632 Fax:(831)462-3697
Internet: www.innatdepothill.com
E-mail: lodging@innatdepothill.com

Circa 1901. Once a railroad depot, this inn offers rooms with
themes to represent different parts of the world: a chic auberge
in St. Tropez, a romantic French hideaway in Paris, an Italian
coastal villa, a summer home on the coast of Holland and a traditional English garden room, to name a few. Most rooms have
garden patios with hot tubs. The rooms have many amenities,
including a fireplace, white marble bathrooms and featherbeds.
Guests are greeted with fresh flowers in their room. Gourmet
breakfast, tea, wine, hors d' oeuvres and dessert are offered daily.

Innkeeper(s): Suzie Lankes & Dan Floyd. $210-295. MC, VISA, AX, DS, TC.
12 rooms with PB, 12 with FP, 4 suites and 1 conference room. Breakfast
and snacks/refreshments included in rates. Beds: KQT. Cable TV, phone, turndown service and VCR in room. Fax and spa on premises. Handicap access.
Amusement parks, antiquing, fishing, golf, live theater, parks, shopping and
water sports nearby.

Publicity: *Country Inn, Santa Cruz Sentinel, McCalls, Choices & Vacation,
San Jose Mercury News, Fresno & Sacramento Bee, San Francisco, Focus,
American Airline Flight and SF Examiner and Sunset Magazine.*

"The highlight of our honeymoon. Five stars in our book!"

Certificate may be used: Monday-Thursday, November through April.
Excludes holidays and special events and week 52 (Christmas/New Years).

Cardiff-By-The-Sea   Q11

Cardiff-By-The-Sea Lodge

142 Chesterfield Dr
Cardiff-By-The-Sea, CA 92007-1922
(760)944-6474 Fax:(760)944-6841
Internet: www.cardifflodge.com

Circa 1990. Each of the guest rooms at this romantic seaside
retreat features an individual theme. For instance, the Santa
Fe room is decorated with a whitewashed, four-poster log
bed, a hand-crafted fireplace and a large Roman tub. This
ocean view room also includes a wet bar. The Sweetheart
room, with its hand-carved bed, heart-shaped whirlpool tub,
fireplace and ocean view is a perfect place for romantics.
Other rooms feature themes such as "Garden View,"
"Victorian," "Summer" and "Paradise." This inn, which offers
convenient access to San Diego, is listed in "The Best Places
to Kiss in Southern California."

Innkeeper(s): James & Jeanette Statser. $105-375. MC, VISA, AX, DS, TC.
17 rooms with PB, 5 with FP. Breakfast included in rates. Type of meal: Cont
plus. Beds: QD. Cable TV, phone and ocean views in room. Air conditioning.
VCR, fax, copier and spa on premises. Amusement parks, antiquing, fishing,
golf, live theater, parks, shopping, tennis and water sports nearby.

Publicity: *Sunset, LA Times, Jeopardy, Wheel of Fortune and Channel 8
and Cable.*

Certificate may be used: January to June, October to December, excludes
holidays and weekends. Excludes Feb. 14 week, Easter week. Monday-
Thursday only.

Carmel   J5

Cobblestone Inn

PO Box 3185
Carmel, CA 93921-3185
(831)625-5222 (800)833-8836 Fax:(831)625-0478

An exterior of wood and cobblestone gathered from the Carmel
River provide a friendly facade for visitors to this bed & breakfast located two blocks from the heart of Carmel. Each guest
room has its own cobblestone fireplace. The inn's English country decor is enhanced with quilts, a col-
orful antique carousel horse and other
early American antiques. In addition to
breakfast and afternoon tea, evening
wine and hors d'oeuvres are served.
Guests can borrow one of the inn's
bicycles to explore the area. The beach
and shopping are nearby. Cobblestone
is one of the Four Sisters Inns.

Innkeeper(s): Sharon Carey. $115-240. 24 rooms with PB, 24 with FP.
Breakfast and afternoon tea included in rates. Types of meals: Full gourmet
bkfst and early coffee/tea. Fax and copier on premises.
Publicity: Country Inns and Honeymoons.
Certificate may be used: December & January; Sunday-Thursday, excluding
holidays & special events.

The Stonehouse Inn

PO Box 2517, 8th below Monte Verde
Carmel, CA 93921-2517
(831)624-4569 (800)748-6618

Circa 1906. This quaint Carmel country house boasts a stone
exterior, made from beach rocks collected and hand shaped by
local Indians at the turn of the century. The original owner,
"Nana" Foster, was hostess to notable artists and writers from
the San Francisco area, including Sinclair Lewis, Jack London
and Lotta Crabtree. The romantic Jack London room features a
dramatic gabled ceiling, a brass bed and a stunning view of the
ocean. Conveniently located, the inn is a short walk from
Carmel Beach and two blocks from the village.

Innkeeper(s): Terri Navailles. $159-207. MC, VISA, AX. 6 rooms. Breakfast
included in rates. Type of meal: Full bkfst. Beds: KQDT. Fishing, live theater,
parks, shopping and water sports nearby.
Publicity: Travel & Leisure and Country Living.
"First time stay at a B&B — GREAT!"
Certificate may be used: Nov. 1 through May 31, Sunday through Thursday,
except special events such as Thanksgiving, Christmas, New Year, AT&T Golf
Tournament.

Chico   E5

The Esplanade B&B

620 The Esplanade
Chico, CA 95926
(530)345-8084

Circa 1914. Each of the rooms at this comfortable bed &
breakfast is named for someone special in innkeeper Lois Kloss'
life. One room includes a Jacuzzi tub and stained-glass window.
Others feature poster beds piled high with feather pillows. Lois
serves a buffet-style breakfast in the morning, and treats guests
to a glass of wine in the afternoons. The home is within walking distance from the university, downtown Chico and the
Chico Museum.

Innkeeper(s): Lois I. Kloss & George Fish. $65-85. MC, VISA, TC. 5 rooms

with PB. Breakfast, afternoon tea and snacks/refreshments included in rates.
Types of meals: Full bkfst and early coffee/tea. Beds: QDT. Cable TV and ceil-
ing fan in room. Air conditioning. Fax on premises. Amusement parks,
antiquing, fishing, three hospitals, live theater, parks, shopping, downhill ski-
ing, cross-country skiing, sporting events and water sports nearby.
Pets Allowed.
Location: City.
Certificate may be used: Sunday-Wednesday, excluding holidays.

L'Abri B&B

13450 Hwy 99
Chico, CA 95973
(530)893-0824 (800)489-3319
Internet: www.now2000.com/labri
E-mail: labrichico@earthlink.net

Circa 1972. This ranch-style house is located on more than
two acres, with a scenic seasonal creek. All three guest rooms
offer a private entrance and each is uniquely decorated. The
pastoral feeling is enhanced with bales of hay and the barnyard
inhabitants: sheep, chickens and an impertinent rooster. Full
breakfasts are offered, often followed by special baked goods
and an occasional peach or berry cobbler when in season.
Cycle the country roads, go horseback riding or go into town
and enjoy light opera and open-air summer concerts.

Innkeeper(s): Sharon & Jeff Bisaga. $65-90. MC, VISA, PC. 3 rooms with
PB. Breakfast and snacks/refreshments included in rates. Types of meals: Full
bkfst, cont plus, country bkfst, veg bkfst and early coffee/tea. Beds: Q. Phone
and ceiling fan in room. Air conditioning. Copier and library on premises.
Antiquing, art galleries, bicycling, canoeing/kayaking, fishing, golf, hiking,
horseback riding, live theater, museums, parks, shopping, downhill skiing,
cross-country skiing, sporting events, tennis and water sports nearby.
Location: Country.
Certificate may be used: Jan. 2-Dec. 1, Sunday-Thursday, except holidays
and special events.

Music Express Inn

1091 El Monte Ave
Chico, CA 95928-9153
(530)345-8376 Fax:(530)893-8521
Internet: www.now2000.com/musicexpress
E-mail: icobeen@aol.com

Circa 1977. Music-lovers will delight in this inn's warmth and
charm. Nine guest rooms, all with private bath and cable TV,
provide country-style comfort to those visiting the college town
of Chico. Jacuzzi tubs, refrigerators and microwaves are among
the amenities. Guests will awake
to the smell of homemade
bread or rolls. Visitors are
welcome to tickle the
ivories of the inn's
Steinway grand piano.
The innkeeper, a music
teacher, is adept at many instruments and plays mandolin in a
local band. The inn's library also lures many guests, and those
who explore the surrounding area will find plenty of opportunities for antiquing and fishing.

Innkeeper(s): Barney & Irene Cobeen. $59-125. MC, VISA, AX, DS, PC, TC. 9
rooms with PB, 1 suite, 1 cottage and 2 conference rooms. Breakfast included
in rates. Type of meal: Full bkfst. Beds: KQDT. Cable TV, phone, ceiling fan,
VCR, microwave, Jacuzzi tubs and refrigerators in room. Air conditioning. Fax,
copier and library on premises. Handicap access. Antiquing, fishing, live theater, parks, shopping, sporting events and water sports nearby.
Certificate may be used: All year, Sunday-Thursday.

Clio
E7

White Sulphur Springs Ranch

PO Box 136
Clio, CA 96106-0136
(916)836-2387 (800)854-1797 Fax:(916)836-2387

Circa 1857. Originally built by partners in the Jamison mine, this stage coach stop serviced the Truckee to Quincy stage. The inn has passed from relative to relative to friend and has not been sold since 1867 when it was purchased by George McLear. Elegantly restored, the rooms still retain many of the original furnishings, now embellished with colorful wallpapers and fabrics. The Marble Room features a moss green velvet fainting couch, marble-topped antiques and a splendid view of the Mohawk Valley. Breakfast is served in the dining room. Mineral waters from five 85-degree springs fill the inn's swimming pool.
Innkeeper(s): Don & Karen Miller, Tom & Linda Vanella. $85-140. MC, VISA, DS, TC. 9 rooms, 3 with PB and 2 conference rooms. Breakfast and afternoon tea included in rates. Types of meals: Full bkfst and early coffee/tea. Beds: KQD. Air conditioning. VCR, fax and copier on premises. Handicap access. Antiquing, fishing, parks, shopping, downhill skiing, cross-country skiing and water sports nearby.
Location: Mountains.
Publicity: *Sacramento Union and Plumas-Sierra.*
"White Sulphur Springs is alive with its past and its present."
Certificate may be used: Sunday-Thursday, September-May, no holidays.

Dana Point
P11

Blue Lantern Inn

34343 Street of the Blue Lantern
Dana Point, CA 92629
(949)661-1304 (800)950-1236 Fax:(949)496-1483

Circa 1990. The four-diamond inn is situated high on a blufftop overlooking a stunning coastline and the blue waters of Dana Point harbor with its pleasure craft, fishing boats and the tall ship, Pilgrim. Each guest room features both a fireplace and a whirlpool tub and many offer private sun decks. Afternoon tea, evening turndown service and bicycles are just a few of the amenities available. In the evening, wine and hors d'oeuvres are served. Shops, restaurants and beaches are nearby, and popular Laguna Beach is just a few miles to the north. Blue Lantern is one of the Four Sisters Inns.
Innkeeper(s): Lin McMahon. $160-500. MC, VISA, AX, DS, TC. 29 rooms with PB, 29 with FP and 3 conference rooms. Breakfast and afternoon tea included in rates. Type of meal: Full gourmet bkfst. Beds: KQD. Phone, turndown service, newspaper and bathrobes in room. Fax, bicycles and exercise room on premises. Handicap access. Amusement parks, antiquing, fishing, beach, Dana Point Harbor, parks, shopping and water sports nearby.
Publicity: *Los Angeles Magazine, Glamour, Oregonian and Orange County Register.*
Certificate may be used: November through February, Monday-Thursday, holidays and special events excluded.

Dunsmuir
B5

Dunsmuir Inn

5423 Dunsmuir Ave
Dunsmuir, CA 96025-2011
(530)235-4543 (888)386-7684 Fax:(530)235-4154

Circa 1925. Set in the Sacramento River Valley, this country-style inn may serve as a base for an assortment of outdoor activities.

At the end of the day, guests can enjoy an old-fashioned soda or ice cream cone. Fishing, available in the crystal-clear waters of the Upper Sacramento River, is within walking distance. The innkeepers can suggest hiking trails and driving tours to mountain lakes, waterfalls, the Castle Crags State Park and Mt. Shasta.
Innkeeper(s): Jerry & Julie Iskra. $65-75. MC, VISA, AX, DC, CB, DS, PC, TC. 5 rooms with PB and 1 suite. Breakfast included in rates. Types of meals: Full bkfst and early coffee/tea. Beds: KD. Turndown service and ceiling fan in room. Air conditioning. VCR and fax on premises. Antiquing, fishing, parks, downhill skiing, cross-country skiing and water sports nearby.
Location: Mountains.
Certificate may be used: October-April.

Eureka
C2

A Weaver's Inn

1440 B St
Eureka, CA 95501-2215
(707)443-8119 (800)992-8119 Fax:(707)443-7923
Internet: www.humboldt1.com/~weavrinn
E-mail: weavrinn@humboldt1.com

Circa 1883. The stately Queen Anne Colonial Revival house features a spacious fenced garden, parlor and gracious dining room. All four guest rooms are furnished with down comforters, fresh flowers from the garden and are decorated to reflect the genteel elegance of the Victorian era. The Pamela Suite has a sitting room and fireplace, while the Marcia Room includes a two-person soaking tub in its private bath. The full breakfast often features home-grown treats from the garden.
Innkeeper(s): Lea L. Montgomery, Shoshana McAvoy. $75-125. MC, VISA, AX, DC, DS. 4 rooms, 3 with PB, 2 with FP and 1 suite. Breakfast included in rates. Type of meal: Full gourmet bkfst. Beds: KQDT.
"It's a charming inn, warm ambiance and very gracious hosts!"
Certificate may be used: Anytime, subject to availability.

Abigail's

1406 C St
Eureka, CA 95501-1765
(707)444-3144 Fax:(707)442-5594
Internet: www.eureka-california.com

Circa 1888. One of Eureka's leading lumber barons built this picturesque home, a National Historic Landmark, from 1,000-year-old virgin redwood. Original wallpapers, wool carpets and antique light fixtures create a wonderfully authentic Victorian ambiance. A tuxedoed butler and your hosts, decked in period attire, greet guests upon arrival. Croquet fields and Victorian gardens surround the inn. The hosts provide complimentary "horseless" carriage rides. The beds in the well-appointed guest  quarters are topped with custom-made mattresses. There is a video library of vintage silent films. The inn has been host to many historic personalities, including actresses Lillie Langtry and Sarah Bernhardt, and many senators and representatives. The Pacific Ocean, beaches and the Giant Redwoods are only a few minutes away.
Innkeeper(s): Doug & Lily Vieyra. $85-215. MC, VISA. 4 rooms, 2 with PB, 1 suite and 1 conference room. Breakfast, afternoon tea and snacks/refreshments included in rates. Types of meals: Cont plus and early coffee/tea. Beds: Q. Phone, turndown service, chocolate truffles and B&B guidebooks in room. Air conditioning. VCR, fax, copier, sauna, bicycles, library, croquet field, antique automobiles and horseless carriages on premises. Antiquing, carriage

rides, bay cruise, horseback riding, sailing, beach, Giant Redwoods, live theater, tennis and water sports nearby.
Location: Redwood Forest.
Publicity: *New York Times, San Francisco Chronicle, Boston Globe, LA Times, Outbreak and Jay Leno.*
Certificate may be used: Standard rooms only, Monday through Thursday during months of January and February only, excluding holidays. Subject to availability no earlier than three days prior to reservation date. Not valid with any other discount.

Cornelius Daly Inn

1125 H St
Eureka, CA 95501-1844
(707)445-3638 (800)321-9656 Fax:(707)444-3636
Internet: www.dalyinn.com
E-mail: innkeeper@dalyinn.com
Circa 1905. This 6,000-square-foot Colonial Revival mansion is located in the historic section of Eureka. The inn's gracious atmosphere includes four wood-burning fireplace and a third floor ballroom. Enjoy the romantic French bedroom suite

with dressing table, armoire and bedstead in Annie Murphey's Room. It offers a fireplace and a view over the Victorian garden and fish pond. Miss Martha's Room features Dutch, bleached-pine antiques and was once the nursery. Breakfast is served fireside in the inn's formal dining room or in the breakfast parlor or garden patio. In the evenings, wine and cheese are served.
Innkeeper(s): Sue & Gene Clinesmith. $85-150. MC, VISA, AX, DS, PC, TC. 5 rooms, 3 with PB, 1 with FP and 2 suites. Breakfast and snacks/refreshments included in rates. Types of meals: Full gourmet bkfst and early coffee/tea. Beds: QT. Turndown service and antiques in room. VCR, fax, copier and library on premises. Antiquing, fishing, redwood park, ocean, live theater and shopping nearby.
Location: Redwoods.
"A genuine delight."
Certificate may be used: Nov. 1-May 1. Holidays & special event weekends excluded.

Ferndale   C2

Gingerbread Mansion Inn

PO Box 40, 400 Berding St
Ferndale, CA 95536-1380
(707)786-4000 (800)952-4136 Fax:(707)786-4381
Internet: gingerbread-mansion.com
E-mail: kenn@humboldt1.com
Circa 1899. Built for Dr. H.J. Ring, the Gingerbread Mansion is now the most photographed of Northern California's inns. Near Eureka, it is in the fairy-tale Victorian village of Ferndale (a National Historical Landmark). Gingerbread Mansion is a unique combination of Queen Anne and Eastlake styles with elaborate gingerbread trim. Inside are spacious and elegant rooms including two suites with "his" and "her" bathtubs. The Empire Suite is said to be the most opulent accommodation in Northern California. Another memorable choice would be "The Veneto," an imaginative experience where guests stay within a piece of artwork. Extensive formal English gardens beautifully surround the

mansion and it is a stroll away to Victorian shops, galleries and restaurants. A Wilderness park and bird sanctuary are a half mile away.
Innkeeper(s): Ken Torbert. $140-350. MC, VISA, AX, PC, TC. 11 rooms with PB, 5 with FP and 5 suites. Breakfast and afternoon tea included in rates. Types of meals: Full bkfst and early coffee/tea. Beds: KQT. Turndown service in room. Library and gardens on premises. Antiquing, fishing, hiking, live theater, parks and shopping nearby.
Location: Village.
Publicity: *San Francisco Focus, Sunset, Travel Holiday, Country Inns, Los Angeles Times, Sunset, Outbreak (Warner Bros.) and PBS (Inn Country USA).*
"Absolutely the most charming, friendly and delightful place we have ever stayed."
Certificate may be used: Nov. 1-March 15, Sunday-Friday, excluding holidays.

Ferndale (Loleta)   C2

Southport Landing

444 Phelan Rd
Ferndale (Loleta), CA 95551
(707)733-5915
Circa 1890. Situated on more than two acres, this early Colonial Revival with its wraparound front porch offers spectacular views of the hills and Humboldt Bay National Wildlife Refuge. Besides the inn's traditional country manor atmosphere with its period antiques, guests will enjoy the uninterrupted silence and the bounty of wildlife. There are five individually decorated guest rooms all with dramatic views of the hillside or the bay. A third-floor game room features a pool table, ping-pong, darts and cards. The country breakfasts include items such as local sausage, homemade muffins and fresh pastry. Snacks are provided in the evening. Hiking, bird-watching, bicycling and kayaking are offered.
Innkeeper(s): Judy & Dana Henderson. $85-125. MC, VISA. 5 rooms, 4 with PB. Breakfast and snacks/refreshments included in rates. Types of meals: Full bkfst and early coffee/tea. Beds: Q. Turndown service in room. VCR, fax, bicycles and library on premises. Antiquing, fishing, golf, kayaking, beach, bird watching, bicycling, hiking, beachcombing, live theater, parks and shopping nearby.
Location: Rural.
"Our greatest B&B experience!"
Certificate may be used: Sunday through Thursday, holidays excluded.

Fish Camp   I8

Karen's B&B Yosemite Inn

PO Box 8
Fish Camp, CA 93623-0008
(209)683-4550
Internet: www.karensyosemitebnb.com
E-mail: karenbnb@sierratel.com
Circa 1988. This contemporary country house enjoys a setting of pine, oak and cedar trees at 5,000 feet. The Rose Room features wicker furniture and a rose motif on quilts and pillows. There's a porch to relax on and in the evening guests enjoy watching raccoons come by for their evening snacks. Cottage-fried potatoes and fresh-baked muffins are a sample of the country breakfast. It's a three-minute drive to the southern gate of Yosemite National Park.
Innkeeper(s): Karen Bergh. $90. 3 rooms. Breakfast included in rates. Type of meal: Full bkfst. Parks nearby.
Publicity: *Contra Costa Times.*
Certificate may be used: Oct. 1-March 31, Sunday through Thursday. Void all holiday periods.

Fort Bragg   E2

Glass Beach B&B

726 N Main St
Fort Bragg, CA 95437-3017
(707)964-6774

Circa 1920. Each of the guest rooms at this Craftsman-style home is decorated in a different theme and named to reflect the decor. The Malaysian and Oriental Jade rooms reflect Asian artistry, while the Forget-Me-Not and Victorian Rose rooms are bright, feminine rooms with walls decked in floral prints. Antiques are found throughout the home and the back cottage, which includes three of the inn's nine guest rooms. The inn also offers a hot tub for guest use. Breakfasts are served in the inn's dining room, but guests are free to take a tray and enjoy the meal in the privacy of their own room.

Innkeeper(s): Nancy & Richard. $100-160. MC, VISA, DS, TC. 9 rooms with PB, 4 with FP and 1 suite. Breakfast included in rates. Type of meal: Full bkfst. Beds: Q. Cable TV and phone in room. Handicap access. Antiquing, fishing, live theater, parks, shopping and water sports nearby.
Location: City.
Certificate may be used: Jan. 5-June 4, Oct. 1-Dec. 31, Sunday-Thursday. Most holidays excluded.

Grey Whale Inn

615 N Main St
Fort Bragg, CA 95437-3240
(707)964-0640 (800)382-7244 Fax:(707)964-4408
Internet: www.greywhaleinn.com
E-mail: stay@greywhaleinn.com

Circa 1915. As the name implies, whales can be seen from many of the inn's vantage points during the creatures' migration season along the West Coast. The stately four-story redwood inn features airy and spacious guest rooms with neighborhood ocean views. Some rooms include a fireplace, whirlpool tub for two or private deck. Near the heart of downtown Fort Bragg, it's an easy

walk to the Skunk Train, shops, galleries, a microbrewery and restaurants. There is also a fireside lounge, TV/VCR room and a recreation area with pool table.

Innkeeper(s): John & Colette Bailey. $90-180. MC, VISA, AX, DS, PC, TC. 14 rooms with PB, 4 with FP and 2 conference rooms. Breakfast included in rates. Type of meal: Full bkfst. Beds: KQDT. Cable TV, phone and coffee maker in room. VCR, fax, copier and library on premises. Handicap access. Antiquing, fishing, whale watching, golf, hiking, bicycling, microbrewery, live theater, parks and shopping nearby.
Location: Small town.
Publicity: *Inn Times, San Francisco Examiner, Travel, Fort Bragg Advocate News, Mendocino Beacon, Los Angeles Times, Sunset* and *Contra Costa Times.*
"We are going to return each year until we have tried each room. Sunrise room is excellent in the morning or evening."
Certificate may be used: October through June, Sunday through Thursday, excluding holiday periods.

Old Stewart House Inn

511 Stewart St
Fort Bragg, CA 95437-3226
(707)961-0775 (800)287-8392

Circa 1876. This is the oldest house in Fort Bragg and was built for the founding partner of the town mill. The Victorian theme is enhanced by rooms that may feature amenities such

as a fireplace or spa, as well as period furnishings. Within a three-block area of the inn are the Skunk Train Depot, restaurants and beaches. Nearby are ocean cliffs, stands of redwood, waterfalls and botanical gardens.

Innkeeper(s): Darrell Galli. $75-125. MC, VISA, DS. 6 rooms with PB, 2 with FP and 2 cabins. Breakfast and snacks/refreshments included in rates. Type of meal: Full bkfst. Beds: Q. Spa and library on premises. Handicap access. Antiquing, fishing, golf, live theater, parks, shopping, tennis and water sports nearby. Pets allowed: in cabins, on approval.
Certificate may be used: Jan. 30-May 10, excluding holidays, Sunday through Thursday only.

Pudding Creek Inn

700 N Main St
Fort Bragg, CA 95437-3017
(707)964-9529 (800)227-9529

Circa 1884. Originally constructed by a Russian count, the inn comprises two picturesque Victorian homes connected by an enclosed garden. There are mounds of begonias, fuchsias and ferns. The Count's Room, in seafoam green and cranberry accents, features inlaid redwood paneling, a stone fireplace and a brass bed. There is a TV/recreation room for guest use. A full buffet breakfast is provided and you can reserve ahead for a picnic lunch. (Guests on a long coastal tour will appreciate the laundry service made available.)

Innkeeper(s): Jacque Woltman. $75-130. MC, VISA, AX. 10 rooms with PB, 3 with FP. Breakfast and afternoon tea included in rates. Type of meal: Full bkfst. Beds: KQDT. Phone in room. Fax on premises. Antiquing, fishing, golf, live theater and tennis nearby.
Publicity: *Evening Outlook.*
"Best stop on our trip!"
Certificate may be used: October-June, midweek Sunday-Thursday only, no holidays.

Geyserville   G4

Hope-Merrill House

21253 Geyserville Ave
Geyserville, CA 95441-9637
(707)857-3356 (800)825-4233 Fax:(707)857-4673

Circa 1885. The Hope-Merrill House is a classic example of the Eastlake Stick style that was so popular during Victorian times. Built entirely from redwood, the house features original wainscoting and silk-screened wallcoverings. A swimming pool, vineyard and gazebo are favorite spots for guests to relax. The Hope-Bosworth House, on the same street, was built in 1904 in the Queen Anne style by an early Geyserville pioneer who lived in the home until the 1960s. The front picket fence is covered with roses. Period details include oak woodwork, sliding doors, polished fir floors and antique light fixtures.

Innkeeper(s): Cosette & Ron Scheiber. $119-215. MC, VISA, AX, DS, PC, TC. 12 rooms with PB, 4 with FP and 1 suite. Breakfast included in rates. Types of meals: Full gourmet bkfst and early coffee/tea. Beds: Q. Ceiling fan in room. Fax and copier on premises. Antiquing, parks, shopping and water sports nearby.
Location: Wine country.
Publicity: *New York Times, San Francisco Chronicles, San Diego Union, Country Homes, Sunset, Sacramento Union, Los Angeles Times* and *Bay Area Back Roads.*
Certificate may be used: Any day, Nov. 2-March 31, otherwise Sunday through Thursday. Holidays excluded.

Grass Valley F6

Murphy's Inn

318 Neal St
Grass Valley, CA 95945-6702
(530)273-6873 (800)895-2488 Fax:(530)273-5157
Internet: www.murphysinn.com
E-mail: murphys@jps.net

Circa 1866. The Gold Rush turned this home's builder into a wealthy man, and he built this Victorian for his new bride. The home is decorated by century-old ivy, and the grounds include a 140-year-old giant  sequoia. Guests can choose from rooms with fireplaces or a skylight, and all rooms are decorated with antiques. Two suites are located in a separate house and one includes a kitchen and living room. The Victorian is located in a Grass Valley historic district and is within walking distance to many local attractions.

Innkeeper(s): Ted & Nancy Daus. $115-165. MC, VISA, AX, TC. 8 rooms with PB, 4 with FP and 3 suites. Breakfast included in rates. Types of meals: Full gourmet bkfst and early coffee/tea. Beds: KQ. Cable TV, phone, ceiling fan and VCR in room. Air conditioning. Fax and video library on premises. Antiquing, fishing, golf, live theater, parks, shopping, downhill skiing, cross-country skiing, tennis and water sports nearby.
Location: Mountains.
Certificate may be used: Jan. 1-April 1.

Groveland H7

The Groveland Hotel

18767 Main St, PO Box 481
Groveland, CA 95321-0481
(209)962-4000 (800)273-3314 Fax:(209)962-6674
Internet: www.groveland.com
E-mail: peggy@groveland.com

Circa 1849. Located 23 miles from Yosemite National Park, the 1992 restoration features both an 1849 adobe building with 18-inch-thick walls constructed during the Gold Rush and a 1914 building erected to  house workers for the Hetch Hetchy Dam. Both feature two-story balconies. There is a Victorian parlor, a gourmet restaurant and a Western saloon. Guest rooms feature European antiques, down comforters and in-room coffee. The feeling is one of casual elegance.

Innkeeper(s): Peggy A. & Grover C. Mosley. $125-200. MC, VISA, AX, DC, CB, DS, PC, TC. 17 rooms with PB, 3 with FP, 3 suites and 1 conference room. Breakfast included in rates. Types of meals: Cont plus and early coffee/tea. Beds: QT. TV, phone and ceiling fan in room. Air conditioning. VCR, fax, copier, library, pet boarding and child care on premises. Handicap access. Antiquing, fishing, golf, parks, shopping, downhill skiing, cross-country skiing, tennis and water sports nearby.
Location: 1/2 hour to Yosemite.
Publicity: *Sonora Union Democrat, Los Angeles Times, Peninsula, Sunset, Stockton Record, Country Inns Magazine (Top 10 inns in U.S.) and Wine Spectator Award of excellence for our wine list.*
Certificate may be used: Oct. 15-April 15, Sunday through Thursday, excluding holidays.

Guerneville G3

Fern Grove Cottages

16650 River Rd
Guerneville, CA 95446-9678
(707)869-8105 Fax:(707)869-1615

Circa 1926. Clustered in a village-like atmosphere and surrounded by redwoods, these craftsman cottages have romantic fireplaces, private entrances, and are individually decorated. The cottages were built in the 1920s and served as little vacation houses for San Francisco families visiting the Russian River. Some units have a kitchen, some have double whirlpool tubs and other cottages are suitable for families. Guests enjoy use of the swimming pool. The cottages are just a few blocks from shops and restaurants, as well as a swimming beach by the river. A state park and winery tour are within three miles of the cottages.

Innkeeper(s): Anne & Simon Lowings. $69-159. MC, VISA, AX, DS, PC, TC. 20 cottages with PB, 11 with FP and 1 conference room. Breakfast included in rates. Type of meal: Cont. Beds: Q. Cable TV in room. Swimming and library on premises. Antiquing, beaches, canoeing/kayaking, fishing, golf, Armstrong Redwater State Park, parks, shopping, tennis, water sports and wineries nearby.
Pets allowed: One per cottage, on leash, clean animals only. $10 charge.
Location: River and vineyards.
Certificate may be used: Sunday-Thursday, Nov. 1-April 30, excludes holidays.

Half Moon Bay I4

Old Thyme Inn

779 Main St
Half Moon Bay, CA 94019-1924
(650)726-1616 (800)720-4277 Fax:(650)726-6394
Internet: www.oldthymeinn.com
E-mail: innkeeper@oldthymeinn.com

Circa 1899. Located on the historic Main Street of Old Town, this fully-restored Queen Anne Victorian is known for its aromatic English garden that includes more than 50 varieties of herbs and flowers. Recently redecorated, rooms are furnished with antiques and fine art and  are named after various herbs found in the garden. Among the amenities available for guests are double Jacuzzis, fireplaces, feather beds and down comforters. Wine, sherry and snacks are served in the afternoon, and in the morning, enjoy a full breakfast. A beautiful crescent-shaped beach is within walking distance, as are fine restaurants, shops and art galleries. Ask the innkeepers to help arrange horseback riding along the shoreline, whale watching cruises or touring elephant seal breeding preserves.

Innkeeper(s): Rick & Kathy Ellis. $100-255. MC, VISA, AX, DS, PC, TC. 7 rooms with PB, 3 with FP. Breakfast included in rates. Type of meal: Full bkfst. Beds: Q. TV, VCR, some with Jacuzzi tubs and fireplaces in room. Fax on premises. Antiquing, fishing, golf, live theater, parks, shopping and water sports nearby.
Location: Mountains.
Publicity: *California Weekends, Los Angeles, San Mateo Times, San Jose Mercury News, Herb Companion and San Francisco Examiner.*
Certificate may be used: Nov. 1 through March 30 (except for Christmas holiday season and Valentine's weekend), Sunday-Thursday.

Healdsburg G4

Madrona Manor, A Country Inn
PO Box 818
Healdsburg, CA 95448-0818
(707)433-4231 (800)258-4003 Fax:(707)433-0703
Circa 1881. The inn is comprised of four historic structures in a national historic district. Surrounded by eight acres of manicured lawns and terraced flower and vegetable gardens, the stately mansion was built for John Paxton, a San Francisco businessman. Embellished with turrets, bay windows, porches, and a mansard roof, it provides a breathtaking view of surrounding vineyards. Elegant antique furnishings and a noteworthy restaurant add to the genuine country inn atmosphere. The Gothic-style Carriage House offers more casual lodging.
Innkeeper(s): Joe & Maria Hadley. $175-330. MC, VISA, AX, DC, CB, DS, PC, TC. 20 rooms with PB, 17 with FP, 3 suites, 1 cottage and 2 conference rooms. Breakfast included in rates. Type of meal: Full gourmet bkfst. Beds: KQDT. Phone in room. Air conditioning. Fax, copier and swimming on premises. Handicap access. Antiquing, fishing, wine tasting, live theater, parks, shopping, sporting events and water sports nearby.
Pets allowed: In select buildings.
Location: Country.
Publicity: *Travel & Leisure, Conde Naste, Gourmet, Woman's Day Home Decorating Ideas, US News, Diversions, Money, Good Housekeeping and Great Country Inns of America.*
"Our fourth visit and better every time."
Certificate may be used: Sunday through Thursday, excluding holidays or special event weekends. All year.

Idyllwild O12

Cedar Street Inn
25870 Cedar
Idyllwild, CA 92549
(909)659-4789 Fax:(909)659-3540
Internet: www.idyllwild.com/cedar.htm
E-mail: cedarstreet@idyllwild.com
Circa 1988. This country-style bed and breakfast is located within walking distance to the village and hiking trails. The complex offers cottage guest rooms, a spacious attic room and a cabin. The decor is country Victorian. While most of the rooms have fireplaces, one boasts a large Roman tub and is a popular honeymoon choice. The Idyllwild Room has knotty pine walls and features furniture made in the '30s in Idyllwild.
Innkeeper(s): Patty & Gary Tompkins. $75-140. MC, VISA, AX, DS, PC, TC. 11 rooms. Type of meal: Early coffee/tea. Beds: KQT. Cable TV, ceiling fan and coffee makers in room. Fax, copier and library on premises. Amusement parks, antiquing, fishing, golf, live theater, shopping and cross-country skiing nearby.
Pets allowed: one cabin only, pet must not be left alone.
Location: Mountains.
Certificate may be used: All year, Sunday-Thursday, except holidays.

The Pine Cove Inn
23481 Hwy 243, PO Box 2181
Idyllwild, CA 92549
(909)659-5033 (888)659-5033 Fax:(909)659-5034
Circa 1935. These rustic, A-frame cottages offer a variety of amenities in a natural, mountain setting. Refrigerators and microwaves have been placed in each unit, several of which include a wood-burning fireplace. One unit has a full kitchen. A full breakfast is served in a separate lodge which dates back to 1935. The village of Idyllwild is three miles down the road, and the surrounding country offers a variety of activities.

Innkeeper(s): Bob & Michelle Bollmann. $70-100. MC, VISA, AX, DS, PC, TC. 10 rooms with PB, 6 with FP, 3 suites and 1 conference room. Breakfast included in rates. Type of meal: Full bkfst. Beds: QT. Ceiling fan and microwave in room. VCR and fax on premises. Antiquing, fishing, hiking, mountain hiking, live theater, parks, shopping and cross-country skiing nearby.
Location: Mountains.
Certificate may be used: Sunday through Thursday only, any dates except Dec. 20 through Jan. 4.

Independence J10

Winnedumah Hotel
211 N Edwards St
Independence, CA 93526
(760)878-2040 Fax:(760)878-2833
Internet: www.winnedumah.com
E-mail: winnedumah@qnet.com
Circa 1927. Located on Highway 395 in the foothills of the Eastern Sierras, this Spanish Colonial hotel boasts comfortable rooms with original furnishings from the Twenties when the inn first started hosting travelers. Handmade quilts add warmth, and there are private baths. The focal point of the lobby is a fieldstone fireplace, a popular gathering spot. Owens Valley and the immediate area offer a trout-filled steam, majestic scenery and hiking and fishing.
Innkeeper(s): Marvey Chapman. $45-70. MC, VISA, TC. 24 rooms, 14 with PB. Breakfast included in rates. Types of meals: Cont plus and cont. Beds: QDT. VCR, fax, copier and bicycles on premises. Antiquing, fishing, hiking, backpacking, cross-country skiing and water sports nearby.
Pets Allowed.
Location: Mountains.
Publicity: *Los Angeles Times, Liberty and Nevada.*
Certificate may be used: January through December, Sunday-Thursday.

Inverness H4

The Patterson House
PO Box 13
Inverness, CA 94937-0013
(415)669-1383
Circa 1916. Views of Tamales Bay with surrounding giant redwood trees, California oaks and Monterey pine trees await guests at this Craftsman-style inn perched on a hill. Guests are invited to read, sip port, plunk on the upright piano or just relax in front of the massive river rock fireplace. The breakfast room, which is next to the common room, has paned windows and French doors that open onto a wraparound deck.
Innkeeper(s): Rosalie & Kraig Patterson. $98-167. MC, VISA, AX, DS. 5 rooms with PB. Breakfast and afternoon tea included in rates. Type of meal: Cont plus. Beds: KQ. Antiquing, fishing and water sports nearby.
Publicity: *Country Inns.*
"Understated elegance, nicest B&B we've ever stayed in."
Certificate may be used: Year-round, Sunday through Thursday, subject to availability.

Rosemary Cottage

PO Box 273
Inverness, CA 94937-0273
(415)663-9338 (800)808-9338
Internet: www.rosemarybb.com
E-mail: rosemarybb@aol.com

Circa 1986. From the windows in this secluded cottage, guests can enjoy views of a wooded canyon and hillside in the Point Reyes National Seashore park. The cottage is a cozy, self-contained unit with a well-equipped kitchen, bedroom, and a living room with a wood-burning stove. The decor is French country, highlighting the wood beams, red oak floors and terra cotta tiles. There is a hot tub in the garden.

Innkeeper(s): Suzanne Storch. $155-250. PC, TC. 3 cottages with PB, 3 with FP. Breakfast included in rates. Type of meal: Full bkfst. Beds: QT. Phone in room. Spa on premises. Antiquing, fishing, parks, shopping and water sports nearby.
Pets Allowed.
Location: Pt. Reyes National Seashore.
Certificate may be used: November through March, Sunday-Thursday, excluding holiday weeks.

Ione   G6

The Heirloom

214 Shakeley Ln, PO Box 322
Ione, CA 95640-9572
(209)274-4468 (888)628-7896
Internet: www.theheirloominn.com

Circa 1863. A two-story Colonial with columns, balconies and a private English garden, the antebellum Heirloom is true to its name. It has many family heirlooms and a square grand piano once owned by Lola Montez. The building was dedicated by the Native Sons of the Golden West as a historic site.

Innkeeper(s): Melisande Hubbs & Patricia Cross. $65-102. MC, VISA, AX, PC, TC. 6 rooms, 4 with PB, 3 with FP and 2 cottages. Breakfast and afternoon tea included in rates. Types of meals: Full gourmet bkfst and early coffee/tea. Beds: KQDT. Air conditioning. Library on premises. Antiquing, fishing, golf, wineries, live theater, parks, shopping and water sports nearby.
Location: Small town, Sierra foothills.
Publicity: *Country Inns, San Francisco Chronicle, Country Living and KSBY-NBC-Dream Vacation.*
"Hospitality was amazing. Truly we've never had such a great time."
Certificate may be used: Jan. 5-March 30 and July 6-Sept. 30. Sunday through Thursday, holidays excluded.

Jackson   G6

Gate House Inn

1330 Jackson Gate Rd
Jackson, CA 95642-9539
(209)223-3500 (800)841-1072 Fax:(209)223-1299
E-mail: info@gatehouseinn.com

Circa 1902. This striking Victorian inn is listed in the National Register of Historic Places. Set on a hillside amid lovely gardens, the inn is within walking distance of a state historic park and several notable eateries. The inn's country setting, comfortable porches and swimming pool offer many opportunities for relaxation. Accommodations include three rooms, a suite and a romantic cottage with wood stove and whirlpool tub. All of the guest rooms feature queen beds and elegant fur-

nishings. Nearby are several lakes, wineries and golf courses.

Innkeeper(s): Keith & Gail Sweet. $110-185. MC, VISA, AX, CB, DS, PC, TC. 6 rooms with PB, 3 with FP, 1 suite and 2 cottages. Breakfast included in rates. Types of meals: Full bkfst and early coffee/tea. Beds: Q. Ceiling fan in room. Air conditioning. Fax, copier and swimming on premises. Antiquing, fishing, live theater, parks, shopping, downhill skiing, cross-country skiing and water sports nearby.
Location: Mountains.
"Most gracious, warm hospitality."
Certificate may be used: Sunday-Thursday, holidays excluded.

Wedgewood Inn

11941 Narcissus Rd
Jackson, CA 95642-9600
(209)296-4300 (800)933-4393 Fax:(209)296-4301
Internet: www.wedgewoodinn.com
E-mail: vic@wedgewoodinn.com

Circa 1987. Located in the heart of Sierra gold country on a secluded, five acres, this Victorian replica is crammed full of sentimental family heirlooms and antiques. Each room has been designed with careful attention to detail. A baby grand piano rests in the parlor. The carriage house is a separate cottage with its own private entrance. It boasts four generations of family heirlooms, a carved canopy bed, a wood-burning stove and a two-person Jacuzzi tub. The innkeepers' 1921 Model-T, "Henry," is located in its own special showroom. Gourmet breakfasts are served on bone china and include specialties such as cheese-filled blintzes, fruit and baked goods. Breakfast is available in selected guest rooms by request. There is a gift shop on the premises.

Innkeeper(s): Vic & Jeannine Beltz. $110-185. MC, VISA, AX, DS, PC, TC. 6 rooms with PB and 1 suite. Breakfast included in rates. Types of meals: Full gourmet bkfst and early coffee/tea. Beds: Q. Turndown service, ceiling fan and Jacuzzi in room. Air conditioning. Fax, copier, croquet, hammocks and horseshoes on premises. Antiquing, fishing, golf, live theater, shopping, downhill skiing and cross-country skiing nearby.
Location: Gold Country Foothills.
Publicity: *San Francisco Chronicle, Contra Costa Times, Stockton Record, Country Magazine and Victorian Magazine.*
Certificate may be used: Sunday through Thursday inclusive, no holiday weekends.

Jamestown   H7

1859 Historic National Hotel, A Country Inn

18183 Main St, PO Box 502
Jamestown, CA 95327
(209)984-3446 (800)894-3446 Fax:(209)984-5620
Internet: www.national-hotel.com
E-mail: info@national-hotel.com

Circa 1859. Located between Yosemite National Park and Lake Tahoe, this is one of the 10 oldest continuously operating hotels in California. In the Gold Country, the inn maintains its original redwood bar where thousands of dollars in gold dust were once spent. Electricity and plumbing were added for the first time when the inn was restored. Original furnish-

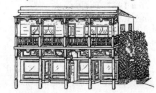

ings, Gold Rush period antiques, as well as brass beds, lace curtains and quilts are among the guest room appointments. A soaking room is an additional amenity, although all rooms have their own private baths. A bountiful continental breakfast is complimentary. Be sure and arrange for romantic dining at the inn's gourmet restaurant, considered to be one of the finest in the Mother Lode. Order a favorite liquor or espresso from the saloon or try the area's wine tasting. Favorite diversions include gold panning, live theatre and antiquing.

Innkeeper(s): Stephen Willey. $80-120. MC, VISA, AX, DC, CB, DS, PC, TC. 9 rooms with PB and 1 conference room. Breakfast included in rates. Types of meals: Cont plus and early coffee/tea. Beds: QT. Cable TV in room. Air conditioning. VCR and fax on premises. Antiquing, fishing, live theater, parks, downhill skiing, cross-country skiing and water sports nearby.
Pets allowed: By arrangement - credit card or cash deposit required.
Location: Mountains.
Publicity: *Bon Appetit, California Magazine, Focus, San Francisco Magazine, Gourmet and Sunset.*
Certificate may be used: Sunday through Thursday nights, holiday periods excluded. Based upon space availability.

Joshua Tree   013

Joshua Tree Inn

61259 29 Palms Hwy, PO Box 340
Joshua Tree, CA 92252-0340
(760)366-1188 (800)366-1444 Fax:(760)366-3805

Circa 1940. The hacienda-style inn was once a '50s motel. It now offers Victorian-style rooms with king-size beds. Antiques and Old West memorabilia add to the decor.

Throughout the inn, local artists display their creations. The inn is one mile from the gateway to the 467,000-acre Joshua Tree National Park.

Innkeeper(s): Dr. Daniel & Evelyn Shirbroun. $85-275. MC, VISA, AX, DC, CB, DS, TC. 10 rooms with PB, 2 suites and 1 conference room. Types of meals: Cont and early coffee/tea. Beds: KQDT. Cable TV, phone and ceiling fan in room. Air conditioning. VCR, fax, copier and swimming on premises. Antiquing, golf, Joshua Tree National Park, live theater, parks, shopping and tennis nearby.
Pets allowed: In designated rooms.
Location: Joshua Tree Natl Park 5 min.
Publicity: *Los Angeles Times and Press Enterprise.*
"Quiet, clean and charming."
Certificate may be used: Any Sunday through Thursday.

Julian   P12

Butterfield B&B

2284 Sunset Dr
Julian, CA 92036
(760)765-2179 (800)379-4262 Fax:(760)765-1229
Internet: butterfieldbandb.com
E-mail: butterfield@abac.com

Circa 1935. Reserve the French Suite here and not only will you have a fireplace, private entrance and sitting area, but you will have the option of having breakfast served in a romantic French antique bed. Located on three acres at the edge of town, the hillside Butterfield B&B also boasts a private cottage, Rose Bud. The inn's breakfast is served in the garden gazebo in the summer and offers specialities such as eggs Benedict and peach and basil crepes. In cool weather, breakfast is served fireside. The innkeepers are able to arrange a private candlelight dinner or a horse-drawn-carriage ride for your special celebrations.

Innkeeper(s): Ed Glass. $115-160. MC, VISA, AX, PC. 5 rooms with PB, 2 with FP and 1 cottage. Breakfast and snacks/refreshments included in rates. Types of meals: Full gourmet bkfst and early coffee/tea. Beds: QD. Cable TV and ceiling fan in room. Library on premises. Antiquing, fishing, golf, live theater, parks, shopping and sporting events nearby.
Location: Mountains.
Publicity: *South Coast and Travel Agent.*
Certificate may be used: Jan. 30-Sept. 30, Sunday-Thursday.

Orchard Hill Country Inn

2502 Washington St, PO Box 425
Julian, CA 92036-0425
(760)765-1700 (800)716-7242
Internet: www.orchardhill.com
E-mail: information@orchardhill.com

This Craftsman-style inn is a perfect country getaway for those seeking solace from the city lights. There are four, 1920s-style cottages, and a new lodge built as a companion. Expansive, individually appointed cottage rooms offer amenities such as fireplaces, whirlpool tubs, hand-knitted afghans and down comforters all surrounded by warm, country decor. Gourmet coffee, tea and cocoa also are provided in each cottage room, as are refrigerators. Guests can enjoy a breakfast of fruits, muffins and a special egg dish in the dining room. Wine and hors d'oeuvres are provided each afternoon. Dinner is served on selected evenings. The expansive grounds boast a variety of gardens highlighting native plants and flowers.

Innkeeper(s): Darrell & Pat Straube. $160-265. MC, VISA, AX, TC. 22 rooms with PB, 11 with FP and 1 conference room. Breakfast and snacks/refreshments included in rates. Types of meals: Full bkfst and early coffee/tea. Beds: KQ. Cable TV, ceiling fan, VCR, whirlpool tub, modem access and wet bar in room. Air conditioning. Fax and copier on premises. Handicap access. Antiquing, fishing, music/art festivals, hiking, horse trails, hiking trails, live theater, parks and shopping nearby.
Location: Heart of historic district, in mountains of Northeast San Diego County.
Publicity: *San Diego Union Tribune, Los Angeles Times, Orange County Register, Orange Coast, San Francisco Chronicle, San Bernardino Sun, Oceanside Blade-Citizen and San Diego and Los Angeles.*
"The quality of the rooms, service and food were beyond our expectations."
Certificate may be used: Monday-Thursday, subject to availability of rooms.

Rockin' A Ranch B&B

1531 Orchard Ln
Julian, CA 92036-9607
(760)765-2820

Circa 1981. This contemporary wood-sided ranch inn found in the countryside outside Julian offers a relaxing getaway for city folk. The inn boasts a private bass fishing facility and guests also visit the farm animals found on the grounds. The three guest rooms have private baths, and amenities include ceiling fans, a fireplace, spa and turndown service. The inn is a very popular anniversary and honeymoon destination. Visitors enjoy a full breakfast and evening snack and will find Julian a fun place to explore in their spare time.

Innkeeper(s): Gil & Dottie Archambeau. $137. MC, VISA. 2 rooms with PB, 2 with FP. Breakfast and snacks/refreshments included in rates. Type of meal: Full bkfst. Beds: QD. Turndown service and ceiling fan in room. VCR, spa and swimming pool (in season) on premises. Antiquing, fishing, live theater, parks, shopping and cross-country skiing nearby.
Location: Mountains.
Certificate may be used: Jan. 2-Dec. 30, Sunday through Thursday excluding holidays.

Kernville   *L10*

Kern River Inn B&B

119 Kern River Dr
Kernville, CA 93238
(760)376-6750 (800)986-4382 Fax:(760)376-6643
Internet: www.virtualcities.com/~virtual/ons/ca/s/cas3501.htm
E-mail: kernriverinn@lightspeed.net

Circa 1991. Located across from Riverside Park and the Kern
River, this country-style inn boasts a wraparound porch with views
and sounds of the river. The Whiskey Flat, Whitewater and Piute
rooms include fireplaces. The Big Blue and Greenhorn rooms offer
whirlpool tubs. All rooms
afford river views.
Breakfast may include the
inn's renowned puffed-
apple pancakes, egg and
cheese dishes or stuffed
French toast.

Innkeeper(s): Jack & Carita Prestwich. $89-109. MC, VISA, AX, PC, TC. 6
rooms with PB. Breakfast and afternoon tea included in rates. Types of meals:
Full bkfst and early coffee/tea. Beds: KQ. VCR, fax and library on premises.
Handicap access. Antiquing, fishing, golf, hiking, whitewater rafting, parks,
shopping, downhill skiing, cross-country skiing and water sports nearby.
Publicity: *Westways, Los Angeles Times, Bakersfield Californian, Kern Valley
Sun, Valley News and Westways.*
"For us, your place is the greatest. So romantic."
Certificate may be used: Nov. 1-March 31, Sunday-Thursday.

Laguna Beach   *P11*

Carriage House

1322 Catalina
Laguna Beach, CA 92651-3153
(949)494-8945 (888)335-8945 Fax:(949)494-6829
Internet: www.carriagehouse.com

Circa 1920. A Laguna Beach historical landmark, this inn has
a Cape Cod clapboard exterior. It housed an art gallery and a
bakery before it was converted into apartments with large
rooms and kitchens. Now
as a cozy inn, each room
has a private parlor.
Outside, the courtyard
fountain is shaded by a
large carrotwood tree with
hanging moss.

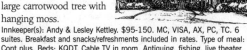

Innkeeper(s): Andy & Lesley Kettley. $95-150. MC, VISA, AX, PC, TC. 6
suites. Breakfast and snacks/refreshments included in rates. Type of meal:
Cont plus. Beds: KQDT. Cable TV in room. Antiquing, fishing, live theater,
parks, shopping and water sports nearby.
Pets allowed: Housebroken & quiet.
Publicity: *Glamour, Los Angeles Times, Orange County Register and Sunset.*
*"A true home away from home with all the extra touches added in.
Reminds me of New Orleans."*
Certificate may be used: Sunday through Thursday, September to June
(as available).

Eiler's Inn

741 S Coast Hwy
Laguna Beach, CA 92651-2722
(949)494-3004 Fax:(949)497-2215

Circa 1940. This New Orleans-style inn surrounds a lush
courtyard and fountain. The rooms are decorated with antiques
and wallpapers. Wine and cheese is served during the evening

in front of the fireplace. Named after Eiler Larsen, famous town
greeter of Laguna, the inn is just a stone's throw from the
beach on the ocean side of Pacific Coast Highway.
Innkeeper(s): Maria Mestas. $100-175. MC, VISA, AX. 12 rooms with PB, 1
with FP and 1 suite. Breakfast included in rates. Type of meal: Cont plus.
Beds: KQD. TV and phone in room. Amusement parks, antiquing, fishing, live
theater and shopping nearby.
Location: City.
Publicity: *California Bride, Los Angeles Magazine, Westways, The Tribune
and Daily News.*
*"Who could find a paradise more relaxing than an old-fashioned bed
and breakfast with Mozart and Vivaldi, a charming fountain, won-
derful fresh-baked bread, ocean air."*
Certificate may be used: October-May, Sunday-Thursday.

Lake Arrowhead   *N11*

Bracken Fern Manor

815 Arrowhead Villas Rd, PO Box 1006
Lake Arrowhead, CA 92352-1006
(909)337-8557 Fax:(909)337-3323

Circa 1929. Opened during the height of the '20s as Lake
Arrowhead's first membership resort, this country inn provided
refuge to Silver Screen heroines, the wealthy and the prominent. Old letters from the Gibson Girls found in the attic
bespoke of elegant parties, dapper gentlemen, the Depression,
Prohibition and homesick hearts. Each room is furnished with
antiques collected from a lifetime of international travel. There
is also a game parlor, wine tasting cellar, library, art gallery and
garden Jacuzzi and sauna. Wine is offered in the afternoon. The
Crestline Historical Society has its own museum and curator
and a map of historical sites you can visit.
Innkeeper(s): Cheryl Weaver. $65-228. MC, VISA, TC. 10 rooms, 9 with PB
and 3 suites. Breakfast included in rates. Types of meals: Full bkfst and early
coffee/tea. Beds: KQDT. VCR, jacuzzi, art gallery and garden & wine cellar on
premises. Antiquing, fishing, live theater, shopping, downhill skiing, cross-
country skiing and water sports nearby.
Location: Mountains.
Publicity: *Mountain Shopper & Historic B&B, The Press Enterprise, Sun
and Lava.*
*"My husband brought me here for my 25th birthday and it was
everything I hoped it would be - peaceful, romantic and so relaxing
.... Thank you for the wonderful memories I will hold close to my
heart always."*
Certificate may be used: March, April, May, January. No holidays.

Lake Tahoe   *F8*

Inn at Heavenly B&B

1261 Ski Run Blvd
Lake Tahoe, CA 96150-8604
(530)544-4244 (800)692-2246 Fax:(530)544-5213
Internet: www.innatheavenly.com
E-mail: mycabin@sierra.net

This inn is just half a mile from the Heavenly Ski Resort and
one mile from Cosmos. Guests will find this log cabin exterior
with theme decorated rooms and rock fireplaces cozy and inviting. Bedchambers offer plenty of amenities, including in-room
coffee makers, refrigerators, microwaves and cable TVs. All
rooms offer VCRs, and there is a complimentary selection of
videos. Guests can reserve to have private use of the hot tub. A
free shuttle goes to casinos and the ski area.
Innkeeper(s): Sue Ogden & Paul Gardner. $125-195. MC, VISA, AX, PC, TC.
15 rooms with PB, 15 with FP, 2 cabins and 1 conference room. Breakfast,
afternoon tea and snacks/refreshments included in rates. Types of meals:

Cont plus and early coffee/tea. Beds: KQD. Cable TV, ceiling fan and VCR in room. Fax, copier, spa, sauna, bicycles, library, park, swings and BBQs on premises. Amusement parks, fishing, live theater, parks, shopping, downhill skiing, cross-country skiing and water sports nearby.
Pets Allowed.
Location: Mountains.
"I've never felt so at home in any lodging. I give 5 stars for hospitality."
Certificate may be used: Early January to Dec. 15, Sunday-Thursday, excluding holidays.

Lakeport   F4

Forbestown B&B Inn

825 N Forbes St
Lakeport, CA 95453-4337
(707)263-7858 Fax:(707)263-7878
Internet: www.innaccess.com/fti
E-mail: forbestowninn@zapcom.net

Circa 1863. Located in the downtown area, this early California farmhouse is just a few blocks from Clear Lake and

the town center. Wisteria drape the front porch. Full breakfasts are served in the dining room with a handsome wall of antique French windows or in the garden as weather permits.

Innkeeper(s): Wally & Pat Kelley. $85-115. MC, VISA, AX, DC, DS, PC, TC. 4 rooms, 2 with PB. Types of meals: Full bkfst and early coffee/tea. Beds: KQ. Ceiling fan in room. VCR, fax, swimming and library on premises. Antiquing, fishing, golf, festivals, local events, parks, shopping, water sports and wineries nearby.
Location: Near Clear Lake.
Certificate may be used: April 15-Nov. 15.

Little River   F2

The Inn at Schoolhouse Creek

7051 N Hwy 1
Little River, CA 95456
(707)937-5525 (800)731-5525 Fax:(707)937-2012
Internet: www.schoolhousecreek.com
E-mail: innkeeper@schoolhousecreek.com

Circa 1860. The Inn at School House Creek offers private cottages and rooms on its eight acres of rose gardens, forests and meadows. (The inn's gardens have been featured in several magazines.) Many cottages include views of the ocean and all offer a fireplace. Located three miles from Mendocino, the inn was a motor court in the '30s. Private beach access to Buckhorn Cove allows guests to enjoy whale watching, sea lions and the crashing waves of the Pacific. Organize your day to include a picnic lunch (available by advance notice) to enjoy at a secluded waterfall in the redwoods. Then take a sunset soak in the inn's ocean view hot tub. The next morning's breakfast may include Fruit Basket Breakfast Pudding with whipped cream, fruit and a variety of freshly baked muffins and breads.

Innkeeper(s): Al & Penny Greenwood. $115-230. MC, VISA, AX, DS, PC, TC. 15 rooms with PB, 15 with FP, 2 suites and 9 cottages. Breakfast included in rates. Types of meals: Cont plus and early coffee/tea. Beds: KQD. Cable TV, phone, VCR, some with whirlpools and kitchens and microwaves in room. Fax, spa and evening hors d'oeuvres on premises. Antiquing, fishing, golf, live theater, parks, shopping, tennis and water sports nearby.
Pets allowed: In designated units, extra fee.
Certificate may be used: Nov. 1-Feb. 28, Sunday-Thursday, holidays and local festivals excluded.

Lucerne   F4

Kristalberg B&B

PO Box 1629
Lucerne, CA 95458-1629
(707)274-8009

This country B&B affords a panoramic view of Clear Lake. Each of the guest rooms is furnished and decorated in a different style. The master suite offers a whirlpool tub and early American decor, other rooms feature French and Spanish decor. The parlor features Victorian and Italian influences. The expansive breakfast is served in the home's formal dining room, and the cuisine features fresh fruit, vegetables and herbs from the garden, and home-baked house specialties. There is a friendly dog in residence.

Innkeeper(s): Merv Myers. $100-165. MC, VISA, AX, DS, PC, TC. 3 rooms. Breakfast included in rates. Type of meal: Full bkfst. Whirlpool tub in master suite in room.
"First rate in food, hospitality, and comfort."
Certificate may be used: November through March and weekdays (Sunday-Friday) April through October.

Mariposa   I8

Rockwood Gardens

5155 Tip Top Rd
Mariposa, CA 95338-9003
(209)742-6817 (800)859-8862 Fax:(209)742-7400

Circa 1989. Nestled among the pines in the Sierra foothills, this five-acre contemporary Prairie-style inn was designed and built to complement the natural beauty found nearby. A creek, oaks, pond and wildflower meadow all are part of the inn's setting. Guests often use the inn as headquarters when exploring the many breath-taking sights of Yosemite National Park. Visitors select from the Rose, Duck and Manzanita rooms. Stroll the grounds and relish the view of evening stars. The inn's suite can accommodate up to four people and is equipped with a dining area, microwave and small refrigerator.

Innkeeper(s): Gerald & Mary Ann Fuller. $65-105. TC. 3 rooms, 1 suite and 1 conference room. Breakfast included in rates. Type of meal: Full bkfst. Beds: KQ. Cable TV, phone, VCR and satellite TV and kitchen in suite in room. Air conditioning. Fax and copier on premises. Antiquing, fishing, Yosemite National Park, parks, shopping, downhill skiing, cross-country skiing and water sports nearby.
Location: Yosemite National Park.
Certificate may be used: Jan. 2 to April 15 & Oct. 1 to Dec. 2, every day.

Mendocino   F2

Brewery Gulch Inn

9350 N Hwy 1
Mendocino, CA 95460-9767
(707)937-4752 (800)578-4454
Internet: www.virtualcities.com

Circa 1864. Located on 12 acres just south of the village, (a one-half-mile walk) there is a spring fed creek, tall pines, wild roses and informal gardens. Beneath an old apple tree, a large copper boiling pot remains from the once active brewery. Guest rooms include some with white-water views, and all have fireplaces. Pecan waffles and cheese blintzes are favorites of returning guests. An abundance of wildlife such as hummingbirds, osprey, woodpeckers, hawks and deer enjoy the property.

Innkeeper(s): Anne Saunders. $75-135. MC, VISA, PC, TC. 5 rooms, 3 with PB, 2 with FP and 2 suites. Breakfast and afternoon tea included in rates.

Type of meal: Full bkfst. Beds: Q. Library on premises. Antiquing, fishing, golf, live theater, parks, shopping, tennis and water sports nearby.
Location: Country.
Publicity: *San Francisco Examiner, Innsider and Home Garden.*
Certificate may be used: Nov. 1 to May 15, Sunday-Thursday, excluding Dec. 23-Jan. 2.

Sea Rock B&B Inn

11101 Lansing St
Mendocino, CA 95460
(707)937-0926 (800)906-0926
Internet: www.searock.com
E-mail: searock@mcn.org

Circa 1930. Enjoy sea breezes and ocean vistas at this inn, which rests on a bluff looking out to the Pacific. Most of the accommodations include a wood-burning Franklin fireplace and featherbed. Four guest rooms are available in the Stratton House, and each affords an ocean view. There are six cottages on the grounds, most offering a sea view. The innkeepers also offer deluxe accommodations in four special suites. Each has an ocean view, wood-burning fireplace, private entrance and a deck. The grounds, which now feature gardens, were the site of an 1870s brewery. The inn is less than half a mile from Mendocino.
Innkeeper(s): Susie & Andy Plocher. $129-259. MC, VISA, AX, DS, PC, TC. 14 rooms with PB, 13 with FP, 8 suites and 6 cottages. Breakfast included in rates. Type of meal: Cont plus. Beds: KQ. Cable TV, phone and VCR in room. Antiquing, fishing, golf, live theater, parks, shopping, tennis and water sports nearby.
Publicity: *California Visitors Review.*
Certificate may be used: Jan. 3-March 1, Monday-Thursday, excluding holiday periods.

Whitegate Inn

499 Howard St
Mendocino, CA 95460
(707)937-4892 (800)531-7282 Fax:(707)937-1131
Internet: www.whitegateinn.com
E-mail: staff@whitegateinn.com

Circa 1883. When it was first built, the local newspaper called Whitegate Inn "one of the most elegant and best appointed residences in town." Its bay windows, steep gabled roof, redwood siding and fish-scale shingles are stunning examples of Victorian architecture. The house's original wallpaper and candelabras adorn the double parlors. There, an antique 1827 piano, at one time part of Alexander Graham Bell's collection, and inlaid pocket doors take you back to a

more gracious time. French and Victorian antique furnishings and fresh flowers add to the inn's elegant hospitality and old world charm. The gourmet breakfasts are artfully presented in the inn's sunlit dining room. The inn is just a block from the ocean, galleries, restaurants and the center of town.
Innkeeper(s): Carol & George Bechtloff. $149-279. MC, VISA, AX, DC, DS, PC, TC. 6 rooms with PB, 6 with FP, 1 suite, 1 cottage and 1 conference room. Breakfast and snacks/refreshments included in rates. Types of meals: Full bkfst and early coffee/tea. Beds: KQT. Cable TV and phone in room. Fax, copier and welcome basket and evening sherry on premises. Antiquing, fishing, golf, horseback riding, whale watching, live theater, parks, shopping, tennis and water sports nearby.
Publicity: *Innsider, Country Inns, Country Home, Glamour, Santa Rosa Press Democrat, San Francisco Chronicle, Bon Appetit, Victoria Magazine, Sunset and San Francisco Examiner.*
Certificate may be used: Nov. 1 through March 30, Sunday-Thursday, no holiday periods, selected rooms.

Montara

The Goose & Turrets B&B

835 George St, PO Box 937
Montara, CA 94037-0937
(650)728-5451 Fax:(650)728-0141
Internet: goose.montara.com
E-mail: rhmgt@montara.com

Circa 1908. In the peaceful setting of horse ranches and strawflower farms, this Italian villa features beautiful gardens surrounded by a 20-foot-high cypress hedge. The gardens

include an orchard, vegetable garden, herb garden, rose garden, fountains, a hammock, swing and plenty of spots to enjoy the sur-
roundings. The large dining and living room areas are filled with art and collectibles. Classical music plays during afternoon tea. Among its many previous uses, the Goose & Turrets once served as Montara's first post office, the town hall and a country club for Spanish-American War veterans.
Innkeeper(s): Raymond & Emily Hoche-Mong. $110-165. MC, VISA, AX, DC, DS, PC, TC. 5 rooms with PB, 3 with FP. Breakfast and afternoon tea included in rates. Beds: KQDT. Turndown service and towel warmer in room. Library, bocce ball court and piano on premises. Antiquing, bicycling, fishing, golf, hiking, horseback riding, nature reserves, whale watching, aero sightseeing, birding, parks and water sports nearby.
Location: Seaside village.
Publicity: *San Diego Union, Tri-Valley, Los Angeles Times, San Jose Mercury, San Jose Mercury News, Half Moon Bay Review, Peninsula Times Tribune, San Mateo Times and Contra Costa Times.*
"You have truly made an art of breakfast and tea-time conversation. We will be back."
Certificate may be used: November through March, Monday through Thursday, holidays excluded.

Monterey

The Jabberwock

598 Laine St
Monterey, CA 93940-1312
(831)372-4777 (888)428-7253 Fax:(831)655-2946
Internet: www.jabberwockinn.com

Circa 1911. Set in a half-acre of gardens, this Craftsman-style inn provides a fabulous view of Monterey Bay with its famous barking seals. When you're ready to settle in for the evening, you'll find huge Victorian beds complete with lace-edged sheets and goose-down comforters. One room includes a Jacuzzi tub. In the late afternoon, hors d'oeuvres and aperitifs are served in an enclosed sun
porch. After dinner, guests are tucked into bed with homemade chocolate chip cookies and milk. To help guests avoid long lines, the innkeepers have tickets available for the popular and nearby Monterey Bay Aquarium.
Innkeeper(s): Joan & John Kiliany. $115-225. MC, VISA. 7 rooms, 5 with PB, 3 with FP. Types of meals: Full gourmet bkfst and early coffee/tea. Beds: KQ. One room with Jacuzzi in room. Fax and copier on premises. Antiquing, fishing, restaurants, live theater, parks, shopping and water sports nearby.
Location: City.
Publicity: *Sunset, Travel & Leisure, Sacramento Bee, San Francisco*

Examiner, Los Angeles Times, Country Inns, San Francisco Chronicle, Diablo and Elmer Dill's KABC-Los Angeles TV.

"Words are not enough to describe the ease and tranquility of the atmosphere of the home, rooms, owners and staff at the Jabberwock."

Certificate may be used: Nov. 1-April 30, Sunday-Thursday.

Mount Shasta   B5

Mount Shasta Ranch B&B

1008 W.A. Barr Rd
Mount Shasta, CA 96067-9465
(530)926-3870 Fax:(530)926-6882
Internet: www.travelassist.com/reg/ca121s.html
E-mail: alpinere@snowcrest.net

Circa 1923. This large two-story ranch house offers a full view of Mt. Shasta from its 60-foot-long redwood porch. Spaciousness abounds from the 1,500-square-foot living room with a massive rock fireplace to the large suites with private bathrooms that include large tubs and roomy showers. A full country breakfast may offer cream cheese-stuffed French toast or fresh, wild blackberry crepes. Just minutes away, Lake Siskiyou boasts superb fishing, sailing, swimming, and 18 hole golf course with public tennis courts.

Innkeeper(s): Bill & Mary Larsen. $50-95. MC, VISA, AX, DS, PC, TC. 9 rooms, 4 with PB, 1 cottage and 1 conference room. Breakfast included in rates. Types of meals: Full bkfst and early coffee/tea. Beds: Q. Cable TV and ceiling fan in room. Air conditioning. VCR, fax, copier, spa and library on premises. Antiquing, fishing, parks, shopping, downhill skiing, cross-country skiing and water sports nearby. Pets Allowed.

Certificate may be used: Sunday through Thursday, holidays excluded.

Murphys   H7

Trade Carriage House

230 Big Trees Rd/600 Algiers St
Murphys, CA 95247
(209)728-3909 (800)800-3408 Fax:(209)728-2527
Internet: www.realtyworld-murphys.com
E-mail: sales@realtyworld-murphys.com

Circa 1930. This little cottage is surrounded by a white picket fence. The structure was built in Stockton and was later moved to Murphys, a historic California town. There are two bedrooms, furnished with antiques and wicker pieces. A second cottage three doors down offers a deck overlooking the treetops. There is no meal service, but the cottages have kitchens. Shops, restaurants and other local sites are within walking distance.

Innkeeper(s): Cynthia Trade. $125. PC, TC. 2 cottages. Beds: QD. Cable TV and phone in room. Air conditioning. Antiquing, fishing, golf, major area for wineries, live theater, parks, shopping, downhill skiing, cross-country skiing, tennis and water sports nearby. Location: Gold Country Foothills.

Certificate may be used: any weekday Tuesday through Thursday, except third Thursday in May.

Napa   H4

1801 Inn

1801 First St
Napa, CA 94581
(707)224-3739 (800)518-0146 Fax:(707)224-3932
Internet: www.napavalley.com/lodging/inns/1801/index.html
E-mail: the1801inn@aol.com

Circa 1903. The innkeepers at this Queen Anne Victorian have created a setting perfect for romance. The guest rooms feature

Victorian decor, Oriental rugs top the hardwood floors, and beds are dressed with fine linens and soft comforters. Each guest bathroom has a large soaking tub, and each bedchamber has a fireplace. The turn-of-the-century inn is located in Old Town Napa and is close to the multitude of wineries in the valley, as well as antique shops and restaurants.

Innkeeper(s): Linda & Chris Craiker. $135-229. MC, VISA, DS, TC. 5 rooms with PB, 5 with FP. Breakfast and snacks/refreshments included in rates. Type of meal: Full gourmet bkfst. Beds: K. Ceiling fan in room. Air conditioning. VCR and fax on premises. Antiquing, fishing, golf, ballooning, hiking, horseback riding, live theater, parks, shopping, tennis and water sports nearby. Location: Wine country.
Publicity: *Sacramento Bee.*

Certificate may be used: Jan. 5-April 30, Sunday-Thursday.

Beazley House

1910 1st St
Napa, CA 94559-2351
(707)257-1649 (800)559-1649 Fax:(707)257-1518
Internet: www.beazleyhouse.com
E-mail: innkeeper@beazleyhouse.com

Circa 1902. Nestled in green lawns and gardens, this graceful shingled mansion is frosted with white trim on its bays and balustrades. Stained-glass windows and polished-wood floors

set the atmosphere in the parlor. There are six rooms in the main house, and the carriage house features five more, many with fireplaces and whirlpool tubs. The venerable Beazley House was Napa's first bed & breakfast inn.

Innkeeper(s): Carol Beazley, Jim Beazley, Scott Beazley, Lorna T. $125-275. MC, VISA, AX, PC. 11 rooms with PB. Breakfast included in rates. Type of meal: Full bkfst. Beds: KQDT. Phone, ceiling fan and fireplaces in room. Central air. Fax and library on premises. Handicap access. Amusement parks, antiquing, art galleries, bicycling, fishing, golf, hiking, horseback riding, museums, parks, shopping, tennis and wineries nearby. Location: Napa Valley wine country.
Publicity: *Los Angeles Times, USA Today, Sacramento Bee, Yellow Brick Road and Emergo.*

"There's a sense of peace & tranquility that hovers over this house, sprinkling magical dream dust & kindness."

Certificate may be used: Dec. 1-23, Sunday-Thursday and Jan. 2-30, Sunday-Thursday.

Belle Epoque

1386 Calistoga Ave
Napa, CA 94559-2552
(707)257-2161 (800)238-8070 Fax:(707)226-6314
Internet: labelleepoque.com
E-mail: innkeeper@labelleepoque.com

Circa 1893. This Queen Anne Victorian has a wine cellar and tasting room where guests can casually sip Napa Valley wines. The inn, which is one of the most unique architectural structures found in the wine country, is located in the heart of Napa's Calistoga Historic District. Beautiful origi-

nal stained-glass windows include a window from an old church. One guest room offers a whirlpool tub. A selection of fine restaurants and shops are within easy walking distance, as well as the riverfront, city parks and the Wine Train Depot. The train, which serves all meals, takes you just beyond St. Helena and back.

Innkeeper(s): Georgia Jump. $170-295. MC, VISA, AX, DS, PC, TC. 6 rooms with PB, 3 with FP, 3 suites and 1 conference room. Breakfast and snacks/refreshments included in rates. Types of meals: Full gourmet bkfst and early coffee/tea. Beds: KQT. Cable TV, phone, ceiling fan, VCR and whirlpools in room. Air conditioning. Fax, copier and spa on premises. Amusement parks, antiquing, golf, live theater, parks, shopping, sporting events and tennis nearby.

Location: Wine country.

"At first I was a bit leery, how can a B&B get consistent rave reviews? After staying here two nights, I am now a believer!"

Certificate may be used: Dec. 1-23, Jan. 1-March 15, Monday-Thursday, holidays excluded.

Hennessey House-Napa's 1889 Queen Anne Victorian B&B

1727 Main St
Napa, CA 94559-1844
(707)226-3774 Fax:(707)226-2975
Internet: www.hennesseyhouse.com
E-mail: inn@hennesseyhouse.com

Circa 1889. Colorful gardens surround this gracious Victorian, once home to Dr. Edwin Hennessey, a Napa County physician. Pristinely renovated, the inn features stained-glass windows and a curving wraparound porch. A hand-
some hand-painted, stamped-tin
ceiling graces the dining room.
The inn's romantic rooms are furnished in antiques and some offer
fireplaces, feather beds and spa
tubs. There is a sauna and a gar-
den fountain. The innkeepers serve gourmet breakfasts and evening wine and cheese. Walk to inviting restaurants and shops. Nearby are the world-famous Napa Valley wineries. Enjoy the area's spas, hot air balloons, cycling and hiking are the most popular activities.

Innkeeper(s): Gilda & Alex Feit. $105-250. MC, VISA, AX, DC, DS. 10 rooms with PB, 5 with FP. Breakfast included in rates. Type of meal: Full bkfst. Beds: KQT. Ceiling fan in room. Air conditioning. Fax, spa and sauna on premises. Antiquing, wine train packages and shopping nearby.

Location: City.

Publicity: *AM-PM Magazine.*

"A great place to relax in Napa!"

Certificate may be used: Nov. 10-March 10, Sunday-Thursday, holidays excluded.

Old World Inn

1301 Jefferson St
Napa, CA 94559-2412
(707)257-0112 (800)966-6624 Fax:(707)257-0118
Internet: www.napavalley.com/oldworld

Circa 1906. The decor in this exquisite bed & breakfast is second to none. In 1981, Macy's sought out the inn to showcase
a new line of fabrics
inspired by Scandinavian
artist Carl Larrson. Each
romantic room is adorned
in bright, welcoming col-
ors and includes special
features such as canopy

beds and clawfoot tubs. The Garden Room boasts three sky-lights, and the Anne Room is a must for honeymoons and romantic retreats. The walls and ceilings are painted in a warm peach and blue, bows are stenciled around the perimeter of the room. A decorated canopy starts at the ceiling in the center of the bed and falls downward producing a curtain-like effect. A buffet breakfast is served each morning and a delicious after-noon tea and wine and cheese social will curb your appetite until dinner. After sampling one of Napa's gourmet eateries, return to the inn where a selection of desserts await you.

Innkeeper(s): Sam Van Hoeve. $135-225. MC, VISA, AX, DS, PC, TC. 10 rooms with PB, 6 with FP, 1 suite and 1 cottage. Breakfast, afternoon tea and snacks/refreshments included in rates. Types of meals: Full gourmet bkfst and early coffee/tea. Beds: KQT. Cable TV, phone, ceiling fan and VCR in room. Air conditioning. Fax and spa on premises. Antiquing, fishing, golf, live theater, parks, shopping, sporting events and tennis nearby.

Location: Wine country.

Publicity: *Napa Valley Traveller.*

"Excellent is an understatement. We'll return."

Certificate may be used: Nov. 15 through March 31, Sunday through Thursday, except holidays.

Stahlecker House B&B Country Inn & Garden

1042 Easum Dr
Napa, CA 94558-5525
(707)257-1588 (800)799-1588 Fax:(707)224-7429
Internet: www.stahleckerhouse.com
E-mail: stahlbnb@aol.com

Circa 1949. This country inn is situated on the banks of tree-lined Napa Creek. The acre and a half of grounds feature rose and orchard gardens, fountains and manicured lawns. Guests
often relax on the sun
deck. There is an antique
refrigerator stocked with
soft drinks and lemonade.
Full, gourmet breakfasts
are served by candlelight
in the glass-wrapped din-
ing room that overlooks
the gardens. In the
evenings, coffee, tea and freshly made choco-
late chip cookies are served. The Napa Wine Train station is five minutes away. Wineries, restaurants, antique shops, bike paths and hiking all are nearby.

Innkeeper(s): Ron & Ethel Stahlecker. $135-279. MC, VISA, AX, DS, TC. 4 rooms with PB, 4 with FP and 1 suite. Breakfast and snacks/refreshments included in rates. Types of meals: Full gourmet bkfst and early coffee/tea. Beds: QT. TV, phone, turndown service and Couple Spa/Couple Shower in room. Air conditioning. Library and ping pong and croquet on premises. Antiquing, fishing, golf, hiking, hot air balloons, live theater, parks, shopping, tennis and wineries nearby.

Location: Wine country.

Publicity: *Brides and Napa Valley Traveler.*

"Friendly hosts and beautiful gardens."

Certificate may be used: Monday-Thursday only, Nov. 1 to April 30 (not valid in summer, no holidays).

Nevada City   F6

Emma Nevada House

528 E Broad St
Nevada City, CA 95959-2213
(530)265-4415 (800)916-3662 Fax:(530)265-4416
Internet: www.nevadacityinns.com
E-mail: emmanev@nevadacityinns.com

Circa 1856. The childhood home of 19th-century opera star
Emma Nevada now serves as an attractive Queen Anne
Victorian inn. English roses line the white picket fence in front,
and the forest-like back garden
has a small stream with bench-
es. The Empress' Chamber is
the most romantic room with
ivory Italian linens atop a
French antique bed, a bay window and a massive French
armoire. Some rooms have
whirlpool baths and TV. Guests
enjoy relaxing in the hexagonal sunroom and on the inn's wrap-
around porches. Empire Mine State Historic Park is nearby.
Innkeeper(s): Ruth Ann Riese. $105-160. MC, VISA, AX, DC, PC, TC. 6
rooms with PB, 2 with FP. Breakfast and afternoon tea included in rates.
Types of meals: Full bkfst and early coffee/tea. Beds: Q. Clawfoot and Jacuzzi
tubs in room. Air conditioning. Fax and library on premises. Antiquing, fishing, live theater, parks, shopping, downhill skiing and water sports nearby.
Location: Town in foothills.
Publicity: *Country Inns, Gold Rush Scene, Sacramento Focus, The Union, Los
Angeles Times, San Jose Mercury News, Sacramento Bee and Karen Browns.*
*"A delightful experience: such airiness and hospitality in the midst of
so much history. We were fascinated by the detail and the faithfulness
of the restoration. This house is a quiet solace for city-weary travel-
ers. There's a grace here."*
Certificate may be used: Jan. 2 to April 30, Monday-Thursday, no holidays.

The Red Castle Inn Historic Lodgings

109 Prospect St
Nevada City, CA 95959-2831
(530)265-5135 (800)761-4766

Circa 1860. The Smithsonian has lauded the restoration of this
four-story brick Gothic Revival known as "The Castle" by
townsfolk. Its roof is laced with wooden icicles and the balconies are adorned with gingerbread. Within, there are intricate
moldings, antiques, Victorian wallpapers, canopy beds and decorative wood stoves. Verandas provide views of the historic city
through cedar, chestnut and walnut trees, and of terraced gardens with a fountain pond. A French chef prepares the inn's
creative breakfasts.
Innkeeper(s): Conley & Mary Louise Weaver. $110-150. MC, VISA, PC, TC. 7
rooms with PB and 3 suites. Breakfast and afternoon tea included in rates.
Types of meals: Full gourmet bkfst and early coffee/tea. Beds: QD. Turndown
service and cassette and radio in room. Air conditioning. Library and phone
upon request on premises. Antiquing, fishing, live theater, parks, shopping,
downhill skiing, cross-country skiing and water sports nearby.
Location: Mountains.
Publicity: *Sunset, Gourmet, Northern California Home & Garden,
Sacramento Bee, Los Angeles Times, Travel Holiday, Victorian Homes,
Innsider, U.S. News & World Report, USAir, McCalls, New York Times,
Brides, San Francisco Focus and Motorland.*
*"The Red Castle Inn would top my list of places to stay. Nothing else
quite compares with it."—Gourmet*
Certificate may be used: Sunday through Thursday, April 1-Aug. 31 except
Easter week and town special events; any day, Jan. 1-March 31 except town
special events.

Nice   F4

Featherbed Railroad Company B&B

2870 Lakeshore Blvd, PO Box 4016
Nice, CA 95464
(707)274-4434 (800)966-6322
Internet: featherbedrailroad.com
E-mail: rooms@featherbedrailroad.com

Circa 1940. Located on five acres on Clear Lake, this unusual
inn features guest rooms in nine luxuriously renovated, painted
and papered cabooses. Each has its own featherbed and private
bath, most have Jacuzzi tubs for two. The Southern Pacific
cabooses have a bay window alcove, while those from the Santa
Fe feature small cupolas.
Innkeeper(s): Lorraine Bassignani. $90-140. MC, VISA, AX, DS. 9 rooms
with PB. Breakfast included in rates. Type of meal: Full bkfst. Beds: QDT.
Cable TV and VCR in room. Spa on premises.
Publicity: *Santa Rosa Press Democrat, Fairfield Daily Republic, London
Times and Travel & Leisure.*
Certificate may be used: Sunday-Thursday, Oct. 15-April 15.

Nipomo   M7

The Kaleidoscope Inn

130 E Dana St
Nipomo, CA 93444-1297
(805)929-5444 Fax:(805)929-5440
Internet: sites.netscape.net/kaleidoscopeinn/homepage
E-mail: kaleidoscope@pronet.net

Circa 1887. The sunlight that streams through the stained-
glass windows of this charming Victorian creates a kaleidoscope
effect and thus the name. The inn is surrounded by one acre of
gardens. Each romantic guest room is dec-
orated with antiques, and the library
offers a fireplace. The parlor includes
an 1886 Steinway upright piano.
Fresh flowers add a special touch.
Breakfast is served either in the dining
room or in the gardens. L.A. Times
readers voted the inn as one of the best
lodging spots for under $100 per night.
Innkeeper(s): Edward & Carol De Leon. $95. MC, VISA, AX, DS. 3 rooms
with PB and 1 conference room. Breakfast included in rates. Types of meals:
Full gourmet bkfst and early coffee/tea. Beds: KQ. Turndown service and ceiling fan in room. VCR and library on premises. Antiquing, fishing, live theater,
parks, shopping and water sports nearby.
Location: Small town.
Publicity: *71 Places To Stay Under $100.00, Santa Maria Times, Los
Angeles Times and Country.*
*"Beautiful room, chocolates, fresh flowers, peaceful night's rest,
great breakfast."*
Certificate may be used: Monday through Thursday, year-round. Holidays
excluded.

Oakland   H4

Dockside Boat & Bed

419 Water St
Oakland, CA 94607
(510)444-5858 (800)436-2574 Fax:(510)444-0420
Internet: www.boatandbed.com

Circa 1980. Enjoy views of San Francisco's skyline at this
unique bed & breakfast, which offers dockside lodging aboard

private motor or sailing yachts. The 14 private yachts vary in size from a 35-foot vessel to a 60-foot yacht. Each boat includes staterooms, galleys, bathrooms and living/dining areas. A continental breakfast is served each morning. Private charters and catered, candlelight dinners can be arranged. The yachts are docked at Pier 39 in San Francisco and Jack London Square in Oakland. A third location is in Long Beach harbor in the Los Angeles area, and it provides a selection of boats within view of the Queen Mary, the new Aquarium, the Long Beach skyline or the Pacific Ocean. All locations are convenient to restaurants, shops and other attractions.

Innkeeper(s): Rob & Mollie Harris. $125-500. MC, VISA, AX, DS, TC. Breakfast included in rates. Type of meal: Cont. Beds: QDT. VCR in room. Fax and copier on premises. Antiquing, fishing, museums, live theater, parks, shopping, sporting events and water sports nearby.
Location: City.
Publicity: *Chicago Tribune, San Francisco Chronicle, San Jose Mercury News, San Francisco Chronicle, Portland Oregonian, Denver Post, Washington Post, Today Show, Channel 2 and 4 & 5 (Bay area).*
Certificate may be used: Sunday through Thursday evenings (maximum six nights per year), Nov. 1-March 30.

Pacific Grove   J5

Centrella B&B Inn

612 Central Ave
Pacific Grove, CA 93950-2611
(408)372-3372 (800)433-4732 Fax:(408)372-2036
Internet: www.centrellainn.com
E-mail: concierge@innsbythesea.com

Circa 1889. Pacific Grove was founded as a Methodist resort in 1875, and this home, built just after the town's incorporation, was billed by a local newspaper as, "the largest, most commodious and pleasantly located boarding house in the Grove." Many a guest is still sure to agree. The rooms are well-appointed in a comfortable, Victorian style. Six guest rooms include fireplaces. The Garden Room has a private entrance, fire-

place, wet bar, Jacuzzi tub and a canopy bed topped with designer linens. Freshly baked croissants or pastries and made-to-order waffles are common fare at the inn's continental buffet breakfast. The inn is within walking distance of the Monterey Bay Aquarium, the beach and many Pacific Grove shops.

Innkeeper(s): Mark Arellano. $109-239. MC, VISA, AX, DS, PC, TC. 26 rooms with PB, 6 with FP, 2 suites and 5 cottages. Breakfast, afternoon tea and snacks/refreshments included in rates. Type of meal: Cont plus. Beds: KQT. Phone in room. VCR, fax, copier and TVs upon request on premises. Antiquing, golf, parks and water sports nearby.
Location: City.
Publicity: *Country Inns, New York Times and San Francisco Examiner.*
"I was ecstatic at the charm that the Centrella has been offering travelers for years and hopefully hundreds of years to come. The bed—perfect! I am forever enthralled by the old beauty and will remember this forever!"
Certificate may be used: Sunday-Thursday excluding July, August, holiday and special events.

Gatehouse Inn

225 Central Ave
Pacific Grove, CA 93950-3017
(831)649-8436 (800)753-1881 Fax:(831)648-8044

Circa 1884. This Italianate Victorian seaside inn is just a block from the Monterey Bay. The inn is decorated with Victorian and 20th-century antiques and touches of Art Deco. Guest rooms feature fireplaces, clawfoot tubs and down comforters. Some rooms have ocean views. The dining room boasts opulent Bradbury & Bradbury Victorian wallpapers as do some of the guest rooms. Afternoon hors d'oeuvres, wine and tea are served. The refrigerator is stocked for snacking.

$110-195. MC, VISA, AX, DS, PC, TC. 9 rooms with PB, 5 with FP. Breakfast, afternoon tea and snacks/refreshments included in rates. Beds: KQT. Phone and turndown service in room. Fax and copier on premises. Antiquing, fishing, live theater, parks, shopping and water sports nearby.
Publicity: *San Francisco Chronicle, Monterey Herald, Time, Newsweek, Inland Empire and Bon Appetit.*
"Thank you for spoiling us."
Certificate may be used: Jan. 1-April 30, Sunday-Thursday.

Gosby House Inn

643 Lighthouse Ave,
Pacific Grove, CA 93950-2643
(831)375-1287 (800)527-8828 Fax:(831)655-9621

Circa 1887. Built as an upscale Victorian inn for those visiting the old Methodist retreat, this sunny yellow mansion features an abundance of gables, turrets and bays. During renovation the innkeeper slept in all the rooms to determine just what antiques were needed and how the beds should be situated. Eleven of the romantic rooms include fireplaces and many offer canopy beds. The Carriage House rooms include fireplaces, decks and spa tubs. Gosby House, which has been open to guests for more than a century, is in the National Register. Gosby House is one of the Four Sisters Inns. The Monterey Bay Aquarium is nearby.

$90-170. MC, VISA, AX, TC. 22 rooms, 20 with PB, 11 with FP. Breakfast and afternoon tea included in rates. Types of meals: Full gourmet bkfst and early coffee/tea. Beds: KQD. Phone, turndown service, bath robes and newspaper in room. Fax, copier and bicycles on premises. Handicap access. Antiquing, aquarium, 17-mile drive and shopping nearby.
Publicity: *San Francisco Chronicle, Oregonian, Los Angeles Times and Travel & Leisure.*
Certificate may be used: November through February, Sunday-Thursday excluding holidays and special events.

Green Gables Inn

104 5th St
Pacific Grove, CA 93950-2903
(831)375-2095 (800)722-1774 Fax:(831)375-5437

Circa 1888. This half-timbered Queen Anne Victorian appears as a fantasy of gables overlooking spectacular Monterey Bay. The parlor has stained-glass panels framing the fireplace and bay windows looking out to the sea. A favorite focal point is an antique carousel

horse. Most of the guest rooms have panoramic views of the ocean, fireplaces, gleaming woodwork, soft quilts and teddy bears, and four rooms have spa tubs. Across the street is the Monterey Bay paved oceanfront cycling path. (Mountain bikes may be borrowed from the inn.) Green Gables is one of the Four Sisters Inns.

Innkeeper(s): Lucia Root. $120-240. MC, VISA, AX, TC. 11 rooms, 7 with PB, 7 with FP and 1 suite. Breakfast and afternoon tea included in rates. Type of meal: Full gourmet bkfst. Beds: KQD. TV, phone, turndown service, terry robes and newspaper in room. Fax, copier and bicycles on premises. Handicap access. Antiquing, aquarium, live theater and shopping nearby.
Publicity: *Travel & Leisure and Country Living.*
Certificate may be used: December and January, Sunday-Thursday excluding holidays and special events.

Palm Springs   O12

Casa Cody Country Inn
175 S Cahuilla Rd
Palm Springs, CA 92262-6331
(760)320-9346 (800)231-2639 Fax:(760)325-8610
Circa 1920. Casa Cody, built by a relative of Wild Bill Cody and situated in the heart of Palm Springs, is the town's oldest continuously operating inn. The San Jacinto Mountains provide a scenic background for  the tree-shaded spa, the pink and purple bougainvillea and the blue waters of the inn's two swimming pools. Each suite has a small kitchen and features red and turquoise Southwestern decor. Several have wood-burning fireplaces. There are Mexican pavers, French doors and private patios. The area offers many activities, including museums, a heritage center, boutiques, a botanical garden, horseback riding and golf.

Innkeeper(s): Elissa Goforth. $79-299. MC, VISA, AX, DC, CB, DS, PC, TC. 23 rooms, 24 with PB, 10 with FP, 8 suites and 2 cottages. Breakfast included in rates. Type of meal: Cont plus. Beds: KQT. Cable TV, phone and ceiling fan in room. Air conditioning. Fax, copier, spa, swimming and library on premises. Antiquing, hiking, horseback riding, tennis, golf, ballooning, polo and live theater nearby.
Pets Allowed.
Location: Heart of village.
Publicity: *New York Times, Washington Post, Los Angeles Times, San Diego Union Tribune, Seattle Times, Portland Oregonian, Los Angeles, San Diego Magazine, Pacific Northwest Magazine, Sunset, Westways and Alaska Airlines Magazine.*
"Outstanding ambiance, friendly relaxed atmosphere."
Certificate may be used: May 3 to Dec. 20, Sunday through Thursday for any large studio or one-bedroom suite, except holidays.

Sakura, Japanese B&B
1677 N Via Miraleste at Vista Chino
Palm Springs, CA 92262
(760)327-0705 (800)200-0705 Fax:(760)327-6847
Circa 1945. An authentic Japanese experience awaits guests of this private home, distinctively decorated with Japanese artwork and antique kimonos. Guests are encouraged to leave their shoes at the door, grab kimonos and slippers and discover what real relaxation is all about. Guests may choose either American or Japanese breakfasts, and Japanese or vegetarian dinners also are available. The Palm Springs area is home to more than 90 golf courses and many fine shops. During the summer months, the innkeepers conduct tours in Japan.

Innkeeper(s): George & Fumiko Cebra. $45-75. 3 rooms, 2 with PB and 1 suite. Breakfast included in rates. Types of meals: Full bkfst & early coffee/tea. Beds: Q. Cable TV, phone & ice pack cooler in room. Air conditioning. VCR, fax, spa, child care & CD player on premises. Amusement parks, antiquing, fishing, live theater, parks, shopping, cross-country skiing, sporting events & water sports nearby.
Location: California desert.
Certificate may be used: All year, Sunday through Thursday.

Pauma Valley   P12

Cupid's Castle B&B
17622 Hwy 76
Pauma Valley, CA 92061
(760)742-3306 Fax:(760)742-3306
Internet: www.cupidscastlebnb.com
E-mail: cupidscastle@1x.netcom.com
Circa 1995. The five acres surrounding this four-story "castle" include gardens with fountains and waterfalls and a fragrant lemon orchard. There's a willow wood love seat swing, as well. Popular for honeymoons and wedding anniversaries, rooms offer Jacuzzi tubs and private balconies, all have canopy beds. The innkeeper collects cupids, and you may spot her collection here and there. A full breakfast is served, and you can make arrangements for a specially prepared dinner such as grilled salmon with buttery pilaf and homemade white chocolate cheesecake. Nearby are wineries, golf courses and Palomar Mountain. Area activities include cycling, ballooning and gambling.

Innkeeper(s): Ted & Connie Vlasis. $175-250. MC, VISA, AX, DS, PC, TC. 4 rooms with PB. Breakfast included in rates. Types of meals: Full bkfst, veg bkfst & early coffee/tea. Beds: KQ. Turndown service, ceiling fan, private balconies and all with Jacuzzi in room. Central air. VCR, fax, copier, spa and library on premises. Handicap access. Amusement parks, antiquing, art galleries, beaches, bicycling, canoeing/kayaking, fishing, golf, hiking, horseback riding, gambling casinos, live theater, museums, parks, shopping, water sports & wineries nearby.
Location: Farm.
Certificate may be used: Anytime when rooms are available.

Petaluma   H4

Cavanagh Inn
10 Keller St
Petaluma, CA 94952-2939
(707)765-4657 (888)765-4658 Fax:(707)769-0466
Internet: www.cavanaghinn.com
E-mail: info@cavanaghinn.com
Circa 1902. Embrace turn-of-the-century California at this picturesque Georgian Revival manor. The garden is filled with beautiful flowers, plants and fruit trees. Innkeeper Jeanne Farris is an award-winning chef and prepares the mouth-watering breakfasts. The innkeepers also serve wine at 5:30 p.m. The parlor and library, which boasts heart-of-redwood paneled walls, is an ideal place to relax. Cavanagh Inn is located at the edge of Petaluma's historic district, and close to shops and the riverfront. Petaluma is 32 miles north of the Golden Gate.

Innkeeper(s): Ray & Jeanne Farris. $100-145. MC, VISA, AX, PC. 7 rooms, 5 with PB and 1 conference room.. Breakfast included in rates. Type of meal: Full gourmet bkfst. Beds: KQDT. Turndown service and electric blankets in room. VCR, fax & library on premises. Antiquing, live theater, parks & shopping nearby.
Location: City.
Publicity: *Argus-Courier, Arizona Daily Star, Travel Today and L.A. Times.*
"This is our first B&B. . .sort of like learning to drive with a Rolls-Royce!"
Certificate may be used: Jan. 2-June 1 and Oct. 1 to Dec. 30, Sunday-Thursday.

Point Reyes Station H4

Carriage House

325 Mesa Rd, PO Box 1239
Point Reyes Station, CA 94956-1239
(415)663-8627 (800)613-8351
Internet: www.carriagehousebb.com

Circa 1960. This remodeled home boasts a view of Inverness Ridge. One guest room and two suites are furnished in antiques and folk art with a private parlor, television, VCR and a fireplace. Children are welcome and cribs and daybeds are available. Point Reyes National Seashore has 100 miles of trails for cycling, hiking or horseback riding. Breakfast items such as freshly squeezed juice, muffins and breads are stocked in your room, so guests may enjoy it at leisure.
Innkeeper(s): Felicity Kirsch. $125-175. 3 rooms with PB, 2 with FP and 2 suites. Breakfast included in rates. Type of meal: Cont plus. Beds: QT. Cable TV and VCR in room. Antiquing, fishing, parks and shopping nearby. Location: Rural.
"What a rejuvenating getaway. We loved it. The smells, sounds and scenery were wonderful."
Certificate may be used: Jan. 3-June 15, Monday-Thursday.

The Tree House

PO Box 1075
Point Reyes Station, CA 94956-1075
(415)663-8720

Circa 1970. This homestay offers an outstanding view of Point Reyes Station from the deck and some of the guest rooms. The King's Room features a king-size waterbed while Queen Quarter boasts its own fireplace. A hot tub is tucked away in a cozy spot of the garden.
Innkeeper(s): Lisa Patsel. $110-145. 3 rooms with PB, 2 with FP and 1 suite. Breakfast included in rates. Type of meal: Cont plus. Phone, ceiling fan and VCR in room. Spa and pet boarding on premises. Antiquing, parks and shopping nearby. Location: Hiking.
Certificate may be used: Sunday through Thursday, January to Dec. 31 (no holidays or weekends).

Rancho Cucamonga O11

Christmas House B&B

9240 Archibald Ave
Rancho Cucamonga, CA 91730-5236
(909)980-6450

Circa 1904. This Queen Anne Victorian has been renovated in period elegance, emphasizing its intricate wood carvings and red and green stained-glass windows. Once surrounded by 80 acres of citrus groves and vineyards, the home, with its wide, sweeping veranda, is still a favorite place for taking in the beautiful lawns and palm trees. The elegant atmosphere attracts the business traveler, romance-seeker and vacationer.
Innkeeper(s): Janice Ilsley. $85-185. MC, VISA, AX, DS. 6 rooms, 4 with PB, 3 with FP, 1 suite and 1 conference room. Breakfast included in rates. Types of meals: Full gourmet bkfst and early coffee/tea. Beds: QD. TV, phone, ceiling fan and VCR in room. Air conditioning. Spa on premises. Antiquing, fishing, live theater, shopping, downhill skiing and sporting events nearby. Location: Foothills.
Publicity: *Country Inns, Los Angeles Times and Elan.*
"Coming to Christmas House is like stepping through a magic door into an enchanted land. Many words come to mind — warmth, serenity, peacefulness."
Certificate may be used: Any night except Saturday night and holidays.

Reedley J8

The Fairweather Inn B&B

259 S Reed Ave
Reedley, CA 93654-2845
(559)638-1918

Circa 1914. This Craftsman-style inn is situated on the bluffs of the Kings River, a half-hour's drive from Sequoia and Kings Canyon national parks. After a restful night in one of the inn's four guest rooms, all with queen beds, visitors will enjoy their gourmet breakfast in the dining room. The antique-filled inn is within walking distance of downtown restaurants and shops, and Reedley also offers a beautiful golf course near the river. Fresno and Visalia are 20 minutes away.
Innkeeper(s): Violet Demyan. $85-95. MC, VISA, AX. 4 rooms, 2 with PB and 1 suite. Breakfast included in rates. Type of meal: Full bkfst. Beds: Q. Air conditioning. Antiquing, fishing, downhill skiing, sporting events and water sports nearby.
"The Fairweather Inn is like an 'Oasis in the Desert'."
Certificate may be used: Jan. 30 through Nov. 15, Sunday-Thursday.

Running Springs O12

Spring Oaks B&B Inn & Mountain Retreat Center

PO Box 2918
Running Springs, CA 92382-2918
(909)867-7797 (800)867-9636
Internet: www.springoaks.com
E-mail: springoaks@webtv.net

Circa 1953. From the hot tub at this B&B guests can see for 100 miles. Aside from viewing far-reaching mountains, guests at this mountain home enjoy cozy bedchambers decorated with country furnishings. Each room is different. One features a white iron bed topped with a quilt, a Victorian dollhouse and a wicker rocking chair. The innkeepers offer a variety of specials, including inn-to-inn hiking trips and massage therapy. Breakfasts are healthy and made from organic ingredients.
Innkeeper(s): Bill & Laura Florian. $85-130. MC, VISA, PC. 3 rooms, 1 with PB. Breakfast and afternoon tea included in rates. Type of meal: Full bkfst. Beds: Q. Ceiling fan in room. Spa on premises. Amusement parks, antiquing, fishing, live theater, parks, shopping, downhill skiing, cross-country skiing and water sports nearby. Location: Mountains.
Certificate may be used: When available, subject to availability.

Sacramento G6

Amber House

1315 22nd St
Sacramento, CA 95816-5717
(916)444-8085 (800)755-6526 Fax:(916)552-6529
Internet: www.amberhouse.com
E-mail: innkeeper@amberhouse.com

Circa 1905. These three historic homes on the city's Historic Preservation Register are in a neighborhood of fine historic homes eight blocks from the capitol. Each room is named for a famous poet, artist or composer and features stained
glass, English antiques,
and amenities such as bath
robes and fresh flowers.
Ask about the Van Gogh

Room where you can soak in the heart-shaped Jacuzzi tub-for-two or enjoy one of the rooms with marble baths and Jacuzzi tubs in either the adjacent 1913 Mediterranean mansion or the 1895 Colonial Revival. A gourmet breakfast can be served in your room or in the dining room at a time you request.
$139-269. MC, VISA, AX, DC, CB, DS, PC, TC. 14 rooms with PB, 3 with FP and 1 conference room. Breakfast included in rates. Types of meals: Full gourmet bkfst and early coffee/tea. Beds: KQ. Cable TV, phone, turndown service and VCR in room. Air conditioning. Fax, bicycles, library and voice mail on premises. Antiquing, fishing, live theater, parks, shopping, downhill skiing, cross-country skiing and water sports nearby.
Location: City.
Publicity: *Travel & Leisure and Village Crier.*
"Your cordial hospitality, the relaxing atmosphere and delicious breakfast made our brief business/pleasure trip so much more enjoyable."
Certificate may be used: Anytime, subject to availability.

San Andreas H7

Robin's Nest

PO Box 1408
San Andreas, CA 95249-1408
(209)754-1076 (888)214-9202 Fax:(209)754-3975
Internet: www.robinest.com
E-mail: info@robinest.com

Circa 1895. Expect to be pampered from the moment you walk through the door at this three-story Queen Anne Victorian. Guests are made to feel at home, and treated to an elegant, gourmet breakfast. The late 19th-century gem includes many fine architectural features, including eight-foot round windows, 12-foot ceilings on the first floor and gabled ceilings with roof windows on the second floor. Antiques decorate the guest rooms, with pieces such as a four-poster, step-up bed. One bathroom includes an original seven-foot bathtub. The grounds boast century-old fruit trees, grapevines, a brick well, windmill and the more modern addition of a hot spa.
Innkeeper(s): Karen & Bill Konietzny. $75-125. 9 rooms, 7 with PB. Breakfast included in rates. Type of meal: Full bkfst. Beds: KQDT. Antiquing, fishing, live theater, downhill skiing, cross-country skiing and water sports nearby.
Publicity: *Stockton Record, In Flight and Westways.*
"An excellent job of making guests feel at home."
Certificate may be used: Jan. 1 to Dec. 31, Sunday through Thursday.

San Diego Q12

Heritage Park Inn

2470 Heritage Park Row
San Diego, CA 92110-2803
(619)299-6832 (800)995-2470 Fax:(619)299-9465
Internet: www.heritageparkinn.com
E-mail: innkeeper@heritageparkinn.com

Circa 1889. Situated on a seven-acre Victorian park in the heart of Old Town, this inn is two of seven preserved classic structures. The main house offers a variety of beautifully appointed guest rooms, decked in traditional Victorian furnishings and decor. The opulent

Manor Suite includes two bedrooms, a Jacuzzi tub and sitting room. Several rooms offer ocean views, and guest also can see the nightly fireworks show at nearby Sea World. A collection of classic movies is available, and a different movie is shown each night in the inn's parlor. Guests are treated to a light afternoon tea, and breakfast is served on fine china on candlelit tables. The home is within walking distance to the many sites, shops and restaurants in the historic Old Town.
Innkeeper(s): Nancy & Charles Helsper. $100-235. MC, VISA, TC. 12 rooms with PB, 1 suite and 1 conference room. Breakfast and afternoon tea included in rates. Types of meals: Full gourmet bkfst and early coffee/tea. Beds: KQT. Phone, turndown service and ceiling fan in room. VCR, fax and copier on premises. Antiquing, fishing, San Diego Zoo, Tijuana, live theater, parks, shopping, sporting events and water sports nearby.
Location: City.
Publicity: *Los Angeles Herald Examiner, Innsider, Los Angeles Times, Orange County Register, San Diego Union, In-Flight, Glamour and Country Inns.*
"A beautiful step back in time. Peaceful and gracious."
Certificate may be used: Call innkeeper for dates. Based on availability.

San Francisco H4

Petite Auberge

863 Bush St.
San Francisco, CA 94108-3312
(415)928-6000 (800)365-3004 Fax:(415)775-5717

Circa 1917. This five-story hotel features an ornate baroque design with curved bay windows. Now transformed to a French country inn, there are antiques, fresh flowers and country accessories. Most rooms also have working fireplaces. It's a short walk to the Powell Street cable car. In the evenings, wine and hors d'oeuvres are served. Petite Auberge is one of the Four Sisters Inns.
Innkeeper(s): Brian Miller. $125-245. MC, VISA, AX, TC. 26 rooms with PB, 17 with FP and 1 suite. Breakfast and afternoon tea included in rates. Types of meals: Full gourmet bkfst and early coffee/tea. Beds: KQ. Phone, turndown service, terry robes and valet parking in room. Fax and copier on premises. Handicap access. Antiquing, historic sites, museums, cable, live theater, parks, shopping and sporting events nearby.
Location: City.
Publicity: *Travel & Leisure, Oregonian, Los Angeles Times and Brides.*
"Breakfast was great, and even better in bed!"
Certificate may be used: November through February, Sunday-Thursday, excluding holidays and special events.

Victorian Inn on The Park

301 Lyon St
San Francisco, CA 94117-2108
(415)931-1830 (800)435-1967 Fax:(415)931-1830
Internet: www.citysearch.com/sfo/victorianinn
E-mail: vicinn@aol.com

Circa 1897. This grand three-story Queen Anne inn, built by William Curlett, has an open belvedere turret with a teahouse roof and Victorian railings. Silk-screened wallpapers, created especially for the inn, are accentuated by intricate mahogany and redwood paneling. The opulent Belvedere Suite features French doors opening to a Roman tub for two. Overlooking Golden Gate Park, the inn is 10 minutes from downtown.

Innkeeper(s): Lisa & William Benau. $139-179. MC, VISA, AX, DC, CB, DS, PC, TC. 12 rooms with PB, 3 with FP and 2 suites. Breakfast included in rates. Types of meals: Cont plus and early coffee/tea. Beds: QT. Phone and balcony in room. Fax, library, child care and refrigerator on premises. Antiquing, museums, live theater, parks and sporting events nearby.
Location: City.
Publicity: *New York Times Sunday Travel, Innsider, Country Inns, Good Housekeeping, Good Morning America, Country Inns USA, Great Country Inns of America, PBS Country Inn Series and Traveling Inn Style.*

"The excitement you have about your building comes from the care you have taken in restoring and maintaining your historic structure."

Certificate may be used: Both nights must be Sunday through Thursday. Holidays excluded. Good Dec. 1 to April 30.

White Swan Inn

845 Bush St.
San Francisco, CA 94108-3300
(415)775-1755 (800)999-9570 Fax:(415)775-5717

Circa 1915. This four-story inn is near Union Square and the Powell Street cable car. Beveled-glass doors open to a reception area with granite floors, an antique carousel horse and English artwork. Bay windows and a rear deck contribute to the feeling of an English garden inn. The guest rooms are decorated with bold English wallpapers and prints. All rooms have fireplaces. Turndown service and complimentary newspapers are included, and in the evenings, wine and hors d'oeuvres are served. White Swan is a Four Sisters Inns.

Innkeeper(s): Brian Miller. $175-250. MC, VISA, AX, TC. 26 rooms with PB, 26 with FP, 3 suites and 1 conference room. Breakfast and afternoon tea included in rates. Types of meals: Full gourmet bkfst and early coffee/tea. Beds: KQT. Phone, turndown service, terry robes and newspaper in room. Fax and copier on premises. Antiquing, museums, live theater, parks, shopping and sporting events nearby.
Location: City.
Publicity: *Travel & Leisure, Victoria and Wine Spectator.*

"Wonderfully accommodating. Absolutely perfect."

Certificate may be used: November through February, Sunday-Thursday, excluding holidays and special events.

San Rafael   H4

Casa Soldavini

531 C St
San Rafael, CA 94901-3809
(415)454-3140

The first Italian settlers in San Rafael built this home. Their grandchildren now own it and proudly hang pictures of their family. Grandfather Joseph, a wine maker, planned and planted what are now the lush gardens surrounding the home. The many Italian antiques throughout the house complement the Italian-style decor. A homemade breakfast is included, and snacks and beverages are served throughout the day.

Innkeeper(s): Linda Soldavini Cassidy. $85-125. 3 rooms. Breakfast included in rates. Type of meal: Cont plus.

Certificate may be used: Anytime, upon availability.

Santa Barbara   N8

Blue Dolphin Inn

420 W Montecito St
Santa Barbara, CA 93101-3879
(805)965-2333 (877)722-3657 Fax:(805)962-4907
Internet: www.sbbluedolphininn.com
E-mail: info@sbbluedolphininn.com

Circa 1920. It's a short walk to the beach and harbor from this Victorian inn, which offers accommodations in the main house and adjacent carriage house. Guest rooms are decorated in period style with antiques. Brass beds, tapestry pillows, and fluffy comforters add a romantic touch. Several rooms include fireplaces, Jacuzzi tubs or private balconies.

Innkeeper(s): Pete Chiarenza, Edward Skolak. $98-225. MC, VISA, AX, PC, TC. 9 rooms, 7 with PB and 2 suites. Breakfast and afternoon tea included in rates. Types of meals: Full gourmet bkfst and veg bkfst. Beds: KQT. Cable TV, phone and VCR in room. Air conditioning. Fax, copier and library on premises. Antiquing, art galleries, beaches, bicycling, golf, hiking, horseback riding, roller skating, live theater, museums, parks, water sports and wineries nearby.
Location: City.
Publicity: *Los Angeles Times.*

Certificate may be used: Year round, Sunday through Thursday, excluding holidays.

Cheshire Cat Inn & Cottages

36 W Valerio St
Santa Barbara, CA 93101-2524
(805)569-1610 Fax:(805)682-1876
Internet: www.cheshirecat.com
E-mail: cheshire@cheshirecat.com

Circa 1894. The Eberle family built two graceful houses side by side, one a Queen Anne, the other a Colonial Revival. President McKinley was entertained here on a visit to Santa Barbara. There is a pagoda-like porch, a square and a curved bay, rose gardens, grassy lawns and a gazebo. Laura Ashley wallpapers and furnishings are featured. Outside, guests will enjoy English flower gardens, an outdoor Jacuzzi, a new deck with sitting areas and fountains.

Innkeeper(s): Christine Dunstan. $140-350. MC, VISA, PC, TC. 17 rooms with PB, 7 suites and 1 conference room. Breakfast included in rates. Type of meal: Full bkfst. Beds: KQT. Cable TV, phone and ceiling fan in room. Spa facilities on premises. Amusement parks, antiquing, fishing, live theater, shopping, sporting events and water sports nearby.
Location: City.
Publicity: *Two on the Town, KABC, Los Angeles Times, Santa Barbara, American In Flight and Elmer Dills Recommends.*

"Romantic and quaint."

Certificate may be used: Jan. 1 to June 30; Sept. 15-Dec. 23. No major holidays. Monday through Thursday.

Glenborough Inn

1327 Bath St
Santa Barbara, CA 93101-3630
(805)966-0589 (800)962-0589 Fax:(805)564-8610
Internet: www.glenboroughinn.com
E-mail: info@glenborough.com

Circa 1885. The Victorian and California Craftsman-style homes that comprise the Glenborough are located in the theatre and arts district. Antiques, rich wood trim and elegant fireplace suites with canopy beds are offered. Some rooms also have mini refrigerators or whirlpools tubs. There's always plenty of hospitality and an invitation to try the secluded garden hot tub. Homemade breakfasts, served in the privacy of your room, have been written up in Bon Appetit and Chocolatier. Bedtime cookies and beverages are served, as well. It's a three-block walk to restaurants, shops and the shuttle to the beach.

Innkeeper(s): Michael & Steve. $100-420. MC, VISA, AX, DC, CB, PC, TC. 13 rooms with PB, 12 with FP, 6 suites and 1 cottage. Breakfast included in rates. Types of meals: Full bkfst and cont. Beds: KQD. Phone, ceiling fan, coffee maker, robes, A/C (some rooms) and mini-fridge (some rooms) in room. Fax and spa on premises. Antiquing, fishing, live theater, parks, shopping, sporting events and water sports nearby.
Location: City.
Publicity: *Houston Post, Los Angeles Times and Pasadena Choice.*

"Only gracious service is offered at the Glenborough Inn."
Certificate may be used: October-June, Sunday-Thursday, except holidays.

The Old Yacht Club Inn

431 Corona Del Mar
Santa Barbara, CA 93103-3601
(805)962-1277 (800)676-1676 Fax:(805)962-3989
Internet: www.oldyachtclubinn.com
E-mail: info@oldyachtclubinn.com

Circa 1912. This California Craftsman house was the home of the Santa Barbara Yacht Club during the Roaring '20s. It was opened as Santa Barbara's first B&B and has become renowned for its gourmet food and superb hospitality. Dinner is offered to guests on Saturday nights. Innkeeper Nancy Donaldson is the author of The Old Yacht Club Inn Cookbook.

Innkeeper(s): Nancy Donaldson. $110-195. MC, VISA, AX, DS, PC, TC. 12 rooms with PB and 1 conference room. Breakfast included in rates. Types of meals: Full gourmet bkfst and early coffee/tea. Beds: KQ. TV and phone in room. Fax, copier and bicycles on premises. Antiquing, fishing, live theater, shopping, sporting events and water sports nearby.
Publicity: *Los Angeles and Valley.*

"Donaldson is one of Santa Barbara's better-kept culinary secrets."
Certificate may be used: November, December, January, February, Monday-Thursday evenings only. Weekend and holiday periods excluded. Reservations taken within two weeks of date requested.

Prufrock's Garden Inn By The Beach

600 Linden Ave
Santa Barbara, CA 93013-2040
(805)566-9696 (877)837-6257 Fax:(805)566-9404
Internet: www.prufrocks.com
E-mail: prufrocksgardeninn@yahoo.com

Circa 1904. A white fence surrounds this California-style cottage, located on a palm-lined small-town main street. The home is one block from a beautiful oceanfront state park, said by some to be the "Best Beach in the West." The inn has been honored by a number of awards, including the L.A. Times "Reader's Favorite" and the Santa Barbara Independent's "Most Romantic Getaway." You can understand all this when you note the Jacuzzis, fireplaces and private sitting areas. Relax on the porch or stroll through the lush gardens. Guests will enjoy the inviting aroma of the inn's busy kitchen, a source for sunset hors d'oeuvres and beach picnics. The innkeeper offers romance and historic themed packages.

Innkeeper(s): Judy & Jim Halvorsen. $119-239. MC, VISA, DS. 7 rooms, 5 with PB. Breakfast, afternoon tea and snacks/refreshments included in rates. Types of meals: Full bkfst, cont and early coffee/tea. Beds: Q. Turndown service, sitting area and daybeds in room. VCR, bicycles and gardens on premises. Antiquing, beaches, bicycling, fishing, hiking, tide pools, live theater, parks, shopping, sporting events and wineries nearby.

Location: Charming seaside town.
Publicity: *Santa Barbara Independent's "Most Romantic Getaway"; Carpinteria's "Community Beautification" award; pictured in Land's End catalog and LA Times "Reader's favorite".*
Certificate may be used: Oct. 1-June 30, Sunday-Thursday.

Secret Garden Inn and Cottages

1908 Bath St
Santa Barbara, CA 93101-2813
(805)687-2300 (800)676-1622 Fax:(805)687-4576
Internet: secretgarden.com
E-mail: garden@secretgarden.com

Circa 1908. The main house and adjacent cottages surround the gardens and are decorated in American and English-Country style. The Hummingbird is a large cottage guest room with a queen-size white iron bed and a private deck with a hot tub for your exclusive use. The three suites have private outdoor hot tubs. Wine and light hors d'oeuvres are served in the late afternoon, and hot apple cider is served each evening.

Innkeeper(s): Jack Greenwald, Christine Dunstan. $115-225. MC, VISA, AX, PC, TC. 11 rooms with PB, 1 with FP, 3 suites and 4 cottages. Breakfast, afternoon tea and snacks/refreshments included in rates. Types of meals: Full bkfst and early coffee/tea. Beds: KQ. TV in room. Fax and copier on premises. Antiquing, fishing, live theater, shopping and water sports nearby.
Location: City.
Publicity: *Los Angeles Times, Santa Barbara and Independant.*

"A romantic little getaway retreat that neither of us will be able to forget. It was far from what we expected to find."
Certificate may be used: Jan. 30-June 30 and Sept. 1-Dec. 17, Sunday-Thursday.

The Upham Hotel & Garden Cottages

1404 De La Vina St
Santa Barbara, CA 93101-3027
(805)962-0058 (800)727-0876 Fax:(805)963-2825
Internet: www.uphamhotel.com
E-mail: innkeeper@vintagehotels.com

Circa 1871. Antiques and period furnishings decorate each of the inn's guest rooms and suites. The inn is the oldest continuously operating hostelry in Southern California. Situated on an acre of gardens in the center of downtown, it's within easy walking distance of restaurants, shops, art galleries and museums. The staff is happy to assist guests in discovering Santa Barbara's varied attractions. Garden cottage units feature porches or secluded patios and several have gas fireplaces.

Innkeeper(s): Jan Martin Winn. $145-395. MC, VISA, AX, DC, DS, TC. 50 rooms with PB, 8 with FP, 4 suites, 3 cottages and 3 conference rooms. Breakfast included in rates. Types of meals: Cont plus and early coffee/tea. Beds: KQ. Cable TV, phone and ceiling fan in room. Fax and copier on premises. Antiquing, golf, live theater, parks, shopping and water sports nearby.
Location: City.
Publicity: *Los Angeles Times, Santa Barbara, Westways, Santa Barbara News-Press and Avenues.*

"Your hotel is truly a charm. Between the cozy gardens and the exquisitely comfortable appointments, The Upham is charm itself."
Certificate may be used: Sunday-Thursday, Jan. 2-Dec. 30.

Santa Clara   I5

Madison Street Inn

1390 Madison St
Santa Clara, CA 95050-4759
(408)249-5541 (800)491-5541 Fax:(408)249-6676
E-mail: madstinn@aol.com

Circa 1890. This Queen Anne Victorian inn still boasts its
original doors and locks, and "No Peddlers or Agents" is
engraved in the cement of the
original carriageway. Guests,
however, always receive a warm
and gracious welcome to high-
ceilinged rooms furnished in
antiques, Oriental rugs and
Victorian wallpaper.

Innkeeper(s): Theresa & Ralph Wigginton. $75-125. MC, VISA, AX, DC, DS,
PC, TC. 6 rooms, 4 with PB. Breakfast, afternoon tea and snacks/refresh-
ments included in rates. Types of meals: Full gourmet bkfst and early
coffee/tea. Beds: QD. Phone and ceiling fan in room. VCR, fax, spa, swimming and bicycles on premises. Amusement parks, antiquing, live theater,
parks, sporting events and water sports nearby.
Pets Allowed.
Location: City.
Publicity: *Discovery.*

*"We spend many nights in hotels that look and feel exactly alike
whether they are in Houston or Boston. Your inn was delightful. It
was wonderful to bask in your warm and gracious hospitality."*
Certificate may be used: Jan. 1 to Dec. 30, Wednesday through Sunday.

Santa Cruz   J5

The Darling House-A B&B Inn By The Sea

314 W Cliff Dr
Santa Cruz, CA 95060-6145
(831)458-1958

Circa 1910. It's difficult to pick a room at this oceanside mansion. The Pacific Ocean Room features a fireplace and a wonderful
ocean view. The Chinese Room might suit you with its silk-
draped, hand-carved rosewood canopy wedding bed. Elegant oak,
ebony, and walnut woodwork is enhanced by the antique decor of
Tiffanys and Chippendales. Roses, beveled glass and libraries add
to the atmosphere. Beyond the ocean-view veranda are landscaped
gardens. Guests often walk to the wharf for dinner.
Innkeeper(s): Karen Darling. $145-170. MC, VISA, AX, DS. 5 rooms and 1
conference room. Breakfast included in rates. Type of meal: Cont. Beds:
KQDT. Turndown service in room. Spa on premises. Amusement parks,
antiquing, fishing, live theater, shopping and sporting events nearby.
Location: City.
Publicity: *Modern Maturity and Pacific.*
"So pretty, so sorry to leave."
Certificate may be used: November-April, Sunday-Thursday, holidays excluded.

Santa Rosa   G4

Pygmalion House B&B Inn

331 Orange St
Santa Rosa, CA 95401-6226
(707)526-3407 Fax:(707)526-3407

Circa 1880. This historic Victorian, which has been restored to
its 19th-century grandeur, is just a few blocks from Santa
Rosa's Old Town, "Railroad Square" and many antique shops,
cafes, coffeehouses and restaurants. The home is filled with a
unique mix of antiques, many of which belonged to famed,

Gypsy Rose Lee. Each of the
Victorian guest rooms includes a
bath with a clawfoot tub. Five different varieties of coffee are blend-
ed each morning for the breakfast
service, which includes home-
made entrees, freshly baked breads and fresh fruit.

Innkeeper(s): Caroline Berry. $89-109. MC, VISA, PC, TC. 6 rooms with PB.
Breakfast and snacks/refreshments included in rates. Type of meal: Full bkfst.
Beds: KQDT. Cable TV in room. Air conditioning. Fax, copier, library, mall and
Railroad Square on premises. Antiquing, fishing, golf, live theater, parks,
shopping and wineries nearby.
Location: City.
Certificate may be used: Jan. 5 to April 30, Sunday-Thursday.

Sequoia   K9

Plantation B&B

33038 Sierra Hwy 198
Sequoia, CA 93244-1700
(559)597-2555 (800)240-1466 Fax:(559)597-2551
Internet: www.plantationbnb.com
E-mail: relax@plantationbnb.com

Circa 1908. The history of orange production is deeply
entwined in the roots of California, and this home is located on
what once was an orange plantation. The original 1908 house
burned in the 1960s, but the current home was built on its
foundation. In keeping with the home's
plantation past, the innkeepers decorated
the bed and breakfast with a "Gone With
the Wind" theme. The comfortable,
country guest rooms sport names such
as the Scarlett O'Hara, the Belle Watling,
and of course, the Rhett Butler. A hot tub
is located in the orchard, and there also
is a heated swimming pool.

Innkeeper(s): Scott & Marie Munger. $69-179. MC, VISA, AX, DC, DS, PC,
TC. 8 rooms, 6 with PB, 2 with FP and 2 suites. Breakfast and
snacks/refreshments included in rates. Types of meals: Full gourmet bkfst and
early coffee/tea. Beds: KQDT. Cable TV, ceiling fan and VCR in room. Air con-
ditioning. Fax, spa and swimming on premises. Antiquing, fishing, golf, parks,
shopping, cross-country skiing, sporting events and water sports nearby.
Location: Mountains.
Publicity: *Exeter Sun, Kaweah Commonwealth, Los Angeles Times, Fresno
Bee and Visalia Delta Times.*
"Scarlett O'Hara would be proud to live on this lovely plantation."
Certificate may be used: Sept. 5-May 17, Sunday through Thursday.

Sonora   H7

Hammons House Inn B&B

22963 Robertson Ranch Rd
Sonora, CA 95370-9555
(209)532-7921 (888)666-5329 Fax:(209)586-4935
Internet: hammonshouseinn.com
E-mail: hammons@hammonshouseinn.com

Circa 1983. This bed & breakfast is secluded on seven wooded
acres from which guests can enjoy splendid panoramic views of
the mountains and foothills of the
Sierras. The Platinum Suite and
The Oak Room each offer a two-
person whirlpool tub, king bed
and private deck. A two-story
bungalow includes a sleeping

loft accessed with an oaken spiral staircase, a full kitchen, bathroom and fireplace. The decor in all accommodations is contemporary in style and comfortable. There is a pool and deck for guests to enjoy as well as a picturesque gazebo often used for weddings. A country breakfast is served in the main inn and is brought to your room or served on your private deck. Wineries, outdoor activities and two historic state parks are nearby.
Innkeeper(s): Linda Hammons. $130-165. MC, VISA, AX, DS, PC, TC. 3 rooms with PB, 2 with FP, 2 suites and 1 cottage. Breakfast and snacks/refreshments included in rates. Types of meals: Full gourmet bkfst, country bkfst and early coffee/tea. Beds: KQ. Phone, ceiling fan and VCR in room. Fax and copier on premises. Antiquing, fishing, golf, live theater, parks, shopping, downhill skiing, cross-country skiing and water sports nearby. Pets Allowed.
Location: Mountains.
Certificate may be used: Jan. 2-Dec. 20, Sunday-Thursday, no holidays.

Lavender Hill B&B

683 S Barretta St
Sonora, CA 95370-5132
(209)532-9024 (800)446-1333
Internet: www.sonnet.com/dancers/bandb
E-mail: lavender@sonnet.com

Circa 1900. In the historic Gold Rush town of Sonora is this Queen Anne Victorian inn. Its four guest rooms include the Lavender Room, which has a mini-suite with desk, sitting area and clawfoot tub and shower. After a busy day fishing, biking, river rafting or exploring nearby Yosemite National Park, guests may relax in the antique-filled parlor or the sitting room. Admiring the inn's gardens from the wraparound porch is also a favorite activity. Be sure to ask about dinner theater packages.
Innkeeper(s): Charlie & Jean Marinelli. $79-99. MC, VISA, AX, PC, TC. 4 rooms with PB and 1 suite. Breakfast included in rates. Types of meals: Full bkfst and early coffee/tea. Beds: KQ. Ceiling fan in room. Air conditioning. Library on premises. Antiquing, fishing, golf, live theater, parks, shopping, downhill skiing, cross-country skiing and water sports nearby.
Location: City.
Publicity: *Roseville Times and Union Democrat.*
Certificate may be used: Jan. 1 to March 31, Sunday through Thursday.

Soquel   J5

Blue Spruce Inn

2815 S Main St
Soquel, CA 95073-2412
(831)464-1137 (800)559-1137 Fax:(831)475-0608
E-mail: innkeeper@bluespruce.com

Circa 1875. Near the north coast of Monterey Bay, this old farmhouse has been freshly renovated and refitted with luxurious touches. The Seascape is a favorite room with its private entrance, wicker furnishings and bow-shaped Jacuzzi for two. The Carriage House offers skylights above the bed, while a heart decor dominates Two Hearts. Local art, Amish quilts and featherbeds are featured throughout. Brunch enchiladas are the inn's speciality. Santa Cruz is four miles away.
Innkeeper(s): Victoria & Thomas Jechart. $95-195. MC, VISA, AX, PC, TC. 6 rooms with PB, 5 with FP. Breakfast included in rates. Types of meals: Full bkfst and early coffee/tea. Beds: KQ. Cable TV, phone, turndown service and four with spa tubs in room. Antiquing, beaches, golf, parks, shopping and wineries nearby.
Location: Resort area.
Publicity: *L.A. Weekly, Aptos Post, San Francisco Examiner and Village View.*
"You offer such graciousness to your guests and a true sense of welcome."
Certificate may be used: Monday-Thursday, all year, subject to availability.

Springville   K9

Annie's B&B

33024 Globe Dr
Springville, CA 93265-9718
(209)539-3827 Fax:(209)539-2179
E-mail: bozanich@lightspeed.net

Circa 1903. Innkeepers Annie and John Bozanich nicknamed their country-style bed & breakfast "Hog Heaven," in honor of their potbellied pigs, Boo and Mr. Magoo and their sow named Fannie. The five-acre grounds boast wonderful views of the Sierra Nevadas. The grounds also include John's custom saddle shop. In keeping with the swine theme, Annie has named one guest quarter Sows Room and another the Boars Room. The third room was named in honor of Annie's grandmother, Ode. Ode's Room features her grandmother's bedroom set and a bedspread crocheted by Ode. This room is located in the back house and has its own private entrance. Annie prepares the multitude of home-baked treats on an antique, wood-burning cookstove. In addition to the ample breakfast, afternoon refreshments are served.
Innkeeper(s): Ann & John Bozanich. $85-95. MC, VISA, AX, DC, TC. 3 rooms with PB. Breakfast, afternoon tea and snacks/refreshments included in rates. Types of meals: Full bkfst and early coffee/tea. Beds: DT. Ceiling fan in room. VCR and spa on premises. Antiquing, fishing, live theater, parks, shopping, cross-country skiing and water sports nearby.
Location: Sierra foothills.
Certificate may be used: Sunday-Thursday only, no holidays or special event days.

Sutter Creek   G6

Grey Gables B&B Inn

161 Hanford St, PO Box 1687
Sutter Creek, CA 95685-1687
(209)267-1039 (800)473-9422 Fax:(209)267-0998

Circa 1897. The innkeepers of this Victorian home offer poetic accommodations both in the delightful decor and by the names of their guest rooms. The Keats, Bronte and Tennyson rooms afford garden views, while the Byron and Browning rooms include clawfoot tubs. The Victorian Suite, which encompasses the top floor, affords views of the garden,  as well as a historic churchyard. All of the guest rooms boast fireplaces. Stroll down brick pathways through the terraced garden or relax in the parlor. A proper English tea is served with cakes and scones. Hors d'oeuvres and libations are served in the evenings.
Innkeeper(s): Roger & Susan Garlick. $100-160. MC, VISA, DS, PC, TC. 8 rooms with PB, 8 with FP. Breakfast, afternoon tea and evening wine and hors d'oeuvres included in rates. Types of meals: Full gourmet bkfst and early coffee/tea. Beds: KQT. Ceiling fan in room. Air conditioning. Fax and copier on premises. Handicap access. Antiquing, fishing, live theater, parks, shopping, downhill skiing, cross-country skiing, water sports and wineries nearby.
Location: Mountains.
Certificate may be used: Jan. 1-Aug. 31, Sunday-Thursday, holidays excluded.

The Hanford House B&B Inn

61 Hanford St Hwy 49
Sutter Creek, CA 95685
(209)267-0747 (800)871-5839 Fax:(209)267-1825
Internet: www.hanfordhouse.com
E-mail: bobkat@hanfordhouse.com

Circa 1929. Hanford House is located on the quiet main street of Sutter Creek, a Gold Rush town. The ivy-covered, brick inn

features spacious, romantic guest rooms, five with a fireplace. The Gold Country Escape includes a Jacuzzi tub, canopy bed, sitting area and a private deck. Guests can enjoy breakfast in their room or in the inn's cheerful breakfast room. Guests can relax in the front of a fire in the Hanford Room, which doubles as facilities for conferences, retreats, weddings and social events. Wineries, antique shops and historic sites are nearby.
Innkeeper(s): Bob & Karen Tierno. $99-185. MC, VISA, DS, PC, TC. 9 rooms with PB, 8 with FP, 3 suites and 1 conference room. Breakfast, afternoon tea and snacks/refreshments included in rates. Types of meals: Full gourmet bkfst and early coffee/tea. Beds: KQ. Phone, ceiling fan and cable TV (most rooms) in room. Air conditioning. VCR and fax on premises. Handicap access. Antiquing, fishing, golf, live theater, shopping, downhill skiing, cross-country skiing and water sports nearby.
Publicity: *Best Places to Kiss.*
Certificate may be used: Jan. 1-Dec. 31; Sunday-Thursday, excluding holidays.

Picturerock Inn

55 Eureka St
Sutter Creek, CA 95685
(209)267-5500 (800)399-2389
Circa 1913. This is an Arts and Crafts-style bungalow with porch, stairways and a low wall constructed of local rock containing mineral deposits that seem to show plant and tree silhouettes. Antiques and art decorate the inn with its original rosewood and redwood beams, built-in cabinets, wainscotting and staircase. If you choose the Eclectic Room, you'll enjoy a view of the hills from your demi-canopied king-size bed. The room also has a wood stove. Nearby are Amador County wineries and gold mine sites.
$65-100. MC, VISA, AX, DS, PC. 5 rooms with PB, 4 with FP. Beds: KQ. Cable TV in room. Air conditioning.
Certificate may be used: Year-round, Sunday-Thursday; Friday included January through March; Friday included July-August; holidays excluded.

Tahoe City
F7

Mayfield House B&B at Lake Tahoe

236 Grove St
Tahoe City, CA 96145-5999
(530)583-1001 (888)518-8898 Fax:(530)581-4104
Internet: www.mayfieldhouse.com
E-mail: innkeeper@mayfieldhouse.com
Circa 1932. This 1890s home has been restored graciously, maintaining many of its Victorian features. Candlelight chandeliers, redwood molding, wainscotting and original fireplaces enhance the turn-of-the-century ambiance, as does the inviting decor. Norman Mayfield, Lake Tahoe's pioneer contractor, built this house of wood and stone, and Julia Morgan, architect of Hearst Castle, was a frequent guest. Many rooms have views of mountains, woods, or the golf course.
Innkeeper(s): Colleen McDevitt. $85-150. MC, VISA, PC. 5 rooms with PB and 1 cottage. Breakfast included in rates. Beds: KQ. TV and one whirlpool tub and one with steam shower in room. Books and CD player on premises. Bicycling, canoeing/kayaking, fishing, hiking, rafting, restaurants, parks, shopping, downhill skiing, cross-country skiing and water sports nearby.
Location: Mountains.
Publicity: *Sierra Heritage, Tahoe Today, San Francisco Chronicle, Reno Air Approach, Reno Gazette and Ski Magazine.*
"This place is charming beyond words, complete with down comforters and wine upon checking in. The breakfast is superb."
Certificate may be used: Sunday-Thursday excluding holidays.

Templeton
L6

Country House Inn

91 S Main St
Templeton, CA 93465-8701
(805)434-1598 (800)362-6032
Circa 1886. This Victorian home, built by the founder of Templeton, is located in rural wine country. Ancient oak trees shade the grounds. The inn was designated as a historic site in San Luis Obispo County.
Innkeeper(s): Dianne Garth. $95-105. MC, VISA, DS, PC. 5 rooms with PB, 1 with FP and 1 suite. Breakfast included in rates. Types of meals: Full gourmet bkfst and early coffee/tea. Beds: KQ. Ceiling fan in room. Antiquing, fishing, live theater, parks, shopping and water sports nearby.
Location: Wine country.
Publicity: *Los Angeles Times, and PM Magazine.*
"A feast for all the senses, an esthetic delight."
Certificate may be used: April-September, Sunday-Thursday; October-March, Sunday-Saturday.

Ukiah
F3

Vichy Hot Springs Resort & Inn

2605 Vichy Springs Rd
Ukiah, CA 95482-3507
(707)462-9515 Fax:(707)462-9516
Internet: www.vichysprings.com
E-mail: vichy@vichysprings.com
Circa 1854. This famous spa, now a California State Historical Landmark (#980), once attracted guests Jack London, Mark Twain, Robert Louis Stevenson, Ulysses Grant and Teddy Roosevelt. Eighteen rooms and four cottages have been renovated for bed & breakfast, while the 1860s naturally warm and carbonated mineral baths remain unchanged. A hot spa and historic, Olympic-size pool await your arrival. A magical waterfall is a 30-minute walk along a year-round stream.
Innkeeper(s): Gilbert & Marjorie Ashoff. $105-235. MC, VISA, AX, DC, CB, DS, PC, TC. 22 rooms with PB, 4 with FP, 4 cottages and 2 conference rooms. Breakfast included in rates. Type of meal: Full bkfst. Beds: QT. Phone in room. Air conditioning. Fax, copier, spa, swimming, massages and facials on premises. Handicap access. Antiquing, fishing, redwood parks, live theater, parks, water sports and wineries nearby.
Location: Country - 700 acres.
Publicity: *Sunset, Sacramento Bee, San Jose Mercury News, Gulliver (Japan), Oregonian, Contra Costa Times, New York Times, San Francisco Chronicle, San Francisco Examiner, Adventure West, Gulliver (italy) and Bay Area Back Roads.*
Certificate may be used: January-February excluding President's weekend & Valentine's weekend.

Visalia
K8

Ben Maddox House B&B

601 N Encina St
Visalia, CA 93291-3603
(559)739-0721 (800)401-9800 Fax:(559)625-0420
Circa 1876. Just 40 minutes away from Sequoia National Park sits this late 19th-century home, constructed completely of gorgeous Sequoia redwood. The parlor, dining room and bedrooms remain in their original state. The house has been tastefully furnished with antiques from the late 1800s to the early 20th century. Breakfast menu choices include

fresh fruit, a selection of homemade breads, eggs and meat. The meal is served either in the historic dining room or on the deck, and it is complemented by flowers, antique china and goldware. The half-acre of grounds includes gardens, a finch aviary, pool and century-old trees.

Innkeeper(s): Diane & Al Muro. $75-95. MC, VISA, AX, DS. 4 rooms with PB. Breakfast included in rates. Types of meals: Full bkfst and early coffee/tea. Beds: KQ. Cable TV and phone in room. Air conditioning. Swimming on premises. Antiquing, fishing, Sequoia National Park, live theater, parks, shopping, cross-country skiing, sporting events and water sports nearby.
Location: Historic District.
Publicity: *Southland and Fresno Bee.*
Certificate may be used: March 1-Jan. 31, Sunday-Friday.

Volcano   G7

St. George Hotel

16104 Main Street
Volcano, CA 95689-0009
(209)296-4458 Fax:(209)296-4457
Internet: www.stgeorgehotel.com
E-mail: stgeorge@stgeorgehotel.com

Circa 1862. Listed in the National Register, this handsome three-story hotel was the most prominent of the Gold Country hotels. Carefully renovated, it features a double-tiered wrap-around porch, and there is a full service restaurant, bar and banquet/parlor. It is situated on an acre of lawns that afford croquet, horseshoes and volleyball. Volcano is a Mother Lode town that has been untouched by supermarkets and modern motels and remains much as it was during the Gold Rush, except that the population has dwindled from 5,000 to 100 today. Modified American Plan (breakfast and dinner) is available. Guests enjoy walking to the local swimming hole or fishing.

Innkeeper(s): Mark & Tracey Berkner. $65-110. MC, VISA, DS, PC, TC. 20 rooms, 15 with PB and 1 conference room. Breakfast included in rates. Type of meal: Cont. Beds: QDT. All original in room. Fax, copier, deck, horseshoes, fire pit, croquet, volleyball and baby sitting on premises. Antiquing, fishing, golf, swimming, mountain lakes, live theater, parks, shopping, downhill skiing, cross-country skiing, tennis and water sports nearby.
Location: Sierra Foothills/Gold Country.

"Quiet, peace, yummy breakfasts and outrageous dinners." C. B., San Francisco
Certificate may be used: Wednesday-Friday, call for availability. Closed first two weeks of January.

Westport   E3

Howard Creek Ranch

40501 N Hwy One, PO Box 121
Westport, CA 95488
(707)964-6725 Fax:(707)964-1603
Internet: www.howardcreekranch.com

Circa 1871. First settled as a land grant of thousands of acres, Howard Creek Ranch is now a 40-acre farm with sweeping views of the Pacific Ocean, sandy beaches and rolling mountains. A 75-foot  bridge spans a creek that flows past barns and outbuildings to the beach 200 yards away. The farmhouse is surrounded by green lawns, an award-winning flower garden, and grazing cows, horses and llama. This rustic rural location offers antiques, a hot tub, sauna and heated pool. A traditional ranch

breakfast is served each morning.

Innkeeper(s): Charles & Sally Grigg. $75-160. MC, VISA, AX, PC, TC. 11 rooms, 10 with PB, 5 with FP, 3 suites and 3 cabins. Breakfast included in rates. Types of meals: Full gourmet bkfst and country bkfst. Beds: KQD. Ceiling fan in room. Fax, spa, swimming, sauna, library and massages on premises. Antiquing, art galleries, beaches, bicycling, canoeing/kayaking, fishing, hiking, horseback riding, farm animals, live theater, museums, shopping and wineries nearby.
Pets allowed: By prior arrangement.
Location: Mountains.
Publicity: *California, Country, Vacations, Forbes, Sunset and Diablo.*
"This is one of the most romantic places on the planet."
Certificate may be used: Oct. 15-May 15, Sunday-Thursday, excluding holiday periods.

Yountville   G4

Maison Fleurie

6529 Yount St.
Yountville, CA 94599-1278
(707)944-2056 (800)788-0369 Fax:(707)944-9342

Circa 1894. Vines cover the two-foot thick brick walls of the Bakery, the Carriage House and the Main House of this French country inn. One of the Four Sisters Inns, it is reminiscent of a bucolic setting in Provence. Rooms are decorated in a warm, romantic style, some with vineyard and garden views. Rooms in the Old Bakery have fireplaces. A pool and outdoor spa are available and you may borrow bicycles for wandering the countryside. In the evenings, wine and hors d'oeuvres are served. Yountville, just north of Napa, offers close access to the multitude of wineries and vineyards in the valley.

Innkeeper(s): Virginia Marzan. $120-260. MC, VISA, AX, TC. 13 rooms with PB, 7 with FP. Breakfast and afternoon tea included in rates. Type of meal: Full gourmet bkfst. Beds: KQD. Phone, turndown service, terry robes and newspaper in room. Fax, spa and bicycles on premises. Handicap access. Antiquing and wineries nearby.
Location: Napa Valley.
"Peaceful surroundings, friendly staff."
Certificate may be used: December through February, Sunday through Thursday, excluding holidays and special events.

Yuba City   F5

Harkey House B&B

212 C St
Yuba City, CA 95991-5014
(530)674-1942 Fax:(530)674-1840

Circa 1875. An essence of romance fills this Victorian Gothic house set in a historic neighborhood. Every inch of the home has been given a special touch, from the knickknacks and photos in the sitting room to the quilts and furnishings in the guest quarters. The Harkey Suite features a poster bed with a down comforter and extras such as an adjoining library room and a gas stove. Full breakfasts of muffins, fresh fruit, juice and freshly ground coffee are served in a glass-paned dining room or on the patio.

Innkeeper(s): Bob & Lee Jones. $80-130. MC, VISA, AX, DS, PC, TC. 4 rooms with PB, 2 with FP, 1 suite and 1 conference room. Breakfast included in rates. Types of meals: Full bkfst and early coffee/tea. Beds: Q. Cable TV, phone, turndown service and ceiling fan in room. Air conditioning. VCR, spa and library on premises. Antiquing, fishing, live theater, parks, shopping and water sports nearby.
Location: Lakes.
Publicity: *Country Magazine.*
"This place is simply marvelous...the most comfortable bed in travel."
Certificate may be used: January to December, Sunday-Thursday.

Colorado

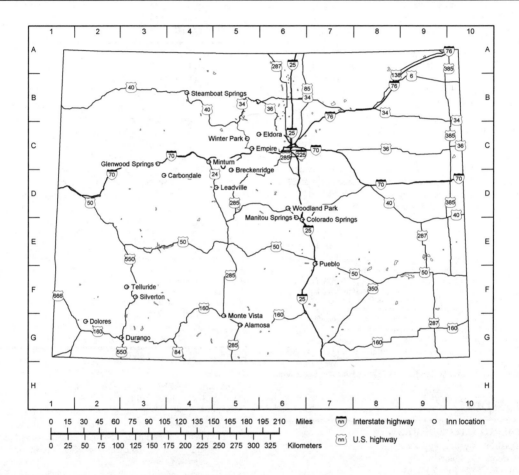

0   15 30 45 60 75 90 105 120 135 150 165 180 195 210 Miles

0   25 50 75 100 125 150 175 200 225 250 275 300 325 Kilometers

nn Interstate highway   o Inn location

nn U.S. highway

Alamosa   G5

Cottonwood Inn & Gallery: A B&B Inn

123 San Juan Ave
Alamosa, CO 81101-2547
(719)589-3882 (800)955-2623 Fax:(719)589-6437
Internet: www.cottonwoodinn.com.
E-mail: julie@cottonwoodinn.com

Circa 1912. This refurbished Colorado bungalow is filled with antiques and paintings by local artists. The Stickley dining room set once belonged to Billy Adams, a Colorado governor in the 1920s. Blue-corn blueberry pancakes, banana crepes with Mexican chocolate are the inn's specialties. A favorite day trip is riding the Cumbres-Toltec Scenic Railroad over the La Magna Pass, site of an Indiana Jones movie.
Innkeeper(s): Deb and Kevin Donaldson. $56-125. MC, VISA, AX, DS, PC, TC. 5 rooms, 3 with PB and 4 suites. Breakfast and afternoon tea included in rates. Types of meals: Full gourmet bkfst. Beds: KQD. Cable TV and phone in room. Fax, library and child care on premises. Antiquing, art galleries, bicycling, fishing, golf, hiking, horseback riding, live theater, museums, parks, shopping, cross-country skiing, sporting events and tennis nearby.
Pets allowed: In two suites with guests present.
Location: Small town.
Publicity: *Colorado Expressions, Rocky Mountain News, Country Inns, Denver Post, Milwaukee Journal, Channel 4 Denver and Colorado Get Away.*
"My husband wants to come over every morning for blueberry pancakes and strawberry rhubarb sauce."
Certificate may be used: Nov. 1-April 30, excluding Crane Festival weekend.

Breckenridge   D5

The Walker House

103 S French St, PO Box 5107
Breckenridge, CO 80424-0509
(970)453-2426

Circa 1875. This three-story log home with Victorian accents is located in a beautiful ski town with a historic past as a mining community. The upstairs rooms have spectacular views of the ski runs, sunsets and a magically lit town at night. While having breakfast in the dining room the sun streams through a stained-glass door. The innkeepers supply flowers and treats to honeymooners and romantic souls.
Innkeeper(s): Sue Ellen Strong. $89-115. MC, VISA. 2 rooms, 1 with PB and 1 suite. Breakfast and afternoon tea included in rates. Type of meal: Early coffee/tea. Beds: KQT. Extra Toiletries in room. Snacks and Tea & Coffee on premises. Antiquing, live theater, shopping, downhill skiing and cross-country skiing nearby.
Location: In mountain area.
Publicity: *State Historic Bus Tour and Summit Colorado Journal.*
Certificate may be used: April 17-19, Thursday to Saturday.

Carbondale   D3

Ambiance Inn

66 N 2nd St
Carbondale, CO 81623-2102
(970)963-3597 (800)350-1515 Fax:(970)963-3130
Internet: www.ambianceinn.com

Circa 1976. This contemporary chalet-style home is located in the beautiful Crystal Valley between Aspen and Glenwood Springs. Each room is individually appointed with amenities

such as four-poster bed or a two-person Jacuzzi. The Aspen Suite features knotty pine paneling and snowshoes hang on the walls, creating a ski lodge atmosphere. Other rooms feature motifs such as Southwestern or Hawaiian style.
Innkeeper(s): Norma & Robert Morris. $60-100. MC, DS, PC. 4 rooms with PB and 1 suite. Breakfast included in rates. Types of meals: Full gourmet bkfst and early coffee/tea. Beds: Q. Cable TV and ceiling fan in room. VCR on premises. Antiquing, fishing, parks, shopping, downhill skiing, cross-country skiing and sporting events nearby.
Certificate may be used: Excludes holidays, Christmas week and peak summer weekends.

Colorado Springs   E6

Black Forest B&B

11170 Black Forest Rd
Colorado Springs, CO 80908-3986
(719)495-4208 (800)809-9901 Fax:(719)495-0688
Internet: www.blackforestbb.com
E-mail: blackforestbandb@msn.com

Circa 1984. Ponderosa pines, golden aspens and fragrant meadows surround this massive log home built on the highest point east of the Rocky Mountains. This rustic mountain setting is complete with 20 acres of beautiful country to explore.

If you want to fully experience mountain living, the innkeepers will be more than happy to share their chores with you, which range from cutting firewood to planting Christmas trees on their tree farm. A greenhouse holds an indoor lap pool, sauna, fitness center and honeymoon suite.
Innkeeper(s): Robert & Susan Putnam. $75-200. MC, VISA, AX, DS, PC, TC. 5 rooms with PB, 2 with FP, 3 suites, 2 cottages and 1 conference room. Breakfast and snacks/refreshments included in rates. Types of meals: Cont plus and early coffee/tea. Beds: KQDT. Phone and ceiling fan in room. VCR, fax and copier on premises. Handicap access. Antiquing, focus on the family, live theater, parks, shopping, cross-country skiing and sporting events nearby.
Location: Mountains.
Certificate may be used: November through April, except Christmas and Thanksgiving holidays.

The Painted Lady

1318 W Colorado Ave
Colorado Springs, CO 80904-4023
(719)473-3165

Circa 1894. Once a popular restaurant in Old Colorado City, the Painted Lady has been remodeled into a bed & breakfast by its new owners. The three-story Victorian is decorated in a warm, romantic manner with lace and floral fabrics. Antique iron and four-poster beds, clawfoot tubs and brass fixtures fill the guest rooms. Hearty breakfasts, served on the veranda in summer, might include seafood quiche or souffles and homemade breads. Afternoon refreshments can be enjoyed in the parlor or on one of the porches.
Innkeeper(s): Valerie Maslowski. $70-150. MC, VISA, AX, DS, PC, TC. 2 suites. Breakfast included in rates. Types of meals: Full bkfst and early coffee/tea. Beds: QDT. Cable TV and ceiling fan in room. Air conditioning. VCR on premises. Antiquing, fishing, uS Air Force Academy, live theater, parks, shopping, downhill skiing, cross-country skiing, sporting events and water sports nearby.
"Calm, peaceful. Our first B&B, very memorable."
Certificate may be used: Nov. 1 to April 30, Sunday-Thursday, excluding holidays.

Serenity Pines Guesthouse

11910 Windmill Rd
Colorado Springs, CO 80908
(719)495-7141 Fax:(719)495-7141
Internet: www.colorado-bnb.com/serenpines
E-mail: serenpines@aol.com

Circa 1998. This spacious private cottage rests among acres of pine trees on park-like grounds in the Pikes Peak area where "America the Beautiful" was written. Up to six guests are welcome to stay in the cottage, and it is especially appealing to families with children because of the neighboring farm where there are baby calves to see and fresh milk, cheese and eggs available. Cook in the country kitchen where there's always a full cookie jar and ingredients for a hearty mountain breakfast. An answering machine, fireplace, shower for two, video library and games are among the amenities. Arrange for an evening campfire with marshmallow and hot dog roasts, or slip into the hot tub and do a little star gazing with the forest as a backdrop. Nearby sites include Garden of the Gods, Pikes Peak, Cave of the Winds, Indian cliff dwellings, Royal Gorge, Buckskin Joe's Old Western Town, Seven Falls, the Air Force Academy, Flying W Ranch and Focus on the Family.

$59-129. MC, VISA, AX, PC, TC. 2 rooms with PB, 1 with FP, 1 suite and 1 cottage. Breakfast and snacks/refreshments included in rates. Type of meal: Cont plus. Beds: QDT. Cable TV, phone, turndown service, ceiling fan, VCR, answer machine, kitchen and microwave in room. Air conditioning. Fax, copier, bicycles, library, pet boarding, child care, hiking, biking, trails and video library on premises. Handicap access. Amusement parks, antiquing, fishing, golf, white water rafting, live theater, parks, shopping, downhill skiing, cross-country skiing, sporting events, tennis and water sports nearby.
Pets allowed: Horses only.
Location: Forest.
Certificate may be used: Sunday-Thursday, Nov. 1 through March 15.

Trout City Berth & Breakfast

12345 Lindsey Lane
Colorado Springs, CO 80908
(719)495-0348 Fax:(719)395-8433
Internet: www.bbinternet.com/troutcity/

Circa 1987. Guests at this unique inn can sleep in an elegantly decorated Victorian Pullman car or in Drover's Caboose. Located on 40 scenic acres of the San Isabel National Forest, the inn offers an 1880 reconstructed depot on its historic narrow-gauge railway site. Although the narrow gauge train is stationary, the locomotive has been used for parades. Depot rooms are furnished in authentic Victorian style. There is a gift shop/museum and a trout stream on the property. The area boasts abundant fishing and hunting in the area as well as a wide variety of outdoor activities, theater and shopping.

Innkeeper(s): Juel & Irene Kjeldsen. $50-70. MC, VISA, AX, TC. 4 rooms with PB and 1 conference room. Breakfast included in rates. Type of meal: Full bkfst. Beds: DT. Peace in room. VCR, movies, Gold panning and hiking on premises. Antiquing, bicycling, fishing, live theater, parks, shopping, tennis and water sports nearby.
Location: Mountains.
Certificate may be used: June 1 to Sept. 1, any day.

Dolores   G2

Mountain View B&B

28050 County Rd P
Dolores, CO 81323
(970)882-7861 (800)228-4592
Internet: subee.com/mtnview/home.html

Circa 1984. This sprawling ranch-type home has a magnificent view of the Mesa Verde National Park, which is 12 miles to its entrance. Besides spending a day or two touring the museum and cliff dwellings in Mesa Verde, guests can step outside this inn to enjoy its 22 acres of trails, woods and a small canyon with creek. In each direction, a short drive will take you to mountains, desert, canyon lands, mesa, forest lakes and world famous archaeological settings.

Innkeeper(s): Brenda & Cecil Dunn. $60-90. MC, VISA, PC, TC. 8 rooms with PB, 4 suites and 1 conference room. Breakfast and snacks/refreshments included in rates. Types of meals: Full bkfst, cont plus and early coffee/tea. Beds: QDT. Ceiling fan in room. Spa, library, barbecue grill, microwave, refrigerator, TV and laundry on premises. Handicap access. Fishing, golf, hiking, hunting, climbing, hunting, biking, parks, shopping, downhill skiing, cross-country skiing and water sports nearby.
Certificate may be used: March 1-May 15, October and November.

Durango   G3

Apple Orchard Inn

7758 County Road 203
Durango, CO 81301-8643
(970)247-0751 (800)426-0751
Internet: www.appleorchardinn.com
E-mail: apple@frontier.net

Circa 1994. As one might assume from the name, this elegant inn and cabins are ideally situated in an apple orchard. The main house is a welcoming farmhouse, and the innkeepers continue the country look inside, as well. Guest rooms offer featherbeds, some with canopies. Four rooms also include fireplaces and Jacuzzi tubs. Hearty, fresh-from-the-oven breakfasts are accompanied with fresh fruits. In the evenings, refreshments are served, and special gourmet dinners are sometimes available upon request.

Innkeeper(s): Celeste & John Gardiner. $75-165. MC, VISA, AX, DS, PC, TC. 10 rooms with PB, 4 with FP, 6 cottages and 1 conference room. Breakfast and snacks/refreshments included in rates. Types of meals: Full gourmet bkfst and early coffee/tea. Beds: KQ. Cable TV, phone and ceiling fan in room. Spa on premises. Handicap access. Fishing, live theater, parks, shopping, downhill skiing, cross-country skiing and water sports nearby.
Location: Mountains.
Publicity: *Colorado Homes & Lifestyles, Albuquerque Journal* and *Denver Post.*
"*A must stay anytime we are in the area.*"
Certificate may be used: Oct. 18-May 15.

Eldora   C5

Goldminer Hotel

601 Klondyke Ave
Eldora, CO 80466-9542
(303)258-7770 (800)422-4629 Fax:(303)258-3850

Circa 1897. This turn-of-the-century National Register hotel is a highlight in the Eldora National Historic District. Suites and rooms are decorated with period antiques. The inn provides packages that include guided jeep, horseback, hiking and fishing tours in the summer and back-country ski tours in the winter.

Innkeeper(s): Scott Bruntjen. $89-229. MC, VISA, AX, DS, TC. 7 rooms, 5 with PB, 1 with FP, 1 suite, 1 cottage and 1 conference room. Breakfast included in rates. Types of meals: Full bkfst and early coffee/tea. Beds: KD. TV in room. VCR, fax, copier, spa, library and cross country skis on premises. Antiquing, fishing, parks, shopping, downhill skiing, cross-country skiing and sporting events nearby.
Pets allowed: Cottage only.
Location: Mountains.
Publicity: *Daily Camera and Mountain Ear.*
Certificate may be used: All except Dec. 23-Jan. 3, May 10-18, Friday-Saturday, June-September.

Empire   C5

Mad Creek B&B

PO Box 404
Empire, CO 80438-0404
(303)569-2003

Circa 1881. This mountain town cottage has just the right combination of Victorian decor with lace, flowers, antiques and gingerbread trim on the facade. Unique touches include door frames of old mineshaft wood, kerosene lamps, Eastlake antiques and complimentary cross-country ski gear and mountain bikes. Relax in front of the rock fireplace while watching a movie, peruse the library filled with local lore, or plan your next adventure with Colorado guides and maps. Empire, which was once a mining town, is conveniently located within 15 to 45 minutes of at least six major ski areas.

Innkeeper(s): Myrna & Tonya Payne. $55-85. MC, VISA, TC. 3 rooms, 1 with PB. Breakfast, afternoon tea and snacks/refreshments included in rates. Types of meals: Full bkfst and early coffee/tea. Beds: KD. Ceiling fan, toiletries and down comforters in room. VCR, bicycles and complimentary ski gear & shoes on premises. Antiquing, fishing, horseback riding, gambling, parks, shopping, downhill skiing, cross-country skiing and water sports nearby.
Location: Rivers.
Certificate may be used: Oct. 15-Nov. 20, Sunday-Thursday; April 16-May 20, Sunday-Thursday.

Glenwood Springs   C3

Kaiser House B&B

932 Cooper Ave # 1952
Glenwood Springs, CO 81601-3630
(970)928-0101 Fax:(970)928-0101

Circa 1902. A welcoming curved porch, gables, stained glass, a rotunda tower and "Painted Lady" palette invite guests to enjoy this Queen Ann Victorian. Light and airy guest rooms are welcome respites after enjoying a long day of skiing, fly fishing, whitewater rafting or rock climbing in the area. Within walking distance are hot springs and vapor caves. Breakfast is served in the dining room in winter and in the rotunda or on the patio in summer.

Innkeeper(s): Joanne DeMars. $105-200. MC, VISA, PC, TC. 8 rooms with PB. Breakfast included in rates. Type of meal: Cont plus. Beds: KQ. Cable TV and ceiling fan in room. Air conditioning. VCR, fax and spa on premises. Antiquing, fishing, golf, parks, shopping, downhill skiing, cross-country skiing, tennis and water sports nearby.
Location: Mountains.
"Outstanding, immaculate clean."
Certificate may be used: Jan. 1 to May 15, Sunday through Thursday nights (not Fridays).

Leadville   D5

Peri & Ed's Mountain Hide Away

201 W 8th St
Leadville, CO 80461-3529
(719)486-0716 (800)933-3715 Fax:(719)486-2181
Internet: www.mountainhideaway.com
E-mail: solder@dsni.net

Circa 1879. This former boarding house was built during the boom days of Leadville. Families can picnic on the large lawn sprinkled with wildflowers under soaring pines. Shoppers and history buffs can enjoy exploring historic Main Street, one block away. The surrounding mountains are a natural playground offering a wide variety of activities, and the innkeepers will be happy to let you know their favorite spots and help with directions. The sunny Augusta Tabor room features a sprawling king-size bed with a warm view of the rugged peaks.

Innkeeper(s): Peri & Ed Solder. $49-107. MC, VISA, AX, DS, PC, TC. 10 rooms with PB, 2 with FP and 2 cottages. Breakfast included in rates. Type of meal: Full bkfst. Beds: KQDT. Ceiling fan in room. VCR, spa and library on premises. Antiquing, fishing, live theater, parks, shopping, downhill skiing and cross-country skiing nearby.
Location: Mountains.
Certificate may be used: October-Dec. 15, April 15-June 30, Monday-Wednesday.

The Ice Palace Inn Bed & Breakfast

813 Spruce St
Leadville, CO 80461-3555
(719)486-8272 (800)754-2840 Fax:(719)486-0345
Internet: icepalaceinn.com
E-mail: ipalace@sni.net

Circa 1899. Innkeeper Kami Kolakowski was born in this historic Colorado town, and it was her dream to one day return and run a bed & breakfast. Now with husband Giles, she has created a restful retreat out of this turn-of-the-century home built with lumber from the famed Leadville Ice Palace. Giles and Kami have filled the home with antiques and pieces of history from the Ice Palace and the town. Guests are treated to a mouth-watering gourmet breakfast with treats such as stuffed French toast or German apple pancakes. After a day enjoying Leadville, come back and enjoy a soak in the hot tub.

Innkeeper(s): Giles & Kami Kolakowski. $79-139. MC, VISA, AX, DC, DS, PC, TC. 8 rooms with PB, 7 with FP. Breakfast, afternoon tea and snacks/refreshments included in rates. Types of meals: Full gourmet bkfst and early coffee/tea. Beds: KQDT. TV, turndown service, ceiling fan and VCR in room. Spa, library and hot tub on premises. Antiquing, fishing, live theater, parks, shopping, downhill skiing, cross-country skiing and water sports nearby.
Location: Mountains.
Publicity: *Herald Democrat.*
Certificate may be used: Dec. 1-March 31, Sunday-Thursday. April and May anytime upon availability. Not valid June-September. October and November anytime upon availability, no holidays.

Manitou Springs   E6

Red Crags B&B Inn

302 El Paso Blvd
Manitou Springs, CO 80829-2308
(719)685-1920 (800)721-2248 Fax:(719)685-1073
Internet: www.redcrags.com
E-mail: info@redcrags.com

Circa 1870. Well-known in this part of Colorado, this unique, four-story Victorian mansion sits on a bluff with a combination of views that includes Pikes Peak, Manitou Valley, Garden of the Gods and the city of Colorado Springs. There are antiques throughout the house. The formal dining room features a rare cherrywood Eastlake fireplace. Two of the suites include double whirlpool tubs.

Outside, guests can walk through beautifully landscaped gardens or enjoy a private picnic area with a barbecue pit and a spectacular view. Wine is served in the evenings.

Innkeeper(s): Howard & Lynda Lerner. $80-180. MC, VISA, AX, DS, PC, TC. 8 rooms with PB, 7 with FP and 5 suites. Breakfast, afternoon tea and snacks/refreshments included in rates. Types of meals: Full bkfst and early coffee/tea. Beds: K. Phone, two jetted tubs for two, clock, feather beds and in room. Fax, copier, spa and TV available upon request on premises. Antiquing, fishing, golf, Pikes Peak, Olympic Training Center, live theater, parks, shopping, cross-country skiing, sporting events and tennis nearby.
Location: Mountains.
Publicity: *Rocky Mountain News, Bridal Guide, Denver Post, Los Angeles Times, Springs Woman and Colorado Springs Gazette.*

"What a beautiful, historical and well-preserved home - exceptional hospitality and comfort. What wonderful people! Highly recommended!"

Certificate may be used: Oct. 15 to April 30, Sunday-Thursday; excluding holidays, subject to availability.

Minturn   C4

Eagle River Inn

PO Box 100
Minturn, CO 81645-0100
(970)827-5761 (800)344-1750 Fax:(970)827-4020
E-mail: eri@vail.net

Circa 1894. Earth red adobe walls, rambling riverside decks, mature willow trees and brilliant flowers enhance the secluded backyard of this Southwestern-style inn. Inside, the lobby features comfortable Santa Fe furniture, an authentic beehive fireplace and a ceiling of traditional latilas and vegas. Baskets, rugs and weavings add warmth. Guest rooms found on two floors have views

of the river or mountains. The innkeepers hold a wine tasting with appetizers each evening. Minturn, which had its beginnings as a stop on the Rio Grande Railroad, is the home of unique and popular restaurants, shops and galleries.

Innkeeper(s): Patty Bidez. $75-215. MC, VISA, AX, DS, PC, TC. 12 rooms with PB. Breakfast and snacks/refreshments included in rates. Type of meal: Full bkfst. Beds: KT. Cable TV in room. Fax and bicycles on premises. Fishing, hot air ballooning, snowmobiling, snowshoeing, shopping, downhill skiing, cross-country skiing and sporting events nearby.
Location: Mountains.
Publicity: *Rocky Mountain News, Denver Post, Dallas Morning, Washington Post, Country Accents, National Geographic Traveler and Travel & Leisure.*

"We love this place and have decided to make it a yearly tradition!"

Certificate may be used: May 27-June 17 and Sept. 27-Nov. 24, Sunday-Thursday.

Monte Vista   G5

The Windmill B&B

4340 W Hwy 160
Monte Vista, CO 81144
(719)852-0438 (800)467-3441

Circa 1959. This Southwestern-style inn affords panoramic views of the surrounding Sangre De Cristo and San Juan moun-

tain ranges. The 22-acre grounds still include the namesake windmill that once was used to irrigate water in the yard and garden. Now it stands guard over the hot tub. Each of the guest rooms is decorated in a different theme, with a few antiques placed here and there. The plentiful country breakfast is served in a dining room with mountain views.

Innkeeper(s): Sharon & Dennis Kay. $65-99. MC, VISA, PC. 4 rooms with PB. Breakfast and snacks/refreshments included in rates. Types of meals: Full gourmet bkfst and early coffee/tea. Beds: KQT. Turndown service in room. Antiquing, fishing, live theater, parks, shopping, downhill skiing and cross-country skiing nearby.
Location: Mountains.
Certificate may be used: Sunday through Friday.

Ouray   F3

Wiesbaden Hot Springs Spa & Lodgings

625 5th St
Ouray, CO 81427
(970)325-4347 Fax:(970)325-4358
E-mail: wiesbaden@gwe.net

Circa 1879. Built directly above mineral hot springs, this old lodge has a European flair. In the basement of the inn, into the side of the mountain, is a vapor cave with a soaking pool, the inn's favorite spot. The water here is a consistent 108 to 110 degrees. Chief Ouray had an adobe on the property, and used the cave for its "sacred waters." Therapeutic massage, facials, acupressure and aromatherapy wraps are offered. Guest rooms are simply decorated with wallpapers and country antiques. Breakfast is not provided. Box Canyon Falls and the Ute Indian reservation are spots to visit in the area.

Innkeeper(s): Linda Wright-Minter. $120-175. MC, VISA, DS, TC. 19 rooms, 18 with PB, 2 with FP, 2 suites and 2 cottages. Type of meal: Early coffee/tea. Beds: KQDT. Cable TV and phone in room. Spa and swimming on premises. Antiquing, fishing, golf, parks, shopping, downhill skiing, cross-country skiing, tennis and water sports nearby.
Location: Mountains.
Publicity: *Travel & Leisure, National Geographics Traveler, Shape, Sunset, Lifestyles and New York Times.*

Certificate may be used: Nov. 15-May 15, Sunday through Thursday excluding all holidays.

Pueblo   E7

Abriendo Inn

300 W Abriendo Ave
Pueblo, CO 81004-1814
(719)544-2703 Fax:(719)542-6544
E-mail: abriendo@rmi.net

Circa 1906. This three-story, 7,000-square-foot four-square-style mansion is embellished with dentil designs and wide porches supported by Ionic columns. Elegantly paneled and carved oak walls and woodwork provide a gracious setting for king-size brass beds, antique armoires and Oriental rugs. Breakfast specialties include raspberry muffins, sunrise egg enchiladas and nut breads. A 24-hour beverage service is offered. Ask for the rooftop room that includes a double whirlpool tub.

Innkeeper(s): Kerrelyn Trent. $59-120. MC, VISA, AX, DC, PC, TC. 10 rooms with PB and 1 suite. Breakfast included in rates. Types of meals: Full gourmet bkfst, cont and early coffee/tea. Beds: KQ. Cable TV, phone, ceiling fan, VCR and whirlpool tub for two in room. Air conditioning. Fax, copier and whirlpool tubs on premises. Antiquing, fishing, golf, parks, shopping, cross-

country skiing, sporting events, tennis and water sports nearby.
Location: City.
Publicity: *Pueblo Chieftain, Rocky Mountain News and Denver Post.*
"This is a great place with the friendliest people. I've been to a lot of B&Bs this one is top drawer."
Certificate may be used: Sunday & Monday only, November through March, holidays excluded.

Silverton   F3

The Wyman Hotel & Inn

1371 Greene St
Silverton, CO 81433
(970)387-5372 (800)609-7845 Fax:(970)387-5745
Circa 1902. Silverton, a Victorian-era mining town in the heart of the San Juan Mountains, is the location for this National Register inn. The historic building still maintains an original tin ceiling and an elevator. However, the elevator is now housed in one of the guest rooms, surrounding a Jacuzzi tub. Other unique features include a stone carving of a mule created by the hotel's builder. The mule is displayed on the roof. One-of-a-kind antiques provide the furnishing for all of the rooms. Aside from the historic ambiance, the innkeepers offer plenty of amenities. Rooms include a TV and VCR, and there are hundreds of movies guests can choose, all free of charge. A gourmet breakfast is served, typically featuring seasonal fruit, freshly baked muffins, breads, cereals, special egg dishes and Silverton Spuds, potatoes baked with onions, peppers, tomatoes and cheese. Tea and homemade cookies are served every afternoon.
Innkeeper(s): Lorraine Lewis. $95-175. MC, VISA, AX, DS, TC. 17 rooms, 18 with PB and 2 suites. Breakfast and afternoon tea included in rates. Types of meals: Full gourmet bkfst and early coffee/tea. Beds: KQ. Cable TV, phone, ceiling fan, VCR, whirlpool tubs, video collection and in room. Fax, copier and library on premises. Antiquing, bicycling, fishing, hiking, hiking, horseback riding, folk festival, jeeping to ghost towns, live theater, parks, shopping and water sports nearby.
Location: Mountains.
Publicity: *Historic Traveler on The Travel Channel.*
Certificate may be used: April and May, except holidays; weekdays in October, except holidays.

Steamboat Springs   B4

The Inn at Steamboat

3070 Columbine Dr
Steamboat Springs, CO 80487
(970)879-2600 (800)872-2601 Fax:(970)879-9270
Internet: www.inn-at-steamboat.com
Circa 1972. Whatever the season, this 33-room inn is near many activities. Skiing is just three blocks away, and in the warm months, guests can hike, bike, go white-water rafting or take a trip through the wilderness on horseback. Most of the guest rooms, which feature country decor, offer views of the ski slopes or surrounding Yampa Valley. In the spring, the grounds are covered with flowers.
Innkeeper(s): Tom & Roxane Miller-Freutel. $39-159. MC, VISA, AX, DS, PC, TC. 34 rooms with PB, 1 suite and 1 conference room. Breakfast and afternoon tea included in rates. Types of meals: Cont plus and early coffee/tea. Beds: KQT. Cable TV and phone in room. Fax, copier, spa, swimming, sauna, bicycles and child care on premises. Handicap access. Fishing, golf, live theater, parks, shopping, downhill skiing, cross-country skiing, tennis and water sports nearby.
Location: Mountains.
"We will treasure the memory of our long weekend at your inn."
Certificate may be used: April 1-May 31 and Oct. 1-Nov. 30 (full non-discounted rates apply, some restrictions apply).

Steamboat Valley Guest House

PO Box 773815
Steamboat Springs, CO 80477-3815
(970)870-9017 (800)530-3866 Fax:(970)879-0361
E-mail: george@steamboatvalley.com
Circa 1957. Enjoy a sleigh ride across snow-covered hills or take in the mountain view from the hot tub at this rustic Colorado home. Logs from the town mill and bricks from an old flour mill were used to construct the home, which features rooms with exposed wooden beams, high ceilings and country furnishings. Beds are covered with fluffy comforters, and several guest rooms  afford magnificent views of this skiing resort town. The innkeepers prepare a varied breakfast menu with staples such as Irish oatmeal to the more gourmet, such as a puffy souffle. The home is located in the Steamboat Springs' historic Old Town area.
Innkeeper(s): George & Alice Lund. $83-148. MC, VISA, AX, DC, CB, DS, PC, TC. 4 rooms with PB, 1 with FP and 1 suite. Breakfast and afternoon tea included in rates. Types of meals: Full bkfst and early coffee/tea. Beds: Q. Phone in room. VCR, fax, copier, spa, library and covered free parking on premises. Fishing, hot air balloon, sleigh and snowmobile rides, hiking, biking, live theater, parks, shopping, downhill skiing, cross-country skiing and water sports nearby.
Location: Mountains.
Publicity: *Best Places to Stay in the Rockies and Steamboat Pilot.*
Certificate may be used: Monday-Thursday, April-June 15, October-Dec. 15.

Telluride   F3

Franklin Manor B&B

627 W Colorado Ave
Telluride, CO 81435
(970)728-4241 (888)728-3351 Fax:(970)728-9668
Internet: www.franklinmanor.com
E-mail: info@franklinmanor.com
Circa 1998. Although recently constructed, this inn features the charming Victorian decor that is such a part of Telluride, with its Old West heritage. The bed & breakfast is named for a young artist, Richard Franklin, who was killed tragically in a plane crash. Evidence of his talent lives on at this inn, which features some of his beautiful paintings as well as other talented artists in its recently completed Franklin Art Gallery. Most rooms in the inn include a balcony that features a mountain view, and guests also enjoy amenities such as whirlpool tubs. Two rooms  offer a fireplace. Additionally, there is a spa tub located on the inn's third-floor deck. Bed & breakfast guests are treated to a gourmet breakfast with items such as asparagus quiche, orange-pecan baked pears and freshly squeezed orange juice. Families might consider reserving the innkeepers' guest house, which offers cooking facilities. Skiing, shopping and hiking are just minutes away. After a busy day in Telluride, guests are pampered with a late afternoon wine tasting.
Innkeeper(s): Lance & Nancy Lee. $110-295. MC, VISA, AX, PC, TC. 5 rooms with PB, 2 with FP, 1 cottage and 1 conference room. Breakfast included in rates. Types of meals: Full gourmet bkfst and early coffee/tea. Beds: KQDT. Cable TV, phone, VCR, original oil & watercolors and Jacuzzi tub in room. Fax, spa, library and art gallery & gift shop on premises. Antiquing,

fishing, golf, wine, jazz, film festivals, hiking, biking, horseback riding, mountain/rock climbing, live theater, parks, shopping, downhill skiing, cross-country skiing, tennis and water sports nearby.

Location: Mountain lake and streams.

Certificate may be used: Sunday-Thursday excluding holidays and special events/festivals.

Winter Park   C5

Alpen Rose

244 Forest Tr, PO Box 769
Winter Park, CO 80482-0769
(970)726-5039 (800)531-1373 Fax:(970)726-0993
Internet: www.bbhost.com/alpenrosebb
E-mail: robinand@rkymtnni.com

Circa 1960. The innkeepers of this European-style mountain B&B like to share their love of the mountains with guests. There is a superb view of the James and Perry Peaks from the large southern deck where you can witness spectacular sunrises and evening alpen glows. The view is enhanced by lofty pines, wildflowers and quaking aspens. Each of the bedrooms is decorated with treasures brought over from Austria, including traditional featherbeds for the queen-size beds. The town of Winter Park is a small, friendly community located 68 miles west of Denver.

Innkeeper(s): Robin & Rupert Sommerauer. $65-135. MC, VISA, AX, DS, PC, TC. 6 rooms with PB. Breakfast and afternoon tea included in rates. Types of meals: Full gourmet bkfst and early coffee/tea. Beds: KQT. VCR, fax, copier and spa on premises. Antiquing, fishing, sledding, sleigh rides, dog sleds, ballooning, river rafting, biking, jeeping, alpine slide, parks, shopping, downhill skiing, cross-country skiing and water sports nearby.

Location: Ski resort.

Publicity: *Denver Post and Rocky Mountain News.*

Certificate may be used: April 15 to Dec. 15, Sunday-Thursday, no holidays.

The Bear Paw Inn

871 Bear Paw Dr, PO Box 334
Winter Park, CO 80482
(970)887-1351 Fax:(970)887-1351
Internet: www.bestinns.net/usa/co/bearpaw.html
E-mail: bearpaw@rkymthhi.com

Circa 1989. This hand-hewn log home is exactly the type of welcoming retreat one might hope to enjoy on a vacation in the Colorado wilderness, and the panoramic views of the Continental Divide and Rocky Mountain National Park are just one reason. The cozy interior is highlighted by wood beams, massive log walls and antiques. There are two guest rooms, both with a Jacuzzi tub. The master

has a private deck with a swing. Guests can snuggle up in feather beds topped with down comforters. Winter Park is a Mecca for skiers, and ski areas are just a few miles from the Bear Paw, as is ice skating, snowmobiling, horse-drawn sleigh rides and other winter activities. For summer guests, there is whitewater rafting, golfing, horseback riding and bike trails. There are 600 miles of bike trials, music festivals and much more.

Innkeeper(s): Rick & Sara Callahan. $140-175. MC, VISA, AX, PC, TC. 2 rooms with PB. Breakfast included in rates. Types of meals: Full gourmet bkfst and early coffee/tea. Beds: Q. TV, turndown service and feather beds in room. VCR, fax and copier on premises. Antiquing, fishing, hot air balloons,

mountain bikes, summer rodeos, live theater, shopping, downhill skiing, cross-country skiing and water sports nearby.

Location: Mountains.

Publicity: *Cape Cod Life, Boston Globe, Los Angeles Times, Continental Airlines Quarterly, Denver Post, Rocky Mountain News, Log Homes Illustrated and Colorado Country Life.*

"Outstanding hospitality."

Certificate may be used: Sunday-Thursday, holidays and special events excluded, Dec. 10-Dec. 31 excluded, June-September excluded and January-March excluded.

Outpost B&B Inn

685 County Rd 517
Winter Park, CO 80482-0041
(970)726-5346 (800)430-4538 Fax:(970)726-5346
Internet: www.outpost-colorado.com
E-mail: outpost@coweblink.net

Circa 1972. Rocky mountain peaks, woods and rolling pastures surround this 40-acre spread, which affords views of the Continental Divide. Guests stay in an antique-filled lodge inn. The inn's atrium includes a hot tub. The innkeepers serve a huge, multi-course feast for breakfast. During the winter months, the innkeepers offer free shuttle service to Winter Park and Mary Jane ski areas.

Innkeeper(s): Ken & Barbara Parker. $120. MC, VISA, AX, DS, PC, TC. 7 rooms with PB. Breakfast included in rates. Types of meals: Full gourmet bkfst and early coffee/tea. Beds: KQDT. VCR, fax, spa, library and cross-country skiing on premises. Antiquing, fishing, golf, snowmobiling, horseback riding, biking, mountain biking, live theater, parks, shopping, downhill skiing, cross-country skiing and water sports nearby.

Location: Ski area.

Publicity: *Denver Post.*

Certificate may be used: Sunday-Thursday; April 1-Dec. 1, Jan. 5-Feb. 1, no holidays.

Woodland Park   D6

Pikes Peak Paradise

236 Pinecrest Rd
Woodland Park, CO 80863
(719)687-6656 (800)728-8282 Fax:(719)687-9008
E-mail: woodlandco@aol.com

Circa 1987. This three-story Georgian Colonial with stately white columns rises unexpectedly from the wooded hills west of Colorado Springs. The south wall of the house has large windows to enhance its splendid views of Pikes Peak. A glass door opens from each guest suite onto a private deck or patio with the same riveting view. Eggs Benedict and baked French apple toast are some of the favorites offered for breakfast.

Innkeeper(s): Rayne & Bart Reese. $120-230. MC, VISA, AX, DS, PC, TC. 5 suites, 4 with FP. Breakfast included in rates. Type of meal: Full bkfst. Beds: KQ. Ceiling fan and deluxe suites have TV/VCR in room. VCR, fax and spa on premises. Handicap access. Amusement parks, antiquing, bicycling, fishing, golf, hiking, horseback riding, gambling, live theater, parks, shopping, cross-country skiing, sporting events and water sports nearby.

Pets allowed: Small pets with prior approval.

Location: Mountains.

Publicity: *Rocky Mountain News.*

Certificate may be used: Nov. 1-April 30 (excluding holidays and weekends).

Connecticut

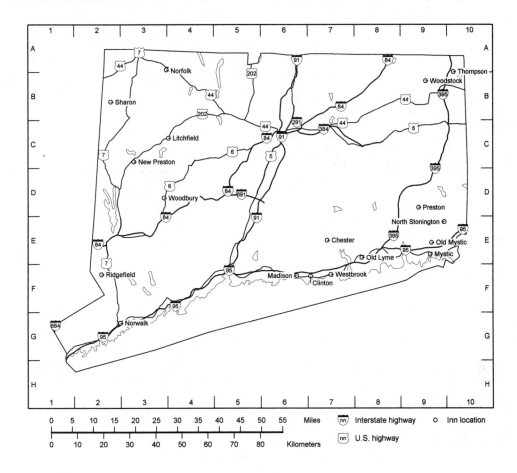

0	5	10	15	20	25	30	35	40	45	50	55	Miles
0	10	20	30	40	50	60	70	80		Kilometers

🛡 Interstate highway   ○ Inn location

🛡 U.S. highway

Chester E7

The Inn at Chester

318 W Main St
Chester, CT 06412-1026
(860)526-9541 (800)949-7829 Fax:(860)526-4387
Internet: www.innatchester.com
E-mail: innkeeper@innatchester.com

Circa 1778. More than 200 years ago, Jeremiah Parmelee built a clapboard farmhouse along a winding road named the Killingworth Turnpike. The Parmelee Homestead stands as a reflection of the past and is an inspiration for the Inn at Chester. Each of the rooms is individually appointed with Eldred Wheeler Reproductions. The Lincoln Suite has a sitting room with a fireplace. Enjoy lively conversation or live music while imbibing your favorite drink at the inn's tavern, Dunk's Landing. Outside Dunk's Landing, a 30-foot fireplace soars into the rafters. Fine dining is offered in the inn's post-and-beam restaurant.

Innkeeper(s): Leonard Lieberman. $105-215. MC, VISA, AX, DS. 42 rooms with PB, 2 with FP, 1 suite and 3 conference rooms. Breakfast included in rates. Type of meal: Cont plus. Beds: KQDT. Cable TV and phone in room. Air conditioning. VCR, fax, copier, sauna, bicycles, tennis, library and pet boarding on premises. Handicap access. Antiquing, fishing, golf, live theater, parks, shopping, downhill skiing, cross-country skiing and water sports nearby.

Pets Allowed.

Location: Country.

Publicity: *New Haven Register, Hartford Courant, Pictorial Gazette, Discover Connecticut, New York Times, Connecticut Magazine and Food Network.*

Certificate may be used: Nov. 1-April 1, Sunday-Thursday.

Clinton F7

Captain Dibbell House

21 Commerce St
Clinton, CT 06413-2054
(860)669-1646 (888)889-6882 Fax:(860)669-2300

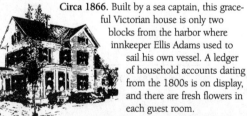

Circa 1866. Built by a sea captain, this graceful Victorian house is only two blocks from the harbor where innkeeper Ellis Adams used to sail his own vessel. A ledger of household accounts dating from the 1800s is on display, and there are fresh flowers in each guest room.

Innkeeper(s): Helen & Ellis Adams. $89-129. MC, VISA, PC, TC. 4 rooms with PB. Breakfast included in rates. Type of meal: Full bkfst. Beds: KQT. Turndown service, ceiling fan and bathrobes in room. Air conditioning. Bicycles on premises. Antiquing, fishing, live theater, parks, shopping and water sports nearby.

Publicity: *Clinton Recorder, New Haven Register and Hartford Courant.*

"This was our first experience with B&Bs and frankly, we didn't know what to expect. It was GREAT!"

Certificate may be used: Sunday through Thursday, holidays, special event weekends and months of July, August and October excluded.

Litchfield C4

Abel Darling B&B

PO Box 1502, 102 West St
Litchfield, CT 06759
(860)567-0384 Fax:(860)567-2638

Circa 1782. The spacious guest rooms in this 1782 colonial home offer a light romantic feel and comfortable beds. Breakfast is served in the sunny dining room and includes home-baked breads and muffins. This bed and breakfast is in the heart of the historic district, and nearby is the village green, hosting many restaurants and boutique shops, and the Litchfield countryside.

Innkeeper(s): Colleen Murphy. $85-125. PC, TC. 2 rooms with PB. Breakfast included in rates. Types of meals: Cont plus and cont. Beds: QD. Table and chairs in room. VCR, fax, copier, bicycles and library on premises. Antiquing, fishing, golf, live theater, parks, shopping, downhill skiing, cross-country skiing and tennis nearby.

Location: Mountains.

Publicity: *Litchfield County Times and New York Times.*

Certificate may be used: Jan. 15-April 30.

Madison F6

Madison Post Road B&B

318 Boston Post Rd
Madison, CT 06443-2936
(203)245-2866 Fax:(203)245-4955
E-mail: duane.harmon@mcione.com

Circa 1830. This farm house was modified to a Greek Revival style and there are now 15 columns and several bay windows. Located on more than an acre, the original homestead included both shoreline salt marsh land and farmland. The innkeepers are parents to nine children, and three of them work at the inn. After enjoying the full breakfast, guests have the choice of outlet or antique shopping, apple picking, scenic drives, bicycling, fishing or boating depending on the season. There are fine restaurants and galleries in several quaint villages nearby.

Innkeeper(s): Duane & Lynette Harmon. $70-110. MC, VISA, AX, PC, TC. 4 rooms with PB. Breakfast included in rates. Type of meal: Full bkfst. Beds: QDT. Cable TV, phone and VCR in room. Air conditioning. Fax and copier on premises. Antiquing, fishing, live theater, parks, shopping, downhill skiing, cross-country skiing, tennis and water sports nearby.

"Your lovely home reflects the comfortable, congenial family you are."

Certificate may be used: Jan. 1 to May 15, Sept. 15 to Dec. 31.

Mystic E9

The Whaler's Inn

20 E Main St
Mystic, CT 06355-2646
(860)536-1506 (800)243-2588 Fax:(860)572-1250
Internet: www.whalersinnmystic.com
E-mail: whalers.inn@riconnect.com

Circa 1901. This classical revival-style inn is built on the historical site of the Hoxie House, the Clinton House and the U.S. Hotel. Just as these famous 19th-century inns offered, the Whaler's Inn has the same charm and convenience for today's visitor to Mystic. Once a booming ship-building center, the town's connection to the sea is ongoing and the sailing schooners still pass beneath the Bascule Drawbridge in the center of town. The inn has indoor and outdoor dining available and more than 75 shops and restaurants are within walking distance.

Innkeeper(s): Richard Prisby. $95-215. MC, VISA, AX, DS, TC. 41 rooms with PB, 1 suite and 1 conference room. Type of meal: Cont plus. Beds: KQD. Cable TV and phone in room. Air conditioning. Fax and copier on premises. Handicap access. Antiquing, fishing, walk to Mystic Seaport, harbor & schooner cruises, parks, shopping and water sports nearby.

Location: City.

Certificate may be used: Nov. 28-March 28, excluding holidays.

New Preston   C3

Boulders Inn

East Shore Rd, Rt 45
New Preston, CT 06777
(860)868-0541 (800)55-BOULDER Fax:(860)868-1925
Internet: www.bouldersinn.com
E-mail: boulders@bouldersinn.com

Circa 1895. Views of Lake Waramaug and its wooded shores can be seen from the living room and most of the guest rooms and cottages of this country inn. The terrace is open in the summer for cocktails, dinner and sunsets over the lake. Antique furnishings, a basement game room, and a beach house with a hanging wicker swing are all part of Boulders Inn. There is a private beach with boats, and bicycles are available.

Innkeeper(s): Kees & Ulla Adema. $225-395. MC, VISA, AX, PC, TC. 17 rooms with PB, 11 with FP, 2 suites, 8 cottages and 1 conference room. Breakfast, afternoon tea and dinner included in rates. Types of meals: Full gourmet bkfst and early coffee/tea. Beds: KQ. TV, phone, turndown service and ceiling fan in room. Air conditioning. VCR, fax, copier, swimming, bicycles and library on premises. Handicap access. Antiquing, fishing, golf, live theater, parks, shopping, downhill skiing, cross-country skiing, tennis and water sports nearby.

Location: Mountains.

Publicity: *New York Times, Travel & Leisure and Country Inns.*

Certificate may be used: Midweek Nov. 1-May 31, excluding Christmas week and holidays.

Norfolk   A3

Manor House

69 Maple Ave
Norfolk, CT 06058-0447
(860)542-5690 Fax:(860)542-5690
Internet: www.manorhouse-norfolk.com
E-mail: tremblay@esslink.com

Circa 1898. Charles Spofford, designer of London's subway, built this home with many gables, exquisite cherry paneling and grand staircase. There are Moorish arches and Tiffany windows. Guests can enjoy hot-mulled cider after a sleigh ride, hay

 ride, or horse and carriage drive along the country lanes nearby. The inn was named by "Discerning Traveler" as Connecticut's most romantic hideaway.

Innkeeper(s): Hank & Diane Tremblay. $100-250. MC, VISA, AX, DS, PC, TC. 9 rooms with PB, 4 with FP, 1 suite and 1 conference room. Breakfast and afternoon tea included in rates. Types of meals: Full gourmet bkfst and early coffee/tea. Beds: KQDT. Ceiling fan and two with double whirlpools in room. Fax and library on premises. Antiquing, fishing, live theater, parks, shopping, downhill skiing, cross-country skiing, sporting events and water sports nearby.

Location: Mountains.

Publicity: *Good Housekeeper, Gourmet, Boston Globe, Philadelphia Inquirer, Innsider, Rhode Island Monthly, Gourmet, National Geographic Traveler and New York Times.*

"Queen Victoria, eat your heart out."

Certificate may be used: Weekdays, excluding holidays and month of October.

North Stonington   E9

Antiques & Accommodations

32 Main St
North Stonington, CT 06359-1709
(860)535-1736 (800)554-7829 Fax:(800)535-2613
Internet: www.visitmystic.com/antiques

Circa 1861. Set amongst the backdrop of an acre of herb, edible flower, perennial and cutting gardens, this Victorian treasure offers a romantic location for a weekend getaway. Rooms filled with antiques boast four-poster canopy beds and fresh flowers surrounded by a soft, pleasing decor. Honeymooners or couples celebrating an anniversary are presented with special amenities such as balloons, champagne and heart-shaped waffles for breakfast. Candlelit breakfasts  include unique items such as edible flowers along with the delicious entrees. Historic Mystic Seaport and Foxwood's Casino are just minutes from the inn.

Innkeeper(s): Ann & Tom Gray. $110-229. MC, VISA. 5 rooms with PB and 1 suite. Breakfast included in rates. Type of meal: Full bkfst. Beds: Q. Cable TV and VCR in room. Air conditioning. Antiquing and fishing nearby.

Publicity: *Country Inns, Woman's Day, New London Day, Connecticut Magazine and Connecticut Public Radio.*

"The building's old-fashioned welcome-all decor made us feel comfortable the moment we stepped in."

Certificate may be used: All year except for legal holidays and weekends.

Arbor House at Kruger's Old Maine Farm

75 Chester Maine Rd
North Stonington, CT 06359-1304
(860)535-4221 Fax:(860)535-4221

Circa 1900. From this restored, turn-of-the-century farmhouse, guests enjoy a view of Connecticut's coastline and picturesque countryside. Spacious guest rooms are decorated in an uncluttered, country style. The farmhouse is surrounded by 37 acres, which includes a vineyard. The old barn has been converted into a winery. Three-course breakfasts are served each morning in the dining room.

Innkeeper(s): Allen & Michelle Kruger. $75-150. MC, VISA, PC, TC. 4 rooms, 2 with PB and 2 suites. Breakfast and afternoon tea included in rates. Types of meals: Full bkfst and early coffee/tea. Beds: Q. Cable TV and turndown service in room. Air conditioning. VCR, fax, stables and pet boarding on premises. Antiquing, fishing, parks, shopping, cross-country skiing and water sports nearby. Pets allowed: Outside.

Location: Country.

Certificate may be used: All year except for legal holidays and weekends.

Norwalk   G2

Silvermine Tavern
194 Perry Ave
Norwalk, CT 06850-1123
(203)847-4558 Fax:(203)847-9171

Circa 1790. The Silvermine consists
of the Old Mill, the Country Store,
the Coach House and the Tavern
itself. Primitive paintings and furnishings, as well as family heirlooms, decorate the inn. Guest rooms and dining rooms overlook the Old Mill, the
waterfall and swans gliding across the
millpond. Some guest rooms offer
items such as canopy bed or private
decks. In the summer, guests can dine
al fresco and gaze at the mill pond.
Innkeeper(s): Frank Whitman, Jr. $110-155. MC, VISA, AX, DC, CB, PC, TC.
10 rooms with PB and 1 suite. Breakfast included in rates. Type of meal:
Cont. Beds: QDT. Some canopied beds in room. Air conditioning. VCR, fax,
copier and handicap access to restaurant on premises. Antiquing, fishing,
parks and shopping nearby.
Location: Residential area.
Certificate may be used: All year, no Friday arrivals, no October.

Old Lyme   E8

Bee and Thistle Inn
100 Lyme St
Old Lyme, CT 06371-1426
(860)434-1667 (800)622-4946 Fax:(860)434-3402
Internet: www.beeandthistle.com
E-mail: info@beeandthistleinn.com

Circa 1756. This stately inn is situated along the banks of the
Lieutenant River. There are five and one-half acres of trees, lawns
and a sunken English garden. The inn is furnished with
Chippendale antiques and reproductions. A guitar duo plays in
the parlor on Friday, and a harpist performs on Saturday
evenings. Bee and Thistle was voted the most romantic inn in
the state, the most romantic dinner spot, and for having the best
restaurant in the state by readers of "Connecticut Magazine."
Innkeeper(s): Bob, Penny, Lori and Jeff Nelson. $79-210. MC, VISA, DC, DS,
PC, TC. 11 rooms with PB, 1 with FP and 1 cottage. Type of meal: Full gourmet
bkfst. Beds: QDT. Phone and ceiling fan in room. Air conditioning. Antiquing, art
galleries, fishing, live theater, museums, parks and shopping nearby.
Location: Village.
Publicity: Countryside, Country Living, Money, New York, U.S. Air, New York
Times and Country Traveler.
Certificate may be used: Sunday through Thursday, excluding holidays and
excluding the months of July, August and October.

Old Mystic   E9

Red Brook Inn
PO Box 237
Old Mystic, CT 06372-0237
(860)572-0349

Circa 1740. If there was no other reason to visit Mystic, a
charming town brimming with activities, the Red Brook Inn
would be reason enough. The Crary Homestead features three
unique rooms with working fireplaces, while the Haley Tavern

offers seven guest rooms, some with canopy beds and fireplaces. Two have whirlpool tubs. Innkeeper Ruth Keyes has
beautiful antiques decorating her inn. Guests are sure to enjoy
her wonderful country breakfasts. A special winter dinner takes
three days to complete and she prepares it over an open hearth.
In addition to a full breakfast, afternoon and evening beverages
are provided. The aquarium, Mystic Seaport Museum, a cider
mill, casinos and many shops are only minutes away.
Innkeeper(s): Ruth Keyes. $189. MC, VISA, AX, DS, PC, TC. 10 rooms with
PB, 7 with FP and 3 conference rooms. Breakfast included in rates. Type of
meal: Full bkfst. Beds: QDT. Whirlpool tub in room. VCR, library, terrace and
parlors on premises. Amusement parks, antiquing, fishing, museums, casino,
live theater, parks, shopping, sporting events and water sports nearby.
Location: Wooded area.
Publicity: Westerly Sun, Travel & Leisure, Yankee, New York, Country
Decorating, Philadelphia Inquirer, National Geographic Traveler and
Discerning Traveler.
"The staff is wonderful. You made us feel at home. Thank you for
your hospitality."
Certificate may be used: Nov. 15 to April 15, Monday, Tuesday, Wednesday,
Thursday. (Not good Friday, Saturday, Sunday).

Preston   D9

Roseledge Farm B&B
418 Rt 164
Preston, CT 06365-8112
(860)892-4739 Fax:(860)892-4739
E-mail: jrogers981@aol.com

Circa 1720. Hearth-cooked New England breakfasts of eggs,
bacon and homemade breads are served in this colonial inn,
one of the oldest homes in Preston. Wide floor boards original
to the home create a feeling of reverence for the finely maintained historic home. There are pegged mortise and tenon
beams and scrolled moldings on the stair treads. Canopy beds
with floaty bed curtains add a romantic touch. There is a stone
tunnel connecting the street with the barn's basement, and
ancient stone walls divide the rolling meadows in view of the
inn's four acres. Guests are invited to help with the farm animals, including gathering eggs.
Innkeeper(s): Gail A. Rogers. $85-125. MC, VISA, AX, DS, PC, TC. 4 rooms,
3 with PB, 4 with FP, 1 suite and 1 conference room. Breakfast, afternoon
tea, dinner and picnic lunch included in rates. Types of meals: Full bkfst and
early coffee/tea. Beds: QD. Phone and turndown service in room. Air conditioning. Fax, pet boarding, child care, limited pet boarding, farm animals, tea
room and antique store on premises. Amusement parks, antiquing, fishing,
golf, Yankee baseball stadium, Mystic area, live theater, parks, shopping,
sporting events, tennis and water sports nearby.
Pets allowed: limited.
Location: Country.
Certificate may be used: Jan. 1 to May 1, Sunday-Thursday.

Ridgefield   F2

West Lane Inn
22 West Ln
Ridgefield, CT 06877-4914
(203)438-7323 Fax:(203)438-7325

Circa 1849. This National Register Victorian mansion on two
acres features an enormous front veranda filled with white whicker
chairs and tables overlooking a manicured lawn. A polished oak
staircase rises to a third-floor landing and lounge. Chandeliers,
wall sconces and floral wallpapers help to establish an intimate
atmosphere. Although the rooms do not have antiques, they feature amenities such as heated towel racks, extra-thick towels, air

conditioning, remote control cable TVs and desks.

Innkeeper(s): Maureen Mayer & Deborah Prieger. $110-175. MC, VISA, AX, DC, CB. 18 rooms with PB, 2 with FP. Breakfast included in rates. Type of meal: Cont. Beds: Q. Phone and ceiling fan in room. Air conditioning. Antiquing, fishing, live theater, shopping and cross-country skiing nearby.

Location: New England town.

Publicity: *Stanford-Advocate, Greenwich Times and Home & Away Connecticut.*

"Thank you for the hospitality you showed us. The rooms are comfortable and quiet. I haven't slept this soundly in weeks."

Certificate may be used: Nov. 30 through April 30, Sunday through Friday, excluding holidays or holiday weekends.

Sharon   B2

1890 Colonial B&B

Rt 41, PO Box 25
Sharon, CT 06069-0025
(860)364-0436
E-mail: colonial@mohawk.net

Circa 1890. Summertime guests can find a cool place to sit on the screened porch of this center-hall Colonial home situated on five park-like acres. Guests visiting in the winter can warm up to any of the main floor fireplaces in the living room, dining room and den. Guest rooms are spacious and have high ceilings. A furnished apartment also is available with private entrance and kitchenette at special weekly rates.

Innkeeper(s): Carole "Kelly" Tangen. $85-112. 3 rooms with PB and 1 suite. Breakfast included in rates. Types of meals: Full bkfst and early coffee/tea. Beds: QT. Cable TV, turndown service and ceiling fan in room. VCR on premises. Antiquing, fishing, live theater, parks, shopping, downhill skiing, cross-country skiing and water sports nearby.

Location: Mountains.

Certificate may be used: Weekdays only.

Thompson   A10

Hickory Ridge Lakefront B&B

1084 Quaddick Town Farm Rd
Thompson, CT 06277-2929
(860)928-9530

Circa 1990. Enjoy three wooded acres in the private rural setting of this spacious post-and-beam home. The inn's property includes a chunk of the Quaddick Lake shoreline and canoes are available for guests. There's plenty of hiking to do with 17 private acres and access to miles of state lands. Quaddick State Park is within walking or bicycling distance. Breakfasts of baked goods and entrees are served at your convenience.

Innkeeper(s): Birdie Olson. $40-85. 3 rooms, 1 with PB, 1 with FP and 1 suite. Breakfast included in rates. Types of meals: Full bkfst and early coffee/tea. Beds: DT. Turndown service in room. VCR and child care on premises. Antiquing, fishing, live theater, shopping and cross-country skiing nearby.

Certificate may be used: Sunday through Thursday, July 1-Oct. 30 (except holidays). Anytime Nov. 1-June 30 (except holidays and graduations).

Westbrook   F7

Westbrook Inn B&B

976 Boston Post Rd
Westbrook, CT 06498-1852
(860)399-4777 Fax:(860)399-8023

Circa 1876. A wraparound porch and flower gardens offer a gracious welcome to this Victorian inn. The innkeeper, an expert in restoring old houses and antiques, has filled the inn

with French and American period antiques, handsome paintings and wall coverings. Home-baked breads accompany a variety of breakfast main dishes. Bike rides and walks to the beach are among guests' most popular activities.

Innkeeper(s): Glenn & Chris. $99-139. MC, VISA, DS. 8 rooms, 1 with FP and 1 cottage. Breakfast, afternoon tea and snacks/refreshments included in rates. Types of meals: Full bkfst and early coffee/tea. Beds: QDT. Cable TV, phone and turndown service in room. Air conditioning. VCR, fax, copier, bicycles and library on premises. Antiquing, fishing, golf, casinos, live theater, parks, shopping, sporting events, tennis and water sports nearby.

Certificate may be used: Oct. 31-April 30, Monday-Thursday.

Woodbury   D3

Merryvale B&B

1204 Main St S
Woodbury, CT 06798-3804
(203)266-0800 Fax:(203)263-4479

Circa 1789. Merryvale, an elegant Colonial inn, is situated in a picturesque New England Village, known as an antique capitol of Connecticut. Guests can enjoy complimentary tea, coffee and biscuits throughout the day. A grand living room invites travelers to relax by the fireplace and enjoy a book from the extensive collection of classics and mysteries. During the week, guests enjoy an ample breakfast buffet and on weekends, the innkeepers prepare a Federal-style breakfast using historic, 18th-century recipes.

Innkeeper(s): Pat Ubaldi Nurnberger. $115-150. MC, VISA, AX, DC. 4 rooms with PB and 2 suites. Breakfast included in rates. Type of meal: Full bkfst. Beds: KQT. Cable TV, phone, wine and homemade cookies in room. Air conditioning. Amusement parks, antiquing, fishing, shopping, downhill skiing and cross-country skiing nearby.

Location: Country town.

Publicity: *Voices, Yankee Traveler, Hartford Courant and Newtown Bee.*

"Your hospitality will always be remembered."

Certificate may be used: Jan. 7-Feb. 28, Monday-Sunday.

Woodstock   B9

Elias Child House B&B

50 Perrin Rd
Woodstock, CT 06281
(860)974-9836 (877)974-9836
Internet: www.eliaschildhouse.com
E-mail: tfelice@compuserve.com

Circa 1700. Nine fireplaces warm this heritage three-story colonial home, referred to as "the mansion house" by early settlers. There are two cooking fireplaces, both walk-in size and a beehive oven. Original floors, twelve-over-twelve windows and paneling remain. A bountiful breakfast is served fireside in the dining room and a screened porch and a patio provide nesting spots for reading and relaxing. The inn's grounds are spacious and offer a pool and hammocks. Woodland walks on the 47 acres and antiquing are popular activities.

Innkeeper(s): Anthony Felice, Jr. & MaryBeth Gorke-Felice. $95-120. MC, VISA, DS, PC, TC. 3 rooms with PB and 1 suite. Breakfast included in rates. Types of meals: Full bkfst and early coffee/tea. Beds: QDT. Turndown service in room. VCR, fax, copier, swimming and bicycles on premises. Cooking demonstrations and cross-country skiing nearby.

Pets allowed: Small dogs with cage.

Location: Country.

Publicity: *Journal Inquirer, Forbes, Hartford Courant, Yankee Traveler and Connecticut Magazine.*

"Comfortable rooms and delightful country ambiance."

Certificate may be used: Sunday through Thursday, except holidays, Valentine's Day.

Delaware

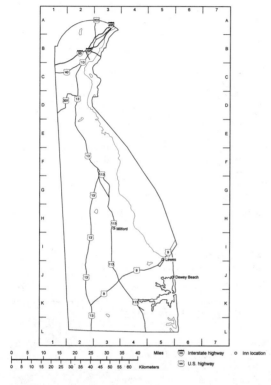

```
0   5   10  15  20  25  30  35  40  Miles        Interstate highway    ○ Inn location
0 5 10 15 20 25 30 35 40 45 50 55 60 Kilometers   U.S. highway
```

Dewey Beach   J5

Barry's Gull Cottage B&B
116 Chesapeake St
Dewey Beach, DE 19971-3403
(302)227-7000 (302)645-1575 Fax:(302)227-7000
Internet: www.gullcottage.com
E-mail: innkeeper@gullcottage.com

Circa 1962. It's only a block and a half to the beach from this
Nantucket-style home, which also affords views of a lake.
Rooms feature antiques, beds covered in quilts, wicker furnishings and stained glass. The innkeepers pamper guests with
treats throughout the day, beginning with a healthy breakfast.
Afternoon tea is served, and the evening is topped off with
sherry, port wine, coffee and luscious award-winning chocolate
cake. Relax in the hot tub illuminated by candlelight. The area
offers plenty of shopping, from outlets to antiques, and good
restaurants are close to this beach retreat.

Innkeeper(s): Vivian & Bob Barry. $120-180. PC, TC. 4 rooms. Breakfast,
afternoon tea and snacks/refreshments included in rates. Types of meals: Full
gourmet bkfst and early coffee/tea. Beds: KQ. Cable TV, turndown service,
ceiling fan and phones some rooms in room. Air conditioning. VCR, fax, copier, spa, bicycles, library, beach chairs and umbrellas, guest refrigerator and
tandem and surrey bicycles on premises. Amusement parks, antiquing, fishing, live theater, parks, shopping and water sports nearby.
Certificate may be used: Monday through Thursday, May 15 to Sept. 30,
excluding July and August.

Lewes   I5

The Bay Moon B&B
128 Kings Hwy
Lewes, DE 19958-1418
(302)644-1802 (800)917-2307 Fax:(302)644-1802

Circa 1887. The exterior of this three-story, cedar Victorian features a front veranda shrouded by the flowers and foliage that also
decorate the front walk. The custom-made, hand-crafted beds in
the guest rooms are topped with feather pillows and down comforters. A champagne turn-
down service is available, and
wine is served each evening.
The innkeeper offers plenty of
amenities. Beach supplies and
a heated outdoor shower are
helpful for guests who want to
enjoy the ocean.

Innkeeper(s): Pamela Rizzo. $95-150. MC, VISA, PC, TC. 4 rooms with PB
and 1 suite. Breakfast included in rates. Types of meals: Full bkfst and early
coffee/tea. Beds: KQ. Cable TV, ceiling fan and VCR in room. Central air. Fax,
spa, library and outdoor Jacuzzi on premises. Antiquing, fishing, beach, live
theater, parks, shopping, sporting events and water sports nearby.
Location: Historic town.
Certificate may be used: Sept. 15-June 15, weekdays Monday-Wednesday
only, no holidays.

New Devon Inn
142 2nd St
Lewes, DE 19958-1396
(302)645-6466 (800)824-8754 Fax:(302)645-7196
Internet: www.beach-net.com/newdevoninn
E-mail: newdevon@dca.net

Circa 1926. In the heart of the historic district, this inn has 24
individually decorated guest rooms. All rooms feature antique
beds and turndown service. The inn, which prefers guests over
the age of 16, also offers conference facilities, catering and convenient access to antiquing, beaches, dining and sightseeing.
Two suites also are available. The shore is just a half-mile from
the inn. Prime Hook National Wildlife Refuge and Cape
Henlopen State Park are nearby.

Innkeeper(s): Suzanne Steele. $50-170. MC, VISA, AX. 18 rooms with PB, 5 suites and 1 conference room. Type of meal: Early coffee/tea. Beds: QDT. Phone and turndown service in room. Air conditioning. Fax and copier on premises. Handicap access. Antiquing, fishing, parks, shopping and water sports nearby.

Location: Historic Maritime Town.

Publicity: *New York Times, Mid-Atlantic Country and National Geographic.*

Certificate may be used: Year-round, Sunday through Thursday, weekends and holidays excluded.

Wild Swan Inn

525 Kings Hwy
Lewes, DE 19958-1421
(302)645-8550 Fax:(302)645-8550

Circa 1900. This Queen Anne Victorian is a whimsical sight, painted in pink with white, green and burgundy trim. The interior is dotted with antiques and dressed in Victorian style. A full, gourmet breakfast and freshly ground coffee are served

each morning. The innkeepers have placed many musical treasures in their inn, including an early Edison phonograph and a Victrola.

Michael often serenades guests on a 1912 player piano during breakfast. Lewes, which was founded in 1631, is the first town in the first state. Wild Swan is within walking distance of downtown where several fine restaurants await you. Nearby Cape Henlopen State Park offers hiking and watersports, and the surrounding countryside is ideal for cycling and other outdoor activities. Listed in the National Trust for Historic Preservation, the inn was 3rd place winner in Jones Dairy Farm National Cooking Contest for B&B Inns.

Innkeeper(s): Michael & Hope Tyler. $85-150. PC, TC. 3 rooms with PB. Breakfast and snacks/refreshments included in rates. Types of meals: Full gourmet bkfst and early coffee/tea. Beds: Q. Turndown service in room. Air conditioning. Swimming, bicycles, library, player piano, Edison & Victrola phonographs and music entertainment on premises. Antiquing, bicycling, fish-

ing, birding, live theater, museums, parks, shopping and water sports nearby.

Location: City.

Publicity: *Country Inns, Country Collectibles, Victorian Lewes, Washington Post, Delaware Today and CNN Travel Guide.*

"The house is beautiful with lovely detailed pieces. Mike and Hope are gracious hosts. You'll sleep like a baby and wake up to a scrumptious breakfast and a great concert!"

Certificate may be used: Nov. 1-May 1, any day except holidays.

Milford   H3

The Towers B&B

101 NW Front St
Milford, DE 19963-1022
(302)422-3814 (800)366-3814
Internet: www.mispillion.com
E-mail: mispillion@ezol.com

Circa 1783. Once a simple colonial house, this ornate Steamboat Gothic fantasy features every imaginable Victorian architectural detail, all added in 1891. There are 10 distinct styles of gingerbread as well as towers, turrets, gables, porches and bays. Inside, chestnut and cherry woodwork, window seats and stained-glass windows are complemented with American and French antiques. The back garden boasts a gazebo porch and swimming pool. Ask for the splendid Tower Room or Rapunzel Suite.

Innkeeper(s): Daniel & Rhonda Bond. $95-135. MC, VISA, AX. 6 rooms with PB and 2 suites. Breakfast included in rates. Beds: QD. TV and ceiling fan in room. Air conditioning. Swimming on premises. Antiquing, fishing, live theater, parks, shopping and water sports nearby.

Location: City.

Publicity: *Washington Post, Baltimore Sun, Washingtonian and Mid-Atlantic Country.*

"I felt as if I were inside a beautiful Victorian Christmas card, surrounded by all the things Christmas should be."

Certificate may be used: Any night of the week throughout the year.

Florida

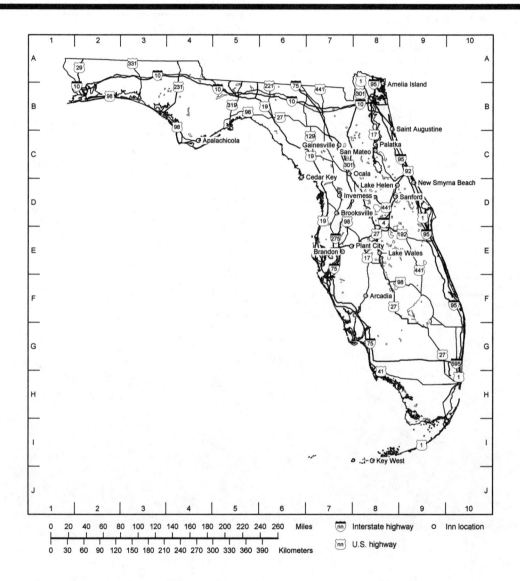

0   20   40   60   80   100 120 140 160 180 200 220 240 260   Miles

0   30   60   90   120 150 180 210 240 270 300 330 360 390   Kilometers

(nn) Interstate highway   o   Inn location

(nn) U.S. highway

Amelia Island   B8

1857 Florida House Inn
PO Box 688, 22 S 3rd St
Amelia Island, FL 32034-4207
(904)261-3300 (800)258-3301 Fax:(904)277-3831
Internet: www.floridahouseinn.com
E-mail: innkeepers@floridahouseinn.com

Circa 1857. Located in the heart of a 50-block historic National Register area, the Florida House Inn is thought to be the oldest continuously operating tourist hotel in Florida. Recently renovated, the inn features a small pub, guest parlor, library and a New Orleans-style courtyard in which guests may enjoy the shade of 200-year-old oaks. Rooms are decorated with country pine and oak antiques, cheerful handmade rugs and quilts, and 10 rooms offer fireplaces and Jacuzzi tubs. The Carnegies, Rockefellers and Ulysses S. Grant have been guests.
Innkeeper(s): Bob & Karen Warner. $70-170. MC, VISA, AX. 15 rooms with PB, 10 with FP, 1 suite and 1 conference room. Breakfast included in rates. Types of meals: Full bkfst and early coffee/tea. Beds: KQT. Cable TV, phone, ceiling fan and 10 Jacuzzi tubs in room. Air conditioning. Fax and copier on premises. Handicap access. Antiquing, fishing, live theater and sporting events nearby.
Location: Village.
Publicity: *Amelia Now, Tampa Tribune, Miami Herald, Toronto Star, Country Living and Ft. Lauderdale Sun Sentinel.*
Certificate may be used: Sunday through Thursday.

Hoyt House B&B
804 Atlantic Ave
Amelia Island, FL 32034-3629
(904)277-4300 (800)432-2085 Fax:(904)277-9626
Internet: www.hoythouse.com
E-mail: hoythouseb&b@net-magic.net

Circa 1905. A wraparound veranda welcomes guests to this three-story, yellow Victorian. Trimmed in blue and white and shaded by large trees, the house is in the National Register. Exuberant color schemes accent the interior architectural features. There are heart-pine floors, handsome woodwork and carved fireplace mantels. Breakfast is served in the lavender and teal dining room under the crystal chandelier. A garden gazebo surrounded by white azaleas boasts a porch swing and old school bell.
Innkeeper(s): Rita & John Kovacevich. $79-159. MC, VISA, AX, DS, PC, TC. 10 rooms with PB, 2 with FP and 1 conference room. Breakfast included in rates. Types of meals: Full gourmet bkfst and early coffee/tea. Beds: KQT. Cable TV, phone, turndown service and ceiling fan in room. Air conditioning. VCR, fax, copier, bicycles, library, hot tub and antique collection on premises. Handicap access. Antiquing, fishing, golf, live theater, parks, shopping, sporting events, tennis and water sports nearby.
Pets allowed: small, with kennel.
Location: Historic district.
Publicity: *The Washington Times, PBS, Southern Living and Intimate Destinations.*
Certificate may be used: July 10-Jan. 31. No holiday periods, Sunday-Thursday.

Apalachicola   C4

The Coombs House Inn
80 6th St
Apalachicola, FL 32320-1750
(850)653-9199
Internet: www.coombshouseinn.com
E-mail: coombsstaff@digitalexp.com

Circa 1905. This Victorian manor was built for James N. Coombs, a wealthy lumber baron who served in the Union Army. Despite his Yankee roots, Coombs was an influential fig-

ure in Apalachicola. The home has been lovingly restored to reflect its previous grandeur. Co-owner Lynn Wilson is a renown interior designer and her talents accent the inn's high ceilings, tiled fireplaces and period antiques. Bright English fabrics decorate windows and Oriental rugs accentuate the hardwood floors.
Innkeeper(s): Pamela Barnes & Anthony Erario. $79-150. MC, VISA, AX, DS, PC, TC. 18 rooms with PB, 3 suites and 1 conference room. Breakfast included in rates. Types of meals: Cont and early coffee/tea. Beds: KQDT. Cable TV, phone and ceiling fan in room. Air conditioning. Fax, copier and bicycles on premises. Handicap access. Antiquing, fishing, parks, shopping and water sports nearby.
Location: Island.
Publicity: *Southern Living, Florida Design and Country Inns Magazine.*
Certificate may be used: Midweek (Sunday-Wednesday), no holidays.

Arcadia   F8

Historic Parker House
427 W Hickory St
Arcadia, FL 34266-3703
(863)494-2499 (800)969-2499

Circa 1895. Period antiques, including a wonderful clock collection, grace the interior of this turn-of-the-century home, which was built by a local cattle baron. Along with two charming rooms and a bright, "yellow" suite, innkeepers Shelly and Bob Baumann added the spacious Blue Room, which offers a white iron and brass bed and clawfoot bathtub. An expanded continental breakfast with pastries, fresh fruits, cereals, muffins and a variety of beverages is offered each morning, and afternoon teas can be prepared on request.
Innkeeper(s): Bob & Shelly Baumann. $69-85. MC, VISA, AX, TC. 4 rooms, 2 with PB, 2 with FP and 1 conference room. Breakfast and afternoon tea included in rates. Types of meals: Cont plus and early coffee/tea. Beds: QDT. Cable TV, phone and ceiling fan in room. Air conditioning. Antiquing, fishing, historical sites, parks, shopping and water sports nearby.
Location: Small country city.
Publicity: *Tampa Tribune, Desoto Sun Herald, Florida Travel & Life, Miami Herald (Palm Beach Edition) and WINK-TV News.*
"Everything was first class and very comfortable."
Certificate may be used: May 1 to Dec. 15, Sunday-Friday.

Sandusky Manor B&B & Victorian Tea Room
606 E Oak St
Arcadia, FL 34266-4630
(941)494-7338 (800)348-5057
Internet: DeSoto.Net
E-mail: d-ccoc@desoto.net

Circa 1913. This bungalow is named for its first resident, Carl Sandusky. The interior is comfortable and eclectic. There are collectibles, photographs, quilts, lanterns and old clocks throughout. Breakfasts with freshly baked biscuits, sweet rolls, fruit and egg dishes are served in the dining room or on the front porch. In the evenings, the innkeepers serve coffee, tea and dessert. Antique shops in historic downtown Arcadia, swamp buggy tours, golf and horseback riding are among the area attractions.
Innkeeper(s): Wayne & Judy Haligus. $65-75. MC, VISA, AX, DC, DS, TC. 4 rooms, 3 with PB. Breakfast and snacks/refreshments included in rates. Types of meals: Full bkfst and early coffee/tea. Beds: KQDT. Ceiling fan and VCR in room. Air conditioning. Small garden w/benches & table for our guests on premises. Antiquing, fishing, golf, canoeing and shopping nearby.
Location: City.
Publicity: *Tampa Tribune.*
"The southern hospitality you provided was to die for!"
Certificate may be used: Sunday-Thursday, May through October.

Brandon   E7

Behind The Fence B&B Inn

1400 Viola Dr at Countryside
Brandon, FL 33511-7327
(813)685-8201 (800)448-2672

Circa 1976. Experience the charm of New England on
Florida's west coast at this secluded country inn surrounded by
tall pines and oaks. Although the frame of the home was built
in the mid-1970s, the innkeepers searched Hillsborough
County for 19th-century and turn-of-the-century artifacts,
including old stairs, doors, windows, a pantry and the back
porch. Guests can stay either in the main house or in a two-
bedroom cottage. All rooms are filled with antique Amish-
county furniture. The innkeepers serve fresh popcorn on cool
nights in front of the fireplace. Breakfast includes fresh fruit,
cereals, juices, coffees and delicious Amish sweet rolls.
Innkeeper(s): Larry & Carolyn Yoss. $79-89. PC, TC. 5 rooms, 3 with PB, 1
suite, 1 cottage and 1 conference room. Breakfast, afternoon tea and
snacks/refreshments included in rates. Types of meals: Cont plus and early
coffee/tea. Beds: DT. Cable TV, phone and VCR in room. Air conditioning.
Swimming on premises. Amusement parks, antiquing, fishing, river canoeing,
horseback riding, parks, shopping, sporting events and water sports nearby.
Location: Subdivision to County Park.
Publicity: *Brandon News, Travel Host and Country Living.*
"One of the best kept secrets in all of Tampa! Thanks again!"
Certificate may be used: August-November, Sunday-Thursday.

Brooksville   D7

Verona House

201 S Main St
Brooksville, FL 34601-3337
(352)796-4001 (800)355-6717 Fax:(352)799-0612
Internet: www.bbhost.com/veronabb/
E-mail: veronabb@gate.net

Circa 1925. In the 1920s, the Verona was one of several styles of
homes available to buyers through the Sears-Roebuck catalog. This
inn arrived by train along with an instruction book. Obviously, its
builder follow the directions, and now guests enjoy this charming
Dutch Colonial. There are four rooms inside the house, and the
innkeepers also offer a cottage with a kitchen and covered deck.
Antique shopping and many outdoor activities are all nearby.
Innkeeper(s): Bob & Jan Boyd. $70-100. MC, VISA, AX, DS, PC, TC. 4 rooms
with PB & 1 cottage. Breakfast & afternoon tea included in rates. Types of meals:
Full bkfst, cont plus, cont & early coffee/tea. Beds: QT. Ceiling fan in room. Air
conditioning. VCR, fax, copier & spa on premises. Handicap access. Antiquing,
fishing, golf, live theater, parks, shopping, tennis & water sports nearby.
Location: Rural city.
Certificate may be used: April 1-Oct. 31, Sunday-Friday.

Cedar Key   C6

Island Hotel

2nd & B St
Cedar Key, FL 32625
(352)543-5111 (800)432-4640
Internet: www.islandhotel-cedarkey.com
E-mail: info@islandhotel-cedarkey.com

Circa 1859. The history of Island Hotel begins at about the
same time as the history of Cedar Key. Constructed from
seashell tabby with oak supports, the hotel and its walls have

withstood wind and weather for a century and a half. Owners
and innkeepers Dawn and Tony Cousins have worked to restore
the home's traditional charm. Some rooms boast views of the
Gulf or Back Bayou. All rooms include access to the inn's balcony, an ideal spot for relaxation. A casual, gourmet seafood
restaurant is located on the premises, promising a delightful
array of local catch, and Neptune Bar, also at the inn, is open
to guests and locals.
Innkeeper(s): Dawn & Tony Cousins. $75-110. MC, VISA, DS, TC. 13 rooms
with PB. Breakfast included in rates. Type of meal: Full gourmet bkfst. Beds:
QD. Air conditioning. Antiquing, fishing, parks, sporting events and water
sports nearby.
Location: Island historic district.
Certificate may be used: June 30-Dec. 15, Sunday-Thursday, no holidays
or festivals.

Gainesville   C7

Magnolia Plantation

309 SE 7th St
Gainesville, FL 32601-6831
Internet: www.magnoliabnb.com
E-mail: info@magnoliabnb.com

Circa 1885. This restored French Second Empire Victorian is
in the National Register. Magnolia trees surround the house.
Five guest rooms are filled with family heirlooms. All bathrooms feature clawfoot
tubs and candles. Guests may enjoy the
gardens, reflecting pond with waterfalls and gazebo. Bicycles are also
available. Evening wine and snacks
are included. The inn is two miles
from the University of Florida.
Innkeeper(s): Joe & Cindy Montalto. $90-
160. MC, VISA, AX. 5 rooms with PB, 5 with FP and 3 cottages. Breakfast
and afternoon tea included in rates. Type of meal: Full bkfst. Beds: Q. TV,
turndown service and ceiling fan in room. Air conditioning. VCR, fax, bicycles
and library on premises. Antiquing, live theater, parks, shopping and sporting
events nearby.
Location: City.
Publicity: *Florida Living Magazine and Inn Country USA.*
"This has been a charming, once-in-a-lifetime experience."
Certificate may be used: Sunday-Thursday or June, July, August last
minute anytime.

Inverness   D7

Crown Hotel

109 N Seminole Ave
Inverness, FL 34450-4100
(352)344-5555 Fax:(352)726-4040

Circa 1890. This 19th-century inn began its life as a general
store. In the 1980s, more than $2 million in renovations trans-
formed it into an elegant hotel. An English ambiance permeates
the interior, including replicas of the Crown Jewels, which are on
display. Paintings of notable English royals and dignitaries follow
guests up the grand staircase. The cozy bedchambers feature
romantic Victorian touches,
from the furnishings to the
flowery wallpapers. There is
an inviting pub, the Fox &
Hounds, where guests can
enjoy a bit of ale and steak

and kidney pie. The hotel's restaurant, Churchill's, serves more formal fare. Outside, a double-decker bus provides added decoration. The inn offers a pool, tennis courts and golf courses are nearby. Orlando and Tampa are 20 miles away.

Innkeeper(s): Jill & Nigel Sumner. $70-85. MC, VISA, AX, DC. 34 rooms with PB, 1 suite and 3 conference rooms. Breakfast included in rates. Type of meal: Cont plus. Beds: QDT. Cable TV and phone in room. Air conditioning. Fax, copier and swimming on premises. Antiquing, fishing, golf, parks, tennis and water sports nearby.
Pets Allowed.
Location: City.
Publicity: *Southern Living, Country Inns and Miami Herald.*
Certificate may be used: Based on availability, April 1-Oct. 31, not available holidays or Saturdays.

The Lake House B&B

8604 E Gospel Island Rd
Inverness, FL 34450
(352)344-3586 Fax:(352)344-3586
E-mail: lakehouse@hitter.net

Circa 1930. The Lake House was built as a fishing lodge, and with its location on Big Lake Henderson, offers picturesque views of woodland and water. Guests usually arrange to be finished with daytime adventures in time to return to the inn for sunset views over the lake. A library and a huge stone fireplace are additional gathering places. Guest rooms are furnished in a French Country decor.

Miles of paved pathways entice roller skaters and cyclers to Withlacoochee State Trail nearby. There are many lakes to choose from for fishing, water-skiing and boating.

Innkeeper(s): Caroline & Blake Jenkins. $70-100. MC, VISA, PC, TC. 5 rooms with PB. Breakfast included in rates. Type of meal: Cont plus. Beds: KQDT. Cable TV and ceiling fan in room. Central air. VCR and library on premises. Amusement parks, antiquing, bicycling, canoeing/kayaking, fishing, golf, hiking, horseback riding, museums, parks, shopping, tennis and water sports nearby.
Pets allowed: small animals.
Publicity: *St. Petersburg Times and Citrus County Chronicle.*
Certificate may be used: Year round, Monday-Thursday, excluding holidays and special event weekends.

Key West   18

The Curry Mansion Inn

511 Caroline St
Key West, FL 33040-6604
(305)294-5349 (800)253-3466 Fax:(305)294-4093
Internet: www.currymansion.com
E-mail: frontdesk@currymansion.com

Circa 1892. This three-story white Victorian was billed as the most elaborate home on Caroline Street when it was built in 1867 by Florida's first millionaire. The inn still contains original features such as bookcases, chandeliers and fireplaces, as well as an abundance of antiques. The innkeepers use the inn to display some of their beautiful collectibles, including a family Limoges service for 120. Guests enjoy Key West's mild weather while enjoying a European-style

breakfast. Piano music serenades guests at a nightly "cocktail" party with hors d'oeuvres and a full open bar.

Innkeeper(s): Albert & Edith Amsterdam. $140-275. MC, VISA, AX, DC, CB, DS, PC, TC. 28 rooms with PB and 10 suites. Breakfast and snacks/refreshments included in rates. Type of meal: Full gourmet bkfst. Beds: KQ. Cable TV, phone and ceiling fan in room. Air conditioning. VCR, fax, copier, spa, swimming, bicycles and library on premises. Handicap access. Antiquing, fishing, swimming, boating, live theater, shopping and water sports nearby.
Pets allowed: under 20 pounds.
Location: Downtown Key West.
Publicity: *Mariner Outboards SLAM, New York Times, Southern Living and Colonial Homes.*

"Everything was so tastefully tended to. We truly felt like 'Royalty'. We certainly will not consider returning to Key West unless we are able to book accommodations at the Curry Mansion."
Certificate may be used: June 1 to Sept. 30, excluding July 4th weekend and Labor Day.

Duval House

815 Duval St
Key West, FL 33040-7405
(305)294-1666 (800)223-8825 Fax:(305)292-1701

Circa 1880. Seven historic houses, painted in island pastel shades, surround a lush tropical garden and a pool. Located on an estate in the heart of the historic Old Town, guests relish the cozy spaces to relax such as the hammock for two, gazebo, sun decks and private balconies. The inn's white picket fences and plentiful porches are bordered by tropical trees, flowers and vines. A continental-plus breakfast is served from the pool house. Rooms have wicker and antique furniture, Victorian armoires and Bahamian fans.

Innkeeper(s): Renner James. $100-315. MC, VISA, AX, DC, DS, TC. 28 rooms, 25 with PB and 4 suites. Breakfast included in rates. Beds: QD. Cable TV and phone in room. Air conditioning. Swimming on premises. Antiquing, spa, historic touring, shopping and water sports nearby.
Publicity: *Palm Beach Post, Cleveland Plain-Dealer, Orlando Sentinel, Brides, Vacations, Honeymoon and Country Living.*

"You certainly will see us again."
Certificate may be used: May 3-Dec. 20, Sunday-Thursday only (excluding holidays and special events).

Paradise Inn

819 Simonton St
Key West, FL 33040-7445
(305)293-8007 (800)888-9648 Fax:(305)293-0807
Internet: www.theparadiseinn.com
E-mail: paradise@keysdigital.com

Circa 1995. Although this inn was constructed recently, its Bahamian architecture is reminiscent of Key West's early days. Rooms are open and spacious, decorated with elegant, contemporary furnishings, such as king-size sleigh beds. Jacuzzi tubs and a bar with a refrigerator are a few of the in-room amenities. There is a fountain-fed pool, Jacuzzi and koi pond on the premises, too. In addition to the modern accommodations, guests also may stay in one of the historic cigar-makers' cottages. The cottages are ideal for families, and each has two bedrooms and two bathrooms. The inn is located in the Key West historic district and is close to the many shops, restaurants and nightclubs on Duval Street.

Innkeeper(s): Shel Segel. $175-545. MC, VISA, AX, DC, CB, DS, TC. 18

rooms with PB, 15 suites and 3 cottages. Breakfast included in rates. Type of meal: Cont. Beds: K. Cable TV, phone, ceiling fan, robes and capes in room. Air conditioning. VCR, fax, copier, spa and swimming on premises. Handicap access. Antiquing, fishing, golf, live theater, parks, shopping, tennis and water sports nearby.
Location: City.
Publicity: *New York Times, Key West Citizen, New Mobility, Travel & Leisure, Conde Nast, Country Inns and Wish You Were Here . . .-BBC.*
"Your fresh rooms and lovely grounds are truly paradise."
Certificate may be used: June through September, Sunday through Thursday.

Lake Helen   D8

Clauser's B&B

201 E Kicklighter Rd
Lake Helen, FL 32744-3514
(904)228-0310 (800)220-0310 Fax:(904)228-2337
Internet: www.clauserinn.com
E-mail: clauserinn@totcon.com

Circa 1890. This three-story, turn-of-the-century vernacular Victorian inn is surrounded by a variety of trees in a quiet, country setting. The inn is listed in the national, state and local historic registers, and offers eight guest rooms, all with private bath. Each room features a different type of country decor, such as Americana, English and prairie. Guests enjoy hot tubbing in the Victorian gazebo or relaxing on the inn's porches,  which feature rockers, a swing and cozy wicker furniture. Borrow a bike to take a closer look at the historic district. Stetson University, fine dining and several state parks are nearby.
Innkeeper(s): Tom & Marge Clauser, Janet Watson. $95-140. MC, VISA, AX, DS, PC, TC. 8 rooms with PB, 1 with FP. Breakfast and snacks/refreshments included in rates. Types of meals: Full bkfst and early coffee/tea. Beds: KQ. Phone, ceiling fan and private screened porch in room. Air conditioning. VCR, fax, copier, spa, bicycles, library and nature trail through forest on premises. Handicap access. Amusement parks, antiquing, fishing, atlantic beaches, live theater, parks, sporting events and water sports nearby.
Location: Small town.
Certificate may be used: April 1-Nov. 30, Sunday-Thursday, excludes holidays.

Lake Wales   E8

Chalet Suzanne Country Inn & Restaurant

3800 Chalet Suzanne Dr
Lake Wales, FL 33853-7060
(863)676-6011 (800)433-6011 Fax:(863)676-1814
Internet: www.chaletsuzanne.com
E-mail: info@chaletsuzanne.com

Circa 1924. Situated on 70 acres adjacent to Lake Suzanne, this country inn's architecture includes gabled roofs, balconies, spires and steeples. The superb restaurant has a glowing reputation and offers a six-course candlelight dinner. Places of interest on the property include the Swiss Room, Wine Dungeon,  Gift Boutique, Autograph Garden, Chapel Antiques, Ceramic Salon, Airstrip and the Soup Cannery. The inn has been transformed into a village of cottages and miniature chateaux, one connected to the other seemingly with no particular order.
Innkeeper(s): Vita Hinshaw & Family. $139-229. MC, VISA, AX, DC, CB, DS, PC, TC. 30 rooms with PB. Breakfast included in rates. Type of meal: Full bkfst. Beds: KDT. Cable TV, phone and ceiling fan in room. Air conditioning. VCR, fax, copier, swimming and library on premises. Handicap access. Amusement parks, antiquing, fishing, golf, live theater, parks, shopping, sporting events, tennis and water sports nearby.
Location: Rural-lakefront.
Publicity: *National Geographic Traveler, Southern Living, Country Inns, Uncle Ben's 1992 award and Country Inn Cooking.*
"I now know why everyone always says, 'Wow!' when they come up from dinner. Please don't change a thing."
Certificate may be used: All year, Sunday through Thursday nights.

New Smyrna Beach   D9

Night Swan Intracoastal B&B

512 S Riverside Dr
New Smyrna Beach, FL 32168-7345
(904)423-4940 (800)465-4261 Fax:(904)427-2814
Internet: www.nightswan.com
E-mail: nightswanb@aol.com

Circa 1906. From the 140-foot dock at this waterside bed & breakfast, guests can gaze at stars, watch as ships pass or perhaps catch site of dolphins. The turn-of-the-century home is decorated with period furnishings, including an antique baby grand piano, which guests are invited to use. Several guest rooms afford views of the Indian River, which is part of the Atlantic Intracoastal Waterway. Seven  rooms include a whirlpool tub. The innkeepers have created several special packages, featuring catered gourmet dinners, boat tours or romantic baskets with chocolate, wine and flowers.
Innkeeper(s): Martha & Chuck Nighswonger. $85-160. MC, VISA, AX, DS, PC, TC. 15 rooms with PB, 4 suites and 1 conference room. Breakfast and snacks/refreshments included in rates. Types of meals: Full bkfst and early coffee/tea. Beds: KQ. Cable TV, phone, ceiling fan and 7 whirlpool tubs in room. Air conditioning. Fax and library on premises. Antiquing, fishing, live theater, parks, shopping and water sports nearby.
Publicity: *Ft. Lauderdale Sun Sentinel and Florida Living.*
Certificate may be used: June 1-Jan. 30, Sunday-Thursday, except holidays.

Ocala   C7

Seven Sisters Inn

820 SE Fort King St
Ocala, FL 34471-2320
(352)867-1170 Fax:(352)867-5266
E-mail: sistersinn@aol.com

Circa 1888. This highly acclaimed Queen Anne-style Victorian is located in the heart of the town's historic district. In 1986, the house was judged "Best Restoration Project" in the state by Florida Trust Historic Preservation Society. Guests may relax on the large covered porches or visit with other guests in the club room. A gourmet breakfast features different entrees daily, which include blueberry French bread, three-cheese stuffed French toast, egg pesto and raspberry-oatmeal pancakes. Inquire about candlelight and murder- mystery dinners.

Innkeeper(s): Ken Oden & Bonnie Morehardt. $115-185. 8 rooms with PB, 3 with FP, 4 suites and 1 conference room. Breakfast and afternoon tea included in rates. Type of meal: Full gourmet bkfst. Beds: KQT. TV, phone, turndown service and ceiling fan in room. Air conditioning. Fax, copier and off-grounds pet boarding available on premises. Antiquing, fishing, golf, national forest, Silver Springs attractions, live theater, shopping and water sports nearby. Pets allowed: Off-grounds pet boarding available.
Location: Historic district.
Publicity: *Southern Living, Glamour, Conde Nast Traveler and Country Inns (one of 12 best).*
Certificate may be used: Sunday-Thursday, no holidays or weekends.

Palatka   C8

Azalea House
220 Madison St
Palatka, FL 32177-3531
(904)325-4547 Fax:(904)325-4547
E-mail: azaleahouse@gbso.net

Circa 1878. Located within the Palatka Historic District, this beautifully embellished Queen Anne Victorian is painted a cheerful yellow with complementing green shutters. Bay windows, gables and verandas have discrete touches of royal blue, gold, white and aqua on the gingerbread trim, a true "Painted Lady." It sits on a green lawn graced with lavish perennial gardens, azaleas and camellias. There are oak, magnolia and palm trees and an 85-year-old, grafted camellia tree with both pink and white blossoms. Double parlors are furnished with period antiques including an arched, floor-to-ceiling mirror. A three-story heart and curly pine staircase leads to the guest rooms. Breakfast is served on fine china in the formal dining room. Two blocks away is the mile-wide north flowing St. John's River. An unaltered golf course designed by Donald Ross in 1925 is nearby, as well as the Ravine State Botanical Garden. It's 25 minutes to Cresent Beach.
Innkeeper(s): Doug & Jill de Leeuw. $75-125. MC, VISA, AX, DS, TC. 6 rooms, 4 with PB. Breakfast and snacks/refreshments included in rates. Types of meals: Full bkfst, cont plus and early coffee/tea. Beds: KQ. Phone, turndown service, ceiling fan and alarm clocks in room. Air conditioning. VCR, fax, spa, swimming and porch swings on premises. Amusement parks, antiquing, fishing, golf, live theater, parks, shopping, sporting events and water sports nearby.
Location: Historic district.
Publicity: *American Treasures.*
Certificate may be used: June 1 to Sept. 30, all days.

Plant City   E7

Rysdon House
702 W Reynolds St
Plant City, FL 33566-4814
(813)752-8717 Fax:(813)752-8717
E-mail: rysdonhous@aol.com

Circa 1910. A lumber baron built this stately home, which features a wide front veranda lined with rocking chairs. The interior still boasts the elegant decor one would expect in the home of a prominent lumberman. The parlor features exposed stone walls, a fireplace, red velvet Victorian furniture and a 200-year-old grand piano. Bedchambers are tastefully appointed, from the masculine hunter green walls in the Kensington room to the iron bed and floral appointments in the Queen Anne suite. There is a pool and spa for guests to use. The home is located in a town historic district.
Innkeeper(s): Claudia Rysdon. $65-105. MC, VISA, AX, DS, PC, TC. 4 rooms with PB, 2 with FP, 1 suite and 1 conference room. Breakfast included in rates. Type of meal: Cont plus. Beds: KQDT. Cable TV, turndown service and ceiling fan in room. Air conditioning. Fax, spa, swimming and bicycles on premises. Antiquing, golf, disney World, Universal Studios and Busch Gardens nearby.
Location: City.
Certificate may be used: June 1 to Oct. 30, seven days a week.

Saint Augustine   B8

Casa De La Paz Bayfront B&B
22 Avenida Menendez
Saint Augustine, FL 32084-3644
(904)829-2915 (800)929-2915
Internet: www.casadelapaz.com
E-mail: delapaz@aug.com

Circa 1915. Overlooking Matanzas Bay, Casa de la Paz was built after the devastating 1914 fire leveled much of the old city. An ornate stucco Mediterranean Revival house, it features clay barrel tile roofing, bracketed eaves, verandas and a lush walled courtyard. The home is listed in the National Register of Historic Places. Guest rooms offer ceiling fans, central air, hardwood floors, antiques, a decanter of sherry, chocolates and complimentary snacks.
Innkeeper(s): Bob & Donna Marriott. $120-225. MC, VISA, DS, PC, TC. 6 rooms with PB, 1 with FP. Breakfast included in rates. Types of meals: Full bkfst and early coffee/tea. Beds: KQ. Cable TV, phone and ceiling fan in room. Air conditioning. Antiquing, fishing, live theater, parks, shopping, sporting events and water sports nearby.
Location: Historic town.
Publicity: *Innsider, US Air Magazine, Southern Living and PBS.*
"We will always recommend your beautifully restored, elegant home."
Certificate may be used: Sunday through Thursday, (holidays and special events excluded) July, August & September, subject to availability.

Castle Garden B&B
15 Shenandoah St
Saint Augustine, FL 32084-2817
(904)829-3839
Internet: www.castlegarden.com
E-mail: castleg@aug.com

Circa 1860. This newly-restored Moorish Revival-style inn was the carriage house to Warden Castle. Among the seven guest rooms are three bridal rooms with in-room Jacuzzi tubs and sunken bedrooms with cathedral ceilings. The innkeepers offer packages including carriage rides, picnic lunches, gift baskets and other enticing possibilities. Guests enjoy a homemade full, country breakfast each morning.
Innkeeper(s): Bruce & Kimmy Kloeckner. $79-155. MC, VISA, AX, DS. 7 rooms with PB and 3 suites. Breakfast included in rates. Types of meals: Full bkfst and early coffee/tea. Beds: KQT. Ceiling fan and TV in some rooms in room. Air conditioning. Common sitting room with cable on premises. Antiquing, fishing, golf, ballooning nearby, live theater, shopping, tennis and water sports nearby.
Location: City.
Certificate may be used: Monday through Thursday. Other times if available.

Old City House Inn & Restaurant
115 Cordova St
Saint Augustine, FL 32084-4413
(904)826-0113 Fax:(904)829-3798
Internet: www.oldcityhouse.com

Circa 1873. Saint Augustine is a treasure bed of history and this inn is strategically located in the center. A red-tile roof covers this former stable, and a veranda and courtyard add to the Spanish atmosphere. Gourmet breakfasts are prepared by innkeeper John Compton, whose recipes have been printed in Food Arts magazine. Inn guests are privy to the expansive breakfasts, but can join others for lunch and dinner in

the restaurant. Appetizers include baked brie and Alligator Fritters. For lunch, unique salads, fresh fish and chicken create the menu, while dinner choices include gourmet standards such as Filet Mignon or a more unusual Seafood Strudel.

Innkeeper(s): John & Darcy Compton. $75-150. MC, VISA, AX, DC, CB, DS. 7 rooms with PB. Breakfast included in rates. Types of meals: Full bkfst and early coffee/tea. Beds: Q. Cable TV and ceiling fan in room. Air conditioning. VCR, fax, copier and bicycles on premises. Handicap access. Antiquing, fishing, live theater, shopping and water sports nearby.

Location: City.

Publicity: *Florida Times Union, Florida Trend and Ft. Lauderdale Sun Sentinal.*

Certificate may be used: Jan. 10-Nov. 15, Sunday-Thursday, all year.

St. Francis Inn

279 Saint George St
Saint Augustine, FL 32084-5031
(904)824-6068 (800)824-6062 Fax:(904)810-5525
Internet: www.stfrancisinn.com
E-mail: innceasd@aug.com

Circa 1791. Long noted for its hospitality, the St. Francis Inn is nearly the oldest house in town. A classic example of Old World architecture, it was built by Gaspar Garcia, who received

a Spanish grant to the plot of land. Coquina was the main building material. A buffet breakfast is served. Some rooms have whirlpool tubs and fireplaces. The city of Saint Augustine was founded in 1565.

Innkeeper(s): Joe Finnegan. $79-189. MC, VISA, AX, PC. 14 rooms, 8 with PB, 4 with FP, 6 suites, 1 cottage and 2 conference rooms. Breakfast included in rates. Type of meal: Full bkfst. Beds: KQDT. Cable TV, phone, ceiling fan and whirlpool tubs in room. Air conditioning. Fax, copier, swimming, bicycles and whirlpool tubs on premises. Antiquing, fishing, parks, shopping, sporting events and water sports nearby.

Location: City.

Publicity: *Orlando Sentinel.*

"We have stayed at many nice hotels but nothing like this. We are really enjoying it."

Certificate may be used: Sunday through Thursday, (excluding holiday periods).

Victorian House B&B

11 Cadiz St
Saint Augustine, FL 32084-4431
(904)824-5214 (877)703-0432

Circa 1897. Enjoy the historic ambiance of Saint Augustine at this turn-of-the-century Victorian, decorated to reflect the grandeur of that genteel era. The heart-of-pine floors are topped with hand-hooked rugs, stenciling highlights the walls, and the innkeepers have filled the guest rooms with canopy beds and period furnishings. The full breakfast includes homemade granola, fresh fruit, hot entree and a variety of freshly made breads.

Innkeeper(s): Ken & Marcia Cerotzke. $89-140. MC, VISA, AX, DS. 8 rooms with PB and 4 suites. Breakfast included in rates. Type of meal: Full bkfst. Beds: KQDT. Ceiling fan and refrigerator (one room) in room. Air conditioning. Antiquing, fine restaurants, live theater, parks and shopping nearby.

Location: City.

Certificate may be used: Monday through Thursday, except holidays.

San Mateo   C8

Ferncourt B&B

150 Central Ave, PO Box 758
San Mateo, FL 32187-0758
(904)329-9755

Circa 1889. This Victorian "painted lady," is one of the few remaining relics from San Mateo's heyday in the early 1900s. Teddy Roosevelt once visited the elegant home. The current owners have restored the Victorian atmosphere with rooms decorated with bright, floral prints and gracious furnishings. Awake to the smells of brewing coffee and the sound of a rooster crowing before settling down to a full gourmet breakfast. Historic Saint Augustine is a quick, 25-mile drive.

Innkeeper(s): Jack & Dee Morgan. $55-85. MC, VISA, PC, TC. 6 rooms, 5 with PB. Breakfast included in rates. Types of meals: Full gourmet bkfst and early coffee/tea. Beds: KQD. Ceiling fan in room. Air conditioning. Bicycles and library on premises. Handicap access. Antiquing, fishing, golf, live theater, parks and shopping nearby.

Location: Rural.

"First class operation! A beautiful house with an impressive history and restoration. Great company and fine food."

Certificate may be used: Anytime as available, except holiday periods.

Sanford   D8

The Higgins House

420 S Oak Ave
Sanford, FL 32771-1826
(407)324-9238 (800)584-0014 Fax:(407)324-5060
Internet: www.higginshouse.com

Circa 1894. This inviting blue Queen Anne-style home features cross gables with patterned wood shingles, bay windows and a charming round window on the second floor. Pine floors, paddle fans and a piano in the parlor, which guests are encouraged to play, create Victorian ambiance. The second-story balcony affords views not only of a charming park and Sanford's oldest church, but of Space Shuttle launches from nearby Cape Canaveral. The Queen Anne room looks out over a Victorian box garden, while

the Wicker Room features a bay window sitting area. The Country Victorian room boasts a 19th-century brass bed. Guests also can opt to stay in Cochran's Cottage, which features two bedrooms and baths, a living room, kitchen and porch. Nature lovers will enjoy close access to Blue Spring State Park, Ocala National Forest, Lake Monroe and the Cape Canaveral National Seashore. And of course, Walt Disney World, Sea World and Universal Studios aren't far away.

Innkeeper(s): Walter & Roberta Padgett. $85-165. MC, VISA, AX, DS, PC, TC. 3 rooms and 1 cottage. Breakfast and snacks/refreshments included in rates. Types of meals: Cont plus and early coffee/tea. Beds: QD. Turndown service and ceiling fan in room. Air conditioning. VCR, spa and bicycles on premises. Antiquing, fishing, parks, shopping and water sports nearby.

Location: Historic district.

Publicity: *Southern Living, Sanford Herald, Connecticut Traveler, LifeTimes, Orlando Sentinel, Southern Accents, Country Inns and Florida Living.*

"The Higgins House is warm and friendly, filled with such pleasant sounds, and if you love beauty and nature, you're certain to enjoy the grounds."

Certificate may be used: Jan. 30-Dec. 31, Sunday-Thursday.

Georgia

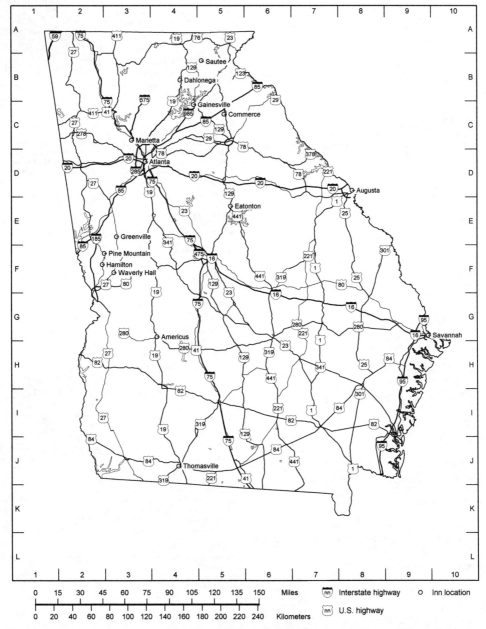

Miles

Kilometers

🄽 Interstate highway   ○ Inn location

🄽 U.S. highway

Americus G4

1906 Pathway Inn B&B

501 S Lee St
Americus, GA 31709-3919
(912)928-2078 (800)889-1466 Fax:(912)928-2078

Circa 1906. This turn-of-the-century inn is located along the Andersonville Trail and not far from the city of Andersonville, a Civil War village with a museum. Located between Andersonville and Plains, the home of former President Jimmy Carter, where you may attend and hear him teach Sunday school. The gracious, wraparound porch is a perfect spot for relaxation. The innkeepers plan the morning meal to accommodate their guests' schedules, serving up a candle-lit breakfast with freshly baked breads using silver, crystal and china. The guest rooms offer romantic amenities such as whirlpools and snug down comforters. Two of the rooms are named in honor of Jimmy and Rosalynn Carter. Late afternoons are reserved for wine and refreshments. Several restaurants are within walking distance.

Innkeeper(s): Angela & Chuck Nolan. $75-125. MC, VISA, AX, DS, PC, TC. 5 rooms with PB, 2 with FP. Breakfast included in rates. Types of meals: Full gourmet bkfst and early coffee/tea. Beds: KQ. Cable TV, phone, turndown service, ceiling fan, VCR and whirlpool tubs in room. Air conditioning. Fax and copier on premises. Antiquing, federal historic sites, live theater and parks nearby.

Pets allowed: With prior approval.

Location: City.

Certificate may be used: Dec. 1-Jan. 20, Sunday-Saturday; year round Sunday-Friday, special events and holidays exempt.

Atlanta D3

Beverly Hills Inn

65 Sheridan Dr NE
Atlanta, GA 30305-3121
(404)233-8520 (800)331-8520 Fax:(404)233-8659
Internet: www.beverlyhillsinn.com
E-mail: info@beverlyhillsinn.com

Circa 1929. Period furniture and polished-wood floors decorate this inn located in the Buckhead neighborhood. There are  private balconies, kitchens and a library with a collection of newspapers and books. The governor's mansion, Neiman-Marcus, Saks and Lord & Taylor are five minutes away.

Innkeeper(s): Mit Amin. $99-160. MC, VISA, AX, DC, DS, PC, TC. 18 suites. Breakfast included in rates. Type of meal: Cont plus. Beds: QD. Cable TV and phone in room. Air conditioning. Health club privileges on premises. Antiquing, parks and shopping nearby.

Pets allowed: With kennels/cages.

Location: City.

Publicity: *Travel & Leisure, Country Inns, Southern Living, Time and CNN.*

"Our only regret is that we had so little time. Next stay we will plan to be here longer."

Certificate may be used: Anytime, subject to availability.

King-Keith House B&B

889 Edgewood Ave NE
Atlanta, GA 30307
(404)688-7330 (800)728-3879 Fax:(404)584-0730
Internet: www.kingkeith.com

Circa 1890. This beautifully restored and preserved Queen Anne Victorian features many wonderful elements, including a whimsical chimney that vividly declares "1890," the year the home was built. Inside, the hardwood floors and intricate woodwork glisten. Walls are painted in deep, rich hues and antiques fill the rooms. Marble-topped tables and delicate love seats decorate the parlor. Each guest room is special, and beds are topped with luxury linens. One room is lit by a colorful stained-glass window, another features a Victorian dollhouse. The opulent home is located in an Atlanta historic district listed in the National Register. It's just two blocks from the subway station.

Innkeeper(s): Jan & Windell Keith. $80-175. MC, VISA, AX, DS, PC, TC. 3 rooms with PB, 1 suite and 1 cottage. Breakfast included in rates. Types of meals: Full gourmet bkfst and early coffee/tea. Beds: KQDT. Cable TV, phone, ceiling fan, hair dryer and cottage with Jacuzzi and fireplace in room. Air conditioning. Fax and gift shop on premises. Amusement parks, antiquing, golf, live theater, parks, shopping, sporting events and tennis nearby.

Location: City.

Certificate may be used: Sunday through Thursday (five days), all year.

Augusta D8

The Azalea Inn

312-334 Greene St
Augusta, GA 30901
(706)724-3454 Fax:(706)724-3454
Internet: www.theazaleainn.com
E-mail: azalea@theazaleainn.com

Circa 1895. Three tastefully restored Victorian homes comprise the Azalea Inn, located in the Olde Town Historic District. Elegantly furnished suites with 11-foot ceilings also  offer fireplaces and large Jacuzzi tubs. Breakfast is delivered to your room in a basket. The inn is within walking distance to the Riverwalk on the Savannah River, fine restaurants, museums, antique shops and unique boutiques.

$79-150. MC, VISA, AX, PC, TC. 21 rooms with PB, 13 with FP, 4 suites and 1 conference room. Type of meal: Cont plus. Beds: KQ. Cable TV, phone, ceiling fan and Jacuzzi tubs in room. Air conditioning. Fax on premises. Handicap access. Antiquing, fishing, golf, historic sites, live theater, parks, shopping, sporting events, tennis and water sports nearby.

Publicity: *Georgia Journal, Augusta Magazine and S.C. State Newspaper.*

"Third time and loved it!"

Certificate may be used: Sunday-Thursday nights, year-round, excluding holidays and April 1-15.

Queen Anne Inn

406 Greene St
Augusta, GA 30901
706-826-7920 (877)460-0045 Fax:(706)826-7920
Circa 1890. This inviting three-story inn, filled with marble-topped antiques, stained glass windows and working fireplaces offers a special family suite in its handsome turret. Shaded by tall trees, the inn's veranda is a favorite spot for relaxing after returning from the Savannah River Walk, which starts three blocks away. Rooms are furnished with antique beds such as a Second Empire, an ornate Eastlake and a high-backed sleigh bed. The parlors offer fringed Victorian pieces, Oriental carpets and original paintings. Breakfast is continental, or you can walk down the tree-shaded street to a local cafe, which provides Queen Anne guests a full hot breakfast. Evening in-suite dining is available by selecting room service dinners from quality restaurants working with the inn. The family tower suite offers parents with children a chance to enjoy an elegant inn, yet have quiet quarters for themselves and their young children in a special section of the inn. Best of all, your well-traveled schoolteacher/innkeepers can arrange baby-sitting services for families. A shuttle service is offered as well.
Innkeeper(s): Val & Bill Mundell. $65-95. 7 rooms with PB. Air conditioning. VCR, fax, bicycles, library and parking on premises. Antiquing, bicycling, canoeing/kayaking, golf, hiking, museums and shopping nearby.
Publicity: *Applause.*
"Thank you so much for taking such good care of my husband on his first trip to Augusta."
Certificate may be used: Year-round, excluding April 1-15 and special events.

Commerce   C5

The Pittman House B&B

81 Homer Rd
Commerce, GA 30529-1806
(706)335-3823
Circa 1890. An hour's drive from Atlanta is this four-square Colonial inn, found in the rolling hills of Northeast Georgia. The inn has four guest rooms, furnished in antiques. The surrounding area offers many activities, including Lake Lanier, Lake Hartwell, Hurricane Shoals, Crawford W. Long Museum, an outlet mall, a winery and a championship golf course. Innkeeper Tom Tomberlin, a woodcarver, has items for sale in an antique shop next to the inn.
Innkeeper(s): Tom & Dot Tomberlin. $55-75. MC, VISA, PC, TC. 4 rooms, 2 with PB. Breakfast included in rates. Types of meals: Full bkfst and early coffee/tea. Beds: D. Ceiling fan in room. Air conditioning. VCR on premises. Antiquing, fishing, parks, shopping, sporting events and water sports nearby.
Location: Foothills NE Ga. Mountains.
Publicity: *Country Extra Magazine.*
Certificate may be used: Sunday through Thursday. No holidays (discount to be used by bearer only).

Dahlonega   B4

Worley Homestead Inn

168 Main St W
Dahlonega, GA 30533-1005
(706)864-7002
Circa 1845. Two blocks from the historic town square is this beautiful old Colonial Revival inn. Several guest rooms are equipped with fireplaces, adding to the romantic atmosphere and Victorian ambiance. All the rooms have private baths, and

feature antique beds. A popular spot for honeymooners and couples celebrating anniversaries, Dahlonega is close to the lures of the Chattahoochee National Forest.
Innkeeper(s): Bill, Francis & Christine. $85-95. MC, VISA. 7 rooms. Breakfast and snacks/refreshments included in rates. Types of meals: Full bkfst and early coffee/tea. Cable TV in room. Air conditioning. Antiquing and shopping nearby.
Location: Small town.
Certificate may be used: January through March, excluding holidays and special events.

Eatonton   E5

The Crockett House

671 Madison Rd
Eatonton, GA 31024-7830
(706)485-2248
Internet: www.bbonline.com/ga/crocketthouse/
Circa 1895. Century-old pecan, oak, pine and magnolia trees shade this alluring Victorian. The sweeping veranda is lined with rockers and wicker for those who wish to relax and enjoy a gentle Georgia breeze. Guests are welcomed with refreshment, and treated to a gourmet, candlelight breakfast. Rooms are decorated with antiques, and exude an old-fashioned, Southern ambiance. The bed & breakfast is located on the historic Antebellum Trail, which stretches from Athens to Macon, and the inn is about midway between both towns. Atlanta is about an hour and 15 minutes away; Augusta is an hour-and-a-half drive.
Innkeeper(s): Christa & Peter Crockett. $85-95. MC, VISA, PC, TC. 6 rooms with PB, 4 with FP. Breakfast included in rates. Types of meals: Full gourmet bkfst and early coffee/tea. Beds: KQD. Cable TV and ceiling fan in room. Air conditioning. Antiquing, fishing, live theater, parks, shopping, sporting events and water sports nearby.
Location: Small town.
Certificate may be used: Sunday-Thursday, January, February, March & August, excluding special events and based on availability.

Gainesville   C4

Dunlap House

635 Green St N W
Gainesville, GA 30501-3319
(770)536-0200 (800)276-2935 Fax:(770)503-7857
Internet: www.dunlaphouse.com
E-mail: dunlaphouse@mindspring.com
Circa 1910. Located on Gainesville's historic Green Street, this inn offers 10 uniquely decorated guest rooms, all featuring period furnishings. Custom-built king or queen beds and remote-controlled cable TV are found in all of the rooms, several of which have romantic fireplaces. Guests may help themselves to coffee, tea and light refreshments in the inn's common area. Breakfast may be enjoyed in guests' rooms or on the picturesque veranda, with its comfortable wicker furniture. Road Atlanta, Mall of Georgia, Lake Lanier, Brenall University, Riverside Academy and the Quinlan Art Center are nearby.
Innkeeper(s): David & Karen Peters. $85-155. MC, VISA, AX, TC. 10 rooms with PB, 2 with FP. Breakfast and snacks/refreshments included in rates. Types of meals: Full bkfst and early coffee/tea. Beds: KQ. Cable TV, phone, laptop computer and phone hook-up in room. Air conditioning. Copier on premises. Handicap access. Antiquing, fishing, golf, Road Atlanta Racing, Lake Lanier, live theater, parks, shopping and water sports nearby.
Location: Mountains.
Publicity: *Southern Living, Atlanta Journal Constitution, Country Inns and North Georgia Journal.*
Certificate may be used: Jan. 1-March 15, Sunday-Friday, except Valentines' weekend; July 1-Sept. 20, Sunday-Thursday.

Greenville
E3

Samples Plantation

15380 Roosevelt Hwy
Greenville, GA 30222
(706)672-4765 Fax:(706)672-9966

Circa 1832. The romance of the South lives on at this Antebellum mansion. The manor originally was part of the Render Plantation, and among the Render family were a Georgia governor, a congressman and a Supreme Court justice. Each guest room has been individually decorated with antiques, lace, satin and romance in mind. Guests are pampered with a homemade plantation-style breakfast. Shopping and other attractions, including Franklin Roosevelt's Little White House, are nearby. Atlanta is 50 miles away, and Callaway Gardens are 17 miles away.

Innkeeper(s): Marjorie Samples. $135-289. MC, VISA, PC, TC. 7 suites, 6 with FP. Breakfast, afternoon tea, snacks/refreshments and picnic lunch included in rates. Types of meals: Full bkfst and early coffee/tea. Beds: KQDT. Turndown service and ceiling fan in room. Air conditioning. VCR, fax, copier, bicycles and library on premises. Amusement parks, antiquing, fishing, live theater, parks, shopping, sporting events and water sports nearby.

Location: City.

Publicity: *Country Inns, Georgia Tour, Georgia Journal, American Inns, Columbia Ledger, Atlanta Journal and Fried Green Tomatoes.*

"Outstanding."

Certificate may be used: June through August.

Hamilton
F2

Magnolia Hall B&B

127 Barnes Mill Rd
Hamilton, GA 31811
(706)628-4566

Circa 1890. Fancy fretwork decorates the wide veranda of this two-story Victorian settled in an acre of magnolias and century-old hollies, near the courthouse. Heart-pine floors, tall ceilings, antiques, a grand piano and china, crystal and silver service for breakfast, set the mood for a gracious inn stay. One of the house specialties is Baked Georgia Croissant with fresh peaches and toasted almonds. It's five miles to Callaway Gardens and 20 miles to Warm Springs.

Innkeeper(s): Dale & Kendrick Smith. $95-115. PC. 5 rooms with PB, 1 with FP and 2 suites. Breakfast and snacks/refreshments included in rates. Types of meals: Full gourmet bkfst and early coffee/tea. Beds: QT. Cable TV, turndown service, VCR and refreshments in rooms in room. Air conditioning. Rockers and porch swing on premises. Handicap access. Amusement parks, antiquing, fishing, golf, Wild Animal Park, FDR Home, live theater, parks, shopping, sporting events, tennis and water sports nearby.

Location: Small town, rural setting.

Publicity: *Victorian Homes, Georgia Journal and Georgia Magazine.*

Certificate may be used: Jan. 7 to Nov. 12, Monday-Thursday.

Marietta
C3

Whitlock Inn

57 Whitlock Ave
Marietta, GA 30064-2343
(770)428-1495 Fax:(770)919-9620
Internet: www.whitlockinn.com

Circa 1900. This cherished Victorian has been restored and is located in a National Register Historic District, one block from the Marietta Square. Amenities even the Ritz doesn't provide are

in every room, and you can rock on the front verandas. An afternoon snack also is served. There is a ballroom grandly suitable for weddings and business meetings.

Innkeeper(s): Alexis Edwards. $100-145. MC, VISA, AX, DS. 5 rooms with PB and 3 conference rooms. Breakfast included in rates. Type of meal: Cont plus. Beds: KQT. Cable TV, phone and ceiling fan in room. Air conditioning. Fax and copier on premises. Amusement parks, antiquing, live theater, parks, shopping and sporting events nearby.

Location: City.

Publicity: *Marietta Daily Journal.*

"This is the most beautiful inn in Georgia and I've seen nearly all of them."

Certificate may be used: All year, Sunday through Thursday, not available on weekends.

Pine Mountain
F3

The Storms House Inn

207 Harris St
Pine Mountain, GA 31822-1011
(706)663-9100 Fax:(706)663-9100

Circa 1895. Shaded by tall trees, this delicate blue and white Queen Ann Victorian is accentuated by a long white picket fence. There is a wraparound first-floor porch and a gallery-style porch on the second floor. The third-story turret provides views, as well. Inside, the inn is decorated with period furnishings and stained woodwork.

Innkeeper(s): Jan & Dallas Storms. $85-300. PC, TC. 12 rooms with PB. Breakfast included in rates. Types of meals: Cont and early coffee/tea. Beds: QDT. Turndown service and ceiling fan in room. Air conditioning. Fax on premises. Handicap access. Antiquing, fishing, golf, parks, shopping, sporting events, tennis and water sports nearby.

Location: Calloway gardens resort.

Certificate may be used: Monday-Wednesday, January through March.

Sautee
B5

The Stovall House

1526 Hwy 255 N
Sautee, GA 30571
(706)878-3355

Circa 1837. This house, built by Moses Harshaw and restored in 1983 by Ham Schwartz, has received two state awards for its restoration. The handsome farmhouse has an extensive wraparound porch providing vistas of 26 acres of cow pastures and mountains. High ceilings, polished walnut woodwork and decorative stenciling provide a pleasant backdrop for the inn's collection of antiques. Victorian bathroom fixtures include pull-chain toilets and pedestal sinks. The inn has its own restaurant.

Innkeeper(s): Ham Schwartz. $72-84. MC, VISA, PC, TC. 5 rooms with PB. Breakfast included in rates. Type of meal: Cont. Beds: KQDT. Ceiling fan in room. Air conditioning. Library on premises. Amusement parks, antiquing, fishing, live theater, parks, shopping and water sports nearby.

Location: Mountains.

Publicity: *Atlanta Journal and GPTV - Historic Inns of Georgia.*

"Great to be home again. Very nostalgic and hospitable."

Certificate may be used: November through September, Sunday through Thursday.

Savannah G9

Broughton Street Bed & Breakfast

511 E Broughton St
Savannah, GA 31401-3501
(912)232-6633 Fax:(912)232-6633
Internet: www.broughtonst.com
E-mail: savbnb@aol.com

Circa 1883. This historic Victorian townhouse offers five guest rooms. Each is decorated with Victorian furnishings, antiques and contemporary artwork. One room includes a Jacuzzi tub and a fireplace. In the afternoons, the innkeepers serve hors d'oeuvres to their guests. Breakfasts feature such items as quiche, homemade Amish bread and fresh fruit.

Innkeeper(s): Tonya & JP Saleeby. $125-225. MC, VISA, AX, DS, PC, TC. 5 rooms, 3 with PB, 2 with FP. Breakfast, afternoon tea and snacks/refreshments included in rates. Type of meal: Full bkfst. Beds: KQ. Cable TV, phone, turndown service, ceiling fan and VCR in room. Air conditioning. Fax, copier, bicycles and library on premises. Antiquing, fishing, golf, live theater, parks, shopping, sporting events, tennis and water sports nearby.

Location: City.

"Our stay was so romantic, we're rejuvenated and ready to take on the world!"

Certificate may be used: June 1-Aug. 30, Sunday-Thursday. Tanner Room only.

Thomasville J4

Serendipity Cottage

339 E Jefferson St
Thomasville, GA 31792-5108
(912)226-8111 (800)383-7377 Fax:(912)226-2656
Internet: www.bbhost.com/serendipity
E-mail: goodnite@rose.com

Circa 1906. A wealthy Northerner hand picked the lumber used to build this Four Square house for his family. The home still maintains its original oak pocket doors and leaded-glass windows. The decor in guest rooms ranges from Victorian with antiques to rooms decorated with wicker furnishings. Breakfasts are hearty and made from scratch, including freshly baked breads and homemade jams. The home is located in a neighborhood of historic houses, and guests can take a walking or driving tour of the town's many historic sites.

Innkeeper(s): Kathy & Ed Middleton. $85-110. MC, VISA, AX, DS, PC, TC. 4 rooms with PB, 2 with FP. Breakfast included in rates. Types of meals: Full bkfst, cont and early coffee/tea. Beds: QD. Cable TV, phone, turndown service, ceiling fan, VCR and complimentary sherry in room. Air conditioning. Bicycles on premises. Antiquing, fishing, plantation tours, live theater, parks, shopping and sporting events nearby.

Location: City.

"Thank you for the wonderful weekend at Serendipity Cottage. The house is absolutely stunning and the food delicious."

Certificate may be used: June 1-Sept. 30, Sunday-Thursday.

Waverly Hall F3

Raintree Farms of Waverly Hall

8060 GA Hwy 208
Waverly Hall, GA 31831-3212
(706)582-3227 (800)433-0627 Fax:(706)582-3227

Circa 1833. Although it now rests on three acres, this early 19th-century home was once part of a large plantation and was later moved to its present location. The grounds include a small lake and a garden. The home is decorated in traditional style with some antiques. In the mornings, items such as almond-orange French toast or eggs and bacon are served.

Innkeeper(s): Sandra R. Lee. $125. DS, PC, TC. 4 rooms, 3 with PB, 4 with FP. Breakfast and afternoon tea included in rates. Type of meal: Full gourmet bkfst. Beds: QDT. Turndown service and ceiling fan in room. Air conditioning. VCR, fax and library on premises. Antiquing, fishing, golf, callaway Gardens, Warm Springs, live theater, parks, shopping, sporting events, tennis and water sports nearby.

Pets allowed: In fenced area only, must bee well behaved and non-aggressive.

Location: Country.

Certificate may be used: Anytime subject to availability.

Hawaii

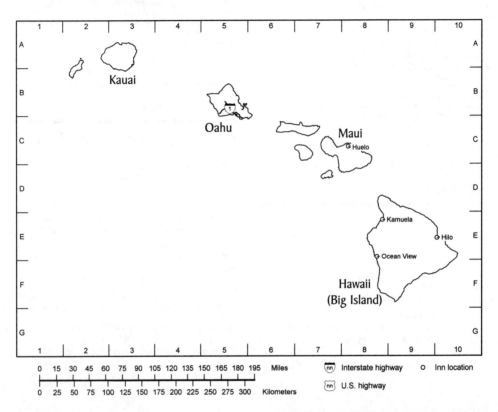

| | 1 | 2 | 3 | 4 | 5 | 6 | 7 | 8 | 9 | 10 |

0   15   30   45   60   75   90   105 120 135 150 165 180 195   Miles

0   25   50   75   100 125 150 175 200 225 250 275 300   Kilometers

nn Interstate highway   o Inn location

nn U.S. highway

Hawaii (Big Island)

Hilo   E10

Lannan's Lihi Kai on Hilo Bay
30 Kahoa Rd
Hilo, HI 96720-2206
(808)935-7865

Circa 1950. The innkeeper here routinely likes to boast about her ocean view of ships, sunsets and whales. A retired cattle-woman, she also lived and worked in Africa for several years before settling down at this cliffside location looking down on the Pacific. This bed and breakfast is like staying with a family friend. Enjoying the swimming pool, coastal walks past water-falls and Hawaiian greenery are the most popular activities here.

Innkeeper(s): Amy Lannan. $60. TC. 2 rooms. Type of meal: Cont plus. Beds: KT. VCR, swimming and above surfing beach on premises. Handicap access. Fishing, golf, parks, sporting events, tennis and water sports nearby.
Certificate may be used: Anytime except Easter Monday week-Merrie Monarch.

Kamuela   E8

Kamuela's Mauna Kea View B&B
PO Box 6375
Kamuela, HI 96743-6375
(808)885-8425 Fax:(808)885-6514
Internet: www.stayhawaii.com

Circa 1988. Guests opt either to stay in a private suite or in a little cottage at this bed & breakfast, which affords views of his-toric Parker Ranch and its namesake mountain, Mauna Kea. The suite and cottage both offer two bedrooms, a living room, fire-place, kitchenette and bathroom, all comfortably decorated. From the decks on both accommodations, guests enjoy mountain views. The bed & breakfast is located on the Big Island, where guests can enjoy plenty of ocean activities, historic sites, horseback riding and much more.

Innkeeper(s): Richard & Deb Mitchell. $65-75. MC, VISA, AX, PC, TC. 2 rooms, 1 suite and 1 cottage. Breakfast included in rates. Type of meal: Cont plus. Beds: QDT. Cable TV, phone, ceiling fan, kitchenette and Deck in room. Spa and barbecue on premises. Antiquing, fishing, golf, white sand beaches, live theater, parks, shopping, downhill skiing, tennis and water sports nearby.

Location: Mountains.

Publicity: *Coffee Times.*

Certificate may be used: Cottage, Sunday-Wednesday, June and September.

Ocean View   E8

Bougainvillea B&B

PO Box 6045
Ocean View, HI 96737-6045
(808)929-7089 (800)688-1763 Fax:(808)929-7089
Internet: hi-inns.com/bougal/www.hawaii-bnb.com/bougvl.html
E-mail: peaceful@interpac.net

Circa 1980. Visitors to this Hawaiian Plantation-style home will be treated to the hospitality of innkeepers who have an extensive background in the travel industry. Guests enjoy a view of South Point, the historic site where the first Polynesians landed. There is a pool and hot tub to enjoy. The innkeepers are full of information about the islands and will share many Hawaii secrets. Green and Black Sand Beach and Volcano National Park are nearby. The bed & breakfast is located midway between Hilo and Kona in the Kau district.

Innkeeper(s): Martie Jean & Don Nitsche. $65. MC, VISA, AX, DC, CB, DS, PC, TC. 4 rooms with PB. Breakfast included in rates. Types of meals: Full gourmet bkfst and cont plus. Beds: Q. Ceiling fan and VCR in room. Fax, copier, spa, swimming, bicycles, satellite TV in common area and movie library on premises. Fishing, hiking, star gazing, parks and water sports nearby.

Location: Country.

"Great food, great people."

Certificate may be used: Jan. 10-Dec. 15, Sunday to Friday.

Maui

Huelo   C8

Hale Huelo

PO Box 1237, Door of Faith Church R
Huelo, HI 96708-1237
(808)572-8669 Fax:(808)573-8403
Internet: www.maui.net/~halehuel
E-mail: halehuel@maui.net

Circa 1997. This contemporary home boasts stunning views of the ocean and surrounding rain forest. The modern home features Asian influences in the design. The interior is definitely Hawaiian, bright tropical prints top the beds and the rooms are airy and bright. Guests can enjoy the view from their own balcony or perhaps while lounging by the pool. For breakfast, the innkeepers serve fruit fresh from the many trees on the property, as well as tropical juices, kona coffee and homemade breads. Hale Huelo is located on the island of Maui, and guests can spend the day hiking to a volcano, snorkeling, surfing or taking a helicopter tour of the scenic area.

Innkeeper(s): Doug Barrett & Seiji Kamijo. $85-125. PC, TC. 3 rooms, 2 with PB and 1 suite. Breakfast included in rates. Types of meals: Cont plus and cont. Beds: Q. Cable TV, ceiling fan, VCR, microwave and coffee maker in room. Fax, copier, spa, swimming and library on premises. Antiquing, fishing, golf, biking, hiking, island tours, live theater, parks, shopping and water sports nearby.

Location: Tropical rain forest valley.

Certificate may be used: Anytime, subject to availability.

Idaho

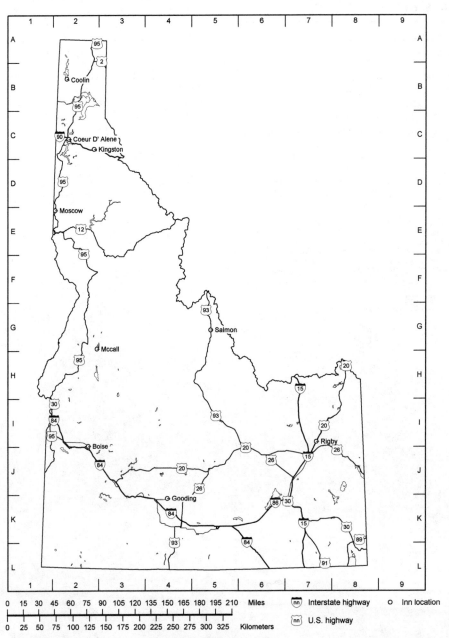

	Miles
0 15 30 45 60 75 90 105 120 135 150 165 180 195 210	Miles

	Kilometers
0 25 50 75 100 125 150 175 200 225 250 275 300 325	Kilometers

Interstate highway   o Inn location

U.S. highway

Visit www.bnbinns.com for photos and more details about each inn.

Boise I2

B&B at Victoria's White House

10325 W Victory Rd
Boise, ID 83709-4079
(208)362-0507 Fax:(208)362-4622
E-mail: boisebandb@aol.com

Circa 1980. Although the inn is not historic, its Colonial Revival-like architecture has incorporated many vintage components saved from local historic

buildings, such as its banister, oak floors and fireplace mantels (gleaned from an old courthouse). Bogus Basin may be seen from the
suite, which features a fireplace, large mirrored tub and parlor. In spring, more than a thousand tulips welcome the new season.

Innkeeper(s): Jeannette T. Baldazo. $95. TC. 2 rooms, 1 with PB, 1 with FP and 1 suite. Breakfast included in rates. Type of meal: Full bkfst. Beds: Q. Cable TV, phone and VCR in room. Air conditioning. Fax, copier and child care on premises. Golf and shopping nearby.

Location: Mountain view.

Certificate may be used: Throughout the year, when open for business.

Coeur d' Alene C2

Country Ranch B&B

1495 S Greenferry Rd
Coeur d' Alene, ID 83814-7606
(208)664-1189 Fax:(208)666-9372
Internet: www.nidlink.com/~countryranch
E-mail: countryranch@nidlink.com

Surrounded by almost 30 acres of woods and rolling hills, this serene retreat is an ideal spot to escape from life's hectic pace. Each of the guest suites features a queen-size poster bed, down

comforters and his and her robes. The Valley View Suite includes a sitting room with a mini-library. A double Jacuzzi tub in the
Mountain View Suite overlooks the ranch's orchard. The scent of freshly baked scones and coffee entices guests to the glass-enclosed morning room or formal dining room where a full, gourmet breakfast is served. In summer, breakfast on the deck overlooking scenic vistas is a tranquil delight. Wine and cheese are offered in the evening.

Innkeeper(s): Ann & Harry Holmberg. $99-135. MC, VISA, PC, TC. 3 rooms with PB and 2 suites. Breakfast included in rates. Types of meals: Full gourmet bkfst and early coffee/tea. Beds: Q. Jacuzzi tub (in Mt. View Suite) in room. Central air. VCR, fax, library, horseshoe pitching and lighted sports court on premises. Amusement parks, antiquing, fishing, golf, factory outlets, golf course with floating green, live theater, parks, shopping, downhill skiing, cross-country skiing and water sports nearby.

Location: Coeur d'Alene City center (4 miles), Spokane, WA (29 miles).

Publicity: *North Idaho Living, The Coeur d'Alene Press, The Spokesman-Review, San Francisco Examiner, Los Angeles Times, Country Magazine and Sunset.*

Certificate may be used: May 1-Sept. 15, Sunday-Thursday, holidays excluded.

Wolf Lodge Creek B&B

715 N Wolf Lodge Creek Rd
Coeur d' Alene, ID 83814-9416
(208)667-5902 (800)919-9653 Fax:(208)667-1133
Internet: www.wolflodge.com
E-mail: wlebb@wolflodge.com

Circa 1994. Secluded on the edge of Coeur d'Alene National Forest, this natural wood home is surrounded by covered porches from which guests can enjoy a stunning view. There's an outdoor hot tub for guests to use after a day of hiking, golfing or skiing. There are four rooms and a suite, and each is individually decorated in a country style. All four rooms include a fireplace. The spacious suite includes an oversized tub, balcony and fireplace. Breakfasts are served buffet style, featuring the innkeeper's special granola, homemade breads, muffins, fresh fruit, yogurt, breakfast meats and entrees such as an oatmeal souffle or egg strata. Lake Coeur d'Alene is just a few minutes away, ski areas are within a half-hour drive, but guests can cross-country ski on the home's surrounding 27 acres.

Innkeeper(s): Terry Cavanaugh, Dave & Tricia Freeman. $100-175. MC, VISA, DS, PC, TC. 5 rooms with PB, 5 with FP and 1 suite. Breakfast included in rates. Type of meal: Full bkfst. Beds: KQ. Ceiling fan in room. VCR, fax, spa and library on premises. Amusement parks, antiquing, fishing, golf, snowmobiling, Horseback Riding, parks, downhill skiing, cross-country skiing and water sports nearby.

Location: Mountains.

Publicity: *Northwest Travel.*

"This place is like a little piece of heaven."

Certificate may be used: Sept. 5 through May 15, Sunday through Friday, excluding holidays.

Coolin B2

Old Northern Inn

PO Box 177, 220 Bayview
Coolin, ID 83821-0177
(208)443-2426 Fax:(208)443-3856
Internet: www.priestlake.com/oldnorthern.html

Circa 1890. This historic inn was built to serve guests riding the Great Northern rail line. Today, travelers come to enjoy trout-filled Priest Lake and all its offerings. The inn is located on the lake shore, and guests enjoy use of a small marina and private beach. There is also a volleyball court, but guests are welcome to simply sit and relax on the spacious deck. The natural surroundings are full of wildlife, and it's not unusual to see deer, caribou and even a moose. The hotel itself is a two-story log and shingle structure, quite at home among the tall cedars. The interior is warm and inviting. There is a common area with a stone fireplace and country furnishings, as well as a view of mountains and the lake. Rooms are decorated with turn-of-the-century antiques, and the suites include a small sitting room. Huckleberry pancakes have been a staple at the inn's breakfast table since the 19th century. In the afternoons, wine, cheese and fruit are served.

$90-140. MC, VISA, PC, TC. 6 rooms with PB and 2 suites. Breakfast included in rates. Types of meals: Full bkfst and early coffee/tea. Beds: Q. Fax, copier and swimming on premises. Handicap access. Antiquing, fishing, golf, shopping, tennis and water sports nearby.

Location: On Priest Lake.

Publicity: *Seattle Times.*

Certificate may be used: Monday through Thursday nights (Friday, Saturday, Sunday nights excluded), valid from June 1-Oct. 15.

Gooding K4

Gooding Hotel Bed & Breakfast

112 Main St
Gooding, ID 83330-1102
(208)934-4374 (888)260-6656

Circa 1906. An early Gooding settler, William B. Kelly, built this historic hotel, which is the oldest building in town. Each of the guest rooms is named in honor of someone significant in the history of Gooding or the hotel. A buffet breakfast is served every morning in the William Kelly Room. The area offers many activities, from golfing and fishing to exploring ice caves or visiting wineries and museums.

Innkeeper(s): Dean & Judee Gooding. $40-65. MC, VISA, AX, PC, TC. 7 rooms and 3 suites. Breakfast included in rates. Types of meals: Full gourmet bkfst and cont. Beds: QDT. Ceiling fan in room. Air conditioning. Copier and bicycles on premises. Antiquing, fishing, golf, hunting, snowmobiling, rafting, wineries, museums, parks, shopping, downhill skiing and cross-country skiing nearby.

Pets allowed: $25 deposit on pets.

Location: Small town.

Certificate may be used: Year-round except Aug.15-31.

Kingston C2

Kingston 5 Ranch B&B

42297 Silver Valley Rd
Kingston, ID 83839-0130
(208)682-4862 (800)254-1852 Fax:(208)682-9445
Internet: www.nidlink.com/~k5ranch
E-mail: k5ranch@nidlink.com

Circa 1930. With the Coeur d'Alene Mountains as its backdrop, this red roofed farmhouse has been renovated with French door and wraparound decks to make the most of its sweeping mountain views and pastoral setting. Innkeepers Walt and Pat Gentry have graced the guest rooms with lace, down comforters, cozy chairs and romantic touches such as four-poster beds. The suites offer  outdoor spas on private decks with mountain views, fireplaces, and baths with whirlpool tubs. The innkeeper is a recipient of several national awards for her recipes. Specialties include Kingston Benedict and stuffed French Toast topped with fresh huckleberry sauce along with freshly baked, prize winning lemon huckleberry muffins. Enjoy activities such as touring two historic gold mines, the Kellogg Gondola, boating or dinner cruises on Lake Coeur d'Alene, skiing,, hiking, fishing, bird watching and driving excursions where you may encounter elk, deer, eagles and other wildlife. Often guests find the greatest pleasure to be watching the horses grazing in the pasture or volunteering to pick fresh strawberries, raspberries or loganberries to top an evening desert of vanilla ice cream.

Innkeeper(s): Walter & Pat Gentry. $100-125. MC, VISA, TC. 2 suites, 2 with FP. Breakfast included in rates. Types of meals: Full bkfst and early coffee/tea. Beds: Q. Digital clocks, fireplaces, Jacuzzi tub and central heat in room. Air conditioning. VCR, fax, copier, spa, stables, bicycles and kennel

one mile off site on premises. Amusement parks, antiquing, fishing, horseback riding, canoeing, mountain biking, live theater, parks, shopping, downhill skiing, cross-country skiing and water sports nearby.

Location: River/mountains.

Publicity: *A Destination Resort.*

Certificate may be used: October, November, January, March through June; Monday, Tuesday and Wednesday, excluding holidays, and holiday periods.

McCall G2

Northwest Passage

201 Rio Vista, PO Box 4208
McCall, ID 83638-8208
(208)634-5349 (800)597-6658 Fax:(208)634-4977

Circa 1938. This mountain country inn rests on five acres and offers six guest rooms, two of them suites. Guests enjoy the inn's two sitting rooms, fireplace and full breakfasts. There are horse corrals on the premises, and most pets can be accommodated when arrangements are made in advance. The inn is furnished in  country decor and provides easy access to a myriad of recreational opportunities found in the area. Payette Lake is just a short distance from the inn, and the Brundage Mountain Ski Area and Ponderosa State Park are nearby.

Innkeeper(s): Steve & Barbara Schott. $70-100. MC, VISA, AX. 6 rooms, 5 with PB, 1 with FP, 2 suites and 1 conference room. Breakfast included in rates. Type of meal: Full bkfst. VCR, fax, television and horse corrals on premises. Antiquing, fishing, live theater, shopping, downhill skiing and cross-country skiing nearby.

Location: Mountains.

Certificate may be used: Year-round, Monday through Thursday, except Winter Carnival (first week in February).

Moscow E2

Paradise Ridge B&B

2455 Blaine Rd
Moscow, ID 83843-7479
(208)882-5292

Circa 1975. Four acres of woods surround this contemporary home, which affords views of buttes and mountains, as well as the town. The decor is a mix of styles, part traditional with a little bit of country. Innkeeper Solveig Miller was a caterer, so she prepares a wonderful breakfast. Huckleberry muffins, scones and oven-puff pancakes are among the homemade offerings.

Innkeeper(s): Jon R. & Solveig L. Miller. $65-95. PC, TC. 3 rooms, 1 with PB and 1 suite. Breakfast included in rates. Types of meals: Full gourmet bkfst and early coffee/tea. Beds: KQ. Ceiling fan in room. Spa on premises. Antiquing, fishing, golf, live theater, parks, shopping, cross-country skiing, sporting events, tennis and water sports nearby.

Location: Forested ridge.

"This certainly rates as one of the best, if not the best, B&B we have stayed in!"

Certificate may be used: Dec. 12 to Jan. 31, any night.

Rigby   I7

Blacksmith Inn

227 N 3900 East
Rigby, ID 83442
(208)745-6208 (888)745-6208 Fax:(208)745-0602

Circa 1996. This contemporary home features unusual architecture. The inn resembles two dome-shaped buildings connected together, and the home is cedar sided. The inn is new, so the innkeepers are constantly adding new items.  Furnishings and decor are country in style, and quilt-topped beds are tucked beside walls painted with murals of Mountain and Western scenes. Breakfasts are served in a cheerful room with a ceiling fan and plants. Scenery of forests and mountain peaks in the Rigby area is outstanding. Guests can ski, fish and hike, and Rigby also offers antique shops, museums and galleries.

Innkeeper(s): Mike & Karla Black. $65-85. MC, VISA, AX, PC, TC. 6 rooms with PB. Breakfast and snacks/refreshments included in rates. Types of meals: Full bkfst and early coffee/tea. Beds: Q. Cable TV, ceiling fan and VCR in room. Fax, copier and stables on premises. Handicap access. Antiquing, fishing, live theater, parks, shopping, downhill skiing, cross-country skiing, sporting events and tennis nearby.

Location: Mountains.

Certificate may be used: Oct. 1-May 15.

Salmon   G5

Greyhouse Inn B&B

HC 61, Box 16
Salmon, ID 83467
(208)756-3968 (800)348-8097
Internet: www.greyhouseinn.com
E-mail: osgoodd@salmoninternet.com

Circa 1894. The scenery at Greyhouse is nothing short of wondrous. In the winter, when mountains are capped in white and the evergreens are shrouded in snow, this Victorian appears as a safe haven from the chilly weather. In the summer, the rocky peaks are a contrast to the whimsical house, which looks like something out of an Old West town. The historic home is known around town as the old maternity hospital, but there is nothing medicinal about it now. The rooms are Victorian in style with antique furnishings. The parlor features deep red walls, floral overstuffed sofas and a dressmaker's model garbed in a brown Victorian gown. Outdoor enthusiasts will find no shortage of activities, from facing the rapids in nearby Salmon River to fishing to horseback riding. The town of Salmon is just 12 miles away.

Innkeeper(s): David & Sharon Osgood. $65-90. MC, VISA, DS, PC, TC. 4 rooms, 2 with PB. Breakfast included in rates. Types of meals: Full bkfst and early coffee/tea. Beds: KQDT. Room fans in room. VCR, bicycles, library and pet boarding on premises. Antiquing, fishing, golf, hiking, horseback riding, float trips, hot springs, mountain biking, parks, shopping, downhill skiing, cross-country skiing and water sports nearby.

Pets allowed: We have a kennel.

Location: Hot springs.

"To come around the corner and find the Greyhouse, as we did, restores my faith! Such a miracle. We had a magical evening here, and we plan to return to stay for a few days. Thanks so much for your kindness and hospitality. We love Idaho!"

Certificate may be used: Oct. 1-May 30.

Illinois

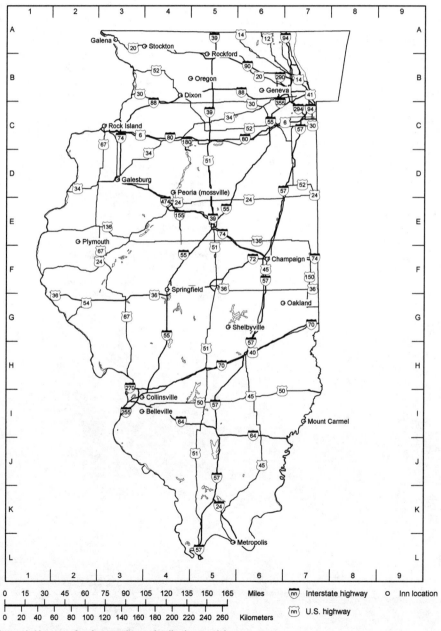

Galena · Stockton · Rockford · Oregon · Dixon · Geneva · Rock Island · Galesburg · Peoria (mossville) · Plymouth · Springfield · Champaign · Oakland · Shelbyville · Collinsville · Belleville · Mount Carmel · Metropolis

0 15 30 45 60 75 90 105 120 135 150 165 Miles

0 20 40 60 80 100 120 140 160 180 200 220 240 260 Kilometers

nn Interstate highway   o Inn location

nn U.S. highway

Belleville
I3

Swans Court B&B

421 Court St
Belleville, IL 62220-1201
(618)233-0779 (800)840-1058 Fax:(618)277-3150
E-mail: mdixon@isbe.accessus.net

Circa 1883. This home, designated by the Department of the Interior as a certified historic structure, was once home to David Baer, known as the "mule king of the world." Baer sold more than 10,000 mules each year to British troops in World War I and to American troops in World War II. The home is furnished almost entirely in antiques. Innkeeper Monty Dixon searched  high and low to fill her B&B with authentic pieces, creating a nostalgic ambiance. The library offers a selection of books, games and puzzles for guests to enjoy. The home is located in a historic neighborhood, within walking distance to shops and restaurants. Belleville is convenient to St. Louis, and there are casinos, historic sites, a racetrack and a state park nearby.

Innkeeper(s): Ms. Monty Dixon. $65-90. MC, VISA, AX, DS, PC, TC. 4 rooms, 2 with PB, 2 with FP. Breakfast and snacks/refreshments included in rates. Type of meal: Full bkfst. Beds: QD. Phone, ceiling fan and folding tables upon request in room. Air conditioning. VCR and library on premises. Handicap access. Antiquing, golf, live theater, shopping, sporting events and tennis nearby.

Location: Town of 45,000.

Publicity: *News Democrat, Country Register and St. Louis Magazine.*

"We feel like we have made a new friend. We appreciated all of the nice little touches, such as the fresh flowers."

Certificate may be used: Jan. 1-Dec. 20, Monday-Thursday.

Champaign
F6

Golds B&B

2065 County Road 525 E
Champaign, IL 61821-9521
(217)586-4345

Circa 1874. Visitors to the University of Illinois area may enjoy a restful experience at this inn, west of town in a peaceful farmhouse setting. Antique country furniture collected by the innkeepers over the past 25 years is showcased in the inn and is beautifully offset by early American stenciling on its walls. An apple tree and garden are on the grounds, and seasonal items are sometimes used as breakfast fare.

Innkeeper(s): Rita & Bob Gold. $45-50. PC, TC. 3 rooms, 1 with PB. Breakfast included in rates. Types of meals: Cont plus and early coffee/tea. Beds: QT. Air conditioning. VCR on premises. Antiquing, fishing, live theater, parks, shopping, cross-country skiing, sporting events and water sports nearby.

Location: Country.

Publicity: *News Gazette.*

Certificate may be used: Anytime except special event weekends.

Collinsville
I3

Maggie's B&B

2102 N Keebler Ave
Collinsville, IL 62234-4713
(618)344-8283

Circa 1900. A rustic two-acre wooded area surrounds this friendly Victorian inn, once a boarding house. Rooms with 14-foot ceilings are furnished with exquisite antiques and art objects collected on worldwide travels. Downtown St. Louis, the Gateway Arch and the Mississippi riverfront are just 10 minutes away.

Innkeeper(s): Maggie Leyda. $45-100. PC, TC. 5 rooms, 3 with PB, 2 with FP and 1 conference room. Breakfast included in rates. Types of meals: Full bkfst and early coffee/tea. Beds: QDT. Cable TV, turndown service, ceiling fan and VCR in room. Air conditioning. Spa and library on premises. Handicap access. Amusement parks, antiquing, fishing, live theater, parks, shopping and sporting events nearby.

Location: Country.

Publicity: *USA Today, Cooking Light, Collinsville Herald Journal, Innsider, Belleville News, Democrat, Saint Louis Homes & Gardens, Edeardsville Intelligences and St. Louis Business Journal.*

"We enjoyed a delightful stay. You've thought of everything. What fun!"

Certificate may be used: Sunday-Thursday, year-round except holidays.

Galena
A3

Eagle's Nest

410 South High St
Galena, IL 61036
(815)777-8400 Fax:(815)777-8446
Internet: www.galenareservations.com
E-mail: lodgings@galenareservations.com

Circa 1842. Furnished with period antiques and carefully restored, this Federal-style brick cottage is tucked into a wooded hillside in the historic district. Enjoy the fireplace and the master bedroom with queen bed. A second bedroom has a double bed. A two-person tub is offered, as well as a fully equipped kitchen. A garden, fountain and patio, complete with barbecue grill, are popular for summertime. Walk to shops and restaurants and most of Galena.

Innkeeper(s): Kate Freeman. $89-169. MC, VISA, AX, DC, DS, PC, TC. 1 cottages, 2 with PB. Breakfast included in rates. Type of meal: Cont. Beds: KD. Cable TV, phone and VCR in room. Air conditioning. Antiquing, fishing, golf, live theater, parks, shopping, downhill skiing, cross-country skiing, tennis and water sports nearby.

Pets allowed: Advance notice and deposit required.

Location: Country.

Certificate may be used: Sunday through Thursday nights. All months except October and Dec. 24-Jan. 3.

Farmers' Guest House

334 Spring St
Galena, IL 61036-2128
(815)777-3456 Fax:(815)777-3514
Internet: www.galenalink.com/farmersguesthouse

Circa 1867. This two-story brick commercial building was built as a bakery and served as a store and hotel, as well. Rows of arched, multi-paned windows add charm to the exterior. The rooms are decorated with antiques, lace curtains and floral wallpapers. The accommodations include seven rooms with queen-size beds, one room with a double bed, the two-room Master Suite and the two-room Queen Suite. There's a bar, featured in the movie "Field of Dreams." A hot tub is offered in the backyard. The inn also has a cabin in the woods available for rent.

Innkeeper(s): Tom & Pam Cummings. $79-150. MC, VISA, AX, DS, PC. 9 rooms with PB and 1 cottage. Breakfast included in rates. Type of meal: Early coffee/tea. Beds: KQD. Cable TV and phone in room. Air conditioning. Fax and spa on premises. Antiquing, fishing, golf, live theater, parks, shopping, downhill skiing, cross-country skiing, sporting events and tennis nearby.

Location: City.

Publicity: *Better Homes & Gardens and Field of Dreams.*

"Neat old place, fantastic breakfasts."

Certificate may be used: All year, Sunday through Thursday.

Galesburg   D3

Seacord House
624 N Cherry St
Galesburg, IL 61401-2731
(309)342-4107

Circa 1891. A former county sheriff and businessman built this Eastlake-style Victorian, which is located in the town's historic district. The home was named for its builder, Wilkens Seacord, a prominent local man whose family is mentioned in Carl Sandburg's autobiography. In keeping with the house's historical prominence, the innkeepers have tried to maintain its turn-of-the-century charm. Victorian wallpapers, lacy curtains and a collection of family antiques grace the guest rooms and living areas. The bedrooms, however, feature the modern amenity of waterbeds. For those celebrating romantic occasions, the innkeepers provide heart-shaped muffins along with regular morning fare.

Innkeeper(s): Gwen and Lyle. $48. MC, VISA, DS. 3 rooms. Breakfast included in rates. Type of meal: Cont plus. Fax on premises.

Certificate may be used: Any day between Nov. 1 and April 1.

Geneva   D3

The Oscar Swan Country Inn
1800 W State St
Geneva, IL 60134-1002
(630)232-0173

Circa 1902. This turn-of-the-century Colonial Revival house rests on seven acres of trees and lawns. Its 6,000 square feet are filled with homey touches. There is a historic barn on the property and a gazebo on the front lawn. A pillared breezeway connects the round garage to the house. The stone pool is round, as well. Nina is a retired home economics teacher and Hans speaks German and was a professor of business administration at Indiana University.

Innkeeper(s): Nina Heymann. $88-150. MC, VISA, AX. 8 rooms, 4 with PB and 3 conference rooms. Breakfast included in rates. Type of meal: Full bkfst. Beds: KQD. Phone and VCR in room. Air conditioning. Antiquing, live theater, shopping and cross-country skiing nearby.

Location: Small town.

Publicity: *Chicago Tribune and Windmill News.*

"Thank you for making our wedding such a beautiful memory. The accommodations were wonderful, the food excellent."

Certificate may be used: Sunday through Thursday, January, February, March, April and November.

Metropolis   L5

Isle of View B&B
205 Metropolis St
Metropolis, IL 62960-2213
(618)524-5838 (800)566-7491
Internet: www.bbonline.com/il/isleofview
E-mail: kimoff@hcis.net

Circa 1889. Metropolis, billed as the "home of Superman," is not a bustling concrete city, but a quaint, country town tucked along the Ohio River. The Isle of View, a stunning Italianate manor, is just a short walk from shops, restaurants and the Players Riverboat Casino. All the guest rooms are appointed in Victorian design with antiques. The Master Suite was originally the home's library and includes a unique coal-burning fireplace, canopy bed and two-person whirlpool tub.

Innkeeper(s): Kim & Gerald Offenburger. $65-125. MC, VISA, AX, DC, CB, DS, TC. 5 rooms with PB. Breakfast included in rates. Types of meals: Full gourmet bkfst and early coffee/tea. Beds: KQD. Cable TV, phone and ceiling fan in room. Air conditioning. Antiquing, fishing, riverboat casino, live theater, parks, shopping and water sports nearby.

Pets allowed: please ask.

Location: Small town.

"You may never want to leave."

Certificate may be used: Sunday-Friday, subject to availability.

Mount Carmel   I7

Living Legacy Homestead
Box 146A, RR 2
Mount Carmel, IL 62863
(618)298-2476

Circa 1870. This turn-of-the-century German homestead features both farmhouse and log house settings. Antiques and period furniture abound, and visitors experience the unique sight of the log house's exposed interior walls and loft. The 10-acre grounds are home to flower, herb and vegetable gardens, and guests also are free to roam the meadows, barnyard and wildlife areas. Nearby are the Beall Woods State Natural Area and the Wabash River. A gift shop featuring antiques, crafts and collectibles is on the premises.

Innkeeper(s): Edna Schmidt Anderson. $50-70. TC. 4 rooms, 2 with PB, 1 cottage and 1 conference room. Breakfast included in rates. Types of meals: Full bkfst and early coffee/tea. Beds: DT. Ceiling fan in room. Air conditioning. Library, attic Treasures Gift Shop in attic loft and nature walks on grounds on premises. Antiquing, fishing, historic village and parks nearby.

Certificate may be used: Feb. 1 to Oct. 31, Sunday through Thursday.

The Poor Farm B&B
Poor Farm Rd
Mount Carmel, IL 62863-9803
(618)262-4663 (800)646-3276 Fax:(618)236-4618
Internet: www.travelassist.com/reg/il102s.html
E-mail: poorfarm@midwest.net

Circa 1915. This uniquely named inn served as a home for the homeless for more than a century. Today, the stately Federal-style structure hosts travelers and visitors to this area of Southeastern Illinois, offering a "gracious glimpse of yesteryear." An antique player piano and a selection of 4,200 in-room movies are available for guests' enjoyment. There are bicycles for those wishing to explore the grounds. The Poor Farm B&B sits adjacent to a recreational park with a well-stocked lake and is within walking distance of an 18-hole golf course and driving range. Riverboat gambling is 45 minutes away in Evansville, Ind.

Innkeeper(s): Liz & John Stelzer. $45-85. MC, VISA, AX, DS, PC, TC. 5 rooms with PB, 2 with FP, 2 suites and 2 conference rooms. Breakfast included in rates. Types of meals: Full bkfst and early coffee/tea. Beds: QDT. Phone, turndown service, ceiling fan and VCR in room. Air conditioning. Fax, copier, bicycles and library on premises. Handicap access. Amusement parks, antiquing, fishing, live theater, parks, shopping, cross-country skiing, sporting events and water sports nearby.

Pets allowed: None inside-outside enclosure.

Location: By an 18-hole golf course.

Certificate may be used: Jan. 10-Nov. 15, Sunday-Thursday, holidays excluded.

Oakland   G6

Inn on The Square

3 Montgomery
Oakland, IL 61943
(217)346-2289 Fax:(217)346-2005

Circa 1878. This inn features hand-carved beams and braided rugs on wide pine flooring. The Tea Room has oak tables, fresh flowers and a hand-laid brick fireplace. Guests may wander in the forest behind the inn or relax in the library with a book or jigsaw puzzle. Guest rooms have oak poster beds and handmade quilts. The Pine Room boasts an heirloom bed with a carved headboard. In addition to guest rooms, the inn houses shops selling ladies apparel, gifts and antiques. The Amish communities of Arthur and Arcola are 14 miles away.

Innkeeper(s): Linda & Gary Miller. $55-65. MC, VISA, PC, TC. 3 rooms with PB, 1 with FP and 1 conference room. Breakfast included in rates. Types of meals: Full bkfst and early coffee/tea. Beds: D. TV, ceiling fan and homemade cookies in room. Air conditioning. VCR and library on premises. Antiquing, golf, Amish Community, forest preserve, Lincoln sites, boating, live theater, parks, shopping, sporting events, tennis and water sports nearby.

Location: small town.

Publicity: *Amish Country News, PM, Midwest Living and Country Living.*

Certificate may be used: Jan. 1 to Dec. 31, Sunday-Thursday only.

Oregon   B4

Patchwork Inn

122 N 3rd St
Oregon, IL 61061
(815)732-4113 Fax:(815)732-6557
Internet: www.essex1.com/people/patchworkinn
E-mail: patchworkinn@essex1.com

Circa 1845. Would you like to sleep where Abraham Lincoln once stayed? This historic inn actually can boast of Mr. Lincoln having "slept here." The Patchwork Inn is the sort you can imagine as providing a speaking platform as well from its two-level veranda across the front facade. Guest rooms feature access to the veranda, and there are high-ceilings and beds with hand-made quilts, the theme of the inn. Guests are pampered at breakfast with a choice of service in your room, the parlor, sun room or on the front porch. A walk away is the river, dam and

tree-lined streets filled with historic houses. Guests often enjoy canoeing on Rock River, picnicking in one of the three state parks or visiting Ronald Reagan's homestead in Dixon.

Innkeeper(s): Michael & Jean McNamara & Ron Bry. $75-115. MC, VISA, DS, TC. 10 rooms with PB and 1 conference room. Breakfast and snacks/refreshments included in rates. Type of meal: Cont. Beds: DT. Cable TV, phone and two rooms have whirlpools in room. Air conditioning. Fax, copier, library and whirlpool tubs in two guest rooms on premises. Antiquing, art galleries, bicycling, canoeing/kayaking, fishing, golf, hiking, horseback riding, live theater, museums, parks, shopping and cross-country skiing nearby.

Location: Rural city.

Certificate may be used: Sunday-Thursday, year round except holidays, subject to availability.

Pinehill B&B

400 Mix St
Oregon, IL 61061-1113
(815)732-2067

Circa 1874. This Italianate country villa is listed in the National Register. Ornate touches include guest rooms with Italian marble fireplaces and French silk-screened mural wallpaper. Outside, guests may enjoy porches, swings and century-old pine trees. Seasonal events include daily chocolate tea parties featuring the inn's own exotic homemade fudge collection.

Innkeeper(s): Susan Koppes. $110-225. MC, VISA, PC, TC. 5 rooms with PB, 3 with FP. Breakfast and afternoon tea included in rates. Types of meals: Full gourmet bkfst and early coffee/tea. Beds: KQD. Turndown service in room. Air conditioning. Antiquing, parks, shopping, sporting events and water sports nearby.

Location: City.

Publicity: *Fox Valley Living, Victorian Sampler, Freeport Journal and Passion of the Automobile.*

"We enjoyed our stay at Pine Hill, your gracious hospitality and the peacefulness. Our thanks to you for a delightful stay. We may have to come again, if just to get some fudge."

Certificate may be used: January, March and April on Sunday, Monday, Tuesday and Wednesday.

Peoria (Mossville)   D4

Old Church House Inn

1416 E Mossville Rd
Peoria (Mossville), IL 61552
(309)579-2300
E-mail: churchhouse@prodigy.net

Circa 1869. Guests will find this restored Colonial a true sanctuary. The inn once served as a country church, but now entices guests with promises of relaxation and hospitality. Each of the guest rooms offers something unique, such as an 1860s carved bedstead, featherbeds, handmade quilts and lacy curtains. Afternoon tea can be enjoyed by a crackling fire or among the garden's menagerie of flowers.

Innkeeper(s): Dean & Holly Ramseyer. $75-115. MC, VISA, DS. 2 rooms, 1 with PB. Breakfast included in rates. Types of meals: Cont plus and early coffee/tea. Beds: Q. Turndown service in room. Air conditioning. Antiquing, fishing, bike trail, live theater, shopping, cross-country skiing, sporting events and water sports nearby.

Location: Village.

Publicity: *Chillicothe Bulletin and Journal Star.*

"Your hospitality, thoughtfulness, the cleanliness, beauty, I should just say everything was the best."

Certificate may be used: Monday-Thursday, anytime on steeple rate only.

Plymouth   E2

Plymouth Rock Roost

201 W Summer St
Plymouth, IL 62367-1104
(309)458-6444 Fax:(309)837-4444
E-mail: plymouthrock@adams.net

Circa 1904. A local banker built this Queen Anne Victorian, which boasts a wraparound veranda, gabled roof and an especially wide turret. The inn is decorated in light Victorian style, with an interesting mix of antiques. One guest room houses a desk that was original to the local post office, another features a huge pencil-post bed. The marble-appointed bathrooms feature oversized tubs and soft, fluffy decorator towels. The innkeepers also run an antique shop on the premises. Western Illinois University is nearby, as are historic sites, golfing and fishing.

Innkeeper(s): Ben Gentry & Joyce Steiner. $59. MC, VISA, PC, TC. 3 rooms and 1 conference room. Breakfast included in rates. Type of meal: Full bkfst. Beds: KD. Cable TV and turndown service in room. Air conditioning. VCR, fax, copier, spa, bicycles and library on premises. Antiquing, fishing, golf, live theater, parks, shopping, downhill skiing, cross-country skiing and sporting events nearby.

Pets allowed: prior approval.

Location: Small town.

Certificate may be used: Anytime we have vacancies.

Rock Island   C3

Potter House B&B

1906 7th Ave
Rock Island, IL 61201-2633
(309)788-1906 (800)747-0339 Fax:(309)794-3947

Circa 1907. This Colonial Revival mansion is in the National Register. Embossed leather wall coverings, mahogany woodwork and stained- and leaded-glass windows are special features. There is a solarium with a tile and marble floor, and there are six fireplaces. A white Chinese carpet, antique beds and a round-tiled shower are features of the Palladian Room. Nearby are the riverboat casinos and a number of excellent restaurants.

Innkeeper(s): Maribeth & Frank Skradski. $75-95. MC, VISA, AX, PC. 5 rooms, 4 with PB, 1 with FP and 1 suite. Breakfast, afternoon tea and snacks/refreshments included in rates. Types of meals: Full bkfst and cont plus. Beds: QD. Cable TV and phone in room. Air conditioning. Fax and bicycles on premises. Amusement parks, antiquing, fishing, golf, casino boats, live theater, parks, shopping, downhill skiing, sporting events and water sports nearby.

Location: City.

Publicity: *Rock Island Argus, Chicago Sun Times, Vacation and Quad-City Times.*

"We love your home and you were so gracious and hospitable."

Certificate may be used: Sunday through Wednesday only. Excludes major holidays. Cannot be used in conjunction with any other promotions or discounts or reservations booked through travel agents. Must mention certificate when making reservations. Subject to availability.

Victorian Inn

702 20th St
Rock Island, IL 61201-2638
(309)788-7068 (800)728-7068 Fax:(309)788-7086
Internet: www.victorianinnbnb.com

Circa 1876. Built as a wedding present for the daughter of a Rock Island liquor baron, the inn's striking features include illuminated stained-glass tower windows. Other examples of the Victorian decor are the living room's beveled-plate-glass French doors and the dining room's Flemish Oak ceiling beams and paneling, crowned by turn-of-the-century tapestries. Standing within sight of three other buildings listed in the National Register, the inn's wooded grounds are home to many songbirds from the area. A glassed-in Florida porch is perfect for relaxing during any season and a patio table in the gardens is a great place to enjoy a glass of pink lemonade on warm evenings.

Innkeeper(s): David & Barbara Parker. $65-125. MC, VISA, AX, PC, TC. 6 rooms with PB, 2 with FP. Breakfast included in rates. Types of meals: Full gourmet bkfst and early coffee/tea. Beds: KQDT. Ceiling fan in room. Air conditioning. Fax, copier and library on premises. Antiquing, fishing, live theater, parks, cross-country skiing, sporting events and water sports nearby.

Location: City.

Certificate may be used: Sunday-Thursday, subject to availability, year round.

Rockford   B5

The Barn of Rockford

6786 Guilford Rd
Rockford, IL 61107-2614
(815)395-8535 (888)378-1729
E-mail: barnrkfd@juno.com

Circa 1886. A large silo marks the entrance to this barn home, surrounded by gardens of perennials. Inside the post and beam building, the original hay track still runs the length of the barn and is incorporated into the first-floor guest room. A great room with a fireplace, library area and heated indoor pool are some of the amenities. Barn-size country breakfasts may include fruit-filled crepes with whipped creme or Scottish eggs served with a hash brown casserole followed with a breakfast dessert.

Innkeeper(s): Ken & Karen Sharp. $65-95. MC, VISA, DS, PC. 4 rooms, 2 with PB. Breakfast included in rates. Types of meals: Full gourmet bkfst and early coffee/tea. Beds: Q. Turndown service and ceiling fan in room. Air conditioning. VCR and swimming on premises. Antiquing, golf, live theater, parks, shopping, sporting events, tennis and water sports nearby.

Location: City.

Publicity: *Rockford Register Star.*

Certificate may be used: Jan. 1-May 31, Sept. 1-Nov. 15, Sunday-Thursday.

Shelbyville   G5

The Shelby Historic House and Inn

816 W Main St
Shelbyville, IL 62565-1354
(217)774-3991 (800)342-9978 Fax:(217)774-2224

This Queen Anne Victorian inn is listed in the National Register of Historic Places. The inn is well known for its conference facilities, and is less than a mile from Lake Shelbyville, one of the state's most popular boating and fishing spots. Guaranteed tee times are available at a neighboring championship golf course. Three state parks are nearby, and the Amish settlement near Arthur is within easy driving distance.

Innkeeper(s): Ken Fry. $52-78. MC, VISA, AX, DC, CB, DS, TC. 38 rooms, 6 suites and 1 conference room. Type of meal: Cont. Beds: K. Cable TV and phone in room. Air conditioning. Fax on premises. Handicap access. Antiquing, fishing, live theater, parks, shopping and water sports nearby.

Certificate may be used: Nov. 1 through May 15.

Springfield   F4

The Inn on Edwards B&B

810 E Edwards St
Springfield, IL 62703
(217)528-0420
E-mail: inn1@juno.com

Circa 1865. The cheerful blue Italianate Victorian displays many original features, from its curving walnut staircase, fine woodwork and fireplace mantel with faux marbling. The home was appointed by a local interior design firm, and rooms feature antiques. The home is adjacent to the Lincoln Home National Historic Site, which includes Abraham Lincoln's family home and several blocks of historic Springfield.

Innkeeper(s): Charles Kirchner. $65-75. MC, VISA, PC. 4 rooms with PB. Breakfast included in rates. Type of meal: Full bkfst. Beds: QT. Cable TV and

ceiling fan in room. Air conditioning. Amusement parks, antiquing, fishing, golf, Muni Opera, State Fair, Lincoln sites, live theater, parks, shopping, sporting events, tennis and water sports nearby.

Location: City.

Publicity: *State Journal Register.*

Certificate may be used: Jan. 1 through Dec. 31, except August 13-22.

Stockton   A3

Maple Lane Country Inn & Resort

3114 S Rush Creek Rd
Stockton, IL 61085-9039
(815)947-3773 Fax:(815)947-3773

Circa 1838. The expansive grounds of this large Colonial Revival mansion, feature a guest house, gazebo, and several farm buildings. The full gourmet breakfasts will delight guests. Historic Galena is within easy driving distance, as are several state parks.

Innkeeper(s): Rose & Bill Stout. $89-150. TC. 22 rooms with PB, 1 with FP, 6 suites and 2 conference rooms. Breakfast included in rates. Type of meal: Full gourmet bkfst. Beds: Q. VCR in room. Air conditioning. Fax, copier, spa, sauna, picnic tables, gazebo, lawn games, Karaoke, sauna, Jacuzzi and fishing on premises. Antiquing, fishing, live theater, parks, shopping, downhill skiing, cross-country skiing, sporting events and water sports nearby.

Location: Scenic country area.

Certificate may be used: Sunday-Thursday, upon availability, except holidays, hunting season and special packages.

Indiana

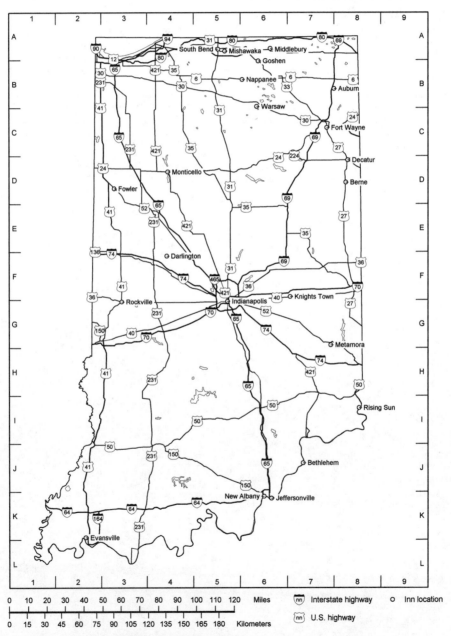

	1	2	3	4	5	6	7	8	9

A — 90, 94, 31, 80, 80, 69; South Bend, Mishawaka, Middlebury

B — 12, 65, 421, 35, 30, 231, 6, 30, 33, 6; Goshen, Nappanee, Auburn

41, Warsaw, 31, 24, 30

C — 65, 231, 421, 35, 24, 69, 27; Fort Wayne

D — 24, 421, 35, 224, Decatur; Monticello, 31, 69, 27, Berne

E — 41, 52, 65, 231, 421, 35, 27; Fowler

F — 136, 74, Darlington, 74, 465, 31, 36, 69, 70; 36

G — 36, 231, 150, 40, 70, 70, 421, 65, 52, 74, 40, 27; Rockville, Indianapolis, Knights Town

H — 41, 231, 421, 74, 50; Metamora, 65, 50

I — 50, 50, 231, 150, 50; Rising Sun

J — 41, 231, 150, 65; Bethlehem

K — 64, 164, 64, 231, 150, 64; New Albany, Jeffersonville, Evansville

	1	2	3	4	5	6	7	8	9

| 0 | 10 | 20 | 30 | 40 | 50 | 60 | 70 | 80 | 90 | 100 | 110 | 120 | Miles |

| 0 | 15 | 30 | 45 | 60 | 75 | 90 | 105 | 120 | 135 | 150 | 165 | 180 | Kilometers |

nn   Interstate highway   o   Inn location

nn   U.S. highway

Berne D8

Schug House Inn

706 W Main St
Berne, IN 46711-1328
(219)589-2303

Circa 1907. This Queen Anne home was built in 1907 by Emanuel Wanner. It was constructed for the Schug family, who occupied the home for 25 years, and whom the innkeepers chose the name of their inn. Victorian features decorate the home, including inlaid floors, pocket doors and a wraparound porch. Guest rooms boast walnut, cherry and oak furnishings. Fruit, cheeses and pastries are served on antique china each morning in the dining room. Horse-drawn carriages from the nearby Old Order Amish community often pass on the street outside.

Innkeeper(s): John Minch. $35-40. MC, VISA. 9 rooms with PB and 1 conference room. Breakfast included in rates. Type of meal: Cont. Beds: KQDT.

Certificate may be used: Jan. 2-Dec. 20, except July 20-27 and Aug. 23-30.

Bethlehem J7

The Inn at Bethlehem

101 Walnut St
Bethlehem, IN 47104
(812)293-3975

Circa 1830. This two-story, Federal-style inn sits atop a bluff overlooking the Ohio River. In its long history, it has seen uses as a grocery, jail and possibly a stop on the Underground Railroad. Rocking chairs and hammocks are ready for those who wish to relax, and there's 26 acres to explore. The inn is furnished with elegant pieces, including some period antiques. One of the innkeepers is an accomplished chef, so the breakfasts are a treat. Guests can make a reservation for a gourmet dinner in the inn's Rustic Lodge. Your menu might include saffron shrimp bisque, garden salad dressed with a balsamic vinaigrette, an appetizer of wild mushroom cream in a beggars purse, then bourbon pecan chicken or perhaps a beef tenderloin wrapped in smoky bacon and served with a Merlot sauce. Guests finish off the meal with a succulent dessert. Sunday brunch also is served.

Innkeeper(s): Gloria Childers. $90-200. MC, TC. 10 rooms with PB, 1 suite and 2 conference rooms. Breakfast included in rates. Types of meals: Full gourmet bkfst and early coffee/tea. Beds: KQDT. Ceiling fan in room. Air conditioning. VCR, fax and bicycles on premises. Antiquing, fishing, parks and shopping nearby.

"We love this place! It is now our little getaway."

Certificate may be used: Nov. 1-April 28, Sunday-Thursday. Holidays excluded.

Darlington F4

Our Country Home

RR 1 Box 103
Darlington, IN 47940
(765)794-3139
E-mail: Ochome@indy.tds.net

Circa 1850. A favorite activity at this country home is a moonlight carriage ride along country roads. (You can opt for carriage driving classes!) Abundant fields of corn and beans surround the 12-acre property, and there are horses and a barn. The innkeepers provide full country breakfasts of muffins, potatoes, eggs, bacon and pancakes. Private candlelight dinners can be reserved as well. Guest rooms are decorated in a country style. There's a bicycle built for two, and guests often cycle the back roads for hours and then come home to soak in the hot tub later that evening under the stars.

Innkeeper(s): Jim & Debbie Smith. $95-205. MC, VISA, AX, DS. 4 rooms. Breakfast included in rates. Type of meal: Full bkfst. Beds: Q. TV, turndown service, ceiling fan and VCR in room. Air conditioning. Spa, swimming, stables, bicycles, library and carriage rides on premises. Bicycling, golf, horseback riding, live theater, museums, shopping and sporting events nearby.

Location: Country.

Publicity: *Journal Review, The Park County Guild and Indianapolis TV Channel 59.*

"Just what the doctor ordered, a very relaxing, rejuvenating and back to nature weekend."

Certificate may be used: Monday-Thursday, excluding holidays.

Decatur D8

Cragwood Inn B&B

303 N 2nd St
Decatur, IN 46733-1329
(219)728-2000
E-mail: cragwood@adamswells.com

Circa 1900. This Queen Anne Victorian with four porches, gingerbread frosting, a turret and a graceful bay facade was built by a Decatur banker. Finely carved oak is magnificently displayed in the paneled ceilings, staircase and pillars of the parlor. Ornate tin ceilings, beveled leaded-glass windows and a crystal chandelier are among other highlights. Twin wicker beds in the Garden Room looks out through a Palladian window. Two other rooms have their own fireplace.

Innkeeper(s): George & Nancy Craig. $60-65. MC, VISA, PC, TC. 4 rooms, 2 with PB, 2 with FP. Breakfast and snacks/refreshments included in rates. Types of meals: Full bkfst and early coffee/tea. Beds: QDT. Air conditioning. VCR, library and beautiful flower gardens on premises. Antiquing and parks nearby.

Location: Small town.

Publicity: *Inside Chicago, Great Lakes Getaway and Christmas Victorian Craft.*

"Your wonderful hospitality, beautiful home and company made my trip that much more enjoyable."

Certificate may be used: Sunday-Thursday, all year.

Evansville K2

Cool Breeze Estate B&B

1240 SE 2nd St
Evansville, IN 47713-1304
(812)422-9635

Circa 1906. This prairie school home is surrounded by more than an acre of grounds, ideal for those in search of peace and quiet. Truck and automobile maker Joseph Graham once lived here, as well as philanthropist Giltner Igleheart. One room features the wallpaper mural, "Scenic America." The same mural was chosen by Jacqueline Kennedy to decorate the White House. The sunny rooms have names such as Margaret Mitchell or Bronte. A zoo, art museum and riverboat casino are among the nearby attractions.

Innkeeper(s): Katelin & David Hills. $85. AX, DC, CB, DS, PC, TC. 3 rooms with PB, 2 suites and 2 conference rooms. Breakfast included in rates. Type of meal: Full bkfst. Beds: QD. TV and phone in room. Air conditioning. VCR and library on premises. Antiquing, university of Southern Indiana, live theater, parks, shopping, sporting events and water sports nearby.

Pets allowed: Must be well trained.

Publicity: *Evansville Courier and Midwest Living.*

"It was so much like discovering something wonderful from the past and disappearing into the warmth of childhood again."

Certificate may be used: Anytime; no restrictions.

Fort Wayne   C7

The Carole Lombard House B&B

704 Rockhill St
Fort Wayne, IN 46802-5918
(219)426-9896 (888)426-9896

Circa 1895. Jane Alice Peters, a.k.a. Carole Lombard, spent her first six years in this turn-of-the-century home located in Ft. Wayne's historic West-Central neighborhood. The innkeepers named two guest rooms in honor of Lombard and her second husband, Clark Gable. Each of these rooms features memorabilia from the Gable-Lombard romance. A video library with a collection of classic movies is available, including many of Lombard's films. The innkeepers provide bicycles for exploring Fort Wayne and also provide information for a self-guided architectural tour of the historic area.

Innkeeper(s): Bev Fiandt. $75-85. MC, VISA, DS, PC, TC. 4 rooms with PB. Breakfast included in rates. Types of meals: Full bkfst and early coffee/tea. Beds: KQDT. Cable TV and phone in room. Air conditioning. VCR and bicycles on premises. Antiquing, live theater, parks and sporting events nearby.

Location: City.

Publicity: *Playboy and Michigan Living.*

"The elegance and ambience are most appreciated."

Certificate may be used: Sunday-Thursday all year.

Fowler   D3

Pheasant Country B&B

900 E 5th St
Fowler, IN 47944-1518
(765)420-8071 Fax:(765)420-8071
E-mail: june@pheasant.com

Circa 1940. This English Colonial-style inn offers its visitors three guest rooms and attentive service. The innkeeper provides early coffee and tea in addition to breakfast. Afternoon tea is featured, and later, an evening snack. Guests also may request room service. The guest rooms, which share two baths, boast many modern amenities. Crepes, scones and egg dishes are the breakfast fare. Visitors may borrow a bicycle for a relaxing ride. Purdue University and the Tippecanoe Battlefield State Monument are within easy driving distance.

Innkeeper(s): June Gaylord. $60-85. MC, VISA, PC, TC. 4 rooms, 1 with PB. Breakfast and snacks/refreshments included in rates. Types of meals: Full bkfst and early coffee/tea. Beds: KQDT. Cable TV, phone, turndown service, ceiling fan and VCR in room. Air conditioning. Fax, bicycles, library and antiques for sale on premises. Antiquing, fishing, golf, live theater, parks, shopping, sporting events, tennis and water sports nearby.

Location: town/village.

Certificate may be used: Jan. 30 to Dec. 30, Sunday-Saturday.

Goshen   B6

Indian Creek B&B

20300 CR 18
Goshen, IN 46528
(219)875-6606 Fax:(219)875-8396
E-mail: 71224,1462@compuserve.com

Circa 1993. This Victorian was built recently, but offers a nostalgic charm reminiscent of its historic architectural style. The comfortable bed rooms are decorated with antiques. The home is located in Amish country, and antique stores, the Shipshewana Flea Market and Notre Dame are nearby.

Innkeeper(s): Jim & Jeanette Vellenga. $69-79. MC, VISA, AX, DS, PC, TC. 1 suites. Breakfast included in rates. Type of meal: Full bkfst. Beds: QDT. Cable TV, phone, turndown service and ceiling fan in room. Air conditioning. VCR, fax, copier and library on premises. Handicap access. Antiquing, fishing, Shipshewana flea market, live theater, parks, shopping, cross-country skiing, sporting events and water sports nearby.

Location: Country.

Certificate may be used: Jan. 1-April 30, Monday-Sunday.

Waterford B&B

3004 S Main St
Goshen, IN 46526-5423
(219)533-6044

This Italianate inn, listed with the National Register, features all Midwest antiques in its furnishing schemes. The innkeeper, an avid antiquer, can provide tips on where to buy in the surrounding area. A full breakfast is served at the Waterford and guests also may relax in the sitting room or in front of the fireplace. The inn is a short distance from the state's chain of lakes, Amish country or famous South Bend, home of the University of Notre Dame.

Innkeeper(s): Judith Forbes. $55-60. 4 rooms. Breakfast included in rates. Type of meal: Full bkfst. Antiquing and shopping nearby.

Certificate may be used: Jan. 1-March 30.

Indianapolis   G5

Speedway B&B

1829 Cunningham Dr
Indianapolis, IN 46224-5338
(317)487-6531 (800)975-3412 Fax:(317)481-1825
Internet: www.speedwaybb.com
E-mail: speedwaybb@msn.com

Circa 1906. This two-story white columned inn reflects a plantation-style architecture. The inn is situated on an acre of lawn and trees. The bed & breakfast has a homey decor that includes a wood-paneled common room and elegantly furnished guest rooms. Breakfast includes items such as homemade coffee cake and Danish or sausage and egg casserole. Nearby attractions include President Harrison's home, the Hall of Fame Museum and the largest city park in the nation, Eagle Creek Park.

Innkeeper(s): Pauline Grothe. $65-135. PC, TC. 5 rooms with PB. Breakfast included in rates. Type of meal: Full bkfst. Beds: KQD. Cable TV and phone in room. Air conditioning. VCR, fax and bicycles on premises. Antiquing, fishing, golf, live theater, parks, shopping, cross-country skiing, sporting events, tennis and water sports nearby.

Location: City.

"It is people like you who have given B&Bs such a good reputation."

Certificate may be used: Monday-Thursday, excluding special events, based upon availability.

The Tranquil Cherub

2164 N Capitol Ave
Indianapolis, IN 46202-1251
(317)923-9036 Fax:(317)923-8676
Internet: www.tranquilcherub.com
E-mail: innkeeper@tranquilcherub.com

Circa 1905. Visitors to the bustling Indianapolis area will appreciate the quiet elegance of the Tranquil Cherub, a Greek Revival home. The morning routine begins with freshly brewed coffee and juice served  prior to breakfast, which is eaten in the oak-paneled dining room or on a back deck overlooking a pond. Guests may choose from the blue and white Victorian Room, with its antique wicker furniture and lace curtains, or the Gatsby Room, highlighted by its Art Deco-era four-poster cannonball bed. The jade-green and navy Rogers Room features stained glass and an oak bedroom set that originated in an old Chicago hotel.

Innkeeper(s): Thom & Barb Feit. $75-125. MC, VISA, AX, PC, TC. 4 rooms with PB and 1 suite. Breakfast and snacks/refreshments included in rates. Types of meals: Full bkfst and early coffee/tea. Beds: KQ. Ceiling fan in room. Air conditioning. VCR, fax and library on premises. Antiquing, golf, live theater, parks, shopping, sporting events, tennis and water sports nearby.

Publicity: *Indianapolis Star.*

Certificate may be used: Jan. 1 through Dec. 31, Sunday-Thursday. Not valid during special local events.

Jeffersonville   K6

1877 House Country Inn

2408 Utica-Sellersburg Rd
Jeffersonville, IN 47130
(812)285-1877 (888)284-1877 Fax:(812)280-1877
E-mail: 1877house@disknet.com

Circa 1877. Sugar maples shade the lawn of this inn located on more than two acres. There are three guest rooms and a cottage available on the property. The renovated farmhouse is decorated with country pieces and memorabilia collected for several years by the innkeepers. German pancakes, savory bread pudding and poppy seed bread are favorites served at the inn that have also been included in the food section of the local paper.

Innkeeper(s): Steve & Carol Stenbro. $75-125. PC, TC. 4 rooms with PB, 4 with FP and 1 cottage. Breakfast, afternoon tea and snacks/refreshments included in rates. Type of meal: Full gourmet bkfst. Beds: QD. Cable TV, ceiling fan and jacuzzi in cottage in room. Air conditioning. VCR, fax, library, child care and outside 8 person hot tub on premises. Amusement parks, antiquing, fishing, golf, live theater, parks, shopping, downhill skiing, sporting events and tennis nearby.

Location: Suburb, country.

Publicity: *Courier Journal and Tribune.*

Certificate may be used: Subject to availability, Sunday-Friday.

Knightstown   F7

Old Hoosier House

7601 S Greensboro Pike
Knightstown, IN 46148-9613
(765)345-2969 (800)775-5315

Circa 1840. The Old Hoosier House was owned by the Elisha Scovell family, who were friends of President Martin Van Buren, and the president stayed overnight in the home. Features of the Victorian house include tall, arched windows and a gabled entrance. Rooms are decorated with antiques and lace curtains. Hearty Hoosier breakfasts include such specialties as a breakfast pizza of egg, sausage and cheese, and Melt-Away Puff Pancakes. The inn's eight acres are wooded, and the deck overlooks a pond on the fourth hole of the adjacent golf course.

Innkeeper(s): Jean & John Butler. $60-70. PC. 4 rooms with PB, 1 with FP and 1 suite. Breakfast, afternoon tea and snacks/refreshments included in rates. Types of meals: Full bkfst and early coffee/tea. Beds: KQT. Phone and ceiling fan in room. Air conditioning. VCR and library on premises. Handicap access. Antiquing, fishing, live theater, parks, shopping and sporting events nearby.

Location: Rural, next to 18 hole golf.

Publicity: *Indianapolis Star News, New Castle Courier-Times and Indianapolis Monthly.*

"We had such a wonderful time at your house. Very many thanks."

Certificate may be used: May through October, subject to availability.

Metamora   G7

The Thorpe House Country Inn

19049 Clayborne St, PO Box 36
Metamora, IN 47030
(765)647-5425 (888)427-7932
E-mail: thorpe_house@hotmail.com

Circa 1840. The steam engine still brings passenger cars and the gristmill still grinds cornmeal in historic Metamora. The Thorpe House is located one block from the canal. Rooms feature original pine and poplar floors, antiques, stenciling and country accessories. Enjoy a hearty breakfast selected from the inn's restaurant menu. (Popular items include homemade biscuits, egg dishes and sourdough pecan rolls.) Walk through the village to explore more than 100 shops.

Innkeeper(s): Mike & Jean Owens. $70-125. MC, VISA, AX, DS, PC, TC. 5 rooms with PB and 1 suite. Breakfast and snacks/refreshments included in rates. Types of meals: Full bkfst and early coffee/tea. Beds: KDT. Air conditioning. Gift shops/pottery studio on premises. Amusement parks, antiquing, fishing, golf, parks, shopping, tennis and water sports nearby.

Pets allowed: by prior arrangement.

Location: Restored 1840 canal-town village.

Publicity: *Cincinnati Enquirer, Chicago Sun-Times and Midwest Living.*

"Thanks to all of you for your kindness and hospitality during our stay."

Certificate may be used: April through November, Sunday through Thursday.

Middlebury   A6

Bee Hive B&B

PO Box 1191
Middlebury, IN 46540-1191
(219)825-5023

Circa 1985. This family home is located on 39 acres in the Amish area of Middlebury and was constructed with hand-sawn lumber. Original primitive paintings by Miss Emma

Schrock are part of the B&B's collectibles. There is also a collection of antique farm equipment. Guest rooms are in the farmhouse with the exception of Honey Comb Cottage which is a guest house with its own bath. If you'd like to help out with some of the farm chores and are an early riser see if you can coax Herb into letting you help. Afterwards you'll be ready for a full farm breakfast including Treva's home made granola and hearty breakfast casseroles. Ask for advice in discovering the best places to visit in the area.

Innkeeper(s): Herb & Treva Swarm. $58-78. MC, VISA, PC, TC. 4 rooms, 1 with PB and 1 cottage. Breakfast and snacks/refreshments included in rates. Types of meals: Full bkfst and early coffee/tea. Beds: QD. Ceiling fan in room. Air conditioning. VCR, fax and copier on premises. Antiquing, fishing, shipshewana Flea Market, live theater, parks, shopping, downhill skiing, cross-country skiing, sporting events and water sports nearby.

Location: Country.

"What a great place to rest the mind, body and soul."

Certificate may be used: Anytime.

Patchwork Quilt Country Inn

11748 CR 2
Middlebury, IN 46540
(219)825-2417 Fax:(219)825-5172
E-mail: rgminn@aol.com

Circa 1800. Located in the heart of Indiana's Amish country, this inn offers comfortable lodging and fine food. Some of the recipes are regionally famous, such as the award-winning Buttermilk Pecan Chicken. All guest rooms feature handsome quilts and country decor, and The Loft treats visitors to a whirlpool tub and kitchenette. Ask about the four-hour guided tour of the surrounding Amish area. The alcohol- and smoke-free inn also is host to a gift shop.

Innkeeper(s): Ray & Rosetta Miller. $70-100. MC, VISA, PC, TC. 15 rooms with PB, 2 suites and 2 conference rooms. Breakfast included in rates. Types of meals: Full bkfst and early coffee/tea. Beds: KQT. Cable TV, have TV and no cable in room. Air conditioning. VCR, fax and copier on premises. Handicap access. Antiquing, fishing, golf, amish buggy rides & tours, live theater, parks, shopping, downhill skiing, cross-country skiing and sporting events nearby.

Location: Amish Country.

Certificate may be used: November, Dec. 1-26, March and April.

Tiffany Powell's Bed & Breakfast

523 South Main St
Middlebury, IN 46540-9004
(219)825-5951
Internet: www.tiffanypowells.com
E-mail: tiff@npcc.net

Circa 1914. The porch of this B&B is a favorite spot for guests to sit and watch Amish buggies pass by, especially on Saturday nights. The inn features leaded and beveled glass and original oak floors and woodwork. Guest rooms reflect a fresh country decor with bright handmade quilts sewn by Judy's grandmother. Known locally and acknowledged nationally on the Oprah show for her hospitality, the innkeeper offers a full breakfast.

Amish Sausage Casserole is a speciality of the house and is served in the dining room. Shipshewana is seven minutes away, and Amish markets and craft shops are nearby.

Innkeeper(s): Judy Powell. $50-80. PC, TC. 5 rooms, 3 with PB, 1 with FP. Breakfast, afternoon tea and snacks/refreshments included in rates. Types of meals: Full bkfst, cont plus and early coffee/tea. Beds: QDT. Cable TV, turn-down service and ceiling fan in room. Air conditioning. VCR and bicycles on premises. Antiquing, fishing, golf, live theater, parks, shopping, cross-country skiing, sporting events, tennis and water sports nearby.

Location: Small town.

Publicity: *South Bend Tribune, Goshen News and Oprah.*

Certificate may be used: Anytime.

Mishawaka   A5

The Beiger Mansion Inn

317 Lincoln Way E
Mishawaka, IN 46544-2012
(219)256-0365 (800)437-0131 Fax:(219)259-2622
Internet: business.michiana.org/beiger/
E-mail: beiger@michiana.org

Circa 1903. This Neoclassical limestone mansion was built to satisfy Susie Beiger's wish to copy a friend's Newport, R.I. estate. Palatial rooms that were once a gathering place for local society now welcome guests who seek gracious accommodations. Notre Dame, St. Mary's and Indiana University in South Bend are nearby.

Innkeeper(s): Ron Montandon. $80-95. MC, VISA, AX, DC, CB, DS, PC, TC. 6 rooms with PB and 1 suite. Breakfast included in rates. Type of meal: Full bkfst. Beds: Q. Cable TV and phone in room. Air conditioning. VCR, fax and copier on premises. Antiquing, fishing, golf, live theater, parks, sporting events and tennis nearby.

Location: City.

Publicity: *Tribune.*

"Can't wait until we return to Mishawaka to stay with you again!."

Certificate may be used: Year round, except Notre Dame home football and special events.

Monticello   D4

The Victoria B&B

206 S Bluff St
Monticello, IN 47960-2309
(219)583-3440

This Queen Anne Victorian was built by innkeeper Karen McClintock's grandfather. Karen and husband, Steve, have filled the home with family antiques and collectibles, including a whimsical cow collection in the breakfast room. A grand, hand-carved oak staircase greets guests as they arrive. Rooms are decorated in a Victorian country theme, setting off the high ceilings and polished wood floors. The grounds boast old magnolia and maple trees and perennials planted by Karen's grandparents.

Innkeeper(s): Karen McClintock. $55-75. 3 rooms. Breakfast included in rates. Type of meal: Cont plus.

Certificate may be used: Oct. 30 to April 30, Monday-Thursday.

Nappanee
B6

Homespun Country Inn

302 N Main St
Nappanee, IN 46550
(219)773-2034 (800)311-2996 Fax:(219)773-3456
Internet: www.homespuninn.com
E-mail: home@hoosierlink.net

Circa 1902. Take your early morning coffee to the porch swing
and you may see a horse and buggy passing by. Stained-glass
windows in the dining room, leaded parlor windows, pocket
doors and quarter-sawn oak woodwork are features of this
Victorian inn. Guest rooms are named for the original occupants and include photos and memorabilia of that era.

Innkeeper(s): Dianne & Dennis Debelak. $59-79. MC, VISA, DS, PC, TC. 5
rooms, 3 with PB. Breakfast and snacks/refreshments included in rates. Types
of meals: Full bkfst and early coffee/tea. Beds: QDT. Cable TV, ceiling fan, VCR
and night lights in room. Air conditioning. Fax and copier on premises.
Antiquing, golf, live theater, parks, shopping, sporting events and tennis nearby.

Location: Amish heritage.

Publicity: *The Elkhart Truth.*

*"We have been telling all our friends about how wonderful your
establishment is."*

Certificate may be used: Any day January-April. Discount based on regular
room rates. No other discount applies.

The Victorian Guest House

302 E Market St
Nappanee, IN 46550-2102
(219)773-4383
Internet: www.victorianb-b.com
E-mail: vghouse@bnin

Circa 1887. Listed in the National Register, this three-story
Queen Anne Victorian inn was built by Frank Coppes, one of
America's first noted kitchen cabinet makers. Nappanee's location
makes it an ideal stopping point for those exploring the heart of
Amish country, or visiting the South Bend or chain of lakes areas.
Visitors may choose from six guest rooms, including the Coppes
Suite, with its original golden oak woodwork, antique tub and
stained glass. Full breakfast is served at the antique 11-foot dining
room table. Amish Acres is just one mile from the inn.

Innkeeper(s): Vickie Hunsberger. $119. MC, VISA, DS. 6 rooms with PB.
Breakfast and afternoon tea included in rates. Types of meals: Full bkfst and
early coffee/tea. Beds: QT. Cable TV, phone, turndown service and ceiling fan
in room. Air conditioning. Antiquing, live theater, shopping, sporting events
and water sports nearby.

Location: City.

Publicity: *Goshen News.*

Certificate may be used: Dec. 1-April 15, Monday-Thursday.

New Albany
K6

Honeymoon Mansion B&B
& Wedding Chapel

1014 E Main St
New Albany, IN 47150-5843
(812)945-0312 (800)759-7270
Internet: www.bbonline.com/in/honeymoon

Circa 1850. The innkeepers at Honeymoon Mansion can provide guests with the flowers, wedding chapel and honeymoon
suite. All you need to bring is a bride or groom. An ordained

minister is on the premises and guests can marry or renew
their vows in the inn's Victorian wedding chapel. However, one
need not be a newlywed to enjoy this bed & breakfast. Canopy
beds, stained-glass windows and heart-shaped rugs are a few of
the romantic touches. Several suites include marble Jacuzzis
flanked on four sides with eight-foot-high marble columns, creating a dramatic and elegant effect. The home itself, a pre-Civil
War Italianate-style home listed in the state and national historic registers, boasts many fine period features. Gingerbread
trim, intricate molding and a grand staircase add to the
Victorian ambiance. Guests are treated to an all-you-can-eat
country breakfast with items such as homemade breads, biscuits and gravy, eggs, sausage and potatoes.

Innkeeper(s): Bill & Donna Stepp. $80-160. MC, VISA, PC, TC. 6 suites, 1
with FP and 2 conference rooms. Breakfast included in rates. Type of meal: Full
bkfst. Beds: Q. Cable TV, ceiling fan and VCR in room. Air conditioning.
Handicap access. Amusement parks, antiquing, fishing, three state parks, three
caves, Culbertson Mansion, riverboat casino, live theater, parks, shopping,
downhill skiing, cross-country skiing, sporting events and water sports nearby.

Location: Mansion Row.

Publicity: *Courier-Journal, Evening News, Tribune and WHAS TV.*

Certificate may be used: Sunday through Thursday, except Derby week, New
Year's and Valentine's, subject to availability.

Rising Sun
I8

The Jelley House Country Inn

222 S Walnut St
Rising Sun, IN 47040-1142
(812)438-2319
E-mail: jmoore@seidata.com

Circa 1847. This pre-Civil War Colonial changed hands many
times before current innkeepers Jeff and Jennifer Moore purchased the place. Antiques decorate the interior, as well as an
old pump organ and a baby grand piano. The front porch is
lined with comfortable chairs for those who wish to relax. The
home is just two blocks from Riverfront Park and the Ohio
River, and the innkeepers offer bikes for guests who wish to
ride around and explore the area.

Innkeeper(s): Jeff & Jennifer Moore. $65-150. MC, VISA, PC, TC. 5 rooms
and 1 suite. Breakfast included in rates. Type of meal: Cont plus. Beds: QDT.
Cable TV and ceiling fan in room. Air conditioning. VCR, bicycles and baby
Grand Piano on premises. Antiquing, fishing, golf, live theater, parks, shopping, downhill skiing, sporting events and water sports nearby.

Pets allowed: Well-behaved, guest responsible for any damage.

Location: City.

Publicity: *Recorded & News.*

*"Beautifully decorated. You have preserved some of the old and
new...enjoyed this home atmosphere."*

Certificate may be used: Jan. 1-Dec. 30, no holidays, limit one coupon per stay.

Rockville
G3

Billie Creek Inn

RR 2, Box 27, Billie Creek Village
Rockville, IN 47872
(765)569-3430 Fax:(765)569-3582

Circa 1996. Although this inn was built recently, it rests on
the outskirts of historic Billie Creek Village. The village is a
non-profit, turn-of-the-century living museum, complete with
30 historic buildings and three covered bridges. Guests can
explore an 1830s cabin, a farmstead, a general store and much

more to experience how Americans lived in the 19th century. The innkeepers take part in the history, dressing in period costume. The inn is decorated in a comfortable, country style. The nine suites include the added amenity of a two-person whirlpool tub. All inn guests receive complimentary admission to Billie Creek Village. Coffee and continental breakfast fare are available around the clock. Special packages include canoeing and bike tours, Civil War Days and covered bridge festivals.

Innkeeper(s): Carol Gum & Doug Weisheit. $49-99. MC, VISA, AX, DS, PC, TC. 31 rooms with PB, 9 suites and 2 conference rooms. Breakfast included in rates. Type of meal: Cont. Beds: KD. Cable TV and phone in room. Air conditioning. VCR, fax, copier, stables, pet boarding, historical village, general store, player piano concerts nightly, ATM, crafts and heated pool May 1 through Nov. 1 on premises. Handicap access. Antiquing, fishing, golf, live theater, parks, shopping, sporting events, tennis and water sports nearby.

Pets allowed: Home to Scott Pet Hotel.

Location: Country.

Publicity: *WTWO, WTHI and WBAK.*

Certificate may be used: Year-round, Sunday through Thursday nights except during special events and the Parke County Covered Bridge festival.

Knoll Inn

317 W High St
Rockville, IN 47872
(765)569-6345 (888)569-6345 Fax:(765)569-3445
Internet: www.coveredbridges.com/knoll-inn/
E-mail: knollinn@abcs.com

Circa 1842. This inn, of Greek Revival and Italianate influence, is situated on one acre of gardens in the historic district. Renovated recently, it offers suites with whirlpool tubs and romantic decor. Farmer's Strada is a favored dish for breakfast, which also includes freshly baked breads and muffins, homemade preserves and fresh fruit such as strawberries and peaches in season. The area offers 32 covered bridges for exploring.

Innkeeper(s): Mark & Sharon Nolin. $85-110. MC, VISA, PC, TC. 3 suites and 1 conference room. Breakfast included in rates. Types of meals: Full bkfst, cont plus, cont and early coffee/tea. Beds: Q. Cable TV, ceiling fan, VCR, two suites with whirlpool spas and in room. Air conditioning. Spa on premises. Antiquing, fishing, golf, covered bridges, parks, shopping, sporting events, tennis and water sports nearby.

Location: small town.

Certificate may be used: Jan. 30 to Dec. 31, Sunday through Wednesday nights. Subject to availability.

Suits Us B&B

514 N College St
Rockville, IN 47872-1511
(765)569-5660 (888)478-4878

Circa 1883. Sixty miles west of Indianapolis is this stately Colonial Revival inn, where Woodrow Wilson, Annie Oakley and James Witcomb Riley were once guests of the Strause Family. The inn offers video library and bicycles. There are 32 covered bridges to visit in the small, surrounding county. Turkey Run State Park is nearby. The Ernie Pyle State Historic Site, Raccoon State Recreation Area and four golf courses are within easy driving distance.

Innkeeper(s): Andy & Lianna Willhite. $60-150. TC. 4 rooms with PB and 1 suite. Breakfast included in rates. Types of meals: Full bkfst and early coffee/tea. Beds: KQD. Cable TV, ceiling fan and VCR in room. Air conditioning. Bicycles, movie library and exercise room on premises. Antiquing, fishing, golf, parks, shopping and water sports nearby.

Location: City.

Publicity: *Touring America and Traces Historic Magazine.*

Certificate may be used: Nov. 1 to March 15; Sunday-Thursday (except special events).

South Bend A5

Oliver Inn

630 W Washington St
South Bend, IN 46601-1444
(219)232-4545 (888)697-4466 Fax:(219)288-9788
Internet: www.oliverinn.com
E-mail: oliver@michiana.org

Circa 1886. This stately Queen Anne Victorian sits amid 30 towering maples and was once home to Josephine Oliver Ford, daughter of James Oliver, of chilled plow fame. Located in South Bend's historic district, this inn offers a comfortable library and nine inviting guest rooms, some with built-in fireplaces or double Jacuzzis. The inn is within walking distance of downtown and is next door to the Tippecanoe Restaurant in the Studebaker Mansion.

Innkeeper(s): Richard & Venera Monahan. $95-145. MC, VISA, AX, DS, PC, TC. 9 rooms, 7 with PB, 2 with FP, 3 suites and 1 conference room. Breakfast and snacks/refreshments included in rates. Types of meals: Full bkfst and early coffee/tea. Beds: KQ. Cable TV, phone and ceiling fan in room. Air conditioning. Fax and baby Grand with computer disk system on premises. Antiquing, canoeing/kayaking, fishing, fine dining, Amish country and Notre Dame, live theater, museums, parks, shopping, cross-country skiing, sporting events and water sports nearby.

Location: Lake Michigan (35 miles), Chicago (90 miles).

Certificate may be used: January through December, Sunday-Thursday.

Warsaw B6

Ramada White Hill Manor

2513 E Center St
Warsaw, IN 46580-3819
(219)269-6933 Fax:(219)268-1936

Circa 1934. This elegantly crafted 4,500-square-foot English Tudor was constructed during the Depression when fine artisans were available at low cost. Handsome arched entryways and ceilings, crown molding and mullioned windows create a gracious intimate atmosphere. The mansion has been carefully renovated and decorated with a combination of traditional furnishings and contemporary English fabrics. The manor is located next to the renowned Ramada Wagon Wheel Theatre. Guests enjoy use of pools, a fitness center and game room at the adjacent Ramada Plaza Hotel.

Innkeeper(s): Melissa Cuningham. $80-139. MC, VISA, AX, DC, DS. 8 rooms with PB. Breakfast included in rates. Type of meal: Full bkfst. Beds: KQ. Handicap access. Antiquing, fishing, trails, watersports and tennis nearby.

Publicity: *Indiana Business and USA Today.*

"It's the perfect place for an at-home getaway."

Certificate may be used: Nov. 1-Feb. 1, Sunday-Friday.

Iowa

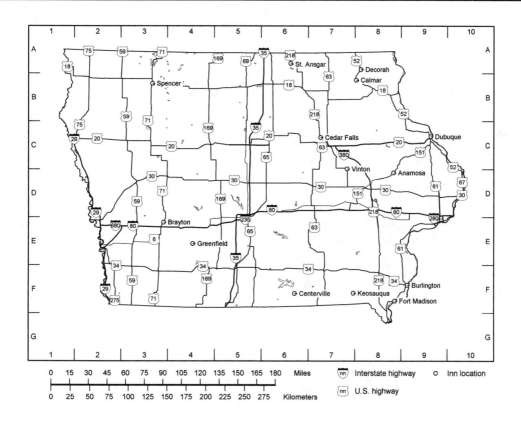

	1	2	3	4	5	6	7	8	9	10	

Scale:
0 15 30 45 60 75 90 105 120 135 150 165 180 Miles
0 25 50 75 100 125 150 175 200 225 250 275 Kilometers

- (nn) Interstate highway
- (nn) U.S. highway
- ○ Inn location

Anamosa   D8

The Shaw House
509 S Oak St
Anamosa, IA 52205-1537
(319)462-4485

Circa 1872. Framed by enormous old oak trees, this three-story
Italianate mansion was built in the style of a Maine sea captain's
house. Bordered by sweeping lawns and situated on a hillside
on 45 acres, the inn provides views of graceful pastureland from
the front porch swing and the tower. Polished oak, walnut and
pine floors highlight the carved woodwork and antique furnishings. Guests can enjoy a short walk to downtown.

Innkeeper(s): Constance & Andy McKean. $70-90. 4 rooms, 2 with PB, 1
with FP, 1 suite and 1 conference room. Breakfast included in rates. Types of
meals: Full bkfst and early coffee/tea. Beds: QDT. TV and phone in room. Air

conditioning. Child care on premises. Antiquing, fishing, live theater, shop-
ping, downhill skiing, cross-country skiing and sporting events nearby.
Location: Hilltop overlooking town.
Publicity: *Cedar Rapids Gazette* and *Anamosa Journal-Eureka.*

"The views were fantastic as was the hospitality."
Certificate may be used: Based on availability.

Brayton   E3

Hallock House B&B
PO Box 19, 3265 Jay Ave
Brayton, IA 50042-0019
(712)549-2449 (800)945-0663

Circa 1882. Innkeeper Ruth Barton's great-great uncle, Isaac
Hallock, built this Queen Anne Victorian. The home is an architectural gem, featuring high ceilings, ornate woodwork, carved

pocket doors and a built-in china cupboard. And as is the Victorian tradition, several porches decorate the exterior. The home is across the street from the site of an old stagecoach stop, which bought an abundance of cattlemen into town, many of whom stayed in the Hallock House. The innkeepers offer stable facilities and an exercise area for guests traveling with horses.

Innkeeper(s): Guy & Ruth Barton. $45. VISA, TC. 2 rooms with PB. Breakfast included in rates. Type of meal: Full bkfst. Beds: QD. Ceiling fan in room. Air conditioning. VCR, bicycles and pet boarding on premises. Antiquing, fishing, parks and shopping nearby.

Pets Allowed.

Location: Country.

Certificate may be used: Anytime except holidays, reservation required.

Burlington   F9

Schramm House B&B

616 Columbia St
Burlington, IA 52601
(800)683-7117 Fax:(319)754-0373

Circa 1866. "Colossal" would be an excellent word to describe this Queen Anne Victorian. The home is an impressive site in this Burlington historic district. The exterior is brick on the first story with clapboard on the second, and a third-story tower is one of the architectural highlights. Inside, the parquet floors and woodwork have been  restored to their 19th-century grandeur. The home was built just after the Civil War by a local department store owner. Additions were made in the 1880s. Eventually, the home was converted into apartments, so the innkeepers took on quite a task refurbishing the place back to its original state. The Victorian is decorated with the innkeepers collection of antiques. One particularly appealing guest room includes an exposed brick wall and tin ceiling. Breakfast might begin with a baked pear topped with toasted almonds and a raspberry sauce. From there, freshly baked muffins arrive, followed by an entree, perhaps a frittata or French toast. All courses are served with fine china and crystal. The home is just six blocks from the Mississippi, and don't pass up a walk down the historic Snake Alley.

Innkeeper(s): Sandy & Bruce Morrison. $85-125. MC, VISA, AX, DS, PC, TC. 4 rooms with PB. Breakfast included in rates. Types of meals: Full bkfst and early coffee/tea. Beds: Q. Turndown service, ceiling fan, robes and hair dryers in room. VCR, fax and library on premises. Antiquing, fishing, golf, parks, shopping and tennis nearby.

Location: Small town historic district.

Publicity: *Hawk Eye.*

Certificate may be used: Sunday-Thursday, all year.

Calmar   B8

Calmar Guesthouse

103 W North St
Calmar, IA 52132-7605
(319)562-3851
E-mail: lbkruse@salamander.com

Circa 1890. This beautifully restored Victorian home was built by John B. Kay, a lawyer and poet. Stained-glass windows, carved moldings, an oak-and-walnut staircase and gleaming woodwork

highlight the gracious interior. A grandfather clock ticks in the living room. In the foyer, a friendship yellow rose is incorporated into the stained-glass window pane. Breakfast is served in the formal dining room. The Laura Ingalls Wilder Museum is nearby in Burr Oak. The Bily Brothers Clock Museum, Smallest Church, Luther College and Norwegian Museum are located nearby.

Innkeeper(s): Lucille Kruse. $59-65. MC, VISA, PC, TC. Breakfast included in rates. Types of meals: Full bkfst and early coffee/tea. Beds: Q. Cable TV in room. Air conditioning. VCR, bicycles and library on premises. Antiquing, fishing, live theater, parks, shopping, downhill skiing, cross-country skiing, sporting events and water sports nearby.

Location: City.

Publicity: *Iowa Farmer Today, Calmar Courier, Minneapolis Star-Tribune, Home and Away* and *Iowan.*

"What a delight it was to stay here. No one could have made our stay more welcome or enjoyable."

Certificate may be used: Monday to Thursday, April to October only.

Cedar Falls   C7

The House By The Side of The Road

6804 Ranchero Rd
Cedar Falls, IA 50613-9689
(319)988-3691

Circa 1901. Located on 80 acres, this inn is a country-style farmhouse. Perfect for those seeking a retreat in the countryside, the rooms in the House by the Side of the Road feature ceiling fans and fireplaces. Corn and soybeans are raised on the property, located near Highway 20, a main link to Dubuque and to the Cedar Rapids area. A dinner boat ride on Shell Rock River can be arranged, and an Amish community is nearby for quilt shopping and crafts.

Innkeeper(s): Harlan S. Hughes. $45. PC, TC. 2 rooms. Breakfast included in rates. Types of meals: Full bkfst and early coffee/tea. Beds: KD. Air conditioning. VCR on premises. Antiquing, fishing, golf, live theater, parks, shopping, sporting events, tennis and water sports nearby.

Location: Many bike trails.

Publicity: *Waterloo-Cedar Falls Courier.*

Certificate may be used: All year, if available.

Centerville   F6

One of A Kind

314 W State St
Centerville, IA 52544
(515)437-4540 Fax:(515)437-4540

Circa 1867. This large, three-story brick home with mansard roof and tall bays is the second oldest house in town. The innkeeper has filled the inn with "One of a Kind" craft and decorative items for sale, created on the premises or by local artisans. There is also a tea room, popular for its chicken soup and homemade croissant sandwiches, so of course you can expect a yummy breakfast, as well. Guest quarters are decorated with antiques and reproductions spiced with a variety of collectibles. The largest fish hatchery in the world is a short drive away at Lake Rathbun, but there is plenty to do within walking distance.

Innkeeper(s): Jack & Joyce Stufflebeem. $35-60. MC, VISA, AX, DS, PC, TC. 5 rooms, 2 with PB and 1 suite. Breakfast and snacks/refreshments included in rates. Types of meals: Full bkfst and early coffee/tea. Beds: DT. Cable TV, turndown service and ceiling fan in room. Air conditioning. VCR, fax and copier on premises. Antiquing, fishing, golf, live theater, parks, shopping, sporting events, tennis and water sports nearby.

Location: Small town.

Certificate may be used: January through December.

Decorah A8

Elmhurst Cottage

3618 - 258th Ave
Decorah, IA 52101
(319)735-5310 (888)413-5600
E-mail: elmcottage@aol.com

Circa 1885. Located on 80 acres, this family cottage provides simple accommodations in a peaceful farm setting. Outdoor activities such as volleyball, horseshoes, tetherball and badminton are available on the property. Area attractions include the Laura Ingalls-Wilder Museum, Norwegian-American Museum, local caves and Amish community tours and shops.

Innkeeper(s): Opal Underbakke. $28-65. MC, VISA, DS, PC. 9 rooms, 1 with PB, 1 suite and 1 cottage. Breakfast included in rates. Types of meals: Full bkfst and early coffee/tea. Beds: KQDT. Alarm clock and wall clock in room. Air conditioning. VCR on premises. Handicap access. Antiquing, canoeing/kayaking, fishing, golf, live theater, parks, shopping, downhill skiing, sporting events and water sports nearby.

Pets allowed: deposit required, restricted areas.

Location: Country.

Certificate may be used: Jan. 1 through Dec. 31, Sunday-Thursday, subject to availability.

Dubuque C9

The Hancock House

1105 Grove Ter
Dubuque, IA 52001-4644
(319)557-8989 Fax:(319)583-0813
Internet: www.thehancockhouse.com

Circa 1891. Victorian splendor can be found at The Hancock House, one of Dubuque's most striking examples of Queen Anne architecture. Rooms feature period furnishings and offer views of the Mississippi River states of Iowa, Illinois and Wisconsin. The Hancock House, listed in the National Register, boasts several unique features, including a fireplace judged blue-ribbon best at the 1893 World's Fair in Chicago. Guests can enjoy the porch swings, wicker furniture and spectacular views from the wraparound front porch.

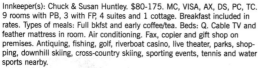

Innkeeper(s): Chuck & Susan Huntley. $80-175. MC, VISA, AX, DS, PC, TC. 9 rooms with PB, 3 with FP, 4 suites and 1 cottage. Breakfast included in rates. Types of meals: Full bkfst and early coffee/tea. Beds: Q. Cable TV and feather mattress in room. Air conditioning. Fax, copier and gift shop on premises. Antiquing, fishing, golf, riverboat casino, live theater, parks, shopping, downhill skiing, cross-country skiing, sporting events, tennis and water sports nearby.

Location: City.

Publicity: *Victorian Sampler (Cover).*

Certificate may be used: Nov. 1 to April 30, Sunday through Thursday.

Lighthouse Valleyview B&B Inn

15937 Lore Mound Rd
Dubuque, IA 52002
(319)583-7327 (800)407-7023 Fax:(319)583-7327

Circa 1963. Although 12 miles from the nearest body of water, this recently built lighthouse has a gift shop inside. To arrive, guests drive past farms and cornfields. Once inside the building, on clear days they can see views from the top that include

three states: Iowa, Illinois and Wisconsin. Other rooms at the hilltop country house are decorated in themes such as Oriental, Safari and Old West. The Nautilus Room offers a collection of decorative lighthouses. There is an indoor pool, hot tub and fireplace for guest use. Coconut Praline French Toast is a favorite breakfast dish.

Innkeeper(s): JoAnn & Bill Klauer. $85-150. MC, VISA, AX, DS, PC, TC. 4 rooms, 1 with PB, 1 with FP and 1 suite. Breakfast and snacks/refreshments included in rates. Types of meals: Full bkfst and early coffee/tea. Beds: KQT. Cable TV, ceiling fan, VCR and coffee service in room. Fax, spa, swimming, sauna, bicycles, library and sauna on premises. Antiquing, fishing, golf, live theater, parks, shopping, downhill skiing, cross-country skiing, tennis and water sports nearby.

Location: country hilltop.

Publicity: *Julien's Journal.*

Certificate may be used: Feb. 28 through Dec. 1, Monday-Thursday.

The Mandolin Inn

199 Loras Blvd
Dubuque, IA 52001-4857
(319)556-0069 (800)524-7996 Fax:(319)556-0587
Internet: www.mandolininn.com
E-mail: innkeeper@mandolininn.com

Circa 1908. This three-story brick Edwardian with Queen Anne wraparound veranda boasts a mosaic-tiled porch floor. Inside are in-laid mahogany and rosewood floors, bay windows and a turret that starts in the parlor and ascends to the second-floor Holly Marie Room, decorated in a wedding motif. This room features a seven-piece French Walnut bedroom suite and a crystal chandelier. A gourmet breakfast is served in the dining room with a fantasy forest mural from the turn-of-the-century. There is an herb garden outside the kitchen. A church is across the street and riverboat gambling is 12 blocks away.

Innkeeper(s): Amy Boynton. $75-135. MC, VISA, AX, DS, PC, TC. 7 rooms, 5 with PB and 2 conference rooms. Breakfast included in rates. Types of meals: Full gourmet bkfst and early coffee/tea. Beds: KQ. Cable TV in room. Central air. Fax on premises. Antiquing, live theater, parks, shopping, downhill skiing, cross-country skiing, sporting events and water sports nearby.

Location: City.

"From the moment we entered the Mandolin, we felt at home. I know we'll be back."

Certificate may be used: Sunday through Thursday. Year-round, except for holidays.

Fort Madison F8

Kingsley Inn

707 Avenue H (Hwy 61)
Fort Madison, IA 52627
(319)372-7074 (800)441-2327 Fax:(319)372-7096
Internet: www.kingsleyinn.com
E-mail: kingsley@interl.net

Circa 1858. Overlooking the Mississippi River, this century-old inn is located in downtown Fort Madison. Though furnished with antiques, all 14 rooms offer modern amenities and private baths (some with whirlpools) as well as river views. A two-bed-

room, two-bath suite also is available. There is a restaurant, Alphas on the Riverfront, and a gift shop on the premises.
Innkeeper(s): Alida Willis. $75-135. MC, VISA, AX, DC, DS. 14 rooms with PB, 1 suite and 1 conference room. Breakfast included in rates. Types of meals: Cont plus and early coffee/tea.
Beds: KQD. Cable TV and phone in room. Air conditioning. Fax on premises. Handicap access. Antiquing, fishing, casino and shopping nearby.
Location: On Mississippi River.
Publicity: *Midwest Living.*
Certificate may be used: November through March, holidays excluded.

Greenfield E4

The Brass Lantern

2446 State Hwy 92
Greenfield, IA 50849-9757
(515)743-2031 (888)743-2031 Fax:(515)343-7500
Internet: www.brasslantern.com
E-mail: info@brasslantern.com

Circa 1918. Located on 20 acres, just minutes from the famous bridges of Madison County, this B&B is highlighted by an indoor pool complex with a curving 40-foot pool. Spacious,

luxuriously appointed guest rooms overlook the pool and rolling countryside and share the use of a fully furnished kitchenette. A hearty breakfast is served next door in the formal dining room of the antique-filled 1918 farm house.
Innkeeper(s): Terry & Margie Moore. $100-195. PC, TC. 3 rooms, 2 with PB. Breakfast included in rates. Types of meals: Full bkfst and early coffee/tea.
Beds: Q. Cable TV and phone in room. Air conditioning. Fax and copier on premises. Antiquing, fishing, golf, hunting and shopping nearby.
Pets allowed: with prior approval.
Location: Country.
"Iowa is a beautiful place and The Brass Lantern is its crown jewel!"
Certificate may be used: Nov. 15-Feb. 15, Monday-Thursday, holidays excluded.

Keosauqua F7

Hotel Manning

100 Van Buren St
Keosauqua, IA 52565
(319)293-3232 (800)728-2718 Fax:(319)293-9960

Circa 1899. This historic riverfront inn offers a peek at bygone days. Its steamboat gothic exterior is joined by an interior that strives for historic authenticity. All bedrooms are furnished with antiques. Lacey-Keosauqua State Park and Lake Sugema are within easy driving distance. Inn guests enjoy a full breakfast. There is a 19-room, modern motel adjacent to the inn.
Innkeeper(s): Ron & Connie Davenport. $35-72. MC, VISA, DS, PC. 18 rooms, 10 with PB, 2 suites and 1 conference room. Breakfast included in

rates. Beds: QD. Ceiling fan in room. Air conditioning. VCR, fax, copier and 19 room modern motel adjacent on premises. Antiquing, fishing, nature trails, parks and shopping nearby.
Location: Small town on riverfront.
Publicity: *Midwest Living.*
Certificate may be used: Sunday-Thursday, May-October; anytime, November to April.

Mason House Inn of Bentonsport

RR 2, Box 237
Keosauqua, IA 52565
(319)592-3133 (800)592-3133

Circa 1846. A Murphy-style copper bathtub folds down out of the wall at this unusual inn built by Mormon craftsmen, who stayed in Bentonsport for one year on their trek to Utah. More than half of the furniture is original to the home, including a nine-foot walnut headboard and a nine-foot mirror. This is the only operating pre-Civil War steamboat inn in Iowa. Guests can imagine the days when steamboats made their way up and down the Des Moines River, while taking in the scenery. A full breakfast is served, but if guests crave a mid-day snack, each room is equipped with its own stocked cookie jar.
Innkeeper(s): William McDermet III. $64-79. MC, VISA. 9 rooms with PB and 1 conference room. Breakfast included in rates. Types of meals: Full bkfst and early coffee/tea. Beds: KQD. Cookie jar filled in room. Air conditioning. Handicap access. Antiquing, shopping and cross-country skiing nearby.
Location: Rural by river.
Publicity: *Des Moines Register, Decatur Herald & Review, AAA Home & Away and Country Magazine.*
"The attention to detail was fantastic, food was wonderful and the setting was fascinating."
Certificate may be used: Sunday through Thursday, all year.

Spencer B3

The Hannah Marie Country Inn

4070 Highway 71
Spencer, IA 51301-2033
(712)262-1286 Fax:(712)262-3294
Internet: www.nwiowabb.com/hannah.htm
E-mail: hmci@rconnect.com

Circa 1907. Enjoy the romance of the country at Hannah Marie's, tucked on a rural highway in the midst of golden fields of corn. Feather beds topped with down comforters, in-room double whirlpool tubs, softened water and bubble bath are some of the luxurious amenities. Each guest room has a special theme. Guests are given parasols for strolling along the grounds, which has herb, flower and vegetable gardens. The innkeepers host themed tea parties, children's etiquette gatherings, herb workshops and afternoon tea. Guests can mingle with the Queen of Hearts or perhaps Queen Elizabeth at a garden party. A butterfly garden also has been added and there's a labyrinth path. The full breakfasts are served by candlelight, or guests can opt for lighter fare delivered to their guest room door in a basket. Early evening refreshments also are included in the rates.

Innkeeper(s): Mary Nichols. $79-115. MC, VISA, DS, PC, TC. 6 rooms with PB and 1 conference room. Breakfast included in rates. Types of meals: Full gourmet bkfst, cont and early coffee/tea. Beds: Q. Ceiling fan and double whirlpools in room. Air conditioning. Amusement parks, antiquing, fishing, live theater, parks, shopping and water sports nearby.

Pets allowed: Outside.

Location: Country.

Publicity: *Midwest Living, Partners, Des Moines Register, Sioux City Journal and Home and Away.*

"Best bed & breakfast in Iowa."—Des Moines Register

Certificate may be used: April, May, November, December, Sunday-Thursday.

St. Ansgar A6

Blue Belle Inn B&B

PO Box 205, 513 W 4th St
St. Ansgar, IA 50472-0205
(515)736-2225 Fax:(515)736-4024
Internet: www.deskmedia.com/~bluebelle
E-mail: bluebelle@smig.net

Circa 1896. This home was purchased from a Knoxville, Tenn., mail-order house. It's difficult to believe that stunning features, such as a tin ceiling, stained-glass windows, intricate woodwork and pocket doors could have come via the mail, but these original items are still

here for guests to admire. Rooms are named after books special to the innkeeper. Four of the rooms include a Jacuzzi tub, and the Never Neverland room has a

clawfoot tub. Other rooms offer a skylight, fireplace or perhaps a white iron bed. During the Christmas season, every room has its own decorated tree. The innkeeper hosts a variety of themed luncheons, dinners and events, such as the April in Paris cooking workshop. Mother's Day brunches, the "Some Enchanted Evening" dinner or the posh "Pomp and Circumstance" dinner are some of the possibilities.

Innkeeper(s): Sherrie Hansen. $65-140. MC, VISA, AX, DS, PC, TC. 6 rooms, 5 with PB, 2 with FP, 2 suites and 2 conference rooms. Breakfast included in rates. Types of meals: Full gourmet bkfst, cont plus, cont and early coffee/tea. Beds: KQT. Cable TV, VCR and jacuzzi for two in room. Air conditioning. Fax, library, kitchenette, Internet access, piano, treadmill and movies on premises. Antiquing, fishing, golf, clay trap shooting, hunting, parks, shopping and water sports nearby.

Location: Small town.

Publicity: *Minneapolis Star Tribune, Post-Bulletin, Midwest Living, Country, AAA Home & Away and Des Moines Register.*

Certificate may be used: Nov. 1-April 30, Monday-Thursday nights only, holidays excluded, Dec. 26-31 excluded, subject to availability.

Vinton C7

Lion & The Lamb B&B

913 2nd Ave
Vinton, IA 52349-1729
(319)472-5086 (888)390-5262 Fax:(319)472-5086
Internet: //members.aol.com/lionlambbb/bnb.htm
E-mail: lionlamb@lionlamb.com

Circa 1892. This Queen Anne Victorian, a true "Painted Lady," boasts a stunning exterior with intricate chimneys, gingerbread trim, gables and turrets. The home still maintains its original pocket doors and parquet flooring, and antiques add to the nostalgic flavor. One room boasts a 150-year-old bedroom set. Breakfasts, as any meal in such fine a house should, are served on china. Succulent French toast topped with powdered sugar and a rich strawberry sauce is a specialty. In the evenings, desserts are served.

Innkeeper(s): Richard & Rachel Waterbury. $75-105. MC, VISA, AX, DS, PC, TC. 4 rooms, 2 with PB, 2 with FP. Breakfast included in rates. Types of meals: Full bkfst and early coffee/tea. Beds: KQ. TV and ceiling fan in room. Air conditioning. VCR, fax and bicycles on premises. Antiquing, fishing, golf, live theater, parks, shopping, cross-country skiing, tennis and water sports nearby.

Location: City.

Publicity: *Cedar Valley Times, Waterloo Courier, Cedar Rapids Gazette and KWWL-Channel 7 Neighborhood News.*

"It is a magical place!"

Certificate may be used: Sunday to Thursday, September to May.

Kansas

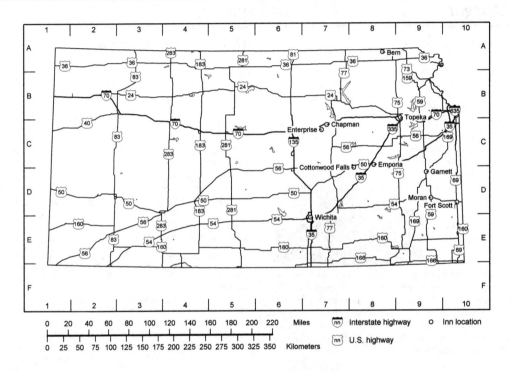

		Miles	
0 20 40 60 80 100 120 140 160 180 200 220	Miles	Interstate highway	o Inn location
0 25 50 75 100 125 150 175 200 225 250 275 300 325 350	Kilometers	U.S. highway	

Bern   A8

Lear Acres B&B

RR 1 Box 31
Bern, KS 66408-9715
(785)336-3903

Circa 1918. A working farm just south of the Nebraska border,
Lear Acres is exactly the down-home setting it appears to be.
The two-story farmhouse features three spacious guest rooms,
all with views of the surrounding countryside. Many of the inn's
furnishings are period pieces from the early 1900s. Guests will
be greeted by a menagerie of farm pets and animals, adding to
the distinctly country atmosphere. The full breakfast features
food from the innkeepers' farm and garden. Fall or winter guests
may ask for Grandma's cozy feather bed.

Innkeeper(s): Toby Lear. $35-38. 3 rooms. Breakfast included in rates. Type of
meal: Full bkfst. Phone, turndown service, ceiling fan, VCR and clock in room.
Air conditioning. Antiquing nearby.

Certificate may be used: Any weekend, except Memorial Day with minimum
of 10-day advance reservation.

Chapman   C7

Windmill Inn B&B

1787 Rain Rd
Chapman, KS 67431-9317
(785)263-8755

Circa 1917. The Windmill Inn is a place of memories. Many were
created by the innkeeper's grandparents, who built the home.
Others are the happy remembrances guests take home. The home
is filled with antiques, family heirlooms. Stained glass and a window seat add to the charm. Evening meals or picnic lunches are
also available. The wraparound porch offers a relaxing swing, and
on starry nights, the outdoor spa is the place to be. Historic
Abilene is just a few miles down the road, offering a glimpse of an
authentic Old West town, located on the Chisolm Trail.

Innkeeper(s): Tim & Deb Sanders. $65-85. 4 rooms. Breakfast included in
rates. Type of meal: Full bkfst.

Certificate may be used: Year-round, Sunday through Thursday, holidays excluded.

Cottonwood Falls   D8

1874 Stonehouse B&B on Mulberry Hill

Rt 1, Box 67A
Cottonwood Falls, KS 66845
(316)273-8481
Internet: www.kansas-stonehouse.com
E-mail: shmh1874@aol.com

Circa 1874. More than 100 acres surround this historic home, which is one of the state's oldest native stone homes that is still in use. Each guest room offers something special. The Rose Room includes a sleigh bed, while the Blue Room and Yellow Room offer views either of the quarry pond or the Flint Hills. Explore the property and you'll see wildlife, an old stone barn and corral ruins. The Cottonwood River runs through the property at one point, offering fishing. The home is five miles from Tallgrass Prairie National Preserve.
Innkeeper(s): Diane Ware. $75-100. MC, VISA, AX. 3 rooms with PB. Breakfast included in rates. Type of meal: Full gourmet bkfst. Beds: KQT. Ceiling fan in room. Air conditioning. VCR, fax and library on premises. Antiquing, fishing, golf, parks and shopping nearby.
Pets allowed: outside kennel only.
Location: Near national park reserve.

"I have never felt so pampered. Our walk around the countryside was so peaceful and beautiful."

Certificate may be used: Sunday-Thursday from Nov. 15-March 14, except holidays.

Emporia   C8

The White Rose Inn

901 Merchant St
Emporia, KS 66801-2813
(316)343-6336

Circa 1902. Emporia is a Midwest college town, and the White Rose Inn is a mere three blocks from Emporia State University. This Queen Anne Victorian home offers three private suites for its guests, all with a sitting room and queen beds. Each morning, guests will be treated to a different and delicious menu. Guests who so desire may have breakfast in bed, and the innkeepers will happily arrange for a massage, manicure or pedicure. The inn also hosts weddings and family reunions.
Innkeeper(s): Samuel & Lisa Tosti. $59-119. MC, VISA, AX, DC, DS, TC. 8 rooms with PB and 4 suites. Breakfast included in rates. Types of meals: Full gourmet bkfst and early coffee/tea. Beds: Q. Cable TV in room. Air conditioning. VCR on premises. Antiquing, fishing, live theater, parks & sporting events nearby.
Location: City.
Certificate may be used: Monday through Thursday, large suites only.

Enterprise   C7

Ehrsam Place B&B

103 S Grant
Enterprise, KS 67441
(785)263-8747 Fax:(785)263-8548
Internet: www.kbba.com

Circa 1879. In its early days, this home and the family who lived in it were the talk of the town. The family held an abundance of well-attended parties, and many rumors were spread about why the Ehrsam company safe was kept in the home's basement. Rumors aside, the home features a variety of architectural styles, leaning toward Georgian, with columns gracing the front entrance. The 20-acre grounds are fun to explore, offering a windmill, silo, stables, a carriage house and creek. The innkeepers encourage guests to explore the home as well, which rises three stories. The basement still houses the illusive safe. Rooms are decorated to reflect the area's history. Guests can enjoy breakfast in bed if they choose. With advance notice, the innkeepers will prepare hors d'oeuvres, picnic lunches and dinners for their guests. Candlelight dinners for two also are available, and turn-down service is one of the romantic amenities.
Innkeeper(s): Mary & William Lambert. $55-85. MC, VISA, PC, TC. 4 suites and 1 conference room. Breakfast, afternoon tea and snacks/refreshments included in rates. Types of meals: Full bkfst and early coffee/tea. Beds: Q. Cable TV, turndown service and ceiling fan in room. Air conditioning. VCR, fax, library and hot tub spa on premises. Antiquing, fishing, golf, eisenhower Museum, Scenic Railroad, live theater, parks, shopping, sporting events and tennis nearby.
Location: near historic Abilene.

"Thank you for history, laughs and most all sharing your treasures with us."

Certificate may be used: All year, if on a weekend, stay must include a Thursday or Sunday night.

Fort Scott   D10

The Chenault Mansion

820 S National Ave
Fort Scott, KS 66701-1321
(316)223-6800

Circa 1887. Curved-glass windows, stained glass, ornate woodwork, pocket doors and fireplaces have been refurbished in this gracious home to reflect its beginnings in the late 19th century. Antiques and a large china and glass collection add ambiance to the elegant rooms. Full breakfasts are served in the well-appointed dining room. The David P. & Mary Josephine Thomas Suite, located in the tower room, boasts a sitting room and wicker furnishings. Other rooms feature special pieces such as a hand-carved walnut bed, and two of the rooms have fireplaces.
Innkeeper(s): Robert Schafer. $65-80. MC, VISA, DS. 5 rooms. Breakfast included in rates. Type of meal: Full bkfst.
Certificate may be used: All year - if stay is on weekend, Thursday or Sunday night must be included.

Lyons' Victorian Mansion

742 S National Ave
Fort Scott, KS 66701-1319
(316)223-3644 (800)784-8378

Circa 1876. This four-story, landmark Italianate manor is one of the first mansions built on the prairie. The home features original chandeliers, which highlight the polished wood floors, family heirlooms and antiques. Innkeeper Pat Lyons serves up an abundant, Southern-style breakfast with treats such as biscuits and gravy or French toast with custard filling. Snacks are always available, and Pat keeps rooms stocked with tea and coffee service. Afternoon teas are served by request, and turndown service is one of the many romantic touches guests will enjoy. Pat has created several special packages for her guests, including her "Mystery in a Parlor" event, which combines gourmet meals with a murder-mystery game.
Innkeeper(s): Pat Lyons. $85-150. MC, VISA, AX, DS. 4 rooms, 3 with PB and 1 suite. Breakfast included in rates. Type of meal: Full bkfst.
Certificate may be used: Dec. 1 to March 31, Sunday-Thursday.

Garnett D9

Kirk House

145 W 4th Ave
Garnett, KS 66032-1313
(785)448-5813 Fax:(785)448-5813
E-mail: khmge@kanza.net

Circa 1913. Those interested in the arts will love Kirk House. The innkeepers have backgrounds as art dealers, and they count weaving and classical music among their other interests. Guests

receive plenty of pampering at this inn, located in eastern Kansas, south of Ottawa. Food preparation and presentation are stressed here, with visitors enjoying gourmet breakfasts, afternoon

teas and evening desserts. The inn also offers turndown service, two sitting rooms and a library for further relaxation.
Innkeeper(s): Robert Cugno & Robert Logan. $100-135. PC, TC. 5 rooms, 1 with PB. Breakfast included in rates. Type of meal: Full gourmet bkfst. Beds: QDT. Turndown service in room. VCR on premises. Antiquing, fishing, live theater, shopping, sporting events and water sports nearby.
Location: City.
Publicity: *Metro News, Kansas, Topeka Capitol Journal, Wichita Eagle, Fox TV and KCPT TV.*
"What a nugget of class, beauty & culture in the middle of Kansas! A feast for the eyes & mouth, too much to absorb in one visit. Gracious, knowledgeable, sensitive innkeepers. We can't rate this wonderful spot too highly."
Certificate may be used: Monday through Thursday, Nov. 1-March 1.

Moran D9

Hedgeapple Acres B&B

4430 US Hwy
Moran, KS 66755-9500
(316)237-4646

Circa 1974. Nestled on 80-acres of farmland, this country home offers comfortable furnishings and plenty of places to relax. One of the bedchambers boasts a whirlpool tub, while another includes a fireplace. Guests not only enjoy a hearty country breakfast, but supper as well. Spend the day exploring the area, which includes historic Fort Scott, or grab your rod and reel and try out the farm's two stocked ponds.
Innkeeper(s): Jack & Ann Donaldson. $59-75. MC, VISA, AX, DS, PC, TC. 4 rooms with PB, 1 with FP and 1 conference room. Breakfast and dinner included in rates. Types of meals: Full bkfst and early coffee/tea. Beds: K. Ceiling fan in room. Air conditioning. VCR on premises. Handicap access. Antiquing, fishing, golf, fishing ponds, walking trails, live theater, parks and shopping nearby.
Location: Country.
Certificate may be used: Sunday to Thursday, Jan. 10-Nov. 10.

Topeka B9

The Elderberry B&B

1035 SW Fillmore St
Topeka, KS 66604
(785)235-6309

Circa 1887. Within walking distance of the state capitol building is this Queen Anne Victorian inn, which once was home to a millinery parlor. The present owners have an impressive collection of hats and other accessories and have furnished the inn with an array of family antiques. Listed in both the State and National Register of Historic Places, the home's historic details include beveled glass and beautiful oak woodwork. Guest rooms are filled with authentic touches of the 1880s. The paisley Holliday Room

is named for the first president of the Atchison, Topeka and Santa Fe Railroad, and the floral Gage Room is named for a famous local sculptor whose work is featured on the capitol grounds.
Innkeeper(s): Carol & Jerry Grant. $55. PC, TC. 2 rooms with PB. Breakfast and snacks/refreshments included in rates. Types of meals: Full bkfst, cont plus, cont and early coffee/tea. Beds: QD. Phone, turndown service and ceiling fan in room. Air conditioning. VCR on premises. Antiquing, fishing, golf, parks, shopping and tennis nearby.
Location: City.
Publicity: *Topeka Metro News and The Capital-Journal.*
"Wonderful hosts, excellent food and beautiful place to stay."
Certificate may be used: Jan. 1-Dec. 31, Sunday-Thursday. Holidays excluded.

Wichita E7

Castle Inn Riverside

1155 N River Blvd
Wichita, KS 67203
(316)263-9300
Internet: www.castleinnriverside.com
E-mail: lcastle@gte.net

Circa 1886. This luxurious inn is a stunning example of Richardsonian Romanesque architecture. The home includes 14 guest rooms, each individually appointed. Twelve of the guest rooms include a fireplace, and six include a double whirlpool tub. Guests are pampered with a gourmet breakfast, and later in the day, with a sampling of wine, cheeses, light hors d'oeuvres, gourmet coffees and teas and homemade desserts. A liqueur cabinet is available for an after-dinner drink or night cap. The inn offers many amenities for its business travelers, including rooms equipped with TVs, VCRs, telephones and dataports. The inn is just a few minutes from downtown Wichita.
Innkeeper(s): Terry & Paula Lowry. $125-275. MC, VISA, DC, CB, DS, PC, TC. 14 rooms with PB, 12 with FP, 1 suite & 1 conference room. Breakfast included in rates. Types of meals: Full gourmet bkfst & snacks/refreshments. Beds: KQ. TV, phone & VCR in room. Air conditioning. Fax & copier on premises. Antiquing, fishing, live theater, parks, shopping, sporting events & water sports nearby.
Location: City.
Publicity: *Country Inns, Midwest Living, Travel Holiday, Runners World, The Wichita Business Journal,* cover of State of Kansas and Wichita travel and event guides, featured in PBS series "A Taste of Kansas."
Certificate may be used: Sunday-Thursday (excluding holidays).

Inn at the Park

3751 E Douglas Ave
Wichita, KS 67218-1002
(316)652-0500 (800)258-1951 Fax:(316)652-0610
Internet: www.innatthepark.com
E-mail: iap@innatthepark.com

Circa 1910. This popular three-story brick mansion offers many special touches, including unique furnishings in each of its 12 guest rooms, three of which are suites. All of the rooms feature fireplaces. The inn's convenient location makes it ideal for business travelers or those interested in exploring Wichita at length. The inn's parkside setting provides additional opportunities for relaxation or recreation. Ask for information about shops and restaurants in Wichita's Old Town.
Innkeeper(s): Judy Hess and/or Jan Lightner. $89-164. MC, VISA, AX, DS. 12 rooms with PB, 8 with FP, 3 suites and 1 conference room. Breakfast included in rates. Types of meals: Cont plus and early coffee/tea. Beds: KQ. Cable TV, phone, turndown service and VCR in room. Air conditioning. Fax, copier and spa on premises. Antiquing, adjacent to conference facility, live theater and shopping nearby.
Location: City.
Publicity: *Wichita Business Journal.*
"This is truly a distinctive hotel. Your attention to detail is surpassed only by your devotion to excellent service."
Certificate may be used: All the time.

Kentucky

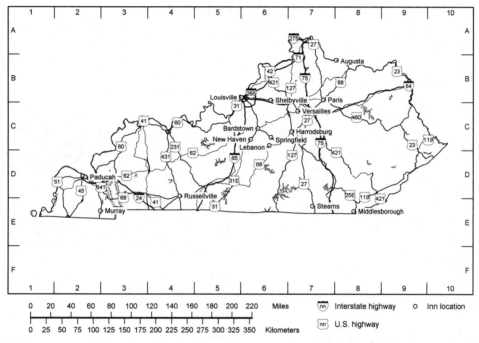

| | | | | | | | | | |
|1|2|3|4|5|6|7|8|9|10|

0 20 40 60 80 100 120 140 160 180 200 220 Miles

0 25 50 75 100 125 150 175 200 225 250 275 300 325 350 Kilometers

Interstate highway   Inn location

U.S. highway

Augusta   B8

Augusta White House Inn

307 Main St
Augusta, KY 41002
(606)756-2004 Fax:(606)756-2004

Circa 1830. The innkeepers of this Victorian hold the actual
house documents from 1850 describing the property, now in the
National Register. The first floor was once a tin shop (appliance
store) and the shopkeepers lived on the upper level. The inn
offers period antiques, crown moldings, Victorian wall coverings
and a two-bedroom cottage. There are rose gardens in the rear of
the house and an architectural antique shop on the property.

Innkeeper(s): Rebecca Spencer. $59-79. MC, VISA, AX, DS, PC, TC. 3
rooms, 1 suite and 1 cottage. Breakfast and afternoon tea included in rates.
Types of meals: Full gourmet bkfst, cont plus, cont and early coffee/tea. Beds:
KDT. Turndown service and ceiling fan in room. VCR, fax, copier, bicycles,
tennis and library on premises. Antiquing, fishing, golf, live theater, parks,
shopping, tennis and water sports nearby.

Publicity: *The Bracken County News.*

"You both truly made us welcome and comfortable in your lovely home."

Certificate may be used: Nov. 1 to May 31.

Bardstown   C6

Arbor Rose B&B

209 E Stephen Foster Ave
Bardstown, KY 40004-1513
(502)349-0014 (888)828-3330 Fax:(502)349-7322
Internet: www.arborrosebardstown.com
E-mail: aborrose@bardstown.com

Circa 1820. This late Victorian style home in the National
Register, is located in the historic district a block and a half
from Courthouse Square. Some of the rooms offer working fireplaces as well as spas or hot tubs. (The inn's fireplaces were
made by Alexander Moore, the master craftsman of "My Old
Kentucky Home.") Full gourmet country breakfasts are served,
often on the outdoor terrace in view of the gardens, Koi pond
and fountain. Smoking is not permitted.

Innkeeper(s): Judy & Derrick Melzer. $99-125. MC, VISA, AX, DS, PC, TC. 5
rooms with PB, 4 with FP and 1 conference room. Breakfast included in rates.
Types of meals: Full gourmet bkfst & early coffee/tea. Beds: K. Cable TV, ceiling
fan & VCR in room. Air conditioning. Fax, copier and spa on premises. Antiquing,
fishing, golf, Stephen Foster musical, live theater, parks, shopping & tennis nearby.
Location: Historic town.

"The food was delicious, our room very attractive and cozy."

Certificate may be used: Nov. 1-June 1, Sunday-Thursday, subject to availability.

Beautiful Dreamer B&B

440 E Stephen Foster Ave
Bardstown, KY 40004-2202
(502)348-4004 (800)811-8312

From one of the porches at this Federal-style inn, guests can view My Old Kentucky Home, the actual house which inspired the famous Stephen Foster song. Civil War troops camped in the vicinity of the home, which is located in a historic district. The home reflects a grandeur of an earlier era. Rooms are furnished elegantly with antiques and reproductions fashioned from cherry wood. One guest room includes a fireplace and Jacuzzi tub, another features a canopy bed and a double Jacuzzi. Guests are encouraged to relax on a porch or the living room. Refreshments and snacks are available in the upstairs sitting area. Coffee and tea are served prior to breakfast. The morning meal is hearty and served family style. Fresh fruit is always available, and home-baked cinnamon or sweet rolls, baked French toast, biscuits and gravy, bacon, grits and egg dishes are among the special treats that change daily.

Innkeeper(s): Lynell Ginter. $99-135. MC, VISA, PC. 4 rooms with PB, 1 with FP. Breakfast included in rates. Types of meals: Full bkfst and early coffee/tea. Beds: Q. Cable TV, phone, ceiling fan and alarm clock in room. Air conditioning. Guest refrigerator in common area on premises. Amusement parks, antiquing, fishing, golf, live theater, parks, shopping and water sports nearby.
Publicity: *Kentucky Standard, Evansville Living, Sauver Gourmet Magazine, Best Places to Stay in the South and Kentucky Living.*
Certificate may be used: Jan. 1-April 15, Sept. 30-xDec. 30. Not valid April 16-Sept. 29 or Dec. 31.

The Mansion Bed & Breakfast

1003 N 3rd St
Bardstown, KY 40004-2616
(502)348-2586 (800)399-2586 Fax:(502)349-6098
Internet: www.bbonline.com/ky/mansion

Circa 1851. The Confederate flag was raised for the first time in Kentucky on this property. The beautifully crafted Greek Revival mansion is in the National Register of Historic Places. Period antiques and hand-crocheted bedspreads, dust ruffles and shams are featured in the guest rooms. There are more than three acres of tall trees and gardens. The Courthouse in historic Bardstown is nine blocks away.

Innkeeper(s): Joseph & Charmaine Downs. $95-140. AX, DS, PC. 7 rooms with PB and 1 conference room. Breakfast included in rates. Type of meal: Cont plus. Beds: KD. Ceiling fan in room. Air conditioning. VCR on premises. Antiquing, fishing, live theater and shopping nearby.
Location: City.
Certificate may be used: All year on stays beginning on Sunday night through Wednesday.

Harrodsburg   C7

Canaan Land Farm B&B

700 Canaan Land Rd
Harrodsburg, KY 40330-9220
(606)734-3984 (888)734-3984
Internet: www.bbonline.com/ky/canaan/

Circa 1795. This National Register farmhouse, one of the oldest brick houses in Kentucky, is appointed with antiques, quilts and featherbeds. Your host is a shepherd/attorney and your hostess is a hand-spinner artist. A large flock of sheep, goats and other assorted barnyard animals graze the pastures at this

working farm. In 1995, the innkeepers reconstructed an 1815, historic log house on the grounds. The log house includes three guest rooms and two working fireplaces.

Innkeeper(s): Theo & Fred Bee. $75-125. PC, TC. 7 rooms with PB, 2 with FP. Breakfast included in rates. Types of meals: Full bkfst and early coffee/tea. Beds: DT. VCR, spa and swimming on premises. Antiquing, fishing, golf, horseback riding, parks, shopping and water sports nearby.
Location: Country.
Publicity: *Danville Advocate and Lexington Herald Leader.*

"You truly have a gift for genuine hospitality."
Certificate may be used: Anytime of year, Sunday-Thursday.

Lebanon   C6

Myrtledene B&B

370 N Spalding Ave
Lebanon, KY 40033-1557
(502)692-2223 (800)391-1721
Internet: www.bbonline.com/ky/myrtledene/

Circa 1833. Once a Confederate general's headquarters at one point during the Civil War, this pink brick inn, located at a bend in the road, has greeted visitors entering Lebanon for more than 150 years. When General John Hunt Morgan returned in 1863 to destroy the town, the white flag hoisted to signal a truce was flown at Myrtledene. A country breakfast usually features ham and biscuits as well as the innkeepers' specialty, peaches and cream French toast.

Innkeeper(s): James F. Spragens. $75. MC, VISA, PC, TC. 4 rooms, 2 with PB, 1 with FP and 1 conference room. Breakfast included in rates. Types of meals: Full gourmet bkfst and early coffee/tea. Beds: DT. Turndown service, Makers Mark bourbon and bourbon chocolates in room. Air conditioning. VCR and library on premises. Antiquing, fishing, live theater, parks, shopping and water sports nearby.
Location: City.
Publicity: *Lebanon Enterprise, Louisville Courier-Journal, Lebanon/Marion County Kentucky and Sunnyside.*

"Our night in the Cabbage Rose Room was an experience of another time, another culture. Your skill in preparing and presenting breakfast was equally elegant! We'll be back!"
Certificate may be used: Anytime except Sept. 27-28.

Louisville   B6

Central Park B&B

1353 S Fourth St
Louisville, KY 40208-2349
(502)638-1505 Fax:(502)638-1525
Internet: ww.centralparkbandb.com
E-mail: centralpar@win.net

Circa 1884. This three-story Second Empire Victorian is listed in the National Register, and it is located in the heart of "Old Louisville," amid America's largest collection of Victorian homes. Enjoy the fine craftsmanship of the home's many amenities, including the reverse-painted glass ceiling of the front porch and the polished woodwork and stained glass. Among its 18 rooms are seven guest rooms. There are 11 fireplaces, some with carved mantels and decorative tile. The third-floor bath boasts a whirlpool tub, and the third-floor suite includes a whirlpool, as well, along with a sitting area. The Carriage House suite has a full kitchen. Antiques are found throughout. The University of Louisville and Spalding University is within easy walking distance. Across the street is Central Park.

Innkeeper(s): Mary & Joseph White. $85-149. MC, VISA, AX, PC, TC. 7 rooms, 5 with PB and 3 suites. Breakfast and snacks/refreshments included in rates. Types of meals: Full bkfst and early coffee/tea. Cable TV, phone, turndown service, hair dryers and computer port in room. Air conditioning. Antiquing, fine dining, live theater, shopping and sporting events nearby.

Location: City.

Certificate may be used: Jan. 1-Dec. 30, Monday-Thursday.

Inn at The Park

1332 S 4th St
Louisville, KY 40208-2314
(502)637-6930 (800)700-7275 Fax:(502)637-2796
Internet: www.innatpark.com
E-mail: innatpark@aol.com

Circa 1886. An impressive sweeping staircase is one of many highlights at this handsome Richardsonian Romanesque inn, in the historic district of Old Louisville. Guests also will appreciate the hardwood floors, 14-foot ceilings and stone balconies on the second and third floors. The seven guest rooms offer a variety of amenities and a view of Central Park.

Innkeeper(s): John & Sandra Mullins. $89-179. MC, VISA, AX, PC, TC. 7 rooms with PB, 5 with FP and 3 suites. Breakfast included in rates. Types of meals: Full bkfst and early coffee/tea. Beds: KQ. Cable TV, phone and ceiling fan in room. Air conditioning. VCR and fax on premises. Amusement parks, antiquing, churchill Downs, live theater, parks, shopping and sporting events nearby.

Location: City.

Publicity: *Country Inns.*

Certificate may be used: Jan. 1-Dec. 31, Monday-Thursday.

The Inn at Woodhaven

401 S Hubbard Ln
Louisville, KY 40207-4074
(502)895-1011 (888)895-1011
Internet: www.innatwoodhaven.com
E-mail: info@innatwoodhaven.com

Circa 1853. This Gothic Revival, painted in a cheerful shade of yellow, is still much the same as it was in the 1850s, when it served as the home on a prominent local farm. The rooms still feature the outstanding carved woodwork, crisscross window designs, winding staircases, decorative mantels and hardwood floors. Guest quarters are tastefully appointed with antiques, suitable for their 12-foot, nine-inch tall ceilings.
Complimentary coffee and tea stations are provided in each room. There are several common areas in the Main House, and guests also take advantage of the inn's porches. Rose Cottage is octagon shaped and features a 25-foot vaulted ceiling, a king bed, fireplace, sitting area, double whirlpool, steam shower and wraparound porch. The National Register home is close to all of Louisville's attractions.

Innkeeper(s): Marsha Burton. $75-175. MC, VISA, AX. 8 rooms with PB, 3 with FP, 2 suites and 1 cottage. Breakfast included in rates. Type of meal: Full gourmet bkfst. Beds: KQDT. Cable TV, phone, ceiling fan, coffee, tea and hot chocolate facility in room. Air conditioning. Fax, copier, library and three rooms with double whirlpools on premises. Handicap access. Amusement parks, antiquing, golf, live theater, parks, shopping, sporting events, tennis and water sports nearby.

Location: City.

Publicity: *Courier Journal, WAVE and WHAS.*

Certificate may be used: Sunday-Thursday, year round.

Middlesborough   E8

The Ridge Runner B&B

208 Arthur Hts
Middlesborough, KY 40965-1728
(606)248-4299

Circa 1890. Bachelor buttons, lilacs and wildflowers line the white picket fence framing this 20-room brick Victorian mansion. Guests enjoy relaxing in its turn-of-the-century library and parlor filled with Victorian antiques. Ask for the President's Room and you'll enjoy the best view of the Cumberland Mountains. (The innkeeper's great, great-grandfather hosted President Lincoln the night before his Gettysburg address, and the inn boasts some heirlooms from that home.) A family-style breakfast is provided and special diets can be accommodated if notified in advance. Cumberland Gap National Park is five miles away, and the inn is two miles from the twin tunnels that pass through the Cumberland Gap. Pine Mountain State Park is 12 miles away. Guests also enjoy a visit to the P. 38 restoration project housed at the local airport.

Innkeeper(s): Susan Richards & Irma Gall. $65-75. PC, TC. 4 rooms, 2 with PB. Breakfast and snacks/refreshments included in rates. Type of meal: Early coffee/tea. Beds: DT. Turndown service and ceiling fan in room. Antiquing, parks and shopping nearby.

Location: Mountains.

Publicity: *Lexington Herald Leader, Blue Ridge Country, Indianapolis Star, Daily News, Courier Journal and Country Inn.*

Certificate may be used: Nov. 15-April 30, Sunday-Thursday, excluding holidays, weekends (i.e. Thanksgiving, Christmas, Labor Day, etc.).

Murray   E2

The Diuguid House B&B

603 Main St
Murray, KY 42071-2034
(270)753-5470 (888)261-3028

Circa 1895. This Victorian house features eight-foot-wide hallways and a golden oak staircase with stained-glass window. There is a sitting area adjoining the portico. Guest rooms are generous in size.

Innkeeper(s): Karen & George Chapman. $40. MC, VISA, DC, PC, TC. 3 rooms. Breakfast included in rates. Types of meals: Full bkfst and early coffee/tea. Beds: QT. Turndown service in room. Air conditioning. Antiquing, fishing, live theater, parks and water sports nearby.

Pets allowed: Advance approval.

Location: Small town.

Publicity: *Murray Ledger & Times.*

"We enjoyed our visit in your beautiful home, and your hospitality was outstanding."

Certificate may be used: Anytime except university graduation, homecoming, parents weekends and last weekend in April.

New Haven   C6

The Sherwood Inn

138 S Main St
New Haven, KY 40051
(502)549-3386 Fax:(502)549-5822

Circa 1914. Since 1875, the Johnson family has owned the Sherwood Inn. A week after the original building burned in 1913, construction for the current building began. In the

National Register, the inn catered to passengers of the nearby L & N (Louisville and Nashville) Railroad. Antiques and reproductions complement some of the inn's original furnishings. The restaurant is open for dinner Wednesday through Saturday. The inn's slogan, first advertised in 1875 remains, "first class table and good accommodations."

Innkeeper(s): Cecilia Johnson. $45-65. MC, VISA, DS. 5 rooms, 3 with PB. Breakfast included in rates. Type of meal: Full bkfst. Beds: D. Ceiling fan in room. Air conditioning. Shopping nearby.

Location: Eleven miles south of Historic Bardstown.

Publicity: *Kentucky Standard.*

"A memorable stop."

Certificate may be used: Upon availability.

Paducah   D2

The 1857's B&B

PO Box 7771 127 Market House Sq
Paducah, KY 42002-7771
(502)444-3960 (800)264-5607 Fax:(502)444-6751

Circa 1857. Paducah's thriving, history-rich commercial district is home to this Folk Victorian inn, located in Market House Square. Guests choose from rooms such as the Master Bedroom, a suite featuring a king-size, four-poster bed or perhaps the Hunt Room, which includes a four-poster, queen-size canopy bed. The popular third-floor game room boasts an impressive mahogany billiard table. There is an outdoor hot tub on the deck. The Ohio River is an easy walk from the inn, and guests also will enjoy an evening stroll along the gas-lit brick sidewalks. The inn occupies the second and third floors of a former clothing store, with an Italian restaurant at street level.

Innkeeper(s): Deborah Bohnert. $65-95. MC, VISA, PC, TC. 3 rooms and 1 suite. Breakfast included in rates. Types of meals: Cont plus and early coffee/tea. Beds: KQDT. Cable TV, phone and ceiling fan in room. Air conditioning. VCR, fax, copier and library on premises. Antiquing, fishing, live theater, shopping and water sports nearby.

Location: City.

Publicity: *Paducah Sun and Paducah Life.*

Certificate may be used: Sunday-Friday, January, February, March, May, June, August, October, November.

Paducah Harbor Plaza B&B

201 Broadway St
Paducah, KY 42001-0711
(502)442-2698 (800)719-7799

This striking, five-story brick structure was known as the Hotel Belvedere at the turn of the century. Guests now choose from four guest rooms on the second floor, where they also will find the arch-windowed Broadway Room, with its views of the Market House District and the Ohio River, just a block away. Breakfast is served in this room, which also contains a 1911 player piano. The guest rooms all feature different color schemes and each is furnished with antique furniture and handmade quilts.

Innkeeper(s): Beverly McKinley. $65-85. MC, VISA, AX. 4 rooms. Breakfast included in rates. Type of meal: Cont plus. Cable TV, phone and ceiling fan in room. Air conditioning. VCR on premises. Antiquing, live theater and shopping nearby.

Certificate may be used: January, February, March, November, December.

Trinity Hills Farm Bed & Breakfast Home-Stained Glass Studio

10455 Old Lovelaceville Rd
Paducah, KY 42001-9304
(270)488-3999 (800)488-3998
Internet: www.trinityhills.com
E-mail: trinity8@apex.net

Circa 1995. This contemporary home is located at the edge of a private fishing lake. Guests can take a stroll and encounter peacocks, ducks, llamas, pygmy goats, miniature donkeys or an Arabian mare. Fishing and boating are other possibilities, or simply relax and enjoy the view from the large deck. Guest rooms are elegantly furnished and are decorated with an interesting mix of collectibles. Each room has access to the kitchenette, and the three suites include a private fireplace, spa or whirlpool tub. There's a treadmill and a movie library. Guests are treated to either country-style or gourmet fare in the mornings, by candlelight. On weekend evenings, desserts are served. Complimentary snacks and beverages are offered during the week, as well. The home is 12 miles west of Paducah. Handicap access is provided.

Innkeeper(s): Mike & Ann Driver. $80-140. MC, VISA, DS, PC, TC. 5 rooms with PB, 4 with FP, 4 suites and 1 guest house. Breakfast included in rates. Types of meals: Full gourmet bkfst and early coffee/tea. Beds: Q. TV, ceiling fan, VCR, table and chairs and robes in room. Air conditioning. Fax, spa, library, treadmill and movie library on premises. Handicap access. Amusement parks, antiquing, golf, live theater, parks, shopping, sporting events, tennis and water sports nearby.

Pets allowed: On ground floor with prior notice (small, in pet taxi).

Location: Country.

Publicity: *Paducah Life, Paducah Sun, Heartland B&Bs and Torchbearer.*

Certificate may be used: Monday through Thursday except holidays and AQS Quilt show.

Paris   B7

Pleasant Place B&B

515 Pleasant St
Paris, KY 40361-1828
(606)987-5546

Circa 1889. Pleasant is an apt description for this Queen Anne Victorian, located in a historic Paris neighborhood. The innkeepers are just the third family to occupy this elegant home, which maintains many original architectural features, including a showpiece staircase. The three guest rooms each are furnished with a variety of fine antiques. Breakfasts feature Kentucky specialties of homemade breads and gourmet casseroles. After a hearty breakfast, guests can explore Kentucky's famed horse country.

Innkeeper(s): Jeanine & Berkeley Scott. $55-75. MC, VISA, DS, PC, TC. 3 rooms, 2 with PB, 3 with FP. Breakfast included in rates. Types of meals: Full gourmet bkfst and early coffee/tea. Beds: KQ. Cable TV and central heating in room. Air conditioning. VCR, fax and library on premises. Antiquing, fishing, golf, parks, shopping and tennis nearby.

Location: Small town.

Publicity: *Bourbon Times and WKYT.*

"Pleasant Place is beautiful and the food was wonderful."

Certificate may be used: Anytime except April and October, subject to availability.

Russellville   D4

The Log House

2139 Franklin Rd
Russellville, KY 42276-9410
(502)726-8483 Fax:(502)726-4610
E-mail: hossom@logantele.com

Circa 1976. This ideal log cabin retreat was built from hand-hewn logs from old cabins and barns in the area. Rooms are full of quilts, early American furnishings and folk art from around the world. The log walls and hardwood floors create an unparalleled atmosphere of country warmth. An impressive kitchen is decorated with an old-fashioned stove and brick floor. The innkeepers create hand-woven garments and hand-spun items in an adjacent studio. Nashville and Opryland are about an hour's drive, and the local area boasts a number of antique shops.
Innkeeper(s): Mike & Sam Hossom. $95. MC, VISA, PC, TC. 4 rooms with PB, 2 with FP. Breakfast included in rates. Type of meal: Full gourmet bkfst. Beds: QDT. Air conditioning. VCR, fax, copier, spa and library on premises. Amusement parks, antiquing, fishing, live theater, parks, shopping, sporting events and water sports nearby.
Location: Countryside woods.
Publicity: *Courier Journal, Nashville Tennessean, WHAS, Louisville; WBKO and Bowling Green.*
Certificate may be used: Anytime. Prior reservations are essential.

Shelbyville   B6

The Wallace House

613 Washington St
Shelbyville, KY 40065-1131
(502)633-2006

Circa 1804. This Federal-style house, midway between Louisville and Frankfort, is listed in the National Register of Historic Places. Its four well-appointed guest suites all feature kitchenettes.
Innkeeper(s): Evelyn Laurent. $65-85. MC, VISA, AX. 4 suites. Type of meal: Cont plus. Beds: Q. Cable TV in room. Air conditioning. Antiquing, fishing, live theater and shopping nearby.
Location: City.
Certificate may be used: Sept. 15 to Dec. 15.

Springfield   C6

Maple Hill Manor

2941 Perryville Rd
Springfield, KY 40069-9611
(606)336-3075 (800)886-7546

Circa 1851. This brick Revival home with Italianate detail is a Kentucky Landmark home and is listed in the National Register of Historic Places. It features 13-1/2-foot ceilings, 10-foot doors, nine-foot windows, a cherry spiral staircase, stenciling in the foyer, a large parlor, period furnishings and a dining room with a fireplace. The library has floor-to-ceiling mahogany bookcases and the Honeymoon Room features a canopy bed and Jacuzzi. A large patio area is set among old maple trees.
Innkeeper(s): Kathleen Carroll. $50-90. MC, VISA, PC, TC. 7 rooms with PB and 1 conference room. Breakfast included in rates. Types of meals: Full bkfst and early coffee/tea. Beds: QDT. Phone, ceiling fan, jacuzzi and honeymoon room in room. Air conditioning. VCR on premises. Antiquing, fishing, murder Mystery, live theater and shopping nearby.
Location: Rural.
Publicity: *Danville's Advocate-Messenger, Springfield Sun, Eastside Weekend and Courier Journal.*
"Thank you again for your friendly and comfortable hospitality."
Certificate may be used: Sunday through Thursday.

Stearns   E7

Marcum-Porter House

35 Hume St
Stearns, KY 42647-0369
(606)376-2242
Internet: http://www.Metronet.com

Circa 1902. This two-story frame home once housed employees of the Stearns Coal & Lumber Company. Many guests like to wander the gardens of the historic inn. Golfers will enjoy a nearby nine-hole course, believed to be the second-oldest course in the state. Be sure to take a ride on the Big South Fork Scenic Railway during your stay. Area attractions include Big South Fork National Recreation Area, Cumberland Falls State Park and Yahoo Falls.
Innkeeper(s): Patricia Porter Newton. $55-65. MC, VISA, PC, TC. 4 rooms, 1 with PB. Breakfast, afternoon tea and snacks/refreshments included in rates. Types of meals: Full gourmet bkfst and early coffee/tea. Beds: D. VCR, library, piano, spacious grounds and porches on premises. Antiquing, fishing, white-water rafting, horseback riding, National & State Parks, parks, shopping and water sports nearby.
Location: Big South Fork National R & R.
Publicity: *McCreary County Record and KET/WKUT.*
Certificate may be used: April through October, Sunday-Thursday.

Versailles   C7

1823 Historic Rose Hill Inn

233 Rose Hill
Versailles, KY 40383-1223
(859)873-5957 (800)307-0460
Internet: www.rosehillinn.com
E-mail: innkeepers@rosehillinn.com

Circa 1823. Both Confederate and Union troops used this manor during the Civil War. The home maintains many elegant features, including original woodwork, 14-foot ceilings and floors fashioned from timber on the property. The decor is comfortable, yet elegant. One guest bath includes a clawfoot bathtub, another includes a double marble Jacuzzi. The innkeepers restored the home's summer kitchen into a private cottage, which now includes a private porch, kitchen and two queen/double beds. Three generations of the Amberg family live and work here, including friendly dogs. The mother/daughter innkeepers serve a hearty, full breakfast, and the cookie jar is always filled with homemade treats. Among the sites are a Shaker Village, antique shops, horse farms, Keeneland Race Track and a wildlife sanctuary.
Innkeeper(s): Sharon Amberg. $85-139. MC, VISA, AX, DS, TC. 4 rooms with PB, 1 suite and 1 cottage. Breakfast included in rates. Types of meals: Full bkfst and early coffee/tea. Beds: KQDT. Cable TV, phone, turndown service and ceiling fan in room. Air conditioning. VCR, bicycles and library on premises. Antiquing, fishing, golf, horse farm tours, Kentucky Horse Park, Shaker Village, parks, shopping and sporting events nearby.
Pets allowed: In cottage with prior approval.
Location: Small town near horse farms.
Certificate may be used: Sunday-Thursday, Nov. 1-March 15 (except holidays).

Louisiana

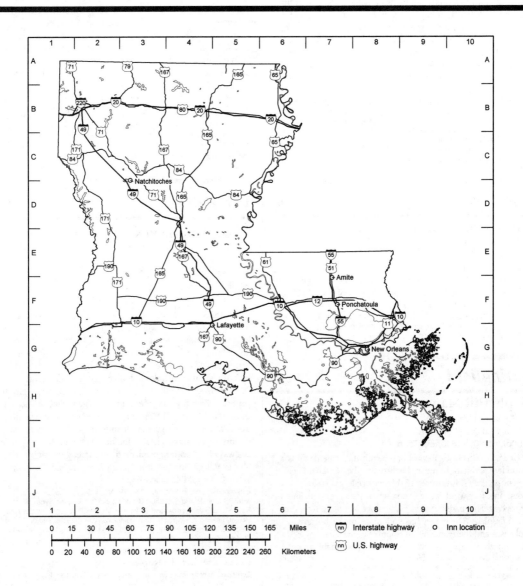

Amite   F7

Blythewood Plantation

PO Box 155, 400 Daniel ST
Amite, LA 70422-0155
(504)748-5886

Circa 1885. The grounds surrounding this majestic plantation home were part of a Spanish land grant. The original home, a pre-Civil War manor, burned, but was rebuilt in the late 19th century. The grand rooms include a gas chandelier, leaded-glass doors and walnut mantels, all original features. In true Louisiana style, guests are served a refreshing mint julep upon arrival. Candlelight dinners can be arranged, as can special teas, parties and weddings.

Innkeeper(s): Nancy, Ipha, Lisa. $89-189. TC. 9 rooms and 2 conference rooms. Breakfast and dinner included in rates. Type of meal: Full gourmet bkfst. Beds: D. Cable TV in room. Air conditioning. VCR on premises. Handicap access. Antiquing, parks and water sports nearby.
Pets Allowed.
Location: City.
Certificate may be used: Jan. 31-Dec. 31.

Elliott House

801 N Duncan Ave
Amite, LA 70422-2222
(504)748-8553 (800)747-8553

Circa 1908. Innkeeper Flora Elliott Landwehr's grandfather, a State Court of Appeals judge, built this Neoclassical home. Flora and husband Joseph painstakingly restored the inheritance, which had deteriorated and was shrouded in overgrown brush. Now, the old pine floors shine and rooms feature Victorian antiques. Two bedchambers have a fireplace. In the mornings, homemade granola, fresh fruit and Louisiana coffee accompany entrees such as eggs Benedict. Guests can spend the day relaxing at the inn and enjoying the five acres. The area offers plenty of outdoor activities, and New Orleans is an hour away.

Innkeeper(s): Joseph and Flora Landwehr. $75-125. MC, VISA, PC, TC. 4 rooms, 3 with PB, 2 with FP, 1 suite and 1 conference room. Breakfast and afternoon tea included in rates. Types of meals: Full gourmet bkfst and early coffee/tea. Beds: KD. Ceiling fan in room. Air conditioning. Bicycles and library on premises. Antiquing, golf, historic sites, wildlife parks, swamp tours, parks, shopping and water sports nearby.
Location: Small town.
Publicity: *Times Picayune, Hammond Star, Country Roads Magazine, Hot Beignets and Warm Boudoirs and PBS.*

"What you are doing and the type of people you are, give folks a memory, not just a place to stay."

Certificate may be used: Jan. 30-Nov. 10, Sunday-Thursday, excluding Mardi Gras and Jazz Fest.

Lafayette   H8

Alida's, A B&B

2631 SE Evangeline Thruway
Lafayette, LA 70508-2168
(337)264-1191 (800)922-5867 Fax:(337)264-6915
E-mail: alidas@iamerica.net

Circa 1902. This home is named for teacher Alida Martin, who along with once owning this Queen Anne house, was responsible for educating many Lafayette citizens, including a few civic leaders. Alida taught at the

house until a one-room schoolhouse was constructed. The innkeepers named a room for Alida, decorated with a 19th-century walnut bed and matching armoire. The bath still features the original clawfoot tub. Other rooms include special antiques, Bavarian collectibles and clawfoot tubs. After breakfast, guests can trek to nearby sites such as the Tabasco Plant and Live Oak Gardens on Jefferson Island.

Innkeeper(s): Tanya & Doug Greenwald. $150-995. MC, VISA, AX, DS, PC, TC. 4 rooms with PB and 1 conference room. Breakfast and snacks/refreshments included in rates. Type of meal: Full gourmet bkfst. Beds: QD. TV, phone, ceiling fan and VCR in room. Air conditioning. Fax and copier on premises. Antiquing, fishing, Cajun dancing & food, parks, shopping and sporting events nearby.
Certificate may be used: November-February, excludes holidays and special events.

Natchitoches   C3

Breazeale House B&B

926 Washington St
Natchitoches, LA 71457-4730
(318)352-5630 (800)352-5631
E-mail: wfreeman@cp-tel.net

Circa 1899. This three-story Victorian home boasts a porch accentuated with white columns on the first level and an expansive balcony with balustrades on the second floor. Stained-and-leaded-glass windows with white shutters and trim offer an inviting exterior. Eleven fireplaces afford a warm backdrop to the inn's antique Victorian furnishings. A popular breakfast menu includes crescent rolls with ham and cheese, eggs, muffins and fruit.

Innkeeper(s): Jack & Willa Freeman. $70-100. MC, VISA, AX, PC. 4 rooms with PB. Breakfast and afternoon tea included in rates. Types of meals: Full bkfst and early coffee/tea. Beds: Q. Ceiling fan in room. Air conditioning. Fax and swimming on premises. Antiquing, fishing, golf, shopping, sporting events, tennis and water sports nearby.
Certificate may be used: Jan. 6 to Nov. 15, Sunday-Thursday.

New Orleans   G8

A Creole House Hotel

1013 Saint Ann St
New Orleans, LA 70116-3012
(504)524-8076 (800)535-7858 Fax:(504)581-3277
Internet: big-easy.org
E-mail: hch5555@aol.com

Circa 1830. The many sites of the French Quarter surround this historic hotel, which was once home to a Voodoo queen. The guest rooms and suites are elegant and decorated in period style. Guided tours, including an evening nightclub tour, stop at the hotel daily. Guests can walk to fine restaurants and boutiques, and Bourbon Street is just two blocks away.

Innkeeper(s): Brent Kovach. $49-189. MC, VISA, AX, DS, TC. 29 rooms. Breakfast included in rates. Type of meal: Cont. Beds: KQ. Cable TV, phone and ceiling fan in room. Air conditioning. Fax and copier on premises. Antiquing, fishing, golf, live theater, parks and sporting events nearby.
Certificate may be used: All year, anytime based on availability, excluding Mardi Gras, Jazz Festival, New Years.

American Creole House

1124 Saint Charles Ave
New Orleans, LA 70130
(504)522-7777 (800)999-7891 Fax:(504)522-7778

Circa 1852. In the French Creole design with wrought iron fence and fret work, this two-story townhouse offers a private balcony overlooking St. Charles Ave. next to the Garden District near Lee Circle. The Creole Balcony Suite has a living room and kitchen. There are Jacuzzi tubs. The I-10 exit is a block away, and of course, the St. Charles Streetcar Line passes in front of the inn.

Innkeeper(s): Marc Cumbow. $75-325. MC, VISA, TC. 3 suites and 1 conference room. Type of meal: Cont. Beds: KQ. Cable TV, phone, ceiling fan and VCR in room. Air conditioning. Fax and copier on premises. Antiquing, fishing, golf, live theater, parks, sporting events, tennis and water sports nearby.
Certificate may be used: May 31-Aug. 31, seven days. Dec. 1-20, Saturday-Saturday.

Bonne Chance B&B

621 Opelousas Ave
New Orleans, LA 70114
(504)367-0798 Fax:(504)368-4643
Internet: www.bonne-chance.com

Circa 1890. This recently renovated two-story Eastlake Victorian boasts balconies and a porch with fretwork and columns painted pastel blue and cream. Antique furnishings and Oriental rugs are found throughout, and fully furnished apartments with kitchens are available. There are gardens and a fountain. A free five-minute ferry boat ride takes you to the French Quarter.
Innkeeper(s): Dolores Watson. $85-175. MC, VISA, AX, PC. 3 suites. Breakfast included in rates. Type of meal: Cont plus. Beds: Q. Cable TV, phone, ceiling fan & three apartments with fully equipped kitchens in room. Air conditioning. VCR, fax, copier & library on premises. Amusement parks, antiquing, fishing, golf, French Quarter, live theater, parks, shopping, sporting events & tennis nearby.
Location: City.
Publicity: *New Orleans.*
Certificate may be used: June 1-Aug. 31, Dec. 1-31.

Fairchild House

1518 Prytania St
New Orleans, LA 70130-4416
(504)524-0154 (800)256-8096 Fax:(504)568-0063
Internet: www.fairchildhouse.com
E-mail: fairchildhou@earthlink.net

Circa 1841. Situated in the oak-lined Lower Garden District of New Orleans, this Greek Revival home was built by architect L.H. Pilie. The house and its guest houses maintain a Victorian ambiance with elegantly appointed guest rooms. Wine and cheese is served upon guests' arrival. Afternoon tea can be served upon request. The bed & breakfast, which is on the Mardi Gras parade route, is 17 blocks from the French Quarter and eight blocks from the convention center. Streetcars are just one block away, as are many local attractions, including paddleboat cruises, Canal Place and Riverwalk shopping, an aquarium, zoo, the Charles Avenue mansions and Tulane and Loyola universities.
Innkeeper(s): Rita Olmo & Beatriz Aprigliano-Ziegler. $75-145. MC, VISA, AX, TC. 14 rooms with PB and 1 suite. Breakfast included in rates. Type of meal: Cont plus. Beds: KQDT. Phone in room. Air conditioning. Fax and copier on premises. Antiquing, live theater and shopping nearby.
Location: City.
"Accommodations were great; staff was great...Hope to see y'all soon!"
Certificate may be used: June 1-Aug. 31, please call during other seasons.

Garden District B&B

2418 Magazine St
New Orleans, LA 70130-5604
(504)895-4302 Fax:(504)895-4306

This restored Victorian home is nestled in New Orleans' Garden District and surrounded by gracious antebellum homes. The innkeepers have restored the pine floors and 12-foot ceilings to their original glory. Rooms include antiques, ceilings fans and Victorian decor. The patio is surrounded by a lush, tropical garden. Guests won't have to walk far to explore the hundreds of antique shops which line Magazine Street.
Innkeeper(s): Joseph Kinsella. $70-80. MC, VISA. 5 rooms. Breakfast included in rates. Type of meal: Cont. Antiquing and French quarter nearby.
Certificate may be used: June, July, August; other months on availability.

Lafitte Guest House

1003 Bourbon St
New Orleans, LA 70116-2707
(504)581-2678 (800)331-7971 Fax:(504)581-2677
Internet: www.lafitteguesthouse.com
E-mail: lafitte@travelbase.com

Circa 1849. This elegant French manor house has been meticulously restored. The house is filled with fine antiques and paintings collected from around the world. Located in the heart of the French Quarter, the inn is near world-famous restaurants, museums, antique shops and rows of Creole and Spanish cottages. Between 5:30 p.m. and 7 p.m., there is a wine and cheese social hour.
Innkeeper(s): Edward G. Dore & Andrew J. Crocchiolo. $129-219. MC, VISA, AX, DC, DS, TC. 14 rooms with PB, 7 with FP and 2 suites. Breakfast included in rates. Type of meal: Cont plus. Beds: KQ. TV, phone and ceiling fan in room. Air conditioning. Fax and copier on premises. Amusement parks, antiquing, fishing, live theater, parks, shopping, sporting events and water sports nearby.
Location: City.
Publicity: *Glamour, Antique Monthly, McCall's, Dixie and Country Living.*
"This old building offers the finest lodgings we have found in the city." — *McCall's Magazine*
Certificate may be used: Last two weeks of August and first two weeks of December, Sunday through Thursday, subject to availability.

Lamothe House

621 Esplanade Ave
New Orleans, LA 70116-2018
(504)947-1161 (800)367-5858 Fax:(504)943-6536
Internet: new-orleans.org
E-mail: lam5675842@aol.com

Circa 1830. A carriageway that formerly cut through the center of many French Quarter buildings was enclosed at the Lamothe House in 1866, and it is now the foyer. Splendid Victorian furnishings enhance moldings, high ceilings and hand-turned mahogany stairway railings. Gilded opulence goes unchecked in the Mallard and Lafayette suites. Registration takes place in the second-story salon above the courtyard.
Innkeeper(s): Carol Chauppette. $75-250. MC, VISA, AX, PC, TC. 20 rooms with PB, 1 with FP, 9 suites, 2 cottages and 1 conference room. Breakfast included in rates. Type of meal: Cont plus. Beds: QDT. Cable TV, phone, turn-down service and ceiling fan in room. Air conditioning. VCR, fax, copier, swimming, child care and free parking on premises. Amusement parks, antiquing, fishing, French Quarter, live theater, parks, shopping and sporting events nearby.
Location: French Quarter.
Publicity: *Southern Living (Cover), Los Angeles Times, Houston Post and Travel & Leisure.*
Certificate may be used: Anytime, subject to availability.

Maison Esplanade

1244 Esplanade Ave
New Orleans, LA 70116-1978
(504)523-8080 (800)892-5529 Fax:(504)527-0040
Internet: www.maisonesplanade.com
E-mail: maison@neworleans.com

Circa 1846. Experience the splendor of New Orleans at this Greek Revival mansion, which is located within walking distance of the French Quarter. Polished wood floors, ceiling fans and 13-foot ceilings highlight this historic district home, which is furnished with antiques and replicas. Bedchambers honor New Orleans' jazz tradition, bearing names such as the Louis Armstrong Suite or Count Basie Room. Cable TV, individual climate control and telephones with dataports and voice mail are among the modern amenities. Continental breakfasts, featuring cereals, bagels, fresh fruit, New Orleans-style chicory coffee, teas and other beverages, are provided each morning. The hosts are full of information about the myriad of tours available in the city, including tours of the French Quarter, plantation homes, historic homes or the city itself. Be sure to ask about the vampire, ghost and swamp tours.

Innkeeper(s): Jarret Marshall. $79-189. MC, VISA, AX, DS, TC. 10 rooms with PB and 2 suites. Breakfast included in rates. Type of meal: Cont. Beds: Q. Phone and ceiling fan in room. Air conditioning. Fax on premises. Antiquing, art galleries, French Quarter, aquarium, casino, concert venue, gourmet dining, lake, live music, movie theater, Superdome, Convention Center, zoo, live theater, museums and shopping nearby.

Pets allowed: in some rooms.

"I had a marvelous visit to New Orleans and your delightful hospitality and friendship made it even more special."

Certificate may be used: Subject to availability.

Mandevilla

7716 Saint Charles Ave
New Orleans, LA 70118
(504)862-6396 (800)288-0484 Fax:(504)866-4104

Circa 1800. Behind a handsome wrought iron fence, the gracious proportions and imposing presence of this Greek Revival assures guests of a truly unique stay. The upper balcony with

columns and shuttered windows provides views of moss laden oak trees. There are fireplaces, private galleries and double whirlpool tubs. Located three blocks from the Mississippi River, the inn is one of the oldest buildings in town.

Innkeeper(s): Martha & Allen Borne. $65-175. MC, VISA, PC, TC. 6 rooms with PB, 2 with FP, 1 suite and 1 conference room. Breakfast included in rates. Types of meals: Cont plus and early coffee/tea. Beds: KQDT. Cable TV, phone, turndown service, ceiling fan, VCR and double whirlpool in room. Air conditioning. Fax, copier, bicycles, library and child care on premises. Amusement parks, antiquing, golf, parks, shopping and tennis nearby.

Location: Mississippi River.

Publicity: *New York Times.*

Certificate may be used: June 1 to Aug. 15, Sunday-Thursday.

The Prytania Park Hotel

1525 Prytania St
New Orleans, LA 70130-4448
(504)524-0427 (800)862-1984 Fax:(504)522-2977
Internet: www.prytaniaparkhotel.com
E-mail: prytaniapk@aol.com

Circa 1850. Prytania Park consists of a historic Greek Revival building and a restored Queen Anne Victorian, located in a National Historic Landmark District. The Greek Revival building includes

rooms decorated with Victorian reproductions, some include fireplaces. A newer section, with 12 Queen Anne-style suites, includes rooms with modern amenities such as refrigerators, microwaves and contemporary decor. The hotel's

historic Victorian mansion is listed in the National Register and maintains original features such as 14-foot ceilings, hardwood floors and intricate fireplace mantels. Several rooms include balconies overlooking Prytania Street. Amenities include shuttle service to the French Quarter and nearby Convention Center.

Innkeeper(s): Edward Halpern. $99-229. MC, VISA, AX, DC, CB, DS, PC,

TC. 74 rooms with PB and 18 suites. Breakfast included in rates. Type of meal: Cont plus. Beds: KQDT. Cable TV, phone, ceiling fan and microwaves in room. Air conditioning. Fax and copier on premises. Antiquing, parks, shopping and sporting events nearby.

Location: National Historic District.

Publicity: *New York Times, Atlanta Constitution and LA Times.*

"A little jewel—Baton Rouge Advocate."

Certificate may be used: Jan. 4 to Dec. 28, Sunday-Thursday.

St. Peter Guest House Hotel

1005 Saint Peter St
New Orleans, LA 70116-3014
(504)524-9232 (800)535-7815 Fax:(504)523-5198
Internet: www.crescent-city.org
E-mail: sp+15678@aol.com

Circa 1800. The St. Peter House, which is ideally situated in the middle of the French Quarter, offers a delightful glance at New Orleans French heritage and 18th-century charm. From the lush courtyards to the gracious balconies, guests will enjoy the view of the busy quarter. Rooms are individually appointed, some with period antiques.

Innkeeper(s): Brent Kovach. $49-225. MC, VISA, AX, DS, PC, TC. 28 rooms with PB and 11 suites. Breakfast included in rates. Type of meal: Cont plus. Beds: KQDT. Cable TV, phone and ceiling fan in room. Air conditioning. Fax on premises. Amusement parks, antiquing, fishing, live theater, parks and shopping nearby.

Location: French Quarter.

Certificate may be used: Anytime, subject to availability.

Ponchatoula F7

Bella Rose Mansion

225 N 8th St
Ponchatoula, LA 70454-3209
(504)386-3857 Fax:(504)386-3857
Internet: cimarron.net/us/la/bella.html

Circa 1942. This Georgian-style mansion boasts a three-story spiral staircase that rises up to a stained-glass dome. Master craftsmen detailed this luxurious manor with mahogany paneling, parquet floors, Waterford crystal chandeliers and a marble-walled solarium with a

fountain. The home once served as a monastery for Jesuit priests. The mansion includes an indoor terrazzo shuffleboard court and heated swimming pool. Gourmet breakfasts feature

entrees such as eggs Benedict complemented with fresh fruits and juices. Ponchatoula's many antique shops have earned its nickname as America's Antique City.

Innkeeper(s): Rose James & Michael-Ray Britton. $125-225. MC, VISA. 4 rooms with PB and 2 suites. Breakfast included in rates. Type of meal: Full gourmet bkfst. Beds: KQ. Ceiling fan in room. Air conditioning. VCR, fax, copier, swimming, bicycles and library on premises. Antiquing, fishing, live theater, parks, shopping, sporting events and water sports nearby.

Publicity: *Houston Chronicle and Sunday Star.*

"What a fabulous place! Your warmth is truly an asset. The peacefulness is just what we needed in our hectic lives."

Certificate may be used: Sunday through Thursday, excluding Mardi Gras and major holidays.

Maine

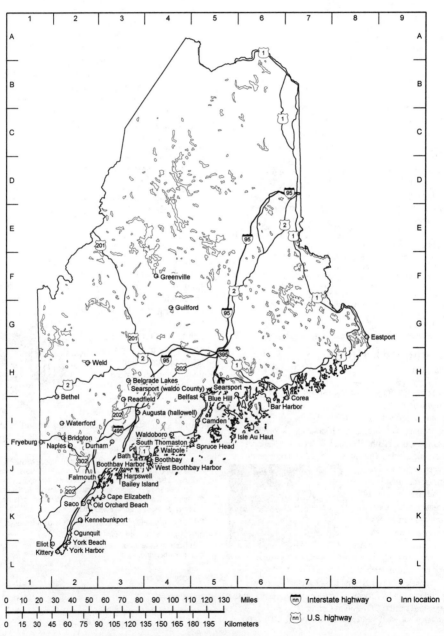

1 2 3 4 5 6 7 8 9

A
B
C
D
E 201
F Greenville
G Guilford 201 Eastport
H Weld 202 Belgrade Lakes 395
Searsport (waldo County) Searsport
Bethel Readfield Belfast Blue Hill Corea
Waterford Augusta (hallowell) Bar Harbor
I Bridgton Camden
Fryeburg Naples Durham Waldoboro Isle Au Haut
South Thomaston
J Walpole
Bath Boothbay Spruce Head
Boothbay Harbor West Boothbay Harbor
Falmouth Harpswell
Bailey Island
Saco Cape Elizabeth
K Old Orchard Beach
Kennebunkport
Ogunquit
L Eliot York Beach
Kittery York Harbor

0 10 20 30 40 50 60 70 80 90 100 110 120 130 Miles
[inn] Interstate highway O Inn location

0 15 30 45 60 75 90 105 120 135 150 165 180 195 Kilometers
[inn] U.S. highway

Augusta (Hallowell)   I3

Maple Hill Farm B&B Inn

RR 1 Box 1145, Outlet Rd
Augusta (Hallowell), ME 04347
(207)622-2708 (800)622-2708 Fax:(207)622-0655
Internet: www.maplebb.com
E-mail: info@maplebb.com

Circa 1890. Visitors to Maine's capitol city have the option of staying at this nearby inn, a peaceful farm setting adjacent to a 550-acre state wildlife management area that is available for canoeing, fishing, hiking and hunting.
This Victorian Shingle-style inn was once a stagecoach stop and dairy farm. The inn's suite includes a double whirlpool tub. The inn, with its 130-acre grounds, easily accommodates confer-

ences, parties and receptions. Guests are welcome to visit the many farm animals. Cobbossee Lake is a five-minute drive from the inn. The center portion of Hallowell is listed as a National Historic District and offers antique shops and restaurants.
Innkeeper(s): Scott Cowger. $50-125. MC, VISA, AX, DC, CB, DS, PC, TC. 7 rooms, 4 with PB, 1 suite and 1 conference room. Breakfast and afternoon tea included in rates. Types of meals: Full bkfst and early coffee/tea. Beds: QD. TV and phone in room. VCR and whirlpool tub on premises. Handicap access. Antiquing, live theater, shopping, cross-country skiing and water sports nearby. Location: Country.
Publicity: *Family Fun, An Explorer's Guide to Maine, The Forecaster, Portland Press Herald, Kennebec Journal and Maine Times.*
"You add many thoughtful touches to your service that set your B&B apart from others, and really make a difference. Best of Maine, hands down!" (Maine Times)
Certificate may be used: May-October, Sunday-Wednesday; November-April, anytime, but not both Friday and Saturday.

Bailey Island   J3

Captain York House B&B

Rt 24, PO Box 298
Bailey Island, ME 04003
(207)833-6224
Internet: www.iwws.com/captainyork
E-mail: athorn7286@aol.com

Circa 1906. Bailey Island is the quaint fisherman's village of stories, poems and movies. Guests cross the world's only cribstone bridge to reach the island, where beautiful sunsets and dinners of fresh Maine lobster are the norm. This shingled, turn-of-the-century, Mansard-style B&B was the home of a famous Maine sea captain, Charles York. Now a homestay-style bed & breakfast, the innkeepers have restored the home to its former glory, filling it with many antiques. Guests at Captain York's enjoy water views from all the guest rooms. Wild Maine blueberries often find a significant place on the breakfast menu.
Innkeeper(s): Alan & Jean Thornton. $68-100. MC, VISA, PC, TC. 5 rooms with PB. Breakfast included in rates. Type of meal: Full bkfst. Beds: QT. VCR on premises. Antiquing, P. McMilan Museum, Maine Maritime Museum, live theater, parks, shopping, sporting events and water sports nearby.
Publicity: *Tri-Town News and Palm Beach Post.*
"Bailey Island turned out to be the hidden treasure of our trip and we hope to return for your great hospitality again."
Certificate may be used: Jan. 30 to May 15, Oct. 15-Dec. 15.

Bar Harbor   I6

The Kedge

112 West St
Bar Harbor, ME 04609-1429
(207)288-5180 (800)597-8306

Circa 1870. Originally, this bed & breakfast was located at the edge of the harbor and served as a social club for gentlemen. In the 1880s, it was moved to its current location on West Street. The home rests on a portion of the street that is listed in the National Register of Historic Places. The interior is Victorian in style, and flowered wallpapers brighten the rooms. One room has a whirlpool tub. The veranda is filled with hunter green wicker furnishings for those who wish to relax. For breakfast, innkeeper Margaret Roberts serves items such as baked peaches with Maine blueberries followed by gingerbread pancakes topped with marmalade syrup.
$60-170. MC, VISA, AX, PC, TC. 3 rooms with PB, 2 with FP. Breakfast included in rates. Types of meals: Full bkfst and early coffee/tea. Beds: KQ. Cable TV in room. Antiquing, golf, museums, oceanarium, concerts, movies, ocean activities, Acadia National Park, live theater, parks, shopping, cross-country skiing, tennis and water sports nearby.
Certificate may be used: Jan. 2-June 15, Oct. 15-Dec. 29, excluding holidays.

Manor House Inn

106 West St
Bar Harbor, ME 04609-1856
(207)288-3759 (800)437-0088 Fax:(207)288-2974
Internet: www.acadia.net/manorhouse
E-mail: manor@acadia.net

Circa 1887. Colonel James Foster built this 22-room Victorian mansion, now in the National Register. It is an example of the tradition of gracious summer living for which Bar Harbor was and is famous. In addition to the main house, there are several charming cottages situated in the extensive gardens on the property.

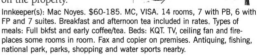

Innkeeper(s): Mac Noyes. $60-185. MC, VISA. 14 rooms, 7 with PB, 6 with FP and 7 suites. Breakfast and afternoon tea included in rates. Types of meals: Full bkfst and early coffee/tea. Beds: KQT. TV, ceiling fan and fireplaces some rooms in room. Fax and copier on premises. Antiquing, fishing, national park, parks, shopping and water sports nearby.
Location: National Park.
Publicity: *Country Folks Art Magazine and Discerning Traveler.*
"Wonderful honeymoon spot! Wonderful inn, elegant, delicious breakfasts, terrific innkeepers. We loved it all! It's our fourth time here and it's wonderful as always."
Certificate may be used: April through mid-June and Oct. 22 through mid-November. Sunday through Thursday.

Mira Monte Inn & Suites

69 Mount Desert St
Bar Harbor, ME 04609-1327
(207)288-4263 (800)553-5109 Fax:(207)288-3115
Internet: www.miramonte.com
E-mail: mburns@acadia.net

Circa 1864. A gracious 18-room Victorian mansion, the Mira Monte has been newly renovated in the style of early Bar Harbor. It features period furnishings, pleasant common rooms, a library and wraparound porches. Situated on estate grounds, there are sweeping lawns, paved terraces and many gardens. The inn was one of the earliest of Bar Harbor's famous summer cottages. The two-room suites each feature canopy beds, two-person whirlpools, a parlor with a sleeper sofa, fireplace and kitchenette unit. The two-bedroom suite includes a full kitchen, dining area and parlor. The suites boast private decks with views of the gardens.

Innkeeper(s): Marian Burns. $145-215. MC, VISA, AX, DC, DS, TC. 16 rooms with PB, 14 with FP and 3 suites. Breakfast and afternoon tea included in rates. Types of meals: Full bkfst and early coffee/tea. Beds: KQT. Cable TV, phone and VCR in room. Air conditioning. Fax and library on premises. Handicap access. Antiquing, fishing, Acadia National Park, live theater, parks and shopping nearby.

Location: Island.

Publicity: *Los Angeles Times.*

"On our third year at your wonderful inn in beautiful Bar Harbor. I think I enjoy it more each year. A perfect place to stay in a perfect environment."

Certificate may be used: April 26-May 20.

The Ridgeway Inn

11 High St
Bar Harbor, ME 04609-1816
(207)288-9682

Circa 1890. Located on a quiet, tree-lined street, this Victorian B&B is a welcome sight for weary travelers. Each of the guest rooms is individually decorated and named after the cottages of the wealthy who made Bar Harbor their summer vacation spot. Many of these homes were destroyed in a 1947 fire, but the innkeepers have preserved their memory. Beds are covered with down comforters. One room includes a Jacuzzi tub, while another offers a private deck. The innkeepers serve an expansive, multi-course breakfast on fireside tables illuminated by candlelight. Freshly baked breads, scones and muffins are followed by a fruit recipe, which all precedes the daily entree.

Innkeeper(s): Lucie Rioux Hollfelder. $70-150. MC, VISA, PC, TC. 5 rooms with PB and 2 suites. Breakfast and afternoon tea included in rates. Types of meals: Full gourmet bkfst and early coffee/tea. Beds: KQ. Amusement parks, antiquing, fishing, hiking, live theater, parks, shopping, cross-country skiing and water sports nearby.

Certificate may be used: May 1-June 15 (excluding Memorial Day weekend). Based on availability.

Bath   J3

Benjamin F. Packard House

45 Pearl St
Bath, ME 04530-2746
(207)443-6069 (800)516-4578
Internet: www.mainecoast.com/packardhouse/
E-mail: packardhouse@clinic.net

Circa 1790. Shipbuilder Benjamin F. Packard purchased this handsome home in 1870. The inn reflects the Victorian influence so prominent in Bath's busiest shipbuilding years. The Packard family, who lived in the house for five generations, left many family mementos. Period furnishings, authentic colors and shipbuilding memorabilia all reflect Bath's romantic past. The mighty Kennebec River is just a block away. A full breakfast is served daily.

Innkeeper(s): Debby & Bill Hayden. $75-100. MC, VISA, AX, DC, DS, PC, TC. 3 rooms with PB and 1 suite. Breakfast included in rates. Type of meal: Full bkfst. Beds: KQT. Library on premises. Antiquing, golf, live theater, parks, shopping and water sports nearby.

Location: City.

Publicity: *Coastal Journal, Times Record and Maine Sunday Telegram.*

"Thanks for being wonderful hosts."

Certificate may be used: Nov. 1-April 30, Sunday-Thursday.

Fairhaven Inn

118 N Bath Rd
Bath, ME 04530
(207)443-4391 (888)443-4391 Fax:(207)443-6412
Internet: www.mainecoast.com/fairhaveninn
E-mail: fairhvn@gwi.net

Circa 1790. With its view of the Kennebec River, this site was so attractive that Pembleton Edgecomb built his Colonial house  where a log cabin had previously stood. His descendants occupied it for the next 125 years. Antiques and country furniture fill the inn. Meadows and lawns, and woods of hemlock, birch and pine cover the inn's 16 acres.

Innkeeper(s): Susie & Dave Reed. $80-120. MC, VISA, DS, PC, TC. 8 rooms, 6 with PB, 1 suite, 1 cottage and 1 conference room. Breakfast included in rates. Types of meals: Full bkfst and early coffee/tea. Beds: KQT. Fax and library on premises. Antiquing, live theater, parks, shopping, cross-country skiing, sporting events and water sports nearby.

Location: River-country setting.

Publicity: *The State and Coastal Journal.*

"The Fairhaven is now marked in our book with a red star, definitely a place to remember and visit again."

Certificate may be used: Sunday-Thursday, Sept. 5-June 30.

The Galen C. Moses House

1009 Washington St
Bath, ME 04530-2759
(207)442-8771 (888)442-8771 Fax:(207)443-6861
Internet: www.galenmoses.com
E-mail: stay@galenmoses.com

Circa 1874. This Victorian mansion is filled with beautiful architectural items, including stained-glass windows, wood-carved and marble fireplaces and a grand staircase. The innkeepers have filled the library, a study, morning room and the parlor with antiques. A corner fireplace warms the dining room, which overlooks the lawns and gardens. Tea is presented in the formal drawing room.

Innkeeper(s): James Haught, Larry Kieft. $79-129. MC, VISA, AX, DS, PC, TC. 4 rooms with PB. Breakfast and afternoon tea included in rates. Types of meals: Full gourmet bkfst and cont. Beds: QDT. Turndown service in room. VCR and library on premises. Antiquing, beaches, fishing, boats, live theater, parks, shopping, cross-country skiing and water sports nearby.

Location: City.

Publicity: *Philadelphia and Back Roads USA.*

"For our first try at B&B lodgings, we've probably started at the top, and nothing else will ever measure up to this. Wonderful food, wonderful home, grounds and wonderful hosts!"

Certificate may be used: Jan. 1-March 30, Sunday-Thursday, holidays excluded.

Belfast   H5

The Alden House Bed & Breakfast

63 Church St
Belfast, ME 04915-6208
(207)338-2151 (877)337-8151 Fax:(207)338-2151
Internet: www.thealdenhouse.com
E-mail: innkeeper@thealdenhouse.com

Circa 1840. This pre-Civil War, pristinely restored Greek Revival manor was built for prominent Belfast citizen Hiram Alden. Alden was editor of the local paper, town postmaster and vice-president of American Telegraph. The interior still boasts grand features, such as marble fireplace mantels, tin ceilings and a hand-carved curved staircase. Early risers enjoy the view from the front porch as they sip a cup of freshly ground coffee. Breakfast begins with juice, fresh fruit and muffins, followed by a special entree. During raspberry season, guests are treated to fresh berries from the inn's grounds.

Innkeeper(s): Bruce & Susan Madara. $86-120. MC, VISA. 7 rooms, 5 with PB, 1 with FP. Breakfast and afternoon tea included in rates. Types of meals: Full bkfst and early coffee/tea. Beds: QDT. Natural body care products, hair dryers and robes in room. VCR, fax and library on premises. Antiquing, fishing, golf, live theater, parks, shopping, downhill skiing, cross-country skiing, tennis and water sports nearby.

Location: City.

Publicity: *Bangor Daily Mews and Waldo Independent.*

Certificate may be used: Nov. 1-May 15.

The Jeweled Turret Inn

40 Pearl St
Belfast, ME 04915-1907
(207)338-2304 (800)696-2304
Internet: www.bbonline.com/me/jeweledturret/

Circa 1898. This grand Victorian is named for the staircase that winds up the turret, lighted by stained- and leaded-glass panels and jewel-like embellishments. It was built for attorney James Harriman. Dark pine beams adorn the ceiling of the den, and the fireplace is constructed of bark and rocks from every state in the Union. Elegant antiques furnish the guest rooms. Guests can relax in one of the inn's four parlors, which are furnished with period antiques, wallpapers, lace and boast fireplaces. Some rooms have a ceiling fan. The verandas feature wicker and iron bistro sets and views of the historic district. The inn is within walking distance of the town and its shops, restaurants and the harbor.

Innkeeper(s): Cathy & Carl Heffentrager. $85-135. MC, VISA, PC, TC. 7 rooms with PB, 1 with FP. Breakfast and afternoon tea included in rates. Types of meals: Full gourmet bkfst and early coffee/tea. Beds: QDT. TV and one room with whirlpool tub in room. Antiquing, fishing, live theater, shopping, downhill skiing, cross-country skiing and water sports nearby.

Location: Small coastal town.

Publicity: *News Herald, Republican Journal, Waterville Sentinel, Los Angels Times, Country Living, Victorian Homes and The Saturday Evening Post.*

"The ambiance was so romantic that we felt like we were on our honeymoon."

Certificate may be used: April, May and November, holidays excluded.

The Thomas Pitcher House B&B

19 Franklin St
Belfast, ME 04915-6518
(207)338-6454 (888)338-6454
Internet: www.thomaspitcherhouse.com
E-mail: tpitcher@acadia.net

Circa 1873. This richly appointed home was considered state-of-the-art back in 1873, for it was one of only a few homes offering central heat and hot or cold running water. Today, innkeepers have added plenty of modern amenities, but kept the ambiance of the Victorian era. Some vanities include original walnut and marble, while another bathroom includes tin ceilings and a step-down bath. Some rooms have cozy reading areas. Guests enjoy a full breakfast each morning with menus that feature specialties such as Maine blueberry buttermilk pancakes or a French toast puff made with homemade raisin bread.

Innkeeper(s): Fran & Ron Kresge. $85-105. MC, VISA, DS, PC, TC. 4 rooms with PB. Breakfast included in rates. Types of meals: Full gourmet bkfst and early coffee/tea. Beds: QDT. Clocks, portable fans and reading bays/areas in room. VCR, library, porch with rockers and deck with wicker furniture on premises. Antiquing, fishing, museums, historic sites, lighthouses, live theater, parks, shopping, downhill skiing, cross-country skiing and water sports nearby.

Location: Historic mid coast town.

Publicity: *Boston Herald, Jackson Clarion-Ledger, Toronto Sunday Sun, Bride's, Knoxville News-Sentinel, Saturday Evening Post, Allentown Morning Call, Waldo Independent and Victorian Homes.*

"A home away from home."

Certificate may be used: September, Oct. 16-June 15 (Sunday through Saturday, excluding holidays).

Belgrade Lakes   H3

Wings Hill

PO Box 386
Belgrade Lakes, ME 04918-0386
(207)495-2400 (800)509-4647

Circa 1800. Antiques and original artwork grace the interior of this restored Cape-style farmhouse. The huge wraparound porch is screened in and an ideal place to relax. Many of the antiques and collectibles are available for sale. The innkeepers serve a country breakfast prepared in the quaint kitchen, an inviting room warmed by a wood burning stove. The innkeepers will help guests plan activities, including rentals for skiing, boating and snowmobiling.

Innkeeper(s): Tammy & Rick Harmon. $80-95. MC, VISA. 8 rooms with PB. Breakfast included in rates. Types of meals: Full bkfst and early coffee/tea. VCR on premises. Antiquing, fishing, live theater, shopping, cross-country skiing, sporting events and water sports nearby.

Certificate may be used: Jan. 1 to Dec. 31, Sunday through Thursday.

Bethel   I2

Abbott House

Rt 26, PO Box 933
Bethel, ME 04217
(207)824-7600 (800)240-2377

Circa 1773. Guests at this 18th-century home are treated to a variety of soothing amenities. Innkeepers Joe Cardello and Penny Bohac-Cardello offer massage service, an outdoor hot tub and will set up goodies such as chocolates and flowers for guests celebrating a special occasion. Penny is an excellent baker and creates all the fresh breads for breakfast and afternoon tea. Her freshly baked treats, such as a succulent blueberry cake, complement Joe's array of breakfast fare. Joe serves up a hearty meal with meats, potatoes, egg dishes and fresh fruit, all garnished with edible flowers from the inn's garden. In warmer months, iced coffees and iced tea are served with the afternoon and evening refreshments.

Innkeeper(s): Joe Cardello, Penny Bohac-Cardello. $75-100. MC, VISA, AX. 3 rooms with PB and 1 suite. Breakfast, afternoon tea and snacks/refreshments included in rates. Types of meals: Full bkfst and early coffee/tea. Beds: QDT. Spa and massage A.M.T.A. certified on premises. Antiquing, fishing, golf, hiking, canoes, parks, shopping, downhill skiing and cross-country skiing nearby.

Location: Country.

Certificate may be used: Not honored between Dec. 15-March 15 and Sept. 15-Oct. 15.

Chapman Inn

PO Box 1067
Bethel, ME 04217-1067
(207)824-2657 (877)359-1498
E-mail: chapman@nxi.com

Circa 1865. As one of the town's oldest buildings, this Federal-style inn has been a store, a tavern and a boarding house known as "The Howard." It was the home of William Rogers Chapman, composer, conductor and founder of the Rubenstein Club and the Metropolitan Musical Society, in addition to the Maine Music Festival. The inn is a convenient place to begin a walking tour of Bethel's historic district.

Innkeeper(s): Sandra & Fred. $25-105. MC, VISA, AX, DS, PC, TC. 10 rooms with PB and 2 suites. Breakfast included in rates. Types of meals: Full bkfst and early coffee/tea. TV and phone in room. Air conditioning. VCR, fax and sauna on premises. Antiquing, fishing, golf, live theater, parks, shopping, downhill skiing, cross-country skiing, tennis and water sports nearby.

Pets Allowed.

Location: In village.

Certificate may be used: March 15-May 15, Oct. 20-Nov. 20.

L'Auberge Country Inn

Mill Hill Rd, PO Box 21
Bethel, ME 04217-0021
(207)824-2774 (800)760-2774 Fax:(207)824-0806

Circa 1870. In the foothills of the White Mountains, surrounded by five acres of gardens and woods, this former carriage house was converted to a guest house in the 1920s. Among its seven guest rooms are two spacious suites. The Theater Suite offers a four-poster queen bed and dressing room. The Family Suite can accommodate up to six guests. Mount Abrahms and Sunday River ski areas are just minutes away.

Innkeeper(s): Tom Rideout. $65-125. MC, VISA, AX, DS. 6 rooms, 2 suites and 1 conference room. Breakfast included in rates. Types of meals: Full bkfst and early coffee/tea. VCR and child care on premises. Antiquing, shopping, downhill skiing and cross-country skiing nearby.

Location: Mountains.

Certificate may be used: Midweek, non-holiday.

Blue Hill   H5

Arcady Down East

HC 64 Box 370
Blue Hill, ME 04614-9603
(207)374-3700

Circa 1834. This attractive Victorian Shingle inn, listed in the National Register, offers many authentic touches, including period antiques and tin ceilings. The inn's seven guest rooms include the Celebration Suite, perfect for honeymooners with its cozy fireplace and sitting area. Another favorite with visitors is the Captain's Quarters, featuring a skylight to help highlight its unique furnishings. The impressive coastal beauty of Acadia National Park is a short drive from the inn.

Innkeeper(s): Mark & Anna Trundy. $85-110. MC, VISA, AX, TC. 7 rooms, 5 with PB, 1 with FP and 1 suite. Breakfast included in rates. Types of meals: Full bkfst and early coffee/tea. Beds: KQDT. Turndown service and ceiling fan in room. Bicycles, child care and ice skating in winter on premises. Antiquing, fishing, live theater, parks, shopping, cross-country skiing and water sports nearby.

Certificate may be used: Oct. 20 through June 1.

Boothbay   J4

Kenniston Hill Inn

Rt 27, PO Box 125
Boothbay, ME 04537-0125
(207)633-2159 (800)992-2915 Fax:(207)633-2159

Circa 1786. The elegant clapboard home is the oldest inn at Boothbay Harbor and was occupied by the Kenniston family for more than a century. Five of the antique-filled bedrooms have fireplaces. After a walk through the gardens or woods, warm up in the parlor next to the elegant, open-hearthed fireplace. Boothbay Harbor offers something for everybody, including whale-watching excursions and dinner theaters.

Innkeeper(s): Susan & David Straight. $60-110. MC, VISA, DS, PC, TC. 10 rooms with PB, 5 with FP. Breakfast and afternoon tea included in rates. Types of meals: Full bkfst and early coffee/tea. Beds: KQDT. Ceiling fan in room. Fax on premises. Antiquing, fishing, live theater, parks, shopping, downhill skiing, cross-country skiing and water sports nearby.

Publicity: Boothbay Register.

"England may be the home of the original bed & breakfast, but Kenniston Hill Inn is where it has been perfected!"

Certificate may be used: January-May, November and December, excluding holiday weekends. Rate is $110 only.

Boothbay Harbor   J4

Harbour Towne Inn on The Waterfront

71 Townsend Ave
Boothbay Harbor, ME 04538-1158
(207)633-4300 (800)722-4240 Fax:(207)633-4300
Internet: www.acadia.net/harbourtowneinn
E-mail: mainco@gwi.net

Circa 1880. This Victorian inn's well-known trademark boasts that it is "the finest B&B on the waterfront." Most of the inn's 12 rooms offer an outside deck and the Penthouse has an outstanding view of the harbor from its private deck. Breakfast is served in the inn's Sunroom, and guests also may relax in the parlor, which has a miniature antique library and a beautiful antique fireplace. A conference area is available for meetings. The inn's meticulous grounds include flower gardens and well-kept shrubs and trees. It's an easy walk to the village and its art galleries, restaurants, shops and boat trips. Special off-season packages are available. Ft. William Henry and the Fisherman's Memorial are nearby.

Innkeeper(s): George Thomas & family. $79-299. MC, VISA, AX, DS, PC, TC. 12 rooms with PB and 1 conference room. Breakfast included in rates. Type of meal: Cont plus. Beds: KQDT. Cable TV and phone in room. Fax and copier on premises. Handicap access. Antiquing, fishing, boating, live theater, parks, shopping, downhill skiing, cross-country skiing and water sports nearby.

Location: Coastal village.

Certificate may be used: November through part of June, excluding all holidays, special events and Friday/Saturday nights. Off rack rates.

Bridgton 12

Tarry-A-While Resort

Box A, Highland Ridge Rd
Bridgton, ME 04009
(207)647-2522 Fax:(207)647-5512
Internet: www.tarryawhile.com
E-mail: tarryayl@megalink.net

Circa 1897. Tarry-A-While offers a variety of comfortable accommodations, including a Victorian inn and cottages. There is also a social hall. The resort is located on a 25-acre hillside and there are plenty of outdoor activities. Tennis and boating are included in the rates, and sailing or waterskiing is available. An 18-hole golf course is a walk away. The inn's dining room, which overlooks Highland Lake and Pleasant Mountain, serves "new American" cuisine as you gaze at the sunset.

Innkeeper(s): Marc & Nancy Stretch. $60-135. MC, VISA, PC, TC. 27 rooms, 22 with PB. Breakfast included in rates. Type of meal: Cont. Beds: KQDT. Air conditioning. Bicycles, tennis, golf course, canoes and rowboats on premises. Antiquing, boats, live theater, shopping and tennis nearby.

"Thanks for sharing this magical place with us! What a wonderful experience."

Certificate may be used: Anytime in June. Aug. 23 through Labor Day.

Camden 15

Captain Swift Inn

72 Elm St
Camden, ME 04843-1907
(207)236-8113 (800)251-0865 Fax:(207)230-0464
Internet: www.swiftinn.com
E-mail: swiftinn@midcoast.com

Circa 1810. This inviting Federal-style home remains much as it did in the 19th century, including the original 12-over-12 windows and a beehive oven. The innkeepers have worked diligently to preserve the historic flavor, and the home's original five fireplaces, handsome wide pine floors, restored moldings and exposed beams add to the warm and cozy interior. Guest rooms are filled with period antiques and reproductions and offer down pillows, handmade quilts and comfortable beds. The only addition to the home was a new section, which includes the innkeeper's quarters, a kitchen and a guest room entirely accessible for guests with wheelchairs. A gourmet, three-course breakfast includes items that sound decadent, but are truly low in fat and cholesterol, such as an apple pancake souffle.

Innkeeper(s): Tom & Kathy Filip. $95-125. MC, VISA, PC, TC. 4 rooms with PB. Breakfast and afternoon tea included in rates. Types of meals: Full gourmet bkfst and early coffee/tea. Beds: QT. Table and chairs in room. Air conditioning. VCR, fax, copier and library on premises. Handicap access. Antiquing, fishing,

golf, schooners, lighthouses, museums, live theater, parks, shopping, downhill skiing, cross-country skiing, tennis and water sports nearby.

Publicity: *Maine Boats & Harbors, Boston Patriot Ledger, Tea-Time Journeys, Secrets of Entertaining and Wake Up & Smell the Coffee.*

"We came intending to stay for one night and ended up staying for five. . .need we say more!"

Certificate may be used: Nov. 1-April 30, Sunday-Saturday. No holidays.

The Elms B&B

84 Elm St
Camden, ME 04843-1907
(207)236-6250 (800)755-3567 Fax:(207)236-7330
Internet: www.elmsinn.net
E-mail: theelms@midcoast.com

Circa 1806. Captain Calvin Curtis built this Colonial a few minutes' stroll from the picturesque harbor. Candlelight shimmers year round from the inn's windows. A sitting room, library and parlor are open for guests. Tastefully appointed bed chambers scattered with antiques are available in both the main house and the carriage house. A cottage garden can be seen beside the carriage house. A lighthouse theme permeates the decor, and there is a wide selection of lighthouse books, collectibles and artwork.

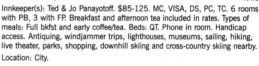

Innkeeper(s): Ted & Jo Panayotoff. $85-125. MC, VISA, DS, PC, TC. 6 rooms with PB, 3 with FP. Breakfast and afternoon tea included in rates. Types of meals: Full bkfst and early coffee/tea. Beds: QT. Phone in room. Handicap access. Antiquing, windjammer trips, lighthouses, museums, sailing, hiking, live theater, parks, shopping, downhill skiing and cross-country skiing nearby.

Location: City.

"If something is worth doing, it's worth doing first class, and your place is definitely first class."

Certificate may be used: Nov. 1 to May 10, all days.

Lord Camden Inn

24 Main St
Camden, ME 04843-1704
(207)236-4325 (800)336-4325 Fax:(207)236-7141
E-mail: lordcam@midcoast.com

Circa 1893. Lord Camden Inn, housed in a century-old brick building, offers the gentle warmth of a seaside inn with all the comforts and services of a modern downtown hotel. Located in the midst of Camden's fine shops and restaurants, the bustling waterfront and beautiful parks, Lord Camden Inn offers splendid views of the harbor, Camden Hill and the village. Amenities include private baths, cable TV, air conditioning, phones and elevator services.

Innkeeper(s): Stuart & Marianne Smith. $88-198. MC, VISA, PC. 31 rooms with PB, 4 suites and 1 conference room. Breakfast included in rates. Types of meals: Cont plus and early coffee/tea. Beds: KQD. Phone, some desks and refrigerators in room. Fax, copier and valet service available in high season on premises. Antiquing, fishing, sailing, fine dining, bicycle rentals, kayaking, hiking, live theater, parks, shopping, downhill skiing, cross-country skiing and water sports nearby.

Publicity: *Portland Magazine and Thinner.*

Certificate may be used: Oct. 16-May 31, Monday-Sunday.

Cape Elizabeth   K3

Inn By The Sea

40 Bowery Beach Rd
Cape Elizabeth, ME 04107-2599
(207)799-3134 (800)888-4287 Fax:(207)799-4779

Circa 1986. This cottage-style resort is like a modern version of
the hotels and inns that dotted Maine's coast in its heyday as a
summer spot. The inn has its own private boardwalk leading to
Crescent Beach. Guests can enjoy swimming, tennis and shuffleboard without leaving the inn's grounds, which also offer a
tea garden and gazebo. The well-appointed rooms are elegant,
but not imposing, with Chippendale furnishings, wicker and floral chintz. Guests opting for one of the inn's cozy garden suites
can grab a book from the inn's library and enjoy it from a rocker
on their own private porch. Cuisine at the inn's gourmet
Audubon Room is full of memorable items. In the summer
months, the inn opens its outdoor West End Cafe and Pool Bar.
Innkeeper(s): Maureen McQuade. $100-390. MC, VISA, AX, DS, TC. 43 suites,
6 with FP and 2 conference rooms. Type of meal: Full bkfst. Beds: KQD. Cable
TV, phone, turndown service, ceiling fan and VCR in room. Fax, copier and bicycles on premises. Amusement parks, antiquing, fishing, live theater, parks, shopping, downhill skiing, cross-country skiing, sporting events & water sports nearby.
Pets Allowed.
Certificate may be used: November-April, excluding holidays, Sunday-Friday.

Corea   I7

The Black Duck Inn on Corea Harbor

PO Box 39 Crowley Island Rd
Corea, ME 04624-0039
(207)963-2689 (877)963-2689 Fax:(207)963-7495
Internet: www.blackduck.com
E-mail: bduck@acadia.net

Circa 1890. Two of the guest rooms at this turn-of-the-century
farmhouse boast harbor views, while another offers a wooded
scene out its windows. The innkeepers have decorated the
home in an eclectic mix of old and new with antiques and contemporary pieces. There are two waterfront cottages for those
who prefer more privacy. The full, gourmet breakfasts include
house specialties, such as "eggs Black Duck" or items such as
orange glazed French toast, blintzes or perhaps eggs Benedict.
Innkeeper(s): Barry Canner & Bob Travers. $85-115. MC, VISA, DS, PC, TC.
6 rooms, 4 with PB, 2 suites, 2 cottages, 2 cabins and 1 conference room.
Breakfast included in rates. Types of meals: Full gourmet bkfst and early cof-
fee/tea. Beds: QDT. VCR, fax, copier and library on premises. Antiquing, art
galleries, beaches, bicycling, canoeing/kayaking, fishing, golf, hiking, live theater, parks, shopping, cross-country skiing and wineries nearby.
Publicity: *Boston Globe and Miami Herald.*

*"Never could we have known how warmly received we would all four
feel and how really restored we would be by the end of the week."*
Certificate may be used: Oct. 15-May 15.

Durham   I3

The Bagley House

1290 Royalsborough Rd
Durham, ME 04222-5225
(207)865-6566 (800)765-1772 Fax:(207)353-5878
Internet: www.bagleyhouse.com
E-mail: bglyhse@aol.com

Circa 1772. Six acres of fields and woods surround the Bagley
House. Once an inn, a store and a schoolhouse, it is the oldest
house in town. Guest rooms are decorated with colonial fur-

nishings and hand-sewn Maine quilts.
For breakfast, guests gather in the
country kitchen in front of a huge
brick fireplace and beehive oven.
Innkeeper(s): Suzanne O'Connor & Susan
Backhouse. $75-150. MC, VISA,
AX, DS, PC, TC. 8 rooms with
PB, 4 with FP and 1 conference
room. Breakfast and afternoon
tea included in rates. Types of meals:
Full bkfst and early coffee/tea. Beds: QDT. Fax and blueberry picking on
premises. Antiquing, live theater, shopping, downhill skiing, cross-country ski-
ing and sporting events nearby.
Location: Country.
Publicity: *Los Angeles Times, New England Getaways, Lewiston Sun and
Springfield Register.*

*"I had the good fortune to stumble on the Bagley House. The rooms
are well-appointed and the innkeepers are charming."*
Certificate may be used: November-June, Sunday-Thursday.

Eastport   G8

The Inn at Eastport

13 Washington St
Eastport, ME 04631-1324
(207)853-4307 Fax:(207)853-6143
E-mail: cbcs@nemaine.com

Circa 1835. Skin-divers consider the waters near this Federal-
style inn among the best in the United States. The innkeepers
are more than happy to assist guests with their sightseeing
efforts in America's most northeasterly city. The inn's antique
furnishings, hardwood floors and black marble hearths will
please visitors. Enjoy a soak in the inn's outdoor hot tub. The
gourmet breakfasts may include wild blueberry pancakes. New
Brunswick is just a 15-minute ferry ride away.
Innkeeper(s): Robert & Brenda Booker. $45-65. MC, VISA, DS, PC, TC. 5
rooms, 4 with PB. Breakfast and afternoon tea included in rates. Types of
meals: Full bkfst and early coffee/tea. Beds: QD. Turndown service in room.
VCR, fax, sauna and hot tub on premises. Antiquing, fishing, golf, parks,
shopping, tennis and water sports nearby.
Pets allowed: If well behaved.

*"Thanks for the great Northern hospitality! It was the best B&B
experience we've ever had!"*
Certificate may be used: January-October.

The Milliken House

29 Washington St
Eastport, ME 04631-1324
(207)853-2955

Circa 1846. This inn is filled with beautiful furnishings and
knickknacks, much of which belonged to the home's first
owner, Benjamin Milliken. Ornately carved, marble-topped
pieces and period decor take guests back in time to the
Victorian Era. Milliken maintained a wharf on Eastport's waterfront from which he serviced the tall trading ships that used
the harbor as a port of entry to the United States. An afternoon
glass of port or sherry and chocolate turn-down service are
among the amenities. Breakfasts are a gourmet treat, served in
the dining room with its carved, antique furnishings.
Innkeeper(s): Joyce Weber. $50-65. MC, VISA, AX, PC, TC. 5 rooms with PB
and 1 conference room. Breakfast included in rates. Type of meal: Full bkfst.
Beds: QT. TV and phone in room.

"A lovely trip back in history to a more gracious time."
Certificate may be used: January-June, October-December, seven days a week.

Weston House

26 Boynton St
Eastport, ME 04631-1305
(207)853-2907 (800)853-2907 Fax:(207)853-0981

Circa 1810. Jonathan Weston, an 1802 Harvard graduate, built this Federal-style house on a hill overlooking Passamaquoddy Bay. John Audubon stayed here as a guest of the Westons while

awaiting passage to Labrador in 1833. Each guest room is furnished with antiques and Oriental rugs. The Weston and Audubon rooms boast views of the bay and gardens. Breakfast menus vary,

including such delectables as heavenly pancakes with hot apricot syrup or freshly baked muffins and coddled eggs. Seasonal brunches are served on weekends and holidays. The area is full of outdoor activities, including whale watching. Nearby Saint Andrews-by-the-Sea offers plenty of shops and restaurants.

Innkeeper(s): Jett & John Peterson. $50-75. PC, TC. 5 rooms, 1 with FP and 1 suite. Breakfast and afternoon tea included in rates. Type of meal: Full gourmet bkfst. Beds: KQDT. Fishing, whale watching, nature, live theater, shopping and tennis nearby.

Location: Coastal New England village.

Publicity: *Down East, Los Angeles Times, Boston Globe, Boston Magazine and New York Times.*

"All parts of ourselves have been nourished."

Certificate may be used: Subject to availability. All months with the exception of the month of August.

Eliot   L2

High Meadows B&B

Rt 101
Eliot, ME 03903
(207)439-0590 Fax:(207)439-6343
E-mail: hymedobb@aol.com

Circa 1740. A ship's captain built this house, now filled with remembrances of colonial days. At one point, it was raised and a floor added underneath, so the upstairs is older than the downstairs. It is conveniently located to factory outlets in Kittery, Maine, and great dining and historic museums in Portsmouth, N.H.

Innkeeper(s): Elaine & Ray. $80-90. MC, VISA, AX, PC, TC. 4 rooms with PB. Breakfast and afternoon tea included in rates. Types of meals: Full bkfst and early coffee/tea. Beds: QDT. Antiquing, fishing, shopping and water sports nearby.

Location: Country.

Publicity: *Portsmouth Herald and York County Focus.*

"High Meadows was the highlight of our trip."

Certificate may be used: Monday-Thursday; April, May, June.

Moses Paul Inn

270 Goodwin Rd
Eliot, ME 03903-1204
(207)439-1861 (800)552-6058

Circa 1780. This Colonial farmhouse is charming and hard to miss, with its barn-red exterior and white trim. The home is truly welcoming. Restored wood floors and woodwork gleam, and rooms, some with exposed beams, are decorated with trea-

sures the innkeepers found at local auctions. Quilts, antiques and country furnishings are among the finds. The restored barn serves as an antique shop. Be sure to ask the innkeepers about a French soldier who may still inhabit the halls in ghostly form. Kittery Outlet Malls and historic Portsmouth are just a few minutes away, as is the coastline.

Innkeeper(s): Joanne Weiss & Larry James. $80-120. MC, VISA, DS, PC, TC. 6 rooms, 3 with PB and 1 suite. Breakfast included in rates. Type of meal: Full bkfst. Beds: QDT. Ceiling fan and suite with fireplace in room. VCR, fax and library on premises. Amusement parks, antiquing, fishing, live theater, parks, shopping, downhill skiing, cross-country skiing, sporting events and water sports nearby.

Certificate may be used: Anytime, subject to availability.

Falmouth   J3

Quaker Tavern B&B

377 Gray Rd # 26/100
Falmouth, ME 04105-2520
(207)797-5540 Fax:(207)797-7599
E-mail: quakerbb@aol.com

Circa 1971. This authentically maintained Federal building was once a tavern run by a descendant of the Halls, the original family of Quakers who settled in Maine. The innkeeper has collected appropriate period furnishings and as an additional enhancement, sometimes dresses in period costume, taking on the role of Experience Hall, once the tavern keeper here. This is usually done along with other historical society members when hosting school children at the inn. The Moses Eaton Jr. room features original stenciling with a pineapple motif applied on wet plaster. There are working fireplaces in each room as well as feather beds, antique four posters and views out over the inn's 15 acres of pasture and woodland. Candlelight breakfasts are offered. The innkeeper also runs Maine Farm Vacations and a reservation service for Maine B&Bs.

Innkeeper(s): Donna Little. $50-80. MC, VISA, PC, TC. 4 rooms, 1 with PB, 1 with FP and 1 conference room. Breakfast included in rates. Types of meals: Cont plus and early coffee/tea. Beds: D. Air conditioning. VCR, fax and copier on premises. Amusement parks, antiquing, fishing, live theater, parks, shopping, downhill skiing, cross-country skiing, sporting events and water sports nearby.

Location: Mountains.

Publicity: *Portland Press Herald.*

Certificate may be used: November-May.

Fryeburg   I1

Admiral Peary House

9 Elm St
Fryeburg, ME 04037-1114
(207)935-3365 (800)237-8080 Fax:(207)935-3365
Internet: www.mountwashingtonvalley.com/admiralpearyhouse
E-mail: admpeary@nxi.com

Circa 1865. Robert E. Peary, the American explorer who discovered the North Pole, once lived in this mid-19th-century home. Each of the guest rooms is named to honor Peary's memory. The North Pole room

includes a scenic mountain view and a king-size brass bed. The Admiral's Quarters include a four-poster bed. Breakfasts are served on tables in the country kitchen and dining room and include such entrees as stuffed French toast, wild blueberry pancakes or the signature dish, Admiral Peary Penguin Pie, a savory combination of cheese, herbs and eggs. In addition to the cozy rooms and hearty breakfasts, the innkeepers offer a variety of amenities. There is a clay tennis court, an outdoor spa, billiard table and, in the winter months, guests can rent or buy snowshoes and traverse the innkeeper's acres of marked snowshoe trails. Guests also can canoe the Saco River, climb to the top of the world's largest boulder, discover covered bridges or visit historic sites.

Innkeeper(s): Ed & Nancy Greenberg. $80-138. MC, VISA, AX, PC, TC. 6 rooms with PB. Breakfast included in rates. Types of meals: Full bkfst, country bkfst, veg bkfst and early coffee/tea. Beds: KQT. Air conditioning. VCR, fax, spa, bicycles, tennis, library, wet bar with complimentary beverages, billiards and snowshoe trail and rentals on premises. Antiquing, beaches, bicycling, canoeing/kayaking, fishing, golf, hiking, horseback riding, snowshoeing, snowmobiling, live theater, museums, parks, shopping, downhill skiing, cross-country skiing, tennis and water sports nearby.

Location: Small village.

Publicity: *Mountain Ear.*

Certificate may be used: Dec. 10-March 20 any day, non-holiday, May 1-June 30 midweek.

Greenville   F4

Greenville Inn

Norris St, PO Box 1194
Greenville, ME 04441-1194
(207)695-2206 (888)695-6000 Fax:(207)695-0335
Internet: www.greenvilleinn.com
E-mail: gvlinn@moosehead.net

Circa 1895. Lumber baron William Shaw built this inn, which sits on a hill overlooking Moosehead Lake and the Squaw Mountains. The inn includes many unique features. Ten years were needed to complete the embellishments on the cherry and mahogany paneling, which is found throughout the inn. A spruce tree is painted on one of the leaded-glass windows on the stairway landing. The inn's six  fireplaces are adorned with carved mantels, English tiles and mosaics. The inn's dining room is ideal for a romantic dinner. Fresh, seasonal ingredients fill the ever-changing menu, and the dining room also offers a variety of wine choices.

Innkeeper(s): Elfi, Michael and Susie Schnetzer. $95-195. MC, VISA, DS, PC, TC. 5 rooms, 12 with PB, 2 with FP, 1 suite and 6 cottages. Type of meal: Cont plus. Beds: KQDT. TV in room.

Publicity: *Maine Times, Portland Monthly, Bangor Daily News and Grays Sporting Journal.*

"The fanciest place in town. It is indeed a splendid place."

Certificate may be used: Nov. 1-April 30, subject to availability, not valid during holiday and winter vacation periods.

Guilford   G4

Trebor Inn

Golda Ct
Guilford, ME 04443
(207)876-4070 (888)487-3267

Circa 1830. Seven guest rooms are available at this stately, turreted Victorian inn, which overlooks Guilford from high on a hill along the Moosehead Trail. Those who enjoy hunting bear,

deer, partridge and pheasant should inquire about the inn's special rates for hunters. Meals are served family-style, and dinners are available on request. The family-oriented inn also accommodates business meetings, family reunions and weddings. Within five minutes of the inn, visitors will find basketball courts, a nine-hole golf course and tennis courts. Peaks-Kenny State Park and Sebec Lake are nearby.

Innkeeper(s): Robert & Larraine Vernal. $50-65. MC, VISA, AX, PC, TC. 7 rooms, 2 with PB. Breakfast included in rates. Types of meals: Full bkfst and early coffee/tea. Beds: QT. VCR on premises. Antiquing, fishing, golf, hunting, snowmobiling, parks, shopping, downhill skiing, cross-country skiing, tennis and water sports nearby.

Location: Town.

Certificate may be used: April 1 to Dec. 1.

Harpswell   J3

The Vicarage By The Sea

RR 1, Box 368B
Harpswell, ME 04079
(207)833-5480 Fax:(207)833-5480
Internet: www.gwi.net/~jmoulton
E-mail: jmoulton@biddeford.com

Circa 1985. This oceanfront inn is located on three acres on an isthmus south of Brunswick. The sun room affords floor-to-ceiling windows looking out through the wooded vistas to the sea. Breakfast is full (egg and cheese casseroles), yet guests still often enjoy a picnic lunch near the water. A favorite activity is walking along the private beach and exploring the shoreline at low tide.

Innkeeper(s): Johanna Wigg. $45-120. VISA, PC, TC. 4 rooms, 2 with PB and 1 suite. Breakfast included in rates. Types of meals: Full gourmet bkfst and early coffee/tea. Beds: QDT. Cable TV, ceiling fan and VCR in room. Fax, copier, swimming, library, pet boarding and canoe on premises. Handicap access. Antiquing, fishing, golf, live theater, parks, shopping, cross-country skiing, sporting events, tennis and water sports nearby.

Pets allowed: downstairs only rooms, well-behaved.

Location: wooded, ocean front.

Certificate may be used: Nov. 1 to March 31, excluding February (Sunday, Monday, Tuesday, Wednesday, Saturday) excluding Friday and Saturday.

Kennebunkport   K2

Cove House

11 S Maine St
Kennebunkport, ME 04046-6313
(207)967-3704

Circa 1793. This roomy Colonial Revival farmhouse overlooks Chick's Cove on the Kennebunk River. The inn's peaceful setting offers easy access to beaches, shops and the town. Three guest rooms serve visitors of this antique-filled home. Guests enjoy full breakfasts, which often include the inn's famous blueberry muffins, in the Flow Blue dining room. A popular gathering spot is the book-lined living room/library. Bicycles may be borrowed for a leisurely ride around the town. A cozy, secluded cottage with a screened front porch is another lodging option.

Innkeeper(s): Katherine Jones. $75-95. MC, VISA, PC, TC. 3 rooms with PB and 1 cottage. Breakfast and afternoon tea included in rates. Types of meals: Full bkfst and early coffee/tea. Beds: QT. VCR, bicycles and library on premises. Antiquing, fishing, whale watching, sailing, live theater, parks, shopping, cross-country skiing and water sports nearby.

Certificate may be used: Nov. 1-May 15, excluding holiday weekends.

Crosstrees

6 South St
Kennebunkport, ME 04046
(207)967-2780 (800)564-1527 Fax:(207)967-2610
Internet: www.crosstrees.com
E-mail: info@crosstrees.com

Circa 1818. Located in Maine's largest historic district, this Federal-style house was built by Daniel Walker, a descendant of an original Kennebunkport family. Later, Maine artist and architect Abbot Graves purchased the property and named it "Crosstrees" for its maple trees. The inn fea-

tures New England antiques and brilliant flower gardens in view of the formal dining room in spring and summer. A full breakfast is provided. Art galleries, beaches, antiquing and golf are nearby.

Innkeeper(s): Dennis Rafferty & Keith Henley. $100-225. MC, VISA, PC, TC. 4 rooms with PB, 3 with FP. Breakfast included in rates. Types of meals: Full bkfst and early coffee/tea. Beds: KQ. Suite with Jacuzzi in room. Antiquing, fishing, ocean, live theater and shopping nearby.

"Absolutely gorgeous inn. You two were wonderful to us. What a great place to relax."

Certificate may be used: Monday-Thursday, mid November to April 30.

English Meadows Inn

141 Port Rd
Kennebunkport, ME 04043
(207)967-5766 (800)272-0698

Circa 1860. Bordered by century-old lilac bushes, this Queen Anne Victorian inn and attached carriage house offer 13 guest rooms. The inn's well-tended grounds, which include apple trees, gardens and lush lawns, invite bird-lovers or those who desire a relaxing stroll. Four-poster beds, afghans and hand-sewn quilts are found in many of the guest rooms. Visitors also will enjoy the talents of local artists, whose works are featured throughout the inn. Guests may eat breakfast in bed before heading out to explore Kennebunkport.

Innkeeper(s): Kathy & Peter Smith. $85-150. MC, VISA, AX, PC, TC. 12 rooms with PB, 1 suite and 1 cottage. Breakfast and afternoon tea included in rates. Types of meals: Full bkfst and early coffee/tea. Beds: KQDT. AC, refrigerator and cable TV in some rooms in room. Amusement parks, antiquing, fishing, live theater, parks, shopping, cross-country skiing and water sports nearby.

"Thanks for the memories! You have a warm Yankee hospitality here!"

Certificate may be used: November-May, Sunday through Thursday.

Kittery   L2

Enchanted Nights B&B

29 Wentworth St, Rt 103
Kittery, ME 03904-1720
(207)439-1489
Internet: www.enchanted-nights-bandb.com
E-mail: info@enchanted-nights-bandb.com

Circa 1890. The innkeepers bill this unique inn as a "Victorian fantasy for the romantic at heart." Each of the guest rooms is unique, from the spacious rooms with double whirlpool tubs to the cozy turret room. A whimsical combination of country

French and Victorian decor permeates the interior. Wrought-iron beds and hand-painted furnishings add to the ambiance. Breakfasts, often with a vegetarian theme, are served with gourmet coffee in the morning room on antique floral china.

Innkeeper(s): Nancy Bogerberger & Peter Lamandia. $52-227. MC, VISA, AX, DC, CB, DS, PC, TC. 6 rooms with PB, 2 with FP and 2 conference rooms. Breakfast included in rates. Types of meals: Full gourmet bkfst, cont plus, cont, veg bkfst and early coffee/tea. Beds: KQDT. Cable TV, ceiling fan, VCR and whirlpool tub in room. Air conditioning. Refrigerator on premises. Handicap access. Antiquing, art galleries, beaches, bicycling, canoeing/kayaking, golf, hiking, horseback riding, outlet shopping, historic homes, whale watching, harbor cruises, live theater, museums, parks, shopping, sporting events, tennis, water sports and wineries nearby.

Pets Allowed.

Location: City.

"The atmosphere was great. Your breakfast was elegant. The breakfast room made us feel we had gone back in time. All in all it was a very enjoyable stay."

Certificate may be used: Nov. 1-June 20, Sunday-Thursday. No holiday weekends.

Naples   J2

Augustus Bove House

Corner Rts 302 & 114, RR 1 Box 501
Naples, ME 04055
(207)693-6365
Internet: www.maineguide.com/naples/augustus
E-mail: augbovehouse@pivot.net

Circa 1830. A long front lawn nestles up against the stone foundation and veranda of this house, once known as the Hotel Naples, one of the area's summer hotels in the 1800s. In the 1920s, the inn was host to a number of prominent guests, including Enrico Caruso, Joseph P. Kennedy and Howard Hughes. The guest rooms are decorated in a Colonial style and modestly furnished with antiques. Many rooms provide a view of Long Lake. A fancy country breakfast is provided.

Innkeeper(s): David & Arlene Stetson. $59-175. MC, VISA, AX, DS, PC, TC. 11 rooms, 7 with PB and 1 suite. Breakfast and afternoon tea included in rates. Types of meals: Full bkfst and early coffee/tea. Beds: KQT. Cable TV and phone in room. Air conditioning. VCR, fax and spa on premises. Antiquing, fishing, live theater, parks, shopping, downhill skiing, cross-country skiing and water sports nearby.

Pets Allowed.

Publicity: *Brighton Times.*

"Beautiful place, rooms, and people."

Certificate may be used: Void July and August, holidays and first week of October, certain rooms apply.

Inn at Long Lake

Lake House Rd, PO Box 806
Naples, ME 04055
(207)693-6226 (800)437-0328
Internet: www.innatlonglake.com
E-mail: innatll@megalink.net

Circa 1906. Reopened in 1988, the inn housed the overflow guests from the Lake House resort about 90 years ago. Guests traveled to the resort via the Oxford-Cumberland Canal, and each room is named for a historic canal boat. The cozy rooms offer fluffy comforters and a warm, country decor in a romantic atmosphere. Warm up in front of a crackling fire in the great room, or enjoy a cool Long Lake breeze on the veranda while watching horses in nearby pastures. The setting is ideal for housing guests for weddings or reunions.

Innkeeper(s): Maynard & Irene Hincks. $49-158. MC, VISA, DS, PC, TC. 16 rooms with PB, 2 suites and 1 conference room. Breakfast included in rates. Types of meals: Cont plus and early coffee/tea. Beds: QDT. TV in room. Air conditioning. Library on premises. Antiquing, fishing, biking, hiking, parks, shopping, downhill skiing, cross-country skiing and water sports nearby.

Publicity: *Bridgton News and Portland Press Herald.*

"Convenient location, tastefully done and the prettiest inn I've ever stayed in."

Certificate may be used: Oct. 16-May 14, Sunday-Thursday.

Ogunquit   K2

Chestnut Tree Inn

PO Box 2201
Ogunquit, ME 03907-2201
(207)646-4529 (800)362-0757
Internet: www.chestnuttreeinn.com
E-mail: mail@chestnuttreeinn.com

Circa 1870. Gable roofs peak out from the top of this Victorian inn, which has greeted guests for more than a century. A smattering of antiques and Victorian decor creates a 19th-century atmosphere. Guests can relax on the porch or head out for a stroll on Marginal Way, a mile-long path set along Maine's scenic coastline. The beach, shops, Ogunquit Playhouse and a variety of restaurants are just a few minutes down the road.

Innkeeper(s): Cynthia Diana & Ronald St. Laurent. $35-125. MC, VISA, AX, TC. 22 rooms, 15 with PB and 1 suite. Type of meal: Cont plus. Beds: QDT. Cable TV and phone in room. Air conditioning. Amusement parks, antiquing, fishing, live theater, parks, shopping, downhill skiing, cross-country skiing, sporting events and water sports nearby.

"Your inn was absolutely beautiful and peaceful. Your kindness will not be forgotten."

Certificate may be used: Monday-Thursday, May 15-June 15 and Sept. 15-Oct. 15.

Hartwell House Inn & Conference Center

118 Shore Rd, PO Box 393
Ogunquit, ME 03907-0393
(207)646-7210 (800)235-8883
Internet: www.hartwellhouseinn.com
E-mail: hartwell@cybertours.com

Circa 1921. Hartwell House offers suites and guest rooms furnished with distinctive early American and English antiques. Many rooms are available with French doors opening to private balconies overlooking sculpted flower gardens. Guests are treated to both a full, gourmet breakfast and afternoon tea. Seasonal dining packages are available. Restaurants, beaches, hiking and outlet shopping is nearby.

Innkeeper(s): Christopher & Tracey Anderson. $90-190. MC, VISA, AX, DS, TC. 16 rooms with PB, 3 suites and 4 conference rooms. Type of meal: Full gourmet bkfst. Beds: QT. TV and ceiling fan in room. Air conditioning. Fax on premises. Antiquing, fishing, restaurants, outlet and boutique shopping, beaches, live theater, parks, shopping, cross-country skiing, sporting events and water sports nearby.

Publicity: *Innsider.*

"This engaging country inn will be reserved for my special clients."

Certificate may be used: Nov. 1-April 30, excluding holidays and special events.

The West Highland Inn

14 Shore Rd
Ogunquit, ME 03907
(207)646-2181

Circa 1890. This Dutch Colonial home features an enclosed front porch, decorated with wicker furnishings, flowers and plants. The interior is Victorian in decor with some elegant traditional touches. In the guest rooms, coordinating prints decorate the windows and the beds. Each room is different from the next. The innkeepers serve a plentiful buffet breakfast, as well as homemade treats in the afternoon. The inn is open from mid-May until mid-October. In addition to the inn rooms, the innkeepers offer three efficiency units.

Innkeeper(s): Steve & Linda Williams. $60-115. MC, VISA, PC, TC. 12 rooms, 10 with PB. Breakfast included in rates. Types of meals: Full bkfst and early coffee/tea. Beds: KQDT. Cable TV in room. Air conditioning. Pet boarding on premises. Amusement parks, antiquing, fishing, golf, beach, live theater, parks, shopping, tennis and water sports nearby.

Pets Allowed.

Location: Small seaside village.

Certificate may be used: April 1-June 15, Sunday-Thursday; Sept. 10-Oct. 15, Sunday-Thursday.

Old Orchard Beach   K2

Atlantic Birches Inn

20 Portland Ave Rt 98
Old Orchard Beach, ME 04064-2212
(207)934-5295 (888)934-5295
Internet: www.atlanticbirches.com
E-mail: info@atlanticbirches.com

Circa 1903. The front porch of this Shingle-style Victorian and 1920s bungalow are shaded by white birch trees. Badminton and croquet are set up on the lawn. The houses are a place for relaxation and enjoyment, uncluttered, simple havens filled with comfortable furnishings. The guest rooms are decorated with a few antiques and pastel wallcoverings. Maine's coast offers an endless amount of activities, from boating to whale watching. It is a five-minute walk to the beach and the pier.

Innkeeper(s): Dan & Cyndi Bolduc. $85-109. MC, VISA, AX, DS, TC. 10 rooms with PB. Breakfast included in rates. Type of meal: Cont plus. Beds: KQDT. Ceiling fan in room. Air conditioning. VCR, copier, swimming and library on premises. Amusement parks, antiquing, fishing, parks, shopping, sporting events and water sports nearby.

"Your home and family are just delightful! What a treat to stay in such a warm & loving home."

Certificate may be used: Sunday-Thursday, Jan. 1-June 17, Oct. 17-Dec. 30.

Readfield   I3

Echo Lake Lodge & Cottages

PO Box 528
Readfield, ME 04355-0528
(207)685-9550

Circa 1938. This waterfront lodge offers knotty pine interiors, large rooms and antiques. There is a screened porch and a fieldstone fireplace. There are 20 acres to explore, and at the inn's boat dock guests may rent small sailboats, canoes and motorboats. The lake offers salmon, trout, bass, and perch.

Innkeeper(s): Eleanor & James McClay. $50-100. PC, TC. 7 rooms, 5 with PB, 15 cottages and 1 conference room. Breakfast included in rates. Type of meal: Cont plus. Beds: KQDT. VCR, fax, copier, swimming, bicycles, library, pet boarding, fishing, hiking, canoeing, sailing and power boating on premises. Amusement parks, antiquing, fishing, golf, ocean, mountains, live theater, parks, shopping, tennis and water sports nearby.

Certificate may be used: May 15 to Nov. 15 no weekends, July and August (Friday & Saturday nights).

Saco   K2

Crown 'n' Anchor Inn

121 North St, PO Box 228
Saco, ME 04072-0228
(207)282-3829 (800)561-8865 Fax:(207)282-7495
E-mail: cnacgwi.net

Circa 1827. This Greek Revival house, listed in the National Register, features both Victorian baroque and colonial antiques. Two rooms include whirlpool tubs. A collection of British coronation memorabilia dis-

played throughout the inn includes 200 items. Guests gather in the Victorian parlor or the formal library. The innkeepers, a college librarian and an academic bookseller, lined the shelves with several thousand volumes, including extensive Civil War and British royal family collections and travel, theater and nautical books. Royal Dalton china, crystal and fresh flowers create a festive breakfast setting.

Innkeeper(s): John Barclay & Martha Forester. $70-120. MC, VISA, AX, PC, TC. 6 rooms with PB, 2 with FP. Breakfast included in rates. Types of meals: Full gourmet bkfst and early coffee/tea. Beds: KQDT. Cable TV and two rooms with whirlpools in room. VCR and library on premises. Amusement parks, antiquing, fishing, live theater, parks, shopping, downhill skiing, cross-country skiing, sporting events and water sports nearby.

Pets allowed: Small or caged.

Location: City.

Publicity: *Yankee, Saco, Biddeford, Old Orchard Beach Courier, Country, Portland Press Herald and HGTV.*

"A delightful interlude! A five star B&B."

Certificate may be used: Year-round, Sunday through Thursday with the exception of July and August.

Searsport   H5

Brass Lantern Inn

81 W Main St
Searsport, ME 04974-3501
(207)548-0150 (800)691-0150
Internet: www.agate.net/~brasslan/brasslantern.html
E-mail: brasslan@agate.net

Circa 1850. This Victorian inn is nestled at the edge of the woods on a rise overlooking Penobscot Bay. Showcased throughout the inn are many collectibles, antiques and family heirlooms, as well as artifacts from innkeeper Maggie Zieg's home in England and two-year stay in Ethiopia. Enjoy breakfast by candlelight in the dining room with its ornate tin ceiling, where you'll feast on Maine blueberry pancakes and other sumptuous treats. Centrally located between Camden and Bar Harbor, Searsport is known as the antique capital of Maine. There are many local attractions, including the Penobscot Marine Museum, fine shops and restaurants, as well as a public boat facility.

Innkeeper(s): Maggie & Dick Zieg. $75-95. MC, VISA, DS, PC, TC. 5 rooms with PB. Breakfast included in rates. Types of meals: Full bkfst and early coffee/tea. Beds: QDT. VCR, library and piano on premises. Antiquing, fishing, live theater, parks, shopping and cross-country skiing nearby.

Location: Penobscot Bay view.

Publicity: *Country Living, Republication Journal, Travel Today, Down East, Saturday Evening Post and AAA Car & Travel.*

"Very elegant surrounding, cozy atmosphere. We felt really spoiled. It was my daughter's first stay at a B&B and she's still praising the blueberry pancakes. Everything was just perfect!"

Certificate may be used: Sept. 1-25, Oct. 20-June 30, Monday-Thursday, no holidays.

Searsport (Waldo County)   H5

Watchtide... by the Sea

190 W Main St, US Rt 1
Searsport (Waldo County), ME 04974-3514
(207)548-6575 (800)698-6575
Internet: www.watchtide.com
E-mail: stay@watchtide.com

Circa 1794. Watch the tides and ships while enjoying a bountiful four-course breakfast overlooking the bay from the sun porch of this historic inn. Once owned by General Henry Knox, first Secretary of War, the inn also was host to several wives of Presidents including Eleanor Roosevelt who visited frequently. There are three seaside acres of lawns and gardens, as well as a bird sanctuary and spectacular views of Penobscot Bay. The rooms offer king-size beds and one has a two-person Jacuzzi. There's an antique/gift shop adjacent to the inn which offers special guest discounts. (The area is known for its excellent antiquing.) Walk to the beach at Moosepoint State Park for swimming, or enjoy the area's lighthouses, sea sports, theater, or golf, boating and fishing. The Penobscot Marine Museum is nearby. Conveniently located between Rockland and Bar Harbor, Watchtide affords easy day trips to everything from Pemiquid Point to Schoodic Point.

Innkeeper(s): Nancy-Linn Nellis & Jack Elliott. $85-175. MC, VISA, DS, PC, TC. 5 rooms with PB. Breakfast and snacks/refreshments included in rates. Types of meals: Full gourmet bkfst and early coffee/tea. Beds: KDT. Turndown service in room. Library and guest lounge with large screen TV and game table on premises. Antiquing, fishing, golf, lighthouses, concerts, whale watching, Acadia National Park, live theater, museums, parks, shopping, sporting events and water sports nearby.

Publicity: *Daily Item, Bangor Daily News, Pilot Tribune, Clarion-Ledger, Sunday Patriot News, Sunday Herald-Times and Deseret News.*

Certificate may be used: Nov. 1-May 15.

South Thomaston   I5

Weskeag at The Water

PO Box 213
South Thomaston, ME 04858-0213
(207)596-6676
Internet: www.midcoast.com/weskeag
E-mail: weskeag@midcoast.com

Circa 1830. The backyard of this three-story house stretches to the edge of Weskeag River and Ballyhac Cove. Fifty yards from the house, there's reversing white-water rapids, created by the 10-foot tide that narrows into the estuary. Guests often sit by the water's edge to watch the birds and the lobster fishermen. Sea kayakers can launch at the inn and explore the nearby coves and then paddle on to the ocean. The inn's furnishings include a mixture of comfortable antiques. Featherbed eggs are a house specialty.

Innkeeper(s): Gray & Lynne Smith. $80-100. 8 rooms, 6 with PB. Breakfast included in rates. Type of meal: Full bkfst. Beds: QD. Ceiling fan in room. VCR on premises. Antiquing, fishing, live theater, shopping, downhill skiing and cross-country skiing nearby.

Location: Tidal saltwater inlet.

Certificate may be used: Oct. 15 through June 15.

Spruce Head   J5

Craignair Inn
533 Clark Island Rd
Spruce Head, ME 04859
(207)594-7644 (800)320-9997 Fax:(207)596-7124
Internet: www.craignair.com
E-mail: innkeeper@craignair.com

Circa 1930. Craignair originally was built to house stonecutters working in nearby granite quarries. Overlooking the docks of the Clark Island Quarry, where granite schooners once were

loaded, this roomy, three-story inn is tastefully decorated with local antiques. A bountiful continental breakfast is served in the inn's dining room which offers scenic ocean and coastline views.

Innkeeper(s): Steve & Neva Joseph. $83-120. MC, VISA, DS, PC, TC. 21 rooms, 12 with PB. Breakfast included in rates. Type of meal: Cont plus. Beds: KQDT. Phone in room. Fax and copier on premises. Antiquing, fishing, live theater, parks, shopping, downhill skiing, cross-country skiing and water sports nearby. Pets Allowed.

Publicity: *Boston Globe, Free Press and Tribune.*

"A coastal oasis of fine food and outstanding service with colonial maritime ambiance!"

Certificate may be used: Oct. 16 to April 30, Tuesday, Wednesday, Thursday, excluding holidays.

Waldoboro   I4

Broad Bay Inn & Gallery
1014 Main St
Waldoboro, ME 04572
(207)832-6668 (800)736-6769

Circa 1830. This Colonial inn lies in the heart of an unspoiled coastal village. You'll find Victorian furnishings throughout and some guest rooms have canopy beds. An established art gallery displays works by renowned artists, as well as limited-edition prints. Television, games and an art library are available in the common room. It's a short walk to restaurants, tennis, churches and the historic Waldo Theatre.

Innkeeper(s): Libby Hopkins. $50-75. MC, VISA, PC, TC. 5 rooms. Breakfast included in rates. Types of meals: Full bkfst & early coffee/tea. Beds: DT. TV in room. VCR, copier, old movies & art library on premises. Antiquing, fishing, live theater, parks, shopping, skiing & water sports nearby.

Location: Village.

Publicity: *Boston Globe, Ford Times, Courier Gazette, Princeton Packet and Better Homes & Gardens Cookbook.*

"Breakfast was so special - I ran to get my camera. Why, there were even flowers on my plate."

Certificate may be used: May-July, September-January, Sunday through Thursday, excludes holidays.

Walpole   J4

Brannon-Bunker Inn
349 S St Rt 129
Walpole, ME 04573
(207)563-5941 (800)563-9225

Circa 1820. This Cape-style house has been a home to many generations of Maine residents, one of whom was captain of a ship that sailed to the Arctic. During the '20s, the barn served as a dance hall. Later, it was converted into comfortable guest rooms. Victorian and American antiques are featured, and there are collections of military and political memorabilia.

Innkeeper(s): Joe & Jeanne Hovance. $60-75. MC, VISA, AX, PC, TC. 8 rooms, 5 with PB and 1 suite. Breakfast included in rates. Type of meal: Cont plus. Beds: QDT. TV in room. VCR, library and child care on premises. Handicap access. Antiquing, fishing, golf, live theater, parks, shopping, cross-country skiing, tennis and water sports nearby.

Location: Country, Damariscotta river.

Publicity: *Times-Beacon Newspaper.*

"Wonderful beds, your gracious hospitality and the very best muffins anywhere made our stay a memorable one."

Certificate may be used: September through June.

Waterford   I2

Kedarburn Inn
Rt 35 Box 61
Waterford, ME 04088
(207)583-6182 Fax:(207)583-6424
Internet: members.aol.com/kedar01
E-mail: kedar01@aol.com

Circa 1858. The innkeepers of this Victorian establishment invite guests to try a taste of olde English hospitality and cuisine at their inn, nestled in the foothills of the White Mountains in Western Maine. Located in a historic village, the

inn sits beside the flowing Kedar Brook, which runs to the shores of Lake Keoka. Each of the spacious rooms is decorated with handmade quilts and dried flowers. Explore the inn's shop

and you'll discover a variety of quilts and crafts, all made by innkeeper Margaret Gibson. Ask about special quilting weekends. With prior reservation, the innkeepers will prepare an English afternoon tea.

Innkeeper(s): Margaret & Derek Gibson. $71-125. MC, VISA, AX, DS, PC, TC. 7 rooms, 5 with PB, 1 suite and 1 conference room. Breakfast included in rates. Types of meals: Full bkfst and early coffee/tea. Beds: KQDT. Air conditioning. VCR and fax on premises. Antiquing, fishing, live theater, shopping, downhill skiing, cross-country skiing and water sports nearby.

Location: Mountains.

Publicity: *Maine Times.*

Certificate may be used: Nov. 1-May 31, except holidays.

Weld
H2

Kawanhee Inn Lakeside Lodge

Rt 142 Webb Lk
Weld, ME 04285
(207)585-2000
Internet: www.lakeinn.com
E-mail: maineinn@somtel.com

Circa 1929. This rustic lodge offers outstanding views of Webb Lake and the surrounding mountains (Tumbledown, Big Jackson, Mt. Blue and Bald Mt.). Four-foot logs are often thrown on the fire in the massive fieldstone fireplace. Both cabins and lodge rooms are available, and if you reserve ahead you may be able to stay in one at the water's edge. Gold panning on the Swift River, enjoying the sandy beach, moose watching, viewing Angel Falls and Smalls Falls and hiking are favorite activities.

Innkeeper(s): Martha Strunk & Sturges Butler. $75-195. MC, VISA. 9 rooms, 5 with PB, 1 suite and 12 cabins. Types of meals: Cont and early coffee/tea. Beds: QDT. Canoe and Kayak rentals on premises. Antiquing, fishing, gold panning, hiking, sandy beach, parks, shopping and tennis nearby.

Pets allowed: Some cabins, not the Inn.

Location: Mountains.

Publicity: *1997 & 1998 Editor Pick Yankee Magazine Travel Guide.*

"It was just great, relaxed and fun!"

Certificate may be used: May 6-July 1.

West Boothbay Harbor
J4

Lawnmeer Inn

PO Box 505
West Boothbay Harbor, ME 04575-0505
(800)633-7645
Internet: www.lawnmeerinn.com
E-mail: cooncat@lawnmeerinn.com

Circa 1899. This pleasant inn sits by the shoreline, providing a picturesque oceanfront setting. Located on a small, wooded island, it is accessed by a lift bridge. Family-oriented rooms are clean and homey, and there is a private honeymoon cottage in the Smoke House. The dining room is waterside and serves continental cuisine with an emphasis on seafood. Boothbay Harbor is two miles away.

Innkeeper(s): Lee & Jim Metzger. $90-195. MC, VISA. 32 rooms with PB, 1 suite and 1 cottage. Types of meals: Full bkfst and early coffee/tea. Beds: KQD. Antiquing, fishing, live theater, shopping and water sports nearby.

Pets allowed: Small pets-one per room.

Publicity: *Los Angeles Times and Getaways for Gourmets.*

"Your hospitality was warm and gracious and the food delectable."

Certificate may be used: Sunday-Thursday, May 25 to Columbus Day, when space available.

York Beach
L2

Homestead Inn B&B

8 S Main St (Rt 1A), PO Box 15
York Beach, ME 03910
(207)363-8952

Circa 1905. This turn-of-the-century boarding house is next to Short Sands Beach. The original hard pine has been retained throughout. Bedrooms have a panoramic view of the ocean and

hills. The house is kept cozy and warm by the heat of a wood stove and fireplace. Guests enjoy the sound of the surf and seagulls. Continental breakfast is offered on the sun deck or in the family dining room.

Innkeeper(s): Daniel Duffy. $49-69. 4 rooms. Breakfast included in rates. Type of meal: Cont plus. Beds: DT. Ceiling fan in room. Bicycles on premises. Amusement parks, antiquing, fishing, live theater, shopping and sporting events nearby.

Certificate may be used: April-June; September and October, Sunday-Thursday (not applicable July-August).

York Harbor
L2

York Harbor Inn

PO Box 573, Rt 1A
York Harbor, ME 03911-0573
(207)363-5119 (800)343-3869 Fax:(207)363-7151
Internet: www.yorkharborinn.com
E-mail: info@yorkharborinn.com

Circa 1800. The core building of the York Harbor Inn is a small log cabin constructed on the Isles of Shoals. Moved and reassembled at this dramatic location overlooking the entrance to York Harbor, the cabin is now a gathering room with a handsome stone fireplace. There is an English-style pub in the cellar, a large ballroom and five meeting rooms. The dining room and many guest rooms overlook the ocean. Several guest rooms have ocean view decks, working fireplaces and Jacuzzi spas. One three-room suite is available.

Innkeeper(s): Joseph & Garry Dominguez. $89-239. MC, VISA, AX, DC, CB, PC, TC. 33 rooms with PB, 4 with FP, 1 suite and 4 conference rooms. Breakfast included in rates. Types of meals: Cont plus, cont and early coffee/tea. Beds: KQD. Cable TV, phone and iron & ironing board in room. Air conditioning. VCR, fax, copier, spa, swimming and child care on premises. Amusement parks, antiquing, fishing, beach, museums, outlet mall, live theater, parks, shopping, cross-country skiing and water sports nearby.

Publicity: *New York Times, Down East, Food & Wine, The Learning Channel, Ladies Home Journal and The Travel Channel's "Great Country Inns of America."*

"It's hard to decide where to stay when you're paging through a book of country inns. This time we chose well."

Certificate may be used: Year-round, except Friday and Saturday in July and August, based on availability.

Maryland

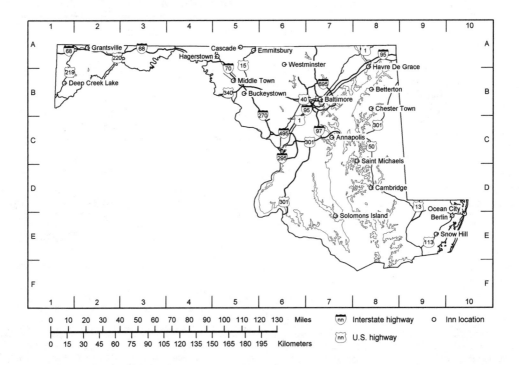

0 10 20 30 40 50 60 70 80 90 100 110 120 130   Miles

0 15 30 45 60 75 90 105 120 135 150 165 180 195   Kilometers

☒ (nn) Interstate highway   ○ Inn location
☒ (nn) U.S. highway

Annapolis   C7

Chesapeake Bay Lighthouse B&B

1423 Sharps Point Rd
Annapolis, MD 21401-6139
(410)757-0248

Circa 1923. Each of the guest rooms in this cottage-style
working lighthouse boasts water views of scenic Chesapeake
Bay. The innkeepers built their unique B&B from designs
found in the National Archives. Grab a pair of binoculars and
enjoy the sites of the Bay Bridge, Thomas Point Lighthouse or
Annapolis harbor entrance and a 300-foot pier. The lighthouse
is only six miles from Annapolis, which is full of historic
attractions, shops and restaurants.

Innkeeper(s): Janice & Bill Costello. $159-220. MC, VISA. 2 rooms. Breakfast
included in rates. Type of meal: Cont plus. Air conditioning.

Publicity: Soundings, Capital and WJZ-TV13 and WMAR-TV2.

Certificate may be used: Jan. 1-March 31, Sunday through Thursday, holidays excluded.

Baltimore   B7

The Inn at Government House

1125 N Calvert St
Baltimore, MD 21202-3801
(410)539-0566 Fax:(410)539-0567

Circa 1883. This is the official guest house for Baltimore's visiting dignitaries, as well as the general public. Three town houses
comprise the inn, located in the Mt. Vernon historic district.
Features include chandeliers, ornate wallpapers and Victorian
antiques. Each bedchamber has its own view.

Innkeeper(s): Barbara Hunter. $55-140. VISA, AX, DC, CB, DS, PC, TC. 21
rooms with PB, 1 suite and 2 conference rooms. Breakfast included in rates.
Types of meals: Cont plus and early coffee/tea. Beds: KQD. Cable TV and
phone in room. Air conditioning. Fax, copier and library on premises.
Handicap access. Antiquing, live theater, shopping and sporting events nearby.
Pets allowed: small, prior approval needed.

Location: City.

Publicity: Travel.

Certificate may be used: Jan. 1 to March 15.

Berlin E10

Merry Sherwood Plantation

8909 Worcester Hwy
Berlin, MD 21811-3016
(410)641-2112 (800)660-0358 Fax:(410)641-9528
Internet: www.merrysherwood.com
E-mail: info@merrysherwood.com

Circa 1859. This magnificent pre-Civil War mansion is a tribute to Southern plantation architecture. The inn features antique period furniture, hand-woven, Victorian era rugs and a square grand piano. The ballroom, now a parlor for guests, boasts twin fireplaces and pier mirrors. (Ask to see the hidden

cupboards behind the fireside bookcases in the library.) Nineteen acres of grounds are beautifully landscaped and feature azaleas, boxwoods and 125 varieties of trees.

Innkeeper(s): Kirk Burbage. $125-175. MC, VISA. 8 rooms, 6 with PB, 4 with FP and 1 suite. Breakfast included in rates. Type of meal: Full gourmet bkfst. Beds: QD. Air conditioning. Amusement parks, antiquing, fishing, shopping and water sports nearby.
Publicity: *Washington Post, Baltimore Sun and Southern Living.*
"Pure elegance and privacy at its finest."
Certificate may be used: Sunday-Thursday nights.

Betterton B8

Lantern Inn

115 Ericsson Ave, PO Box 29
Betterton, MD 21610-9746
(410)348-5809 (800)499-7265 Fax:(410)348-2323
Circa 1904. Framed by a picket fence and a wide two-story front porch, this four-story country inn is located one block from the nettle-free public beach on Chesapeake Bay. Comfortable rooms are furnished with antiques and handmade quilts. The surrounding area is well-known for its wildlife preserves. Antique shops and restaurants are nearby. Kent County offers plenty of cycling possibilities, and there are detailed maps available at the inn for trips that start at the inn and go for 10 to 90 miles. Tennis courts are two blocks away.
Innkeeper(s): Ray & Sandi Sparks. $75-90. MC, VISA, AX. 13 rooms, 4 with PB. Breakfast included in rates. Type of meal: Cont plus. Beds: KQDT. VCR on premises. Antiquing, fishing, horseback riding and sporting clays nearby.
Publicity: *Richland Times-Dispatch, North Carolina Outdoorsman, Washingtonian and Mid-Atlantic Country.*
Certificate may be used: Sunday through Thursday, Jan. 15-Dec. 15, holidays excluded.

Buckeystown B5

The Inn at Buckeystown

3521 Buckeystown Pike Gen Del
Buckeystown, MD 21717
(301)874-5755 (800)272-1190 Fax:(301)831-1355
Circa 1897. Gables, bay windows and a wraparound porch are features of this grand Victorian mansion located on two-and-a-half acres of lawns and gardens (and an ancient cemetery). The inn features a polished staircase, antiques and elegantly decorated guest rooms. Ask for the Deja Vu Suite, which boasts a working fireplace and oak decor. A gourmet dinner is served each Friday,

Saturday and holiday. The inn also hosts weddings, rehearsals and retreats. The village of Buckeystown is in the National Register.

Innkeeper(s): Janet Wells. $90-225. MC, VISA, AX, DS, PC, TC. 7 rooms, 5 with PB. Breakfast and snacks/refreshments included in rates. Types of meals: Full gourmet bkfst, country bkfst, veg bkfst and early coffee/tea. Beds: QD. Cable TV in room. Air conditioning. VCR and fax on premises. Antiquing, art galleries, bicycling, canoeing/kayaking, fishing, golf, live theater, museums, parks, shopping, downhill skiing, sporting events and wineries nearby.
Location: Country.
Publicity: *Mid-Atlantic, Innsider, The Washingtonian, Washington Post and Baltimore Sun.*
"The courtesy of you and your staff were the glue that bound the whole experience together."
Certificate may be used: Year-round, B&B Monday-Tuesday, MAP Wednesday-Thursday.

Catoctin Inn and Conference Center

3613 Buckeystown Pike
Buckeystown, MD 21717
(301)874-5555 (800)730-5550 Fax:(301)874-2026
Internet: www.catoctininn.com
E-mail: catoctin@fred.net

Circa 1780. The inn's four acres of dogwood, magnolias, maples and sweeping lawns overlook the village and the Catoctin Mountains range. Some special features of the inn include a fine-dining restaurant serving breakfast, lunch, dinner and a handsome wraparound veranda. A Victorian carriage house marks the site for weddings, showers and receptions for up to 150 guests. Fifteen of the guest rooms include a fireplace and a whirlpool tub. Nearby villages to visit include Harper's Ferry, Antietam and New Market. Buckeystown's Monocacy River provides canoeing and fishing.
Innkeeper(s): Terry & Sarah MacGillivray. $85-150. MC, VISA, AX, DS, PC. 20 rooms with PB, 15 with FP, 8 suites, 3 cottages and 3 conference rooms. Breakfast included in rates. Type of meal: Full bkfst. Beds: KQ. Cable TV, phone, turndown service and VCR in room. Air conditioning. Antiquing, fishing, hiking, biking, Appalachian Trail, Harper's Ferry, Sugarloaf Mountain, swimming, boating, Civil War history, live theater, shopping, skiing & sporting events nearby.
Location: City.
Certificate may be used: January through April, Monday through Thursday.

Cambridge D8

Glasgow B&B Inn

1500 Hambrooks Blvd
Cambridge, MD 21613
(410)228-0575
Circa 1760. Located along the Choptank River on seven acres, this brick colonial is reached by way of a long tree-lined driveway. The house was built by Dr. William Murray whose son was a friend to Thomas Jefferson and John Quincy Adams. (According to local legend, part of the U.S. Constitution was written here.) The inn is decorated with country colonial antiques and reproductions, enhanced by high ceilings, a mahogany staircase and deep-window seats.
Innkeeper(s): Louiselee Roche & Martha Rayne. $100-150. PC, TC. 7 rooms, 3 with PB, 6 with FP. Breakfast included in rates. Type of meal: Full bkfst. Beds: KQ. TV and phone in room.
Publicity: *Mid-Atlantic Country and Tidewater Times.*
Certificate may be used: Jan. 1-Dec. 31, Monday-Thursday.

Cascade A5

Bluebird on the Mountain

14700 Eyler Ave
Cascade, MD 21719-1938
(301)241-4161 (800)362-9526
Internet: www.bbonline.com/md/bluebird

Circa 1900. In the mountain village of Cascade, this gracious shuttered Georgian manor is situated on two acres of trees and wildflowers. Three suites have double whirlpool tubs. There is an outdoor hot tub as well. The Rose Garden Room and Mt. Magnolia suites have fireplaces and porches overlooking the back garden. The inn is appointed with antiques, lace and white linens, and white wicker. On Sundays, a full breakfast is served. Cascade is located in between Frederick, Md., and Gettysburg, Pa.

Innkeeper(s): Eda Smith-Eley. $105-125. MC, VISA, PC. 5 rooms with PB, 2 with FP and 2 suites. Breakfast included in rates. Types of meals: Full bkfst, cont plus and early coffee/tea. Beds: KQT. Cable TV, turndown service, ceiling fan and VCR in room. Air conditioning. Spa on premises. Antiquing, fishing, hiking, live theater, parks, shopping, downhill skiing, sporting events and water sports nearby.

Location: Mountains.

Publicity: *Warm Welcomes, Baltimore Sun, Frederick News and Washington Post.*

"A wonderful balance of luxury and at-home comfort."

Certificate may be used: Jan. 8 through April 30, Sunday through Thursday, excluding holidays.

Chestertown B8

Great Oak Manor

10568 Cliff Rd
Chestertown, MD 21620-4115
(410)778-5943 (800)504-3098 Fax:(410)778-5943
Internet: www.greatoak.com
E-mail: innkeeper@greatoak.com

Circa 1938. This elegant Georgian mansion anchors vast lawns at the end of a long driveway. Situated directly on the Chesapeake Bay, it is a serene and picturesque country estate. A library with fireplace, den and formal parlors are available to guests. With its grand circular stairway, bayside gazebo, private beach and near-by marina, the Manor is a remarkable setting for events such as weddings and reunions. Chestertown is eight miles away.

Innkeeper(s): Don & Dianne Cantor. $95-175. MC, VISA, PC, TC. 11 rooms with PB, 5 with FP, 1 suite and 2 conference rooms. Breakfast included in rates. Types of meals: Full bkfst and early coffee/tea. Beds: KT. Phone, some VCRs and refrigerator (in suite) in room. Air conditioning. VCR, fax, copier, bicycles, library and computer ready-two rooms on premises. Antiquing, canoeing/kayaking, fishing, golf, Historic Washington College, live theater, shopping and tennis nearby.

Publicity: *Philadelphia, Diversions, Road Best Traveled, Washingtonian, Country Inns, Southern Living, New Choices, Chesapeake Life and Time Magazine.*

"The charming setting, professional service and personal warmth we experienced at Great Oak will long be a pleasant memory. Thanks for everything!"

Certificate may be used: Dec. 1-March 31, Sunday through Thursday.

Lauretum Inn B&B

954 High St
Chestertown, MD 21620-3955
(410)778-3236 (800)742-3236
Internet: www.chestertown.com/lauretum

Circa 1881. At the end of a long winding driveway, this massive Queen Anne Victorian commands a hilltop setting on six acres just outside of town. Inviting parlors and a porch are available to guests. Spacious guest rooms overlook the inn's lawns, often visited by deer in the early morning. Peg, the mother of 16 children, once plied the intracoastal waters on her 40-foot boat and can help you plan your stay in the area.

Innkeeper(s): Peg & Bill Sites. $48-100. MC, VISA, AX, DS, PC. 5 rooms, 3 with PB and 2 suites. Breakfast and afternoon tea included in rates. Types of meals: Cont plus and early coffee/tea. Beds: QDT. Air conditioning. VCR on premises. Antiquing, fishing, golf, live theater, parks, shopping, sporting events and water sports nearby.

Location: Chesapeake Bay.

Certificate may be used: Jan. 2-March 31, excluding holidays.

The Inn at Mitchell House

8796 Maryland Pkwy
Chestertown, MD 21620-4209
(410)778-6500
Internet: www.chestertown.com/mitchell/

Circa 1743. This pristine 18th-century manor house sits as a jewel on 12 acres overlooking Stoneybrook Pond. The guest rooms and the inn's several parlors are preserved and appointed in an authentic Colonial mood, heightened by handsome polished wide-board floors. Eastern Neck Island National Wildlife Refuge, Chesapeake Farms, St. Michaels, Annapolis and nearby Chestertown are all delightful to explore. The Inn at Mitchell House is a popular setting for romantic weddings and small corporate meetings.

Innkeeper(s): Tracy & Jim Stone. $95-120. MC, VISA, PC, TC. 6 rooms, 5 with PB, 4 with FP. Breakfast included in rates. Types of meals: Full bkfst and early coffee/tea. Beds: KQD. Turndown service in room. Air conditioning. VCR on premises. Antiquing, fishing, live theater, shopping, sporting events and water sports nearby.

Location: Country.

Publicity: *Washingtonian, New York Magazine, Glamour, Philadelphia Inquirer, Baltimore Sun, Kent County News, Ten Best Inns in the Country, New York Times. Washington Post and National Geographic Traveler.*

Certificate may be used: Sunday through Thursday, excluding holidays.

Deep Creek Lake B1

Haley Farm B&B and Retreat Center

16766 Garrett Hwy
Deep Creek Lake, MD 21550-4036
(301)387-9050 (888)231-3276 Fax:(301)387-9050
Internet: www.haleyfarm.com
E-mail: kam@haleyfarm.com

Circa 1920. This farmhouse is surrounded by 65 acres of rolling hills and farmland in the mountains of Western Maryland. Inside, the innkeepers have added many elegant touches, transforming the home into a gracious retreat with Chinese carpets, tapestries and European furnishings. There are three luxury suites, which include a heart-shaped Jacuzzi, king-size bed, kitchenette and sitting room with a fireplace. In addition, there are two smaller suites and six deluxe rooms. Croquet and badminton are set up on the grounds. Other popular activities are fishing in the trout pond, soaking in the hot tub, stretching out in the hammock or taking a picnic to the gazebo. The innkeepers can create special romantic packages with flowers and champagne, massages and even horseback riding. A variety of retreats and workshops are offered with subjects ranging from conflict resolution and negotiating strategies to yoga. The farm is three hours from Washington, D.C., and minutes from Deep Creek Lake, five state parks and the WISP ski and golf resort.

Innkeeper(s): Wayne & Kam Gillespie. $100-210. MC, VISA, AX, DS, PC, TC. 11 rooms with PB, 5 with FP and 5 suites. Breakfast included in rates. Type of meal: Full bkfst. Beds: KQ. Ceiling fan in room. Air conditioning. VCR, spa, bicycles, library and trout pond on premises. Antiquing, fishing, white water rafting, parks, shopping, downhill skiing, cross-country skiing and water sports nearby.

Location: Mountains.

"A beautiful setting for a quiet, romantic escape."

Certificate may be used: Sunday-Thursday, not including holidays, all year.

Emmitsbury   A5

The Gallery Suites
304 E Main St
Emmitsbury, MD 21727
(301)447-3292 Fax:(301)447-1666

Circa 1912. This collection of suites is so named because the two are located on the second story of a building that houses an art gallery. Innkeeper Linda Postelle is an artist and her work is featured throughout the suites, including murals on doors and walls. Antiques fill the whimsically decorated rooms. The suites are located in a historic building and were once used as apartments, so the rooms have been completely renovated and restored. Linda delivers breakfast to your door. The Main Street Grill, a local eatery, also is on the premises.

Innkeeper(s): Linda Postelle. $75-100. MC, VISA, PC, TC. 2 suites. Breakfast included in rates. Types of meals: Full gourmet bkfst, cont plus, cont and early coffee/tea. Beds: Q. Cable TV, phone and ceiling fan in room. Air conditioning. Restaurant on premises. Antiquing, golf, parks, downhill skiing and sporting events nearby.

Location: Civil War interests nearby.

Publicity: *Frederick Gazette.*

Certificate may be used: All year except holidays and alumni and parent's weekends at local college.

Grantsville   A2

Walnut Ridge Bed & Breakfast
92 Main St, PO Box 368
Grantsville, MD 21536
(301)895-4248 (888)419-2568 Fax:(301)895-4248
Internet: www.walnutridge.net
E-mail: walnutridge@usa.net

Circa 1864. A grove of walnut trees and a wood-fired hot tub next to a vegetable garden are the unique offerings of this historic farmhouse B&B. The living room is decorated with Amish items and there are country pieces throughout. The accommodations offered include a family suite with full kitchen. The inn's cabin in the woods has its own clawfoot tub, stone fireplace, deck and queen bed. The innkeeper's husband is a local Mennonite minister.

Innkeeper(s): Tim & Candy Fetterly. $75-125. MC, VISA, PC, TC. 4 rooms with PB, 1 suite and 1 cabin. Breakfast included in rates. Types of meals:

Full bkfst and early coffee/tea. Beds: QD. Cable TV and ceiling fan in room. VCR and fax on premises. Antiquing, fishing, golf, parks, shopping, downhill skiing, cross-country skiing, sporting events, tennis and water sports nearby.

Pets allowed: in suite and cabin.

Location: Mountains.

Publicity: *Washington Post and Lancaster Farming.*

"Best nights' sleep I've had this summer."

Certificate may be used: Jan. 2-Dec. 23, Sunday through Thursday, excluding holidays and festivals.

Hagerstown   A5

Beaver Creek House B&B
20432 Beaver Creek Rd
Hagerstown, MD 21740-1514
(301)797-4764 Fax:(301)797-4978
Internet: www.bbonline.com/md/beavercreek

Circa 1905. History buffs enjoy this turn-of-the-century inn located minutes away from Antietam and Harpers Ferry National Historical Parks. The surrounding villages house antique shops and some hold weekend auctions. The inn features a courtyard with a fountain and a country garden. Innkeepers Don and Shirley Day furnished the home with family antiques and memorabilia.  Guests can sip complimentary sherry in the elegant parlor or just relax on the porch and take in the view of South Mountain.

Innkeeper(s): Donald & Shirley Day. $75-95. MC, VISA, AX, PC, TC. 5 rooms with PB and 1 conference room. Breakfast included in rates. Type of meal: Full gourmet bkfst. Beds: DT. Ceiling fan in room. Air conditioning. Copier on premises. Amusement parks, antiquing, fishing, live theater, parks, shopping, downhill skiing, cross-country skiing, sporting events and water sports nearby.

Location: Country.

Publicity: *Baltimore Sun, Hagerstown Journal, Herald Mail, Washington Post and Frederick.*

"Thanks so much for your hospitality. You're wonderful hosts and breakfast was delicious as usual. Don't change a thing."

Certificate may be used: Jan. 30 to Aug. 31, Monday through Thursday. Not valid September and October. Nov. 1 through Dec. 31, not valid on holidays.

Sunday's B&B
39 Broadway
Hagerstown, MD 21740-4019
(301)797-4331 (800)221-4828
Internet: sundaysbnb.com
E-mail: info@sundaysbnb.com

Circa 1890. This Queen Anne Victorian is appropriately appointed with period antiques. Fruit baskets are provided and guests are pampered with a full breakfast, afternoon tea, evening wine and cheese and for late evening, bedside cordials and chocolates. Antietam, Harpers Ferry and the C&O Canal are nearby.

Innkeeper(s): Robert Ferrino. $95-155. MC, VISA, DC. 4 rooms with PB. Breakfast included in rates. Types of meals: Full bkfst and early coffee/tea. Beds: QD. Cable TV, one whirlpool suite, fruit baskets and special soaps in room. Air conditioning. Antiquing, fishing, battlefields, outlets, live theater & parks nearby.

Location: City.

"A four star inn! Every detail perfect, decor and atmosphere astounding."

Certificate may be used: Dec. 1-April 30, Sunday-Thursday except holidays.

Havre De Grace   A8

Spencer Silver Mansion
200 S Union Ave
Havre De Grace, MD 21078-3224
(410)939-1097 (800)780-1485

Circa 1896. This elegant granite Victorian mansion is graced with bays, gables, balconies, a turret and a gazebo veranda. The Victorian decor, with antiques and Oriental rugs, complements the house's carved-oak woodwork, fireplace mantels and parquet floors. The Concord Point Lighthouse (oldest continuously operated lighthouse in America) is only a walk away. In addition to the four rooms in the main house, a romantic carriage house suite is available, featuring an in-room fireplace, TV, whirlpool bath and kitchenette.

Innkeeper(s): Carol Nemeth. $70-140. MC, VISA, AX, DS, PC, TC. 5 rooms, 3 with PB, 1 with FP and 1 cottage. Breakfast included in rates. Types of meals: Full bkfst and early coffee/tea. Beds: QDT. Cable TV, phone and turn-down service in room. Air conditioning. Antiquing, fishing, museums, restaurants, parks, shopping and water sports nearby.

Pets allowed: In Carriage House only.

Location: Small town.

Publicity: Mid-Atlantic Country and Maryland.

"A fabulous find. Beautiful house, excellent hostess. I've stayed at a lot of B&Bs, but this house is the best."

Certificate may be used: Monday through Thursday, all year.

Middletown   B5

Stone Manor
5820 Carroll Boyer Rd
Middletown, MD 21769-6315
(301)473-5454 Fax:(301)371-5622
Internet: www.stonemanor.com
E-mail: themanor@stonemanor.com

Circa 1780. If you're searching for a romantic secluded getaway and hope to be pampered with world-class dining and elegant surroundings, head for this impressive stone estate house. The home is tucked between mountain ranges on 114 acres of picturesque lawns, gardens and working farmland. The interior is intimate and inviting with guest suites decorated in a variety of styles. All include queen-size poster beds and whirlpools baths, and most offer fireplaces and porches that afford tranquil views of flowerbeds, ponds or woods. Be sure and make reservations ahead for the inn's five- and nine-course dinners. Recognized by Washingtonian Magazine's "100 Very Best Restaurants," Wine Spectator Magazine and the Distinguished Restaurants of North America, dinner and lunch are available Tuesday through Sunday. The inn was named as one of the Top Ten Inns in America by Country Inns Magazine.

Innkeeper(s): Judith Harne. $150-275. MC, VISA, AX, TC. 6 rooms with PB, 4 with FP. Breakfast included in rates. Types of meals: Cont plus and early coffee/tea. Beds: Q. Turndown service in room. Air conditioning. VCR, fax and copier on premises. Handicap access. Antiquing, fishing, civil War history, live theater, museums, parks, shopping, cross-country skiing and water sports nearby.

Location: Mountains.

Certificate may be used: Tuesday-Thursday, January-March; July, August, November. Excludes holidays.

Ocean City   E10

Atlantic House B&B
501 N Baltimore Ave
Ocean City, MD 21842-3926
(410)289-2333 Fax:(410)289-2430
Internet: www.atlantichouse.com
E-mail: ocbnb@atlantichouse.com

Circa 1923. From the front porch of this bed & breakfast, guests can partake in ocean and boardwalk views. The rooms are decorated in antique oak and wicker, complementing a relaxing beach stay. The morning's abundant breakfast buffet includes such items as freshly baked muffins and cakes, fruit, egg casseroles, cereals and yogurt. In the afternoons, light refreshments also are served. The inn, nestled in the original Ocean City, is a short walk to the beach, boardwalk and entertainment, but many guests enjoy cycling the scenic trail to Assateague Island. Privileges at a local health club are available.

Innkeeper(s): Paul & Debi Cook. $55-225. MC, VISA, AX, DS, TC. 11 rooms, 7 with PB and 1 suite. Breakfast, afternoon tea and snacks/refreshments included in rates. Types of meals: Full bkfst and early coffee/tea. Beds: QD. Cable TV and ceiling fan in room. Air conditioning. Amusement parks, antiquing, fishing, golf, boardwalk, harness racing, spa and swimming across town, bird watching, biking, live theater, parks, shopping, sporting events and water sports nearby.

Certificate may be used: Labor Day to Memorial Day, Sunday-Thursday.

Saint Michaels   C8

Kemp House Inn
412 Talbot St, PO Box 638
Saint Michaels, MD 21663-0638
(410)745-2243

Circa 1807. This two-story Georgian house was built by Colonel Joseph Kemp, a shipwright and one of the town forefathers. The inn is appointed in period furnishings accentuated by candlelight. Guest rooms include patchwork quilts, a collection of four-poster rope beds and old-fashioned nightshirts. There are several working fireplaces. Robert E. Lee is said to have been a guest.

Innkeeper(s): Diane M. Cooper. $80-120. MC, VISA, DS. 8 rooms, 6 with PB, 4 with FP. Breakfast included in rates. Types of meals: Cont and early coffee/tea. Beds: QDT. Air conditioning. Antiquing, fishing, shopping & water sports nearby.

Pets Allowed.

Location: Small town.

Publicity: Gourmet and Philadelphia.

"It was wonderful. We've stayed in many B&Bs, and this was one of the nicest!"

Certificate may be used: Sunday through Thursday nights, excluding holidays. Year-round.

Parsonage Inn
210 N Talbot St
Saint Michaels, MD 21663-2102
(410)745-5519 (800)394-5519
Internet: www.parsonage-inn.com
E-mail: parsinn@dmv.com

Circa 1883. A striking Victorian steeple rises next to the wide bay of this brick residence, once the home of Henry Clay Dodson, state senator, pharmacist and brickyard owner. The house features brick detail in a variety of patterns and inlays, perhaps a design statement for brick customers. Porches are decorated with filigree and spindled columns. Laura Ashley linens, late Victorian furnishings, fireplaces and decks add to the creature comforts. Six bikes await guests who wish to ride to Tilghman Island or to the ferry that goes to Oxford. Gourmet breakfast is served in the dining room.

Innkeeper(s): Mark & Wendy Tamiso. $100-185. MC, VISA, PC, TC. 8 rooms with PB, 3 with FP. Breakfast included in rates. Type of meal: Full gourmet bkfst. Beds: KQD. Ceiling fan and TV (two rooms) in room. Air conditioning. Bicycles on premises. Handicap access. Antiquing, fishing, Chesapeake Bay Maritime Museum, shopping and water sports nearby.

Location: Main St of Historic Town.

Publicity: *Philadelphia Inquirer Sunday Travel, Wilmington, Delaware News Journal.*

"Striking, extensively renovated."

Certificate may be used: Sunday through Thursday, November until June.

Snow Hill E9

River House Inn

201 E Market St
Snow Hill, MD 21863-2000
(410)632-2722 Fax:(410)632-2866
Internet: www.riverhouseinn.com
E-mail: innkeeper@riverhouseinn.com

Circa 1860. This picturesque Gothic Revival house rests on the banks of the Pocomoke River and boasts its own dock. Its two acres roll down to the river over long tree-studded lawns. Lawn furniture and a hammock add to the invitation to relax as do the inn's porches. Some guest rooms feature faux marble fireplaces. The 17th-century village of Snow Hill boasts old brick sidewalks and historic homes. Canoes can be rented two doors from the inn or you may wish to take a river cruise on the innkeeper's pontoon boat.

Innkeeper(s): Larry & Susanne Knudsen. $120-195. MC, VISA, AX, DS, TC. 10 rooms with PB, 8 with FP, 3 suites and 2 cottages. Breakfast and snacks/refreshments included in rates. Types of meals: Full bkfst and early coffee/tea. Beds: KQT. Ceiling fan in room. Air conditioning. VCR, fax, copier, bicycles, library and child care on premises. Handicap access. Amusement parks, antiquing, fishing, boating, canoeing, beaches, historic sites, shopping and water sports nearby.

Pets allowed: pets considered.

Location: Riverfront.

Publicity: *Newsday, Daily Times, Washington Times, Washingtonian and Washington Post.*

Certificate may be used: Any day of the week, excluding holidays, Nov. 1-March 31, and Sunday-Thursday, excluding holidays, all other months.

Snow Hill Inn

104 E Market St
Snow Hill, MD 21863-1067
(410)632-2102 Fax:(410)632-3623

Circa 1790. Gables, chimneys and blue shutters highlight the exterior of this Victorian country home. Two of the guest rooms include working fireplaces, and all are decorated with period furnishings. Plan on taking a picnic, because the innkeepers will pack up a box or basket filled with gourmet goodies from the inn's restaurant. Walking tours of Snow Hill's historic district, which features more than 100 homes and churches, are popular.

Innkeeper(s): Jim & Kathy Washington. $75. MC, VISA, AX, DS, TC. 3 rooms with PB, 1 with FP. Breakfast included in rates. Type of meal: Cont plus. Beds: QD. Air conditioning. Antiquing, fishing, parks, shopping and water sports nearby.

Certificate may be used: Sunday-Friday, upon availability.

Solomons Island E7

Solomons Victorian Inn

125 Charles Street
Solomons Island, MD 20688-0759
(410)326-4811 Fax:(410)326-0133
Internet: www.chesapeake.net/solomonsvictorianinn
E-mail: solvictinn@chesapeake.net

Circa 1906. The Davis family, renowned for their shipbuilding talents, constructed this elegant Queen Anne Victorian at the turn of the century. Each of the inn's elegant common rooms and bedchambers boasts special touches such as antiques, Oriental rugs and lacy curtains. The inn's suites include whirlpool tubs. The home affords views of Solomons Harbor and its entrance into the picturesque Chesapeake Bay. Guests are treated to an expansive breakfast in a dining room, which overlooks the harbor.

Innkeeper(s): Richard & Helen Bauer. $90-175. MC, VISA, AX, PC. 8 rooms with PB and 3 suites. Breakfast and snacks/refreshments included in rates. Types of meals: Full bkfst and early coffee/tea. Beds: KQ. Whirlpool tub in suite in room. Air conditioning. Fax and library on premises. Antiquing, fishing, live theater, parks, shopping and water sports nearby.

Location: Chesapeake Bay.

"Instead of guests at a place of lodging, you made us feel like welcome friends in your home."

Certificate may be used: Nov. 1 through Feb. 28, Sunday-Thursday.

Westminster A6

The Winchester Country Inn

111 Stoner Ave
Westminster, MD 21157-5451
(410)876-7373 (800)887-3950 Fax:(410)848-7409

Circa 1760. William Winchester, the founder of Westminster, built this unusual English-style house. It has a steeply slanted roof similar to those found in the Tidewater area. A central fireplace opens to both the parlor and the central hall. Colonial-period furnishings prevail, with some items loaned by the local historic society. Community volunteers, historians, craftsmen and designers helped restore the inn, including adding air conditioning throughout. A non-profit agency provides some of the housekeeping and gardening staff from its developmentally disabled program.

Innkeeper(s): Dawn Groom. $40-89. MC, VISA, AX, DS. 5 rooms, 3 with PB. Breakfast included in rates. Type of meal: Full bkfst. Beds: KQDT. TV and working hearth in room. VCR on premises. Handicap access. Antiquing, fishing, live theater, parks and shopping nearby.

Location: Country.

Publicity: *Country Living, Evening Sun, The Towson Flier, The Itinerary, Cracker Barrell and Carroll County Sun.*

"We give your inn an A+. Our stay was perfect."

Certificate may be used: Jan. 1-May 31, Sunday-Saturday; Oct. 1-Dec. 31, Sunday-Saturday. Holidays excluded.

Massachusetts

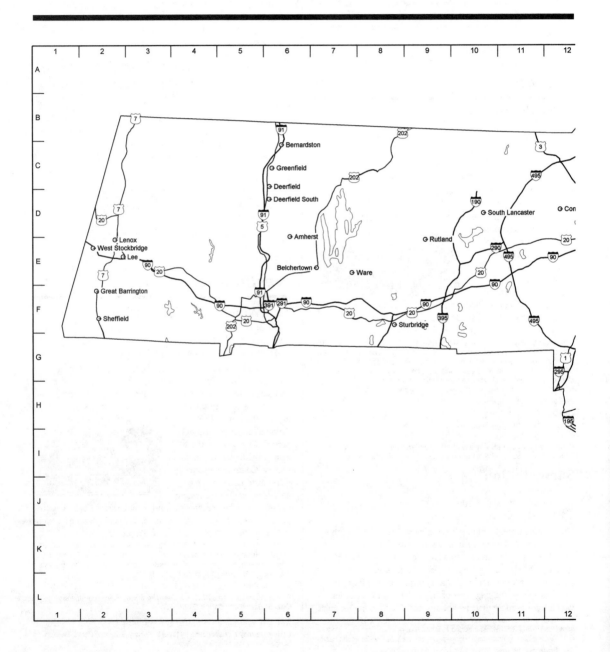

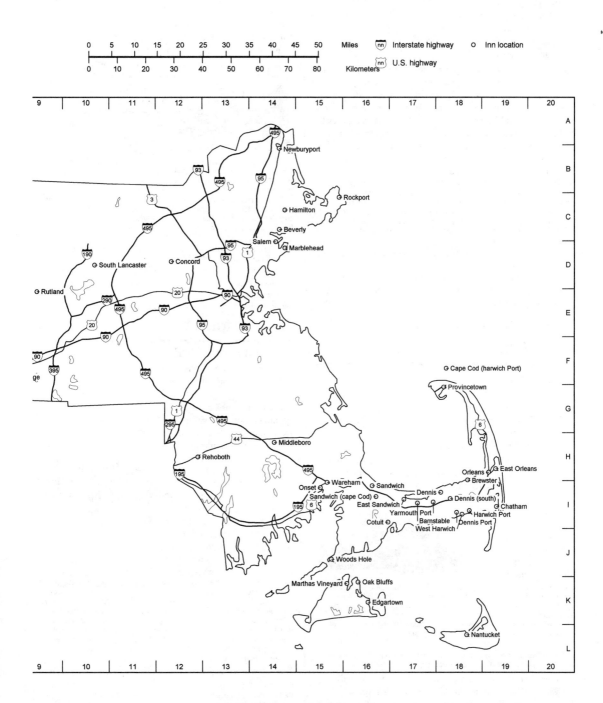

0 5 10 15 20 25 30 35 40 45 50 Miles
0 10 20 30 40 50 60 70 80 Kilometers

⬭ Interstate highway   ○ Inn location
⬭ U.S. highway

9 10 11 12 13 14 15 16 17 18 19 20

A
B
C
D
E
F
G
H
I
J
K
L

Newburyport
Rockport
Hamilton
Beverly
Salem
Marblehead
South Lancaster
Concord
Rutland
ge
Cape Cod (harwich Port)
Provincetown
Middleboro
Rehoboth
Orleans East Orleans
Brewster
Wareham Sandwich
Onset Dennis
Sandwich (cape Cod) Dennis (south)
East Sandwich Chatham
Yarmouth Port Harwich Port
Cotuit Barnstable Dennis Port
West Harwich
Woods Hole
Marthas Vineyard Oak Bluffs
Edgartown
Nantucket

Amherst
D6

Allen House Victorian Inn

599 Main St
Amherst, MA 01002-2409
(413)253-5000
Internet: www.allenhouse.com
E-mail: allenhouse@webtv.net

Circa 1886. This stick-style Queen Anne is much like a Victorian museum with guest rooms that feature period reproduction wallpapers, pedestal sinks, carved golden oak and brass beds, painted wooden floors and plenty of antiques. Among its many other treasures include Eastlake fireplace mantels. Unforgettable breakfasts include specialties such as eggs Benedict or French toast stuffed with rich cream cheese. Afternoon tea is a treat, and the inn offers plenty of examples of poetry from Emily Dickinson, whose home is just across the street from the inn.

Innkeeper(s): Alan & Amanda Zieminski. $75-175. PC, TC. 7 rooms with PB. Breakfast, afternoon tea and snacks/refreshments included in rates. Types of meals: Full bkfst and early coffee/tea. Beds: QDT. Phone, ceiling fan and down comforters & pillows in room. Air conditioning. Fax, copier & library on premises. Amusement parks, antiquing, fishing, golf, live theater, parks, shopping, downhill skiing, cross-country skiing, sporting events, tennis & water sports nearby.

Location: Small college town.

Publicity: *New York Times, Boston Magazine, Bon Appetit, Yankee Travel and Victorian Homes.*

"Our room and adjoining bath were spotlessly clean, charming, and quiet, with good lighting. Our meals were delicious and appetizing, and the casual, family-like atmosphere encouraged discussions among the guests."

Certificate may be used: Jan. 1-April 1, Sunday-Thursday.

Barnstable
I17

Beechwood Inn

2839 Main St, Rt 6A
Barnstable, MA 02630-1017
(508)362-6618 (800)609-6618 Fax:(508)362-0298
Internet: www.beechwoodinn.com
E-mail: info@beechwoodinn.com

Circa 1853. Beechwood is a beautifully restored Queen Anne Victorian offering period furnishings, some rooms with fireplaces or ocean views. Its warmth and elegance make it a favorite hideaway for couples looking for a peaceful and romantic return to the Victorian era. The inn is named for rare old beech trees that shade the veranda.

Innkeeper(s): Debbie & Ken Traugot. $95-180. MC, VISA, AX, DS, PC, TC. 6 rooms with PB, 3 with FP. Breakfast and afternoon tea included in rates. Types of meals: Full bkfst and early coffee/tea. Beds: KQD. Fans, wine glasses and corkscrew in room. Air conditioning. Fax, copier and bicycles on premises. Antiquing, fishing, historic cities, whale watching, bird watching, horseback riding, live theater, parks, shopping, sporting events and water sports nearby.

Publicity: *National Trust Calendar, New England Weekends, Rhode Island Monthly, Cape Cod Life and Boston Magazine.*

"Your inn is pristine in every detail. We concluded that the innkeepers, who are most hospitable, are the best part of Beechwood."

Certificate may be used: November through March, except holiday periods.

Honeysuckle Hill B&B

591 Old Kings Hwy, Rt 6A
Barnstable, MA 02668
(508)362-8418 (800)441-8418 Fax:(508)362-8386
Internet: www.honeysucklehill.com
E-mail: stay@honeysucklehill.com

Circa 1810. This Queen Anne Victorian, which is listed in the National Register, is set on a picturesque acre with gardens.

The interior is decorated with antiques and white wicker furnishings. The hearty breakfasts include items such as Captain's Eggs, homemade granola, fresh fruit and cranberry-orange muffins. Nearby are the dunes of Sandy Neck Beach. Hyannis is 10 minutes away.

Innkeeper(s): Bill & Mary Kilburn. $100-150. MC, VISA, AX, DS, PC, TC. 5 rooms, 4 with PB and 1 suite. Breakfast and snacks/refreshments included in rates. Types of meals: Full gourmet bkfst and early coffee/tea. Beds: QD. Ceiling fan, feather beds, fresh flowers and terry cloth robes in room. Air conditioning. VCR, fax, copier, library, beach towels, chairs and umbrellas, guest refrigerator, fish pond, porch and gardens on premises. Antiquing, art galleries, beaches, bicycling, canoeing/kayaking, fishing, golf, hiking, beach, ferries, whale watching, live theater, museums, parks, shopping, tennis and wineries nearby.

Location: Cape Cod.

Publicity: *Atlanta Constitution, Saint Louis Journal, Prime Time, Cape Cod Travel Guide, Cape Cod Life and Secondhome.*

"The charm, beauty, service and warmth shown to guests are impressive, but the food overwhelms. Breakfasts were divine!—Judy Kaplan, St. Louis Journal."

Certificate may be used: Nov. 1 to April 30, Monday-Thursday.

Belchertown
E7

Ingate Farms B&B

60 Lamson Ave-S. Amherst Line
Belchertown, MA 01007-9710
(413)253-0440 (888)464-2832 Fax:(413)253-0440

Circa 1740. This Cape-style home was built as a bobbin factory, and eventually it was moved and reassembled at its current location on a 400-acre equestrian center. The interior is homey, with an emphasis on early American decor. Guests can relax on the enclosed porch, which is filled with comfortable furnishings. From the porch, guests can watch horses and enjoy the

countryside. The grounds offer an Olympic-size swimming pool, hiking trails, and guests can rent a boat and fish at nearby Quabbin Reservoir. Amherst and Hampshire colleges are nearby, as well as the University of Massachusetts at Amherst.

Innkeeper(s): Virginia Kier & Bill McCormick. $60-90. MC, VISA, AX, PC, TC. 5 rooms, 3 with PB. Breakfast and afternoon tea included in rates. Types of meals: Cont plus and early coffee/tea. Beds: KQT. TV, phone, ceiling fan and ice Water in room. Air conditioning. VCR, fax, copier, swimming, stables, library, pressing/irons, hair dryers, riding and hiking trails, riding lessons and riding summer day camp for children ages 6-14 weekly or daily basis on premises. Amusement parks, antiquing, fishing, golf, live theater, parks, shopping, downhill skiing, cross-country skiing, sporting events and tennis nearby.

Location: Quabbin Reservoir.

"I've felt so at home here this week and also charmed by the calm and loveliness of this place."

Certificate may be used: Jan. 30-April 30, Sunday-Wednesday, Nov. 1-Jan. 29, Sunday-Wednesday.

Bernardston   C6

Falls River Inn

1 Brattleboro Rd
Bernardston, MA 01337-9532
(413)648-9904 Fax:(413)648-0538

Circa 1905. Guests have been welcomed to this site since the late 18th century. The first inn burned down in the 1800s, and the current Federal-style Victorian inn was built in its place. Guests will find various styles of antiques in their comfortable, country rooms, three of which include a fireplace. During the week, a continental breakfast is served, and on weekends, guests are treated to a full breakfast. The inn's restaurant is open Wednesday through Sunday, and features everything

from chicken pot pie to pepper shrimp served on a bed of angel hair pasta and surrounded by an orange cream sauce. Don't forget to try the restaurant's signature "Vampire Chasers."

Innkeeper(s): Kerber Family. $55-93. MC, VISA, AX, DS, PC, TC. 7 rooms with PB, 5 with FP. Breakfast included in rates. Type of meal: Country bkfst. Beds: KQDT. Ceiling fan in room. Antiquing, bicycling, fishing, golf, hiking, live theater, parks, shopping, cross-country skiing, sporting events, tennis and water sports nearby.

Location: Rural village.

Publicity: *Snow Country Magazine, America's Favorite and Franklin County Magazine.*

"The food was excellent, the rooms charming and clean, the whole atmosphere so relaxing."

Certificate may be used: Nov. 10-April 30, Sunday-Friday.

Beverly   C14

Bunny's B&B

17 Kernwood Hgts
Beverly, MA 01915
(978)922-2392 Fax:(978)922-2392

Circa 1940. This Dutch Colonial inn is located on a scenic route along the state's northeastern coast. One room features a decorative fireplace and a handmade Oriental rug. Breakfasts in the formal dining room always feature homemade muffins and the innkeepers will make every effort to meet special dietary needs if notified in advance.

Innkeeper(s): Bunny & Joe Stacey. $65-95. PC, TC. 4 rooms, 2 with PB. Breakfast included in rates. Type of meal: Cont plus. Beds: QDT. TV on premises. Antiquing, historic sites, live theater, parks and shopping nearby.

Certificate may be used: Nov. 20-May 6.

Brewster   H18

Candleberry Inn

1882 Main St
Brewster, MA 02631-1827
(508)896-3300 (800)573-4769 Fax:(508)896-4016
Internet: www.candleberryinn.com
E-mail: candle@cape.com

Circa 1750. The two-acre grounds of this 250-year-old inn feature gardens complete with lawn swings. Wainscoting is dominant in the guest rooms, which feature Oriental rugs

on top of pine-planked floors. Antiques and family heirlooms decorate the inn. Three rooms include working fireplaces and one has a Jacuzzi. A full, gourmet breakfast is served in the dining room, which is also the inn's oldest room. The beach is less than a mile away, and Brewster offers many shops and restaurants.

Innkeeper(s): Gini & David Donnelly. $80-195. MC, VISA, AX, DS, PC, TC. 9 rooms with PB, 3 with FP and 2 suites. Breakfast included in rates. Type of meal: Full gourmet bkfst. Beds: KQDT. Robes and hair dryers in room. Air conditioning. Fax and copier on premises. Antiquing, fishing, golf, bike and nature trails, live theater, parks, shopping, tennis and water sports nearby.

Publicity: *Brewster Oracle and New York Times.*

"Wonderful, relaxing time, don't want to leave."

Certificate may be used: Jan. 30-April 1 and Nov. 1-Jan. 30. Sunday to Thursday, excluding holidays.

Old Sea Pines Inn

2553 Main St, PO Box 1026
Brewster, MA 02631-1959
(508)896-6114 Fax:(508)896-7387
Internet: www.oldseapinesinn.com
E-mail: seapines@c4.net

Circa 1900. This turn-of-the-century mansion on three-and-one-half acres of lawns and trees was formerly the Sea Pines School of Charm and Personality for Young Women, established in 1907. Recently renovated, the inn displays elegant wallpapers and a grand sweeping stairway. It is located near beaches and bike paths, as well as village shops and restaurants.

Innkeeper(s): Michele & Stephen Rowan. $65-125. MC, VISA, AX, DC, DS. 24 rooms, 16 with PB, 3 with FP, 2 suites and 2 conference rooms. Breakfast and afternoon tea included in rates. Types of meals: Full bkfst and early coffee/tea. Beds: QDT. Cable TV and phone in room. Air conditioning. Handicap access. Antiquing, fishing, dinner theatre in summer, live theater, shopping and water sports nearby.

Publicity: *New York Times, Cape Cod Oracle, For Women First, Home Office, Entrepreneur and Boston Magazine.*

"The loving care applied by Steve, Michele and staff is deeply appreciated."

Certificate may be used: Weekdays only March 31-May 31 and Oct. 15-Dec. 21.

Cape Cod   F18

Dunscroft By The Sea Inn & Cottage

24 Pilgrim Rd
Cape Cod, MA 02646
(508)432-0810 (800)432-4345 Fax:(508)432-5134
Internet: www.virtualcities.com/ma/dunscroft.htm
E-mail: alyce@capecod.net

Circa 1920. The innkeepers at this Colonial Revival Inn pride themselves on creating a quiet, romantic retreat for their guests. The Victorian decor includes special touches such as romantic poetry books placed in the

rooms, candles, chocolates and other surprises. Canopy and four-poster beds decorate the graciously appointed bedchambers. Rooms with a fireplace or double Jacuzzi tub also are available. In addition to the inn rooms, the King Suite is located in what was the chauffeur's cottage and includes a fireplace. The inn is located just steps away from a private beach that stretches more than a mile between two harbors. Built as a private summer estate in 1920, the inn has been welcoming guests for nearly half a century. Innkeeper Alyce Cunningham prepares a sumptuous full, country breakfast on a lace-covered table set with elegant china. A short walk will take you to restaurants and shops.

Innkeeper(s): Alyce & Wally Cunningham. $180-250. MC, VISA, AX, PC. 9 rooms with PB, 2 with FP, 1 suite, 1 cottage and 1 conference room. Breakfast included in rates. Type of meal: Full bkfst. Beds: KQ. Ceiling fan in room. Air conditioning. Fax, copier, swimming, tennis and library on premises. Handicap access. Amusement parks, antiquing, fishing, whale watching, natural seashore, live theater, parks, shopping, cross-country skiing, sporting events and water sports nearby.

Location: Village, resort area.

Publicity: *Cape Codder.*

"A quaint and delightful slice of New England. Your generous hospitality is greatly appreciated. Your place is beautiful."

Certificate may be used: Sunday-Thursday, Sept. 20-June 20 on an "as available basis". Excludes holidays.

Chatham
I19

Carriage House Inn

407 Old Harbor Rd
Chatham, MA 02633-2322
(508)945-4688 (800)355-8868 Fax:(508)945-8909
Internet: www.capecodtravel.com/carriagehouse

Circa 1890. This Colonial Revival inn is an easy find as it is located adjacent to Chatham's tallest flagpole. Antiques and family pieces decorate the interior. Chintzes and floral prints permeate the six guest rooms, and the three carriage house

rooms each include a fireplace and an entrance to an outside sitting area. Breakfast items such as fresh fruit, juices, pancakes, French toast, eggs Benedict and quiche can be enjoyed either in the dining room or on the sun porch. Guests can walk to Chatham's Main Street and to shops and galleries, or just relax and enjoy the grounds, which include gardens. Beach towels are furnished for trips to the shore, just a quarter mile away.

Innkeeper(s): Patty & Dennis O'Neill. $95-180. MC, VISA, AX, DS, PC, TC. 6 rooms with PB, 3 with FP. Breakfast and snacks/refreshments included in rates. Types of meals: Full bkfst and early coffee/tea. Beds: Q. Ceiling fan in room. Air conditioning. VCR and fax on premises. Antiquing, fishing, hiking, live theater, parks, shopping and water sports nearby.

Location: Seaside village.

"This might well have been our best B&B experience ever. It was the hosts who made it so memorable."

Certificate may be used: Jan. 2 to April 30, Sunday-Thursday and Oct. 30 to Dec. 30, Sunday-Thursday; excluding all holidays.

Old Harbor Inn

22 Old Harbor Rd
Chatham, MA 02633-2315
(508)945-4434 (800)942-4434 Fax:(508)945-7665
Internet: www.capecod.net/oldharborinn
E-mail: brazohi@capecod.net

Circa 1932. This pristine New England bed & breakfast was once the home of "Doc" Keene, a popular physician in the area. A meticulous renovation has created an elegant, beautifully appointed inn offering antique furnishings, designer linens and lavish amenities in an English country decor. A buffet breakfast, featuring Judy's homemade muffins, is

served in the sunroom or on the deck. The beaches, boutiques and galleries are a walk away and there is an old grist mill, the Chatham Lighthouse, and a railroad museum. Band concerts are offered Friday nights in the summer at Kate Gould Park.

Innkeeper(s): Judy & Ray Braz. $99-239. MC, VISA, PC, TC. 8 rooms with PB, 2 with FP and 1 conference room. Breakfast included in rates. Types of meals: Cont plus and early coffee/tea. Beds: KQT. Ceiling fan, toiletries, welcome package and one with Jacuzzi in room. Air conditioning. Concierge and gift shop on premises. Antiquing, fishing, beaches, art festivals, concerts, golf, tennis, live theater, parks, shopping and water sports nearby.

Location: Seaside Village/National Seashore.

Publicity: *Honeymoon, Cape Cod Life, Boston, Cape Cod Travel Guide and Country Inns.*

Certificate may be used: Nov. 1-April 30, Sunday through Thursday.

Concord
D12

Anderson-Wheeler Homestead

154 Fitchburg Tpke
Concord, MA 01742-5802
(978)369-3756 (800)377-6152
Internet: www.innsandouts.com

Circa 1890. When Route 117 was the main road between Boston and Fitchburg, the Lee family operated a stagecoach stop here. They provided room and board, a change of horses, and a leather and blacksmith shop. The building burned in 1890, and a Victorian house was built by Frank Wheeler, developer of rust-free asparagus. The property has remained in the family, and the veranda overlooks an extensive lawn and the Sudbury River.

Innkeeper(s): Charlotte Anderson. $80-165. MC, VISA, AX, DC, CB, DS, PC, TC. 5 rooms, 2 with PB, 2 with FP and 1 suite. Breakfast and snacks/refreshments included in rates. Type of meal: Cont plus. Beds: KQDT. Cable TV and phone in room. Air conditioning. VCR and library on premises. Antiquing, fishing, golf, live theater, parks, shopping, downhill skiing, cross-country skiing, sporting events and tennis nearby.

Location: Country.

Publicity: *New England Getaways, Concord Journal and PBS.*

"The five nights spent with you were the most comfortable and most congenial of the whole cross-country trip."

Certificate may be used: Oct. 15-March 30, excluding holidays.

Colonel Roger Brown House

1694 Main St
Concord, MA 01742-2831
(978)369-9119 (800)292-1369 Fax:(978)369-1305

Circa 1775. This house was the home of Minuteman Roger Brown, who fought the British at the Old North Bridge. The frame for this center-chimney Colonial was being raised on April 19, 1775, the day the battle took place. Some parts of the house were built as early as 1708. The adjacent Damon Mill houses a fitness club available to guests. Both buildings are in the National Register. Among the many  nearby historic sites are Thoreau's Walden Pond, the Concord Museum, the Alcott House, Old North Bridge, Lexington, the National Heritage Museum, Lowell Mills and much more.

Innkeeper(s): Lauri Berlied. $80-165. MC, VISA, AX, PC, TC. 5 rooms with PB and 1 suite. Breakfast and afternoon tea included in rates. Type of meal: Cont plus. Beds: QDT. Cable TV, phone, color TV and refrigerator upon request in room. Air conditioning. Fax, copier, spa, swimming, sauna, library and data port on premises. Antiquing, fishing, live theater, parks, shopping, downhill skiing, cross-country skiing and water sports nearby.

Location: Town.

Publicity: *Middlesex News, Concord Journal and Washingtonian.*

"The Colonel Roger Brown House makes coming to Concord even more of a treat! Many thanks for your warm hospitality."

Certificate may be used: Nov. 1-April 1, July 1-Aug. 31 on availability.

Hawthorne Inn

462 Lexington Rd
Concord, MA 01742-3729
(978)369-5610 Fax:(978)287-4949
Internet: www.concordmass.com
E-mail: hawthorneinn@concordmass.com

Circa 1870. The Hawthorne Inn is situated on land that once belonged to Ralph Waldo Emerson, the Alcotts and Nathaniel Hawthorne. It was here that Bronson Alcott planted his fruit trees, made pathways to the  Mill Brook, and erected his Bath House. Hawthorne purchased the land and repaired a path leading to his home with trees planted on either side. Two of these trees still stand. Across the road is Hawthorne's House, The Wayside. Next to it is the Alcott's Orchard House and Grapevine Cottage where the Concord grape was developed. Nearby is Sleepy Hollow Cemetery where Emerson, the Alcotts, the Thoreaus and Hawthorne were laid to rest.

Innkeeper(s): Marilyn Mudry & Gregory Burch. $140-215. MC, VISA, AX, DS, PC, TC. 7 rooms with PB. Breakfast and afternoon tea included in rates. Type of meal: Cont plus. Beds: QDT. Phone in room. Air conditioning. Fax, library and piano on premises. Antiquing, fishing, authors homes, parks, shopping and cross-country skiing nearby.

Location: Village.

Publicity: *Yankee, New York Times, Los Angeles Times, Le Monde, Early American Life and Evening.*

"Surely there couldn't be a better or more valuable location for a comfortable, old-fashioned country inn."

Certificate may be used: November-March, Saturday-Thursday (no Fridays).

Cotuit   I16

Salty Dog B&B Inn

451 Main St
Cotuit, MA 02635-3114
(508)428-5228

A 300-year-old oak rests in front of this seaside Victorian inn, which was owned originally by a sea captain. Guest rooms offer four-poster beds surrounded by country decor. The home features wide floor boards, antique moldings and Oriental rugs. Breakfasts of freshly baked muffins and breads are served in the fireplaced common room. Cotuit, known for its picturesque main street, as well as the surrounding Cape Cod, offers plenty of antiquing, shopping and restaurants.

Innkeeper(s): Gerald Goldstein. $75-125. MC, VISA. 5 rooms. Breakfast included in rates. Type of meal: Cont plus.

Certificate may be used: April through December, Sunday through Thursday, excluding holidays.

Deerfield   C6

Deerfield Inn

81 Old Main St
Deerfield, MA 01342-0305
(413)774-5587 (800)926-3865 Fax:(413)775-7221
Internet: www.deerfieldinn.com
E-mail: innkeeper@deerfieldinn.com

Circa 1884. The village of Deerfield was settled in 1670. Farmers in the area still unearth bones and ax and arrow heads from French/Indian massacre of 1704. Now, 50 beautifully restored 18th- and 19th-century homes line the mile-long main street, considered by many to be the loveliest street in New England. Fourteen of these houses are museums of Pioneer Valley decorative arts and are open year-  round to the public. The Memorial Hall Museum, open from May to November, is the oldest museum in New England and full of local antiquities. The inn is situated at the center of this peaceful village, and for those who wish to truly experience New England's past, this is the place. The village has been designated a National Historic Landmark.

Innkeeper(s): Jane & Karl Sabo. $146-241. MC, VISA, AX. 23 rooms with PB and 1 conference room. Breakfast and afternoon tea included in rates. Type of meal: Full bkfst. Beds: T. TV in room. Fax and copier on premises. Handicap access. Antiquing, fishing, live theater and cross-country skiing nearby.

Publicity: *Travel Today, Colonial Homes, Country Living, Country Inns B&B, Yankee and Romantic Homes.*

"We've stayed at many New England inns, but the Deerfield Inn ranks among the best."

Certificate may be used: Sunday-Thursday, based on availability, excluding May, September, October.

Deerfield South   D6

Deerfield's Yellow Gabled House

111 N Main St
Deerfield South, MA 01373-1026
(413)665-4922

Circa 1800. Huge maple trees shade the yard of this historic house, four miles from historic Deerfield and one mile from Route 91. Decorated with antiques, the bed chambers feature coordinating bedspreads and window treatments. One suite includes a sitting room, and canopy beds are another romantic touch. Breakfasts include items such as three-cheese stuffed French toast, an apple puff or fresh fruit topped with a yogurt-cheese sauce. The home is near historic Deerfield, and guests can walk to restaurants. The battle of Bloody Brook Massacre in 1675 occurred at this site, now landscaped with perennial English gardens. Yankee Candle is only one-half mile away.

Innkeeper(s): Edna Julia Stahelek. $75-125. 3 rooms, 1 with PB. Breakfast included in rates. Types of meals: Full gourmet bkfst and early coffee/tea. Beds: QT. Cable TV, phone and ceiling fan in room. Air conditioning. VCR on premises. Antiquing, fishing, biking, live theater, shopping, downhill skiing, cross-country skiing and sporting events nearby.

Location: Rural.

Publicity: *Recorder, Boston Globe and Springfield Republican.*

"We are still speaking of that wonderful weekend and our good fortune in finding you."

Certificate may be used: January, February, and March 30, Sunday-Thursday.

Dennis   I18

Isaiah Hall B&B Inn

152 Whig St, PO Box 1007
Dennis, MA 02638
(508)385-9928 (800)736-0160 Fax:(508)385-5879
Internet: www.isaiahhallinn.com
E-mail: info@isaiahhallinn.com

Circa 1857. Adjacent to the Cape's oldest cranberry bog is this Greek Revival farmhouse built by Isaiah Hall, a cooper. His grandfather was the first cultivator of cranberries in America and Isaiah designed and patented the original barrel for shipping cranberries. In 1948, Dorothy Gripp, an artist, established the inn. Many examples of her artwork remain.

Innkeeper(s): Marie Brophy. $102-170. MC, VISA, AX, DS, TC. 9 rooms, 10 with PB, 1 with FP and 1 suite. Breakfast included in rates. Types of meals: Cont plus and early coffee/tea. Beds: KQDT. Cable TV and phone in room. Air conditioning. Fax on premises. Antiquing, fishing, golf, whale watching, bike paths, live theater, parks, shopping and water sports nearby.

Publicity: *Cape Cod Life, New York Times, Golf and National Geographic Traveler.*

"Your place is so lovely and relaxing."

Certificate may be used: April & May, Sunday-Thursday, holidays excluded.

Dennis (South)   I18

Captain Nickerson Inn

333 Main St
Dennis (South), MA 02660-3643
(508)398-5966 (800)282-1619

Circa 1828. This Queen Anne Victorian inn is located in the mid-Cape area. Guests can relax on the front porch with white wicker rockers and tables. The guest rooms are decorated with period four-poster or white iron queen beds and hand-woven or Oriental-style rugs. The dining room has a fireplace and a stained-glass picture window. The Cape Cod bike Rail Trail, which is more than 20 miles long, is less than a mile away.

Innkeeper(s): Pat & Dave York. $90-150. MC, VISA, DS, PC. 5 rooms with PB and 1 suite. Breakfast included in rates. Type of meal: Full bkfst. Beds: QDT. Ceiling fan and terry robes in room. Air conditioning. VCR, fax, guest refrigerator and bicycles on premises. Antiquing, fishing, beaches, historic sites, museums, bike trails, live theater, parks, shopping and water sports nearby.

Location: Residential.

"Your inn is great!"

Certificate may be used: April 1-May 15; midweek (Sunday to Thursday).

Dennisport   I18

Rose Petal B&B

152 Sea St PO Box 974
Dennisport, MA 02639-2404
(508)398-8470
Internet: www.rosepetalofdennis.com
E-mail: info@rosepetalofdennis.com

Circa 1872. Surrounded by a white picket fence and picturesque gardens, the Rose Petal is situated in the heart of Cape Cod. The Greek Revival-style home was built for Almond Wixon, who was a descendant of the Mayflower and member of a prominent seafaring family. His homestead has been completely restored and offers guest rooms with spacious private baths. Home-baked pastries highlight a full breakfast served in the dining room. Walk through the historic neighborhood past century-old homes to Nantucket Sound's sandy beaches.

Innkeeper(s): Gayle & Dan Kelly. $72-109. MC, VISA, AX. 3 rooms with PB. Breakfast included in rates. Types of meals: Full gourmet bkfst and early coffee/tea. Beds: QT. Air conditioning. Antiquing, fishing, whale watching, live theater, parks, shopping and water sports nearby.

Location: Village.

"Perfect. Every detail was appreciated."

Certificate may be used: January, February, March anytime; April, May, November, Monday, Tuesday, Wednesday, Thursday only.

East Orleans   H19

Ship's Knees Inn

186 Beach Rd, PO Box 756
East Orleans, MA 02643
(508)255-1312 Fax:(508)240-1351
Internet: capecodtravel.com/shipskneesinn

Circa 1820. This 175-year-old restored sea captain's home is a three-minute walk to the ocean. Rooms are decorated in a nautical style with antiques. Several rooms feature authentic ship's knees, hand-painted trunks, old clipper ship models and four-poster beds. Some rooms boast ocean views, and the Master

Suite has a working fireplace. The inn offers swimming and tennis facilities on the grounds. About three  miles away, the innkeepers also offer three rooms, a bedroom efficiency apartment and two heated cottages on the Town Cove. Head into town, or spend the day basking in the beauty of Nauset Beach with its picturesque sand dunes.

Innkeeper(s): Jean & Ken Pitchford. $55-135. MC, VISA. 19 rooms, 9 with PB, 1 with FP. Breakfast included in rates. Type of meal: Cont. Beds: KQDT. Amusement parks, antiquing, fishing, live theater, parks, shopping and water sports nearby.

Publicity: *Boston Globe.*

"Warm, homey and very friendly atmosphere. Very impressed with the beamed ceilings."

Certificate may be used: All year, except July, August and holidays.

East Sandwich   117

Wingscorton Farm Inn

Rt 6A, Olde Kings Hwy
East Sandwich, MA 02537
(508)888-0534

Circa 1763. Wingscorton is a working farm on 13 acres of lawns, gardens and orchards. It adjoins a short walk to a private ocean beach. This Cape Cod manse, built by a Quaker family, is a historical landmark on what once was known as the King's Highway, the oldest historical district in the United States. All the rooms are furnished with antiques and working fireplaces (one with a secret compartment where runaway slaves hid). Breakfast features fresh produce with eggs, meats and vegetables from the farm's livestock and gardens. Pets and children welcome.

Innkeeper(s): Sheila Weyers & Richard Loring. $125-175. MC, VISA, AX, PC, TC. 7 rooms, 7 with FP, 4 suites and 2 cottages. Breakfast included in rates. Type of meal: Full gourmet bkfst. Beds: QDT. TV in room. Swimming, library, child care and private beach on premises. Antiquing, fishing, live theater, parks, shopping, downhill skiing, cross-country skiing, sporting events and water sports nearby.

Pets Allowed.

Location: Country.

Publicity: *US Air and Travel & Leisure.*

"Absolutely wonderful. We will always remember the wonderful time."

Certificate may be used: January to April 30, Monday, Tuesday, Wednesday, Thursday.

Edgartown   K16

Ashley Inn

129 Main St, PO Box 650
Edgartown, MA 02539-0650
(508)627-9655 (800)477-9655

Circa 1860. A retired whaling captain built this gracious Georgian inn on Martha's Vineyard. Guest rooms are furnished in period antiques, brass and wicker. The inn is just four blocks from the beach, and its Main Street location offers easy access to Edgartown's many fine restaurants and shops. Breakfasts are served in the English tea room, and guests find the inn's grounds perfect for an after-meal stroll. Others like to relax in the hammock or in the comfortable sitting room. A special honeymoon package is available.

Innkeeper(s): Fred Hurley. $95-200. MC, VISA, AX. 8 rooms and 1 suite. Breakfast included in rates. Type of meal: Cont. Cable TV in room. Air conditioning. Antiquing and shopping nearby.

Certificate may be used: Oct. 23-April 1, Nov. 1-Dec. 31.

Shiretown Inn on the Island of Martha's Vineyard

44 North Water St
Edgartown, MA 02539-0921
(508)627-3353 (800)541-0090 Fax:(508)627-8478
Internet: shiretowninn.com
E-mail: vacation@shiretowninn.com

Circa 1795. Listed in the National Register of Historic Places, Shiretown Inn is located in a historic district of whaling captain homes on Martha's Vineyard, the famed island seven miles off the coast of Massachusetts. Ask to stay in one of the inn's two 1795 houses where you can choose a traditionally furnished guest room with a variety of amenities such as a canopy bed and an Oriental rug. More modest rooms are available in the Carriage Houses, and there is a cottage with kitchen and living room that is particularly popular for families with small children. The inn's restaurant offers indoor dining or seating on a garden terrace. There's also a pub. Walk one block to the Chappaquiddick Ferry and the harbor. (Make reservations in advance if you plan to bring your car, as there is limited space on the ferry.) Shops, galleries, restaurants and beaches are nearby. Cycling, golf, windsurfing, sailing, tennis and horseback riding are also close.

Innkeeper(s): Gene Strimling. $89-750. MC, VISA, AX, DS. 39 rooms with PB, 5 with FP, 5 suites and 1 cottage. Breakfast included in rates. Type of meal: Cont. Beds: KQDT. Cable TV and phone in room. Air conditioning. Fax on premises. Antiquing, fishing, golf, parks, shopping, tennis and water sports nearby.

Certificate may be used: Nov. 1-May 1, Monday through Thursday except holidays.

Great Barrington   F2

Wainwright Inn

518 Main St
Great Barrington, MA 01230-2006
(413)528-2062

Circa 1766. This pre-Revolutionary War home opened for guests in 1766 as Tory Tavern and Inn, and during the war served as a fort and Colonial armory. The home was also used to lay the groundwork for the commercial use of AC current, when it was owned by Franklin Pope. Pope worked with Thomas Edison and General Electric founder William Stanley. If the history of this inn fails to impress, the rich interior should do the trick. Snuggle up in front of a roaring fire or relax on one of the wraparound porches. Muffins and fresh coffee are delivered to guests each morning. A full breakfast is served later in the fire-lit dining room. Each season brings new activity to the Great Barrington area, which is full of antique shops, orchards to visit, ski slopes and beautiful scenery. The nearby Hancock Shaker Village is a popular attraction.

Innkeeper(s): David Rolland. $50-125. MC, VISA, AX. 8 rooms. Breakfast included in rates. Type of meal: Full bkfst.

Certificate may be used: November-June, Sunday-Thursday.

Greenfield
C6

The Brandt House

29 Highland Ave
Greenfield, MA 01301-3605
(413)774-3329 (800)235-3329 Fax:(413)772-2908
Internet: www.brandthouse.com
E-mail: info@brandthouse.com

Circa 1890. Three-and-a-half-acre lawns surround this impressive three-story Colonial Revival house, situated hilltop. The library and poolroom are popular for lounging, but the favorite gathering areas are the sunroom and the covered north porch. Ask for the aqua and white room with the fireplace, but all the rooms are pleasing. A full breakfast often includes homemade scones and is sometimes available on the slate patio in view of

the expansive lawns and beautiful gardens. A full-time staff provides for guest needs. There is a clay tennis court and nature trails, and in winter, lighted ice skating at a nearby pond. Historic Deerfield and Yankee Candle Company are within five minutes.

Innkeeper(s): Phoebe Compton. $105-195. MC, VISA, AX, DS, TC. 9 rooms, 7 with PB, 2 with FP, 1 suite and 1 conference room. Breakfast included in rates. Types of meals: Full bkfst, cont plus and early coffee/tea. Beds: KQT. Cable TV, phone, ceiling fan, fireplaces in two rooms and microwave in room. Air conditioning. VCR, fax, copier, tennis and library on premises. Antiquing, fishing, Old Deerfield, Lunt Silver, live theater, parks, shopping, downhill skiing, cross-country skiing, sporting events and water sports nearby.

Pets allowed: Call for approval.

Location: Mountains.

Certificate may be used: Nov. 1-April 30, June 1-Aug. 31.

Hamilton
C14

Miles River Country Inn

823 Bay Rd, Box 149
Hamilton, MA 01936
(978)468-7206 Fax:(978)468-3999
Internet: www.milesriver.com

Circa 1789. This rambling colonial inn sits on more than 30 acres of magnificent curving lawns bordered by trees and formal gardens that lead to the Miles River. There are meadows, woodlands and wetlands surrounding the property and available for exploring. The river flows through the property, which is a haven for a wide variety of wildlife. Many of the inn's 12 fireplaces are in the guest rooms. Family heirloom antiques compliment the interior.

Innkeeper(s): Gretel & Peter Clark. $80-210. MC, VISA, AX, PC, TC. 8 rooms, 6 with PB, 4 with FP, 1 suite and 2 conference rooms. Breakfast and afternoon tea included in rates. Types of meals: Full bkfst and early coffee/tea. Beds: QDT. Fans and clocks in room. VCR, fax, copier, bicycles, library, walking trails and gardens on premises. Antiquing, fishing, world class horse events, live theater, parks, shopping, downhill skiing, cross-country skiing, sporting events and water sports nearby.

Location: Rural.

Publicity: *Boston Globe, Beverly Times, Salem Evening News, Local cable TV, Boston Globe, Salem Evening News, Rhode Island Monthly, Beverly Times, Boston Magazine and Yankee.*

Certificate may be used: Most weekdays, weekends November-April, except holiday weekends.

Harwich Port
I18

Captain's Quarters B&B Inn

85 Bank St
Harwich Port, MA 02646-1903
(508)432-1991 (800)992-6550

Circa 1850. This romantic Victorian inn features a classic wrap-around porch and a graceful, curving front stairway. Guest rooms include brass beds and charming decor. A continental breakfast is served each morning. The inn is a three-minute walk to the beach or the village.

Innkeeper(s): Ed Kenney. $89-109. MC, VISA, AX, DS. 5 rooms with PB. Breakfast included in rates. Type of meal: Cont plus. Beds: QT. Cable TV and phone in room. Antiquing, bike trails, whale watching and shopping nearby.

"A great romantic getaway with lovely rooms."

Certificate may be used: May 14 to June 18, Sept. 20 through Oct. 24 (excluding holiday periods).

Lee
E2

Devonfield

85 Stockbridge Rd
Lee, MA 01238-9308
(413)243-3298 (800)664-0880 Fax:(413)243-1360

Circa 1800. The original section of this Federal inn was built by a Revolutionary War soldier. Guest rooms are spacious with charming furniture and patterned wallcoverings. Three of the

rooms feature fireplaces. The one-bedroom cottage has both a fireplace and an efficiency kitchen. Guests are treated to a full breakfast. One need not wander far from the

grounds to find something to do. The innkeepers offer a tennis court, swimming pool and bicycles for guests, and a nine-hole golf course is just across the way. Inside, guests can relax in the living room with its fireplace and library or in the television room. The area is full of boutiques, antique shops and galleries to explore, as well as hiking, fishing and skiing. Tanglewood, summer home of the Boston Symphony, is close by.

Innkeeper(s): Sally & Ben Schenck. $80-275. MC, VISA, AX, DS, PC, TC. 10 rooms with PB, 4 with FP, 4 suites and 1 cottage. Beds: KQT. Cable some rooms in room. Air conditioning. Fax, copier, swimming, bicycles, tennis and library on premises.

Location: Mountains.

Publicity: *Discerning Traveler.*

"A special thank you for your warm and kind hospitality. We feel as though this is our home away from home."

Certificate may be used: Nov. 1-May 31, not including holidays.

Lenox
E2

Brook Farm Inn

15 Hawthorne St
Lenox, MA 01240-2404
(413)637-3013 (800)285-7638 Fax:(413)637-4751
Internet: www.brookfarm.com
E-mail: innkeeper@brookfarm.com

Circa 1870. Brook Farm Inn is named after the original Brook Farm, a literary commune that sought to combine thinker and worker through a society of intelligent, cultivated members. In keeping with that theme, this gracious Victorian inn offers poetry and writing seminars and has a 650-volume poetry library. Canopy beds, Mozart and a swimming pool tend to the spirit.

Innkeeper(s): Joe & Anne Miller. $90-205. MC, VISA, DS, PC, TC. 12 rooms with PB, 6 with FP. Breakfast and afternoon tea included in rates. Types of meals: Full bkfst and early coffee/tea. Beds: KQT. Phone, ceiling fan, fluffy towels and toiletries in room. Air conditioning. Fax, copier, swimming, butler's pantry, round-the-clock coffee and tea on premises. Antiquing, fishing, Tanglewood, live theater, parks, shopping, downhill skiing, cross-country skiing, sporting events and water sports nearby.

Location: Berkshire hills.

Publicity: *Berkshire Eagle, Country Inns, Travel & Leisure and Boston Globe.*

"We've been traveling all our lives and never have we felt more at home."
Certificate may be used: Monday-Thursday, April 1-June 15.

The Gables Inn

81 Walker St, Rt 183
Lenox, MA 01240-2719
(413)637-3416 (800)382-9401

Circa 1885. At one time, this was the home of Pulitzer Prize-winning novelist, Edith Wharton. The Queen Anne-style Berkshire cottage features a handsome eight-sided library and Mrs. Wharton's own four-poster bed. An unusual indoor swimming pool with spa is available in warm weather.

Innkeeper(s): Mary & Frank Newton. $80-225. MC, VISA, DS, PC, TC. 17 rooms with PB, 15 with FP and 4 suites. Breakfast included in rates. Beds: Q. Cable TV and VCR in room. Air conditioning. Fax, swimming and tennis on premises. Antiquing, fishing, live theater, parks, shopping, downhill skiing, cross-country skiing, sporting events and water sports nearby.

Location: Village.

Publicity: *P.M. Magazine and New York Times.*

"You made us feel like old friends and that good feeling enhanced our pleasure. In essence, it was the best part of our trip."
Certificate may be used: Nov. 1 to May 20, Sunday through Thursday only.

Lilac Inn

PO Box 2294, 33 Main St
Lenox, MA 01240-5294
(413)637-2172 Fax:(413)637-2172
Internet: www.berkshireweb.com/lilacinn
E-mail: aliceatlilacinn@msn.com

Circa 1836. Aptly named for a flower, this Italian Revival inn features guest rooms that appear much like a garden. Flowery prints, wicker and antique furnishings and views of Lilac Park from the two porches enhance this cheerful atmosphere. Guests are treated to afternoon refreshments, with a proper mix of savory and sweet tidbits. Breakfasts are bountiful and delicious, yet surprisingly healthy with low-fat, vegetarian versions of treats such as banana nut bread, French toast and vegetable quiche. The library is stocked with books, and the living room, which has a fireplace, is a good place to curl up and relax. The innkeeper also offers a one-bedroom apartment with a kitchen.

Innkeeper(s): Alice Maleski. $100-225. PC. 6 rooms with PB, 1 with FP. Breakfast and afternoon tea included in rates. Types of meals: Full gourmet bkfst and early coffee/tea. Beds: KQT. Turndown service and ceiling fan in room. VCR, fax, copier and library on premises. Handicap access. Antiquing, fishing, golf, outlet shops, live theater, parks, shopping, cross-country skiing and water sports nearby.

Location: Berkshires.

"We are really looking forward to shamelessly overindulging in your breakfasts, and being carried away by the music, the time and the place."
Certificate may be used: Tuesday and Wednesday nights, June 1 to Oct. 31; Nov. 1-May 31, excluding weekends and holidays.

Seven Hills Country Inn & Restaurant

40 Plunkett St
Lenox, MA 01240-2795
(413)637-0060 (800)869-6518 Fax:(413)637-3651
Internet: www.sevenhillsinn.com
E-mail: 7hills@berkshire.net

Circa 1911. Descendants of those who sailed on the Mayflower built this rambling, Tudor-style mansion. The inn's 27 acres of terraced lawns and stunning gardens often serve as the site for weddings, receptions and meetings. The grounds include two tennis courts and a swimming pool. Guest rooms are elegantly appointed with antiques, and the mansion still maintains its hand-carved fireplaces and leaded glass windows. In addition to the original elements, some rooms contain the modern amenity of a jet tub. The inn's chef, whose cuisine has been featured in Gourmet magazine, prepares creative, continental specialties. Seven Hills offers close access to many attractions in the Berkshires.

Innkeeper(s): Patricia & Jim Eder. $85-295. MC, VISA, AX, DC, CB, DS, PC, TC. 52 rooms with PB, 5 with FP, 2 suites and 4 conference rooms. Breakfast included in rates. Types of meals: Full bkfst and cont plus. Beds: KQD. Cable TV and phone in room. Air conditioning. VCR, fax, copier, swimming, tennis and library on premises. Handicap access. Antiquing, fishing, live theater, museums, parks, shopping, downhill skiing, cross-country skiing and water sports nearby.

Pets allowed: Sometimes.

Location: Mountains.

Publicity: *Gourmet and Entrepreneur.*

Certificate may be used: Jan. 1-April 30, all nights; May 1-June 30, Sunday-Friday; July 1-Aug. 31, Monday-Wednesday; Sept. 1-Oct. 26, Sunday-Friday; Oct. 27-Dec. 15, all nights; Dec. 16-31, Sunday-Friday.

Walker House

64 Walker St
Lenox, MA 01240-2718
(413)637-1271 (800)235-3098 Fax:(413)637-2387
Internet: www.walkerhouse.com
E-mail: phoudek@vgernet.net

Circa 1804. This beautiful Federal-style house sits in the center of the village on three acres of graceful woods and restored gardens. Guest rooms have fireplaces and private baths. Each is

named for a favorite composer such as Beethoven, Mozart or Handel. The innkeepers' musical backgrounds include associations with the San Francisco Opera, the New York City Opera, and the Los Angeles Philharmonic. Walker House concerts are scheduled from time to time. The innkeepers offer film and opera screenings nightly on a twelve-foot screen. With prior approval, some pets may be allowed.

Innkeeper(s): Peggy & Richard Houdek. $80-210. PC. 8 rooms with PB, 5 with FP and 1 conference room. Breakfast and afternoon tea included in rates. Types of meals: Cont plus and early coffee/tea. Beds: QDT. TV in room. Air conditioning. VCR, fax, copier, library, theatre with internet access and 100 inch screen on premises. Handicap access. Antiquing, fishing, music, live theater, parks, shopping, downhill skiing, cross-country skiing and water sports nearby.

Pets allowed: With prior approval.

Location: In small village.

Publicity: *Boston Globe, PBS, Los Angeles Times, New York Times & Dog Fancy.*

"We had a grand time staying with fellow music and opera lovers! Breakfasts were lovely."
Certificate may be used: Nov. 1 to April 30, Sunday through Thursday, excluding holiday periods.

Marblehead   D14

A Nesting Place B&B

16 Village St
Marblehead, MA 01945-2213
(781)631-6655
Internet: www.anestingplace.com
E-mail: louisehir@aol.com

Circa 1890. Conveniently located one-half hour away from
Boston and Cape Ann, this turn-of-the-century house located
in a quiet neighborhood offers as much privacy as you require.
Full breakfasts are served and include home baked breads and
muffins and fresh fruit. Discover the world of the early clipper
ships as you walk the narrow winding streets and the beaches
of Marblehead's renowned harbor, only minutes away. There's a
relaxing hot tub to top off a day of browsing through art galleries, antique shops and quaint boutiques. Massages and
facials also are available off premises.

Innkeeper(s): Louise Hirshberg. $65-75. MC, VISA, PC, TC. 2 rooms.
Breakfast included in rates. Types of meals: Cont plus and early coffee/tea.
Beds: KQT. VCR and spa on premises. Antiquing, fishing, historic sites, live
theater, parks, shopping, cross-country skiing, sporting events and water
sports nearby.

Certificate may be used: Nov. 1-April 15, holidays excluded.

Harbor Light Inn

58 Washington
Marblehead, MA 01945
(781)631-2186 Fax:(781)631-2216
Internet: www.harborlightinn.com
E-mail: hli@shore.net

Circa 1729. This early 18th-century inn is an elegant New
England retreat. Oriental rugs, refined furnishings, fine paintings
and items such as four-poster beds create a warm, inviting character. A dozen of the guest rooms include a fireplace, and some
offer sunken Jacuzzi tubs. For
three years, Vacations magazine ranked the inn as one of
the nation's most romantic.
The inn is located within
walking distance of shops and
restaurants, as well as
Marblehead Harbor.

Innkeeper(s): Peter & Suzanne Conway. $105-245. MC, VISA, AX, PC, TC.
22 rooms with PB, 12 with FP, 2 suites, 1 cabin and 1 conference room.
Breakfast included in rates. Type of meal: Cont. Beds: KQT. Cable TV, phone,
VCR and Jacuzzis in room. Air conditioning. Fax, copier, swimming and
sauna on premises.

Publicity: *Vacations.*

Certificate may be used: January-March 10, Sunday-Thursday.

Martha's Vineyard   K16

Nancy's Auberge

98 Main St, PO Box 4433
Martha's Vineyard, MA 02568
(508)693-4434

Circa 1840. This 1840 Greek Revival home affords harbor
views from its spot in a historic neighborhood once home to
early settlers and whaling captains. Three of the antique-filled

rooms include fireplaces, and one of the bedchambers boasts a
harbor view. The inn is just a few blocks from the local ferry.
Bicycle paths and beaches are nearby, as well as restaurants and
a variety of shops.

Innkeeper(s): Nancy Hurd. $98-148. MC, VISA. 3 rooms. Breakfast included
in rates. Type of meal: Cont plus. VCR on premises. Antiquing, live theater
and shopping nearby.
Location: in village.

"It's so picturesque. It's like living on a postcard."

Certificate may be used: Monday through Thursday, November through April,
holidays excluded.

Twin Oaks Inn

8 Edgartown Rd, PO Box 1767
Martha's Vineyard, MA 02568-1767
(508)693-8633 (800)696-8633 Fax:(508)693-5833

Circa 1906. Pastels and floral prints provide a relaxing atmosphere at this Dutch Colonial inn on Martha's Vineyard, which
offers four guest rooms and an apartment with its own kitchen.

The breakfast specialty is apple-
crisp, and guests also enjoy
afternoon tea on the enclosed
wraparound front porch. The
inn is within walking distance of
the bicycle path, downtown
businesses and the ferry, but its

location off the main road affords a more relaxed and sedate
feeling for visitors. The family-oriented inn accommodates family reunions, meetings and weddings, and its fireplace room is
popular with honeymooners.

Innkeeper(s): Doris Clark. $60-200. MC, VISA. 5 rooms, 3 with PB, 2 suites
and 1 conference room. Breakfast included in rates. Types of meals: Cont plus
and early coffee/tea. Beds: QDT. Cable TV and ceiling fan in room. VCR on
premises. Antiquing, fishing, live theater, shopping and water sports nearby.

Publicity: *Detroit Free Press.*

*"We appreciated the wonderful welcome and kind hospitality shown
us for our week's stay on your lovely island."*

Certificate may be used: Jan. 1 to May 15.

Middleboro   H14

On Cranberry Pond B&B

43 Fuller St
Middleboro, MA 02346-1706
(508)946-0768 Fax:(508)947-8221
E-mail: ocpbandb@aol.com

Circa 1989. Nestled in the historic "cranberry capital of the
world," this modern farmhouse rests on a working berry bog
by the shores of its namesake tarn. There are two miles of trails
to meander, and during berry picking season, guests can watch
as buckets of the fruit are collected. Rooms are comfortable and
well appointed. The Master Suite includes a working fireplace.
A 93-foot deck overlooks the cranberry bog. Innkeeper
Jeannine LaBossiere creates breakfasts which begin with fresh
coffee, muffins, cookies and scones.

Innkeeper(s): Jeannine LaBossiere & Tim Dombrowski. $75-140. MC, VISA,
AX, DC, CB, PC, TC. 5 rooms, 3 with PB, 2 with FP, 2 suites and 1 conference room. Breakfast and snacks/refreshments included in rates. Types of
meals: Full gourmet bkfst and early coffee/tea. Beds: QD. Cable TV, phone,
turndown service, ceiling fan and VCR in room. Air conditioning. Fax, copier,
stables, bicycles and library on premises. Amusement parks, antiquing, fishing, live theater, parks, shopping, downhill skiing and water sports nearby.
Location: Countryside.

*"Your dedication to making your guests comfortable is above and
beyond. You are tops in your field."*

Certificate may be used: All year.

Nantucket L18

House of The Seven Gables

32 Cliff Rd
Nantucket, MA 02554-3644
(508)228-4706

Circa 1865. Originally the annex of the Sea Cliff Inn, one of the island's oldest hotels, this three-story Queen Anne Victorian inn offers 10 guest rooms. Beaches, bike rentals, museums, restaurants, shops and tennis courts are all found nearby. The guest rooms are furnished with king or queen beds and period antiques. Breakfast is served each morning in the guest rooms, and often include homemade coffee cake, muffins or Portuguese rolls.

Innkeeper(s): Sue Walton. $85-195. MC, VISA, AX. 10 rooms, 8 with PB. Breakfast included in rates. Type of meal: Cont. Beds: KQ. Antiquing, fishing, live theater, shopping and water sports nearby.
Location: Island.
"You have a beautiful home and one that makes everyone feel relaxed and at home."
Certificate may be used: April 26-June 24, Sunday through Thursday. Aug. 23-Oct. 29, Sunday through Thursday.

Ivy Lodge

2 Chester St
Nantucket, MA 02554-3505
(508)228-7755 Fax:(508)228-0305

Circa 1790. This 18th-century Colonial has spent much of its life serving the needs of travelers. In the 1800s, the home was used both as an inn and a museum. Today, the home serves as a living museum of American history. The home still includes its classic, center chimney, pine floors and fireplaces. Guest rooms are decorated with antiques and beds topped with ornate bedspreads and lacy canopies. Vases filled with flowers add extra color. The Brant Point lighthouse is within walking distance of the inn, and the beach is nearby.

Innkeeper(s): Tuge Roseatra. $75-160. 6 rooms. Breakfast included in rates. Type of meal: Cont plus.
Certificate may be used: Nov. 1-April 30; Oct. 1-30 and May 1-June 15. Excluding holidays and all local festival days and weekends.

Stumble Inne

109 Orange Street
Nantucket, MA 02554-3947
(508)228-4482 (800)649-4482 Fax:(508)228-4752
E-mail: romance@nantucket.net

Circa 1704. This Nantucket Island inn is appointed with fine antiques and period reproductions. Rooms feature wide pine floors, antique beds and ceiling fans. At the back of the inn's hydrangea-filled gardens, there is a two-bedroom cottage that can accommodate up to four people. The cottage also includes a bathroom, kitchen, living room and a private deck. The inn was voted "Best B&B" by Cape Cod Life.

Innkeeper(s): Jeanne & George Todor. $75-250. MC, VISA, AX, TC. 6 rooms with PB and 1 suite. Breakfast included in rates. Types of meals: Cont plus and early coffee/tea. Beds: Q. Cable TV, ceiling fan and VCR in room. Air conditioning. Fax on premises. Antiquing, fishing, restaurants, live theater, shopping and water sports nearby.
Publicity: *Innsider.*
"A relaxing, comfortable week with gracious hosts. Thanks for your Southern hospitality in the Northeast."
Certificate may be used: Oct. 1-May 15, Sunday-Thursday, excluding holiday periods.

The White House

48 Center St
Nantucket, MA 02554-3664
(508)228-4677

Circa 1800. For more than 40 years a favorite hostelry of visitors to Nantucket, The White House is situated ideally in the heart of the historic district and a short walk to the beach and ferry terminal. The first floor houses an antique shop. Guests stay in rooms on the second floor or a housekeeping apartment. Afternoon wine and cheese is served in the garden.

Innkeeper(s): Nina Hellman. $75-130. MC, VISA, AX. 3 rooms with PB and 1 suite. Breakfast included in rates. Type of meal: Cont. Beds: Q. Phone in room. Antiquing, fishing, museums, fine restaurants, live theater, shopping and water sports nearby.
Location: In historic district.
Certificate may be used: Weekdays, mid-April to mid-June and mid-October to mid-November. Anytime mid-November through December. Excludes holidays and special island events.

The Woodbox Inn

29 Fair St
Nantucket, MA 02554-3798
(508)228-0587
Internet: www.woodboxinn.com
E-mail: woodbox@nantucket.net

Circa 1709. In the heart of the historic district, the Woodbox Inn was built in 1709 by Captain George Bunker. Guest rooms are decorated with antiques and reproductions and some have canopy beds. The six suites offer sitting rooms and fireplaces. Walk to Main Street and enjoy fine boutiques and art galleries. Other activities include biking, tennis, golf, whale watching and sandy beaches for sunning. The inn's award-winning gourmet dining room features an early American atmosphere with low-beamed ceilings and pine-paneled walls. (Meals are not included in room rates.).

Innkeeper(s): Dexter Tutein. $175-285. PC, TC. 9 rooms with PB, 6 with FP and 6 suites. Type of meal: Full bkfst. Beds: KQDT. Antiquing, fishing, live theater, parks, shopping, tennis and water sports nearby.
Publicity: *Wharton Alumni, Cape Cod Life, Boston Magazine, Wine Spectator and James Beard Foundation.*
Certificate may be used: Midweek, from mid-October to Jan. 1 and May 1 to Memorial Day, holidays excluded.

Newburyport B14

Clark Currier Inn

45 Green St
Newburyport, MA 01950-2646
(978)465-8363 (800)360-6582

Circa 1803. Once the home of shipbuilder Thomas March Clark, this three-story Federal-style inn provides gracious accommodations to visitors in the Northeast Massachusetts area. Visitors will enjoy the inn's details added by Samuel McEntire, one of the nation's most celebrated home builders and woodcarvers. Breakfast is served in the dining room or garden room, with an afternoon tea offered in the garden room. The inn's grounds also boast a picturesque garden and gazebo. Parker River National Wildlife Refuge and Maudslay State Park are nearby, as well as Plum Island beaches.

Innkeeper(s): Mary & Bob Nolan. $95-155. MC, VISA, AX, DS. 8 rooms with PB. Breakfast and afternoon tea included in rates. Type of meal: Cont plus. Beds: QDT. Phone in room. Air conditioning. Sherry and fruit are available in the library on premises. Amusement parks, antiquing, fishing, many acclaimed and varied restaurants and shops, live theater, parks, shopping, cross-country skiing and water sports nearby.

Location: Historic downtown.

"We had a lovely stay in your B&B! We appreciated your hospitality!"

Certificate may be used: Jan. 1-May 20, excluding holidays. Certificates may be used when space available.

Oak Bluffs   K16

The Oak Bluffs Inn

Circuit and Pequot Ave
Oak Bluffs, MA 02557
(508)693-7171 (800)955-6235

Circa 1870. A widow's walk and gingerbread touches were added to this graceful home to enhance the Victorian atmosphere already prevalent throughout the inn. Rooms are decorated in Victorian style with antiques. Home-baked breads and fresh fruits start off the day. After enjoying the many activities Martha's Vineyard has to offer, return for a scrumptious afternoon tea with scones, tea sandwiches and pastries. Oak Bluffs originally was named Cottage City, and is full of quaint, gingerbread homes to view. Nearby Circuit Avenue offers shopping, ice cream parlors, eateries and the nation's oldest carousel.

Innkeeper(s): Erik & Rhonda Albert. $120-215. MC, VISA, AX. 9 rooms with PB. Breakfast included in rates. Type of meal: Cont plus. Beds: QD. Ceiling fan in room. Air conditioning. Refrigerator/ice maker on premises. Antiquing, fishing, golf, live theater, parks, shopping, tennis and water sports nearby.

Location: on Martha's Vineyard Island.

Certificate may be used: Oct. 1-June 15, Sunday-Thursday.

The Tucker Inn

2 Massasoit Ave
Oak Bluffs, MA 02557-2680
(508)693-1045

Circa 1872. Located on a quiet residential park within walking distance of retail establishments and the town beach, this two-story Victorian Stick/Shingle inn offers visitors to Martha's Vineyard a choice of suites and guest rooms with shared and private baths. The former doctor's residence boasts an attractive veranda that is ideal for reading or relaxing after a busy day exploring the island's many attractions, or a trip to nearby Chappaquiddick. Public transportation and boat lines are a five-minute walk from the inn.

Innkeeper(s): William Reagan. $35-245. MC, VISA. 8 rooms, 5 with PB and 2 suites. Breakfast included in rates. Type of meal: Cont. Beds: QDT. Ceiling fan in room. VCR on premises. Antiquing, fishing, live theater, shopping and water sports nearby.

Location: Residential park.

Certificate may be used: Oct. 1-June 15.

Onset   I15

Onset Pointe Inn

9 Eagle Way, PO Box 1450
Onset, MA 02558-1450
(508)295-8100 (800)356-6738 Fax:(508)295-5241

Circa 1880. This restored Victorian mansion is surrounded by the ocean on Point Independence. Its casually elegant decor is enhanced by sea views, sunlight, bright colors and florals. Spacious verandas, an enclosed circular sun porch and a bay-

side gazebo are available to guests. Accommodations are divided among the main house and two additional buildings. An all-you-can-eat hearty continental breakfast is available in the waterfront dining room. The Onset Pointe Inn received the National Trust first prize for preservation in its B&B category.

Innkeeper(s): Peter Della Monica & Barry Eisenberg. $55-235. MC, VISA, AX, DS, TC. 14 rooms with PB and 6 suites. Breakfast included in rates. Beds: QDT. Phone in room. Fax, copier, swimming and meeting room on premises. Antiquing, fishing, historical sites, live theater, parks, shopping and water sports nearby.

"We've found the B&B we've been looking for!"

Certificate may be used: Oct. 16-April 30, Sunday-Thursday, excluding July & August. Excludes holidays, based on availability. Please mention offer at time of reservation.

Orleans   H19

The Farmhouse at Nauset Beach

163 Beach Rd
Orleans, MA 02653-2732
(508)255-6654

Circa 1870. Feel the intimacy of Orleans and capture the flavor of Cape Cod at this quiet country inn resting in a seashore setting. Rooms in this Greek Revival-style inn are comfortably furnished to depict their 19th-century past. Some rooms offer ocean views, and one includes a decorated fireplace. Nauset Beach is a short walk away. Spend a day charter fishing in Cape Cod Bay or the Atlantic. To make your stay complete, your itinerary can include antiquing, shopping, exploring quiet country lanes or a day at the beach. The inn offers gift certificates and is open year-round.

Innkeeper(s): Dorothy Standish. $52-110. MC, VISA, PC, TC. 8 rooms with PB, 1 with FP. Breakfast included in rates. Type of meal: Cont plus. Beds: KQD. Ceiling fan in some rooms in room. Bike rack on premises. Antiquing, fishing, horseback riding, windsurfing, bike trails, live theater, shopping and water sports nearby.

Location: Mountains.

Certificate may be used: Nov. 1 to April 30, excluding holidays.

Provincetown   G18

Archer Inn

26 Bradford St
Provincetown, MA 02657-1321
(508)487-2529 (800)263-6574

Circa 1800. From the top of a hill, this former sea captain's home affords a panoramic view of Cape Cod Bay. Two suites offer views of the bay, and two other rooms boast harbor views. The innkeepers also offer accommodations in a small cottage adjacent to the main house. A concierge service is available, and guests also can be shuttled to and from the airport or nearby docks.

Innkeeper(s): John Peternell, Rick Golon. $39-189. MC, VISA, AX, TC. 10 rooms, 6 with PB and 1 suite. Breakfast and snacks/refreshments included in rates. Types of meals: Cont and early coffee/tea. Beds: KQD. Cable TV, turndown service and ceiling fan in room. Air conditioning. Copier on premises. Antiquing, fishing, bicycling, Sailing, live theater, parks, shopping and water sports nearby.

Certificate may be used: Sept. 15 to June 30, holidays and special events excluded, space available basis only. Advanced reservations required.

Gabriel's Apartments and Guest Rooms

104 Bradford St
Provincetown, MA 02657-1441
(508)487-3232 (800)969-2643 Fax:(508)487-1605
Internet: www.gabriels.com
E-mail: gabrielsma@aol.com

Circa 1936. For 20 years guests have been enjoying the two homes that comprise Gabriels and both feature gardens and antique furnishings. Each of the guest rooms and apartments at Gabriel's is named after a well-known woman. The Maya Angelou, Katharine Hepburn and Agatha Christie rooms are just a few examples. Some rooms include a fireplace or Jacuzzi tub, or both. The apartments include kitchens, and some have fireplaces and sleeping lofts. Most easily accommodate more than two guests. Guests can use the inn's hot tubs, sauna, steam room or exercise room. The continental-plus breakfasts include homemade muffins and breads, bagels, yogurt, granola, cereals and fresh fruit. Afternoon tea is also served.

Innkeeper(s): Gabriel Brooke. $65-200. MC, VISA, AX, DC, DS, TC. 20 rooms with PB, 8 with FP, 10 suites and 1 conference room. Breakfast included in rates. Type of meal: Cont plus. Beds: QD. Cable TV, phone, ceiling fan and VCR in room. Air conditioning. Fax, copier, spa, sauna, bicycles, library and e-mail on premises. Antiquing, fishing, golf, whale watching, live theater, parks, shopping, cross-country skiing, tennis and water sports nearby.

Pets allowed: In designated rooms.

Certificate may be used: Nov. 1 to April 1. Most midweeks April, May, June, September, October.

Watership Inn

7 Winthrop St
Provincetown, MA 02657-2116
(508)487-0094 (800)330-9413

Circa 1820. This stately manor was built as a home port for a Provincetown sea captain. During the past 10 years, it has been renovated and the original beamed ceilings and polished plank floors provide a background for the inn's antiques and simple decor. Guests enjoy the inn's sun decks and large yard, which offers volleyball and croquet sets.

Innkeeper(s): Richard Conley. $40-205. MC, VISA, AX, DS. 15 rooms with PB. Breakfast included in rates. Type of meal: Cont plus. Beds: QDT. Cable TV in room. Antiquing, beaches, whale watching, museums and parks nearby.

Publicity: *Boston "In".*

"We found your hospitality and charming inn perfect for our brief yet wonderful escape from Boston."

Certificate may be used: Oct. 1-April 30, excluding holidays and special event periods.

Rehoboth H12

Five Bridge Farm Inn

154 Pine St
Rehoboth, MA 02769
(508)252-3190 Fax:(508)252-3190
Internet: www.ici.net/customers/fivbrgin
E-mail: fivbrgin@ici.net

Circa 1985. This Georgian Colonial is centered on 70 acres of New England countryside. The grounds are decorated with English herb and flower gardens and a screened gazebo, where the morning meal is served during warmer months. The decor is that of understated elegance. Polished antiques, chandeliers and a few, simple knickknacks complete the look. The farm

includes a tennis court, lap pool, hiking trails and llamas. Riding stables are located adjacent to the property. However, the hosts provide many places to simply sit and relax.

Innkeeper(s): Ann & Harold Messenger. $78-95. MC, VISA, DC, DS, PC, TC. 5 rooms, 3 with PB, 1 with FP, 1 suite and 1 conference room. Breakfast and picnic lunch included in rates. Types of meals: Full gourmet bkfst and early coffee/tea. Beds: KQT. Cable TV, phone, turndown service and ceiling fan in room. Air conditioning. VCR, fax, copier, swimming, bicycles, tennis, library and pet boarding on premises. Handicap access. Antiquing, fishing, golf, shopping, cross-country skiing and tennis nearby.

Pets allowed: one special room.

Location: Country.

Certificate may be used: Jan. 3-April 1, Sunday-Thursday.

Gilbert's Tree Farm B&B

30 Spring St
Rehoboth, MA 02769-2408
(508)252-6416
E-mail: jeanneg47@aol.com

Circa 1835. This country farmhouse sits on 17 acres of woodland that includes an award-winning tree farm. Cross-country skiing, hiking, and pony-cart rides are found right outside the door. If they choose to, guests can even help with the farm chores, caring for horses and gardening. A swimming pool is open during summer. Three antique-filled bedrooms share a second-floor sitting room. There is a first-floor room with a working fireplace and private bath. The nearby town of Rehoboth is 350 years old.

Innkeeper(s): Jeanne Gilbert. $60-80. PC, TC. 5 rooms. Breakfast, afternoon tea and snacks/refreshments included in rates. Types of meals: Full bkfst and early coffee/tea. Beds: KDT. Fireplace (one room) in room. VCR, copier, swimming, stables, bicycles, library, pet boarding and horse boarding only on premises. Antiquing, fishing, live theater, parks, shopping, cross-country skiing, sporting events and water sports nearby.

Location: Country.

Publicity: *Attleboro Sun Chronicle, Country, Somerset Spectator, Country Gazette and Pawtucket Times.*

"This place has become my second home. Thank you for the family atmosphere of relaxation, fun, spontaneity and natural surroundings."

Certificate may be used: Dec. 1 through February, anytime.

Rockport C15

Sally Webster Inn

34 Mount Pleasant St
Rockport, MA 01966-1713
(978)546-9251 (877)546-9251
Internet: rockportusa.com/sallywebster

Circa 1832. William Choate left this pre-Civil War home to be divided by his nine children. Sally Choate Webster, the ninth child, was to receive several first-floor rooms and the attic chamber, but ended up owning the entire home. Innkeepers Rick and Carolyn Steere have filled the gracious home with antiques and period reproductions, which complement the original pumpkin pine floors, antique door moldings and six fireplaces. Shops, restaurants, the beach and the rocky coast are all within three blocks of the inn. Whale watching, kayaking, antique shops, music festivals, island tours and museums are among the myriad of nearby attractions. In addition to these, Salem is just 15 miles away, and Boston is a 35-mile drive.

Innkeeper(s): Rick & Carolyn Steere. $70-94. MC, VISA, PC, TC. 8 rooms with PB. Breakfast included in rates. Type of meal: Cont plus. Beds: KQDT. TV, guest phone available and air conditioning in room.

"All that a bed and breakfast should be."

Certificate may be used: Sunday-Friday, November-March.

Rutland
E9

The General Rufus Putnam House

344 Main St
Rutland, MA 01543-1303
(508)886-0200 Fax:(508)886-4864
Internet: www.rufusputnamhouse.com

Circa 1750. This restored Federal house, listed in the National Register, was the home of General Rufus Putnam, founder of Marietta, Ohio. A memorial tablet on the house states that "to him it is owing ... that the United States is not now a great slaveholding empire." Surrounded by tall maples and a rambling stone fence, the inn rests on seven acres of woodlands and meadows. There are eight fireplaces, blue Delft tiles and a beehive oven. Afternoon tea and breakfast are served fireside in the keeping room.

Innkeeper(s): Chris & Marcia Warrington. $100-125. DS, TC. 3 rooms, 1 with PB, 3 with FP. Breakfast and snacks/refreshments included in rates. Type of meal: Full bkfst. Beds: KQT. TV and turndown service in room. Fax, copier, swimming and library on premises. Amusement parks, antiquing, fishing, golf, skating, live theater, parks, shopping, downhill skiing, cross-country skiing, sporting events and tennis nearby.

Location: Country, Gentlemen's farm.

Publicity: *Sunday Telegram, The Land Mark and Washusett People.*

"We were thrilled with the beauty and luxury of this B&B and especially the wonderful hospitality."

Certificate may be used: Jan. 1-March 31, Sunday-Thursday.

Salem
D14

The Salem Inn

7 Summer St
Salem, MA 01970-3315
(978)741-0680 (800)446-2995 Fax:(978)744-8924
Internet: www.saleminnma.com
E-mail: saleminn@earthlink.net

Circa 1834. Located in the heart of one of America's oldest cities, the inn's 39 individually decorated guest rooms feature an array of amenities such as antiques, Jacuzzi baths, fireplaces and canopy beds. Luxury suites, as well as comfortable and spacious two-bedroom family suites with kitchenettes, are available. A complimentary continental breakfast is offered. Nearby are other fine restaurants, shops, museums, Pickering Wharf and whale watching boats for cruises.

Innkeeper(s): Richard & Diane Pabich. $129-290. MC, VISA, AX, DC, CB, DS, TC. 39 rooms with PB, 18 with FP and 11 suites. Breakfast included in rates. Types of meals: Cont and early coffee/tea. Beds: KQT. Cable TV and phone in room. Air conditioning. Fax on premises. Antiquing, fishing, live theater, parks, shopping, sporting events and water sports nearby.

Pets Allowed.

Location: City.

Publicity: *New York Times and Boston Sunday Globe.*

Certificate may be used: Nov. 15-April 15, based on availability, exclusive of holidays and special events.

Sandwich
I16

The Dunbar House

1 Water St
Sandwich, MA 02563-2303
(508)833-2485 Fax:(508)833-4713
Internet: www.dunbatrashop.com
E-mail: dunbar@capecod.net

Circa 1741. This Colonial house overlooks Shawme Pond in the charming setting of Cape Cod's oldest town. The three guest rooms are appointed in Colonial style, and all boast a view of the pond. The Ennerdale room has a four-poster bed. Each morning, guests are pampered with a homemade breakfast, and guests receive a voucher for afternoon tea served in the innkeeper's English tea shop. The inn is within walking distance to many historic sites and the beach.

Innkeeper(s): Nancy Iribarren & David Bell. $80-100. MC, VISA, PC, TC. 3 rooms with PB, 3 with FP. Breakfast included in rates. Types of meals: Full gourmet bkfst and early coffee/tea. Beds: KQT. Fans in room. VCR, fax, copier, bicycles, library and canoe on premises. Antiquing, fishing, museums, Heritage Plantation, live theater, parks, shopping and water sports nearby.

Location: Heart of historic district.

Publicity: *Sandwich Broadsider and Cape Cod Times.*

Certificate may be used: Sunday-Thursday, Nov. 1-April 30.

The Summer House

158 Main St
Sandwich, MA 02563-2232
(508)888-4991 (800)241-3609
Internet: www.capecod.net/summerhouse
E-mail: sumhouse@capecod.net

Circa 1835. The Summer House is a handsome Greek Revival in a setting of historic homes and public buildings. (Hiram Dillaway, one of the owners, was a famous mold maker for the Boston & Sandwich Glass Company.) The house is fully restored and decorated with antiques and hand-stitched quilts. Four of the guest rooms have fireplaces. The breakfast room and parlor have black marble fireplaces. The sunporch overlooks an old-fashioned perennial garden, antique rose bushes, and a 70-year-old rhododendron hedge. The inn is open year-round.

Innkeeper(s): Erik Suby & Phyllis Burg. $65-105. MC, VISA, AX, DS, PC, TC. 5 rooms with PB, 4 with FP. Breakfast and afternoon tea included in rates. Types of meals: Full gourmet bkfst and early coffee/tea. Beds: KQT. Window fan in room. Library, lawn & gardens and sunroom on premises. Antiquing, fishing, live theater, parks, shopping, cross-country skiing and water sports nearby.

Location: Cape Cod Village.

Publicity: *Country Living, Boston and Cape Cod Times.*

"An absolutely gorgeous house and a super breakfast! I wish I could've stayed longer! Came for one night, stayed for three! Marvelous welcome."

Certificate may be used: Nov. 1-May 1, Sunday-Thursday.

Sandwich (Cape Cod)
I16

Isaiah Jones Homestead

165 Main St
Sandwich (Cape Cod), MA 02563-2283
(508)888-9115 (800)526-1625

Circa 1849. This fully restored Victorian homestead is situated on Main Street in the village. Eleven-foot ceilings and two bay windows are features of the Gathering Room. Guest rooms contain antique Victorian bedsteads such as the half-canopy bed of burled birch in the Deming Jarves Room, where there is an over-sized whirlpool tub and a fireplace. Candlelight breakfasts are highlighted with the house speciality, freshly baked cornbread, inspired by nearby Sandwich Grist Mill.

Innkeeper(s): Jan & Doug Klapper. $85-155. MC, VISA, AX, DS, PC, TC. 5 rooms with PB, 3 with FP. Breakfast and afternoon tea included in rates. Types of meals: Full bkfst and early coffee/tea. Beds: Q. Three fireplaces and two oversize Jacuzzi tubs in room. Antiquing, beaches, fishing, live theater, parks, shopping and water sports nearby.

Location: Village.

Publicity: *Cape Cod Life, New England Travel and National Geographic Travel.*

"Excellent! The room was a delight, the food wonderful, the hospitality warm & friendly. One of the few times the reality exceeded the expectation."

Certificate may be used: Sunday-Thursday nights, Nov. 1-March 31.

Sheffield F2

Staveleigh House

59 Main St, PO 608
Sheffield, MA 01257-9701
(413)229-2129

Circa 1821. The Reverend Bradford, minister of Old Parish Congregational Church, the oldest church in the Berkshires, built this home for his family. Afternoon tea is served and the inn is especially favored for its four-course breakfasts and gracious hospitality. Located next to the town green, the house is in a historic district in the midst of several fine antique shops. It is also near Tanglewood, skiing and all Berkshire attractions.

Innkeeper(s): Dorothy Marosy & Marion Whitman. $80-125. PC, TC. 5 rooms, 2 with PB. Breakfast and afternoon tea included in rates. Types of meals: Full bkfst and early coffee/tea. Beds: KQDT. Turndown service and ceiling fan in room. Handicap access. Antiquing, fishing, art galleries, live theater, parks, shopping, downhill skiing, cross-country skiing and water sports nearby.

Location: Historic district.

Publicity: *Los Angeles Times and Boston Globe.*

"Our annual needlework workshops are so much fun, we have a waiting list to join our group."

Certificate may be used: Sunday-Thursday, year-round; any day November-March, except holidays.

South Lancaster D10

College Town Inn

PO Box 876, Rt 110
South Lancaster, MA 01561
(978)368-7000 (800)369-2717 Fax:(978)365-5426

Circa 1940. This bed and breakfast offers a country location, and guests may choose a room with a private patio or balcony from which to enjoy it. Rooms are furnished with contempo-rary pieces. In summer, a full breakfast is provided on the patio. Families may prefer the accommodation that has its own kitchen. Nearby are Revolutionary War battlefields, Concord and Longfellow's Wayside Inn.

Innkeeper(s): Jack & Charlotte Creighton. $55-95. MC, VISA, AX, DS, PC, TC. 4 rooms with PB, 1 suite and 1 conference room. Breakfast included in rates. Type of meal: Full bkfst. Beds: KQDT. Cable TV and phone in room. Air conditioning. Fax and copier on premises. Antiquing, fishing, golf, downhill skiing and cross-country skiing nearby.

Certificate may be used: Any nights year-round depending on availability.

Sturbridge F8

Commonwealth Cottage

11 Summit Ave
Sturbridge, MA 01566-1225
(508)347-7708

Circa 1873. This 16-room Queen Anne Victorian house, on an acre near the Quinebaug River, is just a few minutes from Old Sturbridge Village. Both the dining room and parlor have fireplaces. The Baroque theme of the Sal Raciti room makes it one of the guest favorites and it features a queen mahogany bed. Breakfast may be offered on the gazebo porch or in the formal dining room. It includes a variety of homemade specialties, such as freshly baked breads and cakes.

Innkeeper(s): Robert & Wiebke Gilbert. $85-145. PC, TC. 3 rooms with PB. Types of meals: Full bkfst and early coffee/tea. Beds: QDT. Ceiling fan in room. Library on premises. Antiquing, fishing, museum, live theater, parks, shopping and water sports nearby.

Location: Small town.

Publicity: *Long Island Newsday, Villager, WGGB, Springfield and MA.*

"Your home is so warm and welcoming we feel as though we've stepped back in time. Our stay here has helped to make the wedding experience extra special!"

Certificate may be used: December-April, Sunday-Thursday, holiday weekends excluded.

Sturbridge Country Inn

PO Box 60, 530 Main St
Sturbridge, MA 01566-0060
(508)347-5503 Fax:(508)347-5319
Internet: www.sturbridgecountryinn.com
E-mail: info@sturbridgecountryinn.com

Circa 1840. Shaded by an old silver maple, this classic Greek Revival house boasts a two-story columned entrance. The attached carriage house now serves as the lobby and displays the original post-and-beam construction and exposed rafters. All guest rooms have individual fireplaces and whirlpool tubs. They are appointed gracefully in reproduction colonial furnishings, including queen-size, four-posters. A patio and gazebo are favorite summertime retreats.

Innkeeper(s): Patricia Affenito. $59-179. MC, VISA, AX, DS, PC, TC. 9 rooms with PB, 9 with FP, 1 suite and 1 conference room. Breakfast included in rates. Types of meals: Cont and early coffee/tea. Beds: KQ. Cable TV, phone, ceiling fan and VCR in room. Air conditioning. Fax, copier and spa on premises. Antiquing, fishing, old Sturbridge Village, live theater, parks, shopping, downhill skiing, cross-country skiing and water sports nearby.

Location: Rural.

Publicity: *Southbridge Evening News and Worcester Telegram & Gazette.*

"Best lodging I've ever seen."

Certificate may be used: November-August, Sunday-Thursday. No holidays, no special events.

Ware E7

The Wildwood Inn

121 Church St
Ware, MA 01082-1203
(413)967-7798 (800)860-8098

Circa 1880. This yellow Victorian has a wraparound porch and a beveled-glass front door. American primitive antiques include a collection of New England cradles and heirloom quilts, a saddlemaker's bench and a spinning wheel. The inn's two acres are dotted with maple, chestnut and apple trees. Through the woods, you'll find a river.

Innkeeper(s): Fraidell Fenster & Richard Watson. $50-90. MC, VISA, AX, DC, DS, PC, TC. 9 rooms, 7 with PB, 1 suite and 2 conference rooms. Breakfast and afternoon tea included in rates. Types of meals: Full gourmet bkfst and early coffee/tea. Beds: KQDT. Turndown service in room. Air conditioning. Bicycles and library on premises. Handicap access. Amusement parks, antiquing, fishing, horseback riding, hiking, canoeing, kayaking, live theater, parks, shopping, downhill skiing, cross-country skiing and sporting events nearby.

Location: Small town.

Publicity: *Boston Globe, National Geographic Traveler, Country* and *Worcester Telegram & Gazette.*

"Excellent accommodations, not only in rooms, but in the kind and thoughtful way you treat your guests. We'll be back!"

Certificate may be used: All year, excluding holidays, Brimfield Flea Market Weeks and foliage. Please notify of certificate at beginning of phone call.

Wareham I15

Mulberry B&B

257 High St
Wareham, MA 02571-1407
(508)295-0684 Fax:(508)291-2909

Circa 1847. This former blacksmith's house is in the historic district of town and has been featured on the local garden club house tour. Frances, a former school teacher, has decorated the guest rooms in a country style with antiques. A deck, shaded by a tall mulberry tree, looks out to the back garden.

Innkeeper(s): Frances Murphy. $50-75. MC, VISA, AX, DS, PC, TC. 3 rooms. Breakfast included in rates. Type of meal: Full bkfst. Beds: KDT. TV and turndown service in room. Air conditioning. VCR on premises. Antiquing, fishing, whale watching, live theater, parks, shopping, cross-country skiing, sporting events and water sports nearby.

Location: Atlantic Ocean.

Publicity: *Brockton Enterprise and Wareham Courier.*

"Our room was pleasant and I loved the cranberry satin sheets."

Certificate may be used: October through May, except holiday weekends.

West Harwich I18

The Gingerbread House

141 Division St
West Harwich, MA 02671-1005
(508)432-1901 (800)788-1901

Circa 1883. This rambling Queen Anne Victorian is decked with ornate, gingerbread trim and gables. The innkeepers, of Polish descent, have added European flavor to their inn with a

collection of Polish art, crystal and crafts. Aside from the scrumptious breakfasts, the innkeepers offer dinner service at the inn's restaurant. Proper afternoon teas are served in the Tea Room, which is located in the Carriage House. Sandwiches, freshly baked goods and scones are accompanied by Devon clotted cream and a selection of teas. The inn is near many of Cape Cod's shops and restaurants.

Innkeeper(s): Stacia & Les Kostecki. $85-125. MC, VISA, TC. 5 suites, 1 with FP and 1 conference room. Breakfast and afternoon tea included in rates. Types of meals: Full gourmet bkfst, cont and early coffee/tea. Beds: Q. Cable TV and ceiling fan in room. VCR and child care on premises. Handicap access. Antiquing, fishing, live theater, parks and shopping nearby.

Certificate may be used: May 1-Nov. 15, Sunday-Thursday, excluding holidays.

West Stockbridge E2

Card Lake Inn

PO Box 38
West Stockbridge, MA 01266-0038
(413)232-0272 Fax:(413)232-0294
Internet: www.cardlakeinn.com
E-mail: innkeeper@cardlakeinn.com

Circa 1880. Located in the center of town, this Colonial Revival inn features a popular local restaurant on the premises. Norman Rockwell is said to have frequented its tavern. Stroll around historic West Stockbridge then enjoy the inn's deck cafe with its flower boxes and view of the sculpture garden of an art gallery across the street. Original lighting, hardwood floors and antiques are features of the inn. Chesterwood and Tanglewood are within easy driving distance.

Innkeeper(s): Ed & Lisa Robbins. $100-150. MC, VISA, AX, DS. 8 rooms. Breakfast included in rates. Types of meals: Cont and early coffee/tea. Beds: KQ. Ceiling fan in room. Air conditioning. VCR on premises. Amusement parks, antiquing, shopping and sporting events nearby.

Location: Mountains.

Certificate may be used: Anytime excluding holiday weekends and weekends during Tanglewood Season and Foliage.

Woods Hole J15

The Marlborough B&B

PO Box 238
Woods Hole, MA 02543-0238
(508)548-6218 (800)320-2322 Fax:(508)457-7519

Circa 1942. This is a faithful reproduction of a Cape-style cottage complete with picket fence and rambling roses. An English paddle-tennis court and swimming pool are popular spots in summer. In winter, breakfast is served beside a roaring fire. The inn is the closest bed & breakfast to the ferries to Martha's Vineyard and Nantucket.

Innkeeper(s): Al Hammond. $85-175. MC, VISA, AX, PC. 6 rooms with PB and 1 cottage. Breakfast included in rates. Types of meals: Full gourmet bkfst and early coffee/tea. Beds: QD. TV and alarm Clocks in room. Air conditioning. Fax, swimming and tennis on premises. Antiquing, fishing, live theater, shopping and water sports nearby.

Location: Residential.

Publicity: *Cape Cod Standard Times.*

"Our stay at the Marlborough was a little bit of heaven."

Certificate may be used: Nov. 1-May 15, Sunday-Thursday.

Yarmouth Port   117

Old Yarmouth Inn

223 Main St
Yarmouth Port, MA 02675-1717
(508)362-9962 Fax:(508)362-2995
E-mail: oyarminn@capecod.net

Circa 1696. The Old Yarmouth originally was built as a stage stop and is one of America's oldest. There is a guest register from the 1860s when it was called the Sears Hotel. Traveling salesmen often stayed here, and according to the register, they sold such items as Henry's Vermont Linament, lightning rods, sewing machines and drilled-eye needles. Today, this venerable inn has rooms with antiques, but also cable television and air conditioning.

Innkeeper(s): Sheila FitzGerald & Arpad Voros. $100-125. MC, VISA, AX, DC, DS, PC, TC. 4 rooms with PB. Type of meal: Cont. Beds: Q. Air conditioning. Fax and copier on premises. Antiquing, fishing, golf, live theater and shopping nearby.

Publicity: *The Register, Travel News and Cape Cod Travel.*

Certificate may be used: March 15-June 15 and Nov. 1-Dec. 15, Sunday-Thursday, except holiday weekends.

Olde Captain's Inn on The Cape

101 Main St Rt 6A
Yarmouth Port, MA 02675-1709
(508)362-4496 (888)407-7161
Internet: www.oldecaptainsinn.com
E-mail: general@oldecaptainsinn.com

Circa 1812. Located in the historic district and on Captain's Mile, this house is in the National Register. It is decorated in a traditional style, with coordinated wallpapers and carpets, and there are two suites that include kitchens and living rooms. Apple trees, blackberries and raspberries grow on the acre of grounds and often contribute to the breakfast menus. There is a summer veranda overlooking the property. Good restaurants are within walking distance.

Innkeeper(s): Sven Tilly. $60-120. 3 rooms, 1 with PB and 2 suites. Breakfast included in rates. Type of meal: Cont plus. Beds: QD. Cable TV in room. Antiquing, fishing, live theater, shopping, sporting events and water sports nearby.

Location: Historic district.

Certificate may be used: Anytime, Nov. 1-June 1. Sunday through Thursday, June 1-Nov. 1. Excludes holidays.

Michigan

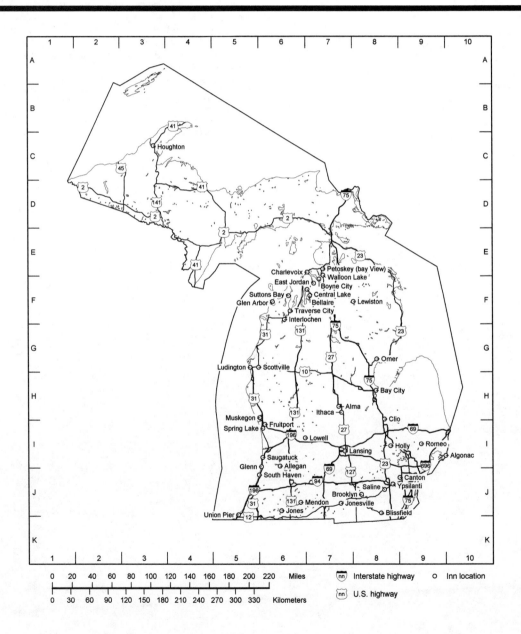

Map labels (north to south):

41 — Houghton
45
2 — 141 — 2 — 2 — 2 — 41 — 75
41
23
Charlevoix — Petoskey (bay View)
Walloon Lake
East Jordan — Boyne City
Suttons Bay — Central Lake
Glen Arbor — Bellaire — Lewiston
Traverse City
Interlochen
131 — 75
31 — 27 — 23
Ludington — Scottville — Omer
10
75
Bay City
31
131 — Ithaca — Alma
Muskegon — Clio
Spring Lake — Fruitport — 69
196 — Lowell — 27 — Holly — Romeo
Lansing — Algonac
Saugatuck — 23
Glenn — Allegan — 69 — 127 — 696 — Canton
South Haven — Saline — Ypsilanti
196 — 94
131 — Brooklyn — 75
31 — Mendon — Jonesville
Union Pier — Jones — Blissfield
12

0 20 40 60 80 100 120 140 160 180 200 220 Miles
0 30 60 90 120 150 180 210 240 270 300 330 Kilometers

nn Interstate highway   o Inn location
nn U.S. highway

Algonac 19

Linda's Lighthouse Inn

5965 PTE. Tremble Rd Box 828
Algonac, MI 48001
(810)794-2992 Fax:(810)794-2992
Internet: www.lindasbnb.com
E-mail: lindasbnb@hotmail.com

Circa 1909. Overlooking Dickerson Island, on the north branch
of the St. Clair River, is this two-story Colonial inn, which once
aided bootleggers who brought in liquor from Canada during
Prohibition. Guests who arrive by
boat and use the inn's 100 feet
of dockage will have transportation to restaurants provided for
them. Guests choose from the
Jacuzzi, Lighthouse, Rose and
Duck rooms, all featuring feather pillows. St. John's Marsh is less
than a half-mile away.

Innkeeper(s): Ron & Linda (Russell) Yetsko. $85-135. MC, VISA. 4 rooms
with PB. Breakfast and snacks/refreshments included in rates. Types of meals:
Full gourmet bkfst and early coffee/tea. Beds: QD. Phone, turndown service,
ceiling fan, robes and flowers in room. Air conditioning. VCR, copier, bicycles
and outside hot tub on premises. Antiquing, fishing, bird watching, hiking,
movies, parks, shopping, cross-country skiing and water sports nearby.
Pets Allowed.

Certificate may be used: May 1-Oct. 31, Monday-Thursday, no holidays.

Allegan 16

Castle In The Country

340 M 40 S
Allegan, MI 49010-9609
(616)673-8054
Internet: www.getaway2smi.com/castle
E-mail: castle@datawise.net

Enjoy refreshing country views from every window at this
three-story Victorian, which was built by a Civil War captain.
Each of the guest quarters offers something special. The
Bittersweet, which has a chandelier and private sitting area,
boasts a view of Bittersweet Mountain. The Rose Gazebo is
located in the home's turret. This unique, round room includes
white, wicker furnishings and flowery linens. Each guest room
is decorated with candles and fresh flowers. Homemade breads
and pastries accompany the full, gourmet breakfasts, which can
be enjoyed in the privacy of your bedchamber or in the formal
dining room. The innkeepers host special events such as murder-mystery weekends and multi-day bicycle tours.

Innkeeper(s): Herb & Ruth Boven. $85-165. MC, VISA. 5 rooms with PB.
Breakfast included in rates. Type of meal: Full bkfst.

Certificate may be used: Sunday-Thursday, Nov. 1-May 31 (excluding holidays).

Winchester Inn

524 Marshall St M-89
Allegan, MI 49010-1632
(616)673-3620 (800)582-5694

Circa 1864. This neo-Italian Renaissance mansion was built of
double-layer brick and has been restored to its original beauty.
Surrounded by a unique, hand-poured iron fence, the inn is

decorated with period antiques, including antique toys and
trains. The innkeeper's love for Christmas and other holidays is
evident. Many christmas decorations remain up throughout the
year. The tree in the dining room is decorated for whatever holiday is near. For instance, around Halloween, pumpkins and
gourds decorate the tree. Each guest room has it's own theme.
One is a Christmas room, another features an angel theme, and
one is decorated for the current holiday.

Innkeeper(s): Denise & Dave Ferber. $70-90. MC, VISA, AX, PC, TC. 4 rooms
with PB. Breakfast included in rates. Types of meals: Full bkfst, cont plus
and early coffee/tea. Beds: KQD. TV, phone and ceiling fan in room.
Antiquing, fishing, golf, live theater, parks, shopping, downhill skiing, cross-
country skiing, sporting events and water sports nearby.
Location: City.
Publicity: *Architectural Digest, Home and Away, Midwest Living, Detroit Free
Press, Cleveland Plain Dealer and Grand Rapids Press.*

"This is one of Michigan's loveliest country inns."

Certificate may be used: Sunday through Thursday, April through October.
Any day November through March. Not during local festivals.

Alma H7

Saravilla

633 N State St
Alma, MI 48801-1640
(517)463-4078
Internet: www.saravilla.com
E-mail: ljdarrow@saravilla.com

Circa 1894. This 11,000-square-foot Dutch Colonial home
with its Queen Anne influences was built as a magnificent wedding gift for lumber baron Ammi W. Wright's only surviving
child, Sara. Wright spared no expense building this mansion
for his daughter, and the innkeepers have spared nothing in
restoring the home to its former prominence. The foyer and
dining room boast imported English oak woodwork. The
foyer's hand-painted canvas wallcoverings and the ballroom's
embossed wallpaper come from France. The home still features
original leaded-glass windows, built-in bookcases, window seats
and light fixtures. In 1993, the innkeepers added a sunroom
with a hot tub that overlooks a formal garden. The full, formal
breakfast includes such treats as homemade granola, freshly
made coffeecakes, breads, muffins and a mix of entrees.

Innkeeper(s): Linda and Jon Darrow. $75-125. MC, VISA, DS, PC, TC. 7
rooms with PB, 3 with FP. Breakfast and afternoon tea included in rates.
Type of meal: Full bkfst. Beds: KQT. Whirlpool tub in room. Antiquing, fishing, canoeing, live theater and cross-country skiing nearby.
Publicity: *Morning Sun, Saginaw News and Sault Sunday.*

*"I suggest we stay longer next time. We are looking forward to
that visit."*

Certificate may be used: Jan. 1-Dec. 31, Sunday-Friday.

Bay City H8

Clements Inn

1712 Center Ave M-25
Bay City, MI 48708-6122
(517)894-4600 (800)442-4605 Fax:(517)891-9442
Internet: www.laketolake.com/clementsinn

Circa 1886. The amber-paned windows and oak ceilings of
this three-story Queen Anne Victorian inn are just a few of its
impressive features. Built by William Clements, the home

joined a number of other impressive estates on Center Avenue, most of which were owned by lumber barons. The inn's well-appointed guest rooms are named for famous authors or fictional characters, continuing a strong tradition started by Clements, a collector of rare books. A winding staircase, original gas lighting fixtures and hand-carved woodwork have impressed many visitors.

Innkeeper(s): Dave & Shirley Roberts. $70-175. MC, VISA, AX, DC, DS, PC, TC. 6 rooms with PB, 3 with FP and 2 suites. Breakfast included in rates. Type of meal: Cont plus. Beds: KQD. Cable TV, phone, VCR and three whirlpool suites in room. Air conditioning. Fax on premises. Antiquing, fishing, planetarium, live theater, parks, shopping, downhill skiing and cross-country skiing nearby.

Certificate may be used: Sunday-Thursday, Nov. 1-April 30.

Bellaire   F7

Grand Victorian B&B Inn

402 N Bridge St
Bellaire, MI 49615-9591
(616)533-6111 (800)336-3860 Fax:(616)533-8197

Circa 1895. It's hard to believe that anything but joy has ever been associated with this beautiful Queen Anne Victorian inn, but its original owner, who built it in anticipation of his upcoming nuptials, left town broken-hearted when his wedding plans fell through. The eye-pleasing inn, with its gables, square corner towers, bays and overhangs, is listed in the National Register of Historic Places. There is much to do in this popular area of Northern Michigan, with its famous nearby skiing and fishing spots, but the inn's impressive interior may entice guests to stay on the premises. Guest rooms are well-appointed with period antiques and lavish touches. Visitors may borrow a bicycle built for two for a relaxing tour of town.

Innkeeper(s): Steve & Glenda Shaffer. $100-130. MC, VISA. 4 rooms with PB. Breakfast and afternoon tea included in rates. Types of meals: Full bkfst and early coffee/tea. Beds: QD. Air conditioning. VCR on premises. Antiquing, fishing, shopping, downhill skiing, cross-country skiing and water sports nearby.

Location: City.

Publicity: *Featured on Nabisco Crackers/Cookies Boxes Promotion, Midwest Living and Country Inns.*

"We certainly enjoyed our visit to the Grand Victorian. It has been our pleasure to stay in B&Bs in several countries, but never one more beautiful and almost never with such genial hosts."

Certificate may be used: Sunday through Thursday, Sept. 15-June 15.

Blissfield   J8

Hiram D. Ellis Inn

415 W Adrian St US Hwy 223
Blissfield, MI 49228-1001
(517)486-3155

Circa 1883. This red brick Italianate house is in a village setting directly across from the 1851 Hathaway House, an elegant historic restaurant. Rooms at the Hiram D. Ellis Inn feature handsome antique bedsteads, armoires and floral wallpapers. Breakfast is served in the inn's common room, and the innkeeper receives rave reviews on her peach and apple dishes. (There

are apple and peach trees on the property.) Bicycles are available for riding around town, or you can walk to the train station and board the murder-mystery dinner train that runs on weekends.

Innkeeper(s): Christine Webster & Frank Seely. $80-100. MC, VISA, AX, PC, TC. 4 rooms with PB. Breakfast included in rates. Types of meals: Full bkfst, cont plus and early coffee/tea. Beds: QD. Cable TV and phone in room. Air conditioning. Bicycles on premises. Antiquing, fishing, golf, live theater, parks, shopping and cross-country skiing nearby.

Pets allowed: small pets only.

Location: Village.

Publicity: *Ann Arbor News and Michigan Living.*

"I have now experienced what it is truly like to have been treated like a queen."

Certificate may be used: Sunday through Thursday, excluding holidays.

Boyne City   F7

Deer Lake Bed & Breakfast

00631 E Deer Lake Rd
Boyne City, MI 49712-9614
(231)582-9039
Internet: www.deerlakebb.com
E-mail: info@deerlakebb.com

Circa 1994. Located in a comfortable, contemporary home, this bed & breakfast offers views from all bedrooms including vistas of lake, pond or forest. Two rooms include private balconies overlooking the lake, and the other three guest quarters share a 40-foot balcony. The house is bright and airy with elegant, country furnishings, French doors and a few lacy touches. Breakfast is served in the parlor at tables embellished with fine china, crystal and candlelight. For those who enjoy the outdoors, the area offers golf, fishing, swimming, sailing, skiing and much more. For those more creatively inclined, the innkeepers, both former jewelers, offer a jewelry class for guests who might enjoy making a 14K gold or sterling ring. Cooking classes are also available in November and in April.

Innkeeper(s): Glenn & Shirley Piepenburg. $80-105. MC, VISA, DS, PC, TC. 5 rooms with PB. Breakfast and snacks/refreshments included in rates. Types of meals: Full bkfst and early coffee/tea. Beds: KQT. Turndown service and ceiling fan in room. Air conditioning. VCR, swimming and sail boat and paddle boat on premises. Antiquing, fishing, golf, parks, shopping, downhill skiing, cross-country skiing and water sports nearby.

Certificate may be used: Sunday through Thursday, excluding holidays, July and August.

Brooklyn   J8

Dewey Lake Manor

11811 Laird Rd
Brooklyn, MI 49230-9035
(517)467-7122
Internet: www.getaway2smi.com/dewey
E-mail: deweylk@frontiernet.net

Circa 1868. This Italianate house overlooks Dewey Lake and is situated on 18 acres in the Irish Hills. The house is furnished in a country Victorian style with antiques. An enclosed porch is a favorite spot to relax and take in the views of the lake while having breakfast. Favorite pastimes include lakeside bonfires in the summertime and ice skating or cross-country skiing in the winter. Canoe and paddleboats are available to guests.

Innkeeper(s): Barb & Joe Phillips. $55-125. MC, VISA, AX. 5 rooms with PB, 5 with FP and 1 conference room. Breakfast included in rates. Types of meals: Full bkfst and early coffee/tea. Beds: QT. Cable TV, phone, ceiling fan and one room has Jacuzzi in room. Air conditioning. VCR on premises. Antiquing, fishing, golf, live theater, shopping, cross-country skiing, sporting events and water sports nearby.

Location: Country.

Publicity: *Ann Arbor News.*

"I came back and brought my friends. It was wonderful."

Certificate may be used: November through April, holidays and special events excluded.

Canton   J9

Willow Brook Inn

44255 Warren Rd
Canton, MI 48187-2147
(734)454-0019 (888)454-1919

Circa 1929. Willow Brook winds its way through the backyard of this aptly named inn, situated on a lush, wooded acre. Innkeepers Bernadette and Michael Van Lenten filled their home with oak and pine country antiques and beds covered with soft quilts. They also added special toys and keepsakes from their own childhood to add a homey touch. After a peaceful rest, guests are invited to partake in the morning meal either in the "Teddy Bear" dining room, in the privacy of their rooms or on the deck. Breakfasts consist of luscious treats such as homemade breads, scones topped with devon cream and a choice of entree.

Innkeeper(s): Bernadette & Michael Van Lenten. $95-125. MC, VISA, AX. 3 suites. Breakfast and snacks/refreshments included in rates. Types of meals: Full gourmet bkfst and early coffee/tea. Beds: KQDT. Cable TV, phone, turn-down service, ceiling fan, VCR and non-cable TV in suite in room. Air conditioning. Fax, copier, bicycles, pet boarding and wood stove on premises. Antiquing, Henry Ford Museum, zoo, live theater, parks, shopping, cross-country skiing, sporting events and water sports nearby.

Pets allowed: Not permitted in bedrooms.

Location: Suburban.

Publicity: *Canton Observer, Canton Eagle, Detroit News and Local PBS station.*

"We've stayed in B&Bs in Europe, Australia and New Zealand, and we put yours at the top of the list for luxury, friendly care and delicious food (especially the scones). We're glad we found you. Thanks."

Certificate may be used: From Nov. 1-May 15, Sunday through Thursday, excluding Feb. 14.

Central Lake   F7

Bridgewalk B&B

2287 S Main, PO Box 399
Central Lake, MI 49622-0399
(231)544-8122
Internet: www.bridgewalkbandb.com

Circa 1895. Secluded on a wooded acre, this three-story Victorian is accessible by crossing a foot bridge over a stream. Guest rooms are simply decorated with Victorian touches, floral prints and fresh flowers. The Garden Suite includes a clawfoot tub. Much of the home's Victorian elements have been restored, including pocket doors and the polished woodwork. Breakfasts begin with such items as a cold fruit soup, freshly baked muffins or scones accompanied with homemade jams and butters. A main dish, perhaps apple-sausage blossoms, tops off the meal.

Innkeeper(s): Janet & Tom Meteer. $85-95. MC, VISA, PC, TC. 5 rooms with PB and 1 suite. Breakfast included in rates. Types of meals: Full bkfst and early coffee/tea. Beds: KQT. Ceiling fan in room. Antiquing, fishing, golf, gourmet restaurants, parks, shopping, downhill skiing and cross-country skiing nearby.

Location: Village.

Certificate may be used: Sunday through Thursday nights.

Torchlight Resort

PO Box 267
Central Lake, MI 49622-0267
(231)544-8263

Circa 1940. These one- and two-bedroom cottages are located on the edge of scenic Torch Lake. The cottages, which all boast lake views, include stocked kitchens and barbeque grills, but towels and linens are not provided. The owners offer docking for private boats, and there is a beach and swimming area.

Innkeeper(s): Robert & Glenda Knott. $85-250. 7 cottages with PB. Beds: D. Fishing nearby.

Certificate may be used: First week of May through third week of June and Labor Day through last week of October; seven days a week. On Torch Lake.

Charlevoix   E7

The Inn at Grey Gables

306 Belvedere Ave
Charlevoix, MI 49720-1413
(616)547-2251 (800)280-4667 Fax:(616)547-1944

Circa 1887. Guests at this attractive two-story inn are just a short walk from a public beach. Visitors have their choice of seven rooms, including two suites. The Pine Suite features a kitchen and private entrance, perfect for honeymooners or for those enjoying a longer-than-usual stay. All of the rooms offer private baths and most have queen beds. Guests may opt to relax and enjoy the beautiful surroundings or take advantage of the many recreational activities available in the Charlevoix area, including Fisherman's Island State Park.

Innkeeper(s): Gary & Kay Anderson. $110-135. MC, VISA, PC, TC. 7 rooms, 5 with PB and 2 suites. Breakfast included in rates. Type of meal: Full bkfst. Beds: KQT. Ceiling fan in room. VCR and fax on premises. Antiquing, fishing, parks, shopping, downhill skiing, cross-country skiing and water sports nearby.

Location: Public beach 1/2 mile.

Publicity: *USA Today.*

Certificate may be used: Nov. 1-May 24, anytime. Sunday-Thursday, June 1-30. Sunday-Thursday, September and Oct. 1-30.

Clio   H8

Cinnamon Stick B&B

12364 Genesee Rd
Clio, MI 48420-9142
(810)686-8391 Fax:(810)686-8094
E-mail: cinstick@tir.com

Circa 1908. Guests enjoy a pastoral setting at this turn-of-the-century farmhouse, which is surrounded by 50 acres. The innkeepers have two Belgian Draft horses, which sometimes take guests on hay or sleigh rides on the scenic property. There are also walking trails and a stocked fishing pond to enjoy. Each of the five guest rooms is decorated in a different country style. The suite includes a sleigh bed and a whirlpool tub. The innkeepers prepare a homemade country breakfast each morning, with dishes such as Belgian waffles, smokey ham and freshly baked poppy seed muffins.

Innkeeper(s): Brian & Carol Powell. $60-125. MC, VISA. 5 rooms, 4 with PB, 1 suite and 1 conference room. Breakfast, afternoon tea, dinner, snacks/refreshments and picnic lunch included in rates. Types of meals: Full gourmet bkfst and early coffee/tea. Beds: QD. Ceiling fan and two-person Jacuzzi in room. Air conditioning. VCR, fax, copier, spa, stables, bicycles, tennis, library, pet boarding, child care and well behaved pets are welcome on premises. Amusement parks, antiquing, fishing, golf, Frenkenmuth & Birch Run Outlet Mall, live theater, parks, shopping, downhill skiing, cross-country skiing, sporting events, tennis and water sports nearby.

Location: Country.

Publicity: *Grand Blanc Business Banner.*

Certificate may be used: Jan. 1-June 1, Sunday-Friday, subject to availability.

East Jordan   F7

Easterly Inn

209 Easterly, PO Box 366
East Jordan, MI 49727-0366
(231)536-3434

Circa 1906. Finely crafted woodwork of cherry, bird's-eye maple and oak are hints that this turn-of-the-century Victorian was built for a lumber merchant. Its three stories and 18 rooms have been carefully restored and furnished with fine antiques and period wallcoverings, which enhance its gleaming hardwood floors and leaded windows. Guest rooms include the Turret Room, which offers a tall, carved walnut and burl queen bed, and the Romantic Lace Room, with Victorian rose prints and a queen canopy bed. Breakfast is served in the semi-circular dining room.

Innkeeper(s): Joan Martin. $60-85. MC, VISA, PC. 4 rooms with PB. Breakfast included in rates. Type of meal: Full bkfst. Beds: QD. Ceiling fan in room. Antiquing, fishing, golf, fine dining, parks, shopping and water sports nearby.

Location: Small town.

"A wonderful inn, full of history and romance. Thank you for sharing yourself with us."

Certificate may be used: May 1-June 20 and Sept. 2-Oct. 30, Monday-Thursday (excluding holiday periods and weekends).

Fruitport   I6

Village Park B&B

60 W Park St
Fruitport, MI 49415-9668
(616)865-6289 (800)469-1118
Internet: www.bbonline.com/mi/villagepark

Circa 1873. Located in the midst of Western Michigan's Tri-Cities area, this inn's small-town village location offers comfort and relaxation to those busy partaking of the many nearby activities. This country classic farmhouse-style inn overlooks Spring Lake and a park where guests may picnic, play tennis, use a pedestrian/bike path and boat launch. There also is a hot tub and exercise room on the premises. The inn offers six guest rooms, all with private bath. A library is just across the street. P.J. Hoffmaster State Park, the Gillette Nature Sand Dune Center are nearby.

Innkeeper(s): John and Linda Hewett. $60-90. MC, VISA, DS, PC, TC. 6 rooms with PB. Breakfast included in rates. Types of meals: Full bkfst, cont plus, cont and early coffee/tea. Beds: KQDT. Cable TV in room. Air conditioning. VCR, fax, sauna, bicycles, exercise room, hot tub and two-person kayak on premises. Amusement parks, antiquing, fishing, museums, nature centre, live theater, parks, shopping, cross-country skiing and water sports nearby.

Location: Village.

Publicity: *Michigan Explorer and Detroit Free Press.*

Certificate may be used: Sunday through Thursday excluding June, July, August and holidays, subject to availability. Excludes corporate rates and packages.

Glen Arbor   F6

White Gull Inn

5926 SW Manitou Tr
Glen Arbor, MI 49636-9702
(231)334-4486 Fax:(231)334-3546
Internet: www.third-coast.net/mi/whitegullinn
E-mail: gullinglen@aol.com

Circa 1900. One of Michigan's most scenic areas is home to the White Gull Inn. With the Sleeping Bear Dunes and alluring Glen Lake just minutes away, visitors will find no shortage of sightseeing or recreational activities during a stay here. The inn's farmhouse setting, country decor and five comfortable guest rooms offer  a relaxing haven no matter what the season. Lake Michigan is a block away, and guests also will enjoy the area's fine dining and shopping opportunities.

Innkeeper(s): Bill & Dotti Thompson. $65-80. MC, VISA, AX, DS, PC. 5 rooms, 1 with FP. Breakfast included in rates. Type of meal: Cont plus. Beds: QDT. Cable TV in room. Air conditioning. Fax on premises. Antiquing, fishing, golf, parks, shopping, downhill skiing, cross-country skiing, tennis and water sports nearby.

Location: Village.

Certificate may be used: Nov. 1-May 15.

Glenn   I6

Will O'Glenn Irish B&B

1286 64th St
Glenn, MI 49416
(616)227-3045 (888)237-3009 Fax:(616)227-3045
Internet: www.irish-inn.com
E-mail: shamrock@irish-inn.com

Circa 1920. With six stables and 17 acres of grounds, a stay at this farmhouse is bit like taking a trip to an Irish country farm. Innkeeper Ward Gahan hails from Ireland, and it is his heritage that is very much in evidence at Will O'Glenn. He and his wife, Shelley, spent months restoring their historic, 4,500-square-foot home, the result is an elegant country decor. Guests enjoy a restful night's sleep under an Irish down comforter before awaking to enjoy a traditional Irish breakfast. The morning fare includes meats and coffee imported from Ward's native land, homemade Irish breads and local items such as fresh fruit and preserves. Lake Michigan is just minutes away, as are parks, wineries, shops and restaurants.

Innkeeper(s): Shelley & Ward Gahan. $79-165. MC, VISA, PC, TC. 4 rooms with PB, 2 with FP. Breakfast included in rates. Types of meals: Full bkfst, cont plus and early coffee/tea. Beds: KQD. Jacuzzi in room. VCR, fax, copier, stables, bicycles, library and Jacuzzi on premises. Antiquing, fishing, golf, live theater, parks, shopping, downhill skiing, cross-country skiing, tennis and water sports nearby.

Location: Country.

"You have mastered the art of running a true Irish B&B."

Certificate may be used: Nov. 1-May 1, Sunday-Sunday; May 1-Nov. 1, Sunday-Thursday.

Holly 18

Holly Crossing B&B

304 S Saginaw St
Holly, MI 48442-1614
(248)634-7075 (800)556-2262 Fax:(248)634-4481
Internet: hollybandb.com
E-mail: hollybb@tir.com

Circa 1900. A unique wraparound veranda fashioned from stones decorates the exterior of this Queen Anne Victorian, which is surrounded by a white picket fence. The interior maintains original fireplace mantels and woodwork. Rooms are Victorian in style and comfortable, offering romantic items such as lacy curtains, silk flowers or perhaps even a double whirlpool tub. The spacious honeymoon suite offers a whirlpool tub, fireplace and a private balcony. All guests enjoy a delicious full breakfast, but guests in the whirlpool rooms have the meal delivered to their door. Holly is a historic railroad village, and the inn is conveniently located within walking distance of shops and restaurants. Battle Alley, a quaint street filled with restored 19th-century buildings, offers many shops and is a popular local attraction. Holly is within 45 minutes of Detroit.

Innkeeper(s): Carl & Nicole Cooper. $50-159. MC, VISA, AX, DS, PC, TC. 5 rooms with PB, 3 with FP and 1 suite. Breakfast included in rates. Type of meal: Full bkfst. Beds: QD. Phone and ceiling fan in room. Air conditioning. Fax, copier and library on premises. Antiquing, golf, live theater, parks, shopping, downhill skiing and cross-country skiing nearby.

Location: Historic railroad village.

Publicity: *Getaways Magazine and The Oakland Press.*

"What a charming Bed & Breakfast! The Oak Room was delightful. My husband and I enjoyed the old world charm mixed in with the modern necessities. This is the nicest B&B we have stayed in thus far."

Certificate may be used: Oct. 1-June 30, Sunday-Friday, excluding holidays.

Houghton C3

Charleston House B&B Inn

918 College Avenue
Houghton, MI 49931-1821
(906)482-7790 (800)482-7404 Fax:(906)482-7068

Circa 1900. Wide verandas on the first and second stories dominate the exterior of this impressive Colonial Revival-style home, which is painted in a light pink hue with white trim. There are ceiling fans and comfortable wicker furnishings on the verandas, and the second-story porch is a private haven for guests staying in the Daughter's Room. Most of the other bedchambers offer a view of the Portage Canal. Mother's Room makes up for its lack of a view by including a bay window, sitting area and clawfoot tub. The scents of brewing coffee and baking muffins will lure you out of your comfortable bed and down to a breakfast with homemade breads and granola, fresh fruit, yogurt and a special daily entree. The inn overlooks the canal, and Lake Superior is nearby, as is the MTU campus, skiing, shops, restaurants and the downtown area.

Innkeeper(s): John & Helen Sullivan. $98-165. MC, VISA, AX, PC, TC. 6 rooms with PB, 2 with FP, 1 suite & 2 conference rooms. Breakfast included in rates. Types of meals: Full bkfst & early coffee/tea. Beds: KQT. Cable TV, phone, turndown service, ceiling fan & microwave/complimentary soft drinks in room. Air conditioning. Fax, copier, library, coffee pots & hair dryers on premises. Amusement parks, antiquing, fishing, golf, Suomi College, live theater, parks, shopping, skiing, sporting events, tennis & water sports nearby.

Location: 7 miles from Lake Superior.

Publicity: *Michigan Explorer.*

"The room and the house was the prettiest I've ever seen."

Certificate may be used: Nov. 1-May 1, Sunday-Friday, with availability.

Interlochen F6

Between The Lakes B&B

4570 Case Blvd Box 280
Interlochen, MI 49643-9534
(616)276-7751 Fax:(616)276-7752

After more than two decades globetrotting as part of the foreign service, the owners of this bed & breakfast decided to become hosts instead of guests. Art, artifacts and furnishings from their world travels decorate the home. Two wooded acres offer privacy, and guests also may use the B&B's heated, indoor swimming pool. The home is within walking distance to Duck and Green lakes as well as the Interlochen Center for the Arts.

Innkeeper(s): Barbara & Gordon Evans. $65-75. MC, VISA, PC. 4 rooms with PB. Breakfast included in rates. Type of meal: Cont plus. Beds: KQT. VCR, fax and swimming on premises. Handicap access. Fishing, parks, shopping, cross-country skiing and water sports nearby.

Pets Allowed.

Location: Rural.

Publicity: *Genevieve Herald and Grand Traverse Business.*

Certificate may be used: Nov. 1 through May 1, Monday through Thursday only.

Ithaca H7

Chaffin Farms B&B

1245 W Washington Rd
Ithaca, MI 48847-9782
(517)875-3410

Circa 1892. Located in central Michigan between Mount Pleasant and Lansing, this inn was once a large dairy farm with 12 barns housing various farm animals. Guests will be impressed with the inn's colorful stone wall, built with rocks hauled in from the surrounding area. The inn is furnished with antiques, and visitors will marvel at the inn's impressive kitchen, which was featured in Country Woman magazine. Antiquing is popular in the area and Alma College is nearby.

Innkeeper(s): Susan Chaffin. $50-55. PC. 2 rooms, 1 with PB. Breakfast included in rates. Types of meals: Full bkfst, cont plus and early coffee/tea. Beds: QT. Air conditioning. Antiquing, parks, shopping and sporting events nearby.

Location: Country.

Certificate may be used: April 15 to Nov. 1.

Jones J6

The Sanctuary at Wildwood

58138 M-40
Jones, MI 49061-9713
(616)244-5910 (800)249-5910 Fax:(616)244-9022
Internet: www.rivercountry.com/saw
E-mail: wildwoodinns@voyager.net

Circa 1972. Travelers in search of relaxation and a little solitude will enjoy the serenity of this estate, surrounded by 95 forested acres. A stroll down the hiking trails introduces guests  to a variety of wildlife, but even inside, guests are pampered by the inn's natural setting. One room, named Medicine Hawk, is adorned with a mural depicting a woodland scene. A mural of a pine forest graces the Quiet Solace room. The Keeper of the Wild Room includes a rustic birch headboard. Each of the rooms includes a fireplace, Jacuzzi and service bar. There also are three cottage suites, situated around a pond. From the dining and great rooms, guests can watch the abundant wildlife. The innkeeper offers a variety of interesting packages. A heated swimming pool is available during the summer months. Wineries are nearby, and the inn is a half hour from Notre Dame and Shipshewana.

Innkeeper(s): Dick & Dolly Buerkle. $139-179. MC, VISA, AX, DS, PC, TC. 14 rooms, 11 suites, 3 cottages and 1 conference room. Breakfast included in rates. Beds: Q. TV and fireplace in room. Air conditioning. Handicap access. Antiquing, fishing, amish communities, shopping, downhill skiing and cross-country skiing nearby.

Location: Rural, wooded countryside.

Publicity: *The Blade.*

Certificate may be used: Nov. 1-April 15, Sunday through Thursday only, excluding holiday periods.

Jonesville J7

Horse & Carriage B&B

7020 Brown Rd
Jonesville, MI 49250-9720
(517)849-2732 Fax:(517)849-2732
E-mail: horsecarriagebb@yahoo.com

Circa 1898. Enjoy a peaceful old-fashioned day on the farm. Milk a cow, gather eggs and cuddle baby chicks. In the winter, families are treated to a horse-drawn sleigh ride at this 18th-century home, which is surrounded by a 700-acre cattle farm. In the warmer months, horse-drawn carriage rides pass down an old country lane past Buck Lake. The innkeeper's family has lived on the property for more than 150 years. The home itself was built as a one-room schoolhouse. A mix of cottage and Mission furnishings decorate the interior. The Rainbow Room, a perfect place for children, offers twin beds and a playroom. Guests are treated to hearty breakfasts made with farm-fresh eggs, fresh fruits and vegetables served on the porch or fireside.

Innkeeper(s): Keith Brown & family. $85-100. PC. 3 rooms, 1 with PB. Breakfast and snacks/refreshments included in rates. Types of meals: Full gourmet bkfst, cont plus, cont and early coffee/tea. Beds: QT. Phone and the inn is air-conditioned in room. Fax, copier, milk a cow, pet lambs, gather eggs and horse/carriage rides on premises. Antiquing, fishing, Jackson Space Center, Speedway, Country Fair, live theater, parks, shopping, cross-country skiing, sporting events and water sports nearby.

Location: Country.

Publicity: *Hillsdale Daily News and MSU Alumni.*

Certificate may be used: Anytime subject to availability.

Munro House B&B

202 Maumee St
Jonesville, MI 49250-1247
(517)849-9292 (800)320-3792

Circa 1840. Ten fireplaces and two Franklin stoves are found in the rooms of the historic Munro House built by George C. Munro, a Civil War brigadier general. The Greek Revival structure, Hillsdale County's first brick house, also served as a safe haven for slaves on the Underground Railroad with a secret room that still exists. Many guests enjoy selecting a book or a movie to spend a quiet evening in front of the fireplace in their room or to enjoy with friends in the library. Seven guest rooms include a fireplace, and two rooms have a whirlpool tub.

Breakfast is enjoyed overlooking the inn's gardens and before an open-hearth fireplace in the 1830's kitchen. Hillsdale College is just five miles away.

Innkeeper(s): Mike & Lori Venturini. $89-179. MC, VISA, AX. 7 rooms with PB, 3 with FP. Breakfast included in rates. Type of meal: Full bkfst. Beds: Q. Cable TV, phone, VCR, Jacuzzi (2 rooms) and Franklin Stove (2 rooms) in room. Air conditioning. Video library & complimentary cookies and soft drinks on premises. Antiquing, bicycling, canoeing/kayaking, golf, horseback riding, massage therapy, reflexology, live theater, shopping, cross-country skiing & sporting events nearby.

Location: City.

"What a delightful stay. Beautiful house, wonderful history and a delightful hostess. Felt like we knew her forever. We will tell all our friends."

Certificate may be used: Any Sunday through Friday.

Lansing J5

Ask Me House

1027 Seymour Ave
Lansing, MI 48906-4836
(517)484-3127 (800)275-6341 Fax:(517)484-4193
Internet: www.askmehouse.com
E-mail: mekiener@aol.com

Circa 1911. This early 20th-century home still includes its original hardwood floors and pocket doors. A hand-painted mural was added to the dining room in the 1940s. Guests can enjoy the unique art during the  breakfasts, which are served on antique Limoges china and Depression glass. The home is near a variety of museums, theaters, a historical village and Michigan State University.

Innkeeper(s): Mary Elaine Kiener & Alex Kruzel. $65. MC, VISA, PC, TC. 2 rooms. Breakfast included in rates. Types of meals: Full gourmet bkfst and early coffee/tea. Beds: DT. Ceiling fan in room. VCR and fax on premises. Antiquing, live theater, parks and sporting events nearby.

Location: City.

Certificate may be used: Anytime except holidays and special events; subject to availability.

Lewiston F8

Gorton House

HCR 3 Box 3738, Wolf Lake Dr
Lewiston, MI 49756-8948
(517)786-2764 Fax:(517)786-2764

Circa 1962. Wolf Lake sits beside this comfortable bed & breakfast. Rooms are filled with antiques and lace. The innkeepers offer a variety of activities including use of a fishing boat and putting green. The grounds boast a lakeside beach and hot tub under a gazebo. Inside, guests can relax near one of three fireplaces or take in a game of pool on the innkeepers' antique pool table. A hearty breakfast with entrees such as omelets or German pancakes is served along with fruits, juices and baked goods. In the summer, morning coffee can be enjoyed in the paddle boat. Freshly baked chocolate chip cookies are always available for a light snack. Antique shopping and golfing are some of the area's offerings.

Innkeeper(s): Lois Gorton. $85-150. MC, VISA, PC, TC. 6 rooms. Breakfast included in rates. Type of meal: Full bkfst.

Certificate may be used: January and February, Monday-Thursday; March-May 15, May 16-Dec. 31, Monday-Thursday, excludes all holidays.

Pine Ridge Lodge

Co Rd 489
Lewiston, MI 49756
(517)786-4789
Internet: www.bbonline.com/mi/pineridge/
E-mail: pineridg@northland.lib.mi.us

Circa 1948. This log lodge is right at home in its natural surroundings, secluded on 37 acres within the AuSable State
Forest. Outdoor enthusiasts are frequent guests, and it's no
wonder. The lodge has its own recreational director, as well as
20 miles of mountain biking trails and 10 kilometers of hiking
and cross-country trails. Exposed log and wood walls add a
rustic touch to the guest rooms and common areas. Each guest
room also includes a log bed. Guests can play darts or shoot
pool in the game room, which also has a fireplace. After a day
of biking, hiking or skiing, come back and relax in the outdoor
hot tub. Breakfasts are always hearty and homemade, a perfect
start to a day full of activity.

Innkeeper(s): Doug Stiles & Suzan Anthony-Stiles. $65-85. PC, TC. 7 rooms, 3
with PB and 1 cabin. Breakfast included in rates. Types of meals: Full bkfst and
early coffee/tea. Beds: QDT. VCR, spa and library on premises. Antiquing, fishing,
golf, parks, shopping, downhill skiing, cross-country skiing & water sports nearby.

Location: Remote wooded.

Publicity: *Ann Arbor News Bureau and The Montmorency County Tribune.*

Certificate may be used: Sunday through Thursday.

Lowell   I6

McGee Homestead B&B

2534 Alden Nash NE
Lowell, MI 49331
(616)897-8142
Internet: www.iserv.net/~mcgeebb
E-mail: mcgeebb@iserv.net

Circa 1880. Just 18 miles from Grand Rapids, travelers will find
the McGee Homestead B&B, an Italianate farmhouse with four
antique-filled guest rooms. Surrounded by orchards, it is one of
the largest farmhouses in the area. Breakfasts feature the inn's
own fresh eggs. Guests may golf at an adjacent course or enjoy
nearby fishing and boating. Lowell is home to Michigan's largest
antique mall, and many historic covered bridges are found in
the surrounding countryside. Travelers who remain on the farm
may relax in a hammock or visit a barn full of petting animals.

Innkeeper(s): Bill & Ardie Barber. $42-62. MC, VISA, AX, DS, PC, TC. 4 rooms
with PB and 1 conference room. Breakfast and snacks/refreshments included in
rates. Types of meals: Full bkfst and early coffee/tea. Beds: KDT. TV and ceiling
fan in room. Air conditioning. VCR and library on premises. Antiquing, fishing,
parks, shopping, downhill skiing and cross-country skiing nearby.

Location: Country.

Certificate may be used: March 1 to Dec. 31, Sunday-Friday.

Ludington   G5

Lamplighter B&B

602 E Ludington Ave
Ludington, MI 49431-2223
(231)843-9792 (800)301-9792 Fax:(231)845-6070
Internet: www.laketolake.com/lamplighter
E-mail: catsup@aol.com

Circa 1895. This Queen Anne home offers convenient access
to Lake Michigan's beaches, the Badger car ferry to Wisconsin
and Ludington State Park. A collection of European antiques,

original paintings and lithographs decorate the inn. The home's center-
piece, a golden oak curved staircase, leads guests up to their
rooms. Two rooms feature
whirlpool tubs, one a fireplace.
The innkeepers have created a
mix of hospitality and conve-
nience that draws both vacationers and busi-
ness travelers. A full, gourmet breakfast is served each morning.
The innkeepers are fluent in German.

Innkeeper(s): Judy & Heinz Bertram. $110-135. MC, VISA, AX, DS, PC, TC.
5 rooms with PB, 1 with FP. Breakfast included in rates. Types of meals: Full
gourmet bkfst and early coffee/tea. Beds: Q. Cable TV, phone, turndown service and whirlpool for two in room. Air conditioning. VCR, fax, copier and
gazebo and terrace on premises. Amusement parks, antiquing, fishing, golf,
parks, shopping, cross-country skiing, tennis and water sports nearby.

Location: City.

*"For my husband's first bed and breakfast experience, it couldn't
have been better."*

Certificate may be used: November through May, holidays excluded.

The Inn at Ludington

701 E Ludington Ave
Ludington, MI 49431-2224
(231)845-7055 (800)845-9170
Internet: www.inn-ludington.com

Circa 1890. This Queen Anne Victorian was built during the
heyday of Ludington's lumber era by a local pharmacist and
doctor. The innkeepers stress relaxation at the inn despite its
elegant exterior with its three-story turret. The rooms are filled
with comfortable, vintage furnishings. Guests can snuggle up
with a book in front of a warming fireplace or enjoy a soak in a
clawfoot tub. A hearty, buffet-style breakfast is served each
morning. The innkeepers take great pride in their cuisine and
are always happy to share some of their award-winning recipes
with guests. After a day of beachcombing, antiquing, cross-
country skiing or perhaps a bike ride, guests return to the inn
to find a chocolate atop their pillow. Don't forget to ask about
the innkeepers' murder-mystery weekends.

Innkeeper(s): Diane & David Nemitz. $75-100. MC, VISA, AX, DS, PC, TC. 6
rooms with PB, 2 with FP and 1 suite. Breakfast included in rates. Types of
meals: Full bkfst and early coffee/tea. Beds: KQD. Cable TV, turndown service
and ceiling fan in room. Air conditioning. Fax, copier and library on premises.
Amusement parks, antiquing, fishing, live theater, parks, shopping, downhill
skiing, cross-country skiing and water sports nearby.

Location: City.

Publicity: *Ludington Daily News, Detroit Free Press, Chicago Tribune,
Country Accents and Michigan Living.*

"Loved the room and everything else about the house."

Certificate may be used: November-April, anytime; May, June, September,
October, weekdays (or weekends as available at last minute).

The Ludington House

501 E Ludington Ave
Ludington, MI 49431-2220
(231)845-7769 (800)827-7869
Internet: www.bbonline.com/mi/tlh

Enjoy the opulence of the Victorian era at this 19th-century
home, which was built by a lumber baron. Grand rooms with
high ceilings, stained glass and polished oak floors are
enhanced by a country collection of period antiques. A showpiece carved, winding staircase and Italian mantels are other

notable architectural features. An antique wedding gown decorates the Bridal Suite. The innkeepers will prepare a picnic lunch, and there are bicycles for guest use. The innkeepers also offer murder-mystery packages.

Innkeeper(s): Virginia Boegner. $80-140. MC, VISA. 8 rooms. Breakfast included in rates. Type of meal: Full bkfst.

Certificate may be used: November to Memorial Day excluding Valentine's Day and New Years Eve.

Welcome Home Inn

716 E Ludington Ave
Ludington, MI 49431-2225
(616)845-7699 (888)253-0982
E-mail: welcome@t-one.net

Circa 1880. The owner of the local dry goods store built this Queen Anne Victorian. It has been restored to its 19th-century elegance. Among the furnishings are antiques such as the fanciful Victorian sofa in the parlor. Guest rooms are romantic. In one room, guests walk up two steps to reach a clawfoot tub located by the bay window. The Enchanted Cottage is the most idyllic with a black iron water bed with a canopy of black chiffon. The bed is draped with a handmade quilt.

Innkeeper(s): Missy & Paula Price. $75-95. MC, VISA, PC, TC. 4 rooms with PB and 1 suite. Breakfast and afternoon tea included in rates. Type of meal: Full gourmet bkfst. Beds: QT. Turndown service and ceiling fan in room. Air conditioning. VCR and child care on premises. Antiquing, fishing, golf, live theater, parks, shopping, tennis and water sports nearby.

Location: small town.

"Thank you so very much for your love and hospitality . . . your place is delightful, but most of all it is a reflection of both you and your precious spirit."

Certificate may be used: Nov. 1-May 31, any day of the week, Sunday-Saturday.

Mendon J6

The Mendon Country Inn

PO Box 98
Mendon, MI 49072-9502
(616)496-8132 (800)304-3366 Fax:(616)496-8403
Internet: www.rivercountry.com/mci
E-mail: wildwoodinns@voyager.net

Circa 1873. This two-story stagecoach inn was constructed with St. Joseph River clay bricks fired on the property. There are eight-foot windows, high ceilings and a walnut staircase. Country antiques are accentuated with woven rugs, collectibles and bright quilts. There are nine antique-filled guest rooms and nine suites which include a fireplace and Jacuzzi tub. Depending on the season,  guests may also borrow a tandem bike or arrange for a canoe trip. Special events are featured throughout the year. The inn's Golden Getaway package includes lodging, a dinner for two and special activity, which might be golfing, a river canoe trip, skiing or perhaps a relaxing massage. A rural Amish community and Shipshewana are nearby.

Innkeeper(s): Geff & Cheryl Clarke. $69-159. MC, VISA, AX, DS, PC, TC. 18 rooms with PB, 14 with FP, 9 suites, 2 cottages and 1 conference room. Breakfast included in rates. Types of meals: Full bkfst and early coffee/tea. Beds: QD. TV, ceiling fan and most rooms with fireplaces in room. Air conditioning. Fax, sauna, bicycles, library and canoeing on premises. Handicap

access. Antiquing, canoeing/kayaking, fishing, shopping, downhill skiing and cross-country skiing nearby.

Location: Rural country.

Publicity: *Innsider, Country Home and Country Magazine.*

"A great experience. Good food and great hosts. Thank you."

Certificate may be used: Nov. 1-April 15, Sunday-Thursday only, excluding holiday periods.

Muskegon H6

Blue Country B&B

1415 Holton Rd
Muskegon, MI 49445-1446
(616)744-2555 (888)569-2050
Internet: www.bbonline.com/mi/bluecountry/

Once known as the Brookside Tea House during Prohibition, this Craftsman home now is known for its family-oriented atmosphere and woodsy setting. Four guest rooms include the Blue Tea Rose Room, with a hand-carved sycamore bed and vanity, and the Whispering Woods Room, featuring wood furnishings and an attractive antique wall print. Guests will enjoy the teapot collection, and they are welcome to try the electronic organ and hammered dulcimer. The inn is just 10 minutes from Lake Michigan. There are numerous area attractions, including Muskegon and Duck Lake state parks.

Innkeeper(s): Barbara Stevens. $64. 2 rooms with PB. Breakfast included in rates. Types of meals: Full bkfst and early coffee/tea. Turndown service in room. Air conditioning. VCR and child care on premises. Amusement parks, antiquing, live theater, shopping, cross-country skiing and sporting events nearby.

Certificate may be used: All year, subject to availability.

Port City Victorian Inn

1259 Lakeshore Dr
Muskegon, MI 49441-1659
(616)759-0205 (800)274-3574 Fax:(616)759-0205
Internet: www.bbonline.com/mi/portcity
E-mail: pcvicinn@gte.net

Circa 1877. Lumber baron and industrialist Alexander Rodgers, Sr. built this Queen Anne-style home. Among its impressive features are the grand entryway with a natural oak staircase and paneling, carved posts and spindles. The curved, leaded-glass windows in the inn's parlor offer a view of Muskegon Lake. Beveled-glass doors enclose the natural wood fireplace in the sitting room, and high ceilings, intricate molding, polished oak floors and  antiques further enhance the charm of this house. Guest rooms offer views of the lake, as well as double whirlpool tubs. A full breakfast is served either on the sun porch, in the dining room or guests can enjoy the meal in the privacy of their room.

Innkeeper(s): Fred & Barbara Schossau. $75-135. MC, VISA, AX, DC, CB, DS, PC, TC. 5 rooms, 3 with PB and 2 suites. Breakfast and snacks/refreshments included in rates. Type of meal: Full bkfst. Beds: D. Cable TV, phone, turndown service, ceiling fan and double whirlpool tubs in room. Air conditioning. VCR, fax, copier, bicycles and second floor sun deck on premises. Amusement parks, antiquing, golf, lake Michigan, Muskegon Lake, cruise ship: Port City Princess, parks and water sports nearby.

Location: City.

Publicity: *Muskegon Chronicle, Michigan Living, PASS and local TV Channel 40.*

"The inn offers only comfort, good food and total peace of mind."

Certificate may be used: November-April, Sunday-Thursday, excluding holidays.

Omer
G8

Rifle River B&B

500 Center Ave
Omer, MI 48749
(517)653-2543

A gathering of maple trees shades this historic home, located in the heart of Omer. The town, which was founded just after the Civil War, has seen a multitude of disasters, and this sturdy home has stood through its fair share of floods, tornadoes and fires. The innkeepers offer four rooms decorated with antiques. Waterbeds and Jacuzzi tubs are relaxing amenities. The home, as its name might suggest, is only two blocks from the Rifle River, which offers fishing and canoeing.

Innkeeper(s): Judy O'Boyle. $38-49. 4 rooms. Breakfast included in rates. Type of meal: Cont.

Certificate may be used: September through April, anytime. May through August, Sunday through Thursday.

Petoskey (Bay View)
E7

Terrace Inn

1549 Glendale
Petoskey (Bay View), MI 49770
(231)347-2410 (800)530-9898 Fax:(231)347-2407
Internet: theterraceinn.com
E-mail: info@theterraceinn.com

Circa 1911. This late Victorian inn is located on what began as a Chautauqua summer resort, surrounded by more than 400 Victorian cottages. Terrace Inn was built in 1911, and most of its furnishings are original to the property. Guests will enjoy stunning views of Lake Michigan and Little Traverse Bay, and they can enjoy the shore at the private Bay View beach. In keeping with the surrounding homes, the guest rooms  are decorated in a romantic-country cottage style. To take guests back in time, there are no televisions or telephones in the rooms. This historic resort town offers many attractions, from swimming and watersports to hiking to summer theater. During the summer season, the inn's restaurant and outdoor veranda are great spots for dinner.

Innkeeper(s): Tom & Denise Erhart. $49-106. MC, VISA, AX. 43 rooms with PB and 2 conference rooms. Breakfast included in rates. Type of meal: Cont plus. Beds: QDT. Air conditioning. VCR, fax, copier, swimming, bicycles, tennis and cross-country skiing on premises. Handicap access. Antiquing, fishing, golf, Chautauqua, live theater, parks, shopping, downhill skiing, cross-country skiing, tennis and water sports nearby.

Location: National historic site.

Publicity: *Oakland Press & Observer Eccentric and Michigan Magazine.*

Certificate may be used: Oct. 20-June 15., Sunday-Thursday.

Romeo
I9

Hess Manor B&B

186 S Main St
Romeo, MI 48065-5128
(810)752-4726 Fax:(810)752-6456
Internet: www.hessmanor.com
E-mail: hessmanor@ees.eesc.com

Circa 1854. This pre-Civil War home is located in a town listed in the National Register. The inn boasts a fireplace and Victorian decor. The innkeepers also renovated the inn's 110-year-old carriage house into an antique and gift shop. At night, guests are encouraged to enjoy the inn's complimentary soda pop and wine while viewing a wide selection free movies. For stargazers, there is a wonderful outdoor Jacuzzi. Much of Romeo's historic sites are within walking distance of Hess Manor, including galleries, antique shops, bookstores and restaurants. Frontier Town, a collection of Old West-style buildings, is a popular attraction.

Innkeeper(s): Thom & Kelly Stephens. $69-80. MC, VISA, AX, PC. 4 rooms, 2 with PB. Breakfast included in rates. Type of meal: Full gourmet bkfst. Beds: Q. Air conditioning. VCR, copier, free video, free beverages and Jacuzzi under stars on premises. Antiquing, fishing, golf, horseback riding, live theater, parks, shopping and water sports nearby.

Location: Historic village.

Certificate may be used: Nov. 1-June 30, all days.

Saline
J8

The Homestead B&B

9279 Macon Rd
Saline, MI 48176-9305
(734)429-9625

Circa 1851. The Homestead is a two-story brick farmhouse situated on 50 acres of fields, woods and river. The house has 15-inch-thick walls and is furnished with Victorian antiques and family heirlooms. This was a favorite camping spot for Native Americans while they salted their fish, and many arrowheads have been found on the farm. Activities include long walks through meadows of wildflowers and cross-country skiing in season. It is 40 minutes from Detroit and Toledo and 10 minutes from Ann Arbor.

Innkeeper(s): Shirley Grossman. $65-70. MC, VISA, AX, DS, PC, TC. 5 rooms and 1 conference room. Breakfast and snacks/refreshments included in rates. Types of meals: Full bkfst and early coffee/tea. Beds: DT. TV in room. Air conditioning. VCR on premises. Antiquing, parks, shopping, cross-country skiing and sporting events nearby.

Location: Country.

Publicity: *Ann Arbor News, Country Focus and Saline Reporter.*

"We're spoiled now and wouldn't want to stay elsewhere! No motel offers deer at dusk and dawn!"

Certificate may be used: From Jan. 2-June 1, Sunday to Friday & Sept. 1-Dec. 30, Sunday to Friday.

Saugatuck I6

Bayside Inn

618 Water St Box 186
Saugatuck, MI 49453
(616)857-4321 Fax:(616)857-1870
Internet: www.baysideinn.net
E-mail: info@baysideinn.net

Circa 1926. Located on the edge of the Kalamazoo River and across from the nature observation tower, this downtown inn was once a boathouse. The common room now has a fire-place and view of the  water. Each guest room has its own deck. The inn is near several restau-rants, shops and beaches. Fishing for salmon, perch and trout is popular.

Innkeeper(s): Kathy Wilson. $65-235. MC, VISA, AX, DS. 10 rooms with PB, 4 with FP, 4 suites and 1 conference room. Breakfast included in rates. Type of meal: Cont plus. Beds: KQD. Cable TV and VCR in room. Air condi-tioning. Fax, copier and spa on premises. Antiquing, fishing, live theater, shopping, cross-country skiing and water sports nearby.

Location: City.

"Our stay was wonderful, more pleasant than anticipated, we were so pleased. As for breakfast, it gets our A 1 rating."

Certificate may be used: November through March, Monday through Thursday excluding holidays.

The Red Dog B&B

132 Mason St
Saugatuck, MI 49453
(616)857-8851 (800)357-3250

Circa 1879. This comfortable, two-story farmhouse is located in the heart of downtown Saugatuck and is just a short walk away from shopping, restaurants and many of the town's seasonal activities. Rooms are furnished with a combination of traditional and antique furnishings. One room includes a fireplace and Jacuzzi tub for two. Guests can relax and enjoy views of the gar-den from the B&B's second-story porch, or warm up next to the fireplace in the living room. The full breakfast includes treats such as baked apple cinnamon French toast or a ham and cheese strata. The innkeepers offer AARP and off-season discounts.

Innkeeper(s): Patrick & Kristine Clark. $85-150. MC, VISA, AX, DC, DS, PC, TC. 6 rooms with PB, 1 with FP and 1 suite. Breakfast included in rates. Types of meals: Full bkfst and early coffee/tea. Beds: QD. Cable TV and ceiling fan in room. Air conditioning. VCR, fax and copier on premises. Antiquing, fishing, live theater, parks, shopping, cross-country skiing and water sports nearby.

Location: City.

Publicity: *South Bend Trio, Michigan Cyclist and Restaurant and Institutions.*

Certificate may be used: November through April.

Twin Oaks Inn

PO Box 867, 227 Griffith St
Saugatuck, MI 49453-0867
(616)857-1600

Circa 1860. This large Queen Anne Victorian inn was a board-ing house for lumbermen at the turn of the century. Now an old-English-style inn, it offers a variety of lodging choices, including a room with its own Jacuzzi and a cozy cottage, which boasts a fireplace and an outdoor hot tub. There are

many diversions at Twin Oaks, including a collection of video-taped movies numbering more than 700. Guests may borrow bicycles or play horseshoes on the inn's grounds.

Innkeeper(s): Jerry & Nancy Horney. $75-125. MC, VISA, DS, TC. 7 rooms with PB and 1 conference room. Types of meals: Full bkfst and early coffee/tea. Beds: KQ. Cable TV and VCR in room. Air conditioning. Antiquing, fishing, live theater, parks, shopping, cross-country skiing and water sports nearby.

Location: Downtown small village.

Publicity: *Home & Away, Cleveland Plain Dealer, South Bend Tribune, Shape, AAA Magazine.*

Certificate may be used: Nov. 1-April 30, Sunday through Thursday.

Scottville G5

Eden Hill B&B

1483 E Chauvez Rd
Scottville, MI 49454-9758
(616)757-2023

Descendants of John Adams have owned this home for more than 120 years, and a special family tree is available for view-ing. This farmhouse is decorated in cheerful, country decor with comfortable furnishings and antiques. Each of the guest rooms is named after relatives who once resided in the house. The full country breakfasts offer a great start to a busy day exploring the Michigan countryside.

Innkeeper(s): Carla Craven. $75-85. PC. 3 rooms. Breakfast included in rates. Type of meal: Full bkfst.

Certificate may be used: Sunday-Thursday, winter and spring, no holidays.

South Haven J5

The Seymour House

1248 Blue Star Hwy
South Haven, MI 49090-9696
(616)227-3918 Fax:(616)227-3010
Internet: www.seymourhouse.com
E-mail: seymour@cybersol.com

Circa 1862. Less than half a mile from the shores of Lake Michigan, this pre-Civil War, Italianate-style home rests upon 11 acres of grounds, complete with nature trails. Each of the guest rooms is named for a state significant in the innkeepers' lives. The Arizona Room, popular with honeymoon-ers, includes a double Jacuzzi tub. Poached pears with raspberry sauce, but-termilk blueberry pan-  cakes and locally made sausages are a few of the items that might appear on the breakfast menu. The inn is midway between Saugatuck and South Haven, which offer plenty of activities. Beaches, Kal-Haven Trail, shopping, horseback riding and winery tours are among the fun destination choices.

Innkeeper(s): Friedl Scimo. $85-145. MC, VISA, PC, TC. 5 rooms with PB, 2 with FP and 1 cabin. Breakfast and afternoon tea included in rates. Types of meals: Full gourmet bkfst and early coffee/tea. Beds: KQ. TV, ceiling fan, VCR and two with jacuzzi in room. Air conditioning. Fax, copier, swimming and library on premises. Antiquing, fishing, golf, live theater, parks, shopping, downhill skiing, cross-country skiing and water sports nearby.

Location: Country setting.

Publicity: *Country and Michigan Living.*

"As one who comes from the land that invented B&Bs, I hope to say that this is a truly superb example."

Certificate may be used: Jan. 1-March 31, Monday-Thursday, holidays excluded.

Victoria Resort B&B

241 Oak St
South Haven, MI 49090-2302
(616)637-6414 (800)473-7376 Fax:(616)637-6127

Circa 1925. Less than two blocks from a sandy beach, this Classical Revival inn offers many recreational opportunities for its guests, who may choose from bicycling, beach and pool swimming, basketball and tennis, among others. The inn's rooms and suites provide visitors several options, including cable TV, fireplaces, whirlpool tubs and ceiling fans. Cottages with maid service, for families or groups traveling together, also are available. A 10-minute stroll down tree-lined streets leads visitors to South Haven's quaint downtown, with its riverfront restaurants and shops.

Innkeeper(s): Bob & Jan Leksich. $49-165. MC, VISA, DS, PC, TC. 9 rooms with PB, 4 with FP, 4 suites and 5 cottages. Breakfast included in rates. Type of meal: Cont plus. Beds: KQ. Cable TV, phone, ceiling fan and VCR in room. Air conditioning. Fax, swimming, bicycles, tennis, library, basketball and volleyball on premises. Antiquing, fishing, horseback riding, parks, shopping, downhill skiing, cross-country skiing and water sports nearby.

Location: City.

Certificate may be used: Sept. 15-May 15, Sunday through Thursday excluding some holidays.

Spring Lake I6

The Royal Pontaluna Inn B&B

1870 Pontaluna Rd
Spring Lake, MI 49456-9614
(231)798-7271 (800)865-3545 Fax:(231)798-7271
Internet: www.bbonline.com/mi/pontaluna
E-mail: fourbuzz@aol.com

Circa 1979. This bed & breakfast is located on 25 acres. There is a tennis court, a whirlpool, sauna and indoor pool to keep guests busy, but travelers are welcome to simply sit and relax in front of the stone fireplace or stroll the wooded grounds. As the innkeepers are named Charles and Di, the two appointed their inn with a regal name. The Royal Suite is a romantic haven with a fireplace and Jacuzzi tub. Three other rooms also include Jacuzzi tubs. Although there is plenty to do at the inn, the area has many lake-related activities, shops, museums and state parks to visit.

Innkeeper(s): Charles & Di Beacham. $109-169. MC, VISA, AX, DS, PC, TC. 5 rooms with PB, 1 with FP, 1 suite and 2 conference rooms. Breakfast included in rates. Types of meals: Full bkfst and early coffee/tea. Beds: Q. Cable TV, phone and VCR in room. Air conditioning. Fax, spa, swimming, sauna, tennis and indoor pool on premises. Amusement parks, antiquing, fishing, golf, live theater, parks, shopping, downhill skiing, cross-country skiing, sporting events and water sports nearby.

Publicity: *Travel News.*

Certificate may be used: Jan. 2-April 30, Nov. 1-Dec. 29, Sunday-Thursday (no holidays).

Suttons Bay F6

Open Windows

PO Box 698, 613 St Marys Ave
Suttons Bay, MI 49682-0698
(231)271-4300 (800)520-3722

Circa 1893. The bay is just two blocks away for guests staying at this bed & breakfast, and those opting for the home's Rose Garden Room enjoy the water view from their quarters. The home's half-acre of grounds is dotted with flower gardens. Adirondack-style chairs, created by the innkeeper, line the front porch. Guests may borrow snowshoes in winter or use the home's grill and picnic table during the warmer months. Locally produced fresh fruits, entrees such as spinach and cheese crepes and homemade breads are among the breakfast fare, which is often served in a room with bay views.

Innkeeper(s): Don & Norma Blumenschine. $95-135. PC, TC. 3 rooms with PB. Breakfast and snacks/refreshments included in rates. Types of meals: Full gourmet bkfst and early coffee/tea. Beds: KQT. Ceiling fan in room. Air conditioning. VCR, bicycles, library, snowshoes, grill, picnic table and refrigerator on premises. Antiquing, fishing, Sleeping Bear Dunes, live theater, parks, shopping, downhill skiing, cross-country skiing and water sports nearby.

Location: Village in rural countryside.

Certificate may be used: Jan. 15-May 15, Monday-Thursday.

Traverse City F6

Historic Victoriana 1898

622 Washington St
Traverse City, MI 49686-2646
(616)929-1009

Circa 1898. Egbert Ferris, a partner in the European Horse Hotel, built this Italianate Victorian manor and a two-story carriage house. Later, the bell tower from the old Central School was moved onto the property and now serves as a handsome Greek Revival gazebo. The house has three parlors, all framed in fretwork. Etched and stained glass is found throughout. Guest rooms are furnished with family heirlooms. The house speciality is Belgian waffles topped with homemade cherry sauce.

Innkeeper(s): Flo & Bob Schermerhorn. $65-90. PC. 3 rooms with PB, 1 with FP and 1 suite. Breakfast and afternoon tea included in rates. Types of meals: Full gourmet bkfst and early coffee/tea. Beds: QD. TV and turndown service in room. Air conditioning. VCR, fax and library on premises. Antiquing, fishing, museums and University Center, live theater, parks, shopping, downhill skiing, cross-country skiing and water sports nearby.

Location: City.

Publicity: *Michigan Living, Minneapolis Star-Tribune, Midwest Living and Oakland Press.*

"In all our B&B experiences, no one can compare with the Victoriana 1898. You're 100% in every category!"

Certificate may be used: Sunday through Thursday, November through April.

Union Pier J5

Pine Garth Inn

15790 Lakeshore Rd
Union Pier, MI 49129-9340
(616)469-1642 Fax:(616)469-0418
Internet: www.pinegarth.com
E-mail: relax@pinegarth.com

Circa 1905. The seven rooms and five guest cottages at this charming bed & breakfast inn are decorated in a country style and each boasts something special. Some have a private deck and a wall of windows that look out to Lake Michigan. Other rooms feature items such as an unusual twig canopy bed, and several have whirlpool tubs. The deluxe cottages offer two queen-size beds, a wood-burning fireplace, VCR, cable TV and an outdoor tub

on a private deck with a gas grill. Rates vary for the cottages. The inn has its own private beach and there are sand dunes, vineyards, forests and miles of beaches in the area.

Innkeeper(s): Paula & Russ Bulin. $115-170. MC, VISA, DS, PC. 7 rooms with PB, 1 with FP, 5 cottages and 1 conference room. Breakfast included in rates. Type of meal: Full gourmet bkfst. Beds: Q. Ceiling fan and VCR in room. Fax, copier, swimming, bicycles and library on premises. Shopping nearby.

Publicity: *Midwest Living/St. Louis News and Channel 16 South Bend.*

"Your warm and courteous reception, attentiveness and helpfulness will never be forgotten."

Certificate may be used: Nov. 1 to May 15, Sunday through Thursday, excluding holidays.

The Inn at Union Pier

9708 Berrien
Union Pier, MI 49129-0222
(616)469-4700 Fax:(616)469-4720
Internet: www.innatunionpier.com

Circa 1920. Set on a shady acre across a country road from Lake Michigan, this inn features unique Swedish ceramic wood-burning fireplaces, a hot tub and sauna, a veranda ringing the house and a large common room with comfortable overstuffed furniture and a grand piano. Rooms offer such  amenities as private balconies and porches, whirlpools, views of the English garden and furniture dating from the early 1900s. Breakfast includes fresh fruit and homemade jams made of fruit from surrounding farms.

Innkeeper(s): Joyce & Mark Pitts. $135-205. MC, VISA, DS, PC, TC. 16 rooms with PB, 12 with FP, 2 suites and 1 conference room. Breakfast and snacks/refreshments included in rates. Types of meals: Full gourmet bkfst, cont and early coffee/tea. Beds: KQT. TV, phone and ceiling fan in room. Air conditioning. VCR, fax, copier, spa, swimming, sauna, bicycles and library on premises. Handicap access. Antiquing, art galleries, bicycling, hiking, wine tasting, parks, cross-country skiing, sporting events, water sports and wineries nearby.

Location: Lakeside resort.

Publicity: *Chicago, Midwest Living, W, Country Living, Travel & Leisure, Bride's, Chicago Tribune, "Chicagoing" on WLS-TV and Romantic-Inns-The Travel Channel.*

"The food, the atmosphere, the accommodations, and of course, the entire staff made this the most relaxing weekend ever."

Certificate may be used: Oct. 1-May 25, Sunday through Thursday only, no holidays.

Walloon Lake   E7

Masters House B&B

2253 N Shore Dr
Walloon Lake, MI 49796
(616)535-2944

Circa 1890. This bed & breakfast once served as the location for the town's first telephone company. There are six comfortably decorated rooms, two with private bath. The home is within walking distance of the beach, shops and restaurants in town.

Innkeeper(s): Joe Breidenstein. $40-90. MC, VISA, PC, TC. 6 rooms, 2 with PB and 1 cottage. Breakfast included in rates. Type of meal: Cont plus. Beds: KQDT. VCR on premises. Antiquing, fishing, snowmobiling, hunting (game and mushrooms), live theater, downhill skiing, cross-country skiing & water sports nearby.

Location: Resort village.

Certificate may be used: Any time, subject to availability, midweek most likely.

Ypsilanti   J8

Parish House Inn

103 S Huron St
Ypsilanti, MI 48197-5421
(734)480-4800 (800)480-4866 Fax:(734)480-7472
Internet: bbhost.com/parish
E-mail: parishinn@aol.com

Circa 1893. This Queen Anne Victorian was named in honor of its service as a parsonage for the First Congregational Church. The home remained a parsonage for more than 50 years after its construction and then served as a church office and Sunday school building. It was moved to its present site in Ypsilanti's historic district in the late 1980s. The rooms are individually decorated with Victorian-style wallpapers and antiques. One guest room includes a two-person Jacuzzi tub. Those in search of a late-night snack need only venture into the kitchen to find drinks and the cookie jar. For special occasions, the innkeepers can arrange trays with flowers, non-alcoholic champagne, chocolates, fruit or cheese. The terrace overlooks the Huron River.

Innkeeper(s): Mrs. Chris Mason. $89-129. MC, VISA, AX, DS, PC, TC. 9 rooms with PB, 2 with FP and 1 conference room. Breakfast and snacks/refreshments included in rates. Types of meals: Full gourmet bkfst, cont and early coffee/tea. Beds: QDT. Cable TV, phone, ceiling fan and VCR in room. Air conditioning. Fax and library on premises. Handicap access. Amusement parks, antiquing, fishing, live theater, parks, shopping, cross-country skiing, sporting events and water sports nearby.

Location: City.

Publicity: *Detroit Free Press and Midwest Living.*

Certificate may be used: December through May, Sunday through Thursday.

Minnesota

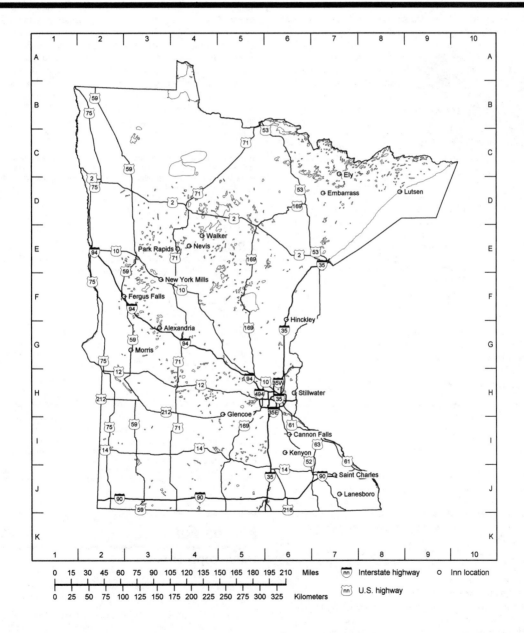

0 15 30 45 60 75 90 105 120 135 150 165 180 195 210 Miles

0 25 50 75 100 125 150 175 200 225 250 275 300 325 Kilometers

Interstate highway   o Inn location

U.S. highway

Alexandria   G3

Cedar Rose Inn

422 7th Ave W
Alexandria, MN 56308
(320)762-8430 (888)203-5333 Fax:(320)762-8044
Internet: www.echopress.com/cedarose
E-mail: cedarose@gctel.com

Circa 1903. Diamond-paned windows, gables, a wraparound porch with a swing for two and stained glass enhance the exterior of this handsome three-story Tudor Revival home in the National Register. Located in what was once referred to as the  "Silk Stocking District," the home was built by the town's mayor. Arched doorways, Tiffany chandeliers, a glorious open staircase, maple floors and oak woodwork set the atmosphere. There's a library, a formal dining room and a parlor with fireplace and window seat. Request the Noah P. Ward room and enjoy the king-size bed and double whirlpool with mood lights for a special celebration. Wake to the aroma of freshly baked caramel rolls, scones or cinnamon buns. Entrees of sausage and quiche are favorites. In the evening, enjoy watching the sunset over Lake Winona. Reserve a mountain bike ahead of time with the innkeeper, or enjoy a day of lake activities, shopping, antiquing or horseback riding.

Innkeeper(s): Aggie & Florian Ledermann. $75-135. MC, VISA, PC. 4 rooms with PB. Breakfast and snacks/refreshments included in rates. Types of meals: Full bkfst and early coffee/tea. Beds: KQ. Air conditioning. Bicycles and library on premises. Antiquing, bicycling, fishing, golf, hiking, live theater, parks, shopping, downhill skiing, cross-country skiing, tennis and water sports nearby.

Location: City.

"The Cedar Rose Inn was more than we imagined it would be. We felt like royalty in your beautiful dining room."

Certificate may be used: Nov. 1-March 31, Sunday-Thursday; April 1-Oct. 31, Sunday-Monday.

Cannon Falls   I6

Quill & Quilt

615 Hoffman St W
Cannon Falls, MN 55009-1923
(507)263-5507 (800)488-3849

Circa 1897. This three-story, gabled Colonial Revival house has six bay windows and several porches and decks. The inn features a well-stocked library, a front parlor with a fireplace, and handsomely decorated guest rooms. A favorite is the room with a double whirlpool tub, two bay windows, a king-size oak canopy bed and Victorian chairs.

Innkeeper(s): Staci Smith. $55-130. MC, VISA. 4 rooms with PB and 1 suite. Breakfast included in rates. Types of meals: Full bkfst and cont. Beds: KQD. TV in room. Spa on premises. Antiquing, downhill skiing, cross-country skiing and water sports nearby.

Publicity: *Minneapolis Tribune and Country Quilts.*

"What a pleasure to find the charm and hospitality of an English country home while on holiday in the United States."

Certificate may be used: Sunday through Thursday, Nov. 1-April 30.

Ely   C7

Burntside Lodge

2755 Burntside Lodge Rd
Ely, MN 55731-8402
(218)365-3894
Internet: www.burntside.com

Circa 1913. "Staying here is like taking a vacation 80 years ago," states innkeeper Lou LaMontagne. Families have come here for more than 80 years to enjoy the waterfront and woodside setting. The lodge and its cabins are in the National Register and much of the original hand-carved furnishings remain from the jazz age. Guests can choose from lodging in rustic cabins that date back to the 1920s, and there also are elegant, renovated cabins that include up to three bedrooms. Fishing, listening to the cry of the loon and boating around the lake's 125 islands are popular activities. Breakfast and dinner are available in the waterside dining room, and there is a lounge, espresso bar and gift shop. The lodge is open from mid-May through September.

Innkeeper(s): Lou & Lonnie LaMontagne. $99-250. MC, VISA, AX, DS. 24 cottages, 1 with FP. Types of meals: Full bkfst and early coffee/tea. Beds: KQDT. Fax, copier, swimming, sauna and library on premises. Antiquing, fishing, parks, shopping and water sports nearby.

Publicity: *Midwest Living and Gourmet Magazine.*

"Unforgettable."

Certificate may be used: May 12 to June 22, Sept. 3-22.

Embarrass   D7

Finnish Heritage Homestead

4776 Waisanen Rd
Embarrass, MN 55732-8347
(218)984-3318 (800)863-6545

Circa 1901. This turn-of-the-century, Finnish-American log house offers outdoor recreation and family-style full breakfasts to visitors, who receive many personal touches, such as bathrobes and slipper socks. Guests also may utilize the inn's relaxing Finnish sauna and enjoy badminton, boccie ball, croquet and horseshoes on the spacious grounds. There are flower and berry gardens, and a gazebo and gift shop are on the premises. Be sure to inquire about the availability of picnic lunches to take along on excursions to nearby historic and mining sites.

Innkeeper(s): Elaine Braginton & Buzz Schultz. $79-105. MC, VISA. 3 rooms and 1 suite. Breakfast included in rates. Types of meals: Full bkfst and early coffee/tea. Beds: QT. Turndown service and ceiling fan in room. VCR, gazebo, horseshoe, badminton and wood fired sauna on premises. Antiquing, fishing, international Wolf Center, historic tours, snowmobiling, parks, shopping and downhill skiing nearby.

Location: Country.

Certificate may be used: Sunday to Thursday only.

Fergus Falls   F3

Bakketopp Hus

RR 2 Box 187A
Fergus Falls, MN 56537-9802
(218)739-2915 (800)739-2915

Circa 1976. From the decks of this wooded home, guests can enjoy the scenery of Long Lake and catch glimpses of wildlife. Antiques, handmade quilts and down comforters decorate the cozy guest rooms. One room includes a private spa and draped canopy bed. Another room includes a fireplace. A bounty of nearby outdoor activities are sure to please nature lovers, and antique shops and restaurants are nearby.

Innkeeper(s): Dennis & Judy Nims. $70-105. MC, VISA, DS, PC, TC. 3 rooms with PB. Breakfast, afternoon tea and snacks/refreshments included in rates. Types of meals: Full gourmet bkfst and early coffee/tea. Beds: Q. Cable TV, phone and ceiling fan in room. Air conditioning. VCR and swimming on premises. Amusement parks, antiquing, fishing, live theater, parks, shopping, downhill skiing, cross-country skiing and water sports nearby.

Publicity: *Minneapolis Tribune.*

Certificate may be used: Sunday through Thursday for months of March, November, December, January, February.

Glencoe   H5

Glencoe Castle B&B

831 13th St E
Glencoe, MN 55336-1503
(320)864-3043 (800)517-3334
Internet: members.aol.com/schoeneck1/home.htm
E-mail: schoenr@hutchtel.net

Circa 1895. Glencoe Castle was built as a wedding promise to lure a bride from New York to Minnesota. She would move to Glencoe only if her husband built her a castle. This grand manor did the trick, with its carved woodwork, stained glass and ornate wood floors. The third floor originally was built as a ballroom. The home is decorated with antiques, Oriental and country pieces. Guests are treated to a lavish candlelight breakfast with such items as baked eggs in cream and Havarti cheese, Canadian bacon, blueberry French toast, homemade bread, pastries and fresh fruit. In the evenings, tea and dessert are served. There is a Victorian gift shop on the premises. For an extra charge, guests can arrange small meetings, parties, group teas, dinner or teas for two. The teas range from a light breakfast tea to the more extravagant Victorian High Tea. Murder-Mystery events also can be arranged.

Innkeeper(s): Becky & Rick Schoeneck. $85-175. MC, VISA, AX, DS, PC. 4 rooms, 1 with PB, 1 with FP. Breakfast and snacks/refreshments included in rates. Type of meal: Full gourmet bkfst. Beds: KD. Air conditioning. VCR on premises. Amusement parks, antiquing, fishing, live theater, parks, shopping, downhill skiing, cross-country skiing and sporting events nearby.

Location: Small town.

Certificate may be used: Year round except holiday weekends and based on room availability.

Hinckley   F6

Dakota Lodge B&B

Rt 3 Box 178
Hinckley, MN 55037-9418
(320)384-6052

Circa 1976. Although this inn is situated between Minneapolis and Duluth on six scenic acres, the innkeepers named their B&B in honor of their birthplace: North Dakota. The guest rooms are named after little known Dakota towns. The Medora and Kathryn rooms include whirlpools and fireplaces. Other rooms include lacy curtains, quilts and special furnishings. The country breakfasts are expansive with egg and meat dishes, fruit and a daily entree. Hinckley offers a variety of activities, including a 32-mile bike trail, a casino and antique shops.

Innkeeper(s): Mike Schmitz & Tad Hilborn. $58-135. MC, VISA, DS, PC, TC.

5 rooms with PB, 4 with FP and 1 cottage. Breakfast included in rates. Types of meals: Full bkfst and early coffee/tea. Beds: KQ. Ceiling fan in room. Air conditioning. VCR, fax, copier and library on premises. Antiquing, fishing, parks, cross-country skiing and water sports nearby.

Location: Country.

Certificate may be used: All year, Sunday-Thursday, excluding holidays.

Kenyon   I6

Grandfather's Woods

3640 450th St
Kenyon, MN 55946-3626
(507)789-6414

Circa 1860. This 440-acre working farm boasts a handsome two-story Scandinavian clapboard home, and off in the woods, the original log cabin built six generations ago by the Langemo family. Abraham Lincoln personally endorsed the original homestead document displayed in the house. Old photos include one of Grandfather Jorgen next to a tiny tree in 1861. The same tree has grown to giant proportions and now shades the entire house. An antique rocking chair, now in the parlor, is seen in an ancient photo of Great-grandmother Karen. The Solarium, one of the bedrooms, has a brass bed and wicker furniture, and it looks out over the fishpond and garden to the fields and woods along the river. There are 65 acres of wooded trails on the property. Guests enjoy the farm's horses and sheep, and in springtime, the young lamb. The inn offers hay and sleigh rides, cross-country skiing, croquet, a large flower garden and a nine-hole golf course across from the hay field. A fancy farm breakfast may include homemade caramel rolls and oven eggs. It is halfway between Minneapolis/St. Paul and Rochester, Minn.

Innkeeper(s): Judy & George Langemo. $70-120. PC. 3 rooms, 2 with PB, 1 with FP and 1 suite. Breakfast and snacks/refreshments included in rates. Types of meals: Full bkfst, cont and early coffee/tea. Beds: QDT. Ceiling fan in room. VCR, stables, bicycles, library and skiis on premises. Antiquing, fishing, golf, sleigh/hay rides, live theater, parks, shopping, downhill skiing, cross-country skiing, sporting events and water sports nearby.

Location: Country.

Publicity: *Rochester Post-Bulletin, Republican Eagle-Red Wing and Life & Leisure.*

Certificate may be used: March 1 to July 30, Sunday-Thursday.

Lanesboro   J7

Mrs. B's Historic Lanesboro Inn & Restaurant

101 Parkway, PO BOX 411
Lanesboro, MN 55949-0411
(507)467-2154 (800)657-4710

Circa 1872. Steep bluffs surround Lanesboro on three sides with hundreds of forested acres, providing spectacular fall colors. Mrs. B's is an old limestone building that was once a furniture store and funeral parlor. Now handsomely renovated and furnished, the inn has a baby grand piano and a well-stocked library in the downstairs lobby. Four-poster and half-canopied beds in the upstairs guest rooms are topped with quilts. Weekend dinner packages are tasty and highly recommended. (Ask for the baked trout with pilaf or fillet of beef tenderloin with Yorkshire pudding.) The inn has a resident story-teller.

Innkeeper(s): Bill Sermeus & Mimi Abell. $50-95. PC. 10 rooms with PB, 2 with FP, 2 suites and 1 conference room. Breakfast included in rates. Type of meal: Full bkfst. Beds: QT. Air conditioning. Library on premises.

Antiquing, fishing, golf, environmental Learning Center, live theater, parks, shopping, cross-country skiing and tennis nearby.

Location: rural town.

Publicity: *Travel & Leisure and Minneapolis Star-Tribune.*

"One of the best B&B stays we have ever had. Outstanding breakfasts!"

Certificate may be used: Oct. 26-May 28, Monday through Thursday.

Lutsen D8

Lindgren's B&B on Lake Superior

5552 County Rd 35, PO Box 56
Lutsen, MN 55612-0056
(218)663-7450

Circa 1926. This '20s log home is in the Superior National Forest on the north shore of Lake Superior. The inn features massive stone fireplaces, a baby grand piano, wildlife decor and a Finnish-style sauna. The living room has tongue-and-groove, Western knotty cedar wood paneling and seven-foot windows offering a view of the lake. In addition to horseshoes and a bonfire pit, guests can gaze at the lake on a swinging love seat.

Innkeeper(s): Shirley Lindgren. $90-135. MC, VISA, PC. 4 rooms with PB, 1 with FP. Breakfast included in rates. Types of meals: Cont plus and early coffee/tea. Beds: KDT. One room with two-person whirlpool in room. VCR, library and CD player on premises. Antiquing, bicycling, canoeing/kayaking, fishing, golf, hiking, horseback riding, fall colors, snowmobiling, state parks, live theater, shopping, downhill skiing, cross-country skiing, tennis and water sports nearby.

Location: Forest Lake.

Publicity: *Country, Brainerd Daily Dispatch, Duluth News-Tribune, Tempo, Midwest Living, Minnesota Monthly, Lake Superior and Minneapolis-St. Paul.*

Certificate may be used: Midweek (Monday-Thursday) April 1-June 1 and Nov. 1-Dec. 15, holidays excluded.

Morris G3

The American House

410 E 3rd St
Morris, MN 56267-1426
(320)589-4054

Circa 1900. One block from the Morris campus of the University of Minnesota, this is a two-story house with a wide veranda. It is decorated in a country style with original stencil designs, stained glass and family heirlooms. The Elizabeth Room holds a Jenny Lind bed with a hand-crocheted bedcover.

Innkeeper(s): Karen Berget. $40-60. MC, VISA, PC, TC. 3 rooms. Breakfast included in rates. Type of meal: Full bkfst. Beds: D. TV and ceiling fan in room. Air conditioning. Bicycles on premises. Fishing, shopping and cross-country skiing nearby.

Location: City.

Publicity: *Forum and Hancock Record.*

"It was most delightful!"

Certificate may be used: Anytime, subject to availability.

Nevis E4

The Park Street Inn

106 Park St
Nevis, MN 56467-9704
(218)652-4500 (800)797-1778
Internet: www.parkstreetinn.com

Circa 1912. This late Victorian home was built by one of Minnesota's many Norwegian immigrants, a prominent businessman. He picked an ideal spot for the home, which overlooks Lake

Belle Taine and sits across from a town park. The suite includes an all-season porch and a double whirlpool tub. The Grotto Room, a new addition, offers an oversize whirlpool and a waterfall. Oak lamposts light the foyer, and the front parlor is highlighted by a Mission oak fireplace. Homemade fare such as waffles, pancakes, savory meats, egg dishes and French toast are served during the inn's daily country breakfast. Bicyclists will appreciate the close access to the Heartland Bike Trail, just half a block away.

Innkeeper(s): Irene & Len Hall. $70-125. MC, VISA, PC, TC. 4 rooms with PB and 1 suite. Breakfast included in rates. Types of meals: Full bkfst and early coffee/tea. Beds: KQD. VCR, spa, bicycles and library on premises. Amusement parks, antiquing, fishing, golf, parks, shopping, cross-country skiing and water sports nearby.

Pets allowed: By arrangement only.

Location: Small town.

"Our favorite respite in the Heartland, where the pace is slow, hospitality is great and food is wonderful."

Certificate may be used: Sept. 15 to May 15, Sunday-Thursday, except holidays.

New York Mills F3

Whistle Stop Inn B&B

RR 1 Box 85
New York Mills, MN 56567-9704
(218)385-2223 (800)328-6315

Circa 1903. A choo-choo theme permeates the atmosphere at this signature Victorian home. Antiques and railroad memorabilia decorate guest rooms with names such as Great Northern or Burlington Northern. The Northern Pacific room includes a bath with a clawfoot tub. For something unusual, try a night in the beautifully restored 19th-century Pullman dining car. It is paneled in mahogany and features floral carpeting as well as a double whirlpool, TV, VCR and refrigerator. A caboose offers a queen-size Murphy bed, whirlpool, TV, VCR and refrigerator. A second Pullman car with the same amenities has just been added and it features a gas-burning fireplace.

Innkeeper(s): Roger & Jann Lee. $65-135. MC, VISA, AX, DS, PC. 5 rooms, 2 with PB, 1 suite and 1 conference room. Breakfast included in rates. Types of meals: Full bkfst, cont and early coffee/tea. Beds: QD. Cable TV, phone, ceiling fan and microwave in room. Bicycles on premises. Antiquing, fishing, golf, snowmobiling trails & cultural center, parks, shopping, cross-country skiing and tennis nearby.

Publicity: *USA Weekend, Minneapolis Tribune, Fargo Forum, ABC-Fargo, WDAY, Fargo, Channel 14 and Fergus Falls.*

Certificate may be used: Year-round, Sunday-Thursday, excluding holidays.

Saint Charles J7

Victorian Lace Inn B&B and Tea Room

1512 Whitewater Ave
Saint Charles, MN 55972-1234
(507)932-4496
Internet: www.bluffcountry.com

Circa 1859. This newly restored brick Victorian features a pleasant front porch where guests often linger to watch an occasional Amish buggy pass by. Lace curtains and antique furnishings are features of the guest rooms.

Innkeeper(s): Sharon Vreeman. $70-85. MC, VISA, AX, PC, TC. 4 rooms. Breakfast included in rates. Types of meals: Full gourmet bkfst and early coffee/tea. Beds: QD. Clock in room. Air conditioning. VCR, bicycles and library on premises. Antiquing, fishing, golf, live theater, parks, shopping, cross-country skiing, tennis and water sports nearby.

"They have thought of everything."

Certificate may be used: January-December, Sunday-Thursday, except holidays.

Stillwater   H6

Cover Park Manor

15330 58th St N
Stillwater, MN 55082-6508
(651)430-9292 (877)430-9292 Fax:(651)430-0034
Internet: www.coverpark.com
E-mail: coverpark@coverpark.com

Circa 1870. Cover Park, a historic Victorian home, rests adjacent to its namesake park on an acre of grounds. Two guest rooms offer a view of the park and the St. Croix River. Each room includes a fireplace and a whirlpool tub. Amenities include items such as refrigerators, stereos and TVs. In addition to the whirlpool and fireplace, Adell's Suite  includes a king-size white iron bed, a sitting room and a private porch. Breakfasts include fresh fruit, one-half-dozen varieties of freshly baked pastries and special entrees. The manor is one mile from historic Stillwater's main street.

Innkeeper(s): Chuck & Judy Dougherty. $89-179. MC, VISA, AX, DC, DS, PC, TC. 4 rooms with PB, 4 with FP and 2 suites. Breakfast and snacks/refreshments included in rates. Types of meals: Full gourmet bkfst and early coffee/tea. Beds: KQ. Cable TV and phone in room. Air conditioning. Fax and copier on premises. Handicap access. Amusement parks, antiquing, fishing, golf, live theater, parks, shopping, downhill skiing, cross-country skiing, sporting events, tennis and water sports nearby.
Publicity: *Pioneer Press, Star Tribune, Country Magazine and Courier.*
Certificate may be used: Jan. 2-Aug. 15, Monday-Thursday, not on holidays.

James A. Mulvey Residence Inn

622 W Churchill
Stillwater, MN 55082
(651)430-8008 (800)820-8008
Internet: www.jamesmulveyinn.com
E-mail: truettldem@aol.com

Circa 1878. A charming river town is home to this Italianate-style inn, just a short distance from the Twin Cities, but far from the metro area in atmosphere. Visitors select from seven guest rooms, many decorated Victorian style. The three suites have Southwest, Art Deco or Country French themes, and there are double Jacuzzi tubs and fireplaces. The inn, just nine blocks from the St. Croix River, is a popular stop for couples celebrating anniversaries. Guests enjoy early coffee or tea service that precedes the full breakfasts. A handsome great room in the vine-covered Carriage House invites relaxation. Antiquing, fishing and skiing are nearby, and there are many picnic spots in the area.

Innkeeper(s): Truett & Jill Lawson. $99-199. MC, VISA, PC, TC. 7 rooms with PB, 7 with FP and 3 suites. Breakfast and afternoon tea included in rates. Types of meals: Full gourmet bkfst and early coffee/tea. Beds: QD. Seven double whirlpool Jacuzzi tubs in room. Air conditioning. Bicycles on premises. Antiquing, fishing, 30 minutes from Mall of America, live theater, parks, shopping, downhill skiing, cross-country skiing and water sports nearby.
Location: City.
Publicity: *Cover of Christian B&B Directory.*
Certificate may be used: Monday-Thursday, excluding September-October.

Walker   E4

Peacecliff

7361 Breezy Point Road NW
Walker, MN 56484-9579
(218)547-2832

Circa 1957. Innkeepers Dave and Kathy Laursen are Minnesota natives, and after years away, returned to their home state and opened this serene, waterfront B&B. The English Tudor affords views of Lake Leech from most of its rooms, which are decorated with a mix of traditional and Victorian furnishings. The Laursens are nature lovers, having trekked across miles of mountain trails and scenic areas. They are happy to point out nearby recreation sites, including the North Country Trail, a 68-mile journey through Chippewa National Forest. There are also 150 miles of paved bike trails to enjoy.

Innkeeper(s): Dave & Kathy Laursen. $65-125. MC, VISA, AX, DS, TC. 5 rooms, 2 with PB, 1 with FP and 1 suite. Breakfast included in rates. Types of meals: Full gourmet bkfst and early coffee/tea. Beds: KQDT. VCR on premises. Amusement parks, antiquing, fishing, bike trails, live theater, parks, shopping, cross-country skiing and water sports nearby.
Certificate may be used: Sunday-Thursday, except holidays.

Mississippi

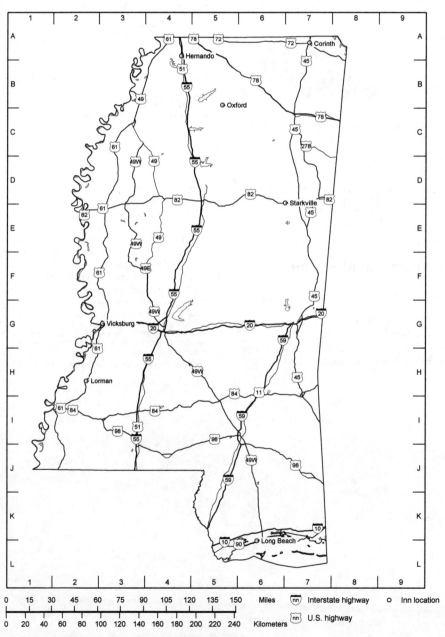

1	2	3	4	5	6	7	8	9

0 15 30 45 60 75 90 105 120 135 150   Miles   🅽🅽 Interstate highway   ○ Inn location

0 20 40 60 80 100 120 140 160 180 200 220 240   Kilometers   🅽🅽 U.S. highway

Corinth A7

Samuel D. Bramlett House

1125 Cruise St
Corinth, MS 38834
(601)286-5370 (800)484-1107 Fax:(601)287-7467
Internet: www.tsixroads.com/corinth/bramlltt.html
E-mail: thom112@avsia.com

Circa 1892. This Queen Anne Victorian boasts several decorated gables and a wraparound porch fringed with intricate fretwork, all beautifully restored. Four verandas are furnished with white wicker rocking chairs and swings, and each has its own ceiling fan. The inn is filled with antiques including an old pump organ. Ornately carved Victorian fireplaces and a staircase add character. Formal gardens surround the house. Nearby attractions include Civil War reenactments, a Civil War walking tour and Shiloh National Military Park.

Innkeeper(s): Cindy & Kevin Thomas. $75-85. MC, VISA, AX, PC, TC. 3 suites, 3 with FP and 2 conference rooms. Breakfast, afternoon tea and snacks/refreshments included in rates. Types of meals: Full gourmet bkfst and early coffee/tea. Beds: DT. Turndown service, ceiling fan, complimentary tea service and private verandas in room. Air conditioning. VCR, fax, copier, library, child care and beautiful gardens on premises. Antiquing, fishing, golf, live theater, parks, shopping, sporting events, tennis and water sports nearby.

Location: Small Southern town.

Publicity: *Country Victorian.*

"This has been a wonderful introduction to the world of B&Bs. Your home has captivated us with its historical beauty and charm."

Certificate may be used: Jan. 1 to Dec. 31, Sunday-Friday.

Hernando A4

Sassafras Inn

785 Hwy 51 S
Hernando, MS 38632-8149
(601)429-5864 (800)882-1897 Fax:(601)429-4591
E-mail: sassyinn@mem.net

Circa 1985. This modern inn offers guests to the state's Northwest corner a delightful respite from their travels or from the hustle and bustle of Memphis, 10 miles south. An impressive indoor swimming pool and spa are guest favorites and visitors also enjoy the cabana room for reading or lounging, or the recreation room with billiards, darts and ping pong. A romantic honeymoon cottage also is available. Arkabutla Lake is an easy drive from the inn.

Innkeeper(s): Dennis & Francee McClanahan. $75-225. MC, VISA, AX, DS, PC, TC. 4 rooms, 3 with PB, 1 suite and 1 cottage. Breakfast, afternoon tea and snacks/refreshments included in rates. Types of meals: Full bkfst and early coffee/tea. Beds: QD. Cable TV, phone, turndown service, ceiling fan and VCR in room. Air conditioning. Fax, copier, spa, swimming, library, indoor pool, basketball and billiards on premises. Antiquing, parks and water sports nearby.

Publicity: *Memphis Commercial Appeal, DeSoto Times, Claridon Ledger, Los Angeles Times and WHBQ Romantic Getaways.*

Certificate may be used: All year, Sunday through Thursday, no holidays.

Long Beach L6

Red Creek Inn, Vineyard & Racing Stable

7416 Red Creek Rd
Long Beach, MS 39560-8804
(228)452-3080 (800)729-9670 Fax:(228)452-4450
Internet: redcreekinn.com
E-mail: info@redcreekinn.com

Circa 1899. This inn was built in the raised French cottage-style by a retired Italian sea captain, who wished to entice his bride to move from her parents' home in New Orleans. There  are two swings on the 64-foot front porch and one swing that hangs from a 300-year-old oak tree. Magnolias and ancient live oaks, some registered with the Live Oak Society of the Louisiana Garden Club, dot 11 acres. The inn features a parlor, six fireplaces, ceiling fans and antiques, including a Victorian organ, wooden radios and a Victrola. The inn's suite includes a Jacuzzi tub.

Innkeeper(s): Karl & Toni Mertz. $49-134. PC. 6 rooms, 5 with PB, 1 with FP, 1 suite and 1 conference room. Breakfast included in rates. Types of meals: Cont plus and early coffee/tea. Beds: QDT. TV in room. Air conditioning. VCR, fax, copier and library on premises. Amusement parks, antiquing, fishing, golf, casinos, live theater, parks, shopping and water sports nearby.

Location: Country.

Publicity: *Jackson Daily News, Innviews, Men's Journal, The Bridal Directory., TV Channel 13 and Mississippi ETV.*

"We loved waking up here on these misty spring mornings. The Old South is here."

Certificate may be used: Sunday-Thursday, May-August and any time September-April (depending upon availability). Holidays usually excluded.

Lorman H2

Rosswood Plantation

Hwy 552 East
Lorman, MS 39096
(601)437-4215 (800)533-5889 Fax:(601)437-6888
Internet: www.rosswood.net
E-mail: whylander@aol.com

Circa 1857. Rosswood is a stately, columned mansion in an original plantation setting. Here, guests may find antiques, buried treasure, ghosts, history of a slave revolt, a Civil War battleground, the first owner's diary and genuine southern hospitality. Voted the "prettiest place in the country" by Farm & Ranch Living, the manor is a Mississippi Landmark and is in the National Register.

Innkeeper(s): Jean & Walt Hylander. $115-135. MC, VISA, AX, DS, PC, TC. 4 rooms with PB, 4 with FP. Breakfast included in rates. Types of meals: Full gourmet bkfst and early coffee/tea. Beds: QDT. Phone, ceiling fan, VCR and tV in room. Air conditioning. Fax, copier, spa, swimming, library, metal detector for treasure hunting and movies on video tape on premises. Antiquing, fishing, deer Hunting, treasure hunting, parks and shopping nearby.

Location: Country.

Publicity: *Southern Living, The New York Times, Mississippi Magazine, Inn Country USA and PBS Series "Inn Country USA"*

Certificate may be used: June, July, August, Sunday through Thursday.

Oxford B5

Oliver-Britt House

512 Van Buren Ave
Oxford, MS 38655-3838
(601)234-8043

Circa 1905. White columns and a picturesque veranda highlight the exterior of this Greek Revival inn shaded by trees. English country comfort is the emphasis in the interior, which includes a collection of antiques. On weekends, guests are treated to a Southern-style breakfast with all the trimmings. A travel service is located on the premises.

Innkeeper(s): Glynn Oliver & Mary Ann Britt. $55-75. MC, VISA, AX, DS, TC. 5 rooms with PB. Breakfast included in rates. Types of meals: Full bkfst and early coffee/tea. Beds: KQ. Cable TV and ceiling fan in room. Air conditioning. Antiquing, parks, shopping and sporting events nearby.

Pets Allowed.

Location: City.

Certificate may be used: Dec. 1-Feb. 28, Sunday-Thursday.

Starkville D7

The Cedars B&B

2173 Oktoc Rd
Starkville, MS 39759-9251
(601)324-7569

Circa 1836. This historic plantation offers a glimpse of life in the 19th-century South. The late Colonial/Greek Revival structure was built primarily by slaves, with construction lasting two years. The inn's 183 acres boast fishing ponds, pasture and woods, and guests love to explore, hike and ride horses. Four guest rooms are available, two with private bath. Visitors enjoy the inn's collection of 19th- and early 20th-century horse and farm equipment. Noxubee Wildlife Refuge and the Tombigbee National Forest are within easy driving distance.

Innkeeper(s): Erin Scanlon. $50-65. TC. 4 rooms, 2 with PB, 4 with FP and 2 conference rooms. Breakfast and snacks/refreshments included in rates. Types of meals: Full bkfst, cont plus, cont and early coffee/tea. Beds: T. Refrigerator by request in room. Air conditioning. Antiquing, fishing, live theater, parks, shopping, sporting events and water sports nearby.

Pets Allowed.

Location: 19th Century plantation.

Certificate may be used: Anytime based on availability.

Vicksburg G3

Balfour House

1002 Crawford St
Vicksburg, MS 39181-0781
(601)638-7113 (800)294-7113
Internet: www.balfourhouse.com

Circa 1835. Writer and former resident Emma Balfour witnessed the Siege of Vicksburg from the window of this Greek Revival

home. Until the Civil War, the home was the site of elegant balls attended by Southern belles in ornate gowns accompanied by Confederate beaus. Innkeepers Bob and Sharon Humble brought back these grand affairs during several re-enactment dances, in which guests dress up in period costume. The National Register home is a piece of history, with stunning architectural features, such as the showpiece, three-story elliptical spiral staircase. The home is an official site on the Civil War Discovery Trail, as well as a Vicksburg and Mississippi landmark.

Innkeeper(s): Bob & Sharon Humble. $85-150. MC, VISA, AX, PC, TC. 4 rooms with PB, 1 with FP and 1 conference room. Breakfast included in rates. Type of meal: Full gourmet bkfst. Beds: KQDT. Cable TV and phone in room. Air conditioning. Amusement parks, antiquing, fishing, live theater, parks and shopping nearby.

Location: City.

Certificate may be used: Sunday-Thursday, no holidays.

Belle of The Bends

508 Klein St
Vicksburg, MS 39180-4004
(601)634-0737 (800)844-2308

Circa 1876. Located in Vicksburg's Historic Garden District, this Victorian, Italianate mansion was built by Mississippi State Sen. Murray F. Smith and his wife, Kate. It is nestled on a bluff overlooking the Mississippi River. The decor includes period antiques, Oriental rugs and memorabilia of the steamboats that plied the river waters in the 1880s and early 1900s. Two bedrooms and the first- and second-story wraparound verandas provide views of the river, as does the third-floor bedroom. A plantation breakfast is served and a tour of the house and history of the steamboats owned by the Morrissey Line is given. Or take a tour of the Victorian Gardens, which always have something in bloom. In addition to the views, there are fountains complete with goldfish.

Innkeeper(s): Wally & Jo Pratt. $85-135. MC, VISA, AX, PC, TC. 6 rooms with PB. Breakfast included in rates. Types of meals: Full bkfst and early coffee/tea. Beds: QD. Cable TV, phone, turndown service and VCR in room. Air conditioning. Library on premises. Antiquing, golf, shopping and tennis nearby.

Location: City.

Publicity: *Natchez Trace News Explorer, Victorian Style and Victoria.*

"Thank you for the personalized tour of the home and area. We greatly enjoyed our stay. This house got us into the spirit of the period."

Certificate may be used: Jan. 30 to March 1, Sunday-Thursday, excluding Valentine's Day weekend. Riverview Room and Captain Tom's Suite.

Missouri

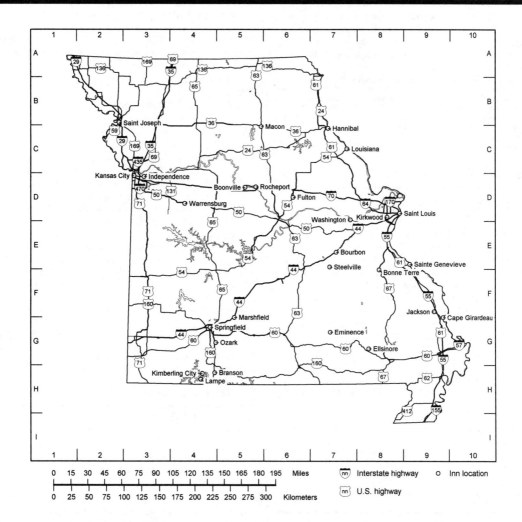

Miles 0 15 30 45 60 75 90 105 120 135 150 165 180 195

Kilometers 0 25 50 75 100 125 150 175 200 225 250 275 300

(nn) Interstate highway   o Inn location

(nn) U.S. highway

Bonne Terre *F8*

Victorian Veranda

207 E School St
Bonne Terre, MO 63628
(573)358-1134 (800)343-1134

Circa 1868. A veranda encircles this blue and white Queen Anne and there are finely crafted decorative details such as porch columns and dentil work. Furnishings in the dining room are country-style enhanced by light floral wallpaper, fine wood paneling and woodwork around the doors, all painted white. Egg casseroles, potatoes and coffee cakes are served here. There are eight state parks in the area and Cherokee Landing offers canoe trips along the river.

Innkeeper(s): Galen & Karen Forney. $70-90. MC, VISA, PC, TC. 4 rooms with PB, 1 with FP and 1 suite. Breakfast, afternoon tea and snacks/refreshments included in rates. Types of meals: Full gourmet bkfst and early coffee/tea. Beds: Q. Phone and ceiling fan in room. Air conditioning. VCR on premises. Antiquing, fishing, golf, scuba diving/cave, live theater, parks, shopping, sporting events, tennis and water sports nearby.

Location: small town.

Certificate may be used: Jan. 2 to Dec. 23, Sunday-Thursday.

Boonville *D5*

Morgan Street Repose B&B

611 E Morgan St
Boonville, MO 65233-1221
(660)882-7195 (800)248-5061

Circa 1869. The historic Missouri River town of Boonville is home to this inn, comprised of two Italianate structures on the site of what once was a hotel that served travelers on the Santa Fe Trail. The inn is listed in the National Register of Historic Places. More than 400 antebellum and Victorian homes and buildings are found in town. Visitors enjoy their gourmet breakfasts in one of three dining rooms or in the Secret Garden. Several state parks are within easy driving distance, and the University of Missouri-Columbia is 20 miles to the east.

Innkeeper(s): Victoria & Todd Dorman. $70-95. MC, VISA, PC. 3 rooms with PB. Breakfast and afternoon tea included in rates. Types of meals: Full bkfst and early coffee/tea. Beds: Q. Ceiling fan in room. Air conditioning. Antiquing and live theater nearby.

Location: Small historic town.

"We had a wonderful, romantic, relaxing honeymoon in the Ashley Suite. The hospitality and atmosphere exceeded our expectations by far. The memory of our stay here will last a lifetime."

Certificate may be used: December through March, Sunday through Thursday, excluding holidays based on availability.

Bourbon *E7*

Meramec Farm Bed and Board

208 Thickety Ford Rd
Bourbon, MO 65441
(573)732-4765
E-mail: mfarmbnb@fidnet.com

Circa 1883. This farmhouse inn and cedar guest cabin are found on a working cattle operation, little more than an hour's drive from St. Louis. Seven generations have lived and worked the farm, which boasts 460 acres. Visitors stay in the 1880s

farmhouse or the cabin, built from cedar cut on the farm. The inn's proximity to the Meramec River and Vilander Bluffs provides excellent views and many outdoor activities. Spring visitors are treated to the sight of baby calves. Meramec Caverns and several state parks are nearby.

Innkeeper(s): Carol Springer. $70-80. 2 rooms, 1 with PB and 1 cottage. Breakfast included in rates. Types of meals: Full bkfst and early coffee/tea. Beds: QDT. Ceiling fan, bBQ, picnic tables and porches in room. Air conditioning. Antiquing and fishing nearby.

Location: Country.

Publicity: *Midwest Motorist, St. Louis Post-Dispatch and St. Louis.*

Certificate may be used: Sunday-Thursday, year-round.

Branson *H4*

Aunt Sadies Garden Glade

163 Fountain St
Branson, MO 65616-9194
(417)335-4063 (800)944-4250 Fax:(417)336-6772
Internet: www.auntsadies.com
E-mail: hovelllin@aol.com

Circa 1965. This secluded home is nestled in a wooded glade, just five minutes from Branson's many activities. The modern ranch home offers two guest rooms in the main house, a cottage that sleeps up to five adults and a private honeymoon suite. Both the Paisley and Rose rooms have private hot tubs, and the Paisley also has a fireplace. Suite Infinity offers a king bed, fireplace and a two-person, heart-shaped whirlpool tub. All rooms have private entrances and some include modern amenities such as coffee makers, refrigerators and microwaves. The inn's big country breakfast, served family style, includes homemade biscuits and gravy, several entrees, fruit and pastry. A large outdoor deck is the perfect place for birdwatching, relaxing or socializing.

Innkeeper(s): Dick & Linda Hovell. $85-95. MC, VISA, AX, DS, PC, TC. 4 rooms, 2 with PB, 2 with FP, 2 suites and 2 cabins. Breakfast and snacks/refreshments included in rates. Types of meals: Full bkfst and early coffee/tea. Beds: KQ. Cable TV, phone, turndown service and ceiling fan in room. Air conditioning. Copier and spa on premises. Amusement parks, antiquing, fishing, golf, live theater, parks, shopping, tennis and water sports nearby.

Certificate may be used: Jan. 30-Sept. 1, Sunday-Thursday.

Cape Girardeau *G9*

Bellevue B&B

312 Bellevue St
Cape Girardeau, MO 63701-7233
(573)335-3302 (800)768-6822 Fax:(573)332-7752
Internet: www.flinthills.com:80/~atway/mo/bellevue.html
E-mail: bellevuebb@compuserv.com

Circa 1891. Within three blocks of Mississippi River front Park, this Queen Anne Victorian with gables and bay windows is in the local historic register. The house is painted deep hunter green with taupe and cranberry trim, emphasizing the historic craftsmanship of its gables, bay windows, balustrades, cornices and stained glass windows. A glider and two wicker rocking chairs sit on the front porch. Inside, the original woodwork remains as well as sev-

eral sets of original pocket doors and fireplaces. Ask for the Parkridge Room where a six-foot high antique headboard is the focal point or for the Shea Lorraine or Dearborn rooms, both with large whirlpool tubs. There's a fireplace on the patio for evening get-togethers. SEMO University is nearby.

Innkeeper(s): Marsha Toll. $70-105. MC, VISA, AX, DS, PC, TC. 4 rooms with PB. Breakfast included in rates. Type of meal: Full bkfst. Beds: Q. Cable TV, ceiling fan, whirlpool and phones in some rooms in room. Air conditioning.

Location: City.

Certificate may be used: All year.

Ellsinore   G8

Alcorn Corner B&B

HCR 3 Box 247
Ellsinore, MO 63937
(573)322-5297

Circa 1904. Surrounded by 20 acres, this simple Victorian farmhouse is the kind of bed & breakfast guests will enjoy sharing with their children. There are farm animals, and the innkeeper, a former teacher, is like a grandma to families. Early American furnishings are found in the two guest rooms, and a family-style breakfast with three menu choices is offered.

Innkeeper(s): Virgie Alcorn Evans. $35-50. TC. 2 rooms. Beds: DT. Turndown service in room. VCR and library on premises. Antiquing, museums, parks and shopping nearby.

Location: Country.

Certificate may be used: May 25 to Nov. 15 Monday-Friday, excluding holidays.

Eminence   G7

Old Blue House B&B

301 S Main St
Eminence, MO 65466-0117
(573)226-3498 (800)474-9695

Circa 1800. This old two-story frame house once was home to a beauty shop, grocery store and pharmacy. There are antiques throughout and framed prints, much of which is for sale. The garden is shaded by maple and magnolia trees and there are peonies, lilacs and roses. Breakfast is continental plus. However, if you'd like a country breakfast with sausage, gravy, scrambled eggs and homemade biscuits there is an extra charge. Eminence is located in the Ozark National Scenic Riverway.

Innkeeper(s): Wanda L. Pummill. $60-85. MC, VISA, AX, DS, PC, TC. 3 rooms with PB. Breakfast and snacks/refreshments included in rates. Types of meals: Full bkfst, cont plus and early coffee/tea. Beds: D. Cable TV and ceiling fan in room. Air conditioning. VCR, badminton and horseshoes on premises. Antiquing, fishing, golf, cross-country trail rides, parks, shopping and water sports nearby.

Location: City.

Publicity: *St. Louis Post Dispatch, Midwest Living and B&B Guest House and Inns of Missouri.*

Certificate may be used: Jan. 1 to Dec. 31, Sunday-Thursday only, no holidays or holiday weekends.

Fulton   D6

Romancing The Past Victorian B&B

830 Court St
Fulton, MO 65251
(573)592-1996 Fax:(573)592-1999
Internet: www.romancingthepast.com
E-mail: innkeepers@sockets.net

Circa 1867. A porch wraps around this pristine Victorian home and offers white wicker furnishings. There's a hammock and hot tub in the garden. Finely crafted and restored fretwork, brackets and bay windows decorate the exterior. Polished woodwork, a gracious staircase and parquet floors are highlighted with well-chosen Victorian antiques. The Renaissance Suite boasts a fainting couch and carved walnut canopy bed, a sitting room and a large bath decorated in the Neoclassical style.

Innkeeper(s): Jim & ReNee Yeager. $100-170. MC, VISA, AX, DS, PC, TC. 3 rooms with PB, 3 with FP. Breakfast, afternoon tea and snacks/refreshments included in rates. Types of meals: Full gourmet bkfst, cont and early coffee/tea. Beds: Q. Phone, turndown service, ceiling fan and clock in room. VCR, fax, copier, spa, bicycles and library on premises. Antiquing, fishing, golf, UMC, bike trails, live theater, parks, shopping, sporting events and tennis nearby.

Pets allowed: pets are not allowed inside the inn.

Location: Small town, beautiful historic neighborhood.

Certificate may be used: Sunday-Thursday.

Hannibal   C7

Fifth Street Mansion B&B

213 S 5th St
Hannibal, MO 63401-4421
(573)221-0445 (800)874-5661 Fax:(573)221-3335
Internet: www.hanmo.com/fifthstreetmansion
E-mail: 5thstbb@nemonet.com

Circa 1858. This 20-room Italianate house listed in the National Register displays extended eaves and heavy brackets, tall windows and decorated lintels. A cupola affords a view of the town. Mark Twain was invited to dinner here by the Garth family and joined Laura Frazer (his Becky Thatcher) for the evening. An enormous stained-glass window lights the stairwell. The library features a stained-glass window with the family crest and is paneled with handgrained walnut.

Innkeeper(s): Donalene & Mike Andreotti. $65-110. MC, VISA, AX, DS, TC. 7 rooms with PB and 1 conference room. Breakfast included in rates. Type of meal: Full bkfst. Beds: Q. TV and phone in room. Air conditioning. VCR and fax on premises. Antiquing, fishing and shopping nearby.

Location: River town.

Publicity: *Insider and Country Inns.*

"We thoroughly enjoyed our visit. Terrific food and hospitality!"

Certificate may be used: Nov. 1 to April 30, Sunday-Thursday.

Independence   D3

Woodstock Inn B&B

1212 W Lexington Ave
Independence, MO 64050-3524
(816)833-2233 (800)276-5202 Fax:(816)461-7226
Internet: www.independence-missouri.com
E-mail: woodstock@independence-missouri.com

Circa 1900. This home, originally built as a doll and quilt factory, is in the perfect location for sightseeing in historic
Independence. Visit the home of Harry S Truman or the
Truman Library and Museum. The Old Jail Museum is another
popular attraction. A large country breakfast is served each
morning featuring malted Belgian waffles and an additional
entree. Independence is less than 30 minutes from Kansas City,
where you may spend the day browsing through the shops at
Country Club Plaza or Halls' Crown Center.

Innkeeper(s): Todd & Patricia Justice. $69-189. MC, VISA, AX, DS, PC, TC.
11 rooms with PB and 2 suites. Breakfast included in rates. Types of meals:
Full bkfst and early coffee/tea. Beds: KQDT. Cable TV, phone, turndown service, VCR and fireplaces in room. Air conditioning. Fax on premises.
Handicap access. Amusement parks, antiquing, art galleries, fishing, golf, live
theater, museums, parks, shopping and sporting events nearby.

Location: City.

Publicity: Country and San Francisco Chronicle.

"Pleasant, accommodating people, a facility of good character."

Certificate may be used: Dec. 1-Feb. 28, anytime, subject to availability.

Jackson   F9

Trisha's B&B

203 Bellevue
Jackson, MO 63755
(573)243-7427

Circa 1905. This inn offers a sitting room, tea room and spacious guest rooms. Some rooms have bay windows and are furnished with antiques and family heirlooms. Trisha provides
unique teas and serves hand-picked fruits and homemade
baked goods.

Innkeeper(s): Trisha Wischmann. $55-80. MC, VISA, AX, DS, TC. 4 rooms with
PB and 2 conference rooms. Breakfast included in rates. Type of meal: Full
gourmet bkfst. Beds: KQD. TV and phone in room. Historic steam train nearby.

Publicity: Cash-Book Journal and Southeast Missourian.

*"You have created a beautiful home so naturally. Your B&B is filled
with love and care—a really special place."*

Certificate may be used: Year-round, Sunday-Thursday.

Kansas City   D3

Dome Ridge

14360 NW Walker Rd
Kansas City, MO 64163-1519
(816)532-4074

Circa 1985. The innkeeper custom-built this inn, a geodesic
dome in a country setting just 10 minutes from the airport.
One guest room boasts a king bed with a white iron and brass
headboard, double spa and separate shower. In the inn's common areas, guests may enjoy a barbecue, CD player, fireplace,
gazebo, library and pool table. The gourmet breakfasts, usually

featuring Belgian waffles or California omelets, are served in the
dining room, but guests are advised that the inn's kitchen is
well worth checking out.

Innkeeper(s): Roberta Faust. $70-95. 4 rooms, 3 with PB. Breakfast includ-
ed in rates. Types of meals: Full bkfst and early coffee/tea. Beds: KQDT. Air
conditioning. VCR, pool table, BBQ and Gazebo on premises. Amusement
parks, antiquing, fishing, live theater, shopping, downhill skiing and sporting
events nearby.

Location: 10 min from airport in country.

Certificate may be used: Sunday through Thursday, all year. Holidays excluded.

Kimberling City   H4

Cinnamon Hill B&B

24 Wildwood Ln
Kimberling City, MO 65686-9515
(417)739-5727 (800)925-1556
Internet: www.bbonline.com/mo/cinnamon

Circa 1984. Cinnamon Hill is a homey place for guests, and it
is especially convenient for those heading to Branson, which is
just a half-hour drive away. There are four guest rooms featuring a comfortable country decor, and each has a private
entrance and access to the deck. Breakfast is a highlight,
innkeeper Shirley DeVrient prepares an abundance of country
fare. Guests feast on fresh fruit, eggs, bacon or sausage, biscuits
& gravy, homemade breads and plenty of coffee, juice and tea.

Innkeeper(s): Shirley DeVrient. $55-65. MC, VISA, PC. 4 rooms with PB.
Breakfast included in rates. Types of meals: Full bkfst and early coffee/tea.
Beds: QDT. Cable TV, phone, turndown service and ceiling fan in room. Air
conditioning. Amusement parks, antiquing, fishing, golf, live theater, shopping, tennis and water sports nearby.

Location: Mountains.

Publicity: Ozark Mountain Visitor.

*"Thanks for the great place to stay! The room is lovely and the break-
fasts were delicious!"*

Certificate may be used: Anytime when there is a vacancy from Jan. 1-May 31.

Kirkwood   D8

Fissy's Place

500 N Kirkwood Rd
Kirkwood, MO 63122-3914
(314)821-4494

Circa 1939. The innkeeper's past is just about as interesting as
the history of this bed & breakfast. A former Miss Missouri, the
innkeeper has acted in movies with the likes of Burt Reynolds
and Robert Redford, and pictures of many movie stars decorate
the home's interior. A trained interior designer, she also shares
this talent in the cheerfully decorated guest rooms. Historic
downtown Kirkwood is within walking distance to the home,
which also offers close access to St. Louis.

Innkeeper(s): Fay Haas. $69-76. MC, VISA, PC, TC. 3 rooms with PB and 1
conference room. Breakfast and snacks/refreshments included in rates. Types
of meals: Full bkfst, cont plus and early coffee/tea. Beds: QDT. Cable TV,
phone, turndown service, ceiling fan and VCR in room. Air conditioning.
Copier on premises. Handicap access. Antiquing, many fine restaurants, live
theater, parks, shopping and sporting events nearby.

Location: Suburb of St. Louis.

Certificate may be used: Sunday-Thursday, January-March.

Lampe   H4

Grandpa's Farm B&B

HC 3, PO Box 476
Lampe, MO 65681-0476
(417)779-5106 (800)280-5106
Internet: www.grandpasfarmbandb.com
E-mail: keithpat@inter-line.net

Circa 1891. This limestone farmhouse in the heart of the
Ozarks offers guests a chance to experience country life in a
relaxed farm setting. Midway between Silver Dollar City and
Eureka Springs, Ark., and close to Branson, the inn boasts several lodging options, including a duplex with suites and a honeymoon suite. The innkeepers are known for their substantial
country breakfast and say guests enjoy comparing how long the
meal lasts before they eat again. Although the inn's 116 acres
are not farmed extensively, domesticated farm animals are on
the premises.

Innkeeper(s): Keith & Pat Lamb. $65-95. MC, VISA, DS, PC, TC. 4 suites.
Breakfast included in rates. Type of meal: Full bkfst. Beds: KQ. Ceiling fan in
room. Air conditioning. VCR, fax, spa and RCA satellite dish with 32-inch TV
screen on premises. Handicap access. Amusement parks, antiquing, fishing,
country western shows, Passion Plays in Branson, live theater, parks, shopping and water sports nearby.

Location: Country.

Certificate may be used: All months except June, July, August, October, no
major holidays.

Louisiana   C7

Meadowcrest Bed & Breakfast

15282 Hwy NN
Louisiana, MO 63353
(573)754-6594 Fax:(573)754-5406
E-mail: reflectionsofmo@big-river.com

Circa 1965. Art lovers will enjoy a stay at this cozy bed &
breakfast, the home of Missouri historian artist John Stoeckley.
Along with his own pieces, he and wife, Karen, have decorated
the home with other fine artwork and a collection of furnishings
acquired on world travels, as well as antiques and family heirlooms. There are 12 wooded acres with hiking trails to explore.
Guests often relax in the sitting room, where a warming fire is
often crackling away. There is a fireplace and classic billiard table
in the home's billiard room, as well. If weather permits, breakfasts, perhaps French toast, country bacon, herbed potatoes,
fruit and homemade muffins, are served in the pavilion. The
innkeepers also have a gallery in town located in an 1837 stagecoach stop. Guests receive a key for the gallery, so they are free
to let themselves in at their leisure. John's artwork, as well as
work from other Missouri artists, is on display. For an extra
charge, special dinners can be arranged at the gallery, and there
is a small conference room there, as well.

Innkeeper(s): John & Karen Stoeckley. $75-85. PC, TC. 2 rooms, 1 with PB.
Breakfast and snacks/refreshments included in rates. Types of meals: Full
gourmet bkfst and early coffee/tea. Beds: QD. Ceiling fan in room. Air conditioning. Fax, spa, sauna, billiards and nature trails on premises. Antiquing,
fishing, golf, live theater, parks, shopping, cross-country skiing, tennis and
water sports nearby.

Location: country.

"What a house. What a gallery. What a meal. We love this place."

Certificate may be used: Jan. 15 to Nov. 30, any days, subject to availability.

Serando's House

918 Georgia St, PO Box 205
Louisiana, MO 63353-1812
(573)754-4067 (800)754-4067

Circa 1876. Southerners traveling up the Mississippi River discovered this lush area in the early 19th century, founded it and
named their little town Louisiana. The town still features many
of the earliest structures in the downtown historic district.
Serando's House still showcases much of its original woodwork
and stained glass. The two guest rooms are comfortably furnished, and one includes a balcony. Guests select their breakfast from a variety of menu items.

Innkeeper(s): Jeannie Serandos. $65-85. MC, VISA, AX, DS, PC, TC. 2
rooms, 1 with PB. Breakfast included in rates. Types of meals: Full bkfst and
early coffee/tea. Beds: Q. Cable TV, ceiling fan and VCR in room. Air conditioning. Spa on premises. Antiquing, fishing, parks, shopping and water
sports nearby.

Location: City.

Publicity: *Discover Mid-America.*

Certificate may be used: Feb. 15-Nov. 20, weekdays, Monday through Thursday.

Macon   C5

St. Agnes Hall B&B

502 Jackson St
Macon, MO 63552-1717
(660)385-2774 Fax:(660)385-4436

Circa 1846. This two-and-a-half story brick home boasts a
rather unique history. As a stop along the Underground
Railroad, it served as a "safe-house" for many slaves seeking
freedom in the North.
During the Civil War, it
was used as Union
headquarters. Eventually
in the 1880s, the home
was converted into a
boarding house and day
school for young
women. In 1895, the home was renovated and used as a private residence. It was the boyhood home of U.S. Sen. James
Preston Kem. Antiques and collectibles decorate the interior, all
surrounded by Victorian decor.

Innkeeper(s): Scott & Carol Phillips. $68-98. MC, VISA, AX, TC. 4 rooms
with PB, 2 with FP and 1 suite. Breakfast included in rates. Types of meals:
Full bkfst and early coffee/tea. Beds: KQ. Cable TV and ceiling fan in room.
Air conditioning. VCR, fax and copier on premises. Antiquing, fishing, golf,
swimming, fine dining, parks, shopping and water sports nearby.

Location: City.

Certificate may be used: Sunday-Friday, excluding special events.

Marshfield   G5

The Dickey House B&B, Ltd.

331 S Clay St
Marshfield, MO 65706-2114
(417)468-3000 (800)450-7444 Fax:(417)859-2775
E-mail: dhousebb1@aol.com

Circa 1913. This Greek Revival mansion is framed by ancient
oak trees and boasts eight massive two-story Ionic columns.
Burled woodwork, beveled glass and polished hardwood floors
accentuate the gracious rooms. Interior columns soar in the

parlor, creating a suitably elegant setting for the innkeeper's outstanding collection of antiques. A queen-size canopy bed, fireplace and sunporch are featured in the Heritage Room. Some rooms offer amenities such as Jacuzzi tubs and a fireplace. All rooms include cable TV and a VCR. The innkeepers also offer a sun room with a hot tub.

Innkeeper(s): Larry & Michaelene Stevens. $65-145. MC, VISA, AX, DS, PC, TC. 7 rooms with PB, 4 suites. Breakfast included in rates. Type of meal: Full gourmet bkfst. Beds: KQD. Cable TV, phone, ceiling fan, VCR and double Jacuzzi (four rooms) in room. Fax, copier, library and new sun room with therapeutic hot tub on premises. Handicap access.

Location: City.

Certificate may be used: Jan. 10 to April 30, Sunday-Friday.

Ozark   G4

Smokey Hollow Lake B&B

880 Cash Spring Rd
Ozark, MO 65721
(417)485-0286 (800)485-0286

Circa 1992. An inviting gazebo sits on a point jutting into the lake on the 187 acres surrounding this B&B. The accommodation is a loft apartment in the barn decorated in a country style. It can sleep six people and boasts a two-person whirlpool. There are hills and streams to explore, and you may see wild turkeys, ducks, deer and the inn's horses and mules. A full breakfast is served, although you also have your own private kitchen.

Innkeeper(s): Brenda & Richard Bilyeu. $90. PC. 1 cottages. Breakfast and snacks/refreshments included in rates. Type of meal: Full bkfst. Beds: QD. Ceiling fan in room. Air conditioning. Fishing, canoes and paddleboats on premises. Fishing, golf, live theater, shopping and water sports nearby.

Location: Country.

Certificate may be used: Jan. 15-Oct. 30, Sunday-Wednesday.

Rocheport   D5

Roby River Run, A B&B

201 N Roby Farm Rd
Rocheport, MO 65279-9315
(573)698-2173 (888)762-9786
Internet: www.bbonline.com/mo/robyriver/

Circa 1854. Moses Payne, known as Boone County's "Millionaire Minister," chose these wooded, 10-acre grounds nestled near the banks of the Missouri River, on which to build his home. The Federal-style manor, which is listed in the National Register, offers three distinctive guest rooms. The Moses U. Payne room offers a cherry, Queen Anne poster bed and a fireplace. The Sarah Payne room, named for Moses' second wife, boasts a rice bed and antique wash-stand. The Hattie McDaniel, named for the Academy Award-winning actress who portrayed Mammy in "Gone With the Wind," offers a peek at the inn's extensive collection of memorabilia from the movie. Homemade breakfasts include eggs, biscuits, country-cured ham and specialties such as marmalade-cream cheese stuffed French toast. Rocheport, a National Register town, offers several antique shops to explore, as well as the Katy Trail, a path for hikers and bikers that winds along the river. As the evening approaches,

guests can head up to Les Bourgeois Vineyards and purchase a picnic basket, a bottle of Missouri wine and watch the sun set over the river or dine at their blufftop restaurant.

Innkeeper(s): Gary Smith & Randall Kilgore. $95-110. MC, VISA, AX, DS, PC. 3 rooms, 1 with PB, 1 with FP. Type of meal: Full bkfst. Beds: Q. Cable TV, phone, turndown service and VCR in room. Air conditioning. Stables on premises. Antiquing and restaurants nearby.

Location: Missouri River.

Certificate may be used: Sunday through Thursday.

School House B&B Inn

504 Third St
Rocheport, MO 65279
(573)698-2022
Internet: www.schoolhousebandb.com
E-mail: innkeeper@schoolhousebandb.com

Circa 1914. This three-story brick building was once a schoolhouse. Now luxuriously appointed as a country inn, it features 13-foot-high ceilings, small print wallpapers and a bridal suite with Victorian furnishings and a private spa. Rooms feature names such as The Spelling Bee and The Schoolmarm. The basement houses an antique bookshop, The Bookseller. Nearby is a winery and a trail along the river providing many scenic miles for cyclists and hikers.

Innkeeper(s): Vicki Ott & Penny Province. $85-205. MC, VISA, DS. 10 rooms with PB, 1 suite and 1 conference room. Breakfast and snacks/refreshments included in rates. Types of meals: Full bkfst, cont plus, cont and early coffee/tea. Beds: KQDT. TV, phone and ceiling fan in room. Air conditioning. Library on premises. Antiquing, fishing, hiking, bicycling, live theater, parks, shopping, art galleries and sporting events nearby.

Location: Village - historic town.

Publicity: Midwest Living, Midwest Motorist, Successful Farming, Hallmark Greeting Cards, Romance of Country Inns, Southern Living and New York Times.

"We are still talking about our great weekend in Rocheport. Thanks for the hospitality, the beautiful room and delicious breakfasts, they were really great."

Certificate may be used: January-April, June-September, November and December, Sunday through Thursday.

Saint Joseph   B2

Shakespeare Chateau B&B

809 Hall St
Saint Joseph, MO 64501
(816)232-2667 Fax:(816)232-0009
Internet: www.ponyexpress.net/~chateau
E-mail: chateau@ponyexpress.net

Circa 1885. This gabeled and turretted confection offers three stories of lavish antique furnishings, carved woodwork and at least 40 original stained-glass windows. The inn is in the Hall Street Historic District, known as "Mansion Hill". All the homes in this area are listed in the National Register. The fireplace in the inn's foyer has boasted a bronze of Shakespeare for more than 100 years and with this as a starting point, the innkeeper has created a Victorian, Shakespearean theme. Two of the inn's room offer whirlpools. A two-course breakfast is served in the romantic dining room.

Innkeeper(s): Terri & Kellie. $100-150. MC, VISA, AX, DS, PC, TC. 7 rooms with PB, 3 suites and 1 conference room. Breakfast and snacks/refreshments included in rates. Type of meal: Full gourmet bkfst. Beds: K. Ceiling fan in room. Air conditioning. VCR, fax and library on premises. Antiquing, golf, live theater, parks, shopping and downhill skiing nearby.

Location: City.

Publicity: Midwest Living.

Certificate may be used: Year-round, Sunday-Friday, subject to availability.

Saint Louis
D8

Lafayette House
2156 Lafayette Ave
Saint Louis, MO 63104-2543
(314)772-4429 (800)641-8965 Fax:(314)664-2156
Internet: www.bbonline.com/mo/laffayette/

Circa 1876. Lafayette House encompasses two historic homes, built by Captain James Eads, the designer and builder of the first trestle bridge to cross the Mississippi. Eads built the homes as wedding gifts for his two daughters. Each home is Victorian in style, and each is decorated with antiques.

Innkeeper(s): Nancy Hammersmith, Anna Millet. $65-150. MC, VISA, AX, DC, CB, DS, PC, TC. 11 rooms, 9 with PB and 2 suites. Breakfast included in rates. Types of meals: Full gourmet bkfst and early coffee/tea. Beds: QDT. Cable TV, phone and jacuzzi in room. Air conditioning. VCR, fax and copier on premises. Antiquing, live theater, parks, shopping and sporting events nearby.
Location: City.

"We had a wonderful stay at your house and enjoyed the furnishings, delicious breakfasts and friendly pets."

Certificate may be used: Jan. 1-April 30, Sunday through Thursday.

Lehmann House B&B
10 Benton Pl
Saint Louis, MO 63104-2411
(314)231-6724

Circa 1893. This National Register manor's most prominent resident, former U.S. Solicitor General Frederick Lehmann, hosted Presidents Taft, Theodore Roosevelt and Coolidge at this gracious home. Several key turn-of-the-century literary figures also visited the Lehmann family. The inn's formal dining room, complete with oak paneling and a fireplace, is a stunning place to enjoy the formal breakfasts. Antiques and gracious furnishings dot the well-appointed guest rooms. The home is located in St. Louis' oldest historic district, Lafayette Square.
Innkeeper(s): Marie & Michael Davies. $70-95. MC, VISA, DS, PC, TC. 4 rooms, 2 with PB, 2 with FP. Breakfast included in rates. Types of meals: Full bkfst and early coffee/tea. Beds: KQDT. Ceiling fan in room. Air conditioning. Swimming, tennis and library on premises. Amusement parks, antiquing, museums, zoos, botanical gardens, live theater, parks, shopping and sporting events nearby.
Location: City.
Publicity: *St. Louis Post Dispatch and KTVI-St. Louis.*

"Wonderful mansion with great future ahead. Thanks for the wonderful hospitality."

Certificate may be used: Nov. 1-March 30, Sunday-Thursday only, holidays and special events excluded.

Sainte Genevieve
E9

Inn St. Gemme Beauvais
78 N Main St
Sainte Genevieve, MO 63670-1336
(573)883-5744 (800)818-5744 Fax:(573)883-3899

Circa 1848. This three-story, Federal-style inn is an impressive site on Ste. Genevieve's Main Street. The town is one of the oldest west of the Mississippi River, and the St. Gemme Beauvais is the oldest operating Missouri bed & breakfast. The rooms are nicely appointed in period style, but there are modern amenities

here, too. The Jacuzzi tubs in some guest rooms are one relaxing example. There is an outdoor hot tub, as well. The romantic carriage house includes a king-size bed, double Jacuzzi tub and a fireplace. Guests are pampered with all sorts of cuisine, including full breakfasts and tea time in the afternoons, wine, hors d'oeuvres and refreshments are served early evenings.
Innkeeper(s): Janet Joggerst. $89-179. MC, VISA, DS, PC, TC. 9 rooms with PB, 1 with FP, 6 suites and 1 conference room. Breakfast, afternoon tea and snacks/refreshments included in rates. Type of meal: Full gourmet bkfst. Beds: KQD. Cable TV and ceiling fan in room. Air conditioning. VCR, fax, copier, spa and bicycles on premises. Antiquing, historic area, parks and shopping nearby.
Location: Historic town.
Certificate may be used: Jan. 30 through Nov. 30, Sunday through Thursday only. No holidays or special weekends. Based on availability.

Main Street Inn
221 North Main St
Sainte Genevieve, MO 63670
(573)883-9199 (800)918-9199
Internet: www.rivervalleyinns.com
E-mail: msinn@ldd.net

Circa 1883. This exquisite inn is one of Missouri's finest bed & breakfast establishments. Built as the Meyer Hotel, the inn has welcomed guests for more than a century. Now completely renovated, each of the individually appointed rooms includes amenities such as bubble bath and flowers. Rooms are subtly decorated, and some have stenciled walls. Beds are topped with vintage quilts and tasteful linens. Two rooms include a whirlpool tub. The morning meal is prepared in a beautiful brick kitchen, which features an unusual blue cookstove, and is served in the elegant dining room. The menu changes from day to day, caramelized French toast is one of the inn's specialties.
Innkeeper(s): Ken & Karen Kulberg. $85-125. MC, VISA, AX, DS, PC, TC. 8 rooms with PB. Breakfast and snacks/refreshments included in rates. Types of meals: Full gourmet bkfst and early coffee/tea. Beds: QDT. Air conditioning. Copier on premises. Antiquing, historic Sites, parks and shopping nearby.
Location: City.
Certificate may be used: Jan. 15-Dec. 15, Sunday-Thursday.

Springfield
G4

Virginia Rose B&B
317 E Glenwood St
Springfield, MO 65807-3543
(417)883-0693

Circa 1906. Three generations of the Botts family lived in this home before it was sold to the current innkeepers, Virginia and Jackie Buck. The grounds still include the rustic red barn. Comfortable, country rooms are named after Buck family members and feature beds covered with quilts. The innkeepers also offer a two-bedroom suite, the Rambling Rose, which is decorated in a sportsman theme in honor of the nearby Bass Pro. Hearty breakfasts are served in the dining room, and the innkeepers will provide low-fat fare on request.
Innkeeper(s): Jackie & Virginia Buck. $50-90. MC, VISA, AX, DS, PC, TC. 5 rooms, 3 with PB and 1 suite. Breakfast included in rates. Types of meals: Full bkfst and early coffee/tea. Beds: QD. Phone and turndown service in room. Air conditioning. VCR and fax on premises. Amusement parks, antiquing, fishing, live theater, parks, shopping, sporting events and water sports nearby.
Location: City.
Publicity: *Auctions & Antiques, Springfield Business Journal and Today's Women Journal.*

"The accommodations are wonderful and the hospitality couldn't be warmer."

Certificate may be used: Any time, subject to availability. Some weekends and holidays excepted.

Walnut Street Inn

900 E Walnut St
Springfield, MO 65806-2603
(417)864-6346 (800)593-6346 Fax:(417)864-6184
Internet: www.walnutstreetinn.com
E-mail: walnutstinn@pcis.net

Circa 1894. This three-story Queen Anne gabled house has cast-iron Corinthian columns and a veranda. Polished wood floors and antiques are featured throughout.

Upstairs you'll find the gathering room with a fireplace. Ask for the McCann guest room with two bay windows, or one of the four rooms with a hot tub. A full breakfast is served, including items such as peach-stuffed French toast.

Innkeeper(s): Gary & Paula Blankenship. $69-159. MC, VISA, AX, DC, DS, PC, TC. 12 rooms with PB, 8 with FP and 1 suite. Breakfast included in rates. Types of meals: Full gourmet bkfst and early coffee/tea. Beds: QD. Cable TV, phone, turndown service, ceiling fan, VCR and coffeemakers and beverage bars in room. Air conditioning. Fax and copier on premises. Handicap access. Amusement parks, antiquing, fishing, live theater, parks, shopping, sporting events and water sports nearby.

Location: City.

Publicity: *Southern Living, Women's World, Midwest Living, Victoria, Country Inns, Innsider, Glamour, Midwest Motorist, Missouri, Saint Louis Post, Kansas City Star and USA Today.*

"Rest assured your establishment's qualities are unmatched and through your commitment to excellence you have won a life-long client."

Certificate may be used: Sunday-Thursday, excluding holidays and certain dates.

Steelville   E7

Frisco Street B&B

305 Frisco St, PO Box 1219
Steelville, MO 65565
(573)775-4247 (888)229-4247
E-mail: friscomone@juno.com

Circa 1871. This Victorian farmhouse is painted baby blue and pink and features a wraparound porch. Breakfast is often served in the gazebo part of the porch. The parlor with armoire, fireplace, floral wallpaper and antique paintings has a Victorian flavor. Ask for the English Rose Garden Suite and you'll have a room with country decor, a canopy bed and a Jacuzzi for two. Upstairs guest rooms all have private balconies. Nearby attractions include three Ozark rivers, Meramac Spring Park, a winery, shops and a country music show.

Innkeeper(s): Sandy Berrier. $68-118. MC, VISA, AX, DS. 4 rooms with PB and 1 suite. Breakfast and snacks/refreshments included in rates. Types of meals: Full gourmet bkfst and early coffee/tea. Beds: Q. Cable TV, phone and ceiling fan in room. Air conditioning. Antiquing, fishing, golf, horseback riding, live theater, parks, shopping, water sports and wineries nearby.

Location: Resort area.

Publicity: *Kansas City Star and Steelville Star.*

"We felt so pampered and special here."

Certificate may be used: June-August, Sunday-Thursday.

Warrensburg   D4

Cedarcroft Farm B&B

431 SE County Rd Y
Warrensburg, MO 64093-8316
(660)747-5728 (800)368-4944
E-mail: bwayne@cedarcroft.com

Circa 1867. John Adams, a Union army veteran, and Sandra's great grandfather, built this house. There are 80 acres of woodlands, meadows and creeks where deer, fox, coyotes and wild turkeys still roam. Two original barns remain. Guests stay in a private, two-bedroom suite, which can accommodate couples or families. Bill participates in Civil War reenactments and is happy to demonstrate clothing, weapons and customs of the era. Sandra cares for her four horses and provides the home-baked, full country breakfasts.

Innkeeper(s): Sandra & Bill Wayne. $75-90. MC, VISA, AX, DS, PC, TC. 1 suites. Breakfast and snacks/refreshments included in rates. Type of meal: Full bkfst. Beds: D. Air conditioning. VCR and stereo on premises. Antiquing, fishing, rodeos, Civil War re-enactment, state fair, horseback riding, live theater, parks and shopping nearby.

Location: Country.

Publicity: *Midwest Motorist, Country America, Entrepreneur, Small Farm Today, Kansas City Star, Daily Star-Journal, Higginsville Advance, KCTV, KMOS, KSHB and CNN.*

"We enjoyed the nostalgia and peacefulness very much. Enjoyed your wonderful hospitality and great food."

Certificate may be used: Sept. 1-April 30, Sunday-Thursday, except holidays.

Washington   D7

Schwegmann House

438 W Front St
Washington, MO 63090-2103
(636)239-5025 (800)949-2262
Internet: www.schwegmannhouse.com
E-mail: cathy@schwegmannhouse.com

Circa 1861. John F. Schwegmann, a native of Germany, built a flour mill on the Missouri riverfront. This stately three-story home was built not only for the miller and his family, but also to provide extra lodging for overnight customers who traveled long hours to the town. Today, weary travelers enjoy the formal gardens and warm atmosphere of this restful home. Patios overlook the river, and the gracious rooms are decorated with antiques and handmade quilts. The new Miller Suite boasts a tub for two and breakfast can be delivered to their door. Guests enjoy full breakfasts complete with house specialties such as German apple pancakes or a three-cheese strata accompanied with homemade breads, meat, juice and fresh fruit. There are 11 wineries nearby, or guests can visit one of the historic districts, many galleries, historic sites, antique shops, excellent restaurants and riverfront park located nearby.

Innkeeper(s): Catherine & Bill Nagel. $85-150. MC, VISA, AX, PC, TC. 9 rooms with PB and 1 suite. Breakfast and snacks/refreshments included in rates. Types of meals: Full gourmet bkfst and early coffee/tea. Beds: QD. Phone and ceiling fan in room. Air conditioning. Antiquing, Missouri River Wine Country and Katy Bike Trail nearby.

Location: Missouri River.

Publicity: *St. Louis Post-Dispatch, West County Journal, Midwest Living, Country Inns, Midwest Motorist and Ozark.*

"Like Grandma's house many years ago."

Certificate may be used: Nov. 1 to April 30, Monday through Thursday.

Montana

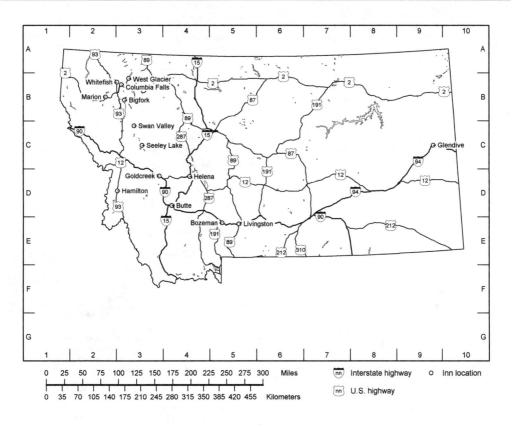

| | Interstate highway | | Inn location |
| nn | U.S. highway | | |

Bigfork   **B3**

Burggraf's Countrylane B&B

Rainbow Drive on Swan Lake
Bigfork, MT 59911
(406)837-4608 (800)525-3344 Fax:(406)837-2468
E-mail: burggraf@digisys.net

Circa 1984. This contemporary log home on Swan Lake,
minutes from Flathead Lake
in the Rockies, offers fine
accommodations in one of
America's most beautiful settings. Upon arrival, visitors
enjoy chilled wine and fresh
fruit. Ceiling fans, clock

radios and turndown service are amenities. Picnic baskets are
available and would be ideal for taking along on a paddle boat
lake excursion. Guests enjoy complimentary use of canoes, lawn
croquet and barbecue grills by the lake. In addition, there is a
small rental cabin, and rental fishing and water ski boats are
available, and all will enjoy the inn's seven scenic acres.

Innkeeper(s): Natalie & RJ Burggraf. $95-130. MC, VISA, PC, TC. 6 rooms
with PB. Breakfast included in rates. Types of meals: Full gourmet bkfst and
early coffee/tea. Beds: KQT. Cable TV, ceiling fan and VCR in room. Fax, copier, swimming, library and pet boarding on premises. Handicap access.
Antiquing, fishing, live theater, parks, shopping, downhill skiing, cross-country
skiing, sporting events and water sports nearby.

Certificate may be used: May, June, September, weekdays only.

Bozeman E5

Chokecherry House

1233 Storymill Rd
Bozeman, MT 59715
(406)587-2657
Internet: www.chokecherry.com
E-mail: nrpope@montana.campus.mci.net

Circa 1939. In the foothills of the Bridger Mountains, this Quonset house was originally built for the schoolteacher of the one-room Storymill Schoolhouse. Now with a bright and airy interior, the home serves as a private two-bedroom guesthouse, decorated in an Americana style and with original art and Western memorabilia. Both innkeepers are professional artists Rick is a professor of art at Montana State University (as well as a licensed fishing guide), and Kimberly is a metalsmith and jeweler. The inn's acre offers great bird watching, and bald eagles are often spotted at nearby Bridger Creek. The house features a kitchen so guests can do their own breakfast.

Innkeeper(s): Rick & Kimberly Pope. $140. PC, TC. 7 rooms and 1 cottage. Beds: QDT. Cable TV and VCR in room. Antiquing, fishing, golf, live theater, parks, shopping, downhill skiing, cross-country skiing, sporting events, tennis and water sports nearby.

Location: fishing creek, golf course.

Certificate may be used: April 15 through June 1, and Oct. 1-Nov. 30 all days of the week.

Lindley House

202 Lindley Pl
Bozeman, MT 59715-4833
(406)587-8403 (800)787-8404 Fax:(406)582-8112
Internet: www.avicom.net/lindley
E-mail: lindley@avicom.net

Circa 1889. The beautiful Montana scenery is a perfect backdrop for this romantic bed & breakfast listed in the National Register. The pampering begins in the beautiful guest rooms,  which offer plenty of soft, down comforters, feather pillows, fluffy robes and a collection of soaps and oils for a long soak in the tub. Each of the rooms is distinct and memorable. The Marie Antoinette Suite boasts a fireplace, sitting room, clawfoot tub and balcony. The Garden Room offers French Provencal decor with a private garden entrance. Other rooms include items such as wicker furnishings, bay windows, lacy curtains, dramatic wall coverings, a French bistro table or brass bed. The gourmet breakfasts, which feature special treats such as crepes, souffles and a variety of breads, yogurt and cereals, are a perfect start to the day.

Innkeeper(s): Stephanie Volz. $75-250. MC, VISA, DS. 6 rooms with PB and 3 suites. Breakfast and afternoon tea included in rates. Type of meal: Full bkfst. Beds: KQT. Antiquing, fishing, live theater, shopping, downhill skiing, cross-country skiing and water sports nearby.

"Elegant, but comfortable. Beautifully restored, wonderful attention to detail."

Certificate may be used: Nov. 1-April 30, Monday through Thursday.

Torch & Toes B&B

309 S 3rd Ave
Bozeman, MT 59715-4636
(406)586-7285 (800)446-2138

Circa 1906. This Colonial Revival home, three blocks from the center of town, boasts an old-fashioned front porch with porch swing and a carriage house. Antique furnishings in the dining room feature a Victrola and a pillared and carved oak fireplace. Ron is a retired professor of architecture at nearby Montana State University and Judy is a weaver.

Innkeeper(s): Ron & Judy Hess. $80-90. MC, VISA, PC, TC. 4 rooms with PB. Breakfast included in rates. Type of meal: Full gourmet bkfst. Beds: KQT. VCR on premises. Antiquing, fishing, live theater, parks, shopping, downhill skiing, cross-country skiing, sporting events and water sports nearby.

Location: Mountains.

Publicity: *Bozeman Chronicle, San Francisco Peninsula Parent and Northwest.*

"Thanks for your warm hospitality."

Certificate may be used: Anytime, subject to availability.

Voss Inn

319 S Willson Ave
Bozeman, MT 59715-4632
(406)587-0982 Fax:(406)585-2964
Internet: www.bozeman-vossinn.com
E-mail: vossinn@imt.net

Circa 1883. The Voss Inn is a restored two-story house with a large front porch and a Victorian parlor. Old-fashioned furnishings include an upright piano and chandelier. Two of the inn's six rooms include air conditioning. A full breakfast is served, with freshly baked rolls kept in a unique warmer that's built into an ornate 1880s radiator.

Innkeeper(s): Bruce & Frankee Muller. $90-110. MC, VISA, AX, PC, TC. 6 rooms with PB. Breakfast and afternoon tea included in rates. Type of meal: Full gourmet bkfst. Beds: KQ. Phone in room. Fax on premises. Antiquing, fishing, golf, hunting, hiking, biking, parks, shopping, downhill skiing, cross-country skiing and water sports nearby.

Location: City.

Publicity: *Sunset, Cosmopolitan, Gourmet, Countryside and Country Inns.*

"First class all the way."

Certificate may be used: January through June, October-Dec. 15. July-September excluded.

Butte D4

Copper King Mansion

219 W Granite St
Butte, MT 59701-9235
(406)782-7580

Circa 1884. This turn-of-the-century marvel was built, as the name indicates, by W.A. Clark, one of the nation's leading copper barons. In the early 1900s, Clark made millions each month hauling copper out of Butte's vast mines. Stained-glass windows, gold leafing on the ceilings and elaborate woodwork are just a few of the opulent touches. Clark commissioned artisans brought in from Germany to carve the intricate staircase, which graces the front hall. The mansion is decked floor to ceiling in antiques collected by the innkeeper's mother and grandmother, who purchased the home from Clark's relatives. A three-room master suite includes two fireplaces, a lavish bedroom, a sitting room and a huge bathroom with a clawfoot tub.

Innkeeper(s): Maria Sigl. $55-95. MC, VISA, AX. 4 rooms. Breakfast included in rates. Type of meal: Full bkfst.

Publicity: *Sunset Magazine.*

Certificate may be used: January, February, March, April, May, September, October, November, December.

Columbia Falls B3

Plum Creek House

985 Vans Ave
Columbia Falls, MT 59912-3203
(406)892-1816 (800)682-1429 Fax:(406)892-1876
Internet: www.wtp.net/go/plumcreek
E-mail: plumcreek@in~tch.com

Incredible views of the Flathead Valley's forests and mountains greet guests at this contemporary riverfront ranch inn. The inn offers something for everyone, even family pets who may stay in the sheltered outdoor kennel. Outdoor recreational opportunities are boundless, but guests who wish to put their feet up and relax also will find this inn to their liking. A heated pool and outdoor spa lure many guests. Glacier National Park can be seen from the inn and is just a short drive away.

Innkeeper(s): Caroline Stevens. $75-115. MC, VISA, AX, DC, DS. 5 rooms and 1 suite. Breakfast included in rates. Types of meals: Full bkfst and early coffee/tea. Cable TV, phone, turndown service, ceiling fan and VCR in room. Air conditioning. Child care on premises. Antiquing, live theater, shopping, downhill skiing and cross-country skiing nearby.

Certificate may be used: Oct. 1 to June 1.

Glendive C9

The Hostetler House B&B

113 N Douglas St
Glendive, MT 59330-1619
(406)377-4505 (800)965-8456 Fax:(406)377-8456

Circa 1912. Casual country decor mixed with handmade and heirloom furnishings are highlights at this Prairie School home. The inn features many comforting touches, such as a romantic hot tub and gazebo, enclosed sun porch and sitting room filled with books. The two guest rooms share a bath, and are furnished by Dea, an interior decorator. The full breakfasts may be enjoyed on Grandma's china in the dining room or on the sun 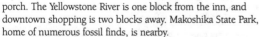 porch. The Yellowstone River is one block from the inn, and downtown shopping is two blocks away. Makoshika State Park, home of numerous fossil finds, is nearby.

Innkeeper(s): Craig & Dea Hostetler. $50. PC, TC. 2 rooms. Breakfast included in rates. Types of meals: Full gourmet bkfst and early coffee/tea. Beds: DT. Ceiling fan and air conditioning in room. VCR, fax, spa, bicycles, library and secretarial service on premises. Antiquing, fishing, fossil and agate hunting, live theater, parks, shopping, cross-country skiing, sporting events and water sports nearby.

Location: Small town.

Publicity: *Ranger Review/Circle Banner.*

"Warmth and loving care are evident throughout your exquisite home. Your attention to small details is uplifting. Thank you for a restful sojourn."

Certificate may be used: Anytime.

Gold Creek D3

LH Ranch B&B

471 Mullan Tr
Gold Creek, MT 59733
(406)288-3436

Circa 1851. Guests can take horseback riding lessons, pan for gold or roll up their sleeves and feed animals or bale hay at this 2,000-acre ranch. Relaxation is another option, and there are plenty of ideal spots. The home is furnished with a collection of family antiques. The LH Ranch is Montana's oldest operating bed & breakfast, open and run by the Lingenfelter family since 1955.

Innkeeper(s): Patti Hansen. $85. 2 rooms, 1 with FP. Breakfast included in rates. Types of meals: Full bkfst, cont plus, cont and early coffee/tea. Beds: D. Amusement parks, antiquing, fishing, live theater, parks, shopping, downhill skiing, cross-country skiing and water sports nearby.

Pets Allowed.

Certificate may be used: Jan. 1-Dec. 11.

Hamilton D3

Deer Crossing B&B

396 Hayes Creek Rd
Hamilton, MT 59840-9744
(406)363-2232 (800)763-2232
Internet: www.wtp.net/go/deercrossing
E-mail: deercros@bitterroot.net

Circa 1980. This Western-style ranch bed & breakfast is located on 25 acres of woods and pastures. One suite includes a double Jacuzzi tub and another has a private balcony. In addition to the suites and guest rooms, travelers also can opt to stay in the bunkhouse, a historic homestead building with a wood-burning stove. The area is full of activities, including horseback riding, hiking, fly fishing and historic sites.

Innkeeper(s): Mary Lynch. $75-125. MC, VISA, AX. 5 rooms with PB and 2 suites. Breakfast and snacks/refreshments included in rates. Types of meals: Full bkfst and early coffee/tea. Beds: KQDT. TV in room. VCR, child care, satellite dish and fireplace on premises. Handicap access. Antiquing, parks, shopping, downhill skiing, cross-country skiing and water sports nearby.

Pets allowed: Horses boarded.

Location: Ranch.

Publicity: *Country Magazine and Montana Handbook.*

"It is so nice to be back after three years and from 5,000 miles away!"

Certificate may be used: Oct. 1 to May 1 any day of the week.

Helena D4

Appleton Inn B&B

1999 Euclid Avenue
Helena, MT 59601-1908
(406)449-7492 (800)956-1999 Fax:(406)449-1261
Internet: www.appletoninn.com
E-mail: appleton@ixi.net

Circa 1890. Montana's first resident dentist called this Victorian his home. It remained in his family until the 1970s when it was transformed into apartments. Fortunately, the innkeepers bought and restored the home, bringing back the original beauty. The innkeepers have their own furniture-making company and have created many of the pieces that decorate the guest rooms. Rooms range from the spacious Master Suite, with its oak, four-poster bed and bath with a claw-foot tub, to the quaint  and cozy Attic Playroom. The inn is a convenient place to enjoy the Helena area, and there are mountain bikes on hand for those who wish to explore.

Innkeeper(s): Tom Woodall & Cheryl Boid. $90-165. MC, VISA, AX, DS, PC, TC. 5 rooms with PB and 1 suite. Breakfast included in rates. Beds: Q. Cable TV and phone in room. Air conditioning. VCR, fax, copier, bicycles and guest pass to athletic pass on premises. Antiquing, fishing, national forest, live theater, parks, shopping, downhill skiing, cross-country skiing, sporting events and water sports nearby.

Pets allowed: Need prior approval.

Location: City.

"Cheryl and Tom have provided a perfect place to call home away from home. The surroundings are delightful - the rooms, the plants, the grounds - and the breakfast very tasty. And they provide lots of helpful information to help you enjoy touring the area. A truly delightful B&B."

Certificate may be used: Nov. 1 to April 30, Sunday-Saturday.

Livingston   E5

The River Inn on The Yellowstone

4950 Hwy 89 S
Livingston, MT 59047
(406)222-2429
Internet: www.wtp.net/go/riverinn
E-mail: riverinn@wtp.net

Circa 1895. Crisp, airy rooms decorated with a Southwestern flavor are just part of the reason why this 100-year-old farmhouse is an ideal getaway. There are five acres to meander, including more than 500 feet of riverfront, and close access to a multitude of outdoor activities. Two rooms have decks boasting views of the river, and the third offers a canyon view. Guests also can stay in Calamity Jane's, a rustic riverside cabin. For an unusual twist, summer guests can opt for Spangler's Wagon and experience life as it was on the range. This is a true, turn-of-the-century sheepherders' wagon and includes a double bed and wood stove. The innkeepers guide a variety of interesting hikes, bike and canoe trips in the summer and fall. The inn is close to many outdoor activities. Don't forget to check out Livingston, just a few miles away. The historic town has been used in several movies and maintains an authentic Old West spirit. The inn is 50 miles from Yellowstone National Park.

Innkeeper(s): Dee Dee VanZyl & Ursula Neese. $40-90. MC, VISA. 3 rooms with PB and 1 cottage. Breakfast included in rates. Types of meals: Full gourmet bkfst and early coffee/tea. Beds: QDT. Table & chairs, private deck and hot tub/Jacuzzi in room. VCR, bicycles, wood stove, fire pit, horse boarding, horseshoes, fishing, BBQ and birdwatching on premises. Antiquing, fishing, museum of the Rockies, historical museum, art galleries, music, live theater, parks, shopping, downhill skiing, cross-country skiing, sporting events and water sports nearby.

Pets allowed: Horses. Dogs permitted in the cabin and wagon only. Other, by arrangement.

Location: Livingston 4 miles.

Certificate may be used: May 1-31, Oct. 1-31.

Marion   B2

Hargrave Ranch

300 Thompson River Rd
Marion, MT 59925-9710
(406)858-2284 (800)933-0696 Fax:(406)858-2444

Circa 1906. If you've ever wondered what it would be like to live on a working cattle ranch, a stay at this 86,000-acre spread will provide a glimpse into this Western lifestyle. Riding lessons, overnight camp-outs and lakeside picnics are just a few of the options available. Guests also may try their hand at cattle herding. Accommodations are unique and varied, and they include a log cabin (formerly a horse stable), the main house or two rustic cottages. The hosts prepare guests for their busy days with huge breakfasts with egg dishes, potatoes, yogurt, fruit, pancakes and other delectables. During the winter months, rates include cross-country skiing.

Innkeeper(s): Leo & Ellen Hargrave. $60-190. MC, VISA, TC. 10 cabins, 3 with PB, 2 with FP and 1 conference room. Breakfast, dinner, snacks/refreshments and picnic lunch included in rates. Types of meals: Full bkfst and early coffee/tea. Beds: KQDT. Ceiling fan in room. VCR, fax, copier, sauna and bicycles on premises. Antiquing, fishing, Glacier National Park, live theater, parks, shopping, downhill skiing, cross-country skiing and water sports nearby.

Location: Ranch.

Certificate may be used: October-May 1.

Seeley Lake   C3

The Emily A. B&B

Hwy 83, Box 350
Seeley Lake, MT 59868
(406)677-3474 (800)977-4639 Fax:(406)677-3474
Internet: www.theemilya.com
E-mail: slk3340@blackfoot.net

Circa 1992. Nestled at the banks of the Clearwater River, this rustic log home was fashioned from local timber. From the lodge, guests enjoy panoramic Rocky Mountain views. Stroll the inn's 158 acres and you'll find hiking trails, wildlife and plenty of places to fish. The home is named for innkeeper Marilyn Shope Peterson's grandmother, a remarkable woman who helped found Montana's Boulder School for the Deaf Mute. Despite being widowed at a young age, Emily managed to support herself and seven children by running a boarding house. Marilyn inherited her grandmother's hospitable skills and she, and husband Keith, pamper their guests. Rooms are decorated with Western furnishings, and beds are topped with feather duvets. There is a collection of Western art on hand, as well.

Innkeeper(s): Marilyn Shope Peterson. $95-150. MC, VISA, TC. 5 rooms, 2 with PB and 1 conference room. Types of meals: Full bkfst, cont plus and early coffee/tea. Beds: KQT. VCR, fax, copier, bicycles and child care on premises. Handicap access. Antiquing, fishing, live theater, parks, shopping, downhill skiing, cross-country skiing, sporting events and water sports nearby.

Location: Mountains, lakes, rivers.

Certificate may be used: Oct. 1-May 1, upon availability.

Swan Valley   C3

Holland Lake Lodge

1947 Holland Lake Rd
Swan Valley, MT 59826
(406)754-2282 Fax:(406)754-2208

Circa 1924. Located in Flathead National Forest, this is a log lodge with 10 acres that border pristine Halland Lake. From the inn you can see the Swan Peaks, Mission Mountains and 100-foot-long Holland Falls. Log pole furnishings add to the authentic feel of the inn, which was constructed on this prime shoreline in the '20s. Accommodations include both lakeside cabins and lodge rooms. In summer, book your room for the cowboy poets' reunion or the fiddlers' jamboree, or take trail rides with the lodge wranglers (or overnights with heated tents!). Winter activities are dog sledding, ice fishing, cross-country skiing and snowmobiling. Fresh salmon and Yankee pot roast are among the dinner offerings.

Innkeeper(s): John Wohlfell. $66-125. MC, VISA, AX, DS, PC, TC. 14 rooms and 5 cabins. Types of meals: Full bkfst and early coffee/tea. Beds: KQDT. Copier, swimming, sauna, stables and espresso Machine on premises. Antiquing, fishing, horse back riding, canoeing, live theater, parks, shopping, cross-country skiing and water sports nearby.

Pets allowed: Cabins only.

Location: Mountains.

Certificate may be used: Sept. 15-May 25, lodge rooms only.

West Glacier   B3

Mountain Timbers Lodge

PO Box 127
West Glacier, MT 59936-0094
(406)387-5830 (800)841-3835 Fax:(406)387-5835

Circa 1973. With the wilderness of Glacier National Park as its backdrop, this rustic, log home is designed for nature lovers. The grounds include miles of professionally designed cross-country ski trails, and guests on a morning walk shouldn't be surprised if they encounter deer or elk sharing the countryside. The inviting interior complements the spectacular scenery. The huge living room is warmed by a rock and stone fireplace and decorated with Southwestern-style furnishings. For those who prefer to simply relax and curl up with a good book, the innkeepers offer a well-stocked library. Beds are topped with down comforters, and guests are further pampered with an outdoor Jacuzzi.

Innkeeper(s): Dave & Betty Rudisill. $75-125. MC, VISA, AX. 6 rooms, 4 with PB and 1 conference room. Breakfast included in rates. Type of meal: Full bkfst. Beds: QDT. Fax, copier and spa on premises. Fishing and cross-country skiing nearby.

Certificate may be used: Jan. 15-May 15 and Oct. 15-Dec. 15.

Whitefish   B3

Crenshaw House

5465 Hwy 93 S
Whitefish, MT 59937-8410
(406)862-3496 (800)453-2863 Fax:(406)862-4742

Circa 1973. This contemporary farmhouse inn offers three guest rooms, all with private bath. Many amenities are found at the inn, including turndown service and a wake-up tray, which precedes the tasty gourmet breakfast prepared by innkeeper Anni Crenshaw-Rieker. Guests also enjoy afternoon tea and an evening snack. The inn also boasts a fireplace and spa, and child care can be arranged. Several state parks are found nearby.

Innkeeper(s): Anni Crenshaw-Rieker. $75-150. MC, VISA, AX, DS, PC, TC. 3 rooms with PB. Breakfast included in rates. Types of meals: Full gourmet bkfst and early coffee/tea. Beds: KQDT. Phone, turndown service, robes & slippers and wake-up tray in room. VCR, fax, copier, spa, library, pet boarding, child care and satellite TV on premises. Antiquing, fishing, live theater, parks, shopping, downhill skiing, cross-country skiing and water sports nearby.

Pets allowed: Only if kept in outside kennel.

Location: Ranchette.

Certificate may be used: Sept. 15-Dec. 15, Jan. 5-June 15, depending on availability. Not Christmas, New Year's.

Nebraska

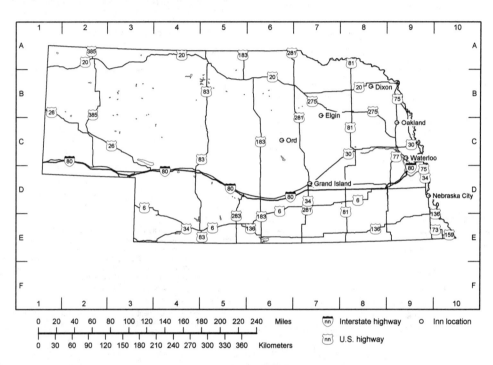

	1	2	3	4	5	6	7	8	9	10

0 20 40 60 80 100 120 140 160 180 200 220 240   Miles

0 30 60 90 120 150 180 210 240 270 300 330 360   Kilometers

(nn) Interstate highway   ○ Inn location

(nn) U.S. highway

Dixon   B8

The George Farm

57759 874 Road
Dixon, NE 68732-3024
(402)584-2625
E-mail: dixonmom@aol.com

Circa 1926. Two miles off Highway 20, west of Sioux City, lies
this air-conditioned farmhouse furnished in country decor.
Although in a rural setting, the farm offers a wide array of activities within easy driving distance. Wayne State College is nearby,
as are an abundance of local crafts and antique establishments.
Marie, an avid antiquer, can provide help for those searching the
area for special items. Relax with a stroll through the farm's 640
acres, or just enjoy some peace and quiet in the library. The inn
accepts children and pets, with prior arrangement.

Innkeeper(s): Marie George. $40-45. PC. 6 rooms. Breakfast included in
rates. Type of meal: Full bkfst. Beds: QD. Air conditioning. VCR on premises.
Pets allowed: By prior arrangement.

Location: Country.

Certificate may be used: Year-round except second weekend in July and first
weekend of pheasant hunting season (usually first weekend of November).

Elgin   B7

Plantation House

401 Plantation St
Elgin, NE 68636-9301
(402)843-2287 Fax:(402)843-2287
Internet: www.rimstarintl.com/plantation
E-mail: plantation@gpcom.net

Circa 1916. This historic mansion sits adjacent to Elgin City
Park, and guests will marvel at its beauty and size. Once a small
Victorian farmhouse, the Plantation House has evolved into a 20-
room Greek Revival treasure. Visitors will be treated to a tour and
a large family-style breakfast, and may venture to the park to play
tennis or horseshoes. The antique-filled guest rooms include the
Stained Glass Room, with
a queen bed and available
twin-bed anteroom, and
the Old Master Bedroom,
with clawfoot tub and
pedestal sink.

Innkeeper(s): Kyle & Deb Warren. $45-75. PC, TC. 5 rooms with PB, 1 cottage and 2 conference rooms. Breakfast included in rates. Types of meals: Full bkfst and early coffee/tea. Beds: QT. Ceiling fan in room. Air conditioning. VCR, fax, copier and library on premises. Antiquing, fishing, historical parks and sites, parks and shopping nearby.
Location: Edge of small town.
Publicity: *Omaha World Herald, Norfolk Daily News, Home & Away and Midwest Living.*
"Gorgeous house! Relaxing atmosphere. Just like going to Mom's house."
Certificate may be used: Jan. 30 to April 30, Sunday-Friday, Oct. 1 to Nov. 15, Sunday-Friday.

Grand Island   D7

Kirschke House B&B

1124 W 3rd St
Grand Island, NE 68801-5834
(308)381-6851 (800)381-6851
Internet: www.gionline.net/~kirschke
E-mail: dawgs098@juno.com

A steeply sloping roofline and a two-story tower mark this distinctive, vine-covered brick Victorian house. Meticulously restored, there are polished wood floors, fresh wallpapers and carefully chosen antiques. The Roses Roses Room is a spacious accommodation with a lace canopy bed, wicker rocking chair and accents of roses and vines. In the old brick wash house is a wooden hot tub. In winter and spring, the area is popular for viewing the migration of sandhill cranes and whooping cranes.
Innkeeper(s): Dennis & Diane Gebers. Call for rates.
Certificate may be used: Anytime.

Nebraska City   D9

Whispering Pines

21st St & 6th Ave
Nebraska City, NE 68410-9802
(402)873-5850
Internet: www.bbonline.com/ne/whispering/
E-mail: wppines@navix.net

Circa 1892. An easy getaway from Kansas City, Lincoln or Omaha, Nebraska City's Whispering Pines offers visitors a relaxing alternative from big-city life. Fresh flowers in each bedroom greet guests at this two-story brick Italianate, furnished with Victorian and country decor. Situated on more than six acres of trees, flowers and ponds, the inn is a birdwatcher's delight. Breakfast is served formally in the dining room, or guests may opt to eat on the deck with its view of the garden and pines. The inn is within easy walking distance to Arbor Lodge, home of the founder of Arbor Day.
Innkeeper(s): W.B. Smulling. $55-75. MC, VISA, DS. 5 rooms, 2 with PB. Breakfast included in rates. Type of meal: Full gourmet bkfst.
Certificate may be used: Jan. 2 to Dec. 15, Sunday-Thursday.

Oakland   C9

Benson B&B

402 N Oakland Ave
Oakland, NE 68045-1135
(402)685-6051
E-mail: sanderson@genesisnet.net

Circa 1905. This inn is on the second floor of the Benson Building, a sturdy, turreted brick structure built of walls nearly 12 inches thick. Decorated throughout in mauve, blue and cream, the Benson B&B features three comfortable guest rooms, and a restful, small-town atmosphere. Guests may visit the Swedish Heritage Center and a nearby city park. An 18-hole golf course is a five-minute drive away. The bed & breakfast features a small gift shop, as well as a collection of soft drink memorabilia. Be sure to ask about the Troll Stroll.
Innkeeper(s): Stan & Norma Anderson. $53-60. DS, PC, TC. 3 rooms. Breakfast and snacks/refreshments included in rates. Types of meals: Full bkfst and early coffee/tea. Beds: QD. Toiletries in room. VCR, spa and library on premises. Antiquing, parks, shopping and sporting events nearby.
Location: City.
Publicity: *KMTV Channel 3 and Omaha.*
Certificate may be used: Anytime, upon availability.

Ord   C6

The Shepherds' Inn, Inc.

Rt 3, Box 108A
Ord, NE 68837
(308)728-3306 (800)901-8649
Internet: www.bbonline.com/ne/shepherd
E-mail: ddvshep@cornhusker.net

Circa 1917. Innkeeper Don Vancura was born in this house, and his grandparents built the early 20th-century farmhouse. The quaint bed & breakfast offers three guest bedrooms, decorated with antiques that are a mix of family pieces and items innkeeper Doris Vancura selected at local auctions. The country setting is ideal for a quiet, secluded getaway. Adults, as well as children, will especially love this inn, as there is a petting zoo on the grounds featuring goats, sheep, a llama and three miniature donkeys. In the mornings, guests enjoy items such as waffles, French toast or egg dishes and fruits.
Innkeeper(s): Don & Doris Vancura. $55-65. MC, VISA, DS, PC, TC. 3 rooms with PB. Breakfast and snacks/refreshments included in rates. Type of meal: Full bkfst. Beds: Q. Turndown service, ceiling fan and alarm clocks in room. Air conditioning. VCR, spa, gift shop and front porch table and chairs on premises. Antiquing, fishing, golf, gift shop, parks, shopping, cross-country skiing, tennis and water sports nearby.
Location: Country.
"We drive hours out of our way just to stay here for a reason—it's home and it's wonderful."
Certificate may be used: Dec. 1-April 1, Sunday-Friday.

Waterloo   C9

J.C. Robinson House B&B

102 E Lincoln Ave, PO Box 190
Waterloo, NE 68069-2004
(402)779-2704

Circa 1905. A short drive from Omaha, the Journey's End is an elegant, Neoclassical Greek Revival home boasting two impressive Ionic columns. The inn, surrounded by large trees, is listed in the national and state historic registers. Antiques, including a stunning clock collection, are found throughout the attractive interior, and the Gone With the Wind Room offers a garden and orchard view. The home, built by seed company founder J.C. Robinson, also features a guest room in his name. Fishing and canoeing are a short walk away or guests may decide to soak up the village's relaxed atmosphere.
Innkeeper(s): John Clark. $50-80. 4 rooms and 1 conference room. Breakfast included in rates. Types of meals: Full bkfst and early coffee/tea.
Certificate may be used: Year-round, Sunday through Thursday, except holiday weekends.

Nevada

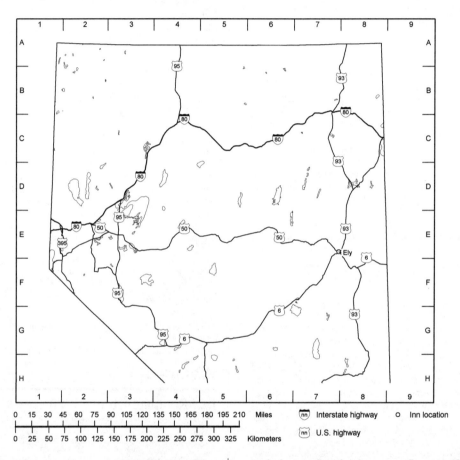

0 15 30 45 60 75 90 105 120 135 150 165 180 195 210   Miles

0 25 50 75 100 125 150 175 200 225 250 275 300 325   Kilometers

Interstate highway   ○ Inn location

U.S. highway

Ely   E7

Steptoe Valley Inn
220 E 11th St, PO Box 150100
Ely, NV 89315-0100
(775)289-8687
Internet: www.nevadaweb.com/steptoe

Circa 1907. Originally a grocery store at the turn of the century, this inn has been lovingly reconstructed and resembles a fancy, Old West-style store. The interior is decorated in Victorian country-cottage style. Five uniquely decorated guest rooms are named for local pioneers. The rooms also have views of the inn's scenic surroundings, and three of them feature

queen beds. A nearby railroad museum offers train rides and Great Basin National Park is 70 miles away. This inn is open from June to October.

Innkeeper(s): Jane & Norman Lindley. $84-95. MC, VISA, AX, PC, TC. 5 rooms with PB and 1 conference room. Breakfast and snacks/refreshments included in rates. Type of meal: Full bkfst. Beds: QT. Cable TV, phone and ceiling fan in room. Air conditioning. VCR, library, jeep rental, gazebo and croquet on premises. Fishing, weekend train rides, four-wheel drive trails, garnet hunting, hiking, casinos and parks nearby.

Location: Small town.

Publicity: *Las Vegas Review Journal, Great Getaways* and *Yellow Brick Road.*

"Everything was so clean and first-rate."

Certificate may be used: Any time March through December, except 4th of July weekend, Labor Day weekend and Arts in the Park weekend (first weekend in August).

New Hampshire

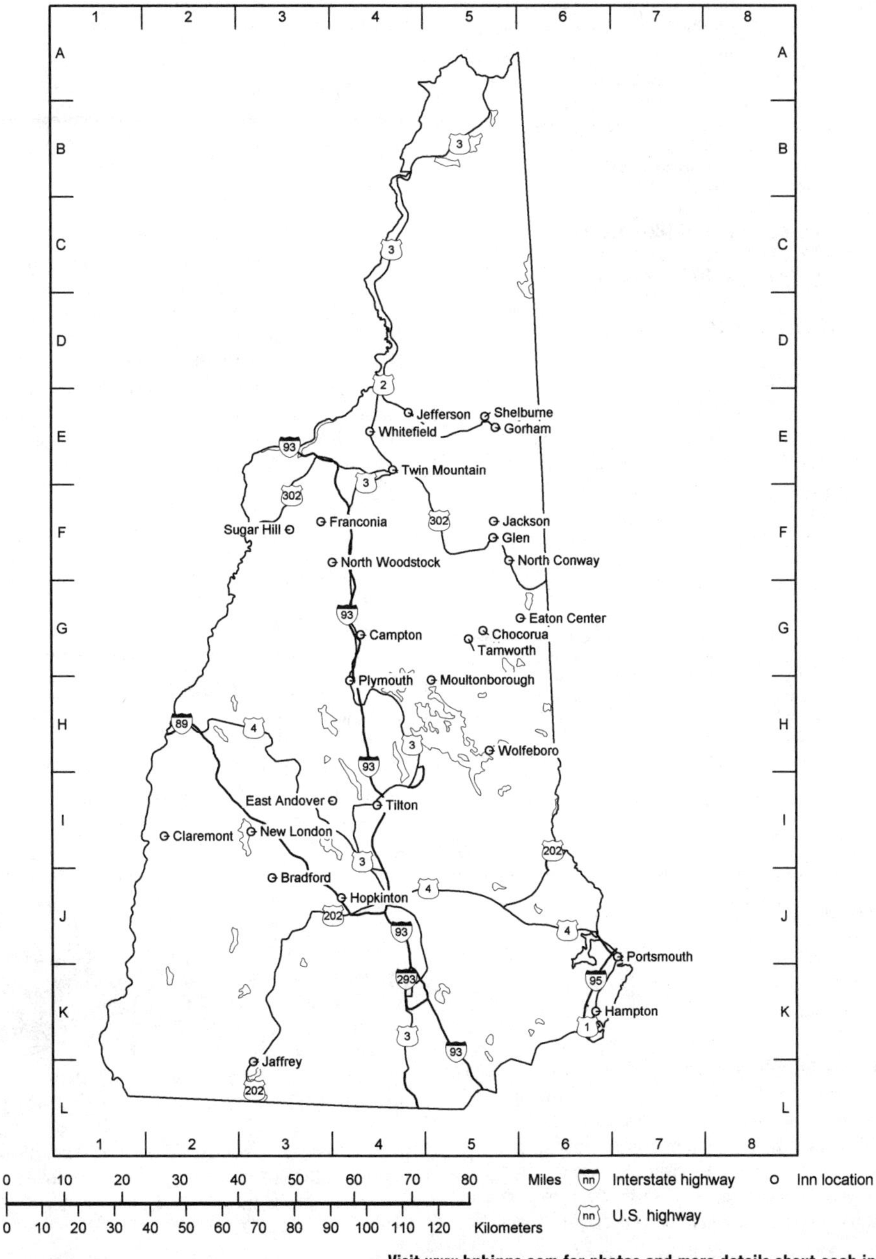

1 2 3 4 5 6 7 8
A B C D E F G H I J K L
Jefferson
Shelburne
Whitefield
Gorham
Twin Mountain
Sugar Hill
Franconia
Jackson
Glen
North Conway
North Woodstock
Eaton Center
Campton
Chocorua
Tamworth
Plymouth
Moultonborough
Wolfeboro
East Andover
Tilton
Claremont
New London
Bradford
Hopkinton
Portsmouth
Hampton
Jaffrey
3 2 93 302 89 4 202 293 95 1
0 10 20 30 40 50 60 70 80 Miles
0 10 20 30 40 50 60 70 80 90 100 110 120 Kilometers
Interstate highway
U.S. highway
Inn location

Bradford
J3

Candlelite Inn

5 Greenhouse Ln
Bradford, NH 03221-3505
(603)938-5571 (888)812-5571
Internet: www.virtualcities.com/ons/nhly/nhyb601.htm

Circa 1897. Nestled on three acres of countryside in the valley of the Lake Sunapee region, this Victorian inn has all of the grace and charm of an era gone by. The inn offers a gazebo porch perfect for sipping lemonade on a summer day. On winter days, keep warm by the parlor's fireplace, while relaxing with a good book. Enjoy a three-course gourmet breakfast, including dessert, in the sun room overlooking the pond. Country roads invite fall strolls, cross-country skiing and snowshoeing.

Innkeeper(s): Les & Marilyn Gordon. $80-110. MC, VISA, AX, DS. 6 rooms with PB. Breakfast included in rates. Types of meals: Full bkfst and early coffee/tea. Beds: Q. Antiquing, live theater, shopping, downhill skiing, cross-country skiing and sporting events nearby.

Location: Small village.

Publicity: Grapevine, InterTown News, Sunday Monitor, N.H. Business Review and The Bradford Bridge.

Certificate may be used: Nov. 1-April 30, excluding holidays.

The Rosewood Country Inn

67 Pleasant View Rd
Bradford, NH 03221-3113
(603)938-5253 Fax:(603)938-5253

Circa 1850. This three-story country Victorian inn in the Sunapee Region treats its guests to a candlelight and crystal breakfast and elegant accommodations that manage to avoid being stuffy. The inn prides itself on special touches. The innkeepers like to keep things interesting with ideas such as theme weekends and special breakfast fare, including cinnamon apple pancakes with cider sauce. Mount Sunapee Ski Area and Lake Sunapee are less than eight minutes away.

Innkeeper(s): Lesley & Dick Marquis. $85-175. MC, VISA, PC, TC. 12 rooms with PB, 1 suite and 1 conference room. Breakfast included in rates. Types of meals: Full gourmet bkfst and early coffee/tea. Beds: QDT. Sherry in room. Fax, cross-country skiing and hiking on premises. Handicap access. Antiquing, fishing, live theater, shopping, downhill skiing, cross-country skiing, sporting events and water sports nearby.

Publicity: Modern Bride, Country Inn, Boston Magazine, Boston Globe, New York Newsday and New York Times.

Certificate may be used: January-June, Sunday-Thursday.

Campton
G4

Mountain-Fare Inn

Mad River Rd, PO Box 553
Campton, NH 03223
(603)726-4283
Internet: www.mountainfareinn.com
E-mail: mtnffareinn@cyberportal.net

Circa 1830. Located in the White Mountains between Franconia Notch and Squam Lake, this white farmhouse is surrounded by flower gardens in the summer and unparalleled foliage in the fall. Mountain-Fare is an early 19th-century village inn in an ideal spot from which to enjoy New Hampshire's many offerings. Each season brings with it different activities, from skiing to biking and hiking or simply taking in the beautiful scenery. Skiers will enjoy the inn's lodge atmosphere during the winter, as well as the close access to ski areas. The inn is appointed in a charming New Hampshire style with country-cottage decor. There's a game room with billiards and a soccer field for playing ball. The hearty breakfast is a favorite of returning guests.

Innkeeper(s): Susan & Nick Preston. $85-135. MC, VISA. 10 rooms, 8 with PB. Breakfast and afternoon tea included in rates. Type of meal: Full bkfst. Beds: QDT. VCR, sauna, game room with billiards and soccer field on premises. Antiquing, fishing, hiking, live theater, parks, downhill skiing, cross-country skiing, sporting events and water sports nearby.

Location: New Hampshire White Mountains.

Publicity: Ski, Skiing and Snow Country.

"Thank you for your unusually caring attitude toward your guests."

Certificate may be used: Sunday through Thursday nights except Dec. 15-Jan. 2 and Sept. 15-Oct 20.

Chocorua
G5

Staffords-In-The-Field

PO Box 270
Chocorua, NH 03817-0270
(603)323-7766 Fax:(603)323-7531

Circa 1778. The main building of Stafford's, home to a prosperous farm family for over 150 years, is Federal style. It became a guest house in the 1890s. An old apple orchard and sugar house remain, and there's a kitchen garden and a nine-hole golf course on the inn's 12 acres. A rocky brook still winds through the rolling fields, and in the adjacent woods, there's a natural swimming hole. Guest rooms are furnished in antiques. A canoe on nearby Lake Chocorua is available to guests.

Innkeeper(s): Fred & Ramona Stafford. $70-170. MC, VISA. 14 rooms, 6 with PB, 1 with FP. Breakfast included in rates. Type of meal: Full gourmet bkfst. Beds: KQDT. TV and phone in room.

Publicity: Esquire, Boston Globe, Seattle Times and Los Angeles Times.

"Delicious food, delightful humor!"

Certificate may be used: May 30 to Sept. 16, Monday-Thursday.

Claremont
I2

Goddard Mansion B&B

25 Hillstead Rd
Claremont, NH 03743-3317
(603)543-0603 (800)736-0603 Fax:(603)543-0001
Internet: www.goddardmansion.com
E-mail: deb@goddardmansion.com

Circa 1905. This English-style manor house and adjacent garden tea house is surrounded by seven acres of lawns and gardens. Each of the guest rooms is decorated in a different style. One features French Country decor, another sports a Victorian look. The living room with its fireplace, window seats and baby  grand piano is a perfect place to relax. Homemade breakfasts, made using natural ingredients and fresh produce, include items such as souffles, pancakes, freshly baked muffins and fruit. The hearty meals are served in the wood paneled dining room highlighted by an antique Wurlitzer jukebox.

Innkeeper(s): Debbie Albee. $75-125. MC, VISA, AX, DS, PC, TC. 10 rooms, 3 with PB, 1 suite and 2 conference rooms. Breakfast included in rates.

Types of meals: Full gourmet bkfst and cont plus. Beds: KQDT. TV, phone, turndown service and some desks in room. Air conditioning. VCR, fax, bicycles, library and child care available on premises. Antiquing, fishing, live theater, parks, shopping, downhill skiing and cross-country skiing nearby.

Location: Rural.

Publicity: *Eagle Times and Yankee (editors pick).*

"A perfect romantic getaway spot."

Certificate may be used: All year, excepting holidays and foliage season. Sunday through Thursday (one weekend night upon availability).

East Andover   I4

Highland Lake Inn B&B

32 Maple St, PO Box 164
East Andover, NH 03231-0164
(603)735-6426 Fax:(603)735-5355
Internet: www.highlandlakeinn.com

Circa 1767. This early Colonial-Victorian inn overlooks three mountains, and all the rooms have views of either the lake or the mountains. Many guest rooms feature handmade quilts and some have four-poster beds. Guests may relax with a book from the inn's library in front of the sitting room fireplace or walk the seven-acre grounds and enjoy old apple and maple trees, as well as the shoreline of the lake. Adjacent to a 21-acre nature conservancy, there are scenic trails and a stream to explore. Highland Lake is stocked with bass and also has trout. Fresh fruit salads, hot entrees, and homemade breads are featured at breakfast.

Innkeeper(s): Mary Petras. $85-125. MC, VISA, AX. 10 rooms with PB. Breakfast included in rates. Type of meal: Full bkfst. Beds: KQT. Ceiling fan in room. VCR on premises. Amusement parks, antiquing, fishing, live theater, shopping, downhill skiing, cross-country skiing, sporting events & water sports nearby.

Location: Mountains.

Publicity: *Andover Beacon.*

Certificate may be used: Nov. 1 to April 1.

Eaton Center   G6

Rockhouse Mountain Farm Inn

PO Box 90
Eaton Center, NH 03832-0090
(603)447-2880

Circa 1900. This handsome old house is framed by maple trees on 450 acres of forests, streams, fields, wildflowers and songbirds. A variety of farm animals provide entertainment for city youngsters of all ages. Three generations of the Edges have operated this inn, and some guests have been coming since 1946, the year it opened. A 250-year-old barn bulges at times with new-mown hay, and there is a private beach nearby with swimming and boating for the exclusive use of guests.

Innkeeper(s): Johnny & Alana Edge. $58-66. PC, TC. 15 rooms, 7 with PB, 1 with FP. Breakfast and dinner included in rates. Type of meal: Full bkfst. Beds: DT. TV in room. Swimming, library and farm animals on premises. Handicap access. Antiquing, fishing, golf, live theater, parks, shopping, tennis and water sports nearby.

Location: Mountains.

Publicity: *New York Times, Family Circle, Woman's Day, Boston Globe and Country Vacations.*

"We have seen many lovely places, but Rockhouse remains the real high spot, the one to which we most want to return."

Certificate may be used: June 17-July 1, Labor Day-Sept. 24.

Franconia   F3

The Inn at Forest Hills

Rt 142, PO Box 783
Franconia, NH 03580
(603)823-9550 (800)280-9550 Fax:(603)823-8701
Internet: www.innatforesthills.com
E-mail: ahi@innfhills.com

Circa 1890. This Tudor-style inn in the White Mountains offers a solarium, a living room with fireplace and a large common room with fireplace and cathedral ceilings. Breakfast is served with a quiet background of classical music in the dining room, where in the winter there's a blazing fireplace, and in summer the French doors open to the scenery. Guest rooms feature a casual country decor with quilts, flowered wall coverings and some four-poster beds. Cross-country ski for free on the inn's property and at the local touring center. Downhill facilities are found at Bretton Woods, Cannon or Loon Mountain. Nearby Franconia Notch Park and the White Mountains feature trails designed for cycling and hiking. Innkeepers are justices of the peace, and will do weddings or a renewal of vows.

Innkeeper(s): Gordon & Joanne Haym. $95-165. MC, VISA, PC, TC. 7 rooms with PB. Breakfast included in rates. Type of meal: Full bkfst. Beds: KQ. VCR, fax, tennis and library on premises. Antiquing, fishing, golf, parks, shopping, downhill skiing, cross-country skiing and water sports nearby.

Location: Mountains.

Publicity: *New York Newsday and Boston Herald.*

"What a delightful inn! I loved the casual country elegance of your B&B and can understand why you are so popular with brides and grooms."

Certificate may be used: Sunday through Thursday, Nov. 1-April 30, except President, Christmas and New Year's weekends.

Franconia Inn

1300 Easton Rd
Franconia, NH 03580-4921
(603)823-5542 (800)473-5299 Fax:(603)823-8078
Internet: www.franconiainn.com
E-mail: info@franconiainn.com

Circa 1934. Beautifully situated on 117 acres below the White Mountain's famous Franconia Notch, this white clapboard inn is three stories high. An oak-paneled library, parlor, rathskeller lounge and two verandas offer relaxing retreats. The inn's rooms are simply decorated in a pleasing style and there is a special honeymoon suite with private Jacuzzi. Bach, classic wines and an elegant American cuisine are featured in the inn's unpretentious dining room.  There's no shortage of activity here. The inn offers four clay tennis courts, horseback riding, a heated swimming pool, croquet, fishing, cross-country ski trails and glider rides among its outdoor amenities.

Innkeeper(s): Alec Morris. $103-188. MC, VISA, AX. 34 rooms, 29 with PB, 3 with FP, 4 suites, 1 cottage and 1 conference room. Breakfast included in rates. Types of meals: Full gourmet bkfst and early coffee/tea. Beds: KQDT. VCR, copier, spa, swimming, bicycles, tennis, child care, sleighs and ice skating on premises. Amusement parks, antiquing, fishing, live theater, parks, shopping, downhill skiing, cross-country skiing and sporting events nearby.

Location: Mountains.

Publicity: *Philadelphia Inquirer, Boston Globe, Travel & Leisure and Powder.*

"The piece de resistance of the Franconia Notch is the Franconia Inn."—Philadelphia Inquirer

Certificate may be used: Midweek (Sunday-Thursday), non-holiday, June, November-March.
Nov. 1-April 30, except President, Christmas and New Years' weekends.

Glen   F5

Bernerhof Inn

Rt 302, PO Box 240
Glen, NH 03838-0240
(603)383-9132 (800)548-8007 Fax:(603)383-0809
Internet: www.bernerhofinn.com
E-mail: stay@bernerhofinn.com

Circa 1880. Built in the late 19th century for travelers passing through Crawford Notch, in the fifties this historic inn was renamed Bernerhof Inn by its proprietors, the Zumsteins, who brought fame to their inn by providing guests with fine accommodations, musical entertainment and cuisine reflecting their Swiss heritage. Today's innkeepers are proud to continue to feature some of the original Swiss recipes (such as Emince de Veau Zurichoise, the national dish of Switzerland), as part of their award-winning menu. The Black Bear Pub, also on the premises, provides more casual fare and a selection of fine brews. Guest rooms are decorated with antiques, and many include two-person Jacuzzi tubs. One offers a fireplace. Novice and experienced chefs alike will enjoy the "Taste of the Mountains Cooking School," where they can pick up many tricks of the trade. The inn's location in the foothills of the White Mountains provides easy access to a variety of outdoor activities including skiing, alpine slides and summer water slides at Attitash Bear Peak. In addition to the historic inn, the innkeepers also offer The Red Apple Inn, a motel-style property. Both properties are non-smoking.

Innkeeper(s): Sharon Wroblewski. $75-150. MC, VISA, AX, DS, PC, TC. 9 rooms with PB and 2 suites. Breakfast included in rates. Types of meals: Full bkfst and early coffee/tea. Beds: KQ. Cable TV, phone, ceiling fan and VCR in room. Air conditioning. Fax, copier and sauna on premises. Amusement parks, antiquing, bicycling, fishing, golf, hiking, rock climbing, ice climbing, snow shoeing, live theater, parks, shopping, downhill skiing and cross-country skiing nearby.

Location: Mountains.

Publicity: *Yankee Magazine, Boston Globe, Bon Appetit, Skiing, Gault Millau, Country New England Inns and Weekends for Two in New England:50 Romantic Getaways Inn Spots & Special Places in New England.*

"When people want to treat themselves, this is where they come."

Certificate may be used: Nov. 1-Dec. 16, Monday-Thursday, standard room. April 1-June 19, Monday-Thursday.

Gorham   E5

The Libby House B&B

55 Main St
Gorham, NH 03581-0267
(603)466-2271 (800)453-0023
E-mail: libbyhouse@worldnet.att.net

Circa 1891. Located across from the town common, this Victorian is in the local historic register. There's a wraparound porch and the three guest rooms are decorated in a comfortable Victorian style. Blueberry pancakes with locally made syrup and cheddar eggs dishes are served frequently.

Innkeeper(s): Margaret & Paul Kuliga. $55-80. MC, VISA, AX, DS, PC, TC. 3 rooms, 2 with PB and 1 suite. Breakfast included in rates. Beds: Q. Ceiling fan in room. VCR, bicycles, library and tennis nearby on premises. Antiquing, fishing, golf, hiking, live theater, parks, shopping, downhill skiing, cross-country skiing, tennis and water sports nearby.

Certificate may be used: November-June, Sunday-Thursday, except holiday weeks, i.e., Christmas, New Year's and winter school vacation.

Hampton   K6

Victoria Inn

430 High St
Hampton, NH 03842-2311
(603)929-1437

Circa 1865. Elegance and style are featured at this Queen Anne Victorian inn just a half-mile from the ocean. A romantic gazebo, spacious guest rooms and Victorian furnishings throughout the inn add to its considerable charm. The Honeymoon Suite and Victoria Room are popular with those seeking privacy and luxury. Guests may borrow the inn's bicycles for a relaxing ride or read a book in its deluxe morning room. Common areas include the living room and the sitting room, with its cozy fireplace.

Innkeeper(s): Bill & Ruth Muzzey. $75-95. MC, VISA, PC, TC. 6 rooms, 3 with PB. Breakfast included in rates. Types of meals: Full bkfst and early coffee/tea. Beds: KQDT. Cable TV, phone, turndown service and ceiling fan in room. Air conditioning. VCR and library on premises. Antiquing, fishing, live theater, parks, shopping, downhill skiing, cross-country skiing, sporting events and water sports nearby.

Certificate may be used: Nov. 1-April 30.

Hopkinton   J4

The Country Porch B&B

281 Moran Rd
Hopkinton, NH 03229
(603)746-6391 Fax:(603)746-6391

Circa 1978. This farmhouse does in fact sport a wraparound covered porch where guests are often found relaxing and enjoying the peaceful 15-acre grounds. The home was built in the late 1970s, but it is a replica of an 18th-century Colonial. There are three guest rooms, decorated in Colonial style. One room has a fireplace, another includes a canopy bed. Whatever the season, guests will find something to do in the Hopkinton area. Guests can visit a restored Shaker Village, shop for antiques, fish, pick berries, ski and much more.

Innkeeper(s): Tom & Wendy Solomon. $60-80. MC, VISA, PC, TC. 3 rooms with PB, 1 with FP and 1 conference room. Breakfast included in rates. Types of meals: Full bkfst and early coffee/tea. Beds: KT. Ceiling fan in room. VCR, fax, copier and swimming on premises. Antiquing, fishing, golf, live theater, parks, shopping, downhill skiing, cross-country skiing, sporting events, tennis and water sports nearby.

Location: Country.

"A highlight of our trip and will be forever a treasured memory."
Certificate may be used: Nov. 1 through April 30, Sunday-Saturday.

Jackson   F5

Dana Place Inn

Rt 16, Pinkham Notch Rd
Jackson, NH 03846
(603)383-6822 (800)537-9276 Fax:(603)383-6022
Internet: www.danaplace.com
E-mail: contact@danaplace.com

Circa 1860. The original owners received this Colonial farmhouse as a wedding present. The warm, cozy atmosphere of the inn is surpassed only by the spectacular mountain views. During autumn, the fall leaves explode with color, and guests can enjoy the surroundings while taking a hike or bike ride through the area. The beautiful Ellis River is the perfect place for an afternoon of fly-fishing or a picnic. After a scrumptious country breakfast, winter guests can step out the door and into skis for a day of cross-country skiing.

Innkeeper(s): The Levine Family. $95-225. MC, VISA, AX, DC, CB, DS, PC, TC. 35 rooms with PB. Breakfast and afternoon tea included in rates. Type of meal: Full bkfst. Beds: KQDT. VCR, fax, copier, spa, swimming, tennis, library and hiking on premises. Amusement parks, antiquing, fishing, golf, White Mountain attractions, live theater, parks, shopping, downhill skiing, cross-country skiing and water sports nearby.

Pets allowed: Exterior rooms.

Location: Mountains.

Publicity: *Travel & Leisure, Inn Spots, Bon Appetit and Country Journal.*

"We had such a delightful time at Dana Place Inn. We will recommend you to everyone."
Certificate may be used: Midweek, year-round, excluding February, August, Sept. 20-Oct. 20 and holiday periods.

Ellis River House

Rt 16, Box 656
Jackson, NH 03846
(603)383-9339 (800)233-8309 Fax:(603)383-4142
Internet: www.erhinn.com
E-mail: innkeeper@erhinn.com

Circa 1893. Andrew Harriman built this farmhouse, as well as the village town hall and three-room schoolhouse where the innkeepers' children attended school. Classic antiques and Laura Ashley prints decorate the guest rooms and riverfront "honeymoon" cottage,

and each window reveals views of magnificent mountains, the vineyard or spectacular Ellis River. In 1993, the innkeepers added 18 rooms, 11 of which feature fireplaces and six offer two-person Jacuzzis. They also added three suites, a heated, outdoor pool, an indoor Jacuzzi and a sauna.

Innkeeper(s): Barry & Barbara Lubao. $89-289. MC, VISA, AX, DC, CB, DS, PC, TC. 18 rooms with PB, 11 with FP, 3 suites, 1 cottage and 1 conference room. Breakfast included in rates. Types of meals: Full bkfst and early coffee/tea. Beds: KQDT. Cable TV and phone in room. Air conditioning. Fax, spa, swimming and sauna on premises. Handicap access. Amusement parks, antiquing, fishing, live theater, parks, shopping, downhill skiing, cross-country skiing, sporting events and water sports nearby.

Location: Mountains.

Publicity: *Philadelphia Inquirer.*

"We have stayed at many B&Bs all over the world and are in agreement that the beauty and hospitality of Ellis River House is that of a world-class bed & breakfast."
Certificate may be used: Midweek, Monday through Thursday; January, March, April, May, November, Dec. 1-15 (non-holiday periods).

Village House

Rt 16 A Box 359
Jackson, NH 03846
(603)383-6666 (800)972-8343 Fax:(603)383-6464

Circa 1860. Village House was built as an annex to the larger Hawthorne Inn, which eventually burned. It is a colonial building, with a porch winding around three sides. The Wildcat River flows by the inn's seven acres, and there is a swimming pool, outdoor Jacuzzi, clay tennis court and shuffleboard set in view of the White Mountains.

Innkeeper(s): Robin Crocker. $65-145. MC, VISA, DS, PC, TC. 9 rooms with PB. Beds: KQ. TV and kitchenettes and Jacuzzi (some rooms) in room. Fax, copier, spa, swimming, tennis and library on premises. Amusement parks, antiquing, canoeing/kayaking, fishing, golf, hiking, horseback riding, live theater, parks, shopping, downhill skiing, cross-country skiing, tennis and water sports nearby.

Pets allowed: In five of our rooms.

Location: Village.

Publicity: *Foxboro Reporter.*

"Your hospitality and warmth made us feel right at home. The little extras, such as turndown service, flowers and baked goods, are all greatly appreciated."
Certificate may be used: Midweek excluding holiday and vacation weeks and Sept. 15-Oct. 15.

Whitneys' Inn Jackson

Rt 16B, PO Box 822
Jackson, NH 03846
(603)383-8916 (800)677-5737 Fax:(603)383-6886
Internet: whitneysinn.com
E-mail: whitneys@ncia.net

Circa 1842. This country inn offers romance, family recreation and a lovely setting at the base of the Black Mountain Ski Area. The inn specializes in recreation, as guests enjoy cookouts, cross-country and downhill skiing, hiking, lawn games, skating, sledding, sleigh rides, swimming and tennis. Popular nearby activities include trying out Jackson's two golf courses and picnicking at Jackson Falls.

Innkeeper(s): Bob Bowman. $70-130. MC, VISA, AX, DC, DS, PC, TC. 30

rooms with PB, 3 with FP, 8 suites, 2 cottages and 2 conference rooms. Breakfast and afternoon tea included in rates. Types of meals: Full bkfst, country bkfst and early coffee/tea. Beds: KQDT. Cable TV and some with refrigerator in room. Air conditioning. VCR, fax, copier, spa, swimming, tennis, library, child care and heated swimming pool on premises. Amusement parks, antiquing, art galleries, bicycling, canoeing/kayaking, fishing, golf, hiking, horseback riding, live theater, shopping, downhill skiing, cross-country skiing, tennis and water sports nearby.

Pets allowed: some rooms and cottages.

Location: Mountains.

Publicity: *Bon Appetit, Ladies Home Journal and Ski.*

Certificate may be used: March 15 to July 14, and Oct. 20 to Dec. 24.

Jaffrey   L3

The Benjamin Prescott Inn

Rt 124 E, 433 Turnpike Rd
Jaffrey, NH 03452
(603)532-6637 (888)950-6637 Fax:(603)532-6637
Internet: www.benjaminprescottinn.com
E-mail: bprescottinn@aol.com

Circa 1853. Colonel Prescott arrived on foot in Jaffrey in 1775 with an ax in his hand and a bag of beans on his back. The family built this classic Greek Revival many years later. Now, candles light the windows, seen from the stonewall-lined lane adjacent to the inn.

Each room bears the name of a Prescott family member and is furnished with antiques.

Innkeeper(s): Mimi and Lee Atwood. $75-150. MC, VISA, AX, PC, TC. 10 rooms with PB and 3 suites. Breakfast included in rates. Types of meals: Full bkfst, country bkfst and early coffee/tea. Beds: KQDT. TV, phone, ceiling fan, toiletries and private label glycerine soaps in room. VCR, fax, copier, library, open cookie jar and tea on premises. Antiquing, art galleries, bicycling, canoeing/kayaking, fishing, golf, hiking, horseback riding, national Shrine, lectures, concerts., live theater, museums, parks, shopping, downhill skiing, cross-country skiing, sporting events and water sports nearby.

Location: Country.

"The coffee and breakfasts were delicious and the hospitality overwhelming."

Certificate may be used: Nov. 1-April 30, excluding holidays, subject to availability.

Jefferson   E4

Applebrook B&B

Rt 115A, PO Box 178
Jefferson, NH 03583-0178
(603)586-7713 (800)545-6504
Internet: www.applebrook.com
E-mail: vacation@applebrook.com

Circa 1797. Panoramic views surround this large Victorian farmhouse nestled in the middle of New Hampshire's White Mountains. Guests can awake to the smell of freshly baked muffins made with locally picked berries. A comfortable, fire-lit sitting room boasts stained glass, a goldfish pool and a beauti-

ful view of Mt. Washington. The innkeeper's newest room, Nellie's Nook, includes a king-size bed and a balcony with views of the mountains and a two-person spa. Test your golfing skills at the nearby 18-hole championship course, or spend the day antique hunting. A trout stream and spring-fed rock pool are nearby. Wintertime guests can ice skate or race through the powder at nearby ski resorts or by way of snowmobile, finish off the day with a moonlight toboggan ride. After a full day, guests can enjoy a soak in the hot tub under the stars, where they might see shooting stars or the Northern Lights.

Innkeeper(s): Sandra Conley & Martin Kelly. $50-90. MC, VISA, PC, TC. 14 rooms, 7 with PB and 1 conference room. Breakfast included in rates. Types of meals: Full bkfst and early coffee/tea. Beds: KQDT. Ceiling fan in room. Spa and library on premises. Amusement parks, antiquing, fishing, live theater, parks, shopping, downhill skiing, cross-country skiing and water sports nearby.

Pets allowed: Two rooms kept pet-free; $6.00/night per pet-half of which is donated to Lancaster Humane Society.

Location: Mountains.

Publicity: *Outside, PriceCostco Connection, New Hampshire Outdoor Companion and Outdoor.*

"We came for a night and stayed for a week."

Certificate may be used: May 15-Oct. 15, Sunday-Thursday.

Moultonborough   H5

Olde Orchard Inn

108 Lee Rd
Moultonborough, NH 03254-9502
(603)476-5004 (800)598-5845 Fax:(603)476-5419
Internet: www.oldeorchardinn.com
E-mail: innkeep@oldeorchardinn.com

Circa 1790. This farmhouse rests next to a mountain brook and pond in the midst of an apple orchard. Nine guest rooms are available, all with private baths. Three rooms have a Jacuzzi tub. After enjoying a large country breakfast, guests may borrow a bicycle for a ride

to Lake Winnipesaukee, just a mile away. The inn is within an hour's drive of five downhill skiing areas, and guests also may cross-country ski nearby. The Castle in the Clouds and the Audubon Loon Center are nearby.

Innkeeper(s): Jim & Mary Senner. $70-175. MC, VISA, DS, PC, TC. 9 rooms with PB, 3 with FP, 1 cottage and 1 conference room. Breakfast included in rates. Types of meals: Full bkfst, country bkfst and veg bkfst. Beds: QDT. Cable TV and Three hot tubs in room. Air conditioning. VCR, fax, copier, spa, sauna, bicycles, library, child care, sauna and Gazebo on premises. Antiquing, beaches, bicycling, canoeing/kayaking, fishing, golf, hiking, horseback riding, live theater, parks, shopping, downhill skiing, cross-country skiing, tennis and water sports nearby.

Pets allowed: In kennel or barn.

Location: Mountains.

Publicity: *Merideth News.*

"What a wonderful getaway we had at your lovely inn. We're so glad we found you on the internet."

Certificate may be used: Nov. 1-May 15, Friday and Saturday excluded.

New London   *I3*

Colonial Farm Inn

Rt 11, PO Box 1053
New London, NH 03257-1053
(603)526-6121 (800)805-8504 Fax:(603)641-0314

Circa 1836. The village of New London holds what should be the world's most popular festival, the Chocolate Fest. The innkeepers at Colonial Farm won the award for top confection, a tangy chocolate-almond pate. The historic home, an example of a center-chimney Colonial, is decorated in a tasteful, period style with a mix of antiques and pieces such as four-poster beds. A memorable breakfast is served, and guests would be wise to save at least one night for dinner at the inn. The dining rooms, with exposed beams and plank floorboards, are cozy and romantic, and the food has drawn many compliments. Specialties include crostini with chicken liver pate and prosciutto, roasted red and green peppers with goat cheese, tenderloin of beef with a burgundy-shallot sauce or, perhaps, chicken stuffed with homemade boursin cheese and walnuts.

Innkeeper(s): Robert & Kathryn Joseph. $85-95. MC, VISA, AX, PC, TC. 5 rooms with PB and 1 conference room. Breakfast included in rates. Type of meal: Full bkfst. Beds: QDT. Air conditioning. VCR, bicycles, library, antique shop and pond on premises. Handicap access. Antiquing, fishing, live theater, parks, shopping, downhill skiing, cross-country skiing, sporting events and water sports nearby.
Location: Country.
Publicity: *New York Times.*

Certificate may be used: Jan. 1-Dec. 31, excluding weekends in the summer. Excluding weekends of April 24, Oct. 2 and Oct. 9.

North Conway   *F5*

The 1785 Inn

3582 White Mountain Hwy
North Conway, NH 03860-1785
(603)356-9025 (800)421-1785 Fax:(603)356-6081
Internet: www.the1785inn.com
E-mail: the1785inn@aol.com

Circa 1785. The main section of this center-chimney house was built by Captain Elijah Dinsmore of the New Hampshire Rangers. He was granted the land for service in the American Revolution. Original hand-hewn beams, corner posts, fireplaces, and a brick oven are still visible and operating. The inn is located at the historical marker popularized by the White Mountain School of Art in the 19th century.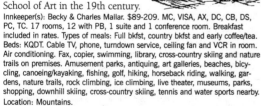

Innkeeper(s): Becky & Charles Mallar. $89-209. MC, VISA, AX, DC, CB, DS, PC, TC. 17 rooms, 12 with PB, 1 suite and 1 conference room. Breakfast included in rates. Types of meals: Full bkfst, country bkfst and early coffee/tea. Beds: KQDT. Cable TV, phone, turndown service, ceiling fan and VCR in room. Air conditioning. Fax, copier, swimming, library, cross-country skiing and nature trails on premises. Amusement parks, antiquing, art galleries, beaches, bicycling, canoeing/kayaking, fishing, golf, hiking, horseback riding, walking, gardens, nature trails, rock climbing, ice climbing, live theater, museums, parks, shopping, downhill skiing, cross-country skiing, tennis and water sports nearby.
Location: Mountains.
Publicity: *Country, Bon Appetit, Travel & Leisure, Valley Visitor, Ski, Travel Holiday, Connecticut and The Wedding Story.*

"Occasionally in our lifetimes is a moment so unexpectedly perfect that we use it as our measure for our unforgettable moments. We just had such an experience at The 1785 Inn."

Certificate may be used: January, March-June, November-December, excluding holidays.

Cranmore Mt Lodge

859 Kearsarge Rd, PO Box 1194
North Conway, NH 03860-1194
(603)356-2044 (800)356-3596 Fax:(603)356-4498
Internet: www.cml1.com
E-mail: c-u@cml1.com

Circa 1860. Babe Ruth was a frequent guest at this old New England farmhouse when his daughter was the owner. There are many rare Babe Ruth photos displayed in the inn and one guest room is still decorated with his furnishings. The barn on the property is held together with wooden pegs and contains dorm rooms.

Innkeeper(s): Garrett & Natalie Blake. $69-159. MC, VISA, AX, DC, DS, PC, TC. 21 rooms, 15 with PB and 1 suite. Breakfast included in rates. Types of meals: Full bkfst and early coffee/tea. Beds: KQDT. Cable TV and ceiling fan in room. Air conditioning. VCR, fax, copier, spa, swimming and tennis on premises. Amusement parks, antiquing, fishing, live theater, parks, shopping, downhill skiing, cross-country skiing and water sports nearby.
Location: Mountains.
Publicity: *Ski, Snow Country, Montreal Gazette and Newsday.*

"Your accommodations are lovely, your breakfasts delicious."

Certificate may be used: Nov. 1-Sept. 15, Sunday through Thursday, excluding holidays and school vacation.

Old Red Inn & Cottages

PO Box 467
North Conway, NH 03860-0467
(603)356-2642 (800)338-1356 Fax:(603)356-6626
Internet: www.oldredinn.com
E-mail: oldredin@nxi.com

Circa 1810. Guests can opt to stay in an early 19th-century home or in one of a collection of cottages at this country inn. The rooms are decorated with handmade quilts and stenciling dots the walls. Several rooms include four-poster or canopy beds. One of the two-bedroom cottages includes a kitchenette, and both feature a screened porch. A hearty, country meal accompanied by freshly baked breads, muffins and homemade preserves starts off the day. The inn is near many of the town's shops, restaurants and outlets.

Innkeeper(s): Dick & Terry Potochniak. $98-178. MC, VISA, AX, DS. 17 rooms, 15 with PB, 1 suite and 10 cottages. Breakfast included in rates. Types of meals: Full bkfst and early coffee/tea. Beds: QDT. Cable TV in room. Air conditioning. Fax, copier and swimming on premises. Amusement parks, antiquing, fishing, golf, live theater, parks, shopping, downhill skiing, cross-country skiing, sporting events, tennis and water sports nearby.
Location: Mountains.

Certificate may be used: Jan. 21-May 21, Sunday-Thursday, (inn rooms only), non-holiday or vacation weeks.

Victorian Harvest Inn

28 Locust Ln, Box 1763
North Conway, NH 03860
(603)356-3548 (800)642-0749 Fax:(603)356-8430
Internet: www.victorianharvestinn.com
E-mail: help@victorianharvestinn.com

Circa 1853. Each guest room at this Victorian inn offers a mountain view, and some have fireplaces. Perched atop a hill in the Mt. Washington Valley, the inn features country Victorian furnishings highlighted by homemade quilts and teddy bears. The Victoria Station Room boasts its own carousel horse, and the Nook & Cranny Room offers a view of the entire Moat Range. Cotswold Hideaway offers a skylight and gas fireplace.

Guests can relax by the pool, lounge in the library while listening to Beethoven, Vivaldi and Bach or hike around the Puddin Pond conservation trail. The grounds include a foot bridge, gardens and the pool. Dutch pannekuchen, Belgian waffles, frittatas or cornmeal and currant pancakes are served at breakfast.

Innkeeper(s): David & Judy Wooster. $75-160. MC, VISA, TC. 8 rooms with PB. Breakfast and afternoon tea included in rates. Type of meal: Full gourmet bkfst. Phone if requested in room. Air conditioning. VCR, fax, copier, swimming and library on premises. Antiquing, canoeing/kayaking, golf, hiking, horseback riding, tubing, outlet shopping, live theater, parks, shopping, downhill skiing, cross-country skiing and water sports nearby.

Location: Mountains.

Certificate may be used: Sunday-Thursday, November-June, no holiday weeks.

North Woodstock F4

Wilderness Inn B&B

Rfd 1, Box 69, Rts 3 & 112
North Woodstock, NH 03262-9710
(603)745-3890 (800)200-9453
Internet: www.thewildernessinn.com
E-mail: info@thewildernessinn.com

Circa 1912. Surrounded by the White Mountain National Forest, this charming shingled home offers a picturesque get-away for every season. Guest rooms are furnished with antiques and Oriental rugs, and the innkeepers also offer family suites and a private cottage with a fireplace, Jacuzzi and a view of Lost River. Breakfast is a delightful affair with choices ranging from fresh muffins to brie cheese omelets, French toast topped with homemade apple syrup, crepes or specialty pancakes. For the children, the innkeepers create teddy bear pancakes or French toast. If you have room, an afternoon tea also is prepared.

Innkeeper(s): Michael & Rosanna Yarnell. $50-135. MC, VISA, AX, PC, TC. 7 rooms with PB and 1 cottage. Breakfast included in rates. Type of meal: Full gourmet bkfst. Beds: QDT. TV in room.

"The stay at your inn, attempting and completing the 3D jig-jaw puzzle, combined with those unforgettable breakfasts, and your combined friendliness, makes the Wilderness Inn a place for special memories."

Certificate may be used: All midweek except holidays and July-October.

Plymouth H4

Colonel Spencer Inn

RR 1, Box 206
Plymouth, NH 03264
(603)536-3438

Circa 1764. This pre-Revolutionary Colonial boasts Indian shutters, gleaming plank floors and a secret hiding place. Joseph Spencer, one of the home's early owners, fought at Bunker Hill and with General Washington. Within view of the river and the mountains, the inn is now a cozy retreat with warm Colonial decor. A suite with a kitchen is also available.

Innkeeper(s): Carolyn & Alan Hill. $45-65. PC, TC. 7 rooms with PB and 1 suite. Breakfast & snacks/refreshments included in rates. Type of meal: Full bkfst. Beds: D. Fans in room. Antiquing, fishing, water parks, live theater, parks, shopping, downhill skiing, cross-country skiing, sporting events & water sports nearby.

Location: Mountains.

"You have something very special here, and we very much enjoyed a little piece of it!"

Certificate may be used: Anytime except holiday weekends and weekends in October.

Crab Apple Inn B&B

PO Box 188
Plymouth, NH 03264-0188
(603)536-4476

Circa 1835. Behind an immaculate, white picket fence is a brick Federal house beside a small brook at the foot of Tenney Mountain. Rooms are appointed with antiques. The two-room suite includes an antique clawfoot tub and a canopy bed. The grounds have gardens and, of course, many crab apple trees.

Innkeeper(s): Christine DeCamp. $70-105. MC, VISA, PC, TC. 5 rooms, 3 with PB. Breakfast and afternoon tea included in rates. Types of meals: Full gourmet bkfst and early coffee/tea. Beds: QDT. Terry robes, candies and down comforters in room. Air conditioning. Amusement parks, antiquing, fishing, hiking, rock climbing, live theater, parks, shopping, downhill skiing, cross-country skiing, sporting events and water sports nearby.

Location: Mountains.

"We are still excited about our trip. The Crab Apple Inn was the unanimous choice for our favorite place to stay."

Certificate may be used: May 1-Sept. 15, midweek only (Tuesday and Wednesday or Wednesday and Thursday).

Portsmouth J7

The Inn at Christian Shore

335 Maplewood Ave
Portsmouth, NH 03801-3536
(603)431-6770 Fax:(603)431-7743

Circa 1800. This handsome Federal-style house combines the convenience of in-town lodging with the charm of a country inn. Minutes from downtown Portsmouth, the inn is located in a diverse neighborhood with historic homes and attractions nearby. The inn offers six tastefully decorated rooms, two of which feature fireplaces. Guests can enjoy a full gourmet breakfast served in our open-beamed dining room appointed with a Harvest table and Windsor chairs.

Innkeeper(s): Mariaelena Koopman. $75-105. MC, VISA, AX, TC. 6 rooms, 4 with PB. Breakfast and afternoon tea included in rates. Types of meals: Full bkfst, cont plus and early coffee/tea. Beds: QDT. Cable TV in room. Air conditioning. VCR on premises. Antiquing, fishing, parks and shopping nearby.

Certificate may be used: Nov. 1 to May 31, Sunday to Friday.

Shelburne E5

The Inn at Shelburne

421 State Rt 2
Shelburne, NH 03581
(603)466-5969 (888)466-5969 Fax:(603)466-5961
Internet: www.shelburne.com
E-mail: innkeeper@shelburneinn.com

Circa 1820. This white Federal building has recently been refurbished by its new owners. The Washington Suite has a four-poster rice bed, other period pieces and a Jacuzzi. There are robes and bath oils in all the rooms. The dining room, open to the public, offers gourmet fireside dining. There are secluded hiking trails on the inn's five acres, or you might prefer to canoe on Reflection Pond.

Innkeeper(s): Mickey & Tina Doucette. $60-189. MC, VISA, AX, DS, TC. 7 rooms, 3 with PB and 4 suites. Breakfast included in rates. Type of meal: Full bkfst. Beds: KQD. Cable TV, phone and VCR in room. Fax, copier, swimming and bicycles on premises. Handicap access. Amusement parks, antiquing, fishing, golf, hiking, biking, canoeing on premises, parks, shopping, downhill skiing, cross-country skiing and water sports nearby.

Pets Allowed.

Location: Mountains.

Publicity: *The Berlin Daily Sun* and *New Hampshire News.*

Certificate may be used: Jan. 1-Jan. 31, March 1-July 31, Oct. 15-Dec. 23.

Sugar Hill   F3

Sunset Hill House

Sunset Hill Rd
Sugar Hill, NH 03585
(603)823-5522 (800)786-4455 Fax:(603)823-5738
Internet: www.sunsethillhouse.com
E-mail: innkeeper@sunsethillhouse.com

Circa 1882. This Second Empire Victorian has views of two
mountain ranges. Three parlors, all with cozy fireplaces, are
favorite gathering spots. The inn's lush grounds offer many
opportunities for recreation or relaxing, and guests often enjoy
special events here, such as the Fields of Lupine Festival. The
Cannon Mountain Ski Area and Franconia Notch State Park are
nearby, and there is 30 kilometers of cross-country ski trails at
the inn. Be sure to inquire about golf and ski packages. By
advance arrangement guests may request maple sugar weekends with history lectures and an after-dinner tea. In the fall, a
Thanksgiving package allows guests to help decorate the inn
for the holidays as well as enjoy Thanksgiving dinner together.
Innkeeper(s): Lon, Nancy, Mary Pearl and Adeline Henderson. $100-350.
MC, VISA, AX, DS, TC. 28 rooms with PB, 5 suites and 1 conference room.
Breakfast included in rates. Types of meals: Full gourmet bkfst and early cof-
fee/tea. Beds: KQDT. Suites with fireplaces and/or whirlpools and ceiling fans
(many rooms) in room. Fax on premises. Antiquing, fishing, golf course, live
theater, parks, shopping, downhill skiing, cross-country skiing and water
sports nearby.

Location: Mountains.

Publicity: *Yankee, Courier, Caledonia Record and Boston Globe.*

"I have visited numerous inns and innkeepers in my 10 years as a
travel writer, but have to admit that few have impressed me as much
as yours and you did."
Certificate may be used: Oct. 21-Dec. 21, March 15-June 15, non-holidays.

Tamworth   G5

Whispering Pines B&B

Rt 113A & Hemenway Road
Tamworth, NH 03886
(603)323-7337

Circa 1901. Bordered on one edge by Hemenway State Forest,
Whispering Pines is set upon 22 acres of woods. The guest
rooms are decorated with antiques, and each is individually
appointed with themes such as Woodlands and Memories.
Items such as baked apple puffs and homemade muffins accompany the morning's breakfast entree. Shops and restaurants are
nearby. There is an abundance of seasonal activities in the area,
including berry picking, hay rides, summer theater, nature trails,
bicycling, a popular farm festival and plenty of antiquing.
Innkeeper(s): Karen & Kim Erickson. $80-100. MC, VISA, DS, PC, TC. 4
rooms, 1 with PB. Breakfast and snacks/refreshments included in rates.
Types of meals: Full bkfst and early coffee/tea. Beds: KQD. Library, hiking
and cross country skiing from door to forest on premises. Antiquing, fishing,
hiking, golf, live theater, parks, shopping, downhill skiing, cross-country skiing and water sports nearby.

Location: Lakes, foothills.

Certificate may be used: July 1-Sept. 29, Sunday-Friday.

Tilton   I4

Tilton Manor

40 Chestnut St
Tilton, NH 03276-5546
(603)286-3457 Fax:(603)286-3308
Internet: www.tiltonmanor.com

Circa 1862. This turn-of-the-century Folk Victorian inn is
just two blocks from downtown Tilton. The inn's comfortable
guest rooms are furnished with antiques and sport handmade
afghans. Guests are treated to a hearty country breakfast featuring freshly baked muffins, and dinner is available with
advance reservations. Visitors enjoy relaxing in the sitting
room, where they may play games, read or watch TV after a
busy day exploring the historic area. Gunstock is nearby and
the Daniel Webster Birthplace and Shaker Village are within
easy driving distance. Shoppers will enjoy Tilton's latest addition — an outlet center.
Innkeeper(s): Chip & Diane. $80. MC, VISA, AX, PC, TC. 4 rooms, 2 with
PB, 1 with FP and 1 suite. Breakfast included in rates. Type of meal: Full
gourmet bkfst. Beds: KDT. Some televisions in room. VCR, fax, copier and
child care on premises. Antiquing, beaches, canoeing/kayaking, fishing, golf,
hiking, horseback riding, outlet mall, parks, shopping, downhill skiing, cross-
country skiing, tennis and water sports nearby.

Pets allowed: Small pets with responsible owners.

Location: Mountains.

Certificate may be used: All days, except holidays.

Twin Mountain   E4

Fieldstone Country Inn

125 Fieldstone Ln
Twin Mountain, NH 03595
(603)846-5646 Fax:(603)846-5646
Internet: www.musar.com/traveler/fieldstone-country-inn.html
E-mail: fieldstone.ctry.inn@worldsurfer.net

Circa 1927. Five acres surround this colonial inn with fieldstone trim. Rooms are decorated country-style, and, in summer,
full country breakfasts are served on the porch with splendid
views of Twin Mountain. In winter the dining room is the site
for breakfast, and there's a fire in the Great Room. Favorite
dishes are Caramel Sticky Buns and Bacon Potato Pie.
Innkeeper(s): Mark & Susan Clark. $55-85. MC, VISA, AX. 7 rooms, 3 with
PB, 1 suite and 1 conference room. Breakfast and snacks/refreshments
included in rates. Type of meal: Full bkfst. Beds: QDT. Cable TV and ceiling
fan in room. VCR and pet boarding on premises. Amusement parks,
antiquing, fishing, golf, live theater, parks, downhill skiing, cross-country skiing and tennis nearby.

Pets Allowed.

Location: Mountains.

Publicity: *Manchester Union.*

Certificate may be used: Sunday-Thursday Oct. 20 to Aug. 25.

Whitefield E4

Spalding Inn & Club

Mountain View Rd
Whitefield, NH 03598
(603)837-2572 (800)368-8439 Fax:(603)837-3062
Internet: www.nettx.com/spalding.htm
E-mail: mflinder@Moose.ncia.

Circa 1865. Guests have enjoyed New England hospitality at
this charming country inn since 1865. Guest rooms are located in the main inn and in the carriage house. There are several private cottages as well, each with one or more bedrooms,
a living room, fireplace and private bath. Laura Ashley decor
and antiques create a romantic atmosphere. The inn is noted
for its cuisine, but the dining room's mountain views are
memorable, too. Breakfasts won't leave you hungry, a variety
of country goodies are prepared. Dinners, served by candlelight, feature a menu which changes daily. The innkeepers
offer a variety of packages, with golf, tennis, family vacation
and theater-lovers as themes.

Innkeeper(s): Diane, April Cockrell, Mike Flinder. $109-119. MC, VISA, PC,
TC. 36 rooms with PB, 6 with FP, 6 suites, 6 cottages and 2 conference

rooms. Breakfast included in rates. Types of meals: Full bkfst and early cof-
fee/tea. Beds: KT. Phone in room. VCR, fax, copier, swimming, tennis, library,
golf, four clay tennis courts and swimming pool on premises. Amusement
parks, antiquing, fishing, live theater and parks nearby.

Pets allowed: In cottages only.

Location: Mountains.

"A special spot in an enchanting setting."
Certificate may be used: June 1 to July 30 & Sept. 1-15.

Wolfeboro H5

Tuc' Me Inn B&B

118 N Main St, PO Box 657, Rt 109 N
Wolfeboro, NH 03894-0657
(603)569-5702
Internet: www.worldpath.net/~tucmeinn/
E-mail: tucmeinn@worldpath.net

This 1850 Federal Colonial-style house features a music room,
parlor and screen porches. Chocolate chip or strawberry pancakes are often presented for breakfast in the dining room or
Victorian Garden Room. The inn is a short walk to the quaint
village of Wolfeboro and the shores of Lake Winnipesaukee.

Innkeeper(s): Terrille Foutz. $75-95. MC, VISA, PC, TC. 7 rooms, 3 with PB.
Breakfast included in rates. Types of meals: Full bkfst and early coffee/tea.
Beds: QT. TV in room. VCR and air conditioning and ceiling fans on premises.
Antiquing, fishing, live theater, shopping, downhill skiing and cross-country
skiing nearby.

Location: City.

Publicity: *Granite State News and Wolfeboro Times.*

Certificate may be used: April 15-Oct. 20, Monday through Thursday; Oct.
21-April 14, anytime.

New Jersey

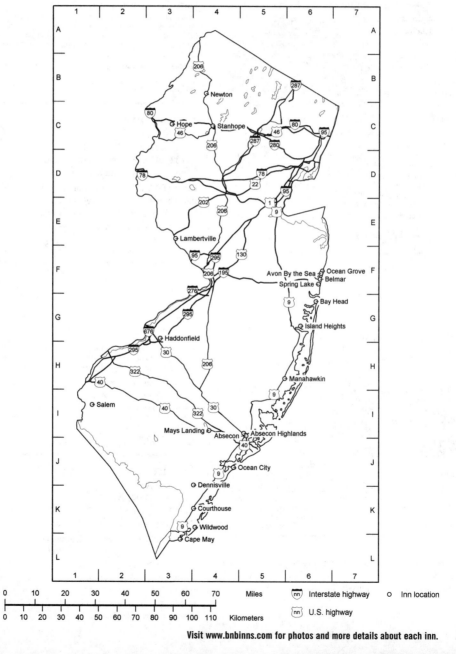

| 0 | 10 | 20 | 30 | 40 | 50 | 60 | 70 | Miles |
| 0 | 10 20 | 30 40 | 50 60 | 70 80 | 90 100 | 110 | Kilometers |

⊡ Interstate highway   ○ Inn location

⬡ U.S. highway

Absecon I5

Dr. Jonathan Pitney House

57 North Shore Rd
Absecon, NJ 08201
(609)569-1799 (888)774-8639 Fax:(609)569-9224
Internet: www.pitneyhouse.com
E-mail: drpitney@bellatlantic.net

Circa 1799. A picket fence surrounds this recently renovated Italianate and Colonial inn. It was the home of Dr. Pitney, considered the Father of Atlantic City. Some of the inn's rooms feature Colonial decor,
while others are in a
Victorian motif. There
are clawfoot tubs,
whirlpools, ceiling fans
and fireplaces. Breakfast
is offered gourmet-style
and features an entree,
freshly baked breads and cakes. Nearby is Atlantic City, Smithville, a winery, beaches, boardwalk, the convention center and a bird sanctuary.

Innkeeper(s): Don Kelly & Vonnie Clark. $100-250. MC, VISA, PC, TC. 10 rooms with PB, 10 with FP and 4 suites. Breakfast and afternoon tea included in rates. Types of meals: Full gourmet bkfst and early coffee/tea. Beds: QD. Cable TV, ceiling fan and VCR in room. Air conditioning. Fax and library on premises. Handicap access. Antiquing, fishing, golf, casinos, parks, shopping, sporting events, tennis and water sports nearby.

Certificate may be used: Sunday through Thursday, Nov. 1 through March 31.

Absecon Highlands I5

White Manor Inn

739 S 2nd Ave
Absecon Highlands, NJ 08201-9542
(609)748-3996 Fax:(609)652-0073

Circa 1932. This quiet country inn was built by the innkeeper's father and includes unique touches throughout, many created by innkeeper Howard Bensel himself, who became a master craftsman from his father's teachings and renovated the

home extensively. Beautiful
flowers and plants adorn
both the lush grounds
and the interior of the
home. Everything is
comfortable and cozy at
this charming B&B, a
relaxing contrast to the
glitz of nearby Atlantic City.

Innkeeper(s): Anna Mae & Howard R. Bensel Jr. $65-105. PC, TC. 7 rooms, 5 with PB, 1 suite and 1 conference room. Breakfast and snacks/refreshments included in rates. Types of meals: Cont plus, cont and early coffee/tea. Beds: QDT. Ceiling fan in room. Air conditioning. VCR on premises. Amusement parks, antiquing, fishing, golf, bird watching, casinos, live theater, parks, shopping, sporting events and water sports nearby.

Location: Country.

"We felt more like relatives than total strangers. By far the most clean inn that I have seen — spotless!"

Certificate may be used: Monday through Thursday, Nov. 1-April 1.

Avon By The Sea F6

The Avon Manor B&B Inn

109 Sylvania Ave
Avon By The Sea, NJ 07717-1338
(732)776-7770

Circa 1907. The Avon Manor was built as a private summer residence in the Colonial Revival style. The handsome facade is graced by a 100-foot wraparound veranda. Light, airy bedrooms are decorated with antiques, wicker and period pieces. Guests breakfast in a sunny dining room or on the veranda.

Innkeeper(s): Greg Dietrich. $75-175. 9 rooms, 7 with PB and 1 suite. Breakfast and afternoon tea included in rates. Type of meal: Full bkfst. Beds: KQT. TV in room. Air conditioning. Child care on premises. Amusement parks, antiquing, fishing, live theater, shopping, sporting events and water sports nearby.

Certificate may be used: Oct. 1 to May 10, not valid holidays or special events.

Bay Head G6

Bentley Inn

694 Main Ave
Bay Head, NJ 08742-5346
(732)892-9589 Fax:(732)701-0030
Internet: www.bentleyinn.com

Circa 1887. Located three houses away from the ocean, this blue shingled inn has a large white wraparound, second-story porch. Rooms are decorated in a Victorian fashion, and the main parlor and library offer wicker furnishings, some antiques and a fireplace. A full breakfast is served in the dining room or screened-in veranda. Afternoon tea is offered during the off season. There is also a restaurant on the premises. Specialties of the house include pasta with a variety of sauces, homemade breads, soups and desserts.

Innkeeper(s): Anthony & Alessandra Matteo. $135-195. MC, VISA, AX, DS, PC, TC. 20 rooms, 13 with PB and 6 suites. Breakfast included in rates. Type of meal: Full bkfst. Beds: QDT. Phone in room. Air conditioning. Amusement parks, antiquing, fishing, golf, parks, shopping, tennis and water sports nearby.

"Many thanks for your thoughtful hospitality. The very best of luck (although you two will not need it.)."

Certificate may be used: Jan. 30 to Dec. 31 Sunday to Thursday except holidays and all of August.

Belmar F6

The Inn at The Shore

301 4th Ave
Belmar, NJ 07719-2104
(732)681-3762 Fax:(732)280-1914
Internet: www.theinnattheshore.com

Circa 1880. This country Victorian actually is near two different shores. Both the ocean and Silver Lake are within easy walking distance of the inn. From the inn's wraparound porch, guests can view swans on the lake. The innkeepers decorated their Victorian home in period style. The inn's patio is set up for barbecues.

Innkeeper(s): Rosemary & Tom Volker. $80-130. MC, VISA, AX. 12 rooms, 3 with PB and 1 conference room. Breakfast included in rates. Type of meal: Full bkfst. Cable TV and phone in room. Air conditioning. VCR, bicycles, aquarium, patio with gas grill, guest pantry w/refrigerator and microwave on premises. Amusement parks, antiquing, fishing, live theater, parks, shopping, sporting events and water sports nearby.

"You both have created a warm, cozy and comfortable refuge for us weary travelers."

Certificate may be used: Sunday to Thursday, May 1-Sept. 30, Sunday to Saturday, Oct. 1-April 30, major holidays excluded.

Cape May   L3

The Abbey Bed & Breakfast

34 Guerney at Columbia Ave
Cape May, NJ 08204
(609)884-4506 Fax:(609)884-2379
Internet: www.abbeybedandbreakfast.com
E-mail: theabbey@bellatlantic.net

Circa 1869. This historic inn consists of two buildings, one a Gothic Revival villa with a 60-foot tower, Gothic arched windows and shaded verandas. Furnishings include floor-to-ceiling mirrors, ornate gas chandeliers, marble-topped dressers and beds of carved walnut, wrought iron and brass. The cottage adjacent to the villa is a classic Second Empire-style cottage with a mansard roof. A full breakfast is served in the dining room in spring and fall and on the veranda in the summer. Late afternoon refreshments and tea are served each day at 5 p.m. The beautiful inn is featured in the town's Grand Christmas Tour, and public tours and tea are offered three times a week in season.

Innkeeper(s): Jay & Marianne Schatz. $100-275. MC, VISA, DS, TC. 14 rooms with PB, 2 suites and 2 conference rooms. Breakfast and afternoon tea included in rates. Type of meal: Full bkfst. Beds: KQD. Ceiling fan, some air conditioning, ceiling fans and desks and antiques in room. Beach chairs and on and off site parking on premises. Antiquing, art galleries, beaches, bicycling, canoeing/kayaking, fishing, hiking, horseback riding, birding, live theater, museums, parks, shopping, tennis and wineries nearby.

Location: National Historic District.

Publicity: *Richmond Times-Dispatch, New York Times, Glamour, Philadelphia Inquirer, National Geographic Traveler. Smithsonian* and *Victorian Homes Magazine.*

"Staying with you folks really makes the difference between a 'nice' vacation and a great one!"

Certificate may be used: Sunday or Monday through Thursday; April, May and October, except Victorian week.

Abigail Adams B&B By The Sea

12 Jackson St
Cape May, NJ 08204-1418
(609)884-1371 (888)827-4354

Circa 1888. This charming Victorian is only 100 feet from the beach which affords refreshing sea breezes and ocean views. There is a free-standing circular staircase, as well as original fireplaces and woodwork throughout. The decor is highlighted with flowered chintz and antiques, and the dining room is hand-stenciled. A full breakfast features the inn's homemade baked sweets.

Innkeeper(s): Kate Emerson. $85-185. MC, VISA, AX, TC. 6 rooms, 3 with PB. Breakfast included in rates. Type of meal: Full bkfst. Beds: QD. Phone and ceiling fan in room. Air conditioning. Amusement parks, antiquing, fishing, live theater and water sports nearby.

"What a wonderful time. Comfortable & homey."

Certificate may be used: Oct. 15-May 15, Sunday-Thursday, excluding holidays.

Captain Mey's B&B Inn

202 Ocean St
Cape May, NJ 08204-2322
(609)884-7793 (800)981-3702
Internet: www.captainmeys.com

Circa 1890. Named after Dutch explorer Capt. Cornelius J. Mey, who named the area, the inn displays its Dutch heritage with table-top Persian rugs, Delft china and imported Dutch lace curtains. The dining room features chestnut and oak Eastlake paneling and a fireplace. One guest room has a double whirlpool tub, another includes a brass-footed, Victorian whirlpool tub. Some guest rooms include both a queen and a single bed. A hearty breakfast is served by candlelight or on the wraparound veranda in the summertime. The ferry and lighthouse are nearby.

Innkeeper(s): George & Kathleen Blinn. $85-225. MC, VISA, AX, PC, TC. 7 rooms with PB and 1 suite. Breakfast and afternoon tea included in rates. Type of meal: Full bkfst. Beds: QT. Ceiling fan and Jacuzzi (some rooms) in room. Air conditioning. Amusement parks, antiquing, fishing, bicycling, bird watching, lighthouse, ferry, live theater, parks, shopping and water sports nearby.

Publicity: *Americana, Country Living, New Jersey Monthly, WKYW News (CBS) Philadelphia, WNJN (N.J. Network News Trenton), New Jersey Country Roads Magazine, Traveller* and *Walking to the Waterline.*

"The innkeepers pamper you so much you wish you could stay forever."

Certificate may be used: April to May & mid-October to Dec. 20, Sunday-Thursday, excluding weekends, holidays and special events.

The Carroll Villa B&B

19 Jackson St
Cape May, NJ 08204-1417
(609)884-9619 Fax:(609)884-0264
Internet: www.carrollvilla.com
E-mail: mbatter@cybernet.net

Circa 1882. This Victorian hotel is located one-half block from the ocean on the oldest street in the historic district of Cape May. Breakfast at the Villa is a memorable event, featuring dishes acclaimed by the New York Times and Frommer's. Homemade fruit breads, Italian omelets and Crab Eggs Benedict are a few specialties. Meals are served in the Mad Batter Restaurant on a European veranda, a secluded garden terrace or in the sky-lit Victorian dining room. The restaurant serves breakfast, lunch and dinner daily. The decor of this inn is decidedly Victorian with period antiques and wallpapers.

Innkeeper(s): Mark Kulkowitz & Pamela Ann Huber. $75-180. MC, VISA, AX, DS, PC. 22 rooms with PB and 2 conference rooms. Breakfast included in rates. Type of meal: Full bkfst. Beds: QD. Phone, ceiling fan and TV and VCR (some rooms) in room. Air conditioning. VCR, fax and copier on premises. Amusement parks, antiquing, fishing, live theater, parks and shopping nearby.

Location: City.

Publicity: *Atlantic City Press, Asbury Press, Frommer's, New York Times* and *Washington Post.*

"Mr. Kulkowitz is a superb host. He strives to accommodate the diverse needs of guests."

Certificate may be used: Sept. 24-May 24, Sunday-Thursday, no holidays, weekends and Christmas week.

Fairthorne B&B

111 Ocean St
Cape May, NJ 08204-2319
(609)884-8791 (800)438-8742 Fax:(609)884-1902
Internet: www.fairthorne.com
E-mail: wehfair@aol.com

Circa 1892. Antiques abound in this three-story Colonial Revival. Lace curtains and a light color scheme complete the charming decor. There is a new, yet historic addition to the

B&B. The innkeepers now offer guest quarters (with fireplaces) in The Fairthorne Cottage, a restored 1880s building adjacent to the inn. The signature breakfasts include special daily entrees along with an assortment of home-baked breads and muffins. A light afternoon tea also is served with refreshments. The proximity to the beach will be much appreciated by guests, and the innkeepers offer the use of beach towels, bicycles and sand chairs. The nearby historic district is full of fun shops and restaurants.

Innkeeper(s): Diane & Ed Hutchinson. $160-230. MC, VISA, AX, DS, TC. 10 rooms and 1 suite. Breakfast and afternoon tea included in rates. Types of meals: Full bkfst and early coffee/tea. Beds: KQ. Ceiling fan in room. Air conditioning. Fax on premises. Antiquing, fishing, historic lighthouse & Victorian architectural tours, live theater, parks, shopping and water sports nearby.

Location: In historic district.

Publicity: *New Jersey Women's Magazine.*

"I feel as if I have come to stay with a dear old friend who has spared no expense to provide me with all that my heart can desire! ... I will savor the memory of your hospitality for years to come. Thanks so much."

Certificate may be used: Nov. 1-May 31, Sunday-Thursday, except holidays.

Gingerbread House

28 Gurney St
Cape May, NJ 08204
(609)884-0211
Internet: gingerbreadinn.com
E-mail: frede@bellatlantic.net

Circa 1869. The Gingerbread is one of eight original Stockton Row Cottages, summer retreats built for families from Philadelphia and Virginia. It is a half-block from the ocean and breezes waft over the wicker-filled porch. The inn is listed in the National Register. It has been meticulously restored and decorated with period antiques and a fine collection of paintings. The inn's woodwork is especially notable, guests enter through handmade teak double doors.

Innkeeper(s): Fred & Joan Echevarria. $90-260. MC, VISA, PC, TC. 6 rooms, 3 with PB and 1 suite. Breakfast and afternoon tea included in rates. Type of meal: Full bkfst. Beds: QD. Air conditioning. Antiquing, fishing, birding. Victorian homes, live theater, parks, shopping and water sports nearby.

Publicity: *Philadelphia Inquirer, New Jersey Monthly and Atlantic City Press Newspaper.*

"The elegance, charm and authenticity of historic Cape May, but more than that, it appeals to us as `home'."

Certificate may be used: Oct. 4-May 26, Monday-Thursday.

The Henry Sawyer Inn

722 Columbia Ave
Cape May, NJ 08204-2332
(609)884-5667 (800)449-5667 Fax:(609)884-9406
Internet: www.beachcomber.com/capemay/bbs/sawyer.html

Circa 1877. This fully restored, three-story peach Victorian home boasts a gingerbread embellished veranda, brick-colored shutters and brown trim. Inside, the parlor features Victorian antiques, a marble fireplace, polished wood floors, an Oriental rug, formal wallcoverings, a crystal chandelier and fresh flowers. Guest rooms have been decorated with careful attention to a romantic and fresh Victorian theme, as well. One room includes a whirlpool tub, one includes a private porch, and another a fireplace.

Innkeeper(s): Mary & Barbara Morris. $85-195. MC, VISA, AX, DC, DS, PC, TC. 5 rooms with PB, 1 with FP and 2 suites. Breakfast and afternoon tea included in rates. Types of meals: Full bkfst and early coffee/tea. Beds: KQT. Cable TV, ceiling fan, whirlpool and private porch in room. Air conditioning. VCR, fax and parking on premises. Antiquing, fishing, golf, carriage, Victorian trolley, live theater, parks, shopping, tennis and water sports nearby.

Location: City.

Certificate may be used: Feb. 15-May 15 & Oct. 15-Dec. 15, Sunday through Thursday, excluding holidays.

The Mason Cottage

625 Columbia Ave
Cape May, NJ 08204-2305
(609)884-3358 (800)716-2766

Circa 1871. Since 1946, this elegant seaside inn has been open to guests. The curved-mansard, wood-shingle roof was built by local shipyard carpenters. Much of the original furniture remains in the house, and it has endured both hurricanes and the 1878 Cape May fire. Two of the inn's suites include a fireplace and whirlpool tub.

Innkeeper(s): Dave & Joan Mason. $95-285. MC, VISA, AX, TC. 9 rooms with PB, 2 with FP, 4 suites and 1 conference room. Breakfast and afternoon tea included in rates. Type of meal: Full bkfst. Beds: QD. Ceiling fan and two with whirlpool tubs in room. Air conditioning. Antiquing, fishing, live theater, parks, shopping and water sports nearby.

Location: Seashore town.

"We relaxed and enjoyed ourselves. You have a beautiful and elegant inn, and serve great breakfasts. We will be back on our next trip to Cape May."

Certificate may be used: April 1-June 15 and Sept. 21-Dec. 15, Monday-Thursday.

The Mission Inn

1117 New Jersey Ave
Cape May, NJ 08204-2638
(609)884-8380 (800)800-8380 Fax:(609)884-4191
Internet: www.mission-inn-nj.com
E-mail: info@mission-inn-nj.com

Circa 1912. In a town filled with gingerbread trim and turrets, The Mission Inn is unusual. The Spanish Mission-style architecture and casual California decor are a departure from the town's notable Victorian flavor. Listed in the National Register, it is included among the 46 original historic structures of  Cape May. In keeping with the more Western appearance, the innkeepers serve treats such as Santa Fe egg rolls for breakfast, along with fresh fruits and biscotti. The meal often is served on the veranda, where guests enjoy a view of the Jersey Shore. The innkeepers provide beach passes and can arrange trolley or house tours, carriage rides, boat cruises and more.

Innkeeper(s): Judith DeOrio & Diane Fischer. $135-235. MC, VISA, AX, TC. 8 rooms with PB, 1 suite and 1 conference room. Breakfast included in rates. Types of meals: Full gourmet bkfst and early coffee/tea. Beds: KQ. Ceiling fan and hair dryers in room. Air conditioning. Fax, copier, wet bar and snacks on premises. Amusement parks, antiquing, fishing, golf, live theater, parks, shopping, tennis and water sports nearby.

Location: City.

Publicity: *Old House Journal.*

"Cape Mays best kept secret."

Certificate may be used: Monday through Thursday, May-June/September-October, holidays excluded.

Poor Richard's Inn

17 Jackson St
Cape May, NJ 08204-1417
(609)884-3536
Internet: www.poorrichardsinn.com

Circa 1882. The unusual design of this Second-Empire house has been accentuated with five colors of paint. Arched gingerbread porches tie together the distinctive bays of the house's facade. The combination of exterior friezes, balustrades and fretwork has earned the inn an individual listing in the National Register. Some rooms sport an eclectic country Victorian decor with patchwork quilts and pine furniture, while others tend toward a more traditional turn-of-the-century ambiance. An apartment suite is available.

Innkeeper(s): Richard Samuelson. $59-147. MC, VISA. 10 rooms with PB and 1 suite. Breakfast included in rates. Types of meals: Cont plus and early coffee/tea. Beds: QDT. Cable TV in room. Air conditioning. Copier on premises. Amusement parks, antiquing, fishing, ocean beach, live theater, parks and water sports nearby.

Publicity: *Washington Post, New York Times, National Geographic Traveler and New Jersey.*

"Hold our spot on the porch. We'll be back before you know it."

Certificate may be used: Sept. 20-June 15, Monday-Thursday.

Queen's Hotel

601 Columbia Ave
Cape May, NJ 08204-2305
(609)884-1613
Internet: www.queenshotel.com

Circa 1876. This charming Victorian hotel is located just a block from the beach in the center of Cape May's historic district. Period decor graces the luxurious guest rooms. The feeling is both romantic and historic. Many of the rooms and suites offer double whirlpool tubs and glass-enclosed marble showers. Other amenities include hair dryers, TV, heated towel bar, air conditioning, coffee makers and mini refrigerators. Some have private balconies and ocean views. As this is a hotel, meals are not included in the rates; however, a multitude of restaurants and cafes are within walking distance or you can ask for the continental breakfast basket for a small charge. The hotel's staff includes professional concierge service. Shops are one block away. There are bicycles on the premises to explore the town and scenic water views.

Innkeeper(s): Dane & Joan Wells. $75-260. MC, VISA, PC. 11 rooms with PB, 1 with FP and 1 suite. Beds: QD. Cable TV, phone, ceiling fan, hair dryer, coffeemaker and heated towel bar in room. Air conditioning. Bicycles on premises. Amusement parks, antiquing, bicycling, fishing, golf, historic tours, live theater, parks and water sports nearby.

Location: City.

Publicity: *Philadelphia Inquirer.*

Certificate may be used: Monday through Thursday, November through March, except holidays and Christmas week.

The Queen Victoria

102 Ocean St
Cape May, NJ 08204-2320
(609)884-8702
Internet: www.queenvictoria.com
E-mail: qvinn@bellatlantic.net

Circa 1881. This nationally acclaimed inn, a block from the ocean and shops in the historic district, is comprised of two beautiful Victorian homes, restored and furnished with antiques. "Victorian Homes" magazine featured 23 color photographs of The Queen Victoria, because of its décor and luxury amenities.

Guest rooms offer handmade quilts, antiques, air conditioning, mini-refrigerators and all have private baths. Some luxury suites include handsome fireplaces and whirlpool tubs. Afternoon tea is enjoyed while rocking on the porch in summer or before a warm fireplace in winter. Breakfast is hearty buffet style and the inn has its own cookbook. The innkeepers keep a fleet of complimentary bicycles available for guests and there are beach chairs and beach towels as well. The inn is open all year with special Christmas festivities and winter packages.

Innkeeper(s): Dane & Joan Wells. $90-290. MC, VISA, PC. 21 rooms with PB and 6 suites. Breakfast and afternoon tea included in rates. Types of meals: Full bkfst and early coffee/tea. Beds: QD. Phones & televisions (some rooms) in room. Air conditioning. Bicycles on premises. Amusement parks, antiquing, beaches, golf, historic tours, parks and water sports nearby.

Publicity: *Philadelphia Inquirer and Travel channel.*

Certificate may be used: Monday through Thursday, November through March, except holidays and Christmas week.

Rhythm of The Sea

1123 Beach Dr
Cape May, NJ 08204-2628
(609)884-7788
Internet: www.rhythmofthesea.com
E-mail: rhythm@algorithms.com

Circa 1915. The apt name of this oceanfront inn describes the soothing sounds of the sea that lull many a happy guest into a restful night's sleep. Watching sunsets, strolling the beach, bird watching and whale watching are popular activities. Many of the features of a Craftsman home are incorporated in this seaside inn, such as light-filled spacious rooms, adjoining dining and living areas and gleaming natural wood floors. Mission oak furnishings compliment the inn's architecture. For guests seeking an especially private stay, ask for the three-room suite and arrange for a private dinner prepared by the innkeeper Wolfgang Wendt, a European trained chef. Full breakfasts are provided each morning. Guests are given complimentary beach towels and chairs. There is free parking and complimentary use of bicycles.

Innkeeper(s): Robyn & Wolfgang Wendt. $99-335. MC, VISA, AX, DS, PC, TC. 7 rooms with PB, 2 with FP and 1 suite. Breakfast and snacks/refreshments included in rates. Type of meal: Full bkfst. Beds: Q. Air conditioning. VCR and bicycles on premises. Amusement parks, antiquing, fishing, live theater, shopping and water sports nearby.

Publicity: *Atlantic City Press, New Jersey Monthly and POV.*

"Your home is lovely, the atmosphere is soothing."

Certificate may be used: October-April, Sunday-Thursday.

Sea Holly B&B Inn

815 Stockton Ave
Cape May, NJ 08204-2446
(609)884-6294 Fax:(609)884-8215
Internet: www.seahollyinn.com
E-mail: seaholly@bellatlantic.com

Circa 1875. The home-baked cuisine at this three-story Gothic cottage is an absolute delight. Innkeepers Patti and Walt Melnick, frequent inngoers themselves, have incorporated their own guest expectations into Sea Holly. The aroma of Patti's special chocolate chip cookies entice guests to search for the dining room. The home is decorated with authentic Renaissance Revival and Eastlake antique pieces. Some rooms boast ocean views. The inn is a wonderful place for a special occasion, and honeymooners or those celebrating an anniversary receive complimentary champagne. In addition to the romantic amenities, the innkeeper provides practical extras such as hair dryers, irons and ironing boards in each room or suite. All rooms and suites include a television. Winter guests should be sure to ask about the inn's midweek winter specials.

Innkeeper(s): Patti & Walt Melnick. $80-200. MC, VISA, AX, TC. 8 rooms with PB and 2 suites. Breakfast and afternoon tea included in rates. Types of meals: Full bkfst and early coffee/tea. Beds: KQ. Ceiling fan, iron & ironing board and cable TV (some rooms) in room. Air conditioning. Fax on premises. Amusement parks, antiquing, fishing, live theater, parks, shopping and water sports nearby.

Publicity: Mid-Atlantic Newsletter, New Jersey Monthly and Fromans.

Certificate may be used: February, March, April, May, Sunday-Thursday; June, September, Monday-Thursday; October, November, December, Sunday-Thursday.

White Dove Cottage

619 Hughes St
Cape May, NJ 08204-2317
(609)884-0613 (800)321-3683
Internet: www.whitedovecottage.com

Circa 1866. The beautiful octagonal slate on the Mansard roof of this Second Empire house is just one of the inn's many handsome details. Bright sunny rooms are furnished in American and European antiques, period wallpapers, paintings, prints and handmade quilts. Rooms with fireplaces or Jacuzzi tub are available. Breakfast is served to the soft music of an antique music box and boasts heirloom crystal, fine china and lace. Located on a quiet, gas-lit street, the inn is two blocks from the beach, restaurants and shops. Ask about mystery weekends and the inn's Honeymoon and Romantic Escape packages.

Innkeeper(s): Frank & Sue Smith. $90-225. 4 rooms with PB and 2 suites. Breakfast and afternoon tea included in rates. Types of meals: Full gourmet bkfst and early coffee/tea. Beds: KQD. Two suites with fireplace and Jacuzzi in room. Antiquing, fishing, live theater, shopping and water sports nearby.

Location: Seashore resort.

Publicity: Bride.

Certificate may be used: After Labor Day through June, Sunday-Thursday. Exclude Victorian week and Christmas week and holidays.

Courthouse   K4

Doctors Inn

2 N Main St
Courthouse, NJ 08210-2118
(609)463-9330 Fax:(609)463-9650

Circa 1854. Several doctors have lived in this pre-Civil War home, including innkeeper Carolyn Crawford, a neonatologist. Each of the romantic guest rooms is named after a doctor and includes a working fireplace and whirlpool tub. There is an emphasis on health here, and the inn includes a spa with sauna, massage and exercise equipment. The inn features a posh restaurant, Bradbury's, and serves a variety of gourmet fare; the seafood is especially noteworthy.

Innkeeper(s): Carolyn Crawford. $125-175. MC, VISA, AX, DC, DS, TC. 6 rooms with PB, 6 with FP, 2 suites and 1 conference room. Breakfast and afternoon tea included in rates. Types of meals: Full bkfst and early coffee/tea. Beds: KQ. Cable TV and phone in room. Air conditioning. Spa and sauna on premises. Handicap access. Amusement parks, antiquing, fishing, live theater, parks, shopping and water sports nearby.

Location: City.

Certificate may be used: Jan. 15-April 30, Sunday-Thursday.

Dennisville   J4

Henry Ludlam Inn

1336 Rt 47
Dennisville, NJ 08214-3608
(609)861-5847

Circa 1804. This country inn borders picturesque Ludlam Lake. Canoeing, birding, biking and fishing are popular activities, and the innkeepers make sure you enjoy these at your peak by providing you with a full country breakfast. Some of the bedrooms have fireplaces, and all feature antique double and queen beds.

Innkeeper(s): Chuck & Pat DeArros. $85-125. MC, VISA, PC, TC. 5 rooms with PB, 3 with FP. Breakfast included in rates. Types of meals: Full gourmet bkfst and early coffee/tea. Beds: QD. TV and ceiling fan in room. Air conditioning. Antiquing, fishing, live theater, parks, shopping and water sports nearby.

Location: Lakefront.

Publicity: Country Inns, Atlantic City Press, New Jersey Outdoors and Bright Side.

"An unforgettable breakfast. Enjoy a piece of history!"

Certificate may be used: Sunday-Thursday, no weekends, no holidays, all year.

Haddonfield   G3

Haddonfield Inn

44 West End Ave
Haddonfield, NJ 08033-2616
(609)428-2195 (800)269-0014 Fax:(609)354-1273
E-mail: qainn@aol.com

This three-story Victorian house, complete with gabled roofs, a turret and veranda, is in the National Trust. Its location is historic Haddonfield, said by Philadelphia Magazine to be the most picturesque village in the Delaware Valley. Handsome heritage homes, fine museums, symphony orchestras, theater and more than 200 shops and restaurants are nearby. Parlors are furnished with antiques and chandeliers, and the guest rooms offer whirlpools and fireplaces, each in the theme of a European country or other culture. Upon arrival, guests are offered snacks and beverages. In the morning, a gourmet breakfast is served before a flickering fireplace in the dining room or on the wraparound veranda overlooking the inn's lawns. For guest convenience, there is an elevator, and the innkeeper provides concierge service. The inn is popular for small meetings and special events. Walk to the train to visit Philadelphia (17 minutes away) and connect to stadiums, the airport and Amtrak.

Innkeeper(s): Nancy & Fred Chorpita. $99-169. MC, VISA, AX, DS, PC, TC. 8 rooms with PB and 1 suite. Breakfast included in rates. Type of meal: Full gourmet bkfst. Cable TV and phone in room. Air conditioning. Handicap access. Golf, swimming, health clubs, parks and tennis nearby.

Pets allowed: Dogs only, subject to restrictions.

Certificate may be used: Sunday-Thursday, holidays excluded.

Hope   C3

The Inn at Millrace Pond

313 Johnsonburg Rd
Hope, NJ 07844
(908)459-4884 (800)746-6467 Fax:(908)459-5276

Circa 1769. The former grist mill buildings house an authentically restored Colonial inn, set in the rolling hills of Northwestern New Jersey. Decorated in the Colonial period, many of the rooms feature original wide-board floors, antiques and Oriental rugs. Rooms in the limestone Grist Mill, a building listed in the National Register of Historic Places, boast hand-crafted American  primitive reproductions and braided rugs. The inn's restaurant features the original millrace room, complete with running water. A former wheel chamber has a staircase that leads to the Tavern Room with its own walk-in fireplace and grain chute.

Innkeeper(s): Cordie & Charles Puttkammer. $110-160. MC, VISA, AX, DC, DS, TC. 17 rooms with PB, 1 with FP, 1 suite and 1 conference room. Breakfast included in rates. Type of meal: Cont plus. Beds: Q. Cable TV and phone in room. Air conditioning. Fax, copier and bicycles on premises. Handicap access. Amusement parks, antiquing, fishing, tennis court on property, parks, shopping and cross-country skiing nearby.

Location: Within historic district.

"The most interesting thing of all is the way these buildings have been restored."

Certificate may be used: All year, Sunday through Thursday, excludes holidays.

Island Heights   G6

Studio of John F. Peto

102 Cedar Ave., PO Box 306
Island Heights, NJ 08732-0306
(732)270-6058

Circa 1889. This Victorian home is listed in the National Register of Historic Places and is of note because it was built by renowned artist John F. Peto. His granddaughter has opened the home for guests. Filled with artifacts, eclectic furnishings, memorabilia and reproductions of his art, the studio is decorated much as it was originally. There is a large screened porch with rocking chairs providing views down the hill to the river. A full breakfast is usually served.

Innkeeper(s): Joy Peto Smiley. $75-95. AX, DS, PC, TC. 4 rooms. Breakfast included in rates. Type of meal: Full bkfst. Beds: DT. Cable TV and phone in room. Air conditioning. Bicycles and library on premises. Amusement parks, antiquing, fishing, parks, shopping and water sports nearby.

Publicity: *Asbury Park Press, House and Gardens Magazine and Observer Entertainer.*

"Breakfast is so great—we won't need any lunch."

Certificate may be used: Year-round except weekends in August.

Lambertville   E3

Chimney Hill Farm Estate & The Ol' Barn Inn

207 Goat Hill Rd
Lambertville, NJ 08530
(609)397-1516 Fax:(609)397-9353
Internet: www.chimneyhillinn.com
E-mail: chbb@erols.com

Circa 1820. Chimney Hill, in the hills above the riverside town of Lambertville, is a grand display of stonework, designed with both Federal and Greek Revival-style architecture. The inn's sunroom is particularly appealing, with its stone walls, fireplaces and French windows looking out to eight  acres of gardens and fields. All eight of the guest rooms in the estate farmhouse include fireplaces, and some have canopied beds. The Ol' Barn has four suites with fireplaces, Jacuzzis, steam rooms, guest pantries, spiral staircases and loft bedrooms. The innkeepers offer adventure, romance and special interest packages for their guests, and the inn is also popular for corporate retreats. There are plenty of seasonal activities nearby, from kayaking to skiing. New Hope is the neighboring town and offers many charming restaurants and shops, as well.

Innkeeper(s): Terry Ann & Richard Anderson. $95-289. MC, VISA, AX, PC, TC. 12 rooms with PB, 8 with FP and 2 conference rooms. Breakfast and snacks/refreshments included in rates. Types of meals: Full bkfst, cont plus and early coffee/tea. Beds: KQD. Phone in room. Air conditioning. Copier, library and butler pantry with snacks on premises. Antiquing, fishing, live theater, parks, shopping, downhill skiing, cross-country skiing, sporting events and water sports nearby.

Location: Countryside.

Publicity: *Country Inns (Cover), Colonial Homes, Country Roads Magazine and New Jersey Network.*

"We would be hard pressed to find a more perfect setting to begin our married life together."

Certificate may be used: Jan. 3-Dec. 20, Sunday through Thursday.

York Street House

42 York St
Lambertville, NJ 08530-2024
(609)397-3007 (888)398-3199 Fax:(609)397-9677
Internet: www.yorkstreethouse.com
E-mail: yorksthse@aol.com

Circa 1909. Built by early industrialist George Massey as a 25th wedding anniversary present for his wife, the gracious manor house is situated on three quarters of an acre in the heart of the Lambertville's historical district. A winding three-story staircase leads to five well-appointed guest rooms decorated with period furnishings. The public rooms are warmed by Mercer Tile fireplaces, original Waterford Crystal chandeliers and a baby grand piano. Breakfast is served in the dining room with its built-in leaded-glass china and large oak servers, looking out over the lawn and sitting porch. Art galleries, antique shops, bookstores and restaurants are all within walking distance from the inn. Lambertville is nestled along the scenic Delaware River and Raritan Canal. Horseback riding, mule-drawn barges and carriage rides are just some of the activities available. A short walk across the Delaware River Bridge brings you to New Hope, Penn., with its many quaint shops.

Innkeeper(s): Nancy Ferguson & Beth Wetterskog. $100-225. MC, VISA, AX, DS, PC, TC. 5 rooms with PB. Breakfast included in rates. Types of meals: Full gourmet bkfst and early coffee/tea. Beds: KQ. Cable TV, ceiling fan and fireplaces in room. Air conditioning. VCR and fax on premises. Antiquing, fishing, live theater, parks and shopping nearby.

Location: Small town.

Certificate may be used: Sunday to Thursday.

Manahawkin   H5

Goose N. Berry Inn

190 N Main St
Manahawkin, NJ 08050-2932
(609)597-6350 Fax:(609)597-6918

Circa 1868. This Queen Anne Victorian, built by an English merchant, has been painstakingly restored and redecorated. Period antiques decorate the guest rooms, each of which has its own personal flair. The Capstan Room features a nautical Victorian theme with paintings in honor of the area's seafaring tradition. Another room is decorated with antique needlepoint samplers, some a cen-

tury old. There are plenty of places to relax, including a library stocked with books. Guests enjoy a wide variety of items during the gourmet buffet breakfast, baked French toast, fresh fruit, homemade breads, egg dishes and gourmet coffee are among the options. The innkeepers have snacks available throughout the day. For those celebrating a special occasions, the innkeepers can prepare a tray with champagne, chocolates or perhaps wine and cheese. The Times-Beacon newspapers voted the inn as the "most romantic getaway" two years in a row.

Innkeeper(s): Tom & Donna Smith. $75-175. TC. 5 rooms with PB, 1 suite and 1 conference room. Breakfast, afternoon tea and snacks/refreshments included in rates. Types of meals: Full gourmet bkfst and early coffee/tea. Beds: D. Turndown service and alarms available in room. Air conditioning. Bicycles and canoe on premises. Amusement parks, antiquing, fishing, gambling & casino shows-Atlantic City, wineries, live theater, parks, shopping and water sports nearby.
Certificate may be used: Sunday to Thursday all year.

Mays Landing   I4
Abbott House
6056 Main St
Mays Landing, NJ 08330-1852
(609)625-4400
Internet: bbianj.com/abbott
E-mail: theabbotthouse@email.msn.com
Circa 1865. Guests at this Victorian-style mansion can relax on the bluff overlooking the Great Egg Harbor River, read on the second-floor veranda with its intricate fretwork or take afternoon tea in the belvedere (cupola) with spectacular views of historic Mays Landing. The inn is within walking distance to Lake Lenape and its various summer attractions. Each room is individually decorated with antiques, wicker, handmade quilts and other special touches. The Victorian Parlor is a place for games, reading and conversation. Refreshments can be enjoyed on one of the many porches and verandas.

Innkeeper(s): Linda Maslanko, Cathy Foschia. $89-119. MC, VISA, AX, DS. 3 rooms and 1 suite. Breakfast included in rates. Type of meal: Full bkfst. Turndown service in room. Air conditioning. Antiquing and shopping nearby.
Certificate may be used: Jan. 1 to Dec. 31, Sunday-Thursday.

Newton   B4
The Wooden Duck B&B
140 Goodale Rd, Andover Township
Newton, NJ 07860-2788
(973)300-0395 Fax:(973)300-0141
Circa 1978. Guests enjoy exploring the 17 acres of wooded grounds and fields that surround this country farmhouse. The innkeepers keep their home filled with things to do. Guests can watch movies, play games or enjoy a good book as they snuggle up next to the huge, double hearth fireplace in the inn's game room. During warm months, guest can use the outdoor pool. Rooms are comfortable and cozy, decorated in country style. The innkeepers display their unique collectibles throughout the home.

Innkeeper(s): Bob & Barbara Hadden. $90-110. MC, VISA, AX, DS, PC, TC. 5 rooms with PB. Breakfast and snacks/refreshments included in rates. Type of meal: Full bkfst. Beds: Q. Cable TV, phone and VCR in room. Air conditioning. Fax, copier, swimming and library on premises. Amusement parks, antiquing, fishing, live theater, parks, shopping, downhill skiing, cross-country skiing, sporting events and water sports nearby.
Location: Country.
Publicity: *New Jersey Country Roads and Bergen Record.*
Certificate may be used: November through March, Sunday through Thursday.

Ocean City   J4
Serendipity B&B
712 E 9th St
Ocean City, NJ 08226-3554
(609)399-1554 (800)842-8544 Fax:(609)399-1527
Internet: www.serendipitynj.com
E-mail: info@serendipitynj.com
Circa 1912. The beach and boardwalk are less than half a block from this renovated inn. Healthy full breakfasts are served, and the innkeepers offer dinners by reservation with a mix of interesting, vegetarian items. In the summer, breakfasts are served on a vine-shaded veranda. The guest rooms are decorated in pastels with wicker pieces.

Innkeeper(s): Clara & Bill Plowfield. $80-159. MC, VISA, AX, DS, PC, TC. 6 rooms, 4 with PB. Breakfast and snacks/refreshments included in rates. Type of meal: Full bkfst. Beds: KQDT. Cable TV, ceiling fan, bathrobes and bottled water in room. Air conditioning. Library and dressing rooms with showers & beach towels on premises. Amusement parks, antiquing, fishing, ocean beach and boardwalk, live theater, parks, shopping and water sports nearby.
"Serendipity is such a gift. For me it's a little like being adopted during vacation time by a caring sister and brother. Your home is a home away from home. You make it so."
Certificate may be used: November-May, Sunday-Thursday. No holidays. May not be combined with any other offers.

Ocean Grove   F6
The Cordova
26 Webb Ave
Ocean Grove, NJ 07756-1334
(732)774-3084 Fax:(212)207-4720
Circa 1885. This century-old Victorian community was founded as a Methodist retreat. Ocean-bathing and cars were not allowed on Sunday until a few years ago. There are no souvenir shops along the white sandy beach and wooden boardwalk. The inn has hosted Presidents Wilson, Cleveland and Roosevelt, who were also speakers at the Great Auditorium with its 7,000 seats. Guests have use of the kitchen, lounge, picnic and barbecue areas, thus making this a popular place for family reunions, retreats, showers and weddings. Ask about the inn's special events. Three suites and two cottage apartments also are available. The Cordova was chosen by New Jersey Magazine as one of the seven best places on the Jersey Shore. For information during the winter season, call (212) 751-9577.

Innkeeper(s): Doris Chernik. $46-159. MC, VISA, PC. 17 rooms, 7 with PB, 3 suites and 2 cottages. Breakfast included in rates. Type of meal: Cont plus. Beds: KQDT. VCR, bicycles, tennis and library on premises. Antiquing, fishing, music concerts, garden tours, dances, shopping and tennis nearby.
Publicity: *New Jersey, Asbury Park Press, St. Martin's Press and "O'New Jersey" by Robert Heide and John Gilman.*
"Warm, helpful and inviting, homey and lived-in atmosphere."
Certificate may be used: anytime between Sept. 15-May 15 (except holidays) and Sunday through Thursday in the summer months.

Pine Tree Inn

10 Main Ave
Ocean Grove, NJ 07756-1324
(732)775-3264 Fax:(732)775-2939
Internet: www.pinetreeinn.com
Circa 1870. This small Victorian inn is operated by a long-standing resident of the area and offers ocean views. Guest rooms are decorated in antiques and all the rooms are equipped with sinks. Bicycles and beach towels are available.
Innkeeper(s): Karen Mason. $55-125. MC, VISA, PC, TC. 12 rooms, 4 with PB and 1 suite. Breakfast and afternoon tea included in rates. Types of meals: Cont plus and early coffee/tea. Beds: QD. Cable TV, phone and ceiling fan in room. Air conditioning. Bicycles on premises. Amusement parks, antiquing, fishing, museums/race tracks, restaurants, PNC Arts Center, live theater, parks, shopping and water sports nearby.
Publicity: *Country Living and USA Today.*
Certificate may be used: All year, Sunday-Thursday only, except on holiday weekends. Must show certificate.

Salem   I1

Brown's Historic Home B&B

41-43 Market St
Salem, NJ 08079
(856)935-8595 Fax:(856)935-8595
Circa 1738. Brown's Historic Home originally was built as a Colonial house. Around 1845, the house was modernized to the Victorian era. The inn is furnished with antiques and heirlooms, including a handmade chess set and quilt. The fireplaces are made of King of Prussia marble. The backyard garden features a lily pond, wildflowers and a waterfall. There is a ferry nearby offering transport to Delaware. On Saturdays, guests can enjoy performances at the Cowtown Rodeo, eight miles away.

Innkeeper(s): William & Margaret Brown. $55-100. MC, VISA, AX, DS, TC. 5 rooms, 3 with PB, 1 with FP and 1 suite. Breakfast and snacks/refreshments included in rates. Types of meals: Full bkfst and country bkfst. Beds: DT. Cable TV, phone, turndown service and ceiling fan in room. Air conditioning. Antiquing, bicycling, fishing, golf, hiking, hunting, bird watching, live theater, museums, parks, shopping and water sports nearby.
Location: Marinas, golf, historic sites.
Publicity: *Newsday, Mid-Atlantic Country, Early American Life and Today's Sunbeam.*
"Down-home-on-the-farm breakfasts with great hospitality."
Certificate may be used: Jan. 10 to Nov. 9, Monday to Friday, except for Sundays and holidays.

Spring Lake   F6

Ashling Cottage

106 Sussex Ave
Spring Lake, NJ 07762-1248
(732)449-3553 (888)274-5464
Internet: www.ashlingcottage.com
E-mail: bmahon@compuserve.com
Circa 1877. Surrounded by shady sycamores on a quiet residential street, this three-story Victorian residence features a mansard-and-gambrel roof with hooded gambrel dormers. One of the two porches has a square, pyramid-roofed pavilion, which has been glass-enclosed and screened. Guests can watch the sun rise over the ocean one block away or set over Spring Lake. A full breakfast can be enjoyed in the plant- and wicker-filled pavilion.
Innkeeper(s): Joanie & Bill Mahon. $99-325. PC, TC. 10 rooms, 8 with PB. Breakfast and afternoon tea included in rates. Types of meals: Full bkfst and early coffee/tea. Beds: Q. Ceiling fan & clock in room. Air conditioning. VCR, bicycles & library on premises. Amusement parks, antiquing, beaches, fishing, race tracks, boardwalk, live theater, parks, shopping, sporting events & water sports nearby.

Location: 1/2 block to lake.
Publicity: *New York Times, New Jersey Monthly, Town & Country, Country Living, New York and Harrods of London.*
Certificate may be used: May 2-June 15 and Sept. 19-Oct. 31, Sunday-Thursday.

Stanhope   C4

Whistling Swan Inn

110 Main St
Stanhope, NJ 07874-2632
(973)347-6369 Fax:(973)347-3391
Internet: www.whistlingswaninn.com
E-mail: wswan@worldnet.att.net
Circa 1905. This Queen Anne Victorian has a limestone wrap-around veranda and a tall, steep-roofed turret. Family antiques fill the rooms and highlight the polished ornate woodwork, pocket doors and winding staircase. It is a little more than a mile from Waterloo Village and the International Trade Center.
Innkeeper(s): Joe Mulay & Paula Williams. $95-150. MC, VISA, AX, DC, DS, PC, TC. 10 rooms with PB, 1 suite and 1 conference room. Breakfast included in rates. Type of meal: Full bkfst. Beds: Q. Cable TV, phone, ceiling fan, VCR, iron and hair dryer in room. Air conditioning. Fax, copier, bicycles, tubs for two and Victorian garden on premises. Antiquing, fishing, golf, hiking, boating, live theater, parks, shopping, sporting events and water sports nearby.
Location: Rural village.
Publicity: *Sunday Herald, New York Times, New Jersey Monthly, Mid-Atlantic Country, Star Ledger, Daily Record, Philadelphia, Country and Chicago Sun Times.*
"Thank you for your outstanding hospitality. We had a delightful time while we were with you and will not hesitate to recommend the inn to our listening audience, friends and anyone else who will listen!" — Joel H. Klein, Travel Editor, WOAI AM
Certificate may be used: Thursday and Friday from January through April, excluding holidays.

Wildwood   K4

Stuart's Once Upon A Time...German B&B

2814 Atlantic Ave
Wildwood, NJ 08260-4902
(609)523-1101 (800)299-6623 Fax:(609)523-1107
E-mail: stuarts-once-upon-a-time@worldnet.att.net
Circa 1905. In the early 20th century, Dr. Henry Tomlin transformed his home into a sanitarium where patients could come for treatment and relaxation. He believed his treatment, along with the sea breezes would invigorate the patients. Today, guests still enjoy the sea air, as well as innkeepers Randall and Christa Stuart's hospitality and fine German cuisine. The spacious home includes six guest rooms and suites, each decorated with European antiques. Breakfasts are served on individual tables and feature fresh cut fruits, homemade breads, cold cuts, cheeses, eggs and imported German coffee. For an additional charge, the innkeepers will prepare a traditional German dinner, complete with soups, appetizers and a main course such as sauerbraten or a sauerkraut platter with bratwurst and mashed potatoes.
Innkeeper(s): Randall & Christa Stuart. $95-185. MC, VISA, TC. 6 rooms with PB, 1 with FP. Breakfast included in rates. Type of meal: Full gourmet bkfst. Beds: QD. Ceiling fan in room. Air conditioning. Fax and heated outdoor shower on premises. Amusement parks, antiquing, fishing, golf, live theater, parks, shopping, tennis and water sports nearby.
Location: City.
Publicity: *Herald News.*
"Superb, as always."
Certificate may be used: June 1-Sept. 30, Sunday-Friday; Oct. 1-May 31, anytime. Not to be combined with any other specials.

New Mexico

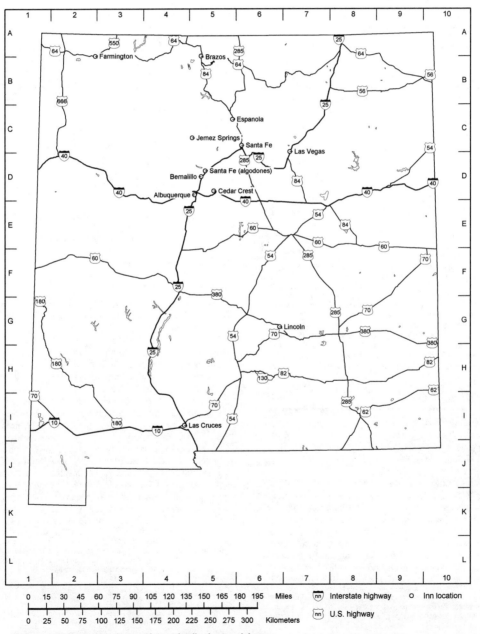

Visit www.bnbinns.com for photos and more details about each inn.

0 15 30 45 60 75 90 105 120 135 150 165 180 195   Miles

0 25 50 75 100 125 150 175 200 225 250 275 300   Kilometers

[nn] Interstate highway   o Inn location

[nn] U.S. highway

Albuquerque D5

Bottger-Koch Mansion B&B

110 San Felipe NW, Old Town
Albuquerque, NM 87104
(505)243-3639 (800)758-3639 Fax:(505)243-4378
Internet: www.bottger.com
E-mail: bottgerk@aol.com

Circa 1912. For Victorian flavor and a superior location close
to Old Town Albuquerque, choose the Bottger-Koch Mansion.
The pink and white exterior is inviting in the dappled shade
from tall trees that shelter the home. The parlor offers a carved

white fireplace, cozy
sitting areas,
Victorian furnish-
ings, art, Oriental
rugs and a chande-
lier shining from an
elaborate ceiling.
Polished wood
floors, light colors and antiques are found throughout. (Ask for
the room with the canopy bed!) Breakfast is served at several
tables in a sun-filled breakfast room. Walk to the New Mexico
Museum of Natural History and Science and the Albuquerque
Museum or to dozens and dozens of restaurants, galleries and
shops in Old Town. A short drive will allow you to visit botanical gardens, the zoo, the Petroglyph National Museum and the
University of New Mexico. Santa Fe is an hour away.

Innkeeper(s): Yvonne & Ron Koch. $99-179. MC, VISA, AX, PC, TC. 8 rooms
with PB and 1 suite. Breakfast, afternoon tea and snacks/refreshments
included in rates. Type of meal: Full gourmet bkfst. Beds: KQT. Ceiling fan in
room. Air conditioning. Fax and copier on premises. Amusement parks,
antiquing, fishing, live theater, parks, shopping, downhill skiing, cross-country
skiing, sporting events and water sports nearby.

Location: City.

Publicity: *PBS Public Television.*

*"Enchanted perfection, the memory of a lifetime. It can't get any bet-
ter than this."*

Certificate may be used: January, February, June, November, December,
Sunday through Thursday, excludes Saturday nights.

Brittania & W.E. Mauger Estate B&B

701 Roma Ave NW
Albuquerque, NM 87102-2038
(505)242-8755 (800)719-9189 Fax:(505)842-8835
Internet: www.maugerbb.com
E-mail: maugerbb@aol.com

Circa 1897. This former boarding house is now an elegantly
restored Victorian in the National Register. Linda Ronstadt and
Martin Sheen have been among some of the inn's notable
guests. Guest rooms include amenities such as refrigerators,
phones with voice mail, coffee makers, a basket with snacks,

and beds topped with
down comforters. The
inn is located four
blocks from the con-
vention center and
business district, and it
is less than one mile
from Old Town.

Innkeeper(s): Mark Brown & Keith Lewis. $89-179. MC, VISA, AX. 8 rooms
with PB and 1 conference room. Breakfast included in rates. Types of meals:
Full bkfst and early coffee/tea. Beds: KQDT. TV, phone, ceiling fan, coffee
maker, iron and hair dryer in room. Air conditioning. VCR, organ and laser
disc player on premises. Amusement parks, antiquing, live theater and shopping nearby.

Location: Old Town.

Publicity: *Albuquerque Journal, Phoenix Home and Garden, Albuquerque
Monthly, National Geographic Traveler, New Mexico Business Week, Golf
Digest and Great Estates.*

*"Because of your hospitality, kindness and warmth, we will always
compare the quality of our experience by the W.E. Mauger Estate."*

Certificate may be used: Nov. 15-March 1, except Thanksgiving and
Christmas, Sunday-Thursday. Friday and Saturday subject to availability.

Casa Del Granjero & El Rancho Guest House

414 C De Baca Ln NW
Albuquerque, NM 87114-1600
(505)897-4144 (800)701-4144 Fax:(505)897-9788
E-mail: granjero@civix.com

Circa 1890. Innkeepers Victoria and Butch Farmer, who appropriately named their home Casa del Granjero, or "the farmer's
house," have designed their bed & breakfast to reflect
Southwestern style with a hint of old Spanish flair. The adobe's
guest rooms all include a rustic, kiva fireplace. Cuarto Allegre is
the largest suite in the main house, and it includes a canopy bed
covered in lace and French doors that open onto a small porch.
Cuarto del Rey affords a mountain view and includes Mexican
furnishings and handmade quilts. Cuarto de Flores also has
quilts, Mexican tile and French doors leading to a private porch.
The innkeepers have a hot tub room for guest use in a special
garden area. The innkeepers also have restored a historic adobe
ranch house across the road. The accommodations here include
three suites and a guest room with a double bed. A kitchen,
common area and wood-burning stove also are located in this
house. A variety of baked goods, New Mexican-style recipes and
fresh fruit are served each morning in the dining room or on the
portal. Several recipes have been featured in a cookbook.

Innkeeper(s): Victoria Farmer. $79-149. MC, VISA. 7 rooms with PB and 5
suites. Breakfast included in rates. Type of meal: Full bkfst. Beds: KQT.
Antiquing, fishing, live theater, downhill skiing, cross-country skiing and
water sports nearby.

Publicity: *Hidden SW.*

"Wonderful place, wonderful people. Thanks so much."

Certificate may be used: January through April, May through December from
Sunday through Thursday. Holidays and special events excluded.

Hacienda Antigua B&B

6708 Tierra Dr NW
Albuquerque, NM 87107-6025
(505)345-5399 (800)201-2986 Fax:(505)345-3855
Internet: www.haciendantigua.com/bnb/
E-mail: antigua@swcp.com

Circa 1780. In the more than 200 years since this Spanish
Colonial-style hacienda was constructed, the current innkeepers
are only the fourth owners. Once a stagecoach stop on the El
Camino Real, it also served as a cantina and mercantile store. It
was built by Don Pablo Yrisarri, who was sent by the King of
Spain to search the area for gold. The home is elegant, yet maintains a rustic, Spanish charm with exposed beams, walls up to
30 inches thick, brick floors and adobe fireplaces. Along with a

sitting room and kiva fireplace, the Don Pablo Suite includes a "ducking door" that leads onto the courtyard. Other rooms have clawfoot tubs, antique iron beds or a private patio. The cuisine is notable and one of the inn's recipes appeared in Culinary Trends magazine. Guests might sample a green chile souffle along with bread pudding and fresh fruit. The inn has been featured on the TV series "Great Country Inns."

Innkeeper(s): Mark Brown & Keith Lewis. $99-189. MC, VISA. 6 rooms with PB, 5 with FP and 1 suite. Breakfast included in rates. Types of meals: Full bkfst and early coffee/tea. Beds: KQT. Phone and ceiling fan in room. Air conditioning. VCR, fax, spa and swimming on premises. Amusement parks, antiquing, fishing, golf, hiking, biking, balloon fiesta, live theater, parks, shopping, downhill skiing, cross-country skiing, sporting events and tennis nearby.

Location: Semi-rural.

Publicity: Culinary Trends, Cavalcade of Enchantment and Great Country Inns.

Certificate may be used: Jan. 3 through Feb. 28.

The W.J. Marsh House Victorian B&B

301 Edith Blvd SE
Albuquerque, NM 87102-3532
(505)247-1001 (888)956-2774 Fax:(505)842-5213
Internet: www.marshhouse.com

Circa 1892. This three-story brick Queen Anne mansion is located in the Huning Highland Historic District. Original redwood doors and trim, porcelain fixtures and an ornate hand-carved fireplace are highlighted by high Victorian decor. A friendly ghost is said to inhabit the house, occasionally opening drawers and rearranging the furniture. The inn is listed in the National and State Historic Registers.

Innkeeper(s): West Burke. $60-120. MC, VISA, TC. 6 rooms, 1 with FP. Breakfast included in rates. Type of meal: Full gourmet bkfst. Beds: QDT. Clocks in room. Brimming with antiques and some for sale on premises. Amusement parks, antiquing, fishing, walking tours, Old Town, zoo, nature center, tramway, live theater, parks, shopping, downhill skiing, cross-country skiing, sporting events and water sports nearby.

Location: Historic District.

Publicity: Albuquerque Monthly.

Certificate may be used: Monday-Thursday except during Balloon Fiesta (first week in October) and major holidays. Certificate valid for Peach or Rose rooms only.

Bernalillo   D5

La Hacienda Grande

21 Baros Ln
Bernalillo, NM 87004
(505)867-1887 (800)353-1887 Fax:(505)771-1436
E-mail: lhg@swcp.com

Circa 1711. The rooms in this historic adobe inn surround a central courtyard. The first European trekked across the grounds as early as 1540. The land was part of a 1711 land grant from Spain, and owned by descendants of the original family until the innkeepers purchased it. The decor is Southwestern, and each bedchamber is filled with beautiful, handcrafted furnishings. One includes an iron high-poster bed and Jacuzzi tub, and others offer a kiva fireplace. Breakfasts are served in a dining room decorated with wood beams and a brick floor.

Innkeeper(s): Rebecca Frey & Shona Zimmerman. $99-129. MC, VISA, AX, DS, TC. 6 rooms with PB, 5 with FP and 1 conference room. Breakfast included in rates. Types of meals: Full bkfst and early coffee/tea. Beds: KQDT. Sitting areas and phone and TV on request in room. Air conditioning. VCR, fax, copier and library on premises. Antiquing, fishing, live theater, parks, shopping, downhill skiing, cross-country skiing and water sports nearby.

Location: Mountains.

Certificate may be used: All dates except holiday weeks and Albuquerque Balloon Festival (first Saturday in October for 10 days).

Brazos   A5

Enchanted Deer Haven B&B

6 Fall Creek Rd
Brazos, NM 87520-0608
(505)588-7535 (800)619-3337 Fax:(505)588-7552
Internet: www.bbhost.com/enchanteddeerhaven
E-mail: edhbb@ravin.net

Circa 1964. Feed the wild mule deer or watch wild turkeys from this inn's location at the 8,000-foot altitude at the base of Brazos Cliffs (which rise to 11,000 feet). Pines, oak and aspen surround the two-story log veneer house. The great room features a fireplace as well as a sunken fire pit surrounded by a large couch. Eighteen-foot windows allow for views of the trees, birds and perhaps a grey tassel-eared squirrel. Guest rooms offer country decor, and some showcase original crafts and artwork by the innkeeper and other artists. Both men and women especially enjoy the Mountain Man room, but there are several more from which to choose. A full breakfast is served in the morning. Afterwards, arrange for a ride on the Cubres & Toltec scenic railroad, or enjoy fishing, cycling or perhaps hiking a back country road.

Innkeeper(s): Garth, Ken, Marth LeClaire. $85-108. MC, VISA, AX, PC, TC. 5 rooms, 3 with PB. Breakfast, afternoon tea and snacks/refreshments included in rates. Types of meals: Full bkfst and early coffee/tea. Beds: QD. Ceiling fan and VCR in room. Fax, copier, bicycles and snow sleds on premises. Fishing, narrow gauge railroad train trip, shopping, cross-country skiing and water sports nearby.

Location: Mountains.

Publicity: Getaway Magazine and Wisconsin Country Life.

"You have mastered the art of comfort. All the perfect little touches make this a dream come true. I only regret that we cannot stay forever."

Certificate may be used: Nov. 1 to Aug. 31, Sunday-Thursday.

Cedar Crest   D5

Elaine's, A B&B

PO Box 444, 72 Snowline Rd Snowline Estates
Cedar Crest, NM 87008-0444
(505)281-2467 (800)821-3092 Fax:(505)281-1384
Internet: www.elainesbnb.com/

Circa 1979. This three-story log home is on four acres of evergreens in the forests of the Sandia Peaks. Rooms are furnished with European country antiques, there are two fireplaces and central air conditioning. Three varieties of hummingbirds visit the property. Guests enjoy views of the mountains from the inn's two balconies. Smoothies and raisin-cinnamon French toast are some of the breakfast items.

Innkeeper(s): Elaine O'Neil. $85-99. MC, VISA, AX, DS, TC. 3 suites. Breakfast included in rates. Type of meal: Full bkfst. Beds: KQ. Air conditioning. Antiquing, golf, parks, shopping, downhill skiing and cross-country skiing nearby.

Location: Mountains.

Publicity: Fodor's, L.A. Times, Albuquerque Journal and New Mexico Magazine.

"Fabulous! Mystical in the spring snow!"

Certificate may be used: Jan. 15-April 15, excluding holidays.

Espanola   C5

Casa del Rio

PO Box 92
Espanola, NM 87532-0092
(505)753-2035 (800)920-1495
Internet: www.virtualcities.com/
E-mail: casadelr@roadrunner.com

Circa 1988. These authentic, replica adobe guest houses are
filled with local handmade crafts, rugs, bed coverings and furniture. Bathrooms boast handmade Mexican tile, and rooms are
decorated in traditional New Mexico style. The guest houses
also boast kiva fireplaces. The patio windows afford a view of
cliffs above the Rio Chama, which is just a short walk from the
home. Casa del Rio is near many attractions, including Indian
pueblos, the many museums of Ghost Ranch, galleries and an
abundance of outdoor activities. The adobe is halfway between
both Taos and Santa Fe.

Innkeeper(s): Eileen Sopanen-Vigil. $100-125. MC, VISA. 4 rooms. Breakfast
included in rates. Type of meal: Full bkfst. Beds: KQT. Bicycling, fishing, hiking, shopping and sporting events nearby.

Certificate may be used: Sunday through Thursday, December through April.

Farmington   A2

Silver River Adobe Inn B&B

3151 W Main, PO Box 3411
Farmington, NM 87499-3411
(505)325-8219 (800)382-9251 Fax:(505)325-5074
Internet: www.cyberport.com/silveradobe
E-mail: sribb@cyberport.com

Circa 1989. Guests at this contemporary adobe house enjoy a
view of the San Juan River from the patio of their room.
Amenities in the suite include a dining/living room, kitchen
with microwave and refrigerator, Mexican tile bathroom, phone
and queen bed. Guests may take a refreshing walk in the nearby cottonwood forest, a perfect spot for birdwatching. The
peaceful setting caters to those wishing to get away from it all,
while those interested in sightseeing will find many opportunities in the area, such as the Aztec and Salmon ruins, Four
Corners Monument and Mesa Verde and Chaco Canyon.

Innkeeper(s): Diana Ohlson & David Beers. $75-105. MC, VISA, AX, PC, TC.
3 rooms, 2 with PB and 1 suite. Breakfast and afternoon tea included in
rates. Types of meals: Full gourmet bkfst and cont plus. Beds: QT. Phone and
ceiling fan in room. Air conditioning. Library on premises. Handicap access.
Antiquing, fishing, golf, ancient Indian ruins, golfing at Pinon Hills, Navajo
art, live theater, parks, shopping, downhill skiing, cross-country skiing, sporting events, tennis and water sports nearby.

Location: High desert/Indian Country.

Publicity: *Cross Currents and Daily Times.*

Certificate may be used: Nov. 1 through Feb. 28.

Jemez Springs   C5

Riverdancer Inn

16445 Hwy 4
Jemez Springs, NM 87025-9424
(505)829-3262 (800)809-3262
Internet: www.riverdance.com
E-mail: info@riverdancer.com

Above a river stocked with rainbow and brown trout and at the
base of Virgin Mesa, which rises 2,000 feet to an ancient pueblo
site, this adobe inn is a welcoming haven for guests seeking a
natural setting. The guest rooms surround the inn's courtyard, a
striking outdoor garden with a flowing birdbath and frequent
visits from hummingbirds. The inn's Southwestern style features
artifacts honoring various Native American tribes as well as pottery, baskets, Mexican tile floors and wooden-beam ceilings.
Each of the rooms is named for a different Native American
nation. The great room is the main gathering area with its two
sitting areas, refreshment bar and kiva fireplace. In the morning
a full breakfast is served here. The inn also offers a four-room
suite with Jacuzzi tub and kitchen. Therapeutic and spa body
treatments also are available, and special healing retreats are
offered. Activities include scenic hikes and visits to the natural
mineral hot springs in the area.

Innkeeper(s): Linsay Locke & Linda Bedre. $109-160. MC, VISA, DS. 6
rooms and 1 suite. Breakfast included in rates. Type of meal: Full bkfst.

Certificate may be used: Nov. 1 to March 15, Sunday-Thursday.

Las Cruces   I4

Lundeen Inn of The Arts

618 S Alameda Blvd
Las Cruces, NM 88005-2817
(505)526-3326 (888)526-3326 Fax:(505)647-1334
Internet: www.innofhearts.com
E-mail: lundeen@innofthearts.com

This restored Mexican territorial inn, in the historic district,
combines an inn with a fine arts gallery. An enormous great
room features polished wood floors, an 18-foot ceiling of
pressed tin, paladian windows and art, of course. Many of the
inn's special features have been designed by innkeeper Jerry, an
architect. Guest rooms have themes centered around New
Mexican and Native American artists. For instance, the Georgia
O'Keeffe room features calla lilies on the fireplace mantel and is
decorated in gray, white and black.

Innkeeper(s): Jerry & Linda Lundeen. $72. MC, VISA, AX, DC, CB, DS, PC,
TC. 24 rooms with PB, 3 with FP and 1 conference room. Breakfast included
in rates. Types of meals: Full bkfst and cont plus. Beds: KQDT. Cable TV,
phone and ceiling fan in room. Air conditioning. Fax, copier and pet boarding
on premises. Handicap access. Golf, parks and shopping nearby.

Pets Allowed.

Location: City.

Publicity: *Country Inns and New Mexico Magazine.*

Certificate may be used: June 1-Oct. 31.

T.R.H. Smith Mansion B&B

909 N Alameda Blvd
Las Cruces, NM 88005-2124
(505)525-2525 (800)526-1914 Fax:(505)524-8227
E-mail: smithmansion@zianet.com

Circa 1914. This Prairie-style mansion with its somewhat notorious past offers nearly 6,000 square feet of living area, making it the largest residence in town. The home, originally built for a local banker whose career ended in disgrace, was later the possible site of the local bordello. The mansion is rumored to house a buried treasure somewhere within its walls. There are four well-appointed guest rooms, each vastly different in style. One room features Southwestern decor with patterned walls, a Mission-style bed and a drum that serves as a table; another room is Polynesian style with a rattan bed decorated with mosquito netting. Guests will enjoy a German-style breakfast of fresh fruit, home-baked breads, smoked meats and cheese.

Innkeeper(s): Marlene & Jay Tebo. $56-132. MC, VISA, AX, DS, PC, TC. 4 rooms with PB, 1 with FP. Breakfast included in rates. Type of meal: Full gourmet bkfst. Beds: KQ. Phone, turndown service, ceiling fan and modem Jacks in room. Air conditioning. VCR, fax, library and pool Table on premises. Antiquing, golf, live theater, parks, shopping, sporting events and tennis nearby.
Publicity: *Las Cruces, N.M. and News.*
Certificate may be used: Jan. 1-Dec. 31, Sunday through Friday.

Las Vegas   C7

Carriage House B&B

925 6th St
Las Vegas, NM 87701-4306
(505)454-1784 (888)221-9689

Circa 1893. A prominent local attorney built this historic Queen Anne Victorian home. The innkeepers offer five comfortable guest rooms, and pamper their guests with a full breakfast and afternoon tea. Las Vegas has an amazing Wild West past, and there are more than 900 buildings in town that are listed in the National Register.

Innkeeper(s): Anne & John Bradford. $59-79. MC, VISA, AX, DS, PC, TC. 5 rooms, 3 with PB. Breakfast included in rates. Type of meal: Cont plus. Beds: Q. VCR on premises. Antiquing, fishing, parks, shopping, downhill skiing, cross-country skiing and sporting events nearby.
Location: Mountains.
Publicity: *Red Dawn.*
Certificate may be used: Sept. 15 to June 15, Sunday-Thursday, subject to availability.

Plaza Hotel

230 Plaza
Las Vegas, NM 87701
(505)425-3591 (800)328-1882 Fax:(505)425-9659
Internet: www.lasvegasnewmex.com/plaza
E-mail: plazahotel@worldplaces.com

Circa 1882. This brick Italianate Victorian hotel, once frequented by the likes of Doc Holliday, Big Nose Kate and members of the James Gang, was renovated in 1982. A stencil pattern found in the dining room inspired the selection of Victorian wallpaper borders in the guest rooms, decorated with a combination of contemporary and period furnishings. Guests are still drawn to the warm, dry air and the hot springs north of town.

Innkeeper(s): Wid & Kak Slick. $59-130. MC, VISA, AX, DC, DS, TC. 37

rooms with PB, 4 suites and 1 conference room. Types of meals: Full gourmet bkfst, cont plus and cont. Beds: KQDT. Cable TV and phone in room. Air conditioning. VCR and copier on premises. Handicap access. Antiquing, fishing, parks, shopping, cross-country skiing and water sports nearby.
Pets allowed: $10 charge.
Certificate may be used: All week, Nov. 1-May 1.

Lincoln   G6

Casa De Patron B&B Inn

PO Box 27, Hwy 380 E
Lincoln, NM 88338-0027
(505)653-4676 (800)524-5202 Fax:(505)653-4671
Internet: www.casaptron.com
E-mail: patron@pvtnetworks.net

Circa 1860. This historic adobe once was used to imprison Billy the Kid and played an integral part in the colorful frontier days of Lincoln County. Shaded courtyards and walled garden add to the authentic Old West atmosphere, and the

comfortable rooms are supplemented by two contemporary adobe casitas. Cleis plays the inn's pipe organ and arranges soap-making workshops for guests.

Innkeeper(s): Jeremy & Cleis Jordan. $84-117. MC, VISA, PC. 7 rooms with PB, 2 with FP, 2 cottages and 1 conference room. Breakfast included in rates. Types of meals: Full bkfst and cont plus. Beds: KQT. Handmade soap, candy; some snacks/refrigerators and one with double Jacuzzi tub in room. VCR, fax and copier on premises. Handicap access. Hiking, casinos, museums, parks, shopping and downhill skiing nearby.
Location: Country.
Publicity: *Bedrooms & Baths, Ruidoso News, Roswell Daily Record, Adventure West Magazine, Tampa Tribune/Times, Recommended Romantic Inns, Country, Southern Living, True West, Historic Traveler, Albuquerque Journal, Preservation News, Albuquerque Journal, Preservation News, Young Guns, Set, Travelin', Rocky Mountain News and Milwaukee Journal.*

"The time with you at Casa de Patron is truly a treasure to me."
Certificate may be used: All year (Sunday through Thursday) with blackout dates: Memorial Day weekend, July 4th weekend, Thanksgiving week and Christmas-New Year's week, first weekend in August.

Santa Fe   C6

Alexander's Inn

529 E Palace Ave
Santa Fe, NM 87501-2200
(505)986-1431 (888)321-5123 Fax:(505)982-8572
Internet: www.collectorsguide.com/alexandinn
E-mail: alexandinn@aol.com

Circa 1903. Twin gables and a massive front porch are prominent features of this Craftsman-style brick and wood inn. French and American country decor, stained-glass windows and a selection of antiques create a light Victorian touch. The inn also features beautiful gardens of roses and lilacs. The exquisite
Southwest adobe casitas are a favorite for families and romantic getaways. Breakfast is often served in the backyard garden. Home-baked treats are offered to guests in the afternoon.

Innkeeper(s): Carolyn Lee. $80-160. MC, VISA, DS, PC, TC. 7 rooms with PB, 5 with FP, 1 suite and 3 cottages. Breakfast and afternoon tea included in rates. Types of meals: Full gourmet bkfst, cont plus and early coffee/tea. Beds: KQT. Cable TV, phone and VCR in room. Fax, spa, library and child care on premises. Antiquing, fishing, museums, Pueblos, live theater, parks, shopping, downhill skiing, cross-country skiing and water sports nearby.
Pets allowed: Well behaved.
Location: City.
Publicity: *New Mexican, Glamour, Southwest Art and San Diego Union Tribune.*
"Thanks to the kindness and thoughtfulness of the staff, our three days in Santa Fe were magical."
Certificate may be used: November through February, Sunday through Thursday, no holidays.

The Madeleine (formerly The Preston House)

106 Faithway St
Santa Fe, NM 87501
(505)982-3465 (888)877-7622 Fax:(505)982-8572
Internet: www.madeleineinn.com
E-mail: madeleineinn@aol.com

Circa 1886. This gracious 19th-century home is the only authentic example of Queen Anne architecture in Santa Fe. This home displays a wonderful Victorian atmosphere with period furnishings, quaint wallpapers and beds covered with down quilts. Afternoon tea is a must, as Carolyn serves up a mouth-watering array of cakes, pies, cookies and tarts. The Madeleine, which is located in downtown Santa Fe, is within walking distance of the Plaza.

Innkeeper(s): Cindy Carano. $70-160. MC, VISA, DS, PC, TC. 8 rooms, 6 with PB, 4 with FP, 2 cottages and 1 conference room. Breakfast and afternoon tea included in rates. Types of meals: Full bkfst and early coffee/tea. Beds: KQDT. Cable TV, phone and ceiling fan in room. Fax and copier on premises. Antiquing, fishing, live theater, parks, shopping, downhill skiing and cross-country skiing nearby.
Pets Allowed.
Location: Mountains.
Publicity: *Country Inns.*
"We were extremely pleased — glad we found you. We shall return."
Certificate may be used: Sunday-Thursday, Nov. 1-May 1, no holidays.

Santa Fe (Algodones)   D5

Hacienda Vargas

PO Box 307
Santa Fe (Algodones), NM 87001-0307
(505)867-9115 (800)261-0006 Fax:(505)867-0640
Internet: www.swcp.com/hacvar//
E-mail: hacvar@swcp.com

Circa 1840. Nestled among the cottonwoods and mesas of the middle Rio Grande Valley, Hacienda Vargas has seen two centuries of Old West history. It once served as a trading post for Native Americans as well as a 19th-century stage-coach stop between Santa Fe and Mesilla. The grounds contain an adobe chapel, courtyard and gardens. The main house features five kiva fireplaces, Southwest antiques, Spanish tile, a library, art gallery and suites with private Jacuzzis.

Innkeeper(s): Paul & Jule De Vargas. $79-149. MC, VISA, PC, TC. 7 rooms with PB, 7 with FP and 4 suites. Breakfast included in rates. Type of meal: Full bkfst. Beds: QT. Ceiling fan and spa in suites in room. Air conditioning. Antiquing, fishing, live theater, shopping, downhill skiing, sporting events and water sports nearby.
Location: Valley.
Publicity: *Albuquerque Journal (Country Inns), Vogue and San Francisco Chronicle.*

"This is the best! Breakfast was the best we've ever had!"
Certificate may be used: Sunday-Thursday except holidays or Balloon Fiesta.

New York

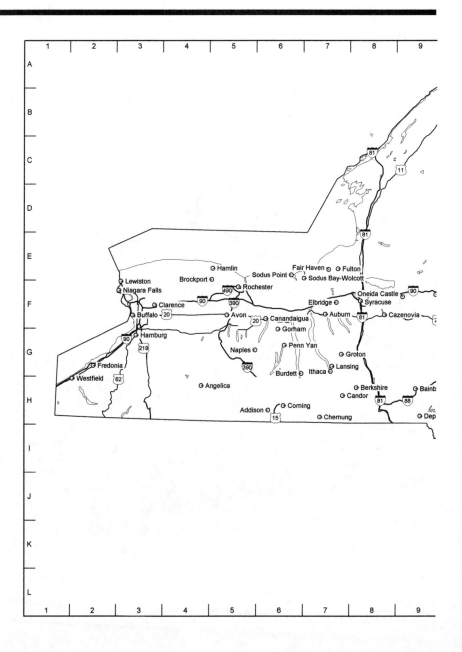

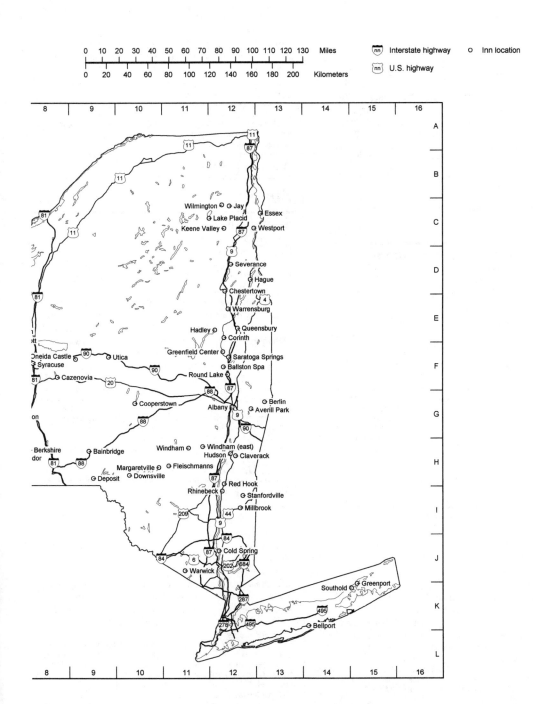

0	10	20	30	40	50	60	70	80	90	100	110	120	130	Miles

0	20	40	60	80	100	120	140	160	180	200	Kilometers

Interstate highway   O Inn location

U.S. highway

Addison
H6

Addison Rose B&B

37 Maple St
Addison, NY 14801-1009
(607)359-4650

Circa 1892. Located on a scenic highway south of the Finger Lakes, this Queen Anne Victorian "painted lady" inn is an easy getaway from Corning or Elmira. The inn, which is listed in the National Register, was built by a doctor for his bride and was presented to her on Christmas Eve, their wedding day. The three guest rooms offer authentic Victorian furnishings. Many fine examples of Victorian architecture exist in Addison. Pinnacle State Park is just east of town.

Innkeeper(s): William & Maryann Peters. $95-115. PC, TC. 3 rooms with PB. Breakfast and afternoon tea included in rates. Types of meals: Full gourmet bkfst and early coffee/tea. Beds: DT. Ceiling fan and private balcony in room. Air conditioning. Library on premises. Antiquing, fishing, parks, shopping and cross-country skiing nearby.

Location: Mountains.

Certificate may be used: November-June, any day, subject to availability.

Albany
G12

Mansion Hill Inn & Restaurant

115 Philip St at Park Avenue
Albany, NY 12202-1747
(518)465-2038 Fax:(518)434-2313

Circa 1861. This Victorian houses guest rooms and apartment suites on the top two floors and a restaurant on the street level. Originally the home of brush maker Daniel Brown, it later served as a bulk grocery store. It is located in the historic district just around the corner from the Governor's Executive Mansion in the Mansion Neighborhood. It is a few minutes' walk to the State Capitol and the downtown Albany business district.

Innkeeper(s): Maryellen, Elizabeth & Stephen Stofelano Jr. $95-155. MC, VISA, AX, DC, CB, DS, PC, TC. 8 rooms with PB and 1 conference room. Breakfast included in rates. Types of meals: Full gourmet bkfst and cont plus. Beds: Q. Cable TV and phone in room. Air conditioning. VCR, fax, copier, pet boarding and child care on premises. Antiquing, fishing, live theater, parks, shopping and sporting events nearby.

Pets Allowed.

Publicity: *Hartford Courant, Albany Review, Hudson Valley Magazine, Albany Times Union and Nation's Business.*

"Rooms were beautiful and comfortable down to the shower curtain."

Certificate may be used: Available year-round on Fridays, Saturdays and Sundays; subject to availability and reservation.

Pine Haven B&B

531 Western Ave
Albany, NY 12203-1721
(518)482-1574

Circa 1896. This turn-of-the-century Victorian is located in Pine Hills, an Albany historic district. In keeping with this history, the innkeepers have tried to preserve the home's 19th-century charm. The rooms offer old-fashioned comfort with Victorian influences. The Capitol Building and other historic sites are nearby.

Innkeeper(s): Janice Tricarico. $64-79. MC, VISA, AX, PC, TC. 5 rooms, 2 with PB. Breakfast included in rates. Types of meals: Cont plus and early coffee/tea. Beds: DT. Phone in room. Air conditioning. Antiquing, live theater, parks, shopping, cross-country skiing and sporting events nearby.

Location: City.

Certificate may be used: Year round, depending only on availability.

Angelica
H4

Angelica Inn

64 E Main St. Box 686
Angelica, NY 14709-8710
(716)466-3063

Circa 1882. Located in the Allegany foothills, the Angelica Inn features stained glass, crystal chandeliers, parquet floors, an oak staircase, carved woodwork, antique furnishings and scented rooms. Guest rooms offer such amenities as fireplaces, a porch and a breakfast alcove area.

Innkeeper(s): Cynthia & Nicholas Petito. $70-100. MC, VISA, DS, PC. 6 suites, 3 with FP and 1 conference room. Breakfast included in rates. Type of meal: Full bkfst. Beds: KQ. Cable TV and ceiling fan in room. Antiquing, fishing, golf, parks and cross-country skiing nearby.

Pets allowed: Country house suites.

Location: Historic village - rural.

"Victorian at its best!"

Certificate may be used: Sunday through Thursday, Jan. 30 to June 1.

Auburn
F7

Springside Inn

PO Box 520, 41-43 W Lake Rd
Auburn, NY 13021-0520
(315)252-7247 Fax:(315)252-4925

Circa 1830. Originally a boy's boarding school run by the first American Missionary to Japan, this four-story Victorian is now a comfortable B&B. The inn's dinner theater, operated Wednesday through Sunday in the summer, is the first dinner theater in the northeastern United States, and it was created by the innkeepers. The Surrey Room is the public dining room, and it boasts beamed cathedral ceilings and a stone fireplace. Guest rooms feature antique beds and print curtains. Breakfast is provided in a basket and consists of muffins, fruit and coffee.

Innkeeper(s): Lois Porten. $65. MC, VISA, AX, TC. 8 rooms, 5 with PB, 3 with FP and 2 conference rooms. Breakfast included in rates. Types of meals: Cont and early coffee/tea. Beds: KT. Ceiling fan in room. Air conditioning. Swimming and bicycles on premises. Handicap access. Antiquing, golf, live theater, parks, downhill skiing and water sports nearby.

Pets allowed: Well-behaved.

Certificate may be used: January, February, March, Wednesday, Thursday.

Averill Park
G12

Ananas Hus B&B

148 South Rd
Averill Park, NY 12018-3414
(518)766-5035

Circa 1963. This ranch home in the mountains east of Albany offers stunning views of the Hudson River Valley. Visitors enjoy gourmet breakfasts and relaxing afternoon teas. There are 29 acres available to guests who wish to hike or play lawn games. The surrounding area offers antiquing, downhill skiing and shopping, and the inn's location provides convenient access to the recreation and sightseeing opportunities of three states. Cherry Plain State Park is nearby.

Innkeeper(s): Clyde & Thelma Olsen Tomlinson. $60-80. AX, PC. 3 rooms. Breakfast included in rates. Types of meals: Full gourmet bkfst and early coffee/tea. Beds: DT. VCR on premises. Antiquing, fishing, live theater, downhill skiing, cross-country skiing and water sports nearby.

Location: Rural.

Publicity: *Discovery Press.*

Certificate may be used: May 1-Dec. 15, Monday through Thursday (excluding holidays).

The Gregory House Country Inn & Restaurant

Rt 43 PO Box 401
Averill Park, NY 12018-0401
(518)674-3774 Fax:(518)674-8916
E-mail: gregoryhse@aol.com

Circa 1830. This colonial house was built in the center of the village by stockbroker Elias Gregory. It became a restaurant in 1976. The historic section of the building now holds the restaurant, while a new portion accommodates overnight guests. It is decorated with Early American braided rugs and four-poster beds.

Innkeeper(s): Bette & Robert Jewell. $80-90. MC, VISA, AX, DC, CB, DS, PC, TC. 12 rooms with PB and 1 conference room. Breakfast included in rates. Type of meal: Cont. Beds: QDT. TV and phone in room. Air conditioning. VCR, fax, copier and swimming on premises. Amusement parks, antiquing, fishing, live theater, parks, shopping, downhill skiing, cross-country skiing, sporting events and water sports nearby.

Location: Village.

Publicity: *Hudson Valley, Albany Times Union, Schenectady Gazette, Courier and Sunday Record.*

"We experienced privacy and quiet, lovely surroundings indoors and out, excellent service, and as much friendliness as we were comfortable with, but no more."

Certificate may be used: Anytime Nov. 1-April 30.

Avon   F5

Avon Inn

55 E Main St
Avon, NY 14414-1438
(716)226-8181 Fax:(716)226-8185

Circa 1820. This Greek Revival mansion, in both the state and national historic registers, has been providing lodging for more than a century. After 1866, the residence was turned into a health center that provided water cures from the local sulphur springs. The guest registry included the likes of Henry Ford, Thomas Edison and Eleanor Roosevelt. Though the inn is no longer a health spa, guests can still relax in the garden with its gazebo and fountain or on the Grecian-pillared front porch. A full-service restaurant and conference facilities are on the premises.

Innkeeper(s): Linda Reusch. $50-85. MC, VISA, AX, DC, CB, DS, TC. 15 rooms with PB. Breakfast included in rates. Types of meals: Cont and early coffee/tea. Beds: KQD. Phone in room. Air conditioning. Fax and copier on premises. Amusement parks, antiquing, fishing, parks, shopping, downhill skiing and cross-country skiing nearby.

Certificate may be used: Not valid Saturdays May 1-Oct. 31. Minimum stay is two nights.

Bainbridge   H9

Berry Hill Gardens B&B

242 Ward Loomis Rd.
Bainbridge, NY 13733
(607)967-8745 (800)497-8745 Fax:(607)967-8745

Circa 1820. Surrounded by flower and herb gardens, this farmhouse presides over 180 acres. Guest rooms are furnished in antiques and decorated with bunches of fresh and dried flow-

ers. Organic gardens provide 100 varieties of annuals and perennials. There are tulips, poppies, lilacs, sweet peas and in May, the fruit trees are in bloom. A full country breakfast is served. By advance reservation you can arrange for a sleigh ride or horse-drawn wagon to take you through the woods and meadows of the Berry Hill Farm, or you may stroll through the gardens and woods on your own.

Innkeeper(s): Jean Fowler & Cecilia Rios. $60-70. MC, VISA, AX, PC, TC. 4 rooms. Breakfast included in rates. Types of meals: Full bkfst and early coffee/tea. Beds: QDT. Ceiling fan in room. VCR, fax, copier and library on premises. Antiquing, fishing, parks, shopping, downhill skiing, cross-country skiing and sporting events nearby.

Location: Rural.

Publicity: *Tri-Town News and Daily Star.*

"The house is just wonderful and our rooms were exceptionally comfortable."

Certificate may be used: Jan. 2-April 30, anytime. May 1-Dec. 20, Sunday through Thursday only. Holidays and special events excluded.

Ballston Spa   F12

Apple Tree B&B

49 W High St
Ballston Spa, NY 12020-1912
(518)885-1113 Fax:(518)885-9758
Internet: www.appletreebb.com
E-mail: mail@appletreebb.com

Circa 1878. A pond, waterfall and a garden decorate the entrance to this Second Empire Victorian, which is located in the historic district of Ballston Spa, a village just a few minutes from Saratoga Springs. Guest rooms feature Victorian and French-country decor, and each has antiques and whirlpool tubs. Guests enjoy fresh fruit, homemade baked goods, a selection of beverages and a daily entree during the breakfast service.

Innkeeper(s): Dolores & Jim Taisey. $85-175. MC, VISA, AX, PC, TC. 5 rooms with PB. Breakfast included in rates. Types of meals: Full bkfst and early coffee/tea. Beds: Q. Cable TV, VCR and whirlpool in room. Central air. Amusement parks, antiquing, fishing, Saratoga Race Course, live theater, parks, shopping, downhill skiing, cross-country skiing, sporting events and water sports nearby.

Location: Village (historic district).

Publicity: *Country Folk Art Magazine.*

Certificate may be used: Midweek, Sunday-Thursday, January-April, and September-December.

Bellport   K14

Great South Bay Inn

160 S Country Rd
Bellport, NY 11713-2516
(516)286-8588 Fax:(516)286-2460

Circa 1890. Long Island's south shore is home to this Cape Cod-style inn filled with turn-of-the-century antiques. Six guest rooms are available, four with private baths and all featuring

original wainscoting. Favorite relaxing spots include the private garden and the parlor with its welcoming fireplace. During the summer months, guests enjoy taking the ferry over to the village's private beach or simply, frequenting one of the local restaurants, which are open all year. The innkeepers are fluent in French and pride themselves on serving guests' individual needs, including pet accommodations or train station pick-ups. Fire Island National Seashore and the Wertheim National Wildlife Refuge are nearby.

Innkeeper(s): Judy Mortimer. $85-125. MC, VISA, TC. 6 rooms, 4 with PB, 1 with FP and 1 suite. Breakfast included in rates. Type of meal: Full bkfst. Beds: QDT. Cable TV, ceiling fan and VCR in room. Air conditioning. Fax and copier on premises. Amusement parks, antiquing, fishing, golf, live theater, parks, shopping, tennis and water sports nearby.

Pets allowed: Must always be with owners, $15 charge.

Certificate may be used: Mid-January to mid-April, Rooms 5 & 6. Other rooms depending on availability.

Berkshire H8

Kinship B&B

12724 Rt 38
Berkshire, NY 13736
(607)657-4455 (800)493-2337

Circa 1809. An antique and collectible doll shop is found on the premises of this farmhouse-style inn. Post-and-beam construction, four fireplaces and plank floors reflect the inn's character. Kinship is centrally located for easy access to the Finger Lakes, upstate New York wineries and Ithaca, Cortland and Binghamton colleges. Four downhill ski areas and cross-country skiing are nearby. In the fall, visitors can enjoy the colors in Fillmore Glen, Treman and Watkins Glen.

Innkeeper(s): John & Carole Shipley. $65-105. MC, VISA, PC, TC. 4 rooms, 1 with FP and 1 suite. Breakfast and snacks/refreshments included in rates. Type of meal: Full gourmet bkfst. Beds: KDT. VCR on premises. Antiquing, fishing, live theater, parks, shopping, downhill skiing, cross-country skiing, sporting events and water sports nearby.

Location: Rural.

Certificate may be used: April-December, Sunday-Saturday (excluding college weekends). Two-night minimum stay.

Berlin G13

Sedgwick Inn

Rt 22, Box 250
Berlin, NY 12022
(518)658-2334 Fax:(518)658-3998

Circa 1791. The Sedgwick Inn sits on 12 acres in the Taconic Valley in the Berkshire Mountains. The main house features guest rooms, the low-ceilinged Coach Room Tavern and a glass-enclosed dining porch facing an English garden. A Colonial-style motel behind the main house sits beside a rushing brook. A converted carriage house with a hard-wood dance floor and hand-hewn beams

serves as a gift shop with prints, paintings, sculptures and a selection of unusual crafts and gourmet items.

Innkeeper(s): Edith Evans. $75-120. MC, VISA, AX, DC, CB, DS, TC. 11 rooms with PB, 1 suite and 1 conference room. Breakfast included in rates. Type of meal: Full bkfst. Beds: KQD. Cable TV, phone and ceiling fan in room. VCR and fax on premises. Antiquing, fishing, golf, live theater, parks, downhill skiing, cross-country skiing and water sports nearby.

Pets allowed: Pets allowed in annex.

Publicity: *Berkshire Eagle, Hudson Valley Magazine, Albany Times Union, Good Housekeeping and US Air.*

"We were absolutely enchanted. We found this to be a charming place, a rare and wonderful treat."

Certificate may be used: Monday-Thursday, year-round. Subject to availability.

Brockport E5

The Portico B&B

3741 Lake Rd N
Brockport, NY 14420-1415
(716)637-0220

Circa 1850. Named for its three porches, called porticos, this Greek Revival inn is situated amid blue spruce, maple and sycamore trees in a historic district. Tall columns and a cupola add to its charm. The interior features three fireplaces. Three antique-filled guest rooms are available to visitors, who enjoy a full Victorian breakfast and kettledrum, also known as afternoon tea. The inn is listed in the National Register, as are several other structures in town. The surrounding area offers many attractions, including the Cobblestone Museum, Darien Lake Amusement Park, George Eastman House and Strasenburgh Planetarium. Several colleges, golf courses and parks are nearby. In winter, sleigh rides also are available nearby.

Innkeeper(s): Anne Klein. $70-80. PC, TC. 3 rooms with PB, 3 with FP. Breakfast included in rates. Types of meals: Full bkfst and early coffee/tea. Turndown service in room. VCR on premises. Amusement parks, antiquing, sleigh rides, live theater, shopping, downhill skiing, cross-country skiing and sporting events nearby.

Location: Suburban - Country.

Certificate may be used: Midweek, Monday through Thursday.

The Victorian B&B

320 S Main St
Brockport, NY 14420-2253
(716)637-7519 Fax:(716)637-7519
Internet: www.victorianbandb.com
E-mail: skehoe@po.brockport.edu

Circa 1890. Within walking distance of the historic Erie Canal, this Queen Anne Victorian inn and its sister house are located on Brockport's Main Street. Visitors select from eight second-floor guest rooms, all with phones, private baths and TVs. Victorian furnishings are found throughout the inn. A favorite spot is the solarium, with its three walls of windows and fireplace, perfect for curling up with a book or magazine. Two first-floor sitting areas with fireplaces also provide relaxing havens for guests. Lake Ontario is just 10 miles away, and visitors will find much to explore in Brockport and Rochester. Brockport is home to the State University of New York.

Innkeeper(s): Sharon Kehoe. $59-98. PC, TC. 8 rooms with PB. Breakfast and afternoon tea included in rates. Type of meal: Full bkfst. Beds: KQDT. Cable TV, phone and jacuzzi tub in room. Air conditioning. VCR, fax and e-mail access on premises. Antiquing, live theater, shopping, cross-country skiing and sporting events nearby.

Location: Village on Erie Canal.

"Memories of another time; hospitality of another era."

Certificate may be used: Nov. 15-April 30.

Buffalo   F3

Beau Fleuve B&B Inn

242 Linwood Ave
Buffalo, NY 14209-1802
(716)882-6116 (800)278-0245
Internet: www.beaufleuve.com
E-mail: beaufleuve@buffnet.net

Circa 1881. Each of the five rooms in this Victorian setting celebrates ethnic groups that settled in the Buffalo area. In the French room, absolute comfort is complete with every touch, from the feather bed that rests atop the Neoclassical king-size bed to Louis XV chairs that are covered with champagne damask with French blue highlights. The Irish room features an antique brass bed, Victorian seating and William Morris chrysanthemum wallcoverings in shades of sage and celery. Other elegant rooms mark the contributions of the German, Italian and Polish immigrants. Artifacts accented by stunning stained-glass windows render homage to the Western New York Native American tribes in the Native American common area. Set in the Linwood Preservation District, this inn is in the middle of everything. Millionaires' Row is only one block from the inn, and museums, art galleries, antique shops and a variety of restaurants are just steps away. A friendly ambiance will remind guests why Buffalo is known as the "City of Good Neighbors." Niagara Falls is a 25-minute drive.

Innkeeper(s): Ramona Pando Whitaker & Rik Whitaker. $75-95. MC, VISA, AX, DS, TC. 3 rooms with PB. Breakfast included in rates. Type of meal: Full bkfst. Beds: KQDT. Antiquing, fishing, concerts/music, live theater, downhill skiing, cross-country skiing, sporting events and water sports nearby.

Publicity: *Buffalo News, New York Daily News, Preservation Coalition Tour House* and *WIVB-TV.*

"Relaxing, comfortable hospitality in beautiful surroundings."

Certificate may be used: From Nov. 1 to April 30, except holidays.

Burdett   G6

The Red House Country Inn

4586 Picnic Area Rd
Burdett, NY 14818-9716
(607)546-8566

Circa 1844. Nestled within the 16,000-acre Finger Lakes National Forest, this old farmstead has an in-ground swimming pool, large veranda overlooking groomed lawns, flower gardens and picnic areas. Pet Samoyeds and goats share the seven acres. Next to the property are acres of wild blueberry patches and stocked fishing ponds. The Red House is near Seneca Lake, world-famous Glen Gorge, and Cornell University.

Innkeeper(s): Sandy Schmanke & Joan Martin. $59-89. MC, VISA, AX, DS, PC. 5 rooms, 1 with FP. Breakfast and afternoon tea included in rates. Types of meals: Full bkfst and early coffee/tea. Beds: QDT. TV in room. Antiquing, fishing, wineries, live theater, parks, shopping, cross-country skiing, sporting events and water sports nearby.

Location: National forest.

Publicity: *New York Alive, Discerning Traveler* and *New York Magazine.*

"An Inn-credible delight. What a wonderful place to stay and a difficult place to leave. It doesn't get any better than this."

Certificate may be used: November-April, Sunday-Thursday.

Canandaigua   F6

Enchanted Rose Inn B&B

7479 Rts 5 & 20
Canandaigua, NY 14424
(716)657-6003 Fax:(716)657-4405
Internet: www.servtech.com/public/enchrose
E-mail: enchrose@servtech.com

Circa 1820. During the restoration of this early 19th-century home, the innkeepers uncovered the many original features, including the wood floors that now glimmer. The fireplace dates back to the 1790s, part of  the original log home. The present structure was built onto the original in the 1820s. The innkeepers are only the fourth owners and have returned the home to its original glory. Freshly cut flowers from the inn's gardens are placed in the guest rooms, which feature antiques and romantic decor. The dining room table is set with beautiful china, a perfect accompaniment to the gourmet breakfasts. Afternoon tea is served in the rose garden or in an inviting parlor with fireplace.

Innkeeper(s): Jan & Howard Buhlmann. $95-135. MC, VISA, AX, DS, PC, TC. 3 rooms with PB and 1 suite. Breakfast included in rates. Types of meals: Full gourmet bkfst and early coffee/tea. Beds: Q. Cable TV, phone, turndown service, VCR, coffee, tea, crackers, cheese and homemade goods in room. Air conditioning. Fax and library on premises. Antiquing, fishing, live theater, parks, shopping, downhill skiing, cross-country skiing, sporting events and water sports nearby.

Location: Edge of village.

Publicity: *WXXI* and *Holiday House Tour.*

"This has been a lovely experience, a wonderful homecoming. You leave no details overlooked."

Certificate may be used: Sunday-Thursday, November-April, no holidays.

Candor   H7

The Edge of Thyme, A B&B Inn

6 Main St
Candor, NY 13743-1615
(607)659-5155 (800)722-7365 Fax:(607)659-5155
Internet: www.wordpro.com/edgeofthyme/

Circa 1840. Originally the summer home of John D. Rockefeller's secretary, this two-story Georgian-style inn offers gracious accommodations a short drive from Ithaca. The inn sports many interesting features, including an impressive stairway, marble fireplaces, parquet floors, pergola (arbor) and windowed porch with leaded glass. Guests may relax in front of the inn's fireplace, catch up with reading in its library or watch television in the sitting room. An authentic turn-of-the-century full breakfast is served, and guests also may arrange for special high teas.

Innkeeper(s): Prof. Frank & Eva Mae Musgrave. $70-135. MC, VISA, AX, TC. 5 rooms, 2 with PB and 2 suites. Breakfast included in rates. Types of meals: Full gourmet bkfst and early coffee/tea. Beds: KQDT. VCR on premises. Antiquing, fishing, live theater, parks, shopping, downhill skiing, cross-country skiing and sporting events nearby.

Location: Village.

Certificate may be used: Sunday through Thursday. Not valid in May, excluding specific weekends.

Cazenovia F8

Brae Loch Inn

5 Albany St
Cazenovia, NY 13035-1403
(315)655-3431 Fax:(315)655-4844
Internet: www.cazenovia.com/braeloch
E-mail: baeloch1@aol.com

Circa 1805. Blue and white awnings accentuate the attractive architecture of the Brae Loch. Since 1946 the inn has been owned and operated by the same family. A Scottish theme is evident throughout, including in the inn's restaurant. Four of the oldest rooms have fireplaces. Stickley, Harden and antique furniture add to the old-world atmosphere, and many rooms offer canopy beds. Guest rooms are on the second and third floors above the restaurant.

Innkeeper(s): Jim & Val Barr. $80-140. MC, VISA, AX, TC. 12 rooms with PB and 1 conference room. Breakfast included in rates. Type of meal: Cont. Beds: KQDT. Cable TV, phone and three rooms with Jacuzzis in room. Air conditioning. Fax and copier on premises. Antiquing, fishing, golf, swimming, parks, shopping, downhill skiing, cross-country skiing, sporting events, tennis and water sports nearby.

Location: Small village by lake.

Publicity: The Globe and Mail, Traveler Magazine and CNY.

"Everything was just perfect. The Brae Loch and staff make you feel as if you were at home."

Certificate may be used: Jan. 2-April 30, Sunday-Friday.

Chemung H7

Halcyon Place B&B

197 Washington St, PO Box 244
Chemung, NY 14825-0244
(607)529-3544
Internet: www.bbonline.com/ny/halcyon
E-mail: herbtique@aol.com

Circa 1820. The innkeepers chose the name "halcyon" because it signifies tranquility and a healing richness. The historic Greek Revival inn and its grounds offer just that to guests, who will appreciate the fine period antiques, paneled doors, six-over-six windows of hand-blown glass and wide plank floors. Two herb garden and screen porch also beckon visitors. Full breakfasts may include omelets with garden ingredients, raspberry muffins, rum sticky buns or waffles. The inn's three guest rooms feature double beds, and one boasts a romantic fire-

place. Fine antiquing and golfing are found nearby. During the summer months, the innkeepers host a Wednesday afternoon herb series and afternoon tea. Also ask about other special packages. The innkeepers opened an herb and antique shop in their restored barn.

Innkeeper(s): Douglas & Yvonne Sloan. $55-85. MC, VISA, PC. 3 rooms, 1 with PB and 1 conference room. Breakfast and snacks/refreshments included in rates. Type of meal: Full gourmet bkfst. Beds: D. Phone and turndown service in room. Air conditioning. Bicycles on premises. Antiquing, art galleries, bicycling, canoeing/kayaking, fishing, golf, hiking, live theater, museums, parks, cross-country skiing, sporting events and tennis nearby.

Location: In a tiny hamlet.

Publicity: Elmira Star Gazette, Chemung Valley Reporter and Evening Star.

Certificate may be used: Sept. 1-May 31, anytime. Subject to availability.

Chestertown D12

The Friends Lake Inn

Friends Lake Rd
Chestertown, NY 12817
(518)494-4751 Fax:(518)494-4616

Circa 1860. Formerly a boardinghouse for tanners who worked in the area, this Mission-style inn now offers its guests elegant accommodations and fine dining. Overlooking Friends Lake, the inn provides easy access to many well-known skiing areas, including Gore Mountain. Guests are welcome to borrow a canoe for a lake outing and use the inn's private beach. Guest rooms are well-appointed and most include four-poster beds. Many have breathtaking lake views or Jacuzzis. Three rooms

have a wood-burning fireplace. An outdoor sauna is a favorite spot after a busy day of recreation. The 32 km Nordic Ski Center is on site with groomed wilderness trails, lessons and rentals. Trails are available for hiking, as well.

Innkeeper(s): Sharon & Greg Taylor. $195-375. MC, VISA, AX, PC, TC. 17 rooms with PB. Breakfast and dinner included in rates. Types of meals: Full bkfst and country bkfst. Beds: KQ. Turndown service in room. Air conditioning. VCR, fax, copier, swimming and library on premises. Amusement parks, antiquing, fishing, live theater, museums, parks, shopping, downhill skiing, cross-country skiing, sporting events and water sports nearby.

Location: Mountains.

Publicity: Country Inns and New York Times.

"Everyone here is so pleasant, you end up feeling like family!"

Certificate may be used: Year round, Sunday-Thursday nights. Not valid on holidays or holiday weekends. Free lodging second night (dinner and breakfast extra charges).

Clarence F3

Asa Ransom House

10529 Main St
Clarence, NY 14031-1684
(716)759-2315 Fax:(716)759-2791
Internet: www.asaransom.com
E-mail: info@asaransom.com

Circa 1853. Set on spacious lawns, behind a white picket fence, the Asa Ransom House rests on the site of the first grist mill built in Erie County. Silversmith Asa Ransom constructed an inn and grist mill here in response to the Holland Land Company's offering of free land to anyone who would start and operate a tavern. A specialty of the dining room is "Veal Perrott" and "Pistachio Banana Muffins."

Innkeeper(s): Robert & Abigail Lenz. $95-155. MC, VISA, DS, PC, TC. 9 rooms with PB, 7 with FP, 2 suites and 1 conference room. Breakfast included in rates. Types of meals: Full bkfst and early coffee/tea. Beds: KQDT. Phone, turndown service and old radio tapes in room. Air conditioning. Fax, copier and library on premises. Handicap access. Antiquing, live theater, parks, shopping and cross-country skiing nearby.

Location: Village.

Publicity: *Toronto Star, Buffalo News, Prevention Magazine, Country Living. Country Inns and Inn Country USA.*

"Popular spot keeps getting better."

Certificate may be used: Feb. 16-May 30, Sept. 1-Dec. 15, Sunday-Thursday.

Claverack   H12

The Martindale B&B Inn

857 Rt-23
Claverack, NY 12513
(518)851-5405 Fax:(518)851-2568
E-mail: solterry@epix.net

Circa 1852. For more than 100 years, this farmhouse remained in the same family. Innkeepers Terry and Soll Berl purchased the home in 1986 and transformed into a small bed & breakfast. Although the exterior features Federal and Colonial architecture, the fancy trim is reminiscent of a Victorian home. The interior definitely favors the Victorian, including antiques, wicker and Oriental rugs. The vast grounds include a pond with a little dock and rowboat, as well as an enclosed gazebo.

Innkeeper(s): Terry & Soll Berl. $85. PC. 4 rooms with PB. Breakfast included in rates. Type of meal: Full bkfst. Beds: DT. Ceiling fan in room. VCR, fax and tennis on premises. Antiquing, fishing, golf, live theater, parks, shopping, downhill skiing and cross-country skiing nearby.

Location: Hudson Valley.

Certificate may be used: Nov. 1-April 30, except holiday seasons.

Cold Spring   J12

Pig Hill Inn

73 Main St
Cold Spring, NY 10516-3014
(914)265-9247 Fax:(914)265-4614
Internet: www.pighillinn.com
E-mail: pighillinn@aol.com

Circa 1808. The antiques at this stately three-story inn can be purchased, and they range from Chippendale to chinoiserie style. Rooms feature formal English and Adirondack decor with special touches such as

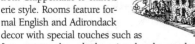

four-poster or brass beds, painted rockers and, of course, pigs. The lawn features a tri-level garden. The delicious breakfasts can be shared with guests in the Victorian conservatory, dining room or garden, or you can take it in the privacy of your room. The inn is about an hour out of New York City, and the train station is only two blocks away.

Innkeeper(s): Kim Teng. $120-170. MC, VISA, AX, TC. 9 rooms, 5 with PB, 6 with FP and 1 conference room. Breakfast included in rates. Type of meal: Full

bkfst. Beds: QDT. Ceiling fan, tea, coffee, ice and glasses in room. Air conditioning. Antiquing, fishing, live theater, shopping and sporting events nearby.

Location: Small Hudson River town.

Publicity: *National Geographic, Woman's Home Journal, Country Inns and Getaways for Gourmets.*

"Some of our fondest memories of New York were at Pig Hill."

Certificate may be used: Monday-Thursday, excluding holidays, May and October.

Cooperstown   G10

Litco Farms B&B

PO Box 1048
Cooperstown, NY 13326-6048
(607)547-2501 Fax:(607)547-7079
Internet: www.heartworksquilts.com
E-mail: litcofarms@stny.rr.com

The 70-acre grounds that surround this Greek Revival farmhouse include 18 acres of mapped wetlands. The natural setting includes trails lined with wildflowers, and guests are sure to spot deer and a variety of birds. On cold days, guests can snuggle up to the wood-burning stove, and there are plenty of ideal spots for picnics during the warmer months. The scent of baking breads and fresh coffee entices guests to the morning meal of country fare. The

innkeepers have been welcoming guests and families with children for more than 16 years. A favorite activity is browsing at Heartworks Quilts and Fabrics, an on-site shop.

Innkeeper(s): Jim & Margaret Wolff. $89-139. 4 rooms. Breakfast included in rates. Type of meal: Full bkfst.

Certificate may be used: April 1-May 15 & Sept. 15-Oct. 30.

Cooperstown (Sharon Springs) G11

Edgefield

Washington St, PO Box 152
Cooperstown (Sharon Springs), NY 13459
(518)284-3339
Internet: www.members.tripod.com/~edgefield

Circa 1865. This home has seen many changes. It began as a farmhouse, a wing was added in the 1880s, and by the turn of the century, it sported an elegant Greek Revival facade. Edgefield is one of a collection of nearby homes used as a family compound for summer vacations. The rooms are decorated with traditional furnishings in a formal English-country style. In the English tradition, afternoon tea is presented with scones, cookies and tea sandwiches. Sharon Springs includes many historic sites, and the town is listed in the National Register.

Innkeeper(s): Daniel Marshall Wood. $95-160. PC, TC. 5 rooms with PB. Types of meals: Full gourmet bkfst and early coffee/tea. Beds: QT. Turndown service and ceiling fan in room. Library, drawing room and veranda on premises. Antiquing, golf, opera, live theater, parks, shopping and water sports nearby.

Location: Village.

Publicity: *Colonial Homes Magazine.*

"Truly what I always imagined the perfect B&B experience to be!"

Certificate may be used: Sept. 8-30, Oct. 20-June 30, Sunday-Thursday.

Corinth
E12

Agape Farm B&B
4894 Rt 9N
Corinth, NY 12822-1704
(518)654-7777

Circa 1870. Amid 33 acres of fields and woods, this Adirondack farmhouse is home to chickens and horses, as well as guests seeking a refreshing getaway. Visitors have their choice of six guest rooms, all with ceiling fans, phones, private baths and views of the tranquil surroundings. The inn's wraparound porch lures many visitors, who often enjoy a glass of icy lemonade. Homemade breads, jams, jellies and muffins are part of the full breakfast served here, and guests are welcome to pick berries or gather a ripe tomato from the garden. A trout-filled stream on the grounds flows to the Hudson River, a mile away.

Innkeeper(s): Fred & Sigrid Koch. $75-175. MC, VISA, DS, PC, TC. 6 rooms with PB and 1 cottage. Breakfast, afternoon tea and snacks/refreshments included in rates. Types of meals: Full bkfst and early coffee/tea. Phone and ceiling fan in room. VCR, library, child care and downstairs HC room and bath on premises. Amusement parks, antiquing, fishing, live theater, parks, shopping, downhill skiing, cross-country skiing, sporting events and water sports nearby.

Location: Hudson River.

"Clean and impeccable, we were treated royally."

Certificate may be used: Sept. 15 to June 15.

Corning
H6

1865 White Birch B&B
69 E 1st St
Corning, NY 14830-2715
(607)962-6355

Circa 1865. This Victorian is a short walk from historic Market Street, the Corning Glass Museum and many restaurants. Guests will appreciate the detailed woodwork, hardwood floors, an impressive winding staircase and many antiques. The rooms are decorated in a cozy, country decor. Home-baked breakfasts provide the perfect start for a day of visiting wineries, antique shops or museums.

Innkeeper(s): Kathy Donahue. $55-85. MC, VISA, AX. 4 rooms, 2 with PB. Breakfast included in rates. Type of meal: Full bkfst. Beds: QT. TV, phone, window fans and comfortable chair in room. Antiquing, fishing, live theater, shopping, cross-country skiing and sporting events nearby.

Location: Between two Finger Lakes.

"This is a beautiful home, decorated to make us feel warm and welcome."

Certificate may be used: January-March, November-December, Sunday through Thursday.

Delevan House
188 Delevan Ave
Corning, NY 14830-3224
(607)962-2347

Circa 1933. Visitors to the Corning area will find a touch of home at this comfortable Colonial Revival house on a hill overlooking town. The inn's screened porch offers the perfect spot for reading, relaxing or sipping a cool drink. A full breakfast is served before guests head out for a day of business, sightseeing or travel. The Finger Lakes are 30 miles away, and just two miles from the inn, visitors will find the city's historic district.

The Mark Twain Home and Pinnacle State Park are nearby.

Innkeeper(s): Mary DePumpo. $60-95. TC. 3 rooms, 1 with PB. Breakfast included in rates. Types of meals: Full gourmet bkfst and early coffee/tea. Beds: D. Cable TV and phone in room. Antiquing, fishing, parks, shopping, downhill skiing, cross-country skiing, sporting events and water sports nearby.

Location: Finger Lakes Area.

Certificate may be used: November to end of March.

Deposit
H9

The White Pillars Inn
82 2nd St
Deposit, NY 13754-1122
(607)467-4191 Fax:(607)467-2264

Circa 1820. Guests are greeted with freshly baked cookies at this exquisite Greek Revival inn. This is only the beginning of a food adventure to remember. After a restful night's sleep on a hand-carved, high-board bed, guests linger over a five-course breakfast, which might include an overstuffed omelette or a baked apple wrapped in pastry and topped with caramel sauce. Dinner is a gourmet's  treat, and all meals are prepared by innkeeper Najla Aswad, whose recipes have been recommended by Gourmet magazine. The inn is decorated with beautiful antiques, rich Persian carpets and colorful floral arrangements.

Innkeeper(s): Najla Aswad. $85-125. MC, VISA, AX, DC, CB, DS. 5 rooms, 3 with PB, 1 suite and 1 conference room. Breakfast included in rates. Type of meal: Full gourmet bkfst. Beds: KDT. Cable TV, phone, turndown service and VCR in room. Air conditioning. Fax and copier on premises. Antiquing, fishing, shopping, downhill skiing, cross-country skiing and sporting events nearby.

Location: Mountains.

Publicity: *Gourmet*.

"The perfect place to do nothing but eat!"

Certificate may be used: November-April.

Downsville
H10

The Victoria Rose B&B
Main St, Box 542
Downsville, NY 13755
(607)363-7838 Fax:(516)928-1780
E-mail: nkeepr@aol.com

Circa 1897. A prominent local doctor built this Victorian home, which boasts original items such as stained-glass windows, a carved mantel and grand staircase. The home is decorated in Victorian style with period antiques and reproductions. Light, lacy curtains shade the windows, and rooms feature flowery wallpapers. There is a covered veranda on one side of the home, offering wicker furnishings for those who want to relax. In addition to breakfast, guests are pampered with afternoon tea. Those in search of outdoor activities will find fishing, hunting, golfing, several state parks and hiking trails all in the area.

Innkeeper(s): Bill & Debby Benzinger. $52-63. MC, VISA, PC. 4 rooms with PB. Breakfast, afternoon tea and snacks/refreshments included in rates. Types of meals: Full gourmet bkfst and early coffee/tea. Beds: QD. Ceiling fan in room. VCR, bicycles and library on premises. Antiquing, fishing, golf, live theater, parks, shopping, cross-country skiing, sporting events, tennis and water sports nearby.

Location: Mountains.

Certificate may be used: June 1-Dec. 31, Sunday-Friday.

Elbridge F7

Fox Ridge Farm B&B

4786 Foster Rd
Elbridge, NY 13060-9770
(315)673-4881 Fax:(315)673-3691
Internet: www.cnylodging.com/foxridge
E-mail: foxridg@dreamscape.com

Circa 1910. Guests shouldn't be surprised to encounter deer or other wildlife at this secluded country home surrounded by woods. The innkeepers have transformed the former farmhouse into an inn with rooms boasting quilts, a four-poster bed and views of the woods or flower garden. Enjoy breakfasts in front of a fire in the large country kitchen. The innkeepers are happy to accommodate dietary needs. Snacks and refreshments always are available for hungry guests in the evening. Nearby Skaneateles Lake offers swimming, boating and other outdoor activities. Dinner cruises, touring wineries and antique shopping are other popular activities.

Innkeeper(s): Marge Sykes. $55-95. MC, VISA, AX, DS, PC, TC. 3 rooms, 1 with PB. Breakfast and snacks/refreshments included in rates. Types of meals: Full gourmet bkfst, cont plus and early coffee/tea. Beds: QD. VCR, grand piano and wood stove on premises. Antiquing, fishing, live theater, parks, shopping, downhill skiing, cross-country skiing, sporting events and water sports nearby.

Location: Rural.

"If I could, I would take Marge Sykes home to Seattle with us. We stayed 7 days for a family reunion. Great company, marvelous hosts and the most delicious breakfasts everyday."

Certificate may be used: Jan. 1 to Dec. 31, Sunday-Thursday, excluding holidays.

Essex C13

The Stone House

PO Box 43
Essex, NY 12936-0043
(518)963-7713 Fax:(518)963-7713

Circa 1826. Just a two-minute walk from the ferry that traverses Lake Champlain, this stately Georgian stone house offers a tranquil English country setting. Breakfast may be eaten in the elegant dining room or on the garden terrace, and guests also enjoy an evening snack and glass of wine by candlelight on the inn's porch. The charming hamlet of Essex, listed in the National Register, is  waiting to be explored, and visitors may do so by borrowing one of the inn's bicycles. Antiquing, fine dining and shopping are found in town, and Lake Champlain and nearby Lake George provide many recreational activities.

Innkeeper(s): Sylvia Hobbs. $75-150. PC, TC. 4 rooms, 2 with PB, 1 suite and 1 cottage. Breakfast, afternoon tea and snacks/refreshments included in rates. Types of meals: Cont plus and early coffee/tea. Beds: QDT. Turndown service in room. VCR, bicycles, library and CD player on premises. Antiquing, fishing, golf, live theater, parks, shopping, tennis and water sports nearby.

Location: Lake Champlain.

"Without a doubt, the highlight of our trip!"

Certificate may be used: May-June, September-October, Sunday to Friday.

Fair Haven E7

Black Creek Farm B&B

PO Box 390
Fair Haven, NY 13064-0390
(315)947-5282

Circa 1888. Pines and towering birch trees frame this Victorian farmhouse inn, filled with an amazing assortment of authentic antiques. Set on 20 acres, Black Creek Farm is a refreshing escape from big-city life. Guests enjoy relaxing in a hammock on the porch or by taking a stroll along the peaceful back roads. A hearty country breakfast features seasonal fruit raised on the grounds as well as home baked date-nut, banana-nut or pumpkin-raisin bread. A new pond-side guest house is an especially popular accommodation for honeymooners and families, offering complete privacy. It features a gas fireplace and double shower. Bring your own breakfast makings and enjoy breakfast sitting on the patio or the porch which overlooks the pond, with ducks and geese, bass and perch. Sometimes turkey or deer may be seen in the meadow. There's a peddle boat on the pond in summer. In winter sledding and snowmobiling are popular. The B&B is two miles from Lake Ontario, Fair Haven Beach State Park and minutes away from Sterling Renaissance Festival.

Innkeeper(s): Bob & Kathy Sarber. $60-125. MC, VISA. 3 rooms with PB. Types of meals: Full bkfst and early coffee/tea. Beds: Q. Air conditioning. VCR, bicycles, pedal boat, satellite disc and movies available on premises. Fishing, snowmobiling, cross-country skiing and water sports nearby.

Location: Country.

Certificate may be used: No weekends (Friday-Sunday) in July and August and other special weekends as determined by innkeeper.

Frost Haven B&B Inn

14380 West Bay Rd, PO Box 241
Fair Haven, NY 13064-0241
(315)947-5331

This Federal-style inn near Lake Ontario offers a relaxing getaway for residents of nearby Rochester and Syracuse. Four guest rooms are available, all furnished with Victorian stylings and featuring bath robes and ceiling fans. Guests enjoy a full breakfast before beginning a busy day of antiquing, fishing, sightseeing, swimming or sunbathing. Fair Haven Beach State Park is nearby, and Fort Ontario is within easy driving distance.

Innkeeper(s): Jean & Glen Spry. $66. MC, VISA. 7 rooms. Ceiling fan in room. VCR on premises. Antiquing nearby.

Location: Village.

Certificate may be used: Weekends July through Labor Day excluded.

Fleischmanns H11

River Run

Main St, Box 9
Fleischmanns, NY 12430
(845)254-4884
Internet: www.catskill.net/riverrun
E-mail: riverrun@catskill.net

Circa 1887. The backyard of this large three-story Victorian gently slopes to the river where the Bushkill and Little Red Kill trout streams meet. Inside, stained-glass windows surround the inn's common areas, shining on the oak-floored dining room and the book-filled parlor. The parlor also includes a fireplace and a piano. Adirondack chairs are situated comfortably on the front porch. Tennis courts, a pool, park, theater and restaurants are within walking distance, as is a country auction held each Saturday night. The inn is two and a half hours out of New York City, 35 minutes west of Woodstock, and accessible by public transportation. Also, the inn was the recipient of the "Catskill Service Award" for best accommodations in the Belleayre Region for 1998 and 1999.

Innkeeper(s): Larry Miller. $70-120. MC, VISA, AX, PC. 10 rooms, 6 with PB and 1 suite. Breakfast and afternoon tea included in rates. Types of meals: Cont plus and early coffee/tea. Beds: KQDT. TV in room. VCR, bicycles, library and refrigerator on premises. Antiquing, fishing, golf, hiking, horseback riding, auctions, flea and farmers markets, live theater, parks, shopping, downhill skiing, cross-country skiing, tennis and water sports nearby.

Pets allowed: Well behaved, fully trained, over one year old.

Location: Mountains.

Publicity: *New York Magazine, Boston Globe, Catskill Mountain News, Kingston Freeman, New York Times, New York Daily News, Philadelphia Inquirer, Inn Country USA and Newsday.*

"We are really happy to know of a place that welcomes all of our family."

Certificate may be used: Weekends March, April, November-December; weekdays all year (all holiday periods excluded). Call for availability of other times.

Fredonia G2

The White Inn

52 E Main St
Fredonia, NY 14063-1836
(716)672-2103 (888)FRE-DONI Fax:(716)672-2107
Internet: www.whiteinn.com
E-mail: inn@whiteinn.com

Circa 1868. This 23-room inn is situated in the center of a historic town. The inn's rooms are pristinely furnished in antiques and reproductions and 11 are spacious suites.

Guests, as well as the public may enjoy gourmet meals at the inn, a charter member of the Duncan Hines "Family of Fine Restaurants." In addition to fine dining and catered events, casual fare and cocktails are offered in the lounge or on the 100-foot-long veranda. Nearby the Chautauqua Institution operates during the summer offering a popular selection of lectures and concert performances. Fredonia State College is another avenue to cultural events as well as sporting events. Wineries, golfing, state parks and shops are nearby. The inn is featured on the front cover.

Innkeeper(s): Robert Contiguglia & Kathleen Dennison. $69-179. MC, VISA, AX, DC, DS, PC, TC. 23 rooms with PB, 2 with FP, 11 suites and 4 conference rooms. Breakfast included in rates. Type of meal: Full bkfst. Beds: KQD. Cable TV and phone in room. Air conditioning. VCR, fax and copier on premises. Handicap access. Antiquing, live theater, parks, shopping and cross-country skiing nearby.

Location: City.

Publicity: *Upstate New York Magazine, Country Living, US Air Magazine and Buffalo News.*

"The perfect mix of old-fashioned charm and modern elegance."

Certificate may be used: November-April, Sunday-Thursday, excluding holidays and holiday weekends.

Fulton E7

Battle Island Inn

2167 State Route 48 N
Fulton, NY 13069-4132
(315)593-3699 Fax:(315)592-5071
Internet: www.battle-island-inn.com
E-mail: battleislandinn@usadatanet.net

Circa 1840. Topped with a gothic cupola, this family farmhouse overlooks the Oswego River and a golf course. There are three antique-filled parlors. Guest accommodations are furnished in a variety of styles including Victorian and Renaissance Revival. There are four wooded  acres with lawns and gardens. Guests are often found relaxing on one of the inn's four porches and enjoying the views. The Honeymoon suite features a canopy bed, full bath and private Jacuzzi.

Innkeeper(s): Richard & Joyce Rice. $60-125. MC, VISA, AX, DS, PC, TC. 5 rooms with PB and 1 suite. Breakfast included in rates. Types of meals: Full gourmet bkfst and early coffee/tea. Beds: QDT. Cable TV, phone and ceiling fan in room. VCR, fax, copier and refrigerator on premises. Handicap access. Fishing, golf, fort, live theater, parks, shopping, cross-country skiing and water sports nearby.

Location: Country.

Publicity: *Lake Effect, Palladium Times, Travel, Journey, Oswego County Business and Valley News.*

"We will certainly never forget our wonderful weeks at Battle Island Inn."

Certificate may be used: Sunday-Thursday.

Gorham G6

The Gorham House

4752 E Swamp Rd
Gorham, NY 14461
(716)526-4402 Fax:(716)526-4402
Internet: www.angelfire.com/biz/GorhamHouse
E-mail: gorham.house@juno.com

Circa 1887. The Gorham House serves as a homey, country place to enjoy New York's Finger Lakes region. The five, secluded acres located between Canandaigua and Seneca lakes, include herb gardens, wildflowers and berry bushes. Part of the home dates back to the early 19th century, but it's the architecture of the 1887 expansion that accounts for the inn's Victorian touches. The interior is warm and cozy with comfortable, country furnishings. Some of the pieces are the innkeepers' family heirlooms. There are more than 50 wineries in the area, as well as a bounty of outdoor activities.

Innkeeper(s): Nancy & Al Rebmann. $89-120. PC, TC. 3 rooms, 1 with PB. Breakfast included in rates. Types of meals: Full gourmet bkfst and early coffee/tea. Beds: QD. Air conditioning. Library on premises. Antiquing, fishing, live theater, parks, shopping, downhill skiing, cross-country skiing, sporting events and water sports nearby.

Location: Heart of the Finger Lakes.

Certificate may be used: Jan. 1-Aug. 1, Sunday-Friday.

Greenfield Center   F12

The Wayside Inn

104 Wilton Rd
Greenfield Center, NY 12833-1705
(518)893-7249 Fax:(518)893-2884

Circa 1786. This Federal-style inn and education center provides a unique atmosphere to visitors of the Saratoga Springs
area. Situated on 10 acres amid a brook, herb gardens, pond,
wildflowers and willows, the inn originally served as a stagecoach tavern. Many interesting pieces, gathered during the
innkeepers' 10 years living abroad, highlight the inn's interior.
Visitors select from the Colonial American, European, Far East
and Middle East rooms. Migrating birds are known to frequent
the inn's picturesque pond.

Innkeeper(s): Karen & Dale Shook. $60-160. MC, VISA, AX, DC, DS. 3
rooms with PB, 1 suite and 2 conference rooms. Breakfast included in rates.
Types of meals: Full bkfst and early coffee/tea. Ceiling fan in room. Air conditioning. VCR and Arts Center - Herb Gardens on premises. Amusement parks,
antiquing, live theater, shopping, downhill skiing, cross-country skiing and
sporting events nearby.

Certificate may be used: January-June, September, December; Sunday,
Monday, Tuesday, Wednesday, Thursday. Space available.

Greenport   K15

The Bartlett House Inn

503 Front St
Greenport, NY 11944-1519
(631)477-0371
Internet: www.greenport.com/bartlett
E-mail: bartletthouseinn@aol.com

Circa 1908. A family residence for more than 60 years and
then a convent for a nearby church, this large Victorian house
became a bed & breakfast in 1982. Features include corinthian
columns, stained-glass windows, two fireplaces and a large
front porch. Period antiques complement the rich interior. The
inn is within walking distance of shops, restaurants, the harbor,
wineries, the Shelter Island Ferry and train station.

Innkeeper(s): Michael & Patricia O'Donoghue. $95-150. MC, VISA, PC, TC.
10 rooms with PB, 1 with FP and 1 conference room. Breakfast included in
rates. Types of meals: Cont plus and early coffee/tea. Beds: QDT. Air conditioning. Antiquing, fishing, maritime museum, outlet shopping, art galleries,
golf, fine restaurants, parks, shopping and water sports nearby.

Location: Historic village.

Publicity: *Suffolk Times, Newsday, New York Times and New York Post.*

Certificate may be used: Monday-Thursday. Nov. 1-June 1, excluding holidays.

Hadley   E12

Saratoga Rose Inn & Restaurant

4274 Rockwell St
Hadley, NY 12835-0238
(518)696-2861 (800)942-5025 Fax:(518)696-5319

Circa 1885. This romantic
Queen Anne Victorian offers a
small, candlelit restaurant perfect for an evening for two.
Breakfast specialties include
Grand Marnier French toast
and eggs Anthony. Rooms are

decorated in period style. The Queen Anne Room, decorated in
blue, boasts a wood and tile fireplace and a quilt-covered bed.
The Garden Room offers a private sunporch and an outside
deck with a Jacuzzi spa. Each of the rooms features something
special. Guests can take in the mountain view or relax on the
veranda while sipping a cocktail.

Innkeeper(s): Nancy Merlino. $135-175. MC, VISA, DS. 6 rooms with PB, 3
with FP. Breakfast included in rates. Type of meal: Full gourmet bkfst. Beds:
KD. Ceiling fan and private hot tubs in room. Air conditioning. VCR and spa
on premises. Amusement parks, antiquing, fishing, live theater, parks, shopping, downhill skiing, cross-country skiing and sporting events nearby.

Location: Mountains.

Publicity: *Getaways for Gourmets.*

"A must for the inn traveler."

Certificate may be used: November-May, Monday-Thursday, may exclude holidays, upon availability.

Hague   D12

Trout House Village Resort

PO Box 510
Hague, NY 12836-0510
(518)543-6088 (800)368-6088 Fax:(518)543-6124
Internet: www.trouthouse.com
E-mail: info@trouthouse.com

Circa 1920. On the shores of beautiful Lake George is this
resort inn, offering accommodations in the lodge, authentic log
cabins or cottages. Many of the guest rooms in the lodge boast
lake views, while the log
cabins offer jetted tubs
and fireplaces. The guest
quarters are furnished
comfortably. The emphasis
here is on the abundance
of outdoor activities.

Outstanding cross-country skiing, downhill skiing and snowmobiling are found nearby. The inn furnishes bicycles, canoes,
kayaks, paddle boats, rowboats, sleds, shuffleboard, skis and
toboggans. Summertime evenings offer games of capture-the-
flag and soccer. Other activities include basketball, horseshoes,
ping pong, a putting green and volleyball.

Innkeeper(s): Scott & Alice Patchett. $45-366. MC, VISA, AX, DS, PC, TC. 9
rooms, 7 with PB, 15 with FP, 15 cottages and 2 conference rooms. Beds:
QDT. Cable TV, phone and VCR in room. Fax, copier, spa, swimming, bicycles
and child care on premises. Handicap access. Amusement parks, antiquing,
art galleries, beaches, bicycling, canoeing/kayaking, fishing, golf, hiking,
horseback riding, museums, parks, shopping, downhill skiing, cross-country
skiing, tennis and water sports nearby.

Pets allowed: During off season.

Location: Adirondack mountains.

*"My wife and I felt the family warmth at this resort. There wasn't
that coldness you get at larger resorts."*

Certificate may be used: Sept. 15-June 5, except holiday weekends.

Hamburg   G3

Sharon's Lake House B&B

4862 Lake Shore Rd
Hamburg, NY 14075-5542
(716)627-7561
E-mail: vdim720905@aol.com

Circa 1935. This historic lakefront house is located 10 miles
from Buffalo and 45 minutes from Niagara Falls. Overlooking
Lake Erie, the West Lake Room and the Upper Lake Room pro-

vide spectacular views. The home's beautiful furnishings offer additional delights.

Innkeeper(s): Sharon & Vince Di Maria. $100-110. PC, TC. 2 rooms, 1 with PB. Breakfast included in rates. Type of meal: Full gourmet bkfst. Beds: D. Cable TV, phone and ceiling fan in room. VCR, swimming and hot tub room & computer room at an hourly rate available on premises. Fishing, live theater, parks, shopping, downhill skiing, cross-country skiing and water sports nearby.

"Spectacular view, exquisitely furnished."

Certificate may be used: Anytime, all year.

Hamlin   E5

Sandy Creek Manor House

1960 Redman Rd
Hamlin, NY 14464-9635
(716)964-7528 (800)594-0400
Internet: www.sandycreekbnb.com
E-mail: agreatbnb@aol.com

Circa 1910. Six acres of woods and perennial gardens provide the setting for this English Tudor house. Stained glass, polished woods and Amish quilts add warmth to the home. The innkeepers have placed many thoughtful amenities in each room, such as clock radios, fluffy robes, slippers and baskets of toiletries. Breakfast is served on the open porch in summer. Fisherman's Landing, on the banks of Sandy Creek, is a stroll away. Bullhead, trout and salmon are popular catches. There is a gift shop, outdoor hot tub and deck on premises. Ask about murder-mystery, sweetheart dinner and spa treatment packages.

Innkeeper(s): Shirley Hollink & James Krempasky. $65-90. MC, VISA, AX, DS, PC, TC. 4 rooms, 1 with PB. Breakfast, afternoon tea and snacks/refreshments included in rates. Types of meals: Full gourmet bkfst, cont plus, cont and early coffee/tea. Beds: KQDT. Cable TV and VCR in room. Air conditioning. Fishing, player piano and guest refrigerator on premises. Antiquing, fishing, farm markets, sky diving, gift shop on premises, parks, shopping, downhill skiing, cross-country skiing, sporting events and water sports nearby.

Pets Allowed.

Location: Country.

Publicity: *Democrat & Chronicle, Buffalo News, Rochester Times Union* and *It's Time To Take Off.*

"Delightful in every way."

Certificate may be used: Anytime.

Hudson   H12

The Inn at Blue Stores

2323 Rt 9
Hudson, NY 12534-0099
(518)537-4277 Fax:(518)537-4277
Internet: www.innatbluestores.com

Circa 1908. A rural Hudson Valley setting may seem an unusual place for a Spanish-style inn, but this former gentlemen's farm now provides a unique setting for those seeking a relaxing

getaway. Visitors enjoy the inn's clay tile roof and stucco exterior, along with its impressive interior, featuring black oak woodwork, leaded-glass entry and stained glass. Visitors are treated to full breakfasts and refreshing afternoon teas. The spacious porch and swimming pool are favorite spots for relaxing and socializing.

Innkeeper(s): Linda & Robert. $99-195. MC, VISA, AX. 5 rooms, 2 with PB and 1 suite. Breakfast included in rates. Types of meals: Full gourmet bkfst and early coffee/tea. Beds: KQT. TV and VCR in room. Air conditioning. Fax and swimming on premises. Antiquing, art galleries, bicycling, canoeing/kayaking, fishing, golf, hiking, horseback riding, historic sites, OLANA, Hyde Park, Clermont Mills Estate, live theater, museums, parks, shopping, cross-country skiing, tennis and wineries nearby.

Location: Country.

Publicity: *Hudson Valley.*

Certificate may be used: Dec. 1-March 31, Monday-Thursday, except holidays.

Ithaca   G7

La Tourelle Country Inn

1150 Danby Rd, Rt 96B
Ithaca, NY 14850-9406
(607)273-2734 (800)765-1492 Fax:(607)273-4821

Circa 1986. This white stucco European-style country inn is located on 70 acres three miles from town, allowing for wildflower walks, cross-country skiing and all-season hiking. Adjacent Buttermilk Falls State Park provides stone paths, waterfalls and streams. The inn is decorated with a hint of European decor and includes fireplace suites and tower suites. For an extra fee, a continental breakfast arrives at your door in a basket, French Provincial style,

and guests often tote it to the patio or gazebo to enjoy views of the rolling countryside. There is also a tennis court available.

Innkeeper(s): Leslie Leonard. $79-150. MC, VISA, AX, TC. 34 rooms with PB, 1 with FP and 1 conference room. Types of meals: Cont and early coffee/tea. Beds: KQ. Cable TV, phone and VCR in room. Air conditioning. Copier, tennis, hiking trails and fishing ponds on premises. Handicap access. Antiquing, fishing, live theater, parks, shopping, downhill skiing, cross-country skiing, sporting events and water sports nearby.

Location: 70 acres hillside, country.

Certificate may be used: Sunday through Thursday not including holidays or college specialty days. No weekends.

Log Country Inn - B&B of Ithaca

PO Box 581
Ithaca, NY 14851-0581
(607)589-4771 (800)274-4771 Fax:(607)589-6151
Internet: www.logtv.com/inn
E-mail: wanda@logtv.com

Circa 1969. As the name indicates, this bed & breakfast is indeed fashioned from logs and rests in a picturesque country setting surrounded by 20 wooded acres. The cozy rooms are rustic with exposed beams and country furnishings. There is also a Jacuzzi. The decor is dotted with a European influence, as is the morning meal. Guests enjoy a full breakfast with blintzes or Russian pancakes. The innkeeper welcomes children.

Innkeeper(s): Wanda Grunberg. $45-200. MC, VISA, AX. 5 rooms, 3 with PB and 1 suite. Breakfast and afternoon tea included in rates. Type of meal: Full bkfst. Beds: QDT. Cable TV and phone in room. VCR, fax, spa, sauna and jacuzzi on premises. Antiquing, fishing, hiking, wine vineyards, parks, shopping, cross-country skiing, sporting events, water sports and wineries nearby.

Pets Allowed.

Location: On the edge of state forest.

Certificate may be used: Jan. 15-May 1, Sunday-Thursday.

Rose Inn

Rt 34N, Box 6576
Ithaca, NY 14851-6576
(607)533-7905 Fax:(607)533-7908
Internet: www.roseinn.com
E-mail: info@roseinn.com

Circa 1842. This classic Italianate mansion has long been famous for its circular staircase of Honduran mahogany. It is owned by Sherry Rosemann, a noted interior designer specializing in mid-19th-century architecture and furniture, and her husband Charles, a hotelier from Germany. On 14 landscaped acres with a large formal garden and wedding chapel, it is 10 minutes from Cornell University. The inn has been the recipient of many awards for its lodging and dining, including a four-star rating eight years in a row.

Innkeeper(s): Charles & Sherry Rosemann. $115-320. MC, VISA, PC, TC. 21 rooms with FP, 7 with FP, 11 suites and 2 conference rooms. Breakfast included in rates. Types of meals: Full gourmet bkfst, cont and early coffee/tea. Beds: KQDT. Cable TV, phone, turndown service, ceiling fan, VCR and eleven suites have Jacuzzi's and seven have fireplaces in room. Air conditioning. Fax, copier and library on premises. Antiquing, art galleries, beaches, bicycling, canoeing/kayaking, fishing, golf, hiking, horseback riding, live theater, museums, parks, shopping, downhill skiing, cross-country skiing, sporting events, tennis, water sports and wineries nearby.

Location: Country.

Publicity: *New York Times, Toronto Globe and Mail and Inn Country USA.*

"The blending of two outstanding talents, which when combined with your warmth, produce the ultimate experience in being away from home. Like staying with friends in their beautiful home."

Certificate may be used: Dec. 1-March 31, Sunday through Friday; April 1-Nov. 30, Monday through Thursday.

Jay   C12

Book and Blanket B&B

Rt 9N, PO Box 164
Jay, NY 12941-0164
(518)946-8323
Internet: www.theadirondacks.com/book&blanket
E-mail: bookinnjay@aol.com

Circa 1860. This Adirondack bed & breakfast served as the town's post office for many years and also as barracks for state troopers. Thankfully, however, it is now a restful bed & breakfast catering to the literary set. Guest rooms are named for authors and there are books in every nook and cranny of the house. Guests may even take a book home with them. Each of the guest rooms is comfortably furnished. The inn is a short walk from the Jay Village Green and the original site of the Historic Jay covered bridge.

Innkeeper(s): Kathy, Fred, Sam & Daisy the Basset Hound. $60-80. AX, PC, TC. 3 rooms, 1 with PB and 1 with FP. Breakfast, afternoon tea and snacks/refreshments included in rates. Types of meals: Full bkfst, veg bkfst and early coffee/tea. Beds: QDT. VCR, whirlpool tub, fireplace and library on premises. Antiquing, art galleries, beaches, bicycling, canoeing/kayaking, fishing, golf, hiking, Olympic venues i.e. bobsled, luge, ski jump, ice skating, parks, downhill skiing, cross-country skiing, sporting events, tennis and water sports nearby.

Location: Small Hamlet.

Certificate may be used: Jan. 15 to June 20, Sunday-Thursday.

Keene Valley   C12

Trail's End Inn

Trail's End Rd, HC 01, Box 103
Keene Valley, NY 12943
(518)576-9860 (800)281-9860 Fax:(518)576-9235
Internet: www.trailsendinn.com
E-mail: innkeeper@trailsendinn.com

Circa 1902. This charming mountain inn is in the heart of the Adirondack's High Peaks. Surrounded by woods and adjacent to a small pond, the inn offers spacious guest rooms with antique furnishings and country quilts. All-you-can-eat morning meals in the glassed-in breakfast room not only provide a lovely look at the countryside, but often a close-up view of various bird species. Fresh air and gorgeous views abound, and  visitors enjoy invigorating hikes, trout fishing and fine cross-country skiing. Downhill skiers will love the challenge of nearby White Mountain, with the longest vertical drop in the East.

Innkeeper(s): Jenny & Curt Borchardt. $49-125. MC, VISA, AX, DS, PC, TC. 10 rooms, 6 with PB, 3 with FP, 2 suites and 1 cottage. Breakfast included in rates. Types of meals: Full bkfst and early coffee/tea. Beds: KQDT. Phone and guest kitchenette in room. VCR, fax, copier, library and child care on premises. Antiquing, fishing, golf, 1980 Olympic headquarters in Lake Placid, rock climbing, ice climbing, major hiking trails, parks, shopping, downhill skiing, cross-country skiing, tennis and water sports nearby.

Location: Mountains.

Publicity: *Outside, Mid-Atlantic and Lake Placid News.*

"Felt like home. What a treasure we found."

Certificate may be used: Jan. 1-June 15 and Oct. 15-Dec. 31; Sunday through Thursday, excluding holiday periods.

Lake Placid   C12

Interlaken Inn

15 Interlaken Ave
Lake Placid, NY 12946-1142
(518)523-3180 (800)428-4369 Fax:(518)523-0117
Internet: www.innbook.com
E-mail: interlkn@northnet.org

Circa 1906. The five-course dinner at this Victorian inn is prepared by innkeeper CIA graduate Kevin Gregg and his talented staff. The high-quality cuisine is rivaled only by the rich decor of this cozy inn. Walnut paneling covers the dining room walls, which are topped with a tin ceiling. Bedrooms are carefully decorated with wallpapers, fresh  flowers and luxurious bed coverings. Spend the afternoon gazing at the mountains and lakes that surround this Adirondack hideaway, or visit the Olympic venues.

Innkeeper(s): Carol & Roy Johnson. $90-180. MC, VISA, AX. 11 rooms with PB and 1 suite. Breakfast included in rates. Types of meals: Full bkfst and early coffee/tea. Beds: KQD. Ceiling fan in room. VCR and fax on premises. Antiquing, fishing, live theater, shopping, downhill skiing, cross-country skiing, sporting events and water sports nearby.

Pets allowed: small, by prior arrangements.

Location: Mountains.

Publicity: *Outside, Country Inns, Wine Trader and PBS.*

Certificate may be used: Jan. 1-June 31, excluding holiday periods, Sunday through Thursday, rates $80-$150 bed & breakfast only. Nov. 1 to Dec. 23 anytime, not valid on weekends.

Lansing   G7

The Federal House B&B

175 Ludlowville Rd
Lansing, NY 14882
(607)533-7362 (800)533-7362 Fax:(607)533-7899
Internet: www.wordpro.com/fedh/fh.htm
E-mail: innkeeper@clarityconnect.com

Circa 1815. Salmon Creek Falls, a well-known fishing spot, is yards away from the inn. The rooms are furnished with antiques, which complement the original woodwork and hand-carved fireplace mantels. Each of the suites includes a television and a fireplace.

Innkeeper(s): Diane Carroll. $55-175. MC, VISA, AX, DS, PC, TC. 4 rooms with PB, 2 with FP and 2 suites. Breakfast included in rates. Type of meal: Full bkfst. Beds: KQT. Air conditioning. Fishing, biking, wineries, Cayuga Lake and State Parks nearby.

Publicity: *Ithaca Journal and Cortland Paper.*

"Your inn is so charming and your food was excellent."

Certificate may be used: January-April, September and November, Monday-Thursday.

Lewiston   F3

The Cameo Inn

4710 Lower River Rd, Rt 18-F
Lewiston, NY 14092-1053
(716)745-3034
Internet: www.cameoinn.com
E-mail: cameoinn@juno.com

Circa 1875. This classic Queen Anne Victorian inn offers a breathtaking view of the lower Niagara River. Located on the Seaway Trail, the inn offers convenient access to sightseeing in this popular region. The inn's interior features family heirlooms and period antiques, and visitors choose from four guest rooms, including a three-room suite overlooking the river. Breakfast is served buffet-style, and the entrees, which change daily, may include German oven pancakes or Grand Marnier French toast. Area attractions include Old Fort Niagara, outlet malls and several state parks.

Innkeeper(s): Gregory Fisher. $65-115. 4 rooms, 2 with PB and 1 suite. Breakfast included in rates. Type of meal: Full bkfst. Beds: QDT. Cable TV and ceiling fan in room. Amusement parks, antiquing, fishing, live theater, shopping, downhill skiing, cross-country skiing, sporting events and water sports nearby.

Publicity: *Country Folk Art, Esquire, Journey, Seaway Trail, Waterways and Buffalo News.*

"I made the right choice when I selected Cameo."

Certificate may be used: Anytime Nov. 15-April 30; Sunday through Thursday May 1-Nov. 14. Holidays and special event periods excluded. All subject to availability.

The Little Blue House B&B

115 Center St
Lewiston, NY 14092-1537
(716)754-9425

Circa 1906. Located in the heart of the village's main street, this Colonial inn offers charming accommodations and convenient access to area activities. Three unique guest rooms are available, including a Chinese-themed room with a king bed and a Victorian-style room with a queen bed. The inn's decor includes antiques, collectibles and contemporary art. Ten minutes away are the American and Canadian Falls.

Innkeeper(s): Michael & Margot Kornfeld. $65-175. AX, PC, TC. 3 rooms, 1 with PB and 1 suite. Breakfast included in rates. Types of meals: Full gourmet bkfst and cont plus. Beds: KQ. Cable TV and ceiling fan in room. Air conditioning. VCR on premises. Amusement parks, antiquing, fishing, live theater, parks, shopping, cross-country skiing and sporting events nearby.

Location: Rural historic village.

Certificate may be used: Nov. 1-April 30, any day except holidays and special events.

Margaretville   H10

Margaretville Mountain Inn B&B

Margaretville Mountain Rd
Margaretville, NY 12455-9735
(914)586-3933
Internet: www.catskill.net/mmibnb
E-mail: mmibnb@catskill.net

Circa 1886. Reminiscent of the Victorian era, this home rests on the site of the nation's first cauliflower farm. The owners have restored the slate roof, elaborate exterior woodwork and decorative interior woodwork. A full breakfast is served in the formal dining room on English china, or guests can enjoy the morning meal on the veranda, which overlooks the Catskill Mountains. The surrounding area offers a variety of activities including antique shopping, ice skating, golf, tennis, swimming, boating, fishing and hiking. The innkeepers offer ski packages.

Innkeeper(s): Carol & Peter Molnar. $55-120. MC, VISA, AX. 7 rooms with PB and 1 suite. Breakfast included in rates. Type of meal: Full gourmet bkfst. Beds: KQDT. TV in room. Fax on premises. Hiking, swimming, downhill skiing and cross-country skiing nearby.

Publicity: *Spotlight and NY Wedding.*

"Truly a step back in time to all that was charming, elegant and wholesome—right here in the 20th century."

Certificate may be used: Sunday-Thursday, non-holidays. Weekends only in March, April and May.

Niagara Falls   F3

The Cameo Manor North

3881 Lower River Rd, Rt 18-F
Niagara Falls, NY 14174
(716)745-3034
Internet: www.cameoinn.com
E-mail: cameoinn@juno.com

Circa 1860. This Colonial Revival inn offers a restful setting ideal for those seeking a peaceful getaway. The inn's three secluded acres add to its romantic setting, as does an interior that features several fireplaces. Visitors select from three suites, which feature private sun rooms, or two guest rooms that share a bath. Popular spots with guests include the library, great room and solarium. Fort Niagara and several state parks are nearby, and the American and Canadian Falls are within easy driving distance of the inn. The inn is actually located about eight miles north of Niagara Falls near the village of Youngstown.

Innkeeper(s): Gregory Fisher. $75-175. 5 rooms. Breakfast included in rates. Type of meal: Full bkfst. Beds: QDT. TV in room. Air conditioning. Amusement parks, antiquing, fishing, live theater, shopping, downhill skiing, cross-country skiing, sporting events and water sports nearby.

Publicity: *Country Folk Art, Esquire, Journey, Seaway Trail, Waterways and Buffalo News.*

"I made the right choice when I selected Cameo."

Certificate may be used: Anytime Nov. 15-April 30; Sunday-Thursday, May 1-Nov. 14, holidays and special event periods excluded. All subject to availability.

Oneida Castle F9

Governors House Bed & Breakfast

50 Seneca Ave
Oneida Castle, NY 13421-2558
(315)363-5643 (800)437-8177 Fax:(315)363-9568

Circa 1848. Built in the hopes of becoming the first residence for the Governor of New York State, this brick Federal house sits on two acres. The inn's finely crafted architecture includes features such as a mansard roof, elegant cupola and handsome porches. Antiques and canopy beds enhance most of the guest rooms, and there are two parlors, a library and a guest kitchen.

Innkeeper(s): Dawn E. Andrews. $76-143. MC, VISA, AX, DC, CB, DS, PC, TC. 5 rooms with PB, 1 suite and 1 conference room. Breakfast, afternoon tea and snacks/refreshments included in rates. Types of meals: Full gourmet bkfst and early coffee/tea. Beds: KQT. Cable TV and phone in room. Air conditioning. VCR, bicycles, library, child care and complimentary guest kitchen on premises. Handicap access. Amusement parks, antiquing, fishing, golf, rural driving and walking routes, live theater, parks, shopping, downhill skiing, cross-country skiing, sporting events, tennis and water sports nearby.

Location: Rural.

Certificate may be used: Nov. 1-April 30, Monday-Sunday (all week).

Penn Yan G6

The Wagener Estate B&B

351 Elm St
Penn Yan, NY 14527-1446
(315)536-4591

Circa 1794. Nestled in the Finger Lakes area on four shaded acres, this 15-room house features a wicker-furnished veranda where guests can relax in solitude or chat with others. Some of the early hand-hewn framing and the original brick fireplace and oven can be seen in the Family Room at the north end of the house. Most of the land, which is known as Penn Yan, was once owned by the original occupants of the home, David Wagener and his wife, Rebecca. David died in 1799, leaving this property to his son, Squire Wagener, who is considered to be the founder of Penn Yan. Some rooms include air conditioning and a television. Gift certificates are available.

Innkeeper(s): Joanne & Scott Murray. $75-95. MC, VISA, AX, DS, PC, TC. 6 rooms, 4 with PB. Breakfast included in rates. Type of meal: Full bkfst. Beds: KQDT. TV in some rooms in room. Antiquing, fishing, parks, cross-country skiing, water sports and wineries nearby.

Publicity: *Finger Lakes Times, Chronicle Express and New York Times.*

"Thanks so much for the wonderful hospitality and the magnificent culinary treats."

Certificate may be used: Dec. 1 to April 15, Sunday-Friday.

Queensbury E12

The Crislip's B&B

693 Ridge Rd
Queensbury, NY 12804-6901
(518)793-6869

Circa 1802. This Federal-style house was built by Quakers and was once owned by the area's first doctor, who used it as a training center for young interns. There's an acre of lawns and annual gardens and a Victorian Italianate veranda overlooks the Green Mountains. The inn is furnished with 18th-century antiques and reproductions, including four-poster canopy beds and highboys. There's a keeping room with a huge fireplace. Historic stone walls flank the property.

Innkeeper(s): Ned & Joyce Crislip. $55-85. MC, VISA, TC. 3 rooms with PB. Breakfast included in rates. Types of meals: Full bkfst and early coffee/tea. Beds: KD. Air conditioning. Amusement parks, antiquing, fishing, civic center, live theater, parks, shopping, downhill skiing, cross-country skiing, sporting events and water sports nearby.

Location: Mountains.

Certificate may be used: November through May, Sunday-Thursday.

Sanford's Ridge B&B

749 Ridge Rd
Queensbury, NY 12804-6903
(518)793-4923

Circa 1797. Visitors to the Adirondacks will find a bit of history and more than a little hospitality at this Federal-style inn, built by David Sanford after the Revolutionary War. The inn has retained its original elegance and added a few modern touches, such as an in-ground swimming pool and a sunny outdoor deck. Visitors select from the Haviland, Sanford and Webster rooms, all with private baths. Each room is decorated in Colonial style with quilt-covered poster beds and antique furnishings. The full breakfasts include a special entree of the day and fruit grown on the premises. Lake George and Saratoga Springs are a short drive away.

Innkeeper(s): Carolyn Rudolph. $65-100. MC, VISA, TC. 3 rooms with PB, 2 with FP. Breakfast included in rates. Type of meal: Full bkfst. Beds: KQT. Air conditioning. Swimming and library on premises. Antiquing, golf, historic sites, live theater, shopping and water sports nearby.

Certificate may be used: November through March, except holiday weekends or holiday periods. Any day of week or weekend.

Red Hook H12

The Grand Dutchess

7571 Old Post Rd
Red Hook, NY 12571-1403
(914)758-5818 Fax:(914)758-3143
Internet: www.granddutchess.com
E-mail: grandut@worldnet.att.net

Circa 1874. This Second Empire Victorian was originally built as the Hoffman Inn. It later served as the town school, a speakeasy and then a lonely hearts club. Twin parlors behind etched glass and wood sliding doors feature hardwood floors, antique chandeliers,

arched marble fireplaces with massive carved mirrors, Oriental rugs and heirloom antiques. Lace curtains decorate the floor-to-ceiling windows. Most of the rooms have queen-sized beds and private baths and are located at the corners of the home to maximize the use of natural light. A full breakfast of homemade breads, a main dish, cereal and fruit is offered. For young guests, the innkeeper will prepare chocolate chip pancakes.

Innkeeper(s): Elizabeth Pagano & Harold Gruber. $95-155. AX, PC, TC. 6 rooms, 4 with PB, 1 suite and 1 conference room. Breakfast included in rates. Types of meals: Full gourmet bkfst and early coffee/tea. Beds: KQDT. Air conditioning. VCR, fax, copier and library on premises. Antiquing, fishing, golf, historic homes, Rhinebeck Aerodrome, live theater, parks, shopping, cross-country skiing and tennis nearby.

Location: Town.

Publicity: *Northeast, Gazette Advertiser, Poughkeepsie Journal and "The Eleanor Affair" an award-winning short film.*

"This place is outrageous! We love this place!"

Certificate may be used: January through April, except holiday weekends. May 1 through Dec. 30, Monday-Thursday.

Rhinebeck   I12

Mansakenning Carriage House

29 Ackert Hook Rd
Rhinebeck, NY 12572
(914)876-3500 Fax:(914)876-6179
Internet: MCHRhinebeck.com
E-mail: Innpeople@aol.com

Circa 1895. Guests are sure to find this National Register Colonial a perfect country inn. Take a walk along the five acres, and you'll find hammocks strung between trees and chairs placed here and there for guests who wish to relax and enjoy the fragrant grounds. Step into any one of the seven guest rooms, and you'll instantly feel as though you've entered a cozy, romantic haven. Ralph Lauren linens dress the beds, which are topped with fluffy comforters. Exposed beams, fireplaces, wood floors and quilts add to the decor of the individually appointed guest rooms. Guests will find robes, specialty bath soaps, a coffee maker, refrigerator,and satellite TV with VCR in their rooms. Innkeeper Michelle Dremann has had several recipes featured in cookbooks, and it is she or the managing innkeeper that prepare the decadent morning feast. Guests have breakfast delivered to their room along with the morning paper. Rhinebeck is full of historic houses and buildings, as well guests can visit antique shops, galleries, wineries, restaurants.

Innkeeper(s): Michelle Dremann. $150-395. PC, TC. 7 rooms with PB, 5 with FP and 5 suites. Breakfast included in rates. Type of meal: Full gourmet bkfst. Beds: KQ. Cable TV, phone, ceiling fan and VCR in room. Air conditioning. Fax, copier and library on premises. Fishing, golf, live theater, parks, shopping, downhill skiing, cross-country skiing, sporting events, tennis and water sports nearby.

Pets allowed: Two rooms only.

Location: Country.

Publicity: *New York Times, Bride's, Hudson Valley Magazine, New York Post, Poughkeepsie Journal, Wingspan, Time Out Magazine, Country Living Magazine and Home and Garden Television.*

Certificate may be used: Jan. 15-June 15, Sunday-Friday.

Rochester   F5

"428 Mt. Vernon" - A B&B Inn

428 Mount Vernon Ave
Rochester, NY 14620-2710
(716)271-0792 (800)836-3159

Circa 1917. Victorian furnishings and decor grace the interior of this stately Irish manor house. Set on two lush acres of shade trees and foliage, this secluded spot is perfect for guests in search of relaxation. Guests can create their morning meals from a varied breakfast menu. The inn is adjacent to Highland Park, a perfect spot for a picnic or birdwatching.

Innkeeper(s): Philip & Claire Lanzatella. $115. MC, VISA, AX, TC. 7 rooms with PB, 3 with FP and 1 conference room. Breakfast included in rates. Types of meals: Full gourmet bkfst and early coffee/tea. Beds: QDT. Cable TV, phone, turndown service and ceiling fan in room. Air conditioning. Amusement parks, antiquing, live theater, parks, shopping and cross-country skiing nearby.

Location: City.

"Everything was wonderful, they took care in every detail."

Certificate may be used: Jan. 15-April 1, Sunday-Thursday.

A Bed & Breakfast at Dartmouth House Inn

215 Dartmouth St
Rochester, NY 14607-3202
(716)271-7872 Fax:(716)473-0778
Internet: www.DartmouthHouse.com
E-mail: stay@DartmouthHouse.com

Circa 1905. The lavish, four-course breakfasts served daily at this beautiful turn-of-the-century Edwardian home are unforgettable. Innkeeper and award-winning, gourmet cook Ellie Klein starts off the meal with special fresh juice, which is served in the parlor. From this point, guests are seated at the candlelit dining table to enjoy a series of delectable dishes,  such as poached pears, a mouth-watering entree, a light, lemon ice and a rich dessert. And each of the courses is served on a separate pattern of Depression Glass. If the breakfast isn't enough, Ellie and husband, Bill, an electrical engineer, have stocked the individually decorated bathrooms with fluffy towels and bathrobes and guests can soak in inviting claw-foot tubs. Each of the bedchambers boasts antique collectibles and fresh flowers. The inn is located in the prestigious turn-of-the-century Park Avenue Historical and Cultural District. The entire area is an architect's dream. Museums, colleges, Eastman School of Music, Highland Park, restaurants and antique shops are among the many nearby attractions.

Innkeeper(s): Elinor & Bill Klein. $85-125. MC, VISA, AX, PC, TC. 4 rooms with PB. Breakfast included in rates. Types of meals: Full bkfst and early coffee/tea. Beds: KQT. TV, phone, ceiling fan, VCR, robe, tape deck and lighted makeup mirror in room. Air conditioning. Fax, bicycles and library on premises. Antiquing, complimentary pass to fitness club, museums, George Eastman Int'l Museum of Photography within walking distance, live theater, museums, parks and shopping nearby.

Location: Cultural & historic district.

Publicity: *Democrat & Chronicle, DAKA, Genesee Country, Seaway Trail, Oneida News, Travelers News, Country Living and The New York Times Travel Section.*

"The food was fabulous, the company fascinating, and the personal attention beyond comparison. You made me feel at home instantly."

Certificate may be used: Jan. 31-April 1, Monday through Thursday, two-night minimum stay.

Round Lake   F12

Olde Stone House Inn
PO Box 451
Round Lake, NY 12151-0451
(518)899-5048

Circa 1820. Ten minutes south of Saratoga Springs, this historic house was constructed of cobblestone, one of about 1,000 remaining in North America. (Ninety percent of these are close to the Rochester area.) The walls are 18 inches thick. Guest rooms offer pine floors, fine linens and garden views. Two acres of grounds include lawns, tall trees and space for badminton, horseshoes and croquet. Breakfast is served fireside in the dining room.

Innkeeper(s): Mary & Walter Zielnicki. $75-150. MC, VISA, PC, TC. 4 rooms, 2 with PB. Breakfast and snacks/refreshments included in rates. Types of meals: Full gourmet bkfst, cont plus and early coffee/tea. Beds: KQT. Ceiling fan and robes in room. Air conditioning. VCR, bicycles, library and complimentary soft drinks and snacks on premises. Amusement parks, antiquing, fishing, golf, live theater, parks, shopping, cross-country skiing, sporting events, tennis and water sports nearby.

Location: Rural.

Publicity: *Hudson Valley Magazine, Daily Gazette and Saratogian.*

Certificate may be used: Any Sunday through Thursday except racing season, holidays and special events.

Saratoga Springs   F12

Westchester House B&B
102 Lincoln Ave
Saratoga Springs, NY 12866-4536
(518)587-7613 (800)581-7613
Internet: www.westchesterhousebandb.com
E-mail: westchester@netheaven.com

Circa 1885. This gracious Queen Anne Victorian has been welcoming vacationers for more than 100 years. Antiques from four generations of the Melvin family grace the high-ceilinged rooms. Oriental rugs top gleaming wood floors, while antique clocks and lace curtains set a graceful tone. Guests gather on the wraparound porch, in the parlors or gardens for an afternoon refreshment of old-fashioned lemonade. Many attractions are within walking distance.

Innkeeper(s): Bob & Stephanie Melvin. $90-275. MC, VISA, AX, PC, TC. 7 rooms with PB and 1 conference room. Breakfast and afternoon tea included in rates. Types of meals: Cont plus and early coffee/tea. Beds: KQT. Phone and ceiling fan in room. Air conditioning. Fax, copier, library and baby grand piano on premises. Antiquing, fishing, opera, ballet, horse racing, race track, Saratoga Performing Arts Center, live theater, parks, shopping, cross-country skiing, sporting events and water sports nearby.

Location: Upstate New York small town.

Publicity: *Getaways for Gourmets, Albany Times Union, Saratogian, Capital, Country Inns, New York Daily News, WNYT, Newsday and Hudson Valley.*

"I adored your B&B and have raved about it to all. One of the most beautiful and welcoming places we've ever visited."

Certificate may be used: Sunday-Thursday, April-June 15, September, November, excluding holiday weekends.

Severance   D12

The Red House
PO Box 125
Severance, NY 12872-0125
(518)532-7734

Circa 1850. Twenty feet from the banks of Paradox Brook, on the West end of Paradox Lake, is this two-story farmhouse inn that boasts a multitude of recreational offerings for its guests, including swimming, tennis, boating and fishing. The inn features three guest rooms, one with private bath. The inn's full breakfasts include homemade breads and regional specialties. Be sure to plan a day trip to Fort Ticonderoga and ride the ferry across Lake Champlain to Vermont. Hiking and cross-country skiing are available nearby.

Innkeeper(s): Helen Wildman & Kelley Head. $55-85. PC. 3 rooms, 1 with PB. Breakfast included in rates. Type of meal: Full bkfst. Beds: KQT. Phone in room. Golf, hiking and canoeing nearby.

Location: By brook.

"Thanks for your wonderful hospitality, we'll definitely be back again."
Certificate may be used: Sunday-Friday, Oct. 1 to June 1.

Sodus Bay-Wolcott   E7

Bonnie Castle Farm B&B
PO Box 188
Sodus Bay-Wolcott, NY 14590-0188
(315)587-2273 (800)587-4006 Fax:(315)587-4003
Internet: www.virtualcities.com/ons/ny/r/nyr9701.htm

Circa 1887. This large, waterfront home is surrounded by expansive lawns and trees, which overlook the east side of Great Sodus Bay, a popular resort at the turn of the century. Accommodations include a suite and large guest rooms with water views. Other rooms feature wainscoting and cathedral ceilings. A full, gourmet breakfast includes a cereal bar, fresh fruit and juices and an assortment of  entrees such as Orange Blossom French toast, sausages, a creamy potato casserole and fresh-baked pastries topped off with teas and Irish creme coffee. Guests can visit many nearby attractions, such as the Renaissance Festival, Erie Canal and Chimney Bluffs State Park.

Innkeeper(s): Eric & Georgia Pendleton. $85-160. MC, VISA, AX, DS, PC, TC. 8 rooms with PB and 1 suite. Breakfast included in rates. Type of meal: Full gourmet bkfst. Beds: KQD. Cable TV, ceiling fan and VCR in room. Air conditioning. Fax, copier, spa and swimming on premises. Antiquing, fishing, live theater, parks, shopping, downhill skiing, cross-country skiing, sporting events and water sports nearby.

Location: Rural.

"We love Bonnie Castle. You have a magnificent establishment. We are just crazy about your place. Hope to see you soon."
Certificate may be used: Anytime except Friday and Saturday from May 15-Sept. 15.

Sodus Point E6

Carriage House Inn

8375 Wickham Blvd
Sodus Point, NY 14555-9608
(315)483-2100 (800)292-2990 Fax:(315)483-2100
Internet: www.carriage-house-inn.com
E-mail: jdendec1@rochester.rr

Circa 1870. The innkeeper at this inn offers accommodations in a historic Victorian home located on four acres in a residential area or in the stone carriage house on the shore of Lake Ontario. The carriage house overlooks the lake and Sodus Point historic lighthouse. The inn offers beach access, and guests can walk to restaurants and charter boats. For an additional cost, the inn will provide sandwiches and thermos.

Innkeeper(s): James Den Decker. $70-95. MC, VISA, AX, DC. 8 rooms with PB. Breakfast included in rates. Type of meal: Country bkfst. Beds: KT. Cable TV and telephone available in room. Refrigerators, gas grills and picnic tables on premises. Antiquing, fishing, golf, snowmobiling, shopping, downhill skiing, cross-country skiing and water sports nearby.

Publicity: *Finger Lakes Times, Democrat and Chronicle, Journey, Outdoor, Travel & Leisure and WTVH.*

"An outstanding inn, beautifully restored and a delightful waterfront historic setting."

Certificate may be used: Dec. 1 through April 15, excluding holidays weekends.

Southold K15

Goose Creek Guesthouse

1475 Waterview Dr, PO Box 377
Southold, NY 11971
(516)765-3356
Internet: www.northfork.com/goosecreek

Circa 1860. Grover Pease left for the Civil War from this house, and after his death, his widow, Harriet, ran a summer boarding house here. The basement actually dates from the 1780s and is constructed of large rocks. The present house was moved here and put on the older foundation. Southold has many beaches and historic homes (a guidebook is provided for visitors). The inn is close to the ferry to New London and the ferries to the South Shore via Shelter Island.

Innkeeper(s): Mary Mooney-Getoff. $70-95. PC, TC. 4 rooms. Breakfast and afternoon tea included in rates. Types of meals: Full gourmet bkfst, country bkfst and early coffee/tea. Beds: KQDT. TV, phone, back rests and feather beds in room. Air conditioning. VCR, library and collection of local books on premises. Amusement parks, antiquing, beaches, fishing, live theater, museums, parks, shopping and water sports nearby.

Location: Rural.

Publicity: *New York Times and Newsday.*

"We will be repeat guests. Count on it!!"

Certificate may be used: Oct. 30-April 30, Sunday-Thursday.

Stanfordville I12

Lakehouse Inn on Golden Pond

Shelley Hill Rd
Stanfordville, NY 12581
(914)266-8093 (800)726-3323 Fax:(914)266-4051
Internet: www.lakehouseinn.com
E-mail: judy@lakehouseinn.com

Circa 1990. Romance abounds at this secluded contemporary home, which is surrounded by breathtaking vistas of woods and Golden Pond. Rest beneath a canopy flanked by lacy curtains as you gaze out the window. Enjoy a long, relaxing bath, or take a stroll around the 22-acre grounds. Each guest room includes a fireplace and whirlpool tub, and most include decks. The decor is a mix with a hint of Victorian, some Asian influences and modern touches that highlight the oak floors and vaulted pine ceilings. The innkeepers start off the day with a gourmet breakfast delivered to your room in a covered basket. Historic mansions and wineries are among the nearby attractions.

Innkeeper(s): Judy & Rich Kohler. $125-650. MC, VISA, PC. 10 rooms with PB, 7 with FP, 7 suites, 1 cottage and 1 conference room. Breakfast included in rates. Beds: KQ. Phone, ceiling fan and VCR in room. Air conditioning. Fax, copier and video library on premises. Antiquing, fishing, boating, live theater, parks, shopping, cross-country skiing, sporting events and water sports nearby.

Publicity: *Newsday, New York Post, New York Magazine and Country Living.*

Certificate may be used: Monday, Tuesday, Wednesday, excluding holidays.

Syracuse F8

Giddings Garden Bed & Breakfast

290 W Seneca Tpke
Syracuse, NY 13207-2639
(315)492-6389 (800)377-3452
Internet: www.giddingsgarden.com
E-mail: giddingsb-b@webtv.net

Circa 1810. Formerly Giddings Tavern, this historic federal-style home offers three guest rooms. The Honey Room features a white iron poster bed and a fireplace, as well as a unique private bath with a marble floor and a marble mirrored shower. The Executive Room is decorated in leather and black moiré fabric with mahogany furnishings, or you might prefer the Country Garden Room with a lace canopy and floral décor. All have marble baths, and there are fireplaces. In the morning, try the menu with Baked Apple Flowers and maple syrup, creamed eggs and hollandaise sauce in a filo cup, and strawberry-filled chocolate cups served with Grand Marnier. Afterwards, relax on the old stone patio that overlooks a fishpond or stroll around the inn's gardens.

Innkeeper(s): Pat & Nancy Roberts. $80-150. MC, VISA, AX, DS, TC. 3 rooms with PB. Breakfast included in rates. Types of meals: Full gourmet bkfst and early coffee/tea. Beds: Q. Cable TV, phone and refrigerator in hall in room. Air conditioning. VCR on premises. Antiquing, fishing, golf, live theater, parks, shopping, downhill skiing, cross-country skiing, sporting events, tennis and water sports nearby.

Location: City.

Certificate may be used: Jan. 30 to Dec. 20, Sunday-Friday subject to availability, holidays excluded.

Utica   F9

Adam Bowman Manor

197 Riverside Dr
Utica, NY 13502-2322
(315)738-0276 Fax:(315)738-0276
E-mail: bargood@msn.com

Circa 1823. The founder of Deerfield, George Weaver, built this graceful brick Federal house for his daughter. It is said to have been a part of the Underground Railroad (there's a secret tunnel) and is in the National Register.
Handsomely landscaped grounds include a fountain, a gazebo, tall oaks and borders of perennials. The late Duke and Dutchess of Windsor were guests here and there are rooms named for them. The Duke's room has French-country furniture, a hand-painted fireplace and a king bed. Enjoy the Drawing Room and library, and in the morning guests are offered a full breakfast in the dining room with china, crystal and silver.

Innkeeper(s): Marion & Barry Goodwin. $40-75. MC, VISA, PC, TC. 4 rooms, 2 with PB, 2 with FP. Breakfast included in rates. Types of meals: Full bkfst, cont plus and cont. Beds: KQD. Air conditioning. VCR, fax and library on premises. Antiquing, golf, live theater, parks, shopping, downhill skiing, cross-country skiing, tennis and water sports nearby.

Location: City.

"Great company, good food and new friends for us."

Certificate may be used: Anytime except months of May, September and October.

Warrensburg   E12

Alynn's Butterfly Inn B&B

Rt 28 PO Box 248
Warrensburg, NY 12885
(518)623-9390 (800)221-9390 Fax:(518)623-9396
Internet: www.alynnsbutterflyinn.com

Circa 1750. This historic Federal-style inn sits on a hill in the six million-acre Adirondack Park and offers four guest rooms with private jet tub baths and showers. After guests are treated to coffee and baked goods in their rooms, they enjoy the inn's full breakfasts in the sunroom, which offers wonderful views of the surrounding fields and woods from its many windows. Cross-country skiing, snowshoeing, biking and hiking may be enjoyed on the spacious grounds, covering 176 acres. Gore Mountain and Whiteface Olympic ski areas are close by, and Lake George is a 10-minute drive.

Innkeeper(s): Al & Lynn Smith. $99-139. MC, VISA, AX, DC, CB, DS, PC, TC. 4 rooms, 3 with PB. Breakfast included in rates. Types of meals: Full gourmet bkfst and early coffee/tea. Beds: Q. Terry robes in room. Air conditioning. VCR, fax, spa and hiking and cross country ski trails on premises. Handicap access. Amusement parks, antiquing, fishing, live theater, parks, shopping, downhill skiing, sporting events and water sports nearby.

Location: Mountains.

Publicity: *Post Star, Chronicle, G.F. Business Journal, Adirondack Journal, Country Victorian, Journal America and Travel.*

Certificate may be used: Sunday through Thursday, all year, and weekends Nov. 15-May 15, subject to availability. Advance reservations required.

Country Road Lodge B&B

115 Hickory Hill Rd
Warrensburg, NY 12885-3912
(518)623-2207 Fax:(518)623-4363
Internet: www.countryroadlodge.com
E-mail: parisibb@netheaven.com

Circa 1929. This simple, rustic farmhouse lodge is situated on 35 acres along the Hudson River at the end of a country road. Rooms are clean and comfortable. A full breakfast is provided with homemade breads and muffins. The sitting room reveals panoramic views of the river and Sugarloaf Mountain. Bird watching, hiking and skiing are popular activities. Groups often reserve all four guest rooms.

Innkeeper(s): Sandi & Steve Parisi. $55-72. PC. 4 rooms, 2 with PB. Breakfast included in rates. Types of meals: Full bkfst & early coffee/tea. Beds: DT. Ceiling fan in room. Air conditioning. Amusement parks, antiquing, fishing, live theater, parks, shopping, downhill skiing, cross-country skiing & water sports nearby.

Location: Mountains.

Publicity: *North Jersey Herald & News.*

"Homey, casual atmosphere. We really had a wonderful time. You're both wonderful hosts and the Lodge is definitely our kind of B&B! We will always feel very special about this place and will always be back."

Certificate may be used: Year-round excluding January and February winter weekend packages and holiday weekends.

The Merrill Magee House

2 Hudson St PO Box 391
Warrensburg, NY 12885-0391
(518)623-2449

Circa 1839. This stately Greek Revival home offers beautiful antique fireplaces in every guest room. The Sage, Rosemary, Thyme and Coriander rooms feature sitting areas. The decor is romantic and distinctly Victorian. Romantic getaway packages include candlelight dinners. The local area hosts art and craft festivals, an antique car show, white-water rafting and Gore Mountain Oktoberfest. Tour the Adirondacks from the sky during September's balloon festival or browse through the world's largest garage sale in early October.

Innkeeper(s): The Carrington Family. $115-215. MC, VISA, AX, DS, TC. 10 rooms with PB, 10 with FP, 1 suite and 2 conference rooms. Breakfast included in rates. Types of meals: Full bkfst and early coffee/tea. Beds: KQDT. Turndown service in room. Air conditioning. Spa, swimming and library on premises. Handicap access. Amusement parks, antiquing, fishing, live theater, parks, shopping, downhill skiing, cross-country skiing, sporting events & water sports nearby.

Location: Small village.

"A really classy and friendly operation—a real joy."

Certificate may be used: Oct. 15 to June 15, Monday-Friday.

Warwick   J11

Warwick Valley Bed & Breakfast

24 Maple Ave
Warwick, NY 10990-1025
(845)987-7255 Fax:(845)988-5318
E-mail: loretta@warwick.net

Circa 1900. This turn-of-the-century Colonial Revival is located in Warwick's historic district among many of the town's other historic gems. The B&B includes four guest rooms decorated with antiques and country furnishings. Breakfasts are a treat with entrees such as eggs Benedict, apple pancakes or a savory potato, cheese and egg bake. Wineries, antique shops and many outdoor activities are nearby, and innkeeper Loretta Orenstein is happy to point guests in the right direction.

Innkeeper(s): Loretta Breedveld. $100-125. MC, VISA, AX, DS, PC, TC. 5 rooms with PB. Breakfast included in rates. Types of meals: Full gourmet bkfst and early coffee/tea. Beds: KQT. TV, phone and sitting area in room. Central air. VCR, fax, copier and bicycles on premises. Amusement parks, antiquing, fishing, golf, wineries, live theater, parks, shopping, downhill skiing, cross-country skiing, sporting events, tennis and water sports nearby.

Location: Historic village.

Publicity: *Warwick Advertiser.*

Certificate may be used: Jan. 15 to April 30, Sunday-Friday, or any weekday stay year-round except holidays.

Westfield   H2

The William Seward Inn

6645 S Portage Rd
Westfield, NY 14787-9602
(716)326-4151 (800)338-4151 Fax:(716)326-4163
Internet: www.williamsewardinn.com
E-mail: wmseward@cecomet.net

Circa 1821. This two-story Greek Revival estate stands on a knoll overlooking Lake Erie. Seward was a Holland Land Company agent before becoming governor of New York. He later served as Lincoln's Secretary of State and is known for the Alaska Purchase. George Patterson bought Seward's home and also became governor of New York. Most of the mansion's furnishings are dated 1790 to 1870 from the Sheraton-Victorian period.

Innkeeper(s): James & Debbie Dahlberg. $70-180. MC, VISA, DS. 12 rooms with PB, 2 with FP. Breakfast included. Type of meal: Full bkfst. Beds: KQT. TV, Jacuzzi & ceiling fans in some rooms. Air conditioning. Fax & library on premises. Handicap access. Amusement parks, antiquing, fishing, parks, shopping, skiing & water sports nearby.

Location: Country.

Publicity: *Intelligencer, Evening Observer, New York-Pennsylvania Collector, Upstate New York Magazine, Pittsburgh Post-Gazette, Toronto Globe & Mail, Lake Erie Magazine and Seaway Trail Magazine.*

"The breakfasts are delicious. The solitude and your hospitality are what the doctor ordered."

Certificate may be used: Anytime, except Friday-Saturday, June 20 through October, some holiday weekends.

Westfield House

E Main Rd, PO Box 505, Rt 20
Westfield, NY 14787
(716)326-6262 Fax:(716)326-2543

Circa 1840. This brick home was built as a homestead on a large property of farmland and vineyards. The next owner constructed the impressive Greek Revival addition. The home also

served guests as a tea room and later as a family-style eatery. Guests will enjoy the elegance of the past, which has been wonderfully preserved at Westfield House. Breakfasts are served on fine china and silver in the home's formal dining room. Wintertime guests enjoy their morning meal in front of a warm fire. Each of the rooms offers something special. The Ruth Thomas Room offers a four-poster bed, high ceilings, antique quilts and a fireplace, while the Rowan Place boasts beautiful furnishings and Gothic crystal windows that look out to maple trees.

Innkeeper(s): Kathleen Grant and Marianne Heck. $75-130. MC, VISA, PC. 7 rooms with PB, 2 suites and 1 conference room. Breakfast included in rates. Type of meal: Full bkfst. Beds: KQDT. TV in room. Air conditioning. VCR on premises. Antiquing, fishing, golf, Chautauqua Institute, live theater, parks, downhill skiing, cross-country skiing and water sports nearby.

Location: Vineyards.

Publicity: *Canadian Leisure Ways and Seaway Trail.*

"Your accommodations and hospitality are wonderful! Simply outstanding. The living room changes its character by the hour."

Certificate may be used: September to June, based on availability.

Westport   C12

The Victorian Lady

57 S Main St
Westport, NY 12993
(518)962-2345 Fax:(518)962-2345
Internet: www.lake-champlain.com/victorianlady
E-mail: victorianlady@lake-champlain.com

Circa 1856. This Second Empire home features all the delicate elements of a true "Painted Lady," from the vivid color scheme to the Eastlake porch that graces the exterior. Delicate it's not, however, having stood for more than a century. Its interior is decked in period style with antiques from this more gracious era. A proper afternoon tea is served, and breakfasts are served by candlelight. More than an  acre of grounds, highlighted by English gardens, surround the home. Lake Champlain is a mere 100 yards from the front door.

Innkeeper(s): Doris & Wayne Deswert. $75-110. PC, TC. 5 rooms, 4 with PB. Breakfast and afternoon tea included in rates. Types of meals: Full gourmet bkfst and early coffee/tea. Beds: KQT. Ceiling fan in room. VCR, fax, copier and library on premises. Antiquing, fishing, golf, live theater, parks, shopping, downhill skiing, cross-country skiing, tennis and water sports nearby.

Location: Historic village.

Publicity: *Victorian Homes Magazine and Toronto Sun.*

Certificate may be used: May 15 to Oct. 15, Monday-Thursday.

Wilmington   C12

Willkommen Hof

Rt 86, PO Box 240
Wilmington, NY 12997
(518)946-7669 (800)541-9119 Fax:(518)946-7626
Internet: lakeplacid.net/willkommenhof
E-mail: willkommenhof@whiteface.net

Circa 1925. This turn-of-the-century farmhouse served as an inn during the 1920s, but little else is known about its past. The innkeepers have created a cozy atmosphere, perfect for relaxation after a day exploring the Adirondack Mountain area. A large selection of books and a roaring fire greet guests who choose to settle down in the reading room. The innkeepers also offer a large selection of movies. Relax in the sauna or outdoor spa or simply enjoy the comfort of your bedchamber.

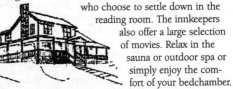

Innkeeper(s): Heike & Bert Yost. $57-154. MC, VISA, PC, TC. 6 rooms, 3 with PB and 1 suite. Breakfast and afternoon tea included in rates. Type of meal: Full bkfst. Beds: KQDT. Ceiling fan and one room with whirlpool bath in room. VCR, fax, spa, sauna, bicycles and pet boarding on premises. Antiquing, fishing, rock climbing, mountain biking, parks, shopping, downhill skiing, cross-country skiing and water sports nearby.

Pets allowed: Pets must stay in kennel when guests are gone. Kennels available for rent.

Location: Mountains.

"Vielen Dank! Alles war sehr schoen and the breakfasts were delicious."

Certificate may be used: Midweek, non-holiday, year-round.

Windham   H11

Albergo Allegria B&B

Rt 296, PO Box 267
Windham, NY 12496-0267
(518)734-5560 Fax:(518)734-5570
Internet: www.albergousa.com
E-mail: mail@albergousa.com

Circa 1892. Two former boarding houses were joined to create this luxurious, Victorian bed & breakfast whose name means "the inn of happiness." Guest quarters, laced with a Victorian theme, are decorated with period wallpapers and antique furnishings. One master suite includes an enormous Jacuzzi tub. There are plenty of relaxing options at Albergo Allegria, including a rustic lounge with a large fireplace and overstuffed couches. A second-story library, decorated with plants and wicker furnishings, is still another location to relax with a good book. Guests also can choose from more than 300 videos in the innkeeper's movie collection. Located just a few feet behind the inn are the Carriage House Suites, each of which includes a double whirlpool tub, gas fireplace, king-size bed and cathedral ceilings with skylights. The innkeepers came to the area originally to open a deluxe, gourmet restaurant. Their com-

mand of cuisine is evident each morning as guests feast on a variety of home-baked muffins and pastries, gourmet omelettes, waffles and other tempting treats. The inn is a registered historic site.

Innkeeper(s): Leslie & Marianna LEman. $73-233. MC, VISA, TC. 21 rooms with PB, 8 with FP and 9 suites. Breakfast included in rates. Type of meal: Full gourmet bkfst. Beds: KQT. Cable TV, phone, ceiling fan & VCR in room. Air conditioning. Fax, copier and bicycles on premises. Handicap access. Amusement parks, antiquing, bicycling, fishing, hiking, bird watching, waterfalls, parks, shopping, downhill skiing, cross-country skiing, tennis & water sports nearby.
Location: Mountains.
Publicity: *Yankee.*
Certificate may be used: Year round, Sunday-Thursday. non-holidays.

Country Suite B&B

Rt 23 W, PO Box 700
Windham, NY 12496-0700
(518)734-4079
E-mail: ctrysuite@aol.com

Circa 1875. This spacious country farmhouse in the Catskill Mountains offers easy access to the many scenic attractions of the region. Five guest rooms, all with private baths, are available to visitors. The inn's country-style furnishings include antiques and family heirlooms. After a busy day of exploring the area, guests often gather in the inn's comfortable living room to relax. Ski Windham is just two miles from the inn and several other ski areas are within a 30-minute drive.

Innkeeper(s): Lorraine Seidel. $99-149. AX. 5 rooms with PB. Breakfast included in rates. Type of meal: Full gourmet bkfst. Antiquing and downhill skiing nearby.
Location: Catskill Mountains.

"Country elegance with a distinctly urban flair. A treasure to be discovered over and over again."
Certificate may be used: April through Nov. 1, Sunday-Thursday.

Danske Hus

361 South St, PO Box 893
Windham, NY 12496
(518)734-6335
Internet: www.windham-area.com/danskehus.htm

Circa 1865. Located just across the road from Ski Windham and nestled between two golf courses, this farmhouse-style inn offers countryside and mountain views to its guests, as well as a taste of Scandinavian hospitality. Breakfast may be enjoyed in the heirloom-filled dining room or outside on a picturesque deck complete with the sounds of a babbling brook. Guests also enjoy a large living room, piano, wood-burning fireplace and a sauna. The Catskills provide many other tourist attractions, including caverns, fairs and ethnic festivals, as well as shopping, antiquing and sporting activities. The innkeeper welcomes families with children, and with prior arrangement, dogs may be allowed.

Innkeeper(s): Barbara Jensen. $65-95. AX, DS. 4 rooms, 3 with PB. Breakfast and afternoon tea included in rates. Type of meal: Full bkfst. Beds: KQDT. Air conditioning. Sauna and library on premises. Amusement parks, antiquing, fishing, horseback riding, golf, hiking, parks, shopping, skiing & water sports nearby.
Pets allowed: Dogs only.
Location: Mountains.

"Your warm and cozy home is surpassed only by your warm and friendly smile. Breakfast - Wow - it can't be beat!"
Certificate may be used: Anytime, except holidays, holiday weekends and Dec. 13-March 13.

Windham (East)   H11

Point Lookout Mountain Inn

The Mohican Trail, Rt 23
Windham (East), NY 12439
(518)734-3381 Fax:(518)734-6526
Internet: www.bestinns.net/usa/ny/plm/html
E-mail: romaint@worldnet.att.net

Circa 1965. This cliffside inn offers a panoramic view stretching for more than 180 miles to the northeast and encompassing the mountain ranges of five states. Guest rooms feature spectacular views of the sunrise, sunset and moonrise. The inn features two of the area's most popular restaurants on its premises: The Rainbow Cafe and Cliffside Deck. They offer breakfast, lunch, snacks  and homemade ice cream while the Bella Vista Restaurant features fireside dining and a dinner menu influenced by the cuisines of the Mediterranean and Southwest. A variety of local microbrewed beers and variety of wine are featured in the Tap Room. The innkeepers are both professional chefs with more than 40 years of combined experience. Outdoor gardens, arbors, decks and unparalleled views make the Point Lookout Mountain Inn a favorite spot for wedding receptions and group functions.

Innkeeper(s): Rosemary Jensen, Mariana DiToro. $70-145. MC, VISA, AX, DS, PC, TC. 19 rooms, 14 with PB, 5 suites and 3 conference rooms. Breakfast included in rates. Types of meals: Full gourmet bkfst, cont plus and early coffee/tea. Beds: QD. Cable TV and ceiling fan in room. VCR, fax, copier, library and pet boarding on premises. Handicap access. Amusement parks, antiquing, fishing, golf, bicycling, live theater, parks, shopping, downhill skiing, cross-country skiing, tennis and water sports nearby.
Pets allowed: Not left alone for long periods. Bring own bedding. On leash in bldg.
Location: Cliffside.
Publicity: *Wonderful Weekends, Albany Times Union, Poughkeepsie Journal, Hudson Valley Magazine and Albany - Channel 10 Guest Chef.*
"Just wanted to thank you, once again, for a great time."
Certificate may be used: Sunday-Thursday, non-holidays.

North Carolina

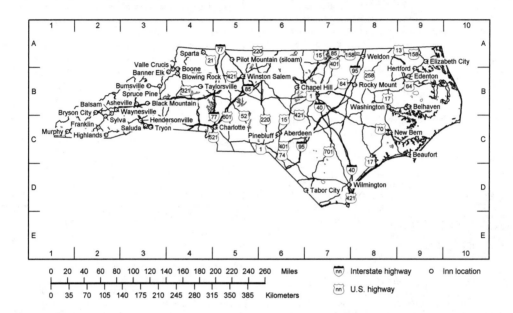

```
                  1      2      3      4      5      6      7      8      9     10
              ┌──────────────────────────────────────────────────────────────────┐
           A  │                           Sparta ─77─      220      ─15─ ─85─  13  │  A
              │              Valle Crucis  ─21─    Pilot Mountain (siloam) ─401─ 158─ Weldon  158  │
              │              Banner Elk ○○ Boone               ─95─   Hertford ○─ Elizabeth City │
           B  │           Burnsville ○─  Blowing Rock ─421─ Winston Salem  258  ○ Edenton │  B
              │              Spruce Pine ─321─  Taylorsville  ─85─  ○ Chapel Hill  64  ○ Rocky Mount  64 │
              │           Balsam  Asheville ○─ Black Mountain     ─1─          17        │
              │        Bryson City ○○○ Waynesville  ─77─ ─601─ ─52─  ─40─ Washington ○─ Belhaven │
              │           Franklin ○ Sylva ─ Hendersonville  220  ─15─ ─421─   ─70─ New Bern │
           C  │        Murphy ○─ Saluda ○─ Tryon  ─521─  Charlotte  Pinebluff ○ Aberdeen  ─17─ Beaufort │  C
              │           Highlands ○      ─1─  ─401─ ─95─ ─701─      ─40─        │
              │                          ─74─              ─17─  Wilmington       │
           D  │                    ○ Tabor City        ─421─                     │  D
              │                                                                    │
           E  │                                                                    │  E
              └──────────────────────────────────────────────────────────────────┘
                  1      2      3      4      5      6      7      8      9     10
```

0 20 40 60 80 100 120 140 160 180 200 220 240 260   Miles

0 35 70 105 140 175 210 245 280 315 350 385   Kilometers

🛡(nn) Interstate highway   ○ Inn location

🛡(nn) U.S. highway

Aberdeen   C6

The Inn at Bryant House
214 N Poplar St
Aberdeen, NC 28315-2812
(910)944-3300 (800)453-4019 Fax:(910)944-8898
Internet: innatbryanthouse.com
E-mail: lsteele@eclipsetel.com

Circa 1913. This Colonial Revival inn has been completely
restored to its original Southern splendor. Pastel colors flow
through the entire house, and the sitting, dining and living
rooms open to one another for easy access. Breakfast is served
in the dining or garden room. With advance notice, lunches
and dinners can be served for small business meetings, wedding parties, family gatherings, club activities and weekend
retreats. The Pinehurst area is known for its quiet rolling hills
and more than 30 championship-quality golf courses.

Innkeeper(s): Lee & Sharon Steele. $70-105. MC, VISA, AX, DS. 9 rooms,
8 with PB. Breakfast included in rates. Type of meal: Full bkfst. Beds: QDT.
Air conditioning. VCR on premises. Antiquing, golf, live theater and shopping nearby.

Location: Historic district.

Certificate may be used: Any time of the year, when available.

Asheville   B3

Beaufort House Victorian B&B
61 N Liberty St
Asheville, NC 28801-1829
(828)254-8334 (800)261-2221 Fax:(828)251-2082
Internet: www.beauforthouse.com
E-mail: rob@beauforthouse.com

Circa 1894. In the Queen Anne Victorian style, this inn rests
on two acres of beautifully landscaped grounds, including a tea
garden. Offering views of the mountains, the full wraparound
porch is festooned with gingerbread trim. Most guest rooms
feature Jacuzzi tubs. Ask for the Sarah Davidson Suite where
light streams through a handsome fan window onto a king-size
canopy bed decked in white Battenburg Lace. There is a sitting
area with wing back chairs and a Queen Anne desk. Guests are
pampered with a lavish, gourmet breakfast.

Innkeeper(s): Robert & Jacqueline Glasgow. $75-225. MC, VISA, PC, TC. 11
rooms. Breakfast and afternoon tea included in rates. Types of meals: Full
gourmet bkfst and early coffee/tea. Beds: KQD. Cable TV, phone, ceiling fan
and VCR in room. Air conditioning. Fax and bicycles on premises.
Amusement parks, antiquing, fishing, golf, live theater, parks, shopping,
downhill skiing, sporting events and tennis nearby.

Location: Mountains.

Certificate may be used: Jan. 1-Feb. 28, Sunday-Thursday.

Carolina B&B

177 Cumberland Ave
Asheville, NC 28801-1736
(828)254-3608 (888)254-3608 Fax:(828)252-0640
Internet: www.bbonline.com/nc/carolina/index.html
E-mail: cesaul@aol.com

Circa 1900. Architect Richard Sharp Smith, whose credits
include creating homes for such tycoons as George Vanderbilt,
designed this home in Asheville's historic Montford district.

Bay windows and porches
decorate Carolina's exterior,
as do innkeeper and land-
scape architect Sam
Fain's well-attended
grounds. Inside, rooms
feature pine floors, high
ceilings and many fire-
places. Guest rooms are furnished with antiques and unique
collectibles, such as ice skates, lace collars and evening bags.
The expansive breakfasts include fresh breads, fruits, egg dishes
and breakfast meats.

Innkeeper(s): Connie Stahl. $95-180. MC, VISA, DS, PC, TC. 7 rooms, 6 with
PB, 5 with FP and 1 cottage. Breakfast and afternoon tea included in rates.
Types of meals: Full gourmet bkfst and early coffee/tea. Beds: Q. Cable TV and
ceiling fan in room. Air conditioning. Fax, copier and spa on premises.
Antiquing, golf, live theater, parks, shopping, downhill skiing and tennis nearby.

Location: Mountains.

Publicity: *Orange County Register, Asheville Citizen-Times, Charlotte and
Mid-Atlantic Country.*

*"It was like a dream, exactly as we pictured the perfect honeymoon.
Excellent host & hostess, very helpful and informative as to local
area. Food was wonderful. Rated an A-plus."*

Certificate may be used: Jan. 3-March 30, anytime except holidays; April 1-
Sept. 30, Sunday-Wednesday except holidays.

Corner Oak Manor

53 Saint Dunstans Rd
Asheville, NC 28803-2620
(828)253-3525 (888)633-3525

Circa 1920. Surrounded by oak, maple and pine trees, this
English Tudor inn is decorated with many fine oak antiques
and handmade items. Innkeeper Karen Spradley has hand-
stitched something special for each room, and the house features handmade items by local artisans. Breakfast delights
include entrees such as Blueberry Ricotta Pancakes, Four
Cheese and Herb Quiche and Orange French Toast. When you
aren't enjoying local activities, you can sit on the shady deck,
relax in the Jacuzzi, play a few songs on the piano or curl up
with a good book.

Innkeeper(s): Karen & Andy Spradley. $100-160. MC, VISA, AX, DS, PC, TC.
3 rooms with PB, 1 with FP and 1 cottage. Breakfast included in rates. Type
of meal: Full gourmet bkfst. Beds: Q. Ceiling fan and one cottage with fireplace in room. Air conditioning. Jacuzzi (outdoor) on premises. Antiquing,
fishing, live theater, parks, shopping and downhill skiing nearby.

Location: Quiet neighborhood.

*"Great food, comfortable bed, quiet, restful atmosphere, you provided
it all and we enjoyed it all!"*

Certificate may be used: January-March anytime except holidays, April
through September & November, Sunday-Thursday only. No holidays, October
& December excluded.

Dogwood Cottage

40 Canterbury Rd N
Asheville, NC 28801-1560
(828)258-9725

Circa 1910. This Carolina mountain home is located a mile-
and-a-half from downtown Asheville, on Sunset Mountain. The
veranda, filled with white wicker and floral chintz prints, is the
focal point of the inn during summer. It affords tree-top views
of the Blue Ridge Mountains. Wing chairs and country pieces
accent the inn's gleaming hardwood floors. Breakfast is served
in the formal dining room or on the covered porch.

Innkeeper(s): Joan & Don Tracy. $110-125. MC, VISA, AX, PC. 4 rooms with
PB, 3 with FP. Breakfast included in rates. Types of meals: Full gourmet bkfst
and early coffee/tea. Beds: Q. Ceiling fan in room. Air conditioning. Pet
boarding on premises. Handicap access. Antiquing, fishing, live theater,
parks, shopping, downhill skiing, sporting events and water sports nearby.

Pets Allowed.

Location: Mountains.

"Cozy, warm and gracious."

Certificate may be used: Sunday through Thursday only, not in July, October,
December, not during a holiday weekend.

The Lion & The Rose

276 Montford Ave
Asheville, NC 28801-1660
(828)255-7673 (800)546-6988
Internet: www.lion-rose.com
E-mail: info@lion-rose.com

Circa 1895. Asheville's Montford Historic District wouldn't be
complete without this Queen Anne Georgian, listed in the
National Register. Innkeepers Lisa and Rice Yordy preserve the
history of this home with the period decor. The interior is gracious, showcasing the original leaded- and stained-glass windows and tiger oak wood. A wonderful afternoon tea is served
each day, often on the inn's wraparound veranda. Lisa prepares
the memorable breakfasts, which are served on English china
with silver. Fresh flowers and chocolates welcome guests to
their well-appointed rooms.

Innkeeper(s): Rice & Lisa Yordy. $135-225. MC, VISA, AX, DS, TC. 5 rooms
with PB and 1 suite. Breakfast and afternoon tea included in rates. Type of
meal: Full gourmet bkfst. Beds: QT. Cable TV, turndown service and ceiling
fan in room. Air conditioning. Antiquing, restaurants, live theater, parks,
shopping and water sports nearby.

Location: Mountains.

Certificate may be used: Jan. 7-March 31, Sunday through Thursday.

The Inn on Montford

296 Montford Ave
Asheville, NC 28801-1660
(828)254-9569 (800)254-9569 Fax:(828)254-9518
Internet: innonmontford.com
E-mail: info@innonmontford.com

Circa 1900. This National Register home was one of a few
Asheville homes designed by Richard Sharp Smith, who also

served as the supervising
architect for the lavish
Biltmore Estate. The exterior is
a simple and pleasing Arts &
Crafts design flanked by a
wide veranda, where guests
can relax and enjoy the quiet
neighborhood. There are four

well-appointed guest rooms highlighted by beautiful antique beds. Three rooms include a whirlpool tub, and the fourth offers a clawfoot tub. All four have a fireplace. English and American antiques fill the elegant inn. Breakfasts include a special fruit dish, such as a baked banana soufflé, freshly baked pastries and a special daily entree. Spend the day touring historic homes, take a trip to the Biltmore Estate or enjoy hiking and rafting in nearby wilderness areas.

Innkeeper(s): Ron and Lynn Carlson. $145-210. MC, VISA, AX, DS, PC, TC. 4 rooms with PB, 4 with FP. Breakfast included in rates. Types of meals: Full gourmet bkfst and early coffee/tea. Beds: Q. Phone in room. Air conditioning. VCR, fax, copier and library on premises. Amusement parks, antiquing, fishing, golf, live theater, parks, shopping, downhill skiing, sporting events, tennis and water sports nearby.

Location: City.

Certificate may be used: Jan. 30-Sept. 30, Sunday-Thursday.

Balsam   B2

Balsam Mountain Inn

Balsam Mountain Rd
Balsam, NC 28707-0040
(828)456-9498 (800)224-9498 Fax:(828)456-9298
Internet: www.balsaminn.com
E-mail: balsaminn@earthlink.net

Circa 1905. This inn, just a quarter mile from the famed Blue Ridge Parkway, is surrounded by the majestic Smoky Mountains. The inn was built in the Neoclassical style and overlooks the scenic hamlet of Balsam. The inn is listed in the National Register of Historic Places and is designated a Jackson County Historic Site. It features a mansard roof and wraparound porches with mountain views. A complimentary full breakfast is served daily, and dinner also is available daily.

Innkeeper(s): Merrily Teasley. $95-160. MC, VISA, DS, TC. 50 rooms with PB and 8 suites. Breakfast included in rates. Types of meals: Full gourmet bkfst and early coffee/tea. Beds: KD. Fax, copier, hiking trails and wildflower walks on premises. Handicap access. Antiquing, fishing, whitewater rafting, hiking, Blue Ridge Pkwy, parks, shopping and downhill skiing nearby.

Location: Mountains.

"What wonderful memories we have of this beautiful inn."

Certificate may be used: Sunday through Thursday, November through June & September, excluding holiday periods.

Banner Elk   B4

Beech Alpen Inn

700 Beech Mountain Pkwy
Banner Elk, NC 28604-8015
(704)387-2252 Fax:(704)387-2229

Circa 1968. This rustic inn is a Bavarian delight affording scenic vistas of the Blue Ridge Mountains. The innkeepers offer accommodations at Top of the Beech, a Swiss-style ski chalet with views of nearby slopes. The interiors of both properties are inviting. At the Beech Alpen, several guest rooms have stone fireplaces or French doors that open onto a balcony. Top of the Beech's great room is a wonderful place to relax, with a huge stone fireplace and comfortable furnishings. The Beech Alpen Restaurant serves a variety of dinner fare.

Innkeeper(s): Lisa & Taylor Rees. $49-149. MC, VISA, AX, TC. 25 rooms with PB, 4 with FP. Breakfast included in rates. Types of meals: Cont and early coffee/tea. Beds: KQD. Cable TV in room. Fax and copier on premises. Antiquing, fishing, live theater, parks, shopping, downhill skiing, cross-country skiing and sporting events nearby.

Location: Mountains.

Certificate may be used: Sunday-Thursday, Jan. 3-Dec. 14.

Hummingbird Lodge B&B

8778 NC Hwy 194 South
Banner Elk, NC 28604
(704)963-7210 Fax:(704)963-7210
Internet: www.ingetaways.com/nc/features/humming.html
E-mail: hummingbird@boone.net

Circa 1991. Perched on the side of a mountain, on more than five acres, Hummingbird Lodge is an Appalachian log home constructed of red cedar. There is a spacious, open dining room that overlooks the valley as well as an outside breakfast terrace. Breakfast specialties include dishes such as eggs Benedict, hash brown casseroles, homemade breads and blueberry pancakes. A variety of ski resorts are nearby such as Ski Beech on Beech Mountain and Sugar Mountain. The Banner Elk area also offers river rafting, trout fishing, golf, gemstone mining and horseback riding. Be sure not to miss Grandfather Mountain Park and its mile-high swinging bridge.

Innkeeper(s): Randy & Susan Hutchins. $89-110. MC, VISA, DS, PC, TC. 4 rooms, 3 with PB and 1 suite. Breakfast included in rates. Type of meal: Full bkfst. Beds: QT. Turndown service and ceiling fan in room. VCR, fax, copier and hiking trails on premises. Amusement parks, antiquing, fishing, golf, hiking, horseback riding, live theater, parks, shopping, downhill skiing, sporting events, tennis and water sports nearby.

Location: Mountains.

Certificate may be used: Jan. 1-Dec. 31, Sunday-Thursday.

Beaufort   C9

Pecan Tree Inn B&B

116 Queen St
Beaufort, NC 28516-2214
(252)728-6733
Internet: www.pecantree.com
E-mail: pecantreeinn@coastalnet.com

Circa 1866. Originally built as a Masonic lodge, this state historic landmark is in the heart of Beaufort's historic district. Gingerbread trim, Victorian porches, turrets and two-century-old pecan trees grace the exterior. Guests can relax in the parlor, on the porches, or pay a visit to the flower and herb gardens. The Bridal Suite and "Wow" suite boast a king-size, canopied bed and two-person Jacuzzi.

Innkeeper(s): Susan & Joe Johnson. $75-145. MC, VISA, AX, DS, PC, TC. 7 rooms with PB and 1 suite. Breakfast included in rates. Types of meals: Cont plus and early coffee/tea. Beds: KQ. Ceiling fan in room. Air conditioning. Bicycles and library on premises. Amusement parks, antiquing, fishing, jogging, biking, hiking, tennis, historical sites, parks, shopping and water sports nearby.

Publicity: *Raleigh News & Observer, Rocky Mtn Telegram, Jacksonville Scale, Southern Getaway, This Week, Conde Nast, State, Video - NC's Best 50 Inns and ABC - Greenville NC.*

Certificate may be used: October through April, Sunday through Thursday.

Belhaven   B9

River Forest Manor

738 E Main St
Belhaven, NC 27810-1622
(252)943-2151 (800)346-2151 Fax:(252)943-6628

Circa 1899. Both Twiggy and Walter Cronkite have passed through the two-story, pillared rotunda entrance of this white mansion located on the Atlantic Intracoastal Waterway. Ornate, carved ceilings, cut and leaded-glass windows and crystal chandeliers grace the inn. Antiques are found throughout. Each evening a smorgasbord buffet features more than 50 items from the inn's kitchen.

Innkeeper(s): Melba, Axson Jr. & Mark Smith. $65-95. MC, VISA, AX. 12 rooms with PB. Breakfast included in rates. Types of meals: Full bkfst and cont. Beds: KQD. Cable TV and phone in room. Air conditioning. VCR, fax and copier on premises. Antiquing, fishing, beach, Wildlife Center and water sports nearby.

Location: Intracoastal Waterway.

Publicity: *Southern Living, National Geographic, North Carolina Accommodations, Country Inns, State and Historical Inns.*

"River Forest Manor is our favorite place in east North Carolina."

Certificate may be used: April 1-30, Sunday through Thursday.

Black Mountain · B3

Red Rocker Country Inn

136 N Dougherty St
Black Mountain, NC 28711-3326
(828)669-5991 (888)669-5991 Fax:(828)669-5560
Internet: www.redrockerinn.com
E-mail: redrockerinn.com

Circa 1896. An expansive wraparound porch surrounds this three-story country inn located on one acre of landscaped grounds. Guest rooms such as the Preacher's Room, the Anniversary Room, Savannah and Elizabeth's Attic are part of the "grandma's place" feel to the inn. Mountain dinners served in the inn's restaurant include Carolina pot roast pie topped with puff pastry with fruit cobblers for dessert.

Innkeeper(s): Craig & Margie Lindberg. $85-145. PC, TC. 17 rooms with PB, 3 with FP. Breakfast, afternoon tea and snacks/refreshments included in rates. Types of meals: Full bkfst and early coffee/tea. Beds: KQD. Ceiling fan in room. Air conditioning. Fax and library on premises. Antiquing, fishing, golf, live theater, parks, shopping, downhill skiing, tennis and water sports nearby.

Location: Mountains.

Certificate may be used: Feb. 1 to March 31, Sunday-Thursday; Nov. 1 to Dec. 20, Sunday-Thursday.

Blowing Rock · B4

Victorian Inn

242 Ransom St
Blowing Rock, NC 28605
(828)295-0034
Internet: www.the-victorian-inn.com

Circa 1932. This two-story pale green and brown Victorian is set off with white trim and borders of white impatiens. Baskets of flowers hang from the balconies and each suite has a private entrance, ceiling fan and small refrigerator. Two baths have garden tubs as well as separate showers. Shops and restaurants are within walking distance. Blowing Rock has been a Blue Ridge resort for more than 100 years and is named for a rock that hangs over a cliff.

Innkeeper(s): Ron Branch. $99-139. MC, VISA, PC, TC. 6 rooms with PB. Beds: KQ. Cable TV, turndown service, ceiling fan, VCR and fireplace & Jacuzzi tubs in room. Air conditioning. Copier on premises. Amusement parks, antiquing, fishing, golf, horseback riding, hiking, canoeing, craft shows, live theater, parks, shopping, downhill skiing, cross-country skiing, sporting events, tennis and water sports nearby.

Location: Downtown Blowing Rock.

Certificate may be used: Jan. 3-April 30, Sunday through Thursday.

Bryson City · B2

Charleston Inn

208 Arlington Ave, PO Box 880
Bryson City, NC 28713
(828)488-4644 (888)285-1555
Internet: www.charlestoninn.com
E-mail: chasinn@dnet.net

Circa 1926. Framed by a stone wall and shaded by tall trees, Charleston Inn offers rooms in both the original house and the three-story wings, added more recently. Guest rooms feature period reproductions mixed with art and antiques, and each features a stained-glass door created by the innkeepers. There are Jacuzzis, porches set among treetops and a cottage with a fireplace and Jacuzzi. Apple crunch with ice cream and caramel sauce, club omelets, hash brown casserole and buttermilk biscuits are favorites at breakfast. The inn's two acres include gardens with a gazebo and a deck with a hot tub overlooking the mountains. Near the southern end of the Blue Ridge Parkway and close to the Great Smoky Mountains National Park, there are opportunities for white-water rafting, hiking, mountain biking and mining for gems.

Innkeeper(s): Rollon/Sherry Smith. $89-145. MC, VISA, AX, DC, CB, DS, PC, TC. 20 rooms, 18 with PB, 1 with FP and 1 cabin. Breakfast and snacks/refreshments included in rates. Types of meals: Full gourmet bkfst and early coffee/tea. Beds: KQ. Cable TV and ceiling fan in room. Air conditioning. VCR, spa, bicycles, library, pet boarding and child care on premises. Amusement parks, antiquing, fishing, golf, parks, shopping, downhill skiing, cross-country skiing, sporting events and water sports nearby.

Location: Mountains.

Publicity: *Southern Living.*

Certificate may be used: May to June, August, September, Sunday-Thursday.

Randolph House Country Inn

223 Fryemont Rd PO Box 816
Bryson City, NC 28713-0816
(828)488-3472 (800)480-3472

Circa 1895. Randolph House is a mountain estate tucked among pine trees and dogwoods, near the entrance of Great Smoky Mountain National Park. Antiques, some original to the house, fill this National Register home. Each guest room is appointed in a different color scheme. The house provides an unforgettable experience, not the least of which is the gourmet dining provided on the terrace or in the dining room.

Innkeeper(s): Bill & Ruth Randolph Adams. $130-160. MC, VISA, AX, DS, PC, TC. 7 rooms, 3 with PB, 2 with FP, 2 suites, 1 cottage and 1 conference room. Breakfast and dinner included in rates. Types of meals: Full bkfst and early coffee/tea. Beds: KQDT. Cable TV in room. Air conditioning. Library on premises. Handicap access. Antiquing, fishing, parks, shopping and water sports nearby.

Location: Mountains.

Publicity: *New York Times and Tourist News.*

"Very enjoyable, great food."

Certificate may be used: May and September, weekdays only. Bed & Breakfast rates $85-$95 only.

Burnsville   B3

A Little Bit of Heaven

937 Bear Wallow Br
Burnsville, NC 28714-6539
(828)675-5379 Fax:(828)675-0364

Circa 1970. This ranch-style house, on grounds with 50 dog-wood trees and gardens, is located in the mountains about 15 miles from the Blue Ridge Parkway. The home is partial stone and features several wide dormers. At the back, there's a second-story deck over the patio. From there, views extend out over the lawns and Pisgah National Forest to Celo Knob, at 6,200 feet, one of the highest points east of the Mississippi.
Innkeeper(s): John & Shelley Johnson. $65-75. 4 rooms with PB. Breakfast and snacks/refreshments included in rates. Type of meal: Full gourmet bkfst. Beds: KQT. Turndown service and ceiling fan in room. VCR and fax on premises. Antiquing, fishing, golf, live theater, shopping and tennis nearby. Pets allowed: Outdoors only.

Location: Mountains.

"Views are spectacular. Excellent service and attention to detail."
Certificate may be used: All year; exclusions: Holidays, first weekend in August and the month of October.

Chapel Hill   B6

The Inn at Bingham School

PO Box 267
Chapel Hill, NC 27514-0267
(919)563-5583 (800)566-5583 Fax:(919)563-9826
Internet: www.chapel-hill-inn.com
E-mail: fdeprez@aol.com

Circa 1790. This inn served as one of the locations of the famed Bingham School. This particular campus was the site of a liberal arts preparatory school for those aspiring to attend the University at Chapel Hill. The inn is listed as a National Trust

property and has garnered awards for its restoration. The property still includes many historic structures including a 1790s log home, an 1801 Federal addition, an 1835 Greek Revival home, the headmaster's office, which was built in 1845, and a well house, smokehouse and milk house. Original heart of pine floors are found throughout the inn. Guests can opt to stay in the Log Room, located in the log cabin, with a tight-winder staircase and fireplace. Other possibilities include Rusty's Room with two antique rope beds. The suite offers a bedroom glassed in on three sides. A mix of breakfasts are served, often including pear almond Belgian waffles, quiche or souffles.
Innkeeper(s): Francois & Christina Deprez. $75-120. MC, VISA, AX, DS, PC, TC. 5 rooms with PB, 4 with FP, 1 suite, 1 cottage and 1 conference room. Breakfast and snacks/refreshments included in rates. Types of meals: Full gourmet bkfst and early coffee/tea. Beds: QD. Phone, hair dryers and robes in room. Air conditioning. VCR, fax, library, trails and hammocks on premises. Antiquing, fishing, live theater, parks, shopping, sporting events and water sports nearby.

Location: 11 miles west of Chapel Hill.

Publicity: *Southern Inns, Mebane Enterprise, Burlington Times, Times News and Washington Post.*

Certificate may be used: Dec. 1-March 31, Sunday-Thursday only.

Charlotte   C5

The Homeplace B&B

5901 Sardis Rd
Charlotte, NC 28270-5369
(704)365-1936

Circa 1902. Situated on two-and-one-half wooded acres in Southeast Charlotte, this peaceful setting is an oasis in one of the South's fastest-growing cities. Bedrooms have 10-foot ceilings, heart-of-pine floors and blends of Country/Victorian decor. Special touches include quilts, fine linens, handmade accessories, family antiques and original primitive paintings by innkeeper Peggy Dearien's father. Spend the afternoon or evening relaxing on the porches or walking the secluded gardens. While touring the grounds, you will see a 1930s log barn that was moved to the property in 1991.
Innkeeper(s): Margaret and Frank Dearien. $98-135. MC, VISA, AX. 4 rooms, 2 with PB and 1 suite. Breakfast included in rates. Types of meals: Full bkfst and early coffee/tea. Beds: QT. TV, phone and ceiling fan in room. Air conditioning. Antiquing, shopping and sporting events nearby.

Location: City.

Publicity: *Charlotte Observer, Birmingham News, Country and Southern Living's Weekend Vacations.*

"Everything was perfect. The room was superb, the food excellent!"
Certificate may be used: January, February, March, July and August, Sunday through Thursday only.

Edenton   B9

The Lords Proprietors' Inn

300 N Broad St
Edenton, NC 27932-1905
(919)482-3641 (800)348-8933 Fax:(919)482-2432

Circa 1801. Since 1982, this elegant inn has been welcoming guests. There are 20 guest rooms spread among three houses, all located in Edenton's historic district. Dining is a separate building on a garden patio, where guests can enjoy gourmet dinners Tuesday through Saturday courtesy of Chef Kevin Yokley. On Albemarle Sound, Edenton was one of the Colonial capitols of North Carolina. Guided walking tours of area museum homes begin at the nearby visitor's center.

Innkeeper(s): Arch & Jane Edwards. $225-275. PC, TC. 20 rooms with PB and 1 conference room. Breakfast and dinner included in rates. Types of meals: Full bkfst and early coffee/tea. Beds: KQT. Cable TV, ceiling fan and VCR in room. Air conditioning. Fax and child care on premises. Handicap access. Antiquing, fishing, swimming, golf and shopping nearby.

Location: Historic waterfront town.

Publicity: *Virginia Pilor, Washington Post, House Beautiful, Southern Living, Mid-Atlantic Country and PBS - Inn Country USA & Inn Country Chefs.*

"One of the friendliest and best-managed inns I have ever visited."
Certificate may be used: Anytime, except holidays and special weekends (i.e. Christmas candlelight tour, etc).

Trestle House Inn

RR 4, Box 370, 632 Soundside Rd
Edenton, NC 27932-9668
(252)482-2282 (800)645-8466 Fax:(252)482-7003
Internet: www.edenton.com/trestlehouse
E-mail: thinn@coastalnet.com

Circa 1968. Trestle House is located on a six acres with a lake and a pond filled with large-mouth bass. The interior is unique as it features beams that were actually trestles that once belonged to the Southern Railway Company. Rooms are named for different birds, such as the Osprey and Mallard rooms. Two rooms have a sleigh bed. The morning meal includes homemade breads, breakfast casseroles and fresh orange juice.
Innkeeper(s): Peter L. Bogus. $85-110. MC, VISA, AX, PC, TC. 5 rooms with PB and 1 suite. Breakfast included in rates. Type of meal: Full bkfst. Beds: KQDT. Cable TV, phone, ceiling fan and VCR in room. Air conditioning. Fax, swimming, bicycles and tennis on premises. Antiquing, fishing, golf, live theater, parks, shopping, sporting events, tennis and water sports nearby.

"We have stayed at many B&B, but yours is special because it brings us close to nature. Your breakfast are wonderful and relaxing while eating and watching wildlife in their natural habitat!"

Certificate may be used: Nov. 1-March 31, excluding holidays and holiday weekends.

Elizabeth City   A9

Culpepper Inn

609 W Main St
Elizabeth City, NC 27909-4256
(919)335-1993 Fax:(919)335-1555
E-mail: culpepperinn@ecsu.campus.mci.net

Circa 1935. The inn is the town's most impressive brick Colonial Revival-style house. It was built by William and Alice Culpepper. Guests can come here to pick a peach from the tree, sit by the pool or in a hammock, read a book by the goldfish pond or relax by the fireplace. A Roman-style swimming pool was added in the mid-1980s. The town is situated on the Pasquotank River in the heart of the historical  Albemarle area and is home to the Museum of the Albemarle, numerous antique stores, historic homes and restaurants.
Innkeeper(s): Robert & Julia Russell. $90-110. MC, VISA, AX, PC, TC. 11 rooms, 10 with PB, 4 with FP, 1 suite and 1 conference room. Breakfast, afternoon tea and snacks/refreshments included in rates. Types of meals: Full bkfst and early coffee/tea. Beds: KQT. Cable TV, phone, ceiling fan and phones in room. Air conditioning. VCR, fax, copier, swimming and library on premises. Handicap access. Antiquing, fishing, golf, shopping and water sports nearby.
Location: Small town.

Certificate may be used: Year round.

Franklin   C2

Buttonwood Inn

50 Admiral Dr
Franklin, NC 28734-1981
(828)369-8985 (888)368-8985

Circa 1927. Trees surround this two-story batten board house located adjacent to the Franklin Golf Course. Local crafts and handmade family quilts accent the country decor. Wonderful breakfasts are served here—often eggs Benedict, baked peaches and sausage and freshly baked scones with homemade lemon butter. On a sunny morning, enjoy breakfast on the deck and savor the Smoky Mountain vistas. Afterward, you'll be ready for white-water rafting, hiking and fishing.
Innkeeper(s): Liz Oehser. $60-90. PC, TC. 4 rooms with PB. Breakfast and afternoon tea included in rates. Types of meals: Full bkfst and early coffee/tea. Beds: KDT. Ceiling fan in room. Antiquing, fishing, parks and shopping nearby.
Location: County city line.

Certificate may be used: Sunday-Thursday, except October, no weekends or holidays.

Hendersonville   C3

Echo Mountain Inn

2849 Laurel Park Hwy
Hendersonville, NC 28739-8925
(828)693-9626 (888)324-6466 Fax:(828)697-2047
Internet: www.echoinn.com

Circa 1896. Sitting on top of Echo Mountain, this large stone and wood inn has spectacular views, especially from the dining room and many of the guest rooms. Rooms are decorated with antiques and reproductions and many include a fireplace. The historic town of Hendersonville is three miles away. Gourmet dining includes an added touch of the city lights below. Guests may want to partake in refreshments of their choice served in the inn's fireside tavern.
Innkeeper(s): Peter & Shirley Demaras. $50-175. MC, VISA, AX. 37 rooms with PB, 8 with FP, 2 suites and 1 conference room. Breakfast included in rates. Types of meals: Cont and early coffee/tea. Beds: KQDT. Cable TV and phone in room. Air conditioning. Antiquing, fishing, golf, live theater, shopping and downhill skiing nearby.
Location: Mountains.

"It was quite fabulous and the food entirely too rich."

Certificate may be used: January-December, Sunday-Thursday. Holidays, holiday weeks and special events excluded.

Mountain Home B&B

PO Box 234
Hendersonville, NC 28758-0234
(828)697-9090 (800)397-0066

Circa 1915. This home and its surrounding grounds have quite a history behind them. Although the inn itself was built in 1915, a plantation home once stood in this area, holding court over an enormous spread, which included a dairy, blacksmith shop, race track and stables. The plantation home was burnt at the end of the Civil War, and it was not until the early 1900s that a hotel was built on a 640-acre parcel of the property. This, too, burnt, and in 1941, a local dentist built his family home out of the hotel's remains. Today, the guests once again travel to this picturesque spot to enjoy Southern hospitality. Rooms are romantically appointed with items such as a four-poster rice bed, a sleigh bed, skylights, fireplace or Jacuzzi tub. The front porch, with its rockers, is ready for those who wish to relax. Guests also are pampered with a hearty breakfast; raspberry stuffed French toast is a specialty. The innkeepers offer a variety of getaway packages.
Innkeeper(s): Mike & Joanie Hockspiel. $85-195. MC, VISA, AX, PC. 7 rooms with PB, 1 with FP, 1 suite and 1 conference room. Breakfast and

snacks/refreshments included in rates. Types of meals: Full gourmet bkfst and early coffee/tea. Beds: KQD. Cable TV and phone in room. Air conditioning. Handicap access. Antiquing, fishing, live theater, parks and shopping nearby.

Location: Mountains.

Publicity: *Arts & Entertainment.*

"Thanks for showing us what 'Southern hospitality' is like."
Certificate may be used: Sunday-Thursday, January-March.

The Waverly Inn

783 N Main St
Hendersonville, NC 28792-3622
(828)693-9193 (800)537-8195 Fax:(828)692-1010
Internet: www.waverlyinn.com
E-mail: waverlyinn@ioa.com

Circa 1898. In the National Register, this three-story Victorian and Colonial Revival house has a two-tiered, sawn work trimmed porch and widow's walk. A beautifully carved Eastlake staircase and an original registration desk grace the inn. There are four-poster canopy beds and clawfoot tubs.

Breakfast is served in the handsome dining room. The Waverly is the oldest surviving inn in Hendersonville.

Innkeeper(s): John & Diane Sheiry, Darla Olmstead. $109-195. MC, VISA, AX, DC, CB, DS, PC. 14 rooms with PB and 1 suite. Breakfast and snacks/refreshments included in rates. Type of meal: Full bkfst. Beds: KQDT. Cable TV, phone and ceiling fan in room. Air conditioning. Fax on premises. Antiquing, fishing, hiking, live theater, parks, shopping and cross-country skiing nearby.

Location: In town near mountains.

Publicity: *New York Times, Country, Blue Ridge Country, Vogue, Southern Living and Travel South.*

"Our main topic of conversation while driving back was what a great time we had at your place."
Certificate may be used: January, February, March anytime. November, December, April, May, September, Sunday-Thursday.

Hertford   B9

1812 on The Perquimans B&B Inn

Rt 3, Box 10
Hertford, NC 27944-9502
(919)426-1812

Circa 1790. William and Sarah Fletcher were the first residents of this Federal-style plantation home, and the house is still in the family today. The Fletchers were Quakers and the first North Carolina residents to not only free their slaves, but also offered to pay the way for workers who wished to return to Africa. The farm rests along the banks of the Perquimans River, and the grounds retain many original outbuildings, including a brick dairy, smokehouse and a 19th-century frame barn. Inside, the mantels, marble and woodwork have been restored.

Innkeeper(s): Peter & Nancy Rascoe. $75-85. MC, VISA. 5 rooms. Breakfast included in rates. Type of meal: Full bkfst.

Certificate may be used: All year, weekdays.

Highlands   C2

Morning Star Inn

480 Flat Mountain Estates Rd
Highlands, NC 28741-8325
(704)526-1009

Circa 1960. For anyone hoping to enjoy the serenity and scenery of North Carolina, this inn is an ideal place for that and more. Hammocks and rockers are found here and there on the two-acre grounds, dotted with gardens and fountains. There is a parlor with a stone fireplace and a wicker-filled sunporch. Rooms are decorated in a romantic and elegant style. Beds are dressed with fine linens and down comforters. To top off the amenities, one of the innkeepers is a culinary school graduate and prepares the mouthwatering cuisine guests enjoy at breakfast. On the weekends, afternoon refreshments and a selection of hors d'oeuvres and wine are served. The innkeeper also is working on a cookbook, which will no doubt include tidbits such as Southwestern eggs and fresh fruit with amaretto cream sauce. For those interested in improving their culinary skills, cooking classes sometimes are available.

Innkeeper(s): Pat & Pat Allen. $140-165. MC, VISA, PC, TC. 5 rooms with PB and 1 suite. Breakfast included in rates. Type of meal: Full gourmet bkfst. Beds: KQ. Turndown service, ceiling fan and tVs in some rooms in room. Air conditioning. Sunroom with mountain view, hammock, swings, rockers and porches with hammocks on premises. Antiquing, fishing, golf, hiking, bird watching, rafting, mountain climbing, Auction waterfalls, live theater, shopping, downhill skiing and tennis nearby.

Location: Mountains.

Publicity: *Victoria Magazine, Southern Living Magazine and Tampa Tribune.*

Certificate may be used: January-May, Sunday through Thursday.

Murphy   C1

Huntington Hall B&B

500 Valley River Ave
Murphy, NC 28906-2829
(828)837-9567 (800)824-6189 Fax:(828)837-2527
Internet: bed-breakfast-inn.com/
E-mail: huntington@grove.net

Circa 1881. This two-story country Victorian home was built by J.H. Dillard, the town mayor and twice a member of the House of Representatives. Clapboard siding and tall columns accent the large front porch. An English country theme is highlighted throughout. Afternoon refreshments and evening turndown service are included. Breakfast is served on the sun porch. Murder-mystery, summer-theater, and white-water-rafting packages are available.

Innkeeper(s): Curt & Nancy Harris. $65-125. MC, VISA, AX, DS, PC, TC. 5 rooms with PB. Breakfast included in rates. Types of meals: Full gourmet bkfst and early coffee/tea. Beds: KQDT. Cable TV, turndown service and ceiling fan in room. Air conditioning. VCR, fax, copier and library on premises. Antiquing, fishing, live theater, parks, shopping, tennis and water sports nearby.

Location: Small town.

Publicity: *Atlanta Journal, Petersen's 4-Wheel and New York Times.*

"A bed and breakfast well done."
Certificate may be used: Sunday through Thursday any month.

New Bern
C8

Harmony House Inn

215 Pollock St
New Bern, NC 28560-4942
(252)636-3810 (800)636-3113 Fax:(252)636-3810
Internet: www.harmonyhouseinn.com
E-mail: harmony@cconnect.net

Circa 1850. Long ago, this two-story Greek Revival was sawed in half and the west side moved nine feet to accommodate new hallways, additional rooms and a staircase. A wall was then built to divide the house into two sections. The rooms are decorated with antiques, the innkeeper's collection of handmade crafts and other collectibles. One of the suites includes a heart-shaped Jacuzzi tub. Offshore breezes sway blossoms in the lush garden. Cross the street to an excellent restaurant or take a picnic to the shore.

Innkeeper(s): Ed & Sooki Kirkpatrick. $109-150. MC, VISA, DS, PC, TC. 7 rooms, 10 with PB, 10 with FP, 3 suites and 2 conference rooms. Breakfast and snacks/refreshments included in rates. Types of meals: Full bkfst and early coffee/tea. Beds: KQT. Cable TV, phone and ceiling fan in room. Air conditioning. Fax on premises. Antiquing, parks, shopping and water sports nearby.

Publicity: *Atlanta Constitution, Raleigh News, Bon Appetit and Observer.*

"We feel nourished even now, six months after our visit to Harmony House."

Certificate may be used: Year-round, Sunday through Thursday. Weekends November-February, excluding holidays and special events.

King's Arms Inn

212 Pollock St
New Bern, NC 28560-4943
(919)638-4409 (800)872-9306 Fax:(919)638-2191

Circa 1848. Three blocks from the Tryon Palace, in the heart of the New Bern Historic District, this Colonial-style inn features a mansard roof and touches of Victorian architecture. Guest rooms are decorated with antiques, canopy and four-poster beds and decorative fireplaces. An old tavern in town was the inspiration for the name of the inn. Guests can enjoy a candlelight continental-plus breakfast served in their room.

Innkeeper(s): Richard & Pat Gulley. $100-145. MC, VISA, AX, PC, TC. 8 rooms, 7 with PB and 1 suite. Breakfast included in rates. Types of meals: Full bkfst and early coffee/tea. Beds: KQD. Cable TV, phone and ceiling fan in room. Air conditioning. Fax on premises. Antiquing, fishing, golf, historic sites, live theater, parks, shopping, tennis and water sports nearby.

Location: City.

Publicity: *Raleigh News-Observer, Washington Post, Southern Living and Sun Journal.*

"Delightful. Wonderful breakfast. Beautiful old home. Marvelous muffins."

Certificate may be used: Sunday-Thursday only, no holidays.

Pilot Mountain (Siloam)
A5

The Blue Fawn B&B

3052 Siloam Rd
Pilot Mountain (Siloam), NC 27041
(336)374-2064 (800)948-7716

Circa 1892. This Greek Revival-style house, with its four two-story columns, is bordered by an old stone fence. Located 10 minutes from town, the Blue Fawn B&B offers a friendly stay in a small tobacco farming community. There are three porches, and one is off the second-story guest rooms, which are decorated comfortably with many quilts. Spinach blue cheese strudel, Irish soda bread and fruit or homemade biscuits served with sausage gravy, fried potatoes and baked garlic cheese grits are some of the breakfast offerings. It's a tenth of a mile to the Yadkin River.

Innkeeper(s): Geno & Terri Cella. $65-85. MC, VISA, PC. 3 rooms with PB and 1 suite. Breakfast, afternoon tea and snacks/refreshments included in rates. Types of meals: Full gourmet bkfst and early coffee/tea. Beds: KQDT. Cable TV, turndown service, ceiling fan, second story porch off rooms and quilts in room. Air conditioning. VCR, bicycles, library and three porches on premises. Antiquing, fishing, golf, horseback riding, hiking, live theater, parks, shopping and water sports nearby.

Location: Country.

Publicity: *Mt. Airy News.*

"Words could never express how welcome and at home you have made our family feel."

Certificate may be used: January-December.

Pinebluff
C6

Pine Cone Manor

450 E Philadelphia Ave
Pinebluff, NC 28375
(910)281-5307

Circa 1912. The family that built this home lived here for more than 60 years, finally selling it in the 1970s. Today the house is a comfortable B&B set on private, wooded acres that include a variety of the namesake pines. The front porch is an ideal place to relax, offering a collection of rockers and a swing. The area is full of interesting sites, NASCAR and horse racing tracks are just a few. There are dozens of golf courses and the World Golf Hall of Fame.

Innkeeper(s): Virginia H. Keith. $60-65. MC, VISA, PC, TC. 3 rooms with PB, 1 with FP and 1 cottage. Breakfast included in rates. Types of meals: Cont plus and early coffee/tea. Beds: KQDT. Cable TV, phone and ceiling fan in room. Air conditioning. Library on premises. Antiquing, parks, shopping and sporting events nearby.

Certificate may be used: Anytime subject to availability.

Rocky Mount
B8

Sunset Inn B&B

1210 Sunset Ave
Rocky Mount, NC 27804-5126
(252)446-9524 (800)786-7386

Circa 1920. This Georgian inn is an impressive site from its spot on Sunset Avenue. The innkeepers filled the home with antiques and vast collections of art. Each of the guest rooms is appointed with Victorian furnishings and decor. With advance notice, the innkeepers can accommodate pets.

Innkeeper(s): Dale & Herbert Fuerst. $60-100. PC. 5 rooms with PB and 2 conference rooms. Breakfast included in rates. Types of meals: Full bkfst and early coffee/tea. Beds: KQT. Cable TV and phone in room. Air conditioning. Copier on premises. Amusement parks, antiquing and parks nearby.

Pets Allowed.

Location: City.

Certificate may be used: All year, when available.

Saluda C3

Orchard Inn

PO Box 725
Saluda, NC 28773-0725
(828)749-5471 (800)581-3800 Fax:(828)749-9805
Internet: www.orchardinn.com
E-mail: Orchard@SaludaTDS.com

Circa 1908. This inn combines the casual feel of a country
farmhouse with the elegance of a Southern plantation. The spacious living room features Oriental rugs, original artwork, quilts
and a cozy stone fireplace. In addition to the nine comfortably
furnished guest rooms, there
are three cottages with fireplaces, whirlpool baths and
private decks. A full
breakfast is served every
morning, and dinner is
available by reservation
Tuesday through
Saturday. Guests can explore the area on superb country roads
recently designated a scenic by-way. Southern Living, Raleigh
News & Observer, Tryon Daily Bulletin and State.

Innkeeper(s): Kathy & Bob Thompson. $119. MC, VISA, DS, PC, TC. 12
rooms, 9 with PB, 3 with FP, 3 cottages and 1 conference room. Breakfast
included in rates. Types of meals: Full bkfst and early coffee/tea. Beds: Q.
Ceiling fan in room. VCR, fax and hiking trails on premises. Antiquing, fishing, golf, Biltmore Estate, parks, shopping, tennis and water sports nearby.

Location: Mountains.

Publicity: *Southern Living, Raleigh News & Observer, Tryon Daily Bulletin
and State.*

*"We enjoyed the peace and tranquility, the fine food and good friends
we made."*

Certificate may be used: Jan. 1 through April 1, Sunday through Thursday.

Sparta A4

Mountain Hearth Inn B&B

110 Mountain Hearth Dr
Sparta, NC 28675
(336)372-8743
E-mail: mthearth@skybest.com

Circa 1989. Located on 10 acres, this lodge offers log cabins
overlooking the creek or mountains. They feature double
Jacuzzi tubs and gas fireplaces and are decorated with country
antiques. Lodge rooms also are available. A frequently served
breakfast is French herb mushroom omelets with grits or potatoes. Stay for dinner at the inn's restaurant and you'll probably
want to order mountain trout and potato pancakes.

Innkeeper(s): Virginia & Judy Williams, Susan W. Vanderbilt. $65-125. MC,
VISA, PC, TC. 7 rooms, 3 with PB, 1 suite and 3 cabins. Breakfast included
in rates. Type of meal: Full bkfst. Beds: QD. Ceiling fan, cassette player and
gas fireplace (in cabin and suite) in room. VCR on premises. Antiquing, fishing, golf, canoeing, hiking, parks, shopping and cross-country skiing nearby.

Pets Allowed.

Location: Mountains.

Certificate may be used: Sunday through Thursday, non-holiday weekends.

Spruce Pine B3

Richmond Inn B&B

51 Pine Ave
Spruce Pine, NC 28777-2733
(828)765-6993 (877)765-6993

Circa 1939. The scent of freshly baked muffins and steaming
coffee serves as a pleasing wake-up call for guests staying at this
country mountain home. More than an acre of wooded grounds
surround the inn, which overlooks the Toe River valley. Rooms
are decorated with family heirlooms and antiques. Several guest
rooms include four-poster beds. Crackling flames from the stone
fireplace warm the living room, a perfect place to relax. The
innkeepers keep a guest refrigerator in the butler's pantry.

Innkeeper(s): Carmen Mazzagatti. $65-110. MC, VISA, DS, TC. 8 rooms with
PB, 1 with FP and 1 suite. Breakfast included in rates. Types of meals: Full
bkfst and early coffee/tea. Beds: QT. Ceiling fan and Jacuzzi in suite in room.
VCR and fax on premises. Antiquing, golf, gem mining, crafts, parks, shopping, downhill skiing and cross-country skiing nearby.

Location: Mountains.

Certificate may be used: January-April, Sunday-Thursday.

Sylva C2

The Freeze House B&B

71 Sylvan Heights
Sylva, NC 28779-2523
(828)586-8161 Fax:(828)631-0714
Internet: www.dnet.net/~freezeh
E-mail: freezeh@dnet.net

Circa 1917. Two-hundred-year-old oak trees shade this brick
cottage, one of the oldest buildings in the village. There's a
comfortable porch for enjoying the relaxing views. Guests
might enjoy water rafting or taking a train through the
Tuckasiegee Valley or the Nantahala Gorge. Guests may breakfast on cheese grits, country sausage and scrambled eggs with
sauteed mushrooms and tomatoes on the side.

Innkeeper(s): Patrick & Mary Ellen Montague. $65-100. PC, TC. 4 rooms, 3
with PB and 1 cottage. Breakfast included in rates. Type of meal: Full
gourmet bkfst. Beds: D. Cable TV in room. Air conditioning. VCR, fax and
library on premises. Antiquing, art galleries, bicycling, canoeing/kayaking,
fishing, hiking, live theater, museums, parks, shopping, tennis and water
sports nearby.

Location: Mountains.

Certificate may be used: March 1-Nov. 30, Monday-Thursday.

Mountain Brook

208 Mountain Brook Rd #19
Sylva, NC 28779-9659
(828)586-4329
Internet: www.mountainbrook.com
E-mail: vacation@mountainbrook.com

Circa 1930. Located in the Great Smokies, Mountain Brook
consists of 12 cottages on a hillside amid rhododendron, elm,
maple and oak trees. The resort's 200-acre terrain is criss-
crossed with brooks and waterfalls, contains a trout-stocked
pond and nature trail. Two cottages are constructed with logs
from the property, while nine are made from native stone. They
feature fireplaces and porch swings and have brass, four-poster
and canopy beds, quilts and rocking chairs, and some have
bubble tubs.

Innkeeper(s): Gus, Michele & Maqelle McMahon. $90-140. TC. 12 cottages with PB, 12 with FP. Type of meal: Early coffee/tea. Beds: KD. Sauna, game room and spa/sauna bungalow on premises. Handicap access. Amusement parks, antiquing, fishing, golf, casino, Great Smokies National Park, railroad. nature trail, live theater, shopping, downhill skiing, sporting events, tennis and water sports nearby.

Location: Rural.

Publicity: *Brides Magazine, Today and The Hudspeth Report.*

"The cottage was delightfully cozy, and our privacy was not interrupted even once."

Certificate may be used: Jan. 1 to Oct. 1, Nov. 1 to Dec. 20.

Tabor City   D7

Four Rooster Inn

403 Pireway Rd/Rt 904
Tabor City, NC 28463-2519
(910)653-3878 (800)653-5008 Fax:(910)653-3878
Internet: www.bbonline.com/nc/rooster/
E-mail: 4rooster@intrstar.net

Circa 1949. This inn is surrounded by more than an acre of lush grounds, featuring camellias and azaleas planted by the innkeeper's father. Antiques, fine linens and tables set with china and crystal await to pamper you. Afternoon tea is served in the parlor. The innkeepers place a tray with steaming fresh coffee or tea and the newspaper beside your guest room door in the morning. After a good night's sleep and coffee, guests settle down to a lavish, gourmet Southern breakfast, served in the inn's formal dining room. Sherried fruit compote, warm yam bread and succulent French toast stuffed with cheese are just a few of the possible items guests might enjoy. Myrtle Beach offers outlet shopping, beaches, and more than 100 golf courses, the first of which is just four miles from the inn.

Innkeeper(s): Gloria & Bob Rogers. $55-85. MC, VISA, AX, DC, DS, PC, TC. 4 rooms, 2 with PB. Breakfast, afternoon tea and snacks/refreshments included in rates. Types of meals: Full gourmet bkfst and early coffee/tea. Beds: QD. Phone and turndown service in room. Air conditioning. VCR on premises. Amusement parks, antiquing, fishing, outlets, live theater, parks, shopping, sporting events and water sports nearby.

"Such a fine place, we crowed over their outstanding hospitality, beautiful antiques and excellent food" Southern Living Magazine."

Certificate may be used: Anytime, subject to availability.

Taylorsville   B4

Barkley House B&B

2522 NC Hwy 16 S
Taylorsville, NC 28681-8952
(704)632-9060 (888)270-9060

Circa 1896. This 19th-century home is decorated in a country Victorian motif with antiques and family heirlooms, including the wedding dress that belonged to the innkeeper's mother, which is on display in the parlor. Breakfast is a lavish, Southern affair. Guests are pampered with entrees such as breakfast casseroles or stuffed French toast served with hot chocolate or hot apple cider, biscuits and gravy, grits, juice and fresh fruit. The area offers galleries, historic mansions and the Emerald Hollow Gem Mine, where guests can dig for precious gems. Guests enjoy a personal brandy cabinet and there are brandy tastings around 5 p.m.

Innkeeper(s): Phyllis Barkley. $59. MC, VISA, AX, DS, PC, TC. 4 rooms with PB, 1 with FP. Breakfast and snacks/refreshments included in rates. Types of

meals: Full gourmet bkfst, cont plus and early coffee/tea. Beds: KQDT. Cable TV, phone, turndown service, ceiling fan and feather beds in room. Air conditioning. VCR, spa, library and private brandy chess on premises. Antiquing, fishing, shopping and sporting events nearby.

Pets allowed: Restricted to room.

Location: Foothills.

Certificate may be used: January-December, Sunday-Thursday, no major holidays or Blue Grass festival.

Tryon   C3

Foxtrot Inn

PO Box 1561, 800 Lynn Rd
Tryon, NC 28782-2708
(828)859-9706 (888)676-8050
Internet: www.foxtrotinn.com

Circa 1915. Located on six acres in town, this turn-of-the-century home features mountain views and large guest rooms. There is a private guest cottage with its own kitchen and a hanging deck. The rooms are furnished with antiques. The Cherry Room in the main house has a four-poster, queen-size canopy bed with a sitting area overlooking the inn's swimming pool. The Oak Suite includes a wood-paneled sitting room. A cozy fireplace warms the lobby.

Innkeeper(s): Wim & Tiffany Woody. $75-125. PC. 4 rooms with PB, 2 suites and 1 cottage. Breakfast included in rates. Type of meal: Full bkfst. Beds: QDT. Air conditioning. Swimming on premises. Antiquing, fishing, parks, shopping and water sports nearby.

Pets allowed: Pets allowed in cottage by special arrangement.

Certificate may be used: Year-round, subject to availability, excluding October. For inn only, not guest cottage.

Mimosa Inn

Mimosa Inn Dr
Tryon, NC 28782
(828)859-7688

Circa 1903. The Mimosa is situated on the southern slope of the Blue Ridge Mountains. With its long rolling lawns and large columned veranda, the inn has been a landmark and social gathering place for almost a century. Breakfasts are served either in the dining room or on the columned veranda.

Innkeeper(s): Jim & Stephanie Ott. $95. MC, VISA, PC, TC. 10 rooms with PB and 1 conference room. Breakfast included in rates. Types of meals: Full bkfst and early coffee/tea. Beds: QT. Air conditioning. Library on premises. Amusement parks, antiquing, fishing, live theater, parks and shopping nearby.

Location: Mountains.

"Thanks for your hospitality. We could just feel that Southern charm."
Certificate may be used: January-March, Sunday-Thursday. April-December, Monday-Thursday, except holidays and special events.

Tryon Old South B&B

107 Markham Rd
Tryon, NC 28782-3054
(828)859-6965 (800)288-7966 Fax:(828)859-6965
Internet: www.tryonoldsouth.com

Circa 1910. This Colonial Revival inn is located just two blocks from downtown and Trade Street's antique and gift shops. Located in the Thermal Belt, Tryon is known for its pleasant, mild weather. Guests don't go away hungry

from innkeeper Pat Grogan's large Southern-style breakfasts. Unique woodwork abounds in this inn and equally as impressive is a curving staircase. Behind the property is a large wooded area and several waterfalls are just a couple of miles away. The inn is close to Asheville attractions.

Innkeeper(s): Tony & Pat Grogan. $55-125. MC, VISA, PC, TC. 4 rooms with PB and 2 cottages. Breakfast included in rates. Types of meals: Full bkfst and early coffee/tea. Beds: QDT. Air conditioning. VCR, fax and copier on premises. Antiquing, fishing, live theater, parks and shopping nearby.

Location: Small town.

Certificate may be used: Anytime except for the months of August, September, and October.

Valle Crucis   B4

Mast Farm Inn

PO Box 704
Valle Crucis, NC 28691-0704
(828)963-5857 (888)963-5857 Fax:(828)963-6404
E-mail: stay@mastfarminn.com

Circa 1885. Listed in the National Register of Historic Places, this 18-acre farmstead includes a main house and seven outbuildings. The inn features a wraparound porch with rocking chairs, swings  and a view of the mountain valley. Rooms are furnished with antiques, quilts and mountain crafts. In addition to the inn rooms, there are four cottages available, some with kitchens. Flowers and vegetables from the garden are specialties. Early morning coffee can be delivered to your room. Dinners feature contemporary regional cuisine.

Innkeeper(s): Wanda Hinshaw & Kay Philipp. $110-215. MC, VISA, AX, DS, TC. 9 rooms with PB and 4 cottages. Breakfast included in rates. Type of meal: Full bkfst. Beds: KQD. Ceiling fan in room. Fax on premises. Handicap access. Antiquing, galleries, bike trails, hiking, river sports, live theater, downhill skiing, sporting events and water sports nearby.

Location: Mountain Valley-Rural.

Publicity: Blue Ridge Country and Southern Living.

"We want to live here!"

Certificate may be used: January-April, September, November-December Monday-Wednesday, excluding holidays and special events.

Washington   B8

Acadian House B&B

129 Van Norden St
Washington, NC 27889-4846
(252)975-3967 (888)975-3393 Fax:(252)975-1148
E-mail: acadianbb@aol.com

Circa 1902. This turn-of-the-century Victorian is listed in the National Register of Historic Places and is located in a historic district. The exterior boasts high ceilings and heart pine floors. Rooms are simple and comfortably furnished with Victorian touches. The innkeepers both hail from New Orleans and often serve Creole specialties for breakfast, including beignets and café au lait. Shops and restaurants are within walking distance to downtown. The beautiful Pamlico River is just one block away.

Innkeeper(s): Johanna & Leonard Huber. $60-110. MC, VISA, AX, PC, TC. 4 rooms with PB, 3 with FP and 1 suite. Breakfast included in rates. Types of meals: Full bkfst and early coffee/tea. Beds: KQT. TV, phone, ceiling fan and

central heat and air in room. Fax, bicycles and library on premises. Antiquing, fishing, golf, boating, live theater, parks, shopping, tennis and water sports nearby.

"We really enjoyed the comfortable atmosphere and the food was delectable."

Certificate may be used: Feb. 1-March 31, Sunday-Thursday; July, Sunday-Thursday; Nov. 1-Dec. 15, Sunday-Thursday.

Waynesville   B2

Belle Meade Inn

1534 S Main St
Waynesville, NC 28786-1319
(828)456-3234 Fax:(828)452-5617
E-mail: aldinc@juno.com

Circa 1908. Located near Asheville in the mountains of the Western part of the state, this Craftsman-style home was named Belle Meade, a French phrase meaning "beautiful meadow." Chestnut woodwork provides the background for antiques and traditional furnishings. A fieldstone fireplace is featured in the living room. The Great Smoky Mountain Railroad ride is nearby.

Innkeeper(s): Gloria & Al DiNofa. $70-80. MC, VISA, AX, DS, PC, TC. 4 rooms with PB, 2 with FP. Breakfast and afternoon tea included in rates. Types of meals: Full bkfst and early coffee/tea. Beds: QD. Cable TV and ceiling fan in room. Air conditioning. VCR, fax and copier on premises. Amusement parks, antiquing, fishing, golf, live theater, parks, shopping, downhill skiing, cross-country skiing, sporting events and tennis nearby.

Location: Mountains.

Publicity: Blue Ridge Magazine, Asheville Citizen Times and St. Petersburg Times.

"Immaculately clean. Distinctively furnished. Friendly atmosphere."

Certificate may be used: Jan. 1-May 15.

Grandview Lodge

466 Lickstone Rd
Waynesville, NC 28786
(828)456-5212 (800)255-7826 Fax:(828)452-5432
Internet: www.grandviewlodgenc.com
E-mail: sarnold@haywood.main.nc.us

Circa 1890. Grandview Lodge is located on two-and-a-half acres in the Smoky Mountains. The land surrounding the lodge has an apple orchard, rhubarb patch, grape arbor and vegetable garden for the inn's kitchen. Rooms are available in the main lodge and in a newer addition. The inn's dining room is known throughout the region and Linda, a home economist, has written "Recipes from Grandview Lodge," and its sequel, "More Recipes from Grandview Lodge."

Innkeeper(s): Stan & Linda Arnold. $110-120. MC, VISA, PC, TC. 9 rooms with PB, 3 with FP and 2 suites. Breakfast and dinner included in rates. Types of meals: Full bkfst and early coffee/tea. Beds: KQDT. Cable TV, fans and refrigerator in apartments in room. Air conditioning. VCR, fax and library on premises. Amusement parks, antiquing, fishing, golf, live theater, parks, shopping, downhill skiing and water sports nearby.

Location: Mountains.

Publicity: *Asheville Citizen, Winston-Salem Journal, Raleigh News & Observer and Atlanta Journal & Constitution.*

"It's easy to see why family and friends have been enjoying trips to Grandview."

Certificate may be used: November, January through May, anytime; June, July, September, Sunday through Thursday; not participating August, October and December.

Weldon   A8

Weldon Place Inn

500 Washington Ave
Weldon, NC 27890-1644
(252)536-4582 (800)831-4470 Fax:(252)536-4708

Circa 1913. Blueberry buckle and strawberry blintzes are a pleasant way to start your morning at this Colonial Revival home. Located in a National Historic District, it is two miles from I-95. Wedding showers and other celebrations are popular here. There are beveled-glass windows, canopy beds and Italian fireplaces. Most of the inn's antiques are original to the house, including a horse-hair stuffed couch with its original upholstery. Select the Romantic Retreat package and you'll enjoy sweets, other treats, a gift bag, sparkling cider, a whirlpool tub and breakfast in bed.

Innkeeper(s): Bill & Cathy Eleczko. $65-89. MC, VISA, AX, DS, TC. 4 rooms with PB. Breakfast included in rates. Type of meal: Full bkfst. Beds: D. Cable TV and phone in room. Air conditioning. VCR on premises. Antiquing, fishing, live theater and shopping nearby.

Location: Historic small town.

Certificate may be used: Anytime, based upon availability.

Wilmington   D7

The Inn on Orange

410 Orange St
Wilmington, NC 28401-4527
(910)815-0035 (800)381-4666 Fax:(910)815-6617
E-mail: innonorang@aol.com

Circa 1875. Burgundy paint accentuates the trim of this blue and white Italianate Victorian B&B. Surrounded by a white picket fence, the inn's landscaping is enhanced by azaleas, roses and 40-foot-tall crepe myrtle. Spacious guest rooms feature canopy beds and European linens, antiques, fireplaces, ceiling fans, Russian art and Persian carpets. Twelve-foot ceilings are found throughout, including the dining room where four-course breakfasts are served by candlelight with fine china, silver and crystal. Walk to restaurants, nightclubs and shops, or enjoy the Riverwalk, a waterfront park. In addition to the neighborhoods of stately homes, guests often ride the sternwheel paddleboat or horse-drawn carriage to further enjoy the Southern atmosphere.

Innkeeper(s): Vargas Family. $85-125. MC, VISA, AX, DS, PC, TC. 4 rooms, 2 with PB, 4 with FP and 2 suites. Breakfast included in rates. Types of meals: Full gourmet bkfst and early coffee/tea. Beds: KQDT. Cable TV, phone, ceiling fan and claw footed tubs in room. Air conditioning. Fax, copier, swimming, library and stocked refrigerators on premises. Amusement parks, antiquing, fishing, golf, Atlantic Ocean, Cape Fear River, live theater, parks, shopping, sporting events, tennis and water sports nearby.

Location: City.

Publicity: *Travelhost.*

"A relaxing atmosphere with a touch of elegance."

Certificate may be used: Oct. 1-April 1, Sunday-Thursday.

Winston-Salem   B5

Augustus T. Zevely Inn

803 S Main St
Winston-Salem, NC 27101-5332
(336)748-9299 (800)928-9299 Fax:(336)721-2211
Internet: www.winston-salem.inn.com

Circa 1844. The Zevely Inn is the only lodging in Old Salem. Each of the rooms at this charming pre-Civil War inn have a view of historic Old Salem. Moravian furnishings and fixtures permeate the decor of each of the guest quarters, some of which boast working fireplaces. The home's architecture is reminiscent of many structures built in Old Salem during the second quarter of the 19th century. The formal dining room and parlor have wood burning fireplaces. The two-story porch offers visitors a view of the period gardens and a beautiful magnolia tree. A line of Old Salem furniture has been created by Lexington Furniture Industries, and several pieces were created especially for the Zevely Inn.

Innkeeper(s): Lori Long. $80-205. MC, VISA, AX, PC, TC. 12 rooms with PB, 3 with FP and 1 suite. Breakfast and snacks/refreshments included in rates. Beds: KQDT. Cable TV, phone and whirlpool tub in room. Air conditioning. Fax and copier on premises. Antiquing, Old Salem Historic District, live theater, shopping and sporting events nearby.

Location: City.

Publicity: *Washington Post Travel, Salem Star, Winston-Salem Journal, Tasteful, Country Living, National Trust for Historic Preservation, Homes and Gardens, Homes Across America, Southern Living and Home & Gardens Network Show.*

"Colonial charm with modern conveniences, great food. Very nice! Everything was superb."

Certificate may be used: November, December, January, February on Sunday, Monday, excluding seasonal events.

Colonel Ludlow Inn

434 Summit at W 5th
Winston-Salem, NC 27101
(336)777-1887 (800)301-1887 Fax:(336)777-0518
Internet: www.bbinn.com
E-mail: innkeeper@bbinn.com

Circa 1887. Located in a historic urban residential neighborhood, this inn is comprised of two adjacent Victorian homes. Both homes are listed in the National Register and boast such features as wraparound porches, gabled roofs, ornate entrances, beautiful windows and high ceilings. Guest rooms are decorated with Victorian antiques, and each includes a double whirlpool tub. The innkeepers provide many thoughtful amenities, such as stocked mini-refrigerators, microwaves, coffee makers, stereos, TVs with VCRs and free movies, irons, bathrobes and hair dryers. There is a Nautilus exercise room and a billiards room. Two gourmet restaurants in historic homes are only two blocks away.

Innkeeper(s): Constance Creasman. $89-209. MC, VISA, AX, DC, DS, PC, TC. 10 rooms with PB, 5 with FP. Breakfast included in rates. Types of meals: Full bkfst and early coffee/tea. Beds: K. Cable TV, phone, ceiling fan, VCR, towel warmer and hair dryer in room. Air conditioning. Antiquing, live theater, parks, shopping and sporting events nearby.

Location: City.

Publicity: *Winston-Salem Journal, Charlotte Observer, Mid-Atlantic Country, Southern Living, Southern Accents, USA Today and American Way.*

"I have never seen anything like the meticulous and thorough attention to detail." — Dannye Romine, The Charlotte Observer

Certificate may be used: Sunday-Monday.

North Dakota

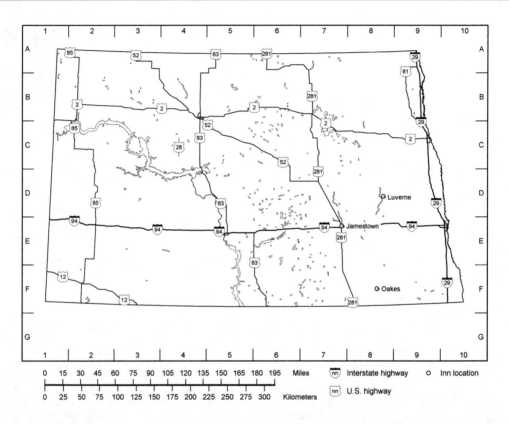

	1	2	3	4	5	6	7	8	9	10	

0 15 30 45 60 75 90 105 120 135 150 165 180 195   Miles

0   25   50   75   100 125 150 175 200 225 250 275 300   Kilometers

nn Interstate highway   O Inn location

nn U.S. highway

Jamestown   E7

Country Charm B&B
7717 35th St. SE
Jamestown, ND 58401
(701)251-1372

Circa 1897. Jamestown not only offers convenience — centrally located at the intersection of the state's east-west interstate and main north-south highway — it features the Country Charm, a prairie farmhouse six miles from town and a short hop from I-94. The inn's tranquil setting is accented by the surrounding pines and cottonwood trees. The blue-dominated Patches and Lace Room features a multi-shaded patchwork quilt. Activities and places of interest abound in the Jamestown area, including Frontier Village and North Dakota's oldest courthouse.

Innkeeper(s): Tom & Ethel Oxtoby. $50-75. 4 rooms. Breakfast included in

rates. Type of meal: Full bkfst. Ceiling fan in room. Air conditioning. VCR on premises. Antiquing, fishing, live theater, shopping, cross-country skiing and sporting events nearby.

Location: Country.

Certificate may be used: Monday through Thursday no holidays.

Luverne   D8

Volden Farm
11943 County Rd 26
Luverne, ND 58056
(701)769-2275 Fax:(701)769-2610
Internet: www.broadvu.com/voldenfarm
E-mail: voldenfarm-bb@broadvu.com

Circa 1926. Perennial gardens and a hedge of lilacs surround this redwood house with its newer addition. A favorite room is the North Room with a lace canopy bed, an old pie safe and a

Texas Star quilt made by the host's grandmother. Guests enjoy soaking in the clawfoot tub while looking out over the hills. There are two libraries, a music room and game room. The innkeepers also offer lodging in the Law Office, which dates to 1885 and is a separate little prairie house ideal for families. A stream, bordered by old oaks and formed by a natural spring, meanders through the property. The chickens here lay green and blue eggs. Dinner is available by advanced arrangement. Hiking, birdwatching, snowshoeing and skiing are nearby.

Innkeeper(s): Jim & JoAnne Wold. $60-95. PC. 2 rooms and 1 cottage. Breakfast and snacks/refreshments included in rates. Types of meals: Full gourmet bkfst and early coffee/tea. Beds: KDT. Bicycles and library on premises. Antiquing, fishing, hiking, golf, canoeing, snowshoeing, bird watching, downhill skiing and cross-country skiing nearby.

Pets allowed: Outside.

Location: Country.

Publicity: *Fargo Forum, Horizons, Grand Forks Herald, Mid-West Living and Getaways.*

"Very pleasant indeed! Jim & JoAnne make you feel good. There's so much to do, and the hospitality is amazing!"

Certificate may be used: Anytime, holidays excluded.

Oakes
F8

House of 29
215 S 7th St
Oakes, ND 58474-1621
(701)742-2227

Circa 1923. Donated by a man whose son had polio, this 29-room mansion was used by Sister Kinney as a hospital for 25 years. The construction includes double brick walls, and there are porches, dormers and stained glass. The innkeeper has decorated the house with antiques, many collected during the years she ran an antique shop. Ask for the large master bedroom or the room with the king-size tub. A full breakfast is provided and may include carrot muffins, a specialty of the inn. The lower floor of the three-story house offers a small gift shop.

Innkeeper(s): Grace J. Johnson. $50-60. 4 rooms, 1 with PB.

Location: City.

Publicity: *Fargo Forum.*

"Staying with you in your lovely home was indeed a highlight of the trip."

Certificate may be used: Anytime, based on availability.

Ohio

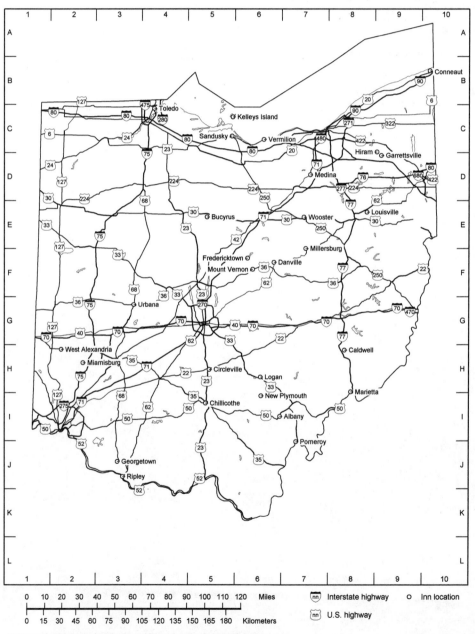

0 10 20 30 40 50 60 70 80 90 100 110 120 Miles

0 15 30 45 60 75 90 105 120 135 150 165 180 Kilometers

| | Interstate highway | o | Inn location |
| | U.S. highway | | |

Albany I6

Albany House

9 Clinton St
Albany, OH 45710
(740)698-6311 (888)212-8163

Circa 1860. Located seven miles from Ohio University in a quaint village setting, this inn is filled with antiques, quilts, Oriental rugs and collectibles. Because of four two-story columns, it is often referred to as "Tara North." A new addition includes an indoor pool, fireplace, showers and changing room.
Innkeeper(s): Sarah & Ted Hutchins. $75-135. PC, TC. 7 rooms with PB and 1 conference room. Breakfast and snacks/refreshments included in rates. Types of meals: Full gourmet bkfst and early coffee/tea. Beds: QDT. Antiquing, fishing, live theater, parks, shopping and water sports nearby.
Publicity: *Post, A. News and S.E. Ohio Magazine.*
Certificate may be used: Weekdays, Sunday-Thursday; weekends if available.

Bucyrus E5

Hide Away B&B

1601 SR 4
Bucyrus, OH 44820-9587
(419)562-3013 Fax:(419)562-3003

Circa 1938. This aptly named B&B sits on six acres, which afford views of the nearby Little Scioto River. The home was built by inventor S.H. Smith, who among his patents, was responsible for creating transistor radios used in World War II aircraft. Guest rooms are decorated in a comfortable country motif with special antiques and amenities such as a feathertick. The grounds include a swimming pool and relaxing Jacuzzi.
Innkeeper(s): Steve & Debbie Miller. $77-255. MC, VISA, AX, DS, TC. 6 rooms with PB and 2 conference rooms. Types of meals: Full gourmet bkfst, cont plus, cont and early coffee/tea. Beds: KQ. Phone, turndown service, VCR and satellite in room. Air conditioning. Fax, copier, spa, bicycles and child care on premises. Amusement parks, antiquing, live theater, parks, shopping, downhill skiing and water sports nearby.
Certificate may be used: Sunday-Thursday, excluding holidays and special event dates.

Caldwell H8

Harkins House Inn

715 West St
Caldwell, OH 43724-1230
(740)732-7347

Circa 1905. Innkeeper Stacey Lucas' great-grandfather built this turn-of-the-century home, which features many Victorian elements. He was a founder of the town's First National Bank. High ceilings, intricate moldings and original woodwork remain, as does the grand staircase. The decor includes brightly painted walls and flowery wallpapers. The second-story hall features Victorian furnishings, rose walls with teal stenciling and carpeting. Guests choose their own breakfast fare from a daily menu, which features items such as bacon, eggs, homemade muffins and coffee cake. State parks, antique shops and historic sites are nearby.
Innkeeper(s): Jeff & Stacey Lucas. $30-75. MC, VISA, AX, PC, TC. 2 rooms with PB. Breakfast included in rates. Types of meals: Full bkfst and early coffee/tea. Beds: DT. Cable TV in room. Air conditioning. VCR, library and child care on premises. Antiquing, fishing, golf, live theater, parks and shopping nearby.
Location: Village.
Publicity: *Journal-Leader.*

"Lucky for us we found your most interesting and beautiful home."
Certificate may be used: Sunday-Thursday.

Chillicothe I5

Chillicothe B&B

202 S Paint St
Chillicothe, OH 45601-3827
(740)772-6848

Circa 1864. This National Register home, which was constructed while the nation struggled with the Civil War, was built by the owner of the town's first paper mill. Innkeepers Katie and Jack Sullivan furnished the home with antiques and collectibles, including a collection of vintage clothing. Clothing is somewhat of a passion for Katie, who has created costumes for many local theatrical productions. Jack, an artist and photographer, will provide a tour of his studio to interested guests. Chillicothe, once the capital of Ohio, is full of many historic homes.
Innkeeper(s): Katie & Jack Sullivan. $50-70. MC, VISA, AX. 4 rooms. Breakfast included in rates. Type of meal: Full bkfst.
Certificate may be used: Sunday through Thursday, year-round.

Circleville H5

Penguin Crossing B&B

3291 Sr 56 W
Circleville, OH 43113-9622
(740)477-6222 (800)736-4846 Fax:(740)420-6060
Internet: www.penguin.cc
E-mail: innkeeper@penguin.cc

Circa 1820. Once a stagecoach stop, now a romantic country getaway, this B&B offers amenities in the rooms such as a wood-burning fireplace, brass bed or a heart-shaped Jacuzzi.

As the name might suggest, the innkeepers have a collection of penguins on display. Breakfasts include a selection of natural foods, and the innkeeper is happy to cater to special dietary needs.

Innkeeper(s): Ross & Tracey Irvin. $100-225. MC, VISA, AX, DS, PC, TC. 5 rooms with PB, 2 with FP. Breakfast included in rates. Types of meals: Cont and early coffee/tea. Beds: KQDT. Phone and Jacuzzi (four rooms) in room. Air conditioning. VCR and fax on premises. Handicap access. Antiquing, fishing, live theater, parks, shopping and water sports nearby.
Location: Country.

"If I had to describe this home in one word, it would be — enchanting."
Certificate may be used: All year, Monday-Thursday, except Valentine's Day.

Conneaut B10

Campbell Braemar

390 State St
Conneaut, OH 44030-2510
(216)599-7362

Circa 1927. This little Colonial Revival house is decorated in a Scottish style, and a Scottish breakfast is provided. Guests are invited to use the kitchen for light cooking as the hosts live next door. Wineries, golf, fishing, sandy beaches of Lake Erie and hunting are nearby. The innkeepers also offer a fully furnished apartment with two large bedrooms, a living room, cable TV and a fully equipped kitchen.

Innkeeper(s): Mary & Andrew Campbell. $78-98. PC, TC. 3 rooms. Breakfast and afternoon tea included in rates. Types of meals: Full bkfst, cont plus, cont and early coffee/tea. Beds: KQD. Air conditioning. Antiquing, fishing, parks and water sports nearby.

Certificate may be used: Monday-Friday, January through June, September through December, except holidays.

Danville   F6

Red Fox Country Inn

26367 Danville Amity Rd, PO Box 717
Danville, OH 43014-0746
(740)599-7369

Circa 1830. This inn, located on 15 scenic central Ohio acres, was built originally to house those traveling on the Danville-Amity Wagon Road and later became a farm home. Amish woven rag rugs and country antiques decorate the guest rooms. Some of the furnishings belonged to early owners, and some date to the 18th century. Three rooms include Amish-made oak beds and the fourth an 1880s brass and iron double bed. Breakfasts include fresh pastries, fruits, coffee and a variety of delectable entrees. Special dietary needs usually can be accommodated. There are books and games available in the inn's sitting room, and guests also are invited to relax on the front porch. Golfing, canoeing, fishing, horseback riding, hiking, biking, skiing and Mohican State Park are nearby, and the inn is 30 minutes from the largest Amish community in the United States.

Innkeeper(s): Sue & Denny Simpkins. $75-85. MC, VISA, AX, DS, PC, TC. 4 rooms with PB. Breakfast included in rates. Beds: QD. Air conditioning. Library on premises.

Location: Small town.

Publicity: *Dealers Automotive, Columbus Dispatch, Mount Vernon News and Cincinnati Enquirer.*

"Our dinner and breakfast were '5 star'. Thank you for the gracious hospitality and special kindness you showed us."

Certificate may be used: Weekdays all year round. Weekends Dec. 1-March 31. Excludes holidays and events at area colleges.

The White Oak Inn

29683 Walhonding Rd, SR 715
Danville, OH 43014
(740)599-6107
Internet: whiteoakinn.com
E-mail: yvonne@ecr.net

Circa 1915. Large oaks and ivy surround the wide front porch of this three-story farmhouse situated on 13 green acres. It is located on the former Indian trail and pioneer road that runs along the Kokosing River, and an Indian mound has been discovered on the property. The inn's woodwork is all original white oak, and guest rooms are furnished in antiques. Visitors often shop for maple syrup, cheese and handicrafts at nearby Amish farms. Three cozy fireplace rooms provide the perfect setting for romantic evenings.

Innkeeper(s): Yvonne & Ian Martin. $80-140. MC, VISA, AX, DS, PC, TC. 10 rooms with PB, 3 with FP and 1 conference room. Breakfast & snacks/refreshments included in rates. Types of meals: Full bkfst and early coffee/tea. Beds: QDT. Phone, ceiling fan and TV Jacks in room. Air condi-

tioning. Bicycles, library, guest refrigerator and piano on premises. Antiquing, fishing, horseback riding, Amish area/museums, parks, shopping and water sports nearby.

Location: Rural.

Publicity: *Ladies Home Journal, Columbus Monthly, Cleveland Plain Dealer, Country, Glamour, Columbus Dispatch, Midwest Living and PBS - Country Inn Cooking.*

"The dinner was just fabulous and we enjoyed playing the antique grand piano."

Certificate may be used: Sunday to Thursday nights all year-round.

Fredericktown   F6

Heartland Country Resort

2994 Township Rd 190
Fredericktown, OH 43019
(419)768-9300 (800)230-7030

Circa 1878. This remodeled farmhouse and luxury log cabin offer guests a serene country setting with hills, woods, pastures, fields, wooded trails, barns, horse stables and riding arenas. The four suites include a fireplace and Jacuzzi tub. With full run of the huge house, guests also have their choice of a wide variety of recreation. Horseback riding is the recreation of choice for most visitors. Innkeeper Dorene Henschen tells guests not to miss the beauty of the woods as seen on the guided trail rides.

Innkeeper(s): Dorene Henschen. $80-175. MC, VISA, DS, TC. 6 rooms with PB and 4 suites. Breakfast and afternoon tea included in rates. Type of meal: Cont plus. Beds: KQT. Jacuzzis in suites in room. Antiquing, fishing, downhill skiing, cross-country skiing and water sports nearby.

Pets Allowed.

Publicity: *Columbus Dispatch, Country Extra, One Tank Trips and Getaways.*

"Warm hospitality . . . Beautiful surroundings and pure peace & quiet. What more could one want from a B&B in the country? Thank you for an excellent memory!"

Certificate may be used: Monday through Thursday.

Garrettsville   D9

Blueberry Hill B&B

11085 North St (Rt 88)
Garrettsville, OH 44231
(330)527-5068

Although this restored Victorian is just minutes from downtown Garrettsville, the landscaped grounds create a secluded, pastoral setting. Relax in front of a wood-burning fireplace or stroll through nearby woods. Rooms are decorated in Laura Ashley prints with Victorian touches and the innkeepers own an impressive collection of artwork. The home is located on the outskirts of one of the largest Amish towns in the United States, and it is near both Hiram College and Kent State University.

Innkeeper(s): Deborah Darling. $75. 2 rooms. Breakfast included in rates. Type of meal: Cont.

Certificate may be used: All year, Monday through Thursday, except holidays.

Georgetown J3

Bailey House

112 N Water St
Georgetown, OH 45121-1332
(937)378-3087

Circa 1830. The stately columns of this three-story Greek Revival house once greeted Ulysses S. Grant, a frequent visitor during his boyhood when he was sent to buy milk from the Bailey's. A story is told that Grant accidentally overheard that the Bailey boy was leaving West Point. Grant immediately ran through the woods to the home of Congressman Thomas Hamer and petitioned an appointment in Bailey's place which he received, thus launching his military career. The inn has double parlors, pegged oak floors and Federal-style fireplace mantels. Antique washstands, chests and beds are found in the large guest rooms.

Innkeeper(s): Nancy Purdy & Jane Sininger. $55. PC. 4 rooms, 2 with FP. Breakfast and afternoon tea included in rates. Types of meals: Full bkfst and early coffee/tea. Beds: QD. Phone, fireplace (two rooms) and desk (one room) in room. Air conditioning. Swimming, library, herb garden and gift shop on premises. Antiquing, fishing, golf, private tours of U.S. Grant Home, historic sites, John Ruthven Art Gallery, parks, shopping, tennis and water sports nearby.

Pets Allowed.

Location: Historic District town.

"Thank you for your warm hospitality, from the comfortable house to the delicious breakfast."

Certificate may be used: Sunday-Thursday, Jan. 2 to Sept. 10.

Hiram C9

The Lily Ponds B&B

PO Box 322, 6720 Wakefield Rd
Hiram, OH 44234-0322
(330)569-3222 (800)325-5087 Fax:(330)569-3223

Circa 1940. This homestay is located on 20 acres of woodland dotted with rhododendron and mountain laurel. There are two large ponds and an old stone bridge. Your hostess works with a tour company and has traveled around the world. The inn's decor includes her collections of Eskimo art and artifacts and a variety of antiques. Pecan waffles served with locally harvested maple syrup are a favorite breakfast. Guests enjoy borrowing the canoe or hiking the inn's trails. Sea World is a 15-minute drive away.

Innkeeper(s): Marilane Spencer. $55-85. MC, VISA, PC. 3 rooms with PB. Breakfast included in rates. Types of meals: Full bkfst and early coffee/tea. Beds: KQT. Cable TV in room. Air conditioning. VCR, bicycles, library, child care, canoeing and skiing on premises. Amusement parks, antiquing, fishing, parks, shopping, downhill skiing, cross-country skiing and water sports nearby.

Location: Village, on pond.

Publicity: *Local newspaper, Record-Courier and Record-News.*

"We felt like we were staying with friends from the very start."

Certificate may be used: Any weekday, year-round, weekends Oct. 31-April 30.

Kelleys Island C5

Fly Inn B&B

PO Box 471, Dwelle Ln
Kelleys Island, OH 43438-0471
(419)746-2525 (800)359-4661 Fax:(419)746-2525

Circa 1988. Kelleys Island, for those not familiar with Ohio, encompasses a 2,800-acre patch of land in Lake Erie, all designated a historic district in the National Register. One acre of this wooded island encircles this rustic B&B, adjacent to the airport. Guests can watch as light planes cruise by or visit the island's historic sites and winery. The guest rooms are comfortable and homey, with modern decor. During the summer, guests can dive into the inn's swimming pool, and the innkeepers offer bicycles for touring the area.

Innkeeper(s): Rob & Heidi Quinn. $110-155. MC, VISA. 4 rooms with PB and 1 conference room. Breakfast included in rates. Type of meal: Cont. Beds: KQ. Air conditioning. VCR, fax, bicycles and golf carts available on premises. Handicap access. Amusement parks, fishing, parks, shopping and water sports nearby.

Location: Island on Lake Erie.

Certificate may be used: Off season only, weekdays, eight months of the year. Open all year.

The Inn on Kelleys Island

PO Box 489
Kelleys Island, OH 43438-0011
(419)746-2258
Internet: aves.net/the-inn

Circa 1876. With a private deck on the shore of Lake Erie, this waterfront Victorian offers an acre of grounds. Built by the innkeeper's ancestor, Captain Frank Hamilton, the house features a black marble fireplace and a porch with a spectacular Lake Erie view. The Pilot House is a room with large windows looking out to the lake. The inn is close to the ferry and downtown with restaurants, taverns and shops.

Innkeeper(s): Lori & Pat Hayes. $65-95. 4 rooms. Breakfast included in rates. Types of meals: Cont and early coffee/tea. Beds: Q. Ceiling fan in room. VCR on premises. Amusement parks, antiquing, fishing and shopping nearby.

Certificate may be used: Sunday-Thursday during months of May, June, September, October and November; excluding holidays and festivals.

Logan H6

The Inn At Cedar Falls

21190 SR 374
Logan, OH 43138
(740)385-7489 (800)653-2557 Fax:(740)385-0820
Internet: www.innatcedarfalls.com

Circa 1987. This barn-style inn was constructed on 75 acres adjacent to Hocking State Parks and one-half mile from the waterfalls. The kitchen and dining room is in a 19th-century log house with a wood-burning stove and 18-inch-wide plank floor. Accommodations in the new barn building are simple and comfortable,

each furnished with antiques. There are also six, fully equipped log cabins available, each individually decorated. Verandas provide sweeping views of woodland and meadow. The grounds include organic gardens for the inn's gourmet dinners, and animals that have been spotted include bobcat, red fox, wild turkey and whitetail deer.

Innkeeper(s): Ellen Grinsfelder. $75-240. MC, VISA, PC. 9 rooms with PB, 6 cabins and 2 conference rooms. Breakfast included in rates. Types of meals: Full gourmet bkfst and early coffee/tea. Beds: QT. Gas log stoves in room. Air conditioning. Fax, copier and library on premises. Handicap access. Antiquing, fishing, live theater, parks, shopping and cross-country skiing nearby.

Location: Country.

Publicity: *Ohio Magazine, Columbus Dispatch, Country, Post., Channel 4 and Ed Johnson.*

"Very peaceful, relaxing and friendly. Couldn't be nicer."

Certificate may be used: Sunday through Thursday beginning Dec. 1 and ending April 30, no holidays included, rooms and cabins.

Louisville   E8

The Mainstay B&B

1320 E Main St
Louisville, OH 44641-1910
(330)875-1021
Internet: www.bbonline.com/oh/mainstay
E-mail: mainstay@cannet.com

Circa 1886. Built by a Civil War veteran, this Victorian still has the original fish scale on its gables, and inside, it features carved-oak woodwork and oak doors. Guests are treated to a complimentary basket of fruit and cheese in their air-conditioned rooms. Outside are flower gardens with birdbaths and a water fountain. Nearby colleges are Malone, Walsh, Mount Union and Kent State University.

Innkeeper(s): Mary & Joe Shurilla. $50-65. MC, VISA, PC. 3 rooms with PB. Breakfast and snacks/refreshments included in rates. Types of meals: Full bkfst and early coffee/tea. Beds: QDT. Whirlpools in room. Air conditioning. VCR on premises. Antiquing, parks and downhill skiing nearby.

Certificate may be used: Sunday through Thursday, no holidays or Pro Football H.O.F. week Aug. 2-9.

Marietta   H8

The Buckley House

332 Front St
Marietta, OH 45750-2913
(614)373-3080 Fax:(614)373-8000
E-mail: dnicholas@wscc.edu

Circa 1879. A double veranda accents this historic, gablefront Greek Revival home and provides views of Muskingum Park and the river, as well as Lookout Point and the "Valley Gem," a traditional Mississippi river boat. The grounds include a New Orleans-style garden with a fish pond and gazebo. Museums, a mound cemetery, the W.P. Snyder Jr. Sternwheeler, boat rides, trolley tours, shops and restaurants are within walking distance.

Innkeeper(s): Dell & Alf Nicholas. $75-85. MC, VISA, DS, PC, TC. 3 rooms with PB, 1 with FP and 1 suite. Breakfast included in rates. Types of meals: Full bkfst and early coffee/tea. Beds: KDT. Ceiling fan in room. Air conditioning. VCR, fax, spa and library on premises. Antiquing, fishing, live theater, parks, shopping and water sports nearby.

Certificate may be used: Nov. 15-March 31, Monday-Thursday.

Medina   D7

Livery Building

254 E Smith Rd
Medina, OH 44256-2623
(330)722-1332

This three-story Queen Anne, which once housed a local livery horse business, offers one immense suite featuring antique furnishings, small parlor and kitchenette with a wet bar. The wood-burning stove adds country charm. The innkeepers offer a full breakfast made from organic ingredients. The bed & breakfast is within walking distance of Medina's restored Victorian town square and historic district.

Innkeeper(s): Candace Hutton. $65. 1 rooms. Breakfast included in rates. Type of meal: Full bkfst.

Certificate may be used: December-February, except holidays.

Miamisburg   H2

English Manor B&B

505 E Linden Ave
Miamisburg, OH 45342-2850
(937)866-2288 (800)676-9456

Circa 1924. This is a beautiful English Tudor mansion situated on a tree-lined street of Victorian homes. Well-chosen antiques combined with the innkeepers' personal heirlooms added to the inn's polished floors, sparkling leaded-and stained-glass windows, make this an elegant retreat. Breakfast is served in the formal dining room. Tea is served in the afternoon. Fine restaurants, a water park, baseball, air force museum and theater are close by, as is The River Corridor bikeway on the banks of the Great Miami River.

Innkeeper(s): Ken & Jeannette Huelsman. $65-95. MC, VISA, AX, DC, CB, DS. 5 rooms and 1 conference room. Breakfast included in rates. Type of meal: Full bkfst. Phone and turndown service in room. Air conditioning. VCR on premises. Amusement parks, antiquing, live theater, shopping and sporting events nearby.

Certificate may be used: Sunday through Thursday.

Millersburg   F7

Bigham House

151 S Washington St
Millersburg, OH 44654-1315
(800)689-6950
Internet: www.bbonline.com/bighamhs

Circa 1869. Located in a quiet village in the heart of Amish Country, Holmes County, this immaculately restored inn fancies itself not only a bed & breakfast but also an authentic English Tea Room where guests can enjoy traditional tea in grand Victorian style. Each guest chamber and suite are distinctly decorated in antiques, Victorian reproductions and carefully selected traditional fabrics and wallcoverings. Tea is served by the inn's own British gentleman, by reservation only.

Innkeeper(s): Winnie & John Ellis. $75-130. MC, VISA. 5 rooms with PB, 1 with FP and 1 suite. Breakfast included in rates. Type of meal: Full bkfst. Beds: Q.

Publicity: *Holmes County Traveler, Cleveland Plain Dealer, Amish Heartland and North Central Business Traveler.*

Certificate may be used: November-April, Sunday-Thursday.

Mount Vernon   F6

Tuck'er Inn
12059 Tucker Rd
Mount Vernon, OH 43050-9650
(740)392-5659

Circa 1969. There are 12 woodland acres to explore here. Guests can hike ravines or enjoy the scenery around Granny Creek. There are two guest rooms in the main house, which was built in Colonial style. There is also a guest house in the woods with two bedrooms and a wood-burning stove. The guest house can sleep up to five people. The inn is a few minutes away from the Mt. Vernon Nazarene College and Kenyon College in Gambier, and within an hour of Columbus, as well as Amish country. Because of its location it is popular for church and private retreats. Guests also can visit the Siberian Tiger Foundation, nearby.

Innkeeper(s): Bill & Marian Cleland. $50-125. PC, TC. 2 rooms and 1 cottage. Breakfast included in rates. Type of meal: Cont plus. Beds: QD. Air conditioning. VCR, library, sun room, recreation room, ping pong, darts and hot tub on premises. Antiquing, fishing, Siberian Tiger Foundation, live theater, parks, shopping, downhill skiing, cross-country skiing and sporting events nearby.

Location: Rural country on Granny creek.

Publicity: *Mount Vernon News.*

"I had such a sweet night at your inn. Many, many thanks."

Certificate may be used: November-April, June, July; seven days subject to availability. Guesthouse $125 a night.

New Plymouth   I6

Ravenwood Castle
65666 Bethel Rd
New Plymouth, OH 45654-9707
(740)596-2606 (800)477-1541
Internet: www.ravenwoodcastle.com
E-mail: ravenwood@ohiohills.com

Circa 1995. Although this is a newer construction, the architect modeled the inn after a 12th-century, Norman-style castle, offering a glimpse back at Medieval England. A Great Hall with massive stone fireplace, dramatic rooms and suites with antique stained-glass windows and gas fireplaces make for a unique getaway. The castle, which overlooks Vinton County's Swan township, is surrounded by 50 acres of forest and large rock formations and is reached by a half-mile private road. There is a tea room and gift shop on the premises, opened from May 1 to Oct. 31.

Innkeeper(s): Jim & Sue Maxwell. $95-175. MC, VISA, DS. 6 rooms with PB, 2 suites and 4 cottages. Breakfast included in rates. Types of meals: Full bkfst and early coffee/tea. Beds: KQD. Ceiling fan in room. Air conditioning. VCR, fax and copier on premises. Handicap access. Antiquing, fishing, near caves, waterfalls, shopping and water sports nearby.

Location: Forested.

Publicity: *Columbus Dispatch, Cincinnati Enquirer, Midwest Living, USA Today, Honeymoon, Ohio Magazine, Milwaukee Journal Sentinel, Copley News Service, PBS-TV and "Country Inn Cooking with Gail Greco."*

"The atmosphere is romantic, the food excellent, the hospitality super!"

Certificate may be used: Nov. 1-March 31, Sunday-Thursday, except holidays and Christmas week.

Pomeroy   J7

Holly Hill Inn
114 Butternut Ave
Pomeroy, OH 45769-1295
(614)992-5657

Circa 1836. This gracious clapboard inn with its many shuttered windows is shaded by giant holly trees. Original window panes of blown glass remain, as well as wide-board floors, mantels and fireplaces. The family's antique collection includes a crocheted canopy bed in the Honeymoon Room overlooking a working fireplace. Dozens of antique quilts are displayed and for sale. Guests are invited to borrow an antique bike to ride through the countryside.

Innkeeper(s): George Stewart. $59-89. MC, VISA. 4 rooms, 2 with FP and 1 conference room. Breakfast included in rates. Type of meal: Full bkfst. Beds: DT. Cable TV, phone and VCR in room. Antiquing, shopping and sporting events nearby.

Publicity: *Sunday Times-Sentinel.*

"Your inn is so beautiful, and it has so much historic charm."

Certificate may be used: Sunday through Thursday. Some weekends, based on availability. Not special weekends and holidays.

Ripley   J3

Baird House B&B
201 N 2nd St
Ripley, OH 45167-1002
(937)392-4918

Circa 1825. A lacy wrought-iron porch and balcony decorate the front facade of this historic house, while the second-floor porch at the rear offers views of the Ohio River, 500 feet away. There are nine marble fireplaces and an enormous chandelier in the parlor. A full breakfast is served.

Innkeeper(s): Patricia Kittle. $85-125. PC, TC. 3 rooms, 2 with PB, 3 with FP and 1 suite. Breakfast included in rates. Types of meals: Full gourmet bkfst and early coffee/tea. Beds: KDT. Phone, turndown service, ceiling fan and electric blankets in winter in room. Air conditioning. Organ, swings and porches on premises. Antiquing, shopping and sporting events nearby.

Location: Ohio River.

Publicity: *Ohio Magazine.*

"Thanks for a wonderful memory."

Certificate may be used: All year Monday through Thursday, based on availability.

The Signal House
234 N Front St
Ripley, OH 45167-1015
(937)392-1640 Fax:(937)392-1640
E-mail: signalhouse@webtv.net

Circa 1830. This Greek Italianate home is said to have been used to aid the Underground Railroad. A light in the attic told Rev. John Rankin, a dedicated abolitionist, that it was safe to transport slaves to freedom. Located within a 55-acre historical district, guests can take a glance back in time, exploring museums and antique shops. Twelve-foot ceilings with ornate plaster-work grace the parlor, and guests can sit on any of three porches anticipating paddlewheelers traversing the Ohio River.

Innkeeper(s): Vic & Betsy Billingsley. $75. MC, VISA, DS, PC, TC. 2 rooms. Breakfast included in rates. Types of meals: Full bkfst and early coffee/tea. Beds: Q. Ceiling fan in room. Central air. VCR, fax, copier and library on premises. Antiquing, bicycling, canoeing/kayaking, fishing, golf, hiking, horseback riding, museums, parks, shopping, tennis, water sports and wineries nearby.

Publicity: *Cincinnati Enquirer, Ohio Columbus Dispatch, Ohio Off the Beaten Path, Cincinnati Magazine, Cincinnati Post, Dayton Daily News, Ohio Magazine & Country Almanac, Cleveland Plain Dealer, Husband's first car in "Lost in Yonkers", Channel 12- "One Tank Trip" and WKRC.*

Certificate may be used: Monday-Thursday.

Sandusky   C5

Wagner's 1844 Inn

230 E Washington St
Sandusky, OH 44870-2611
(419)626-1726
Internet: www.lrbcg.com/wagnersinn
E-mail: wagnersinn@sanduskyohio.com

Circa 1844. This inn originally was constructed as a log cabin. Additions and renovations were made, and the house evolved 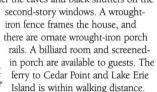 into Italianate style accented with brackets under the eaves and black shutters on the second-story windows. A wrought-iron fence frames the house, and there are ornate wrought-iron porch rails. A billiard room and screened-in porch are available to guests. The ferry to Cedar Point and Lake Erie Island is within walking distance.

Innkeeper(s): Barb Wagner. $70-120. MC, VISA, DS. 3 rooms with PB, 2 with FP. Breakfast included in rates. Type of meal: Cont. Beds: Q. TV in room. Air conditioning. Library on premises. Amusement parks, antiquing, fishing, Lake Erie Islands, golf, parks and shopping nearby.

Pets allowed: Some limitations.

Location: City.

Publicity: *Lorain Journal and Sandusky Register.*

"This B&B rates in our Top 10."

Certificate may be used: Nov. 1 to May 1.

Toledo   C4

The William Cummings House B&B

1022 N Superior St
Toledo, OH 43604
(419)244-3219 (888)708-6998 Fax:(419)244-3219
E-mail: BnBToledo@aol.com

Circa 1857. This Second Empire Victorian, which is listed in the National Register, is located in the historic Vistula neighborhood. The inn's fine appointments, collected for several years, include period antiques, Victorian chandeliers, mirrors, wallcoverings and draperies. The hosts are classical musicians of renown. Sometimes the inn is the location for chamber music, poetry readings and other cultural events.

Innkeeper(s): Lowell Greer, Lorelei Crawford. $40-90. PC, TC. 3 rooms and 1 suite. Breakfast & snacks/refreshments included in rates. Type of meal: Cont plus. Beds: KQDT. TV, ceiling fan, VCR, fresh flowers, robes & house chocolates in room. Air conditioning. Fax, copier, library, video library & refrigerator on premises. Amusement parks, antiquing, fishing, Toledo Art Museum, Toledo Zoo, science center, live theater, parks, shopping, sporting events & water sports nearby.

Location: City.

"We will never forget our wedding night at your B&B. We'll try to be in the area next anniversary."

Certificate may be used: Oct. 1 through May 31, Sunday-Thursday.

Urbana   G3

Northern Plantation B&B

3421 E RR 296
Urbana, OH 43078
(937)652-1782 (800)652-1782

Circa 1913. This Victorian farmhouse, located on 100 acres, is occupied by fourth-generation family members. (Marsha's father was born in the downstairs bedroom in 1914.) The Homestead Library is decorated traditionally and has a handsome fireplace, while the dining room features a dining set and a china cabinet made by the innkeeper's great-grandfather. Most of the guest rooms have canopy beds. A large country breakfast is served. On the property is a fishing pond, corn fields, soybeans and woods with a creek. Nearby are Ohio Caverns and Indian Lake.

Innkeeper(s): Marsha J. Martin. $85-105. MC, VISA, DS. 4 rooms, 1 with PB. Breakfast included in rates. Types of meals: Full bkfst and cont plus. Beds: KD. Air conditioning. VCR and library on premises. Antiquing, parks, shopping and cross-country skiing nearby.

Location: Country.

Certificate may be used: Any day, except holidays.

Vermilion   C6

Gilchrist Guesthouse

5662 Huron St
Vermilion, OH 44089-1000
(216)967-1237

Captain J.C. Gilchrist, owner of the largest fleet of ships on the Great Lakes, built this charming 1885 Victorian, which is listed in the National Register. From the wraparound porch, guests can relax and enjoy the view. The grounds, nestled near Lake Erie's southern shore, are surrounded by gracious old buckeye trees. Guest rooms are filled with antiques. The innkeepers transformed the second-story ballroom into a comfortable common room filled with games and a TV. The large, continental breakfasts feature sweet rolls and muffins from Vermilion's century-old family bakery. The innkeepers also offer kitchen suites for those planning longer stays. The home is only 400 feet from city docks and the beach, and a two-block walk takes guests into the downtown area with its many shops and restaurants. A maritime museum and historic lighthouse are next door.

Innkeeper(s): Dan Roth. $85-115. MC, VISA, AX. 4 rooms. Breakfast included in rates. Type of meal: Cont plus.

Certificate may be used: Nov. 30 to May 15, excluding Saturday and holidays.

West Alexandria   H2

Twin Creek Country B&B

5353 Enterprise Rd
West Alexandria, OH 45381-9518
(513)787-3990

Circa 1835. This brick farmhouse is the oldest house in the township and the 170 acres surrounding the home were part of a land grant signed by Thomas Jefferson. Beautiful rich woodwork highlights the interior, which has an old-fashioned, country appeal. Innkeepers Mark and Carolyn Ulrich live in an adjacent home, providing their guests with extra privacy. The grounds offer more than 70 acres of woods to hike through. The innkeepers also own Twin Creek Townehouse B&B, an Italianate-style home that includes a tea room and catering business. The two upstairs guest rooms are decorated with local antiques. The tea room is an impressive feature, with a carved ceiling, marble fireplace and walls painted in a deep teal hue with rose trim.

Innkeeper(s): Dr. Mark & Carolyn Ulrich. $69-89. MC, VISA, AX, DS, PC, TC. 2 rooms with PB and 1 suite. Breakfast and snacks/refreshments included in rates. Type of meal: Full bkfst. Beds: DT. Phone in room. Air conditioning. Amusement parks, antiquing, fishing, live theater, parks, shopping, sporting events and water sports nearby.

Location: Country.

Certificate may be used: No holidays; good Monday through Thursday, subject to availability.

Wooster   E7

Historic Overholt House B&B

1473 Beall Ave
Wooster, OH 44691-2303
(330)263-6300 (800)992-0643 Fax:(330)263-9378

Circa 1874. This burgundy Victorian with its peaked roofs and colorful trim literally was saved from the wrecking ball. Several concerned locals fought to have the home moved to another location rather than face demolition in order to make way for a parking lot. The current owners later purchased the historic home and furnished it with beautiful wall coverings, antiques and Victorian touches. The focal point of the interior is a mag-

nificent walnut "flying staircase" that rises three stories. The innkeepers provide plenty of ways to spend a comfortable evening. The common room is stocked with games, reading material, classic movies and a cassette collection of vintage radio shows. Autumn and winter guests are invited to snuggle up in front of a roaring fire while sipping a hot drink and munching on homemade cookies. The area boasts many craft, antique and gift shops, as well as Amish country sites and activities at the College of Wooster, which is adjacent to the Overholt House. After a busy day, come back to the home and enjoy a soak in the hot tub.

Innkeeper(s): Sandy Pohalski & Bobbie Walton. $63-70. MC, VISA, DS, PC. 4 rooms with PB and 1 suite. Breakfast and snacks/refreshments included in rates. Types of meals: Cont plus and early coffee/tea. Beds: QDT. Cable TV, ceiling fan and VCR in room. Air conditioning. Fax and spa on premises. Amusement parks, antiquing, Ohio Light Opera, live theater, parks and shopping nearby.

Location: City.

Publicity: *Exchange, Daily Record, Pathways and Akron Beacon Journal.*

"A real retreat. So quiet, clean and friendly. I feel pampered! An old penny always returns."

Certificate may be used: Jan. 1 to June 1, Monday-Thursday.

Oklahoma

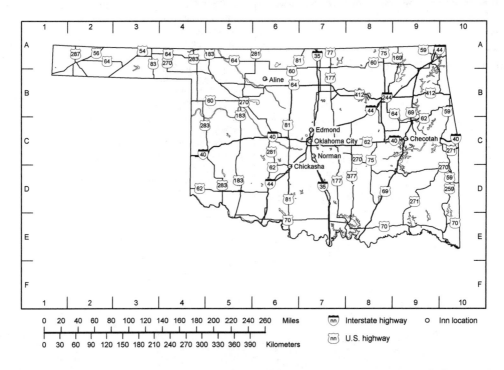

Map legend:
- [nn] Interstate highway
- ○ Inn location
- [nn] U.S. highway

```
0  20  40  60  80  100 120 140 160 180 200 220 240 260  Miles
0  30  60  90  120 150 180 210 240 270 300 330 360 390  Kilometers
```

Aline   B6

Heritage Manor

RR 3 Box 33
Aline, OK 73716-9118
(580)463-2563 (800)295-2563

Circa 1903. This inn provides a way to enjoy and experience
the ambiance of the turn of the century. Explore and relax in
the inn's peaceful gardens and 80-acre wildlife habitat and
watch song birds, butterflies, long-haired cattle, donkeys and
ostriches. The inn invites visitors to enjoy its more than 5,000-
volume library and more than a 100 channels on Primestar TV.
Guests can walk the suspension bridge to two roof-top decks
and a widow's walk to view the stars and sunsets. There is also
an out-door hot tub for soaking. Dine in the parlor, gazebo,
courtyard or tree-top-level deck where the choice of time and
menu is entirely up to the guest.

Innkeeper(s): A.J. & Carolyn Rexroat. $55-150. PC, TC. 4 rooms, 2 suites and 2
conference rooms. Breakfast and snacks/refreshments included in rates. Types of
meals: Full bkfst and early coffee/tea. Beds: D. Cable TV and phone in room. Air

conditioning. VCR, spa and library on premises. Handicap access. Antiquing,
fishing, live theater, parks, shopping, sporting events and water sports nearby.
Pets Allowed.

Location: Country.

Publicity: *Country, Enid Morning News and Daily Oklahoman.*

Certificate may be used: Anytime available.

Checotah   C9

Sharpe House

301 NW 2nd St
Checotah, OK 74426-2240
(918)473-2832

Circa 1911. Built on land originally bought from a Creek
Indian, this Southern plantation-style inn was a teacherage—the
rooming house for single female teachers. It is furnished with
heirlooms from the innkeepers' families and hand-crafted accessories. The look of the house is antebellum, but the specialty of
the kitchen is Mexican cuisine. Family-style evening meals are
available upon request. Checotah is located at the junction of I-
40 and U.S. 69. This makes it the ideal base for your day trips

of exploration or recreation in Green Country.

Innkeeper(s): Kay Kindt. $35-50. PC, TC. 3 rooms with PB and 1 suite. Breakfast included in rates. Types of meals: Full bkfst, cont plus, cont and early coffee/tea. Beds: D. Cable TV and ceiling fan in room. Air conditioning. Library and child care on premises. Amusement parks, antiquing, fishing, parks, shopping and water sports nearby.

Pets Allowed.

Location: small town, Lake Eufaula.

Certificate may be used: Anytime, space available.

Chickasha   D6

Campbell-Richison House B&B

1428 Kansas
Chickasha, OK 73018
(405)222-1754

Circa 1909. Upon entering this prairie-style home, guests will notice a spacious entryway with a gracious stairway ascending to the second-floor guest rooms. The front parlor is a wonderful spot for relaxing, reading or just soaking up the history of the home. The dining room has a stained-glass window that gives off a kaleidoscope of beautiful colors when the morning sun shines through. A spacious yard encompasses one-quarter of a city block and has large shade trees that can be enjoyed from the wicker-lined porch.

Innkeeper(s): Kami & David Ratcliff. $50-70. 3 rooms with PB. Breakfast included in rates. Types of meals: Full bkfst and early coffee/tea. Beds: KQD. Phone and sitting area in room. Air conditioning. VCR on premises. Antiquing, shopping and sporting events nearby.

Location: City.

Publicity: *Oklahoma Today, Chickasha Express, Cache Times Weekly and Chickasha Star.*

"We enjoyed our stay at your lovely B&B! It was just the getaway we needed to unwind from a stressful few weeks. Your hospitality fellowship and food were just wonderful."

Certificate may be used: Anytime, except December weekends and swap-meet weekends.

Edmond   C7

The Arcadian Inn B&B

328 E 1st St
Edmond, OK 73034-4543
(405)348-6347 (800)299-6347 Fax:(405)348-6347
Internet: www.bbonline.com/ok/arcadian

Circa 1908. Unwind in the garden spa of this Victorian inn or on the wraparound porch to enjoy the Oklahoma breeze. Breakfast may be served privately in your suite or in the dining room flooded with morning sunlight, beneath the ceiling paintings of angels and Christ done by a local artisan. Located next to the University of Central Oklahoma, the inn is four blocks from downtown antique shopping. Guests will enjoy the private baths with Jacuzzis and clawfoot tubs.

c. 1908

Innkeeper(s): Martha & Gary Hall. $99-179. MC, VISA, AX, DS, TC. 8 rooms with PB and 4 suites. Breakfast included in rates. Type of meal: Full bkfst. Beds: KQ. Cable TV, phone and ceiling fan in room. Air conditioning. Fax and spa on premises. Amusement parks, antiquing, fishing, live theater, parks, shopping, sporting events and water sports nearby.

Location: City.

Publicity: *Daily Oklahoman and Antique Traveler.*

Certificate may be used: Sunday through Thursday, excluding holidays.

Norman   C7

Holmberg House B&B

766 Debarr Ave
Norman, OK 73069-4908
(405)321-6221 (877)621-6221 Fax:(405)321-6221
E-mail: info@holmberghouse.com

Circa 1914. Professor Fredrik Holmberg and his wife Signy built this Craftsman-style home across the street from the University of Oklahoma. Each of the antique-filled rooms has

its own individual decor and style. The Blue Danube and Bed & Bath rooms are romantic retreats and both include a two-person whirlpool tub. The Garden Room includes a clawfoot tub.

The Sundance Room is ideal for friends traveling together, as it includes both a queen and twin bed. The parlor and front porch are perfect places to relax with friends, and the lush grounds include a cottage garden. Aside from close access to the university, Holmberg House is within walking distance to more than a dozen restaurants.

Innkeeper(s): Eddie & Bernie Flax. $85-120. MC, VISA, PC, TC. 4 rooms with PB. Breakfast included in rates. Types of meals: Full gourmet bkfst and early coffee/tea. Beds: QT. Cable TV and ceiling fan in room. Air conditioning. Fax, copier and library on premises. Antiquing, live theater, parks, shopping and sporting events nearby.

Location: City.

Publicity: *Metro Norman, Oklahoma City Journal Record, Norman Transcript and Country Inns.*

"Your hospitality and the delicious food were just super."

Certificate may be used: All year, one night must include Sunday-Thursday.

Oklahoma City   C7

Ambrosia Rose B&B

2718 NW 14th St
Oklahoma City, OK 73107
(405)942-7319 Fax:(405)942-7319
Internet: www.travelok.com
E-mail: arosebb@aol.com

Circa 1910. This Queen Anne Cottage-style home was the first homestead on the 160 acres now known as the Miller Neighborhood. The-two-and-a-half-story home offers two parlors, a wraparound porch and a balcony off the upstairs sitting room. A variety of collections and family memorabilia such as a salt and pepper collection, lace and fringe punctuate the home's décor. Breakfast is served with candles, silver, crystal, stemware and china, and may include "Cornbread Sausage Apple Pie" or "Grandma's (heart-shaped) Waffles" served with fresh strawberries and cream.

Innkeeper(s): Don & Shirley Bray. $65. PC, TC. 2 rooms with PB. Breakfast and snacks/refreshments included in rates. Types of meals: Cont plus and early coffee/tea. Beds: D. Phone, turndown service and ceiling fan in room. Air conditioning. VCR, fax, garden sitting areas and wrap-a-round porch on premises. Amusement parks, antiquing, golf, live theater, parks, shopping, sporting events and tennis nearby.

Publicity: *Daily Oklahoman.*

Certificate may be used: Jan. 1 to Dec. 31, Sunday-Friday.

The Grandison at Maney Park

1200 N Shartel Ave
Oklahoma City, OK 73103-2402
(405)232-8778 (800)240-4667 Fax:(405)232-5039
Internet: www.bbonline.com/ok/grandison
E-mail: grandison@juno.com

Circa 1904. This spacious Victorian has been graciously restored and maintains its original mahogany woodwork, stained glass, brass fixtures and a grand staircase. Several rooms include a Jacuzzi, and all have their own unique decor. The Treehouse Hideaway includes a queen bed that is meant to look like a hammock and walls are painted with a blue sky and stars. The Jacuzzi tub rests beneath a skylight. The home is located north of downtown Oklahoma City in a historic neighborhood listed in the National Register.

Innkeeper(s): Claudia & Bob Wright. $75-150. MC, VISA, AX, DS, PC, TC. 9 rooms with PB, 3 suites and 1 conference room. Breakfast and snacks/refreshments included in rates. Types of meals: Full bkfst, cont plus and early coffee/tea. Beds: KQT. Cable TV, phone, ceiling fan and VCR in room. Air conditioning. Fax, copier, workout room and video library on premises. Handicap access. Antiquing, live theater, parks and sporting events nearby.

Location: City.

Publicity: *Daily Oklahoman, Oklahoma Pride, Oklahoma Gazette, Discover Oklahoma and Discover Oklahoma.*

"Like going home to Grandma's!"

Certificate may be used: Anytime.

Oregon

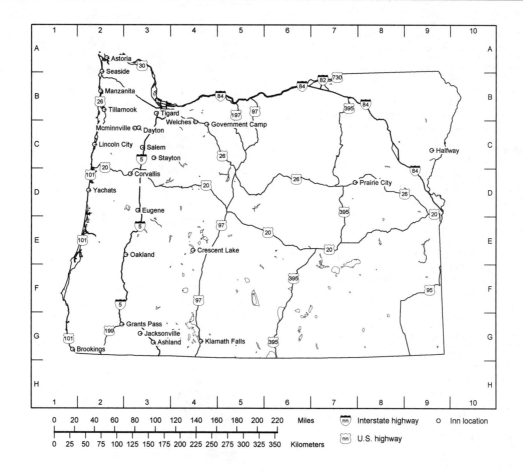

| | | | | | | | | | |
|1|2|3|4|5|6|7|8|9|10|

Astoria
30
Seaside
Manzanita
26
Tillamook
Mcminnville
Tigard
Welches
Government Camp
Dayton
Lincoln City
Salem
Stayton
26
Corvallis
101
20
Yachats
20
Eugene
5
Oakland
Crescent Lake
97
Grants Pass
199
Jacksonville
Ashland
Klamath Falls
101
Brookings

84
197
97
82 730
84
395
84
Halfway
26
Prairie City
26
20
395
20
20
395
95
395

0 20 40 60 80 100 120 140 160 180 200 220   Miles

0 25 50 75 100 125 150 175 200 225 250 275 300 325 350   Kilometers

nn Interstate highway   o Inn location

nn U.S. highway

Ashland
G3

Chanticleer B&B Inn

120 Gresham St
Ashland, OR 97520-2807
(541)482-1919 (800)898-1950 Fax:(541)488-4810
Internet: www.ashlandbnb.com
E-mail: innkeeper@ashlandbnb.com

Circa 1920. This clapboard, Craftsman-style house has been totally renovated and several rooms added. The inn is light and airy and decorated with antiques. Special features include the open hearth fireplace and bricked patio garden.

Innkeeper(s): Pebby Kuan. $95-350. MC, VISA, AX. 6 rooms with PB, 1 with FP & 1 suite. Breakfast included in rates. Types of meals: Full gourmet bkfst & early coffee/tea. Beds: QT. TV and phone in room. Air conditioning. Antiquing, live theater, shopping, downhill skiing, cross-country skiing & sporting events nearby.
Location: Village/town.
Publicity: *Country Home and Pacific Northwest.*

"Chanticleer has set the standard by which all others will be judged."
Certificate may be used: Nov. 1-March 31, excluding weekends and holidays.

Iris Inn

59 Manzanita St
Ashland, OR 97520-2615
(541)488-2286 (800)460-7650 Fax:(541)488-3709
Internet: www.irisinnbb.com
E-mail: irisinnbb@aol.com

Circa 1905. The Iris Inn is a restored Victorian set on a large flower-filled yard. It features simple American country antiques. The upstairs guest rooms have views of the valley and mountains. Evening sips of wine often are taken out on the large deck overlooking a rose garden. Breakfast boasts an elegant presentation with dishes such as buttermilk scones and eggs Benedict with smoked salmon.

Innkeeper(s): Vicki & Greg Capp. $60-120. MC, VISA. 5 rooms with PB. Breakfast included in rates. Type of meal: Full bkfst. Beds: QT. Turndown service and ceiling fan in room. Air conditioning. Fax and large deck in garden on premises. Antiquing, fishing, golf, live theater, shopping, downhill skiing, cross-country skiing, sporting events and water sports nearby.
Location: Small town.
Publicity: *Sunset and Oregonian.*

"A favorite place to be pampered since 1982."
Certificate may be used: October, Sunday-Thursday only; any night November-February; March-May, Sunday-Thursday only. Based on availability.

Mousetrap Inn

312 Helman St
Ashland, OR 97520-1138
(541)482-9228 (800)460-5453

Circa 1895. The century-old farmhouse is furnished with antiques and decorated with modern art and pottery created by the innkeepers. Breakfasts often feature organically grown foods and include treats such as juice smoothies, fresh fruit, baked goods and frittatas. The grounds are dotted with gardens and there is a swing on the inn's porch. The inn is located in Ashland's historic Railroad District.

Innkeeper(s): Johnny & Amy Ma. $90-110. MC, VISA, PC. 6 rooms with PB. Breakfast included in rates. Types of meals: Full bkfst and early coffee/tea. Beds: Q. Ceiling fan in room. Air conditioning. Fishing, river trips, bicycling, live theater, parks, shopping and water sports nearby.
Pets allowed: On a limited basis.
Location: Railroad district, small town.
Certificate may be used: Jan. 1-May 31 and Oct. 15-Oct. 31.

Oak Hill Country B&B

2190 Siskiyou Blvd
Ashland, OR 97520-2531
(541)482-1554 (800)888-7434 Fax:(541)482-1378
Internet: www.bbonline.com/or/oakhill
E-mail: oakhill@mind.net

Circa 1910. Decorated with hints of French country, this Craftsman farmhouse has a fine front porch and expansive sunny deck in back creating relaxing areas for enjoying the less crowded south end of town. A hearty country gourmet breakfast is served family style in the dining room. There are bicycles for exploring the area. With advance notice, the innkeepers can prepare picnic lunches. Ski packages are available.

Innkeeper(s): Linda Johnson. $65-105. MC, VISA, PC, TC. 6 rooms with PB. Breakfast included in rates. Type of meal: Early coffee/tea. Turndown service in room. Air conditioning. VCR, fax and copier on premises. Antiquing, fishing, river rafting, biking, live theater, parks, shopping, downhill skiing and cross-country skiing nearby.

"You definitely have the beauty of spirit-It shows in everything from the exquisite breakfasts to the wonderful decor."
Certificate may be used: November-March, Monday-Thursday.

The Woods House B&B

333 N Main St
Ashland, OR 97520-1703
(541)488-1598 (800)435-8260 Fax:(541)482-8027
Internet: www.mind.net/woodshouse/
E-mail: woodshse@mind.net

Circa 1908. Built and occupied for almost 40 years by a prominent Ashland physician, each room of this Craftsman-style inn boasts special detail. Many guest rooms offer canopied beds and skylights. Full breakfasts are served either in the sunny dining room or in the garden under a spreading walnut tree. After breakfast, take a stroll through the half-acre of terraced, English gardens. Located in the historic district, the inn is four blocks from Ashland's Shakespearean theaters.

Innkeeper(s): Francoise Roddy. $85-125. MC, VISA. 6 rooms with PB. Breakfast included in rates. Types of meals: Full bkfst and early coffee/tea. Beds: KQT. Books, magazines, shampoo and etc in room. Air conditioning. VCR, fax, copier and gardens for quiet parties on premises. Antiquing, live theater, shopping, downhill skiing and cross-country skiing nearby.
Location: City.
Publicity: *Seattle Times, Oregonian, San Francisco Examiner, American Visions Magazine, Emerge Magazine, Black Conventions Magazine and New York Times.*

"Within this house lies much hospitality, friendship and laughter. What more could a home ask to be?."
Certificate may be used: October-March, any nights. Excluding holidays.

Brookings $\qquad$ G1

Chetco River Inn/Lavender Bee Farm

21202 High Prairie Rd
Brookings, OR 97415-8200
(541)670-1645
Internet: www.chetcoriverinn.com

Circa 1987. Situated on 40 wooded acres and the Chetco River, this modern bed & breakfast offers a cedar lodge exterior and a marble- and antique-filled interior. A collection of crafts, Oriental rugs and leather sofas add to your enjoyment. Breakfast and goodies served to guests include the addition of the farm's honey. Enjoy the sounds of the rushing river without interruption, or stroll through the acres of lavender. (Because it's 18 miles from Brookings, the property is out of the summer coastal fog.) Hiking the many inviting trails, exploring the Kalmiopsis Wilderness area and steelhead fishing are the favorite activities.

Innkeeper(s): Sandra Brugger. $115-135. PC, TC. 5 rooms with PB and 1 cottage. Breakfast included in rates. Types of meals: Full bkfst and early coffee/tea. Beds: KT. Views in room. Library, darts and horseshoes and other outdoor games on premises. Antiquing, fishing, live theater, parks, shopping and water sports nearby.

Location: Riverfront in mountain.

Publicity: Country, Oregon Coast, Midford Newspaper, Tribune and Sunset.

Certificate may be used: April through June and September through December, except for holidays.

South Coast Inn B&B

516 Redwood St
Brookings, OR 97415-9672
(541)469-5557 (800)525-9273 Fax:(541)469-6615
Internet: www.southcoastinn.com
E-mail: innkeeper@southcoastinn.com

Circa 1917. Enjoy panoramic views of the Pacific Ocean at this Craftsman-style inn designed by renowned San Francisco architect Bernard Maybeck. All rooms are furnished with antiques, ceiling fans, VCRs and TVs. Two guest rooms afford panoramic views of the coastline and there is a separate cottage. A floor-to-ceiling stone fireplace and beamed ceilings make the parlor a great place to gather with friends. There are sun decks, a strolling garden, and an indoor hot tub and sauna. The Brookings area offers something for everyone. Outdoor activities include hiking, boating, golfing, digging for clams or simply enjoying a stroll along the spectacular coastline. Concerts, galleries, museums, antiques, specialty shops and fine restaurants all can be found within the area.

Innkeeper(s): Ken Raith & Keith Pepper. $84-109. MC, VISA, AX, DS, PC, TC. 4 rooms with PB and 1 cottage. Breakfast included in rates. Types of meals: Full gourmet bkfst and early coffee/tea. Beds: KQ. Cable TV, ceiling fan, VCR, hair dryers in baths and 1 with gas fireplace/stove in room. Fax, spa, sauna and library on premises. Antiquing, fishing, live theater, parks, shopping and water sports nearby.

Location: City.

"Thank you for your special brand of magic. What a place!"
Certificate may be used: November-April, except holidays.

Corvallis $\qquad$ D3

Harrison House

2310 NW Harrison Blvd
Corvallis, OR 97330-5402
(541)752-6248 (800)233-6248
Internet: www.proaxis.com/~harrisonhouse/
E-mail: harrisonhouse@proaxis.com

Circa 1939. This Dutch-Colonial-style house, adjacent to Oregon State University, was built by the Allison family who lived here until 1990. Upon its conversion to a bed & breakfast, it was graciously restored. The rooms are large and comfortable, decorated and furnished in Williamsburg-style family antiques. The favorite guest room overlooks a side yard with beds of flowers and fruit trees. The full breakfast begins with a fruit course and features either eggs Benedict, various stuffed crepes or other regional fare. Antiques, fishing, hiking, shopping, skiing, sporting events and theater are nearby.

Innkeeper(s): Maria Tomlinson. $90-100. MC, VISA, AX, DS. 4 rooms with PB. Type of meal: Early coffee/tea. Beds: KQD. Cable TV and phone in room. Amusement parks, antiquing, fishing, live theater, shopping, downhill skiing, cross-country skiing and sporting events nearby.

Location: Small town-next to OSU Univ.

"What an exceptional weekend!"
Certificate may be used: Dec. 1 to Feb. 28, Sunday-Thursday.

Crescent Lake $\qquad$ E4

Willamette Pass Inn & RV

PO Box 35
Crescent Lake, OR 97425-0035
(541)433-2211 (888)433-2211 Fax:(541)433-2211

Circa 1984. Each of the guest rooms at this rustic, comfortable lodge includes a fireplace and pine furnishings. Beds are topped with flannel sheets. Turndown service is a real treat, guests return from dinner to find cookies and muffins waiting. The inn is located in a national forest, ancient Indian grounds and more than one dozen lakes are nearby.

Innkeeper(s): George & Alicia Primgore. $68-98. MC, VISA, DS, PC, TC. 12 rooms with PB, 10 with FP. Snacks/refreshments included in rates. Beds: Q. Cable TV, phone, turndown service and VCR in room. Fax and library on premises. Handicap access. Fishing, snowmobiling, parks, shopping, downhill skiing, cross-country skiing and water sports nearby.

Pets allowed: $15 non-refundable/small pets only.

Location: 17 lakes within 30 miles.

Certificate may be used: Jan. 5-Dec. 15, except holidays and Saturday nights.

Dayton $\qquad$ C3

Wine Country Farm

6855 NE Breyman Orchards Rd
Dayton, OR 97114-7220
(503)864-3446 (800)261-3446 Fax:(503)864-3109
Internet: www.winecountryfarm.com
E-mail: winecountryfarm@webtv.net

Circa 1910. Surrounded by vineyards and orchards, Wine Country Farm is an eclectic French house sitting on a hill overlooking the Cascade Mountain Range. Arabian horses are raised here, and five varieties of grapes are grown. Request the master bedroom and you'll enjoy a fireplace. The innkeepers can arrange for a horse-drawn buggy ride and picnic or horseback through the vineyards and forests to other wineries. There are outdoor wedding facilities and a new wine tasting room, where guests can sample wine from the vineyard. Downtown Portland and the Oregon coast are each an hour away.

Innkeeper(s): Joan Davenport. $85-125. MC, VISA, PC. 7 rooms with PB, 2 with FP, 1 suite and 1 conference room. Breakfast included in rates. Types of meals: Full gourmet bkfst and early coffee/tea. Beds: KQDT. Air conditioning. VCR, fax, copier, stables and library on premises. Antiquing, fishing, live theater, parks, shopping, downhill skiing, cross-country skiing, sporting events and water sports nearby.

Location: One hour to ocean.

Publicity: *Wine Spectator.*

Certificate may be used: Dec. 1 through April 30, Monday-Thursday.

Eugene D3

Campbell House, A City Inn

252 Pearl St
Eugene, OR 97401-2366
(541)343-1119 (800)264-2519 Fax:(541)343-2258
Internet: www.campbellhouse.com
E-mail: campbellhouse@campbellhouse.com

Circa 1892. An acre of grounds surrounds this Victorian inn, built by a local timber owner and gold miner. The guest quarters range from a ground-level room featuring fly-fishing paraphernalia and knotty-pine paneling to an elegant two-room honeymoon suite on the second floor, complete with fireplace, jetted bathtub for two and a view of the mountains. The Campbell House, located in Eugene's historic Skinner Butte District, is within walking distance of restaurants, the Hult Center for the Performing Arts, the 5th Street Public Market and antique shops. Outdoor activities include jogging or biking along riverside paths.

Innkeeper(s): Myra Plant. $86-350. MC, VISA, AX, DS, TC. 18 rooms with PB, 7 with FP, 1 suite and 2 conference rooms. Breakfast included in rates. Types of meals: Full bkfst and early coffee/tea. Beds: KQDT. Cable TV, phone, turndown service, ceiling fan, VCR and jetted or clawfoot tubs in room. Air conditioning. Fax, copier and library on premises. Handicap access. Antiquing, bicycling, fishing, golf, hiking, rock climbing, live theater, parks, sporting events and water sports nearby.

Location: On Skinner's Butte (hiking).

Publicity: *Oregon Business, American Travels, B&B Innkeepers Journal, Eugene Register Guard, Country Inns, Oregonian, Sunset, Good Evening Show, KVAL & KAUW News.*

"I guess we've never felt so pampered! Thank you so much. The room is beautiful! We had a wonderful getaway."

Certificate may be used: January through March (not valid during events, holidays or conferences).

Kjaer's House In Woods

814 Lorane Hwy
Eugene, OR 97405-2321
(541)343-3234 (800)437-4501
Internet: Eugene_BedandBreakfast.com

Circa 1910. This handsome Craftsman house on two landscaped acres was built by a Minnesota lawyer. It was originally accessible by streetcar. Antiques include a square grand piano of

rosewood and a collection of antique wedding photos. The house is attractively furnished and surrounded by flower gardens.

Innkeeper(s): George & Eunice Kjaer. $65-80. PC, TC. 2 rooms with PB and 1 conference room. Breakfast included in rates. Types of meals: Full gourmet bkfst, cont and early coffee/tea. Beds: Q. VCR and library on premises. Antiquing, fishing, live theater, parks, shopping and sporting events nearby.

Location: City.

Publicity: *Register Guard and Oregonian.*

"Lovely ambiance and greatest sleep ever. Delicious and beautiful food presentation."

Certificate may be used: Nov. 1-May 10, Sunday-Friday.

Pookie's B&B on College Hill

2013 Charnelton St
Eugene, OR 97405-2819
(541)343-0383 (800)558-0383 Fax:(541)431-0967
Internet: www.pookiesbandblodging.com
E-mail: dougwalling@aol.com

Circa 1918. Pookie's is a charming Craftsman house with "yester-year charm." Surrounded by maple and fir trees, the B&B is located in an older, quiet neighborhood. Mahogany and oak antiques decorate the rooms. The innkeeper worked

for many years in the area as a concierge and can offer you expert help with excursion planning or business needs.

Innkeeper(s): Pookie & Doug Walling. $80-115. PC, TC. 3 rooms, 2 with PB and 1 suite. Breakfast included in rates. Types of meals: Full bkfst, cont plus, cont and early coffee/tea. Beds: KQT. Cable TV, phone and ceiling fan in room. VCR, fax and copier on premises. Antiquing, fishing, baseball stadium, live theater, parks, shopping, sporting events and water sports nearby.

Location: City.

Publicity: *Oregon Wine.*

"I love the attention to detail. The welcoming touches: flowers, the 'convenience basket' of necessary items . . . I'm happy to have discovered your lovely home."

Certificate may be used: Jan. 15-May 1, Sunday-Wednesday, suite only.

The Oval Door

988 Lawrence St
Eugene, OR 97401-2827
(541)683-3160 (800)882-3160
Internet: www.ovaldoor.com
E-mail: ovaldoor@ovaldoor.com

Circa 1990. This recently constructed New England farm-style house comes complete with wraparound porch. It is located in a residential neighborhood 15 blocks from the University of Oregon. A welcoming parlor boasts a fireplace and plush furniture. Guest rooms feature ceiling fans and antiques. There is both a whirlpool room with music and a library. Breakfast can be made to order for special dietary needs, but the regular gourmet offerings are especially good. Homemade breads and local fruits and berries are also featured. Arrive in time to enjoy afternoon tea and freshly baked cookies or sweets.

Innkeeper(s): Nicole Wergeland, Melissa Coray. $75-125. MC, VISA, AX. 4 rooms with PB. Beds: QT. TV, phone, turndown service, ceiling fan and VCR in room. Fax and library on premises.

Location: City.

Certificate may be used: November-April, Sunday-Thursday. Not valid during special events, holidays or conferences.

Government Camp (Mt. Hood) C4

Falcon's Crest Inn

87287 Government Camp Loop Hwy
Government Camp (Mt. Hood), OR 97028
(503)272-3403 (800)624-7384 Fax:(503)272-3454
Internet: www.falconscrest.com
E-mail: falconscrest@earthlink.net

Circa 1983. This chalet-style home is located in an old growth forest in the scenic Mt. Hood area. Skiers enjoy close access to local slopes, and there is plenty of space to store equipment.

Guests enjoy a view of the ski mountain from the Great Room, which includes a wood-burning stove. There are two other common areas for guests to use in this 6,500-square-foot home, which is somewhat like staying in an intimate mountain lodge. Guest

rooms feature unique themes. The Cat Ballou Room is done in an Old West country style with an iron bed and an exposed cedar wall. The Safari Suite, complete with palm tree, is reminiscent of the jungle, with a large rattan chair and a bamboo bed draped with netting. One suite is dedicated to the innkeepers' grandmother, and others are done in French-country or Southwestern style. A family-style breakfast is included in the rates, but guests also can reserve a six-course gourmet dinner. The Saltimbocca, veal with prosciutto and mozzarella, is a specialty. The inn is located just off what was the Oregon Trail.

Innkeeper(s): BJ & Melody Johnson. $95-179. MC, VISA, AX, DS, PC, TC. 3 rooms with PB, 2 suites and 1 conference room. Breakfast included in rates. Types of meals: Full bkfst, cont plus and early coffee/tea. Beds: KQT. Phone and turndown service in room. VCR, fax, copier and bicycles on premises. Antiquing, fishing, golf, live theater, parks, shopping, downhill skiing, cross-country skiing, tennis and water sports nearby.

Location: Mountains.

Publicity: Sunset Magazine, Northwest Travel., AM Northwest-Channel 2, Northwest Discoveries and Channel 12.

Certificate may be used: Sunday through Thursday except holiday periods, subject to availability. (Not valid with any other discount card, coupon or certificate.).

Grants Pass G2

Lawnridge House

1304 N W Lawnridge Ave
Grants Pass, OR 97526-1218
(541)476-8518

Circa 1909. This inn, a graceful, gabled clapboard house is shaded by 200-year-old oaks. The home features spacious rooms with comfortable antiques, canopy beds and beamed ceilings. Mini refrigerators, TVs and VCRs are among the amenities. A family suite accommodates up to six people and includes one or two bedrooms, a sitting room and bathroom. The innkeeper serves Northwest regional cuisine for the full breakfasts. The Rogue River is five minutes away, and the Ashland Shakespearean Festival is a 45-minute drive.

Innkeeper(s): Barbara Head. $70-85. PC, TC. 2 suites. Breakfast included in rates. Type of meal: Full bkfst. Beds: KQ. Air conditioning. Antiquing, fishing, live theater and water sports nearby.

Location: City.

Publicity: Grants Pass Courier, This Week and CBS TV.

"Thank you for your incredible friendliness, warmth, and energy expended on our behalf! I've never felt so nestled in the lap of luxury - what a pleasure!"

Certificate may be used: Jan. 6-May 15, space available basis only same day, no advance reservations. Ask for special Canadian discounts.

Pine Meadow Inn Bed & Breakfast

1000 Crow Rd
Grants Pass, OR 97532
(541)471-6277 (800)554-0806 Fax:(541)471-6277
Internet: www.pinemeadowinn.com
E-mail: pmi@pinemeadowinn.com

Circa 1991. Built on a wooded knoll, this handsome yellow farmhouse looks out on a four-acre meadow, which the innkeepers call their front yard. Five acres of private forest feature walking paths, and there are vegetable and flower gardens and private sitting areas.

(Breakfast includes seasonal fruits and vegetables raised on the grounds.) The home's wraparound porch offers wicker furniture, and there is a large deck and hot tub under towering pines. There also is a koi pond and waterfall where one can relax and contemplate. The inn is easily accessible from I-5, yet it feels worlds away.

Innkeeper(s): Nancy & Maloy Murdock. $85-120. MC, VISA, AX, DS, PC. 4 rooms with PB. Breakfast included in rates. Types of meals: Full gourmet bkfst and early coffee/tea. Beds: Q. Phone, turndown service, ceiling fan and clock in room. Air conditioning. Spa, library and koi pond on premises. Antiquing, fishing, redwoods, Crater Lake, live theater, parks, shopping and water sports nearby.

Location: Secluded countryside.

Publicity: Medford Tribune, Daily Courier and Good News Christmas.

Certificate may be used: October-April, Sunday-Thursday.

Weasku Inn

5560 Rogue River Hwy
Grants Pass, OR 97527
(541)471-8000 (800)334-4567 Fax:(541)471-7038
Internet: www.weasku.com
E-mail: info@weasku.com

Circa 1924. Built as a secluded fishing lodge, this historic inn once hosted the likes of President Herbert Hoover, Zane Grey, Walt Disney, Clark Gable and Carole Lombard. It is said that after Lombard's death, Gable spent several weeks here, lamenting the loss of his beloved wife. A complete restoration took place in the early 1990s, reviving the inn back to its former glory. The log exterior, surrounding by towering trees and 10 fragrant acres, is a welcoming site. Inside, crackling fires from the inn's rock fireplaces

warm the common rooms. Vaulted ceilings and exposed log beams add a cozy, rustic touch to the pristine, airy rooms all decorated in

Pacific Northwest style. Many rooms include a whirlpool tub and river rock fireplace, and several offer excellent views of the Rogue River, which runs through the inn's grounds. In addition to the inn rooms, there are riverfront cabins, offering an especially romantic setting. In the evenings, guests are treated to a wine and cheese reception, and in the mornings, a continental breakfast is served. The staff can help plan many activities, including fishing and white-water rafting trips.

Innkeeper(s): Dayle Sedgemore. $85-295. MC, VISA, AX, DC, CB, DS, TC. 21 rooms, 19 with PB, 13 with FP, 3 suites, 12 cabins, 1 guest house and 1 conference room. Breakfast and snacks/refreshments included in rates. Type of meal: Cont plus. Beds: KQT. Cable TV, phone and ceiling fan in room. Central air. Fax on premises. Handicap access. Antiquing, canoeing/kayaking, fishing, golf, hiking, jet boat excursions/wildlife park, live theater, museums, parks, shopping, water sports and wineries nearby.

Location: On the Rogue River.

Publicity: *Travel & Leisure Magazine and LA Magazine.*

Certificate may be used: Sunday-Thursday, subject to availability.

Halfway   C9

Birch Leaf Farm

Rt 1, Box 91
Halfway, OR 97834-9704
(541)742-2990

Circa 1905. Nestled in the middle of a 42-acre farm near the Oregon Trail and halfway between the Eagle Cap Wilderness and Hells Canyon, this National Register farmhouse boasts original woodwork and hardwood floors. Each guest room has a view of the Wallowa Mountains. A country-style breakfast is served complete with locally made jams and honey. Nearby activities include white-water rafting, jet-boat trips, pack trips and skiing through local mountains.

Innkeeper(s): Maryellen Olson. $65-70. VISA. 4 rooms, 1 with PB and 1 conference room. Breakfast included in rates. Types of meals: Full bkfst and early coffee/tea. Beds: KQDT. TV and phone in room. Antiquing, fishing, shopping, downhill skiing and cross-country skiing nearby.

Location: Mountains.

Publicity: *Hells Canyon Journal.*

"I will always remember the warmth and quiet comfort of your place."
Certificate may be used: All days except July 4, Labor Day and Christmas.

Jacksonville   G3

Touvelle House

455 N Oregon St
Jacksonville, OR 97530-1891
(541)899-8938 (800)846-8422 Fax:(541)899-3992
Internet: www.touvellehouse.com
E-mail: touvelle@wave.net

Circa 1916. This Craftsman inn is two blocks away from the main street of this old Gold Rush town. The common areas of this Craftsman inn include The Library, which has a TV and VCR; The Great Room, featuring a large-stoned fireplace; The Sunroom, which consists of many windows; and The Dining Room, featuring an intricate built-in buffet. Guests can relax on either of two spacious covered verandas.

Innkeeper(s): Nick Williamson, Steven Harris. $110-195. 6 rooms with PB and

1 suite. Breakfast included in rates. Type of meal: Full bkfst. Beds: KQDT. Antiquing, fishing, festival, live theater, downhill skiing, cross-country skiing and water sports nearby.

Publicity: *ABC News.*

"The accommodations are beautiful, the atmosphere superb, the breakfast and other goodies delightful, but it is the warmth and caring of the host that will make the difference in this B&B!!"
Certificate may be used: Jan. 1-April 30, Nov. 1-Dec. 20, Sunday-Thursday night, except holidays.

Klamath Falls   G4

Thompsons' B&B

1420 Wild Plum Ct
Klamath Falls, OR 97601-1983
(541)882-7938
E-mail: tompohll@aol.com

Circa 1987. The huge picture windows in this comfortable retreat look out to a spectacular view of Klamath Lake and nearby mountains. Innkeeper Mary Pohll has a collection of dolls and clowns. Popular Moore Park is next door, providing a day of hiking, picnicking or relaxing at the marina. The inn is a perfect site to just relax and enjoy the view. Bird watching is a must, as the inn is home to pelicans, snow geese, bald eagles and many varieties of wild ducks.

Innkeeper(s): Mary & Bill Pohll. $70-80. PC, TC. 4 rooms with PB. Breakfast included in rates. Types of meals: Full bkfst and early coffee/tea. Beds: K. Cable TV and phone in room. Air conditioning. Antiquing, parks and water sports nearby.

"Hospitality as glorious as your surroundings."
Certificate may be used: November through February, Sunday through Saturday.

Lincoln City   C2

Brey House "Ocean View" B&B

3725 NW Keel Ave
Lincoln City, OR 97367
(541)994-7123
Internet: www.moriah.com/breyhouse

Circa 1941. The innkeepers at this three-story, Cape Cod-style house claim that when you stay with them it's like staying with Aunt Shirley and Uncle Milt. Guest rooms include some with ocean views and private entrances, and the Deluxe Suite offers a living room with fireplace, two baths and a kitchen. The Admiral's Room on the third floor has knotty pine walls, a skylight, fireplace and the best view.

Innkeeper(s): Milt & Shirley Brey. $75-135. MC, VISA, DS, TC. 4 rooms with PB, 3 with FP and 2 suites. Breakfast included in rates. Types of meals: Full gourmet bkfst and early coffee/tea. Beds: KQ. Cable TV, ceiling fan and VCR in room. Antiquing, fishing, golf, indian casino, live theater, parks, shopping, tennis and water sports nearby.

Location: City.

Certificate may be used: Not honored June, July, August. January to June and September to December good Sunday through Thursday.

The Enchanted Cottage

4507 SW Coast Ave
Lincoln City, OR 97367
(541)996-4101 Fax:(541)996-2682
Internet: www.lincolncity.com/tec
E-mail: daythia@wcn.net

Circa 1940. This 4,000-square-foot house is 300 feet from the beach and a short walk from Siletz Bay with its herd of sea lions. Victoria's Secret is a favorite romantic guest room that features a queen canopy bed, antique furnishings and, best of all, the sounds of the Pacific surf. Ask for Sir Arthur's View if you must see and hear the ocean. This two-room suite also has a private deck and a living room with a fireplace and wet bar. Homemade breakfast casseroles are a specialty during the morning meal, which is served either in the dining room or on the deck overlooking the Pacific. Pets are allowed with some restrictions.

Innkeeper(s): David & Cynthia Gale Fitton. $100-175. MC, VISA, PC, TC. 3 rooms with PB, 1 with FP and 1 suite. Breakfast and snacks/refreshments included in rates. Types of meals: Full gourmet bkfst and early coffee/tea. Beds: KQ. Cable TV in room. VCR, fax, copier and library on premises. Handicap access. Amusement parks, antiquing, fishing, golf, Oregon Coast Aquarium, live theater, parks, shopping, tennis and water sports nearby.

Pets allowed: With some restrictions. Prefer small pets. Must have own pet bed.

Publicity: *Oregonian & L C Newsguard.*

Certificate may be used: October through April, Sunday-Friday; May through September, Sunday-Thursday, no holidays.

Manzanita   B2

The Arbors at Manzanita

78 Idaho Ave, PO Box 68
Manzanita, OR 97130-0068
(503)368-7566

Circa 1920. This old-English-style cottage is a half block from the wide sandy beaches that the area is known for. The Neakahnie Mountains are in view as well as the panoramic stretches of the Pacific coastline. Ask for the Waves View room to enjoy the largest view. Enjoy the library, garden and the innkeeper's evening snacks.

Innkeeper(s): H.L. Burrow. $90-105. 2 rooms. Breakfast included in rates. Type of meal: Full gourmet bkfst. Beds: QT. VCR on premises. Antiquing, fishing and shopping nearby.

Certificate may be used: November through April 15, Sunday through Thursday.

McMinnville   C3

Baker Street B&B

129 S Baker St
McMinnville, OR 97128-6035
(503)472-5575 (800)870-5575
Internet: www.bakerstreetinn.com

Circa 1914. The natural wood that graces the interior of this Craftsman inn has been restored to its original luster. Vintage Victorian antiques and memorabilia decorate the rooms. Several guest rooms include clawfoot tubs, each features a different color scheme. Couples traveling together or those planning longer visits, might consider the Carnation Cottage, which includes two bedrooms, a bathroom, living room, kitchen and laundry facilities. The breakfast table is set with china and silver. The B&B is one hour from Portland and the coast, and there are gourmet restaurants and 40 wineries nearby.

Innkeeper(s): Cheryl Collins. $75-85. MC, VISA, AX, DS, PC, TC. 4 rooms with PB and 1 cottage. Type of meal: Full bkfst. Beds: KQDT. VCR in room. Air conditioning. Antiquing, restaurants & 40 wineries, parks and shopping nearby.

Location: Small town.

Certificate may be used: November-April.

Oakland   E3

The Beckley House

PO Box 198
Oakland, OR 97462-0198
(541)459-9320

Local merchant Charles Beckley built this two-story home, a historic example of late 19th-century Classic Revival architecture. Rooms are furnished in Victorian style with period antiques, including a rare Victrola. One of the guest rooms boasts a white, iron bed. Fresh flowers brighten the rooms and add to the home's garden setting. Breakfasts are a treat, featuring entrees such as apple dumplings with cheese or Grand Marnier French toast. Enjoy a glass of wine or iced tea on the canopied swing or on the plant-filled patio. Walking tours of the historic town are available, as are romantic carriage rides.

Innkeeper(s): Karene Biedermann. $70-85. MC, VISA, AX, DS. 2 rooms. Breakfast included in rates. Type of meal: Cont.

Certificate may be used: October-April, excluding holidays, based upon availability.

Prairie City   D7

Strawberry Mountain Inn

HCR 77 Box 940
Prairie City, OR 97869
(541)820-4522 (800)545-6913 Fax:(541)820-4622
Internet: www.moriah.com/strawberry
E-mail: linda@highdesertnet.com

Circa 1910. Vistas of Strawberry Mountain are a highlight of a getaway to this peaceful inn, set on three acres of farmland. The home, the largest in Grant County, was built by a man who bred and raised horses for the U.S. Cavalry. The interior is spacious and comfortable, a place where guests are made to feel at home. There is a library offering a wide selection of books, and guests can relax on the front porch or enjoy a game of chess in the parlor. A deep-dish apple puff pancake or croissant French  toast might appear on the breakfast table, served by candlelight while classical melodies play out in the background.

Innkeeper(s): Bill & Linda Harrington. $65-125. MC, VISA, AX, DS, PC, TC. 4 rooms, 2 with PB. Breakfast included in rates. Type of meal: Full gourmet bkfst. Beds: KQDT. VCR, fax, copier, spa, stables, library, pet boarding and child care on premises. Antiquing, fishing, golf, John Day Fossil Beds National Monument, historic museums, Kamwah Chung Chinese museums, parks, shopping, cross-country skiing and water sports nearby.

Pets allowed: Not inside the inn, separate facility.

Location: Wilderness area.

Certificate may be used: From Nov. 15 to March 15, excluding holidays.

Salem   C3

A Creekside Inn, The Marquee House

333 Wyatt Ct NE
Salem, OR 97301-4269
(503)391-0837
Internet: www.marqueehouse.com/rickiemh
E-mail: rickiemh@open.org

Circa 1938. Each room in this Mt. Vernon Colonial replica of
George Washington's house is named after a famous old-time
movie. Consider the Auntie Mame room. This gracious view
room features a fireplace, fainting couch, costumes, collectibles
and a private bath. The four other upstairs guest rooms offer
similar themes. There are regular evening movie screenings
complete with popcorn in the common room. The extensive
gardens offer guests an opportunity to stroll along historic Mill
Creek or enjoy a round of croquet in the spacious backyard,
weather permitting. Hazelnut waffles, confetti hash and oatmeal
custard are a few of the breakfast specialties. The inn is just
two blocks from the Chemeketa Historic District.

Innkeeper(s): Ms. Rickie Hart. $65-90. MC, VISA, DS, DC, PC, TC. 5 rooms,
3 with PB, 1 with FP. Breakfast and snacks/refreshments included in rates.
Types of meals: Full gourmet bkfst and early coffee/tea. Beds: QT. VCR and
bicycles on premises. Amusement parks, antiquing, golf, wine country tours,
wineries, live theater, parks, shopping and sporting events nearby.

Location: City.

Publicity: *Statesman Journal* and *The Christian Science Monitor.*

*"We all agreed that you were the best hostess yet for one of our
weekends!"*

Certificate may be used: Oct. 15 to June 15, Sunday-Friday.

Seaside   A2

Custer House B&B

811 1st Ave
Seaside, OR 97138-6803
(503)738-7825 (800)738-7852 Fax:(503)738-4324
Internet: www.clatsop.com/custer
E-mail: custerbb@seasurf.com

Circa 1900. Wicker furnishings and a clawfoot tub are features
of one of the rooms in this farmhouse-style B&B. It is located
four blocks from the ocean and two blocks from the Seaside
Convention Center. Your host is retired from the Air Force.
Enjoy exploring the area's historic forts and beaches.

Innkeeper(s): Skip & Helen Custer. $55-75. MC, VISA, AX, DC, CB, DS, TC.
3 rooms, 1 with PB and 1 conference room. Breakfast included in rates. Type
of meal: Full bkfst. Beds: QT. VCR and bicycles on premises. Antiquing, fishing, live theater, parks, shopping and water sports nearby.

Location: City.

Publicity: *Oregon Adventures.*

Certificate may be used: Oct. 15-May 15.

Sand Dollar B&B

606 N Holladay Dr
Seaside, OR 97138-6926
(503)738-3491 (800)738-3491

Circa 1920. This Craftsman-style home looks a bit like a
seashell, painted in light pink with dark pink trim. In fact, one
of the guest rooms bears the name Sea Shell, filled with bright
quilts and wicker. The Driftwood Room can be used as a two-

bedroom suite for families, and there is also a cottage on the
river. As the room names suggest, the house is decorated in a
beach theme, graced by innkeeper Nita Hempfling's stained
glasswork. Before breakfast is served, coffee or tea is delivered
to the rooms.

Innkeeper(s): Robert & Nita Hempfling. $55-125. MC, VISA, AX, DS, TC. 3
rooms, 2 with PB and 1 suite. Breakfast and snacks/refreshments included in
rates. Beds: KQT. Cable TV, ceiling fan and VCR in room. Bicycles and canoe
on premises. Antiquing, fishing, parks, shopping and water sports nearby.

Certificate may be used: Sept. 15-May 15, Sunday-Thursday.

Sea Side Inn

581 S Promenade
Seaside, OR 97138-7138
(503)738-6403 (800)772-7766 Fax:(503)738-6634
Internet: www.seasideinn.com

Circa 1994. This four-story inn is oceanfront on the
Promenade. If you've never tried sleeping in a round bed, ask
for the Clock Tower Room, which also offers a whirlpool tub for
two in a marble bathroom and a fireplace. The Rock and Roll
Room boasts a '59 Oldsmobile bed. Many rooms have white-
water views and special amenities. There's an elevator in the
inn, and the Shell Seeker is a beautiful handicap accessible
room. Enjoy the oceanfront patio and the inn's gathering rooms.

Innkeeper(s): Susan K. Peters. $115-245. MC, VISA, DS, PC, TC. 14 rooms
with PB, 6 with FP, 2 suites and 1 conference room. Breakfast included in
rates. Types of meals: Full bkfst and early coffee/tea. Beds: KQT. Cable TV,
phone, ceiling fan and VCR in room. Air conditioning. Fax, copier, spa and
library on premises. Handicap access. Amusement parks, antiquing, fishing,
golf, horseback riding, helicopters, live theater, parks, shopping, tennis and
water sports nearby.

Location: Waterfront.

Certificate may be used: Sunday through Thursday, non-holidays November,
December, January.

The Guest House B&B

486 Necanicum Dr
Seaside, OR 97138
(503)717-0495 (800)340-8150 Fax:(503)717-9385
E-mail: guesthouse@clatsop.com

Circa 1981. Across the street from the city historic museum,
this B&B is situated behind a picket fence. Although the inn is
of contemporary construction, all the guest rooms here offer
antique beds and historical touches such as old area photos.
Breakfast is served in the dining room where guests enjoy views
of the Necanicum River. The Lewis and Clark Trail ends in the
town of Seaside. The house is two blocks from the beach and
near shops, restaurants and many outdoor activities. Portland is
an hour and a half away, and Seattle is about three and a half
hours from Seaside.

Innkeeper(s): Nancy & Ken Bailey. $60-95. MC, VISA, DS, PC, TC. 4 rooms
with PB, 1 with FP. Breakfast and snacks/refreshments included in rates.
Types of meals: Full bkfst and early coffee/tea. Beds: QDT. Cable TV and ceiling fan in room. Fax, spa, library and pet boarding on premises. Amusement
parks, antiquing, fishing, golf, live theater, parks, shopping, tennis and water
sports nearby.

Pets allowed: In garage or fenced yard, not indoors.

Certificate may be used: Oct. 15 to April 15 any day of the week.

Stayton   C3

The Inn at Gardner House Bed & Breakfast

633 N 3rd Ave
Stayton, OR 97383-1731
(503)769-6331

Circa 1893. A former Stayton postmaster and city councilman built this home, which features a wraparound veranda. Accommodations include a suite with a small kitchen and dining room. Each guest room is comfortably furnished, with some antiques. The innkeeper prepares creative breakfasts with homemade breads, fresh fruit and entrees such as asparagus quiche or breakfast burritos topped with salsa.

Innkeeper(s): Dick Jungwirth. $55-65. MC, VISA, AX, DC, CB, DS, PC, TC. 2 rooms with PB and 1 suite. Breakfast included in rates. Types of meals: Full gourmet bkfst and early coffee/tea. Beds: QT. Cable TV, phone and VCR in room. Copier and library on premises. Antiquing, fishing, live theater, parks, shopping, downhill skiing, cross-country skiing, sporting events and water sports nearby.

Pets Allowed.

Location: Mountains.

Certificate may be used: Jan. 1 to Dec. 31.

Tigard   B3

The Woven Glass Inn

14645 SW Beef Bend Rd
Tigard, OR 97224
(503)590-6040

Circa 1938. This comfortable farmhouse is surrounded by more than an acre of grounds, including a sunken garden. The French Room includes a four-poster, king bed and a private deck. Guests staying in the Garden Suite enjoy a view of the garden. Beds in both guest rooms include fluffy down pillows and fine linens. The inn is 20 minutes from Portland, and the area offers a variety of wineries to visit. There is a friendly cat in residence.

Innkeeper(s): Paul & Renee Giroux. $65-75. MC, VISA, AX, DS, PC, TC. 2 rooms with PB, 2 with FP and 1 suite. Breakfast included in rates. Type of meal: Full bkfst. Beds: KQ. Phone, turndown service and fans in room. Library and sitting room with limited kitchen facilities on premises. Amusement parks, antiquing, fishing, golf, alpaca farm, ballooning, bicycling, water parks, rivers, live theater, parks, shopping, downhill skiing, cross-country skiing, sporting events, tennis and water sports nearby.

Location: Country.

Publicity: *Wine Press.*

"We needed a little rest and relaxation and we found it here. We loved everything."

Certificate may be used: Oct. 1-April 30, Sunday-Thursday.

Tillamook   B2

Blue Haven Inn

3025 Gienger Rd
Tillamook, OR 97141-8258
(503)842-2265 Fax:(503)842-2265

Circa 1916. This Craftsman-style home has been refurbished and filled with antiques and collectibles. Guest rooms feature limited-edition plate series as themes. Tall evergreens, lawns and flower gardens add to the setting.

Innkeeper(s): Joy Still. $70-85. PC, TC. 3 rooms, 1 with PB. Breakfast

included in rates. Types of meals: Full gourmet bkfst and early coffee/tea. Beds: QD. VCR, fax, bicycles and library on premises. Antiquing, fishing, parks, shopping and water sports nearby.

Location: Country.

Publicity: *Oakland Tribune.*

"Your home is like a present to the eyes."

Certificate may be used: Sunday-Thursday, November-June, excluding holidays.

Welches   C4

Old Welches Inn B&B

26401 E Welches Rd
Welches, OR 97067-9701
(503)622-3754 Fax:(503)622-5370
Internet: www.innsandouts.com/property/old_welches.inn.html

Circa 1890. This two-story colonial building, behind a picket fence, was originally the first hotel to be built in the Mt. Hood area. Reconstructed in the '30s, the building now has shutters and French windows. The inn's two acres offer a plethora of flower beds and views of the Salmon River and Hunchback Mountain. Rooms are named for wildflowers and include antiques. If traveling with children or friends try Lilybank, a private cottage which overlooks the first hole of Three Nines. There are two bedrooms, a kitchen and a river rock fireplace.

Innkeeper(s): Judith & Ted Mondun. $75-130. MC, VISA, AX, DS, PC, TC. 4 rooms and 1 cottage. Breakfast and snacks/refreshments included in rates. Types of meals: Full bkfst and early coffee/tea. Beds: QD. Turndown service in room. VCR, fax and pet boarding on premises. Antiquing, fishing, golf, parks, shopping, downhill skiing, cross-country skiing, sporting events and tennis nearby.

Pets allowed: House broken, well behaved in cottage only.

Location: Mountains.

Publicity: *Oregonian, Sunset and Northwest Best Places.*

Certificate may be used: Jan. 31-May 15 and Oct. 1-Nov. 15; Sunday through Thursday.

Yachats   D2

Sea Quest

95354 Hwy 101 S
Yachats, OR 97498-9713
(541)547-3782 (800)341-4878 Fax:(541)547-3719

Circa 1990. This 6,000-square-foot cedar and glass house is only 100 feet from the ocean, located on two-and-one-half acres. Each guest room has a Jacuzzi tub and outside entrance. The second-floor breakfast room is distinguished by wide views of the ocean, forest and Ten Mile Creek. Guests are often found relaxing in front of the home's

floor-to-ceiling brick fireplace. More adventuresome guests may enjoy the Oregon coast and nearby aquariums.

Innkeeper(s): George & Elaine. $150-245. MC, VISA, DS, PC. 5 rooms with PB. Breakfast included in rates. Types of meals: Full bkfst and early coffee/tea. Beds: Q. Fax, spa, sauna and library on premises. Antiquing, fishing, horseback riding, Oregon Coast Aquarium, Cape Perpetua, Devil's Churn, parks, shopping and water sports nearby.

Certificate may be used: Jan. 5 to May 5, Sunday-Thursday, no holidays.

Pennsylvania

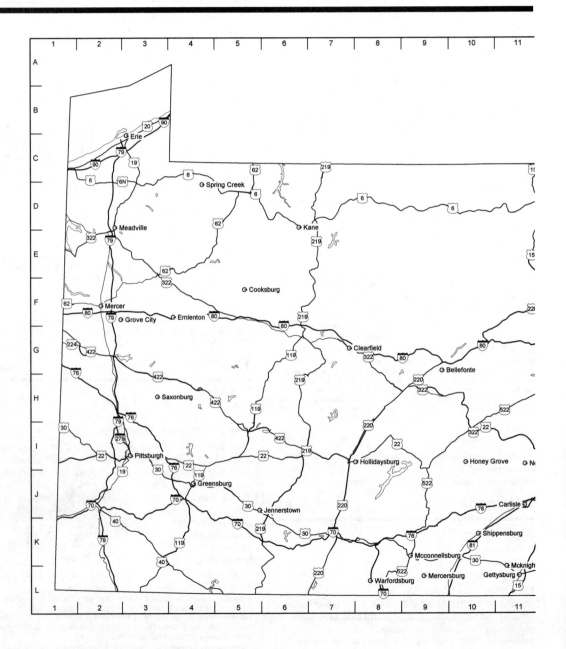

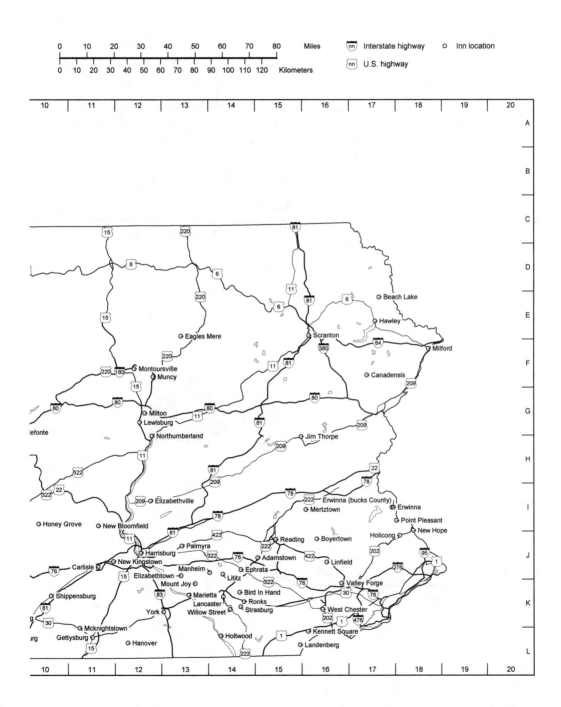

0   10   20   30   40   50   60   70   80   Miles

[nn] Interstate highway   ○ Inn location

0 10 20 30 40 50 60 70 80 90 100 110 120   Kilometers

[nn] U.S. highway

Adamstown   K12

Adamstown Inn

62 W Main St
Adamstown, PA 19501
(717)484-0800 (800)594-4808
Internet: www.adamstown.com

Circa 1830. This square brick house, with its 1850s pump organ found in the large parlor and other local folk art, fits right into this community known as one of the antique capitals of America (3,000 antique dealers). Other decorations include family heirlooms, Victorian wallpaper, handmade quilts and lace curtains. Before breakfast, coffee, tea or hot chocolate is brought to your room. For outlet mall fans, Adamstown is 10 miles from Reading, which offers a vast assortment of top-quality merchandise.

Innkeeper(s): Tom & Wanda Berman. $70-135. MC, VISA, PC, TC. 4 rooms with PB and 1 suite. Breakfast, afternoon tea and snacks/refreshments included in rates. Types of meals: Cont plus and early coffee/tea. Beds: Q. Ceiling fan and Jacuzzi (two rooms) in room. Air conditioning. Copier and library on premises. Amusement parks, antiquing, fishing, live theater, parks and shopping nearby.

Location: Small town, population 1,100.

Publicity: *Country Victorian, Lancaster Intelligencer, Reading Eagle, Travel & Leisure and Country Almanac.*

"Your warm hospitality and lovely home left us with such pleasant memories."

Certificate may be used: Nov. 1-April 15, Sunday through Thursday.

Beach Lake   E17

East Shore House B&B

100 3rd Street
Beach Lake, PA 18405-9726
(570)729-8523 Fax:(570)729-8080

Circa 1901. This Victorian-style home boasts a wraparound porch perfect for rest and relaxation. The gazebo, which sits on top of a bubbling brook, offers another enchanting rest spot. Rooms feature decor typical of turn-of-the-century boarding-house rooms. Each season brings a host of new activities. In warm months, enjoy canoeing and hiking at nearby Delaware River. The "Fall Foliage Express" takes tourists on a train excursion through the local countryside. In winter, guests can snuggle up by the wood stove after a day of skiing or ice skating.

Innkeeper(s): Amy Wood. $50-75. MC, VISA. 6 rooms, 4 with PB. Breakfast included in rates. Type of meal: Full bkfst. Beds: D. Ceiling fan in room. Amusement parks, antiquing, fishing, shopping and downhill skiing nearby.

Certificate may be used: Sunday through Thursday, except holidays, year-round.

Bellefonte   G9

Reynolds Mansion B&B

101 W Linn St
Bellefonte, PA 16823-1622
(814)353-8407 (800)899-3929
Internet: www.bellefonte.com/rmbb
E-mail: jheidt@bellefonte.com

Circa 1885. Bellefonte is a town with many impressive, historic homes, and this exquisite stone mansion is no exception. The home, a combination of late Victorian and Gothic styles, fea-

tures extraordinary, hand-crafted woodwork and intricately laid wood floors, as well as 10 fireplaces. Five guest rooms include a fireplace and a Jacuzzi tub. All enjoy a romantic atmosphere, heightened by candles, fresh flowers and the poshest of furnishings and decor. There also is a billiards room and library for guests to enjoy. Baked, stuffed French toast served with bacon or sausage is among the breakfast specialties accompanied by muffins, juices, cereals and a fruit compote created with more than a half dozen different fresh fruits. For an excellent lunch or dinner, the innkeepers suggest the nearby Gamble Mill Tavern, a 200-year-old mill listed in the National Register.

Innkeeper(s): Joseph & Charlotte Heidt. $95-165. MC, VISA, AX, PC, TC. 6 suites, 5 with FP. Breakfast included in rates. Types of meals: Full gourmet bkfst, cont plus and early coffee/tea. Beds: KQ. Jacuzzi tubs and Jacuzzi steam shower in room. VCR, fax, copier, library and billiards room on premises. Antiquing, fishing, golf, victorian architecture, live theater, parks, shopping, downhill skiing, cross-country skiing, sporting events and water sports nearby.

Location: Small Victorian town.

"Your bed & breakfast is such an inspiration to us."

Certificate may be used: Monday-Thursday, garden room.

Bird-in-Hand   K14

Mill Creek Homestead B&B

2578 Old Philadelphia Pike
Bird-in-Hand, PA 17505-9796
(717)291-6419 (800)771-2578 Fax:(717)291-2171
Internet: www.800padutch.com/millcree.html
E-mail: valfone@concentric.net

Circa 1790. This 18th-century fieldstone farmhouse is one of the oldest homes in Bird-in-the-Hand. Located in the Pennsylvania Dutch Heartland, the inn is decorated for comfort

with Amish influences represented throughout. There are four guest rooms with private baths and fireplaces or stoves. Guests are invited to lounge by the outdoor pool or sit on the porch and watch the horse-

drawn buggies go by. A full breakfast is served in the formal dining room, while afternoon refreshments are in the common rooms. The inn is within walking distance of shops, museums, farmers market, antiques and crafts.

Innkeeper(s): Vicki & Frank Alfone. $99-129. MC, VISA, DS, PC, TC. 4 rooms with PB. Breakfast, afternoon tea and snacks/refreshments included in rates. Types of meals: Full bkfst and early coffee/tea. Beds: QT. Turndown service and ceiling fan in room. Air conditioning. Swimming and library on premises. Amusement parks, antiquing, fishing, golf, live theater, parks, shopping, tennis and water sports nearby.

Location: Country, rural.

Publicity: *Country Inns and Lancaster County Magazine.*

"Thank you for sharing your wonderful home with us. I knew this place would be perfect!"

Certificate may be used: Tuesday-Thursday, Jan. 2-Feb. 28, excluding holidays.

Boyertown   J16

The Enchanted Cottage

22 Deer Run Rd, Rd 4
Boyertown, PA 19512-8312
(610)845-8845

Circa 1984. This timber and stone cottage looks much like one might imagine the woodcutter's tiny house in the fairy tale "Hansel and Gretel." Ivy covers the front of the main house, which guests reach via a little brick path. Inside, exposed wood beams, a bay window and a wood stove create a cozy, romantic ambiance in the living room. The first floor also includes a kitchenette. Upstairs, guests will find a quilt-topped double bed and a bathroom with a clawfoot tub. The innkeepers live in a nearby home where gourmet breakfasts are served. The cottage is near many attractions, including historic sites such as the Daniel Boone Home, Dupont Estate, Longwood Gardens, museums, Amish farms and a restored mining village. Outlet shopping in Reading is a popular activity.

Innkeeper(s): Peg & Richard Groff. $85-90. PC, TC. 1 cottages with PB, 1 with FP. Breakfast included in rates. Type of meal: Full gourmet bkfst. Beds: D. Phone, ceiling fan and kitchenette in room. Air conditioning. Amusement parks, antiquing, golf, many historic sights & sites, auctions, parks, downhill skiing and tennis nearby.

Location: Country, wooded clearing.

Publicity: *Boyertown Area Times, Allentown News, Pottstown Mercury, Reading Times and New York Times.*

"The Enchanted Cottage is a place you've seen in dreams."

Certificate may be used: April 1-Sept. 30, Monday-Thursday.

Canadensis   F17

Brookview Manor B&B Inn

RR 1 Box 365
Canadensis, PA 18325-9740
(570)595-2451 (800)585-7974 Fax:(570)595-5065

Circa 1911. By the side of the road, hanging from a tall evergreen, is the welcoming sign to this forest retreat. There are brightly decorated common rooms and four fireplaces. The carriage house has three rooms. There are two rooms with Jacuzzi tubs. The innkeepers like to share a "secret waterfall" within a 30-minute walk from the inn.

Innkeeper(s): Mary Anne Buckley. $100-150. MC, VISA, AX, DS, PC, TC. 10 rooms with PB, 1 with FP and 2 suites. Breakfast and afternoon tea included in rates. Types of meals: Full bkfst and early coffee/tea. Fax and copier on premises. Amusement parks, antiquing, fishing, hiking, live theater, parks, shopping, downhill skiing, cross-country skiing and water sports nearby.

Location: Mountains.

Publicity: *Mid-Atlantic Country and Bridal Guide.*

"Thanks for a great wedding weekend. Everything was perfect."

Certificate may be used: Year-round weekdays only, Sunday-Thursday evenings.

The Merry Inn

PO Box 757, Rt 390
Canadensis, PA 18325-0757
(717)595-2011 (800)858-4182

Circa 1942. Set in the picturesque Pocono Mountains, this bed & breakfast is a 90-minute drive from the metropolitan New York and Philadelphia areas. The turn-of-the-century,

mountainside home was built by two sisters and at one time was used as a boarding house. Current owners and innkeepers Meredyth and Chris Huggard have decorated their B&B using an eclectic mix of styles. Each guest room is individually appointed, with styles ranging from Victorian to country. Guests enjoy use of an outdoor Jacuzzi set into the mountainside. Bedrooms are set up to accommodate families, and children are welcome here.

Innkeeper(s): Meredyth & Christopher Huggard. $75-95. MC, VISA, PC, TC. 6 rooms with PB. Breakfast included in rates. Type of meal: Full bkfst. Beds: KQDT. Cable TV and VCR in room. Jacuzzi (outdoor) on premises. Antiquing, fishing, golf, live theater, parks, shopping, downhill skiing, cross-country skiing and water sports nearby.

Pets allowed: Dogs must be trained, $25 deposit.

Location: Mountains.

Certificate may be used: Anytime midweek, weekends Nov. 15-April 15. No holidays.

Carlisle   J11

Line Limousin Farmhouse B&B

2070 Ritner Hwy
Carlisle, PA 17013-9303
(717)243-1281

Circa 1864. The grandchildren of Bob and Joan are the ninth generation of Lines to enjoy this 200-year-old homestead. A stone and brick exterior accents the farmhouse's graceful style, while inside, family heirlooms attest to the home's longevity. This is a breeding stock farm of 110 acres and the cattle raised here, Limousin, originate from the Limoges area of France. Giant maples shade the lawn and there are woods and stone fences.

Innkeeper(s): Bob & Joan Line. $65-85. PC. 4 rooms, 2 with PB. Breakfast included in rates. Type of meal: Full bkfst. Beds: KQT. Cable TV and phone in room. Air conditioning. VCR and guest refrigerator on premises. Amusement parks, antiquing, fishing, golf, live theater, parks, shopping, cross-country skiing and sporting events nearby.

Location: Country.

"Returning to your home each evening was like returning to our own home, that's how comfortable and warm it was."

Certificate may be used: March 20-Nov. 20, Monday-Thursday, except special events. Smoking prohibited.

Pheasant Field B&B

150 Hickorytown Rd
Carlisle, PA 17013-9732
(717)258-0717 Fax:(717)258-0717
Internet: www.pa.net/pheasant
E-mail: pheasant@pa.net

Circa 1800. Located on eight acres of central Pennsylvania farmland, this brick, two-story Federal-style farmhouse features wooden shutters and a covered front porch. Most rooms include a TV and telephone. An early 19th-century stone barn is on the property, and horse boarding often is available. The

Appalachian Trail is less than a mile away. Fly-fishing is popular at Yellow Breeches and Letort Spring. Dickinson College and Carlisle Fairgrounds are other points of interest.

Innkeeper(s): Denise Fegan. $85-120. MC, VISA, AX. 4 rooms with PB. Breakfast included in rates. Types of meals: Full bkfst and early coffee/tea.

Beds: KQT. Cable TV and phone in room. Air conditioning. VCR, fax and piano on premises. Amusement parks, antiquing, fishing, live theater, downhill skiing and cross-country skiing nearby.
Location: Country.
Publicity: *Outdoor Traveler and Harrisburg Magazine.*

"You have an outstanding, charming and warm house. I felt for the first time as being home."
Certificate may be used: November through March.

Clearfield   G7

Christopher Kratzer House

101 E Cherry St
Clearfield, PA 16830-2315
(814)765-5024 (888)252-2632
E-mail: bbaggett@uplink.net

Circa 1840. This inn is the oldest home in town, built by a carpenter and architect who also started Clearfield's first newspaper. The innkeepers keep a book of history about the house and town for interested guests. The interior is a mix of antiques from different eras, many are family pieces. There are collections of art and musical instruments. Two guest rooms afford views of the Susquehanna River. Refreshments and a glass of wine are served in the afternoons. The inn's Bridal Suite Special includes complimentary champagne, fruit and snacks, and breakfast may be served in the privacy of your room. Small wedding receptions, brunches and parties are hosted at the inn.
Innkeeper(s): Bruce & Ginny Baggett. $65-80. MC, VISA, DS, PC, TC. 4 rooms, 2 with PB. Breakfast, afternoon tea and snacks/refreshments included in rates. Types of meals: Full gourmet bkfst and early coffee/tea. Beds: KQT. Cable TV, phone and ceiling fan in room. Air conditioning. Library on premises. Antiquing, fishing, hiking, biking, playground across street, live theater, parks, shopping, cross-country skiing and sporting events nearby.
Location: Small town.
Publicity: *Local PA newspapers.*

"Past and present joyously intermingle in this place."
Certificate may be used: Nov. 30-Aug. 31, Sunday-Saturday.

Victorian Loft B&B

216 S Front St
Clearfield, PA 16830-2218
(814)765-4805 (800)798-0456 Fax:(814)765-9596
Internet: www.virtualcities.com/pa/victorianloft.htm
E-mail: pdurant@csrlink.net

Circa 1894. Accommodations at this bed & breakfast are available in either a historic Victorian home on the riverfront or in a private, three-bedroom cabin. The white brick home is dressed with colorful, gingerbread trim, and inside, a grand staircase, stained glass and antique furnishings add to the Victorian charm. The suite is ideal for families as it contains two bedrooms, a living room, dining room, kitchen and a bath with a whirlpool tub. The cabin, Cedarwood Lodge, sleeps six and is located on eight, wooded acres near Parker Dam State Park and Elliot State Park. This is a favorite setting for small groups.
Innkeeper(s): Tim & Peggy Durant. $55-125. MC, VISA, DS, PC, TC. 3 rooms, 1 with PB, 2 suites and 1 cottage. Breakfast included in rates. Types of meals: Full bkfst and early coffee/tea. Beds: QD. Phone and VCR in room. Whirlpool on premises. Antiquing, fishing, live theater, parks, shopping, cross-country skiing, sporting events and water sports nearby.
Pets allowed: By prior arrangement.
Location: Small town.
Publicity: *Clearfield Progress and Tri-County.*

"A feeling of old-fashioned beauty. The elegance of roses and lace. All wrapped up into a romantic moment."
Certificate may be used: Sunday through Thursday only, based on availability.

Cooksburg   F5

Clarion River Lodge

HC 1 Box 22D
Cooksburg, PA 16217-9704
(814)744-8171 (800)648-6743 Fax:(814)744-8553

Circa 1964. This lodge is a rustic retreat above the Clarion River and surrounded by Cook Forest. Its pegged-oak flooring, oak beams, pine ceiling, wild cherry and butternut paneling and fieldstone fireplace add to the lodge's natural character. A distinctive glassed-in breezeway leads from the main building to the guest wing. Rooms are decorated with modern Scandinavian decor. Dinner and continental breakfast packages available.
Innkeeper(s): Ellen O'Day. $72-129. MC, VISA, AX, TC. 20 rooms with PB and 1 conference room. Breakfast included in rates. Type of meal: Cont. Beds: KQ. Cable TV and phone in room. Air conditioning. VCR and fax on premises. Antiquing, fishing, live theater, parks and shopping nearby.
Location: River.
Publicity: *Pittsburgh Press and Pittsburgh Women's Journal.*

"If your idea of Paradise is a secluded rustic retreat surrounded by the most beautiful country this side of the Rockies, search no more."
Certificate may be used: November-April, Sunday-Thursday, no holidays.

Eagles Mere   E13

Crestmont Inn

Crestmont Dr
Eagles Mere, PA 17731
(570)525-3519 (800)522-8767
Internet: www.crestmont-inn.com
E-mail: crestmnt@epix.net

Eagles Mere has been a vacation site since the late 19th century and still abounds with Victorian charm. The Crestmont Inn is no exception. The rooms are tastefully decorated with Oriental rugs, flowers and elegant furnishings. Suites include two-person whirlpool tubs, and one has a fireplace. A hearty country breakfast is served each morning, and guests also are treated to a five-course dinner in the candle-lit dining room. Savor a variety of mouth-watering entrees and finish off the evening with scrumptious desserts such as fresh fruit pies, English trifle or Orange Charlotte. The cocktail lounge is a perfect place to mingle and enjoy hors d'oeuvres, wines and spirits. The inn grounds offer a large swimming pool, tennis and shuffleboard courts. The Wyoming State Forest borders the property, and golfing is just minutes away.
Innkeeper(s): Karen Oliver & Doug Rider. $90-178. MC, VISA. 14 rooms. Breakfast included in rates. Type of meal: Full bkfst.
Certificate may be used: Monday through Thursday.

Shady Lane B&B

Allegheny Ave, PO Box 314
Eagles Mere, PA 17731-0314
(717)525-3394 (800)524-1248

Circa 1947. This ranch-style house rests on two mountaintop acres. Eagles Mere is a Victorian town with gaslights and old-fashioned village shops. Crystal clear Eagles Mere Lake is surrounded by Laurel Path, a popular scenic walk. The Endless Mountains provide cross-country skiing, fishing and hiking. Tobogganing is popular on the Eagles Mere Toboggan Slide.

Innkeeper(s): Pat & Dennis Dougherty. $85. TC. 8 rooms, 7 with PB and 1 suite. Breakfast and afternoon tea included in rates. Type of meal: Full gourmet bkfst. Beds: KQDT. Ceiling fan in room. Antiquing, fishing, lake, parks, shopping and cross-country skiing nearby.

Location: Mountains.

Certificate may be used: Sunday through Thursday from Sept. 1-June 30 (not in July or August).

East Berlin (Gettysburg Area) *K12*

Bechtel Victorian Mansion B&B Inn

400 W King St
East Berlin (Gettysburg Area), PA 17316
(717)259-7760 (800)579-1108
Internet: www.bbonline.com/pa/bechtel/

Circa 1897. The town of East Berlin, near Lancaster and 18 miles east of Gettysburg, was settled by Pennsylvania Germans prior to the American Revolution. William Leas, a wealthy banker, built this many-gabled romantic Queen Anne mansion, now listed in the National Register. The inn is furnished with an abundance of museum-quality antiques and collections. Floral comforters top many of the handsome bedsteads.

Innkeeper(s): Richard & Carol Carlson. $70-150. MC, VISA, AX, DS, PC, TC. 7 rooms with PB and 2 suites. Breakfast included in rates. Types of meals: Full bkfst and early coffee/tea. Beds: KQD. Turndown service in room. Air conditioning. VCR on premises. Amusement parks, antiquing, bicycling, fishing, golf, hiking, live theater, museums, shopping, downhill skiing and wineries nearby.

Location: Historic district-German town.

Publicity: *Washington Post and Richmond Times.*

Certificate may be used: November through Sept. 15, Sunday through Thursday. Non-holiday Fridays and Saturdays, when rooms are available.

East Petersburg (Lancaster County) *K14*

The George Zahm House

6070 Main St
East Petersburg (Lancaster County), PA 17520-1266
(717)569-6026

Circa 1856. The bright red exterior of this Federal-style inn is a landmark in this village. The home is named for its builder and first resident, who constructed his sturdy dwelling with 18-inch-thick brick walls. Innkeeping is a family affair for owners Robyn Kemple-Keeports and husband, Jeff Keeports, who run the inn along with Robyn's mother, Daneen. The rooms are inviting and comfortable, yet elegant. Beautiful drapery, rich wallpapers and a collection of antique furniture combine to give the house an opulent feel. Many of the pieces are family heirlooms. Breakfasts with homemade specialty cakes, breads, Belgian waffles and fresh fruits are served in the dining room on a table set with Blue Willow china.

Innkeeper(s): Robyn & Jeff Keeports. $65-85. MC, VISA, PC, TC. 4 rooms, 3 with PB and 1 suite. Breakfast and afternoon tea included in rates. Type of meal: Cont plus. Beds: KQDT. Ceiling fan and antiques in room. Air conditioning. Iron, ironing board and guest refrigerator on premises. Handicap access. Amusement parks, antiquing, outlets, Farmer's Markets, Amish countryside, live theater, parks, shopping and sporting events nearby.

Location: small village.

"An oasis - truly a wonderful place. Most charming."
Certificate may be used: Year-round, Sunday-Thursday.

Elizabethtown *J13*

West Ridge Guest House

1285 W Ridge Rd
Elizabethtown, PA 17022-9739
(717)367-7783 (877)367-7783 Fax:(717)367-8468
Internet: www.westridgebandb.com
E-mail: wridgeroad@aol.com

Circa 1890. Guests at this country home have many choices. They may opt to relax and enjoy the view from the gazebo, or perhaps work out in the inn's exercise room. The hot tub provides yet another soothing possibility. Ask about rooms with whirlpool tubs. The 20-acre grounds also include two fishing ponds. The innkeepers pass out a breakfast menu to their guests, allowing them to choose the time they prefer to eat and a choice of entrees. Along with the traditional fruit, muffins or coffeecake and meats, guests choose items such as omelets, waffles or pancakes.

Innkeeper(s): Alice P. Heisey. $60-120. MC, VISA, AX. 9 rooms with PB, 3 with FP and 2 suites. Breakfast included in rates. Type of meal: Full bkfst. Beds: KQ. Cable TV, phone, ceiling fan and VCR in room. Air conditioning. Fax, copier and spa on premises. Antiquing, fishing, parks and shopping nearby.

Location: Rural, country setting.

Certificate may be used: All year, Sunday-Thursday, no holidays.

Elizabethville *I12*

The Inn at Elizabethville

30 W Main St, Box V
Elizabethville, PA 17023
(717)362-3476 Fax:(717)362-4571

Circa 1883. This comfortable, two-story house was owned by a Civil War veteran and founder of a local wagon company. The owners decided to buy and fix up the house to help support their other business, renovating old houses. The conference room features an unusual fireplace with cabinets and painted decorations. Rooms are filled with antiques and Mission oak-style furniture. County auctions, local craft fairs and outdoor activities entice guests. Comfortable living rooms, porches and a sun parlor are available for relaxation.

Innkeeper(s): Jennifer Kutzor. $49-65. MC, VISA, AX, TC. 7 rooms with PB and 1 conference room. Breakfast included in rates. Type of meal: Cont. Beds: DT. Ceiling fan in room. Air conditioning. VCR, fax and copier on premises. Antiquing, fishing, parks, shopping and water sports nearby.

Location: City.

Publicity: *Harrisburg Patriot-News and Upper Dauphin Sentinel.*

Certificate may be used: Anytime with prior notice.

Ephrata *J14*

Doneckers, The Guesthouse, Inns

409 N State St
Ephrata, PA 17522
(717)738-9502 Fax:(717)738-9554

Circa 1777. Jacob Gorgas, a devout member of the Ephrata Cloister and a clock maker, noted for crafting 150 eight-day Gorgas grandfather clocks, built this stately Dutch Colonial-style home. Guests can opt to stay in one of four antique-filled homes. The 1777 House, which includes 12 rooms, features hand-stenciled walls, suites with whirlpool baths, fireplaces,

original stone masonry and an antique tiled floor. The home served as a tavern in the 1800s and an elegant inn in the early 1900s. The Homestead includes four rooms some with fireplaces and amenities such as Jacuzzis, sitting areas and four-poster beds. The Guesthouse features a variety of beautifully decorated rooms each named and themed in honor of local landmarks or significant citizens. The Gerhart House memorializes prominent innkeepers or hotel owners in Ephrata's history. All guests enjoy an expansive breakfast with freshly squeezed juice, fruits, breakfast cheeses and other delicacies. The homes are part of the Donecker Community, which features upscale fashion stores, art galleries and a restaurant within walking distance of the 1777 House.

Innkeeper(s): Mary DeSimone. $65-210. MC, VISA, AX, DC, CB, DS, PC, TC. 40 rooms, 39 with PB and 13 suites. Breakfast included in rates. Types of meals: Full gourmet bkfst and cont plus. Beds: KQDT. Phone and cable music in room. Central air. VCR and fax on premises. Amusement parks, antiquing, art galleries, golf, live theater, museums, parks, shopping and wineries nearby.

Location: Small town.

Publicity: *Daily News and Country Inns.*

"A peaceful refuge."

Certificate may be used: Sunday-Thursday, except holidays, year round.

Erwinna   117

Golden Pheasant Inn

763 River Rd
Erwinna, PA 18920-9254
(610)294-9595 (800)830-4474 Fax:(610)294-9882
Internet: www.goldenpheasant.com
E-mail: barbara@goldenpheasant.com

Circa 1857. The Golden Pheasant is well established as the location of a wonderful, gourmet restaurant, but it is also home to six charming guest rooms decorated by Barbara Faure. Four-poster canopy beds and antiques

decorate the rooms, which offer views of the canal and river. The fieldstone inn was built as a mule-barge stop for travelers heading down the Delaware Canal. The five-acre grounds resemble a French-country estate, and guests can enjoy the lush surroundings in a plant-filled greenhouse dining room. There are two other dining rooms, including an original fieldstone room with exposed beams and stone walls with decorative copper pots hanging here and there. The restaurant's French cuisine, prepared by chef Michel Faure, is outstanding. One might start off with Michel's special pheasant pate, followed by a savory onion soup baked with three cheeses. A mix of greens dressed in vinaigrette cleanses the palate before one samples roast duck in a luxurious raspberry, ginger and rum sauce or perhaps a sirloin steak flamed in cognac.

Innkeeper(s): Barbara & Michel Faure. $95-195. MC, VISA, AX, DC, CB, DS, PC, TC. 6 rooms with PB, 2 with FP, 1 suite, 1 cottage and 3 conference rooms. Breakfast included in rates. Types of meals: Cont plus and early coffee/tea. Beds: Q. Phone, ceiling fan and jacuzzi tub/fireplaces in room. Air conditioning. Fax, copier, library and canal path for walking on premises. Antiquing, art galleries, bicycling, canoeing/kayaking, fishing, golf, hiking, horseback riding, historic Doylestown, New Hope, Washington Crossing, live theater, museums, parks, shopping, cross-country skiing, tennis, water sports and wineries nearby.

Pets allowed: cottage only.

Location: Country.

Publicity: *The Philadelphia Inquirer, New York Times, Philadelphia Magazine., Food Network and Fox.*

"A more stunningly romantic spot is hard to imagine. A taste of France on the banks of the Delaware."

Certificate may be used: Sunday-Thursday, excluding holidays.

Erwinna (Bucks County)   117

Evermay-On-The-Delaware

River Rd, PO Box 60
Erwinna (Bucks County), PA 18920
(610)294-9100 Fax:(610)294-8249
Internet: www.evermay.com
E-mail: moffly@evermay.com

Circa 1700. Twenty-five acres of Bucks County at its best — rolling green meadows, lawns, stately maples and the silvery Delaware River, surround this three-story manor. Serving as an inn since 1871, it has hosted such guests as the Barrymore family. Rich walnut wainscoting, a grandfather clock and twin fireplaces warm the parlor, scented by vases of roses or gladiolus. Antique-filled guest rooms overlook the river or gardens.

Innkeeper(s): Bill & Danielle Moffly. $135-350. MC, VISA, PC, TC. 18 rooms with PB, 1 suite, 2 cottages and 2 conference rooms. Breakfast and afternoon tea included in rates. Type of meal: Cont plus. Beds: QD. Phone and turndown service in room. Air conditioning. VCR, fax, copier and library on premises. Handicap access. Antiquing, fishing, live theater, parks, shopping, cross-country skiing, sporting events and water sports nearby.

Location: Rural Bucks County.

Publicity: *New York Times, Philadelphia, Travel & Leisure, Food and Wine, Child, Colonial Homes and USAir Magazine.*

"It was pure perfection. Everything from the flowers to the wonderful food."

Certificate may be used: Sunday-Thursday, excluding holidays.

Gettysburg   L11

James Gettys Hotel

27 Chambersburg St
Gettysburg, PA 17325
(717)337-1334 Fax:(717)334-2103
Internet: www.jamesgettyshotel.com
E-mail: jghotel@mail.cvn.net

Circa 1803. Listed in the National Register, this newly renovated four-story hotel once served as a tavern through the Battle of Gettysburg and was used as a hospital for soldiers. Outfitted with cranberry colored awnings and a gold painted entrance, the hotel offers a tea room, nature store and gallery on the street level. From the lobby, a polished chestnut staircase leads to the guest quarters. All accommodations are suites with living rooms appointed with home furnishings, and each has its own kitchenette. Breakfasts of home-baked scones and coffee cake are brought to your room.

Innkeeper(s): Stephanie McSherry. $125-145. MC, VISA, AX, DS, PC, TC. 11 suites. Breakfast included in rates. Type of meal: Cont. Beds: QD. Cable TV, phone and turndown service in room. Air conditioning. VCR and fax on premises. Handicap access. Amusement parks, antiquing, art galleries, bicycling, fishing, golf, hiking, horseback riding, museums, parks, shopping, downhill skiing, cross-country skiing, tennis and wineries nearby.

Location: Small historic town.

Certificate may be used: Monday through Thursday, excluding holidays and special events, Jan. 1-Dec. 30.

Keystone Inn B&B

231 Hanover St
Gettysburg, PA 17325-1913
(717)337-3888

Circa 1913. Furniture maker Clayton Reaser constructed this three-story brick Victorian with a wide-columned porch hugging the north and west sides. Cut stone graces every door and window sill, each with a keystone. A chestnut staircase ascends the full three stories, and the interior is decorated with comfortable furnishings, ruffles and lace.

Innkeeper(s): Wilmer & Doris Martin. $69-109. MC, VISA, DS. 5 rooms with PB and 1 suite. Breakfast and afternoon tea included in rates. Types of meals: Full bkfst and early coffee/tea. Beds: KQDT. Phone in room. Air conditioning. Library on premises. Amusement parks, antiquing, fishing, Civil War Battlefield, historic sites, live theater, parks, shopping, downhill skiing and cross-country skiing nearby.

Location: Small town.

Publicity: *Lancaster Sunday News, York Sunday News, Hanover Sun, Allentown Morning Call, Gettysburg Times, York Sunday News, Pennsylvania, Lancaster Sunday News, Los Angeles Times., York Sunday News, Pennsylvania, Lancaster Sunday News and Los Angeles Times.*

"We slept like lambs. This home has a warmth that is soothing."
Certificate may be used: November-April, Monday-Thursday.

Greensburg   J4

Huntland Farm B&B

RD 9, Box 21
Greensburg, PA 15601-9232
(724)834-8483 Fax:(724)838-8253

Circa 1848. Porches and flower gardens surround the three-story, columned, brick Georgian manor that presides over the inn's 100 acres. Corner bedrooms are furnished with English antiques. Fallingwater, the Frank Lloyd Wright house, is nearby. Other attractions include Hidden Valley, Ohiopyle water rafting, Bushy Run and Fort Ligonier.

Innkeeper(s): Robert & Elizabeth Weidlein. $75-85. AX, PC, TC. 4 rooms, 2 with FP. Breakfast included in rates. Type of meal: Full bkfst. Beds: KQDT. Ceiling fan in room. VCR, fax, copier and library on premises. Antiquing, live theater, parks and shopping nearby.

Location: Country.

Publicity: *Tribune Review.*

Certificate may be used: All year. Nov. 1-May 1, any day; May 1-Oct. 31, weekdays only.

Grove City   F2

Snow Goose Inn

112 E Main St
Grove City, PA 16127
(412)458-4644 (800)317-4644
Internet: www.bbonline.com/pa/snowgoose/

Circa 1895. This home was built as a residence for young women attending Grove City College. It was later used as a family home and offices for a local doctor. Eventually, it was transformed into an intimate bed & breakfast, offering four homey guest rooms. The interior is comfortable, decorated in country style with stenciling, collectibles and a few of the signature geese on display. Museums, shops, Amish farms and several state parks are in the vicinity, offering many activities.

Innkeeper(s): Orvil & Dorothy McMillen. $65. MC, VISA. 4 rooms with PB. Breakfast and snacks/refreshments included in rates. Types of meals: Full gourmet bkfst and early coffee/tea. Beds: QD. Air conditioning. VCR on premises. Amusement parks, antiquing, fishing, golf, live theater, parks, shopping, downhill skiing, cross-country skiing, sporting events, tennis and water sports nearby.

Location: City.

Publicity: *Allied News.*

"Your thoughtful touches and "homey" atmosphere were a balm to our chaotic lives."

Certificate may be used: All year.

Hanover   L12

Beechmont B&B Inn

315 Broadway
Hanover, PA 17331-2505
(717)632-3013 (800)553-7009

Circa 1834. This gracious Georgian inn was a witness to the Civil War's first major battle on free soil, the Battle of Hanover. Decorated in Federal-period antiques, several guest rooms are named for the battle's commanders. The romantic Diller Suite contains a marble fireplace and queen canopy bed. The inn is noted for elegant breakfasts.

Innkeeper(s): William & Susan Day. $80-135. MC, VISA, AX, DS, PC, TC. 7 rooms with PB, 3 with FP, 3 suites and 1 conference room. Breakfast, afternoon tea and snacks/refreshments included in rates. Types of meals: Full gourmet bkfst and early coffee/tea. Beds: QD. Cable TV, phone and ceiling fan in room. Air conditioning. Copier and library on premises. Amusement parks, antiquing, fishing, live theater, parks, shopping, downhill skiing, cross-country skiing, sporting events and water sports nearby.

Location: City.

Publicity: *Evening Sun and York Daily Record.*

"I had a marvelous time at your charming, lovely inn."
Certificate may be used: Sunday-Thursday, except holidays.

Harrisburg   J12

Abide With Me B&B

2601 Walnut St
Harrisburg, PA 17103-1952
(717)236-5873
Internet: www.user.pa.net/~adamsew/abidebb

Circa 1870. A city historical site, this B&B is a brick Second Empire Victorian. There are three stories with shuttered windows, a large bay and a rounded front veranda. Oak, parquet and wide-plank floors and fireplaces add to the interest inside. Modestly furnished, the B&B offers some antiques and country pieces. The Harrisburg State Capital is a mile-and-a-half away.

Innkeeper(s): Don & Joyce Adams. $56. PC. 4 rooms. Breakfast included in rates. Types of meals: Full gourmet bkfst and early coffee/tea. Beds: QDT. Air conditioning. VCR on premises. Amusement parks, antiquing, fishing, live theater, parks, shopping, sporting events and water sports nearby.

Certificate may be used: Anytime available except Auto Show week in October.

Hawley E17

Academy Street B&B

528 Academy St
Hawley, PA 18428-1434
(570)226-3430 Fax:(570)226-1910
Internet: www.academybb.com
E-mail: shlazan@worldnet.att.net

Circa 1863. This restored Civil War Victorian home boasts a mahogany front door with the original glass paneling, two large fireplaces (one in mosaic, the other in fine polished marble) and a living room with oak sideboard, polished marble mantel and yellow pine floor. The airy guest rooms have canopied brass beds. Guests are welcome to afternoon tea, which includes an array of cakes and pastries. Full, gourmet breakfasts are served on weekends.

Innkeeper(s): Judith Lazan. $65-90. MC, VISA. 7 rooms, 4 with PB. Breakfast and afternoon tea included in rates. Type of meal: Early coffee/tea. Beds: QDT. Cable TV and ceiling fan in room. Air conditioning. VCR on premises. Amusement parks, antiquing, fishing, live theater, parks, shopping and water sports nearby.

Publicity: *Wayne Independent and Citizens' Voice.*

"Truly wonderful everything!"

Certificate may be used: Monday through Friday.

Holicong J18

Barley Sheaf Farm

5281 York Rd, Rt 202 Box 10
Holicong, PA 18928
(215)794-5104 Fax:(215)794-5332
Internet: www.barleysheaf.com
E-mail: info@barleysheaf.com

Circa 1740. Situated on part of the original William Penn land grant, this beautiful stone house with ebony green shuttered windows and mansard roof is set on 30 acres of farmland. Once owned by noted playwright George Kaufman, it was the gathering place for the Marx Brothers, Lillian Hellman and S.J. Perlman. The bank barn, pond and majestic old trees round out a beautiful setting.

Innkeeper(s): Peter Suess. $105-235. MC, VISA, AX, PC, TC. 12 rooms with PB, 3 with FP, 4 suites and 3 conference rooms. Breakfast and afternoon tea included in rates. Types of meals: Full bkfst and early coffee/tea. Beds: KQD. Phone in room. Air conditioning. VCR, fax, copier and swimming on premises. Handicap access. Amusement parks, antiquing, fishing, museums, live theater, parks, shopping, downhill skiing, cross-country skiing and water sports nearby.

Location: Country.

Publicity: *Country Living, Romantic Inns of America and CNC Business Channel.*
Certificate may be used: Sunday through Thursday, no holidays.

Hollidaysburg I8

Hoenstine's B&B

418 N Montgomery St
Hollidaysburg, PA 16648-1432
(814)695-0632 (888)550-9655 Fax:(814)696-7310

Circa 1830. This inn is an antique-lover's dream, as it boasts many pieces of original furniture. Stained-glass windows and the 10-foot-high ceilings add to the atmosphere. Breakfast is served in the home's formal dining room. Guests will sleep well in the comfortable and beautifully decorated rooms, especially knowing that the house is being protected by innkeeper Barbara Hoenstine's black standard poodle, Dickens, who is a happy guide and escort around the canal-era town. The B&B is within walking distance of shops, restaurants and the downtown historic district.

Innkeeper(s): Barbara Hoenstine. $50-70. MC, VISA, PC, TC. 4 rooms, 1 with PB. Breakfast included in rates. Type of meal: Full bkfst. Beds: QDT. Cable TV, ceiling fan and VCR in room. Fax, copier and library on premises. Amusement parks, antiquing, fishing, golf, hiking-rails to trails, live theater, parks, shopping, downhill skiing, cross-country skiing, sporting events, tennis and water sports nearby.

Location: Small town.

"Thank you for a truly calm and quiet week. This was our first B&B experience and it won't be our last."

Certificate may be used: Monday-Friday anytime, or last minute (same day).

Holtwood L14

Country Cottage

163 Magnolia Dr
Holtwood, PA 17532-9773
(717)284-2559 (800)560-3801

This simple brick cottage is adjacent to a main house where the innkeepers live. There are two comfortably furnished bedrooms, a dining room, small kitchen and a family room with a large stone fireplace. Two stained-glass windows flank the front door. Guests have use of an outdoor deck and spa. The innkeepers offer homemade muffins and coffee cake in the mornings. The cottage is close to many Pennsylvania Dutch country attractions.

Innkeeper(s): Donald & Jo Davis. $95. PC. 2 rooms, 1 with PB, 1 with FP and 1 cottage. Breakfast included in rates. Type of meal: Cont. Beds: QD. Phone, ceiling fan and VCR in room. Air conditioning. Spa on premises. Amusement parks, antiquing, fishing, golf, fishing, live theater, parks, shopping, downhill skiing, cross-country skiing, sporting events, tennis and water sports nearby.

Pets allowed: Well-behaved.

Location: woods also.

Certificate may be used: Sunday-Friday, all year except Thanksgiving & Christmas holidays.

Honey Grove   *I10*

The Inn at McCullochs Mills

RR 1, Box 194
Honey Grove, PA 17035-9801
(717)734-3628 (800)377-5106
Internet: www.mcinn.com

Circa 1890. Innkeepers Verne and Christine Penner spent several years restoring their inn, once home to a local millmaster. The original home burned, and this charming 1882 Victorian was built in its place. The Penners offer a multitude of romantic amenities and extras that will make any getaway memorable. Carriage rides and moonlight sleigh rides are among the choices. Guests are pampered with gourmet breakfasts served by candlelight, chocolates, fresh flowers and more. Some rooms include clawfoot or Jacuzzi tubs.

Innkeeper(s): Verne & Christine Penner. $59-89. MC, VISA, DS, PC. 5 rooms with PB. Breakfast, afternoon tea and snacks/refreshments included in rates. Types of meals: Full gourmet bkfst and early coffee/tea. Beds: QD. Turndown service, ceiling fan and 2 private Jacuzzis for two in room. Air conditioning. Antiquing, canoeing/kayaking, fishing, golf, country sightseeing, shopping and cross-country skiing nearby.

Location: Trout stream on property.

Publicity: *Pennsylvania Magazine.*

Certificate may be used: Any weekday, Monday-Thursday.

Intercourse (Lancaster County)   *K14*

Carriage Corner

3705 E Newport Rd, PO Box 371
Intercourse (Lancaster County), PA 17534-0371
(717)768-3059
Internet: www.bbonline.com/pa/carriagecorner/

Circa 1981. Located in the heart of Amish farmland, this two-story Colonial rests on two, pastural acres. Homemade, country breakfasts are served, often including innkeeper Gordon Schuit's special recipe for oatmeal pancakes. A five-minute walk will take guests into the village where they'll find Amish buggies traveling down the lanes and more than 100 shops displaying local crafts, pottery, quilts and furniture, as well as art galleries. The innkeepers can arrange for dinners in an Amish home, buggy rides and working Amish farm tours. Longwood Gardens, Hershey's Chocolate World and Gettysburg are also nearby.

Innkeeper(s): Gordon & Gwen Schuit. $72-90. MC, VISA, PC. 5 rooms with PB. Breakfast included in rates. Type of meal: Full bkfst. Beds: Q. Cable TV in room. Air conditioning. Antiquing, hub of Amish farmland, Amish dinners arranged, buggy rides, working Amish farm tours, Strasbury Steam Railroad, Railroad Museum of PA, "Noah" at sight and sound, festivals and auctions, craft and quilt fairs, farmers' markets and roadside stands, Longwood Gardens, Hershey's Chocolate World, Gettysburg and shopping nearby.

Location: Amish Farmland.

Certificate may be used: January and February, excluding holiday weekends. March-May, November, December, Sunday through Wednesday, excluding special events.

Jennerstown   *J5*

The Olde Stage Coach B&B

1760 Lincoln Hwy
Jennerstown, PA 15547
(814)629-7440
Internet: www.oldestagecoachbandb.com
E-mail: carol@oldestagecoachbandb.com

Circa 1752. This renovated two-story Country Victorian farmhouse, located in the Laurel Mountains on historical Lincoln Highway, once served as a stagecoach rest stop. The yellow house has white trim and a wraparound porch overlooking the inn's acre. The common room features Victorian antiques, and guest rooms offer a fresh country decor. Blueberry French toast is a specialty of the innkeepers as well as home-baked breads and apple pancakes. The immediate area boasts the Mountain Playhouse, three golf courses within three miles, trout streams and lakes, hiking, skiing and outlet shopping — something for all generations.

Innkeeper(s): Carol & George Neuhof. $70-85. MC, VISA, PC, TC. 4 rooms with PB. Breakfast and snacks/refreshments included in rates. Types of meals: Full bkfst and early coffee/tea. Beds: QDT. Ceiling fan, chair and table in room. VCR, fax, library and wrap-around porch with swing on premises. Amusement parks, antiquing, fishing, golf, Nascar racing, live theater, parks, shopping, downhill skiing and cross-country skiing nearby.

Location: Mountains.

Certificate may be used: Jan. 2 through Dec. 31, Sunday-Thursday except special holidays.

Jim Thorpe   *H15*

Harry Packer Mansion

Packer Hill, PO Box 458
Jim Thorpe, PA 18229
(570)325-8566
Internet: www.murdermansion.com
E-mail: mystery@murdermansion.com

Circa 1874. This extravagant Second Empire mansion was used as the model for the haunted mansion in Disney World. It was constructed of New England sandstone, and local brick and stone trimmed in cast iron. Past ornately carved columns on the front veranda, guests enter 400-pound, solid walnut doors. The opulent interior includes marble mantels, hand-painted ceilings and elegant antiques. Murder-mystery weekends are a mansion specialty, and Victorian Balls are held in June and December.

Innkeeper(s): Robert & Patricia Handwerk. $85-175. MC, VISA, TC. 13 rooms, 11 with PB, 3 suites and 3 conference rooms. Breakfast included in rates. Types of meals: Full gourmet bkfst and early coffee/tea. Beds: QD. Turndown service and ceiling fan in room. Air conditioning. VCR on premises. Antiquing, fishing, parks, shopping, downhill skiing, cross-country skiing and water sports nearby.

Location: Mountains.

Publicity: *Philadelphia Inquirer, New York, Victorian Homes and Washington Post.*

"What a beautiful place and your hospitality was wonderful. We will see you again soon."

Certificate may be used: Sunday through Thursday night except for holidays.

The Inn at Jim Thorpe

24 Broadway
Jim Thorpe, PA 18229
(570)325-2599 (800)329-2599 Fax:(570)325-9145
Internet: www.innjt.com
E-mail: innjt@ptd.net

Circa 1848. This massive New Orleans-style structure, now restored, hosted some colorful 19th-century guests, including Thomas Edison, John D. Rockefeller and Buffalo Bill. All rooms

are appointed with Victorian furnishings and have private baths with pedestal sinks and marble floors. The suites include fireplaces and whirlpool tubs. Also on the premises are a Victorian dining Room, Irish pub and a conference center. The inn is situated in the heart of Jim Thorpe, a quaint Victorian town that was known at the turn of the century as the "Switzerland of America." Historic mansion tours, museums and art galleries are nearby, and mountain biking and whitewater rafting are among the outdoor activities.

Innkeeper(s): David Drury. $85-250. MC, VISA, AX, DC, DS, TC. 37 rooms with PB, 8 suites and 2 conference rooms. Breakfast included in rates. Type of meal: Cont plus. Beds: KQ. Cable TV, phone and 8 suites with whirlpools and fireplaces in room. Air conditioning. Fax, copier, game room and exercise room on premises. Handicap access. Antiquing, art galleries, bicycling, canoeing/kayaking, fishing, golf, hiking, horseback riding, museums, parks, shopping, downhill skiing and wineries nearby.

Publicity: *Philadelphia Inquirer, Pennsylvania Magazine and Allentown Morning Call.*

"We had the opportunity to spend a weekend at your lovely inn. Your staff is extremely friendly, helpful, and courteous. I can't remember when we felt so relaxed, we hope to come back again soon."

Certificate may be used: Nov. 1-June 30, Sunday-Thursday, excluding holidays and Dec. 24-28.

The Victorian

68 Broadway
Jim Thorpe, PA 18229-2022
(570)325-8107 Fax:(570)325-8107

Circa 1860. Historic Millionaire's Row is the site of this Victorian, which is painted a deep red hue with blue trim. Innkeeper Louise Ogilvie preserves the 19th-century ambiance throughout the home, decorating the place with Victorian furnishings and bright wallpapers. Most rooms are European in style and share a bath. The two suites include a private bath. The grounds include a garden. Louise's history is as fascinating as the historic home's past. She was an actress and cabaret singer in New York and was proprietor of a renown nightclub in San Juan, Puerto Rico.

Innkeeper(s): Louise Ogilvie. $55-85. MC, VISA, AX, DS, TC. 8 rooms, 2 with PB, 2 suites and 1 conference room. Breakfast included in rates. Type of meal: Full bkfst. Beds: KQDT. Cable TV, turndown service and ceiling fan in room. Air conditioning. VCR, fax, copier and library on premises. Antiquing, fishing, golf, parks, shopping, downhill skiing, cross-country skiing, tennis and water sports nearby.

Location: Mountains.

Publicity: *Times News.*

"We never thought our weekend would turn out to be such a wonderful adventure. Thank you for opening your inn to us."

Certificate may be used: Jan. 30-Dec. 31, Sunday-Thursday.

Kane   D6

Kane Manor Country Inn

230 Clay St
Kane, PA 16735-1410
(814)837-6522 (888)550-652 Fax:(814)837-6664
E-mail: kanemanor@aol.com

Circa 1896. This Georgian Revival inn, on 250 acres of woods and trails, was built for Dr. Elizabeth Kane, the first female doctor to practice in the area. Many of the family's possessions dating back to the American Revolution and the Civil War remain. Decor is a mixture

of old family items in an unpretentious country style. There is a pub, popular with locals, on the premises. The building is in the National Register.

Innkeeper(s): Joyce Benek. $89-99. MC, VISA, AX, DS, PC, TC. 10 rooms, 6 with PB. Breakfast included in rates. Types of meals: Full bkfst, cont plus, cont and early coffee/tea. Beds: DT. Cable TV in room. VCR, fax, copier and library on premises. Antiquing, fishing, parks, shopping, downhill skiing, cross-country skiing and water sports nearby.

Location: Mountains.

Publicity: *Pittsburgh Press, News Herald, Cleveland Plain Dealer and Youngstown Indicator.*

"It's a place I want to return to often, for rest and relaxation."

Certificate may be used: Jan. 1-Sept. 15 and Dec. 1-29.

Kennett Square   L16

Scarlett House

503 W State St
Kennett Square, PA 19348-3028
(610)444-9592 (800)820-9592

Circa 1910. This granite American four-square home features an extensive wraparound porch, a front door surrounded by leaded-glass windows and magnificent chestnut woodwork. Beyond the foyer are two downstairs parlors with fireplaces, while a second-floor parlor provides a sunny setting for afternoon tea. Rooms are furnished in romantic Victorian decor with period antiques and Oriental carpets. An elegant gourmet breakfast is served with fine china, silver, crystal and lace linens. Mushroom-shaped chocolate chip scones are a novel breakfast specialty at the inn—a reminder that this is the acclaimed mushroom capital of the world.

Innkeeper(s): Jane & Sam Snyder. $89-139. MC, VISA, AX, DS, TC. 4 rooms, 2 with PB, 1 suite and 1 conference room. Breakfast, afternoon tea and snacks/refreshments included in rates. Types of meals: Full gourmet bkfst and early coffee/tea. Beds: QD. Phone and ceiling fan in room. Central air. Longwood Gardens, Brandywine Valley attractions and Amish country nearby.

Location: Historic small town.

"Truly an enchanting place."

Certificate may be used: No holidays or holiday weekends. Jan. 1-Feb. 28, all week; March 1-Dec. 31, Sunday-Thursday only.

Lancaster   K14

1725 Historic Witmer's Tavern Inn & Museum

2014 Old Philadelphia Pike
Lancaster, PA 17602-3413
(717)299-5305
Internet: www.800padutch.com/1725histwit.html

Circa 1725. This pre-Revolutionary War inn is the oldest and most complete Pennsylvania inn still lodging travelers in its original building. Designated a Federal Landmark, the property has been restored to its original, pioneer style with hand-fashioned hardware and "bubbly" glass nine-over-six windows. There is even an Indian escape tunnel. Guest rooms feature antiques, fresh flowers, antique quilts and original wood-burning fireplaces. Revolutionary and Colonial dignitaries like Washington, Lafayette, Jefferson and Adams were entertained here. The Witmers gave provisions to hundreds of immigrants as they set up Conestoga Wagon trains and headed for western and southern homestead regions. Amish farmland is adjacent to and in the rear of the inn, and a lovely park is located across the street. The innkeeper, native to the area, can provide an abundance of local information. He can also plan extra touches for a special occasion, and guests also can make an appointment for a therapeutic massage.

Innkeeper(s): Brant Hartung. $70-110. PC. 7 rooms, 2 with PB, 5 with FP. Breakfast included in rates. Type of meal: Cont plus. Beds: D. Seven rooms with wood-burning fireplaces in room. Air conditioning. Tavern on premises. Amusement parks, antiquing, fishing, golf, nature preserves, auctions, Amish farms and villages, live theater, shopping, sporting events, tennis and water sports nearby.

Location: Edge of Amish farm.

Publicity: *Stuart News, Pennsylvania, Antique, Travel & Leisure, Mid-Atlantic, Country Living, Early American Life, Colonial Homes and USA Today.*

"Your personal attention and enthusiastic knowledge of the area and Witmer's history made it come alive and gave us the good feelings we came looking for."

Certificate may be used: December-April, Sunday through Thursday only, excluding all holidays.

Flowers & Thyme B&B

238 Strasburg Pike
Lancaster, PA 17602-1326
(717)393-1460 Fax:(717)399-1986
Internet: www.members.aol.com/padutchbnb
E-mail: Padutchbnb@aol.com

Circa 1941. This home was built by an Amish carpenter for a Mennonite minister and his family in a farming community. The innkeepers grew up among Amish and Mennonite communities and are full of knowledge about the area and its history. Fresh flowers from the inn's beautiful gardens are placed

in the guest rooms in season. A country breakfast is served in the breakfast room overlooking the herb garden. The inn is only minutes away from outlet stores and plenty of outdoor activities.

Innkeeper(s): Don & Ruth Harnish. $85-115. PC, TC. 3 rooms with PB. Breakfast included in rates. Type of meal: Full bkfst. Beds: Q. Ceiling fan in room. Air conditioning. Library and jacuzzi in one room on premises. Amusement parks, antiquing, live theater, parks, shopping, sporting events and water sports nearby.

Location: Rural country setting.

Publicity: *Lancaster newspapers, Allentown Morning Call and Birds & Bloom Magazine.*

Certificate may be used: January-June, Sunday-Thursday, excluding holidays.

Homestead Lodging

184 Eastbrook Rd
Lancaster, PA 17576-9701
(717)393-6927 Fax:(717)393-1424
Internet: www.virtualcities.com/ons/pa/r/par4801/.htm

Circa 1984. An Amish farm rests adjacent to this newer brick Colonial, and from this bed & breakfast, guests can enjoy Pennsylvania Dutch country. Farmers' markets, antique shops, museums and restaurants all are nearby. Guest rooms include a refrigerator and cable TV. Children are welcome.

Innkeeper(s): Robert & Lori Kepiro. $42-69. MC, VISA, AX, DS, TC. 5 rooms with PB. Breakfast included in rates. Type of meal: Cont. Beds: QD. Cable TV, ceiling fan and hair dryer in room. Air conditioning. Microwave oven on premises. Amusement parks, antiquing, golf, museums, farmer's market, quilt shops, outlets, auctions, live theater, parks, shopping, tennis and water sports nearby.

Location: Countryside.

"Your hospitality and immaculate lodge stay with us long after we leave."

Certificate may be used: November-March, Sunday-Wednesday, excluding holidays and holiday weekends.

New Life Homestead B&B

1400 E King St, Rt 462
Lancaster, PA 17602-3240
(717)396-8928
Internet: www.800padutch.com/newlife.htm1

Circa 1912. This two-and-a-half story brick home is situated within one mile of Amish Farms, and it's less than two miles from the city of Lancaster. Innkeepers Carol and Bill Giersch, both Mennonites, host evening discussions about the culture and history of Amish and Mennonite people. Carol's homemade breakfasts are made with local produce.

Innkeeper(s): Carol Giersch. $65-85. 3 rooms, 2 with PB and 1 suite. Breakfast included in rates. Type of meal: Full bkfst. Beds: QDT. VCR on premises. Amusement parks, antiquing, fishing, live theater, shopping and sporting events nearby.

Location: Suburban.

Publicity: *Keystone Gazette and Pennsylvania Dutch Traveler.*

"Reminded me of my childhood at home."

Certificate may be used: January, February, March, anytime.

O'Flaherty's Dingeldein House B&B

1105 E King St
Lancaster, PA 17602-3233
(717)293-1723 (800)779-7765 Fax:(717)293-1947
Internet: www.800padutch.com/ofhouse.html
E-mail: oflahbb@lancnews.infi.net

Circa 1910. This Dutch Colonial home was once residence to the Armstrong family, who acquired fame and fortune in the tile floor industry. Springtime guests will brighten at the sight of this home's beautiful flowers. During winter months, innkeepers Jack and Sue Flatley deck the halls with plenty of seasonal decorations. Breakfast by candlelight might include fresh-baked muffins, fruits, the innkeepers' special blend of coffee and mouth-watering omelets, pancakes or French toast. Cozy rooms include comfortable furnishings and cheery wall coverings. With advance notice, the innkeepers can arrange for guests to enjoy dinner at the home of one of their Amish friends.

Innkeeper(s): Jack & Sue Flatley. $95-120. MC, VISA, DS, PC, TC. 4 rooms with PB and 1 suite. Breakfast included in rates. Types of meals: Full gourmet bkfst and early coffee/tea. Beds: QT. Ceiling fan in room. Air conditioning. VCR, fax, copier and library on premises. Amusement parks, antiquing, fishing, live theater, parks, shopping and sporting events nearby.

Location: Residential.

Publicity: *Gourmet.*

Certificate may be used: All year except April, July, August and October, Sunday through Thursday.

The King's Cottage, A B&B Inn

1049 E King St
Lancaster, PA 17602-3231
(717)397-1017 (800)747-8717 Fax:(717)397-3447
Internet: www.innbook.com/inns/kings/
E-mail: kingscottage@earthlink.net

Circa 1913. This Mission Revival house features a red-tile roof and stucco walls, common in many stately turn-of-the-century houses in California and New Mexico. Its elegant interiors

include a sweeping staircase, a library with marble fireplace, stained-glass windows and a solarium. The inn is appointed with Oriental rugs and antiques and fine 18th-century English reproductions. The Carriage House features the same lovely furnishings with the addition of a fireplace and Jacuzzi. The formal dining room provides the location for gourmet morning meals.

Innkeeper(s): Karen Owens. $105-220. MC, VISA, DS. 9 rooms with PB and 1 conference room. Breakfast and afternoon tea included in rates. Type of meal: Full bkfst. Beds: KQ. TV, turndown service and TV upon request in room. Amusement parks, antiquing, fishing, live theater, shopping, cross-country skiing and sporting events nearby.

Location: Residential neighborhood.

Publicity: *Country, USA Weekend, Bon Appetit, Intelligencer Journal and Times.*

"I appreciate your attention to all our needs and look forward to recommending your inn to friends."

Certificate may be used: November-July, Monday-Thursday.

Landenberg   L15

Cornerstone B&B Inn

300 Buttonwood Rd
Landenberg, PA 19350-9398
(610)274-2143 Fax:(610)274-0734
Internet: www.belmar.com/cornerstone
E-mail: corner3000@aol.com

Circa 1704. The Cornerstone is a fine 18th-century country manor house filled with antique furnishings. Two fireplaces make the parlor inviting. Wing chairs, fresh flowers and working fireplaces add enjoyment to the guest rooms.

Perennial gardens, a water garden and swimming pool with hot tub are additional amenities.

Innkeeper(s): Linda Chamberlin & Marty Mulligan. $75-250. MC, VISA, DS, PC, TC. 8 rooms with PB, 5 with FP, 1 suite and 6 cottages. Breakfast included in rates. Types of meals: Full bkfst and early coffee/tea. Beds: KQT. Cable TV in room. Air conditioning. VCR, fax, spa and swimming on premises. Amusement parks, antiquing, live theater, parks, shopping and sporting events nearby.

Location: Country.

Certificate may be used: Sunday-Thursday, Jan. 2-Dec. 15. No holiday weekdays.

Lewisburg   G12

Brookpark Farm B&B

100 Reitz Rd
Lewisburg, PA 17837-9653
(717)523-0220

Circa 1914. Twenty-five acres surround this three-story brick house. The innkeepers operate the Pennsylvania House Gallery in their enormous barn on the property. The inn, therefore, includes traditional, transitional and country designs from these furniture collections including cherry, pine and mahogany woods.

Innkeeper(s): Crystale & Todd Moyer. $63-68. MC, VISA. 7 rooms, 3 suites and 2 conference rooms. Breakfast and afternoon tea included in rates. Types of meals: Full gourmet bkfst and early coffee/tea. Beds: Q. Air conditioning. Amusement parks, antiquing, fishing, live theater, parks, shopping and sporting events nearby.

Certificate may be used: No restrictions, anytime.

Linfield   J16

Shearer Elegance

1154 Main St
Linfield, PA 19468-1139
(610)495-7429 (800)861-0308 Fax:(610)495-7814
Internet: //members.aol.com/shearerc/shirley1.htm
E-mail: shearerc@aol.com

Circa 1897. This stone Queen Anne mansion is the height of Victorian opulence and style. Peaked roofs, intricate trim and a stenciled wraparound porch grace the exterior. Guests enter the

home via a marble entry, which boasts a three-story staircase. Stained-glass windows and carved mantels are other notable features. The Victorian furnishings and decor complement the ornate workmanship, and

lacy curtains are a romantic touch. The bedrooms feature hand-carved, built-in wardrobes. The grounds are dotted with gardens. The inn is located in the village of Linfield, about 15 minutes from Valley Forge.

Innkeeper(s): Shirley & Malcolm Shearer & Beth Smith. $90-140. AX, PC, TC. 7 rooms with PB, 3 suites and 3 conference rooms. Types of meals: Full bkfst and early coffee/tea. Beds: KQ. Cable TV, ceiling fan and VCR in room. Air conditioning. Fax, copier and library on premises. Amusement parks, antiquing, fishing, golf, outlets, live theater, parks, shopping, downhill skiing, sporting events and tennis nearby.

Location: Country.

Publicity: *Reading, Norristown, Pottstown and Local.*

"Thank you for creating such a beautiful place to escape reality."

Certificate may be used: Anytime, excluding holidays.

Lititz J14

Casual Corners B&B

301 N Broad St
Lititz, PA 17543
(717)626-5299 (800)464-6764
Internet: www.bbonline.com/pa/casual
E-mail: ccbb@redrose.net

Circa 1904. This three-story home has a dormer window, shutters and a wide wraparound porch filled with hanging ferns and wicker furnishings. There is a second-floor sitting room for guests. A country breakfast often includes poached pears and caramel apple French toast. Walk to the Wilbur Chocolate Company or the country's first pretzel bakery.

Innkeeper(s): Glenn & Ruth Lehman. $65-85. MC, VISA, PC, TC. 4 rooms, 2 with PB and 1 suite. Breakfast included in rates. Types of meals: Full bkfst, country bkfst, veg bkfst and early coffee/tea. Beds: QD. Turndown service and ceiling fan in room. Air conditioning. Amusement parks, antiquing, art galleries, bicycling, golf, hiking, live theater, museums, parks, shopping, tennis and wineries nearby.

Location: City.

Certificate may be used: Sunday night-Thursday night.

The Alden House

62 E Main St
Lititz, PA 17543-1947
(717)627-3363 (800)584-0753
Internet: www.aldenhouse.com
E-mail: inn@aldenhouse.com

Circa 1850. For more than 200 years, breezes have carried the sound of church bells to the stately brick homes lining Main Street. The Alden House is a brick Victorian in the center of this historic district and within walking distance of the Pretzel House (first in the country) and the chocolate factory. A favorite room is the suite with a loft dressing room and private bath. A full breakfast is served, often carried to one of the inn's three porches.

Innkeeper(s): Tom & Lillian Vazquez. $90-120. MC, VISA, PC, TC. 5 rooms with PB, 1 with FP and 3 suites. Breakfast included in rates. Type of meal: Full bkfst. Beds: Q. Cable TV and ceiling fan in room. Air conditioning. Amusement parks, antiquing, live theater, parks and shopping nearby.

Location: Small town.

Publicity: *Travel Holiday, Rockland Journal News, Penn Dutch Traveler, Now in Lancaster County* and *Philadelphia Inquirer.*

"Truly represents what bed & breakfast hospitality is all about. You are special innkeepers. Thanks for caring so much about your guests. It's like being home."

Certificate may be used: Sunday night to Thursday night, year-round, except holiday weeks.

Manheim J14

Country Comforts of Jonde Lane Farm

1103 Auction Rd
Manheim, PA 17545-9143
(717)665-4231

Circa 1859. Cows graze and chickens cackle on this working, "hands-on" farm. The farm has been in the innkeepers' family since its construction in the mid-19th century. Guests can pitch in and help with the chores or just relax and enjoy the serene countryside. Children are welcome, and there's plenty

for them to do, such as bottle feeding a calf, milking a goat, gathering eggs and helping feed chickens. Hay and pony rides are available, and there is a play area in the backyard. The rooms feature a comfortable, country decor, and some bathrooms are shared. The innkeepers are Mennonite and begin each morning with special prayer, songs and then a hearty full breakfast. On Sundays, homemade continental fare is provided, and guests have the option of attending church with the family. The farm is close to Lancaster and other Pennsylvania Dutch country sites.

Innkeeper(s): John & Elaine Nissley. $50-70. MC, VISA, PC, TC. 6 rooms. Breakfast included in rates. Types of meals: Full bkfst and early coffee/tea. Beds: QDT. Clocks and reading area in room. Amusement parks, antiquing, fishing, golf, pony rides, hay rides, live theater, parks, shopping and tennis nearby.

Location: Country.

Publicity: *In Pittsburgh, Family Fun* and *Los Angeles Times.*

"We all agreed, our stay with you was the highlight of our trip."

Certificate may be used: Nov. 1-March 30, Monday-Thursday, excluding holiday weekends.

Rose Manor B&B Tea Room and Herbal Gift Shop

124 S Linden St
Manheim, PA 17545-1616
(717)664-4932 (800)666-4932 Fax:(717)664-1611

Circa 1905. A local mill owner built this manor house, and it still maintains original light fixtures, woodwork and cabinetry. The grounds are decorated with roses and herb gardens. An herb theme is played out in the guest rooms, which feature names such as the Parsley, Sage, Rosemary and Thyme rooms. The fifth room is named the Basil, and its spacious quarters encompass the third story and feature the roof's angled ceiling. One room offers a whirlpool and another a fireplace. The decor is a comfortable Victorian style with some antiques. Afternoon tea is available by prior reservation and there is a gift shop on the premises. The inn's location provides close access to many Pennsylvania Dutch country attractions.

Innkeeper(s): Susan & Anne Jenal. $70-120. MC, VISA, PC. 5 rooms, 3 with PB, 1 with FP. Breakfast included in rates. Type of meal: Full bkfst. Beds: QDT. Cable TV, ceiling fan and whirlpool tub (one room) in room. Air conditioning. Fax, copier and library on premises. Amusement parks, antiquing, fishing, live theater, parks and shopping nearby.

Location: Small village.

Publicity: *Harrisburg Patriot, Lancaster County Magazine* and *Central Pennsylvania Life.*

Certificate may be used: Jan. 1-May 31; Nov. 1-30; Sunday-Thursday, except holidays.

Marietta K13

Railroad House Restaurant B&B

280 W Front St
Marietta, PA 17547-1405
(717)426-4141
Internet: www.lancnews.com/railroadhouse

Circa 1820. The Railroad House, a sprawling old hotel, conjures up memories of the days when riding the rail was the way to travel. The house was built as a refuge for weary men who were working along the Susquehanna River. When the railroad finally made its way through Marietta, the rail station's waiting room and ticket office were located in what's now known as the Railroad House. The restored rooms feature antiques, Oriental rugs, Victorian decor and rustic touches such as exposed brick walls. The chefs at the inn's restaurant create a menu of American and continental dishes using spices and produce from the beautifully restored gardens. The innovative recipes have been featured in Bon Appetit. The innkeepers also host a variety of special events and weekends, including murder mysteries and clambakes serenaded by jazz bands. Carriage rides and special walking tours of Marietta can be arranged.

Innkeeper(s): Richard & Donna Chambers. $89-119. MC, VISA, TC. 8 rooms with PB, 1 cottage and 1 conference room. Breakfast included in rates. Types of meals: Full gourmet bkfst and early coffee/tea. Beds: QDT. Air conditioning. Copier, bicycles and gardens and yard games on premises. Amusement parks, antiquing, fishing, music box museum, live theater, parks, shopping, downhill skiing, sporting events and water sports nearby.

Location: Small town.

Certificate may be used: Anytime.

River Inn

258 W Front St
Marietta, PA 17547-1405
(717)426-2290 (888)824-6622 Fax:(717)426-2966

Circa 1790. This Colonial has more than 200 years of history within its walls. The home is listed in the National Register and located in Marietta's historic district. Herb and flower gardens decorate the grounds. Relaxing in front of a fireplace is an easy task since the inn offers six, one of which resides in a guest room. Colonial decor and antiques permeate the interior. The inn is within walking distance to the Susquehanna River.

Innkeeper(s): Joyce & Bob Heiserman. $65-85. MC, VISA, DC, CB, DS, PC, TC. 3 rooms with PB, 1 with FP. Breakfast included in rates. Types of meals: Full bkfst and early coffee/tea. Beds: QT. Air conditioning. Bicycles and library on premises. Amusement parks, antiquing, fishing, museum, live theater, parks, shopping and water sports nearby.

Location: Small town.

Publicity: *Colonial Homes 1984 - previous owner.*

Certificate may be used: Year-round, Sunday-Thursday.

McConnellsburg   K9

The McConnellsburg Inn

131 W Market St
McConnellsburg, PA 17233-1007
(717)485-5495
Internet: www.bbhost.com/mcinn
E-mail: mcinn@cvn.net

Circa 1903. This turn-of-the-century inn was built by a retired Union officer of the Civil War. Guest rooms include four-poster and canopy beds. Spiced apple crepes, savory ham and freshly baked fruit muffins are among the breakfast specialties. The inn is located in the McConnellsburg National Register Historic District. Gettysburg, East Broad Top Railroad, Cowans Gap State Park and Buchanan State Forest are nearby, as is Whitetail Ski Resort. Pennsylvania.

Innkeeper(s): Tim & Margie Taylor. $70. MC, VISA, AX, PC, TC. 3 rooms with

PB. Breakfast included in rates. Type of meal: Full gourmet bkfst. Beds: QD. Cable TV in room. Air conditioning. Fax, copier and library on premises. Antiquing, fishing, nature photography, country auctions, hiking, country auctions, downhill skiing, cross-country skiing and water sports nearby.

Pets allowed: Sometimes.

Location: Mountains.

Publicity: *Pennsylvania.*

Certificate may be used: Anytime there is availability.

McKnightstown   L11

Country Escape

275 Old Rt 30, PO Box 195
McKnightstown, PA 17343
(717)338-0611 (800)484-3244 Fax:(717)334-5227
Internet: www.gettysburgaddress.com/htmls/b&b.html
E-mail: merry@innernet.net

Circa 1867. This country Victorian, a brick structure featuring a porch decked in gingerbread trim, rests on the route that Confederate soldiers took on their way to nearby Gettysburg.

The home itself was built just a few years after the Civil War. There are three comfortable guest rooms, decorated in country style. For an extra fee, business travelers can use the inn's typing, copying, faxing or desktop publishing services.

All guests can enjoy the outdoor hot tub. There is also a children's play area outside. A traditional American breakfast is served, with such hearty items as eggs, pancakes, bacon and sausage. The inn offers close access to the famous battlefield, as well as other historic sites.

Innkeeper(s): Merry Bush & Ross Hetrick. $65-85. MC, VISA, AX, DC, DS, PC, TC. 3 rooms, 1 with PB and 1 suite. Breakfast and snacks/refreshments included in rates. Types of meals: Full bkfst, country bkfst and veg bkfst. Beds: Q. Air conditioning. VCR, fax, copier, spa, gift shop, children's play area and gardens on premises. Antiquing, bicycling, golf, horseback riding, battlefield - Gettysburg, live theater, museums, parks, shopping, downhill skiing and wineries nearby.

Location: Country/rural.

Publicity: *Gettysburg Times and Hanover Evening Sun.*

Certificate may be used: Jan. 1 through May 15 and Aug. 1 through Dec. 30, Sunday-Friday.

Meadville   D2

Fountainside B&B

628 Highland Ave
Meadville, PA 16335-1938
(814)337-7447

Circa 1855. A long front porch extends across the front of this farmhouse-style B&B. A full breakfast is served on the weekends, a continental breakfast during the week. Both Victorian and modern pieces are combined to furnish the rooms. Allegheny College is next door.

Innkeeper(s): Maureen Boyle. $50-65. MC, VISA, AX, DS. 5 rooms and 1 conference room. Breakfast included in rates. Types of meals: Full bkfst, cont and early coffee/tea. Turndown service and ceiling fan in room. Amusement parks, antiquing, live theater, shopping, cross-country skiing and sporting events nearby.

Certificate may be used: Anytime room is available.

Mechanicsburg J12

Kanaga House B&B

US Rt 11 6940 Carlisle Pike
Mechanicsburg, PA 17055
(717)697-2714

Circa 1775. This gracious three-story German stone house is built of limestone. The innkeepers have gathered historic information that links the builder of the home, Joseph Junkin, with the Revolutionary War, the Puritans and the first Covenater's Communion. A Joseph Junkin letter to his son, commander of the Battle of Brandywine, is in the parlor. The Elizabeth Junkin Room features a hope chest dated 1796, while the Eleanor Junkin Room offers a canopy bed with rose and blue bed hangings. Outside, an enormous gazebo creates a focal point for garden weddings.

Innkeeper(s): Mary Jane & Dave Kretzing. $75-95. MC, VISA, AX. 6 rooms with PB, 1 with FP and 1 conference room. Breakfast included in rates. Types of meals: Full bkfst and early coffee/tea. Beds: Q. Air conditioning. VCR, copier and gazebo with table and chairs on premises. Amusement parks, antiquing, live theater, shopping and downhill skiing nearby.

Location: Rural setting.

Certificate may be used: Sunday-Thursday, all year.

Mercer F2

The Magoffin Inn

129 S Pitt St
Mercer, PA 16137-1211
(412)662-4611 (800)841-0824

Circa 1884. Dr. Magoffin built this house for his Pittsburgh bride, Henrietta Boulevard. The Queen Anne style is characterized by patterned brick masonry, gable detailing, bay windows and a wraparound porch. The technique of marbleizing was used on six of the nine fireplaces. Magoffin Muffins are featured each morning. Dinner is available Friday and Saturday.

Innkeeper(s): Jacque McClelland. $115-125. MC, VISA, AX, PC, TC. 5 rooms with PB, 5 with FP and 1 suite. Breakfast and snacks/refreshments included in rates. Types of meals: Full bkfst and early coffee/tea. Beds: QD. Cable TV in room. Air conditioning. Antiquing, parks and shopping nearby.

Location: Town.

Publicity: *Western Reserve and Youngstown Vindicator.*

"While in Arizona we met a family from Africa who had stopped at the Magoffin House. After crossing the United States they said the Magoffin House was quite the nicest place they had stayed."

Certificate may be used: Sunday through Thursday nights.

Mercersburg L9

The Mercersburg Inn

405 S Main St
Mercersburg, PA 17236-9517
(717)328-5231 Fax:(717)328-3403
Internet: www.mercersburginn.com

Circa 1909. Situated on a hill overlooking the Tuscorora Mountains, the valley and village, this 20,000-square-foot Georgian Revival mansion was built for industrialist Harry Byron. Six massive columns mark the entrance, which opens to a majestic hall featuring chestnut wainscoting and an elegant double stairway and rare scagliola (marbleized) columns. All

the rooms are furnished with antiques and reproductions. A local craftsman built the inn's four-poster, canopied king-size beds. Many of the rooms have their own balconies and a few have fireplaces. During the weekends, the inn's chef prepares noteworthy, elegant five-course dinners, which feature an array of seasonal specialties.

Innkeeper(s): Walt & Sandy Filkowski. $120-235. MC, VISA, DS. 15 rooms with PB, 3 with FP and 1 conference room. Breakfast included in rates. Type of meal: Full gourmet bkfst. Beds: KQT. TV and phone in room. Air conditioning. VCR and bicycles on premises. Antiquing, fishing, golf, live theater, shopping, downhill skiing, cross-country skiing and water sports nearby.

Location: Cumberland Valley.

Publicity: *Mid-Atlantic Country, Washington Post, The Herald-Mail, Richmond News Leader, Washingtonian, Philadelphia Inquirer and Pittsburgh.*

"Elegance personified! Outstanding ambiance and warm hospitality."

Certificate may be used: Sunday-Thursday, non-holidays.

Mertztown I16

Longswamp B&B

1605 State St
Mertztown, PA 19539-8912
(610)682-6197 Fax:(610)682-4854

Circa 1789. Country gentleman Colonel Trexler added a mansard roof to this stately Federal mansion in 1860. Inside is a magnificent walnut staircase and pegged wood floors. As the story goes, the colonel discovered his unmarried daughter having an affair and shot her lover. He escaped hanging, but it was said that after his death his ghost could be seen in the upstairs bedroom watching the road. In 1905, an exorcism was reported to have sent his spirit to a nearby mountaintop.

Innkeeper(s): Elsa Dimick. $83-88. MC, VISA, AX. 10 rooms, 6 with PB, 2 with FP and 2 suites. Breakfast and afternoon tea included in rates. Types of meals: Full gourmet bkfst and early coffee/tea. Beds: QT. TV, phone and ceiling fan in room. Air conditioning. VCR and bicycles on premises. Antiquing, fishing, shopping, cross-country skiing and sporting events nearby.

Location: Country.

Publicity: *Washingtonian, Weekend Travel and The Sun.*

"The warm country atmosphere turns strangers into friends."

Certificate may be used: November-April.

Milford F18

Cliff Park Inn & Golf Course

155 Cliff Park Rd
Milford, PA 18337-9708
(570)296-6491 (800)225-6535 Fax:(570)296-3982
Internet: www.cliffparkinn.com
E-mail: info@cliffparkinn.com

Circa 1820. This historic country inn is located on a 600-acre family estate, bordering the Delaware River. It has been in the Buchanan family since 1820. Rooms are spacious with individual climate control, telephone and Victorian-style furnishings. Cliff Park features both a full-service restaurant and golf school. The inn's golf course, established in 1913, is one of the oldest in the United States. Cliff Park's picturesque setting is popular for country weddings and

private business conferences. Both B&B or MAP plans are offered.

Innkeeper(s): Harry W. Buchanan III. $93-160. MC, VISA, AX, DC, CB, DS. 18 rooms with PB and 1 conference room. Breakfast included in rates. Type of meal: Full bkfst. Beds: KQDT. Fax on premises. Handicap access. Cross-country skiing and water sports nearby.

"Cliff Park Inn is the sort of inn I look for in the English countryside. It has that authentic charm that comes from History."

Certificate may be used: Nov. 1-May 20, Sunday-Thursday.

Milton   G12

Pau-Lyn's Country B&B

RR 3 Box 676
Milton, PA 17847-9506
(570)742-4110

Circa 1850. This Victorian brick home offers a formal dining room with a fireplace and antique musical instruments. This restful haven offers a porch and patio overlooking the large lawn. Nearby are working farms and dairies, covered bridges, mountains, rivers and valleys and underground railroad stops.

Innkeeper(s): Paul & Evelyn Landis. $60-65. 7 rooms and 2 suites. Breakfast included in rates. Type of meal: Full bkfst. Air conditioning. Large lawn and patio on premises. Amusement parks, antiquing, bicycling, golf, hiking, museum, underground railroad, little league field and shopping nearby.

Location: Near small town.

Certificate may be used: Year-round, Sunday through Thursday, some weekends. All depends on availability.

Tomlinson Manor B&B

250 Broadway St
Milton, PA 17847-1706
(717)742-3657
Internet: www.sunlink.net/~tmbandb/
E-mail: tmbandb@sunlink.net

Circa 1927. In the Georgian style, this appealing three-story stone manor was designed by Dr. Charles Tomlinson, a local physician and amateur architect. Shutters border the small-paned windows, and there are gardens all around. All the rooms, including the library, are furnished with antiques. Next door to the B&B is a dinner theater.

Innkeeper(s): Mike & Nancy Slease. $60. MC, VISA. 3 rooms. Breakfast included in rates. Type of meal: Full bkfst. Air conditioning. VCR on premises. Antiquing, live theater, shopping and sporting events nearby.

Location: Town.

Certificate may be used: Anytime except college weekends.

Montoursville   F12

The Carriage House at Stonegate

RR 1 Box 11A
Montoursville, PA 17754-9801
(717)433-4340 Fax:(717)433-4653

Circa 1850. President Herbert Hoover was a descendant of the original settlers of this old homestead in the Loyalsock Creek Valley. Indians burned the original house, but the present farmhouse and numerous outbuildings date from the early 1800s. The Carriage House is set next to a brook.

Innkeeper(s): Harold & Dena Mesaris. $50-70. PC. 2 rooms. Breakfast included in rates. Type of meal: Cont plus. Beds: QD. Cable TV and phone in room. Fax, library, pet boarding and child care on premises. Amusement parks, antiquing, fishing, live theater, parks, shopping, downhill skiing, cross-country skiing, sporting events and water sports nearby.

Pets Allowed.

"A very fine B&B — the best that can be found. Gracious hosts."

Certificate may be used: Monday through Thursday nights, all months.

Mount Joy   K13

Cedar Hill Farm

305 Longenecker Rd
Mount Joy, PA 17552-8404
(717)653-4655 Fax:(717)653-9242
Internet: www.cedarhillfarm.com

Circa 1817. Situated on 51 acres overlooking Chiques Creek, this stone farmhouse boasts a two-tiered front veranda affording pastoral views of the surrounding fields. The host was born  in the house and is the third generation to have lived here since the Swarr family first purchased it in 1878. Family heirlooms and antiques include an elaborately carved walnut bedstead, a marble-topped washstand and a "tumbling block" quilt. In the kitchen, a copper kettle, bread paddle and baskets of dried herbs accentuate the walk-in fireplace, where guests often linger over breakfast. Cedar Hill is a working poultry and grain farm.

Innkeeper(s): Russel & Gladys Swarr. $75-95. MC, VISA, AX, DS, PC, TC. 5 rooms with PB. Breakfast included in rates. Types of meals: Cont plus and early coffee/tea. Beds: KQDT. Whirlpool tub in room. Central air conditioning. Internet access, fax, VCR, picnic table, meadows and stream on premises. Amusement parks, antiquing, fishing, amish country, live theater, parks, shopping, cross-country skiing, sporting events and water sports nearby.

Location: Midway between Lancaster and Hershey.

Publicity: *Women's World, Lancaster Farming, Philadelphia, New York Times, Ladies Home Journal and Lancaster County Heritage.*

"Dorothy can have Kansas, Scarlett can take Tara, Rick can keep Paris — I've stayed at Cedar Hill Farm."

Certificate may be used: Nov. 1-April 1, Sunday through Thursday, holidays excluded.

Hillside Farm B&B

607 Eby Chiques Rd
Mount Joy, PA 17552-8819
(717)653-6697 (888)249-3406 Fax:(717)653-9775
Internet: www.hillsidefarmbandb.com
E-mail: hillside3@juno.com

Circa 1863. This comfortable farm has a relaxing homey feel to it. Rooms are simply decorated and special extras such as handmade quilts and antiques add an elegant country touch. A new guest cottage offers a king bed, whirlpool tub for two, fireplace, wet bar and deck overlooking a bucolic meadow. The home is a true monument to the cow. Dairy antiques, cow knickknacks and antique milk bottles abound. Some of the bottles were found during the renovation of the home and its grounds. Spend the day hunting for bargains in nearby antique shops, malls and factory outlets, or tour local Amish and Pennsylvania Dutch attractions. The farm is a good vacation spot for families with children above the age of 10.

Innkeeper(s): Gary & Deborah Lintner. $70-185. MC, VISA, DS, PC, TC. 3 rooms with PB, 1 suite and 1 cottage. Breakfast and snacks/refreshments included in rates. Types of meals: Full bkfst and early coffee/tea. Beds: KQDT. Ceiling fan, wet bar in cottage, heat thermostats and magazines in room. Central air. VCR, spa, library, barn to explore, balcony and one two bedroom suite on premises. Amusement parks, antiquing, fishing, dinner with the Amish available with advance reservation. Hiking and biking trails, live theater, parks, shopping and water sports nearby.

Location: Country.

Certificate may be used: December through March, Sunday-Thursday. Country Cottage excluded.

The Olde Square Inn

127 E Main St
Mount Joy, PA 17552-1513
(717)653-4525 (800)742-3533 Fax:(717)653-0976

Circa 1917. Located on the town square, this Neoclassical house features handsome columned fireplaces and leaded-glass windows. The innkeeper starts off the day with breakfast items such as baked oatmeal, cherry cobbler, homemade breads and pancakes with a side of sausage. Amish farms and marketplaces are nearby. The town of Mount Joy offers restaurants, shops and parks all accessible with a short walk.

Innkeeper(s): Fran & Dave Hand. $95-125. MC, VISA, PC, TC. 4 rooms with PB. Breakfast included in rates. Types of meals: Full bkfst and early coffee/tea. Beds: QD. Cable TV, phone and VCR in room. Air conditioning. Fax on premises. Amusement parks, antiquing, fishing, live theater, parks, shopping and sporting events nearby.

Location: Small town.

Certificate may be used: Nov. 1 through April 30.

Muncy   F12

The Bodine House B&B

307 S Main St
Muncy, PA 17756-1507
(570)546-8949 Fax:(570)546-0607
E-mail: Bodine@pcspower.net

Circa 1805. This Federal-style townhouse, framed by a white picket fence, is in the National Register. Antique and reproduction furnishings highlight the inn's four fireplaces, the parlor, study and library. A favorite guest room features a walnut canopy bed, hand-stenciled and bordered walls, and a framed sampler by the innkeeper's great-great-great-grandmother. Candlelight breakfasts are served beside the fireplace in a gracious Colonial dining room. Also available is a guest cottage with kitchenette.

Innkeeper(s): David & Marie Louise Smith. $65-125. MC, VISA, AX, DS, PC, TC. 3 rooms with PB, 1 with FP and 1 cottage. Breakfast included in rates. Types of meals: Full bkfst and early coffee/tea. Beds: QDT. Cable TV and turndown service in room. Air conditioning. VCR, fax, bicycles and library on premises. Antiquing, fishing, parks, shopping, canoeing, cross-country skiing and sporting events nearby.

Location: Village.

Publicity: *Colonial Homes and Philadelphia Inquirer.*

"What an experience, made special by your wonderful hospitality."
Certificate may be used: Sunday through Thursday, year-round, subject to availability.

New Bloomfield   I11

Tressler House B&B

PO Box 38, 41 W Main St
New Bloomfield, PA 17068-0038
(717)582-2914
E-mail: dulsh@pa.net

Circa 1830. A white picket fence frames the acre of lawn surrounding this Federal-period home. A spider web window transom marks the front entrance. Oriental rugs, coordinated fabrics and wallcoverings fill the 22 rooms. Old mill stones, collected by the former owner, are woven into the brick patio and sidewalk. There is a covered porch filled with antique wicker, and a walled duck pond. Smoked turkey sausages and blueberry pancakes often are featured at breakfast.

Innkeeper(s): David & Carol Ulsh. $70-80. 4 rooms, 2 with PB. Types of meals: Full bkfst and early coffee/tea. Beds: DT. Cable TV in room. Air conditioning.

Location: Small town.

Publicity: *Perry County Times, Perry County Shopper and Antiques & Auction News.*

Certificate may be used: Sunday-Thursday, upon availability, all year.

New Hope   I18

Aaron Burr House Inn & Conference Center

80 W Bridge St
New Hope, PA 18938-1303
(215)862-2570
Internet: www.new-hope-inn.com
E-mail: stay@new-hope-inn.com

Circa 1870. Aaron Burr hid in this Bucks County house after his infamous duel with Alexander Hamilton. The home also is one of the Wedgwood Collection inns. A Victorian Shingle style, it is in the National Register. Its three stories, including the spacious parlor, are appointed with antiques and reproductions. Guest rooms offer amenities such as private baths, telephones and TVs, and many have two-person whirlpool tubs and fireplaces. Within walking distance are fine restaurants, shops and art galleries. The grounds offer two gazebos, stately old trees, a screened-in flagstone patio and a barn perfect for bicycle storage.

Innkeeper(s): Carl Glassman & Nadine Silnutzer. $95-255. MC, VISA, AX, PC, TC. 12 rooms with PB, 6 with FP, 6 suites, 1 cottage and 3 conference rooms. Breakfast, afternoon tea and snacks/refreshments included in rates. Types of meals: Cont plus and early coffee/tea. Beds: KQT. Phone, turndown service, ceiling fan and canopy beds in room. Air conditioning. VCR, fax, swimming, tennis and pet boarding on premises. Handicap access. Antiquing, fishing, covered bridge, live theater, parks, shopping, downhill skiing, cross-country skiing, sporting events and water sports nearby.

Location: Art colony/village.

Publicity: *The Intelligencer Record and Bucks County Courier Times.*

Certificate may be used: Monday-Thursday, December-April, holidays excluded.

Hollileif B&B

677 Durham Rd (Rt 413)
New Hope, PA 18940
(215)598-3100
Internet: www.bbhost.com/hollileif
E-mail: hollileif@aol.com

Circa 1700. This handsome former farmhouse sits on more than five rolling acres of scenic Bucks County countryside. The name "hollileif," which means "beloved tree," refers to the 40-foot holly trees that grace the entrance. Bedrooms are appointed with lace and fresh flowers. Afternoon refreshments in the parlor or patio are provided, as well as evening turndown service.

Innkeeper(s): Ellen & Richard Butkus. $85-160. MC, VISA, AX, DS, PC, TC. 5 rooms with PB, 2 with FP and 1 conference room. Breakfast and afternoon tea included in rates. Types of meals: Full gourmet bkfst and early coffee/tea. Beds: QD. Cable TV, turndown service and ceiling fan in room. Central air. VCR, fax, copier and library on premises. Antiquing, art galleries, bicycling, canoeing/kayaking, fishing, golf, hiking, horseback riding, live theater, museums, parks, shopping, downhill skiing, cross-country skiing, tennis, water sports and wineries nearby.

Location: Country.

Publicity: *Long Island Newsday, Bucks County Courier Times, Trentonian, Bucks County Courier Times and Philadelphia Inquirer.*

"The accommodations were lovely and the breakfasts delicious and unusual, but it is really the graciousness of our hosts that made the weekend memorable."

Certificate may be used: Sunday through Thursday except (1) during month of October, (2) holidays and holiday periods, (3) Dec. 26-31.

The Whitehall Inn

1370 Pineville Rd
New Hope, PA 18938-9495
(215)598-7945

Circa 1794. This white-plastered stone farmhouse is located on 13 country acres studded with stately maple and chestnut trees. Inside, a winding walnut staircase leads to antique-furnished guest rooms that offer wide pine floors, wavy-glass windows, high ceilings and some fireplaces. An antique clock collection, Oriental rugs and late Victorian furnishings are found throughout. Afternoon tea, evening chocolates and candlelight breakfasts served with heirloom china and sterling reflect the inn's many amenities. There are stables on the property and horseback riding may be arranged.

Innkeeper(s): Mike Wass. $140-200. MC, VISA, AX, DC, CB, DS. 6 rooms. Breakfast included in rates. Types of meals: Full bkfst and early coffee/tea. Turndown service and clocks in room. Air conditioning. Amusement parks, antiquing, live theater, shopping and cross-country skiing nearby.

Location: Country.

Certificate may be used: January-September, Monday-Thursday.

Northumberland   H12

Campbell's B&B

707 Duke St
Northumberland, PA 17857-1709
(717)473-3276

Circa 1859. This old farmhouse has three stories and there are porches overlooking the well-planted grounds and rose gardens. A few antiques and reproductions add to the country decor. Lake Augusta is a mile away for fishing and boating.

Innkeeper(s): Bob & Millie Campbell. $60-70. 3 rooms, 2 with PB, 1 suite and 1 conference room. Breakfast, afternoon tea and snacks/refreshments included

in rates. Types of meals: Full bkfst and early coffee/tea. Beds: QT. Cable TV, phone, turndown service and ceiling fan in room. Air conditioning. VCR and swimming on premises. Amusement parks, antiquing, fishing, historic sites, live theater, parks, shopping, cross-country skiing and water sports nearby.

Certificate may be used: Anytime except local college weekends. Monday through Thursday.

Palmyra   J13

The Hen-Apple B&B

409 S Lingle Ave
Palmyra, PA 17078-9321
(717)838-8282
Internet: www.visithc.com/henapple.html

Circa 1825. Located at the edge of town, this Georgian farmhouse is surrounded by an acre of lawns and gardens. There are antiques and country pieces throughout. Breakfast is served to guests in the dining room or on the screened veranda. Hershey is two miles away, Lancaster and Gettysburg are nearby.

Innkeeper(s): Flo & Harold Eckert. $55-75. MC, VISA, AX, DS, TC. 6 rooms with PB. Breakfast included in rates. Types of meals: Full bkfst and cont. Beds: QDT. Ceiling fan in room. Air conditioning. Amusement parks, antiquing, fishing, live theater, parks, shopping, sporting events and water sports nearby.

Location: Edge of small town.

Publicity: *Pennsylvania Magazine.*

Certificate may be used: March 1 to March 30, Sunday-Friday.

Pittsburgh   I3

The Priory

614 Pressley St
Pittsburgh, PA 15212-5616
(412)231-3338 Fax:(412)231-4838
Internet: www.sgi.net/thepriory/

Circa 1888. The Priory, now a European-style hotel, was built to provide lodging for Benedictine priests traveling through Pittsburgh. It is adjacent to Pittsburgh's Grand Hall at the Priory in historic East Allegheny. The inn's design and maze of rooms and corridors give it a distinctly Old World flavor. All rooms are decorated with Victorian furnishings.

Innkeeper(s): Ed & Mary Ann Graf. $114-150. MC, VISA, AX, DC, DS. 24 rooms with PB, 3 suites and 1 conference room. Breakfast included in rates. Type of meal: Cont plus. Beds: QDT. Handicap access. Live theater nearby.

Publicity: *Pittsburgh Press, US Air, Country Inns, Innsider, Youngstown Vindicator, Travel & Leisure, Gourmet and Mid-Atlantic Country.*

"Although we had been told that the place was elegant, we were hardly prepared for the richness of detail. We felt as though we were guests in a manor."

Certificate may be used: December-March, excludes New Year's Eve and Valentine's Day.

Point Pleasant   I18

Tattersall Inn

16 Cafferty Rd, PO Box 569
Point Pleasant, PA 18950
(215)297-8233 (800)297-4988 Fax:(215)297-5093
Internet: www.bbhost.com/tattersall_inn

Circa 1750. This Bucks County plastered fieldstone house with its 18-inch-thick walls, broad porches and wainscoted entry hall was the home of local mill owners for 150 years. Today it offers a peaceful place to relax, rebuild and enjoy the bucolic surroundings in Olde Bucks. Breakfast is served in the dining room or brought to your room. The Colonial-style common room features a beamed ceiling and walk-in fireplace where guests gather for apple cider, cheese and crackers and tea or coffee in the late afternoon.

Innkeeper(s): Donna & Bob Trevorrow. $90-140. MC, VISA, DS. 6 rooms with PB, 2 with FP, 1 suite and 1 conference room. Breakfast and afternoon tea included in rates. Type of meal: Full bkfst. Beds: Q. Air conditioning. Fax, copier, library and refrigerator on premises. Antiquing, fishing, live theater, parks, shopping, cross-country skiing and water sports nearby.

Location: Bucks County, eight miles north of New Hope on River Road, Rt 32.

Publicity: *Courier Times, Philadelphia, New York Times and WYOU.*

"Thank you for your hospitality and warm welcome. The inn is charming and has a wonderful ambiance."

Certificate may be used: All year, Sunday-Thursday, holidays excluded.

Reading   J15

Hunter House Bed & Breakfast

118 S Fifth St
Reading, PA 19602-1626
(610)374-6608 Fax:(610)372-7888
Internet: members.aol.com/hunterhous
E-mail: hunterhous@aol.com

Circa 1846. This inn is a fine example of Greek Revival architecture and features many European touches, such as antique furnishings and elaborate 13-foot ceilings topped with ornate plaster moldings. Guests will find shopping here to be some of the best in the nation, with antique shops and world-famous outlet stores within minutes of the inn. Other attractions include the Hawk Mountain Sanctuary, and the historic Daniel Boone Homestead.

Innkeeper(s): Bill D. Solliday. $95-125. MC, VISA, AX, DS, PC, TC. 4 rooms, 3 with PB and 3 suites. Breakfast, afternoon tea and snacks/refreshments included in rates. Type of meal: Full bkfst. Beds: QT. Cable TV, phone, turndown service and ceiling fan in room. Air conditioning. Fax and copier on premises. Amusement parks, antiquing, fishing, golf, outlet shopping, live theater, parks, shopping, downhill skiing, sporting events, tennis and water sports nearby.

Location: City.

"The accommodations are lovely, and the hospitality is exceptional."

Certificate may be used: Jan. 8-11, Jan. 15-18, Jan. 29-Feb. 1, Feb. 5-8, March 5-8, March 12-15, Dec. 3-6, Dec. 10-13.

Ronks   K14

Candlelight Inn B&B

2574 Lincoln Hwy E
Ronks, PA 17572-9771
(717)299-6005 (800)772-2635 Fax:(717)299-6397
E-mail: candleinn@aol.com

Circa 1920. Located in the Pennsylvania Dutch area, this Federal-style house offers a side porch for enjoying the home's acre and a half of tall trees and surrounding Amish farmland. Guest rooms feature Victorian decor. Two rooms include a Jacuzzi tub and fireplace. The inn's gourmet breakfast, which might include a creme caramel French toast, is served by candlelight. The innkeepers are professional classical musicians. Lancaster is five miles to the east.

Innkeeper(s): Tim & Heidi Soberick. $79-139. MC, VISA, DS, PC, TC. 7 rooms with PB, 2 with FP and 2 suites. Breakfast included in rates. Type of meal: Full gourmet bkfst. Beds: KQT. Amaretto, robes, Jacuzzi and fireplaces in room. Air conditioning. Fax, badminton and croquet on premises. Amusement parks, antiquing, fishing, live theater, parks, shopping, downhill skiing, cross-country skiing, sporting events and water sports nearby.

Location: Suburban-surrounded by farms.

Publicity: *Lancaster Daily News, Pennsylvania Dutch Traveler and Pennsylvania Intelligencer Journal.*

Certificate may be used: December through April, excluding holidays, Sunday through Thursday.

Saxonburg   H3

The Main Stay B&B of Saxonburg

214 Main St, PO Box 547
Saxonburg, PA 16056
(724)352-9363
Internet: www.mainstay.cjb.net
E-mail: mainbnb@hotmail.com

Recently restored, this handsome Federal-style home offers a light and airy decor with touches of English Country. There is a private garden, a library and parlor. Ask for the Nelizibeth Room for a hand painted chest and romantic iron bed. Another favorite room is the room with the four-poster bed and floral wall covering, or consider the newly created loft. It's an apartment with full kitchen and living room that offers original beamed ceilings and a skylight in the bedroom. Full breakfasts are served by candlelight in the cozy dining room. Pittsburgh is 20 miles away.

Innkeeper(s): Judith Focareta. $70-95. MC, VISA, PC, TC. 5 rooms, 4 with PB, 1 suite and 1 conference room. Breakfast and snacks/refreshments included in rates. Type of meal: Full bkfst. Beds: Q. Turndown service in room. Air conditioning. Fax, copier and library on premises. Antiquing, golf, live theater, parks, shopping and sporting events nearby.

"Even though I grew up here, I've never felt more at home than I have while staying with you."

Certificate may be used: Throughout the year, all days of the week.

Scranton   E16

The Weeping Willow Inn

308 N Eaton Rd
Scranton, PA 18657
(570)836-7257
E-mail: oaktree1@epix.net

Circa 1836. This Colonial, set on 22 acres, is filled with beautiful antiques and an elegant traditional decor. The home's original pine floor is topped with Oriental rugs. Breakfasts, with a fresh fruit parfait and perhaps apple-cinnamon French toast, are

served by candlelight. The nearby Susquehanna River and mountains provide ample activities, from hiking to fishing and canoeing. Antique and craft shops also are plentiful in the area.
Innkeeper(s): Patty & Randy Ehrenzeller. $70-80. MC, VISA, PC, TC. 3 rooms with PB. Breakfast included in rates. Type of meal: Full bkfst. Beds: QD. Phone and turndown service in room. Air conditioning. Antiquing, fishing, golf, parks, shopping, downhill skiing, cross-country skiing, tennis and water sports nearby.
Location: Mountains.
Publicity: *WNEP TV.*
Certificate may be used: Sunday through Thursday, no holidays, Jan. 3-Dec. 20.

Shippensburg   K10

Field & Pine B&B

2155 Ritner Hwy
Shippensburg, PA 17257-9756
(717)776-7179
Internet: cvbednbreakfasts.com
E-mail: fieldpine@aol.com

Circa 1790. Local limestone was used to build this stone house, located on the main wagon road to Baltimore and Washington. Originally, it was a tavern and weigh station. The house is surrounded by stately pines, and sheep graze on the inn's 80 acres. The bedrooms are hand-stenciled and furnished with quilts and antiques.
Innkeeper(s): Mary Ellen & Allan Williams. $70-80. MC, VISA, PC, TC. 3 rooms, 1 with PB, 1 with FP and 1 suite. Breakfast and snacks/refreshments included in rates. Types of meals: Full gourmet bkfst and early coffee/tea. Beds: QDT. TV and turndown service in room. Air conditioning. VCR on premises. Antiquing, fishing, parks and shopping nearby.
Location: Country.
Publicity: *Central Pennsylvania Magazine.*

"Our visit in this lovely country home has been most delightful. The ambiance of antiques and tasteful decorating exemplifies real country living."
Certificate may be used: Sunday through Thursday, year-round.

Spring Creek   D4

Spring Valley B&B

RR Box 117
Spring Creek, PA 16436-9507
(814)489-3695 (800)382-1324
E-mail: springvalley@penn.com

Circa 1820. Although located on Pennsylvania's Allegheny Plateau, this 105-acre spread feels more like a Western-style ranch. Deer and other wildlife roam the grounds, and there are hiking and cross-country ski trails on the premises. The land is adjacent to more than 8,000 acres of state game lands. There are two suites available in the main house as well as a log and cedar cottage. The cottage sleeps six and includes a fireplace and deck overlooking the woods. Four guests can stay comfortably in the Parlor Suite, which includes a corn-burning stove and clawfoot tub. For an additional fee, guests can enjoy guided, horseback trail rides.
Innkeeper(s): Kate & Clyde Miles. $75-130. MC, VISA, DS, PC, TC. 3 rooms and 2 cottages. Breakfast included in rates. Types of meals: Full gourmet bkfst, cont plus, cont and early coffee/tea. Beds: QD. Cable TV and ceiling fan in room. VCR, fax, copier, stables, bicycles, library, child care and compaq on premises. Handicap access. Antiquing, fishing, live theater, parks, shopping, downhill skiing, cross-country skiing and water sports nearby.
Location: Mountains.
Publicity: *Pennsylvania.*
Certificate may be used: All year except October, Dec. 24-Jan. 4. Weekdays only, except holiday weekends, upon availability.

Strasburg   K14

Strasburg Village Inn

1 W Main St, Centre Sq
Strasburg, PA 17579
(717)687-0900 (800)541-1055
Internet: strasburg.com
E-mail: foraroom@strasburg.com

Circa 1788. Located on historic Strasburg's Centre Square, this brick inn offers guests a glimpse of early Americana, in the center of the Amish country. Despite the old-fashioned charm, two suites offer the romantic, albeit modern, amenity of Jacuzzi tubs. The inn is adjacent to the Strasburg Country Store and Creamery, the town's oldest operating store. The shop offers a variety of baked goods, a 19th-century soda fountain, a deli with homemade ice cream, penny candy and plenty of collectibles. Guests are treated to a full breakfast at The Creamery. The inn is surrounded by many Pennsylvania Dutch sites, including Amish farms, antique stores and historic villages. Sight and Sound Theater, the Strasburg Railroad and Dutch Wonderland Amusement Park are nearby.
Innkeeper(s): Helen Pyott. $70-150. MC, VISA, AX, DS, PC, TC. 10 rooms with PB and 2 suites. Breakfast included in rates. Types of meals: Full bkfst and early coffee/tea. Beds: KQD. Cable TV in room. Air conditioning. Restaurant on premises. Several outlet malls nearby nearby.
Location: City.
Certificate may be used: Sunday-Thursday, Nov. 1-May 21, excluding holidays.

Valley Forge   K16

The Great Valley House of Valley Forge

1475 Swedesford Rd
Valley Forge, PA 19355
(610)644-6759 Fax:(610)644-7019
Internet: www.greatvalleyhouse.com
E-mail: info@greatvalleyhouse.com

Circa 1691. This 300-year-old Colonial stone farmhouse sits on four acres just two miles from Valley Forge Park. Boxwoods line the walkway, and ancient trees surround the house. Each of the three antique-filled guest rooms is hand-stenciled and features a canopied or brass bed topped with handmade quilts. Guests enjoy a full breakfast before a 14-foot fireplace in the "summer kitchen," the oldest part of the house. On the grounds are a swimming pool, walking and hiking trails and the home's original smokehouse.
Innkeeper(s): Pattye Benson. $75-95. MC, VISA, DS, PC, TC. 3 rooms, 2 with PB. Breakfast included in rates. Types of meals: Full gourmet bkfst and early coffee/tea. Beds: QDT. Cable TV, phone and turndown service in room. Air conditioning. Fax, swimming and grand piano on premises. Antiquing, fishing, live theater, parks, shopping, cross-country skiing, sporting events and water sports nearby.
Location: Rural/suburban setting.
Publicity: *Main Line Philadelphia, Philadelphia Inquirer, Washington Post, New York Times, Suburban Newspaper and Travel cable network.*

"As a business traveler, Patty's enthusiasm and warm welcome makes you feel just like you're home."
Certificate may be used: Year-round. Both nights must be Sunday-Thursday. Excludes holidays.

Warfordsburg   L8

Buck Valley Ranch

1344 Negro Mountain Rd
Warfordsburg, PA 17267
(717)294-3759 (800)294-3759 Fax:(717)294-6413

Circa 1930. Trail riding is a popular activity on the ranch's 64 acres in the Appalachian Mountains of South Central Pennsylvania. State game lands and forests border the ranch. The guest house, decorated in a ranch/cowboy style, is a private farmhouse that can accommodate eight people. Meals are prepared using homegrown vegetables and locally raised meats. Rates also include horseback riding.

Innkeeper(s): Nadine & Leon Fox. $125. MC, VISA, DS, PC, TC. 4 rooms. Breakfast, dinner, snacks/refreshments and picnic lunch included in rates. Types of meals: Full gourmet bkfst and early coffee/tea. Beds: DT. Air conditioning. Fax, copier, spa, swimming, sauna and stables on premises. Amusement parks, antiquing, fishing, C&O Canal, steam train rides, 2 trail rides, parks, shopping, downhill skiing, cross-country skiing and water sports nearby.

Location: Mountains.

Publicity: *Washington Post, Pittsburgh Press, PA bride, Baltimore Sun and Potomac.*

Certificate may be used: Jan. 1-Dec. 31, Sunday-Thursday, excluding weekends and holidays.

West Chester   K16

Bankhouse B&B

875 Hillsdale Rd
West Chester, PA 19382-1975
(610)344-7388

Circa 1765. Built into the bank of a quiet country road, this 18th-century house overlooks a 10-acre horse farm and pond. The interior is decorated with country antiques, stenciling and folk art. Guests have a private entrance and porch. Two bedrooms share a common sitting room library. Hearty country breakfasts include German apple souffle pancakes, custard French toast and nearly 100 other recipes. West Chester and the Brandywine Valley attractions are conveniently close.

Innkeeper(s): Diana & Michael Bove. $70-90. TC. 2 rooms and 1 suite. Breakfast and snacks/refreshments included in rates. Types of meals: Full gourmet bkfst and early coffee/tea. Beds: DT. Phone in room. Central air. Antiquing, live theater, parks, shopping, cross-country skiing and sporting events nearby.

Location: Country/suburb.

Publicity: *Philadelphia Inquirer, Mercury, Bucks County Town & Country Living, Chester County Living and Washington Post.*

"Everything was so warm and inviting. One of my favorite places to keep coming back to."

Certificate may be used: Sunday-Thursday, January-April and November-December.

Willow Street   K14

The Inn at Hayward Heath B&B

2048 Silver Ln
Willow Street, PA 17584-9729
(717)464-0994 (800)482-6432
Internet: www.ristenbatt.com/hayward/

Circa 1887. Located in Southern Lancaster Country, this graceful brick Colonial house overlooks two acres of lawns and gardens. There are high ceilings, wide window sills and oak and cherry grained woodwork. There is a walk-in fireplace in the former summer kitchen, now a family room furnished with antiques. The Shaker Room offers a queen-size canopy bed, and one room offers a double whirlpool tub. Baked apples, stuffed French toast and egg dishes are served in the dining room. Amish farms, craft shops, outlet malls, restaurants and farmers markets are popular Lancaster County attractions.

Innkeeper(s): David & Joan Smith. $86-120. MC, VISA, DS, PC. 4 rooms, 3 with PB. Breakfast included in rates. Type of meal: Full bkfst. Beds: QD. Ceiling fan and 2-person Jacuzzi in room. Air conditioning. Porch on premises. Amusement parks, antiquing, golf, live theater, parks, shopping and tennis nearby.

Publicity: *Lancaster Country Magazine.*

Certificate may be used: Nov. 1-April 30, Sunday-Thursday, excluding holidays.

York   K13

Friendship House B&B

728 E Philadelphia St
York, PA 17403-1609
(717)843-8299

Circa 1897. A walk down East Philadelphia Street takes visitors past an unassuming row of 19th-century townhouses. The Friendship House is a welcoming site with its light blue shutters and pink trim. Innkeepers Becky Detwiler and Karen Maust have added a shot of Victorian influence to their charming townhouse B&B, decorating with wallcoverings and lacy curtains. A country feast is prepared some mornings with choices ranging from quiche to French toast accompanied with items such as baked apples, smoked sausage and homemade breads. Most items are selected carefully from a nearby farmer's market. Becky and Karen make sure guests never leave their friendly home empty-handed, offering a bottle of Pennsylvania's finest maple syrup upon departure.

Innkeeper(s): Becky Detwiler & Karen Maust. $55-65. 3 rooms, 2 with PB and 1 suite. Breakfast and snacks/refreshments included in rates. Types of meals: Full bkfst and cont plus. Beds: Q. Air conditioning. VCR on premises. Antiquing, fishing, museums, live theater, parks and shopping nearby.

Location: City.

Certificate may be used: Jan. 2-Feb. 28.

Rhode Island

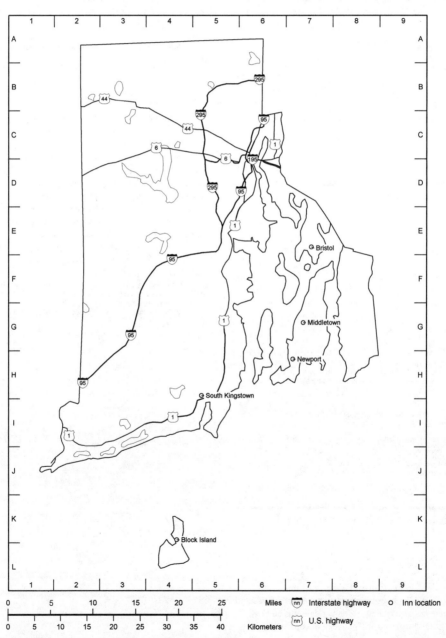

Miles   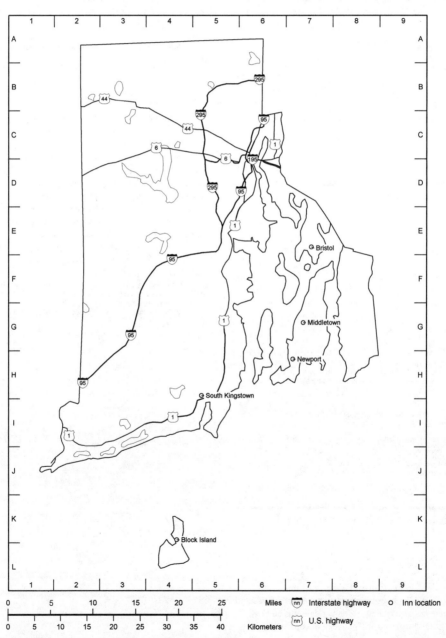 Interstate highway   ○ Inn location

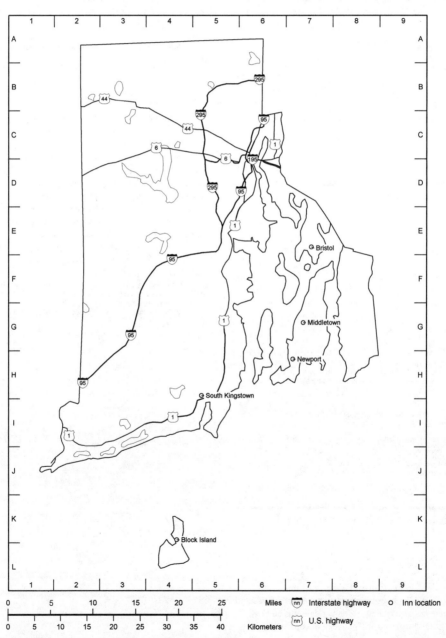 U.S. highway

Kilometers

   Visit www.bnbinns.com for photos and more details about each inn.

Block Island
K4

Blue Dory Inn

PO Box 488, Dodge St
Block Island, RI 02807-0488
(401)466-5891 (800)992-7290 Fax:(401)466-9910
Internet: www.blockislandinns.com
E-mail: rendezvous@aol.com

Circa 1887. This Shingle Victorian inn on Crescent Beach offers many guest rooms with ocean views. The Cottage, The Doll House and The Tea House are separate structures for those desiring more room or privacy. Antiques and Victorian touches are featured throughout. Year-round car ferry service, taking approximately one hour, is found at Point Judith, R.I. The island also may be reached by air on New England Airlines or by charter. Mohegan Bluffs Scenic Natural Area is nearby.

Innkeeper(s): Ann Loedy. $65-225. MC, VISA, AX, DS, PC, TC. 12 rooms with PB, 3 suites, 4 cottages and 1 conference room. Breakfast and afternoon tea included in rates. Types of meals: Cont plus and early coffee/tea. Beds: KQDT. Phone, some air conditioning, VCRs and Cable TV in room. VCR, fax, copier, swimming and child care on premises. Antiquing, beaches, fishing, live theater, parks, shopping and water sports nearby.

Pets allowed: Restricted to certain cottages.

"The Blue Dory is a wonderful place to stay. The room was lovely, the view spectacular and the sound of surf was both restful and tranquil."

Certificate may be used: Midweek Sept. 15-June 15, Sunday through Thursday.

Sheffield House Bed & Breakfast

PO Box 1557, High St
Block Island, RI 02807
(401)466-2494 Fax:(401)466-8890
Internet: www.sheffieldhouse.com
E-mail: info@sheffieldhouse.com

Circa 1888. Step off the ferry and step into a bygone era at this Queen Anne Victorian, which overlooks the Old Harbor district. Relax on one of the front porch rockers or enjoy the fragrance as you stroll through the private garden. Guest rooms are furnished with antiques and family pieces; each is individually decorated.

Innkeeper(s): Molly & Chris O'Neill. $50-165. MC, VISA, AX, PC, TC. 7 rooms, 5 with PB. Breakfast, afternoon tea and snacks/refreshments included in rates. Types of meals: Cont and early coffee/tea. Beds: Q. Ceiling fan in room. Antiquing, fishing, ocean, beaches, nature, restaurants, parks, shopping and water sports nearby.

Certificate may be used: Oct. 15-May 15, Sunday-Thursday.

The Bellevue House

PO Box 1198, High St
Block Island, RI 02807-1198
(401)466-2912

Circa 1882. Offering a hilltop perch, meadow-like setting and ocean views, this Colonial Revival farmhouse inn in the Block Island Historic District has served guests for more than a century. A variety of accommodations includes eight guest rooms, three with private bath, four suites and two cottages. The Old Harbor Ferry, restaurants and shops are just a five-minute walk from the inn. Guests may use ferries from New London, Conn., Montauk Point, N.Y., and Newport, Point Judith and Providence, R.I., to reach the island. Beaches, Block Island

National Wildlife Reserve and Rodmans Hollow Nature Area are nearby. Children are welcome.

Innkeeper(s): Neva Flaherty. $65-170. MC, VISA, PC, TC. 8 rooms, 4 suites and 2 cottages. Breakfast included in rates. Type of meal: Cont. Beds: KQD. Library, gas grills and picnic tables on premises. Fishing, parks, shopping and water sports nearby.

Location: 12 miles from mainland Rhode Island.

Certificate may be used: Sunday-Thursday, May 14-June 22, Sept. 10-Oct. 5.

Bristol
E7

William's Grant Inn

154 High St
Bristol, RI 02809-2123
(401)253-4222 (800)596-4222

Circa 1808. This handsome Federal Colonial home was built by Governor William Bradford for his grandson. There are two beehive ovens and seven fireplaces as well as original wideboard pine floors and paired interior chimneys. Antique furnishings and folk art make the guest rooms inviting. The backyard is an ideal spot for relaxation with its patios, water garden and quaint stone walls.

Innkeeper(s): Warren & Diane, Matthew & Janet Poehler. $95-110. MC, VISA, AX, DS, PC, TC. 5 rooms, 3 with PB, 5 with FP. Breakfast included in rates. Type of meal: Full gourmet bkfst. Beds: QD. Turndown service and ceiling fan in room. Air conditioning. Bicycles and goldfish pond with waterfall on premises. Antiquing, fishing, parks, shopping, sporting events and water sports nearby.

Location: Historic downtown district.

Publicity: *New York Times, Sun Sentinel, Providence Journal and Bristol Phoenix.*

"We felt better than at home with the wonderful treats (the breakfasts were fabulous), the lovely rooms, the inn is full of inspiration and innovation . . ."

Certificate may be used: November-May, Sunday-Thursday, based on availability.

Middletown
G7

Lindsey's Guest House

6 James St
Middletown, RI 02842-5932
(401)846-9386

Circa 1955. This contemporary split-level home in a residential area features three guest rooms, including one on the ground level that boasts a private entrance and is handicap-accessible. Breakfast is served in the dining room and usually includes cereal, coffee cake, fruit, juice, muffins and jam, and coffee or beverage of choice. The innkeeper has worked in the hospitality industry for more than 30 years and is happy to offer sightseeing tips. The Norman Bird Sanctuary and Sachuest Point National Wildlife Reserve are nearby.

Innkeeper(s): Anne T. Lindsey. $40-75. MC, VISA, AX, PC, TC. 2 rooms with PB. Breakfast included in rates. Type of meal: Cont plus. Beds: KD. Phone and ceiling fan in room. VCR and tV on premises. Handicap access. Antiquing, fishing, mansions, boat & bus tours, live theater, parks, shopping and water sports nearby.

Certificate may be used: Sunday through Thursday, all year, except July and August.

Newport
H7

Halidon Hill Guest House

Halidon Ave
Newport, RI 02840
(401)847-8318 (800)227-2130

Circa 1969. This contemporary, two-story Georgian-style inn offers a convenient location and comfortable accommodations for those exploring the Newport area. The two spacious suites both boast kitchenettes. The inn is just a 10-minute walk to Hammersmith Farm and provides easy access to the area's mansions, restaurants and shopping. Guests will enjoy lounging on the roomy deck near the in-ground pool, or in front of the fireplace in cooler weather. Newport Harbor and the Tennis Hall of Fame are nearby.

Innkeeper(s): Helen & Paul Burke. $75-200. AX, DC, DS, PC, TC. 2 suites. Types of meals: Full bkfst and early coffee/tea. Beds: KQDT. Cable TV and ceiling fan in room. Air conditioning. VCR and swimming on premises. Antiquing, fishing, golf, live theater, parks, shopping, sporting events, tennis and water sports nearby.

Location: City.

Certificate may be used: Weekdays, from May 1-Nov. 1. Weekdays or weekends from Nov. 1-May 1.

Hammett House Inn

505 Thames St
Newport, RI 02840-6723
(401)848-0593 (800)548-9417 Fax:(401)848-2258
E-mail: CIS 76470,3440

Circa 1758. This three-story Georgian Federal-style home has watched the nation grow and prosper from its little nook on Thames Street. The rooms are decorated with romance in mind. Especially picturesque are the Rose and Windward rooms, which afford views of Newport Harbor. The Pewter Room includes a unique metal canopy bed. The inn is a short walk from shops, restaurants and the waterfront.

Innkeeper(s): Marianne Spaziano. $95-195. MC, VISA, AX, DS, TC. 5 rooms with PB. Breakfast included in rates. Type of meal: Cont plus. Beds: Q. Cable TV in room. Air conditioning. Fax on premises. Antiquing, fishing, newport mansion tours, live theater, parks, shopping and water sports nearby.

Location: City.

Certificate may be used: Anytime Nov. 16-April 1; April-June, Tuesday-Thursday only.

Hydrangea House Inn

16 Bellevue Ave
Newport, RI 02840-3206
(401)846-4435 (800)945-4667 Fax:(401)846-6602
Internet: www.hydrangeahouse.com
E-mail: hydrangeahouse@home.com

The scent of fresh flowers welcomes guests into their cheery rooms at this B&B, which once housed a school of music. After abdicating his throne, King Edward was a guest at this home. Romance is emphasized by the decor in each of the individually appointed guest rooms, which feature wicker and antique furnishings. Breakfasts are served on the veranda, with its view of the gardens. In cooler weather, the breakfast buffet is set up in the art gallery, which features many original works.

Innkeeper(s): Grant Edmondson. $125-280. MC, VISA, AX. 6 rooms. Breakfast included in rates. Type of meal: Full bkfst.

Certificate may be used: Nov. 1-April 30, Sunday-Wednesday.

Inntowne Inn

6 Mary St
Newport, RI 02840-3028
(401)846-9200 (800)457-7803 Fax:(401)846-1534

Circa 1935. This Colonial-style inn is an elegant spot from which to enjoy the seaside town of Newport. Waverly and Laura Ashley prints decorate the individually appointed guest rooms, some of which have four-poster or canopy beds. The innkeeper serves an expanded continental breakfast with items such as fresh fruit, quiche and ham and cheese croissants. Afternoon tea also is served. A day in Newport offers many activities, including touring the Tennis Hall of Fame, taking a cruise through the harbor, shopping for antiques or perhaps taking a trek down Cliff Walk, a one-and-a-half-mile path offering the ocean on one side and historic mansions on the other. Parking is included in the rates.

Innkeeper(s): Carmella Gardner. $95-224. MC, VISA, AX. 26 rooms with PB and 1 suite. Afternoon tea included in rates. Type of meal: Cont plus. Beds: KQDT. Phone in room. Air conditioning. VCR, fax, copier and parking included in rates on premises. Antiquing, parks and shopping nearby.

"Thank you for your excellent service with a smile."

Certificate may be used: Nov. 1-Feb. 28, Sunday through Thursday.

Jailhouse Inn

13 Marlborough St
Newport, RI 02840-2545
(401)847-4638 (800)427-9444 Fax:(401)849-0605
Internet: historicinnsofnewport.com
E-mail: vacation@jailhouse.com

Circa 1772. Built in 1772, this restored Colonial jail maintains just a touch of jail flavor as a backdrop to comfort and convenience. Prison-striped bed coverings and tin cups and plates for breakfast express the jailhouse motif. Guests can stay in the Cell Block, Maximum Security or Solitary Confinement, each on a separate level of the inn. Nevertheless, because guests pay for their time here, there are luxuries in abundance. A complimentary continental breakfast buffet and afternoon tea service is offered daily.

Innkeeper(s): Susan P. Mauro. $55-250. VISA, AX, DC. 22 rooms with PB. Breakfast and afternoon tea included in rates. Beds: KQ. Cable TV and phone in room. Air conditioning. Copier and parking on premises on premises. Handicap access. Antiquing, fishing, shopping and water sports nearby.

Location: City.

Publicity: *Providence Journal.*

"I found this very relaxing and a great pleasure."

Certificate may be used: Nov. 10-May 10, Sunday through Friday.

The Inn at Shadow Lawn

120 Miantonomi Ave
Newport, RI 02842-5450
(401)847-0902 (800)352-3750 Fax:(401)848-6529
Internet: www.shadowlawn.com
E-mail: randy@shadowlawn.com

Circa 1856. This elegant, three-story Stick Victorian inn, listed in the National Register, offers a glimpse of fine living in an earlier age. The innkeepers' attention to detail is evident throughout, with French crystal chandeliers, stained-glass windows and parquet floors in the library as a few of the highlights. Parlors are found on each of the inn's floors. Newport's many attractions, including the Art Museum, sailing and the world famous Newport mansions are just a short drive from the inn.

Innkeeper(s): Randy & Selma Fabricant. $85-225. MC, VISA, AX, TC. 8 rooms with PB, 8 with FP and 3 conference rooms. Breakfast included in rates. Types of meals: Full bkfst and cont plus. Beds: KQ. Cable TV, phone and VCR in room. Air conditioning. Fax, copier and library on premises. Antiquing and mansions and sailing nearby.

Location: City.

Publicity: *Newport Daily News, Providence Journal, West Essex Tribune and Mr. Smith.*

"A dream come true! Thanks for everything! We'll be back."

Certificate may be used: Jan. 20-April 30, Monday-Thursday, no holidays, festivals.

The Melville House

39 Clarke St
Newport, RI 02840-3023
(401)847-0640 Fax:(401)847-0956
Internet: www.melvillehouse.com
E-mail: innkeeper@ids.net

Circa 1750. This attractive, National Register two-story Colonial inn once housed aides to General Rochambeau during the American Revolution. Early American furnishings decorate the interior. There is also an unusual collection of old appliances, including a cherry-pitter, mincer and dough maker. A full break-

fast includes Portuguese Quiche, Jonnycakes, homemade bread and berry-stuffed French toast. The inn is a pleasant walk from the waterfront and historic sites.

Innkeeper(s): Christine Leone. $110-165. MC, VISA, AX, DS, PC, TC. 7 rooms, 5 with PB, 1 with FP and 1 suite. Breakfast and afternoon tea included in rates. Types of meals: Full gourmet bkfst and early coffee/tea. Beds: KDT. Air conditioning. Fax and bicycles on premises. Antiquing, fishing, live theater, parks, shopping and water sports nearby.

Location: City.

Publicity: *Country Inns, "Lodging Pick" for Newport, Good Housekeeping and New York Post.*

"Comfortable with a quiet elegance."

Certificate may be used: January-March, anytime, 50% off full price. November-December and April-May, no Saturdays or holidays. Call for additional summer weekday discounts.

Victorian Ladies Inn

63 Memorial Blvd
Newport, RI 02840-3629
(401)849-9960 Fax:(401)849-9960

Circa 1850. Guests of this restored three-story Victorian building can stroll to Newport's beaches, the Cliff Walk, the Colonial town and the harbor front. At the Victorian Ladies, a charming latticed courtyard connects the main house to the smaller house in back. Reproduction period furniture, crystal and lush floral prints add to the Victorian ambiance in the rooms that innkeeper Helene O'Neill decorated.

Innkeeper(s): Donald & Helene O'Neill. $95-225. MC, VISA. 11 rooms with PB. Breakfast included in rates. Type of meal: Full gourmet bkfst. Beds: KQ. Cable TV and phone in room. Air conditioning. Fax and copier on premises. Antiquing, fishing, golf, live theater, parks, shopping, sporting events and tennis nearby.

Location: Three blocks from shopping.

Publicity: *Country Inns, Glamour, Bride Magazine, L. A. Times and Country Victorian.*

"We want to move in!"

Certificate may be used: Feb. 15 to Dec. 15, Sunday-Thursday, (months of July and August excluded).

South Kingstown   H5

Admiral Dewey Inn

668 Matunuck Beach Rd
South Kingstown, RI 02879-7053
(401)783-2090 (800)457-2090
Internet: www.admiraldeweyinn.com

Circa 1898. Although the prices have risen a bit since this inn's days as a boarding house (the rate was 50 cents per night), this Stick-style home still offers hospitality and comfort. The National Register inn is within walking distance of Matunuck Beach. Guests can enjoy the sea breeze from the inn's wraparound porch. Period antiques decorate the guest rooms, some of which offer ocean views.

Innkeeper(s): Joan Lebel. $100-150. MC, VISA, PC. 10 rooms, 8 with PB. Breakfast included in rates. Types of meals: Cont plus and early coffee/tea. Beds: QDT. VCR, fax and copier on premises. Antiquing, fishing, live theater, parks, shopping and water sports nearby.

Location: Free access to town beach.

Publicity: *Yankee Traveler and Rhode Island Monthly.*

Certificate may be used: October to May.

South Carolina

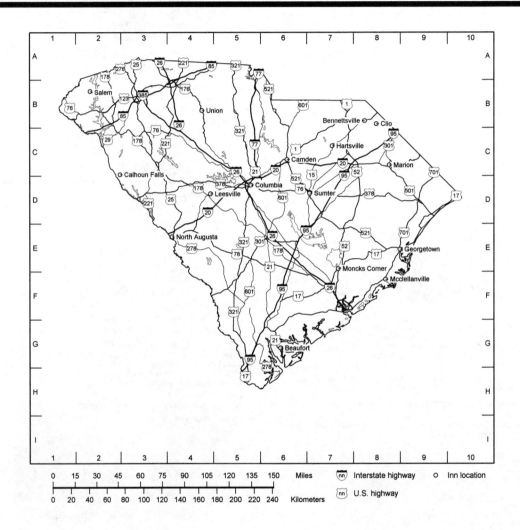

0   15   30   45   60   75   90   105 120 135 150   Miles

0   20   40   60   80 100 120 140 160 180 200 220 240   Kilometers

Interstate highway   O   Inn location

U.S. highway

Beaufort G6

The Beaufort Inn

809 Port Republic St
Beaufort, SC 29901-1257
(843)521-9000 Fax:(843)521-9500
Internet: www.beaufortinn.com
E-mail: bftinn@hargray.com

Circa 1897. Every inch of this breathtaking inn offers something special. The interior is decorated to the hilt with lovely furnishings, plants, beautiful rugs and warm, inviting tones. Rooms include four-poster and canopy beds combined with the modern amenities such as fireplaces, wet bars and stocked refrigerators. Enjoy a complimentary full breakfast at the inn's gourmet restaurant. The chef offers everything from a light breakfast of fresh fruit, cereal and a bagel to heartier treats such as pecan peach pancakes and Belgium waffles served with fresh fruit and crisp bacon.

Innkeeper(s): Russell & Debbie Fielden. $125-225. MC, VISA, AX, DS, PC, TC. 17 rooms with PB, 4 with FP, 1 suite and 1 conference room. Breakfast included in rates. Types of meals: Full gourmet bkfst and early coffee/tea. Beds: KQ. Cable TV, phone, turndown service, ceiling fan and VCR in room. Air conditioning. Fax, copier and bicycles on premises. Handicap access. Antiquing, fishing, live theater, parks, shopping and water sports nearby.
Location: Historic Landmark District.
Publicity: Beaufort, Southern Living, Country Inns, Carolina Style, US Air and Town & Country.
Certificate may be used: December, January and February, Sunday through Wednesday night only. Good only for four rooms which have a rate of $195 or higher.

The Cuthbert House Inn B&B

1203 Bay St
Beaufort, SC 29902-5401
(843)521-1315 (800)327-9275 Fax:(843)521-1314
Internet: www.cuthberthouseinn.com
E-mail: cuthbert@hargray.com

Circa 1790. This 18th-century waterfront mansion, listed in the National Register, boasts a veranda overlooking Beaufort Bay. The home was built during Washington's presidency, and General W.T. Sherman was once a guest here. The home has been lovingly restored to its original grandeur. Rich painted walls are highlighted by fine molding. Hardwood floors are topped with Oriental rugs and elegant 19th-century furnishings. The morning meal is served in a breakfast room that overlooks the water. The surrounding area offers plenty of activities in every season, and for those celebrating a new marriage, a honeymoon package is available.

Innkeeper(s): Gary & Sharon Groves. $135-225. MC, VISA, AX, DS, PC, TC. 7 rooms with PB, 2 suites and 2 conference rooms. Breakfast included in rates. Types of meals: Full bkfst, cont and early coffee/tea. Beds: KQDT. Cable TV, phone, turndown service, mini bar, robes, hair dryers and data port in room. Air conditioning. VCR, fax, bicycles, library, whirlpool, off street parking and beach towels on premises. Antiquing, fishing, Parris Island USMC Depot, Ace Basin Tours, National Historic District tours, parks and water sports nearby.
Location: Beaufort Bay-waterfront.
Publicity: Charleston Post Courier, Beaufort Gazette, Atlanta Journal-Constitution, Glamour, Travel & Leisure, Delta Airlines Sky Magazine., White Squall and House & Garden Channel.
Certificate may be used: Jan. 10-Feb. 10, June 10-30; Sunday-Wednesday.

The Rhett House Inn

1009 Craven St
Beaufort, SC 29902-5577
(843)524-9030 (888)480-9530 Fax:(843)524-1310
Internet: www.innbook.com/rhett.html
E-mail: rhetthse@hargray.com

Circa 1820. Most people cannot pass this stunning two-story clapboard house without wanting to step up to the long veranda and try the hammock. Guest rooms are furnished in antiques with quilts and orchids. Eight of the rooms offer private Jacuzzi tubs. Many bedrooms have fireplaces, and some have a history of famous  guests such as Ben Affleck, Sandra Bullock, Gwyneth Paltrow and Barbra Streisand. Handsome gardens feature a fountain and are often the site for romantic weddings. (The innkeeper is available to perform the ceremony.)

Innkeeper(s): Stephen Harrison. $150-250. MC, VISA, AX, TC. 17 rooms with PB, 8 with FP. Breakfast and afternoon tea included in rates. Types of meals: Full bkfst and early coffee/tea. Beds: KQ. Cable TV, phone, turndown service, ceiling fan and eight rooms with Jacuzzi tubs in room. Air conditioning. Fax on premises. Handicap access. Antiquing, fishing, golf, live theater, tennis and water sports nearby.
Location: In a historic district.
Publicity: New York Times, Vogue, Elle, Conde Nast Traveler, Travel & Leisure, Self, Brides and Martha Stewart.
Certificate may be used: January, February, June through September and December, Sunday through Thursday, good only for rooms $175 and over.

Bennettsville B8

The Breeden Inn & Carriage House

404 E Main St
Bennettsville, SC 29512
(843)479-3665 (888)335-2996
Internet: www.bbonline.com/sc/breeden/
E-mail: breedeninn@mecsc.net

Circa 1886. One especially bountiful cotton crop paid for the construction of this mansion, which local attorney Thomas Bouchier presented to his bride as a wedding gift. The exterior is graced with more than two dozen columns and the interior boasts a carved oak archway in the center hall. Stained and beveled glass are found throughout the home, along with original light fixtures. Breakfasts can be served in the formal dining room or on the veranda. The innkeepers also offer accommodations in two restored guest houses, which include a gathering room, kitchens and front porches lined with rocking chairs and swings.

Innkeeper(s): Wesley & Bonnie Park. $95-135. MC, VISA, AX, PC, TC. 10 rooms with PB, 8 with FP, 3 suites, 2 cottages and 1 conference room. Breakfast and afternoon tea included in rates. Types of meals: Full bkfst and early coffee/tea. Beds: QDT. Cable TV, phone, ceiling fan and private phone lines with data port in room. Air conditioning. VCR, fax, copier and swimming on premises. Antiquing, fishing, golf, walking trails, swimming, historic tours, live theater, museums, shopping and tennis nearby.

"We have so much enjoyed our stay here in your charming and comfortable inn."
Certificate may be used: Year-round. Excludes special event dates and holidays.

Calhoun Falls   C2

Latimer Inn

1379 Highway 81
Calhoun Falls, SC 29268
(864)391-2747 Fax:(864)391-2747

Circa 1907. Thirty-seven acres surround this three-story
Colonial inn. There is a tree-shaded porch and a balcony that
stretches across the second story offering views out over the
grounds. Some guest rooms offer high ceilings and whirlpool
tubs and all have television and private baths. Guests may use
the washer and dryer, fish cleaning area, boat hookups and the
gas grill on the patio. A continental breakfast is provided.
Calhoun Falls State Park is a mile away.

Innkeeper(s): Harrison & Anne Sawyer. $49-129. MC, VISA, AX, DS, PC, TC.
17 rooms with PB, 1 with FP, 3 suites and 1 conference room. Types of
meals: Full gourmet bkfst, cont plus and cont. Beds: QDT. Cable TV, phone,
ceiling fan and VCR in room. Air conditioning. Fax, copier, spa, swimming
and tennis on premises. Antiquing, fishing, golf, historical Abbeville, SC, live
theater, parks, shopping, sporting events, tennis and water sports nearby.

Location: Historical Abbeville, SC.

"We felt very welcome, enjoyed our stay, and will return."

Certificate may be used: June 1-Feb. 28, Sunday-Friday.

Camden   C6

A Camden, SC Bed & Breakfast

127 Union St
Camden, SC 29020-2700
(803)432-2366
Internet: www.tech-tech.com/b&bonlyweb
E-mail: jerixon@tech-tech.com

Circa 1920. This Federal-style home is built on what was a
battlefield during the Revolutionary and Civil wars. The home
originally served as the residence for a local judge. Rooms are
decorated in a country style with many antiques. Guest will
find poster beds topped with antique quilts, as well as quilts
decorating the walls. Guests can stay in one of the rooms in
the main house or in the adjacent cottage, which served as the
judge's law library. Homemade breads and jam, savory egg
dishes and fresh fruit are presented in the mornings on a breakfast table set with fine linens.

Innkeeper(s): Janie Erickson. $85-225. MC, VISA, AX, DC, CB, DS, PC, TC.
3 suites, 2 with FP and 2 cottages. Breakfast included in rates. Types of
meals: Full gourmet bkfst, cont plus, cont and early coffee/tea. Beds: QT.
Turndown service in room. Air conditioning. Fax and internet access on
premises. Antiquing, fishing, golf, live theater, parks, shopping, tennis and
water sports nearby.

Pets Allowed.

Location: Historic town.

"It was great being pampered by you."

Certificate may be used: July 1-Aug. 30, Sunday-Thursday.

Candlelight Inn

1904 Broad St
Camden, SC 29020-2606
(803)424-1057

Circa 1933. Two acres of camellias, azaleas and oak trees surround this Cape Cod-style home. As per the name, the innkeepers keep a candle in each window, welcoming guests to this
homey bed & breakfast. The decor is a delightful and tasteful

mix of country, with quilts, hand-crafted samplers, poster beds,
family antiques and traditional furnishings. Each of the rooms is
named for someone significant in the innkeeper's life, and a picture of the special person decorates each room. Guests will enjoy
the hearty breakfast, which changes daily. Several of innkeeper Jo
Ann Celani's recipes have been featured in a cookbook, and one
recipe won a blue ribbon at the Michigan State Fair.

Innkeeper(s): Jo Ann & George Celani. $75-125. MC, VISA, AX, DS, PC, TC. 3
rooms, 2 with PB and 1 suite. Breakfast and snacks/refreshments included in
rates. Types of meals: Full bkfst and early coffee/tea. Beds: QT. Phone and turndown service in room. Air conditioning. Library on premises. Antiquing, fishing,
golf, two steeplechase races, live theater, parks, shopping and tennis nearby.

Location: Historic town.

Publicity: Chronicle-Independent, Sandlapper and Southern Inns and B&Bs.

"You have captured the true spirit of a bed & breakfast."

Certificate may be used: Based on availability excluding race weekends.

Clio   B8

Henry Bennett House

301 Red Bluff St
Clio, SC 29525-3009
(843)586-9290
Internet: www.bennetthouse.net
E-mail: hbhbbemarlboroelectric.net

A huge veranda, decorated with whimsical gingerbread trim,
rambles around the exterior of this Victorian, which was built
by a cotton farmer. A turret and widow's walk also grace the
home. Clawfoot tubs and working fireplaces are some of the
amenities found in the comfortable guest rooms. The area
offers several golf courses and antiquing.

Innkeeper(s): Connie Hodgkinson. $55. MC, VISA. 3 rooms. Breakfast includ-
ed in rates. Type of meal: Full bkfst.

Certificate may be used: April-October.

Columbia   D5

Chesnut Cottage B&B

1718 Hampton St
Columbia, SC 29201-3420
(803)256-1718

Circa 1850. This inn was originally the home of Confederate
General James Chesnut and his wife, writer Mary Boykin Miller
Chesnut. She authored "A Diary From Dixie," written during
the Civil War but published posthumously in 1905. The white
frame one-and-a-half-story house has a central dormer with an
arched window above the main entrance. The small porch has
four octagonal columns and an ironwork balustrade. Hearty
breakfasts are served in the privacy of your room, on the porch
or in the main dining room. The innkeepers can provide you
with sightseeing information, make advance dinner reservations,
as well as cater to any other special interests you might have.

Innkeeper(s): Diane & Gale Garrett. $65-150. MC, VISA, AX, DC, DS, TC. 4
rooms with PB and 1 suite. Breakfast and snacks/refreshments included in
rates. Types of meals: Full gourmet bkfst, cont plus and early coffee/tea.
Beds: KQ. Phone, turndown service, ceiling fan and VCR in room. Air conditioning. Fax and bicycles on premises. Antiquing, fishing, live theater, parks,
shopping, sporting events and water sports nearby.

Location: City.

Publicity: Sandlapper, London Financial Times and TV show "Breakfast
with Christie."

"You really know how to pamper and spoil. Chesnut Cottage is a
great place to stay."

Certificate may be used: All year, Sunday through Thursday.

Georgetown E8

1790 House B&B Inn

630 Highmarket St
Georgetown, SC 29440-3652
(843)546-4821 (800)890-7432
Internet: www.1790house.com
E-mail: jwiley5211@aol

Circa 1790. Located in the heart of a historic district, this beautifully restored West Indies Colonial just celebrated its 200th birthday. The spacious rooms feature 11-foot ceilings and seven fireplaces, three in the guest bedrooms. The inn's decor reflects the plantations of a bygone era. Guests can stay in former slave quarters, renovated to include a queen bedroom and sitting area. Each of the romantic rooms features special touches, such as the Rice Planters' Room with its four-poster, canopy bed and window seat. The Dependency Cottage is a perfect honeymoon hideaway with a Jacuzzi tub and a private entrance enhanced with gardens and a patio. The inn is located one hour north of Charleston and 45 minutes south of Myrtle Beach.

Innkeeper(s): John & Patricia Wiley. $95-135. MC, VISA, AX, DS, PC, TC. 6 rooms with PB, 1 with FP and 1 cottage. Breakfast and snacks/refreshments included in rates. Type of meal: Full gourmet bkfst. Beds: KQT. Cable TV, phone and ceiling fan in room. Air conditioning. VCR, bicycles, hammock, ping pong table and board games on premises. Antiquing, fishing, tours, boats, tram, live theater, parks and shopping nearby.

Publicity: *Brides, Georgetown Times, Sun News, Charlotte Observer, Southern Living. USAir, Augusta, Pee Dee and Sandlapper.*

"The 1790 House always amazes me with its beauty. A warm welcome in a lovingly maintained home. Breakfasts were a joy to the palate."

Certificate may be used: Anytime in December-February. Sunday-Thursday for March-November.

Ashfield Manor

3030 S Island Rd
Georgetown, SC 29440-4422
(843)546-0464
E-mail: ashfield@sscoast.net

Circa 1960. Breakfast with many homemade items is served in guests' rooms, the parlor or on the inn's long, screened porch. Georgetown is conveniently located 30 miles from Myrtle Beach and 60 miles from Charleston. A beautiful public beach is 15 minutes away at Pawleys Island. Located on Winyah Bay, the town's seaport offers area restaurants with abundant fresh seafood. Many homes and churches date back to the 1700s and can be seen on a walking tour or by carriage or tour train. Also available are harbor tours that allow you to see Georgetown and its plantations from the water.

Innkeeper(s): Carol Ashenfelder. $50-75. MC, VISA, DC, DS, TC. 4 rooms. Breakfast included in rates. Type of meal: Cont. Beds: Q. TV and ceiling fan in room. Air conditioning. Amusement parks, antiquing, fishing, live theater and shopping nearby.

Certificate may be used: Based upon availability, except July 4th weekend and Labor Day weekend.

Du Pre House LLC

921 Prince St
Georgetown, SC 29440-3549
(803)546-0298 (800)921-3877 Fax:(803)520-0771

Circa 1740. The lot upon which this pre-Revolutionary War gem stands was partitioned off in 1734, and the home built six years later. Three guest rooms have fireplaces, and all are

decorated with a poster bed. A full breakfast is prepared featuring such items as French toast, specialty egg dishes, fresh fruit and home-baked muffins. For those who love history, Georgetown, South Carolina's third oldest city, offers more than 60 registered National Historic Landmarks.

Innkeeper(s): Marshall Wile. $75-115. MC, VISA, AX, PC, TC. 5 rooms with PB, 3 with FP. Breakfast, afternoon tea and snacks/refreshments included in rates. Types of meals: Full bkfst, cont plus and early coffee/tea. Beds: Q. Turndown service, ceiling fan and bathrobes in room. Air conditioning. Fax, copier, spa, swimming and library on premises. Amusement parks, antiquing, fishing, Myrtle Beach, plantation tours, live theater, parks, shopping and water sports nearby.

Certificate may be used: Nov. 15-May 15, Sunday-Thursday.

King's Inn at Georgetown

230 Broad St
Georgetown, SC 29440-3604
(843)527-6937 (800)251-8805 Fax:(843)527-6937

Circa 1825. Enjoy the height of elegance, as well as basking in history at this Federal-style mansion. Union troops seized the house and used it as headquarters during the Civil War. The home boasts features such as magnificent moldings, crystal chandeliers, beautifully restored original floors and three, antique-filled parlors. Individually decorated guest rooms include luxurious items such as canopy beds, private piazzas or perhaps an in-room double Jacuzzi. In 1995, Country Inns magazine named King's Inn as one of the year's Top 12. Gourmet breakfasts are served in the garden breakfast room, which overlooks the lap pool. Tables are set with fine linens, china, silver and crystal. The beach and Brookgreen, one of the world's largest outdoor sculpture gardens, are nearby.

Innkeeper(s): Marilyn & Jerry Burkhardt. $89-139. MC, VISA, AX. 7 rooms with PB. Breakfast and afternoon tea included in rates. Types of meals: Full bkfst and early coffee/tea. Beds: KQDT. Phone and jacuzzi for two in one room in room. VCR, bicycles, child care, screened porch, individual breakfast tables and modems on premises. Antiquing, fishing, golf, museums, beach, live theater, parks, shopping and sporting events nearby.

Location: City.

Publicity: *Country Inns Magazine Top 12 Inns for 1995, Georgetown Times, The Myrtle Beach Sun News and Southern Living.*

"Wonderful effect in every room with the brilliant use of color."

Certificate may be used: Sunday-Friday, all year.

Live Oak Inn B&B

515 Prince St
Georgetown, SC 29440
(843)545-8658 (888)730-6004 Fax:(843)545-8948
Internet: www.liveoakinn.com
E-mail: info@liveoakinn.com

Said to have lived five centuries, two live oaks spread their branches over this recently renovated Victorian. Some of the turn-of-the-century treasures in the home are its grand carved stairway, its columned entry and inlaid hardwood floors. There's a whirlpool in most of the guest rooms, and furnishings include family antiques and collections. (Sam's Rooms features quilts made by the family's grandmothers.)

Innkeeper(s): Fred & Jackie Hoelscher. $75-125. MC, VISA, AX. 4 rooms with PB, 4 with FP. Beds: KQ. TV and fireplace in room. Bicycles, fireplace, parlor games, TV, baby grand piano and 300 kites on premises. Antiquing, fishing, bicycling, canoeing/kayaking, golf, tennis and shopping nearby.

Certificate may be used: No restrictions.

The Shaw House B&B

613 Cypress Ct
Georgetown, SC 29440-3349
(843)546-9663

Circa 1972. Near Georgetown's historical district is the Shaw House. It features a beautiful view of the Willowbank marsh, which stretches out for more than 1000 acres. Sometimes giant turtles come up and lay eggs on the lawn. Guests enjoy rocking on the inn's front and back porches and identifying the large variety of birds that live here. A Southern home-cooked breakfast often includes grits, quiche and Mary's heart-shaped biscuits.
Innkeeper(s): Mary & Joe Shaw. $55-75. PC, TC. 3 rooms with PB. Breakfast included in rates. Types of meals: Full bkfst and early coffee/tea. Beds: KQ. Cable TV, phone, turndown service and ceiling fan in room. Air conditioning. Bicycles and library on premises. Amusement parks, antiquing, fishing, live theater, parks, shopping and water sports nearby.
Location: City.
Publicity: *Charlotte Observer and Country.*

"Your home speaks of abundance and comfort and joy."
Certificate may be used: Sunday-Friday, any time available.

Hartsville   C7

Missouri Inn B&B

314 E Home Ave
Hartsville, SC 29550-3716
(843)383-9553 Fax:(843)383-9553
E-mail: stay@missouriinn.com

Circa 1901. It is from the third owners of this Federal-style inn that it derives its name. The home was at that time owned by the innkeepers' grandparents, F.E. and Emily Fitchett, and "Missouri" was the nickname given to Emily by her son-in-law. The entire house, including the five guest rooms, are decorated with antiques, and features wallpaper original to the home. The continental breakfasts are hearty and homemade. Don't forget to sample afternoon tea, which features scones, tarts, miniature quiche and tea sandwiches. The home, located in the town historic district, is across the street from Coker College and four blocks from downtown Hartsville.
Innkeeper(s): Kyle & Kenny Segars. $75-85. MC, VISA, AX, PC, TC. 5 rooms with PB, 3 with FP. Breakfast and afternoon tea included in rates. Types of meals: Full gourmet bkfst, cont plus and early coffee/tea. Beds: KQT. Cable TV, phone, ceiling fan, robes, flowers, mints and heated towel racks in room. Air conditioning. VCR, fax, copier and library on premises. Handicap access. Antiquing, fishing, golf, parks, tennis and water sports nearby.
Location: Small town, Historic District.
Certificate may be used: All days except Nascar weekends (March 20-22 and Labor Day weekend).

Leesville   D4

The Able House Inn

244 E Columbia Ave
Leesville, SC 29070-9284
(803)532-2763 Fax:(803)532-2763

Circa 1939. This elegant, white brick home was built by a local druggist. Relax in the tastefully decorated living room or lounge on a comfy wicker chair among the large plants in the sunroom. Guest rooms, named after various relatives, boast beautiful amenities such as a canopied bed or window seats. Jennifer's Room opens into a sitting room with a window seat so large, some guests have snuggled down for a restful night's

sleep instead of the large, brass and enamel four-poster bed. Innkeepers offer guests a fresh fruit basket and turndown service each night. Wake to freshly ground coffee before taking on the day. During the warmer months, innkeepers offer guests the use of their swimming pool.
Innkeeper(s): Jack & Annabelle Wright. $65-75. MC, VISA, PC, TC. 5 rooms with PB and 1 suite. Breakfast and snacks/refreshments included in rates. Types of meals: Cont plus and early coffee/tea. Beds: QD. Cable TV, phone, turndown service and ceiling fan in room. Air conditioning. VCR, fax, copier and swimming on premises. Antiquing, fishing, golf, live theater, shopping, sporting events, tennis and water sports nearby.
Location: City.
Publicity: *Sandlapper and State Newspaper.*

"Thank you for the warm Southern welcome. Your place is absolutely beautiful, very inviting. The food was extraordinary!"
Certificate may be used: Sept. 1 to April 1.

Marion   C8

Montgomery's Grove

408 Harlee St
Marion, SC 29571-3144
(843)423-5220 (877)646-7721
Internet: www.bbonline.com/sc/montgomery

Circa 1893. The stunning rooms of this majestic Eastlake-style manor are adorned in Victorian tradition with Oriental rugs, polished hardwood floors, chandeliers and gracious furnishings. High ceilings and fireplaces in each room complete the elegant look. Guest rooms are filled with antiques and magazines or books from the 1890s. Hearty full breakfasts are served each day, and candlelight dinner packages can be arranged. Guests will appreciate this inn's five acres of century-old trees and gardens. The inn is about a half-hour drive to famous Myrtle Beach and minutes from I-95.
Innkeeper(s): Coreen & Richard Roberts. $80-100. 5 rooms, 3 with PB and 1 suite. Breakfast included in rates. Type of meal: Full bkfst. Beds: KQ. Antiquing, fishing, live theater and water sports nearby.
Publicity: *Pee Dee Magazine, Sandlapper, Marion Star, Palmetto Places TV and Country Living.*
Certificate may be used: Anytime.

McClellanville   F8

Laurel Hill Plantation B&B

8913 N Hwy 17
McClellanville, SC 29458-9423
(843)887-3708 (888)887-3708 Fax:(843)887-3878
Internet: www.bbonline.com/sc/laurelhill/

Circa 1991. The wraparound porches at this plantation home provide a view of salt marshes, islands and the Atlantic

Ocean. The home was destroyed in 1989 by Hurricane Hugo, but has been totally reconstructed in its original Low Country style. It is furnished with antiques, local crafts and folk art.

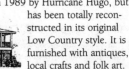

Innkeeper(s): Jackie & Lee Morrison. $100-125. MC, VISA, AX, DC, DS, PC, TC. 4 rooms with PB. Breakfast included in rates. Types of meals: Full bkfst, country bkfst and early coffee/tea. Beds: QD. TV, phone and ceiling fan in room. Central air. Antiquing, beaches, canoeing/kayaking, fishing, golf, hiking and horseback riding nearby.

Publicity: *Atlanta Journal, Country Living, Seabreeze, Pee Dee and State.*

Certificate may be used: December, January, February; Monday-Thursday.

Moncks Corner   E7

Rice Hope Plantation Inn

206 Rice Hope Dr
Moncks Corner, SC 29461-9781
(843)761-4832 (800)569-4038 Fax:(843)884-0223

Circa 1840. Resting on 11 acres of natural beauty, the inn is set among live oaks on a bluff overlooking the Cooper River. On the property are formal gardens that boast a 200-year-old camellia and many varieties of azaleas and other trees and plants. Nearby attractions include the Trappist Monastery at Mepkin Plantation, Francis Marion National Forest, Cypress Gardens and historic Charleston. Outdoor occasions are great because of the inn's formal gardens and the Cooper River backdrop.

Innkeeper(s): Doris Kasprak. $60-95. MC, VISA, AX. 5 rooms, 3 with PB and 1 conference room. Breakfast included in rates. Types of meals: Full bkfst, cont plus and early coffee/tea. Beds: QD. Ceiling fan in room. Air conditioning. Antiquing and fishing nearby.

Certificate may be used: Sunday-Thursday, all year.

North Augusta   E4

Rosemary & Lookaway Halls

804 Carolina Ave
North Augusta, SC 29841-3436
(803)278-6222 (800)531-5578 Fax:(803)278-4877

Circa 1902. These historic homes are gracious examples of Southern elegance and charm. Manicured lawns adorn the exterior of both homes, which appear almost as a vision out of "Gone With the Wind." The Rosemary Hall boasts a spectacular heart-of-pine staircase. The homes stand as living museums, filled to the brim with beautiful furnishings and elegant decor, all highlighted by stained-glass windows, chandeliers and lacy touches. Some guest rooms include Jacuzzis, while others offer verandas. A proper afternoon tea is served each afternoon at Rosemary Hall. The Southern hospitality begins during the morning meal. The opulent gourmet fare might include baked orange-pecan English muffins served with Canadian bacon or, perhaps, a Southern strata with cheese and bacon. The catering menu is even more tasteful, and many weddings, showers and parties are hosted at these inns.

Innkeeper(s): Geneva Robinson. $75-195. MC, VISA, AX, DC, CB, DS, PC, TC. 23 rooms with PB and 2 conference rooms. Breakfast and snacks/refreshments included in rates. Types of meals: Full bkfst, cont plus and early coffee/tea. Beds: KQDT. Cable TV, phone and turndown service in room. Air conditioning. Fax and copier on premises. Handicap access. Antiquing, fishing, parks, shopping, sporting events and water sports nearby. Location: City.

Certificate may be used: Jan. 3-April 1, April 20-Sept. 1, Sunday-Tuesday. Does not include April 2-19.

Pawleys Island   E9

Litchfield Plantation

King's River Rd, PO Box 290
Pawleys Island, SC 29585
(843)237-9121 (800)869-1410 Fax:(843)237-1041
Internet: www.litchfieldplantation.com
E-mail: vacation@litchfieldplantation.com

Circa 1750. Live oaks line the drive that leads to this antebellum mansion, and in one glance, guests can imagine a time when this 600-acre estate was a prosperous rice plantation. The interior boasts many original features, and although the decor is more modern than it was in 1750, it still maintains charm and elegance. Four-poster and canopy beds, as well as a collection of traditional furnishings, grace the

guest rooms, which are located in a variety of lodging options. Guests can stay in a plantation house suite or opt for a room in the Guest House. There are two- and three-bedroom cottages available, too. The cottages are particularly suited to adult families or couples traveling together and include amenities such as a fireplace, kitchen and washer and dryer. The inn's dining room, located in the Carriage House, is a wonderful place for a romantic dinner. Start off with appetizers such as Terrine al Fresco, followed by a Caesar salad and an entree such as medallions of pork or the Carriage House Grooper. Guests enjoy privileges at the oceanfront Pawleys Island Beach House, and there are tennis courts and a swimming pool on the plantation premises. Many golf courses are nearby. Be sure to ask about the inn's packages.

Innkeeper(s): Karl W Friedrich. $186-582. MC, VISA, AX, DS, TC. 38 rooms with PB, 7 with FP, 10 suites, 8 cottages and 3 conference rooms. Breakfast included in rates. Types of meals: Cont plus. Beds: KQT. Cable TV and phone in room. Air conditioning. Fax, copier, swimming, tennis, library and oceanfront beach clubhouse on premises. Amusement parks, antiquing, fishing, golf, live theater, parks, shopping and water sports nearby.

Publicity: *Tales of the South Carolina Low Country, Golf Week, Augusta Magazine, PeeDee Magazine, Hidden Carolinas and Rice Plantations of Georgetown.*

"What a wonderful, relaxing place to stay! Your accommodations were excellent—first class."

Certificate may be used: Dec. 1 through Feb. 28, Sunday through Thursdays, except holidays. (Not applicable for Plantation House Suites.)

Salem   B2

Sunrise Farm B&B

325 Sunrise Dr
Salem, SC 29676-3444
(864)944-0121 (888)991-0121
Internet: www.bbonline.com/sc/sunrisefarm
E-mail: sfbb@bellsouth.net

Circa 1890. Situated on the remaining part of a 1,000-acre cotton plantation, this country Victorian features large porches with rockers and wicker. Guest rooms are furnished with period antiques, thick comforters, extra pillows and family heirlooms. The "corn crib" cottage is located in the original farm structure used for storing corn. It has a fully equipped kitchen, sitting area and bedroom with tub and shower. The June Rose Garden Cottage includes a river rock fireplace and full kitchen, as well as pastoral and mountain views. The inn offers a full breakfast and country picnic baskets.

Innkeeper(s): Barbara Laughter. $75-120. MC, VISA, TC. 4 rooms with PB and 2 cottages. Breakfast and snacks/refreshments included in rates. Types of meals: Full bkfst and cont plus. Beds: Q. TV, ceiling fan, VCR and free movies in room. Air conditioning. Antiquing, fishing, parks, sporting events & water sports nearby. Pets allowed: With advanced notice.
Location: Mountains.
Publicity: *National Geographic Traveler and Palmetto Places.*

"Saying thank you doesn't do our gratitude justice."

Certificate may be used: Jan. 1-March 30, Nov. 1-Dec. 1, cottages only.

Sumter   D7

Magnolia House

230 Church St
Sumter, SC 29150-4256
(803)775-6694 (888)666-0296
E-mail: magnoliahouse@sumter.net

Circa 1907. Each room of this Greek Revival home with its five fireplaces is decorated in antiques from a different era. Also gracing the inn are inlaid oak floors and stained-glass windows. Sumter's historic district includes neighborhood heroes such as George Franklin Haynesworth, who fired the first shot of The War Between the States. Guests may enjoy an afternoon refreshment in the formal backyard garden. Breakfast is served in the large dining room with massive French antiques.

Innkeeper(s): Pierre & Liz Tremblay. $85-135. MC, VISA, AX, PC, TC. 5 rooms, 4 with PB and 1 suite. Breakfast included in rates. Types of meals: Full gourmet bkfst and early coffee/tea. Beds: QDT. TV, phone, turndown service and ceiling fan in room. Air conditioning. VCR, bicycles and english gardens with fountains on premises. Antiquing, fishing, golf, kayaking, canoeing, live theater, parks and shopping nearby.
Pets allowed: Call inn first.
Location: City.

Certificate may be used: Anytime except Celtic Festival, Memorial Day weekend, 4th of July, Iris Festival and Labor Day weekend.

Union   B4

The Inn at Merridun

100 Merridun Pl
Union, SC 29379-2200
(864)427-7052 (888)892-6020 Fax:(864)429-0373
Internet: www.merridun.com
E-mail: info@merridun.com

Circa 1855. Nestled on nine acres of wooded ground, this Greek Revival inn is in a small Southern college town. During spring, see the South in its colorful splendor with blooming azaleas, magnolias and wisteria. Sip an iced drink on the inn's marble verandas and relive memories of a bygone era. Soft strains of Mozart and Beethoven, as well as the smell of freshly baked cookies and country suppers, fill the air of this antebellum country inn. In addition to a complimentary breakfast, guest will enjoy the inn's dessert selection offered every evening.

Innkeeper(s): Jim & Peggy Waller & JD the inn cat. $89-125. MC, VISA, AX, DS, PC, TC. 5 rooms with PB and 3 conference rooms. Breakfast included in rates. Types of meals: Full gourmet bkfst and early coffee/tea. Beds: KQT. Cable TV, phone, ceiling fan and hair dryers in room. Air conditioning. VCR, fax, copier, library, refrigerator on each floor for guest use, evening dessert and Miss Fannie's Tea Room on premises. Amusement parks, antiquing, fishing, parks, shopping, sporting events and water sports nearby.
Location: City.
Publicity: *Charlotte Observer, Bed & Breakfast, Spartanburg Herald, SCETV, Prime Time Live, BBC Documentary and Marshall Tucker Band Music Video.*

Certificate may be used: Jan. 15-Nov. 15, Sunday-Friday.

South Dakota

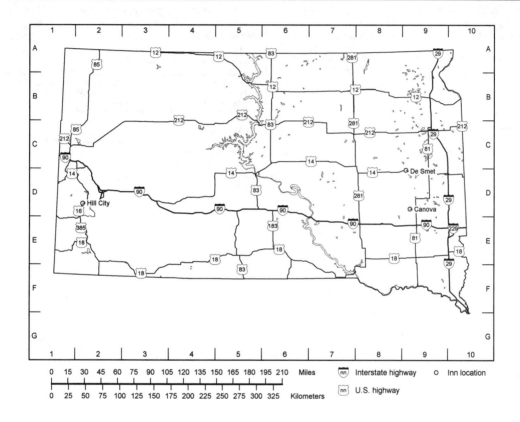

0 15 30 45 60 75 90 105 120 135 150 165 180 195 210 Miles

0 25 50 75 100 125 150 175 200 225 250 275 300 325 Kilometers

Interstate highway   o   Inn location

U.S. highway

Canova D9

B&B at Skoglund Farm

24375 438 Avenue
Canova, SD 57321-9726
(605)247-3445

Circa 1917. This is a working farm on the South Dakota prairie. Peacocks stroll around the farm along with cattle, chickens, emu and other fowl. Guests can enjoy an evening meal with the family. The innkeepers offer special rates for families with children. The farm's rates are $30 per adult, $25 per teen-ager and $20 per child. Children age five and younger stay for free.

Innkeeper(s): Alden & Delores Skoglund. $60. PC. 4 rooms. Breakfast and dinner included in rates. Types of meals: Full bkfst and early coffee/tea. Beds: QDT. TV in room. VCR and library on premises. Antiquing, fishing, parks, shopping, sporting events and water sports nearby.

Pets Allowed.

Location: Country.

"Thanks for the down-home hospitality and good food."

Certificate may be used: April 1-Dec. 1.

Hill City D2

High Country Ranch B&B Trail Rides

12172 Deerfield Rd
Hill City, SD 57745
(605)574-9003 (888)222-4628 Fax:(605)574-9003
Internet: www.rapidnet.com/~hcranch

Circa 1994. Ten cabins set on a grassy meadow offer skylights and private decks. Some have full kitchens, and there are special honeymoon and anniversary accommodations. The inn's special use permit allows guests to enjoy the Black Hills National Forest on horseback with half-day and full-day rides available. The dining room looks like a covered wagon. The ranch is close to Mount Rushmore.

Innkeeper(s): Larry and Bonnie McCaskell. $65-225. VISA, PC, TC. 10 cabins, 1 with FP. Breakfast included in rates. Types of meals: Full bkfst and early coffee/tea. Beds: Q. Cable TV, ceiling fan and VCR in room. Air conditioning. Fax, copier, spa and stables on premises. Handicap access. Fishing, golf, deer and turkey hunting, horse back riding, close to Mt Rushmore, live theater, parks, shopping, downhill skiing, cross-country skiing, tennis and water sports nearby.

Pets allowed: small pets are allowed deposit required, limited units.

Location: Guest Ranch.

Publicity: *Minnesota Monthly.*

Certificate may be used: Sept. 25-May 1.

Tennessee

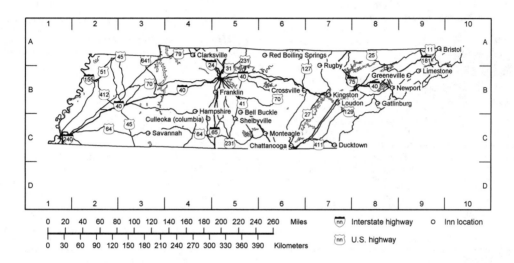

	1	2	3	4	5	6	7	8	9	10	

0 20 40 60 80 100 120 140 160 180 200 220 240 260   Miles

0 30 60 90 120 150 180 210 240 270 300 330 360 390   Kilometers

(nn) Interstate highway   o Inn location

(nn) U.S. highway

Bell Buckle   B5

Spring House B&B

201 Hinkle Hill, PO Box 363
Bell Buckle, TN 37020
(931)389-6400

Circa 1920. This country home was built as a boarding house, and the innkeepers have hosted several of the former boarders as guests. Guests are encouraged to relax at this comfortable house. From the front porch, guests can rock away the hours and watch as rail cars pass. Each of the rooms has a different theme. The Sewing Room contains a dress form, while the Western Room commemorates the Native American and Cowboy traditions.

Innkeeper(s): George Glover. $55-65. AX. 4 rooms. Breakfast included in rates. Type of meal: Full gourmet bkfst. Beds: QDT. Fishing nearby.
Publicity: *Tullahoma News and Guardian.*

Certificate may be used: All months except August.

Bristol   A9

New Hope B&B

822 Georgia Ave
Bristol, TN 37620-4024
(423)989-3343 (888)989-3343
Internet: www.bbonline.com/tn/newhope/
E-mail: newhope@preferred.com

Circa 1892. Abram Reynolds, older brother of R.J. Reynolds, once owned the property that surrounds this inn, and one of the guest rooms is named in his honor. Each of the rooms has been creatively decorated with bright prints and cheerful wall-coverings, emphasizing the high ceilings and wood floors. Clawfoot tubs, transoms over the doors and distinctive wood-work are some of the period elements featured in this late Victorian home. Bristol is known as a birthplace for country music, and the innkeepers pay homage to the history with the whimsically decorated Tennessee Ernie Ford hallway. Ford got his start in Bristol, and pictures, record jackets, books and wall-paper fashioned from sheet music bedeck the hallway. The home is located in the historic Fairmount area, and a guided walking tour begins at New Hope. Half of the town of Bristol is located in Tennessee and the other half in Virginia.

Innkeeper(s): Tom & Tonda Fluke. $95-155. MC, VISA, AX, PC, TC. 4 rooms with PB, 1 with FP. Breakfast and snacks/refreshments included in rates. Types of meals: Full bkfst and early coffee/tea. Beds: KQT. Cable TV, phone, ceiling fan and whirlpool tub for two in room. Air conditioning. Library and large game room on premises. Antiquing, fishing, golf, live theater, parks, shopping and downhill skiing nearby.

Location: Blue Ridge Mtn, Caverns.

Publicity: *Tennessee Getaways. Bristol Herald Courier.*

"It was like a second home in such a short time."

Certificate may be used: All year, Sunday through Thursday.

Chattanooga   C6

Adams Hilborne Mansion Inn & Restaurant

801 Vine St
Chattanooga, TN 37403-2318
(423)265-5000 Fax:(423)265-5555
Internet: www.innjoy.com

Circa 1889. This former mayor's mansion of Tudor and Romanesque design was presented with the 1997 award for Excellence in Preservation by the National Trust. The interior of this gracious home boasts 16-foot ceilings and floors patterned from three different woods. The large entrance hall features carved cornices, a coiffured ceiling and a fireplace. Every room offers something special, from Tiffany windows and beveled glass to the mansion's eight fireplaces and luxurious ballroom. The cornerstone of the Fortwood Historic District, Chattanooga's finest historic residential area, the mansion has also received the coveted City Beautiful Award.

Innkeeper(s): Wendy & Dave Adams. $100-275. MC, VISA, AX, TC. 10 rooms with PB, 4 with FP and 3 suites. Breakfast included in rates. Types of meals: Cont plus and early coffee/tea. Beds: KQD. Cable TV, phone, turndown service and VCR in room. Air conditioning. Fax, copier, library and smoking pub bar on premises. Amusement parks, antiquing, fishing, live theater, parks, shopping, sporting events and water sports nearby.

Location: City.

Publicity: Chatanooga News Free, Nashville Tennessean, Southern Accents, National Geographic, Preservation Magazine, Traveler, News Free Press., PBS, CBS and NBC.

Certificate may be used: Sunday-Thursday, January, February, March except Valentine's Day and other special times.

Clarksville   A4

Hachland Hill Inn

1601 Madison St
Clarksville, TN 37043-4980
(931)647-4084 Fax:(931)552-3454

Circa 1795. This log cabin contains a dining room and, in a stone-walled chamber, a place where pioneers sought refuge during Indian attacks. Three of Clarksville's oldest log houses have been reconstructed in the garden where old-fashioned barbeque suppers and square dances are held. Newly built rooms are available in the brick building, so request the log cabin if you want authentic historic atmosphere.

Innkeeper(s): Phila Hach. $95. MC, VISA, AX. 20 rooms, 10 with PB, 3 with FP and 1 conference room. Type of meal: Full bkfst. Beds: D. Fax on premises. Handicap access.

Certificate may be used: Anytime on availability. Breakfast served for extra charge.

Crossville   B6

An-Jen Inn

8654 Hwy 127 North
Crossville, TN 38555-9700
(931)456-0515

Circa 1910. Innkeeper Sandra Monk-Goldston's family has lived on this 25-acre spread for seven generations. She was born in the turn-of-the-century house that now serves as a six-

room bed & breakfast. She named her inn after two nieces, Andrea and Jennifer, and they each have a room named after them, as well. The inn is decorated in a nostalgic Victorian theme, with antiques and family pieces. In addition to the inn, Sandra operates the Fantasy Wedding Chapel in a adjacent building that resembles a tiny country church.

Innkeeper(s): Sandra & Ron Goldston. $60. PC. 6 rooms. Breakfast included in rates. Types of meals: Full bkfst and early coffee/tea. Beds: D. Cable TV, phone, turndown service, ceiling fan and VCR in room. Air conditioning. Spa, swimming and wedding chapel on premises. Amusement parks, antiquing, fishing, golf, live theater, parks, shopping, sporting events, tennis and water sports nearby.

Location: Mountains.

Publicity: Tennessee Living.

Certificate may be used: Monday-Thursday, November through February.

Culleoka (Columbia)   C4

Sweetwater Inn B&B

2436 Campbells Station Rd
Culleoka (Columbia), TN 38451-2304
(931)987-3077 Fax:(931)987-2525
Internet: www.bbonline.com/tn/sweetwater/

Circa 1900. This turn-of-the-century Gothic Steamboat-style country home, set in the middle of Tennessee, is a perfect base to explore the surrounding country-side. There are two wraparound porches and lots of rocking chairs to sit in while viewing the breathtaking vistas of soft rolling hills. Each of the four individually decorated guest rooms has access to the second-floor porch, where guests can watch the sunrise with an early-morning cup of coffee or tea. A sumptuous gourmet breakfast is served daily.

Innkeeper(s): Melissa McEwen. $100-135. MC, VISA, DS, PC, TC. 4 rooms with PB and 2 suites. Breakfast, afternoon tea and snacks/refreshments included in rates. Type of meal: Full gourmet bkfst. Beds: Q. Turndown service and ceiling fan in room. Air conditioning. VCR, fax and copier on premises. Antiquing, fishing, golf, live theater, parks, shopping and tennis nearby.

Location: Rolling countryside.

Publicity: Nashville Woman.

"Exceptional, beautiful, and so worthy of praise! It seemed a magical beginning to awaken in such a "timeless" place."

Certificate may be used: Sunday through Thursday, April 1-Sept. 30; Oct. 1-March 30, anytime.

Ducktown   C7

The White House B&B

104 Main St, PO Box 668
Ducktown, TN 37326-0668
(423)496-4166 (800)775-4166 Fax:(423)496-9778
Internet: www.bbonline.com/tn/whitehouse
E-mail: mardan@tds.net

Circa 1898. This Queen Anne Victorian boasts a wraparound porch with a swing. Rooms are decorated in traditional style with family antiques. Innkeepers pamper their guests with Tennessee hospitality, a hearty country breakfast and a mouth-watering sundae bar in the evenings. The innkeepers also help guests plan daily activities, and the area is bursting with possibilities. Hiking, horseback riding, panning for gold and driving tours are only a few choices. The Ocoee River is the perfect place for a river float trip or take on the challenge of roaring rapids.

The river was selected as the site of the 1996 Summer Olympic Whitewater Slalom events.

Innkeeper(s): Dan & Mardee Kauffman. $69-79. MC, VISA, DS, PC, TC. 3 rooms, 1 with PB. Breakfast, afternoon tea and snacks/refreshments included in rates. Types of meals: Full gourmet bkfst and early coffee/tea. Beds: QT. Ceiling fan and central heat in room. Central air. VCR, fax and library on premises. Antiquing, fishing, parks, shopping and water sports nearby.
Location: Small town in the mountains.
Publicity: *Southern Living.*

"We wanted a relaxing couple of days in the mountains and that's what we got. Thank you."

Certificate may be used: Sunday through Thursday, April-November. Everyday, December through March. Holidays and special events excluded.

Franklin   B5

Namaste Acres Country Ranch Inn

5436 Leipers Creek Rd
Franklin, TN 37064-9208
(615)791-0333

Circa 1993. This handsome Dutch Colonial is directly across the street from the original Natchez Trace. As the B&B is within walking distance of miles of hiking and horseback riding trails. Each of the suites includes private entrances and features individual themes. One room boasts rustic, cowboy decor with a clawfoot tub, hand-crafted furnishings, log and rope beds, and rough sawn lumber walls. The innkeepers chose the name Namaste from an Indian word, and carry an Indian theme in one of the guest rooms. Namaste Acres is just 12 miles outside of historic Franklin, which offers plenty of shops, a self-guided walking tour, Civil War sites and the largest assortment of antique dealers in the United States.

Innkeeper(s): Lisa Winters. $75-85. MC, VISA, AX, DS, PC. 3 rooms. Type of meal: Full bkfst. Beds: Q. Spa & swimming on premises. Guided trail rides nearby.
Publicity: *Southern Living, Western Horseman and Horse Illustrated.*

Certificate may be used: Year-round, Sunday-Thursday only. No holidays.

Gatlinburg   B8

7th Heaven Log Inn on The Golf Resort

3944 Castle Rd
Gatlinburg, TN 37738-6321
(423)430-5000 (800)248-2923 Fax:(423)436-7748
E-mail: heaveninn@aol.com

Circa 1991. This log inn is located on the seventh green of the Bent Creek Golf Resort within scenic Smoky Mountain National Park. Four of the five rooms are located on the same level as the golf course and open into a common area with a kitchen, fireplace, pool table and plenty of games and books. A wraparound deck offers a view of the golf course and surrounding mountains. One guest room, Laura's Lit'l Heaven, has a whirlpool tub, private entrance and a deck. There is a log gazebo with a hot tub. Aside from the many outdoor activities available in and around the national park, Dollywood, a casino, country music theaters and outlet shopping are nearby.

Innkeeper(s): Cheryl & Donald Roese. $97-137. MC, VISA, PC, TC. 5 rooms with PB and 1 suite. Breakfast and snacks/refreshments included in rates. Types of meals: Full bkfst and early coffee/tea. Beds: KQD. Ceiling fan, cable TV and VCR in suite in room. Air conditioning. VCR, fax, copier, sauna, kitchen, pool table, card table, bumper pool and books on premises. Amusement parks, antiquing, fishing, live theater, parks, shopping, downhill skiing, sporting events and water sports nearby.
Location: On golf course.

"Five days was not enough. We'll be back."

Certificate may be used: Nov. 1-June 1, Sunday-Thursday, excluding holidays.

Greeneville   B9

Hilltop House B&B

6 Sanford Cir
Greeneville, TN 37743-4022
(423)639-8202

Circa 1920. Situated on a bluff overlooking the Nolichuckey River valley, this manor home boasts mountain views from each of the guest rooms. The Elizabeth Noel room, named for the original owner, includes among its treasures a canopy bed, sitting room and a private veranda, a perfect spot to watch the sunsets. After a hearty breakfast, take a stroll across the beautifully landscaped grounds. Innkeeper Denise Ashworth is a landscape architect and guests will marvel at her wonderful gardens. Ashworth sponsors several gardening workshops each year at the inn, covering topics such as flower arranging, Christmas decorations and landscaping your home grounds.

Innkeeper(s): Denise Ashworth. $75-80. MC, VISA, AX, PC, TC. 3 rooms with PB. Breakfast and afternoon tea included in rates. Types of meals: Full gourmet bkfst and early coffee/tea. Beds: KQD. Cable TV, phone, turndown service and VCR in room. Air conditioning. Library and exercise room on premises. Antiquing, fishing, golf, hiking, horseback riding, live theater, parks, shopping and water sports nearby.
Location: Mountains.
Publicity: *Country Inns.*

"Peaceful and comfortable, great change of pace."

Certificate may be used: Jan. 1-March 31.

Nolichuckey Bluffs

400 Kinser Park Lane
Greeneville, TN 37743-4748
(423)787-7947 (800)842-4690 Fax:(423)787-9247
Internet: www.usit.net/cabins
E-mail: cabins@usit.net

Circa 1997. Comprised of six cabins and three B&B guest rooms, this inn boasts 16 wooded acres overlooking the river. Redbud Cabin, for instance, offers two bedrooms, a kitchen, dining area and living room. Six can sleep here, and there are generously-sized decks and a fireplace, (air conditioning, too). In the main house, Pamela's Room has a queen bed, Jacuzzi and a mountain view. A full breakfast is served. Best of all is the hot tub/gazebo perched high on the blufftop over the river.

Innkeeper(s): Patricia & Brooke Sadler. $70-95. MC, VISA, DS, PC, TC. 7 rooms with PB, 3 with FP and 6 cottages. Breakfast and snacks/refreshments included in rates. Types of meals: Full bkfst and early coffee/tea. Beds: KQDT. Cable TV, phone, turndown service, ceiling fan and VCR in room. Air conditioning. Fax, copier, spa, bicycles and library on premises. Antiquing, fishing, golf, parks, shopping and tennis nearby.
Pets allowed: In one cabin only.
Location: Mountains.

Certificate may be used: Sunday through Thursday nights all months except October.

Hampshire   B4

Ridgetop B&B

Hwy 412 W, PO Box 193
Hampshire, TN 38461-0193
(615)285-2777 (800)377-2770
E-mail: natcheztrace@worldnet.att.net

Circa 1979. This contemporary Western cedar house rests on 20 cleared acres along the top of the ridge. A quarter-mile below is a waterfall. Blueberries grow in abundance on the property and guests may pick them in summer. These provide the filling for luscious breakfast muffins, waffles and pancakes year-round. There are 170 acres in all, mostly wooded. Picture windows and a deck provide views of the trees and wildlife: flying squirrels, birds, raccoons and deer. The inn is handicap-accessible. The innkeepers will help guests plan excursions on the Natchez Trace, including biking trips.

Innkeeper(s): Bill & Kay Jones. $75-95. MC, VISA, PC, TC. 3 rooms, 1 with FP, 1 cottage and 1 cabin. Breakfast included in rates. Types of meals: Full bkfst and early coffee/tea. Beds: DT. Ceiling fan in room. Air conditioning. Handicap access. Antiquing, fishing, antebellum homes, parks, shopping and water sports nearby.

Pets allowed: In outbuilding.

Location: Countryside.

Publicity: *Columbia Daily Herald.*

"What a delightful visit! Thank you for creating such a peaceful, immaculate, interesting environment for us!"

Certificate may be used: Nov. 15-March 15; July 6-Aug. 31, excluding holidays.

Kingston B7

Whitestone Country Inn

1200 Paint Rock Rd
Kingston, TN 37763-5843
(423)376-0113 (888)247-2464 Fax:(423)376-4454
Internet: www.whitestones.com
E-mail: moreinfo@whitestones.com

Circa 1995. This regal farmhouse sits majestically on a hilltop overlooking miles of countryside and Watts Bar Lake. The inn is surrounded by 360 acres, some of which borders a scenic lake, where guests can enjoy fishing or simply communing with nature. There are eight miles of hiking trails, and the many porches and decks are perfect places to relax. The inn's interior is as pleasing as the exterior surroundings.  Guest rooms are elegantly appointed, and each includes a fireplace and whirlpool tub. Guests are treated to a hearty, country-style breakfast, and dinners and lunch are available by reservation. The inn is one hour from Chattanooga, Knoxville and the Great Smoky Mountains National Park.

Innkeeper(s): Paul & Jean Cowell. $105-200. MC, VISA, AX, DS, PC, TC. 16 rooms with PB, 16 with FP and 2 conference rooms. Breakfast included in rates. Type of meal: Full bkfst. Beds: KQ. Cable TV, phone, turndown service, ceiling fan and VCR in room. Air conditioning. Fax, copier, spa, sauna and library on premises. Handicap access. Antiquing, fishing, golf, shopping and water sports nearby.

Location: Mountains.

"Not only have you built a place of beauty, you have established a sanctuary of rest. An escape from the noise and hurry of everyday life."

Certificate may be used: Jan. 1 to March 31, Sunday-Thursday.

Limestone B9

Snapp Inn B&B

1990 Davy Crockett Park Rd
Limestone, TN 37681-6026
(423)257-2482

Circa 1815. From the second-story porch of this brick Federal, guests enjoy views of local farmland as well as the sounds of Big Limestone Creek. The Smoky Mountains are seen from the back

porch. Decorated with locally gathered antiques, the home is within walking distance of Davy Crockett Birthplace State Park. A full country breakfast often includes Ruth's homemade biscuits.

Innkeeper(s): Ruth & Dan Dorgan. $65. MC, VISA, PC, TC. 2 rooms with PB. Breakfast included in rates. Types of meals: Full bkfst and early coffee/tea. Beds: QD. Air conditioning. VCR, library and pool table on premises. Antiquing, fishing, golf, swimming, hiking, live theater, parks, shopping and water sports nearby.

Pets Allowed.

Location: River & creek.

Publicity: *Greenville Sun.*

Certificate may be used: Anytime, subject to availability.

Loudon B7

The Mason Place B&B

600 Commerce St
Loudon, TN 37774-1101
(865)458-3921 Fax:(865)458-6092
Internet: www.themasonplace.com
E-mail: thempbb@aol.com

Circa 1865. In the National Register, Mason Place is acclaimed for its award-winning restoration. In the Greek Revival style, the inn has a red slate roof and graceful columns. Three porches overlook three acres of  lawns, trees and gardens. Inside, guests are welcomed to a grand entrance hall and tasteful antiques. There are 10 working fireplaces in the mansion's 7,000 square feet. Guests enjoy the Grecian swimming pool, gazebo and wisteria-covered arbor. A favorite honeymoon getaway has been created from the old smokehouse. It features brick walls and floors, a library loft, feather bed, wood burning Franklin fireplace and a tin bathtub (once feature in the movie Maverick).

Innkeeper(s): Bob & Donna Siewert. $96-135. PC, TC. 5 rooms with PB, 5 with FP. Breakfast included in rates. Types of meals: Full gourmet bkfst and early coffee/tea. Beds: Q. Air conditioning. Horseshoe and croquet on premises. Amusement parks, antiquing, fishing, white water rafting, parks, shopping, tennis and wineries nearby.

Location: Quaint civil war town of 5000.

Publicity: *Country Inn, Country Side, Country Travels, Tennessee Cross Roads, Antiquing in Tennessee, Knox-Chattanooga, Oak Ridge and Detroit Magazine.*

"Absolutely wonderful in every way. You are in for a treat! The best getaway ever!"

Certificate may be used: January, February, March, Sunday-Thursday.

Monteagle C6

Adams Edgeworth Inn

Monteagle Assembly
Monteagle, TN 37356
(931)924-4000 Fax:(931)924-3236
Internet: www.innjoy.com
E-mail: innjoy@blomand.com

Built in 1896 this National Register Victorian inn recently has been refurbished in a country-chintz style. Original paintings, sculptures and country antiques are found throughout. Wide verandas are filled with wicker furnishings and breezy hammocks, and there's an award-winning chef

who will prepare candle-lit five-course dinners. You can stroll through the 96-acre Victorian village that surrounds the inn and enjoy rolling hills, creeks and Victorian cottages. Waterfalls, natural caves and scenic overlooks are along the 150 miles of hiking trails of nearby South Cumberland State Park.

Innkeeper(s): Wendy Adams. $100-275. MC, VISA, AX. 12 rooms with PB, 4 with FP, 1 suite and 1 conference room. Breakfast included in rates. Type of meal: Full bkfst. Beds: KQD. Phone, air-conditioning and ceiling fan and TV (some rooms) in room. VCR, fax and copier on premises. Antiquing, fishing, hiking, caving, historic architecture, live theater, parks, shopping and sporting events nearby.

Location: Mountains.

Publicity: *Country Inns, Chattanooga News Free Press, Tempo, Gourmet, Victorian Homes, Brides, Tennessean, Southern Living, National Geographic, Inn Country., PBS Crossroads, ABC TV, CBS TV and Travel Channel.*

Certificate may be used: January, February, March, November and December, Sunday-Thursday (except special events such as Valentine's, New Year's, etc. and subject to availability).

Newport   B8

Christopher Place - An Intimate Resort

1500 Pinnacles Way
Newport, TN 37821-7308
(423)623-6555 (800)595-9441 Fax:(423)613-4771
Internet: www.christopherplace.com
E-mail: thebestinn@aol.com

Circa 1976. Although it was built in the mid-1970s, this mansion has the appearance of a great Antebellum estate. The inn is surrounded by more than 200 acres and offers views of the Great Smoky Mountains. The inn's interior, as well as its reputation for hospitality and service, earned it a four-diamond award. Country Inns magazine and Waverly chose Christopher Place's Stargazer as the 1995 Room of the Year. Each of the guest rooms is decorated with a different theme in mind. The Roman Holiday room is a romantic retreat with an iron canopy bed draped with a sheer, dramatic canopy. There is a fireplace and a whirlpool tub for two. Papaw's Suite is a rustic room with a hand-carved bed and hot tub. In addition to the inn's transfixing decor, guests are further pampered with on-site tennis courts, a sauna, swimming pool, billiards and library. As well, Gatlinburg and Pigeon Forge aren't far away.

Innkeeper(s): Tim Hall. $150-300. MC, VISA, AX, DS, PC, TC. 8 rooms with PB, 2 with FP, 6 suites and 1 conference room. Breakfast included in rates. Types of meals: Full bkfst and early coffee/tea. Beds: KQD. Cable TV, phone, turndown service, ceiling fan and VCR in room. Air conditioning. Fax, copier, swimming, sauna, tennis, library, billiard room and hiking trails on premises. Handicap access. Amusement parks, antiquing, fishing, golf, parks, shopping, downhill skiing, tennis and water sports nearby.

Location: Mountains.

Publicity: *Knox News, Country Inns, Sentinel and Country Almanac.*

Certificate may be used: Jan. 1-May 31, Sunday-Thursday check-in.

Red Boiling Springs   A6

Armours Hotel

321 E Main St
Red Boiling Springs, TN 37150-2322
(615)699-2180 Fax:(615)699-5111
Internet: www.armours.homestead.com
E-mail: armours@mindspring.com

Circa 1924. As Tennessee's only remaining mineral bathhouse, this two-story, National Historic Register house is tucked away in the rolling hills of the Cumberland Plateau. Whether resting in one of the 23 antique-furnished guest rooms, listening to the babbling creek from the second-floor veranda, strolling under covered bridges, or simply enjoying the sunrise in a rocking chair on the porch before breakfast, tranquillity awaits each guest. Spend the afternoon in the gazebo

with your favorite book from the library next door, or get in a game of tennis at the park across the street before dinner.

Innkeeper(s): Joy B Pike. $45. MC, VISA, AX, PC, TC. 23 rooms with PB and 3 suites. Breakfast and dinner included in rates. Type of meal: Country bkfst. Beds: KQDT. Air conditioning. VCR, fax, copier, tennis, library, volleyball, steam and mineral baths, massage room and badminton on premises. Antiquing, bicycling, fishing, golf, hiking, parks, shopping and tennis nearby.

Location: Country.

Publicity: *Southern Living and Country Crossroads.*

Certificate may be used: January through April.

Rugby   A7

Newbury House at Historic Rugby

Hwy 52, PO Box 8
Rugby, TN 37733-0008
(423)628-2430 Fax:(423)628-2266

Circa 1880. Mansard-roofed Newbury House first lodged visitors traveling to this English village when author and social reformer Thomas Hughes founded Rugby. Filled with authentic Victorian antiques, the inn includes some furnishings that are original to the colony. There are also several restored cottages on the property, and there is a two-room suite with a queen bed, two twin beds and a private bathroom.

Innkeeper(s): Historic Rugby. $65-89. MC, VISA, PC, TC. 6 rooms, 4 with PB, 1 suite and 2 cottages. Types of meals: Full bkfst and early coffee/tea. Beds: QDT. Ceiling fan in room. Air conditioning. Library and veranda on premises. Antiquing, fishing, hiking, historic village, building tours, parks, shopping and water sports nearby.

Location: Tiny village on Cumberland Pl.

Publicity: *New York Times, Americana, USA Weekend, Tennessean, Southern Living, Atlanta Journal-Constitution, Victorian Homes and A&E History Channel.*

"I love the peaceful atmosphere here and the beauty of nature surrounding Rugby."

Certificate may be used: June 1-Sept. 30 and Nov. 1-April 30, excluding Friday and Saturday nights.

Savannah   C3

White Elephant B&B Inn

304 Church St
Savannah, TN 38372
(901)925-6410
Internet: www.bbonline.com/tn/elephant/

Circa 1901. Guests will know they've arrived at the right place
when they spot the white elephants on the front lawn of this
Queen Anne Victorian. Listed in the National Register as part
of the Savannah Historic District, it offers a wraparound veranda, back porch swing and shade from tall sugar maples. There
are curved bay windows and, of course, a tower. Guest rooms
feature antiques (ask for the Poppy Room) and bathrooms with
clawfoot tubs. At breakfast, in addition to the silver, crystal and
fine service, guests may find French toast made in the shape of
an elephant. Afternoon refreshments are served and include the
innkeeper's award-winning cookies. Turndown service is another special addition. Innkeeper Ken Hansgen offers guided tours
of nearby Shiloh National Military park.

Innkeeper(s): Ken & Sharon Hansgen. $90-110. PC, TC. 3 rooms with PB.
Breakfast and snacks/refreshments included in rates. Types of meals: Full
bkfst and early coffee/tea. Beds: Q. Ceiling fan in room. Central air. VCR,
library, croquet, radio, CD player and pump organ on premises. Antiquing,
bicycling, canoeing/kayaking, fishing, golf, hiking, Natchez Trace, live theater,
museums, parks, shopping, sporting events, tennis and water sports nearby.

Location: City.

Publicity: *Nashville Tennessean, Jackson Sun, Birmingham News,
Savannah Courier, Memphis Commercial Appeal, Tennessee Magazine
and Country Magazine.*

Certificate may be used: Jan. 1-Dec. 31, Sunday-Thursday.

Shelbyville   C5

Cinnamon Ridge B&B

799 Whitthorne St
Shelbyville, TN 37160-3501
(931)685-9200 (877)685-9200 Fax:(931)684-0978
Internet: www.bbonline.com/tn/cinnamon/

Circa 1927. Tennessee offers many reasons to visit, not the
least of which is this hospitable home. The light scent of cinnamon permeates the home, which is decorated with antiques in
a mix of Colonial and Traditional styles. Innkeeper Pat Sherrill
loves to pamper guests, especially with food. The full breakfasts
are accompanied by candlelight and soft, soothing music. Pat
serves afternoon teas and has created a few special events,
including her Chocolate Lovers' Paradise, where guests enjoy a
variety of cocoa-laden delicacies.

Innkeeper(s): Bill & Pat Sherrill. $65-75. MC, VISA, AX, TC. 5 rooms with
PB and 1 conference room. Breakfast, afternoon tea and snacks/refreshments
included in rates. Types of meals: Full bkfst and early coffee/tea. Beds: KD.
Cable TV, phone, ceiling fan and central heat in room. Central air. VCR, fax
and bicycles on premises. Amusement parks, antiquing, fishing, live theater,
parks, shopping and water sports nearby.

Location: Rolling hills, historic area.

Certificate may be used: Jan. 7-Nov. 13, Sunday through Wednesday.

Texas

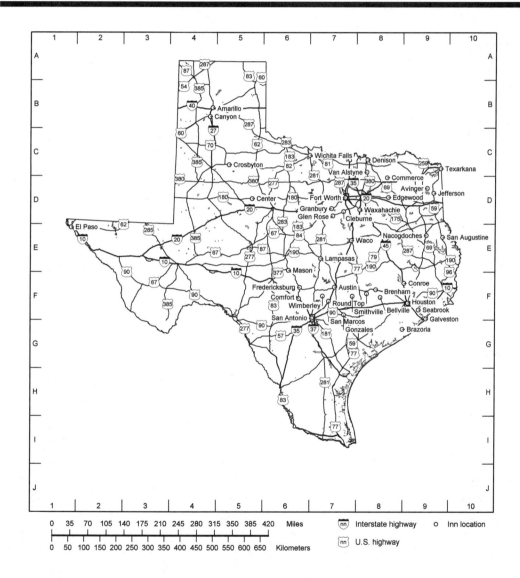

	1	2	3	4	5	6	7	8	9	10

Legend:
- 🛡 Interstate highway
- ○ Inn location
- 🛡 U.S. highway

Miles scale: 0 35 70 105 140 175 210 245 280 315 350 385 420

Kilometers scale: 0 50 100 150 200 250 300 350 400 450 500 550 600 650

Amarillo   B4

Parkview House B&B

1311 S Jefferson St
Amarillo, TX 79101-4029
(806)373-9464
Internet: hometown.aol.com/Parkviewbb/index.htm
E-mail: parkviewbb@aol.com

Circa 1908. Ionic columns support the wraparound wicker-
filled front porch of this prairie Victorian. Herb and rose gardens, highlighted by statuary and Victorian gazing ball, surround the property. Antique mahogany, walnut and oak pieces
are found throughout. Guest rooms all feature draped bedsteads and romantic decor. A gourmet, full or continental-plus
breakfast is served in an Andy Warhol-style kitchen or in the
formal dining room. Guests can relax and enjoy the fireplaces,
there's one in the kitchen and another in the common room.
After a day of sightseeing, guests can enjoy a soak under the
stars in the inn's hot tub or borrow a bicycle for a tour of the
historic neighborhood. There are a multitude of area attractions, including shopping for antiques along historic Route 66,
hiking in Palo Duro Canyon, touring historic homes and museums, hiking, birdwatching or perhaps attending the ballet,
opera, symphony or a performance of "Texas," an outdoor
musical drama presented nearby.

Innkeeper(s): Carol & Nabil Dia. $65-135. MC, VISA, AX, PC, TC. 5 rooms, 3
with PB, 1 suite and 1 cottage. Breakfast included in rates. Types of meals:
Full gourmet bkfst, cont plus and early coffee/tea. Beds: QD. TV, some ceiling
fans, desks and telephones in room. Air conditioning. VCR, fax and bicycles on
premises. Amusement parks, antiquing, bicycling, hiking, horseback riding,
bird watching, live theater, parks, shopping, tennis and water sports nearby.

Location: City.

Publicity: Lubbock Avalanche, Amarillo Globe News, Accent West, Sunday
Telegraph Review and Channel 7.

"You are what give B&Bs such a wonderful reputation. Thanks very
much for the wonderful stay! The hospitality was warm and the
ambiance incredible."

Certificate may be used: Anytime, excluding holidays or weekends, Christmas,
New Year's, Valentine's, Memorial Day, Mother's and Father's Day, etc.

Austin   F7

Carrington's Bluff

1900 David St
Austin, TX 78705-5312
(512)479-0638 (800)871-8908 Fax:(512)476-4769
Internet: www.citysearch.com/aus/carringtonbluff
E-mail: governorsinn@earthlink.net

Circa 1877. Situated on a tree-covered bluff in the heart of
Austin, this inn sits next to a 500-year-old oak tree. The
innkeepers, one a Texan, the other British, combine down-
home hospitality with English charm. The house is filled with
English and American antiques and handmade quilts. Rooms
are carefully decorated with dried flowers, inviting colors and
antique beds, such as the oak barley twist bed in the Martha
Hill Carrington Room. After a hearty breakfast, relax on a 35-
foot-long porch that overlooks the bluff. The Austin area is
booming with things to do.

Innkeeper(s): Lisa Kloss. $69-109. MC, VISA, AX, DC, CB, DS, PC, TC. 8
rooms with PB, 1 suite, 1 cottage and 1 conference room. Breakfast and
snacks/refreshments included in rates. Types of meals: Full gourmet bkfst and

early coffee/tea. Beds: KQDT. Cable TV, phone and ceiling fan in room. Air
conditioning. VCR, fax, copier, library and child care on premises.
Amusement parks, antiquing, fishing, live theater, parks, shopping, sporting
events and water sports nearby.

Location: City.

Publicity: PBS Special.

"Victorian writer's dream place."

Certificate may be used: Jan. 2-Dec. 1, Sunday-Thursday only.

Governors' Inn

611 W 22nd St
Austin, TX 78705-5115
(512)479-0638 (800)871-8908 Fax:(512)476-4769
Internet: www.governorsinnaustin.com
E-mail: governorsinn@earthlink.net

Circa 1897. This Neoclassical Victorian is just a few blocks
from the University of Texas campus and three blocks from the
State Capitol. Guests can enjoy the view of two acres of trees
and foliage from the porches that decorate each story of the
inn. The innkeepers have decorated the guest rooms with
antiques and named them after former Texas governors. Several
of the bathrooms include clawfoot tubs.

Innkeeper(s): Lisa Kloss. $59-119. MC, VISA, AX, DC, CB, DS, TC. 10
rooms with PB, 5 with FP and 1 conference room. Breakfast, afternoon tea
and snacks/refreshments included in rates. Types of meals: Full gourmet bkfst
and early coffee/tea. Beds: KQ. Cable TV, phone, turndown service, ceiling
fan, hair dryers and robes in room. Air conditioning. VCR, fax and copier on
premises. Handicap access. Antiquing, fishing, live theater, parks, shopping,
sporting events and water sports nearby.

Pets Allowed.

Location: City.

Publicity: Romantic Inns of America.

Certificate may be used: Jan. 2-Dec. 1, Sunday-Thursday only.

Woodburn House B&B

4401 Avenue D
Austin, TX 78751-3714
(512)458-4335 (888)690-9763 Fax:(512)458-4319
Internet: www.woodburnhouse.com
E-mail: woodburn@iamerica.net

Circa 1909. This stately home was named for Bettie Hamilton
Woodburn, who bought the house in 1920. Hamilton's father
was once the provisional governor of Texas and a friend of
Abraham Lincoln. The home
once was slated for demolition
and saved in 1979 when George
Boutwell bought the home for $1
and moved it to its present location. Guests will be taken immediately by the warmth of the home
surrounded by old trees. The home is furnished with period
antiques. Breakfasts are served formally in the dining room.

Innkeeper(s): Herb & Sandra Dickson. $80-130. MC, VISA, AX, PC, TC. 4
rooms with PB and 1 suite. Breakfast included in rates. Types of meals: Full
gourmet bkfst and early coffee/tea. Beds: KQT. Phone, ceiling fan, whirlpool
for two, double vanity, sitting room with sofa and and TV in suite in room. Air
conditioning. VCR, fax and amenities for the deaf on premises. Antiquing,
fishing, museum, live theater, parks, shopping and sporting events nearby.

Publicity: Austin Chronicle, Dallas Morning News, Usa Today and Hard Promises.

"The comfort, the breakfasts and the hospitality were excellent and
greatly appreciated."

Certificate may be used: Sunday-Thursday, no holidays, excluding February,
March, April, October & November.

Avinger   D9

McKenzie Manor

Rt 1 Box 440
Avinger, TX 75630-9648
(903)755-2240

Circa 1964. Nature trails with private ponds are right outside
the door of this rustic, rock lodge set on the shore of Lake O'
The Pines. Guests can sit on wide decks and watch eagles soar,
beavers build dams and deer graze. Relax in the gazebo or by
the large rock fireplace with a good book from the private
library of innkeeper, historian and author Fred McKenzie. This
four-generation family home is designed with a large meeting
room, vaulted ceilings and stained-glass windows. All rooms
are adjacent to sitting areas and each room is decorated in its
own unique style with antiques and family possessions.
Innkeeper(s): Anne & Fred McKenzie. $65-95. MC, VISA, PC, TC. 7 rooms, 5
with PB, 1 with FP, 1 suite and 1 conference room. Breakfast and afternoon
tea included in rates. Types of meals: Full bkfst, cont plus and early
coffee/tea. Beds: KQD. Ceiling fan in room. Air conditioning. Swimming,
library and canoe & fishing boat on premises. Handicap access. Antiquing,
fishing, live theater, shopping and water sports nearby.
Certificate may be used: Jan. 15-Feb. 15, Feb. 25-April 28, July 1-Nov. 21,
Dec. 15-21.

Bellville   F8

High Cotton Inn

214 S Live Oak St
Bellville, TX 77418-2340
(409)865-9796 (800)321-9796 Fax:(409)865-5588

Use of the downstairs parlor, fenced swimming pool and bottomless cookie jar is encouraged at this Victorian B&B. Porch
swings are strategically located on the balcony and front porch.
There's a cozy upstairs sitting room for reading, television or
conversation. Around 9 a.m. each morning, guests gather in
the old family dining room for a full Southern-style breakfast.
Innkeepers can provide information on excursions to Blue Bell
Creamery, Winedale, Round Top and Festival Hill.
Innkeeper(s): Anna Horton. $60-75. 5 rooms. Breakfast included in rates. Type
of meal: Full bkfst. Ceiling fan in room. Air conditioning. Antiquing nearby.
Certificate may be used: Sunday through Thursday.

Brazoria   G8

Roses & The River

7074 CR 506
Brazoria, TX 77422
(409)798-1070 (800)610-1070 Fax:(409)798-1070
E-mail: hosack@tgn.net

Circa 1980. This Texas farmhouse rests beside the banks of the
San Bernard River. There is a sweeping veranda lined with rockers, and the two-acre grounds are well landscaped with an
impressive rose garden. Each of the three guest rooms has been
decorated with a rose theme. Rooms are named New Dawn,
Rainbow's End and Rise 'n Shine. Two rooms view the river
and one views the rose gardens. Breakfasts include unique
treats such as a "blushing orange cooler," grapefruit baked
Alaska, homemade sweet rolls and savory egg dishes. The area
offers many attractions, including two wildlife refuges, Sea

Center Texas, where guests can learn about marine life, the
Center for the Arts and Sciences and several historical sites.
Innkeeper(s): Mary Jo & Dick Hosack. $125. MC, VISA, AX, DS. 3 rooms
with PB. Breakfast included in rates. Types of meals: Full gourmet bkfst and
early coffee/tea. Beds: Q. Cable TV, phone, ceiling fan and VCR in room. Air
conditioning. Fax, copier and library on premises. Amusement parks,
antiquing, fishing, golf, live theater, parks, shopping and water sports nearby.
Publicity: *Brazosport Facts.*
Certificate may be used: Sunday through Thursday any months of the year.

Brenham   F8

Mariposa Ranch B&B

8904 Mariposa Ln
Brenham, TX 77833-8906
(979)836-4737 (877)647-4774
Internet: www.mariposaranch.com
E-mail: info@mariposaranch.com

Circa 1870. Several buildings comprise the inn: a Victorian, an
1820 log cabin, a quaint cottage, a farmhouse and a 1836
Greek Revival home. Guests relax on the veranda, stroll through
the Live Oaks or explore the ranch's 100 acres of fields and
meadows. The inn is furnished with fine antiques. Ask for the
Texas Ranger Cabin and enjoy a massive stone fireplace, sofa,
clawfoot tub and loft with queen bed. Jennifer's Suite boasts a
king canopy bed and two fireplaces. The "Enchanted Evening"
package offers champagne, fruit, flowers, candlelight, candy and
an optional massage. Guests can select a room with a Jacuzzi for
two or a clawfoot tub for additional luxury.
Innkeeper(s): Johnna & Charles Chamberlain. $90-165. MC, VISA, PC, TC.
10 rooms with PB, 8 with FP, 3 suites, 3 cottages, 1 cabin and 1 conference
room. Breakfast included in rates. Types of meals: Full gourmet bkfst and early
coffee/tea. Beds: KQDT. TV, ceiling fan, VCR and microwaves in room. Air conditioning. Fax, copier and library on premises. Handicap access. Antiquing,
fishing, golf, live theater, parks, shopping, tennis and water sports nearby.
Location: Texas hill country.
Publicity: *Southern Living and Texas Monthly.*
Certificate may be used: From May 1-March 15, Sunday-Thursday.

Canyon   B4

Country Home B&B

RR 1 Box 447
Canyon, TX 79015-9743
(806)655-7636 (800)664-7636

Circa 1989. This bed & breakfast is, as the title suggests, a
quaint country home located on an acre of grounds that offer a
restful porch swing and a gazebo. Each of the two guest rooms
shares a bath with a clawfoot tub. Flowered prints, iron beds,
candles, family heirlooms and antiques add to the country
ambiance. Guests enjoy use of an outdoor hot tub. Homemade
muffins, fresh fruit and specialties such as quiche often appear
at the breakfast table.
Innkeeper(s): Tammy & Dennis Brooks. $200. MC, VISA, AX, DS, PC, TC. 2
rooms, 1 suite and 1 cottage. Breakfast and snacks/refreshments included in
rates. Types of meals: Full bkfst, cont plus and early coffee/tea. Beds: D. Air
conditioning. VCR, spa and bicycles on premises. Amusement parks,
antiquing, live theater, parks and shopping nearby.
Location: Country.
Publicity: *Country Magazine and Accent West.*
Certificate may be used: October-April, Sunday-Thursday.

Historical Hudspeth House

1905 4th Ave
Canyon, TX 79015-4023
(806)655-9800 (800)655-9809 Fax:(806)655-7457
Internet: www.hudspethinn.com

Circa 1909. Artist Georgia O'Keefe was once a guest at this three-story prairie home, which serves as a bed & breakfast. The home boasts many impressive architectural features, including an expansive entry with stained glass and a grandfather clock. The parlor boasts 12-foot ceilings and antiques, other rooms include chandeliers and huge fireplaces. Guests can arrange to have a candlelight dinner in their room.

Innkeeper(s): Mark & Mary Clark. $55-110. MC, VISA, AX, DS, PC, TC. 8 rooms with PB, 5 with FP, 2 suites and 2 conference rooms. Breakfast included in rates. Type of meal: Early coffee/tea. Beds: KQ. Cable TV, phone, ceiling fan and fireplaces in five rooms in room. Air conditioning. Fax, copier and spa on premises. Amusement parks, antiquing, live theater, parks and sporting events nearby.

Location: City.

Publicity: *Southern Living and Valentine Getaways.*

Certificate may be used: January, March, September, October, Sunday-Thursday only.

Center   D5

Pine Colony Inn

500 Shelbyville St
Center, TX 75935-3732
(409)598-7700

Circa 1940. This inn is a restored hotel with more than 8,000 square feet of antique-filled rooms. Artwork from local artist Woodrow Foster adorns the walls. These limited-edition prints are framed and sold by the innkeepers. The town is located between Toledo Bend, which has one of the largest man-made lakes in the United States, and Lake Pinkston, where the state record bass (just under 17 pounds) was caught in 1986. Ask the innkeepers about all the little-out-of-the-way places to see either by foot, bicycle or car.

Innkeeper(s): Marcille Hughes. $55-75. MC, VISA. 10 rooms with PB and 4 suites. Breakfast included in rates. Types of meals: Full bkfst and early coffee/tea. Cable TV, phone, turndown service, ceiling fan and VCR in room. Air conditioning. Amusement parks, antiquing, fishing, parks, shopping, sporting events and water sports nearby.

Certificate may be used: All days except Thanksgiving Day, Christmas Eve. All other days are acceptable.

Cleburne   D7

Anglin Queen Anne B&B

723 N Anglin St
Cleburne, TX 76031-3905
(817)645-5555

Circa 1892. This home, which was once owned by a cattle baron, is dominated by a three-story cupola set between two second-story porches. The first story includes a large round veranda with porch posts and gingerbread fretwork. The mansion's interior is embellished with wood paneling, molding and fancy carvings. Two main staircases have elaborate grillwork, paneling and stained glass. The dining rooms include a Northwind dining set, Oriental warlord's chair and a carved chair set from a European guest house.

Innkeeper(s): Billie Anne Leach. $49-149. 5 rooms, 1 suite and 1 conference room. Breakfast included in rates. Types of meals: Cont plus and early coffee/tea. Phone, ceiling fan and VCR in room. Air conditioning. Murder Mystery Dinner for 8 on premises. Amusement parks, antiquing, live theater, shopping and sporting events nearby.

Certificate may be used: Yearly.

Comfort   F6

Idlewilde

115 Hwy 473
Comfort, TX 78013
(830)995-3844

Circa 1902. This Western-style farmhouse and its cottages have come to be known as "Haven in the Hills." The home and surrounding grounds were a girls' summer camp for more than 60 years. The inn has no set check-in or check-out times. The innkeepers offer breakfast either in the main house dining area or at your specified spot (which could be breakfast in bed). The large, unique hallways and center rooms are open and airy with lots of windows. Antiques and country French furniture decorate the entire lodge.

Innkeeper(s): Hank Engel & Connie Engel. $77-93. 2 cottages. Breakfast included in rates. Type of meal: Full bkfst. Beds: Q. Amusement parks, antiquing, fishing, golf, shopping, sporting events and water sports nearby.

Pets Allowed.

Publicity: *Austin Chronicle and Hill Country Recorder.*

Certificate may be used: Any night, year-round, except holidays.

Commerce   D8

Bois D'arc B&B

2212 Charity Rd
Commerce, TX 75428-3914
(903)886-7705
E-mail: stinnett@unicomp.net

Circa 1984. Wake to the comforting aroma of gingerbread scones baking in the kitchen of this home, which is located on more than two pecan-shaded acres. The brick home offers three bedrooms on a separate wing of the house. Request the Lodge Room for rustic lodge-type furnishings, including a bed topped with a flannel patchwork quilt, or if you enjoy woodland views, ask for the Sunflower Room, which offers a king bed. A hearty Southwestern breakfast features huevos rancheros and homemade rancheros sauce.

Innkeeper(s): Jim & Frances Stinnett. $60. AX, PC. 3 rooms, 2 with PB. Breakfast and snacks/refreshments included in rates. Types of meals: Cont plus and early coffee/tea. Beds: DT. Ceiling fan in room. Air conditioning. Copier, bicycles and Apple II GS on premises. Antiquing, fishing, live theater, sporting events and water sports nearby.

Location: Small town.

Certificate may be used: Summer, anytime.

Conroe   F9

Heather's Glen . . . A B&B & More

200 E Phillips St
Conroe, TX 77301-2646
(936)441-6611 (800)665-2643 Fax:(936)441-6603
Internet: www.heathersglen.com

Circa 1900. This turn-of-the-century mansion still maintains many of its original features, such as heart-of-pine flooring, gracious staircases and antique glass windows. Verandas and covered porches decorate the exterior, creating ideal places to relax. Guest rooms are decorated in a romantic, country flavor. One room has a bed draped with a lacy canopy, and five rooms include double Jacuzzi tubs. Antique shops, an outlet mall and Lake Conroe are nearby, and the home is within an hour of Houston.

Innkeeper(s): Ed & Jamie George. $75-195. MC, VISA, AX, DS, PC, TC. 8 rooms with PB, 3 with FP and 3 conference rooms. Breakfast, afternoon tea and snacks/refreshments included in rates. Types of meals: Full gourmet bkfst and early coffee/tea. Beds: QD. Cable TV, phone, turndown service and ceiling fan in room. Air conditioning. Fax and copier on premises. Handicap access. Amusement parks, antiquing, fishing, auctions weekly, live theater, parks, shopping, downhill skiing, sporting events and water sports nearby.

Certificate may be used: Jan. 1-Dec. 31, Sunday-Friday, upon availability.

Denison C8

Ivy Blue B&B
1100 W Sears St
Denison, TX 75020-3326
(903)463-2479 (888)489-2583 Fax:(903)465-6773
Internet: www.ivyblue.com

Circa 1899. This Victorian charmer is set on a manicured lawn and shaded by several large trees. Guest rooms are named in honor of previous owners. Some of the furnishings and antiques that decorate the rooms are original to the home. Old newspaper clippings, antique dress patterns, historical documents and a time capsule are among the unique surprises guests might discover in their rooms. Fragrant soaps, lotions and chocolates add a touch of romance. Breakfasts are served on tables set with lace and antique china. Such items as banana almond waffles or mango coconut pancakes get the morning off to a great start. The inn's carriage house, which contains Lois' Cottage and the Field Suite, is an ideal spot for those who prefer a bit more privacy. Carriage house guests may opt to enjoy breakfast in their room. Besides privacy, the Garden Suite offers a Jacuzzi tub, CD player and VCR. Guests are encouraged to ask about the murder mystery dinners, sunset cruises and carriage rides.

Innkeeper(s): Lane & Tammy Segerstrom. $65-150. MC, VISA, AX, DS, PC, TC. 6 rooms with PB, 3 suites and 3 cottages. Breakfast included in rates. Types of meals: Full gourmet bkfst and early coffee/tea. Cable TV, phone and ceiling fan in room. Air conditioning. Fax, swimming, library and waverunners on premises. Handicap access. Antiquing, fishing, Lake Texoma, horseback riding, parks, shopping and water sports nearby.

Publicity: *Dallas Morning News, Park Cities News and KXII Channel 21.*

Certificate may be used: Anytime except holidays.

Edgewood D8

Crooked Creek Farm B&B
RR 1 Box 180
Edgewood, TX 75117-9709
(903)896-1284 (800)766-0790

Circa 1977. This traditional brick house, which is found in a rural community of 1,300, is nestled on the edge of the East Texas timberline. Not far from the Greater Dallas area, the farm covers more than 100 acres where cattle graze and hay is grown and baled. Trees, a creek, nature trails, and four fishing ponds are on the property. A hearty country breakfast may feature ham and bacon, eggs, seasoned hash browns, biscuits and gravy as well as a fruit dish served with home baked sweet breads. The menu varies daily. In town, Heritage Park Museum

offers turn-of-the-century restored buildings furnished to represent the rural life of a century ago.

Innkeeper(s): Dorthy Thornton. $75. 6 rooms. Breakfast included in rates. Types of meals: Full bkfst and early coffee/tea. Ceiling fan in room. Air conditioning. VCR and outdoor games and fishing on premises. Antiquing and shopping nearby.

Location: Country.

"We love B&Bs, and probably never stayed anywhere else that had better breakfasts."

Certificate may be used: All year, except "Canton Texas First Monday Trade Days" weekend each month.

El Paso E1

Sunset Heights B&B
717 W Yandell Dr
El Paso, TX 79902-3837
(915)544-1743 Fax:(915)544-5119

Circa 1905. This luxurious inn is accentuated by palm trees and Spanish-style arches. Inside, bedrooms are filled with antiques and boast brass and four-poster beds. Breakfast is a five- to eight-course feast pre-pared by innkeeper Richard Barnett. On any morning, a guest might awake to sample a breakfast with Southwestern flair, including Eggs Chillquillas and pit-smoked Machakas, a combination of smoked beef, avocado and onion. Juice, fresh coffee, tea, dessert and fresh fruits top off the meal, which might begin with caviar and quiche. Enjoy the morning meal in the dining room or spend breakfast in bed.

Innkeeper(s): Mrs. Mel Martinez. $75-150. MC, VISA, AX, DS, PC, TC. 5 rooms with PB, 1 with FP, 1 suite, 1 cottage and 1 conference room. Breakfast included in rates. Type of meal: Full gourmet bkfst. Beds: KQD. Cable TV, phone, turndown service, ceiling fan and VCR in room. Air conditioning. Fax, copier, spa and swimming on premises. Amusement parks, antiquing, parks, shopping and sporting events nearby.

Pets allowed: Outdoor cat.

Location: City.

Publicity: *Southwest Profile and Pony Soldiers.*

Certificate may be used: Year-round, except weekends and holidays.

Fort Worth D7

Miss Molly's Hotel
109 1/2 W Exchange Ave
Fort Worth, TX 76106-8508
(817)626-1522 (800)996-6559 Fax:(817)625-2723
Internet: www.missmollys.com
E-mail: missmollys@travelbase.com

Circa 1910. An Old West ambiance permeates this hotel, which once was a house of ill repute. Miss Josie's Room, named for the former madame, is decked with elaborate wall and ceiling coverings and carved oak furniture. The Gunslinger Room is filled with pictures of famous and infamous gunfighters. Rodeo memorabilia decorates the Rodeo Room, and twin iron beds and a pot belly stove add flair to the Cowboy's Room. Telephones and TV sets are the only things missing from the rooms, as the innkeeper hopes to preserve the flavor of the past.

Innkeeper(s): Mark & Alice Hancock. $75-170. MC, VISA, AX, DC, CB, DS, PC, TC. 8 rooms, 1 with PB. Breakfast included in rates. Types of meals: Cont plus and early coffee/tea. Beds: DT. Ceiling fan in room. Air conditioning. Fax and copier on premises. Amusement parks, antiquing, stockyards National Historic district, live theater, shopping and sporting events nearby.

Publicity: *British Bulldog, Arkansas Gazette, Dallas Morning News, Fort Worth Star-Telegram, Continental Profiles and Eyes Of Texas.*

Certificate may be used: Year-round, Sunday through Thursday excluding holidays and Stockyards annual special event dates.

Texas White House B&B

1417 8th Ave
Fort Worth, TX 76104-4111
(817)923-3597 (800)279-6491 Fax:(817)923-0410
Internet: www.texaswhitehouse.com
E-mail: txwhitehou@aol.com

Circa 1910. A spacious encircling veranda shaded by an old elm tree, graces the front of this two-story home located within five minutes of downtown, TCU, the zoo and many other area attractions. The inn's parlor and living room with fireplace and gleaming hardwood floors are the most popular spots for relaxing when not lingering on the porch. Guest rooms are equipped with phones and television, and early morning coffee is provided before the inn's full breakfast at a time convenient to your personal schedule. Baked egg casseroles and freshly made breads are served to your room or in the dining room. The owners are Fort Worth experts and keep abreast of cultural attractions and are happy to help with reservations and planning. The inn is popular with business travelers — secretarial services are available, etc. — during the week and appealing to couples on weekends.

Innkeeper(s): Grover & Jamie McMains. $105-125. MC, VISA, AX, DC, DS, PC, TC. 3 rooms with PB and 1 conference room. Breakfast and snacks/refreshments included in rates. Types of meals: Full gourmet bkfst and early coffee/tea. Beds: Q. Cable TV, phone, turndown service, ceiling fan and VCR in room. Central air. Fax on premises. Antiquing, art galleries, golf, live theater, museums and parks nearby.

Location: City.

Certificate may be used: Sunday-Thursday, no holidays. Nights must be consecutive; June 1-Aug. 31.

Fredericksburg   F6

Alte Welt Gasthof (Old World Inn)

PO Box 628
Fredericksburg, TX 78624
(830)997-0443 (888)991-6749 Fax:(830)997-0040
Internet: www.texas-bed-n-breakfast.com
E-mail: stay@texas-bed-n-breakfast.com

Circa 1915. Located on the second floor above a Main Street shop, Alte Welt is in a Basse Block building in the historic district. The entryway opens to an antique-filled foyer. A three-room suite offers a white sofa, silver accents including a silver, tin ceiling, wood floors and an antique iron four-poster bed draped in soft gauze. An armoire with TV and a small refrigerator and microwave add convenience. The innkeeper collects antique, crocheted and embroidered linens for the guest rooms. There is a spacious deck with hot tub adjoining one of the suites. Together, the two suites can accommodate as many as 10 people, so it is popular with families and small groups, who enjoy the freedom of simply going downstairs to Main Street and all its boutiques, shops and restaurants.

Innkeeper(s): Ron & Donna Maddux. $135-150. MC, VISA, AX, DS, PC, TC. 2 suites. Breakfast included in rates. Types of meals: Cont and early coffee/tea. Beds: Q. Cable TV, phone, ceiling fan, microwave, coffee bar and in room. Air conditioning. Antiquing, fishing, golf, museums, hunting, parks, shopping and tennis nearby.

Certificate may be used: Jan. 2 to Feb. 5 and Sept. 1-30, Sunday-Thursday, suite No. 1 only.

Fredericksburg (Luckenbach)   F6

The Luckenbach Inn

3234 Luckenbach Rd
Fredericksburg (Luckenbach), TX 78624-9729
(830)997-2205 (800)997-1124 Fax:(830)997-1115
Internet: www.luckenbachtx.com
E-mail: theinn@luckenbachtx.com

Circa 1867. This rustic bed & breakfast inn actually is located about 10 minutes from Fredericksburg in the town of Luckenbach. The homestead originally belonged to Luckenbach's founding citizen, and his 1867 log cabin remains for guests to enjoy today. The cabin offers two bedrooms and a shared bath. Guests also can opt to stay in Old Smokehouse, another cottage. Other accommodations include two rooms and a suite. The suite has a full kitchen and private porch. The rooms offer a whirlpool tub, and one has a fireplace. Breakfasts are hearty and include items such as eggs Luckenbach, apple-smoked bacon, banana walnut pancakes, fresh fruit and other treats. The town is famous for its historic dance hall.

Innkeeper(s): Capt. Matt & Eva Marie Carinhas. $95-125. MC, VISA, AX, DS, PC, TC. 6 rooms, 4 with PB, 2 with FP, 1 suite and 1 cottage. Breakfast included in rates. Types of meals: Full bkfst and early coffee/tea. Beds: Q. Ceiling fan, jacuzzi tubs and fireplaces in room. Air conditioning. Fax, copier, pet boarding and wine cellar on premises. Amusement parks, antiquing, fishing, golf, parks, shopping and water sports nearby.

Pets allowed: Call first.

Location: Hill country with creek.

Publicity: *Dallas Morning News, San Antonio Express News, Southern Living Texas Vacation and KXAN - San Antonio.*

"We had an excellent weekend at your inn."

Certificate may be used: Any, Sunday-Thursday.

Galveston   F9

Carousel Inn

712 Tenth St
Galveston, TX 77550-5116
(409)762-2166

Circa 1886. The Carousel Inn stands as a testament to Texas stamina. The home, located in a historic Galveston neighborhood, was one of a few left standing after a fierce storm ripped through the Gulf in 1900. The inn's namesake, a hand-carved carousel horse, decorates the parlor. The guest rooms are inviting with special touches such as leaf pine walls, a private porch swing or a roomy pineapple bed. The carriage house offers the added amenity of a sitting area, private entrance and antique walnut bed. The innkeepers offer a variety of home-baked treats each morning, served up in the cheerful breakfast room. The home is near many Galveston attractions including a rail museum, a tall ship and many shops and restaurants.

Innkeeper(s): Jim & Kathy Hughes. $95-130. MC, VISA, AX, DS, PC, TC. 4 rooms with PB and 1 suite. Breakfast included in rates. Types of meals: Cont plus and early coffee/tea. Beds: KQD. Ceiling fan in room. Air conditioning. Bicycles, library, player piano and hand-crank phonograph on premises. Amusement parks, antiquing, fishing, historical points of interest, live theater, shopping and water sports nearby.

Location: City.

Certificate may be used: All year, Sunday through Thursday nights.

Glen Rose   D7

Ye Ole' Maple Inn
PO Box 1141
Glen Rose, TX 76043-1141
(254)897-3456

Circa 1950. Pecan trees shade this comfortable home, which overlooks the Paluxy River. The interior is decorated with a variety of antiques, including a grandfather clock imported from Germany. The innkeepers also keep on display a Santa Claus collection. The fireplaced den offers a large selection of reading material. One of the bedrooms, decked in pink and gray hues, includes an iron and brass bed and wicker furnishings. The other features Victorian decor and a four-poster bed. Breakfasts include specialties such as oatmeal waffles with pecan sauce or an egg, sausage and apple casserole. Innkeeper Roberta Maple also serves up a mouth-watering selection of evening desserts such as peanut butter pie and Texas brownies.

Innkeeper(s): Roberta Maple. $85. MC, VISA, AX, PC, TC. 2 rooms with PB. Breakfast and snacks/refreshments included in rates. Type of meal: Full bkfst. Beds: Q. Ceiling fan in room. VCR and library on premises. Handicap access. Antiquing, fishing, live theater, shopping and water sports nearby.

Location: Brazos River.

Certificate may be used: Monday through Thursday, January to December.

Gonzales   F7

St. James Inn
723 Saint James St
Gonzales, TX 78629-3411
(830)672-7066 Fax:(830)672-7787
Internet: www.stjamesinn.com
E-mail: email@stjamesinn.com

Circa 1914. Ann and J.R. Covert spent three years restoring this massive Texas Hill Country mansion, once owned by a cattle baron. On the main floor is a tiled solarium, living room, reception hall, dining room, butler's pantry and kitchen. The second-

floor guest rooms all have working fireplaces and porches. The top-level room has a unique wind tunnel—a long crawl space with windows on either end—which once provided natural air conditioning to the original occupants of the home. Gourmet candlelight dinners in addition to the full breakfasts make this an elegant getaway.

Innkeeper(s): Ann & J.R. Covert. $85-100. MC, VISA, AX, PC, TC. 5 rooms with PB, 5 with FP, 2 suites and 1 conference room. Breakfast and afternoon tea included in rates. Types of meals: Full gourmet bkfst and early coffee/tea. Beds: KQ. Cable TV, phone, turndown service and ceiling fan in room. Air conditioning. Screen porch on premises. Antiquing, fishing, live theater, parks, shopping and water sports nearby.

Location: City.

Publicity: *Gonzales Inquirer, Houston Chronicle, Victoria Advocate, Austin American Statesman and San Antonio Express-News.*

"We had a wonderful weekend. It's a marvelous home and your hospitality is superb. We'll be back."

Certificate may be used: Jan. 30-Aug. 1 and Nov. 1-15, Sunday-Friday, or call for other choices if possible.

Granbury   D7

Dabney House B&B
106 S Jones St
Granbury, TX 76048-1905
(817)579-1260 (800)566-1260
E-mail: safe-dabney@flash.net

Circa 1907. Built during the Mission Period, this Craftsman-style country manor boasts original hardwood floors, stained-glass windows and some of the original light fixtures. The parlor and dining rooms have large, exposed, wooden beams and the ceilings throughout are 10-feet high. The Dabney Suite has a private entrance into an enclosed sun porch with rattan table and chairs that allow for a private breakfast or a candlelight dinner by advance reservation. The bedroom of this suite is furnished with a four-post tester bed with drapes and an 1800 wardrobe.

Innkeeper(s): John & Gwen Hurley. $70-105. MC, VISA, AX, PC, TC. 4 rooms with PB and 1 suite. Breakfast and snacks/refreshments included in rates. Type of meal: Full bkfst. Beds: Q. Ceiling fan in room. Air conditioning. VCR, spa, library, hot tub and evening beverage on premises. Antiquing, fishing, live theater, parks, shopping and water sports nearby.

Location: Small town.

Publicity: *Fort Worth Star Telegram and Dallas Morning News.*

Certificate may be used: Sunday through Friday, all year, does not apply on major holidays or special events.

Pearl Street Inn B&B
319 W Pearl St
Granbury, TX 76048-2437
(817)579-7465 (888)732-7578

Circa 1911. Known historically as the B. M. Estes House, the inn is decorated with a mix of English, French and American antiques. The Pearl Room boasts a king-size antique Victorian half canopy bed, a restored clawfoot tub and wall sink. The water closet is a few steps from the guest room door. Other guest rooms include clawfoot tubs, crystal lamps and an outdoor hot tub.

Innkeeper(s): Danette D. Hebda. $59-119. PC, TC. 5 rooms with PB and 1 suite. Breakfast included in rates. Types of meals: Full gourmet bkfst and early coffee/tea. Beds: KD. Ceiling fan and table and chairs in room. Central air. VCR, copier, complimentary coffee and tea and cocoa on premises. Antiquing, fishing, golf, drive-in movie, live theater, parks, shopping and water sports nearby.

Location: City.

Publicity: *Fort Worth Star Telegram, Dallas Morning News and New York Times.*

"Needless to say, we want to stay forever! We had a grand time and highly enjoyed conversations and hospitality."

Certificate may be used: Sunday-Thursday, excluding special events.

Houston   F9

Angel Arbor B&B Inn
848 Heights Blvd
Houston, TX 77007-1507
(713)868-4654 (800)722-8788
Internet: www.angelarbor.com

Circa 1922. Each of the rooms at Angel Arbor has a heavenly name and elegant decor. The Angelique Room offers a cherry sleigh bed and a balcony overlooking the garden. Canopy or poster beds grace the other rooms and suite, named Gabriel, Raphael and Michael. The Georgian-style home is located in the historic Houston Heights neighborhood and was built by a prominent local family. The innkeeper, a cookbook author, prepares a mouthwatering homemade breakfast each morning. Ask about the innkeeper's special murder-mystery dinner parties.

Innkeeper(s): Marguerite Swanson. $95-125. MC, VISA, AX, DS, PC, TC. 5

rooms with PB and 1 conference room. Breakfast included in rates. Types of meals: Full gourmet bkfst and early coffee/tea. Beds: Q. Phone, turndown service, ceiling fan and VCR in room. Air conditioning. Fax and library on premises. Amusement parks, antiquing, fishing, jogging, live theater, parks, shopping, sporting events and water sports nearby.
Location: City.
Certificate may be used: Jan. 2-Dec. 15, Sunday-Thursday.

Robin's Nest

4104 Greeley St
Houston, TX 77006-5609
(713)528-5821 (800)622-8343 Fax:(713)521-2154
Internet: www.houstonbnb.com
E-mail: robin@hypercon.com

Circa 1898. Robin's Nest is the oldest home in Houston's historic Montrose District. A two-story wooden Queen Anne Victorian, the historic home features original pine hardwoods, tall windows, high ceilings and a wraparound veranda.
Luxurious fabrics, all custom sewn, warm the interior, which also boasts wall murals.  The home originally was a dairy farm and now rests on an urban lot surrounded by dozens of rose bushes and azaleas. Located in the city's museum and arts district, the inn offers close proximity to downtown Houston, theaters and gourmet restaurants. Galveston and Johnson Space Center are about an hour away.
Innkeeper(s): Robin Smith. $75-120. MC, VISA, AX, DS. 4 rooms with PB and 1 conference room. Breakfast included in rates. Type of meal: Full bkfst. Beds: QT. Cable TV, phone, ceiling fan and baths in room. Air conditioning. Amusement parks, antiquing, fishing, live theater, museums, shopping, sporting events and water sports nearby.
Location: Inside 610 Loop very near downtown, George R. Brown Convention Center and Texas Medical Center.
Publicity: *Houston Home and Garden, Houston Business Journal, Woman's Day, Houston Metropolitan, Houston Post, Southern Living, Texas Monthly, Houston Chronicle and Inside Houston.*

"Fanciful and beautiful, comfortable and happy. We saw a whole new side of Houston, thanks to you."
Certificate may be used: Sunday-Thursday, all year.

Jefferson   D9

1st Bed & Breakfast in Texas Pride House

409 Broadway
Jefferson, TX 75657
(800)894-3526 Fax:(903)665-3901
Internet: www.jeffersontexas.com
E-mail: jefftx@mind.net

Circa 1889. Mr. Brown, a sawmill owner, built this Victorian house using fine hardwoods, sometimes three layers deep. The windows are nine-feet tall on both the lower level and upstairs. The rooms include amenities such as fireplaces, balconies, canopy beds and private entrances. Most boast original stained-glass windows, and each room is named after a steamboat that once docked in Jefferson. One room is decorated in crimson reds and features a gigantic clawfoot tub that has received an award from Houston Style Magazine for "best bath in Texas." A wide veranda stretches around two sides of the house.
Innkeeper(s): Carol Abernathy & Christel Frederick. $85-200. MC, VISA, PC, TC. 11 rooms with PB, 3 with FP, 1 suite and 1 cottage. Types of meals: Full

gourmet bkfst and early coffee/tea. Beds: KQT. Phone, ceiling fan and some fireplaces in room. Air conditioning. TV (by request) on premises. Handicap access. Antiquing, canoeing/kayaking, fishing, steamboat tours, home tours, water skiing, steam train, antebellum home tours and live theater nearby.
Location: City.
Publicity: *Woman's Day, Country Home, Texas Highways and Texas Homes.*
"No five star hotel can compare to the hospitality of Pride House."
Certificate may be used: Sunday-Thursday, some restrictions apply.

McKay House

306 E Delta St
Jefferson, TX 75657-2026
(903)665-7322 (800)468-2627

Circa 1851. For more than 15 years, the McKay House has been widely acclaimed for its high standards, personal service and satisfied guests. Both Lady Bird Johnson and Alex Haley have enjoyed the gracious Southern hospitality offered at the McKay House. Accented by a Williamsburg-style picket fence, the Greek Revival cottage features a front porch with pillars. Heart-of-pine floors, 14-foot ceilings and documented wallpapers complement antique furnishings. A full "gentleman's" breakfast is served in the garden conservatory by the gable fireplace. Orange-pecan French toast, home-baked muffins and shirred eggs are a few of the house specialties. In each of the seven bedchambers you find a Victorian nightgown and old-fashioned nightshirt laid out for you. History abounds in Jefferson, considered the "Williamsburg of the Southwest."
Innkeeper(s): Lisa & Roger Cantrell. $89-169. MC, VISA, AX, PC, TC. 8 rooms with PB, 6 with FP and 1 cottage. Breakfast included in rates. Types of meals: Full gourmet bkfst and early coffee/tea. Beds: QD. Cable TV, phone, ceiling fan and suites also in room. Air conditioning. Refrigerator in common rooms on premises. Antiquing, fishing, live theater, parks, shopping & water sports nearby.
Location: City.
Publicity: *Southern Accents, Dallas Morning News, Country Home and Bride.*
"The facilities of the McKay House are exceeded only by the service and dedication of the owners."
Certificate may be used: Sunday through Thursday, not including spring break or festivals/holidays; space available, reserved one week in advance please.

Lampasas   E7

Historic Moses Hughes B&B

RR 2 Box 31
Lampasas, TX 76550-9601
(512)556-5923
Internet: www.moseshughesranch.com
E-mail: mhrbb@n-link.com

Circa 1856. Nestled among ancient oaks in the heart of the Texas Hill Country, this native stone ranch house rests on 45 acres that include springs, a creek, wildlife and other natural beauty. The ranch was built by Moses Hughes, the first white settler and founder of Lampasas. He and his wife decided to stay in the area after her health dramatically improved after visiting the springs. Guests can join the innkeepers on the stone patio or upstairs wooden porch for a taste of Texas Hill Country life.
Innkeeper(s): Al & Beverly Solomon. $75-90. MC, VISA, PC, TC. 3 rooms with PB. Breakfast included in rates. Type of meal: Full gourmet bkfst. Beds: QD. Air conditioning. VCR, library and creek & springs on premises. Antiquing, fishing, birding, hiking,hunting, caves, parks and water sports nearby.
Location: Ranch.
Publicity: *Spiegel Catalog, Dallas Morning News, Discover, Texas Highway., Texas Film Commission, CBS and ABC.*
"What a delightful respite! Thank you for sharing your very interesting philosophies and personalities with us at this very special B&B. We hate to leave."
Certificate may be used: Year-round, Sunday-Thursday, no holidays.

Mason E6

Hasse House and Ranch

PO Box 779
Mason, TX 76856
(888)414-2773

Circa 1883. Guests may explore the 320-acre Hasse ranch, which is a working ranch where deer, wild turkey, feral hogs, quail and a bounty of wildflowers and bluebonnets are common sights. After purchasing the land, Henry Hasse and his wife lived in a log cabin on the property before building the sandstone home 23 years later. Three generations of Hasses have lived here, and today it is owned by a great-granddaughter who restored the home in 1980. The house is located in the small German village of Art, Texas, which is located six miles east of Mason. The innkeepers rent the two-bedroom National Register home out to only one group or guest at a time, host free. The home is filled with period furniture and accessories, yet offers the modern convenience of an on-site washer and dryer and a fully stocked kitchen. The ranch grounds include a two-mile nature trail perfect for nature lovers.

Innkeeper(s): Laverne Lee. $95. MC, VISA, PC, TC. 2 rooms with PB. Type of meal: Cont plus. Beds: D. TV, ceiling fan, dishwasher, microwave and etc in room. Air conditioning. Library, washer, dryer, stove, microwave and patio on premises. Handicap access. Antiquing, bicycle routes, 2 mile nature trail on ranch, bird-watching, wildflower viewing, parks, shopping & water sports nearby.
Location: 320-acre ranch.
Publicity: *San Angelo and Tx Special & "Eyes of Texas"*
"We enjoyed every aspect of our stay; the atmosphere, sense of history, rustic setting with a touch of class. We would love to return the same time next year!."
Certificate may be used: June 1 through Nov. 4.

Mason Square B&B

134 Ft McKavett, PO Box 298
Mason, TX 76856-0298
(915)347-6398 (800)369-0405

Circa 1901. A fine collection of framed, historically significant maps of Texas and the Southwest that span centuries of discovery and settlement are throughout the guest rooms and hallway of this inn. Located on the second floor of a historic commercial building, the B&B has original pressed-tin ceilings, Victorian woodwork and doors, stained-glass transoms and oak floors. Guests can step outside for a stroll down memory lane as the inn is part of the courthouse square with buildings dating from 1879. Several antique shops, galleries and some local businesses have occupied the same buildings for generations.

Innkeeper(s): Brent Hinckley. $55-65. 3 rooms. Breakfast included in rates. Type of meal: Cont plus. Ceiling fan in room. Air conditioning. VCR on premises. Antiquing nearby.
Certificate may be used: All times, except holidays.

Nacogdoches E9

Llano Grande Plantation

RR 4 Box 9400
Nacogdoches, TX 75964-9276
(409)569-1249
Internet: www.llanogrande.com
E-mail: llanogr@inu.net

Circa 1840. A collection of three lodgings sit on this 600 acres of creeks and pine forest. The accommodations are located on what was called the Llano Grande land grant, given to Pedro

Jose Esparza in 1779. Among the buildings is the Tol Barret House, which was the home of the person who drilled the first producing oil well in Texas. It is both a Texas Historic Landmark and listed in the National Register. This home includes a bedroom with four beds, as well as a kitchen and fireplace. The Sparks House, which dates to the mid-1800s, is another option. The Texas Landmark home has two bedrooms, a fireplace, wood-burning stove and sitting area. Rosewild is an 1855 plantation home in the antebellum style and features a columned portico, Oriental rugs, crystal chandeliers and a square grand piano. In all of the homes, carefully chosen antiques resemble those of the original owners.

Innkeeper(s): Captain Charles & Ann Phillips. $75-95. PC, TC. 4 suites, 4 with FP. Breakfast included in rates. Types of meals: Full bkfst and cont plus. Phone and clocks in room. Air conditioning. Antiquing, fishing, live theater, parks, shopping, sporting events and water sports nearby.
Location: in 600 acre forest.
Certificate may be used: April to Feb. 28, Sunday-Thursday, except local college (SFASU) events (homecoming, parents weekend, etc.).

Round Top F8

Heart of My Heart Ranch B&B

PO Box 106
Round Top, TX 78954-0106
(800)327-1242 Fax:(409)249-3171

Circa 1825. This log frontier home was built by Jared Groce, known as the father of Texas agriculture. Groce planted the state's first cotton, and built the first cotton gin in Texas. Well-appointed rooms feature antiques such as a cannonball or canopy bed. The Lone Star and Brookfield rooms boast fireplaces. The Lone Star has a unique staircase that leads up to the second-story Harwood Room. The innkeepers also offer accommodations in the charming carriage house, and a rustic setting in the 170-year-old log cabin. The cabin boasts a sleeping loft, stone fireplace, clawfoot tub and a complete kitchen. Rockers have been set up on the expansive front porch, perfect for relaxing. The lush grounds offer a swimming pool, Jacuzzi, fruit tree orchard and gardens. A hearty, country breakfast is served each morning, and for an extra charge, the innkeepers will prepare a picnic lunch.

Innkeeper(s): Frances Harris. $65-135. MC, VISA, AX, DS. 17 rooms. Breakfast included in rates. Type of meal: Full bkfst.
Certificate may be used: Sunday-Thursday.

San Antonio F7

B&B on The River

129 Woodward Pl
San Antonio, TX 78204-1120
(210)225-6333 (800)730-0019 Fax:(210)271-3992
Internet: www.hotx.com/sa/bb/
E-mail: adz@swbell.net

Circa 1916. Located in a restored river home, the inn is encircled by an iron fence and shaded by a tall pecan tree. There are gables and a wraparound porch. Inside are polished pine floors and tall ceilings. Antiques, Jacuzzi tubs, fireplaces and private porches are among the guest room offerings. A third-floor penthouse offers French doors opening to a private balcony. There is a large Jacuzzi and king-size bed. Stroll to the Riverwalk for scenic shopping, restaurants and entertainment. The Convention Center is four blocks away.

Innkeeper(s): A.D. Zucht. $99-175. MC, VISA, AX, DS, PC, TC. 12 rooms with PB, 2 with FP. Breakfast included in rates. Type of meal: Full bkfst. Beds: KQT. Cable TV, phone, ceiling fan, one room w/refrigerator, 4 w/spa and in room. Air conditioning. Fax and copier on premises. Antiquing, river, museums, live theater, parks and shopping nearby.

Pets allowed: Pets on discretion of owner.

Location: City.

Certificate may be used: Jan. 1 to Feb. 28 and June 1-Sept. 30.

Brackenridge House

230 Madison
San Antonio, TX 78204-1320
(210)271-3442 (800)221-1412 Fax:(210)226-3139
Internet: www.brackenridgehouse.com
E-mail: benniesueb@aol.com

Circa 1901. Each of the guest rooms at Brackenridge House is individually decorated. Clawfoot tubs, iron beds and a private veranda are a few of the items that guests might discover. Several rooms include kitchenettes. Blansett Barn, often rented by families or those on an extended stay, includes two bedrooms, a bathroom, a full kitchen and living and dining areas. Many of San Antonio's interesting sites are nearby. The San Antonio Mission Trail begins just a block away, and trolleys will take you to the Alamo, the River Walk, convention center and more. Coffeehouses, restaurants and antique stores all are within walking distance. Small pets are welcome in Blansett Barn.

Innkeeper(s): Bennie & Sue Blansett. $89-175. MC, VISA, DC, DS, PC, TC. 6 rooms with PB, 2 suites and 1 cottage. Breakfast included in rates. Types of meals: Full gourmet bkfst and early coffee/tea. Beds: KQD. Cable TV, phone, ceiling fan, VCR, microwave, irons and ironing boards and hair dryers in room. Air conditioning. Fax, copier and spa on premises. Amusement parks, antiquing, fishing, golf, live theater, parks, shopping, sporting events and tennis nearby.

Pets allowed: Small pets in carriage house.

Location: 1/2 miles to Alamo & Riverwal.

"Innkeeper was very nice, very helpful."

Certificate may be used: All year, no holidays or fiesta, Monday-Thursday.

Christmas House B&B

2307 McCullough
San Antonio, TX 78212
(210)737-2786 (800)268-4187 Fax:(210)734-5712
Internet: www.travelpages-usa.com/christmashouse

Circa 1908. Located in Monte Vista historic district, this two-story white inn has a natural wood balcony built over the front porch. The window trim is in red and green, starting the Christmas theme of the inn. (There's a Christmas tree decorated all year long.) Guest rooms open out to pecan-shaded balconies. The Victorian Bedroom offers pink and mauve touches mixed with the room's gold and black decor. The Blue & Silver Room is handicap accessible and is on the first floor. Antique furnishings in the inn are available for sale.

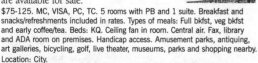

$75-125. MC, VISA, PC, TC. 5 rooms with PB and 1 suite. Breakfast and snacks/refreshments included in rates. Types of meals: Full bkfst, veg bkfst and early coffee/tea. Beds: KQ. Ceiling fan in room. Central air. Fax, library and ADA room on premises. Handicap access. Amusement parks, antiquing, art galleries, bicycling, golf, live theater, museums, parks and shopping nearby.

Location: City.

Publicity: *Fort Worth Star Telegram.*

"What a treat to rise to the sweet smell of candied pecans and a tasty breakfast."

Certificate may be used: Sunday-Thursday, year-round.

Noble Inns

107 Madison
San Antonio, TX 78204-1319
(210)225-4045 (800)221-4045 Fax:(210)227-0877
Internet: www.nobleinns.com
E-mail: nobleinns@aol.com

Circa 1894. Two historic homes, both designated city historic structures, comprise the Noble Inns collection. Both are located in the King William Historic District. The Jackson House is a brick and limestone Victorian. It offers a conservatory of stained and leaded glass enclosing a heated spa. Breakfast is served in the dining room and there is a parlor. The Pancoast Carriage House provides individual suites with full kitchens and stocked continental breakfasts. There is a swimming pool as well as spa. Both inns are furnished with Victorian-era antiques. There are fireplaces, marble baths, clawfoot tubs or whirlpools. Fresh flowers and fluffy monogrammed robes greet guests when they enter their rooms. Transportation in a classic 1960 Rolls Royce Silver Cloud II is available upon request. Call ahead for rates.

Innkeeper(s): Don & Liesl Noble. $130-190. MC, VISA, AX, DS, PC, TC. 9 rooms with PB, 9 with FP and 4 suites. Breakfast and afternoon tea included in rates. Type of meal: Full bkfst. Beds: KQ. Cable TV, phone, turndown service and ceiling fan in room. Air conditioning. Fax, spa, library and voice mail on premises. Antiquing, live theater, parks, shopping and sporting events nearby.

Location: City.

"It couldn't have been better if we dreamed it! Thank you."

Certificate may be used: Jan. 3-Feb. 12, Monday-Thursday and June 1-Aug. 28, Monday-Thursday; holidays excluded.

San Augustine E9

The Wade House

202 E Livingston St, PO Box 695
San Augustine, TX 75972
(409)275-5489 Fax:(409)275-5489
E-mail: jhwade@netdot.com

Circa 1940. The Wade House is a Mount Vernon-style red brick house located two blocks from the old courthouse square. Guest rooms are decorated in a mixture of contemporary and antique furnishings and are cooled by both ceiling fans and air conditioning. The nearby Mission Park commemorates the 1717 Spanish Mission Nuestra Senora de los Dolores de los Ais.

Innkeeper(s): Nelsyn & Julia Wade. $50-90. PC, TC. 6 rooms, 2 with PB, 1 suite and 1 conference room. Breakfast included in rates. Type of meal: Cont. Beds: KQDT. Cable TV, ceiling fan and VCR in room. Air conditioning. Handicap access.

Location: Small town.

Publicity: *San Augustine Tribune and Dallas Morning News.*

"The house is one of the most beautiful in the area. Each room is decorated to the utmost excellence."

Certificate may be used: Feb. 15-Nov. 20, excluding holidays.

San Marcos F7

Crystal River Inn

326 W Hopkins St
San Marcos, TX 78666-4404
(512)396-3739 (888)396-3739 Fax:(512)353-3248
E-mail: chrystalriverinn@

Circa 1883. This Greek Revival inn with its tall white columns has a fireside dining room with piano and wet bar. Innkeepers encourage a varied itinerary, including sleeping until noon and

having breakfast in bed to participating in a hilarious murder mystery. Guests can rock the afternoon away on the veranda or curl up by the fireplace in their bedroom. Guest rooms include clawfoot tubs, four-poster and canopied beds. Texas' largest outlet mall, not too far away, features more than 150 designer stores.
Innkeeper(s): Mike, Cathy & Sarah Dillon. $75-150. MC, VISA, AX, DC, CB, DS, PC, TC. 13 rooms with PB, 4 with FP, 3 suites, 1 cottage, 1 cabin and 1 conference room. Breakfast included in rates. Types of meals: Full gourmet bkfst, cont plus, cont and early coffee/tea. Beds: KQDT. Cable TV, phone and ceiling fan in room. Air conditioning. Fax, copier, bicycles, child care, gardens, fish pond and verandah on premises. Handicap access. Amusement parks, antiquing, fishing, golf, live theater, parks, shopping, sporting events and water sports nearby.
Location: small town.
Publicity: *Texas Monthly Press, Vacations, Country Inns, Southern Living and Dallas Morning News.*
"Thanks for a smashing good time! We really can't remember having more fun anywhere, ever!"
Certificate may be used: Sunday-Thursday, year-round, except for holiday weeks (Thanksgiving, Memorial Day, July 4th, etc.).

Seabrook F9

Pelican House B&B Inn

1302 First St
Seabrook, TX 77586-3802
(281)474-5295 Fax:(281)474-7840
Circa 1902. An acre of lawns with live oak and pecan trees stretch to the banks of Old Seabrook's Back Bay from this cozy yellow country house. Just beyond a white picket fence, the inn's salmon shutters and inviting front porch welcome guests. Inside, there are two dining areas and a sitting room. Bed chambers feature queen-size beds and a nautical, whimsical decor. Baked eggs in pastry is a favorite morning entree. In April and September, great white pelicans assemble on the bay and fish for mullet. Ospreys and other shore birds are seen most of the year. Within walking distance are antique shops and restaurants. The Nasa Space Center is three miles away.
Innkeeper(s): Suzanne Silver. $85-95. MC, VISA, AX, DS, PC, TC. 4 rooms with PB. Breakfast included in rates. Type of meal: Full gourmet bkfst. Beds: Q. Ceiling fan in room. Air conditioning. VCR, fax and copier on premises. Antiquing, fishing, golf, parks, shopping, tennis and water sports nearby.
Publicity: *Houston Life and Texas Highways.*
Certificate may be used: Monday-Thursday, all year.

Smithville F7

The Katy House

201 Ramona St, PO Box 803
Smithville, TX 78957-0803
(512)237-4262 (800)843-5289 Fax:(512)237-2239
Internet: www.katyhouse.com
E-mail: thekatyh@onr.com
Circa 1909. Shaded by tall trees, the Katy House's Italianate exterior is graced by an arched portico over the bay-windowed living room. Georgian columns reflect the inn's turn-of-the-century origin. Long leaf pine floors, pocket doors and a graceful stairway accent the completely refurbished interior. The inn is decorated almost exclusively in American antique oak and railroad memorabilia. Historic Main Street is one block away with a fine collection of antique shops. Also available are maps that outline walking or biking tours and

point out scenic views such as that of the Colorado River from the city park. Guests usually come back from walking tours with pockets full of pecans found around town. Smithville was the hometown location for the movie "Hope Floats."
Innkeeper(s): Bruce & Sallie Blalock. $56-110. MC, VISA, AX, PC, TC. 5 rooms with PB, 1 suite and 2 cottages. Breakfast included in rates. Types of meals: Full bkfst and early coffee/tea. Beds: Q. TV, ceiling fan and VCR in room. Air conditioning. Fax and bicycles on premises. Antiquing, fishing, parks and shopping nearby.
Pets allowed: With advance notice, in certain rooms.
Location: Small town.
Certificate may be used: Sunday through Thursday.

Texarkana C9

Mansion on Main B&B

802 Main St
Texarkana, TX 75501-5104
(903)792-1835 Fax:(903)793-0878
Internet: www.bbonline.com/tx/mansion/
E-mail: mansiononmain@aol.com
Circa 1895. Spectacular two-story columns salvaged from the St. Louis World's Fair accent the exterior of this Neoclassical-style inn. Victorian nightgowns and sleepshirts are provided, and whether you are on a business trip or your honeymoon, expect to be pampered. Five bedchambers, all furnished with antiques and period appointments. Awake to the aroma of dark roast cajun coffee, and then enjoy a full "gentleman's" breakfast in the parquet dining room. The inn is located in the downtown historic area. Enjoy a cup of rich coffee or a cool lemonade on the veranda. The inn offers plenty of amenities for the business traveler, including fax machine, desks and modem connections.
Innkeeper(s): Laura Gentry.. $65-109. MC, VISA, AX, PC, TC. 5 rooms with PB. Breakfast included in rates. Types of meals: Full bkfst and early coffee/tea. Beds: QD. Cable TV, phone, ceiling fan and Victorian sleepware in room. Air conditioning. Veranda, courtyard and gardens on premises. Antiquing, fishing, live theater and shopping nearby.
Location: City.
Publicity: *Arkansas Democrat, Texarkana Gazette and Dallas Morning News.*
Certificate may be used: Anytime, except holidays.

Van Alstyne C8

Durning House B&B

205 W Stephens, PO Box 1173
Van Alstyne, TX 75495-1173
(903)482-5188
Circa 1900. Decorated with American oak and antiques, the inn has been host to many events, including weddings, office parties, Christmas parties, club meetings and murder-mystery dinners. Three life-size pigs grace the east garden. The innkeepers have published a cookbook titled "Hog Heaven" that includes more than 400 recipes featured at the inn. Your hosts also appear regularly on a TV show preparing recipes from "Hog Heaven."
Innkeeper(s): Brenda Hix & Sherry Heath. $110-135. MC, VISA, TC. 2 rooms. Type of meal: Cont. Beds: QD. Ceiling fan, jacuzzi and in room. Air conditioning. Massage therapy on premises. Handicap access. Antiquing, fishing, live theater, shopping, sporting events and water sports nearby.
Location: Small town.
Certificate may be used: Jan. 30-Nov. 20, Sunday-Friday.

Waco E7

The Judge Baylor House

908 Speight Ave
Waco, TX 76706-2343
(254)756-0273 (888)522-9567 Fax:(254)756-0711
Internet: www.eyeweb.com/jbaylor
E-mail: jbaylor@iamerica.net

Circa 1940. This home was built by the head of the chemistry department at Baylor University, which is just one block away. There are five well-appointed guest rooms, each decorated with English antiques. Each room
has something special. In one room, guests will discover French doors leading out to a patio. In another, there is a poster bed and hand-painted pedestal sink. Aside from the university and Elizabeth Barrett

& Robert Browning Library, the home is near the Brazos Riverwalk, Lake Waco, the Texas Sports Hall of Fame, antique shops, historic homes and more.

Innkeeper(s): Bruce & Dorothy Dyer. $72-105. MC, VISA, AX, PC, TC. 5 rooms, 4 with PB and 1 suite. Breakfast and afternoon tea included in rates. Types of meals: Full bkfst and early coffee/tea. Beds: KQT. Ceiling fan in room. Air conditioning. VCR, fax, copier and library on premises. Antiquing, fishing, golf, live theater, parks, shopping, sporting events and tennis nearby.

Location: City.

Publicity: *Star-Telegram and Dallas Morning Star.*

Certificate may be used: Sunday through Thursday.

Waxahachie D8

The BonnyNook

414 W Main St
Waxahachie, TX 75165-3234
(972)938-7207 (800)486-5936 Fax:(972)937-7700

Circa 1887. Each of the five guest rooms at this Queen Anne "Painted Lady" is filled with plants and antiques from around the world. The Sterling Room, a large octagon-shaped chamber, features a hand-carved mahogany canopy bed. The Morrow Room boasts a 100-year-old sleigh bed and an antique clawfoot tub with a shower. Three of the guest baths offer whirlpool tubs. Bon Appetit featured BonnyNook as part of an article on bed & breakfasts. The hearty breakfasts feature such notable items as blueberry pudding coffeecake or Southern crepes filled with vegetables and eggs. Innkeeper Bonnie Franks keeps a special Coffee Nook filled with teas, coffee, hot cocoa and a refrigerator for her guests. Don't forget to ask about the inn's special cookies. BonnyNook is only two blocks from antique shops, boutiques and restaurants. Gourmet, six-course meals are available by reservation. Massage also is available by reservation.

Innkeeper(s): Vaughn & Bonnie Franks. $85-125. MC, VISA, AX, DC, DS. 5 rooms with PB. Breakfast and snacks/refreshments included in rates. Types of meals: Full bkfst, cont and early coffee/tea. Beds: KQD. Phone, ceiling fan

and some rooms have Jacuzzis in room. Air conditioning. Fax, copier, coffee nook with refrigerator and ice buckets/ice on premises. Antiquing, parks and shopping nearby.

Location: Small town.

Publicity: *Texas Highways, Dallas Morning News, Forbes, Texas People & Places and Bon Appetit.*

"This was a wonderful retreat from the everyday hustle and bustle and we didn't hear a phone ring once!"

Certificate may be used: Sunday-Thursday.

Wichita Falls C6

Harrison House B&B

2014 11th St
Wichita Falls, TX 76301-4905
(940)322-2299 (800)327-2299

This prairie-style inn features 10-foot ceilings, narrow-board oak floors, a hand-carved mantelpiece, gumwood paneling and detailed molding. The home was built by oilman, developer and philanthropist N.H. Martin. After the discovery of oil on the family ranch in nearby Jolly, Martin and his partner went on to build the Country Club Estates. They donated the land on which Hardin Junior College (now Midwestern State University) was built. The inn also caters to special occasions as many as 200 guests can be accommodated for a stand-up buffet.

Innkeeper(s): Suzanne Staha. $55-125. MC, VISA, AX. 4 rooms and 1 suite. Breakfast included in rates. Type of meal: Full bkfst. Ceiling fan in room. Air conditioning. VCR on premises. Antiquing and shopping nearby.

Certificate may be used: Anytime with advance notice.

Wimberley F7

Southwind

2701 FM 3237
Wimberley, TX 78676-5511
(512)847-5277 (800)508-5277
Internet: www.southwindbedandbreak.com
E-mail: jerry@wimberley.net

Circa 1985. Located three miles northeast of the quaint village of Wimberley, this early Texas-style inn sits on 25 wooded acres along with three secluded rustic cedar cabins, each with Jacuzzi tub, kitchen, fireplace and porch. Roam the unspoiled acres and discover deer crossing your path and armadillos, raccoons and foxes skittering just beyond your footsteps. During the wet season, enjoy clear natural springs with access to the swimming hole. The inn offers a library/lounge with a fireplace, or you can take advantage of the panoramic valley views from the porch hot tub or from one of the rocking chairs. The parlor is a cool retreat in the summer and provides a warm fireplace in winter weather. Two cabins feature wheelchair access. Cabin guests are invited to enjoy the inn, library and hot tub. Gourmet dinners may be enjoyed by advance reservation.

Innkeeper(s): Jerry McGhee. $80-105. MC, VISA, AX, DS, PC, TC. 6 rooms with PB, 4 with FP. Breakfast included in rates. Types of meals: Full gourmet bkfst and early coffee/tea. Beds: KQ. Ceiling fan in room. Air conditioning. Spa and library on premises. Handicap access. Amusement parks, antiquing, canoeing/kayaking, fishing, hiking, hiking, massage therapist on call by request, swimming, live theater, parks, shopping, sporting events and water sports nearby.

Pets allowed: in cabins.

Location: Rural Texas Hill Country.

Certificate may be used: Sunday through Thursday nights only, except holidays and April, June and July.

Utah

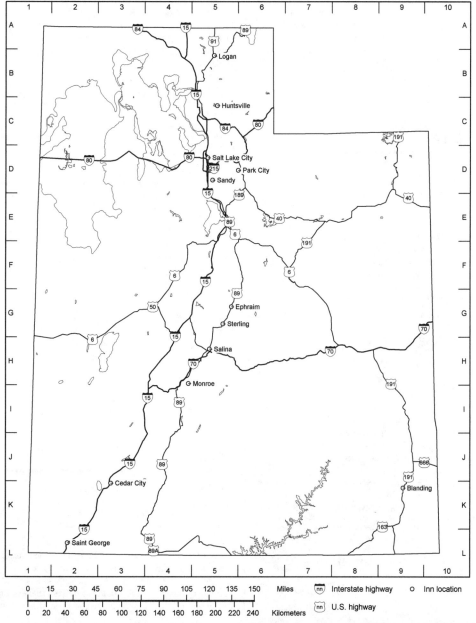

	Miles	nn Interstate highway	o Inn location
0 15 30 45 60 75 90 105 120 135 150			
0 20 40 60 80 100 120 140 160 180 200 220 240	Kilometers	nn U.S. highway	

Blanding K9

The Grayson Country Inn B&B

118 E 300 S
Blanding, UT 84511-2908
(435)678-2388 (800)365-0868

Circa 1908. Over the years, The Grayson Country Inn has served a number of purposes, including a small hotel and boarding house. The inn is the perfect location to enjoy the many sites in the area, and is within walking distance from a pottery factory and gift shops. The area abounds with outdoor activities, as many national parks are nearby. Edge of the Cedars State Park is only a mile from the inn. A three-bedroom cottage is available for groups and/or families.

Innkeeper(s): Dennis & Lurlene Gutke. $47-69. MC, VISA, AX. 8 rooms with PB and 1 cottage. Breakfast included in rates. Type of meal: Full bkfst. Beds: Q. Cable TV and ceiling fan in room. Air conditioning. Library on premises. Fishing, hiking, parks and water sports nearby.

Location: Country.
Publicity: *Salt Lake Tribune.*

Certificate may be used: Anytime, with availability.

Cedar City K3

Bard's Inn

150 S 100 W
Cedar City, UT 84720-3276
(801)586-6612

Circa 1910. This handsome bungalow features stained-glass windows, a wide front porch and a second-story porch. The Katharina Room has an antique, high-back queen bed and a twin-size walnut sleigh bed. Homemade pastries and fruit are served on the porch or in the formal dining room.

Innkeeper(s): Jack & Audrey Whipple. $85. MC, VISA, AX. 7 rooms with PB. Breakfast included in rates. Type of meal: Full bkfst. Beds: QT. Air conditioning. Antiquing, live theater, parks, shopping, downhill skiing, cross-country skiing and sporting events nearby.

Location: City.

Certificate may be used: Oct. 16 to May 15, based on availability.

Paxman's House B&B

170 N 400 W
Cedar City, UT 84720-2421
(435)586-3755

Circa 1900. This steeply-gabled, turn-of-the-century Victorian offers a small veranda overlooking a residential street, two blocks from the Shakespearean Festival. Early Mormon pioneer pieces furnish the Pine Room, while walnut and marble Victorian furnishings fill the Walnut Room. Breakfast includes fruit, cereals, rolls and beverages. Brian Head Ski Resort and Zion National Park are a short drive away.

Innkeeper(s): Karlene Paxman. $69-85. MC, VISA, AX. 3 rooms. Breakfast included in rates. TV in room. Air conditioning. VCR on premises. Antiquing, live theater, shopping, downhill skiing, cross-country skiing and sporting events nearby.

Location: City.

Certificate may be used: Nov. 1 to May 15, everyday except holidays, based upon availability.

Ephraim G5

Ephraim Homestead

135 W 100 N (43-2)
Ephraim, UT 84627-1131
(435)283-6367

Circa 1880. Three buildings comprise this Mormon pioneer homestead. The Granary, circa 1860, is furnished in Mormon pioneer items and resembles a museum reproduction with its fireplace, cast-iron cookstove, rustic kitchen, antique beds and cradle. The barn offers two rustic rooms on the top floor, while the Victorian Gothic house, fashioned of adobe, is furnished in Eastlake antiques. It features Scandinavian/Victorian stencilings in its two tiny guest rooms located up steep stairs off the kitchen. Apple muffins and French toast are prepared on the wood stove for guests.

Innkeeper(s): Sherron Andreasen. $55-95. 2 rooms and 1 cottage. Breakfast included in rates. Type of meal: Full bkfst. Phone, antique parlor and cookstoves in room. Air conditioning. Garden, swings, porches and patio on premises. Antiquing, live theater, shopping, cross-country skiing and sporting events nearby.

Location: near mountains.

Certificate may be used: All year, every day, excluding third and fourth weeks of June.

Huntsville C5

Jackson Fork Inn LLC

7345 E 900 S
Huntsville, UT 84317-9778
(801)745-0051 (800)255-0672

Circa 1938. This former dairy barn was named after the hay fork that was used to transport hay into the loft of the barn. The inn has eight guest rooms, all in a two-story configuration with lofts and spiral staircases. Four rooms include two-person Jacuzzi tubs, and all are cozy and comfortable. A self-serve continental breakfast is prepared each day with muffins and fresh coffee. There's a restaurant on the first floor that offers fish, chicken and steak. The inn is ideal for skiers with its location near Powder Mountain, Nordic Valley and Snowbasin ski resorts.

Innkeeper(s): Vicki Petersen. $60-120. MC, VISA, AX, DS, PC, TC. 8 rooms with PB. Breakfast included in rates. Type of meal: Cont. Beds: Q. Ceiling fan in room. Full breakfast on Sunday on premises. Fishing, parks, shopping, downhill skiing, cross-country skiing and water sports nearby.

Pets allowed: With $20 fee - must be kept on leash.
Location: Mountains.

Certificate may be used: Monday through Thursday, excluding holidays.

Logan B5

Center Street B&B

169 E Center St
Logan, UT 84321-4606
(435)752-3443
Internet: www.centerstreetinn.com

Circa 1879. Imagine wandering through a castle until you come to a room lit by the amber glow from the fireplace. A canopy bed awaits and above, Michelangelo's glorious works decorate the ceiling. If this doesn't spark your interest, pretend you've traveled back in time to the Old West in a suite with pine walls, a pool table, moose head and a pressed-brass ceiling. These are just two of the options at this most unusual bed & breakfast. Each of the rooms has its own theme, from the above mentioned Castle and Jesse James motifs to the bedchambers with names such as Caribbean Sea Cave, Space Odyssey, Amazon Rain Forest or perhaps the Arabian Nights Suite. Fireplaces and Jacuzzis (some heart-shaped) are among the amenities. Guests in three rooms each reserve a private time at the indoor pool, with walls adorned with murals of whales and sea creatures.

$57-180. MC, VISA, AX, PC, TC. 16 suites, 7 with FP. Breakfast included in rates. Type of meal: Cont plus. Beds: KQ. Cable TV, phone and VCR in room. Air conditioning. Spa and swimming on premises. Antiquing, fishing, golf, live theater, parks, shopping, downhill skiing, cross-country skiing, sporting events, tennis and water sports nearby.

Location: Mountains.

Certificate may be used: Oct. 1-June 1, Sunday-Thursday except holidays and Dec. 20-Jan. 2. Subject to availability.

Monroe   H4

Peterson's B&B

PO Box 142
Monroe, UT 84754-0142
(435)527-4830

Circa 1895. Although it appears to be a modern ranch house, this home has sections more than 100 years old. For more than two decades Mary Ann has hosted bed & breakfast guests here. A former cooking teacher, she offers breakfasts of Hawaiian French toast and Eggs Benedict. The fenced yard, shaded by an apple tree offers outdoor furnishings for relaxation. Open from April through October, the inn is near five national parks and four national forests. Visit Fremont Indian State Park and discover petroglyphs and pictographs carved into the cliffs, as well as pit dwellings. Monroe is halfway between Denver and Los Angeles.

Innkeeper(s): Mary Ann Peterson. $65-75. PC. 3 rooms, 1 with PB and 1 suite. Breakfast included in rates. Types of meals: Full gourmet bkfst and early coffee/tea. Beds: KDT. Cable TV in room. Air conditioning. Library and outdoor furniture in shaded yard on premises. Fishing, golf, swimming, live entertainment, natural hot springs, live theater, parks, shopping, cross-country skiing and tennis nearby.

Location: Mountains.

Publicity: *Salt Lake Tribune and Desert News.*

Certificate may be used: April 1 to Oct. 30.

Park City   D6

The 1904 Imperial Hotel-A B&B

221 Main St, PO Box 1628
Park City, UT 84060-1628
(435)649-1904 (800)669-8824 Fax:(435)645-7421
Internet: www.1904imperial.com
E-mail: stay@1904imperial.com

Circa 1904. The Imperial, a historic turn-of-the-century hotel, is decorated in a "Western" Victorian style. Several guest rooms include amenities like clawfoot or Roman tubs and sitting areas. A few overlook Park City's historic Main Street. The inn's largest suite includes a bedroom and a spiral staircase leading up to

a cozy loft area. There are ski lockers and a Jacuzzi on-site. Transportation to area ski lifts are located nearby.

Innkeeper(s): Nancy McLaughlin & Karen Hart. $80-245. MC, VISA, AX, DS, TC. 10 rooms with PB and 2 suites. Breakfast included in rates. Type of meal: Full bkfst. Beds: KQT. Cable TV and phone in room. Fax and copier on premises. Antiquing, fishing, live theater, parks, shopping, downhill skiing, cross-country skiing, sporting events and water sports nearby.

Location: Mountains.

Certificate may be used: April 15-June 15; Sept. 15-Nov. 15, space available.

The Old Miners' Lodge - A B&B Inn

615 Woodside Ave, PO Box 2639
Park City, UT 84060-2639
(435)645-8068 (800)648-8068 Fax:(435)645-7420
Internet: www.oldminerslodge.com
E-mail: stay@oldminerslodge.com

Circa 1889. This originally was established as a miners' boarding house by E. P. Ferry, owner of the Woodside-Norfolk silver

mines. A two-story Victorian with Western flavor, the lodge is a significant structure in the Park City National Historic District. Just on the edge of the woods is a deck and a steaming hot tub.

Innkeeper(s): Susan Wynne & Liza Simpson. $70-275. MC, VISA, AX, DC, CB, DS, PC, TC. 12 rooms with PB, 3 suites and 3 conference rooms. Breakfast and snacks/refreshments included in rates. Types of meals: Full bkfst and early coffee/tea. Beds: KQDT. Turndown service, ceiling fan, robes and clock in room. Fax, copier, spa and library on premises. Antiquing, fishing, live theater, parks, shopping, downhill skiing and cross-country skiing nearby.

Location: Mountains.

Publicity: *Boston Herald, Los Angeles Times, Detroit Free Press, Washington Post, Ski, Bon Appetit and ESPN.*

"This is the creme de la creme. The most wonderful place I have stayed at bar none, including ski country in the U.S. and Europe."

Certificate may be used: April 15-June 15, Sept. 15-Nov. 15, subject to availability.

Saint George   L2

Greene Gate Village Historic B&B Inn

76 W Tabernacle St
Saint George, UT 84770-3420
(435)628-6999 (800)350-6999 Fax:(435)628-6989
Internet: www.greenegate.com
E-mail: stay@greenegate.com

Circa 1876. This is a cluster of nine restored pioneer homes all located within one block. The Bentley House has comfortable Victorian decor. The Orson Pratt House and the Tolley House are other choices, all carefully restored. The fifth house contains three bedrooms each with private bath, a kitchen, living room and two fireplaces. Six of the bedrooms have large whirlpool tubs.

Innkeeper(s): Durk & Jane Johnson. $65-129. MC, VISA, AX, DC, DS, PC, TC. 16 rooms with PB, 8 with FP, 6 suites, 1 cottage and 1 conference room. Breakfast included in rates. Type of meal: Full bkfst. Beds: KQDT. Cable TV, ceiling fan, courtyard and porches in room. Central air. VCR, fax, spa and swimming on premises. Handicap access. Antiquing, art galleries, bicycling, fishing, golf, hiking, horseback riding, live theater, museums, parks, shopping, tennis and water sports nearby.

Location: Mountains.

Publicity: *Deseret News, Spectrum, Better Homes & Garden, Sunset and Country.*

"You not only provided me with rest, comfort and wonderful food, but you fed my soul."

Certificate may be used: Sunday-Thursday.

Salina   H5

The Victorian Inn

190 W Main St
Salina, UT 84654-1153
(435)529-7342 (800)972-7183

A courtyard filled with a rose garden, stained-glass windows and fine wood floors and moldings set the tone for this Victorian experience. The inn has down comforters, king beds and antique clawfoot tubs. Abundant Grandmother-type servings are offered at breakfast. The valley, surrounded by mountains as high as 12,000 feet, offers close spots for fishing, hunting and snowmobiling.

Innkeeper(s): Debbie Van Horn. $75-90. MC, VISA. 3 rooms. Breakfast included in rates. Type of meal: Full bkfst. Air conditioning. Cross-country skiing nearby.

Location: Small town.

Certificate may be used: Mid-June through mid-August, Sunday-Thursday only.

Salt Lake City   D5

Saltair B&B

164 S 900 E
Salt Lake City, UT 84102-4103
(801)533-8184 (800)733-8184 Fax:(801)595-0332
Internet: www.saltlakebandb.com
E-mail: saltair@saltlakebandb.com

Circa 1903. The Saltair is the oldest continuously operating bed & breakfast in Utah and offers a prime location to enjoy Salt Lake City. The simply decorated rooms include light, airy window dressings, charming furnishings and special touches. Breakfasts, especially the delicious Saltair Eggs Benedict topped with avocado, sour creme and salsa, are memorable. The inn is within walking distance to four historic districts and only one mile from Temple Square and the Governor's Mansion. Day trips include treks to several national and state parks and the Wasatch Front ski areas.

Innkeeper(s): Nancy Saxton & Jan Bartlett. $75-149. MC, VISA, AX, DC, CB, DS. 7 rooms, 4 with PB. Breakfast and snacks/refreshments included in rates. Types of meals: Full gourmet bkfst and early coffee/tea. Beds: QT. Fresh flowers in room. Air conditioning. VCR, fax and spa on premises. Antiquing, fishing, live theater, parks, shopping, downhill skiing, cross-country skiing, sporting events and water sports nearby.

Location: City.

Publicity: *Mobil, Logan Sun and Sunset.*

"Your swing and Saltair Muffins were fabulous."

Certificate may be used: April-July, September-November, Dec. 1-15.

The Anton Boxrud B&B

57 S 600 E
Salt Lake City, UT 84102-1006
(801)363-8035 (800)524-5511 Fax:(801)596-1316
Internet: www.netoriginals.com/antonboxrud/
E-mail: antonboxrud@earthlink.net

Circa 1901. One of Salt Lake City's grand old homes, this Victorian home with eclectic style is on the register of the Salt Lake City Historical Society. The interior is furnished with antiques from around the country and Old World details. In the sitting and dining rooms, guests will find chairs with intricate carvings, a table with carved swans for support, embossed brass door knobs and stained and beveled glass. There is an out-door  hot tub available to guests. The inn is located just a half-block south of the Utah Governor's Mansion in the historic district. A full homemade breakfast and evening snack are provided.

Innkeeper(s): Jane Johnson. $69-140. MC, VISA, AX, DC, DS. 7 rooms, 5 with PB and 1 suite. Breakfast included in rates. Types of meals: Full bkfst and early coffee/tea. Beds: KQT. Amusement parks, antiquing, fishing, live theater, shopping, downhill skiing, cross-country skiing, sporting events and water sports nearby.

Location: City.

Publicity: *Salt Lake Tribune.*

"Made us feel at home and well-fed. Can you adopt us?."

Certificate may be used: April through November.

Wildflowers B&B

936 E 1700 S
Salt Lake City, UT 84105-3329
(801)466-0600 (800)569-0009 Fax:(801)484-7832

Circa 1891. Holding true to its name, the grounds surrounding this Victorian home are covered with all sorts of flowers ranging from wild geraniums to coreopsis to meadow rue. The outside beauty only serves to complement the magnificence on the inside of this historic residence. Hand-carved staircases, stained-glass windows, clawfoot bathtubs and original chandeliers make up just some of the touches that will make a stay here memorable. Situated in the heart of Salt Lake City, this home offers all the comfort one could ask for and the convenience of being just a few minutes away from skiing or a trip downtown. Like this classic residence, 10 nearby homes are also listed in the National Register of Historic Places.

Innkeeper(s): Jeri Parker & Cill Sparks. $70-125. MC, VISA, AX. 5 rooms with PB, 2 suites and 1 conference room. Breakfast included in rates. Type of meal: Full gourmet bkfst. Beds: KQD. Cable TV, phone, ceiling fan and VCR in room. Air conditioning. Fax, copier, bicycles and art on premises. Amusement parks, antiquing, fishing, museums, live theater, parks, shopping, downhill skiing, cross-country skiing, sporting events and water sports nearby.

Location: 5 minutes to mountains.

Publicity: *Salt Lake Tribune.*

"Service above and beyond my expectations with people that I'll remember."

Certificate may be used: Not February, March, holidays. All other times depending on availability.

Sandy D5

Mountain Hollow B&B Inn

10209 S Dimple Dell Rd
Sandy, UT 84092-4536
(801)942-3428 (800)757-3428 Fax:(801)733-7187
Internet: www.mountainhollow.com
E-mail: kpl@aos.net

Circa 1973. Located just outside of Salt Lake City, this contemporary home is surrounded by the beautiful scenery of Little Cottonwood Canyon and the Watsatch Mountains. Ski and hiking areas are about 15 minutes away, and after a day on the slopes, guests can relax in their comfortable, country-style rooms; enjoy a soak in the outdoor hot tub; or take on a round of table tennis or pool in the game room. In warm weather, the breakfasts of fresh breads, fruit, cheese, hard-boiled eggs and other treats are served on the patio. In cool weather, the morning meal is presented fireside indoors.

Innkeeper(s): Kathy & Doug Larson. $75-275. MC, VISA, AX, DS, PC, TC. 10 rooms, 5 with PB, 1 with FP and 5 suites. Breakfast and snacks/refreshments included in rates. Type of meal: Cont plus. Beds: KQT. Air conditioning. VCR, fax, spa and library on premises. Amusement parks, antiquing, fishing, live theater, parks, shopping, downhill skiing, cross-country skiing, sporting events and water sports nearby.

Location: Suburban rural.

Certificate may be used: April 15-Nov. 15.

Sterling G5

Cedar Crest Inn

819 Palisade Rd
Sterling, UT 84665
(801)835-6352

Circa 1903. Several structures comprise the Cedar Crest Inn, including the Swiss-style Lindenhaus, named for a giant linden tree adjacent to the home. The tree was brought to America from Germany as a seedling. Guests also can opt to stay in Linderhof, which offers three beautiful suites. The third structure on this 18-acre property is the popular Cedar Crest Restaurant, which serves a variety of gourmet entrees, including lobster, chicken Cordon Bleu and Filet Mignon. The grounds are beautiful, and on cold nights, guests can stay indoors and watch a favorite movie. The innkeepers have a selection of more than 300.

Innkeeper(s): Ron & Don Kelsch. $52-100. MC, VISA, AX, DS. 12 rooms, 9 with PB, 2 suites and 1 conference room. Breakfast included in rates. Types of meals: Full gourmet bkfst and early coffee/tea. Beds: KQD. Cable TV and VCR in room. Air conditioning. Spa and bicycles on premises. Antiquing, parks, shopping, cross-country skiing and water sports nearby.

Location: Mountains.

Certificate may be used: Jan. 30 to Nov. 30, Saturday-Thursday. Excludes holidays and special events.

Vermont

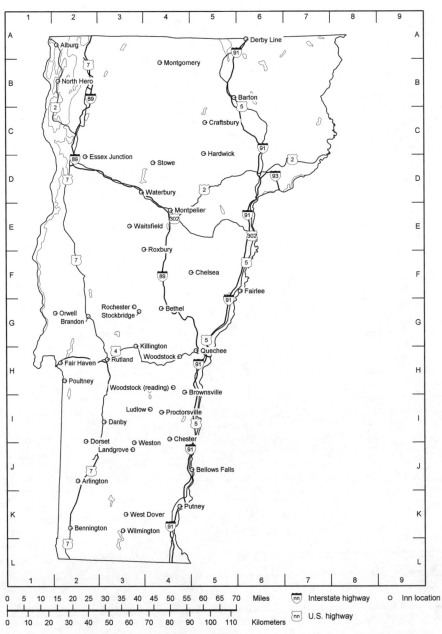

Map legend:
- nn Interstate highway
- nn U.S. highway
- ○ Inn location

Miles scale: 0 5 10 15 20 25 30 35 40 45 50 55 60 65 70 Miles

Kilometers scale: 0 10 20 30 40 50 60 70 80 90 100 110 Kilometers

Alburg A2

Thomas Mott Homestead B&B

63 Blue Rock Rd on Lake Champlain
Alburg, VT 05440-4002
(800)348-0843 Fax:(802)796-3736
Internet: www.thomas-mott-bb.com
E-mail: tmott@together.net

Circa 1838. Each room in this restored farmhouse provides a special view of Lake Champlain, yet guests often may be found enjoying the view from the sitting room as they warm by the fireplace. There are also full views of Mt. Mansfield and nearby Jay Peak. Montreal Island is one hour away. Guests are sure to enjoy the complimentary Ben & Jerry's ice cream. Patrick is a noted wine consul-

tant and holds Master's Degrees in criminology, sociology and the classical arts. A boat dock, extending 75 feet onto the lake, recently has been added to the property.

Innkeeper(s): Patrick Schallert. $79-109. MC, VISA, AX, DC, CB, DS, PC, TC. 5 rooms with PB, 1 with FP, 2 suites and 3 conference rooms. Breakfast and snacks/refreshments included in rates. Types of meals: Full gourmet bkfst and early coffee/tea. Beds: KQ. Turndown service and ceiling fan in room. Fax, copier and library on premises. Amusement parks, antiquing, fishing, live theater, parks, shopping, downhill skiing, cross-country skiing, sporting events and water sports nearby.

Publicity: *Los Angeles Times, St. Alban's Messenger, Yankee Traveler, Boston Globe, Elle, Outside, Prime Time and Vermont Life.*

"One of the greatest surprises was to open the freezer in the kitchen and find 15 flavors of Ben & Jerry's ice cream compliments of the host, available to anyone at anytime. We all enjoyed."

Certificate may be used: Nov. 1-Dec. 15 and Jan. 2-April 30.

Arlington J2

Arlington Manor House B&B

Cor. Buck Hill & Salter Hill Rd
Arlington, VT 05250-8648
(802)375-6784
Internet: www.arlingtonmanorhouse.com
E-mail: kitandal@arlingtonmanorhouse.com

Circa 1908. A view of Mt. Equinox is enjoyed from the spacious terrace of this Dutch Colonial inn in the Battenkill River Valley. The inn also sports its own tennis court and is within easy walking distance of the Battenkill River, where canoeing, fishing and river tubing are popular activities. A variety of accommodations is offered, and two of the inn's guest rooms have romantic fireplaces. A bikers' workshop and bench stand are on the premises.

Innkeeper(s): Al & Kit McAllister. $85-145. MC, VISA, AX, PC, TC. 5 rooms, 3 with PB, 2 with FP, 1 suite and 2 conference rooms. Breakfast and afternoon tea included in rates. Types of meals: Full bkfst and early coffee/tea. Beds: KQDT. TV in room. Air conditioning. VCR, tennis, library, workbench, shops and satellite Prime-star on premises. Antiquing, fishing, live theater, parks, shopping, downhill skiing, cross-country skiing and water sports nearby.

Location: Battenkill River nearby.

Certificate may be used: All year except holiday weeks, Sunday through Friday.

Hill Farm Inn

458 HIll Farm Rd
Arlington, VT 05250-9311
(802)375-2269 (800)882-2545 Fax:(802)375-9918
Internet: hillfarminn.com
E-mail: hillfarm@vermontel.com

Circa 1790. One of Vermont's original land grant farmsteads, Hill Farm Inn has welcomed guests since 1905 when the widow Mettie Hill opened her home to summer vacationers.

The farm is surrounded by 50 peaceful acres that border the Battenkill River. Guests can relax and enjoy the simple life and visit the inn's sheep, goats and chickens or soak in the 360-degree views of the mountains. Accommodations are charming and cozy, and summer guests have the option of staying in one of four cabins. A large, country breakfast of homemade fare starts off each day.

Innkeeper(s): Kathleen & Craig Yanez. $70-155. MC, VISA, AX, DS. 15 rooms with PB and 2 suites. Breakfast and afternoon tea included in rates. Types of meals: Full bkfst and early coffee/tea. Beds: KQDT. TV and one kitchenette in room. Fax and copier on premises. Antiquing, bicycling, fishing, families welcome, parks, shopping, downhill skiing and cross-country skiing nearby.

Location: River borders property.

Publicity: *Providence Journal, Boston Globe, Innsider and Country.*

"I have already taken the liberty of changing the meaning of relaxation in the dictionary to "Hill Farm Inn". Thank you . . . It was great."

Certificate may be used: Nov. 1-Sept. 15, Sunday-Thursday; excluding holiday periods.

Ira Allen House

Rd 2, Box 2485
Arlington, VT 05250-9317
(802)362-2284 Fax:(802)362-0928
Internet: www.iraallenhouse.com
E-mail: stay@iraallenhouse.com

Circa 1770. Built by Ethan Allen's brother, this Colonial Revival inn is a state historic site. Hand-blown glass panes, hand-hewn beams, handmade bricks and wide-board floors provide evidence of the inn's longevity. Surrounded by farms and forest, the inn's setting is perfect for those searching for some peace and quiet. Plenty of recreational activities also are found nearby, including fine trout fishing in the Battenkill River just across the

road, yet still on the property. Saturday-night dinners are available in winter, and guests are welcome to raid the living room fridge, where they will find soda and other refreshments.

Innkeeper(s): Sandy & Ray Walters. $75-100. 9 rooms and 2 suites. Breakfast included in rates. Type of meal: Full bkfst. Air conditioning. VCR on premises. Antiquing, canoeing/kayaking, live theater, shopping, downhill skiing and cross-country skiing nearby.

Location: River across street.

Certificate may be used: Year-round except foliage season (last week September-last week October) and holidays.

Barton
B5

Anglin B&B
202 Lakeside Ln
Barton, VT 05822
(802)525-4546 Fax:(802)525-8840
Internet: http://www.bartonareachamber.org
E-mail: bac@conriv.net

Circa 1923. This is a large Cape-style home located on an acre of lakefront on Crystal Lake. A green lawn, porch and waterside deck claim most guests' hours. Some elect to fish right at the dock or take a canoe or boat out to explore the scenic setting. All of the guest rooms have lake views and are decorated in a country style. Full breakfasts of French toast, Vermont maple syrup and locally cured bacon are served in the dining room or out on the porch. Your host is a life-long Vermonter and encourages moonlight canoeing as well as star gazing so guests enjoy the full Vermont experience. In winter, there's ice fishing on the premises available by advance reservations.
Innkeeper(s): Fay U. Valley. $75. PC, TC. 3 rooms with PB. Breakfast and snacks/refreshments included in rates. Type of meal: Full gourmet bkfst. Beds: KQT. Phone in room. VCR, fax, copier, swimming, bicycles, library, child care, boat rental and water skiing on premises. Amusement parks, antiquing, art galleries, beaches, bicycling, canoeing/kayaking, fishing, golf, hiking, horseback riding, ice fishing, live theater, museums, parks, shopping, downhill skiing, cross-country skiing, tennis and water sports nearby.
Location: Country.
Certificate may be used: Oct. 15 through June 15, Sunday-Thursday.

Bellows Falls
J5

River Mist B&B
7 Burt St
Bellows Falls, VT 05101-1401
(802)463-9023 (888)463-9023 Fax:(802)463-1571
Internet: www.river-mist.com
E-mail: rmistbnb@vermontel.net

Circa 1880. The scenic village of Bellows Falls is home to this late 19th-century Queen Anne Victorian inn, with its inviting wraparound porch and country Victorian interior. Guests may relax in any of three sitting rooms or in front of the fireplace. Enjoy a day of antiquing, skiing or just wandering around the picturesque environs. Be sure to take a ride on the Green Mountain Flyer before leaving town.
Innkeeper(s): John & Linda Maresca. $69-89. 3 rooms. Breakfast included in rates. Type of meal: Full bkfst. Amusement parks, antiquing, live theater, shopping, downhill skiing and cross-country skiing nearby.
Location: Village.
Certificate may be used: Anytime except foliage season weekends, Sept. 1-Oct. 31, and holiday weekends.

Bennington
K2

Alexandra B&B
Rt 7A Orchard Rd
Bennington, VT 05201
(802)442-5619 (888)207-9386 Fax:(802)442-5592
Internet: www.alexandrainn.com
E-mail: alexandra@sover.net

Circa 1859. Located on two acres at the edge of town, Alexandra is a Colonial-style inn. There are king or queen beds in all the rooms, as well as fireplaces and views of Bennington Monument and the Green Mountains. Each bath offers water jets and showers. A full gourmet breakfast is served. Bennington College and the business district are five minutes from the inn.
Innkeeper(s): Alex Koks & Andra Erickson. $100-150. MC, VISA, AX, DS, TC. 13 rooms with PB, 12 with FP, 7 suites and 1 conference room. Breakfast included in rates. Types of meals: Full gourmet bkfst and early coffee/tea. Beds: KQ. Cable TV, phone and VCR in room. Air conditioning. Fax and copier on premises. Antiquing, art galleries, bicycling, canoeing/kayaking, fishing, golf, hiking, horseback riding, live theater, museums, parks, shopping, downhill skiing, cross-country skiing, tennis, water sports and wineries nearby.
Pets allowed: Discuss.
Location: Country.
Certificate may be used: Jan. 2-July 1, weekdays only.

Four Chimneys Inn
21 West Rd
Bennington, VT 05201-2145
(802)447-3500 (800)649-3503 Fax:(802)447-3692
Internet: www.fourchimneys.com
E-mail: judy@4chimneys.com

Circa 1783. The inn's four distinctive chimneys rise from the roofline of this three-story Georgian Revival manor on 11 acres. Most guest rooms offer fireplaces and Jacuzzis and all have television. Accommodations are also available in the carriage house and ice house. The inn's formal gardens with fountain are often the site for elegant weddings. There's a well-known restaurant on the premises. (Try the beef Wellington or Lamb Rack) Nearby activities include white-water rafting, canoeing and antiquing.
Innkeeper(s): Ronald & Judith Schefkind. $110-185. MC, VISA, AX, DC, CB, DS. 11 rooms with PB, 8 with FP and 1 suite. Breakfast included in rates. Type of meal: Cont plus. Beds: KQT. Cable TV, phone, ceiling fan and jacuzzi jets in tubs in room. Air conditioning. VCR, fax, copier and bicycles on premises. Handicap access. Antiquing, fishing, golf, live theater, parks, shopping, downhill skiing, cross-country skiing, tennis and water sports nearby.
Location: historic village.
Certificate may be used: Sunday-Thursday Jan. 15-May 15.

Bethel
G4

Greenhurst Inn
River St, Rd 2, Box 60
Bethel, VT 05032-9404
(802)234-9474 (800)510-2553

Circa 1890. In the National Register of Historic Places, Greenhurst is a gracious Victorian mansion built for the Harringtons of Philadelphia. Overlooking the White River, the inn's opulent interiors include etched windows once featured on the cover of Vermont Life. There are eight masterpiece fireplaces and a north and south parlor.
Innkeeper(s): Lyle & Claire Wolf. $50-100. MC, VISA, DS, PC, TC. 13 rooms, 7 with PB, 4 with FP. Breakfast included in rates. Types of meals: Cont plus, cont and early coffee/tea. Beds: QDT. VCR and library on premises. Antiquing, fishing, live theater, parks, shopping, downhill skiing, cross-country skiing and water sports nearby.
Pets allowed: Dogs only.
Publicity: *Best Country Inns of New England, Victorian Homes, Washington Post, Boston Globe, Bride's Magazine, Los Angeles Times, Time, New York Times, Vermont Life.* and *The Man Who Corrupted Hadleyburg.*

"The inn is magnificent! The hospitality unforgettable."
Certificate may be used: Sunday-Thursday except Sept. 15-Oct. 15.

Brandon   G2

Hivue B&B Tree Farm

730 High Pond Rd
Brandon, VT 05733-8514
(802)247-3042 (800)880-3042

Circa 1960. There are meadows and woods to meander
through, and a stream stocked with trout winds its way
through the 76-acre grounds at this raised ranch-style home.
Accommodations are comfortable, a bit like an old country
farmhouse. Guests enjoy views of the surrounding Green
Mountains. Brandon, a historic little village, is just a few miles
down the road.

Innkeeper(s): Winifred Reuschle. $60. PC, TC. 2 rooms with PB. Breakfast
included in rates. Type of meal: Full bkfst. TV and VCR in room. Antiquing,
bicycling, canoeing/kayaking, fishing, parks, shopping, downhill skiing, cross-
country skiing and water sports nearby.

Pets Allowed.

Location: Rural.

Certificate may be used: Jan. 1-May 19, Monday-Thursday; June 17-July 1,
Monday-Wednesday; July 12-Aug. 26, Wednesday-Friday; Aug. 31-Sept. 19,
Tuesday & Thursday; Oct. 13-Dec. 16, Wednesday-Thursday.

Moffett House

69 Park St
Brandon, VT 05733-1121
(802)247-3843 (800)394-7239

Circa 1856. This graceful French Second Empire house has a
mansard roof and a Queen Anne Victorian veranda that was
added in 1880. Widow walks top the roof, and gingerbread
trim adds to the street-side appeal of Moffett House. The inn
was named after Hugh Moffett, Time-Life editor and Vermont
legislator. A country breakfast is served in the dining room. The
Kellington-Pico ski area is nearby.

Innkeeper(s): Mary Bowers. $65-125. MC, VISA. 7 rooms, 3 with PB and 1
suite. Breakfast included in rates. Types of meals: Full bkfst and early
coffee/tea. Beds: KQDT. Cable TV and ceiling fan in room. Antiquing, fishing,
live theater, parks, shopping, downhill skiing, cross-country skiing and water
sports nearby.

Pets Allowed.

Location: Small town.

Publicity: *Rutland Business Journal.*

*"My mother, aunt, cousin and I were all delighted with the lovely
accommodations and the delicious breakfasts."*

Certificate may be used: Sunday-Friday, excludes holidays and foliage season.

Rosebelle's Victorian Inn

31 Franklin St
Brandon, VT 05733-0370
(802)247-0098 (888)767-3235 Fax:(802)247-4552
Internet: www.rosebelles.com
E-mail: rosebel@together.net

Circa 1839. This elegant Second Empire Victorian inn with
mansard roof is listed in the National Register of Historic
Places. The home was part of the Underground Railroad.
Impressive both inside and out, the inn and
its six guest rooms have been lovingly
furnished with authentic Victorian
pieces by the innkeepers. Favorite
gathering spots include the comfortable common rooms and the wick-
er-filled porch. Guests also enjoy strolling the lush grounds
where they often experience close encounters with butterflies
and hummingbirds. The innkeepers, who speak French, offer
gift certificates and special packages. The inn is near
Middlebury College and minutes from major ski areas.

Innkeeper(s): Ginette & Norm Milot. $65-95. MC, VISA, AX, PC, TC. 6
rooms, 4 with PB. Breakfast included in rates. Type of meal: Full bkfst. Beds:
QDT. Ceiling fan in room. VCR, storage barn for bikes and skis on premises.
Antiquing, fishing, hiking, snow shoeing, Bluegrass Festival and underground
railroad site, live theater, parks, shopping, downhill skiing, cross-country skiing, sporting events and water sports nearby.

Location: Historic town/village.

"You have captured a beautiful part of our history."

Certificate may be used: Jan. 30 to Sept. 1, Sunday-Thursday, except holiday weekends-Memorial Day, 4th of July, Labor Day, Valentine week. Call for
possible weekend availability.

The Gazebo Inn

On Rt 7 (25 Grove St)
Brandon, VT 05733
(802)247-3235 (888)858-3235
Internet: www.brandon.org/gazebo.htm
E-mail: gazebo@sover.net

Circa 1865. This National Register home is like a little museum with antique tools, toys, glass, bottles, musical instruments
and other collectibles placed throughout the rooms. In the
summer and fall months, the innkeepers open an antique shop
on the premises, and the area is bursting with places to hunt
for antiques and crafts. A variety of dishes, from traditional
pancakes with locally produced maple syrup to huevos
rancheros, are served each morning in the dining room. Guests
are invited to simply sit and relax in the gazebo, on the porch
or in front of a wood-burning stove.

Innkeeper(s): Janet & Joel Mondlak. $55-85. MC, VISA, AX, DS, TC. 4 rooms
with PB. Breakfast included in rates. Beds: QDT. Copier, bicycles and antique
shop on premises. Antiquing, fishing, live theater, parks, shopping, downhill
skiing, cross-country skiing, sporting events and water sports nearby.

Location: Small town/village.

*"Thank you for your hospitality. We had a wonderful time. We will
try to make this an annual event."*

Certificate may be used: Always, except fall foliage and holiday weekends.

Brownsville   H4

Mill Brook B&B

PO Box 410
Brownsville, VT 05037-0410
(802)484-7283

Circa 1878. Once known as the House of Seven Gables, Mill
Brook has been in constant use as a family home and for a
while, a boarding house for mill loggers. Old German Fraktur
paintings decorate the woodwork and there are three sitting
rooms for guests. Antique furnishings are found throughout.
Popular activities in the area include hang gliding, bike tours
and canoeing.

Innkeeper(s): K. Carriere. $69-129. MC, VISA. 5 rooms, 2 with PB and 3
suites. Breakfast included in rates. Types of meals: Full bkfst and early cof-
fee/tea. Beds: QDT. TV, phone and ceiling fan in room. VCR on premises.
Antiquing, live theater, shopping, downhill skiing, cross-country skiing and
sporting events nearby.

Pets Allowed.

Location: Rural village.

"Splendid hospitality. Your B&B was beyond our expectation."

Certificate may be used: March-August and November, Monday-Thursday,
excluding holidays.

Chelsea   F5

Shire Inn

Main St, PO Box 37
Chelsea, VT 05038
(802)685-3031 (800)441-6908 Fax:(802)685-3871
Internet: www.shireinn.com
E-mail: keepers@shireinn.com

Circa 1832. Granite lintels over the windows and a sunburst light over the entry highlight this Adams-style brick home. The romantic inn, which is located in a 210-year-old historic village, has a grand spiral staircase ascend-

ing from wide-plank pumpkin pine floors in the entryway. Guest rooms include antique canopied beds, tall windows and 10-foot ceilings. Most have wood-burn-ing fireplaces. Included on the property's 23 acres are granite post fencing, perennial gardens dating from the 19th century, and a broad, rocky stream spanned by a farm bridge. On most evenings a five-course gourmet dinner is available.

Innkeeper(s): Jay & Karen Keller. $105-155. MC, VISA, DS, PC, TC. 6 rooms with PB, 4 with FP and 1 cottage. Breakfast included in rates. Types of meals: Full bkfst and early coffee/tea. Beds: KQD. Fax, copier, bicycles and library on premises. Antiquing, fishing, hiking, live theater, parks, shopping, downhill skiing, cross-country skiing and water sports nearby.

Location: Country village.

Publicity: *Country Inn Review, Vermont Life and PBS.*

"What an inn should be! Absolutely delicious food - great hospitality! The rooms are filled with romance."

Certificate may be used: Anytime except Sept. 10-Oct. 20 and holidays.

Chester   I4

Hugging Bear Inn & Shoppe

244 Main St
Chester, VT 05143
(802)875-2412 (800)325-0519 Fax:(802)875-3823
Internet: huggingbear.com
E-mail: inn@huggingbear.com

Circa 1850. Among the 9,000 teddy bear inhabitants of this white Victorian inn, several peek out from the third-story windows of the octagonal tower. There is a teddy bear shop on the premises and children and adults can borrow a bear to take to bed with them. Rooms are deco-rated with antiques and comfortable furniture. A bear puppet show is often staged during breakfast.

Innkeeper(s): Georgette Thomas. $62-125. MC, VISA, AX, DS, PC, TC. 6 rooms with PB. Breakfast included in rates. Types of meals: Full gourmet bkfst and early coffee/tea. Beds: QDT. Teddy bear in room. Air conditioning. VCR and library on premises. Antiquing, fishing, golf, swimming, parks, shopping, downhill skiing and cross-country skiing nearby.

Location: Mountains.

Publicity: *Rutland Daily Herald, Exxon Travel, Teddy Bear Review, Teddy Bear Scene and Teddy Bear Tribune.*

Certificate may be used: Monday through Thursday, November through May except holiday weeks (Christmas to New Year's and Presidents' weeks).

Craftsbury   C5

Craftsbury Inn

Main St, Box 36
Craftsbury, VT 05826-0036
(802)586-2848 (800)336-2848

Circa 1850. Bird's-eye maple woodwork and embossed tin ceilings testify to the history of this Greek Revival inn, which also features random-width floors with square nails. The foun-dation and porch steps were made of bull's-eye granite, quar-ried in town. The living room fireplace once graced the first post office in Montpelier. Guest rooms sport country antiques and handmade quilts. The dining room is open to the public by advance reservation and features four dinner seatings.

Innkeeper(s): Blake & Rebecca Gleason. $60-160. MC, VISA, TC. 10 rooms, 6 with PB and 1 conference room. Breakfast included in rates. Type of meal: Full bkfst. Beds: DT. VCR on premises. Antiquing, fishing, shopping, downhill skiing, cross-country skiing and water sports nearby.

Location: Village.

Publicity: *Boston Globe and New York Times.*

"Very comfortable - the dining was a special treat!"

Certificate may be used: Sunday through Thursday, January-December, except during foliage season.

Danby   I3

Quail's Nest B&B

81 S Main Street
Danby, VT 05739
(802)293-5099 (800)599-6444 Fax:(802)293-6300

Circa 1835. Located in the village, this Greek Revival inn fea-tures six guest rooms all with private baths and on each bed is found a handmade quilt. Full breakfasts are made to order by the innkeepers, and Nancy serves it in period clothing. Also provided is early morning coffee or tea, afternoon tea and an evening snack. The Green Mountain National Forest is just to the east of the inn, providing many outstanding recreational opportunities. Outlet shopping is found just a few miles south in Manchester, and Alpine skiing is enjoyed at Bromley, Killington, Okemo, Pico and Stratton ski areas, all within easy driving distance.

Innkeeper(s): Greg & Nancy Diaz. $60-120. MC, VISA, AX, DS, PC, TC. 6 rooms with PB and 1 conference room. Breakfast and afternoon tea includ-ed in rates. Types of meals: Full bkfst and early coffee/tea. Beds: KQT. VCR on premises. Antiquing, fishing, swimming, biking, hiking, live theater, shopping, downhill skiing, cross-country skiing, sporting events and water sports nearby.

Location: Mountains.

Publicity: *Vermont.*

Certificate may be used: Sunday-Thursday; January-August, November, December, excluding our own special promotions.

Derby Line   A6

Derby Village Inn

440 Main St, PO Box 1085
Derby Line, VT 05830
(802)873-3604 Fax:(802)873-3047
Internet: www.together.net/~dvibandb
E-mail: dvibandb@together.net

Circa 1900. This turn-of-the-century Neoclassical inn is just off the Canadian border in the village of Derby Line. Elegant rooms are individually decorated. Guests are pampered with a homemade breakfast. The inn is near to many activities, including downhill and cross-country skiing, hiking, snowmobiling, fishing and a variety of water sports. Antique shops are nearby, and an international library and opera house are within walking distance.

Innkeeper(s): Catherine McCormick & Sheila Steplar. $75-100. MC, VISA, AX, DS, PC, TC. 5 rooms with PB, 1 with FP, 1 suite and 1 conference room. Breakfast included in rates. Types of meals: Full bkfst and early coffee/tea. Beds: KQT. VCR, fax, copier and library on premises. Antiquing, bicycling, fishing, golf, snowmobiling, ice fishing, auctions, live theater, downhill skiing, cross-country skiing and water sports nearby.

Location: Village.

Certificate may be used: Anytime except Saturdays and Sept. 1-Oct. 31.

Dorset
I2

Marble West Inn
PO Box 847, Dorset West Rd
Dorset, VT 05251-0847
(802)867-4155 (800)453-7629 Fax:(802)867-5731
Internet: www.marblewestinn.com
E-mail: marwest@sover.net

Circa 1840. This historic Greek Revival inn boasts many elegant touches, including stenciling in its entrance hallways done by one of the nation's top craftspeople. Guests also will enjoy Oriental rugs, handsome marble fireplaces and polished dark oak floors. Visitors delight at the many stunning views enjoyed at the inn, including Green Peak and Owl's Head mountains, flower-filled gardens and meadows and two trout-stocked ponds. Emerald Lake State Park is nearby.

Innkeeper(s): Bonnie & Paul Quinn. $90-175. MC, VISA, AX, PC. 8 rooms with PB, 4 with FP and 1 suite. Breakfast and afternoon tea included in rates. Type of meal: Full bkfst. Beds: KQDT. Turndown service in room. Library on premises. Antiquing, fishing, designer outlet shopping, horseback riding, art galleries, biking, golf, tennis, fine dining, live theater, parks, shopping, downhill skiing, cross-country skiing and water sports nearby.

Location: Mountains.

"A charming inn with wonderful hospitality. The room was comfortable, immaculate, and furnished with every imaginable need and comfort."

Certificate may be used: Jan. 1-Sept. 1, Nov. 1-Dec. 15, Sunday-Thursday.

Essex Junction
D2

The Inn at Essex
70 Essex Way
Essex Junction, VT 05452-3383
(802)878-1100 Fax:(802)878-0063
Internet: www.innatessex.com
E-mail: innfo@innatessex.com

Elegant furnishings and decor, each in a different style, grace the guest rooms at this luxurious Colonial inn, which carries a four-diamond rating. Several guest suites include whirlpool tubs, and 50 of the rooms include wood-burning fireplaces. The two restaurants are operated by New England Culinary Institute, one a gourmet restaurant and the other a more casual tavern. The inn also includes a swimming pool, library, art gallery and a bakery.

Innkeeper(s): Jim Lamberti. $175-499. MC, VISA, AX, DC, CB, DS. 120 rooms. Breakfast included in rates. Type of meal: Cont. Art gallery, ice skating in winter and volleyball in summer on premises.

Certificate may be used: November-July, Sunday-Thursday.

Fair Haven
H2

Maplewood Inn
Rt 22A S
Fair Haven, VT 05743
(802)265-8039 (800)253-7729 Fax:(802)265-8210
Internet: www.sover.net/~maplewd
E-mail: maplewd@sover.net

Circa 1843. This beautifully restored Greek Revival house, which is in the National Register, was once the family home of the founder of Maplewood Dairy, Isaac Wood. Period antiques and reproductions grace the inn's spacious rooms and suites. Some rooms boast fireplaces and all have sitting areas. A collection of antique spinning wheels and yarn winders is displayed. A porch wing, built around 1795, was a tavern formerly located down the road. Overlooking three acres of lawn, the inn offers an idyllic setting. The parlor's cordial bar and evening turndown service are among the many amenities offered by the innkeepers.

Innkeeper(s): Lisa NeJame Osborne & Don Osborne. $80-145. MC, VISA, AX, PC, TC. 5 rooms with PB, 4 with FP, 2 suites and 1 conference room. Breakfast included in rates. Beds: QD. Cable TV, phone and turndown service in room. Air conditioning. Fax, copier, library, complimentary cordial bar, hot beverage bar and snacks on premises. Amusement parks, antiquing, fishing, live theater, parks, shopping, downhill skiing, cross-country skiing, sporting events and water sports nearby.

Location: Rural countryside.

Publicity: *New England Getaways, Country, Americana and Innsider.*

"Your inn is perfection. Leaving under protest."

Certificate may be used: Jan. 3-April 30 and Nov. 1-Dec. 23, Sunday-Thursday.

Fairlee
F6

Silver Maple Lodge & Cottages
520 US Rt 5 South
Fairlee, VT 05045
(802)333-4326 (800)666-1946
Internet: www.silvermaplelodge.com
E-mail: scott@silvermaplelodge.com

Circa 1790. This old Cape farmhouse was expanded in the 1850s and became an inn in the '20s when Elmer & Della Batchelder opened their home to guests. It became so successful that several cottages, built from lumber on the property, were added. For 60 years, the Batchelder family continued the operation. They misnamed the lodge, however, mistaking silver poplar trees on the property for what they thought were silver maples. Guest rooms are decorated with many of the inn's original furnishings, and the new innkeepers have carefully restored the rooms and added several bathrooms. A screened-in porch surrounds two sides of the house. Three of the cottages include working fireplaces and one is handicap accessible.

Innkeeper(s): Scott & Sharon Wright. $56-86. MC, VISA, AX, DS, PC, TC. 16 rooms, 14 with PB, 3 with FP and 8 cottages. Breakfast included in rates. Type of meal: Cont. Beds: KQDT. TV in room. VCR, copier and bicycles on premises. Handicap access. Antiquing, fishing, live theater, parks, shopping, downhill skiing, cross-country skiing and water sports nearby.

Pets allowed: Cottage rooms only.

Location: Country.

Publicity: *Boston Globe, Vermont Country Sampler, Travel Holiday, Travel America and New York Times.*

"Your gracious hospitality and attractive home all add up to a pleasant experience."

Certificate may be used: Sunday-Thursday, Oct. 20-Sept. 20.

Hardwick   C5

Carolyn's Victorian Inn

15 Church St, PO Box 1087
Hardwick, VT 05843-1087
(802)472-6338

Guests are treated to English tea and sweets upon arrival at this historic home, which boasts natural hardwood floors, original cherry woodwork and porches decorated with wicker. A cypress staircase leads up to the guest rooms, which have feather beds and quilts. The home's antiques are steeped in Vermont history. Carolyn serves up luscious breakfasts in the dining room on tables set with lacy tablecloths and fine linens. The special entrees include delectables such as banana-walnut pancakes, souffles or Yorkshire pudding with raspberry sauce.

Innkeeper(s): Carolyn Richter. $85-150. MC, VISA. 5 rooms. Breakfast included in rates. Type of meal: Full bkfst.

Certificate may be used: January, April, May, Nov. 1-20, Dec. 1-15.

Somerset House B&B

130 Highland Ave, PO Box 1098
Hardwick, VT 05843-1098
(802)472-5484 (800)838-8074
Internet: www.somersethousebb.com

Circa 1894. After having been away for two years in England, the innkeepers returned home to Vermont and settled in this gracious Victorian house to provide lodging for those visiting this beautiful part of the country. The home is located in the heart of the village and set amid lawns and flower gardens. Breakfast is served in the dining room.

Innkeeper(s): Ruth & David Gaillard. $79-99. MC, VISA, PC, TC. 4 rooms. Breakfast included in rates. Type of meal: Full gourmet bkfst. Beds: QT. Library on premises. Antiquing, bicycling, fishing, hiking, horseback riding, live theater, shopping, downhill skiing, cross-country skiing and water sports nearby.

Location: Village.

"We found a treasure. C'est super fun."

Certificate may be used: Anytime except June-October and holidays.

Killington   G3

The Cascades Lodge & Restaurant

Killington Village, 58 Old Mill Rd
Killington, VT 05751-9710
(802)422-3731 (800)345-0113 Fax:(802)422-3351
Internet: www.cascadeslodge.com
E-mail: info@cascadeslodge.com

Circa 1980. Breathtaking views and modern amenities are found at this contemporary three-story country lodge in the heart of the Green Mountains. Guests enjoy an exercise area,

indoor pool with sundeck, sauna and whirlpool. A bar and award-winning restaurant are on the premises, and the inn's amenities make it an ideal spot for meetings, reunions or weddings. Within walking distance is an 18-hole golf course and the Killington Summer Theater.

Innkeeper(s): Bob, Vickie & Andrew MacKenzie. $59-299. MC, VISA, AX, DS, TC. 46 rooms, 45 with PB and 6 suites. Breakfast included in rates. Types of meals: Full bkfst and early coffee/tea. Beds: QD. Cable TV and phone in room. VCR, fax, copier, spa and sauna on premises. Handicap access. Antiquing, fishing, live theater, parks, shopping, downhill skiing and cross-country skiing nearby.

Pets Allowed.

Location: Walk to slopes and golf.

Certificate may be used: May 1 to Nov. 1.

The Peak Chalet

PO Box 511, 184 South View Path
Killington, VT 05751-0511
(802)422-4278

Circa 1978. This contemporary chalet-style inn is located in the heart of the Killington Ski Resort. That convenience is matched by the inn's elegant accommodations and attention to detail. Guest rooms feature either a four-poster, iron, panel or sleigh bed, all queen-size. The living room, with its impressive stone fireplace and view of the Green Mountains, is a favorite gathering spot for those not on the slopes.

Innkeeper(s): Greg & Diane Becker. $61-121. MC, VISA, AX, DC, PC, TC. 4 rooms with PB. Breakfast included in rates. Type of meal: Cont plus. Beds: QT. VCR on premises. Antiquing, bicycling, fishing, golf, live theater, parks, shopping, downhill skiing, cross-country skiing, tennis and water sports nearby.

Location: Mountains.

Certificate may be used: Jan. 1-Sept. 21 and Oct. 15-Dec. 21, Sunday-Thursday, holidays excluded.

The Vermont Inn

Rt 4
Killington, VT 05751
(802)775-0708 (800)541-7795 Fax:(802)773-2440
Internet: www.vermontinn.com
E-mail: vtinn@together.net

Circa 1840. Surrounded by mountain views, this rambling red and white farmhouse has provided lodging and superb cuisine

for many years. Exposed beams add to the atmosphere in the living and game rooms. The award-winning dining room provides candlelight tables beside a huge fieldstone fireplace.

Innkeeper(s): Megan & Greg Smith. $50-185. MC, VISA, AX, DC, PC, TC. 18 rooms with PB, 2 with FP. Breakfast and afternoon tea included in rates. Types of meals: Full bkfst and early coffee/tea. Beds: QDT. TV and ceiling fan in room. Air conditioning. VCR, fax, copier, spa, swimming, sauna, tennis, library and screened porch on premises. Handicap access. Antiquing, fishing, live theater, parks, shopping, downhill skiing, cross-country skiing and water sports nearby.

Location: Mountains.

Publicity: *New York Daily News, New Jersey Star Leader, Rutland Business Journal, Bridgeport Post Telegram, New York Times, Boston, Vermont and Asbury Park Press.*

"We had a wonderful time. The inn is breathtaking. Hope to be back."

Certificate may be used: Jan. 1-Sept. 15, Sunday-Thursday.

Landgrove
J3

Landgrove Inn
Rd Box 215, Landgrove Rd
Landgrove, VT 05148
(802)824-6673 (800)669-8466 Fax:(802)824-3055
Internet: www.vermont.com/business/landgroveinn
E-mail: vtinn@sover.net

Circa 1820. This rambling inn is located along a country lane in the valley of Landgrove in the Green Mountain National Forest. The Rafter Room is a lounge and pub with a fireside sofa for 12. Breakfast and dinner are served in the newly renovated and stenciled dining room. Evening sleigh or hay rides are often arranged. Rooms vary in style and bedding arrangements, including some newly decorated rooms with country decor, so inquire when making your reservation.

Innkeeper(s): Kathy & Jay Snyder. $95-140. MC, VISA, AX, DS, TC. 18 rooms, 16 with PB and 1 conference room. Breakfast included in rates. Type of meal: Full bkfst. Beds: QD. Phone in room. VCR, fax, copier and spa on premises. Antiquing, fishing, live theater, parks, shopping, downhill skiing and cross-country skiing nearby.

Location: Rural country.

"A true country inn with great food — we'll be back."

Certificate may be used: May 20-Sept. 20 and Dec. 20-April 1, Sunday through Thursday, non-holidays.

Ludlow
I4

Echo Lake Inn
PO Box 154
Ludlow, VT 05149-0154
(802)228-8602 (800)356-6844 Fax:(802)228-3075
E-mail: echolkinn@aol.com

Circa 1840. Just minutes from Killington and Okemo ski areas, this New England country-style inn offers gourmet candlelight dining, a full country breakfast, library and parlor. Guests also may borrow canoes and are allowed to pick wildflowers and berries in season. Guests will find golf, horseback riding, waterfalls and wineries within easy walking distance. The inn is located in Tyson, five miles north of Ludlow.

Innkeeper(s): Laurence & Beth and Christopher & Diane Jeffrey. $109-299. MC, VISA, AX. 23 rooms, 18 with PB and 2 suites. Breakfast and dinner included in rates. Types of meals: Full bkfst and early coffee/tea. Beds: QDT. Ceiling fan in room. Fax, spa, swimming, sauna, tennis and library on premises. Antiquing, fishing, live theater, shopping, downhill skiing, cross-country skiing and water sports nearby.

Location: Mountains.

Publicity: *Vermont, Bon Appetit and Gourmet.*

"Very special! We've decided to make the Echo Lake Inn a yearly tradition for our family."

Certificate may be used: May 1-Sept. 20, Nov. 20-Dec. 23, Jan. 5-Feb. 12, Feb. 23-March 30, Sunday-Thursday, non-holiday.

Montgomery
B4

Black Lantern Inn
Rt 118
Montgomery, VT 05470
(802)326-4507 (800)255-8661 Fax:(802)326-4077

Circa 1803. This brick inn and restaurant originally served as a stagecoach stop. Vermont antiques enhance the carefully decorated rooms, and there are six suites with fireplaces and whirlpool tubs. An outdoor hot tub is popular on starry nights. The inn's restaurant offers entrees such as horseradish potato crusted salmon, roast duck and lamb marguerite. A few minutes from the inn, skiers (novice and expert) can ride the tramway to the top of Jay Peak. Montgomery Village is known also for its seven covered bridges. Hiking the Long Trail is popular as is fishing and mountain biking.

Innkeeper(s): Rita & Allen Kalsmith. $85-145. MC, VISA, AX, DS, PC, TC. 16 rooms, 10 with PB and 6 suites. Breakfast included in rates. Type of meal: Full bkfst. Beds: KQDT. TV, ceiling fan and VCR in room. Fax on premises. Antiquing, fishing, downhill skiing and cross-country skiing nearby.

Location: Village.

Publicity: *Burlington Free Press, Los Angeles Times, Bon Appetit, Ottawa Citizen. and Travel - CJCF Montreal.*

"...one of the four or five great meals of your life."-Jay Stone, Ottawa Citizen

Certificate may be used: Anytime except holiday (Christmas) and fall foliage.

Montpelier
E4

Betsy's B&B
74 E State St
Montpelier, VT 05602-3112
(802)229-0466 Fax:(802)229-5412
Internet: www.central-vt.com/web/betsybb
E-mail: betsybb@together.net

Circa 1895. Within walking distance of downtown and located in the state's largest historic preservation district, this Queen Anne Victorian with romantic turret and carriage house features lavish Victorian antiques throughout its interior. Bay windows, carved woodwork, high ceilings, lace curtains and wood floors add to the authenticity. The full breakfast varies in content but not quality, and guest favorites include orange pancakes.

Innkeeper(s): Jon & Betsy Anderson. $60-100. MC, VISA, AX, DS, PC, TC. 12 rooms with PB. Breakfast included in rates. Type of meal: Full bkfst. Beds: QDT. Cable TV and phone in room. VCR, fax and laundry on premises. Antiquing, fishing, art & history museums, live theater, parks, shopping, downhill skiing, cross-country skiing and water sports nearby.

Location: Residential in small city.

Certificate may be used: Nov. 1-April 30, holiday weekends excluded.

North Hero
B2

North Hero House
Rt 2 Box 155, Champlain Islands
North Hero, VT 05474
(802)372-4732 (888)525-3644
Internet: www.northherohouse.com
E-mail: nhhlake@aol.com

Circa 1891. Open year-round, this restored property overlooks Lake Champlain and Vermont's highest peak, Mt. Mansfield. The inn comprises 26 rooms housed in a variety of historic buildings with amenities such as data ports, private baths, television and the timeless inspiration of Lake Champlain water views. Some accommodations offer waterfront porches.

Innkeeper(s): John Martinez. $69-249. MC, VISA. 26 rooms with PB. Breakfast included in rates. Type of meal: Cont. Beds: KQDT. TV and phone in room. Sauna on premises. Handicap access.

Publicity: *Gourmet.*

"We have visited many inns and this house was by far the best, due mostly to the staff!"

Certificate may be used: All of May and June; Sunday, Monday, Tuesday, Wednesday-July, August, September and October.

Orwell G2

Historic Brookside Farms Country Inn & Antique Shop

PO Box 36, Route 22A
Orwell, VT 05760
(802)948-2727 Fax:(802)948-2800
Internet: brooksideinnvt.com
E-mail: hbfinnvt@aol.com

Circa 1789. More than 300 acres of lush meadows and scenic trails surround this National Register home. In a Neoclassical Greek Revival style designed by architect James Lamb, there are

nineteen stately Ionic columns that grace the front of the mansion. This is a working farm with Hereford cattle, Hampshire sheep, maple syrup production and poultry. Miles of trails invite cross-country skiing and hiking, while a 26-acre pond offers opportunities for boating and fishing. Lawn games are popular as well. There's an antique shop on the property with seven rooms full of 18th and early 19th-century furnishings and accessories. A full country breakfast is served. The farm is owned and operated by the Korda family.

Innkeeper(s): The Korda Family. $95-175. 7 rooms, 3 with PB, 1 suite and 1 conference room. Breakfast and afternoon tea included in rates. Types of meals: Full gourmet bkfst and early coffee/tea. Beds: DT. Welcome tray w/ VT products in room. VCR, fax, copier, fishing, cross-country skiing and child care available on premises. Handicap access. Antiquing, live theater and downhill skiing nearby.

Location: Village.

Publicity: *New York Times, Burlington Free Press, Los Angeles Times and Preservation Magazine Antiques.*

Certificate may be used: Jan. 1-May 15, June 1-Aug. 31, Nov. 1-Dec. 15.

Poultney H2

Tower Hall B&B

399 Bentley Ave
Poultney, VT 05764-1176
(802)287-4004 (800)894-4004

Circa 1895. A three-story peaked turret lends the name to this Queen Anne inn located next to Green Mountain College. Stained glass, polished woodwork and original fireplace mantels add to the Victorian atmosphere, and the guest rooms are furnished with antiques of the period. A sitting room adjacent to the guest rooms has its own fireplace. Kathy's cranberry nut and date nut breads are especially popular breakfast items.

Innkeeper(s): Pat Perrine. $60-80. MC, VISA, TC. 3 rooms, 1 with PB. Breakfast included in rates. Types of meals: Cont plus and early coffee/tea. Beds: D. Cable TV in room. Bicycles on premises. Antiquing, fishing, parks, shopping, cross-country skiing and water sports nearby.

Location: Small rural college town.

Publicity: *Rutland Herald and Rutland Business Journal.*

"Your beautiful home was delightful and just the best place to stay!"

Certificate may be used: Nov. 1-April 30, Sunday-Saturday.

Proctorsville I4

Golden Stage Inn

399 Depot St, PO Box 218
Proctorsville, VT 05153
(802)226-7744 (800)253-8226 Fax:(802)226-7882
Internet: www.goldenstageinn.com
E-mail: goldenstageinn@tds.net

Circa 1780. The Golden Stage Inn was a stagecoach stop built shortly before Vermont became a state. It served as a link in the Underground Railroad and was the home of Cornelia Otis

Skinner. Cornelia's Room still offers its original polished wide-pine floors and view of Okemo Mountain, and now there's a four-poster cherry bed, farm animal border, wainscoting and a comforter filled with wool from the inn's sheep. Outside are gardens of wildflowers, a little pen with two sheep, a swimming pool and blueberries and raspberries for the picking. Breakfast offerings include an often-requested recipe, Golden Stage Granola. Home-baked breakfast dishes are garnished with Johnny-jump-ups and nasturtiums from the garden. Guests can indulge anytime by reaching into the inn's bottomless cookie jar. Okemo Mountain Resort base lodge is four miles away and it's a 15 minute drive to Killington.

Innkeeper(s): Sandy & Peter Gregg. $79-199. MC, VISA, PC. 10 rooms, 6 with PB and 1 suite. Breakfast included in rates. Type of meal: Full bkfst. Beds: KQDT. VCR, fax, copier, swimming and library on premises. Antiquing, fishing, golf, live theater, shopping, downhill skiing and cross-country skiing nearby.

Location: Mountains.

Publicity: *Journal Inquirer, Gourmet and Los Angeles Times.*

"The essence of a country inn!"

Certificate may be used: April 1-30, Sunday-Saturday.

Putney K4

The Putney Inn

PO Box 181
Putney, VT 05346-0181
(802)387-5517 (800)653-5517 Fax:(802)387-5211
Internet: www.putneyinn.com
E-mail: putneyin@sover.net

Circa 1790. The property surrounding this New England farmhouse was deeded to an English Army Captain by King George in 1790. The grounds' first home

burned in a fire, and this inn was constructed on the original foundation. Eventually it became a Catholic seminary, and then an elegant country inn. Rooms are located in a 1960s building, adjacent to the main historic farmhouse. The rooms are decorated in a Colonial style with antiques. The inn's dining room, headed by renown chef Ann Cooper, features New England cuisine. The ingredients are fresh and locally produced, and might include appetizers such as smoked salmon on Johnnycakes with an apple cider vinaigrette. Entrees such as a mixed grill of local venison and game hen flavored by an apple-horseradish marinade follow. Craft and antique shops, hiking, skiing and biking are among the local activities.

Innkeeper(s): Randi Ziter. $78-158. MC, VISA, AX, DS, PC, TC. 25 rooms with PB and 4 conference rooms. Breakfast included in rates. Types of meals: Full gourmet bkfst, cont plus, cont and early coffee/tea. Beds: Q. Cable TV and phone in room. Air conditioning. VCR, fax, copier and full dining restaurant on premises. Handicap access. Amusement parks, antiquing, fishing, golf, national forest; nature hikes, biking, live theater, shopping, downhill skiing, cross-country skiing, tennis and water sports nearby.

Pets allowed: Smaller than a cow, not left alone in room.

Location: walk to village and river.

Publicity: *Chicago Tribune, Boston Herald, Culinary Arts, US Air, Travel & Leisure, Vermont Life, Vermont Magazine. and Dine-Around.*

Certificate may be used: November through April. Holidays excluded. May through June, Sunday through Thursday. Not in conjunction with any other promotion.

Quechee   H5

Parker House Inn
1792 Quechee Main St
Quechee, VT 05059
(802)295-6077
Internet: www.theparkerhouseinn.com
E-mail: parker-house_inn@valley.net

Circa 1857. State Sen. Joseph C. Parker built this riverside manor in 1857, and three of the guest rooms are named in honor of his family. Mornings at the inn begin with a delicious country breakfast served in the Parker House Restaurant's cozy dining rooms. The chefs are justifiably proud of their "comfort food" cuisine. Guests can stroll next door to watch the art of glass blowing, or take a walk along the Ottauquechee River. The surroundings of this historic town provide hours of activity for nature-lovers and shutterbugs. Fall foliage, of course, is an autumnal delight.

Innkeeper(s): Barbara & Walt Forrester. $115-140. MC, VISA, AX, PC, TC. 7 rooms with PB. Breakfast included in rates. Type of meal: Full gourmet bkfst. Beds: KQ. Ceiling fan in room. Air conditioning. VCR, fax and bicycles on premises. Antiquing, fishing, golf, live theater, downhill skiing, cross-country skiing and water sports nearby.

Location: Rural.

Publicity: *Vermont Magazine and Quechee Times.*

"The inn is lovely, the innkeepers are the greatest, excellent food and heavenly bed!"

Certificate may be used: Anytime, Nov. 1-April 30, except Christmas week and President's weekend.

Rochester   G3

Liberty Hill Farm
511 Liberty Hill Rd
Rochester, VT 05767-9501
(802)767-3926
Internet: www.libertyhillfarm.com
E-mail: beth@libertyhillfarm.com

Circa 1825. A working dairy farm with a herd of registered Holsteins, this farmhouse offers a country setting and easy access to recreational activities. The inn's location, between the

White River and the Green Mountains, is ideal for outdoor enthusiasts and animal lovers. Stroll to the barn, feed the calves or climb up to the hayloft and read or play with the kittens. Fishing, hiking, skiing and swimming are popular pastimes of guests, who are treated to a family-style dinner and full breakfast, both featuring many delicious homemade specialties.

Innkeeper(s): Robert & Beth Kennett. $140. PC, TC. 7 rooms. Breakfast and dinner included in rates. Types of meals: Full bkfst and early coffee/tea. Beds: QDT. VCR, swimming, library and child care on premises. Antiquing, fishing, live theater, parks, shopping, downhill skiing, cross-country skiing, sporting events and water sports nearby.

Location: Mountains.

Publicity: *New York Times, Boston Globe, Vermont Life, Family Circle, Family Fun, Woman's Day, Country Home, Boston Chronicle and Good Morning America.*

"We had a wonderful time exploring your farm and the countryside. The food was great."

Certificate may be used: Jan. 1 to May 20, Sunday-Friday.

Roxbury   E4

Johnnycake Flats
Carrie Howe Rd
Roxbury, VT 05669
(802)485-8961
E-mail: jcflats@tds.net

Circa 1806. Johnnycake Flats is an unpretentious and delightfully small bed and breakfast that offers guests a quiet escape from the hectic pace of metropolitan life. The guest rooms in this registered historical site include family antiques, Shaker baskets and handmade quilts. The innkeepers can help you identify local wildflowers and birds. In winter, enjoy cross-country skiing or snowshoeing and come home to sip hot cider beside the fire.

Innkeeper(s): Debra & Jim Rogler. $65-85. DS, PC, TC. 4 rooms, 1 with PB. Breakfast and afternoon tea included in rates. Types of meals: Cont plus, cont and early coffee/tea. Beds: DT. Bicycles, library and snowshoes on premises. Antiquing, bicycling, fishing, snowshoeing, live theater, parks, shopping, downhill skiing, cross-country skiing, sporting events and water sports nearby.

Location: Mountains.

Publicity: *Local area newspapers.*

"You've nurtured a bit of paradise here, thanks for the lovely stay."

Certificate may be used: Sunday-Thursday, except holidays, special events and foliage season.

Rutland   H3

The Inn at Rutland
70 N Main St
Rutland, VT 05701-3249
(802)773-0575 (800)808-0575

Circa 1890. This distinctive Victorian mansion is filled with many period details, from high, plaster-worked ceilings to leather wainscoting in the dining room. Leaded windows and interesting woodwork are found throughout. Guest rooms have been decorated to maintain Victorian charm without a loss of modern comforts. A wicker-filled porch and common rooms are available to guests. Located in central Vermont, The Inn at Rutland is only 15 minutes from the Killington and Pico ski areas.

Innkeeper(s): Bob & Tanya Liberman. $59-209. MC, VISA, AX, DC, CB, DS, TC. 12 rooms with PB, 1 suite and 2 conference rooms. Breakfast included in rates. Type of meal: Full bkfst. Beds: KQD. Phone and clocks in room. Air conditioning. VCR, fax, copier and bicycles on premises. Antiquing, fishing, museum (Norman Rockwell), live theater, parks, shopping, downhill skiing, cross-country skiing and water sports nearby.

Location: Views of valley & mountains.

"A lovely page in the 'memory album' of our minds."

Certificate may be used: April 1-Aug. 31, Nov. 1-Dec. 15, Sunday-Thursday, excluding holidays.

Stockbridge G3

Stockbridge Inn B&B

PO Box 45
Stockbridge, VT 05772-0045
(802)746-8165 (800)588-8165

This Italianate inn has a history involving Justin Morgan, who was instrumental in developing the Morgan horse breed. The inn's location is in the countryside outside of Stockbridge and provides easy access to the nearby White River, famed for its canoeing, trout fishing and white-water rafting. Killington Mountain skiing is within easy driving distance, and autumn colors in the surrounding area are hard to beat.

Innkeeper(s): Janice Hughes. $40-90. MC, VISA. 6 rooms. Breakfast included in rates. Type of meal: Full bkfst. VCR on premises. Antiquing, live theater, shopping, downhill skiing and cross-country skiing nearby.

Certificate may be used: Anytime except holiday weeks/weekends and fall foliage.

Stowe D4

Brass Lantern Inn

717 Maple St
Stowe, VT 05672-4250
(802)253-2229 (800)729-2980 Fax:(802)253-7425
Internet: www.brasslanterninn.com
E-mail: brasslntrn@aol.com

Circa 1810. This rambling farmhouse and carriage barn rests at the foot of Mt. Mansfield. A recent award-winning renovation has brought a new shine to the inn, from the gleaming plank floors to the polished woodwork and crackling fireplaces and soothing whirlpool tubs. Quilts and antiques fill the guest rooms, and some, like the Honeymoon Room, have their own fireplace, whirlpool tub and mountain view. A complimentary afternoon and evening tea is provided along with a full Vermont-style breakfast. A new two-bedroom cottage is now available, as well. The inn is a multi-time winner of the Golden Fork Award from the Gourmet Dinners Society of North America.

Innkeeper(s): Andy Aldrich. $80-225. MC, VISA, AX. 9 rooms with PB, 3 with FP. Breakfast and afternoon tea included in rates. Types of meals: Full bkfst and early coffee/tea. Beds: QDT. TV and whirlpool tubs in 6 rooms in room. Air conditioning. VCR, fax, copier, library, gardens and patio on premises. Antiquing, fishing, tours, live theater, parks, shopping, downhill skiing, cross-country skiing, sporting events and water sports nearby.

Location: Village/country.

Publicity: *Vermont, Vermont Life, Innsider, Discerning Traveler and Ski.*

"The little things made us glad we stopped."

Certificate may be used: Midweek and limited weekends during April, May and to mid-June; late October, November and to mid-December excluding holidays.

Ye Olde England Inne

433 Mountain Rd
Stowe, VT 05672-4628
(802)253-7558 (800)477-3771 Fax:(802)253-8944
Internet: www.oldeenglandinne.com
E-mail: englandinn@aol.com

Circa 1890. Originally a farmhouse, Ye Olde England Inne has acquired a Tudor facade, interior beams and stone work. Each guest room is different. One cozy room includes hunter green carpeting and cheerful wallcoverings with red flowers. A matching comforter tops the lace canopy bed and a massive wardrobe further decorates the room. Other rooms are more traditional style. The suites

and cottages include a whirlpool tub, and many offer a mountain view and a private porch from which to enjoy it. The inn has a variety of getaway packages. A popular honeymoon package includes French champagne, a complete spa treatment and in winter, a sleigh ride. Mr. Pickwick's, which resembles an English pub, is an ideal spot to relax and enjoy ale or a glass or wine. The inn also offers Copperfields, where guests can enjoy a romantic dinner. Guests can spend their days hiking, skiing, relaxing by the inn's pool or exploring Stowe.

Innkeeper(s): Christopher & Linda Francis. $98-375. MC, VISA, AX. 30 rooms with PB, 13 with FP, 12 suites and 1 conference room. Breakfast included in rates. Type of meal: Full gourmet bkfst. Beds: QDT. Cable TV, phone and ceiling fan in room. Air conditioning. Fax, copier and spa on premises. Antiquing, live theater, parks, shopping, downhill skiing, cross-country skiing and sporting events nearby.

Location: Mountains.

Publicity: *National Geographic Traveler and Channel 5 TV in Boston.*

Certificate may be used: Midweek, non-holiday, subject to advance reservations and availability.

Waitsfield E3

Lareau Farm Country Inn

PO Box 563, RT 100
Waitsfield, VT 05673-0563
(802)496-4949 (800)833-0766
Internet: www.lareaufarminn.com
E-mail: lareau@lareaufarminn.com

Circa 1794. This Greek Revival house was built by Simeon Stoddard, the town's first physician. Old-fashioned roses, lilacs, delphiniums, iris and peonies fill the gardens. The inn sits in a wide meadow next to the crystal-clear Mad River. A canoe trip or a refreshing swim are possibilities here.

Innkeeper(s): Susan Easley. $80-135. MC, VISA, PC, TC. 13 rooms, 11 with PB, 1 suite and 1 conference room. Breakfast included in rates. Types of meals: Full gourmet bkfst and early coffee/tea. Beds: QD. TV in room. Swimming and library on premises. Antiquing, fishing, live theater, shopping, downhill skiing and cross-country skiing nearby.

Location: Country.

Publicity: *Pittsburgh Press, Philadelphia Inquirer and Los Angeles Times.*

"Hospitality is a gift. Thank you for sharing your gift so freely with us."

Certificate may be used: Dec. 15-April 1 and May 1-June 29, weekdays, holiday weeks excluded.

Mad River Inn

Tremblay Rd, PO Box 75
Waitsfield, VT 05673
(802)496-7900 (800)832-8278 Fax:(802)496-5390

Circa 1860. Surrounded by the Green Mountains, this Queen Anne Victorian sits on seven scenic acres along the Mad River. The charming inn boasts attractive woodwork throughout, highlighted by ash, bird's-eye maple and cherry. Guest rooms feature European featherbeds and include the Hayden Breeze Room,  with a king brass bed, large windows and sea relics, and the Abner Doubleday Room, with a queen ash bed and mementos of baseball's glory days. The inn sports a billiard table, gazebo, organic gardens and a Jacuzzi overlooking the mountains. Guests can walk to a recreation path along the river.

Innkeeper(s): Luc Maranda. $95-135. MC, VISA, AX. 10 rooms with PB. Breakfast and afternoon tea included in rates. Type of meal: Full gourmet bkfst. Beds: KQ. Turndown service and ceiling fan in room. VCR, fax, spa, stables and child care on premises. Antiquing, fishing, live theater, shopping,

downhill skiing, cross-country skiing, sporting events and water sports nearby.
Location: Mountains.
Publicity: *Innsider, Victorian Homes, Let's Live, Skiing, AAA Home & Away, Tea Time at the Inn and Travel & Leisure.*

"Your hospitality was appreciated, beautiful house and accommodations, great food & friendly people, just to name a few things. We plan to return and we recommend the Mad River Inn to friends & family."
Certificate may be used: Sunday-Thursday, except Dec. 21-31, Sept. 21-Oct 15.

Waitsfield Inn

Rt 100, PO Box 969
Waitsfield, VT 05673-0969
(802)496-3979 (800)758-3801 Fax:(802)496-3970
Internet: www.waitsfieldinn.com
E-mail: waitsfieldinn@madriver.com

Circa 1825. This Federal-style inn once served as a parsonage and was home to several state senators of the Richardson family. Pink and yellow flower beds frame the rambling inn. The 1839 barn offers a Great Room with fireplace and wood-plank floors, or in winter you may enjoy sipping spiced Vermont apple cider and munching on fresh cookies in the sitting room. Guest quarters are furnished with period antiques, quilts or comforters and some rooms have exposed beams or hand stenciling. A full breakfast is served in the dining room, with fresh-baked breads, fruit, muffins and a main dish. As the inn is in the village of Waitsfield, the entire town's sites are nearby including a beautiful covered bridge. Visit Glen Moss Waterfall, fly fish, canoe, try a glider, golf or watch a polo match. Snowshoeing, skiing and visits to the New England Culinary Institute and Ben & Jerry's Ice Cream Factory are popular activities.
Innkeeper(s): Jim & Pat Masson. $79-135. MC, VISA, AX, DS, PC, TC. 14 rooms with PB. Breakfast included in rates. Type of meal: Full bkfst. Beds: QDT. Antiquing, fishing, golf, canoeing, live theater, shopping, skiing nearby.
Location: Village.

Certificate may be used: Sunday-Thursday, January-March, July 1-Sept. 16, anytime. April-June, November-December, all holiday weeks excluded.

Waterbury   D3

Grunberg Haus B&B & Cabins

94 Pine St, Rt 100 South
Waterbury, VT 05676-9621
(802)244-7726 (800)800-7760
Internet: www.waterbury.org/grunberg
E-mail: grunhaus@aol.com

Circa 1972. This hillside Tyrolean chalet was hand-built by George and Irene Ballschneider. The Grunberg Haus captures the rustic charm of country guest homes in Austria with its wall of windows overlooking the Green Mountains, a massive fieldstone fireplace and a self-service Austrian pub. Rooms are decorated with antique furniture and cozy quilts. All rooms open onto the second-floor balcony that surrounds the chalet. Attractions in Stowe, the Mad River Valley, Montpelier and the Lake Champlain region are close at hand.
Innkeeper(s): Jeff & Linda Connor. $59-145. MC, VISA, DS, PC, TC. 14 rooms, 9 with PB, 2 with FP, 2 cabins & 1 conf. room. Types of meals: Full gourmet bkfst, country bkfst, veg bkfst and early coffee/tea. Beds: QD. Balconies and antiques in room. Spa, sauna, grand piano, walking & skiing trails & BYOB pub on premises. Antiquing, art galleries, beaches, bicycling, canoeing/kayaking, fishing, golf, hiking, horseback riding, Ben & Jerry's Factory, covered bridges, live theater, museums, parks, shopping, skiing, sporting events, tennis & water sports nearby.
Location: Country.
Publicity: *New York Times, St. Louis Dispatch, Yankee and Connecticut Public Television Travel Channel.*

"You made an ordinary overnight stay extraordinary."
Certificate may be used: April 1-June 15 (daily), Oct. 23-Dec. 20 (daily), January, February and March (Sunday-Thursday).

Thatcher Brook Inn

PO Box 490, Rt 100 N
Waterbury, VT 05676-0490
(802)244-5911 (800)292-5911 Fax:(802)244-1294
Internet: www.thatcherbrook.com
E-mail: info@thatcherbrook.com

Circa 1899. Listed in the Vermont Register of Historic Buildings, this restored Victorian mansion features a rambling porch with twin gazebos. A covered walkway leads to the historic Wheeler House. Guest
rooms are decorated in classic country style. Four rooms have fireplaces, and six have whirlpool tubs. The inn's restaurant and tavern are located in the main inn. Guests can dine fireside or by candlelight.
Innkeeper(s): Lisa & John Fischer. $80-185. MC, VISA, AX, DC, DS, PC, TC. 22 rooms with PB, 4 with FP, 1 suite and 1 conference room. Breakfast included in rates. Type of meal: Full bkfst. Beds: KQDT. Phone, ceiling fan and 6 rooms have whirlpools in room. Air conditioning. Fax and copier on premises. Handicap access. Antiquing, bicycling, fishing, hiking, live theater, parks, shopping, downhill skiing, cross-country skiing and water sports nearby.
Location: City.

"I'd have to put on a black tie in Long Island to find food as good as this and best of all it's in a relaxed country atmosphere. Meals are underpriced."
Certificate may be used: November through August, Sunday through Thursday.

The Inn at Blush Hill

784 Blush Hill Rd
Waterbury, VT 05676
(802)244-7529 (800)736-7522 Fax:(802)244-7314
Internet: www.blushhill.com
E-mail: innatbh@aol.com

Circa 1790. This shingled Cape-style house was once a stagecoach stop en route to Stowe and is the oldest inn in Waterbury. A 12-foot-long pine farmhand's table is set near the
double fireplace and the kitchen bay window, revealing views of the Worcester Mountains. A favorite summertime breakfast, served gardenside, is pancakes with fresh blueberries, topped with ice cream and maple syrup.
Innkeeper(s): Pam Gosselin. $75-130. MC, VISA, AX, DS, PC, TC. 5 rooms with PB, 1 with FP. Breakfast, afternoon tea and snacks/refreshments included in rates. Types of meals: Full gourmet bkfst and early coffee/tea. Beds: QT. TV, turndown service and ceiling fan in room. Air conditioning. Fax and library on premises. Antiquing, fishing, golf, Ben & Jerry's ice cream factory, live theater, parks, shopping, downhill skiing, cross-country skiing and water sports nearby.
Location: Mountains.
Publicity: *Vermont, Charlotte Observer, Yankee, New York Times, Ski, New York Post and WCAX Television.*

"Our room was wonderful — especially the fireplace. Everything was so cozy and warm."
Certificate may be used: Sunday through Thursday, January to June; November-December (excluding holidays).

West Dover — K3

Austin Hill Inn

Rt 100, Box 859
West Dover, VT 05356
(802)464-5281 (800)332-7352 Fax:(802)464-1229
E-mail: austinhi@sovernet.com

Circa 1930. This family-owned and operated inn is situated between Mt. Snow and Haystack Mountains just outside the historic village of West Dover. Guest rooms feature country decor and furnishings. Romantic amenities include in-room fireplaces and votive candles at turndown. Guests are treated to a hearty New England breakfast, as well as afternoon wine and cheese or home-baked treats. In cool weather, guests enjoy the warm glow of the inn's fireplaces in the common rooms. The Austin Hill Inn is notable for its attention to detail and superior hospitality.

Innkeeper(s): John & Deborah Bailey. $100-165. MC, VISA, DS, PC, TC. 10 rooms with PB, 1 suite and 1 conference room. Breakfast and snacks/refreshments included in rates. Type of meal: Full bkfst. Beds: KQDT. Fax and copier on premises. Antiquing, bicycling, canoeing/kayaking, fishing, golf, hiking, chamber music, live theater, parks, downhill skiing and cross-country skiing nearby.

Location: Mountains.

Publicity: *Country Inns, Getaways and Greenwich Magazine.*

Certificate may be used: Sunday through Thursday, non-holidays excluding Sept. 22-Oct. 20.

Weston — J3

Darling Family Inn

815 Rt 100
Weston, VT 05161-5404
(802)824-3223

This two-story inn also features two cottages. Located in the Green Mountains, just minutes from Bromley, Okemo, Magic and Stratton ski areas, the inn provides a taste of life from the early Colonial days. Guest rooms feature handmade quilts crafted locally. The cottages include kitchenettes, and pets are welcome in the cottages if prior arrangements are made.

Innkeeper(s): Chapin & Joan Darling. $85-145. PC, TC. 5 rooms with PB and 2 cottages. Breakfast included in rates. Type of meal: Full bkfst. Turndown service in room. VCR and swimming on premises. Antiquing, live theater, shopping, downhill skiing and cross-country skiing nearby.

Location: Mountains.

Certificate may be used: Sunday through Thursday, excluding Sundays of holiday weekends; January through June; Sept. 1-15; Oct. 15-Dec. 23.

Wilder Homestead Inn

25 Lawrence Hill Rd
Weston, VT 05161-5600
(802)824-8172 Fax:(802)824-5054
Internet: www.wilderhomestead.com
E-mail: wilder@sover.net

Circa 1827. Located in historic Weston and within walking distance of the Green Mountain National Forest, this inn has both Federal and Greek Revival stylings and features seven guest rooms, all with private baths and views. Five of the rooms have decorative fireplaces and three feature original

Moses Eaton stenciling. Afternoon tea and romantic candlelight dinners are offered. Breakfast may include fresh fruit, eggs and homemade biscuits with jam, hot cakes with genuine Vermont maple syrup, Lumberjack mush or sausage. There's an old English pub and a craft shop is on the premises.

Innkeeper(s): Peter & Patsy McKay. $85-150. MC, VISA. 7 rooms with PB. Breakfast included in rates. Types of meals: Full bkfst and country bkfst. Beds: KQDT. Ceiling fan in room. VCR on premises. Antiquing, fishing, live theater, shopping, downhill skiing, cross-country skiing and sporting events nearby.

Location: Village.

Publicity: *Gourmet, Country, Boston Globe and New York Times.*

Certificate may be used: Sunday through Thursday, non-holidays. January-March; May and June; November through Dec. 19.

Wilmington — K3

White House of Wilmington

178 Rt 9 East
Wilmington, VT 05363
(802)464-2135 (800)541-2135 Fax:(802)464-5295
Internet: www.whitehouseinn.com
E-mail: whitehse@sover.net

Circa 1915. The White House was built as a summer home for a wealthy lumber baron, and he spared no expense. The inn has 14 fireplaces, rich woodwork and hand-crafted French doors. Nine of the guest rooms include fireplaces, and some have a balcony, terrace or whirlpool tub. Seven guest rooms are located in an adjacent guest house. There is an outdoor swimming pool, and the spa includes an indoor pool, whirlpool and sauna. Guests are treated to breakfast, and award-winning, gourmet dinners are available in the dining rooms.

Innkeeper(s): Bob Grinold. $118-195. MC, VISA, AX, DC, DS, PC, TC. 23 rooms with PB, 9 with FP, 1 suite and 2 conference rooms. Breakfast included in rates. Type of meal: Full bkfst. Beds: KQDT. VCR, fax, copier, spa, swimming and sauna on premises. Handicap access. Antiquing, fishing, golf, live theater, parks, shopping, downhill skiing, cross-country skiing, tennis and water sports nearby.

Location: Mountains.

Publicity: *New York Times, Boston Herald, Vermont Magazine, Yankee Travel Guide, PM Magazine and Good Morning America.*

Certificate may be used: Jan. 3-31, March 1-Sept. 25, and Oct. 25-Dec. 21, all midweek reservations.

Woodstock — H4

Ardmore Inn

23 Pleasant St
Woodstock, VT 05091
(802)457-3887 (800)497-9652 Fax:(802)457-9006
Internet: www.ardmorein.com
E-mail: ardmoreinn@aol.com

Circa 1850. This Greek Revival-style inn offers a gentle welcome with its pretty shutters and graceful entrance. Located on an acre in a village setting, it is furnished elegantly. For instance, the Tully Room has four eyebrow windows shedding sunlight on its four-poster queen bed, and there's a sitting area and marble bath. Enjoy breakfasts of Vermont flat bread served with truffle eggs, apple-smoked sausage and asparagus spears.

$110-175. MC, VISA, AX, PC, TC. 5 suites, 1 with FP. Breakfast and after-noon tea included in rates. Type of meal: Full gourmet bkfst. Beds: KQD. Air conditioning. Fax, copier and bicycles on premises. Antiquing, fishing, golf, mountain biking, fly fishing, live theater, parks, shopping, downhill skiing, cross-country skiing and tennis nearby.

Location: Village.

Certificate may be used: Jan. 30-Sept. 1, certain holidays excluded.

Carriage House of Woodstock

455 Woodstock Road, Rt 4 W
Woodstock, VT 05091-1253
(802)457-4322 (800)791-8045 Fax:(802)457-4322
Internet: www.carriagehousewoodstock.com
E-mail: stanglin@sover.net

Circa 1830. This century-old home has been generously refurbished and features rooms filled with period antiques and individual decor. Those in search of relaxation will find

plenty of possibilities, from quiet music and conversation in the parlor to relaxing on the wraparound porch over-looking the picturesque views. Antique shopping, galleries, the historic Billings Farm Museum and

plenty of outdoor activities are found in the Woodstock area. Fall and spring bring an explosion of color, and scenic drives will take you under covered bridges.

Innkeeper(s): Debbie & Mark Stanglin. $95-170. MC, VISA, AX, DS, PC, TC. 9 rooms with PB, 1 with FP. Breakfast and snacks/refreshments included in rates. Type of meal: Full bkfst. Beds: KQT. Cable TV and individual heat in room. Air conditioning. VCR, fax, refrigerator and microwave on premises. Antiquing, fishing, live theater, parks, shopping, downhill skiing, cross-coun-try skiing, sporting events and water sports nearby.

Certificate may be used: Sunday-Thursday, Nov. 1-Aug. 1, except holidays and holiday weekends.

Charleston House

21 Pleasant St
Woodstock, VT 05091-1131
(802)457-3843
Internet: charlestonhouse.com
E-mail: nohl@together.net

Circa 1810. This authentically restored brick Greek Revival town house, in the National Register, welcomes guests with shuttered many-paned windows and window boxes filled with pink blooms. Guest rooms are appointed with period antiques and reproduc-tions, an art collection and Oriental rugs. Most of the rooms boast four-poster beds, and some feature fireplaces and Jacuzzis. A hearty full breakfast starts off the day in the candle-lit dining room, and the innkeepers serve afternoon refreshments, as well. Area offerings include winter sleigh rides, snow skiing, auctions, fly fishing, golfing and summer stock theater, to name a few.

Innkeeper(s): Dieter & Willa Nohl. $110-195. MC, VISA, AX. 9 rooms with PB. Breakfast included in rates. Type of meal: Full bkfst. Beds: QT. TV in room. Jacuzzis and fireplaces on premises. Antiquing, fishing, golf, downhill skiing and cross-country skiing nearby.

Publicity: *Harbor News, Boston Business Journal, Weekend Getaway, Inn Spots and Special Places.*

Certificate may be used: Nov. 1 to June 30, except holidays.

Woodstocker B&B

61 River St
Woodstock, VT 05091-1227
(802)457-3896 Fax:(802)457-3897
Internet: www.scenesofvermont.com/woodstocker/index.html

Circa 1830. This early 19th-century, Cape-style inn is located at the base of Mt. Tom at the edge of the village of Woodstock. Hand-hewn wood beams create a rustic effect. The seven guest

rooms and two suites are individually appointed. Buffet-style, full breakfasts get the day off to a great start. Guests can take a short walk across a covered bridge to reach shops and

restaurants. Hikers will enjoy trails that wind up and around Mt. Tom. After a busy winter day, come back and enjoy a soak in the five-person whirlpool.

Innkeeper(s): Tom & Nancy Blackford. $85-155. MC, VISA, AX. 9 rooms with PB and 2 suites. Breakfast included in rates. Types of meals: Full bkfst and early coffee/tea. Beds: QD. Cable TV and ceiling fan in room. Air condi-tioning. VCR, fax and copier on premises. Antiquing, fishing, live theater, shopping, downhill skiing, cross-country skiing, sporting events and water sports nearby.

Location: Village.

"You have truly opened your home and heart to create a comfortable and memorable stay."

Certificate may be used: Sunday through Thursday, except July 1-Oct. 20 and Dec. 20-Jan. 1.

Woodstock (Reading)   H4

Bailey's Mills B&B

1347 Bailey's Mills Rd
Woodstock (Reading), VT 05062
(802)484-7809 (800)639-3437
Internet: bbonline.com/vt/baileysmills/

Circa 1820. This Federal-style inn features grand porches, 11 fireplaces, a "good-morning" staircase and a ballroom on the third floor. Four generations of Baileys lived in the home, as well as housing mill workers. There also was once a country store on the premises. Guests can learn much about the home and history of the people who lived here through the innkeep-ers. Two of the guest rooms include a fireplace, and the suite has a private solarium. There's plenty to do here, from explor-ing the surrounding 48 acres to relaxing with a book on the porch swing or in a hammock. If you forgot your favorite novel, borrow a book from the inn's 2,200-volume library.

Innkeeper(s): Barbara Thaeder & Don Whitaker. $90-140. MC, VISA, PC, TC. 3 rooms with PB, 2 with FP and 1 suite. Breakfast included in rates. Types of meals: Cont plus and early coffee/tea. Beds: KQ. Fireplace (two rooms) in room. Swimming, library, pond, stream and graveyard on premises. Antiquing, fishing, live theater, parks, shopping, downhill skiing and cross-country skiing nearby.

Pets allowed: Small, polite, innkeeper approval required.

Location: Country.

Publicity: *Carnie Show.*

"If words could encapsulate what a wonderful weekend would be, it would have to be 'Bailey's Mills B&B.' Your home is beautiful. It is elegant yet homey."

Certificate may be used: November-May, Sunday-Thursday or call anytime for last-minute openings.

Virginia

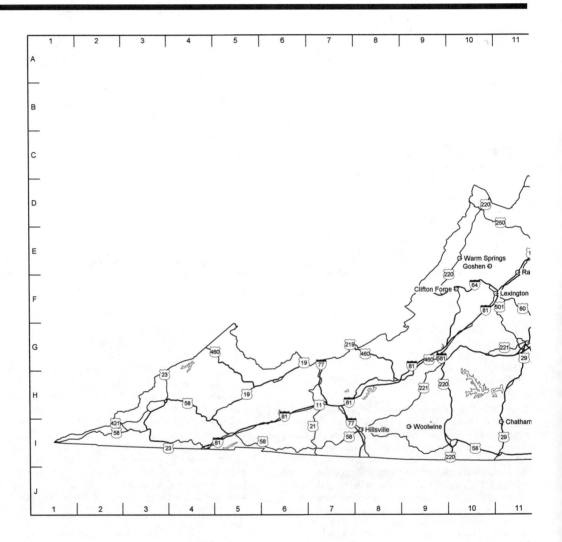

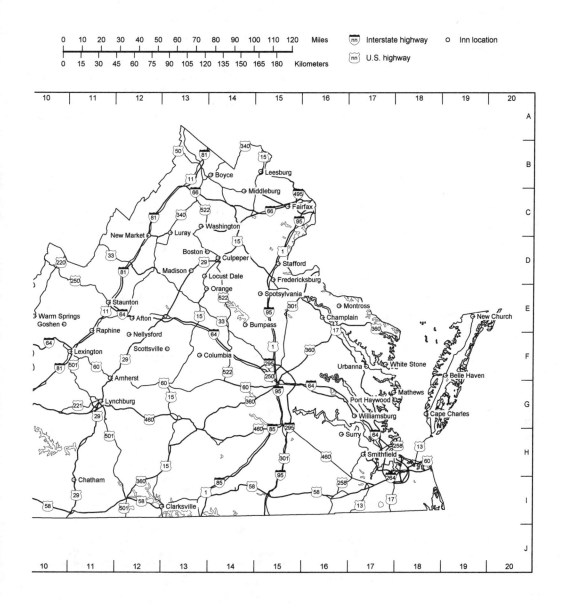

| 0 | 10 | 20 | 30 | 40 | 50 | 60 | 70 | 80 | 90 | 100 | 110 | 120 | Miles |

| 0 | 15 | 30 | 45 | 60 | 75 | 90 | 105 | 120 | 135 | 150 | 165 | 180 | Kilometers |

Interstate highway   o Inn location

U.S. highway

Afton   E12

Looking Glass House B&B

10273 Rockfish Valley Hwy
Afton, VA 22920-9802
(540)456-6844 (800)769-6844 Fax:(540)456-7112
Internet: www.symweb.com/rockfish/lookingglass.html
E-mail: lookingglass@symweb.com

Circa 1848. Romantic 120-year-old oaks surround this
Victorian-style farmhouse located on 10 acres with views of the
Blue Ridge Valley and mountain range. A gazebo framed by a
formal rose garden is the focal point of the flower-filled landscape. Past antique wicker furnishings on the wide front porch,
a stained glass door leads inside. The drawing room and library
are furnished with family antiques from the 1800s and 1900s.
The innkeeper's dried flower arrangements add an inviting
touch to the fireplace mantels. Guest rooms offer large size beds
and antiques. At 8 a.m., early morning coffee is set up on an
antique server in the upstairs hallway. Breakfast, presented in
the dining room, includes gourmet fare such as egg frittatas,
apple super-puff pancakes and raspberry almond croissant
French toast. Favorite activities are enjoying the sunsets over the
valley and doing a few moonlight laps in the swimming pool.
Murder mysteries, receptions and weddings are popular here.

Innkeeper(s): Janet & Earl Hampton. $80-95. MC, VISA, AX, DC, PC, TC. 4
rooms with PB. Breakfast, afternoon tea and snacks/refreshments included in
rates. Types of meals: Full gourmet bkfst and early coffee/tea. Beds: KQT.
Ceiling fan in room. Air conditioning. VCR, fax, copier, swimming and library
on premises. Antiquing, fishing, golf, hiking, horseback riding, live theater,
parks, shopping, downhill skiing, cross-country skiing, sporting events, tennis, water sports and wineries nearby.

Location: Mountains.

"I'll never want to stay in a motel again!"

Certificate may be used: Jan. 5-April 27 and June 5-Sept. 30, Sunday-
Thursday. Nov. 1-Dec. 14, Sunday-Thursday, no holidays.

Amherst   F11

Dulwich Manor B&B Inn

550 Richmond Hwy
Amherst, VA 24521-3962
(804)946-7207 (800)571-9011
Internet: thedulwichmanor.com
E-mail: mfarmer@iwinet.com

Circa 1912. This red Flemish brick and white columned
English Manor sits on five secluded acres at the end of a country lane and in the midst of 93 acres of woodland and meadow.
The Blue Ridge Parkway is minutes away. The entry features a
large center hall and a wide oak staircase. Walls are 14 inches
thick. The 18 rooms include a 50-foot-long ballroom on the
third floor. The inn is decorated with a creative mix of antiques,
traditional furniture and collectibles.

Innkeeper(s): Mike & Georgie Farmer. $80-110. MC, VISA, PC, TC. 6 rooms with
PB, 3 with FP. Breakfast included in rates. Types of meals: Full bkfst and early
coffee/tea. Beds: KQ. Phone, ceiling fan and two rooms with whirlpool tub in
room. Air conditioning. Spa on premises. Antiquing, fishing, hiking, historic sites,
Monticello, Appomattox Court House and natural bridge nearby, live theater,
parks, shopping, downhill skiing, sporting events, water sports & wineries nearby.

Location: Countryside.

Publicity: *Country Inn and Scene.*

Certificate may be used: Sunday-Thursday, except May and October, holidays and holiday eves. Anytime, December-February, except holidays and
holiday eves.

Belle Haven   F19

Bay View Waterfront B&B

35350 Copes Dr
Belle Haven, VA 23306-1952
(757)442-6963 (800)442-6966
Internet: www.bbhost.com/bvwaterfront
E-mail: browning@shore.intercom.net

Circa 1800. This rambling inn stretches more than 100 feet
across and has five roof levels. There are heart-pine floors, high
ceilings and several fireplaces. The hillside location affords bay
breezes and wide views of the Chesapeake, Occohannock
Creek and the inn's surrounding 140 acres. The innkeepers are
descendants of several generations who have owned and operated Bay View. If you come by water to the inn's deep water
dock, look behind Channel Marker 16. Guests can arrange to
enjoy a boat tour along the Chesapeake Bay or Atlantic Ocean
led by the innkeepers' daughter, U.S. Coast Guard-approved
Capt. Mary.

Innkeeper(s): Wayne & Mary Will Browning. $95. PC, TC. 3 rooms, 1 with PB,
1 with FP. Breakfast included in rates. Type of meal: Full bkfst. Beds: D. Phone
in room. Air conditioning. VCR, swimming, bicycles and library on premises.
Antiquing, fishing, live theater, parks, shopping and water sports nearby.

Location: Country.

Publicity: *Rural Living and City.*

*"We loved staying in your home, and especially in the room with a
beautiful view of the bay. You have a lovely home and a beautiful
location. Thank you so much for your hospitality."*

Certificate may be used: Sunday-Thursday, Sept. 15-May 15 excluding holidays and special events.

Boston   D13

Thistle Hill B&B

5541 Sperryville Pike
Boston, VA 22713
(540)987-9142 Fax:(540)987-9122

The inn, an antique shop and restaurant combine to create
this restful bed & breakfast. The rambling home rests alongside
a former military turnpike used during the Civil War. There are
10 acres of woods to stroll through, a stream, hot tub and a
gazebo. Rooms are furnished with antiques and reproductions.
The Little Thistle House, a romantic, cozy cottage, offers a
sleigh bed, fireplace and sitting room for those seeking solitude. Breakfasts are huge—freshly baked muffins, fruit and coffee accompany the day's entree. Dinners are served by candlelight, and guests can arrange a private dinner for two.

Innkeeper(s): Charles & Marianne Wilson. $95-145. MC, VISA, DS. 5 rooms,
4 with PB, 1 with FP and 1 conference room. Breakfast and afternoon tea
included in rates. Type of meal: Full bkfst. Beds: Q. TV and phone in room.
Fax and spa on premises. Handicap access.

Publicity: *Washington Post.*

Certificate may be used: Sunday through Thursday, excluding holidays.

Boyce   **B14**

L'Auberge Provencale

13630 Lord Fairfax Highway
Boyce, VA 22620
(540)837-1375 (800)638-1702 Fax:(540)837-2004
Internet: www.laubergeprovencale.com
E-mail: cborel@shentel.net

Circa 1753. This farmhouse was built with fieldstones gathered from the area. Hessian soldiers crafted the woodwork of the main house, Mt. Airy. As the name suggests, a French influence is prominent throughout the inn. Victorian and European antiques fill the elegant guest rooms, several of which include fireplaces. Innkeeper Alain Borel hails from a long line of master chefs, his expertise creates many happy culinary memories guests cherish. Many of the French-influenced items served at the inn's four-diamond restaurant, include ingredients from the inn's gardens, and Alain has been hailed by James Beard as a Great Country Inn Chef. The innkeepers also offer accommodations three miles away at Villa La Campagnette, an 1890 restored home. The home includes two suites and the Grand Master bedroom. Guests enjoy 18 acres with a swimming pool, hot tub and stables.

Innkeeper(s): Alain & Celeste Borel. $145-250. MC, VISA, AX, DC, DS, PC, TC. 11 rooms with PB, 6 with FP, 3 suites and 1 conference room. Breakfast included in rates. Type of meal: Full gourmet bkfst. Beds: KQD. Air conditioning. Fax and copier on premises. Antiquing, bicycling, canoeing/kayaking, fishing, golf, hiking, horseback riding, live theater, museums, parks, shopping, tennis and wineries nearby.

Location: Country.

Publicity: *Food & Wine, Romantic Homes, Bon Appetit, Glamour, Washington Dossier, Washington Post, Baltimore, Richmond Times., Great Chefs of the East and Great Country Inns.*

"Peaceful view and atmosphere, extraordinary food and wines. Honeymoon and heaven all in one!"

Certificate may be used: Wednesday through Friday, no May or October or holidays.

Bumpass   **E14**

Rockland Farm Retreat

3609 Lewiston Rd
Bumpass, VA 23024-9659
(540)895-5098
Internet: www.rocklandretreat.com

Circa 1820. The 75 acres of Rockland Farm include pasture land, livestock, vineyard, crops and a farm pond for fishing. The grounds here are said to have spawned Alex Haley's "Roots." Guests can study documents and explore local cemeteries describing life under slavery in the area surrounding this historic home and 18th-century farmlands.

Innkeeper(s): Roy E. Mixon. $69-79. AX, PC. 4 rooms, 3 with PB, 1 suite and 2 conference rooms. Breakfast included in rates. Type of meal: Full bkfst. Beds: DT. Air conditioning. VCR on premises. Amusement parks, antiquing, fishing, parks, shopping and water sports nearby.

Pets Allowed.

Location: Country.

Publicity: *Washington Post and Free Lance-Star.*

Certificate may be used: Non-holiday weekends.

Cape Charles   **G18**

Cape Charles House

645 Tazewell Ave
Cape Charles, VA 23310-3313
(757)331-4920 Fax:(757)331-4960
Internet: capecharleshouse.com
E-mail: stay@capecharleshouse.com

Circa 1912. The Cape Charles House was the recipient of the 2000 Governor's Award for Virginia Hospitality. A Cape Charles attorney built this Colonial Revival home on the site of the town's first schoolhouse. Each room is named for someone important to Cape Charles  history. The Julia Wilkins Room is especially picturesque. Rich blue walls and white woodwork are accented by blue and white pastoral print draperies, a private bath with whirlpool and a balcony. There is a seamstress dress form with an antique dress, rocking chair and chaise. Other rooms are decorated with the same skill and style, with fine window dressings, artwork and carefully placed collectibles. Oriental rugs top the wood floors, and among the fine furnishings are family heirlooms. Breakfasts are gourmet and served in the formal dining room. Innkeeper Carol Evans prepares breakfast items such as chilled melon with a lime glaze and lemon yogurt topping, egg quesadillas, rosemary roasted potatoes and freshly baked muffins. From time to time, cooking classes and murder-mystery events are available. There are many attractions in the area, including sunset sails, historic walking tours of Cape Charles, antique shops, golfing, beach and The Nature Conservancy.

Innkeeper(s): Bruce & Carol Evans. $85-120. MC, VISA, AX, DS, PC, TC. 5 rooms with PB. Breakfast, afternoon tea and snacks/refreshments included in rates. Types of meals: Full gourmet bkfst and early coffee/tea. Beds: KQ. Ceiling fan and Jacuzzi (two rooms) in room. Air conditioning. VCR, fax, copier and bicycles on premises. Antiquing, fishing, golf, live theater, parks, shopping, tennis and water sports nearby.

Location: Small Town.

Publicity: *Southern Inns.*

"Cape Charles House is first and foremost a home and we were made to feel 'at home'."

Certificate may be used: November through March, Sunday-Thursday.

Champlain   **E16**

Linden House B&B & Plantation

PO Box 23
Champlain, VA 22438-0023
(804)443-1170 (800)622-1202

Circa 1750. This restored planters home is designated a state landmark and listed in the National Register. The lush grounds boast walking trails, a pond, an English garden, patio with fountain, gazebo, arbor and five porches. Each of the accommodations offers something special. The Carriage Suite features country decor, antiques, a private porch and a fireplace. The Robert E. Lee room has a high-poster bed, fireplace and private bath. The Jefferson Davis room has a luxurious bath with a Jacuzzi and steam room. The fourth-floor Linden Room affords a view of the countryside and features a queen-size bed and an alcove with a day bed adjoining the private bath. Other rooms also promise an enchanting experience. All rooms have their own television and refrigerator. With its new reception hall and verandas, the inn is popular for weddings, conferences and meetings.

Innkeeper(s): Ken & Sandra Pounsberry. $85-135. MC, VISA, AX, PC, TC. 7 rooms with PB and 2 suites. Breakfast included in rates. Types of meals: Full gourmet bkfst and early coffee/tea. Beds: Q. Phone, turndown service, ceiling fan and VCR in room. Air conditioning. Stables, bicycles and library on premises. Handicap access. Amusement parks, antiquing, fishing, boarding school, live theater, parks, shopping and water sports nearby.

Location: Plantation.

Publicity: *Washington Times Dispatch and Rappahannock-Journal Times.*

Certificate may be used: Jan. 2 through Dec. 30.

Chatham   I11

Eldon, The Inn at Chatham

SR 685, 1037 Chalk Level Rd
Chatham, VA 24531
(804)432-0935

Circa 1835. Beautiful gardens and white oaks surround this former tobacco plantation home set among the backdrop of the Blue Ridge Mountains. Stroll the grounds and discover sculptures and an array of flowers and plants. Southern hospitality reigns at this charming home filled with Empire antiques. Guest rooms are light and airy and tastefully decorated with beautiful linens, Oriental rugs and antiques. Fresh flowers accentuate the bright, cheerful rooms. A lavish, Southern-style breakfast is served up each morning, and dinners at Eldon feature the gourmet creations of Chef Joel Wesley, a graduate of the Culinary Institute of America. Eldon is a popular location for weddings and parties.

Innkeeper(s): Joy & Bob Lemm. $80-130. MC, VISA, PC, TC. 4 rooms, 3 with PB and 1 suite. Breakfast included in rates. Types of meals: Full gourmet bkfst, cont plus and early coffee/tea. Beds: QDT. Cable TV, phone and turndown service in room. Air conditioning. Swimming and library on premises. Handicap access. Antiquing, Chatham Hall, parks, shopping and water sports nearby.

Location: Rural country.

Publicity: *Danville Register, Richmond Times and Chatham Star Tribune.*

"The food, the ambiance, your wonderful hospitality made for a most charming weekend."

Certificate may be used: January, February, March-anytime; April, May, June, July, August, Sunday-Thursday; Friday and Saturday as available.

Sims-Mitchell House B&B

PO Box 429
Chatham, VA 24531-0429
(804)432-0595 (800)967-2867
Internet: www.victorianvilla.com
E-mail: answers@victorianvilla.com

Circa 1870. This Italianate house has 11 fireplaces, original horsehair-based plaster, furnishings from several generations of Mitchells and original art by Southern artists. (Art created by your host also is displayed.) There is a two-bedroom suite and a separate two-bedroom cottage at the side yard offering pastoral views. Hargrave Military Academy and Chatham Hall are within a five-block walk. Patricia, a food historian, has more than 50 books in print and husband Henry is her editor.

Innkeeper(s): Patricia & Henry Mitchell. $60-70. MC, VISA, PC, TC. 2 suites. Breakfast included in rates. Type of meal: Cont plus. Phone in room. Air conditioning. Antiquing nearby.

Location: Rural edge of small town.

Certificate may be used: Monday through Wednesday nights.

Clifton Forge   F10

Longdale Inn

6209 Longdale Furnace Rd
Clifton Forge, VA 24422-3618
(540)862-0892 (800)862-0386 Fax:(540)862-3554
Internet: www.longdale-inn.com
E-mail: bnbinns@longdale-inn.com

Circa 1873. This Victorian was built by the ironmaster of the Longdale Furnace Company and is located in a state historic district named for the firm. The home boasts many unusual features, including a wraparound porch that includes a built-in gazebo. There are more than 12 acres to enjoy, as well as views of the surrounding Shenandoah Valley and the Allegheny Mountains. Rooms are cheerfully appointed in a Victorian style and include ceiling fans and fireplaces. Civil War sites, museums, plantations, zoos, shopping and plenty of outdoor activities are in the area.

Innkeeper(s): Bob Cormier. $80-140. MC, VISA, AX, DS, PC, TC. 11 rooms, 6 with PB, 5 with FP, 1 suite and 1 cottage. Breakfast included in rates. Types of meals: Full bkfst and early coffee/tea. Beds: KQDT. Phone and ceiling fan in room. VCR, fax, copier, bicycles and library on premises. Antiquing, fishing, golf, live theater, parks, shopping, downhill skiing, cross-country skiing and water sports nearby.

Pets allowed: First floor suite and cottages, with notice.

Location: Mountains.

"We'll catch your dreams."

Certificate may be used: Jan. 2-April 30, all days.

Columbia   F13

Upper Byrd Farm B&B

6452 River Rd W
Columbia, VA 23038-2002
(804)842-2240

Circa 1890. This 26-acre farm rests on top of a hill overlooking the James River. The scenic location is dotted with trees and wildflowers. Innkeeper Ivona Kaz-Jepsen, a native of Lithuania, had her work cut out for her when she began renovation of the house, which was inhabited by college students. She transformed the home into an artist's retreat, filling it with antiques and her own artwork. The breakfast table is set with a beautiful mix of china, and the meal is served by candlelight.

Innkeeper(s): Ivona Kaz-Jepsen. $70. 3 rooms, 2 with FP. Breakfast included in rates. Types of meals: Full gourmet bkfst and early coffee/tea. Beds: KT. Air conditioning. VCR on premises. Antiquing, fishing and water sports nearby.

Location: Country.

Certificate may be used: June 15-Aug. 20, Sunday-Friday.

Fairfax   C15

Bailiwick Inn

4023 Chain Bridge Rd
Fairfax, VA 22030-4101
(703)691-2266 (800)366-7666 Fax:(703)934-2112
Internet: www.bailiwickinn.com
E-mail: theinn@baliwickinn.com

Circa 1800. Located across from the county courthouse where George Washington's will is filed, this distinguished three-story Federal brick house recently has been renovated. The first Civil War casualty occurred on what is now the inn's lawn. The elegant, early Virginia decor is reminiscent of the state's fine plantation mansions. Ask to stay in the Thomas Jefferson Room, a replica of Mr. Jefferson's bedroom at Monticello. Five-course "Wine Master Dinners" at the inn are featured once a month on Tuesdays and

include the opportunity for a special package rate for rooms. Every Thursday and Sunday, afternoon teas are featured.

$205-330. MC, VISA, AX. 14 rooms with PB, 4 with FP, 1 suite and 1 conference room. Breakfast and afternoon tea included in rates. Types of meals: Full gourmet bkfst and early coffee/tea. Beds: KQT. Cable TV, phone and turndown service in room. Air conditioning. VCR, fax and copier on premises. Antiquing, live theater, parks, shopping and sporting events nearby.

Location: City.

Publicity: *Washington Post, Journal, Fairfax Connection, Inn Times, Mid-Atlantic Country, Victoria, Country Inns, Colonial Homes, Great Country Inns TV Program and Romancing America TV Program.*

"A visit to your establishment clearly transcends any lodging experience that I can recall."

Certificate may be used: Sunday-Thursday, January, February, March, July, August, September.

Fredericksburg   D15

La Vista Plantation

4420 Guinea Station Rd
Fredericksburg, VA 22408-8850
(540)898-8444 (800)529-2823
Internet: www.bbonline.com/va/lavista/
E-mail: lavistabb@aol.com

Circa 1838. La Vista has a long and unusual past, rich in Civil War history. Both Confederate and Union armies camped here, and this is where the Ninth Cavalry was sworn in. It is no wonder then that the house is listed in the National Register of Historic Places. The house, a Classical Revival structure with high ceilings and wide pine floors, sits on 10 acres of pasture and woods. The grounds include a pond stocked with bass. Guest quarters include a spacious room with a king-size, four-poster bed, fireplace and Empire furniture or a two-bedroom apartment that can accommodate up to six guests and includes a fireplace. Breakfasts feature homemade egg dishes from hens raised on the property.

Innkeeper(s): Michele & Edward Schiesser. $105. MC, VISA, PC, TC. 1 rooms with PB. Breakfast included in rates. Types of meals: Full bkfst & early coffee/tea. Beds: KQDT. TV and phone in room. Air conditioning. Copier & library on premises. Amusement parks, antiquing, fishing, horseback riding, pond, rowboat & birdwatching, live theater, parks, shopping, sporting events & water sports nearby.

Location: Country.

Publicity: *Mid-Atlantic Country, Free Lance Star and Richmond Times Dispatch.*

"Coming here was an excellent choice. La Vista is charming, quiet and restful, all qualities we were seeking. Breakfast was delicious."

Certificate may be used: January and February, Monday-Thursday.

Goshen   E10

The Hummingbird Inn

PO Box 147, 30 Wood Ln
Goshen, VA 24439-0147
(540)997-9065 (800)397-3214 Fax:(540)997-0289
Internet: www.hummingbirdinn.com
E-mail: hmgbird@cfw.com

Circa 1853. This early Victorian villa is located in the Shenandoah Valley against the backdrop of the Allegheny Mountains. Both the first and second floors offer wraparound verandas. Furnished with antiques, the inn features a library and

sitting room with fireplaces. The rustic den and one guest room comprise the oldest portions of the inn, built around 1780. Four-course dinners, which include wine, are available by advance reservation. An old barn and babbling creek are on the grounds.

Innkeeper(s): Diana & Jeremy Robinson. $95-145. MC, VISA, AX, DS, PC, TC. 5 rooms with PB, 2 with FP. Breakfast included in rates. Types of meals: Full bkfst and early coffee/tea. Beds: Q. TV and ceiling fan in room. Air conditioning. VCR, fax, library and satellite TV on premises. Handicap access. Antiquing, fishing, live theater, shopping, downhill skiing and cross-country skiing nearby.

Pets allowed: Dogs with prior arrangements.

Location: Mountains.

Publicity: *Blue Ridge Country and Inn Spots and Special Places.*

"We enjoyed our stay so much that we returned two weeks later on our way back for a delicious home-cooked dinner, comfortable attractive atmosphere, and familiar faces to welcome us after a long journey."

Certificate may be used: Nov. 15-April 15, Monday-Thursday.

Leesburg   B15

The Norris House Inn & Stone House Tea Room

108 Loudoun St SW
Leesburg, VA 20175
(703)777-1806 (800)644-1806 Fax:(703)771-8051
Internet: norrishouse.com
E-mail: inn@norrishouse.com

Circa 1760. The Norris brothers, Northern Virginia's foremost architects and builders, purchased this building in 1850 and began extensive renovations several years later. They used the finest wood and brick available, remodeling the exterior to an Eastlake style. Beautifully restored, the inn features built-in bookcases in the library and a cherry fireplace mantel. Evening libations are served.

Innkeeper(s): Pamela & Don McMurray. $80-145. MC, VISA, AX, DC, CB, DS, PC, TC. 6 rooms, 3 with FP and 3 conference rooms. Breakfast included in rates. Types of meals: Full bkfst and early coffee/tea. Beds: QD. Turndown service in room. Air conditioning. Fax and library on premises. Antiquing, fishing, hiking, biking, parks, shopping and water sports nearby.

Location: Historic district.

Publicity: *New York Times, Better Homes & Gardens, Washingtonian and Country Home.*

"Thank you for your gracious hospitality. We enjoyed everything about your lovely home, especially the extra little touches that really make the difference."

Certificate may be used: Sunday through Thursday only.

Lexington   F11

Brierley Hill B&B Inn

985 Borden Rd
Lexington, VA 24450
(540)464-8421 (800)422-4925 Fax:(540)464-8925
Internet: www.brierleyhill.com
E-mail: brierley@cfw.com

Circa 1993. Visitors to this inn, which is set on eight acres, enjoy a spectacular view of the Shenandoah Valley and Blue Ridge Mountains. The natural setting aside, the interior is reason enough for a stay. The rooms are decorated in light, romantic colors, reminiscent of a field of wildflowers. Antiques and poster beds blend with flowery prints, light wallpapers and knickknacks. The suites include a Jacuzzi. Breakfasts, weather permitting, are served on the veranda, which offers a wonderful view.

Innkeeper(s): Al & Jeanne Perkins. $95-160. MC, VISA, TC. 5 rooms with PB, 3 with FP and 2 suites. Breakfast and snacks/refreshments included in rates. Types of meals: Full bkfst and early coffee/tea. Beds: KQ. TV, ceiling fan and Jacuzzi (suites) in room. Air conditioning. Fax and copier on premises. Antiquing, fishing, live theater, parks, shopping, downhill skiing, cross-country skiing, sporting events and water sports nearby.

Location: Historic town.

Publicity: *Blue Ridge Country.*

Certificate may be used: All year except May and October, holidays excluded, Sunday through Wednesday.

Maple Hall

3111 N Lee Hwy
Lexington, VA 24450-8842
(540)463-2044 (877)463-2044 Fax:(540)463-6693

Circa 1850. Maple Hall is one of the Historic Country Inns of Lexington, an elegant ensemble of some of Virginia's notable mansions and homes. The red brick manor, flanked by stately columns, remained in the original owner's family until the mid-1980s. Many of the rooms include working fireplaces and all are individually decorated with antiques. A restored guest house, dating prior to the 1850 main house, includes three bedrooms, a kitchen and living room. Secluded accommodations also are available at Pond House, which includes four mini-suites and a back veranda with a view of the pond and surrounding countryside. The home rests on a 56-acre estate with boxwoods, walking trails, a fishing pond, swimming pool and tennis courts. Breakfast and evening wine is included. Gourmet dining, with specialties such as lobster bisque, prime rib or poached Alaskan salmon, is available at the inn's restaurant.

Innkeeper(s): Don Fredenburg. $95-160. MC, VISA, PC. 21 rooms with PB, 16 with FP, 5 suites, 2 cottages and 1 conference room. Breakfast included in rates. Type of meal: Cont plus. Beds: QDT. Phone and clocks in room. Air conditioning. VCR, fax, copier, swimming, tennis, walking trails and fishing pond on premises. Antiquing, fishing, live theater, parks, shopping and sporting events nearby.

Location: Mountains.

"The view from the back balcony was so peaceful and serene. What a perfect weekend!"

Certificate may be used: July and August, November and December (except first week), January-March.

The Inn at Union Run

Union Run Rd
Lexington, VA 24450
(540)463-9715 (800)528-6466 Fax:(540)463-3526
Internet: www.unionrun.com
E-mail: unionrun@cfw.com

Circa 1883. This inn was named for the spring-fed creek that meanders in front of this restored farmhouse. Union troops, specifically the 2nd and 4th Michigan Calvary, camped on the grounds during the Civil War. The home is surrounded by 10 acres with a fishing pond and brook. The innkeepers have traveled extensively throughout Europe and have brought the influence into their inn. The furnishings, many of which were fashioned out of oak, are a mix of American and Victorian styles.

Innkeeper(s): Roger & Jeanette Serens. $95-130. MC, VISA, AX, TC. 8 rooms with PB, 4 with FP and 1 conference room. Breakfast and afternoon tea included in rates. Types of meals: Full bkfst and early coffee/tea. Beds: Q. Phone, turndown service, ceiling fan and Jacuzzis (6 rooms) in room. Air conditioning. Handicap access. Antiquing, fishing, Civil War sites, live theater, museums, parks, shopping, cross-country skiing and water sports nearby.

Pets allowed: Call first.

Location: Creek-front mountainside property.

Publicity: *News Gazette, Blue Ridge Country and Insider Guide of Virginia.*

Certificate may be used: January to December, excluding October, excludes holidays, Sundays to Thursdays.

Locust Dale   D13

The Inn at Meander Plantation

HC 5, Box 460A
Locust Dale, VA 22948-9701
(540)672-4912 (800)385-4936 Fax:(540)672-0405
Internet: www.meander.net
E-mail: inn@meander.net

Circa 1766. This elegant country estate was built by Henry Fry, close friend of Thomas Jefferson, who often stopped here on his way to Monticello. Ancient formal boxwood gardens, woodland and meadows are enjoyed by guests as well as views of the Blue Ridge Mountains from the rockers on the back porches. The mansion is decorated serenely with elegant

antiques and period reproductions, including queen-size, four-poster beds. The innkeeper is a food writer and will prepare special breakfasts for individual diets. Full dinner service and picnic baskets are available with advance reservations.

Innkeeper(s): Bob & Suzie Blanchard, Suzanne Thomas. $110-200. MC, VISA, AX, PC, TC. 8 rooms with PB, 5 with FP, 4 suites and 1 conference room. Breakfast included in rates. Types of meals: Full bkfst and early coffee/tea. Beds: KQD. Air conditioning. VCR, fax, stables, library, pet boarding and child care on premises. Antiquing, fishing, live theater, parks, shopping, downhill skiing, cross-country skiing and sporting events nearby.

Pets allowed: In dependencies only. Stabling for horses available.

Location: Country.

"Staying at the Inn at Meander Plantation feels like being immersed in another century while having the luxuries and amenities available today."

Certificate may be used: Year-round, Sunday through Thursday, excluding holidays.

Luray   C13

Spring Farm B&B

13 Wallace Ave
Luray, VA 22835-9067
(540)743-4701 (800)203-2814 Fax:(540)743-7851

Circa 1795. Spring Farm is on 10 acres two miles from Luray
Caverns. Hite's Springs run through the land. The Greek Revival
home has double front and back verandas. Rooms feature a mix

of antique and new furnishings, and
there is a fireplace in the living
room. Ask the innkeepers for
advice on shopping, dining
and activities in the
Shenandoah and they'll be
happy to help you plan a getaway you'll long remember.

Innkeeper(s): Thelma Mayes & Susan Murphy. $75-150. MC, VISA, DC, DS,
PC, TC. 4 rooms, 2 with PB and 1 cottage. Breakfast, afternoon tea and
snacks/refreshments included in rates. Types of meals: Full bkfst and early
coffee/tea. Beds: QD. Air conditioning. VCR and fax on premises. Antiquing,
fishing, parks, shopping, downhill skiing and water sports nearby.

Publicity: *Christmas Tour-Page Courier.*

"Our first, but definitely not our last, visit."

Certificate may be used: Weekdays only during April through December
(Tuesday-Thursday).

The Ruffner House

440 Ruffner House Rd
Luray, VA 22835-9704
(540)743-7855 (800)969-7855

Circa 1840. Situated on a farm nestled in the heart of the
Shenandoah Valley, this stately manor was built by Peter
Ruffner, the first settler of Page Valley and Luray. Ruffner family
members discovered a cavern opposite the entrance to the
Luray Caverns, which were found later. Purebred Arabian hors-
es graze in the pasture on this 23-acre estate.

Innkeeper(s): Sonia Croucher. $98-150. PC, TC. 6 rooms with PB, 2 with FP.
Breakfast included in rates. Types of meals: Full bkfst and early coffee/tea.
Beds: QD. TV and ceiling fan in room. Air conditioning. VCR and spa on
premises. Antiquing, canoeing/kayaking, fishing, golf, parks, shopping, downhill skiing, cross-country skiing and sporting events nearby.

Location: Horse breeding farm.

Publicity: *Page News & Courier and Virginian Pilot.*

*"This is the loveliest inn we have ever stayed in. We were made to feel
very welcome and at ease."*

Certificate may be used: Jan. 15-Sept. 15, Monday-Thursday. Nov. 1-Dec.
15, Monday-Thursday.

Lynchburg   G11

Federal Crest Inn

1101 Federal St
Lynchburg, VA 24504-3018
(804)845-6155 (800)818-6155 Fax:(804)845-1445
Internet: www.federalcrest.com

Circa 1909. The guest rooms at Federal Crest are named for
the many varieties of trees and flowers native to Virginia. This
handsome red brick home, a fine example of Georgian Revival
architecture, features a commanding front entrance flanked by
columns that hold up the second-story veranda. A grand stair-

case, carved woodwork,
polished floors topped
with fine rugs and more
columns create an aura of
elegance. Each guest
room offers something
special and romantic,
from a mountain view to
a Jacuzzi tub. Breakfasts
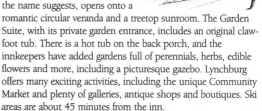
are served on fine china, and the first course is always a freshly
baked muffin with a secret message inside.

Innkeeper(s): Ann & Phil Ripley. $95-125. MC, VISA, AX, DS, PC, TC. 5
rooms, 4 with PB, 3 with FP, 2 suites and 1 conference room. Breakfast,
afternoon tea and snacks/refreshments included in rates. Types of meals: Full
bkfst and early coffee/tea. Beds: Q. Cable TV, turndown service, portable telephone and portable VCR in room. Air conditioning. Fax, copier, library, conference theater with 60-inch TV (Ballroom) with stage and 50's cafe with
antique jukebox on premises. Antiquing, fishing, golf, live theater, parks,
shopping, sporting events and tennis nearby.

Location: Central Virginia.

Publicity: *Washington Post, News & Advance, Scene and Local ABC.*

*"What a wonderful place to celebrate our birthdays and enjoy our
last romantic getaway before the birth of our first child."*

Certificate may be used: All year, Sunday-Thursday.

Lynchburg Mansion Inn B&B

405 Madison St
Lynchburg, VA 24504-2455
(804)528-5400 (800)352-1199 Fax:(804)847-2545
Internet: www.lynchburgmansioninn.com
E-mail: mansioninn@aol.com

Circa 1914. This regal, Georgian mansion, with its majestic
Greek Revival columns, is located on a brick-paved street in the
Garland Hill Historic District. The grand hall showcases an oak
and cherry staircase that leads up to the solarium. Breakfasts are
served in the formal dining room on
antique china. Romantic rooms feature
inviting touches such as a four-
poster beds, Laura Ashley and
Ralph Lauren linens, Battenburg
lace pillows and some include
fireplaces. The Veranda Suite, as
the name suggests, opens onto a
romantic circular veranda and a treetop sunroom. The Garden
Suite, with its private garden entrance, includes an original clawfoot tub. There is a hot tub on the back porch, and the
innkeepers have added gardens full of perennials, herbs, edible
flowers and more, including a picturesque gazebo. Lynchburg
offers many exciting activities, including the unique Community
Market and plenty of galleries, antique shops and boutiques. Ski
areas are about 45 minutes from the inn.

Innkeeper(s): Mauranna and Bob Sherman. $109-144. MC, VISA, AX, DC. 5
rooms with PB, 3 with FP, 2 suites and 1 conference room. Breakfast included in rates. Types of meals: Full gourmet bkfst and early coffee/tea. Beds:
KQ. Cable TV, phone and turndown service in room. Air conditioning. Period
library on premises. Handicap access. Antiquing, live theater, shopping,
downhill skiing and sporting events nearby.

Location: City.

Publicity: *News & Advance and Roanoker.*

*"The Lynchburg Mansion Inn is the creme de la creme. You have
earned all sorts of pats on the back for the restoration and hospitality
you offer. It is truly elegant."*

Certificate may be used: Year-round, excluding holidays, holiday eves and
weekends around holidays; excludes weekends in April, May, June, August
and October.

Madison   D13

Dulaney Hollow at Old Rag Mountain Inn & Antiques

HC 6 Box 215 - Scenic VA Byway, Rt 231
Madison, VA 22727
(540)923-4470 Fax:(540)923-4841
E-mail: oldragmtninn@tidalwave.net

Circa 1903. Period furnishings decorate this Victorian manor house on 15 acres in the foothills of the Blue Ridge Mountains. There is also a cabin and hayloft suite available amid the shaded lawns and old farm buildings. A country breakfast is served, and picnic baskets may be packed for you to take on a bicycle jaunt or for hiking the hills around the Shenandoah River and National Park. A walk up the inn's pasture provides a great view of the Blue Ridge. Monticello, Charlottesville and Montpelier are within an hour's drive.

Innkeeper(s): Susan & Louis Cable. $80-130. PC, TC. 6 rooms, 4 with PB and 2 cottages. Breakfast included in rates. Types of meals: Full gourmet bkfst, cont plus and early coffee/tea. Beds: QD. Ceiling fan in room. Air conditioning. VCR, fax, copier, swimming, bicycles, pet boarding and Internet access on premises. Antiquing, fishing, golf, Civil War sites, historic sites and battlefields, Shenandoah National Park, wildlife preserve, live theater, parks, shopping, downhill skiing, cross-country skiing, sporting events, tennis, water sports and wineries nearby.
Pets allowed: for a fee.

Location: Mountains.

Publicity: *Madison Eagle and Charlottesville Daily Progress.*

Certificate may be used: Jan. 1 through Dec. 31 (seven days a week), except holidays, holiday weekends (Friday, Saturday, Sunday) and all weekends (Friday, Saturday) in September, October and November.

Mathews   G17

Ravenswood Inn

PO Box 1430
Mathews, VA 23109-1430
(804)725-7272

Circa 1913. This intimate waterfront home is located on five acres along the banks of the East River, where passing boats still harvest crabs and oysters. A long screened porch captures river breezes. Most rooms feature a river view and are decorated in Victorian, country, nautical or wicker. Williamsburg, Jamestown and Yorktown are within an hour.

Innkeeper(s): Mrs. Ricky Durham. $70-120. MC, VISA, TC. 5 rooms with PB. Breakfast included in rates. Types of meals: Full gourmet bkfst and early coffee/tea. Beds: KQ. Ceiling fan in room. Air conditioning. VCR and spa on premises. Amusement parks, antiquing, live theater, shopping, sporting events and water sports nearby.

Publicity: *Virginian Pilot and Daily Press.*

"While Ravenswood is one of the most beautiful places we've ever been, it is your love, caring and friendship that has made it such a special place for us."

Certificate may be used: April-November, Sunday-Thursday.

Middleburg   C14

Red Fox Inn

2 E Washington St
Middleburg, VA 22117-0385
(540)687-6301 (800)223-1728 Fax:(540)687-6053
Internet: www.redfox.com
E-mail: innkeeper@redfox.com

Circa 1728. Originally Chinn's Ordinary, the inn was a popular stopping place for travelers between Winchester and Alexandria. During the Civil War, Colonel John Mosby and General Jeb Stuart met here. Guest rooms are furnished in 18th-century decor and most feature four-poster canopy beds.

Innkeeper(s): F. Turner Reuter, Jr. $140-250. MC, VISA, AX, DS, TC. 24 rooms with PB and 4 conference rooms. Breakfast included in rates. Type of meal: Cont. Beds: KQ. Cable TV and phone in room. Air conditioning. Fax and copier on premises. Handicap access. Antiquing nearby.

Location: Historic town.

Publicity: *Washingtonian, Southern Living, Washington Bride and Virginia Wine Publications.*

Certificate may be used: Sunday-Thursday, all year.

Montross   E16

The Inn at Montross

21 Polk Street
Montross, VA 22520
(804)493-0573 Fax:(804)493-9118
E-mail: chefcin@aol.com

Circa 1684. Montross was rebuilt in 1800 on the site of a 17th-century tavern. Operating as an "ordinary" since 1683, parts of the structure have been in continuous use for more than 300 years. It was visited by Burgesses and Justices of the Court (Washington, Lee and Jefferson). The guest rooms feature canopy beds and colonial furnishings. Smoking is allowed here.

Innkeeper(s): Scott Massidda & Cindy Brigman. $65-100. MC, VISA, AX, PC, TC. 5 rooms with PB and 1 conference room. Breakfast included in rates. Type of meal: Full gourmet bkfst. Beds: Q. Air conditioning. VCR, fax, tennis, library, pet boarding and in-house certified therapeutic massage on premises. Amusement parks, antiquing, fishing, golf, parks, shopping, tennis and water sports nearby.
Pets Allowed.

Location: Historic County/town.

Publicity: *Virginian-Pilot, Travel, Richmond Times-Dispatch, Washington Post and New York Times.*

"Hospitality is Inn!"

Certificate may be used: Feb. 8-Jan. 3, Sunday-Thursday.

Nellysford   F12

The Mark Addy

56 Rodes Farm Dr
Nellysford, VA 22958-9526
(804)361-1101 (800)278-2154
Internet: www.symweb.com/rockfish/mark.html
E-mail: markaddy@symweb.com

Circa 1837. It's not hard to understand why Dr. John Everett, the son of Thomas Jefferson's physician, chose this picturesque, Blue Mountain setting for his home. Everett expanded the simple, four-room farmhouse already present into a gracious manor. The well-appointed guest rooms feature double whirlpool baths, double showers or a clawfoot tub. Beds are covered with vintage linens, feather pillows and cozy, down comforters. There are plenty of relaxing possibilities, including five porches and a hammock set among the trees.

Innkeeper(s): John Storck Maddox. $90-145. MC, VISA, PC, TC. 9 rooms with PB and 1 suite. Types of meals: Full gourmet bkfst, cont and early coffee/tea. Beds: KQDT. Ceiling fan and jacuzzi in room. Air conditioning. VCR and library on premises. Handicap access. Antiquing, fishing, horseback riding, hiking, live theater, parks, shopping, downhill skiing and sporting events nearby.

Location: Mountains.

Publicity: *Local paper.*

Certificate may be used: January, March, July-August, December, Sunday to Thursday.

New Church E19

The Garden and The Sea Inn

4188 Nelson Rd, #275
New Church, VA 23415-0275
(757)824-0672 (800)824-0672
Internet: www.gardenandseainn.com
E-mail: baker@shore.intercom.net

Circa 1802. Gingerbread trim, a pair of brightly colored gables and two, adjacent verandas adorn the exterior of this Victorian. A warm, rich Victorian decor permeates the antique-filled guest rooms, an ideal setting for romance. Several rooms include whirlpool tubs. The inn's dining room serves gourmet dinners with an emphasis on fresh catches from the waters of the Eastern shore, but many continental items are featured as well.
Innkeeper(s): Tom & Sara Baker. $75-175. MC, VISA, AX, DS, PC, TC. 6 rooms with PB and 1 conference room. Breakfast included in rates. Type of meal: Cont plus. Beds: Q. Ceiling fan in room. Air conditioning. VCR, fax, copier and library on premises. Handicap access. Antiquing, fishing, beach, parks, shopping and water sports nearby.

Pets allowed: quiet and leashed outside.

Location: Country.

Publicity: *Washington Post and Modern Bride.*

Certificate may be used: Sunday through Thursday, in March, April, May, June, October and November.

New Market C12

Cross Roads Inn B&B

9222 John Sevier Rd
New Market, VA 22844-9649
(540)740-4157
Internet: www.crossroadsinnva.com
E-mail: freisitz@shentel.net

Circa 1925. This Victorian is full of Southern hospitality and European charm. The innkeepers serve imported Austrian coffee alongside the homemade breakfasts, and strudel is served as an afternoon refreshment. The home is decorated like an English garden, laced with antiques, some of which are family pieces. Four-poster and canopy beds are topped with fluffy, down comforters. The historic downtown area is within walking distance.
Innkeeper(s): Mary Lloyd & Roland Freisitzer. $55-100. MC, VISA, TC. 6 rooms with PB, 1 with FP and 1 conference room. Breakfast, afternoon tea and snacks/refreshments included in rates. Types of meals: Full gourmet bkfst and early coffee/tea. Beds: KQDT. Turndown service in room. Air conditioning. VCR, fax and copier on premises. Handicap access. Antiquing, fishing, musical summer festivals, live theater, parks, shopping, downhill skiing, sporting events and water sports nearby.

Location: Small town.

Certificate may be used: November to September, Sunday-Thursday.

Orange E13

Hidden Inn

249 Caroline St
Orange, VA 22960-1529
(540)672-3625 Fax:(540)672-5029

Circa 1880. Acres of huge old trees can be seen from the wraparound veranda of this Victorian inn nestled in the Virginia countryside. Guests are pampered with afternoon tea, and a candlelight picnic can be ordered. Monticello, Montpelier, wineries, shopping and antiquing all are nearby. After a day of exploring the area, guests can return to the inn for afternoon refreshments and then head out for dinner at a local restaurant.
Innkeeper(s): Barbara & Ray Lonick, Chrys Dermody. $99-169. MC, VISA, AX, PC, TC. 10 rooms with PB, 2 with FP and 2 cottages. Breakfast and afternoon tea included in rates. Types of meals: Full bkfst and early coffee/tea. Beds: KQDT. TV in room. Fax on premises. Antiquing, fishing, Monticello, Montpelier Civil War sites, wineries, live theater, shopping, sporting events and water sports nearby.

Location: Small village.

Publicity: *Forbes, Washington Post, Country Inns, Learning Channel, Inn Country USA., Great Country Inns, Inn Country USA, TLC and The Learning Channel.*

"It just doesn't get any better than this!"

Certificate may be used: Monday-Thursday, except May and October. No holidays.

Willow Grove Inn

14079 Plantation Way
Orange, VA 22960
(540)672-5982 (800)349-1778 Fax:(540)672-3674

Circa 1778. The exterior of this inn is Classical Revival style, while the interior retains Federal simplicity. Located in Orange County, Virginia, the inn is listed in the National Register of Historic Places and has been designated a Virginia Historic Landmark. The mansion, nestled on 37 acres, has survived two wars. Generals Wayne and Muhlenberg camped here during the Revolution, and the mansion was under siege during the Civil War. Trenches and breastworks are visible near the manor house, and a cannonball was removed from the eaves not too long ago.
Innkeeper(s): Angela Malloy. $225-330. MC, VISA, AX. 10 rooms, 5 with PB and 2 suites. Breakfast included in rates. Type of meal: Full bkfst. Beds: QDT. Antiquing, fishing, live theater and water sports nearby.

Publicity: *Southern Living, Country Inns, Victorian Homes, Countryside, Virginia, Washington Post, Washington Times, Country Accents, Baltimore Sun and Washingtonian.*

"Your congenial staff, excellent food, elegant and historical ambiance ... meticulous attention to detail, and of course your gracious hospitality, overwhelmingly delighted our senses and contributed to an experience we will never forget."

Certificate may be used: Tuesday, Wednesday, Thursday, MAP only, breakfast and dinner included. Four-course dinner off menu, excluding holidays and weekends.

Port Haywood G18

Tabb's Creek Inn

PO Box 219 Rt 14 Mathews Co
Port Haywood, VA 23138-0219
(804)725-5136 Fax:(804)725-5136

Circa 1820. Surrounded by 30 acres of woods and located on the banks of Tabb's Creek, this post-Colonial farm features a detached guest cottage. There are maple, elm, magnolia trees and 150 rose bushes on the property. The suites and guest rooms feature fireplaces and antiques. Boats for rowing and canoeing, docks, a swimming pool, and private waterview porches make this an especially attractive getaway for those seeking a dose of seclusion.

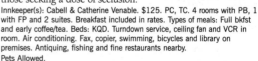

Innkeeper(s): Cabell & Catherine Venable. $125. PC, TC. 4 rooms with PB, 1 with FP and 2 suites. Breakfast included in rates. Types of meals: Full bkfst and early coffee/tea. Beds: KQD. Turndown service, ceiling fan and VCR in room. Air conditioning. Fax, copier, swimming, bicycles and library on premises. Antiquing, fishing and fine restaurants nearby.

Pets Allowed.

Location: Country.

"A spot of tea with a bit of heaven. Truly exceptional hosts. The best B&Bs I've happened across!"

Certificate may be used: All year.

Raphine   E11

Oak Spring Farm B&B

5895 Borden Grant Tr
Raphine, VA 24472-2615
(540)377-2398 (800)841-8813

Circa 1826. A willow tree droops gracefully over a pond at Oak Spring Farm. Guests can take a stroll through the grounds with a perennial garden, lawn and orchard. The historic plantation house features porch views of the Blue Ridge Mountains and has been pristinely renovated. Guest rooms are decorated with family heirlooms, contemporary touches and fresh flowers. Friendly exotic animals belonging to the Natural Bridge Zoo live here.
Innkeeper(s): Frank & Sally Harrelson. $75-145. MC, VISA, AX, DC, DS, PC, TC. 4 rooms with PB, 3 with FP & 1 suite. Breakfast & afternoon tea included in rates. Types of meals: Full gourmet bkfst & early coffee/tea. Beds: Q. Air conditioning. Antiquing, fishing, live theater, shopping, downhill skiing & sporting events nearby.
Location: Mountains.
Publicity: *The News-Gazette, The News and County Press and Mid-Atlantic Country.*
"The good taste, the privacy, the decor and the hosts were unbeatable!"
Certificate may be used: Sunday-Thursday, Jan. 1-Dec. 1. Excludes holidays.

Scottsville   F13

High Meadows Vineyard & Mtn Sunset Inn

Highmeadows Ln
Scottsville, VA 24590
(804)286-2218 (800)232-1832 Fax:(804)286-2124
Internet: www.highmeadows.com
E-mail: peterhmi@aol.com

Circa 1832. Minutes from Charlottesville on the Constitution Highway (Route 20), High Meadows stands on 50 acres of gardens, forests, ponds, a creek and a vineyard. Listed in the National Register, it is actually two historic homes joined by a breezeway as well as a turn-of-the-century Queen Anne manor house. The inn is furnished in Federal and  Victorian styles. Guests are treated to gracious Virginia hospitality in an elegant and peaceful setting with wine tasting and a romantic candlelight dinner every evening. There are two private hot tubs on the grounds.
Innkeeper(s): Peter Sushka & Mary Jae Abbitt. $84-195. MC, VISA, AX, DS. 14 rooms with PB, 12 with FP, 5 suites and 1 conference room. Breakfast included in rates. Type of meal: Full gourmet bkfst. Beds: KQDT. Turndown service and ceiling fan in room. Air conditioning. Spa on premises. Handicap access. Antiquing, fishing, live theater, shopping, downhill skiing, cross-country skiing, sporting events and water sports nearby.
Location: Rural countryside.
Publicity: *Washington Times, Cavalier Daily, Daily Progress, Washington Post, Richmond Times Dispatch, Mid-Atlantic and Washingtonian.*
Certificate may be used: All year, Sunday-Thursday, non-holidays; Sunday-Friday, Dec. 1-March 1, non-holidays.

Smithfield   H17

Four Square Plantation

13357 Foursquare Rd
Smithfield, VA 23430-8643
(757)365-0749 Fax:(757)365-0749

Circa 1807. Located in the historic James River area, the original land grant, "Four Square" was established in 1664 and consisted of 640 acres. Now in the National Register and a Virginia Historic

Landmark, the Federal style home is called Plantation Plain by Virginia preservationists. The inn is furnished with family period pieces and antiques. The Vaughan Room offers a fireplace, Empire furnishings and access by private staircase. Breakfast is served in the dining room. The inn's four acres provide a setting for weddings and special events. Tour Williamsburg, Jamestown, the James River Plantations and Yorktown nearby.
Innkeeper(s): Roger & Amelia Healey. $75-85. MC, VISA, AX, PC, TC. 3 rooms with PB, 3 with FP. Breakfast included in rates. Types of meals: Full gourmet bkfst and early coffee/tea. Beds: KQT. Cable TV, phone, turndown service and ceiling fan in room. Air conditioning. VCR, fax and copier on premises. Antiquing, golf and shopping nearby.
Pets allowed: small, well behaved pets allowed with a deposit.
Location: Country.
Publicity: *Daily Press and Virginia Pilot.*
Certificate may be used: Sunday-Thursday, Jan. 1-March 31, July 10-Sept. 30, Nov. 1-Dec. 23, no holidays.

Isle of Wight Inn

1607 S Church St
Smithfield, VA 23430-1831
(757)357-3176 (800)357-3245

Circa 1980. This Colonial inn is located in a historic seaside town, boasting more than 60 homes that date back to the mid-18th century. St. Luke's Church, the oldest in the United States, dating back to 1632, is located near the inn. Antiques and reproductions fill the rooms, the suites offer the added amenities of fireplaces and whirlpool tubs. The inn also houses a gift boutique and one of the area's finest antique shops, featuring old clocks and period furniture.
Innkeeper(s): Jackie Madrigel & Bob Hart. $59-119. MC, VISA, AX, DS, TC. 9 rooms with PB, 3 with FP, 2 suites and 1 conference room. Breakfast included in rates. Types of meals: Full bkfst and early coffee/tea. Beds: QDT. Cable TV, phone, fireplace three rooms and Jacuzzis in room. Air conditioning. VCR and library on premises. Handicap access. Amusement parks, antiquing, fishing, Air & Space Museum, Norticus, live theater, parks, shopping and water sports nearby.
Location: Historic small town.
Certificate may be used: Sunday through Thursday, all year, space available.

Spotsylvania   E15

Roxbury Mill B&B

6908 S Roxbury Mill Rd
Spotsylvania, VA 22553-2438
(540)582-6611
Internet: members.aol.com/roxburymil
E-mail: roxburymil@aol.com

Circa 1723. Once a working mill for the Roxbury Plantation, this early 18th-century home has seen the formation of a nation and the wars that would follow. Civil War relics have been found on the property, which includes a dam and millpond. The innkeepers strive to maintain a sense of history at their B&B, keeping the decor in Colonial to pre-Civil War styles. The large master suite affords a view of the river from its private deck, and the bed is an 18th-century antique. All guest rooms offer a view, private porch and antique furnishings. Traditional Southern-Colonial fare, from family recipes, fills the breakfast menu. Cornpone topped with slab bacon or country ham and biscuits are some of the appetizing choices. For late risers, the innkeepers also offer brunch.
Innkeeper(s): Joyce B. Ackerman. $75-150. MC, VISA, TC. 3 rooms, 2 with PB & 1 suite. Breakfast & afternoon tea included in rates. Types of meals: Full gourmet bkfst and early coffee/tea. Beds: QD. Cable TV, turndown service and ceiling fan in room. Air conditioning. VCR on premises. Amusement parks, antiquing, fishing, Civil War battlefields, museum, parks, shopping and water sports nearby.
Pets Allowed.
Certificate may be used: Nov. 1-March 15, Sunday through Thursday.

Stafford D15

Courthouse Road B&B

2247 Courthouse Rd
Stafford, VA 22554-5508
(540)720-3785 (800)720-3784 Fax:(540)720-3785
E-mail: courthouseinkeep@juno.com

Circa 1990. Of recent construction, this inn resembles Mount Vernon, the home of George Washington, 20 miles away. A breezeway filled with sunlight and a common room with fireplace invite guests to linger. The Fairfax suite includes two floors, and in addition to a vaulted ceiling and Jacuzzi, it has a private sitting room. Full breakfast and afternoon tea are served. Three acres of grounds include flower gardens, a gazebo, fountain and rose arbor. The area offers several Civil War battlefields, Presidential homes and Virginia wineries.

Innkeeper(s): Charlotte Patnode. $65-175. MC, VISA, PC, TC. 4 rooms, 2 with PB, 1 with FP and 1 suite. Breakfast and afternoon tea included in rates. Type of meal: Full bkfst. Beds: KQDT. Ceiling fan in room. Air conditioning. Fax and copier on premises. Antiquing, golf, parks and shopping nearby.
Location: Rural.
Publicity: *Courthouse Chronicle.*
Certificate may be used: Sunday-Thursday, no three-day weekend holidays.

Staunton E11

Ashton Country House

1205 Middlebrook Ave
Staunton, VA 24401-4546
(540)885-7819 (800)296-7819 Fax:(540)885-6029
Internet: www.bbhost.com/ashtonbnb

Circa 1860. This Greek Revival home is surrounded by 25 explorable acres where cows roam and birds frolic in the trees. A mix of traditional and Victorian antiques grace the interior. Four of the guest rooms include a fireplace, and each is appointed individually. The inn's porches, where afternoon tea often is served, are lined with chairs for those who seek relaxation and the scenery of rolling hills. Woodrow Wilson's  birthplace is among the town's notable attractions.

Innkeeper(s): Dorie & Vince Di Stefano. $70-125. MC, VISA, AX, PC, TC. 6 rooms with PB. Breakfast, afternoon tea and snacks/refreshments included in rates. Beds: Q. Ceiling fan and fireplaces (four bedrooms) in room. Central air. VCR on premises. Handicap access. Antiquing, fishing, museums, parks, shopping and water sports nearby.
Pets allowed: with prior arrangement.
Location: Country.
Certificate may be used: April 1 to Nov. 30, Sunday-Thursday.

Thornrose House at Gypsy Hill

531 Thornrose Ave
Staunton, VA 24401-3161
(540)885-7026 (800)861-4338

Circa 1912. A columned veranda wraps around two sides of this gracious red brick Georgian-style house. Two sets of Greek pergolas grace the lawns and there are gardens of azalea, rhododendron and hydrangea. The inn is furnished with a mix of antique oak and walnut period pieces and overstuffed English country chairs.

Bircher muesli, and hot-off-the-griddle whole grain banana pecan pancakes are popular breakfast items, served in the dining room (fireside on cool days). Across the street is a 300-acre park with lighted tennis courts, an 18-hole golf course and swimming pool.

Innkeeper(s): Otis & Suzy Huston. $69-89. 5 rooms with PB. Breakfast and afternoon tea included in rates. Type of meal: Full bkfst. Beds: KQDT. Turndown service and ceiling fan in room. Air conditioning. Antiquing, fishing, live theater, shopping and sporting events nearby.
"We enjoyed ourselves beyond measure, the accommodations, the food, your helpfulness, but most of all your gracious spirits."
Certificate may be used: Dec. 1-March 31, Sunday through Thursday, no holidays.

Surry H16

Seward House B&B

193 Colonial Trail E
Surry, VA 23883
(757)294-3810

Circa 1901. A long white porch, festooned with gingerbread and flowers, invites you to an old-fashioned visit at "Grandma's house." Family pieces and collections from three generations include toys, needlework and china. Ask for the Seward House omelet, a house specialty. Afterwards, enjoy the Chippokes Plantation State Park or cross the James River by ferry and visit Colonial Williamsburg.

Innkeeper(s): Jackie Bayer & Cindy Erskine. $65-80. AX, DS, PC, TC. 4 rooms, 2 with PB and 1 suite. Breakfast included in rates. Types of meals: Full bkfst and early coffee/tea. Beds: QDT. Ceiling fan in room. Air conditioning. VCR and bicycles on premises. Amusement parks, antiquing, parks and shopping nearby.
Location: Small town - agricultural.
Certificate may be used: Any day during promotion, except holidays.

Urbanna F17

Hewick Plantation

VSH 602/615, Box 82
Urbanna, VA 23175
(804)758-4214 Fax:(804)758-3115
Internet: www.hewick.com
E-mail: hewick1@oasisonline.com

Circa 1678. The innkeepers at Hewick Plantation are 10th- and 11th-generation descendants of Christopher Robinson, builder of Hewick Plantation and an original trustee of the College of William and Mary. Built of Flemish bond brick, this two-story Colonial home served as the base for a tobacco plantation. At one time, the property was a village unto itself with blacksmith, carpenter, cobbler and butcher shops. A driveway lined with large oak trees leads to the manor house. Now containing 66 acres, there is an ancient  family cemetery on the grounds. Quarters near the river housed plantation slaves. River docks were used for loading shipments of tobacco to England and receiving manufactured goods. A cross-stitch kit of Hewick Plantation, made by the Heirloom Needlecraft company, is available at the inn. The historic "Urbanna" coverlet is another unique item on display.

Innkeeper(s): Helen Battleson. $99-158. MC, VISA, AX, DS, PC, TC. 2 rooms with PB, 2 with FP. Breakfast included in rates. Type of meal: Cont plus. Beds: QDT. Cable TV and phone in room. Air conditioning. Fax and stables on premises. Sailing, antiquing, fishing, parks and shopping nearby.
Publicity: *Richmond Times, Dispatch, Washington Post, Daily Press, Pleasant Living., Channel 8 - Richmond, WRIC-TV and TV-Tokyo.*
Certificate may be used: Nov. 15-April 15, Monday through Wednesday.

Warm Springs   E10

Three Hills Inn

PO Box 9
Warm Springs, VA 24484-0009
(540)839-5381 (888)234-4557 Fax:(540)839-5199
Internet: www.3hills.com
E-mail: inn@3hills.com

Circa 1913. Mary Johnston, who wrote the book "To Have and to Hold," built this inn, which rests on 38 mountainous acres. In 1917, Mary and her sisters opened the home to guests, earning a reputation for the home's view of the Allegheny Mountains and Warm Springs Gap. The innkeepers now offer lodging in the antique-filled main house or adjacent cottages. Some rooms include private decks, while others have fireplaces or clawfoot tubs. Each of the cottages includes a kitchen; one has a working fireplace, while another offers a wood-burning stove.
Innkeeper(s): Julie Miller. $69-189. MC, VISA, DS, PC, TC. 10 rooms with PB, 3 with FP, 7 suites and 2 cottages. Breakfast included in rates. Type of meal: Full bkfst. Beds: KQDT. Cable TV in room. VCR, fax, copier, child care, boardroom that seats 12, and a conference center that seats 80 and hiking on premises. Antiquing, fishing, hiking, thermal "spa" warm spring pools, live theater, parks, shopping, downhill skiing and cross-country skiing nearby.
Pets allowed: In rooms with outside door.
Location: Mountains.
Publicity: *Listed on "Women of Virginia Historic Trail".*
Certificate may be used: Anytime, except weekends July-October and major (legal) holidays.

Washington   C13

Caledonia Farm - 1812

47 Dearing Rd (Flint Hill)
Washington, VA 22627
(540)675-3693 (800)262-1812 Fax:(540)675-3693
Internet: www.bnb-n-va.com/cale1812.htm

Circa 1812. This gracious Federal-style stone house in the National Register is beautifully situated on 52 acres adjacent to Shenandoah National Park. It was built by a Revolutionary War officer, and his musket is displayed over a mantel. The house, a Virginia Historic Landmark, has been restored with the original Colonial color scheme retained. All rooms have

working fireplaces and provide views of Skyline Drive and the Blue Ridge Mountains. The innkeeper is a retired broadcaster.
Innkeeper(s): Phil Irwin. $140. MC, VISA, DS, PC, TC. 2 suites, 3 with FP and 1 conference room. Breakfast and snacks/refreshments included in rates. Types of meals: Full gourmet bkfst and early coffee/tea. Beds: D. Phone, turndown service, VCR and skyline Drive View in room. Air conditioning. Fax, copier, spa, bicycles, library, hayride and lawn games on premises. Antiquing, fishing, wineries, caves, stables, battlefields, live theater, parks, shopping, downhill skiing, cross-country skiing and water sports nearby.
Location: Mountains.
Publicity: *Country, Country Almanac, Country Living, Blue Ridge Country, Discovery, Washington Post, Baltimore Sun and Pen TV/Cable 15/PBS X3.*
"We've stayed at many, many B&Bs. This is by far the best!"
Certificate may be used: Non-holiday, Sunday-Wednesday, Jan. 2-Sept. 15.

Fairlea Farm Bed & Breakfast

636 Mt Salem Ave, PO Box 124
Washington, VA 22747-0124
(540)675-3679 Fax:(540)675-1064
E-mail: longyear@shentel.net

Circa 1960. View acres of rolling hills, farmland and the Blue Ridge Mountains from this fieldstone house. Rooms are decorated with crocheted canopies and four-poster beds. Plants and floral bedcovers add a homey feel. The stone terrace is set up for relaxing with chairs lined along the edge. As a young surveyor, George Washington inspected the boundaries of this historic village, which is just a short walk from Fairlea Farm, a working sheep and cattle farm.
Innkeeper(s): Susan & Walt Longyear. $85-135. PC, TC. 3 rooms with PB and 1 suite. Breakfast and afternoon tea included in rates. Types of meals: Full gourmet bkfst and early coffee/tea. Beds: QT. Turndown service in room. Air conditioning. VCR, fax and copier on premises. Antiquing, fishing, horseback riding, vineyards, Shenandoah National Park, Civil War battlefields and live theater nearby.
Location: Village/working farm.
Certificate may be used: All year, suite only: Sunday through Thursday, except holidays.

Gay Street Inn

160 Gay St
Washington, VA 22747
(540)675-3288 Fax:(540)675-1070
E-mail: gaystinn@shentel.net

Circa 1855. After a day of Skyline Drive, Shenandoah National Park and the caverns of Luray and Front Royal, come home to this stucco, gabled farmhouse. If you've booked the fireplace room, a canopy bed will await you. Furnishings include period Shaker pieces. The innkeepers will be happy to steer you to the most interesting vineyards, organic "pick-your-own"

fruit and vegetable farms and Made-In-Virginia food and craft shops. Breakfast and afternoon tea are served in the garden conservatory. Five-star dining is within walking distance at The Inn at Little Washington. The innkeepers can arrange for child care.
Innkeeper(s): Robin & Donna Kevis. $95-135. MC, VISA, AX, PC, TC. 4 rooms with PB, 1 with FP and 1 suite. Breakfast and afternoon tea included in rates. Types of meals: Full gourmet bkfst, cont plus and early coffee/tea. Beds: Q. Air conditioning. Child care available and limited on premises. Handicap access. Antiquing, fishing, golf, horseback riding, vineyards, live theater, parks, shopping and water sports nearby.
Pets Allowed.
Location: Rural town.
Publicity: *Blue Ridge Country and Food Art.*
"Thank you for a wonderful visit. Your hospitality was superb."
Certificate may be used: Sunday through Thursday, excluding holidays and three-day weekends.

White Stone   F17

Flowering Fields B&B

232 Flowering Field
White Stone, VA 22578-9722
(804)435-6238 Fax:(804)435-6238

Circa 1790. Guests will find plenty to do at this Victorian bed & breakfast. The game room is stocked with a pool table, games, darts, cable TV and a fireplace. The grounds are shared by the innkeepers friendly dogs, cat and several horses. The parlor is a bit more formal, and the music room includes a baby grand piano.

Complimentary beverages are available around the clock. The morning begins with a huge breakfast. Innkeeper Lloyd Niziol's famous crab cakes, fresh fruit, omelets, French toast and fried apples are among the possibilities. The innkeepers will plan the meal around guests' dietary restrictions. Guest rooms include items such as a four-poster rice bed, antiques, Queen Anne chairs and Oriental rugs. The innkeepers welcome families with children.

Innkeeper(s): Lloyd Niziol & Susan Moenssens. $75-120. PC, TC. 5 rooms, 2 with PB, 1 suite and 1 conference room. Breakfast, afternoon tea and snacks/refreshments included in rates. Types of meals: Full gourmet bkfst and early coffee/tea. Beds: KQDT. Ceiling fan, some cable, some desks and sitting area in room. Air conditioning. VCR, fax, copier, bicycles, library, advance notification for handicap access and first floor room with private bath on premises. Antiquing, fishing, Williamsburg, parks, shopping & water sports nearby.

Certificate may be used: Jan. 1-Dec. 31, Sunday-Thursday, excluding holiday weekends (Thanksgiving, Fourth of July, Memorial, Labor Day, Christmas).

Williamsburg   G17

Cedars

616 Jamestown Rd
Williamsburg, VA 23185-3945
(757)229-3591 (800)296-3591

Circa 1930. This three-story brick Georgian home is a short walk from Colonial Williamsburg and is located across from William and Mary College. Rooms are decorated with Traditional antiques, Colonial reproductions, fireplaces and four-poster or canopy beds. The bountiful breakfasts include a hearty entree, fresh fruits, breads, muffins and cereals.

Innkeeper(s): Carol, Jim & Brona Malecha. $76-180. MC, VISA, PC, TC. 8 rooms with PB, 2 with FP, 2 suites and 1 cottage. Breakfast included in rates. Types of meals: Full bkfst and early coffee/tea. Beds: KQT. TV and ceiling fan in room. Air conditioning. Library on premises. Amusement parks, antiquing, historic sites, parks and shopping nearby.

Location: Colonial Williamsburg.

Certificate may be used: Jan. 2-March 13, excluding holiday weekends.

Homestay B&B

517 Richmond Rd
Williamsburg, VA 23185-3537
(757)229-7468 (800)836-7468 Fax:(757)229-0126
Internet: www.williamsburg-virginia.com/homestay

Circa 1933. This Colonial Revival house is decorated with Victorian pieces inherited from the innkeeper's family. A screened back porch and fireplace in the living room are gathering spots. Collections of hand-crafted Noah's arks may be found throughout the house. The College of William and Mary is adjacent, and Colonial Williamsburg's is four blocks away.

Innkeeper(s): James Thomassen. $90-100. MC, VISA. 3 rooms with PB. Breakfast included in rates. Type of meal: Full bkfst. Beds: KT. Ceiling fan in room. Air conditioning. VCR on premises. Amusement parks, antiquing, live theater and sporting events nearby.

"Our stay at your inn has been wonderful. Thank you so much for your warm and gracious welcome."

Certificate may be used: Jan. & Feb., except holidays. March through December, Sunday-Thursday, except holidays & special events. Pre-payment by check only.

Williamsburg Sampler

922 Jamestown Rd
Williamsburg, VA 23185-3917
(757)253-0398 (800)722-1169 Fax:(757)253-2669
Internet: www.williamsburgsampler.com
E-mail: WbgSampler@aol.com

Circa 1976. Although this 18th-century-style home was built in the year of the bicentennial, it captures the early American spirit of Colonial Williamsburg. The rooms serve as wonderful replicas

of an elegant Colonial home, with antiques, pewter and framed American and English samplers found throughout the inn. Bedchambers, which include suites with fireplaces, TV and "Roof Top Garden," are cozy with rice-carved, four-poster beds and Colonial decor. Guests can test their skill at checkers or curl up with a book in the 1827 armchair in the Tavern Reading Room, or watch premium cable TV in the Common Keeping Room. The innkeepers term the morning meal at the Rooster's Den a "Skip Lunch® breakfast," an apt description of the colossal menu. If guests can move after this wonderful meal, they head out for a day exploring historic Williamsburg. Virginia's Governor has proclaimed Williamsburg Sampler as "Inn of the Year."

Innkeeper(s): Helen & Ike Sisane. $110-160. PC. 4 rooms with PB, 2 with FP and 2 suites. Breakfast included in rates. Type of meal: Full bkfst. Beds: KQ. Cable TV, ceiling fan, VCR, refrigerator and fireplace (suites) in room. Air conditioning. Fax and copier on premises. Amusement parks, antiquing, fishing, golf, live theater, parks, shopping, sporting events, tennis and water sports nearby.

Certificate may be used: Midweek only (Monday-Thursday), Jan. 3-27, Feb. 1-24 (holidays excluded).

Woolwine   I9

The Mountain Rose B&B Inn

1787 Charity Hwy
Woolwine, VA 24185
(540)930-1057 Fax:(540)930-2165
Internet: www.mountainrose-inn.com
E-mail: mtrosein@swva.net

Circa 1901. This historic Victorian inn, once the home of the Mountain Rose Distillery, sits on 100 acres of forested hills with plenty of hiking trails. A trout-stocked stream goes through the property and a swimming pool pro-vides recreation. Each room has an antique manteled fireplace, some of which have been converted to gas logs. Guests can relax by the pool or in rocking chairs on one of the six porches. The innkeepers look forward to providing guests with casually elegant hospitality in the Blue Ridge Mountains. The Blue Ridge Parkway, Mabury Mill, The Reynolds Homestead, Laurel Hill J. EB Stuart Birthplace, Patrick County Courthouse and the Patrick County Historical Museum are located nearby. A three-course breakfast is offered every morning.

Innkeeper(s): Melodie Pogue & Reeves Simms. $89-119. MC, VISA, DS, PC, TC. 5 rooms with PB, 5 with FP. Breakfast and afternoon tea included in rates. Types of meals: Full gourmet bkfst and early coffee/tea. Beds: KQDT. Air conditioning. VCR, fax, copier, swimming, bicycles and trout-stocked creek on premises. Antiquing, fishing, golf, hiking, Nascar racing, parks, shopping, tennis, water sports and wineries nearby.

Location: Mountains.

Publicity: *Enterprise, Bill Mountain Bugle, New York Times, The Parkway Edition and City Magazine.*

Certificate may be used: Nov. 1-May 30, Sunday-Thursday.

Washington

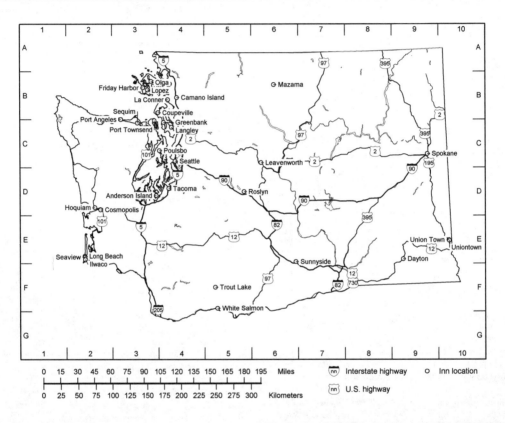

	1	2	3	4	5	6	7	8	9	10	

Map locations: Olga, Friday Harbor, Lopez, La Conner, Camano Island, Mazama, Sequim, Coupeville, Port Angeles, Greenbank, Port Townsend, Langley, Poulsbo, Seattle, Leavenworth, Spokane, Tacoma, Anderson Island, Roslyn, Hoquiam, Cosmopolis, Union Town, Uniontown, Seaview, Long Beach, Ilwaco, Sunnyside, Dayton, Trout Lake, White Salmon

| 0 15 30 45 60 75 90 105 120 135 150 165 180 195 | Miles |
| 0 25 50 75 100 125 150 175 200 225 250 275 300 | Kilometers |

Interstate highway Inn location
U.S. highway

Anderson Island   D3

The Inn at Burg's Landing

8808 Villa Beach Rd
Anderson Island, WA 98303-9785
(206)884-9185 Fax:(206)488-8682
E-mail: innatburgslanding@mailexcite.com

Circa 1987. A short ferry trip from Steilacoom and Tacoma, this
log homestead boasts beautiful views of Mt. Rainier, Puget
Sound and the Cascade Mountains.
The master bedroom features
a skylight and a private
whirlpool bath. After a full
breakfast, guests can spend
the day at the inn's private
beach. Golf, hiking and fresh-

water lakes are nearby, and the area has many seasonal activities,
including Fourth of July fireworks, the Anderson Island fair and
parade in September.

Innkeeper(s): Ken & Annie Burg. $75-110. MC, VISA, PC, TC. 4 rooms, 2
with PB. Breakfast included in rates. Type of meal: Full bkfst. Beds: Q. VCR in
room. Spa on premises. Amusement parks, fishing, parks, shopping and
downhill skiing nearby.

Location: Puget Sound.

Publicity: *Sunset, Tacoma News Tribune, Portland Oregonian and Seattle Times.*

Certificate may be used: Sunday-Thursday, May 1-Sept. 30, Oct. 1-April
30, anytime.

Camano Island   B4

The Inn at Barnum Point

464 S Barnum Rd
Camano Island, WA 98292-8510
(360)387-2256 (800)910-2256 Fax:(360)387-2256
Internet: www.whidbey.com/inn/
E-mail: barnum@camano.net

Circa 1991. This Cape Cod-style house is located on the bay.
Guests enjoy listening to the water lap at the shoreline, watching deer in the orchard and sneaking a kiss under the apple
tree. (The orchard was planted by the innkeeper's family in
1904.) The newest accommodation is the 900-square-foot
Shorebird Room with deck, fireplace and soaking tub overlooking Port Susan Bay and the Cascade Mountains.

Innkeeper(s): Carolin Barnum Dilorenzo. $89-185. MC, VISA, DS, PC, TC. 3
rooms with PB, 3 with FP. Breakfast included in rates. Types of meals: Full
gourmet bkfst and early coffee/tea. Beds: Q. TV, phone and VCR in room.
Fax, copier, swimming and child care on premises. Antiquing, golf, live theater, parks, shopping, downhill skiing and water sports nearby.

Certificate may be used: Oct. 15-March 15, Sunday through Thursday,
no holidays.

Cosmopolis   D2

Cooney Mansion B&B

PO Box 54, 1705 Fifth St
Cosmopolis, WA 98537-0054
(360)533-0602
Internet: www.come.to/cooneymansion
E-mail: cooney@techline.com

Circa 1908. This former lumber magnate's home, in a wooded
setting, boasts 37 rooms. In the National Register, it was built
with a ballroom in the daylight basement, nine bedrooms and
eight bathrooms. There are soaking tubs in all of the rooms. The
inn features original mission furnishings, and the Cooney suite
has a fireplace, TV and VCR and original "rainfall" shower. Guests
can enjoy the National Award Winning Lumber Baron's Breakfast.

Innkeeper(s): Judi & Jim Lohr. $75-185. MC, VISA, DC, DS. 8 rooms, 5 with
PB, 1 with FP, 1 suite and 1 conference room. Breakfast and afternoon tea
included in rates. Types of meals: Full bkfst and early coffee/tea. Beds: KQDT.
VCR, fax, spa, sauna and golf on premises. Antiquing, fishing, golf, whale
watching, rain forest, live theater, parks, shopping, sporting events, tennis
and water sports nearby.

Location: Small town on river.

Publicity: *Sunset Magazine, Travel & Leisure, Country Inns and Northwest Travel.*

*"A good B&B should offer the comforts of home, serenity, relaxation
and good company. You gave us all we expected and more. Thanks for
a romantic weekend."*

Certificate may be used: Sept. 15-May 15, Sunday-Friday, holidays excluded.

Coupeville   B4

Captain Whidbey Inn

2072 W Captain Whidbey Inn Rd
Coupeville, WA 98239
(360)678-4097 (800)366-4097 Fax:(360)678-4110

Circa 1907. Overlooking Whidbey Island's Penn Cove, this
log inn has comfortable rooms featuring down comforters,
feather beds and views of lagoons and gardens. The dining

room also has a magnifi-
cent view and guests can
enjoy their meals by the
fireplace. The chef uti-
lizes local catches such
as steelhead, salmon,
spot prawns and Penn
Cove mussels. The
proprietor is also a sail-
ing captain, and guests can book an afternoon on his 52-
foot ketch, Cutty Sark. The proprietor's family has run the
inn for more than 30 years.

Innkeeper(s): Dennis A. Argent. $95-225. MC, VISA, AX, DC, DS. 32 rooms,
20 with PB, 7 with FP and 1 conference room. Breakfast included in rates.
Type of meal: Full bkfst. Beds: KQD. Phone in room. Fax, copier, sailing and
fishing on premises. Antiquing, museums and shopping nearby.

Publicity: *Gourmet Magazine and USA-Weekend.*

"I visit and stay here once a year and love it."

Certificate may be used: October-May, Sunday-Thursday, excluding special
events/holidays.

Colonel Crockett Farm

1012 S Fort Casey Rd
Coupeville, WA 98239-9753
(360)678-3711
Internet: www.crockettfarm.com
E-mail: email@crockettfarm.com

Circa 1855. In the National Register, this Victorian farmhouse
presides over 40 island acres of lawns, meadows and country
gardens. Sweeping views of Crockett Lake and Admiralty Inlet
may be enjoyed from the inn and its grounds. The Crockett
Room, a favorite of newlyweds, has a blue chintz canopied bed
and fainting couch. Danny DeVito, Michael Douglas and
Kathleen Turner stayed at the inn during the Coupeville filming
of War of the Roses.

Innkeeper(s): Bob & Beulah Whitlow. $75-105. MC, VISA. 5 rooms with PB.
Breakfast included in rates. Type of meal: Full bkfst. Beds: KQD. Antiquing,
live theater and shopping nearby.

Location: Country.

Publicity: *Peninsula, Portland Oregonian, Country Inns and Glamour.*

"Everyone felt quite at home...such a beautiful spot."

Certificate may be used: October through April, Sunday (except on three-day
holiday weekends) through Thursday (except Thanksgiving and Christmas).

Inn at Penn Cove

702 N Main, PO Box 85
Coupeville, WA 98239-0085
(360)678-8000 (800)688-2683

Circa 1887. Two restored historic houses, one a fanciful white
and peach Italianate confection in the National Register, comprise
the inn. Each house contains only three guest rooms affording a
variety of small parlors for guests to enjoy. The most romantic
accommodation is Desiree's Room with a fireplace, a whirlpool
tub for two and mesmerizing views of Puget Sound and Mt. Baker.

Innkeeper(s): Gladys & Mitchell Howard. $75-125. MC, VISA, AX, DS, PC,
TC. 6 rooms, 4 with PB, 3 with FP and 1 conference room. Type of meal:
Full bkfst. Beds: KQ. TV, phone and ceiling fan in room. VCR, game room,
puzzles and board games on premises. Antiquing and shopping nearby.

Location: Waterside village.

Publicity: *Whidbey News-Times, Country Inns and Glamour.*

*"Our hosts were warm and friendly, but also gave us plenty of space
and privacy - a good combination."*

Certificate may be used: Oct. 15-March 15, Sunday-Friday; March 15-June
15, Sunday-Thursday.

The Victorian B&B

602 N Main
Coupeville, WA 98239-0761
(360)678-5305

Circa 1889. This graceful Italianate Victorian sits in the heart of one of the nation's few historic reserves. It was built for German immigrant Jacob Jenne, who became the proprietor of the Central Hotel on Front Street. Noted for having the first running water on the island, the house's old wooden water tower stands in the back garden. An old-fashioned storefront, once the local dentist's office, sits demurely behind a picket fence, now a private hideaway for guests.

Innkeeper(s): Alfred Sasso. $65-100. MC, VISA. 3 rooms with PB and 1 suite. Breakfast included in rates. Type of meal: Full bkfst. Beds: Q. TV and phone in room. VCR on premises. Antiquing, fishing, live theater and shopping nearby.
Location: City.

Publicity: *Seattle Times and Country Inns.*

"If kindness and generosity are the precursors to success (and I certainly hope they are!), your success is assured."

Certificate may be used: October through May, Sunday through Friday.

Dayton
E9

The Purple House

415 E Clay St
Dayton, WA 99328-1348
(509)382-3159 (800)486-2574

Circa 1882. History buffs will adore this aptly named bed & breakfast, colored in deep purple tones with white, gingerbread trim. The home, listed in the National Register, is the perfect place to enjoy Dayton, which boasts two historic districts and a multitude of preserved Victorian homes. Innkeeper Christine Williscroft has filled the home with antiques and artwork. A highly praised cook, Christine prepares the European-style full breakfasts, as well as mouthwatering afternoon refreshments. Guests can relax in the richly appointed parlor or library, and the grounds also include a swimming pool.

Innkeeper(s): D. Christine Williscroft. $85-125. MC, VISA. 4 rooms, 2 with PB, 1 with FP and 1 suite. Breakfast and afternoon tea included in rates. Types of meals: Full gourmet bkfst and early coffee/tea. Beds: QD. Phone and ceiling fan in room. Air conditioning. VCR, swimming, library and pet boarding on premises. Handicap access. Antiquing, fishing, live theater, parks, shopping, downhill skiing, cross-country skiing, sporting events and water sports nearby.
Pets Allowed.
Location: City.
Publicity: *Sunset.*

"You have accomplished so very much with your bed & breakfast to make it a very special place to stay."

Certificate may be used: Monday through Thursday.

Weinhard Hotel

235 E Main St
Dayton, WA 99328-1352
(509)382-4032 Fax:(509)382-2640
Internet: www.weinhard.com

Circa 1890. This luxurious Victorian bed & breakfast, tucked at the base of the scenic Blue Mountains, originally served up spirits as the Weinhard Saloon and Lodge Hall. Guests are transported back to the genteel Victorian era during their stay. After a restful sleep among period pieces, ornate carpeting and ceilings fans, guests might imagine the days when horses and buggies road through town. While the innkeepers have worked to preserve the history of the hotel, they didn't forget such modern luxuries as Jacuzzi tubs in the private baths. The hotel boasts a beautiful Victorian roof garden, a perfect place to relax with a cup of tea or gourmet coffee. For a unique weekend, try the hotel's special Romantic Getaway package. Guests are presented with sparkling wine or champagne and a dozen roses. The package also includes a five-course meal.

Innkeeper(s): Virginia Butler. $70-125. MC, VISA. 15 rooms with PB. Breakfast included in rates. Beds: Q.
Pets Allowed.
Publicity: *Seattle Times, Daily Journal of Commerce, Sunset Magazine, Lewiston Morning Tribune, San Francisco Examiner and Spokesman Review.*
"It's spectacular! Thank you so much for all your kindness and caring hospitality."

Certificate may be used: Sunday-Thursday, year-round, except May 26-29, July 14-17, Sept. 1-5, excluding special events and holidays.

Friday Harbor
B3

San Juan Inn B&B

50 Spring St, Box 776
Friday Harbor, WA 98250-0776
(360)378-2070 (800)742-8210 Fax:(360)378-6437

Circa 1873. In the National Register, this old European-style hotel is filled with stained glass, old photographs and flowers picked from the inn's garden. A Victorian settee is situated under a cherry tree within sniffing distance of the lilacs and roses. It's a half-block to the ferry landing. The innkeeper speaks Danish, German, Norwegian, French, Swedish and English.

Innkeeper(s): Annette & Skip Metzger, Linda Francis. $65-225. MC, VISA, AX, DS, PC, TC. 10 rooms, 4 with PB and 2 suites. Breakfast included in rates. Type of meal: Cont plus. Beds: KQDT. Cable TV, ceiling fan and VCR in room. Fax and spa on premises. Fishing, live theater, parks, shopping and water sports nearby.
Pets allowed: Small dogs under 40 pounds.
Location: City.

Certificate may be used: Oct. 15-April 30, Sunday-Thursday.

States Inn

2039 W Valley Rd
Friday Harbor, WA 98250-9211
(360)378-6240 Fax:(360)378-6241
Internet: www.karuna.com/statesinn
E-mail: paschal@rockisland.com

Circa 1910. This sprawling ranch home has ten guest rooms, each named and themed for a particular state. The Arizona and New Mexico rooms, often booked by families or couples traveling together, can be combined to create a private suite with two bedrooms, a bathroom and a sitting area. The oldest part of the  house was built as a country school and later used as a dance hall, before it was relocated to its current 60-acre spread. Baked French toast, accompanied by fresh fruit topped with yogurt sauce and homemade muffins are typical breakfast fare.

Innkeeper(s): Alan & Julia Paschal. $85-125. MC, VISA, PC, TC. 10 rooms, 8 with PB, 1 with FP and 1 suite. Breakfast included in rates. Type of meal: Full bkfst. Beds: KQDT. Fax and stables on premises. Handicap access. Antiquing, fishing, golf, kayaks, whale watching, live theater, parks, shopping and water sports nearby.
Location: Country.
Publicity: *Glamour, Conde Nast and USA Today.*
Certificate may be used: Oct. 1 to March 31, entire week.

Tucker House B&B With Cottages

260 B St
Friday Harbor, WA 98250-8074
(360)378-2783 (800)965-0123 Fax:(360)378-6437
Internet: www.tuckerhouse.com
E-mail: info@tuckerhouse.com

Circa 1898. Only one block from the ferry landing, the white picket fence bordering Tucker House is a welcome sight for guests. The spindled entrance leads to the parlor. The home includes three guest rooms that share a bath. The rooms are decorated with antiques. The innkeepers also offer self-contained cottages that include private baths, kitchenettes, queen beds, TVs and VCRs. All guests enjoy use of the outdoor hot tub. The inn's breakfasts are served in the solarium.

Innkeeper(s): Alan & Julia Paschal. $115-200. MC, VISA, PC, TC. 6 rooms, 2 suites and 3 cottages. Breakfast included in rates. Type of meal: Full bkfst. Beds: Q. Cable TV and VCR in room. Spa on premises. Antiquing, fishing, live theater, parks, shopping and water sports nearby.

Pets allowed: Dogs under 40 pounds; $15 per evening per dog, limit two.

Publicity: *Sunset, Pacific Northwest Magazine and Western Boatman.*

"A lovely place, the perfect getaway. We'll be back."

Certificate may be used: Oct. 16-April 15.

Greenbank   C4

Guest House Log Cottages

24371-SR 525, Whidbey Island
Greenbank, WA 98253
(360)678-3115
Internet: www.whidbey.net/logcottages
E-mail: guesthse@whidbey.net

These storybook cottages and log home are nestled within a peaceful forest on 25 acres. The log cabin features stained-glass and criss-cross paned windows that give it the feel of a gingerbread house. Four of the cottages are log construction. Ask for the Lodge and enjoy a private setting with a pond just beyond the deck. Inside are two Jacuzzi tubs, a stone fireplace, king bed, antiques and a luxurious atmosphere.

Innkeeper(s): Don & Mary Jane Creger. $125. MC, VISA, AX, DS, PC, TC. 6 cottages. Breakfast included in rates. Type of meal: Full bkfst. Beds: KQ. Ceiling fan, VCR, kitchen and Jacuzzi in room. Air conditioning. Fax, copier, spa and swimming on premises. Antiquing, fishing, golf, parks, shopping and tennis nearby.

Location: Island - wooded.

Publicity: *Los Angeles Times, Woman's Day, Sunset, Country Inns and Bride's.*

"The wonderful thing is to be by yourselves and rediscover what's important."

Certificate may be used: Midweek Monday, Tuesday, Wednesday, Thursday, either Farm Guest or Carriage House cottages, Nov. 1-March 15.

Hoquiam   D2

Lytle House

509 Chenault Ave
Hoquiam, WA 98550-1821
(360)533-2320 Fax:(360)533-4025

Circa 1900. Set high on a hill overlooking the harbor, this massive three-story Queen Anne Victorian was built by a lumberman. There are graceful sun porches, arches and gingerbread trim. The Treehouse Room is shaded by a 100-foot copper beech tree, while the Rose Room offers a view of the harbor.

Afternoon tea is available. The innkeepers will host a murder-mystery dinner party or elegant high tea by prior arrangement.

Innkeeper(s): Robert Bencala. $65-125. MC, VISA, AX. 8 rooms and 1 suite. Breakfast included in rates. Types of meals: Full bkfst and early coffee/tea. VCR on premises. Antiquing, live theater and shopping nearby.

Location: Harbor view.

Certificate may be used: Sept. 15-May 1, excluding holidays. Some restrictions may apply.

Ilwaco   E2

Chick A Dee Inn at Ilwaco

120 NE Williams
Ilwaco, WA 98624
(360)642-8686 (888)244-2523 Fax:(360)642-8642

Circa 1879. A weathered, shingled New England-style building, the Inn at Ilwaco was originally the Community Presbyterian Church. The former sanctuary is now used for weddings, seminars, concerts and reunions. Some rooms have views of a stream that meanders by and the Columbia River seaport is two blocks away. Excursions include salmon fishing charters, clam digging, horseback riding, and visiting the cranberry bogs.

Innkeeper(s): Ed & Karen Bussone. $79-189. MC, VISA. 9 rooms with PB, 2 with FP, 3 suites and 2 conference rooms. Breakfast and picnic lunch included in rates. Types of meals: Full gourmet bkfst and early coffee/tea. Beds: KQ. Cable TV in room. VCR, fax, copier, bicycles and library on premises. Amusement parks, antiquing, fishing, golf, beach, live theater, parks, shopping, tennis and water sports nearby.

Location: Lighthouses, forts.

Certificate may be used: Nov. 1-April 30.

La Conner   B4

Katy's Inn

503 S Third
La Conner, WA 98257-0869
(360)466-3366 (800)914-7767
Internet: home.ncia.com/katysinn/
E-mail: katysinn@juno.com

Circa 1882. This pristinely renovated farmhouse is framed by flower gardens and a white picket fence. Victorian wallpapers enhance a collection of antique furnishings. Each guest room opens to the veranda or balcony, providing a view of the countryside. Bicycles and boats can be rented from the village two blocks away.

Innkeeper(s): Bruce & Kathie Hubbard. $90-125. MC, VISA, DS. 4 rooms with PB. Breakfast and snacks/refreshments included in rates. Types of meals: Full bkfst and early coffee/tea. Beds: QD. Spa on premises. Antiquing, fishing, museum, ferry to San Juan Island, parks, shopping and water sports nearby.

"The most charming and warmest of the B&Bs in which we stayed."

Certificate may be used: January & February, Sunday-Thursday.

The White Swan Guest House

15872 Moore Rd
La Conner, WA 98273-9249
(360)445-6805

Circa 1898. Guests will marvel at innkeeper Peter Goldfarb's beautiful gardens as they wind up the driveway to reach this charming, yellow Victorian farmhouse. Inside, guests are greeted with luscious home-baked chocolate chip cookies in the bright, cheery kitchen and a vegetarian breakfast in the morning. Guest rooms are filled with comfortable, Victorian furnishings, and there's even a cozy Garden Cottage to stay in, complete with its own kitchen and private sun deck. Each April, the area is host to the Skagit Valley Tulip festival. La Conner, a nearby fishing village, is full of shops and galleries to explore.

Innkeeper(s): Peter Goldfarb. $75-150. MC, VISA, PC, TC. 3 rooms and 1 cottage. Breakfast included in rates. Types of meals: Cont plus and early coffee/tea. Beds: KQD. Turndown service in room. Antiquing, fishing, art museum and galleries, parks and shopping nearby.

Location: Country.

Publicity: *Country Home, Bird & Blooms and Ernst Commercial.*

"This has been a very pleasant interlude. What a beautiful, comfortable place you have here. We will be back."

Certificate may be used: October-March, Sunday-Friday in main house only.

Langley   C4

Island Tyme, Bed & Breakfast Inn

4940 S Bayview Rd
Langley, WA 98260-9778
(360)221-5078 (800)898-8963

Circa 1993. Located on Whidbey Island, this Victorian is a whimsical mix of colors topped with gingerbread trim and a turret. The inn's 10 acres ensure solitude, and romantic amenities abound. The Heirloom Suite boasts both a fireplace and a Jacuzzi tub for two. The Turret room is tucked into the inn's tower and also offers a Jacuzzi tub for two. Quilts, antiques and collectibles are found throughout the guest rooms. The dining room, where the country breakfasts are served, is located in the inn's turret.

Innkeeper(s): Lyn & Phil Fauth. $90-140. MC, VISA, AX, PC, TC. 5 rooms with PB, 2 with FP and 1 suite. Breakfast and snacks/refreshments included in rates. Types of meals: Full gourmet bkfst and early coffee/tea. Beds: KQ. Cable TV, phone, turndown service, ceiling fan, VCR and fireplace in two rooms in room. Library, pet boarding and child care on premises. Handicap access. Antiquing, fishing, live theater, parks, shopping and water sports nearby.

Pets allowed: In Keepsake Room only.

Location: Small lake 1/2 mile away.

Publicity: *Whidbey Record.*

Certificate may be used: Nov. 1 to April 15, except third weekend of February. No holidays.

Saratoga Inn

PO Box 428
Langley, WA 98260
(360)221-5801 (800)698-2910 Fax:(360)221-5804

This romantic, island inn is located away from the hustle and bustle of Seattle. To reach the inn, guests hop aboard a ferry and take a 20-minute journey from the city to quiet Whidbey Island. The inn offers 15 elegantly appointed guest rooms, each with a fireplace. Each room also boasts a water view. Guests enjoy a full breakfast and afternoon tea with a variety of goodies. Guests can spend the day exploring the island, or hop aboard the ferry to visit the sites of Seattle. Saratoga Inn is a Four Sisters Inn.

Innkeeper(s): Jessica Anderegg. $110-250. MC, VISA, AX. 15 rooms with PB, 15 with FP. Breakfast and afternoon tea included in rates. Types of meals: Full gourmet bkfst and early coffee/tea. Beds: KQ. Phone and turndown service in room. Fax and bicycles on premises. Handicap access.

Certificate may be used: November through June, Sunday through Thursday, excluding holidays and special events.

Twickenham House B&B Inn

5023 S Langley Rd
Langley, WA 98260-9609
(360)221-2334
Internet: www.nwculture.com
E-mail: twcknham@whidbey.com

Circa 1990. If the beauty of Puget Sound isn't enough, this island inn will be sure to satisfy. The inn offers comfortable rooms with French Canadian and European pine furniture, and a gourmet, three-course breakfast is served each morning. The home has three living rooms with fireplaces and a British pub area. The inn shares the expansive 10-acre grounds with Northwest evergreens, ducks, sheep, hens and roosters. The island has many restaurants, boutiques and shops. Langley holds several seasonal events, including a country fair and a mystery weekend.

Innkeeper(s): Maureen & Ray Cooke. $85-120. MC, VISA. 6 rooms with PB and 2 suites. Breakfast included in rates. Types of meals: Full gourmet bkfst and early coffee/tea. Beds: Q. VCR on premises. Antiquing, fishing, british pub, live theater, shopping and water sports nearby.

Location: Country.

Publicity: *Sunset, Country Living, Oregonian and Odyssey.*

"Gracious and friendly hosts."

Certificate may be used: Monday-Thursday, excluding holiday periods.

Leavenworth   C6

Autumn Pond B&B

10388 Titus Rd
Leavenworth, WA 98826-9509
(509)548-4482 (800)222-9661
Internet: www.autumnpond.com
E-mail: info@autumnpond.com

Circa 1992. This modern ranch-style home is set at the base of the Cascade Mountains and offers stunning views, which one can enjoy from the outdoor hot tub. The interior is welcoming, with bright, flowery prints on the beds and country furnishings. Exposed beams add a rustic touch to the dining area and living room. Guests can feed the ducks at the pond or fish for trout. After a homemade breakfast, head into Leavenworth and explore the shops and sites of this historic Bavarian town.

Innkeeper(s): John & Jennifer Lorenz. $69-99. MC, VISA, AX, PC. 6 rooms with PB. Breakfast included in rates. Types of meals: Full bkfst and early coffee/tea. Beds: Q. Air conditioning. Pond on premises. Antiquing, fishing, golf, whitewater rafting, cross country skiing, hiking, mountain biking, live theater, parks, shopping, downhill skiing, cross-country skiing and water sports nearby.

Location: Mountains.

Certificate may be used: Year-round, Sunday-Thursday, except August, no festivals/holidays.

Haus Rohrbach Pension

12882 Ranger Rd
Leavenworth, WA 98826-9503
(509)548-7024 (800)548-4477 Fax:(509)548-5038
Internet: www.hausrohrbach.com
E-mail: info@hausrohrbach.com

Circa 1975. This inn is located two minutes away from the village. Private fireplaces and whirlpools for two are features of each of three suites. Sourdough pancakes and cinnamon rolls are specialties of the house. Guests often take breakfast out to the deck to enjoy pastoral views that include grazing sheep and a pleasant pond. In the evening, return from white-water rafting, tobogganing, skiing or sleigh rides to soak in the hot tub or indulge in the inn's complimentary desserts served in front of the wood stove.

Innkeeper(s): Kathryn Harrild. $85-175. MC, VISA, AX, DS, PC, TC. 10 rooms, 8 with PB, 3 with FP, 3 suites and 2 conference rooms. Breakfast included in rates. Types of meals: Full bkfst and early coffee/tea. Beds: KQD. Air conditioning. Handicap access. Antiquing, fishing, horseback riding, shopping, downhill skiing and cross-country skiing nearby.

Location: Theme town.

Certificate may be used: Jan. 7 to May 7, Sept. 10 to Oct. 31, Sunday through Thursday. Holiday and festival times are excluded.

Long Beach   *E2*

Scandinavian Gardens Inn

1610 California St
Long Beach, WA 98631-9801
(360)642-8877 (800)988-9277 Fax:(360)642-8764

You are asked to honor a Scandinavian custom of removing your shoes upon entering this B&B. White wool carpeting and blond-wood pieces decorate the living room. A recreation room offers a hot tub and Finnish sauna. The Icelandic Room has an antique armoire and hand-painted cabinets, while the Swedish Suite features a two-person soaking tub tucked into a private nook. Breakfast items such as creamed rice, shrimp au gratin and Danish pastries are served smorgasbord-style with the hosts in costume.

Innkeeper(s): Marilyn Dakan, Rod Dakan. $105-145. MC, VISA. 4 rooms and 1 suite. Breakfast included in rates. Type of meal: Full bkfst. Turndown service in room. Antiquing and shopping nearby.

Certificate may be used: Sunday-Thursday, holidays and festivals excluded.

Lopez   *B3*

MacKaye Harbor Inn

949 MacKaye Harbor Rd
Lopez, WA 98261
(360)468-2253 (888)314-6140 Fax:(360)468-2393
Internet: www.san-juan.net/mackayeharbor
E-mail: mckay@pacificrim.net

Circa 1927. Launching a kayak from the inn's sandy beach is a favorite activity here, as well as watching otters, seals and eagles from the waterfront parlor. Four of the guest rooms boast views of the bay, and there are eight acres to explore, including a quarter mile of beach. The home was the first house on the island to have electric lights, as well as its first inn. In the evenings, guests are treated to chocolate truffles and an aperitif to enhance the sunset views. The innkeepers also take care of two luxurious carriage houses next door, popular for families with children and for couples seeking more seclusion. Complimentary mountain bikes are offered for cycling around the island.

Innkeeper(s): Robin & Mike. $89-175. MC, VISA, PC, TC. 5 rooms, 3 with PB, 1 with FP, 1 suite and 1 conference room. Breakfast included in rates. Types of meals: Full gourmet bkfst and early coffee/tea. Beds: KQDT. Turndown service in room. Fax, copier and BBQs on premises. Antiquing, bicycling, canoeing/kayaking, fishing, golf, parks and tennis nearby.

Location: Sandy beach.

Publicity: *Los Angeles Times, Sunset, Northwest and Coastal Living.*

Certificate may be used: Oct. 20-March 30, Sunday-Friday, excluding holidays.

Mazama   *B6*

Mazama Country Inn

42 Lost River Rd, HCR 74 Box B-9
Mazama, WA 98833-9700
(509)996-2681 (800)843-7951 Fax:(509)996-2646
Internet: www.mazamacountryinn.com
E-mail: mazamacountryinn@methow.com

Circa 1985. With its log beams and cedar siding, this inn is a rustic retreat in an old mining town secluded in the beauty of the North Cascades. There are guest rooms in the inn and accommodations in cabins, which sleep up to six or eight people (ideal for families). In the winter season, all three meals are included in the rates for inn guests. A hearty breakfast is served, and guests can pack their own lunch from a selection of items, then return to the lodge in the evening for a family-style dinner. On cold nights, the lounge's huge Russian fireplace is a perfect place to relax. Guests enjoy use of a sauna and hot tub, as well.

Innkeeper(s): George Turner. $80-190. MC, VISA, DS, PC, TC. 14 rooms with PB and 6 cottages. Type of meal: Full bkfst. Beds: QDT. Air conditioning (three rooms) in room. VCR, fax, copier, spa, sauna, tennis and library on premises. Handicap access. Antiquing, bicycling, fishing, golf, hiking, horseback riding, parks, shopping, cross-country skiing and tennis nearby.

Location: Methow River.

Publicity: *New York Times and NW Best Places.*

"Comfortable accommodations, great food, great staff — thanks!"

Certificate may be used: Oct. 1-Dec. 15 and March 15-June 15.

Olga   *B3*

Buck Bay Farm

716 Pt Lawrence Rd
Olga, WA 98279
(360)376-2908 (888)422-2825
Internet: www.buckbayfarm.com

Circa 1920. This farmhouse is secluded on five acres and is decorated in country style. Down pillows and comforters are a few homey touches. Homemade breakfasts include items like freshly baked muffins, scones and biscuits still steaming from the oven.

Innkeeper(s): Rick & Janet Bronkey. $85-125. MC, VISA, AX, DS, PC, TC. 5 rooms, 4 with PB and 1 suite. Breakfast included in rates. Types of meals: Full bkfst and early coffee/tea. Beds: Q. Spa on premises. Handicap access. Antiquing, canoeing/kayaking, fishing, hiking, whale watching, live theater, parks and shopping nearby.

Location: Country.

Publicity: *Island's Sounder.*

Certificate may be used: Oct. 15-April 15, everyday except holiday weekends.

Port Angeles   *C3*

5 SeaSuns B&B Inn

1005 S Lincoln St
Port Angeles, WA 98362-7826
(360)452-8248 (800)708-0777 Fax:(360)417-0465
Internet: www.seasuns.com
E-mail: seasuns@olypen.com

Circa 1926. Five SeaSuns was built by a local attorney and later purchased by a prominent area family who hosted many social gatherings here. The restored home maintains much of its historic ambiance with guest rooms decorated in 1920s style with

period antiques. Guest rooms include amenities such as whirlpool or soaking tubs, balconies and water or mountain views. Picturesque gardens highlight the estate like grounds. Artfully presented gourmet breakfasts are served with fine china, silver and candlelight.

Innkeeper(s): Jan & Bob Harbick. $75-135. MC, VISA, AX, PC, TC. 5 rooms with PB, 1 suite and 1 cottage. Breakfast, afternoon tea and snacks/refreshments included in rates. Types of meals: Full bkfst, veg bkfst and early coffee/tea. Beds: QD. Turndown service in room. VCR and fax on premises. Antiquing, art galleries, beaches, bicycling, canoeing/kayaking, fishing, hiking, live theater, museums, parks, shopping, cross-country skiing and wineries nearby.

Location: City.

Certificate may be used: Oct. 15 to May 15, Sunday-Thursday.

Port Townsend   C3

Ann Starrett Mansion

744 Clay St
Port Townsend, WA 98368-5808
(888)385-3205
Internet: www.starrettmansion.com

Circa 1889. George Starrett came from Maine to Port Townsend and became the major residential builder. By 1889, he had constructed one house a week, totaling more than 350 houses. The Smithsonian believes the Ann Starrett's elaborate free-hung spiral staircase is the only one of its type in the United States. A frescoed dome atop the octagonal tower depicts four seasons and four virtues. On the first day of each season, the sun causes a ruby red light to point toward the appropriate painting. The mansion won a "Great American Home Award" from the National Trust for Historic Preservation.

Innkeeper(s): Edel Sokol. $133-225. MC, VISA, AX, DS, PC, TC. 11 rooms with PB, 2 with FP, 2 suites, 2 cottages and 2 conference rooms. Breakfast included in rates. Type of meal: Full bkfst. Beds: KQDT. Cable TV, phone and one room includes spa in room. VCR and fax on premises. Antiquing, fishing, live theater, parks, shopping, cross-country skiing and water sports nearby.

Location: Seaport Village.

Publicity: *Peninsula, New York Times, Vancouver Sun, San Francisco Examiner, London Times, Colonial Homes, Elle, Leader, Japanese Travel, National Geographic Traveler, Victorian, Historic American Trails, Day Boy Night Girl,* voted "Best Historic Inn" by Sunset Magazine and PBS.

"Staying here was like a dream come true."

Certificate may be used: November-April, Sunday through Thursday, must mention certificate at time of reservation.

Holly Hill House B&B

611 Polk St
Port Townsend, WA 98368-6531
(360)385-5619 (800)435-1454
Internet: www/acies.com/hollyhill/
E-mail: hollyhill@olympus.net

Circa 1872. A unique "upside-down" century-old Camperdown elm and several holly trees surround this aptly named bed & breakfast, built by Robert C. Hill, the co-founder of the First National Bank of Port Townsend. The cozy, romantic rooms are decorated with florals and lace. Billie's Room affords a view of Admiralty Inlet and Mt. Baker, while Lizette's Room offers Victorian decor and a view of the garden. The Skyview Room includes a wonderful skylight. The spacious Colonel's

Room features a picture window with water and mountain views, and the Morning Glory Room is a cozy retreat with lace-trimmed quilts. Expansive breakfasts are served in the dining room, and coffee and tea are always available. The inn's gardens are surrounded by a picket fence and nearly 200 rose bushes.

Innkeeper(s): Lynne Sterling. $78-145. 5 rooms with PB and 1 suite. Breakfast included in rates. Types of meals: Full bkfst and early coffee/tea. Beds: KQT. Turndown service in room. Library on premises. Antiquing, fishing, whale watching, live theater, parks and shopping nearby.

Location: Mountains.

Certificate may be used: Oct. 31-April 30, Sunday to Thursday.

Lizzie's

731 Pierce St
Port Townsend, WA 98368-8042
(360)385-4168 (800)700-4168
Internet: www.kolke.com/lizzies
E-mail: wickline@olympus.net

Circa 1887. Named for Lizzie Grant, a sea captain's wife, this Italianate Victorian is elegant and airy. In addition to the gracious interiors, some rooms command an outstanding view of Port Townsend Bay, Puget Sound, and the Olympic and Cascade mountain ranges. Each room is filled with antiques dating from 1840 to the turn of the century. The grounds boast colorful gardens, and the dog's house is a one-quarter scale replica of the original house. Lizzie's is known for its elaborate breakfasts, where guests are encouraged to help themselves to seconds. The inn was recently named Western Washington's favorite B&B by Seattle's Channel 5 TV.

Innkeeper(s): Patricia Wickline. $70-135. MC, VISA, DS, PC, TC. 7 rooms with PB. Breakfast included in rates. Type of meal: Full bkfst. Beds: KQ.

Publicity: *Travel & Leisure and Victorian Homes.*

"As they say in show biz, you're a hard act to follow."

Certificate may be used: October through May, Sunday through Thursday.

Manresa Castle

PO Box 564, 7th & Sheridan
Port Townsend, WA 98368-0564
(360)385-5750 (800)732-1281 Fax:(360)385-5883

Circa 1892. When businessman Charles Eisenbeis built the largest private residence in Port Townsend, locals dubbed it "Eisenbeis Castle," because it resembled the castles in Eisenbeis' native Prussia. The home is truly a royal delight to behold, both inside and out. Luxurious European antiques and hand-painted wall coverings decorate the dining room and many of the castle's stately guest rooms. The turret suites are unique and many of the rooms have mountain and water views, but beware of the third floor. Rumors of ghosts in the upper floor have frightened some, but others seek out the "haunted" rooms for a spooky stay. Port Townsend offers a variety of galleries, gift shops and antiquing.

Innkeeper(s): Roger O'Connor. $80-175. MC, VISA, DS. 40 rooms with PB and 1 conference room. Breakfast included in rates. Types of meals: Full gourmet bkfst and cont. Beds: KQD. Cable TV and phone in room. Antiquing, fishing, live theater, shopping and water sports nearby.

Location: Mountains.

Publicity: *Island Independent, Leader News, Province Showcase and Sunset Magazine.*

Certificate may be used: Sunday through Friday, October through May.

Palace Hotel

1004 Water St
Port Townsend, WA 98368-6706
(360)385-0773 (800)962-0741 Fax:(360)385-0780

Circa 1889. This old brick hotel has been restored and refurbished in a Victorian style. The Miss Rose Room has a Jacuzzi tub and is on the third floor. Some rooms have kitchenettes. Miss Kitty's Room, with its antique bed and wood-burning stove has great views of Puget Sound and downtown.

Innkeeper(s): Phoebe Mason. $49-159. MC, VISA, AX, DS. 16 rooms. Breakfast included in rates. Type of meal: Cont plus. Beds: KQDT. TV in room. Small conference room on premises.

Pets Allowed.

Certificate may be used: October to May, except Friday and Saturday nights, excludes holidays.

Ravenscroft Inn

533 Quincy St
Port Townsend, WA 98368-5839
(360)385-2784 (800)782-2691 Fax:(360)385-6724
Internet: www.ravenscroftinn.com
E-mail: ravenscroft@olympus.net

Circa 1987. A second suite has been added to this relaxing inn, which includes a fireplace and six-foot soaking tub. From the suite's large window seat, guests can enjoy the view of Mt. Baker. The room has an Impressionist touch, decorated in Monet colors. Other rooms are equally interesting, all individually decorated with Colonial influences. The inn is just three blocks from the water.

Innkeeper(s): Leah Hammer. $65-185. MC, VISA, AX, DS, PC, TC. 8 rooms with PB, 3 with FP, 2 suites and 1 conference room. Breakfast, afternoon tea and snacks/refreshments included in rates. Type of meal: Full gourmet bkfst. Beds: KQT. Turndown service, soaking tubs and clocks in room. VCR, fax and library on premises. Antiquing, fishing, golf, hiking, bicycling, music festivals/jazz/fiddle tunes blues, live theater, parks, shopping, cross-country skiing, tennis and water sports nearby.

Publicity: *Accent, Better Homes & Gardens and Travel Channel.*

Certificate may be used: Oct. 15-May 15, Sunday-Thursday, except holidays and special event dates.

The English Inn

718 F St
Port Townsend, WA 98368-5211
(360)385-5302 (800)254-5302 Fax:(360)385-5302
Internet: www.English-Inn.com
E-mail: Nancy@Macaid.com

Circa 1885. This Italianate Victorian was built during Port Townsend's 19th-century heyday, when the town served the railroad and shipping industries. The home overlooks the Olympic Mountains, and several guest rooms offer mountain views. The rooms are named in honor of English poets. There is a four-person Jacuzzi tub secluded in the garden. Guests often enjoy sunsets and scenic vistas in the gazebo, and many weddings take place at this picturesque spot. All rooms have Internet access. Breakfasts are seasonal and creative, offering such items as raspberry strudel muffins, herbed poached eggs on crumpets, artichoke frittatas or broiled grapefruit with brandy sauce.

Innkeeper(s): Mark & Deborah Raney. $65-95. MC, VISA, AX, DC, DS, PC, TC. 5 rooms with PB and 2 conference rooms. Breakfast included in rates. Types of meals: Full gourmet bkfst and early coffee/tea. Beds: KQ. Ceiling fan in room. VCR, fax, copier, spa and bicycles on premises. Antiquing, fishing, mountain biking, live theater, parks, shopping and water sports nearby.

Certificate may be used: Jan. 1-June 30 & Oct. 1-Dec. 31, Sunday-Thursday.

Poulsbo   C4

Foxbridge B&B

30680 Hwy 3 NE
Poulsbo, WA 98370
(360)598-5599 Fax:(360)598-3588
Internet: www.sfox.com/foxbridge
E-mail: foxbridge@sprintmail.com

Circa 1993. The innkeepers at this Georgian-style home have taken the words bed & breakfast to heart. Each of the comfortable rooms has an individual theme. The Country Garden room is a floral delight with a canopy bed. The Old World room includes a sleigh bed and down comforter. The Foxhunt room is done up in masculine hues with a four-poster  bed. Antiques are placed throughout the home. As for the breakfast, each morning brings a new menu. Heart-shaped waffles topped with blueberries and cream might be the fare one morning, while another day could bring eggs Benedict or a smoked-salmon quiche. All are served with cereals and a special starter, perhaps baked nectarines with cream Ambrose.

Innkeeper(s): Beverly Higgins. $90. MC, VISA, DS, PC. 3 rooms with PB. Breakfast and afternoon tea included in rates. Types of meals: Full gourmet bkfst and early coffee/tea. Beds: Q. Turndown service in room. Fax and library on premises. Antiquing, fishing, museums, live theater, parks, shopping, cross-country skiing and water sports nearby.

Location: Country.

Certificate may be used: Nov. 1 to May 15, excluding holidays.

Roslyn   D5

Hummingbird Inn

106 E Pennsylvania Ave PO Box 984
Roslyn, WA 98941
(509)649-2758
Internet: www.pocc.com/~hummingbirdinn

Circa 1890. This little blue house, located on an acre, has steep gables, a small front porch and a white picket fence. Once the local mine manager's house, it's decorated in country Victorian furnishings in keeping with its architecture. Breakfast burritos and Dutch babies are served with homemade berry jam and baked goods. Both hosts are registered nurses.

Innkeeper(s): Roberta Spinazola. $60-75. MC, VISA, DS, PC, TC. 3 rooms, 1 with PB. Breakfast and snacks/refreshments included in rates. Types of meals: Full bkfst and early coffee/tea. Beds: Q. Child care, CD player & CDs, snow shoes and piano on premises. Antiquing, fishing, golf, national/historic town, rodeo over labor day, small 50-seat movie house, parks, shopping, downhill skiing, cross-country skiing and water sports nearby.

Location: Cascade foothills.

"Your friendliness was infectious and we love the place. We will definitely be back."

Certificate may be used: All year except Saturday nights.

Seaview   E2

Shelburne Inn
4415 Pacific Way, PO Box 250
Seaview, WA 98644
(360)642-2442 Fax:(360)642-8904
Internet: www.theshelburneinn.com

Circa 1896. The Shelburne is known as the oldest continuously operating hotel in the state of Washington, and it is listed in the National Register. The front desk at the hotel is a former church altar. Art nouveau stained-glass windows rescued from a church torn down in Morecambe, England, now shed light and color on the dining room. The guest rooms are appointed in antiques. Just a 10-minute walk from the ocean, the inn is situated on the Long Beach Peninsula, a 28-mile stretch of seacoast that includes bird sanctuaries and lighthouses. The inn offers a full gourmet breakfast.

Innkeeper(s): David Campiche & Laurie Anderson. $109-249. MC, VISA, AX. 15 rooms with PB, 2 suites and 1 conference room. Breakfast included in rates. Type of meal: Full gourmet bkfst. Beds: QD. Fax and copier on premises. Handicap access. Antiquing and fishing nearby.
Publicity: *Better Homes & Gardens, Bon Appetit, Conde Nast Traveler, Esquire, Gourmet and Food & Wine.*
"Fabulous food. Homey but elegant atmosphere. Hospitable service, like being a guest in an elegant home."
Certificate may be used: Midweek, October through May, excluding holidays.

Sequim   C3

Greywolf Inn
395 Keeler Rd
Sequim, WA 98382-9024
(360)683-5889 (800)914-9653 Fax:(360)683-1487
Internet: www.greywolfinn.com
E-mail: info@greywolfinn.com

Built in a farmhouse style, this house is located on five acres. If you prefer a canopy bed, request the Pamela Room and enjoy Bavarian decor. Salmon and egg dishes are presented at breakfast. Decks surround the house, affording views of an occasional eagle, ducks in the pond and Mount Baker. A nature trail provides a pleasant walk through the fields, tall fir trees and over a small stream. Birdwatching and beachcombing are popular on the Dungeness Spit.

Innkeeper(s): Peggy Melang. $70-135. MC, VISA, AX, DS. 5 rooms and 1 suite. Breakfast included in rates. Type of meal: Full bkfst. Cable TV, phone and ceiling fan in room. VCR on premises. Antiquing, fishing, golf, hiking, casino, live theater, shopping, downhill skiing and cross-country skiing nearby.
Certificate may be used: Anytime from Oct. 15-May 15, excluding holiday weekends. Offer limited to three rooms.

Spokane   C9

Fotheringham House
2128 W 2nd Ave
Spokane, WA 99204-0916
(509)838-1891 Fax:(509)838-1807
Internet: www.ior.com/fotheringham
E-mail: fotheringham.bnb@ior.com

A vintage Victorian in the National Register, this inn was built by the first mayor of Spokane, David Fotheringham. There are tin ceilings, a carved staircase, gabled porches and polished wood-

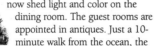

work. Victorian furnishings and stained-glass pieces are featured. Across the street is Coeur d'Alene Park and the Patsy Clark Mansion, a favorite Spokane restaurant. Walk two blocks to the Elk Public House.
Innkeeper(s): Jackie & Graham Johnson. $90-105. MC, VISA, AX, DS. 4 rooms. Breakfast included in rates. Types of meals: Full bkfst and early coffee/tea. Chocolates and amenities in room. Player piano on premises. Antiquing, live theater, shopping and sporting events nearby.
Location: City.
Certificate may be used: Consecutive nights Sunday through Thursday, November through April.

Marianna Stoltz House
427 E Indiana Ave
Spokane, WA 99207-2324
(509)483-4316 (800)978-6587 Fax:(509)483-6773
Internet: www.aimcomm.com/stoltzhouse

Circa 1908. Located on a tree-lined street, two miles from downtown Spokane, is this American Four Square Victorian. It is in the local historic register and features a wraparound porch, high ceilings and leaded-glass windows. Furnishings include Oriental rugs and period pieces. Peach Melba Parfait and Stoltz House Strada are breakfast specialties.
Innkeeper(s): Phyllis & Jim Maguire. $69-99. MC, VISA, AX, DC, DS, PC, TC. 4 rooms, 2 with PB and 1 suite. Breakfast included in rates. Types of meals: Full bkfst and early coffee/tea. Beds: KQT. Cable TV and phone in room. Air conditioning. Fax, copier & piano on premises. Amusement parks, fishing, live theater, parks, shopping, downhill skiing, cross-country skiing & sporting events nearby.
Location: City.
Certificate may be used: Sunday through Thursday, Nov. 15-March 15, holidays excluded.

Sunnyside   E6

Sunnyside Inn B&B
800 E Edison Ave
Sunnyside, WA 98944-2206
(509)839-5557 (800)221-4195
Internet: www.sunnysideinn.com
E-mail: sunnyside@sunnysideinn.com

Circa 1919. This wine country inn offers spacious rooms, decorated in a comfortable, country style. Most of the rooms include baths with double Jacuzzi tubs. The one bedroom without a Jacuzzi, includes the home's original early 20th-century fixtures. Two rooms offer fireplaces. A full breakfast is served, as well as evening snacks.
Innkeeper(s): Karen & Don Vlieger. $69-109. MC, VISA, AX, DS, TC. 13 rooms with PB, 2 with FP. Breakfast & snacks/refreshments included in rates. Type of meal: Full bkfst. Beds: KQ. Cable TV, phone & ceiling fan in room. Air conditioning. Antiquing, fishing, golf, live theater, parks, shopping & cross-country skiing nearby.
Location: City.
Certificate may be used: Nov. 1-June 30, Sunday-Thursday.

Tacoma   D4

Chinaberry Hill - An 1889 Grand Victorian Inn
302 Tacoma Ave N
Tacoma, WA 98403
(253)272-1282 Fax:(253)272-1335
Internet: www.chinaberryhill.com
E-mail: chinaberry@wa.net

Circa 1889. In the 19th century, this Queen Anne was known as far away as China for its wondrous gardens, one of the earliest examples of landscape gardening in the Pacific Northwest.

The home, a wedding present from a husband to his bride, is listed in the National Register. The innkeepers have selected a unique assortment of antiques and collectibles to decorate the manor. The house offers two Jacuzzi suites and a guest room, all eclectically decorated with items such as a four-poster rice bed or a canopy bed. There are two lodging options in the Catchpenny Cottage, a restored carriage house steps away from the manor. Guests can stay either in the romantic carriage suite or the Hay Loft, which includes a bedroom, sitting room, clawfoot tub and a unique hay chute. In the mornings, as the innkeepers say, guests enjoy "hearty breakfasts and serious coffee." Not a bad start to a day exploring Antique Row or Pt. Defiance, a 698-acre protected rain forest park with an aquarium, gardens, beaches and a zoo. Seattle is 30 minutes away.

Innkeeper(s): Cecil & Yarrow Wayman. $95-195. MC, VISA, AX, DS, PC, TC. 5 rooms with PB, 1 with FP, 4 suites, 1 cottage and 2 conference rooms. Breakfast and snacks/refreshments included in rates. Types of meals: Full gourmet bkfst, cont plus and early coffee/tea. Beds: Q. Cable TV, phone, turn-down service, ceiling fan, VCR, down comforters, terrycloth robes and double Jacuzzi in room. Fax, copier, library, guest refrigerator, snack area, porch and kitchen in carriage house on premises. Antiquing, fishing, golf, zoo, aquarium, museums, billiards, kayaking, Victorian conservatory, live theater, parks, shopping, sporting events, tennis and water sports nearby.

Location: 6 blocks to downtown.

Publicity: News Tribune, Habitat, Olympian, Oregonian, Seattle Magazine and Tacoma Weekly.

". . . the highlight of our trip so far - wonderful . . .the company, the food, the accommodations, all the best."

Certificate may be used: January-March, Sunday-Thursday.

Commencement Bay B&B

3312 N Union Ave
Tacoma, WA 98407-6055
(253)752-8175 Fax:(253)759-4025
Internet: www.great-views.com
E-mail: greatviews@aol.com

Circa 1937. Watch boats sail across the bay while enjoying breakfast served with gourmet coffee at this Colonial Revival inn. All guest rooms feature bay views and each is unique and individually decorated. The surrounding area includes historic sites, antique shops, waterfront restaurants, wooded nature trails and Pt. Defiance Zoo and Aquarium. Relax in a secluded hot tub and deck area or in the fireside room for reading and the romantic view. The innkeepers also offer an exercise room and video/book library. Business travelers will appreciate amenities such as an office work area and dataports, free e-mail and cable Internet access. The B&B is centrally located, 30 miles from both Seattle and Mt. Rainier park.

Innkeeper(s): Sharon & Bill Kaufmann. $85-125. MC, VISA, AX, DS, PC, TC. 3 rooms with PB and 2 conference rooms. Breakfast, afternoon tea and snacks/refreshments included in rates. Types of meals: Full bkfst and early coffee/tea. Beds: Q. Cable TV, phone, VCR and robes in room. Fax, spa, bicycles, computer data ports, exercise room, massages and exercise room on premises. Antiquing, fishing, Washington State Historic Museum, botanical parks, the International Glass Museum, restaurants, live theater, parks, shopping, sporting events and water sports nearby.

Location: Historic area.

Publicity: Tacoma Weekly, News Tribune, Tacoma Reporter, Oregonian, NW Best Places and NBC "Evening Magazine."

"Perfect in every detail! The setting, breathtaking; the food, scrumptious and beautifully presented; the warmth and friendship here."

Certificate may be used: Sept. 1-May 31, Sunday-Thursday.

Trout Lake · F5

The Farm Bed & Breakfast

490 Sunnyside Rd
Trout Lake, WA 98650-9715
(509)395-2488

Circa 1890. Four acres surround this three-story yellow farmhouse, 25 miles north of the Columbia Gorge and Hood River. The old rail fence, meadow and forested foothills of Mount Adams create a pastoral scene appropriate for the inn's herd of Cashmere goats. A big farm breakfast is served. Inside, entertainment centers around the player piano, wood stove and satellite dish. Outdoors, take a flight from Trout Lake into Mount St. Helens, or gear up for huckleberry picking, trout fishing and hiking at nearby Gifford Pinchot National Forest. Ask the innkeepers about the fairs, rodeos and Saturday markets.

Innkeeper(s): Rosie & Dean Hostetter. $75-85. PC. 2 rooms. Breakfast included in rates. Types of meals: Full bkfst and early coffee/tea. Beds: QD. VCR, bicycles and perennial flower gardens on premises. Antiquing, fishing, shopping, downhill skiing, cross-country skiing and water sports nearby.

Certificate may be used: Oct. 15-May 31.

Uniontown · E10

Churchyard Inn

206 Saint Boniface St
Uniontown, WA 99179
(509)229-3200 Fax:(509)229-3213
Internet: www.pullman-wa.com/housing/chrchbb.htm
E-mail: cyi@inlandnet.com

Circa 1905. Not surprisingly, this historic inn is located adjacent to a church. From 1913 until 1972, the home served as a convent. The three-story brick home is adorned with a second-story portico supported by two columns. The innkeepers restored the home to its turn-of-the-century grace and added a new wing. The inn's restored red fir woodwork is a highlight. The seven guest rooms include a spacious third-floor suite with a kitchen and fireplace. The home is listed in the National Register of Historic Places.

Innkeeper(s): Marvin J. & Linda J. Entel. $60-150. MC, VISA, DS. 7 rooms with PB, 1 with FP, 1 suite and 1 conference room. Breakfast included in rates. Types of meals: Full bkfst, cont and early coffee/tea. Beds: KQDT. Phone, ceiling fan and window fans in room. VCR and fax on premises. Handicap access. Antiquing, fishing, golf, parks, shopping, sporting events and water sports nearby.

Location: Country.

Publicity: Lewiston Tribune, Colfax Gazette, Moscow Daily News, Weekend Getaways., KHQ Channel 6 Northwest Edition and Channel 10 PBS.

"Beautiful property, location and setting. I would recommend this wonderful B&B to anyone coming to the area."

Certificate may be used: Jan. 5 through Nov. 30.

White Salmon · F5

Llama Ranch B&B

1980 Hwy 141
White Salmon, WA 98672-8032
(509)395-2786

Llamas abound at this unique, picturesque ranch, which affords views of Mt. Adams. Innkeeper Jerry Stone offers nature walks through the woods accompanied by some of their friendly llamas. Jerry also offers the unusual amenity of llama boarding. The White Salmon area, located in between the Mt. Adams Wilderness Area and Columbia Gorge, is full of interesting activities, including white-water rafting, horseback riding and berry picking.

Innkeeper(s): Jerry Stone. $79-99. MC, VISA, AX, DS. 7 rooms. Breakfast included in rates. Type of meal: Full bkfst.

Certificate may be used: Oct. 1-April 30.

Washington, D.C.

Aaron Shipman House

PO Box 12011
Washington, DC 20005-0911
202-328-3510 Fax:(202)332-3885

Circa 1887. This three-story Victorian townhouse was built by Aaron Shipman, who owned one of the first construction companies in the city. The turn-of-the-century revitalization of Washington began in Logan Circle, considered to be the city's first truly residential area. During the house's restoration, flower gardens, terraces and fountains were added. Victorian antiques, original wood paneling, stained glass, chandeliers, as well as practical amenities such as air conditioning and laundry facilities, make this a comfortable stay. There is a furnished apartment available, as well.

Innkeeper(s): Charles & Jackie Reed. $65-150. MC, VISA, AX, DS, TC. 6 rooms, 5 with PB, 3 with FP and 1 suite. Breakfast included in rates. Type of meal: Cont plus. Beds: QD. Cable TV, phone, Jacuzzi (one room) and player piano in room. Air conditioning. Antiquing, live theater, parks, shopping and sporting events nearby.

Location: City.

"This home was the highlight of our stay in Washington! This was a superb home and location. The Reeds treated us better than family."
Certificate may be used: Jan. 1-March 15, not valid holiday weekends or special events.

Adams Inn

1744 Lanier Pl NW
Washington, DC 20009-2118
(202)745-3600 (800)578-6807 Fax:(202)319-7958
Internet: www.adamsinn.com
E-mail: adamsinn@adamsinn.com

Circa 1908. These restored town houses have fireplaces, a library and parlor, all furnished home-style, as are the guest rooms. Former residents of this neighborhood include Tallulah Bankhead,

Woodrow Wilson and Al Jolson. The Adams-Morgan area is home to diplomats, radio and television personalities and government workers. A notable firehouse across the street holds the record for the fastest response of a horse-drawn fire apparatus. Located in the restaurant area, over 100 restaurants and shops are within walking distance.

Innkeeper(s): Gene & Nancy Thompson, Anne Owens. $55-70. MC, VISA, AX, DC, CB, DS, TC. 24 rooms, 14 with PB. Breakfast included in rates. Types of meals: Cont plus and early coffee/tea. Beds:

QDT. TV in room. Air conditioning. Library on premises. Antiquing, walking distance to Metro and buses and parks nearby.

Location: City.

Publicity: *Travel Host.*

"We enjoyed your friendly hospitality and the home-like atmosphere. Your suggestions on restaurants and help in planning our visit were appreciated."
Certificate may be used: Dec. 1-March 1, Sunday-Thursday.

The Embassy Inn

1627 16th St NW
Washington, DC 20009-3063
(202)234-7800 (800)423-9111 Fax:(202)234-3309

Circa 1910. This restored inn is furnished in a Federalist style. The comfortable lobby offers books and evening sherry. Conveniently located, the inn is seven blocks from the Adams Morgan area of ethnic restaurants. The Embassy's philosophy of innkeeping includes providing personal attention and cheerful hospitality. Concierge services are available. The inn does not have an elevator.

Innkeeper(s): Susan Stiles. $79-150. MC, VISA, AX, DC, CB, TC. 38 rooms with PB. Breakfast included in rates. Type of meal: Cont plus. Beds: DT. Cable TV, phone and free HBO in room. Air conditioning. Fax, copier and Washington Post daily on premises. Antiquing, white House, live theater, museums & parks nearby.

Location: City.

Publicity: *Los Angeles Times, Inn Times, Business Review and N.Y. Times.*

"When I return to D.C., I'll be back at the Embassy."
Certificate may be used: Jan. 1-March 31, June 1-Sept. 15, Nov. 1-Dec. 29.

The Windsor Inn

1842 16th St NW
Washington, DC 20009-3316
(202)667-0300 (800)423-9111 Fax:(202)667-4503

Circa 1910. Recently renovated and situated in a neighborhood of renovated townhouses, the Windsor Inn is the sister property to the Embassy Inn. It is larger and offers suites as well as a small meeting room. The refurbished lobby is in an Art Deco style and a private club atmosphere prevails. It is six blocks to the Metro station at Dupont Circle. There are no elevators.

Innkeeper(s): Susan Stiles. $89-199. MC, VISA, AX, DC, CB, TC. 45 rooms with PB, 2 suites and 1 conference room. Breakfast included in rates. Type of meal: Cont plus. Beds: QDT. TV, phone and some refrigerators in room. Air conditioning. Fax, copier and Washington Post daily on premises. Antiquing, live theater and parks nearby.

Location: City.

Publicity: *Los Angeles Times, Inn Times, Sunday Telegram, WCUA Press Release and New York Times.*

"Being here was like being home. Excellent service, would recommend."
Certificate may be used: Jan. 1-March 31, June 15-Sept. 15, Nov. 1-Dec. 28 always based on availability.

West Virginia

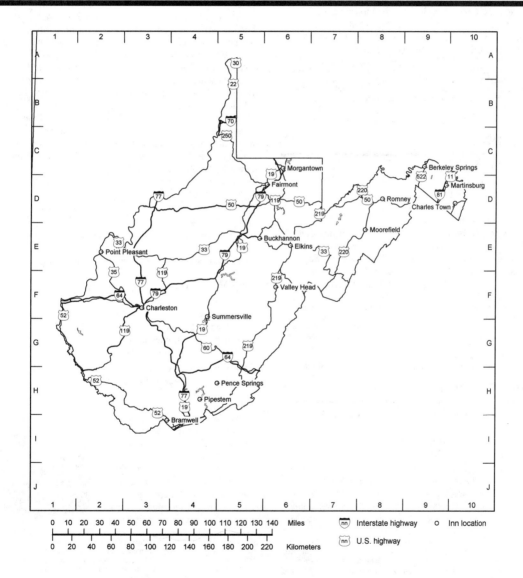

	Miles	
0 10 20 30 40 50 60 70 80 90 100 110 120 130 140		
0 20 40 60 80 100 120 140 160 180 200 220	Kilometers	

- nn — Interstate highway
- O — Inn location
- nn — U.S. highway

Berkeley Springs   C9

The Manor Inn

415 Fairfax St
Berkeley Springs, WV 25411-1607
(304)258-1552 (800)225-5982

Circa 1878. In the National Register, this Second Empire Victorian features 12-foot ceilings, a mansard roof, large porch and French doors. The innkeeper is a quilter and collects antique quilts. George Washington is said to have bathed in the warm mineral springs in town where he owned a property a block from the Manor Inn. Roman and Turkish baths are featured in The Baths, a West Virginia State Park.
Innkeeper(s): Don Trask. $75-130. MC, VISA, PC, TC. 4 rooms, 3 with PB and 1 suite. Breakfast included in rates. Types of meals: Full gourmet bkfst and early coffee/tea. Beds: QD. Cable TV and ceiling fan in room. Air conditioning. VCR on premises. Antiquing, fishing, live theater, parks, shopping, downhill skiing, cross-country skiing and water sports nearby.
Location: Small town in foothills.
Certificate may be used: Sunday through Thursday, non-holiday weeks.

Bramwell   I3

Perry House B&B

Main St, PO Box 188
Bramwell, WV 24715-0248
(304)248-8145 (800)328-0248
E-mail: perryhouse@netlinkcorp.com

Circa 1902. This brick Victorian was built by a bank cashier and remained in the family for 80 years. The rooms are decorated in period style with antiques. Although a small village, Bramwell once was home to more than a dozen millionaires, and some of these families' homes are located on the town walking tour. The inn is listed in the National Register.
Innkeeper(s): Joyce & Jim Bishop. $55-85. MC, VISA, PC, TC. 4 rooms, 1 with PB. Breakfast included in rates. Types of meals: Cont and early coffee/tea. Beds: QDT. Phone and ceiling fan in room. Air conditioning. Copier on premises. Antiquing, fishing, live theater, parks, shopping, downhill skiing and water sports nearby.
Location: Mountains.
Certificate may be used: Sunday through Friday nights, except major holidays.

Buckhannon   E5

Post Mansion Inn Bed & Breakfast

8 Island Ave
Buckhannon, WV 26201-2822
(304)472-8959 (800)301-9309

Circa 1860. This massive Neoclassical Revival mansion is constructed of brick and precision-cut stone. An attached three-story stone tower resembles a medieval castle. Located on six acres, this National Register inn is bordered by the Buckhannon River on the front and back of the grounds. Victorian antiques furnish the inn.
Innkeeper(s): Lawrence & Suzanne Reger. $80. PC, TC. 3 rooms, 1 with PB and 1 conference room. Breakfast and snacks/refreshments included in rates. Types of meals: Full bkfst and early coffee/tea. Beds: QD. Air conditioning. Cable TV and VCR on premises. Antiquing, golf, parks, downhill skiing and water sports nearby.
Publicity: The Inter-Mountain and The Record Delta.
"We were so pleased with everything and all the guests couldn't say enough about your beautiful home."
Certificate may be used: Jan. 30 to Jan. 1.

Charles Town   D10

Gilbert House B&B of Middleway

PO Box 1104
Charles Town, WV 25414-7104
(304)725-0637
E-mail: gilberthouse@hotmail.com

Circa 1760. A magnificent graystone of early Georgian design, the Gilbert House is located in one of the state's oldest European settlements. Elegant appointments include fine Oriental rugs, tasteful art and antique furnishings. During restoration, graffiti found on the upstairs bedroom walls included an 1832 drawing of the future President James Polk and a child's growth chart from the 1800s. The inn is located in the Colonial era mill village of Middleway, which contains one of the country's best collections of log houses. The village is a mill site on the original settlers' trail into Shenandoah Valley ("Philadelphia Waggon Road" on Peter Jefferson's 1755 map of Virginia). Middleway was also the site of "wizard clip" hauntings during the last decade of the 1700s. The region was home to members of "Virginia Blues," commanded by Daniel Morgan during the Revolutionary War.
Innkeeper(s): Bernie Heiler. $100-140. MC, VISA, AX, PC, TC. 3 rooms with PB, 2 with FP and 1 suite. Breakfast included in rates. Type of meal: Full gourmet bkfst. Beds: QT. Air conditioning. VCR and library on premises. Antiquing, sports car racing, slots, live theater, parks and shopping nearby.
Location: 18th century village.
"We have stayed at inns for fifteen years, and yours is at the top of the list as best ever!"
Certificate may be used: At base rate from Nov. 30 through Aug. 15.

The Washington House Inn

216 S George St
Charles Town, WV 25414-1632
(304)725-7923 (800)297-6957 Fax:(304)728-5150
Internet: www.washingtonhouseinnwv.com
E-mail: emailus@washingtonhouseinnwv.com

Circa 1899. This three-story brick Victorian was built by the descendants of President Washington's brothers, John Augustine and Samuel. Carved oak mantels, spacious guest rooms, antique furnishings and refreshments served on the wraparound veranda or gazebo make the inn memorable. For business travelers, dataports are available. Harpers Ferry National Historic Park, Antietam, and the Shenandoah and Potomac rivers are all within a 15-minute drive, as is Martinsburg outlet shopping. Thoroughbred racing and car racing are some of the popular area attractions.
Innkeeper(s): Mel & Nina Vogel. $75-125. MC, VISA, AX, DS, PC, TC. 6 rooms with PB, 1 suite and 1 conference room. Breakfast and snacks/refreshments included in rates. Types of meals: Full bkfst, cont plus, cont and early coffee/tea. Beds: QT. Cable TV, phone and ceiling fan in room. Air conditioning. VCR, fax, copier, data ports, internet and antiques and collectibles for sale on premises. Antiquing, fishing, golf, history museums, horse racing, car racing, live theater, parks, shopping and water sports nearby.
Location: City.
Certificate may be used: Sunday-Thursday, Nov. 1-Aug. 31.

Charleston   F3

Benedict Haid Farm

8 Hale St
Charleston, WV 25301-2806
(304)346-1054

Circa 1869. Although no breakfast is served, we couldn't help including this farm on 350-mountain-top acres because it specializes in raising exotic animals that include llamas, guanacos and black mountain sheep, as well as donkeys and cows. There are two rustic cabins for those looking for an economical stay. Most will prefer the main German-built, hand-hewn log lodge, which features antique furnishings and a large screened-in deck with fireplace and hot tub. There is a stocked pond. Bring your own breakfast.

Innkeeper(s): Steve Jones. $150-200. MC, VISA, TC. 3 rooms and 1 cottage. Beds: D. TV in room. Air conditioning. VCR and bicycles on premises. Fishing, horseshoes, croquet, volleyball and cross-country skiing nearby.

Location: Mountains.

Publicity: *Television Travel Show.*

"Like stepping back in time."

Certificate may be used: Anytime, based on availability.

Brass Pineapple B&B

1611 Virginia St E
Charleston, WV 25311-2113
(304)344-0748 (800)CALL-WVA Fax:(304)344-0748
Internet: www.wvweb.com/brasspineapplebandb
E-mail: pineapp104@aol.com

Circa 1910. This elegant smoke-free inn is situated in Charleston's historic district, one-half block from the Capitol Complex. Original oak paneling and leaded and stained glass are among the architectural highlights. Thoughtful amenities such as terry robes and hair dryers have been placed in each guest room. In-room phones offer voice mail. A typical breakfast may include juice, fruit, muffins, cinnamon pecan waffles with warm maple syrup, fluffy scrambled eggs, cottage fries and basil tomatoes. Freshly ground coffee or Twinings tea are served in the parlor or on the front porch in season. Honeymooners can have breakfast delivered to their room on a silver tray. Limited airport pick-up and delivery is available, and the inn hosts small business meetings.

Innkeeper(s): Bill & Sue Pepper. $59-109. MC, VISA, AX, DC, DS, PC, TC. 6 rooms with PB and 1 suite. Breakfast, afternoon tea and snacks/refreshments included in rates. Types of meals: Full bkfst, cont plus and early coffee/tea. Beds: KQT. Cable TV, phone, VCR, robes and voice mail in room. Air conditioning. Fax, copier and bicycles on premises. Antiquing, fishing, golf, horseback riding, river cruises, live theater, parks, shopping, sporting events, tennis and water sports nearby.

Location: City.

Publicity: *Mid-Atlantic Country, Country Inns, Gourmet, Charlestonian, Charleston Daily Mail, Gourmet, Southern Living, Recommended Country Inns and News 8.*

"Charming, convenient location, lovely antiques, appealing decor. Extremely clean; excellent service from Sue and her staff."

Certificate may be used: Anytime, except major holidays and vacation periods.

Elkins   E6

Tunnel Mountain B&B

Rt 1, Box 59-1
Elkins, WV 26241-9711
(304)636-1684 (888)211-9123

Circa 1939. Nestled on five acres of wooded land, this three-story Fieldstone home offers privacy in a peaceful setting. Rooms are tastefully decorated with antiques, collectibles and crafts. Each bedroom boasts a view of the surrounding mountains. The chestnut and knotty pine woodwork accentuate the decor. The fireplace in the large common room is a great place for warming up after a day of touring or skiing. The area is home to a number of interesting events, including a Dulcimer festival and the state's largest festival, the Mountain State Forest Festival.

Innkeeper(s): Anne & Paul Beardslee. $75-80. PC, TC. 3 rooms with PB, 1 with FP. Breakfast included in rates. Types of meals: Full bkfst and country bkfst. Beds: QD. Cable TV in room. Air conditioning. One great room on premises. Antiquing, art galleries, beaches, bicycling, canoeing/kayaking, fishing, golf, hiking, horseback riding, rock climbing, live theater, museums, parks, shopping, downhill skiing, cross-country skiing, sporting events, tennis and water sports nearby.

Location: Mountains.

Publicity: *Blue Ridge Country, Washington Post and WBOY.*

Certificate may be used: November to May, Sunday-Thursday.

Fairmont   D6

Acacia House

158 Locust Ave
Fairmont, WV 26554-1630
(304)367-1000 (888)269-9541 Fax:(304)367-1000
Internet: www.acaciahousewv.com
E-mail: acacia@acaciahousewv.com

Circa 1917. Two maple trees frame this four-story brown brick home built in the Neoclassical style. As an antique dealer, innkeeper Kathy Sprowls has filled her home with a memorable assortment of collectibles, including butter pats, pill boxes and stone eggs from around the world. There's an antique store on the premises and items found in the inn are also available for purchase. Guest rooms are handsomely furnished with antiques, of course. Kathy and her husband, George, serve a country breakfast in the dining room with Texas French toast or puffed pancakes, hot pepper bacon or West Virginia sausage and a fruit cup. As with most bed & breakfasts, smoking is not allowed.

Innkeeper(s): Kathy & George Sprowls. $45-70. MC, VISA, AX, DC, DS, PC, TC. 4 rooms, 2 with PB. Breakfast included in rates. Types of meals: Full bkfst, cont plus, cont and early coffee/tea. Beds: QDT. TV in room. Air conditioning. VCR, fax and library on premises. Antiquing, bicycling, fishing, golf, live theater, parks, shopping, sporting events and water sports nearby.

Location: City.

Certificate may be used: No weekends June through November.

Martinsburg   D9

Pulpit & Palette Inn

516 W John St
Martinsburg, WV 25401-2635
(304)263-7012

Circa 1870. Listed in the National Register, this Victorian inn is set off by a handsome iron fence. The interior is filled with a mix of American antiques, Tibetan rugs and art, setting off moldings and other architectural details in the library, drawing room and upstairs veranda. Your British-born innkeeper prepares afternoon tea for guests. The Blue Ridge Outlet Center is one block away.

Innkeeper(s): Bill & Janet Starr. $80. MC, VISA, TC. 2 rooms. Breakfast, afternoon tea and snacks/refreshments included in rates. Types of meals: Full gourmet bkfst and early coffee/tea. Beds: Q. Turndown service in room. Air conditioning. Antiquing, canoeing, live theater, parks and shopping nearby.

Location: City.

Publicity: Morning Herald, Antique Traveler and Journal.

"You have set an ideal standard for comfort and company."

Certificate may be used: March 1 to May 21 and Nov. 1 to Dec. 31, Sunday-Thursday, except for holiday periods.

Moorefield   E8

McMechen Inn

109 N Main St
Moorefield, WV 26836-1154
(304)538-7173 (800)298-2466 Fax:(304)538-7841

Circa 1853. This handsomely restored three-story brick Greek Revival townhouse is in the National Register. There are polished pine floors, a spectacular cherry staircase winding up to the third floor, walnut doors and woodwork, cranberry glass light fixtures and indoor folding shutters. Two parlors and a library add to the gracious dining room that houses the inn's restaurant. From May through September, guests can enjoy meals outdoors at the inn's Green Shutters Cafe. There is an antique, book and gift shop on the premises. The inn is often the site of weddings and receptions.

Innkeeper(s): Linda & Bob Curtis. $85-115. MC, VISA, AX, DC, PC, TC. 5 rooms with PB. Breakfast, afternoon tea and snacks/refreshments included in rates. Types of meals: Full bkfst and early coffee/tea. Beds: D. Alarm clocks and some ceiling fans and phones in room. Air conditioning. VCR, fax, copier, library and television on premises. Antiquing, fishing, live theater, parks and downhill skiing nearby.

Publicity: Mid-Atlantic Country and Blue Ridge Country.

Certificate may be used: Jan. 30-Aug. 30, Sunday-Friday.

Morgantown   C6

Almost Heaven B&B

391 Scott Ave
Morgantown, WV 26505-8804
(304)296-4007 Fax:(304)296-4007
Internet: www.surfinusa.net/almostheaven
E-mail: vid@surfinusa.net

Circa 1990. A burgundy-colored door and steps add a hint of color to this white Federal-style house, which is set on two landscaped acres. Inside, guests will find Victorian decor and soft, feather beds. Innkeeper Cookie Coombs prepares a veritable feast for breakfast, with items such as biscuits and gravy, fried potatoes, apple dumplings, fresh fruit and pastries. The inn offers close access to West Virginia University.

Innkeeper(s): Cookie Coombs. $65-150. MC, VISA, AX, DC, CB, DS, PC, TC. 5 rooms with PB and 1 suite. Breakfast included in rates. Type of meal: Full bkfst. Beds: KQ. Cable TV, phone, ceiling fan and VCR in room. Air conditioning. Fax and library on premises. Antiquing, fishing, golf, live theater, parks, shopping, cross-country skiing, sporting events, tennis and water sports nearby.

Location: Woods.

Publicity: Dominion Post.

Certificate may be used: Jan. 1-March 15, Sunday-Friday.

Pence Springs   H5

The Pence Springs Hotel

St Rts 3 & 12, PO Box 90
Pence Springs, WV 24962-0090
(304)445-2606 (800)826-1829 Fax:(304)445-2204

Circa 1918. Listed in the National Register, this inn is known as one of the "historic springs of the Virginias." Mineral waters from Pence Springs captured a silver medal at the 1904 World's  Fair. After the fair, the healing properties of the waters drew many guests. From 1947 until the mid-1980s, the property was used as a state prison for women. A restoration effort began in 1986, and the inn once again welcomes guests. The inn's Art Deco-style furnishings and decor are reminiscent of the hotel's heyday in the 1920s when prominent and wealthy guests flocked to the hotel. Guests enjoy a full breakfast, and during the summer months, Sunday brunch is available. There are two restaurants in the hotel that serve dinner. The area boasts many outdoor activities, beautiful scenery and plenty of antique shopping.

Innkeeper(s): O. Ashby Berkley & Rosa Lee Berkley Miller. $70-100. MC, VISA, AX, DC, CB, DS, PC, TC. 25 rooms, 15 with PB, 3 suites and 3 conference rooms. Breakfast included in rates. Type of meal: Full gourmet bkfst. Beds: KDT. TV on request in room. Air conditioning. VCR, fax, copier, swimming, stables, bicycles, child care and antique shop on premises. Handicap access. Antiquing, fishing, parks, live theater, parks, shopping, downhill skiing and water sports nearby.

Pets allowed: Cannot be left in room; kennel space in basement.

Location: Mountains.

Publicity: Gourmet, Southern Living, Mid-Atlantic Country, West Virginia Quarterly, MIT Press Journal, Goldenseal and Travel Host.

"As always, I left your place rejuvenated. The property grows even more beautiful year after year."

Certificate may be used: April through December, Sunday through Thursday, non-holiday.

Pipestem   H4

Walnut Grove Inn

HC 78 Box 260
Pipestem, WV 25979-9702
(304)466-6119 (800)701-1237

Circa 1850. Located on 38 acres, this red shingled country farmhouse has a century-old log barn and ancient cemetery with graves of Confederate soldiers and others prior to the Civil War. The farmhouse is decorated eclectically, and the front porch is furnished with rocking chairs and a swing. Swimming, basketball, badminton and horseshoes are available. A gourmet breakfast of biscuits and gravy, fresh eggs and homemade preserves is served in the dining room or screen room.

Innkeeper(s): Bonnie & Larry Graham. $80. MC, VISA, AX, DS. 5 rooms with PB. Breakfast, afternoon tea and snacks/refreshments included in rates. Types of meals: Full gourmet bkfst, cont plus and early coffee/tea. Beds: KQDT. Air conditioning. Swimming on premises. Antiquing, fishing, whitewater rafting, golf, hiking trails, live theater, parks, shopping, downhill skiing, cross-country skiing and water sports nearby.

Certificate may be used: Weekdays Monday through Thursday, all year; weekdays and weekends, Nov. 1-May 1.

Point Pleasant
E2

Stone Manor

12 Main St
Point Pleasant, WV 25550-1026
(304)675-3442 Fax:(304)675-7323

Circa 1887. This stone Victorian sits on the banks of the Kanawha River with a front porch that faces the river. Point Pleasant Battle Monument Park, adjacent to the inn, was built to commemorate the location of the first battle of the Revolutionary War. In the National Register, the inn was once the home of a family who ran a ferry boat crossing for the Ohio and Kanawha rivers. Now restored, the house is decorated with Victorian antiques and offers a pleasant garden with a Victorian fish pond and fountain.

Innkeeper(s): Janice & Tom Vance. $50. PC. 3 rooms, 3 with FP. Breakfast included in rates. Type of meal: Full bkfst. Beds: QD. VCR in room. Air conditioning.

Location: Junction of two rivers on property.

Certificate may be used: Anytime except Oct. 9-11, Friday-Sunday.

Romney
D8

Hampshire House 1884

165 N Grafton St
Romney, WV 26757-1616
(304)822-7171

Circa 1884. Located near the south branch of the Potomac River, the garden here has old boxwoods and walnut trees. The inn features ornate brickwork; tall, narrow windows; and fireplaces with handsome period mantels. A sitting room with a well-stocked library, a cozy patio and a music room with an antique pump organ are favorite places. The spa room includes on-site massage.

Innkeeper(s): Jane & Scott Simmons. $70-95. MC, VISA, AX, DC, DS, PC, TC. 5 rooms with PB, 3 with FP and 1 conference room. Breakfast included in rates. Types of meals: Full bkfst and early coffee/tea. Beds: QDT. Cable TV and phone in room. Air conditioning. Bicycles and therapeutic massage on premises. Antiquing, fishing, canoeing, hiking, massage, shopping, Civil War museum and water sports nearby.

Location: South branch Potomac River.

Publicity: *Hampshire Review, Mid-Atlantic Country and Weekend Journal.*

"Your personal attention made us feel at home immediately."

Certificate may be used: November-May 1; weekdays only May 2-Sept. 30 (not honored in October).

Summersville
F4

Historic Brock House B&B Inn

1400 Webster Rd
Summersville, WV 26651-1524
(304)872-4887

Circa 1890. This Queen Anne farmhouse is the second venture into the bed & breakfast business for innkeepers Margie and Jim Martin. The exterior looks friendly and inviting, perhaps because of its long history of welcoming guests. The National Register inn originally served as a hotel and later as a boarding house. Margie has a degree in design, and her skills are evident in the cheerful, country rooms. Each of the guest rooms has a different color scheme and decor. One is decked in deep blue, another is appointed with flowery bedspreads and pastel curtains.

Innkeeper(s): Margie N. Martin. $70-90. MC, VISA, PC, TC. 6 rooms, 4 with PB, 1 suite and 1 conference room. Breakfast, afternoon tea and snacks/refreshments included in rates. Types of meals: Full gourmet bkfst, cont and early coffee/tea. Beds: QT. Turndown service in room. Air conditioning. VCR, fax and library on premises. Antiquing, fishing, white water, boating, biking, live theater, parks, shopping and water sports nearby.

Location: Mountains.

Certificate may be used: Feb. 1 to Nov. 22, Sunday through Friday.

Valley Head
F6

Nakiska Chalet B&B

HC 73 Box 24
Valley Head, WV 26294-9504
(304)339-6309 (800)225-5982

Circa 1982. On the way to this bed & breakfast, you'll be traveling the mountainous roads of West Virginia, and the hosts remind you to slow down and enjoy the scenery. Their A-frame house on 11 acres is surrounded by forests of sugar maples that display the best of foliage in autumn. Breakfast, served buffet-style, often includes local maple syrup atop blueberry pancakes. Wild turkey, deer, fox and grouse have been spotted from the deck.

Innkeeper(s): Joyce & Doug Cooper. $60-75. MC, VISA. 3 rooms, 1 with PB. Breakfast and snacks/refreshments included in rates. Type of meal: Full bkfst. Beds: KQT. Ceiling fan in room. Spa, sauna and library on premises. Fishing, biking, hiking, downhill skiing and cross-country skiing nearby.

Certificate may be used: Sunday through Thursday nights, excluding holidays, subject to availability.

Wisconsin

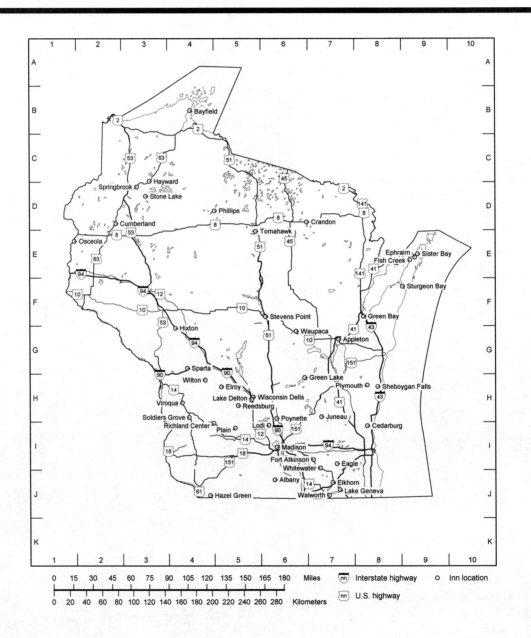

Albany   J6

Albany House

405 S Mill St
Albany, WI 53502-9502
(608)862-3636 Fax:(608)862-1837

Circa 1908. The brick walkway, French-tiled foyer, over-stuffed furniture and abundance of flowers both inside and out set the comfortable tone for this three-story inn. A baby grand piano in the large foyer and fireplace in the living room also add to the pleasant atmosphere. The guest rooms have large windows overlooking the garden and are furnished with many antiques and collectibles. Outside, maple and black walnut trees and various gardens grace the inn's two-acre property. Guests can tour New Glarus, a village known as America's Little Switzerland, which is a short drive away. Guests also can enjoy a bicycle ride on the nearby Sugar River Trail or canoe on the Sugar River.

Innkeeper(s): Ken & Margie Stoup. $65-95. MC, VISA, PC. 6 rooms, 4 with PB, 1 with FP. Breakfast included in rates. Types of meals: Full bkfst and early coffee/tea. Beds: KQD. Ceiling fan in room. Air conditioning. VCR, library, swings, hammock and horseshoe on premises. Antiquing, bicycling, canoeing/kayaking, fishing, parks and cross-country skiing nearby.

Location: Village.

Publicity: *Madison, Monroe Evening Times, Silent Sports and Video: A Video Tour of Wisconsin's Bed & Breakfasts.*

"Was even more than I expected."

Certificate may be used: Monday-Thursday, May-October. Anytime, November-April.

Oak Hill Manor

401 E Main St
Albany, WI 53502-9797
(608)862-1400 Fax:(608)862-1403
Internet: www.oakhillmanor.com

Circa 1908. The state's scenic Hidden Valley region is home to this American four-square inn, just 30 minutes south of Madison. Sylvia's Room boasts a five-foot iron and brass headboard on its queen bed, a view of the garden and a fireplace. The romantic Judith's Room features a heart-shaped queen canopy bed. Guests enjoy a three-course gourmet breakfast, including a sample of some of the area's outstanding cheeses. Nearby recreational activities include canoeing the Sugar River, hiking the Ice Age Trail or riding the inn's bikes on the Sugar River Trail.

Innkeeper(s): Donna & Glen Rothe. $65-85. MC, VISA, PC, TC. 4 rooms with PB, 1 with FP. Breakfast, afternoon tea and snacks/refreshments included in rates. Types of meals: Full gourmet bkfst and early coffee/tea. Beds: Q. Air conditioning. Bicycles, library and gazebo on premises. Antiquing, fishing, bicycle trail, parks, shopping, cross-country skiing and water sports nearby.

Location: Small village.

Publicity: *Monroe Times and Janesville Gazette.*

Certificate may be used: Sunday-Thursday, subject to availability.

Appleton   G7

The Queen Anne B&B

837 E College Ave
Appleton, WI 54911-5619
(920)831-9903 (888)241-0419

Circa 1895. On a tree-lined street, The Queen Anne features polished oak, pine and maple floors, and beveled- and stained-glass windows. The dining area has bay windows. Furnishings include Victorian, Louis XV, Eastlake and Empire.

Innkeeper(s): Emilie & Tom Sabol. $85-150. 4 rooms, 2 with PB and 1 conference room. Type of meal: Full bkfst. Beds: Q. TV in room.

Publicity: *The Post Crescent and Valleysun.*

"The Queen Anne is an expression of your warmth & hospitality and a delightful place to be."

Certificate may be used: Monday-Thursday, January-March.

Bayfield   B4

Apple Tree Inn

Rt 1, Box 251, Hwy 135
Bayfield, WI 54814-9767
(715)779-5572 (800)400-6532

Circa 1911. The Apple Tree Inn is a fully restored farmhouse overlooking Lake Superior. It was once owned by a dairy farmer and landscape artist. A hearty, country-style breakfast is served in the sunroom, which boasts a panoramic view of Madeline Island and Lake Superior. Guest rooms are furnished in early Americana style and three have lake views.

Innkeeper(s): Ellen & Rick Melcher. $85-95. MC, VISA, PC. 5 rooms with PB. Breakfast included in rates. Types of meals: Full gourmet bkfst and early coffee/tea. Beds: KQD. Ceiling fan in room. Air conditioning. VCR on premises. Antiquing, canoeing/kayaking, fishing, sailing, live theater, parks, shopping, downhill skiing, cross-country skiing and water sports nearby.

Pets allowed: Please check with innkeeper.

Location: Country.

Publicity: *Lake Superior.*

"You made us feel like old friends rather than guests."

Certificate may be used: Nov. 1-April 30, anytime, void with any other discount offer.

Thimbleberry Inn B&B

15021 Pagent Rd, PO Box 1007
Bayfield, WI 54814-1007
(715)779-5757

Circa 1992. The waters of Lake Superior sparkle beside the 400-foot shoreline adjacent to this natural wood home. The peaceful forest setting adds to the romance of the rooms, which include fireplaces. Innkeeper Sharon Locey writes a food column and currently is writing her first cookbook. Her culinary expertise makes breakfast a gourmet treat. While enjoying your morning meal, watch for wildlife and bald eagles as they soar over the Loceys' 40 acres. The deck features a cedar hot tub perfect for relaxing after skiing, hiking or just spending the day by the lake's side.

Innkeeper(s): Sharon Locey. $79-139. 3 rooms with PB, 3 with FP and 1 suite. Breakfast included in rates. Types of meals: Full bkfst and early coffee/tea. Beds: KQ. Antiquing, fishing, sailboat, shopping, downhill skiing and cross-country skiing nearby.

Location: On Lake Superior.

Certificate may be used: Jan. 2-May 15, Nov. 1-Dec. 15, Sunday-Thursday.

Cedarburg I8

The Washington House Inn

W 62 N 573 Washington Ave
Cedarburg, WI 53012-1941
(262)375-3550 (800)554-4717 Fax:(262)375-9422
Internet: www.washingtonhouseinn.com
E-mail: whinn@execpc.com

Circa 1886. Completely renovated, this three-story cream city brick building is in the National Register. Rooms are appointed in a country Victorian style and feature antiques, whirlpool baths, vases of flowers and fireplaces. The original guest registry, more than 100 years old, is displayed proudly in the lobby, and a marble trimmed fireplace is often lit for the afternoon wine and cheese hour. Breakfast is continental and is available in the gathering room, often including recipes from a historic Cedarburg cookbook for items such as homemade muffins, cakes and breads.

Innkeeper(s): Wendy Porterfield. $79-209. MC, VISA, AX, DC, DS, TC. 34 rooms with PB, 3 suites and 1 conference room. Breakfast included in rates. Type of meal: Cont plus. Beds: KQD. Cable TV, phone, ceiling fan and VCR in room. Air conditioning. Fax, copier and sauna on premises. Antiquing, fishing, live theater, parks, shopping, cross-country skiing and sporting events nearby.

Location: Historic district.

Publicity: *Country Home and Chicago Sun-Times.*

Certificate may be used: Sunday through Thursday on $119-$209 rooms, no holidays.

Crandon D6

Courthouse Square B&B

210 E Polk St
Crandon, WI 54520-1436
(715)478-2549 Fax:(715)478-2549
E-mail: bb@newnorth.net

Circa 1905. Situated on the shores of Surprise Lake, this Victorian Shingle also manages to provide the conveniences of town with its location. The inn features antique and country furnishings, and each of its guest rooms offers a lake or park view. The area provides excellent antiquing and shopping opportunities, in addition to cross-country and downhill skiing. Visitors also enjoy borrowing a bike to explore the town, relaxing on the inn's porch or venturing across the street to a city park.

Innkeeper(s): Les & Bess Aho. $52-70. AX. 3 rooms, 1 with PB. Breakfast included in rates. Types of meals: Full gourmet bkfst and early coffee/tea. Beds: QDT. Ceiling fan, fresh flowers and sweets in room. VCR on premises. Antiquing, fishing, parks, shopping, downhill skiing, cross-country skiing and water sports nearby.

Location: Small town.

Certificate may be used: Sunday to Thursday, year-round, except holidays & special events.

Cumberland D2

The Rectory

1575 Second Ave, Box 1042
Cumberland, WI 54829
(715)822-3151

Circa 1905. This city's unique island setting makes it an ideal stopping point for those exploring the state's lake-rich Northwest. The German Gothic inn, once home to the parish priest, features charming guest rooms, all filled with antiques, heirlooms and items of interest. The Mae Jenet Room, with its striking corner turret, features a doll collection and other unique toys. Breakfasts, served in the roomy parlor, often feature the inn's famous Breakfast Pie. A gaming casino is nearby, and 50 lakes are found within a 10-mile radius of Cumberland.

Innkeeper(s): Jerry & Ethel Anderson. $60-75. MC, VISA. 4 rooms, 2 with PB. Ceiling fan in room. VCR, piano and garage on premises. Antiquing, live theater, shopping and cross-country skiing nearby.

Location: Island.

Certificate may be used: Sunday-Thursday, excluding holidays and special events.

Eagle I7

Novels Country Inn

PO Box 456, 229 E Main St
Eagle, WI 53119-0456
(414)594-3729 Fax:(414)962-2920

Circa 1895. The interior of this late 19th-century home boasts beautiful woodwork, from the carved staircase to the French doors that open into the living room. The interior features many Arts & Crafts-style pieces, as well as traditional furnishings. The coach house includes rooms with whirlpool tubs and fireplaces. Homemade breads, fresh fruit, yogurt and egg dishes are among the breakfast fare. The area offers plenty of activities, such as cross-country skiing, horseback riding and shopping for antiques.

Innkeeper(s): Tom & Karrie Houlton. $70-125. VISA, PC, TC. 9 rooms, 6 with PB, 3 with FP. Types of meals: Full bkfst, cont plus and early coffee/tea. Beds: KQT. Cable TV, phone, ceiling fan and VCR in room. Air conditioning. Fax and library on premises. Handicap access. Antiquing, fishing, golf, old World Wisconsin, bicycling, live theater, parks, shopping, cross-country skiing, sporting events and water sports nearby.

Location: state park.

"Quiet, great breakfast. Will come back again soon."

Certificate may be used: Jan. 1 to March 30, except Valentine's Day.

Elkhorn J7

Ye Olde Manor House

N7622 US Hwy 12
Elkhorn, WI 53121
(262)742-2450 Fax:(262)742-2450
Internet: www.insite.com//inns/a000252

Circa 1905. Located on three tree-shaded acres, this country manor house offers travelers all the simple comforts of home. The guest rooms, living room and dining room are decorated with a variety of antiques and

comfortable furniture that inspires a family atmosphere. One room offers a porch and views of Lauderdale Lakes. The B&B offers a full gourmet breakfast each morning.

Innkeeper(s): Babette & Marvin Henschel. $50-100. MC, VISA, AX, PC, TC. 4 rooms, 2 with PB, 1 suite and 1 conference room. Breakfast included in rates. Types of meals: Full gourmet bkfst and early coffee/tea. Beds: QDT. Cable TV in room. VCR, fax and copier on premises. Antiquing, fishing, golf, live theater, parks, shopping, downhill skiing, cross-country skiing and water sports nearby.

Location: Country.

Certificate may be used: Sunday through Thursday, except holiday weekends, and from October to May 15 any day that rooms are open.

Elroy   H5

East View B&B
33620 County P Rd
Elroy, WI 53929
(608)463-7564
Internet: www.outspokinadventures.com/eastview

Circa 1994. This comfortable ranch house offers splendid views of the countryside, with its rolling hills covered with woods. Autumn is a particularly scenic time for a visit, when the trees explode in color. The three guest rooms are simply furnished in a homey, country style with quilts topping the beds. Each room offers a pleasing view. Breakfast comes in several courses, with fresh fruit, homemade breads, a daily entree and finally a dessert. The area provides opportunities for hiking, biking, canoeing or browsing at local craft stores.

Innkeeper(s): Dom & Bev Puechner. $65-75. MC, VISA. 3 rooms with PB. Breakfast included in rates. Types of meals: Full bkfst and early coffee/tea. Beds: QD. Phone, turndown service and ceiling fan in room. Air conditioning. Walking trails on premises. Amusement parks, antiquing, golf, shopping and cross-country skiing nearby.

Pets allowed: Caged and cared for by pet owner.

Location: Country.

Publicity: *Country Inns.*

"What a wonderful treat it was to stay at East View. The view was magnificent and the breakfasts superb."

Certificate may be used: Sunday through Thursday, Jan. 2-Dec. 31 except Holy Saturday, Easter Sunday, Thanksgiving, Christmas Eve, Christmas Day.

Ephraim   E9

Hillside Hotel B&B
9980 Hwy 42, PO Box 17
Ephraim, WI 54211-0017
(920)854-2417 (800)423-7023 Fax:(920)854-4240
Internet: www.hillsidehotel.com
E-mail: mcneil@juno.com

Circa 1854. In the National Register, this Victorian country house is the last remaining "grand hotel" of the turn-of-the-century hotels in the area. On the waterfront, Hillside provides views of Eagle Harbor and Green Bay from most of the rooms and the 100-foot veranda. There is a private beach and moorings for small craft. Guest rooms feature antiques, feather beds and four-poster beds. Afternoon tea is offered with scones, petit fours and tea breads, while eggs Benedict is often found on the breakfast menu along with specialty items found locally.

Innkeeper(s): David & Karen McNeil. $79-94. MC, VISA, DS, PC, TC. 12 rooms, 2 with FP, 2 cottages and 1 conference room. Breakfast and afternoon tea included in rates. Type of meal: Full gourmet bkfst. Beds: QD. Turndown service, ceiling fan, fireplace and AC and refrigerator in cottages in room.

VCR, fax, copier, swimming, private beach and small boat moorings available on premises. Amusement parks, antiquing, fishing, golf, world-class galleries, musical events, live theater, parks, shopping, cross-country skiing, sporting events, tennis and water sports nearby.

Publicity: *Milwaukee Journal, Chicago Tribune and Wisconsin Restaurant Magazine.*

"You have a very nice inn and the breakfasts were great. You all made us feel at home (without the chores) and it was like we'd known you for a long time."

Certificate may be used: From Nov. 1 to May 1, Sunday-Friday.

Fish Creek   E9

Thorp House Inn & Cottages
4135 Bluff Ln, PO Box 490
Fish Creek, WI 54212
(920)868-2444
Internet: www.thorphouseinn.com
E-mail: innkeeper@thorphouseinn.com

Circa 1902. Freeman Thorp picked the site for this home because of its view of Green Bay and the village. Before his house was finished, however, he perished in the bay when the Erie L. Hackley sank. His wife completed it as a guest house. Each room is decorated with English or Victorian antiques. A stone fireplace is the focal point of the parlor, and four of the cottages on the property have fireplaces. Some cottages have whirlpools and all have kitchens, cable TVs and VCRs. Listed in the National Register of Historic Places, everything upon which the eye might rest in the inn must be "of the era." Breakfast is not included in the rates for cottage guests.

Innkeeper(s): Christine & Sverre Falck-Pedersen. $85-185. PC, TC. 6 cottages with PB. Breakfast included in rates. Types of meals: Cont plus and early coffee/tea. Beds: KQDT. Ceiling fan in room. Bicycles on premises. Antiquing, fishing, summer art school, music festival, live theater, parks, shopping, cross-country skiing and water sports nearby.

Location: Small village.

Publicity: *Green Bay Press-Gazette, Milwaukee Journal/Sentinel, McCall's, Minnesota Monthly and Madison PM.*

"Amazing attention to detail from restoration to the furnishings. A very first-class experience."

Certificate may be used: Sunday through Thursday nights, Nov. 6 through May, holidays excluded.

Fort Atkinson   I7

Lamp Post Inn
408 S Main St
Fort Atkinson, WI 53538-2231
(920)563-6561
Internet: www.thelamppostinn.com

Circa 1878. Prepare to enjoy an authentic Victorian experience at this charming, restored home. Innkeepers Debra and Mike Rusch get into the spirit of things by donning Victorian ware. Each of the guest rooms includes a working Victrola, which guests are encourage to use and enjoy. Debra and Mike pamper guests with fresh flowers and chocolates. Rooms are furnished completely with antiques. Breakfasts include specialties such as jelly-filled muffins, scones, Swedish puff pancakes and strawberry sorbet.

Innkeeper(s): Debra & Mike Rusch. $70-105. PC, TC. 3 rooms, 2 with PB. Breakfast included in rates. Types of meals: Full gourmet bkfst and early coffee/tea. Beds: D. Phone, VCR and jacuzzi in room. Air conditioning.

Location: Small town.

Certificate may be used: Sunday through Thursday, excluding holidays.

Green Bay F8

The Astor House B&B

637 S Monroe Ave
Green Bay, WI 54301-3614
(920)432-3585 (888)303-6370
Internet: www.astorhouse.com
E-mail: astor@execpc.com

Circa 1888. Located in the Astor Historic District, the Astor House is completely surrounded by Victorian homes. Guests have their choice of five rooms, each uniquely decorated for a range of ambiance, from the Vienna Balconies to the Marseilles Garden to the Hong Kong Retreat. The parlor, veranda and many suites feature a grand view of City Centre's lighted church towers. This home is also the first and only B&B in Green Bay and received the Mayor's Award for Remodeling and Restoration. Business travelers should take notice of the private phone lines in each room, as well as the ability to hook up a modem.

Innkeeper(s): Greg & Barbara Robinson. $115-152. MC, VISA, AX, DC, DS. 5 rooms with PB, 4 with FP and 3 suites. Breakfast included in rates. Type of meal: Cont plus. Beds: KQDT. Cable TV, phone, VCR, gas fireplaces and double whirlpool tub (4 of 5 rooms) in room. Air conditioning. Amusement parks, antiquing, fishing, live theater, parks, shopping, cross-country skiing, sporting events and water sports nearby.

Location: City.

Publicity: *Chicago Sun-Times and Corporate Reports.*

Certificate may be used: Monday-Thursday.

Green Lake H6

McConnell Inn

497 S Lawson Dr
Green Lake, WI 54941-8700
(414)294-6430

Circa 1901. This stately home features many of its original features, including leaded windows, woodwork, leather wainscoting and parquet floors. Each of the guest rooms includes beds covered with handmade quilts and clawfoot tubs. The grand, master suite comprises the entire third floor and boasts 14-foot vaulted beam ceilings, Victorian walnut furnishings, a Jacuzzi and six-foot oak buffet now converted into a unique bathroom vanity. Innkeeper Mary Jo Johnson, a pastry chef, creates the wonderful pastries that accompany an expansive breakfast with fresh fruit, granola and delectable entrees.

Innkeeper(s): Mary Jo Johnson. $80-130. MC, VISA. 5 rooms. Breakfast included in rates. Type of meal: Full bkfst.

Certificate may be used: November-April.

Hayward C3

Lumberman's Mansion Inn

204 E Fourth St
Hayward, WI 54843-0885
(715)634-3012 Fax:(715)634-5724
Internet: www.haywardlakes.com/mansion.htm

Circa 1887. This Queen Anne Victorian, once the home of a local lumber baron, sits on a hill overlooking the city, park and pond. An oak staircase, maple floors, tiled fireplaces, pocket doors and a carriage stoop are among the finely restored details. Antique furnishings blend with modern amenities such as whirlpool tubs and a video library. Wild rice pancakes, Wisconsin sausages and freshly squeezed cranberry juice are some of the regional specialties featured for breakfast. The innkeepers host many seasonal events and evening lectures. Plays are sometimes performed on the front porch.

Innkeeper(s): Jan Hinrichs Blaedel & Wendy Hinrichs Sanders. $70-100. MC, VISA, PC, TC. 5 rooms with PB, 2 suites and 1 conference room. Breakfast included in rates. Type of meal: Full bkfst. Beds: Q. Spa and bicycles on premises. Antiquing, fishing, golf, biking, cross-country skiing and water sports nearby.

Publicity: *Sawyer County Record, Chicago Sun Times, Wisconsin Trails, Minneapolis Star Tribune and Wisconsin Country Life.*

"The food was excellent. And the extra personal touches (chocolate on the pillow, cookies & pie at night, muffins in the morning, etc.) were especially nice. This is definitely the best B&B we've ever been to."

Certificate may be used: Sunday-Thursday.

Hazel Green J4

De Winters of Hazel Green

2225 Main St, PO Box 384
Hazel Green, WI 53811-0384
(608)854-2768

Circa 1847. This Federal and Greek Revival home dates back to pre-Civil War times. Innkeeper Don Simison was born in the home and his family heirlooms fill the house. A hearty homemade breakfast is served each morning. Explore Hazel Green or just relax at the inn. The city hosts some interesting attractions including a parade and open house of historic homes early in December.

Innkeeper(s): Don & Cari Simison. $45-75. TC. 3 rooms, 1 with PB. Breakfast included in rates. Type of meal: Full bkfst. Beds: D. Air conditioning. Library on premises. Antiquing, fishing, live theater, parks, shopping and downhill skiing nearby.

Location: Small town near Galena, IL.

"Good food and fun."

Certificate may be used: Jan. 30 to Oct. 1, Nov. 1 to Jan. 30.

Wisconsin House Stagecoach Inn

2105 Main, PO Box 71
Hazel Green, WI 53811-0071
(608)854-2233
Internet: wisconsinhouse.com
E-mail: wishouse@mhtc.net

Circa 1846. Located in southwest Wisconsin's historic lead mining region, this one-time stagecoach stop will delight antique-lovers. The spacious two-story inn once hosted Ulysses S. Grant, whose home is just across the border in Illinois. One of the inn's guest rooms bears his name and features a walnut four-poster bed. Don't miss the chance to join the Dischs on a Saturday evening for their gourmet dinner, served by reservation only.

Innkeeper(s): Ken & Pat Disch. $55-110. MC, VISA, AX, DS, PC. 8 rooms, 6 with PB and 2 suites. Breakfast included in rates. Types of meals: Full gourmet bkfst and early coffee/tea. Beds: KQDT. Air conditioning. Copier, bicycles and library on premises. Antiquing, fishing, live theater, parks, downhill skiing and cross-country skiing nearby.

Location: City.

Publicity: *Travel & Leisure, Milwaukee Magazine, Chicago Magazine and Milwaukee Journal.*

Certificate may be used: May through October anytime, rooms with shared baths only. Other months all rooms available.

Hixton G4

Triple R Resort

N11818 Hixton-Levis Rd
Hixton, WI 54635
(715)964-8777 (888)963-8777 Fax:(715)964-7777

Circa 1971. Located on 525 acres, this rustic lodge was formerly a youth horse camp. There's a five-acre lake just steps away from the inn, offering a little dock. A fireplace in the gathering area is a popular spot for guests to discuss the day's activities. A campground is also on the property. Scrambled eggs, sausage, gravy with biscuits and hash browns are only part of a typical breakfast here.

$54-73. MC, VISA, DS, PC, TC. 6 rooms, 4 with PB and 1 suite. Breakfast included in rates. Type of meal: Full bkfst. Beds: KDT. Turndown service in room. Air conditioning. VCR, fax, copier, swimming, horseshoes, camping, volleyball and hiking on premises. Antiquing, fishing, golf, live theater, parks, shopping, cross-country skiing and water sports nearby.

Pets allowed: must be accompanied by owner at all times.

Location: Country.

Publicity: *Banner Journal and WEAU Channel 13.*

Certificate may be used: May 15 to Nov. 15, Sunday to Thursday, excluding holiday weeks.

Juneau H7

Country Retreat B&B on Primrose

N4589 Primrose Ln
Juneau, WI 53039-9787
(920)386-2912 (800)434-3910
E-mail: mlroth@nconnect.net

The most interesting room in this contemporary two-story house is the sunroom overlooking gardens and the home's 10 acres. There's also a sauna, pool table and exercise equipment to use. The largest guest room offers a whirlpool tub and a king-size bed.

Innkeeper(s): Mark & Linda Roth. $36-80. MC, VISA, AX, DS, PC, TC. 4 rooms, 1 with PB. Breakfast included in rates. Types of meals: Full bkfst, cont plus and early coffee/tea. Beds: KQT. Air conditioning. Spa, sauna, library, pool table and exercise equip on premises. Antiquing, golf, wild Goose State Trail and cross-country skiing nearby.

Location: Country.

Certificate may be used: Jan. 30 to Dec. 31, Saturday-Thursday.

Lake Delton H5

The Swallow's Nest B&B

141 Sarrington, PO Box 418
Lake Delton, WI 53940-0418
(608)254-6900

Circa 1988. This inn has a picturesque view of the Wisconsin Dells and Lake Delton. The Swallow's Nest features a two-story atrium with skylights, and cathedral windows and ceiling. Guests may relax on the screened deck, in the library by the fireplace or in the gazebo by the waterfall. The inn is furnished with English period furniture, rocking chairs, lace curtains, handmade quilts and goose-down comforters.

Innkeeper(s): Mary Ann Stemo. $65-70. MC, VISA. 4 rooms with PB, 2 with FP. Breakfast included in rates. Type of meal: Full bkfst. Beds: QDT. Phone in room. Air conditioning. Amusement parks, antiquing, live theater, shopping, downhill skiing, cross-country skiing and sporting events nearby.

Publicity: *Milwaukee Journal and Wisconsin Trails.*

"Your home is beautiful, and the breakfasts were wonderful!"

Certificate may be used: Monday through Thursday, no holidays or holiday weekends.

Lake Geneva J7

T.C. Smith Historic Inn B&B

865 W Main St
Lake Geneva, WI 53147-1804
(414)248-1097 (800)423-0233 Fax:(414)248-1672
Internet: www.tcsmithinn.com

Circa 1845. Listed in the National Register of Historic Places, this High Victorian inn blends elements of Greek Revival and Italianate architecture. The inn has massive carved wooden doors, hand-painted moldings and woodwork, a high-ceilinged foyer, an original parquet floor, Oriental carpets, museum-quality period antiques and European oil paintings. Guests enjoy tea in the Grand Parlor by a marble fireplace, sipping morning coffee while taking in the view from the rooftop balcony and breakfasting on an open veranda overlooking Lake Geneva. The grounds are also impressive, boasting formal Victorian gardens, a spacious gazebo, a water garden and an exotic fish pool.

Innkeeper(s): The Marks Family. $135-375. MC, VISA, AX, DC, DS, PC, TC. 8 rooms with PB, 5 with FP, 2 suites and 2 conference rooms. Breakfast, afternoon tea and snacks/refreshments included in rates. Types of meals: Full gourmet bkfst and early coffee/tea. Beds: KQD. Ceiling fan, VCR and four with whirlpools in room. Air conditioning. Fax, copier and bicycles on premises. Antiquing, fishing, live theater, parks, downhill skiing, cross-country skiing and water sports nearby.

Pets allowed: In specific rooms only.

Location: Downtown Lake Geneva.

Publicity: *Keystone Country Peddler and Pioneer Press Publication.*

"As much as we wanted to be on the beach, we found it impossible to leave the house. It's so beautiful and relaxing."

Certificate may be used: Monday through Thursday, Nov. 15-April 15, no holidays.

Lodi I6

Prairie Garden B&B

W13172 Hwy 188
Lodi, WI 53555
(608)592-5187 (800)380-8427
Internet: www.mailbag.com/users/prairiegarden/
E-mail: prairiegarden@bigfoot.com

This 19th-century farmhouse offers four guest rooms, each decorated in a pleasant Victorian style. Innkeeper Todd Olson includes family pictures and his aunt's artwork within the decor. In the mornings, he or partner Dennis Stocks, deliver a delicious homemade breakfast to their guests' rooms. The B&B is closed to many attractions, including skiing, a nude beach, a casino, winery and Lake Wisconsin.

Innkeeper(s): Todd Olson & Dennis Stocks. $55-115. MC, VISA, DS, PC. 4 rooms, 1 with PB. Breakfast and afternoon tea included in rates. Type of meal: Full bkfst. Beds: D. Cable TV, turndown service and ceiling fan in room. Air conditioning. VCR, fax, spa, stables and bicycles on premises. Handicap access. Amusement parks, antiquing, fishing, golf, live theater, parks, shopping, downhill skiing, cross-country skiing, sporting events, tennis and water sports nearby.

Pets Allowed.

Location: Country.

Publicity: *In Step Newsmagazine.*

Certificate may be used: Nov. 1-April 30, Sunday through Thursday.

Madison I6

Arbor House, An Environmental Inn

3402 Monroe St
Madison, WI 53711-1702
(608)238-2981
Internet: www.arbor-house.com

Circa 1853. Nature-lovers not only will enjoy the inn's close access to a 1,280-acre nature preserve, they will appreciate the innkeepers' ecological theme. Organic sheets and towels are offered for guests as well as environmentally safe bath products. Arbor House is one of Madison's oldest existing homes and features plenty of historic features, such as romantic reading chairs and antiques, mixed with modern amenities and unique touches. Five guest rooms include a whirlpool tub and three have fireplaces. The Annex guest rooms include private balconies. The innkeepers offer many amenities for business travelers, including value-added corporate rates. The award-winning inn has been recognized as a model of urban ecology. Lake Wingra is within walking distance as are biking and nature trails, bird watching and a host of other outdoor activities. Guests enjoy complimentary canoeing and use of mountain bikes.

Innkeeper(s): John & Cathie Imes. $89-210. MC, VISA, AX, PC, TC. 8 rooms with PB, 3 with FP, 1 suite and 1 conference room. Breakfast included in rates. Types of meals: Full bkfst and cont plus. Beds: KQ. Cable TV, phone, ceiling fan and VCR in room. Air conditioning. Fax and copier on premises. Handicap access. Antiquing, fishing, parks, shopping, cross-country skiing, sporting events and water sports nearby.

Location: City.

Publicity: *Money Magazine, Coop America and E.*

"What a delightful treat in the middle of Madison. Absolutely, unquestionably, the best time I've spent in a hotel or otherwise. B&Bs are the only way to go! Thank you!"

Certificate may be used: January-March, Sunday-Thursday, excluding holidays. John Nolen & Cozy Rose guest rooms only.

Osceola E1

St. Croix River Inn

305 River St, PO Box 356
Osceola, WI 54020-0356
(715)294-4248 (800)645-8820
Internet: www.stcroixriverinn.co

Circa 1908. This stone house is poised on a bluff overlooking the St. Croix River. The sitting room overlooks the river. All guest rooms have whirlpool baths. Rooms feature such amenities as four-poster canopy beds, a tile fireplace, a Palladian window that stretches from floor to ceiling, stenciling, bull's-eye moldings and private balconies. Breakfast is served in room.

Innkeeper(s): Sonja Schmitt. $100-200. MC, VISA, AX, DC, CB, DS, PC, TC. 7 rooms with PB and 2 suites. Breakfast and snacks/refreshments included in rates. Types of meals: Full bkfst, cont, country bkfst and early coffee/tea. Beds: Q. TV, phone, turndown service and VCR in room. Central air. Spa on premises. Handicap access. Antiquing, beaches, bicycling, canoeing/kayaking, golf, hiking, live theater, shopping, downhill skiing, cross-country skiing and water sports nearby.

Location: Country.

Publicity: *Chicago Sun-Times, Skyway News and St. Paul Pioneer Press.*

Certificate may be used: Sunday-Thursday, all year. Excludes holidays.

Phillips D5

East Highland School House B&B

West 4342, Hwy D
Phillips, WI 54555
(715)339-3492

Guests are invited to ring the bell at this restored one-room schoolhouse. An addition to the building in 1920 features rooms with rustic exposed beams, brick walls and original light fixtures. Innkeepers Jeanne and Russ Kirchmeyer filled the home with family antiques and turn-of-the-century pieces. Lacy curtains, doilies and hand-hooked rugs lend to the romantic, country atmosphere. Two museums featuring a 1900s kit area, school area and old logging and farming tools have been added to the inn; one in the basement and one in the barn across the street. The kitchen, which once served as a stage for the school, is now where Jeanne prepares the expansive morning meals.

Innkeeper(s): Russ & Jeanne Kirchmeyer. $45-60. 4 rooms. Breakfast included in rates. Type of meal: Full bkfst.

Certificate may be used: Year-round, weekends if available.

Plain I5

Bettinger House B&B

855 Wachter Ave, Hwy 23
Plain, WI 53577
(608)546-2951 Fax:(608)546-2951

Circa 1904. This two-story brick inn once was home to the town's midwife, (and the innkeeper's grandmother) who delivered more than 300 babies here. The current innkeepers are just as eager to bring new guests into their home. The Elizabeth Room, named for the midwife, boasts a round king-size bed and private bath. Lavish country breakfasts often include potatoes dug from the innkeeper's off-site farm, sour cream cucumbers, breakfast pie with eggs and sausage, rhubarb coffeecake and sorbet. Area attractions are plentiful, including the House on the Rock, St. Anne's Shrine and the Wisconsin River. Be sure to visit the nearby Cedar Grove Cheese Factory.

Innkeeper(s): Marie Neider. $55-75. MC, VISA. 5 rooms, 3 with PB. Breakfast included in rates. Type of meal: Full bkfst. Beds: KQ. Ceiling fan in room. Air conditioning. VCR, fax and copier on premises. Antiquing, fishing, live theater, parks, shopping, cross-country skiing and water sports nearby.

Location: Village.

Certificate may be used: Sunday through Thursday, except holidays.

Plymouth H8

Hillwind Farm B&B

N 4922 Hillwind Rd
Plymouth, WI 53073
(920)892-2199
Internet: www.execpc.com/hillwind

Circa 1856. Hillwind, a charming Victorian, is one of the oldest farmhouses in the county, built prior to the Civil War. The rooms are decorated in a romantic Victorian style with antiques, colorful wallpapers and luxurious linens. Three of the rooms offer a fireplace and double whirlpool tub. There are private porches for those who wish to relax and enjoy the pastoral setting. The breakfasts are sometimes served on the covered front veranda.

Innkeeper(s): Kim & Art Jasso. $140. MC, VISA, PC. 4 rooms with PB, 3 with FP and 1 suite. Breakfast included in rates. Beds: Q. Cable TV, ceiling fan, VCR, double whirlpool tubs and outside sitting porches in room. Air conditioning. Antiquing, fishing, golf, parks, shopping, cross-country skiing, tennis and water sports nearby.

Location: Country setting old farmstead.

"Thank you for a weekend we'll both never forget. We're engaged!"

Certificate may be used: Monday-Thursday, November through April, excludes month of February and holidays.

Yankee Hill Inn B&B

405 Collins St
Plymouth, WI 53073-2361
(920)892-2222
Internet: www.yankeehillinn.com

Circa 1870. Two outstanding examples of 19th-century architecture comprise this inn, one a striking Italianate Gothic listed in the National Register, and the other a Queen Anne Victorian with many custom touches. Between the two impressive structures, visitors will choose from 12 spacious guest rooms, featuring antique furnishings and handmade quilts. Visitors can walk to downtown, where they will find an antique mall, shopping and fine dining.

Innkeeper(s): Peg Stahlman. $78-106. MC, VISA. 12 rooms with PB. Breakfast included in rates. Types of meals: Full bkfst and early coffee/tea. Beds: QD. VCR on premises. Antiquing, fishing, bicycling, hiking, shopping and cross-country skiing nearby.

Location: Small city.

Publicity: *Wisconsin Country Life, Milwaukee Journal, Plymouth Review and Wisconsin Trails.*

"You have mastered the art of comfort. All the perfect little touches make this a dream come true. I only regret that we cannot stay forever."

Certificate may be used: Nov. 1-April 30, anytime except holidays or holiday weekends. May 1-Oct. 31, Monday through Thursday only.

Poynette   H6

Jamieson House

407 N Franklin St
Poynette, WI 53955-9490
(608)635-4100 Fax:(608)635-2292

Circa 1879. Victorian elegance and proximity to recreational activities and sightseeing attractions help bring enthusiastic guests to this inn, which consists of three different structures. A main house, guest house and schoolhouse are furnished with antiques gathered from the entire Midwest. Four of the rooms have whirlpool tubs, and the inn's breakfast fare is noteworthy. Water sports are just a few miles away on Lake Wisconsin, and Baraboo's Circus World Museum, Madison and the Wisconsin Dells are within easy driving distance.

Innkeeper(s): Heidemarie Hutchison. $65-155. MC, VISA, AX, DS. 11 rooms with PB, 1 with FP and 1 conference room. Breakfast included in rates. Type of meal: Full bkfst. Beds: KQDT. TV and phone in room.

Publicity: *Capital Times, North West News and Poynette Press.*

Certificate may be used: Sunday-Thursday, anytime, excluding holidays.

Reedsburg   H5

Parkview B&B

211 N Park St
Reedsburg, WI 53959-1652
(608)524-4333
Internet: www.jvlnet.com/~parkview
E-mail: parkview@jvlnet.com

Circa 1895. Tantalizingly close to Baraboo and Spring Green, this central Wisconsin inn overlooks a city park in the historic district. The gracious innkeepers delight in tending to their guests' desires and offer wake-up coffee and a morning paper. The home's first owners were in the hardware business, so there are many original, unique fixtures, in addition to hardwood floors, intricate woodwork, leaded and etched windows and a suitors' window. The downtown business district is just a block away.

Innkeeper(s): Tom & Donna Hofmann. $65-80. MC, VISA, AX. 4 rooms, 2 with PB. Breakfast included in rates. Types of meals: Full gourmet bkfst and early coffee/tea. Beds: QT. TV and ceiling fan in room. Air conditioning. Antiquing, biking, hiking, State Parks, parks and shopping nearby.

Location: City.

Publicity: *Reedsburg Report and Reedsburg Times-Press.*

"Your hospitality was great! You all made us feel right at home."

Certificate may be used: Sunday-Thursday, Nov. 1-April 30.

Richland Center   I4

The Mansion

323 S Central Ave
Richland Center, WI 53581-2500
(608)647-2808

Circa 1916. As the birthplace of Frank Lloyd Wright, Richland Center attracts its share of visitors. Guests at this Mission Inn, with its Prairie-style overtones, are within walking distance of the Warehouse, designed by Wright during his Mayan period. The Warehouse also is home to the Frank Lloyd Wright Museum. Other fine examples of Wright's work are found less than a half-hour's drive in Spring Green, site of his home and school, Taliesin. The inn's visitors select from the Mandarin, Meadowlands, Oakwood and Scandia guest rooms. Summer visitors enjoy the Farmer's Market, a short walk from the inn.

Innkeeper(s): Beth Caulkins & Harvey Glanzer. $45-55. PC. 4 rooms, 1 with FP, 1 suite and 1 conference room. Breakfast included in rates. Types of meals: Cont plus and early coffee/tea. Beds: QDT. Air conditioning. VCR, library and refrigerator in guest area on premises. Antiquing, fishing, golf, cinema on next block, live theater, parks, shopping, cross-country skiing and tennis nearby.

Pets allowed: By arrangement.

Certificate may be used: May 1 to Nov. 10, Sunday to Friday.

Sheboygan Falls   H8

The Rochester Inn

504 Water St
Sheboygan Falls, WI 53085-1455
(920)467-3123
Internet: www.classicinns.com
E-mail: rochesterinn@excel.net

Circa 1848. This Greek Revival inn is furnished with Queen Anne Victorian antiques, wet bars and four-poster beds. The most romantic offerings are the 600-square-foot suites. They include living rooms with camel back couches and wing back chairs on the first floor and bedrooms with double whirlpool tubs on the second floor. Sheboygan Falls is one mile from the village of Kohler.

Innkeeper(s): Sean & Jacquelyn O'Dwanny. $99-160. MC, VISA, AX, PC, TC. 6 suites. Breakfast included in rates. Types of meals: Full gourmet bkfst, cont plus and early coffee/tea. Beds: Q. Cable TV, phone, VCR and whirlpool in room. Air conditioning. Antiquing, fishing, golf, black Wolf Run, Kohler, WI, parks, shopping, cross-country skiing, tennis and water sports nearby.

Location: small town.

Certificate may be used: Sunday-Thursday, Nov. 1-May 1, some restrictions apply.

Sister Bay   E9

The Wooden Heart Inn

11086 Hwy 42
Sister Bay, WI 54234
(920)854-9097

This contemporary log home in the woods of beautiful Door County offers antique furnishings, ceiling fans and queen beds. An adjoining loft is available to read, relax or watch television. Guests frequently convene in the greatroom before the stone fireplace. The full country breakfasts are served in the great room. A gift shop specializing in hearts is on the premises.

Innkeeper(s): Mike Hagerman. $90-95. MC, VISA. 3 rooms. Breakfast included in rates. Types of meals: Full bkfst and early coffee/tea. Ceiling fan in room. Air conditioning. VCR on premises. Amusement parks, antiquing, live theater, shopping and cross-country skiing nearby.

Certificate may be used: Nov. 1-April 30, Sunday through Thursday.

Soldiers Grove   H4

Old Oak Inn & Acorn Pub

Rt 1, Box 1500, Hwy 131 S
Soldiers Grove, WI 54655-9777
(608)624-5217

Circa 1900. Guests will find lodging and dining at this spacious Queen Anne Victorian turreted inn, a mile from town. Beautiful etched and stained glass and woodcarving dominate the interior, while the guest rooms boast antique-style furnishings and imported woodwork. The area is well-known for its antiquing, cross-country skiing and fishing, and many visitors just enjoy soaking up the abundant local scenery. The inn's facilities make it a natural location for meetings and receptions, and it also is popular with those celebrating anniversaries.

Innkeeper(s): Karen Kovars. $48-62. MC, VISA. 7 rooms. Types of meals: Full gourmet bkfst, cont plus and early coffee/tea. Beds: KDT. Cable TV in room. Air conditioning. VCR on premises. Antiquing, fishing, parks, shopping, downhill skiing, cross-country skiing and water sports nearby.

Location: Small town.

Certificate may be used: Nov. 1-March 1, anytime; March 1-Oct. 31, Sunday through Thursday, with reservations.

Sparta   G4

Justin Trails B&B Resort

7452 Kathryn Ave
Sparta, WI 54656-9729
(608)269-4522 (800)488-4521 Fax:(608)269-3280
Internet: www.justintrails.com
E-mail: justntrailsbb@centuryinter.net

Circa 1920. Nestled in a scenic valley sits this 200-acre farm. Guests are encouraged to explore the hiking, snowshoe and cross-country ski trails. The innkeepers offer ski and snowshoe

rentals and lessons for both adults and children. In addition to delightfully decorated rooms in the farmhouse, there are two Scandinavian log houses and a plush, restored granary for those desiring more privacy. Each of these cottages includes a whirlpool bath and a fireplace. There also is a suite in the farmhouse with a fireplace and whirlpool. The well-cared-for grounds and buildings reflect the innkeepers' pride in their home, which was built by Don's grandfather. Guests will find cats, kittens, rabbits, chickens, a pygmy goat named Peter, and Heidi, a Siberian Husky dog on the premises.

Innkeeper(s): Don & Donna Justin. $80-300. MC, VISA, AX, DS, PC, TC. 7 rooms with PB, 5 with FP, 3 cottages and 1 conference room. Breakfast included in rates. Type of meal: Full bkfst. Beds: KQT. Ceiling fan in room. Air conditioning. Disc golf on premises. Antiquing, fishing, golf, amish, snowshoe trails, parks, shopping, downhill skiing and cross-country skiing nearby.

Pets allowed: $10 per pet per day.

Location: Country.

Publicity: *Milwaukee Journal/Sentinel, Wisconsin Trails, Travel America, Family Fun and Family Life.*

Certificate may be used: Nov. 1-June 30, Monday-Thursday, except holidays.

Springbrook   D3

The Stout Trout B&B

W4244 Cty F
Springbrook, WI 54875-9801
(715)466-2790

Circa 1900. Located on 40 acres of rolling, wooded countryside, The Stout Trout overlooks a lily-ringed bay on Gull Lake. The lake can be viewed from the living room, dining areas and second-floor guest rooms. The inn features wood-plank floors, folk art, classic prints and country-style furniture. Homemade jams and maple syrup are served.

Innkeeper(s): Kathleen Fredricks. $65-75. 4 rooms with PB. Breakfast included in rates. Type of meal: Full bkfst. Beds: QD. TV and phone in room. Antiquing, fishing, shopping, cross-country skiing and sporting events nearby.

Publicity: *Chicago Tribune and Wisconsin West Magazine.*

"Thank you again for the comfortable setting, great food and gracious hospitality!"

Certificate may be used: Nov. 1-May 30, Sunday through Thursday.

Stevens Point   F6

Dreams of Yesteryear B&B

1100 Brawley St
Stevens Point, WI 54481-3536
(715)341-4525 Fax:(715)344-3047
Internet: dreamsofyesteryear.com
E-mail: bonnie@dreamsofyesteryear.com

Circa 1901. This elegant, three-story, 4,000-square-foot Queen Anne home is within walking distance of downtown, the Wisconsin River and the University of Wisconsin. The inn features golden oak woodwork, hardwood floors and leaded glass. Each guest room offers exquisite decor; the third-floor Ballroom Suite boasts a whirlpool. Gourmet breakfasts are served in the inn's formal dining room. An excellent hiking trail is just a block from the inn.

Innkeeper(s): Bonnie & Bill Maher. $58-142. MC, VISA, AX, DS, PC, TC. 6 rooms, 4 with PB and 2 suites. Breakfast, afternoon tea and snacks/refreshments included in rates. Types of meals: Full gourmet bkfst and early coffee/tea. Beds: KQDT. Cable TV and phone in room. Air conditioning. VCR, library, piano and victrolas on premises. Amusement parks, antiquing, fishing, historical attractions, hiking trails, live theater, parks, shopping, downhill skiing, cross-country skiing, sporting events and water sports nearby.

Location: City.

Publicity: *Victorian Homes, Reach, Stevens Point Journal and News WAOW Channel 9.*

"Something from a Hans Christian Anderson fairy tale."

Certificate may be used: Nov. 15-March 1, Monday-Thursday, except Christmas, New Year's and Valentine's Day.

Stone Lake   D3

Lake House

5793 Division (on the lake)
Stone Lake, WI 54876
(715)865-6803
E-mail: tweldon@win.bright.net

Circa 1917. This bed & breakfast is the oldest building in town and began its life as a hotel in Stone Lake's downtown area. Several years later, it was moved to its present lakeside location. Innkeepers Maxine Mashek and Terri Weldon renovated the homes interior, decorating it with antiques. There are plenty of places to relax, including common areas with fireplaces, a porch or on the deck overlooking the water. In addition to the B&B, there is an art gallery on the premises, featuring works of local artists.

Innkeeper(s): Maxine Mashek & Terri Weldon. $55-75. MC, VISA, PC, TC. 4 rooms, 2 with PB, 1 with FP. Breakfast and afternoon tea included in rates. Types of meals: Full gourmet bkfst and early coffee/tea. Beds: QD. Ceiling fan and VCR in room. Air conditioning. Fax, swimming, bicycles and library on premises. Handicap access. Amusement parks, antiquing, fishing, golf, live theater, parks, shopping, downhill skiing, cross-country skiing and water sports nearby.

Publicity: *Four Seasons.*

Certificate may be used: March 1 through June 15, Sunday through Thursday.

Sturgeon Bay   F9

Inn at Cedar Crossing

336 Louisiana St
Sturgeon Bay, WI 54235-2422
(920)743-4200 Fax:(920)743-4422
Internet: www.innatcedarcrossing.com
E-mail: innkeeper@innatcedarcrossing.com

Circa 1884. This historic hotel, in the National Register, is a downtown two-story brick building that once housed street-level shops with second-floor apartments for the tailors, shopkeepers and pharmacists who worked below. The upstairs, now guest rooms, is decorated with rich fabrics and wallpapers and fine antiques. The Anniversary Room has a mahogany bed, fireplace and double whirlpool tub. The Victorian-era dining room and pub, both with fireplaces, are on the lower level. The waterfront is three blocks away.

Innkeeper(s): Terry Smith. $115-180. MC, VISA, AX, DS, PC, TC. 9 rooms with PB, 6 with FP. Breakfast and snacks/refreshments included in rates.

Types of meals: Full gourmet bkfst, cont plus and early coffee/tea. Beds: KQ. Cable TV, phone, VCR, double whirlpool tubs and some fireplaces in room. Air conditioning. Fax, copier and library on premises. Antiquing, fishing, art galleries, great biking, live theater, parks, shopping, downhill skiing, cross-country skiing and water sports nearby.

Publicity: *New Month, New York Times, Chicago Sun-Times, Country Inns, Bon Appetit, Gourmet, Green Bay Press Gazette, Midwest Living, Milwaukee Journal, Wisconsin Trails and New York Times.*

"The second-year stay at the inn was even better than the first. I couldn't have found a more romantic place."

Certificate may be used: November through April, Sunday through Thursday (excludes holiday stays).

Scofield House B&B

908 Michigan St
Sturgeon Bay, WI 54235-1849
(920)743-7727 (888)463-0204 Fax:(920)743-7727
Internet: www.scofieldhouse.com
E-mail: cpietrek@doorpi.net

Circa 1902. Mayor Herbert Scofield, prominent locally in the lumber and hardware business, built this late-Victorian house with a sturdy square tower and inlaid floors that feature intricate borders patterned in cherry, birch, maple, walnut, and red and white oak. Oak moldings throughout the house boast raised designs of bows, ribbons, swags and flowers. Equally lavish decor is featured in the guest rooms with fluffy flowered comforters and cabbage rose wallpapers highlighting romantic antique bedsteads. Baked apple-cinnamon French toast is a house specialty. Modern amenities include many suites with fireplaces and double whirlpools. "Room at the Top" is a sky-lit 900-square-foot suite occupying the whole third floor and furnished with Victorian antiques.

Innkeeper(s): Mike & Carolyn Pietrek. $98-202. PC, TC. 6 rooms with PB, 5 with FP. Breakfast and afternoon tea included in rates. Type of meal: Full gourmet bkfst. Beds: Q. Cable TV, ceiling fan, VCR and double whirlpools in room. Air conditioning. Fax, copier and movie library (free) on premises. Amusement parks, antiquing, fishing, live theater, parks, shopping, downhill skiing, cross-country skiing, sporting events and water sports nearby.

Location: Surrounded by 250 miles of shoreline.

Publicity: *Insider, Glamour, Country, Wisconsin Trails, Green Bay Press Gazette, Chicago Tribune, Milwaukee Sentinel-Journal, Midwest Living, Victorian Decorating & Lifestyle, Country Inns and National Geographic Traveler.*

"You've introduced us to the fabulous world of B&Bs. I loved the porch swing and would have been content on it for the entire weekend."

Certificate may be used: Sunday through Thursday, Nov. 15-April 30 (except holiday week of Christmas, New Year's).

The Reynolds House B&B

111 So 7th Ave
Sturgeon Bay, WI 54235
(920)746-9771 Fax:(920)746-9441
Internet: www.reynoldshousebandb.com

Circa 1900. A three-story, red-roofed Queen Anne Victorian house, the Reynolds House is painted in two shades of teal and yellow with white trim on its balustrades and brackets. Leaded-glass windows and a stone veranda that wraps around the front of the house are features. Rooms are cheerfully decorated and offer antique beds, attractive bed coverings and wallpapers. Tucked under the gable, the Winesap Suite includes a whirlpool, sitting room and fireplace. The innkeeper's kitchen garden furnishes fresh herbs to accent breakfast dishes, as well as flowers for the table.

Innkeeper(s): Stan & Jan Sekula. $75-155. MC, VISA, AX, DS. 4 rooms with PB, 3 with FP and 1 suite. Breakfast and snacks/refreshments included in rates. Types of meals: Full gourmet bkfst and early coffee/tea. Beds: Q. Cable TV and ceiling fan in room. Central air. VCR, fax, copier and library on premises. Antiquing, art galleries, beaches, bicycling, fishing, golf, hiking, horseback riding, live theater, museums, parks, shopping, cross-country skiing, tennis and wineries nearby.
Location: City.
Publicity: *Door County Magazine.*

"Sometimes the last minute things in life are the best!"

Certificate may be used: Nov. 1 through April 30, Sunday-Thursday.

White Lace Inn

16 N 5th Ave
Sturgeon Bay, WI 54235-1795
(920)743-1105
Internet: www.whitelaceinn.com
E-mail: romance@whitelaceinn.com

Circa 1903. White Lace Inn is four Victorian houses, one an ornate Queen Anne. It is adjacent to two districts listed in the National Register. Often the site for romantic anniversary celebrations, a favorite suite has a two-sided fireplace, magnificent walnut Eastlake bed, English country fabrics and a two-person whirlpool tub. There are 12 rooms that offer whirlpool tubs, 15 feature fireplaces and nine rooms have both whirlpool tubs and fireplaces. Enjoy the landscaped gardens and gazebo.

Innkeeper(s): Dennis & Bonnie Statz. $58-229. MC, VISA, AX, DS. 18 rooms with PB, 15 with FP and 5 suites. Breakfast included in rates. Type of meal: Full bkfst. Beds: KQ. Phone, 12 with whirlpool tubs and 9 with fireplace and whirlpool in room. Handicap access. Antiquing, fishing, live theater, cross-country skiing and water sports nearby.
Publicity: *Milwaukee Sentinel, Brides, National Geographic Traveler, Wisconsin Trails, Milwaukee, Country Home and Midwest Living.*

"Each guest room is an overwhelming visual feast, a dazzling fusion of colors, textures and beautiful objects. It is one of these rare gems that established a tradition the day it opened." — Wisconsin Trails

Certificate may be used: November-April, Sunday through Thursday, holidays excluded.

Tomahawk   E5

Swan Song B&B

PO Box 582
Tomahawk, WI 54487
(715)453-1173
Internet: www.newnorth.net/~swansong
E-mail: swansong@newnorth.net

Circa 1913. Popular with cyclists, this white farm house is located on 18 acres near forests and lakes and offers scenic back roads for exploring. Entrance is through an enclosed porch with a blue floor, and the inn's decor shows touches of the owners' Swedish heritage. The innkeepers are avid snowmobilers, skiers and bicyclists, and they frequently coordinate cycle tours from inn to inn. Full breakfasts are offered.

$50-60. PC. 3 rooms. Breakfast included in rates. Types of meals: Full bkfst and early coffee/tea. Beds: KT. Cable TV and turndown service in room. Air conditioning. Antiquing, fishing, golf, biking, live theater, parks, shopping, cross-country skiing, tennis and water sports nearby.
Location: country.
Certificate may be used: All year.

Viroqua   H4

Viroqua Heritage Inn B&B's

217 & 220 E Jefferson St
Viroqua, WI 54665
(608)637-3306 (888)443-7466
E-mail: rhodsent@mwt.net

Circa 1890. The three-story turret of this gabled Queen Anne mansion houses the sitting room of a guest chamber and the formal first-floor parlor. Columns and assorted gingerbread spice the exterior, while beveled glass, ornate fireplaces and crystal gaslight chandeliers grace the interior. The home was previously owned by silent movie star Coleen Moore. An antique baby grand piano and Victrola reside in the music room. A full breakfast is served on the original carved-oak dining table, on the balcony or on the front porch.

Innkeeper(s): Nancy Rhodes. $60-120. MC, VISA, DS, PC, TC. 9 rooms, 5 with PB, 1 with FP and 1 suite. Breakfast included in rates. Types of meals: Full bkfst and early coffee/tea. Beds: KQD. TV, phone and coffee pots in room. Air conditioning. VCR, bicycles, library, child care, refrigerator, exercise club, whirlpool tub, organic cooking and healing and nurturing spa on premises. Antiquing, fishing, Amish shopping, community built city park, live theater, parks, shopping, downhill skiing, cross-country skiing and water sports nearby.
Location: Wisconsin "Main Street" Town.
Publicity: *Smithsonian Magazine and Readers' Digest. Milwaukee Magazine.*
"Wonderful house, great hosts."
Certificate may be used: Weekdays, all year, except September-October. All week, November-March, except holidays.

Walworth   J7

Arscott House B&B

PO Box 875, 241 S Main
Walworth, WI 53184-0875
(414)275-3233

Circa 1903. Built by a master carpenter at the turn of the century, this turreted Queen Anne Victorian has been lovingly restored to its original stylings. A new addition is the inn's Arizona Apartment, with Southwestern decor, a spacious sitting room, kitchen and a private, outside entrance. A roomy front porch and two outside decks are favorite relaxing spots, and a full breakfast is available to guests. The inn is just minutes from Lake Geneva's many attractions.

Innkeeper(s): Valerie C. Dudek. $45-165. MC, VISA, DS, PC, TC. 2 rooms. Breakfast included in rates. Types of meals: Full bkfst and early coffee/tea. Beds: QDT. Cable TV, turndown service, ceiling fan, VCR and front porch & two decks in room. Air conditioning. Video library and bike rental on premises. Antiquing, fishing, live theater, parks, shopping, downhill skiing, cross-country skiing and water sports nearby.
"Enjoyed your gracious hospitality. Loved the breakfast. Loved your house. We'll be back again. Thank you for making our first anniversary such an enjoyable one."
Certificate may be used: Nov. 1-April 30, Sunday-Friday.

Waupaca   G6

Crystal River B&B

E1369 Rural Rd
Waupaca, WI 54981-8246
(715)258-5333

Circa 1853. The stately beauty of this historic Greek Revival farmhouse is rivaled only by its riverside setting. Each room features a view of the water, garden, woods or all three. A Victorian gazebo, down comforters and delicious breakfasts, with pecan sticky buns, a special favorite, add to guests' enjoyment. Exploring the village of Rural, which is in the National Register, will delight those interested in bygone days. Recreational activities abound, with the Chain O'Lakes and a state park nearby.

Innkeeper(s): Lois Sorenson. $65-125. MC, VISA. 7 rooms, 2 with PB. Breakfast included in rates. Type of meal: Full bkfst. Beds: Q. TV, phone and ceiling fan in room. Air conditioning. Antiquing, shopping, downhill skiing, cross-country skiing and sporting events nearby.

Location: 23 Lakes.

Publicity: *Resorter, Stevens Point Journal and Wisconsin Trail.*

"It was like being king for a day."

Certificate may be used: Nov. 1 through June 30, Sunday-Friday.

Thomas Pipe Inn

11032 Pipe Rd
Waupaca, WI 54981-8604
(715)824-3161

Circa 1854. A former stagecoach stop in the pre-railroad days, this historic Greek Revival inn offers four elegant guest rooms to visitors, many who have come to explore the Chain O'Lakes and its many attractions. Elizabeth's Room boasts a clawfoot tub and canopy bed, while the Florence Pipe Room features a brass bed loaded with pillows. The Thomas Pipe Room has a beautiful view of the woods, and Marjorie's Suite has an antique bed and sitting room with sleeper sofa and fireplace. Hartman's Creek State Park is a 10-minute drive from the inn.

Innkeeper(s): Marcella Windisch. $65-125. MC, VISA. 5 rooms and 1 suite. Breakfast included in rates. Type of meal: Full bkfst. Air conditioning. VCR on premises. Antiquing, shopping and cross-country skiing nearby.

Certificate may be used: November through June.

Walkers Barn B&B

E1268 Cleghorn Rd
Waupaca, WI 54981
(715)258-5235 (800)870-0737

Circa 1985. Three acres surround this country house with a log facade. The inn boasts interiors of barn-board walls and Amish furnishings and quilts. For instance, there are some hand-crafted bedsteads including a four-poster. A large stone fireplace in the living room and woodland views from the dining room enhance the country setting. Dutch pancakes with apple topping and maple butter is a favorite breakfast item. Nearby are antique shops, art galleries, streams for canoeing and back roads for cycling.

Innkeeper(s): Bob & Linda Yerkes. $65-110. MC, VISA, DS, PC. 4 rooms, 2 with PB, 2 with FP. Breakfast included in rates. Types of meals: Full bkfst and early coffee/tea. Beds: QT. Turndown service and ceiling fan in room. Air conditioning. VCR on premises. Antiquing, fishing, golf, parks, shopping, cross-country skiing and water sports nearby.

Location: Rural.

Certificate may be used: Sept. 1 to June 15, Sunday-Friday.

Whitewater   I7

Victoria-On-Main B&B

622 W Main St
Whitewater, WI 53190-1855
(414)473-8400

Circa 1895. This graceful Queen Anne Victorian, shaded by a tall birch tree, is in the heart of Whitewater National Historic District, adjacent to the University of Wisconsin. It was built for Edward Engebretson, mayor of Whitewater. Yellow tulip and sunny daf-

fodils fill the spring flower beds, while fuchsias and geraniums bloom in summertime behind a picket fence. The inn's gables, flower-filled veranda and three-story turret feature a handsome green tin roof. Each guest room is named for a Wisconsin hardwood. The Red Oak Room, Cherry Room and Bird's Eye Maple Room all offer handsome antiques in their corresponding wood, Laura Ashley prints, antique sheets, pristine heirloom-laced pillowcases and down comforters. A hearty breakfast is sometimes served on the wraparound veranda, and there are kitchen facilities available for light meal preparation. Whitewater Lake and Kettle Moraine State Forest are five minutes away.

Innkeeper(s): Nancy Wendt. $65-75. MC, VISA. 3 rooms, 1 with PB, 1 with FP. Breakfast included in rates. Types of meals: Full bkfst and early coffee/tea. Beds: D. Ceiling fan in room. Air conditioning. Antiquing, fishing, live theater, parks, shopping, cross-country skiing and water sports nearby.

Location: City.

"We loved it. Wonderful hospitality."

Certificate may be used: June through September and January, Sunday through Thursday.

Wilton   H4

Rice's Whispering Pines B&B

RR 2, Box 225
Wilton, WI 54670
(608)435-6531

Circa 1896. Guests will find this pleasant place for a getaway. There are 60 acres surrounding the main farmhouse, ensuring tranquility during one's stay. Tucked behind the century-old farmhouse are a bright red barn and grain elevators, adding to the rural setting. Although not a working farm, the property has chickens and horses. The comfortable home has been in the Rice family for three generations. There are three guest rooms, decorated in a homey country style. One room has a wilderness scene on the wall behind the white iron and brass bed. In another room, a swash of fabric, decorated with cream-colored tassels, is draped at the headboard of the bed, which rests on a backdrop of a tree. The third room offers two twin beds, a queen-size bed and a day bed, all dressed in coordinating fabrics. The homestay is close to Amish communities and the Elroy-Sparta Bicycle Trail.

Innkeeper(s): Bill & Marilyn Rice. $60-70. PC, TC. 3 rooms. Breakfast included in rates. Types of meals: Full bkfst and early coffee/tea. Beds: QT. Air conditioning. Antiquing, fishing, parks, shopping, downhill skiing and cross-country skiing nearby.

Location: Hills and valleys.

Publicity: *Summer Fun.*

"We loved the peace and quiet of Whispering Pines."

Certificate may be used: Nov. 1-March 30, Sunday-Monday, seven days a week.

Wisconsin Dells   H5

Historic Bennett House

825 Oak St
Wisconsin Dells, WI 53965-1418
(608)254-2500

Circa 1863. This handsomely restored Greek Revival-style home, framed by a white picket fence, once housed the Henry Bennetts. Mr. Bennett's work, displayed in the Smithsonian, is noted for being the first stop-action photography. His family recently donated the Bennett photographic studio, located in town, to the state. It will open as a museum, the ninth historical site in Wisconsin. The National Register home is decorated in European and Victorian styles and its flower-filled grounds offer sun and shade gardens.

Innkeeper(s): Gail & Rich Obermeyer. $70-95. PC, TC. 3 rooms, 1 with PB and 1 suite. Breakfast included in rates. Types of meals: Full gourmet bkfst and early coffee/tea. Beds: QD. Cable TV, ceiling fan, VCR, designer bedding, antiques and armoires in room. Air conditioning. Library, gardens, fountain, benches and picnic table on premises. Amusement parks, antiquing, river tours, museums, crane and eagles, casino, greyhound racing, indian mounds, live theater, parks, shopping, downhill skiing, cross-country skiing and water sports nearby.

Location: City.

Publicity: *Milwaukee Journal, Wisconsin State Journal, Midwest Living, Country Life and Travel & Leisure.*

"We felt we were visiting relatives for the weekend and the visit was too short."

Certificate may be used: October through May, Sunday through Thursday.

Terrace Hill B&B

922 River Rd
Wisconsin Dells, WI 53965-1423
(608)253-9363

Circa 1900. With a park bordering one edge and the Wisconsin River just across the street, Terrace Hill guests are treated to pleasant surroundings both inside and out. The interior is a cheerful mix of Victorian and country decor. The Park View suite includes a canopy bed and a clawfoot tub, other rooms offer views and cozy surroundings. There is a barbecue grill and picnic table available for guest use. The inn is just a block and a half from downtown Wisconsin Dells.

Innkeeper(s): Len, Cookie, Lenard & Lynn Novak. $55-140. PC, TC. 5 rooms with PB and 1 suite. Breakfast and afternoon tea included in rates. Types of meals: Full bkfst and early coffee/tea. Beds: Q. Cable TV in one room in room. Air conditioning. VCR and library on premises. Amusement parks, antiquing, fishing, live theater, parks, shopping, downhill skiing, cross-country skiing and water sports nearby.

Location: City.

Certificate may be used: Sept. 20 to June 30.

Wisconsin Dells Thunder Valley B&B Inn

W15344 Waubeek Rd
Wisconsin Dells, WI 53965-9005
(608)254-4145

Circa 1870. The Wisconsin Dells area is full of both Scandinavian and Native American heritage, and the innkeeper of this country inn has tried to honor the traditions. The inn even features a Scandinavian gift shop. Chief Yellow Thunder, for whom this inn is named, often camped out on the grounds and surrounding area. The inn's restaurant is highly acclaimed. Everything is fresh, including the wheat the innkeepers grind for the morning pancakes and rolls. There is a good selection of Wisconsin beer and wine, as well. Guests can stay in the farmhouse, Guest Hus, or Wee Hus, all of which offer microwaves and refrigerators.

Innkeeper(s): Anita, Kari & Sigrid Nelson. $65-105. MC, VISA. 4 rooms with PB. Breakfast included in rates. Type of meal: Full bkfst. Beds: KQD. Air conditioning. Handicap access. International Crane Foundation, Circus Museum, House on Rock, casino and farm animals and dairy nearby.

Location: Country.

Publicity: *Wisconsin Trails Magazine, Country Inns, Midwest Living Magazine, Chicago Sun-Times, Milwaukee Journal-Sentinel and National Geographic Travel Magazine.*

"Thunder Valley is a favorite of Firstar Club members — delicious food served in a charming atmosphere with warm Scandinavian hospitality."

Certificate may be used: Sunday through Thursday, Nov. 1-May 1, except holidays and upon availability.

Wyoming

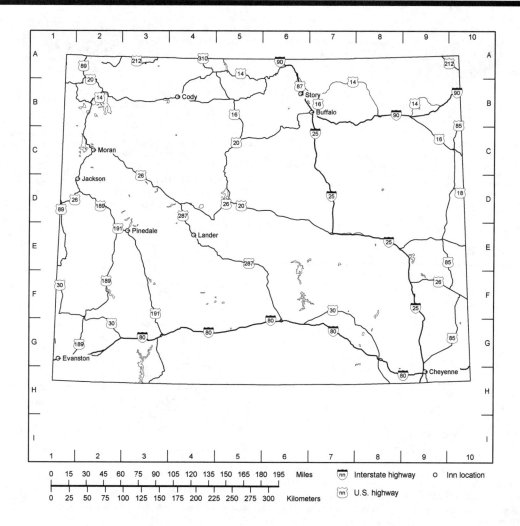

Buffalo   B7

Cloud Peak Inn

590 N Burritt Ave
Buffalo, WY 82834-1610
(307)684-5794 (800)715-5794 Fax:(307)684-7653

Circa 1906. Built at the turn of the century by a wealthy rancher, this inn features a graceful staircase, elegant parlor and spacious bedrooms. At the end of the day, guests can relax in

front of the "fossilized" fireplace, soak in the Jacuzzi or unwind on the porch or balcony. Arrangements can be made for dinner although there are some excellent restaurants in the area. A fine golf course is only two blocks from the inn. The innkeepers will tell you about the secret fishing spots in the mountains that are sure bets. Geologic tours of the area can be arranged with prior notice.

Innkeeper(s): Rick & Kathy Brus. $55-85. MC, VISA, AX, PC, TC. 5 rooms, 3 with PB and 1 conference room. Breakfast included in rates. Types of meals: Full gourmet bkfst and early coffee/tea. Beds: KQDT. Ceiling fan in room. VCR, fax, copier, spa and library on premises. Amusement parks, antiquing, fishing, parks, shopping, downhill skiing, cross-country skiing and water sports nearby.

Location: Mountains.

Publicity: *Billings Gazette, Los Angeles Times and Sheridan Press.*

Certificate may be used: All year.

Cheyenne   H9

A. Drummonds Ranch B&B

399 Happy Jack Rd, Hwy 210
Cheyenne, WY 82007
(307)634-6042 Fax:(307)634-6042
Internet: www.cruising-america.com/drummond.html
E-mail: adrummond@juno.com

Circa 1990. With 120 acres of Wyoming wilderness and a nearby National Forest and State Park, this Old English-style farmhouse offers a quiet retreat. Private, outdoor Jacuzzis provide views of the surrounding area and evening skies filled with stars. Some

rooms include private entrances, window seats, a fireplace or a steam sauna. One unit is completely self-contained and includes a small kitchen. Homemade snacks, beverages and fresh fruit always are available for guests. Boarding is available for those traveling with horses and pets. A. Drummonds Ranch is located halfway between Cheyenne and Laramie.

Innkeeper(s): Taydie Drummond. $60-175. MC, VISA, PC, TC. 4 rooms, 2 with PB, 1 FP and 1 suite. Breakfast, afternoon tea and snacks/refreshments included in rates. Types of meals: Full gourmet bkfst and early coffee/tea. Beds: QDT. TV, phone and turndown service in room. VCR, fax, copier, sauna, bicycles, library, pet boarding and child care on premises. Fishing, live theater, parks, cross-country skiing, sporting events and water sports nearby.

Pets allowed: Pets must be kennelled in our facilities.

Location: Mountains.

Publicity: *Country Inns, Country Extra, Inn Times and Adventures West.*

Certificate may be used: October-December, January-April, Monday nights through Thursday nights.

Adventurers' Country B&B
Raven Cry Ranch

3803 I-80 Service Rd
Cheyenne, WY 82009-8785
(307)632-4087 Fax:(307)632-4087
E-mail: fwhite1@juno.com

Circa 1985. Situated behind an adobe fence, this Southwestern-style inn rests on a knoll overlooking 102 acres of prairie. Guests enjoy the tree-lined adobe courtyard, flower

gardens and a front veranda filled with rocking chairs and swings. The inn offers murder-mystery weekends and

a Western Adventure package. Weekly rodeos, a scenic rail excursion, and crystal and granite lakes are nearby.

Innkeeper(s): Fern White. $50-140. 5 rooms, 4 with PB, 1 with FP and 1 suite. Breakfast included in rates. Types of meals: Full bkfst and early coffee/tea. Beds: KQ. Phone and turndown service in room. VCR and horseback activities on premises. Antiquing, live theater, parks, shopping, downhill skiing, cross-country skiing and sporting events nearby.

Location: Ranch.

"The service was superbly personalized with great attention to detail and a great down-home cowboy atmosphere."

Certificate may be used: Jan. 1-Dec. 31, except for July 23-Aug. 2.

Porch Swing

712 E 20th St
Cheyenne, WY 82001-3806
(307)778-7182 Fax:(307)778-7182
Internet: www.cruising-america.com/porch.html
E-mail: porchswing@juno.com

At this Victorian inn, breakfast is served on the back porch in summer and by the dining room fire in cold weather. Guests can enjoy items like yeast waffles with maple syrup and fresh

strawberries, orange pecan French toast and German pancakes with Swiss honey butter. All these recipes and more are found in the innkeepers' cookbook available for sale. The property's summer gardens are colorful and fragrant with a variety of perennials, aromatic and culinary herbs, wildflowers and annuals. The innkeepers would be happy to send you home with a cutting or seeds of something that's taken your fancy.

Innkeeper(s): Carole Eppler. $39-66. MC, VISA. 3 rooms. Breakfast included in rates. Types of meals: Full bkfst and early coffee/tea. VCR on premises. Antiquing, shopping, downhill skiing and sporting events nearby.

Location: 25 minutes from mountains.

Certificate may be used: November-March, Sunday-Thursday except July 15-30.

Cody
B4

Cody Guest Houses

1525 Beck Ave
Cody, WY 82414-3920
(307)587-6000 (800)587-6560 Fax:(307)587-8048
Internet: www.awaywest.com/accoms/cghouses

Circa 1905. As long as innkeepers Daren and Kathy Singer are in town, Cody's past will be preserved. This diligent couple have restored several historic local buildings, including the home of Cody's first mayor who later became a Wyoming governor. The Mayor's Inn, built in 1901, houses an antique shop on its first floor, and offers three guest rooms with a freshwater spa, double shower and luxury linens. A continental breakfast is served to Mayor's Inn guests. The guest houses also include a 1906 Victorian home, two cottages and a brick home dating to 1926.

Rooms are well-appointed in a variety of styles, from Victorian to Old West. Although breakfast is not included in the rates, guests are offered plenty of other amenities. Daily housekeeping, kitchens, laundry facilities, freshwater spas, fireplaces and in-room stereos, CD players and televisions are among the offerings.

Innkeeper(s): Kathy & Daren Singer. $50-450. MC, VISA, DS, PC, TC. 10 rooms with PB, 1 with FP, 8 suites, 3 cottages and 3 conference rooms. Beds: KQD. Cable TV, phone, ceiling fan and VCR in room. Air conditioning. Hot tubs and fresh water spa on premises. Fishing, golf, horseback riding, museums, Yellowstone National Park, Buffalo Bill Center, parks, shopping, downhill skiing, cross-country skiing, tennis and water sports nearby.

Location: Mountains.

Publicity: *Cody Enterprise.*

"Understated western elegance!"

Certificate may be used: Jan. 1-June 1 and October-December.

Parson's Pillow B&B

1202 14th St
Cody, WY 82414-3720
(307)587-2382 (800)377-2348 Fax:(307)587-6372
Internet: www.cruising-america.com/parsonspillow
E-mail: ppbb@trib.com

Circa 1991. This historic building originally served as the Methodist-Episcopal Church, Cody's first church. Guests are free to practice a tune on the piano in the home's parlor, which also offers a TV and VCR. Guest rooms feature antiques and quilts. Clawfoot and oak-framed prairie tubs add to the nostalgia. The Buffalo Bill Historical Center and the Cody Historic Walking Tour are nearby.

Innkeeper(s): Lee & Elly Larabee. $65-85. MC, VISA, AX, DS, PC. 4 rooms with PB. Breakfast included in rates. Types of meals: Full gourmet bkfst and early coffee/tea. Beds: Q. Turndown service and ceiling fan in room. VCR, library and computer port on premises. Antiquing, fishing, golf, white water rafting, parks, shopping, downhill skiing, cross-country skiing, tennis and water sports nearby.

Location: City.

Certificate may be used: September through May, any day of the week. Subject to availability.

The Lockhart B&B Inn

109 W Yellowstone Ave
Cody, WY 82414-8723
(307)587-6074 (800)377-7255 Fax:(307)587-8644
E-mail: cbaldwin@wyoming.com

Circa 1890. Once the home of author and journalist Caroline Lockhart, this Victorian inn has beautiful mountain views from its veranda. The deck affords a view of the Shoshone River.

Rooms are decorated with antiques, old-fashioned beds and a clawfoot tub. Breakfast is served on fine china at your private table in the dining room. Airport pick-up service is offered, as well as making reservations for dining, river rafting, golfing, rodeo events and more.

Innkeeper(s): Don Kramer & Cindy Baldwin Kramer. $78-95. MC, VISA, DS. 7 rooms with PB. Breakfast included in rates. Type of meal: Full bkfst. Beds: QT. Cable TV, phone and ceiling fan in room. Air conditioning. Piano on premises. Antiquing, fishing, live theater, shopping, downhill skiing, cross-country skiing, sporting events and water sports nearby.

Location: overlooking river.

Publicity: *Glamour, AAA Today, National Geographic Traveler, Windsurf, New York Times, Houston Post and Los Angeles Times.*

"Just like going to grandma's house, like coming home to family — home away from home."

Certificate may be used: January-May, Sept. 15-Dec. 31, excluding holidays.

Evanston
G1

Pine Gables Inn B&B

1049 Center St
Evanston, WY 82930-3432
(307)789-2069 (800)789-2069

Circa 1883. This Eastlake Victorian was built by A.V. Quinn, who ran the company store in town for the Union Pacific railroad. The rooms of this National Register home are filled with antiques, and the carved handmade beds are a highlight. The guest rooms are cheerful with romantic touches. One room features a beautiful antique bed decorated with a hint of ivy and bathroom with a pedestal sink and hand-stenciled walls. The inn's parlor is particularly inviting. Rich, rose-colored walls and white molding are enhanced by stenciling and an ornate ceiling. French doors lead out to the porch. In the mornings, guests feast on items such as waffles, omelets, quiche, fresh fruit and homemade muffins.

Innkeeper(s): Nephi & Ruby Jensen. $55-135. MC, VISA, AX, DS, PC, TC. 5 rooms with PB, 3 with FP. Breakfast included in rates. Types of meals: Full bkfst and early coffee/tea. Beds: KQD. Cable TV, phone, ceiling fan, clawfoot tubs and one with Jacuzzi in room. Antiquing, fishing, golf, live theater, parks, shopping, cross-country skiing and tennis nearby.

Certificate may be used: October to March, Sunday-Thursday.

Jackson D2

Sassy Moose Inn

HC 362, Teton Village Rd
Jackson, WY 83001
(307)733-1277 (800)356-1277 Fax:(307)739-0793
E-mail: ckelley@wyoming.com

Circa 1992. All of the rooms at this log-house-style inn have spectacular Teton views. The Mountain Room has a rock fireplace, queen bed and mountain cabin decor. The River Room's decor is dominated by the colors of the Snake River and accented with antiques. The inn is five minutes from Teton Village and the Jackson Hole Ski Resort. Teton Pines Golf Course and Nordic Trails are just across the road. After a day of activities, enjoy sharing your experiences over tea or relaxing in the large hot tub.

Innkeeper(s): Polly Kelley. $109-154. MC, VISA, AX, DS. 5 rooms with PB, 4 with FP and 1 suite. Breakfast included in rates. Types of meals: Full bkfst and early coffee/tea. Beds: KQT. VCR, fax, copier, spa, pet boarding and child care on premises. Fishing, live theater, parks, shopping, downhill skiing, cross-country skiing and water sports nearby.

Pets Allowed.

Location: Snake River.

Certificate may be used: Anytime except January-February and June-September.

Lander E4

Piece of Cake B&B

2343 Baldwin Creek Rd
Lander, WY 82520-0866
(307)332-7608

Circa 1991. View roaming wildlife and the breathtaking Wind River Mountains from more than 1,000 square feet of deck attached to this lodge-style log home. Guest rooms include a Jacuzzi tub in a private bath. The inn is open year-round and winter guests can enjoy the Continental Divide Snowmobile Trail and the inn's 10,000 acres. In the summer, mountain bikes are available.

Innkeeper(s): Sarah & David Love. $80-90. PC, TC. 6 rooms with PB, 1 suite and 2 conference rooms. Breakfast and snacks/refreshments included in rates. Types of meals: Full gourmet bkfst and early coffee/tea. Beds: QDT. Turndown service in room. VCR, fax, spa, pet boarding and satellite dish on premises. Antiquing, fishing, parks, shopping, downhill skiing, cross-country skiing and water sports nearby.

Pets allowed: Pets allowed in one cabin.

Publicity: *Los Angeles Times.*

Certificate may be used: Oct. 1-March 30.

Moran C2

Diamond D Ranch-Outfitters

Buffalo Valley Rd, Box 211
Moran, WY 83013
(307)543-2479

Located on the scenic Buffalo Valley Road, this log house inn serves many purposes, including being an old hunting lodge, guest ranch, pack trip outfitter, cross-country skiing lodge, and snowmobile and base lodge for touring Yellowstone and Grand Teton national parks. There's a relaxed atmosphere with a flexible schedule. The main lodge has two units each with private baths, and the cabins have two units also with private baths. The staff teaches Western

horsemanship and has horses for each guest's ability.

Innkeeper(s): Rod Doty. $99. 16 rooms and 2 suites. Breakfast included in rates. Type of meal: Full bkfst. Cable TV in room. Cross-country skiing nearby.

Location: Guest ranch.

Certificate may be used: Nov. 1 to Dec. 15, Jan. 5 to May 15. Sunday through Thursday.

Pinedale E3

Window on The Winds

10151 Hwy 191, PO Box 996
Pinedale, WY 82941
(307)367-2600 (888)367-1345 Fax:(307)367-2395
Internet: www.cruising-america.com/windowonwinds
E-mail: lmcclain@wyoming.com

Circa 1968. At the base of the Wind River Mountains, this log house inn has lodgepole pine queen beds, down comforters and western-style furnishings. All rooms feature scenic mountain views, and the balcony has views of "the Winds." A hot tub is set among flowers, ivy and culinary herbs. Guests enjoy gourmet breakfasts. Pinedale is the trailhead into the Wind River Mountains for hiking, fishing, skiing and snowmobiling and is on the route to Jackson and Yellowstone.

Innkeeper(s): Leanne & Doug Rellstab. $50-125. MC, VISA, AX, DS, PC, TC. 4 rooms with PB and 1 conference room. Breakfast included in rates. Types of meals: Full bkfst and early coffee/tea. Beds: QT. Fax, copier, spa, stables and pet boarding on premises. Fishing, shopping, downhill skiing, cross-country skiing and water sports nearby.

Location: Mountains.

Certificate may be used: Sept. 1-May 31, all days of the week.

Story B6

Piney Creek Inn B&B

11 Skylark Ln, PO Box 456
Story, WY 82842
(307)683-2911
Internet: www.pineycreekinn.com
E-mail: pineyinn@cyberhighway.net

Circa 1956. There's an abundance of wildlife on the property of this secluded log-house-style inn nestled in the Big Horn Mountains. For the Old West buff, historic sites that are only minutes away include Fort Phil Kearny, Bozeman Trail, Little Big Horn Battlefield, numerous Indian battle sites and museums and galleries. Ranch experiences and trail ride packages are favorites. At the end of the day, relax on the deck or in the common area, where visitors will find a television, books, magazines and games. Guests also can relax by the campfire for conversation and viewing the stars. Historical tours, ranch adventures and trail-ride packages are available.

Innkeeper(s): Vicky Hoff. $65-150. MC, VISA, PC, TC. 4 rooms, 3 with PB and 2 cabins. Breakfast and snacks/refreshments included in rates. Types of meals: Full bkfst, cont and early coffee/tea. Beds: KQDT. Ceiling fan in room. VCR, spa, library, hot tub, campfire and refrigerator on premises. Handicap access. Antiquing, fishing, golf, trail rides, historical tours, live theater and shopping nearby.

Location: Mountains.

Publicity: *Country.*

Certificate may be used: Nov. 1-April 30, excluding holidays.

U.S. Territories

Puerto Rico

Ceiba

Ceiba Country Inn

PO Box 1067
Ceiba, PR 00735-1067
(787)885-0471 Fax:(787)885-0471
Internet: www.golf.net/about/webpressure/cci/
E-mail: prinn@juno.com

Circa 1950. A large Spanish patio is available at this tropical country inn perched on rolling, green hills. Situated 500 feet above the valley floor, the inn affords a view of the ocean with the isle of Culebra on  the horizon. A continental buffet is served in the warm and sunny breakfast room. The inn is four miles from Puerto Del Rey, the largest marina in the Caribbean, and 10 miles from Luquillo Beach, which is a mile of white sand, dotted with coconut palms.

Innkeeper(s): Sue Newbauer & Dick Bray. $75. MC, VISA, AX, DS, TC. 9 rooms with PB. Breakfast included in rates. Type of meal: Cont plus. Beds: QT. Phone in room. Air conditioning. Fax and library on premises. Handicap access. Fishing, golf, hiking, snorkeling, shopping and water sports nearby.
Location: Mountains.
Certificate may be used: May-November.

Canada

British Columbia

Crawford Bay

Wedgwood Manor Country Inn

16002 Crawford Creek Rd, PO Box 135
Crawford Bay, BC V0B 1E0
(250)227-9233 (800)862-0022 Fax:(250)227-9233
E-mail: wedgwood@lightwave.bc.ca

Circa 1912. Set against a magical forest on 50 acres, this English manor house boasts gables, multi-paned windows and a steep red roof. It was built for a member of the Wedgwood china family. Favorite spots include the library, veranda and parlor. Breakfast is served fireside in the dining room and often features just-picked berries with whipped cream, freshly baked scones and Eggs Wedgwood (poached eggs over Black Forest ham over English muffins with an herb sauce from the inn's gardens). The innkeeper is a botanist and is a resource for the area's birds and wildlife. Wedgwood's park-like grounds include flower beds, wildflowers, a stream, ponds and a fountain. Across the road is the Kokanee springs Golf Resort.

Innkeeper(s): Joan Huiberts & John Edwards. $69-110. MC, VISA, TC. 6 rooms with PB, 1 with FP. Breakfast, afternoon tea and snacks/refreshments included in rates. Types of meals: Full gourmet bkfst and early coffee/tea. Beds: QDT. Fax, bicycles and library on premises. Antiquing, fishing, golf, hiking, mountain biking, birding, live theater, parks, shopping, tennis and water sports nearby.

Location: Mountains.

Publicity: *Calgary Herald* and *Vancouver Sun*.

"We really appreciate the way you spoil and pamper us. Wish we could just move in."

Certificate may be used: April 12 to June 25 and Sept. 30 to Oct. 8. Sunday-Thursday.

Nanoose Bay

Lookout at Schooner Cove

3381 Dolphin Dr
Nanoose Bay, BC V9P 9H7
(250)468-9796 Fax:(250)468-9796
Internet: www.bbcanada.com/490.html
E-mail: thelookout@webtv.net

Circa 1972. Massive rocks, tall trees and a winding path lead to this West Coast contemporary house overlooking Georgia Strait and the mountains. Schooner Cove and its marina are within 500 yards. Located on Vancouver Island, halfway between Victoria and Tofino, the inn offers a wraparound deck the favorite spot for enjoying lingering sunsets, Alaskan cruise ships, eagles, otters and sea lions. Reserve early to get one of the two rooms with private bath.

Innkeeper(s): Marj & Herb Wilkie. $65-95. PC, TC. 3 rooms, 1 with PB, 1 with FP and 1 suite. Breakfast included in rates. Type of meal: Full bkfst. Beds: Q. Cable TV, phone, ceiling fan and VCR in room. Fax, copier and library on premises. Amusement parks, antiquing, fishing, golf, live theater, parks, shopping, downhill skiing, cross-country skiing, sporting events, tennis and water sports nearby.

"I must say, we had the most relaxing time with you. Moreover, you served the best breakfast."

Certificate may be used: May 1-June 30, Sunday-Thursday; September, Sunday-Thursday, subject to availability, holidays excluded.

North Vancouver

Laburnum Cottage B&B

1388 Terrace Ave
North Vancouver, BC V7R 1B4
(604)988-4877 Fax:(604)988-4877

Set in one-half acre of beautifully kept English gardens, this country-style inn is surrounded by virgin forest, yet is only 15 minutes from downtown Vancouver. Afternoon tea is offered on the covered porch overlooking the award-winning gardens and meandering creek. In addition to the guest rooms, there are two self-contained cottages. Both cottages include a fireplace, kitchen facilities and a private bath. Check-in time is flexible and two major bus routes are only two blocks away.

Innkeeper(s): Delphine Masterton. $100-175. MC, VISA. 4 rooms with PB and 2 cottages. Breakfast included in rates. Type of meal: Full bkfst. VCR on premises. Shopping, downhill skiing and cross-country skiing nearby.

Location: Mountains.

Certificate may be used: Year-round, Sunday-Friday, space available.

Salt Spring Island

Anne's Oceanfront Hideaway B&B

168 Simson Rd
Salt Spring Island, BC V8K 1E2
(250)537-0851 (888)474-2663 Fax:(250)537-0861
Internet: www.bbcanada.com/annesoceanfront
E-mail: annes@saltspring.com

Circa 1995. The exquisite views of the blue Pacific from the wraparound veranda, living room and guest rooms are the most rewarding feature of this 7,000-square-foot Country Victorian inn. However, even without the magnificent setting, you could luxuriate in the amenities, which include a library, fine linens, hydro massage tub, canopy bed or fireplace. A four-course breakfast is served in the dining room. (Ask about the egg blossom and lamb patty entree.) The quiet setting of oak and arbutus trees, and the ocean path

that leads to the sandstone beach are additional pleasures. The inn is also wheelchair accessible, and there's an elevator.

Innkeeper(s): Rick & Ruth-Anne Broad. $150-230. MC, VISA, AX, TC. 4 rooms with PB, 1 with FP. Breakfast included in rates. Types of meals: Full bkfst and early coffee/tea. Beds: KQT. Turndown service and robes and slippers in room. Air conditioning. VCR, fax, copier, bicycles and library on premises. Handicap access. Art galleries, fishing, golf, studio tours, live theater, parks, shopping, tennis and water sports nearby.

Publicity: *Island.*

"We leave relaxed, refreshed and anxious to return. You've thought of every detail and we've so enjoyed the results."

Certificate may be used: Oct. 1 to May 1, Sunday to Friday, (excluding holidays and long weekends), subject to availability.

Shawnigan Lake

Marifield Manor, an Edwardian B&B

2039 Merrifield Ln, RR 1
Shawnigan Lake, BC V0R 2W0
(250)743-9930 Fax:(250)743-1667
Internet: www.marifieldmanor.com
E-mail: mariman@pccinternet.com

Circa 1910. Overlooking Shawnigan Lake, this Edwardian mansion features wraparound verandahs. Guest rooms offer clawfoot tubs, antiques and fine, old linens. Most have views of the mountains and lake through the trees. Tea is served fireside or on the veranda, if weather permits. Tapestries and antiques are found throughout. The inn's artfully presented, gourmet breakfasts are served in the dining room or al fresco. The inn has become popular for meetings, workshops and retreats as well as receptions and family gathering, recently hosting visitors on Heritage House Tour.

Innkeeper(s): Cathy Basskin. $75-175. TC. 6 rooms with PB, 2 suites and 1 conference room. Breakfast and afternoon tea included in rates. Types of meals: Full gourmet bkfst, cont plus and early coffee/tea. Beds: QDT. Turndown service in room. Air conditioning. VCR, fax, copier, sauna, bicycles, library and e-mail on premises. Antiquing, bicycling, canoeing/kayaking, golf, rowing, host of Shawnigan Lake Writers Village, boarding schools, live theater, parks, downhill skiing, water sports and wineries nearby.

Location: Rural.

"To a new and wonderful friend. Thank you for sharing your little slice of paradise."

Certificate may be used: Year-round. Not during rowing regattas, long weekends. Best to reserve well in advance.

Sooke

Ocean Wilderness Inn & Spa Retreat

109 W Coast Rd, RR 2
Sooke, BC V0S 1N0
(250)646-2116 (800)323-2116 Fax:(250)646-2317
Internet: www.sookenet.com/ocean
E-mail: ocean@sookenet.com

Circa 1940. The hot tub spa of this log house inn is in a Japanese gazebo overlooking the ocean. Reserve your time for a private soak, terry bathrobes are supplied. Experience massage

and mud treatments, ocean treatments and herbal wraps while meditation enhances your creative expression. The inn will arrange fishing charters, nature walks and beachcombing. Coffee is delivered to your room each morning on a silver ser-

vice. Guests are invited to enjoy breakfast in their room or in the dining lounge. Rooms include antiques, sitting areas and canopy beds. Two of the rooms have hot tubs for two with spectacular ocean and Olympic Mountain views.

Innkeeper(s): Marion J. Rolston. $85-175. MC, VISA, AX, TC. 9 rooms with PB. Breakfast included in rates. Types of meals: Full bkfst and early coffee/tea. Beds: KQT. Fax and copier on premises. Handicap access. Antiquing, fishing, whale watching, live theater, parks and shopping nearby.

Pets allowed: By arrangement.

Publicity: *Puget Sound Business Journal, Getaways from Vancouver and Travel Holiday Magazine.*

"Thank you for the most wonderful hospitality and accommodations of our entire vacation."

Certificate may be used: Oct. 1 to June 30.

Valemount

Rainbow Retreat B&B

PO Box 138
Valemount, BC V0E 2Z0
(250)566-9747

This authentically fashioned log cabin home rests beside an old fur-trader's route nestled in the Canadian Rockies and surrounded by woods. Guests are sure to see plenty of birds and wildlife, including the occasional deer that march across the grounds. The innkeepers have kept the rustic touch, but added Victorian flair such as stained glass and a grand piano. Hearty breakfasts start off the day and gourmet dinners are made-to-order. The secluded retreat is just a few minutes from Mount Robson Provincial Park, and it's just a short walk to Fraser River, especially popular during the annual salmon spawning run.

Innkeeper(s): Keith Burchnall. $50-70. 2 rooms. Breakfast included in rates. Type of meal: Full bkfst.

Certificate may be used: Anytime, except July and August.

Vernon

Richmond House 1894

4008 Pleasant Valley Rd
Vernon, BC V1T 4M2
(250)549-1767

Because of its central location, this Victorian inn is an ideal spot for outdoor enthusiasts to base their daily activities. The ski area of Silverstar Mountain is a 30-minute drive and two major lakes (Okanagan and Kalamalka) are 10 minutes from the inn. Internationally renowned Predator Ridge golf course is 20 minutes away. A fireplace in the living room brings warmth in the winter months, and an outdoor deck and hot tub are enjoyed year-round. The innkeeper can direct you to adventure travel packages and local wineries. Breakfasts include a variety of quiche or stuffed French toast with peach sauce.

Innkeeper(s): Keith Brookes & Colleen Couves. $65-75. MC, VISA. 3 rooms. Breakfast included in rates. Type of meal: Full bkfst. Ceiling fan in room. Library and lounge on premises. Antiquing, golf, shopping, downhill skiing and cross-country skiing nearby.

Certificate may be used: Anytime, except for Canadian holiday weekends.

Victoria

Claddagh House B&B

1761 Lee Ave
Victoria, BC V8R 4W7
(250)370-2816 Fax:(250)592-0228
Internet: www.accommodationsbc.com/claddaghhouse.html

Circa 1913. This historic home offers three comfortable guest rooms, one with a private bath. The Rostrevor Room opens out to the garden, offering a picturesque site. The innkeepers prepare an Irish-style breakfast with a variety of savory fare. Although tucked away in a quiet residential neighborhood, the attractions of Victoria are close by.

Innkeeper(s): Elaine & Ken Brown. $149-249. MC, VISA, AX, PC, TC. 3 rooms, 2 with PB and 1 suite. Breakfast, afternoon tea and snacks/refreshments included in rates. Types of meals: Full gourmet bkfst, cont plus and early coffee/tea. Beds: KQDT. Ceiling fan in room. VCR, fax, copier, bicycles and library on premises. Antiquing, fishing, whale watching, castle tours, gardens, live theater, parks, shopping and water sports nearby.
Pets allowed: Small short haired pets, one room only.
Location: Residential.
Certificate may be used: Oct. 1 to May 1, Sunday-Thursday, excluding holidays.

Gregory's Guest House

5373 Patricia Bay Hwy
Victoria, BC V8Y 2N9
(250)658-8404 (888)658-8404 Fax:(250)658-4604
Internet: www.bctravel.com/gregorys.html
E-mail: gregorys@direct.ca

Circa 1919. The two acres of this historic hobby farm are just across the street from Elk Lake, six miles from downtown Victoria and near Butchart Gardens. All the rooms are decorated in antiques and duvets, and they feature garden and lake views. The grounds include water gardens, a waterfall and a pond. A traditional, full Canadian breakfast is served, and after the meal, guests can enjoy the hobby farm and animals or perhaps rent a boat at the lake.

Innkeeper(s): Paul & Elizabeth Gregory. $79-89. MC, VISA, PC, TC. 3 rooms, 2 with PB. Breakfast included in rates. Type of meal: Full bkfst. Beds: DT. Fax, library and parlor with fireplace on premises. Antiquing, fishing, Victoria Butchart Gardens, live theater, parks, sporting events and water sports nearby.
"Our family felt very welcome, loved the house and especially liked the super breakfasts."
Certificate may be used: Oct. 15-March 30. May not be used with other off-season specials.

Rose Cottage B&B

3059 Washington Ave
Victoria, BC V9A 1P7
(250)381-5985 Fax:(250)592-5221

The well-traveled hosts of this Folk-Victorian inn know the value their visitors place on a warm welcome. The innkeepers have plenty of inside information about Victoria to make your visit as adventurous or as relaxing as you want. The inn sits on a peaceful street close to downtown and a short distance from the Gorge Park Waterway. The decor includes large, high ceilings, period furniture, a guest parlor that boasts a nautical theme and a large dining room with library.

Innkeeper(s): Robert Bishop. $65-80. MC, VISA. 3 rooms. Breakfast included in rates. Type of meal: Full bkfst. Phone and turndown service in room. VCR on premises. Antiquing and shopping nearby.
Certificate may be used: Sept. 15 through May 31.

Scholefield House B&B

731 Vancouver St
Victoria, BC V8V 3-V4
(250)385-2025 (800)661-1623 Fax:(250)383-3036
Internet: scholefieldhouse.com
E-mail: mail@scholefieldhouse.com

Circa 1892. The innkeeper at this two-story Queen Anne Victorian is an author, who enjoys the connection to the original owner of the house who founded the library in the Legislature Building. Located on a tree-lined street a short walk from the Empress Hotel, a picket fence and gabled front entrance welcome guests. Rooms are furnished with antiques, elegant draperies and period decor, and there are clawfoot soaker tubs. Edible flowers decorate the abundant servings of eggs Florentine, french toast with Brie, smoked salmon and other entrees of the five-course champagne breakfasts served fireside in the parlor. The house is listed in the historical heritage register.

Innkeeper(s): Tana Dineen. $100-150. MC, VISA, PC, TC. 3 rooms with PB, 1 with FP and 1 suite. Breakfast included in rates. Type of meal: Full gourmet bkfst. Beds: KQ. Turndown service and ceiling fan in room. VCR, fax and library on premises. Antiquing, canoeing/kayaking, fishing, golf, whale watching, salmon fishing, gardens, English high tea, live theater, museums and shopping nearby.
Location: City.
Certificate may be used: Nov. 1-April 30.

Whistler

Golden Dreams B&B

6412 Easy St
Whistler, BC V0N 1B6
(604)932-2667 (800)668-7055 Fax:(604)932-7055
E-mail: goldendreams@whistlerweb.net

Circa 1986. This private homestay is located two hours from Vancouver in the famed resort town of Whistler. The Victorian, Oriental and Aztec guest rooms feature duvets, sherry and bath robes. Enjoy views of the mountains and the herb and flower gardens. There is an outdoor hot tub and a fireside family room, as well as a full guest kitchen. The home is a mile from ski lifts, and the valley trail system and bus route are just outside the door. The innkeepers have on-site bicycle rentals. The innkeepers also offer condos within walking distance to ski lifts. The condos have fireplaces, a full kitchen, underground parking and spa access.

Innkeeper(s): Ann & Terry Spence. $85-125. MC, VISA. 3 rooms, 1 with PB and 2 suites. Breakfast included in rates. Type of meal: Full gourmet bkfst. Beds: QD. Bath robes and slippers in room. VCR, fax, spa, bicycles and library on premises. Fishing, horseback, rafting and canoeing, parks, downhill skiing, cross-country skiing, sporting events and water sports nearby.
Location: Mountains.
"Great house, great food, terrific people."
Certificate may be used: April 15-June 15 and Sept. 15-Nov. 15, except holidays.

New Brunswick

Saint Andrews

Kingsbrae Arms Relais & Chateaux

219 King St
Saint Andrews, NB E5B 1Y1
(506)529-1897 Fax:(506)529-1197
Internet: www.kingsbrae.com
E-mail: kingbrae@nbnet.nb.ca

Circa 1897. With its splendid ocean views and ridgeline location, this shingle-style was built at the turn of the century on a
choice piece of land. Today a trip to the manor house is a bit
like traveling to a welcoming English country estate. The five
guest rooms and three suites have been decorated with the
utmost of elegance. Each room has a fireplace, and beds are
dressed with fine linens and puffy comforters. Guests might
find a room with a canopy bed draped with velvet or perhaps a
bath with a clawfoot tub, marble walls and a wood floor. For
those who wish to relax, the library is a masculine retreat with
a fireplace and dark, exposed wood beams. Guests also can
take a swim in the outdoor, heated swimming pool. The
innkeepers pamper you with a gourmet morning feast and tea
in the afternoon. One also can arrange to enjoy a five-course
dinner, as rates are MAP. The inn has a Canada Select five-star
rating and holds a four-star rating from Mobile. It has been
selected as a Grand Award Winner of Andrew Harper's
Hideaways of the Year."

Innkeeper(s): Harry Chancey & David Oxford. $375-525. MC, VISA, PC. 8
rooms with PB, 8 with FP, 3 suites and 1 conference room. Breakfast, after-
noon tea, dinner and snacks/refreshments included in rates. Types of meals:
Full gourmet bkfst and early coffee/tea. Beds: KQ. Cable TV, phone, turndown
service, ceiling fan, VCR, whirlpools and Jacuzzi in room. Air conditioning.
Fax, copier, swimming, bicycles, library, patio and piano on premises.
Antiquing, fishing, golf, whale watching, parks, shopping, cross-country ski-
ing, tennis and water sports nearby.
Pets allowed: With advance permission.
Publicity: *Boston Globe, Atlantic Monthly, Canadian House & Home and
CBC TV & Radio.*
Certificate may be used: Nov. 15-April 15, Monday-Thursday.

Nova Scotia

Liverpool

Lane's Privateer Inn & B&B

27-33 Bristol Ave, PO Box 509
Liverpool, NS B0T 1K0
(902)354-3456 (800)794-3332 Fax:(902)354-7220
Internet: www3.nssympatico.ca/ron.lane
E-mail: ron.lane@ns.sympatico.ca

Circa 1798. For more than 30 years, three generations of the
Lane family have run this historic lodge nestled among Nova
Scotia's scenic coast and forests. The inn is a participant in "A
Taste of Nova Scotia," which features a group of fine eateries
that meet strict government standards. Lane's hosts a "Sip and
Savour" series throughout the year, featuring wine tastings and
gourmet meals. Breakfast at the inn is a treat with specialty
menus featuring such items as haddock cakes and eggs

Benedict. Nearby Kejimkujik National Park offers plenty of out-
door activities, and beaches are only a few miles away.
Liverpool offers many fine shops and restaurants to enjoy.
Innkeeper(s): The Lane Family, Ron, Carol, Susan & Terry. $50-85. MC, VISA,
AX, DC, DS. 30 rooms, 27 with PB. Breakfast included in rates. Beds: QDT.
Antiquing, fishing, live theater, cross-country skiing and water sports nearby.
Publicity: *Encore Travel, Providence and Rhode Island News.*
"Warm and relaxed atmosphere!"
Certificate may be used: Oct. 31-June 1, based on availability.

Ontario

Alymer

Ye Olde Apple Yard B&B

49450 College Line, RR 4
Alymer, ON N5H 2R3
(519)765-2708

This Italianate farmhouse is set on acres of secluded countryside. Guests can stroll through the apple orchard or simply
relax with a picnic under the trees. Romantic dinners for two
can be arranged. Guests can also enjoy the company of the resident farm animals, or simply sit and relax by the fireplace. The
area offers many interesting shops and Amish farms.
Innkeeper(s): Tino Smiaris. $60. 2 rooms. Breakfast included in rates. Type
of meal: Full bkfst.
Certificate may be used: Monday to Thursday, Nov. 1-April 30.

Collingwood

Pretty River Valley Country Inn

RR 1
Collingwood, ON L0M 1P0
(705)445-7598 Fax:(705)445-7598
Internet: www.prettyriverinn.com
E-mail: inn@cois.on.ca

Circa 1980. Each of the guest rooms at this log inn includes a
fireplace, and suites have the added amenity of a double
whirlpool tub. The secluded, 120-acre estate offers views of the
Pretty River Valley as well as the Blue Mountains. The innkeepers provide an ample breakfast, highlighted by items such as
eggs Benedict. A collection of menus from local restaurants is
kept on hand. Each season brings outdoor fun. Downhill and
cross-country skiing, water sports on the bay and golfing are
nearby, and there are plenty of antique shops to explore.
Innkeeper(s): Steve & Diane Szelestowski. $89-120. MC, VISA, AX, DC, TC.
8 rooms with PB, 8 with FP, 2 suites and 1 conference room. Breakfast
included in rates. Type of meal: Full bkfst. Beds: QT. Whirlpool two rooms in
room. Air conditioning. Fax, spa and pet boarding on premises. Antiquing,
bicycling, fishing, golf, hiking, kennel across street, parks, shopping, downhill
skiing, cross-country skiing, tennis and water sports nearby.
Pets allowed: Boarding for pets across road.
Location: In valley surrounded by hills.
Publicity: *Toronto Sun and Century Homes.*
Certificate may be used: April-June 30, (Sunday-Thursday).

Elora

Cedarbrook Farm B&B

RR 2
Elora, ON N0B 1S0
(519)843-3481

Circa 1876. A 100-acre working farm surrounds this simple stone farmhouse where guests enjoy eating breakfast overlooking fields of cattle and Arabian horses. A stream and trails on the property may be explored or visit the nearby Mennonite communities of Elmira and St. Jacobs. The town of Elora and the Elora Gorge are a few minutes away. Select a full or continental breakfast or choose a vegetarian repast.

Innkeeper(s): Thilo Elste. $60. 2 rooms. Breakfast included in rates. Types of meals: Full bkfst and cont.

"Very comfortable house, lovely countryside, thank you for all of your hospitality."

Certificate may be used: Nov. 1-April 30 all week.

Gananoque

Manse Lane B&B

465 Stone St S
Gananoque, ON K7G 2A7
(613)382-8642 (888)565-6379
Internet: www.bbcanada.com/942.html

Circa 1860. Four comfortable guest rooms, two with a private bath, are available at this bed & breakfast. Breakfasts include items such as cereal, fruit, yogurt, cheeses, breads, bacon and eggs. Guests are within walking distance of local attractions.

Innkeeper(s): Jocelyn & George Bounds. $53-130. MC, VISA, AX, TC. 4 rooms, 2 with PB. Breakfast included in rates. Types of meals: Full bkfst and early coffee/tea. Beds: QT. Air conditioning. Swimming on premises. Antiquing, fishing, golf, boat cruises, festivals, live theater, parks, cross-country skiing, tennis and water sports nearby.

"Thoroughly enjoyed the stay. It was great to see you again."

Certificate may be used: Oct. 1 through April 30.

Kingston

The North Nook B&B

83 Earl St
Kingston, ON K7L 2G8
(613)547-8061 Fax:(613)547-2818

Circa 1849. Recently restored, this two-story limestone house has exposed stone and brick walls, gleaming pine floors and original tin ceilings and a tin roof. It was originally built as a market. Antiques now fill the rooms. Breakfast is served in the dining room and often includes orange French toast.

Innkeeper(s): Mary Ellen North. $85-135. MC, VISA, AX. 4 rooms with PB. Breakfast and afternoon tea included in rates. Types of meals: Cont plus and early coffee/tea. Beds: QD. Cable TV, phone, turndown service, ceiling fan and VCR in room. Air conditioning. Fax on premises. Antiquing, fishing, golf, live theater, parks, shopping, downhill skiing, cross-country skiing, tennis and water sports nearby.

Pets Allowed.

Location: City.

Certificate may be used: Nov. 1 to March 31.

New Hamburg

The Waterlot

17 Huron St
New Hamburg, ON N0B 2G0
(519)662-2020 Fax:(519)662-2114
E-mail: waterlotesympatico.ca

Circa 1844. Located beside a mill pond, this Victorian home boasts an imaginative architecture with gothic gables frosted with gingerbread trim and an  unusual cupola. It houses the inn's most important asset, a French-country restaurant, Le Bistro, which seats 125 people. Overlooking the Nith River as it flows through the backyard, the restaurant has been well-known for more than two decades. Guest rooms are simple and housed beneath each of the inn's twin gables.

Innkeeper(s): Gord & Leslie Elkeer. $75-115. MC, VISA, AX, DC, PC, TC. 3 rooms, 1 suite and 2 conference rooms. Breakfast included in rates. Type of meal: Cont plus. Beds: KQD. Fax and copier on premises. Amusement parks, antiquing, fishing, golf, live theater, parks, shopping, downhill skiing, cross-country skiing and tennis nearby.

Certificate may be used: April 1-Feb. 28, (closed March).

Niagara Falls

Butterfly Manor

4917 River Rd
Niagara Falls, ON L2E 3G5
(416)358-8988 Fax:(905)358-8988

Circa 1985. Within walking distance of Niagara Falls, this Tudor-style inn overlooks the Niagara River. The inn is also a short drive from Niagara-on-the-Lake and a five-minute walk from the train and bus stations. Many points of interest on both sides of the U.S.-Canadian border are minutes away. The warm kitchen with fireplace delights guests with home-baked smells and pleasant atmosphere. The hostess will help you find a good place to dine and make suggestions on what you should include on your itinerary.

Innkeeper(s): L. Siciliano. $110-125. MC, VISA, AX, DC, PC, TC. 7 rooms with PB, 1 with FP and 2 suites. Breakfast included in rates. Type of meal: Full bkfst. Cable TV in room. Air conditioning. Amusement parks, antiquing, golf, live theater, parks, shopping and water sports nearby.

Certificate may be used: Nov. 1 to April 30, excluding Valentine's Day weekend.

Ottawa

Rideau View Inn

177 Frank St
Ottawa, ON K2P 0X4
(613)236-9309 (800)658-3564 Fax:(613)237-6842
Internet: home.istar.ca/~rideau/
E-mail: rideau@istar.ca

Circa 1907. This large Edwardian home is located on a quiet residential street near the Rideau Canal. A hearty breakfast is served in the dining room. Guests are encouraged to relax in front of the fireplace in the living room.

Innkeeper(s): Richard Colling. $63-87. MC, VISA, AX, DC, TC. 7 rooms, 2 with PB, 1 with FP. Breakfast included in rates. Type of meal: Full bkfst.

Beds: QDT. Phone in room. Air conditioning. VCR, fax and copier on premises. Antiquing, tourist attractions, live theater, parks, shopping, downhill skiing, cross-country skiing and sporting events nearby.

Location: City.

Publicity: *Ottawa Citizen.*

Certificate may be used: Nov. 1-April 30, Sunday-Saturday.

Peterborough

King Bethune Guest House

270 King St
Peterborough, ON K9J 2S2
(705)743-4101 (800)574-3664 Fax:(705)743-8446
Internet: www.bbcanada.com/165
E-mail: marlis@sympatico.ca

Circa 1893. This brick Victorian is downtown on a quiet tree-shaded street. Restored hardwood floors, original trim throughout, tall ceilings and handsome windows grace the interiors. Guest rooms are large and offer antiques, as well as desks, data

ports, TVs and VCRs. The Executive Suite has a king bed and private entrance as well as a private hot tub, sauna and steam bath. There's a private walled garden with reflecting pool, fountain and fireplace, a favorite spot for breakfast. Plan ahead, and you can arrange for a roast beef dinner complete with yorkshire pudding.

Innkeeper(s): Marlis Lindsay. $74-156. MC, VISA, AX, PC, TC. 3 rooms with PB. Breakfast included in rates. Types of meals: Full gourmet bkfst and early coffee/tea. Beds: KQ. Cable TV, phone, turndown service, ceiling fan, VCR, sauna and garden hot tub in room. Fax, spa, sauna, bicycles, library and english courtyard garden on premises. Amusement parks, antiquing, fishing, golf, live theater, parks, shopping, downhill skiing, cross-country skiing, sporting events, tennis and water sports nearby.

Pets allowed: owner supervised.

Location: City.

Publicity: *Canadian Country and Examiner.*

"We still have not found better accommodations anywhere."

Certificate may be used: Jan. 30-Nov. 30, Sunday-Monday.

Westport

Stepping Stone Inn

328 Centreville Rd, RR 2
Westport, ON K0G 1X0
(613)273-3806 Fax:(613)273-3331
Internet: www.steppingstoneinn.com
E-mail: stepping@rideau.net

Circa 1840. Multi-colored limestone warms in the afternoon sun on this historic house located on more than 150 acres. Flower beds surround the wraparound veranda decorated in

white gingerbread and fretwork. Rooms are furnished with antiques, and there is a solarium and dining room that overlook flower gardens, a picturesque swimming pond and waterfall. Guest rooms include luxury suites with Jacuzzis, fireplaces and private entrances. Plan ahead and the inn's chef will create a custom menu for you. Stepping Stone is popular for garden weddings and corporate meetings. The grounds offer a beaver pond, pastures, an ostrich farm and nature trails. Nearby is the Rideau Canal System and many lakes.

Innkeeper(s): Madeleine Saunders. $75-150. MC, VISA, AX, TC. 6 rooms, 4 with PB, 3 with FP, 1 suite, 1 cabin and 1 conference room. Breakfast and afternoon tea included in rates. Types of meals: Full gourmet bkfst and early coffee/tea. Beds: QT. Air conditioning. Fax, swimming and library on premises. Handicap access. Antiquing, fishing, golf, live theater, parks, shopping, cross-country skiing, tennis and water sports nearby.

Certificate may be used: Feb. 1 to Dec. 15, Sunday to Thursday, subject to availability.

Quebec

North Hatley

Cedar Gables B&B

Box 355, 4080 Magog Rd
North Hatley, QB J0B 2C0
(819)842-4120

Circa 1896. Bordering Lake Massiwippi, this gabled home boasts a wooded country setting. The inn's dock, canoes and rowboat are available to guests. Some bedrooms have lake views. Breakfast is served out on the veranda, weather permitting. The village is a five-minute walk from the inn.

Innkeeper(s): Ann & Don Fleischer. $80-104. MC, VISA, AX, PC, TC. 5 rooms with PB, 1 with FP and 1 suite. Breakfast and afternoon tea included in rates. Types of meals: Full gourmet bkfst, cont plus and early coffee/tea. Beds: K. Cable TV, VCR and electric blankets in room. Swimming and library on premises. Handicap access. Antiquing, fishing, live theater, parks, downhill skiing, cross-country skiing, sporting events and water sports nearby.

Pets Allowed.

Location: Village.

Publicity: *Montreal Gazette.*

"We felt comfortable and at home the minute we stepped in the door."

Certificate may be used: Nov. 1-May 15, except holidays.

Inns of Interest

African American History

Wingscorton Farm Inn . . . . .East Sandwich, Mass.
Munro House B&B . . . . .Jonesville, Mich.
Signal House . . . . .Ripley, Ohio
1790 House B&B Inn . . . . . . .Georgetown, S.C.
Golden Stage Inn . . . . .Proctorsville, Vt.
Rockland Farm Retreat . . . . .Bumpass, Va.

Animals

Alligators, giant turtles
Shaw House . . . . .Georgetown, S.C.
Armadillo
Southwind B&B . . . . .Wimberley, Texas

Barns

Old Church House Inn . . . . .Mossville, Ill.
Barn of Rockford . . . . .Rockford, Ill.
Watchtide, B&B By the Sea . . . . .Searsport, Maine
Candlelite Inn . . . . .Bradford, N.H.
Inn at Cedar Falls . . . . .Logan, Ohio
Conerstone B&B Inn . . . . .Landenberg, Pa.
Jackson Fork Inn . . . . .Huntsville, Utah
Waitsfield Inn . . . . .Waitsfield, Vt.

Boats

Dockside Boat & Bed . . . . .Oakland, Calif.

Castles

Castle Inn Riverside . . . . .Wichita, Kan.
Manresa Castle . . . . .Port Townsend, Wash.

Churches

Old Church House Inn . . . . .Mossville, Ill.
Parsonage Inn . . . . .St. Michaels, Md.
The Abbey . . . . .Cape May, N.J.
Parson's Pillow . . . . .Cody, Wyo.

Civil War

The Mansion B&B . . . . .Bardstown, Ky.
Myrtledene . . . . .Lebanon, Ky.
Munro House . . . . .Jonesville, Mich.
The Sedgwick Inn . . . . .Berlin, N.Y.
Goose Creek Guesthouse . . . . . . .Southold, N.Y.
James Getty Hotel . . . . .Gettysburg, Pa.
La Vista Plantation . . . . .Fredericksburg, Va.

Cookbooks

"The Old Yacht Club Inn Cookbook"
The Old Yacht Club Inn . . . . .Santa Barbara, Calif.
"Sea Holly Bed and Breakfast, A Sharing of Secrets"
Sea Holly Inn . . . . .Cape May, N.J.
"Recipes from Grandview Lodge"
Grandview Lodge . . . . .Waynesville, N.C.
"Hog Heaven"
The Durning House B&B and Tea Room
. . . . .Van Alstyne, Texas

"Recipes from the Kitchen of"
Hill Farm Inn . . . . .Arlington, Vt.
"Waking Up Down South"
"Well Bless Your Heart," Vols. I & II
"Butter'em While They're Hot"
Sims-Mitchell House B&B . . . . . . .Chatham, Va.
"Breakfast with Bunny"
Bombay House . . . . . . .Bainbridge Island, Wash.
"Something's CookInn"
Ravenscroft Inn . . . . .Port Townsend, Wash.
"With Lots of Love"
A. Drummonds Ranch . . . . .Cheyenne, Wyo.

Farms and Orchards

Apple Blossom Inn B&B . . . . . . .Ahwahnee, Calif.
Apple Lane Inn . . . . .Aptos, Calif.
Rockin' A B&B . . . . .Julian, Calif.
Howard Creek Ranch . . . . .Westport, Calif.
Apple Orchard Inn . . . . .Durango, Colo.
Kingston 5 Ranch B&B . . . . .Kingston, Id.
The Shaw House . . . . .Anamosa, Iowa
Lear Acres B&B . . . . .Bern, Kan.
Peaceful Acres B&B . . . . .Great Bend, Kan.
Canaan Land Farm B&B . . . . . .Harrodsburg, KY
Maple Hill Farm B&B Inn
. . . . .Hallowell/Augusta, Maine
On Cranberry Pond B&B . . . .Middleboro, Mass.
Gilbert's Tree Farm B&B . . . . . .Rehoboth, Mass.
Wingscorton Farm Inn . . . . .Sandwich, Mass.
Steep Acres Farm . . . . .Williamstown, Mass.
Grandpa's Farm . . . . .Lampe, Mo.
Rockhouse Mountain Farm Inn
. . . . .Eaton Center, N.H.
Ellis River B&B . . . . .Jackson, N.H.
Olde Orchard Inn . . . . . .Moultonborough, N.H.
Volden Farm . . . . .Lucerne, N.D.
Wine Country Farm . . . . .Dayton, Ore.
Line Limousin Farmhouse B&B . . . . .Carlisle, Pa.
Huntland Farm . . . . .Greensburg, Pa.
Barley Sheaf Farm . . . . .Holicong, Pa.
Cedar Hill Farm . . . . .Mount Joy, Pa.
Field & Pine B&B . . . . .Shippensburg, Pa.
B&B at Skogland Farm . . . . .Canova, S.D.
Llano Grande Plantation . . . . .Nacogdoches, Texas
Hill Farm Inn . . . . .Arlington, Vt.
Historic Brookside Farms . . . . .Orwell, Vt.
Liberty Hill Farm . . . . .Rochester, Vt.
Rockland Farm Retreat . . . . .Bumpass, Va.
Upper Byrd Farm . . . . .Columbia, Va.
Colonel Crockett Farm . . . . . . .Coupeville, Wash.
Just-N-Trails B&B . . . . .Sparta, Wis.

Glacier Viewing

Pearson's Pond Luxury Inn . . . . . .Juneau, Alaska

Gold Mines & Gold Panning

Pearson's Pond Luxury Inn . . . . . .Juneau, Alaska

Hot Springs

Vichy Hot Springs Resort & Inn . . . . .Ukiah, Calif.

Inns Built Prior to 1799

1678 Hewick Plantation . . . . .Urbanna, Va.
1684 The Inn at Montross . . . . . .Montross, Va.
1691 The Great Valley House of Valley Forge
. . . . .Valley Forge, Pa.
1696 Old Yarmouth Inn . . . .Yarmouth Port, Mass.
1700 Elias Child House B&B . .Woodstock, Conn.
1700 Evermay-On-The-Delaware . . . .Erwinna, Pa.
1700 Hollileif B&B . . . . .New Hope, Pa.
1704 Stumble Inne . . . . .Nantucket, Mass.
1704 Cornerstone B&B Inn . . . .Landenberg, Pa.
1709 The Woodbox Inn . . . . . .Nantucket, Mass.
1711 La Hacienda Grande . . . . . .Bernalillo, N.M.
1720 Roseledge Farm B&B . . . . . .Preston, Conn.
1723 Roxbury Mill B&B . . . . . . .Spotsylvania, Va.
1725 1725 Historic Witmer's Tavern Inn
. . . . .Lancaster, Pa.
1728 Red Fox Inn . . . . .Middleburg, Va.
1729 Harbor Light Inn . . . . . .Marblehead, Mass.
1738 Brown's Historic Home B&B . .Salem, N.J.
1740 Red Brook Inn . . . . .Old Mystic, Conn.
1740 High Meadows B&B . . . . .Eliot, Maine
1740 Ingate Farms B&B . . . .Belchertown, Mass.
1740 Barley Sheaf Farm . . . . .Holicong, Pa.
1740 Du Pre House LLC . . . . . .Georgetown, S.C.
1741 The Dunbar House . . . . .Sandwich, Mass.
1743 The Inn at Mitchell House
. . . . .Chestertown, Md.
1750 Candleberry Inn . . . . .Brewster, Mass.
1750 The General Rufus Putnam House
. . . . .Rutland, Mass.
1750 Alynn's Butterfly Inn B&B
. . . . .Warrensburg, N.Y.
1750 Tattersall Inn . . . . .Point Pleasant, Pa.
1750 The Melville House . . . . . . .Newport, R.I.
1750 Litchfield Plantation . . .Pawleys Islands, S.C.
1750 Linden House B&B & Plantation
. . . . .Champlain, Va.
1752 The Olde Stage Coach B&B
. . . . .Jennerstown, Pa.
1753 L'Auberge Provencale . . . . .White Post, Va.
1756 Bee and Thistle Inn . . . . .Old Lyme, Conn.
1758 Hammett House Inn . . . . . . .Newport, R.I.
1760 Glasgow B&B Inn . . . . . . .Cambridge, Md.
1760 The Winchester Country Inn
. . . . .Westminster, Md.
1760 The Norris House Inn . . . . . .Leesburg, Va.
1760 Gilbert House B&B of Middleway
. . . . .Charles Town, W.Va.
1763 Wingscorton Farm Inn
. . . . .East Sandwich, Mass.
1764 Colonel Spencer Inn . . . . . .Plymouth, N.H.
1765 Bankhouse B&B . . . . .West Chester, Pa.
1766 Wainwright Inn . . . .Great Barrington, Mass.
1766 The Inn at Meander Plantation
. . . . .Locust Dale, Va.

1767 Highland Lake Inn B&B
. . . . .East Andover, N.H.
1769 The Inn at Millrace Pond . . . . . .Hope, N.J.
1770 Ira Allen House . . . . .Arlington, Vt.
1772 The Bagley House . . . . . . .Durham, Maine
1772 Jailhouse Inn . . . . .Newport, R.I.
1773 Abbott House . . . . .Bethel, Maine
1775 Colonel Roger Brown House
. . . . .Concord, Mass.
1775 Kanaga House B&B . . . .Mechanicsburg, Pa.
1777 Doneckers, The Guesthouse, Inns
. . . . .Ephrata, Pa.
1778 The Inn at Chester . . . . . . .Chester, Conn.
1778 Staffords-In-The-Field . . . . .Chocorua, N.H.
1778 Willow Grove Inn . . . . .Orange, Va.
1780 Moses Paul Inn . . . . .Eliot, Maine
1780 Catoctin Inn and Conference Center
. . . . .Buckeystown, Md.
1780 Stone Manor . . . . .Middletown, Md.
1780 Hacienda Antigua B&B .Albuquerque, N.M.
1780 Golden Stage Inn . . . . . . .Proctorsville, Vt.
1782 Abel Darling B&B . . . . . . .Litchfield, Conn.
1783 The Towers B&B . . . . .Milford, Del.
1783 Four Chimneys Inn . . . . . .Bennington, Vt.
1785 The 1785 Inn . . . . . . .North Conway, N.H.
1786 Kenniston Hill Inn . . . . . . .Boothbay, Maine
1786 The Wayside Inn . . .Greenfield Center, N.Y.
1788 Strasburg Village Inn . . . . . .Strasburg, Pa.
1789 Merryvale B&B . . . . . . .Woodbury, Conn.
1789 Miles River Country Inn . . .Hamilton, Mass.
1789 Longswamp B&B . . . . .Mertztown, Pa.
1789 Historic Brookside Farms Country Inn
. . . . .Orwell, Vt.
1790 Silvermine Tavern . . . . . . .Norwalk, Conn.
1790 Fairhaven Inn . . . . .Bath, Maine
1790 Benjamin F. Packard House . . . .Bath, Maine
1790 Ivy Lodge . . . . .Nantucket, Mass.
1790 Snow Hill Inn . . . . .Snow Hill, Md.
1790 The Inn at Bingham School
. . . . .Chapel Hill, N.C.
1790 1812 on The Perquimans B&B Inn
. . . . .Hertford, N.C.
1790 Olde Orchard Inn . .Moultonborough, N.H.
1790 Mill Creek Homestead B&B
. . . . .Bird-in-Hand, Pa.
1790 River Inn . . . . .Marietta, Pa.
1790 Field & Pine B&B . . . . . .Shippensburg, Pa.
1790 The Cuthbert House Inn B&B
. . . . .Beaufort, S.C.
1790 1790 House B&B Inn . . .Georgetown, S.C.
1790 Red Shutter Farmhouse B&B
. . . . .New Market, Va.
1790 Flowering Fields B&B . . . .White Stone, Va.
1790 Hill Farm Inn . . . . .Arlington, Vt.
1790 Silver Maple Lodge & Cottages . .Fairlee, Vt.
1790 The Putney Inn . . . . .Putney, Vt.
1790 The Inn at Blush Hill . . . . . .Waterbury, Vt.
1791 St. Francis Inn . . . . . .Saint Augustine, Fla.
1791 Sedgwick Inn . . . . .Berlin, N.Y.
1793 Cove House . . . . . .Kennebunkport, Maine
1794 Watchtide... by the Sea . .Searsport, Maine
1794 The Wagener Estate B&B . . .Penn Yan, N.Y.
1794 The Whitehall Inn . . . . . . .New Hope, Pa.
1794 Lareau Farm Country Inn . . .Waitsfield, Vt.
1795 Canaan Land Farm B&B .Harrodsburg, Ky.
1795 Shiretown Inn on the Island of Martha's
Vineyard . . . . .Edgartown, Mass.

1795 Hachland Hill Inn . . . . . .Clarksville, Tenn.
1795 Spring Farm B&B . . . . .Luray, Va.
1797 Applebrook B&B . . . . . .Jefferson, N.H.
1797 Sanford's Ridge B&B . . . .Queensbury, N.Y.
1798 Lane's Privateer Inn & B&B
. . . . .Liverpool, Nova Scotia

Jail House

Casa de Patron . . . . .Lincoln, N.M.

Literary Figures Associated With Inns

Louisa May Alcott, Ralph Waldo Emerson,
Nathaniel Hawthorne
Hawthorne Inn . . . . .Concord, Mass..
Jack London
Vichy Hot Springs Resort Inn . . . . . .Ukiah, Calif.
Becky Thatcher
Fifth Street Mansion B&B . . . . .Hannibal, Mo.
Mark Twain/Samuel Clemens
Vichy Hot Springs Resort & Inn . . . .Ukiah, Calif.
Fifth Street Mansion B&B . . . . .Hannibal, Mo.
Edith Wharton
The Gables Inn . . . . .Lenox, Mass.

Llama Ranches

Canaan Land Farm B&B . . . . . .Harrodsburg, Ky.
Rockhouse Mountain Farm Inn
. . . . .Eaton Center, N.H.
Llama Ranch B&B . . . . .White Salmon, Wash.

Log Houses/Cabins

Ocean Wilderness Country Inn
. . . . .Sooke, British Columbia
Old Carson Inn . . . . .Lake City, Colo.
The Log House . . . . .Russellville, Ky.
Lindgren's B&B . . . . .Lutsen, Minn.
Trout House Village Resort . . . . . . .Hague, N.Y.
Log Country Inn- B&B of Ithaca . . . .Ithaca, N.Y.
Inn at Cedar Falls . . . . .Logan, Oh.
The Inn at Burg's Landing
. . . . .Anderson Island, Wash.
A. Drummonds Ranch . . . . .Cheyenne, Wyo.

Movies Filmed at Inns

Maverick
The Mason Place B&B . . . . .Loudon, Tenn.

Old Mills

Lodge at Manuel Mill . . . . .Arnold, Calif.
Silvermine Tavern . . . . .Norwalk, Conn.
Arbor Rose B&B . . . . .Stockbridge, Mass.
Asa Ransom House . . . . .Clarence, N.Y.

Old Taverns

Red Brook Inn . . . . .Old Mystic, Conn.
Silvermine Tavern . . . . .Norwalk, Conn.
Witmer's Tavern-Historic 1725 Inn
. . . . .Lancaster, Pa.
Red Fox Inn . . . . .Middleburg, Va.

Oldest Continuously Operated Inns

1859 Historic National Hotel B&B
. . . . .Jamestown, Calif.
1857 Florida House Inn . . . . .Amelia Island, Fla.

Candlelite Inn . . . . .Bradford, N.H.
The Bellevue House . . . . .Block Island, R.I.

Plantations

Merry Sherwood Plantation . . . . .Berlin, Md.
Laurel Hill Plantation . . . . . .McClellanville, S.C.
Inn at La Vista Plantation . . . . .Fredericksburg, Va.
Inn at Meander Plantation . . . . .Locust Dale, Va.

Ranches

Howard Creek Ranch . . . . .Westport, Calif.
Wine Country Farm . . . . .Dayton, Ore.
Hasse House and Ranch . . . . . . .Mason, Texas
A. Drummonds Ranch . . . . .Cheyenne, Wyo.

Revolutionary War

Colonel Roger Brown House . . . .Concord, Mass.
The Melville House . . . . .Newport, R.I.
Gilbert House B&B of Middleway
. . . . .Charles Town, W.Va.

Schoolhouses

The Bagley House . . . . .Durham, Maine
Old Sea Pines Inn . . . . .Brewster, Mass.
School House B&B . . . . .Rocheport, Mo.
The Inn at Bingham School . . . .Chapel Hill, N.C.
East Highland School House B&B . . .Phillips, Wis.

Space Shuttle Launches

The Higgins House . . . . .Sanford, Fla.

Stagecoach Stops

Maple Hill Farm B&B Inn . . . . .Hallowell, Maine
Hacienda Antigua B&B . . . . .Albuquerque, N.M.
Hacienda Vargas . . . . .Algodones/Santa Fe, N.M.
The Inn at Bingham School . . . .Chapel Hill, N.C.
Mountain Home B&B . . . . .Mountain Home, N.C.
Penguin Crossing B&B . . . . .Circleville, Ohio
The Olde Stage Coach B&B . . . .Jennerstown, Pa.
The Golden Stage Inn . . . . .Proctorsville, Vt.
Inn at Blush Hill . . . . .Waterbury, Vt.
Old Stagecoach Inn . . . . .Waterbury, Vt.
Wisconsin House Stagecoach Inn
. . . . .Hazel Green, Wis.

Still in the Family

The Sherwood Inn . . . . .New Haven, Ky.
Cedarcroft Farm B&B . . . . . . .Warrensburg, Mo.
Rockhouse Mountain Farm Inn
. . . . .Eaton Center, N.H.
Line Limousin Farmhouse B&B . . . . .Carlisle, Pa.
Cedar Hill Farm . . . . .Mount Joy, Pa.
Hasse House and Ranch . . . . .Mason, Texas
Bay View Waterfront B&B . . . . . .Belle Haven, Va.
Hewick Plantation . . . . .Urbanna, Va.
Inn at Barnum Point . . . . . .Camano Island, Wash.

Taverns

Red Brook Inn . . . . .Old Mystic, Conn.
Silvermine Tavern . . . . .Norwalk, Conn.
Giddings . . . . .Syracuse, N.Y.
James Getty Hotel . . . . .Gettysburg, Pa.
1725 Historic Witmer's Tavern . . . .Lancaster, Pa.

Train Stations & Renovated Rail Cars

The Inn at Depot Hill
. . . . .Capitola-by-the-Sea, Calif.
Trout City Berth & Breakfast . . .Buena Vista, Colo.

Tunnels, Secret Passageways, Caves

Merry Sherwood Plantation . . . . . . .Berlin, Maine
Wingscorton Farm . . . . . . .East Sandwich, Mass.
Munro House B&B . . . . .Jonesville, Mich.
Colonel Spencer Inn . . . . .Plymouth, N.H.
Witmer's Tavern-Historic 1725 Inn
. . . . .Lancaster, Pa.
Lynchburg Mansion Inn . . . . .Lynchburg, Va.

Unusual Architecture

The Oscar Swan Country Inn . . . . . . .Geneva, Ill.

Unusual Sleeping Places

On a yacht
Dockside Boat & Bed . . . . .Oakland, Calif.
In a barn
The Barn of Rockford . . . . .Rockford, Ill.
50 yards from reversing whitewater rapids
The Weskeag Inn . . . . . . .South Tomaston, Maine
In a trading post
Hacienda Vargas . . . . .Santa Fe, N.M.
On or next to an archaelogical dig site
The White Oak Inn . . . . .Danville, Ohio
Hewick Plantation . . . . .Urbanna, Va.

Waterfalls

Inn at Cedar Falls . . . . .Logan, Ohio

Who Slept/Visited Here

John Adams
Witmer's Tavern-Historic 1725 Inn
. . . . .Lancaster, Pa.

Ben Affleck
The Rhett House Inn . . . . .Beaufort, S.C.
John James Audubon
Weston House . . . . .Eastport, Maine
The Barrymore family
Evermay-on-the-Delaware . . . . .Erwinna, Pa.
Henry Bennett, photographer
Historic Bennett House . . . .Wisconsin Dells, Wis.
Sarah Bernhardt
Abigail's "Elegant Victorian Mansion"
. . . . .Eureka, Calif.
Big Nose Katy
Plaza Hotel . . . . .Las Vegas, N.M.
Billy the Kid
Plaza Hotel . . . . .Las Vegas, N.M.
Casa de Patron . . . . .Lincoln, N.M.
Sandra Bullock
The Rhett House Inn . . . . .Beaufort, S.C.
Grover Cleveland
Cordova . . . . .Ocean Grove, N.J.
Danny DeVito, Michael Douglas
Colonel Crockett Farm . . . . . . .Coupeville, Wash.
Clark Gable
Gold Mountain Manor Historic B&B
. . . . .Big Bear, Calif.
Mrs. Warren Harding
Watchtide, B&B By the Sea . . . . .Searsport, Maine
Lillian Hellman
Barley Sheaf Farm . . . . .Holicong, Pa.
Doc Holliday
Plaza Hotel . . . . .Las Vegas, N.M.
Herbert Hoover
The Carriage House at Stonegate
. . . . .Montoursville, Pa.
Mrs. Herbert Hoover
Watchtide, B&B By the Sea . . . . .Searsport, Maine
Thomas Jefferson
1725 Historic Witmer's Tavern . . . .Lancaster, Pa.
Inn at Meander Plantation . . . . .Locust Dale, Va.

Lillie Langtry
Abigail's "Elegant Victorian Mansion"
. . . . .Eureka, Calif.
Carole Lombard
Gold Mountain Manor House B&B
. . . . .Big Bear Lake, Calif.
Jack London
Vichy Hot Springs Resort & Inn . . . .Ukiah, Calif.
Marx brothers
Barley Sheaf Farm . . . . .Holicong, Pa.
Captain Cornelius J. Mey
Captain Mey's B&B Inn . . . . . . .Cape May, N.J.
Gwyneth Paltrow
The Rhett House Inn . . . . .Beaufort, S.C.
S.J. Perlman
Barley Sheaf Farm . . . . .Holicong, Pa.
Eleanor Roosevelt
Watchtide, B&B By the Sea . . . . .Searsport, Maine
Theodore Roosevelt
Vichy Hot Springs Resort & Inn . . . . .Ukiah, Calif.
Lillian Russell
Bayview Hotel B&B Inn . . . . .Aptos, Calif.
Babe Ruth
Cranmore Mt. Lodge . . . . . . .North Conway, N.H.
William Seward
The William Seward Inn . . . . .Westfield, N.Y.
General W.T. Sherman
Cuthbert House Inn B&B . . . . . . .Beaufort, S.C.
Barbra Streisand
The Rhett House Inn . . . . .Beaufort, S.C.
Kathleen Turner
Colonel Crockett Farm . . . . . . .Coupeville, Wash.
Mark Twain
Vichy Hot Springs Resort & Inn . . . . .Ukiah, Calif.
Martin Van Buren
Old Hoosier House . . . . .Knightstown, Ind.
1725 Historic Witmer's Tavern . . . . .Lancaster, Pa.
Woodrow Wilson
The Cordova . . . . .Ocean Grove, N.J.

INN EVALUATION FORM

Please copy and complete this form for each stay and mail to the address shown. Since 1981 we have maintained files that include thousands of evaluations from inngoers who have sent this form to us. This information helps us evaluate and update the inns listed in this guide.

Name of Inn: _____

City and State: _____

Date of Stay: _____

Your Name: _____

Address: _____

City/State/Zip: _____

Phone: (__ __ __) __ __ __ – __ __ __ __

E-mail: _____

Please use the following rating scale for the next items.
1: Outstanding.   2: Good.   3: Average.   4: Fair.   5: Poor.

Location	1	2	3	4	5
Cleanliness	1	2	3	4	5
Food Service	1	2	3	4	5
Privacy	1	2	3	4	5
Beds	1	2	3	4	5
Bathrooms	1	2	3	4	5
Parking	1	2	3	4	5
Handling of reservations	1	2	3	4	5
Attitude of staff	1	2	3	4	5
Overall rating	1	2	3	4	5

Comments on Above: _____

_____

_____

_____

_____

MAIL THE COMPLETED FORM TO:
American Historic Inns, Inc.
PO Box 669
Dana Point, CA 92629-0669
(949) 499-8070
www.bnbinns.com

Publications From American Historic Inns

Bed & Breakfast and Country Inns, 12th Edition

By Deborah Edwards Sakach

Imagine the thrill of receiving this unique book with its FREE night certificate as a gift. Now you can let someone else experience the magic of America's country inns with this unmatched offer. *Bed & Breakfasts and Country Inns* is the most talked about guide among inngoers.

This fabulous guide features more than 1,500 inns from across the United States and Canada. Best of all, no other bookstore guide offers a FREE night certificate.* This certificate can be used at any one of the inns featured in the guide.

American Historic Inns, Inc. has been publishing books about bed & breakfasts since 1981. Its books and the FREE night offer have been recommended by many travel writers and editors, and featured in: *The New York Times, Washington Post, Los Angeles Times, Boston Globe, Chicago Sun Times, USA Today, Orange County Register, Baltimore Sun, McCalls, Good Housekeeping, Cosmopolitan, Consumer Reports* and more.

*With purchase of one night at the regular rate required. Subject to limitations.

416 pages, paperback, 500 illustrations.   **Price $21.95**

The Official Guide to American Historic Inns

Completely Revised and Updated, Seventh Edition

By Deborah Sakach

Open the door to America's past with this fascinating guide to historic inns that reflect our colorful heritage. From Dutch Colonials to Queen Anne Victorians, these bed & breakfasts and country inns offer experiences of a lifetime.

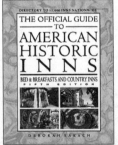

This special edition guide includes certified American Historic Inns that provide the utmost in hospitality, beauty, authentic restoration and preservation. Inns have been carefully selected so as to provide readers with the opportunity to visit genuine masterpieces.

With Inns dating back to as early as 1649, this guide is filled with treasures waiting to be discovered. Full descriptions, illustrations, guest comments and recommendations all are included to let you know what's in store for you before choosing one of America's Historic Inns.

528 pages, paperback, 1,000 illustrations.   **Price $15.95**

How To Start & Run Your Own Bed & Breakfast Inn

By Ripley Hotch & Carl Glassman

In this book you'll discover the secrets of the best inns. Learn how to decide whether owning or leasing an inn is right for you. Find out what business strategies characterize a successful inn and learn how to incorporate them in your own business.

If you've always dreamed of owning a bed & breakfast, then this book is for you!

182 pages, paperback.   **Price $15.95**

The Bed & Breakfast Encyclopedia
Completely Revised and Updated, Second Edition

By Deborah Edwards Sakach & Tiffany Crosswy

This massive guide is the most comprehensive guide on the market today. Packed with detailed listings to more than 2,300 bed & breakfasts and country inns, the Encyclopedia also includes an index to an additional 13,000 inns, detailed state maps and more than 1,200 illustrations. Recipes, helpful phone numbers, information about reservation services and informative articles about bed & breakfast hot spots, the best bed & breakfasts, inns of interest, how to start your own B&B and much, much more.

If you're planning a getaway, this all-inclusive guide is a must!

992 pages, paperback, 1,200 illustrations　　　　　　　　　　　　**Price $18.95**

Bed & Breakfast and Country Inn Travel Club
Membership From American Historic Inns, Inc.

SAVE! SAVE! SAVE! We offer an exclusive discount club that lets you enjoy the excitement of bed & breakfast and country inn travel again and again. As a member of this special club, you'll receive benefits that include savings of 25% to 50% off every night's stay!

Your membership card will entitle you to tremendous savings at some of the finest inns in America. Members receive a guide with more than 1,100 participating bed & breakfasts and country inns to choose from. Plan affordable getaways to inns nearby or visit an area of the country you've always wanted to experience.

The best part of being an American Historic Inns Travel Club Member is that the card can be used as many times as you like.

In addition to your card, you will get a FREE night's stay certificate—truly a club membership that's hard to pass up!

All travel club members receive:
- Travel club card entitling holder to 25% to 50% off lodging.
- FREE night's stay certificate.
- Guide to more than 1,100 participating inns across America.

Membership is good for one year. Free night's stay with purchase of one night at the regular rate. Discount and certificate cannot be combined.

Introductory price with full benefits (Reg. $59.95)　　　　　　　　**$49.95**

Golf Across America Club Membership

Introducing the best way to get free greens fees and other discounts at more than 700 courses nationwide! Golf Across America club discounts include:

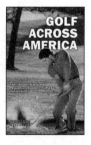

- Free greens fees
- Buy-One-Get-One-Free greens fees
- 50% off greens fees.
- Plus More!

A one-year membership also includes a 2/1 bucket of balls certificate good at an additional 100 Family Golf Center Driving Ranges. Plus, your Golf Across America membership card can be used as many times as you like. The average Golf Across America club member saves between $200-$400 each year. Get your one-year club membership and start saving today!

Introductory price with full benefits　　　　　　　　　　　　　　**$39.95**

**AMERICAN
HISTORIC
INNS**
INCORPORATED

PO Box 669
Dana Point
California
92629-0669
(949) 499-8070
Fax (949) 499-4022
www.bnbinns.com

Order Form

Date: __ __ / __ __ / __ __   Shipped: __ __ / __ __ / __ __

Name: _____

Street: _____

City/State/Zip: _____

Phone: (__ __ __) __ __ __ – __ __ __ __   E-mail: _____

QTY.	Prod. No.	Description	Amount	Total
_____	AHI12	Bed & Breakfasts and Country Inns	$21.95	_____
_____	AHIH7	The Official Guide to American Historic Inns	$15.95	_____
_____	AHIE2	Bed & Breakfast Encyclopedia	$18.95	_____
_____	AHIC2	Bed & Breakfast and Country Inn Travel Club	$49.95	_____
_____	CB03	How to Start Your Own B&B	$15.95	_____
_____	GOLF	Golf Across America Club Membership	$39.95	_____

Subtotal _____

California buyers add 7.75% sales tax _____

Shipping and Handling on Encyclopedia Book Orders
STANDARD (10-20 days): $3 for first book. Add $1 for each additional copy.
PRIORITY (3-5 days): $5. Add $2 each add'l copy. 2ND-DAY AIR: $7.50. Add $4.50 each add'l copy.

Shipping and Handling on Other Book and Travel Club Orders
STANDARD (10-20 days): $2.25 for first book. Add 75¢ for each additional copy.
PRIORITY (3-5 days): $3.75. Add $2 each add'l copy. 2ND-DAY AIR: $7.50. Add $4.50 each add'l copy _____

TOTAL _____

❑ Check/Money Order   ❑ Discover   ❑ Mastercard   ❑ Visa   ❑ American Express

Account Number __ __ __ __ __ __ __ __ __ __ __ __ __ __ __ __   Exp. Date __ __ / __ __

Name on card _____

Signature _____